AN
ENGLISH-READER'S
DICTIONARY

AN
ENGLISH-READER'S
DICTIONARY

Regino Manuel Roque Bergara

A. S. HORNBY AND E. C. PARNWELL

SECOND EDITION
Revised and enlarged

LONDON
OXFORD UNIVERSITY PRESS

Oxford University Press, Ely House, London W. 1

GLASGOW NEW YORK TORONTO MELBOURNE WELLINGTON
CAPE TOWN IBADAN NAIROBI DAR ES SALAAM LUSAKA ADDIS ABABA
DELHI BOMBAY CALCUTTA MADRAS KARACHI LAHORE DACCA
KUALA LUMPUR SINGAPORE HONG KONG TOKYO

ISBN 0 19 431116 3

© *Oxford University Press 1969*

First Published 1952
Reprinted seventeen times
Second Edition 1969
Third Impression 1973
(with corrections)

Printed in Great Britain
at the University Press, Oxford
by Vivian Ridler
Printer to the University

PREFACE

An English-Reader's Dictionary is designed for use by learners of the English language, more especially where no adequate bilingual dictionary exists. It sets out to help students who have completed an elementary Course to read books written in everyday English, to write straightforward, idiomatic compositions, and to converse naturally.

With this special purpose in view the dictionary defines words in the simplest English terms that are consistent with accuracy and gives particular attention to the usage of structural words.

The compilers have had continually before them the needs of the students whom they wish to serve. They have striven always to be mindful of how much—or how little—these students know. They have had to bear in mind, also, the limits of length that the Publisher fixed in order to publish the dictionary at a price in keeping with its grade.

In this Second Edition the system of phonetic transcription has been changed to the more generally used broad transcription of the International Phonetic Association; the headwords have been syllabified; the entries generally have been re-examined, and have been improved and amplified wherever desirable. Structural and other high-frequency words that were left undefined in the First Edition have now been treated more fully.

A. S. H.
E. C. P.

September 1968

NOTES ON THE USE OF THIS DICTIONARY

The proper use of a dictionary requires care and patience. If the definition of a word is not at first clearly understood, the user should turn up the entries of the words used in that definition, in order to make certain that he knows what they mean. If used in this manner an English dictionary will extend and improve the student's knowledge of the language far beyond the range of his textbooks.

When a word has several senses, the definition of each is numbered. The student must decide for himself, by referring to the sentence in which the word appears, which definition fits that sentence best.

When a word used in a definition has more than one meaning, a number in brackets after the word indicates the particular meaning used in that definition. Thus, under **pay**, the verb *discharge* (4) is used for the definition of *pay sb. off*. The figure (4) indicates that the sense of *discharge* here is that given in the definition so numbered.

When a headword has several quite unrelated meanings, each one is shown by a raised number printed in front of the headword and given a separate entry. (See **¹refuse, ²refuse**.)

Italic Type

When a word or words are printed in italic type as a part of the definition, this indicates the construction to be used. Thus, under the entry for **persuade,** the italic type shows the possible constructions *persuade somebody to do something, persuade somebody of the truth, importance, etc., of something,* and *persuade somebody that something is true.*

The entries (*-bb-*), (*-dd-*), (*-gg-*), (*-mm-*), (*-nn-*), (*-ll-*), (*-rr-*), and (*-tt-*), indicate a doubling of the consonant in the past tense, etc., of certain verbs, and in the comparative and superlative forms of some adjectives, as in *rob, robbed; beg, begging; big, bigger, biggest.*

Word Division

Headwords are divided into syllables by dots. These show where a hyphen can be put when a word has to be split at the end of a line; but a word should not be split if either part of it would be less than one syllable of two letters. For example, **ob·scure, glad·ly,** can be split, but not **a·bly, jump·y.** A syllable whether it is part of a word or a whole word, should not be split. Thus **pre·cious** will be divided (at the dot), but not **flour, cruel, bought, cleanse.**

Pronunciation

Pronunciation is indicated by a phonetic re-spelling (in square brackets). The sounds represented by the letters used within these square brackets are shown on p. vii.

Pronunciation varies from region to region. Although the phonetic transcription in this dictionary records what Daniel Jones called 'Received Pronunciation', this is not put forward as the only 'correct' pronunciation.

Stress

The upright marks inserted in phonetic re-spellings show on what syllable or syllables stress is laid. The stress falls on the syllable following the upright mark. Thus:

table ['teibl]   *because* [bi'kɔz]

Where there are two unequal stresses in one word, the primary stress is placed above the line and the secondary one below, thus:

regulation [ˌregju'leiʃən]

Where the mark ~ is used in derivates (in *-y, -ly, -en, -ness*, etc.), the stress mark is not given, as these endings are always unstressed. In compounds for which no phonetic transcription is given, stress marks are given with the ordinary spelling, or with the mark ~ and the added word. Thus, under *head*, we have:

'~'*master* (two primary stresses)
'~*phones* (one primary stress)

Under *heart* we have:

'~-ˌ*breaking* (one primary stress and one secondary stress).

Key to Pronunciation

Phonetic Symbol	Word	(Transcription)	Phonetic Symbol	Word	(Transcription)
ɑː	*father*	'fɑːðə*	ŋ	*long*	lɔŋ
æ	*bad*	bæd	ŋg	*longer*	'lɔŋgə*
ai	*cry*	krai	ə	*hot*	hɔt
au	*how*	hau	o	*obey*	ə'bei, ou'bei
b	*back*	bæk	ɔː	*saw*	sɔː
d	*day*	dei	ɔə¹	*more*	mɔə*, mɔː*
dʒ	*page*	peidʒ	ɔi	*boy*	bɔi
ð	*then*	ðen	ou	*so, sew, sow*	sou
e	*wet*	wet	p	*put*	put
ɛə	*hair*	hɛə*	r	*red*	red
ei	*day*	dei	s	*sit, this*	sit, ðis
əː	*bird*	bəːd	ʃ	*show, wish*	ʃou, wiʃ
ə	*ago, ladder*	ə'gou, 'lædə*	t	*tin, hit*	tin, hit
f	*full, physics*	ful, 'fiziks	tʃ	*church*	tʃəːtʃ
g	*get*	get	θ	*thin*	θin
h	*hot*	hɔt	uː	*boot*	buːt
iː	*meet*	miːt	u	*good, put*	gud, put
i	*sit*	sit	uə	*sure*	ʃuə*
iə	*hear*	hiə*	v	*very*	'veri
j	*yes*	jes	ʌ	*cup*	kʌp
k	*cold, kill*	kould, kil	w	*wet*	wet
l	*like, fill*	laik, fil	z	*zero, his*	'ziərou, hiz
m	*make*	meik	ʒ	*pleasure*	'pleʒə*
n	*not*	nɔt			

¹ Many speakers replace [ɔə] by [ɔː]

Vowels weakly accented within a word are often omitted. Thus, the syllable *-tion*, which is transcribed in this dictionary [-ʃən], is usually [-ʃn]. So *adoption* may be either [ə'dɔpʃən] or [ə'dɔpʃn]. Where an italic letter is printed in a phonetic re-spelling, it indicates a sound which may be omitted. Thus *pinch* is transcribed [pintʃ]. This means that *pinch* may be pronounced as [pintʃ] or, in more rapid speech, as [pinʃ].

The asterisk (*) is used to indicate possible r-linking. Thus the word *father* is transcribed ['fɑːðə*]. When a word beginning with a consonant sound follows, the pronunciation is ['fɑːðə]. When a word beginning with a vowel sound follows, the pronunciation is ['fɑːðər], as in 'the father of these children' [ðə 'fɑːðər əv ðiːz 'tʃildrən].

Abbreviations and Symbols

In a short dictionary it is necessary to economize in space. Many more words have been included through the use of the following symbols and shortened forms, which (like the phonetic symbols) the student should learn to recognize before the dictionary is used:

&	and	*opp.*	opposite in meaning
abbr.	abbreviation	*pl.*	plural
adj.	adjective	*poet.*	poetical style
adv.	adverb	*poss.*	possessive
attrib.	attributive(ly)	*p.p.*	past participle
aux.	auxiliary	*ppl.*	participial
bibl.	biblical style	*pred.*	predicative
cf.	compare	*prep.*	preposition
chem.	chemistry	*pres. t.*	present tense
colloq.	colloquial	*pron.*	pronoun
comp.	comparative	*p.t.*	past tense
conj.	conjunction	*q.v.*	refer to the entry for
e.g.	for example		this word in the
esp.	especial(ly)		dictionary
etc.	et cetera, and others	*rel.*	relative
fig.	figurative(ly)	*R.*	River
Fr.	French	*R.C.*	Roman Catholic
Gt. Brit.	Great Britain	*sb.*	somebody
humor.	humorous(ly)	*Scot.*	Scotch, Scottish
i.e.	that is	*sing.*	singular
inf.	infinitive	*sth.*	something
int.	interjection	*superl.*	superlative
interr.	interrogative	*U.S.A.*	American usage
lb.	pound(s) weight	*usu.*	usually
lit.	literal(ly)	*v.*	verb
liter.	literary style	*v.i.*	verb intransitive
maths.	mathematics	*v.t.*	verb transitive
n., nn.	noun, nouns	*v.t. & i.*	verb transitive and
neg.	negative		intransitive

The mark ~ indicates the complete word at the beginning of an entry. Thus, under *moist*, ~*en* stands for *moisten*.

A

A1 [ei'wʌn] *adj.* classified as first rate; excellent.

a [ei, ə], **an** [æn, ən] *indefinite article.* **1.** one (cf. *some, any, a few,* with pl. nouns): *I have a pen* (pl. *some pens*). **2.** (with adj. & pron. of number and quantity): *a great many friends* ; *a lot of money.* **3.** that which is called; any; every: *A horse is an animal* (pl. *Horses are animals*). **4.** each; every: *twice a day; two shillings a pound; sixty miles an hour.*

a·back [ə'bæk] *adv.* taken ~, surprised.

ab·a·cus ['æbəkəs] *n.* frame with balls on wires, used in eastern countries for working with numbers.

a·ban·don [ə'bændən] *v.t.* **1.** leave, go away from (not intending to return to). **2.** give up: *Don't ~ hope yet. ~ oneself to,* give oneself up to; cease to control (one's feelings, etc.). **a·ban·doned** *adj.* given up to bad ways.

a·base [ə'beis] *v.t.* bring or make lower (in rank, honour, or self-respect). **~ment** *n.*

a·bashed [ə'bæʃt] *adj.* confused; embarrassed.

a·bate [ə'beit] *v.t. & i.* **1.** make or become less. **2.** (law) put a stop to.

ab·at·toir ['æbətwɑ:*] *n.* place where animals are killed for use as food.

ab·bess ['æbis] *n.* woman at the head of a nunnery; Mother Superior.

ab·bey ['æbi] *n.* (pl. ~s). **1.** society of men (called monks) or women (called nuns) living apart from others in the service of God. **2.** building(s) in which they live(d). **3.** church of an ~.

ab·bot ['æbət] *n.* man at the head of a monastery; Father Superior.

ab·bre·vi·ate [ə'bri:vieit] *v.t.* make (a word, story, etc.) shorter. **ab·bre·vi·a·tion** [ə,bri:vi'eiʃən] *n.* shortening; short form (esp. of a word), e.g. *Mon.* for *Monday.*

ab·di·cate ['æbdikeit] *v.t. & i.* give up (a throne, right, position of authority). **ab·di·ca·tion** [,æbdi'keiʃən] *n.*

ab·do·men ['æbdəmən, æb'doumen] *n.* **1.** (colloq. *belly*) lower front part of the body including the stomach and bowels. **2.** last of the three divisions of an insect's body. **ab·dom·i·nal** [æb'dɔminl] *adj.* in or of the ~: *abdominal pains.*

ab·duct [æb'dʌkt] *v.t.* carry off or lead away (sb.) unlawfully. **ab·duc·tion** *n.* unlawful carrying away (esp. of a young woman).

a·bet [ə'bet] *v.t.* (-tt-). aid and abet, help and encourage (to do wrong).

a·bey·ance [ə'beiəns] *n.* in ~, condition of not being in force or in use for a time.

ab·hor [əb'hɔ:*] *v.t.* (-rr-). feel hatred or disgust for. **~rence** [əb'hɔrəns] *n.* extreme hatred or disgust; sth. for which ~rence is felt. **~rent** *adj.* causing horror.

a·bide [ə'baid] *v.i. & t.* (p.t. & p.p. abode [ə'boud]). **1.** ~ by, be true and faithful to (a promise, etc.). **2.** (old use) live or stay (at or in). **3.** put up with; endure: *I can't ~ that woman.*

a·bil·i·ty [ə'biliti] *n.* **1.** power (esp. of mind) to do things: *a man of great (not much) ~; to the best of my ~.* **2.** (pl.) cleverness of mind.

ab·ject ['æbdʒekt] *adj.* **1.** unreserved; without self-respect: *an ~ apology (confession).* **2.** deserving contempt: ~ *behaviour.* **3.** (of conditions) wretched: *in ~ poverty.*

ab·jure [əb'dʒuə*] *v.t.* swear or promise publicly and solemnly to give up (a belief, opinion, right, etc.).

a·blaze [ə'bleiz] *adv. & pred. adj.* on fire; bright as if on fire.

a·ble ['eibl] *adj.* **1.** be ~ to do sth., have the power, time, etc. to do something: *I hope you will be ~ to come tomorrow.* (Cf. *can, could.*) **2.** clever; showing skill and knowledge: *an ~ speech (speaker).* ~-bodied sea·man, one who has been trained. **a·bly** *adv.*

ab·lu·tion [ə'bluːʃən] *n.* (usu. pl.) a washing of the body (esp. as an act of religion).

ab·nor·mal [æb'nɔːml] *adj.* not normal; different from what is ordinary, usual, or expected. ~·i·ty [ˌæbnɔː'mæliti] *n.* being ~; sth. ~.

a·board [ə'bɔːd] *adv. & prep.* on (to) or in(to) a ship or aircraft.

a·bode [ə'boud] *n.* (old use) house; living-place. *v.i.* p.t. & p.p. of *abide.*

a·bol·ish [ə'bɔliʃ] *v.t.* stop altogether; put an end to (e.g. war, slavery). **ab·o·li·tion** [ˌæbə'liʃən] *n.* act of ~ing; being ~ed.

a·bom·i·na·ble [ə'bɔminəbl] *adj.* causing horror and disgust. **a·bom·i·nate** [ə'bɔmineit] *v.t.* feel hatred or disgust for. **a·bom·i·na·tion** [əˌbɔmi'neiʃən] *n.*

ab·o·rig·i·nes [ˌæbə'ridʒiniːz] *n. pl.* earliest known inhabitants of a country. **ab·o·rig·i·nal** [ˌæbə'ridʒinl] *adj.* of ~; existing (in a place, country) from the earliest times. *n.* sing. form of ~.

a·bor·tion [ə'bɔːʃən] *n.* **1.** delivery of a baby before it can live; (deliberate act) bringing this about. **2.** creature so produced, usu. misshapen. **a·bor·tive** [ə'bɔːtiv] *adj.* of ~; coming too soon and therefore unsuccessful; imperfect.

a·bound [ə'baund] *v.i.* **1.** be plentiful. **2.** ~ in, ~ with, have in great numbers or quantity.

a·bout [ə'baut] *prep. & adv.* **I. prep. 1.** (*go*, etc.) in various directions; to various places. **2.** (*be*, etc.) in various places in or on: *Men were standing ~ the street corners.* **3.** near to: *They live somewhere ~ here.* **4.** in connexion with; regarding: *We know nothing ~ her. How ~? What ~?*, used at the beginning of a question seeking an opinion, proposing an action, etc.: *How ~ buying ourselves a drink? He's a handsome man, but what ~ his character?* **5.** ~ to, just going to: *The telephone rang as I was ~ to leave the office.* **II. adv. 1.** a little more or less; a little before or after: *She's ~ ten years old. It's ~ five o'clock.* **2.** (*move*, etc.) to various places, in various directions: *Children usually rush ~.* **3.** (*be, sit, lie,* etc.) here and there: *People were sitting ~ on the grass.* **4.** *come ~,* happen; *bring ~,* cause (sth.) to happen. **5.** facing round; in the opposite direction: *A~ turn!*, military command to turn round and face the opposite direction.

a·bove [ə'bʌv] *prep. & adv.* **I. prep. 1.** higher than: *The sun rose ~ the horizon. Your name comes ~ mine on the list.* **2.** greater in number, price, weight, etc.: *The temperature has not risen ~ 10° C. all day.* **3.** more than: *A good soldier values honour ~ life. ~ all,* more than anything else. **4.** too good, great, proud, etc.: *If we want to learn, we should not be ~ asking questions.* **5.** *This book is ~ me* (too difficult for me, beyond my understanding). *He's living ~ his income* (spending more than he receives). **II. adv. 1.** *Seen from ~, the houses and fields looked quite flat.* **2.** earlier (in a book, article, etc.): *I must repeat what I wrote ~.* ~-board [ə'bʌvbɔːd] *pred. adj. & adv.* straightforward(ly); hiding nothing.

a·bra·sive [ə'breisiv] *adj.* that rubs harshly or scrapes. *n.* substance (like emery or sandpaper) used for smoothing a rough surface.

a·breast [ə'brest] *adv.* (of persons, ships, etc.) (moving) side by side (in the same direction). ~ *of*, level with : ~ *of the times*, up to date.

a·bridge [ə'brɪdʒ] *v.t.* make shorter, esp. by using fewer words ; cut short (a discussion, the time sth. lasts). ~·ment *n.* making shorter ; sth. (esp. a book or play) made shorter.

a·broad [ə'brɔːd] *adv.* **1.** to or in other countries. **2.** everywhere ; in all directions.

ab·ro·gate [ˈæbrougeit] *v.t.* put an end to (a law, custom). **ab·ro·ga·tion** [ˌæbrouˈgeiʃən] *n.*

ab·rupt [ə'brʌpt] *adj.* **1.** sudden ; unexpected : ~ *turns in a road.* **2.** (of speech, writing, behaviour) sudden ; rough. ~·ly *adv.*

ab·scess [ˈæbsis] *n.* collection of thick yellowish-white liquid (called *pus*) or other poisonous matter in a hollow place in the body.

ab·scond [əbˈskɔnd] *v.i.* go away (*with* sth.) suddenly, secretly, and aware of having done wrong.

ab·sence [ˈæbsəns] *n.* being away (*from*) : ~ *from school through illness.*

ab·sent [ˈæbsənt] *adj.* not present. [əbˈsent] *v.t.* ~ *oneself from*, not be present at. ~·minded [ˈæbsəntˈmaindid] *adj.* not thinking of what one is doing. **ab·sen·tee** [ˌæbsənˈtiː] *n.* one who is ~.

ab·so·lute [ˈæbsəljuːt] *adj.* **1.** complete ; perfect. **2.** having complete power : *an* ~ *ruler.* ~·ly *adv.*

ab·solve [əbˈzɔlv] *v.t.* set or declare free (from blame, guilt, a promise, duty, or the consequences of past sin). **ab·so·lu·tion** [ˌæbsəˈluːʃən] *n.* forgiveness (through a religious act) for past wrongdoing.

ab·sorb [əbˈsɔːb, əbˈzː] *v.t.* **1.** take in or up ; soak up. **2.** take up or occupy (time, attention) : ~*ed in a book.* **ab·sor·bent** [əbˈsɔːbənt] *adj.* able to ~. *n.* substance that ~s moisture. ~·ing *adj.* taking up the

thoughts, attention, etc., completely.

ab·stain [əbˈstein] *v.i.* do without (esp. alcoholic drinks) ; hold oneself back (*from*). ~·er *n.* total ~*er*, one who ~s completely from alcoholic drinks. **ab·sti·nence** [ˈæbstinəns] *n.* ~·ing (*from* food, drink, enjoyment). *total abstinence*, ~ing completely from alcoholic drinks.

ab·ste·mi·ous [əbˈstiːmiəs] *adj.* sparing or moderate in the use of enjoyable things (esp. good food, wine).

ab·sten·tion [əbˈstenʃən] *n.* abstaining (*from* sth.), esp. not using one's vote at an election ; instance of this.

ab·stract [ˈæbstrækt] *adj.* opposite to what is material or concrete. *n.* short account (of the chief ideas in a book, speech, etc.). [æbˈstrækt] *v.t.* take away ; separate from ; make an ~ of. **ab·stract·ed** *adj.* not paying attention. **ab·strac·tion** *n.* state of being ~ed or lost in thought ; idea not concerned with material things, e.g. *truth, whiteness.*

ab·struse [æb-, əbˈstruːs] *adj.* whose meaning or answer is hidden ; difficult to understand. ~·ly *adv.*

ab·surd [əbˈsəːd] *adj.* foolish ; causing laughter ; far from what is usual and normal. ~·i·ty *n.* state of being ~ ; ~ idea or thing. ~·ly *adv.*

a·bun·dance [əˈbʌndəns] *n.* **1.** great plenty : *food in* ~. **2.** number or quantity which is more than enough : *an* ~ *of good things.* **a·bun·dant** *adj.* more than enough ; plentiful ; rich (*in*). **a·bun·dant·ly** *adv.*

a·buse [əˈbjuːs] *n.* **1.** wrong, rough, or harmful treatment. **2.** angry complaint(s) against sb. or sth. : *a stream of* ~. **3.** wrong or unjust custom, practice, or use : *put an end to* ~*s* ; *an* ~ *of trust.* [əˈbjuːz] *v.t.* make wrong use of ; treat badly ; say severe and harsh things to or about. **a·bu·sive** *adj.* containing, using, ~. **a·bu·sive·ly** *adv.*

a·byss [ə'bis] *n.* great hole so deep as to appear bottomless; hell. **a·bys·mal** [ə'bizməl] *adj.* (often fig.) deep: *abysmal ignorance.*

a·cad·e·my [ə'kædəmi] *n.* 1. school for higher learning, usu. for a special subject or purpose: *a military ~.* 2. society of learned men: *the Royal Academy.* **ac·a·dem·ic** [,ækə'demik] *adj.* of schools, colleges, learning, or teaching; concerned with theory rather than with practice.

ac·cede [ək'si:d] *v.i.* 1. agree (*to* a proposal, etc.). 2. come or succeed (*to* a position of authority): *When did he ~ to the throne?*

ac·cel·er·ate [ək'seləreit] *v.t. & i.* increase the speed of; become quicker; make sth. happen sooner. **ac·cel·er·a·tor** *n.* (esp.) pedal in a motor-car which increases the speed when pressed down.

ac·cent ['æksnt] *n.* 1. (in speaking) extra force or stress given to one part of a word of more than one syllable, or to certain words in a sentence. 2. printed mark above or below a letter, as *é, è.* 3. particular way of speaking or pronouncing a language: *speaking English with a Scottish ~.* [ək'sent] *v.t.* add stress to; mark with a written or printed *~.* **ac·cen·tu·ate** [æk'sentjueit] *v.t.* give more force or importance to. **ac·cen·tu·a·tion** [æk,sentju'eifən] *n.*

ac·cept [ək'sept] *v.t.* (agree to) take what is offered. **~·a·ble** *adj.* worth ~ing; pleasing and satisfactory. **~·ance** *n.* act of ~ing.

ac·cess ['ækses] *n.* 1. way (in)to a place: *easy of ~,* easy to get at or in. 2. right of reaching, using, speaking to. **ac·ces·si·ble** [ək'sesibl] *adj.* easy to reach or approach.

ac·ces·sa·ry [æk'sesəri] *n.* one who helps in any act, esp. in crime.

ac·ces·sion [æk'sefən] *n.* 1. coming to or reaching power or

a position. 2. (an) addition; (an) increase.

ac·ces·so·ry [æk'sesəri] *n.* sth. extra, helpful and useful, but not an original part: *accessories of a bicycle* (e.g. lamps, pump).

ac·ci·dent ['æksidənt] *n.* chance happening; unfortunate or disastrous event. **ac·ci·den·tal** [,æksi'dentl] *adj.* happening by chance. **ac·ci·den·tal·ly** *adv.*

ac·claim [ə'kleim] *v.t.* 1. welcome (with shouts of approval). 2. make (sb.) ruler with loud cries: *~ a man king.* **ac·cla·ma·tion** [,æklə'meifən] *n.* loud cries of satisfaction or praise.

ac·cli·ma·tize [ə'klaimətaiz] *v.t.* get (oneself or an animal or plant) used *to* a new climate.

ac·com·mo·date [ə'kɔmədeit] *v.t.* 1. have or provide room(s) for. 2. get (plans, etc.) into adjustment or agreement. **ac·com·mo·da·ting** *adj.* willing to fit in with the wishes of others. **ac·com·mo·da·tion** [ə,kɔmə'deifən] *n.* room(s), etc., provided for visitors.

ac·com·pa·ny [ə'kʌmpəni] *v.t.* 1. go with; happen or do at the same time as. 2. play music to support a singer or other performer. **ac·com·pa·ni·ment** *n.* sth. that accompanies, esp. (e.g. piano) music to support a voice or solo instrument. **ac·com·pa·nist** *n.* one who plays an accompaniment.

ac·com·plice [ə'kʌmplis] *n.* helper or companion in wrongdoing.

ac·com·plish [ə'kʌmplif] *v.t.* finish successfully. **ac·com·plished** *adj.* skilled (esp. in such social arts as music, painting, talking). **~·ment** *n.* 1. finishing. 2. sth. done well; sth. one can do well, e.g. playing the piano.

ac·cord [ə'kɔ:d] *n.* agreement (e.g. between two countries). *of one's own ~,* without being forced or requested. *v.t. & i.* give (a welcome, etc.); be in harmony (*with*). **ac·cord·ing to** *prep.* on the authority of; in a manner that suits or is fitting.

~·ance *n.* agreement. **~·ing·ly** *adv.* for that reason.
ac·cor·dion [əˈkɔːdjən] *n.* see the picture.

An accordion

ac·cost [əˈkɔst] *v.t.* speak to (esp. a stranger in the street).

ac·count [əˈkaunt] *v.i. & t.* **1.** ~ *for,* explain satisfactorily; give reasons for; keep or give a written statement about (money or goods). **2.** consider: ~ *a man innocent.* *n.* **1.** written statement(s) with details (esp. of money received and paid, articles bought and sold, etc.). *on* ~, in part payment. **2.** story or description. **3.** reason; cause: *on no (not on any)* ~, for no reason; *on this* ~, for this reason. **4.** use; profit; importance: *of no* ~, useless; worthless; *take into* ~, consider; *take no* ~ *of,* pay no attention to; *on one's own* ~, by and for oneself. **~·a·ble** *adj.* responsible; expected to give an explanation: *A madman is not ~able for his actions.* **~·an·cy** *n.* the work of keeping ~s (1). **~·ant** *n.* person who keeps ~s (1).

ac·cred·it [əˈkredit] *v.t.* send (an ambassador) with an official introduction (*to* a foreign government or ruler).

ac·crue [əˈkruː] *v.i.* come (*to* sb., *from . . .*) as a natural development (esp. of interest on money).

ac·cu·mu·late [əˈkjuːmjuleit] *v.t. & i.* come or gather together; become, cause to become, greater in number or amount. **ac·cu·mu·la·tion** [əˌkjuːmjuˈleiʃən] *n.* **ac·cu·mu·la·tor** *n.* apparatus for storing electricity.

ac·cu·rate [ˈækjurit] *adj.* careful and exact (in doing things); free from error. **ac·cu·ra·cy** *n.*

ac·cursed, ac·curst [əˈkəːst] *adj.* under a curse; hateful.

ac·cuse [əˈkjuːz] *v.t.* say (sb.) is guilty (*of* sth.). *the ~d,* the person ~d in a law court. **ac·cu·sa·tion** [ˌækjuˈzeiʃən] *n.* **ac·cus·er** *n.*

ac·cus·tom [əˈkʌstəm] *v.t.* get used (*to*). **ac·cus·tomed** *adj.* usual.

ace [eis] *n.* playing-card with one mark on it: *the ace of spades.* *within an ace of,* very close to.

a·ce·tic [əˈsiːtik] *adj.* of vinegar.

a·cet·y·lene [əˈsetiliːn] *n.* a colourless gas that burns with a bright flame.

ache [eik] *n.* continuous pain. *v.i.* have an ~.

a·chieve [əˈtʃiːv] *v.t.* finish; reach; carry out successfully. **~·ment** *n.* achieving; sth. ~d.

a·cid [ˈæsid] *n.* **1.** strong, sour liquid. **2.** (chem.) one of a class of substances containing hydrogen, turning blue litmus-paper red. *adj.* with the properties of an acid; sour; sharp-tasting. ~ *test,* one that proves the true value of sth. **a·cid·i·ty** [əˈsiditi] *n.* ~ quality.

ac·knowl·edge [əkˈnɔlidʒ] *v.t.* **1.** agree, admit (that sth. is true). **2.** send news that one has received sth. **3.** regard (as): *He is ~d to be an expert on this subject.* **~·ment** *n.* act of acknowledging; letter, etc., given or sent to ~ sth. received.

ac·me [ˈækmi] *n.* highest point: *the ~ of good behaviour.*

a·corn [ˈeikɔːn] *n.* seed or fruit of the oak-tree.

a·cous·tic [əˈkuːstik] *adj.* of the sense of hearing. **a·cous·tics** *n.* the science of sound; the ~ properties (of a hall, etc.).

ac·quaint [əˈkweint] *v.t.* make aware; make familiar (*with*): *to ~ oneself with one's new duties;* *be ~ed with,* have met personally. **~·ance** *n.* **1.** slight personal knowledge. **2.** sb. whom one has met a few times.

ac·qui·esce [ˌækwiˈes] *v.i.* agree without protest: *He ~d in the arrangements.* **ac·qui·es·cence**

n. **ac·qui·es·cent** *adj.* willing to ~.

ac·quire [ə'kwaiə*] *v.t.* become the owner of; gain for oneself by skill or ability. **~ment** *n.* acquiring; sth. ~d; a skill or ability. **ac·qui·si·tion** [ˌækwi-'ziʃən] *n.* 1. ~ment. 2. thing ~d. **ac·quis·i·tive** [ə'kwizitiv] *adj.* eager to ~; in the habit of acquiring.

ac·quit [ə'kwit] *v.t.* (*-tt-*). 1. say that (sb.) has not done wrong, is not guilty (of a crime). 2. ~ oneself (well, etc.), do one's work or duty (well, etc.). **~tal** *n.*

a·cre ['eikə*] *n.* area of 4,840 square yards, or about 4,000 square metres.

ac·rid ['ækrid] *adj.* (of smell or taste) sharp, bitter.

ac·ri·mo·ni·ous [ˌækri'mouniəs] *adj.* (of words, temper, etc.) bitter.

ac·ro·bat ['ækrəbæt] *n.* person who can do clever things with his body, such as balancing on a rope. **~ic** [ˌækrə'bætik] *adj.* **~ics** *n. pl.* tricks of, or like those of, an ~.

a·cross [ə'krɔs] *prep. & adv.* **I. prep. 1.** from side to side of: *The child ran ~ the road without looking.* **2.** on the other side of: *There is a garage just ~ the street.* **3.** so as to cross or to form a cross: *She lay with her arms ~ her breast.* **II. adv.** *The river is a mile ~ (wide) at that point.*

act [ækt] *v.i. & t.* **1.** perform actions, do sth.: *If we are to save her life we must act now!* **2.** do what is usual, expected, or required: *The front brake on my bicycle won't act.* **3.** take part in a play on the stage, etc. **4.** pretend: *I know you're not really crying, you're just acting.* **5.** act as, do the work or duty of. *act upon* (advice, a suggestion), do (what is advised, suggested). *act (up)on*, have an effect on: *This medicine acts upon the nerves.* *n.* **1.** thing done: *a cruel act; little acts of kindness; caught in the act of stealing.* **2.** (*Act*) bill (3) passed

by Parliament. **act·ing** *adj.* doing the work usu. done by another: *the acting manager of a business.*

ac·tion ['ækʃən] *n.* **1.** movement; (way of) moving or working (limbs); doing; using energy, influence, etc.: *a time for ~; a man of ~; out of ~,* not fit to work, to be used, etc. **2.** effect: *the ~ of an acid.* **3.** sth. done: *judge a man by his ~s.* **4.** fighting; a battle: *killed in ~; break off an ~.* **5.** (law) *bring an ~ (against),* seek judgement (against), in a law court.

ac·ti·vate ['æktiveit] *v.t.* make active.

ac·tive ['æktiv] *adj.* **1.** working; at work; in the habit of moving quickly: *an ~ brain (life).* **2.** practical; effective: *taking an ~ part in local affairs; on ~ service* (of a soldier engaged in fighting). **3.** *~ voice,* the form of the verb which shows that the subject of the verb is doing sth. (Cf. *passive.*) **~ly** *adv.*

ac·tiv·i·ty [æk'tiviti] *n.* being ~; purpose about which sb. is ~: *classroom (outdoor) activities.*

ac·tor ['æktə*] *n.* man who acts (in plays (2) and films (3)). **ac·tress** ['æktris] *n.* woman ~.

ac·tu·al ['æktjuəl] *adj.* real; present; not imagined. **~ly** *adv.* really; in truth; for the time being.

ac·tu·ate ['æktjueit] *v.t.* cause (sb. or sth.) to act or do sth.

a·cute [ə'kjuːt] *adj.* **1.** (of pain, etc.) sharp. **2.** (of feelings, senses) keen, delicate. **3.** responding quickly; clever; clear-sighted: *an ~ brain; an ~ observer.* **4.** (of an illness) coming quickly to a turning-point or crisis. **5.** *~ angle,* less than 90°.

ad·age ['ædidʒ] *n.* old and wise saying; proverb.

ad·a·mant ['ædəmənt] *adj.* like a hard substance that cannot be cut or broken; strongly resisting persuasion.

a·dapt [ə'dæpt] *v.t.* change in order to make suitable (*for a new purpose*). **~·a·ble** *adj.* able

to ~ or be ~ed. **ad·ap·ta·tion**
[ˌædæpˈteiʃən] *n.* ~ing; result
of ~ing. ~·er *n.* person who
~s (a play, a book, etc.). ~·or
n. attachment that enables sth.
(esp. electrical apparatus) to be
used for a new purpose.

add [æd] *v.t. & i.* **1.** put one
thing together with another: *If
you add 5 and 5 you get 10. If
the tea is too strong, add more
hot water.* **2.** find the total of:
Add up these figures. **3.** make
a total of: *These figures add up
to* 912. **4.** say sth. more: '*And
now, go away*', *he added.* (See
addition.)

ad·den·dum [əˈdendəm] (Latin)
n. (pl. *addenda*). something which
is to be added.

ad·der [ˈædə*] *n.* small poisonous
snake.

ad·dict [əˈdikt] *v.t.* ~ed *to*, (of
a person) in the habit of applying or devoting himself to; given
up to: ~ed *to taking drugs
(smoking).* [ˈædikt] *n.* person
~ed to (the thing, practice, etc.
named): *drug* ~s.

ad·di·tion [əˈdiʃən] *n.* adding;
sth. (to be) added. *in* ~ (*to*),
further; besides. ~·al *adj.*
extra.

ad·dle [ˈædl] *v.i.* (of eggs) become unfit for food; go bad.

ad·dress [əˈdres] *v.t.* **1.** direct
(send) a written or spoken message; deliver a speech to. **2.** ~
oneself to (a piece of work), be
busy with; give one's attention
to. *n.* **1.** particulars of the town,
street, etc., where a person may
be found or to which his letters,
etc., may be sent. **2.** speech to
an audience. **3.** way of speaking
and behaving: *a man of pleasing*
~. **4.** (pl.) *pay one's* ~es *to*,
show by words and behaviour
that one wants the favour of.
ad·dres·see [ˌædreˈsiː] *n.* person
to whom a letter is addressed.

ad·duce [əˈdjuːs] *v.t.* show or
bring forward (as a reason, an
example).

ad·ept [ˈædept] *n.* one who is
skilled (*in*, *at*). [əˈdept] *adj.*
expert.

ad·e·quate [ˈædikwit] *adj.*

enough; having the qualities
needed. **a·de·qua·cy** *n.*

ad·here [ədˈhiə*] *v.i.* **1.** become
or stay stuck fast (*to*) (e.g. with
paste or glue). **2.** be faithful (*to*);
give support (*to* a religion, party,
etc.). **ad·her·ence** *n.* **ad·her·**
ent *n.* supporter.

ad·he·sive [ədˈhiːsiv] *adj.* sticky:
~ *tape.* *n.* glue, paste (3).
ad·he·sion [ədˈhiːʒn] *n.* being
or becoming stuck.

a·dieu [əˈdjuː] *int.* good-bye.

ad·ja·cent [əˈdʒeisənt] *adj.* next
(*to*) but not necessarily touching.

ad·jec·tive [ˈædʒiktiv] *n.* word
that names a quality, as *large,
red, good.* **ad·jec·ti·val** [ˌædʒik-
ˈtaivl] *adj.* of or like an ~: *an
adjectival clause.*

ad·join [əˈdʒoin] *v.t.* be next or
nearest to; be touching: *the
~ing room (field).*

ad·journ [əˈdʒəːn] *v.t. & i.* **1.**
break off (a meeting, etc.) for
a time or to a later date. **2.** (of
a group of persons, a meeting)
stop doing sth. and separate
or go to another place: *We ~ed
to the next room.* ~·ment *n.*

ad·ju·di·cate [əˈdʒuːdikeit] *v.t.
& i.* give a judgement or decision (*upon* sth.) (settling a
quarrel, claim, or competition);
sit in judgement. **ad·ju·di·ca·**
tion [əˌdʒuːdiˈkeiʃən] *n.*

ad·junct [ˈædʒʌŋkt] *n.* sth.
joined to a more important
thing.

ad·jure [əˈdʒuə*] *v.t.* ask (sb.)
earnestly or solemnly; request
(sb.) under penalty.

ad·just [əˈdʒʌst] *v.t.* put in order
or agreement; make suitable
or convenient. ~·a·ble *adj.*
~·ment *n.* ~ing or being ~ed;
part by which sth. (in a machine)
is ~ed.

ad·ju·tant [ˈædʒutənt] *n.* army
officer who does administrative
work for a superior officer.

ad·min·is·ter [ədˈministə*] *v.t.*
1. control, manage, look after
(an estate, business affairs, etc.).
2. put (the law) into operation;
give (justice, punishment, etc.).
3. cause sb. to take: *to* ~ *an
oath to sb.*; *to* ~ *medicine.*

ad·min·is·tra·tion [əd‚minis-'treiʃən] *n.* **1.** management (of affairs, business, etc.). **2.** government (of a country). *the Administration*, the Ministry; the Government. **3.** giving of relief, justice, an oath, etc.. **ad·min·is·tra·tive** [əd'minis-trətiv] *adj.* of administration: *administrative work (ability).* **ad·min·is·tra·tor** [əd'minis-treitə*] *n.* one who ~s.

ad·mi·ra·ble ['ædmərəbl] *adj.* causing admiration; excellent. **ad·mi·ra·bly** *adv.*

ad·mir·al ['ædmərəl] *n.* naval officer of highest rank; officer who commands a fleet of warships. ~**ty** *n.* branch of government controlling the navy. *the Admiralty*, the building in London where ~ty officials work.

ad·mire [əd'maiə*] *v.t.* look at with pleasure; have a high opinion of. **ad·mi·ra·tion** [‚ædmi'reiʃən] *n.* feeling of pleasure, satisfaction, or respect.

ad·mit [əd'mit] *v.t. & i.* (*-tt-*). **1.** allow to enter: *to ~ sb. into a house; windows to ~ light and air.* **2.** say unwillingly; confess; agree (that sth. is true): *He ~ted having stolen the chicken.* **3.** ~ *of*, leave room for: *It ~s of No doubt.* **ad·mis·si·ble** [əd'misəbl] *adj.* that can be allowed or considered. **ad·mis·sion** [əd'miʃən] *n.* **1.** ~ting or being ~ted: *admission free.* **2.** statement ~ting (2) sth.: *an unwise admission; on his own admission.* ~**tance** [əd'mitəns] *n.* ~ting or being ~ted (to a place): *No ~tance except on business.* **ad·mit·ted·ly** [əd'mitidli] *adv.* as people generally ~ (2).

ad·mix·ture [əd'mikstʃə*]. *n.* action of mixing things; sth. which is the result of mixing.

ad·mon·ish [əd'mɔniʃ] *v.t.* advise (sb.) to do right; warn (sb.) against doing what is wrong. **ad·mo·ni·tion** [‚ædmə'niʃən] *n.* advice or warning about behaviour.

a·do [ə'du:] *n.* activity, usu. causing excitement.

ad·o·les·cent [‚ædə'lesnt] *n. &*

adj. (boy or girl) growing up (between the ages of about 13 and 20). **ad·o·les·cence** *n.*

a·dopt [ə'dɔpt] *v.t.* **1.** take (sb.) into one's own family and treat as one's own child. **2.** follow or use (sb. else's method(s), idea(s), belief(s), etc.). **a·dop·tion** [ə'dɔpʃən] *n.* act of ~ing.

a·dore [ə'dɔ:*] *v.t.* **1.** worship (God); love deeply and respect highly. **2.** (colloq.) be fond of. **a·dor·a·ble** *adj.* fit to be ~d. **ad·o·ra·tion** [‚ædə'reiʃən] *n.* worship; deep love and respect.

a·dorn [ə'dɔ:n] *v.t.* add beauty or ornaments to. ~**ment** *n.* ~ing; sth. used for ~ing.

a·drift [ə'drift] *adv. & pred. adj.* (of ships and boats) not under control and driven by wind and water. *turn ~,* send away (from home or employment).

a·droit [ə'drɔit] *adj.* clever; skilful. ~**ly** *adv.*

ad·u·la·tion [‚ædju'leiʃən] *n.* praise or respect (foolishly or excessively given, esp. to win favour).

a·dult [ə'dʌlt] *adj. & n.* (also ['ædʌlt]). (person or animal) grown to full size and strength; (law) person who is over 21 years old.

a·dul·ter·ate [ə'dʌltəreit] *v.t.* make poorer in quality, make impure, by adding sth. of less value. **a·dul·ter·a·tion** [ə‚dʌl-tə'reiʃən] *n.*

a·dul·ter·y [ə'dʌltəri] *n.* (of a husband or wife) act which breaks the marriage vow of faithfulness. **a·dul·ter·er** *n.* man guilty of ~. **a·dul·ter·ess** *n.* woman guilty of ~.

ad·vance [əd'va:ns] *v.i. & v.t.* **1.** come, go, put or help, forward: *The army ~d five miles. The general ~d his infantry.* **2.** (of prices, rates) make or become higher. **3.** pay (money) before it is due; lend (money). *n.* **1.** forward movement. *in ~ (of),* in front (of); sooner. **2.** rise in price or value. **3.** sum of money asked for, paid, or given, before it is due. **4.** (pl.) attempts to become a friend or lover. **ad·vanced** *adj.* (of persons, their ideas, views, etc.) leading others. ~**ment** *n.* advancing; progress.

ad·van·tage [əd'vɑ:ntidʒ] *n.* better position; profit; sth. likely to bring success. *take ~ of*, make use of (fairly or unfairly); *turn to ~*, use so as to profit from; *(seen) to ~*, in a way that shows the good points; *to the ~ of*, so as to help or profit. **ad·van·ta·geous** [ˌædvən'teidʒəs] *adj.* useful; helpful; profitable.

ad·vent ['ædvent] *n.* coming or arrival (usu. of an important person or event); *A~*, the season (with four Sundays) before Christmas; the coming of Christ.

ad·ven·ti·tious [ˌædven'tiʃəs] *adj.* coming by chance; accidental.

ad·ven·ture [əd'ventʃə*] *n.* unusual, exciting, or dangerous journey or activity : *~s in the jungle; a story of ~.* **ad·ven·tur·er** *n.* **1.** person who seeks ~. **2.** person ready to make a profit for himself by risky and sometimes dishonest means. **ad·ven·tur·ous** *adj.* fond of, ready for, ~; full of danger and excitement : *an adventurous voyage.*

ad·verb ['ædvə:b] *n.* word which answers questions beginning *how, when, where.* **ad·ver·bi·al** [əd'və:biəl] *adj.* of or like an ~ : *an ~ial clause.*

ad·ver·sa·ry ['ædvəsəri] *n.* enemy.

ad·verse ['ædvə:s] *adj.* unfavourable; against one's interests : *~ winds.* **ad·ver·si·ty** [əd-'və:siti] *n.* trouble.

ad·ver·tise ['ædvətaiz] *v.t. & i.* **1.** make known to people by printed notices (in newspapers, magazines, etc.), or by other methods, usu. for the purpose of trade. **2.** ask for by a public notice : *to ~ for a servant (a lost dog).* **ad·ver·tis·er** *n.* **ad·ver·tise·ment** [əd'və:tismənt] *n.* advertising; statement or other thing which ~s.

ad·vice [əd'vais] *n.* **1.** opinion given about what to do, how to act, etc. : *to follow the doctor's ~ ; a piece of ~.* **2.** (usu. pl.) news, esp. commercial.

ad·vise [əd'vaiz] *v.t.* **1.** give advice to. **2.** (business) inform. *ill-advised,* unwise. *well-advised,* wise. **ad·vi·sa·ble** *adj.* wise; to be advised. **ad·vi·so·ry** [əd'vaizəri] *adj.* having the right to ~ ; giving advice.

ad·vo·cate ['ædvəkit] *n.* one who speaks (esp. in a law court) in favour of a person or cause. ['ædvəkeit] *v.t.* support; speak in favour of (ideas, causes). **ad·vo·ca·cy** ['ædvəkəsi] *n.* pleading in support of sb. or sth.

adze [ædz] *n.* tool with a curved blade for shaping large pieces of wood.

aer·ate ['eiəreit] *v.t.* let air or put gas into (a substance).

aer·i·al ['ɛəriəl] *n.* wire(s), etc. for receiving or sending radio signals. (also [ei'iəriəl]) *adj.* of or in the air; flimsy; imaginary.

aer·o- ['ɛərou-] *prefix.* of air; of flying or aviation. **aer·o·drome** ['ɛərədroum] *n.* flying-ground. **aer·o·plane** ['ɛərəplein] *n.* aircraft; flying-machine. **aer·o·naut·i·cal** [ˌɛərə'nɔ:tikl] *adj.* of aircraft and their control.

aes·thet·ic [i:s'θetik] *adj.* concerning beauty in nature, art, literature, music; able to appreciate such beauty; showing good taste (in art, etc.). **aes·thet·ics** *n.* study of the principles of beauty.

a·far [ə'fɑ:*] *adv.* far off.

af·fa·ble ['æfəbl] *adj.* friendly; good-humoured; pleasant and easy to talk to. **af·fa·bly** *adv.* **af·fa·bil·i·ty** [ˌæfə'biliti] *n.*

af·fair [ə'fɛə*] *n.* **1.** sth. done or thought about; business matter : *That is my ~, not yours.* **2.** (pl.) business; events: *a man of ~s,* a business man; *mind one's own ~s,* not ask questions about, not interfere in, the business of others. *Foreign Affairs,* relations with foreign countries. **3.** event; happening; thing : *The picnic was a pleasant ~. ~ of honour,* duel.

¹**af·fect** [ə'fekt] *v.t.* **1.** have a

result or effect on: *The climate ~ed his health.* **2.** move the feelings of: *deeply ~ed by the sad news.* **~·ing** *adj.* moving the feelings: *~ing scenes.*

¹af·fect [ə'fekt] *v.t.* **1.** pretend to have, be, feel, or do: *to ~ ignorance.* **2.** show a liking for: *to ~ bright colours* (e.g. by wearing brightly-coloured clothes). **~·ed** *adj.* not natural or genuine. **af·fec·ta·tion** [ˌæfek'teiʃən] *n.* behaviour, show of feeling, which is not natural or genuine.

af·fec·tion [ə'fekʃən] *n.* **1.** love; kindly feeling: *to win sb.'s ~(s); in need of ~.* **2.** illness or disease: *an ~ of the stomach.* **~·ate** *adj.* loving; showing a feeling of love. **~·ate·ly** *adv.*

af·fi·da·vit [ˌæfi'deivit] *n.* written statement made on one's oath.

af·fil·i·ate [ə'filieit] *v.t. & i.* accept as a member or branch of a society; become connected (*with*). **af·fil·i·a·tion** [əˌfili'eiʃən] *n.*

af·fin·i·ty [ə'finiti] *n.* **1.** close connexion (e.g. between animals, plants, languages). **2.** family relation through marriage. **3.** attraction: *the ~ of common salt for water.*

af·firm [ə'fə:m] *v.t.* declare firmly. **af·fir·ma·tion** [ˌæfə-'meiʃən] *n.* **~·ing; sth. ~ed,** esp. (law) a solemn declaration made by sb. not wishing to take an oath. **af·fir·ma·tive** [ə'fə:-mətiv] *adj. & n.* (answering) 'yes'.

af·fix ['æfiks] *n.* suffix or prefix. [ə'fiks] *v.t.* fix or fasten (sth. *to* or *on*); put on (e.g. a postage stamp).

af·flict [ə'flikt] *v.t.* cause pain, trouble, or suffering to. **af·flic·tion** *n.* (cause of) suffering.

af·flu·ent ['æfluənt] *adj.* wealthy; well off. **af·flu·ence** *n.* being *~: living in affluence,* having plenty of money for one's needs.

af·ford [ə'fɔ:d] *v.t.* **1.** (usu. with *can, could, be able to*) spare or find enough (money or time for). **2.** (of things) give; provide.

af·for·est [ə'fɔrist] *v.t.* make into forest land; plant with trees. **af·for·es·ta·tion** [əˌfɔris'teiʃən] *n.*

af·fray [ə'frei] *n.* fight in a public place, esp. one that disturbs people.

af·fright [ə'frait] *v.t.* frighten.

af·front [ə'frant] *v.t.* hurt sb.'s feelings or self-respect, esp. in public. *n.* public insult: *to offer an ~ to sb.*

a·field [ə'fi:ld] *adv.* far away from home; to or at a distance.

a·fire [ə'faiə*] *adv. & pred. adj.* aflame.

a·flame [ə'fleim] *adv. & pred. adj.* on fire; burning: (fig.) *~ with passion.*

a·float [ə'flout] *adv. & pred. adj.* **1.** resting on the surface of the sea, etc. **2.** at sea; on board ship. **3.** (of a business) started. **4.** (of rumours, etc.) spreading about.

a·foot [ə'fut] *adv. & pred. adj.* in progress; taking place: *There's mischief ~. I wish I knew what's ~.*

a·fore [ə'fɔ:*] *adv.* (in combinations), as *a'fore'mentioned, a'fore-said* (i.e. mentioned or named earlier).

a·fraid [ə'freid] *pred. adj.* **1.** frightened; feeling fear: *Are you ~? There's nothing to be ~ of. I was ~ of hurting his feelings* (because I had no wish to do so). Cf. *I was ~ to offend him* (because he might hit me). **2.** *I'm ~ . . .,* polite way of giving information that will not be welcome: *I'm ~ your wife has been taken ill. I can't meet you, I'm ~.*

a·fresh [ə'freʃ] *adv.* again; in a new way.

aft [ɑ:ft] *adv.* at or towards the rear of a ship: *to go aft; aft of the mast.*

af·ter ['ɑ:ftə*] *prep., adv. & conj.* **I.** *prep.* **1.** following in time; later than: *~ dinner; soon ~ 2 o'clock; ~ that,* then, next. **2.** next in order; following: *Put the direct object ~ the verb.* **3.** behind (in place): *Shut the door ~ you as you go out.* **4.** because of: *A~ his rudeness to you, he ought to apologize.* **5.** in spite of: *A~ all (his efforts), he has failed.* **6.** one *~ another, bus ~ bus,* in turn, in succession. **7.** in search of, in pursuit of: *The police are ~ the man who broke into the Bank.* **II. adv.** later in time: *He fell ill on Monday and died a week ~.* **III. conj.** at or during a time later than: *He arrived ~ I had gone home.*

af·ter·math ['ɑːftəmæθ] *n.* (fig.) what follows; the outcome of (an event, etc.): *Misery is often the ~ of war.*

af·ter·noon [ˌɑːftə'nuːn] *n.* period of time between morning and evening.

af·ter·thought ['ɑːftəθɔːt] *n.* thought or explanation that comes to the mind after something has happened.

af·ter·wards ['ɑːftəwədz] *adv.* after; later: *I did not realize what had happened till ~.*

a·gain [ə'gein] *adv.* **1.** once more; a second time: *I did not hear what you said, please say it ~. now and ~,* occasionally. *~ and ~, time and ~,* repeatedly; very often. **2.** as before: *She will soon be well ~.* **3.** *as much ~, as many ~,* twice as much (many). **4.** further; on the other hand: *I did not know him well enough to interfere, and ~, I might have been unwise to do so.*

a·gainst [ə'geinst] *prep.* **1.** *There were twenty votes ~ the proposal and only fourteen in favour of it, so it was abandoned.* **2.** *We rowed hard ~ the current, but made little progress.* **3.** *I have hit my head ~ a wall and hurt myself.* **4.** in preparation for: *Save money ~ a time of need.* **5.** *I left the ladder leaning ~ a wall* (which supported it). *The piano stood ~ the wall* (close to it, alongside).

a·gape [ə'geip] *adv. & pred. adj.* with the mouth wide open (in wonder, surprise, or yawning).

age [eidʒ] *n.* **1.** length of time sb. or sth. has existed. **2.** *come (be) of age,* be (over) 21 years old; *under age,* not yet 21. **3.** long period of time: *the age we live in; the Stone Age; the Middle Ages* (in Europe, from A.D. 600 to 1450). **4.** (colloq.) a long time:

We've been waiting for ages. v.i. & t. (cause to) grow old; begin to look old: *He's ag(e)ing fast.* **aged** [eidʒd] *pred. adj.* of the age of: *a boy aged five.* ['eidʒid] *ppl. adj.* having lived long: *an aged man.* **age·less** *adj.* never fading. **age·long** *adj.* going on for an age (3).

a·gen·cy ['eidʒənsi] *n.* **1.** the business, work, or office of an agent. **2.** action, operation: *the ~ of water on rocks.* **3.** a means: *through the ~ of friends.*

a·gen·da [ə'dʒendə] *n.* (list of) things to be done or discussed (esp. at a meeting).

a·gent ['eidʒənt] *n.* **1.** person who acts for, or who manages the business affairs of, another: *house·~* (who buys, sells, and lets houses for others); *shipping or forwarding ~.* **2.** person or thing producing an effect: *Rain and frost are natural ~s which wear away rocks.*

ag·gra·vate ['ægrəveit] *v.t.* make (sth.) more serious; (colloq.) annoy. **ag·gra·va·tion** [ˌægrə'veiʃən] *n.*

ag·gre·gate ['ægrigit] *n. & adj.* total. *in the ~,* taken as a whole.

ag·gres·sion [ə'greʃən] *n.* act of attacking; an attack made without just cause: *a country guilty of ~ against its neighbours.* **ag·gres·sive** [ə'gresiv] *adj.* fond of attacking; likely to attack without just cause; of or for the purpose of attack: *aggressive weapons.* **ag·gres·sor** *n.* person or country making an aggressive attack.

ag·grieved [ə'griːvd] *adj.* hurt in the feelings; conscious of unjust treatment.

a·ghast [ə'gɑːst] *pred. adj.* filled with terror or surprise.

ag·ile ['ædʒail] *adj.* (of living things) quick-moving; active. **a·gil·i·ty** [ə'dʒiliti] *n.*

ag·i·tate ['ædʒiteit] *v.t. & i.* **1.** (of liquids) move; shake. **2.** disturb; cause anxiety to (a person, his feelings). **3.** *~ for,* keep on trying to get (a change in conditions, etc.): *They ~d for* *higher wages.* **ag·i·ta·tion** [ˌædʒi-'teiʃən] *n.* **ag·i·ta·tor** *n.*

a·glow [ə'glou] *adv. & pred. adj.* showing warmth from exercise or excitement; giving out light and heat.

ag·nos·tic [æg'nɔstik] *n.* one who believes that nothing can be known about God or of anything except material things. *adj.* of this belief.

a·go [ə'gou] *adv.* measured back in past time: *The train went out ten minutes ago.* (Cf. *It is ten minutes since the train went out.*)

a·gog [ə'gɔg] *adv. & pred. adj.* eager; excited; full of interest: *all ~ to know what had happened.*

ag·o·ny ['ægəni] *n.* great pain or suffering (of mind or body). **ag·o·niz·ing** ['ægənaiziŋ] *adj.* causing ~.

a·gree [ə'gri:] *v.i.* 1. say 'yes'; consent. 2. have the same opinion. 3. (of two or more persons) be happy together. 4. ~ *with*, be in harmony with; suit the health of; be good for. **~·a·ble** *adj.* pleasing; ready to ~. **~·ment** *n.*

ag·ri·cul·ture ['ægrikʌltʃə*] *n.* science or practice of farming. **ag·ri·cul·tur·al** [ˌægri'kʌltʃərəl] *adj.*

a·ground [ə'graund] *adv. & pred. adj.* (of ships) touching the bottom in shallow water: *to be (run, go) ~.*

a·gue ['eigju:] *n.* malarial fever.

ah [ɑː], **a·ha** [ə'hɑː] *int.* cry of surprise, pleasure, triumph, etc.

a·head [ə'hed] *adv. & pred. adj.* in front (*of*). (ships) *in line ~*, sailing one in front of another. *look ~*, think of and prepare for the future. *go ~*, make progress; (colloq.) go on.

a·hem [ə'hem] *int.* (usual spelling for) noise made when clearing the throat (uttered to call attention or to give a slight warning).

a·hoy [ə'hɔi] *int.* greeting or warning cry used by seamen.

aid [eid] *v.t. & n.* help; sth. that gives help: *raising funds in aid of the sick; first aid,* treatment given at once to a sick or injured person.

aide-de-camp ['eiddəkɔŋ] *n.* officer who helps a General.

ail [eil] *v.t. & i.* trouble; afflict; be ill: *What ails him?* **ail·ment** *n.* illness; sickness.

aim [eim] *v.t. & i.* 1. point (a gun, etc.) (*at*). 2. send (a blow, object, etc.) (*at* or *towards*). 3. have in view as a purpose or design. *n.* act of aiming; purpose. **aim·less** *adj.* without purpose.

ain't [eint] vulgar form of *am not, is not, are not.*

air [ɛə*]. 1. mixture of gases that surrounds the earth and which we breathe. (special uses only) *by air,* in an aircraft; *air force,* all the aircraft owned by a country for use in war; *on the air,* through or by means of the radio: *What's on the air this evening? air letter,* printed form on which to write a letter for posting by air at a reduced rate. 2. appearance; way of behaving: *an air of importance; a triumphant air; put on (give oneself) airs,* behave unnaturally, trying to appear better or more important than one really is. 3. tune; melody (2). *v.t.* 1. put (clothing, bedding, etc.) into the open air or into a warm place to dry it. 2. let air come into. 3. cause others to know (one's opinions, etc.).

air- *prefix.* **'air·borne** *adj.* (of an aircraft) off the ground; (of troops, etc.) carried by air. **'air-con·di·tioned** *adj.* supplied with pure air at a comfortable temperature. **'air·craft** *n.* (sing. & pl.) flying-machine. **'air·field** *n.* aerodrome. **'air·host·ess** *n.* stewardess on an airliner. **'air·line** *n.* air transport system or company. **'air·lin·er** *n.* aircraft carrying passengers on a regular route. **'air·mail** *n.* mail (to be) carried by air. **'air·man** *n.* man who flies aircraft. **'air·port** *n.* public flying-ground for commercial use, with a custom-house, etc. **'air·screw** *n.* propeller of an aircraft. **'air·tight** *adj.* not allowing air to enter or escape.

air·y ['ɛəri] *adj.* 1. with air entering freely. 2. of or like air; gay; cheerful; not serious. **air·i·ly** *adv.*

aisle [ail] *n.* passage separating blocks of seats (esp. in a church).

aitch [eitʃ] *n.* the letter H.

a·jar [ə'dʒɑː*] *adv.* (of a door) slightly open.

a·kim·bo [ə'kimbou] *adv. with arms* ~, with the hands on the hips and the elbows bent outwards.

a·kin [ə'kin] *pred. adj.* belonging to the same family. ~ *to*, (fig.) like : *Pity is often* ~ *to love.*

al·a·bas·ter ['æləbɑːstə*] *n.* (name for several kinds of) hard white stone used for making ornaments.

a·lac·ri·ty [ə'lækriti] *n.* quick and willing eagerness.

a·larm [ə'lɑːm] *n.* 1. sound or signal giving a warning; apparatus used to make such a sound. ~ *clock,* one with a bell which rings to wake a sleeping person. 2. fear or excitement caused by real or imagined danger. *v.t.* give a warning or feeling of danger to. ~**ing** *adj.* **a·larmed** *adj.*

a·las [ə'læs, ə'lɑːs] *int.* cry of sorrow or anxiety.

al·ba·tross ['ælbətrɔs] *n.* very large white sea-bird common in the Pacific and Southern Oceans.

al·bi·no [æl'biːnou] *n.* animal or human being born without natural colouring matter in skin and hair (which are white).

al·bum ['ælbəm] *n.* book in which a collection of photographs, postage stamps, etc., can be kept.

al·bu·men ['ælbjumen] *n.* (substance found in) white of egg.

al·chem·y ['ælkəmi] *n.* early form of chemistry whose chief object was to find how to change other metals into gold. **al·chem·ist** *n.*

al·co·hol ['ælkəhɔl] *n.* 1. (pure, colourless, intoxicating liquid present in) such drinks as beer, wine, whisky. 2. (chem.) large group of compounds of the same type as the ~ in wine. ~**ic**

[,ælkə'hɔlik] *adj.* containing ~. *n.* person in a diseased condition caused by drinking ~.

al·cove ['ælkouv] *n.* small space in a room formed by a break in the line of a wall, etc., e.g., one occupied by a bed or seat(s).

al·der·man ['ɔːldəmən] *n.* one of the senior members of a city or county council in England.

ale [eil] *n.* pale beer.

a·lert [ə'ləːt] *adj.* watchful; fully awake. *n. on the* ~, on the lookout. *v.t.* put (troops, etc.) on the ~.

al·fres·co [æl'freskou] *adv. & adj.* outdoors; open-air: *an* ~ *lunch* ; *to lunch* ~.

al·ge·bra ['ældʒibrə] *n.* branch of mathematics using signs and letters to represent quantities.

a·li·as ['eiliəs] *n.* name which a person uses instead of (usu. to hide) his real name: *The thief had several* ~*es.*

al·i·bi ['ælibai] *n.* the argument or proof that (when an act, esp. a crime, took place) one was in another place.

a·lien ['eiliən] *adj.* 1. of another race, nation, or country. 2. ~ *to,* out of harmony with : *Cruelty was quite* ~ *to his nature.* *n.* person of another nation or country ; foreigner.

a·lien·ate ['eiliəneit] *v.t.* 1. lose, turn away, the love or affection of. 2. transfer (property) to the ownership of another : *Enemy property is usually* ~*d in time of war.* **a·lien·a·tion** [,eiliə'neiʃən] *n.*

¹**a·light** [ə'lait] *pred. adj.* burning ; lighted up ; (fig.) bright-looking and cheerful : *faces* ~ *with happiness.*

²**a·light** [ə'lait] *v.i.* 1. get down from or off (a bus, train, etc.). 2. come down to rest from the air : *The bird* ~*ed on a branch.*

a·lign [ə'lain] *v.t.* put, bring, three or more things or persons (e.g. soldiers) into a straight line. ~**ment** *n.* arrangement in a straight line : *These desks are in (out of)* ~*ment.*

a·like [ə'laik] *pred. adj.* like one another. *adv.* in the same way.

al·i·men·ta·ry [ˌæli'mentəri] *adj.*
~ *canal*, series of organs and
channels along which food passes
through an animal body.

a·live [ə'laiv] *pred. adj.* 1. living.
2. in force; in existence: *to keep
a claim* ~. 3. ~ *to*, fully aware
of: ~ *to the dangers of a situation.*

al·ka·li ['ælkəlai] *n.* (chem.) one
of a number of substances (e.g.
soda, potash, ammonia) which
combine with acids to form
salts. **al·ka·line** *adj.*

all [ɔ:l] *adj., pron., adv. & n.*
I. *adj.* (with pl. nn.) the whole
number of; (with sing. nn.) the
whole extent or amount of:
*All horses are animals but not all
animals are horses. All five men
were killed in the car crash. He
has lived all his life in France.
All the butter has been eaten.* II.
pron. 1. everything: *He wants
all or nothing.* 2. everyone, the
whole: *All of us want to go.
Take all of it. We all want to go.
Take it all.* 3. *All* (= All that)
I want is rest and peace. 4. (in
prepositional phrases) *above all*,
more than anything else: *Above
all, I want rest.* **after all**, in
spite of our efforts: *After all
we lost the train.* **at all**: *If you
are at all worried* (worried in any
way or in the least degree) *consult a lawyer. I am not at all comfortable* (I am very uncomfortable). **once and for all**, for the
last or the only time: *I tell you
once and for all, you must not
do this thing.* **all in**, exhausted:
I'm all in. **all out**: *We must
go all out* (try our hardest) *to
win.* **all in all**: *All in all* (considering everything) *they did
well. The boy and girl are all in
all to each other* (deeply in love).
not . . . all that: *I'm not as ill
as all that* (as ill as you seem to
think I am). **all together**: *Now,
all together* (united, and at the
same time), *pull!* III. *adv.* 1.
quite; entirely: *They were
dressed all in black.* **all for**:
I'm all for accepting this offer
(anxious to accept it). **all over**,
(a) in every part of: *He has
travelled all over Europe;* (b) at

an end: *You've come too late, the
party is all over.* **all right**,
(a) well; safe: *I'm all right,
thank you;* (b) (in answer to a
suggestion) yes, I agree. IV. *n.*
We lost our all (everything we
possessed) *in the flood.* V. (in
compounds): *an all-round
sportsman,* good at many games,
etc. *an all-time high* (*low*), the
highest (lowest) speed, etc., ever
recorded.

al·lay [ə'lei] *v.t.* make (pain,
trouble, excitement) less.

al·lege [ə'ledʒ] *v.t.* put forward
a statement as a fact; claim sth.
to be true: *to* ~ *that sb. is a
thief; to* ~ *illness as a reason for
not going to work.* **al·le·ga·tion**
[ˌæle'geiʃən] *n.*

al·le·giance [ə'li:dʒəns] *n.* duty,
support, or loyalty that is due
(to a ruler, government, or
country).

al·le·go·ry ['æligəri] *n.* story in
which, e.g., Patience, Purity,
Truth appear as living characters.
al·le·gor·i·cal [ˌæle'gorikl] *adj.*

al·le·lu·ia *int.* = hallelujah.

al·ler·gy ['ælədʒi] *n.* (condition
of) being unusually sensitive to
certain foods, pollen, etc. **al·
ler·gic** [ə'lə:dʒik] *adj.* having
an ~ to sth; (colloq.) having a
dislike of (sth. or sb.).

al·le·vi·ate [ə'li:vieit] *v.t.* make
(pain or suffering) less, or easier
to bear. **al·le·vi·a·tion** [ə,li:vi-
'eiʃən] *n.*

al·ley ['æli] *n.* narrow passage
between buildings. *blind* ~, one
with a closed end.

al·li·ance [ə'laiəns] *n.* union of
persons, parties, or states, for a
special purpose. *in* ~ (*with*),
united (with).

al·lied, see *ally*.

al·li·ga·tor ['æligeitə*] *n.* reptile
like a crocodile, living in lakes
and rivers of America.

al·lit·er·a·tion [ə,litə'reiʃən] *n.*
succession of words in which the
same sound or letter is repeated:
apt ~*'s artful aid; safe and
sound.*

al·lo·cate ['æləkeit] *v.t.* decide to
put (money, supplies, etc.) to
a (given) purpose. **al·lo·ca·tion**

[ˌælə'keiʃən] *n.* **1.** allocating. **2.** sth. ~d (*to* sb., *for* a purpose).

al·lot [ə'lɔt] *v.t.* (*-tt-*). decide a person's share of; make a distribution of. ~'ment *n.* that which is ~ted, esp. (in England) a small area of land rented for growing vegetables, etc.

al·low [ə'lau] *v.t. & i.* **1.** permit; let: *Smoking is not ~ed.* **2.** agree (that a statement is correct). **3.** agree to give (money, time): *to ~ sb. one pound a week for pocket money.* **4.** ~ *for*, take into account; think about and provide for; leave enough space for. ~'ance *n.* amount (of money, etc.)~ed to sb. regularly. *make ~ances for*, not be too severe in judging sb.: *We must make ~ances for his youth.*

al·loy ['æloi] *n.* mixture of two or more metals, esp. of different values. [ə'loi] *v.t.* mix (metals).

al·lude [ə'lu:d] *v.i.* ~ *to*, refer to; speak or write of indirectly; hint at. al·lu·sion [ə'lu:ʒən] *n.*

al·lure [ə'luə*] *v.t.* attract; tempt. ~'ment *n.* that which ~s: *the ~ments of a big town.*

al·lu·vi·al [ə'lu:viəl] *adj.* made up of sand, earth, etc., washed down by rain or rivers: ~ *soil.*

al·ly [ə'lai, 'ælai] *v.t.* **1.** join, unite (for a special purpose): *countries which were allied during the war.* **2.** *be allied* (*to*), be connected (with): *The English language is allied to German.* ['ælai] *n.* person or country allied to another. al·lied ['ælaid] *adj.* joined by agreement, common interest, etc.

al·ma·nac ['ɔ:lmənæk] *n.* book or calendar with notes on coming events (e.g. public holidays), information about the sun, moon, tides, etc.

al·might·y [ɔ:l'maiti] *adj.* powerful beyond measure. *The A~*, God.

al·mond ['ɑ:mənd] *n.* nut or seed of a tree allied to the peach and plum; the tree.

al·most ['ɔ:lmoust] *adv.* **1.** nearly: *He slipped and ~ fell to the ground. Dinner is ~ (will soon be) ready.* **2.** (with *no, none*,

nothing, never): *The speaker said ~ nothing* (a few words of little importance).

alms [ɑ:mz] *n.* money, clothes, food, etc., given to poor people. ~·house *n.* house in which poor people, no longer able to earn money, may live without paying rent.

al·oe ['ælou] *n.* plant with thick, sharp-pointed leaves from which a bitter juice is obtained for medicine.

a·loft [ə'lɔft] *adv. & pred. adj.* high up; overhead; (in a ship) up the mast(s).

a·lone [ə'loun] *adv. & pred. adj.* **1.** without anyone else present; without help: *I sat ~. I went ~. I did the job ~.* **2.** with no other(s) near: *The house stood ~ on the hillside.* **3.** (following a noun or pronoun) and no other: *Smith ~ knows the answer.* **4.** *let sth. or sb. ~*, not touch or interfere with it (him).

a·long [ə'lɔŋ] *prep.* from one end to the other end of; through any part of the length of: *We walked ~ the road. There are trees all ~ the riverside. adv. Run ~, now!* (Go away!) *Come ~!* (Hurry up! Come with me!) ~·side [ə'lɔŋsaid] *adv. & prep.* against the side of (a ship, pier).

a·loof [ə'lu:f] *adv. & pred. adj.* apart; separately. ~·ness [ə'lu:fnis] *n.*

a·loud [ə'laud] *adv.* so as to be heard; not in a whisper.

al·pac·a [æl'pækə] *n.* animal of Peru, larger than a goat, with long soft hair; (cloth made from) its wool: *an ~ coat.*

al·pha ['ælfə] *n.* the first letter (A) in the Greek alphabet.

al·pha·bet ['ælfəbet] *n.* the letters of a language. ~·i·cal [ˌælfə'betikl] *adj.* of the ~: *in ~ical order.*

al·pine ['ælpain] *adj.* of a mountain or mountain-side: ~ *flowers.*

al·read·y [ɔ:l'redi] *adv.* by this (that) time; before now: *The postman has ~ been* (has been ~). *Has the postman been ~* (so soon)? *I've been there ~, so I don't want to go again.*

al·so [ˈɔːlsou] *adv.* too ; besides ; as well.

al·tar [ˈɔː(ː)ltə*] *n.* **1.** raised place (table or platform) on which offerings are made to a god. **2.** (in a Christian church) Communion table : *lead a woman to the ~,* marry her.

al·ter [ˈɔː(ː)ltə*] *v.t. & i.* make or become different ; change. **al·ter·a·tion** [ˌɔː(ː)ltəˈreiʃən] *n.* change ; act of changing.

al·ter·ca·tion [ˌɔː(ː)ltəˈkeiʃən] *n.* quarrelling ; quarrel ; noisy argument.

al·ter·nate [ɔː(ː)lˈtəːnit] *adj.* (of two things or two kinds) in turn, first one and then the other : ~ *laughter and tears* ; (of days, numbers) first and third, second and fourth, etc. : *They met on ~ days* (Monday, Wednesday, etc.). [ˈɔːltəneit] *v.t. & i.* **1.** (of things of two kinds) come, do, put, arrange, by turns ; replace (one thing) with (the other): *Wet days ~d with fine days.* *to ~ kindness with severity.* **2.** (of two things) keep coming, one after the other. *alternating current,* electric current that travels first one way and then the other along a wire. **al·ter·na·tion** [ˌɔː(ː)ltəˈneiʃən] *n.* **al·ter·na·tive** [ɔː(ː)lˈtəːnətiv] *adj.* offering the choice between two things. *n.* second or later choice or possibility that can be made other than one's first choice : *I had to go ; there was no alternative.*

al·though, see *though.*

al·ti·me·ter [ˈæltimiːtə*] *n.* instrument for measuring height above sea level.

al·ti·tude [ˈæltitjuːd] *n.* height (esp. height above sea level).

al·to [ˈæltou] *n.* (person having) singing voice between tenor and treble ; lower of two female voices.

al·to·geth·er [ˌɔːltəˈgeðə*] *adv.* **1.** entirely ; wholly : *I don't ~ agree. It's ~ wrong to ill-treat animals.* **2.** on the whole : *The weather was bad and the trains were crowded ; ~, we wished we had not gone out.*

al·tru·ism [ˈæltruizm] *n.* principle of considering the well-being and happiness of others first. **al·tru·ist** *n.* **al·tru·is·tic** [ˌæltruˈistik] *adj.*

al·u·min·i·um [ˌæljuˈminiəm] *n.* silver-white metal, very light, not affected by the oxygen in the air.

al·ways [ˈɔːlwəz] *adv.* at all times ; with no exception : *The sun ~ rises in the east.* **2.** again and again ; repeatedly : *Why are you ~ finding fault with me?*

am, see *be.*

a·mal·gam [əˈmælgəm] *n.* mixture of mercury and another metal.

a·mal·ga·mate [əˈmælgəmeit] *v.t. & i.* join together ; unite ; mix. **a·mal·ga·ma·tion** [əˌmælgəˈmeiʃən] *n.*

a·mass [əˈmæs] *v.t.* pile up, heap together (esp. riches).

am·a·teur [ˈæmətə:*, ˈæmətjuə*] *n.* person who paints pictures, performs music, plays, etc., for the love of it and not for money ; person playing a game, taking part in sports, etc., without being paid for doing so. (Cf. *professional.*) ~**ish** [ˌæməˈtəːriʃ] *adj.* not expert.

a·maze [əˈmeiz] *v.t.* fill with great surprise or wonder. ~**ment** *n.*

am·bas·sa·dor [æmˈbæsədə*] *n.* political representative of the Government of one country who conducts its business with the Government of another.

am·ber [ˈæmbə*] *n.* clear, hard, yellowish gum used for making ornaments ; its colour.

am·bi·gu·i·ty [ˌæmbiˈgjuiti] *n.* (word, phrase, etc.) having more than one possible meaning. **am·big·u·ous** [æmˈbigjuəs] *adj.* of doubtful meaning or nature. **am·big·u·ous·ly** *adv.*

am·bi·tion [æmˈbiʃən] *n.* **1.** strong desire (to be successful, famous, etc., or to do sth.). **2.** that which one desires to do. **am·bi·tious** [æmˈbiʃəs] *adj.* **am·bi·tious·ly** *adv.*

am·ble [ˈæmbl] *v.i.* (of a horse) move along without hurrying, lifting the two feet on one side together; (of a person) move slowly. *n.* a slow, easy pace.

am·bu·lance ['æmbjuləns] *n.* motor van or carriage for carrying wounded, injured, or sick persons.

am·bush ['æmbuʃ] *n.* (the placing of) men in hiding for making a surprise attack. *v.t. & i.* wait in ~ for; place in ~; attack from a place of ~.

a·me·li·o·rate [ə'mi:liəreit] *v.t. & i.* make or become better. **a·me·li·o·ra·tion** [ə,mi:liə-'reiʃən] *n.*

a·men ['ɑ:'men, 'ei'men] *n. & int.* word used at the end of a prayer or hymn, meaning 'May it be so'.

a·me·na·ble [ə'mi:nəbl] *adj.* ~ to. 1. (of persons) willing to be guided or persuaded by. 2. (of things) able to be tested by: *The case is not ~ to ordinary rules.*

a·mend [ə'mend] *v.t.* 1. improve; correct; make free from faults: *You must ~ your ways.* 2. make changes in (laws, rules). ~·ment *n.* alteration (to laws, etc.). **a·mends** *n.* compensation: *make ~s for sth.*

a·me·ni·ty [ə'mi:niti] *n.* 1. pleasantness: *the ~ of the climate.* 2. sth. that makes life pleasant: *the amenities of town life* (e.g. concerts, public libraries).

am·e·thyst ['æmiθist] *n.* precious stone, purple or violet.

am·ia·ble ['eimjəbl] *adj.* lovable; good-tempered; kind-hearted. **am·ia·bil·i·ty** [,eimjə'biliti] *n.*

am·i·ca·ble ['æmikəbl] *adj.* friendly; peaceful: *to settle a question in an ~ way.* **am·i·ca·bly** *adv.*

a·mid(st) [ə'mid(st)] *prep.* in(to) the middle of. **a·mid·ships** *adv.* Our cabin is amidships.

a·miss [ə'mis] *pred. adj. & adv.* wrong(ly); out of order: *There's not much ~ with it.* take sth. ~, feel offended at sth.

am·i·ty ['æmiti] *n.* friendship; friendly behaviour.

am·me·ter ['æmitə*] *n.* meter for the measurement of electric current in amperes.

am·mo·nia [ə'mounjə] *n.* colour-

less gas with a strong, sharp smell; this gas dissolved in water, used for cleaning.

am·mu·ni·tion [,æmju'niʃən] *n.* military stores, esp. shells, bombs, etc., to be used against the enemy in battle.

am·nes·ty ['æmnəsti] *n.* general pardon of those who have committed crimes (esp. in a rising against a ruler or government).

a·moe·ba [ə'mi:bə] *n.* (pl. -bae [-bi:]). simple form of living matter, always changing shape and too small to be seen except through a microscope. **a·moe·bic** *adj.*

a·mok = *amuck.*

a·mong(st) [ə'mʌŋ(st)] *prep.* 1. surrounded by; in the middle of: *a mother sitting ~ her small children.* (Note the pl. noun. Cf. *between.*) *A~ those present was the Mayor.* 2. (with a superlative) one of: *The Amazon is ~ the longest rivers in the world.* 3. (indicating a sharing of possessions, activity, etc.) *The rich merchant divided his property ~ his four sons. Settle this matter ~ yourselves. There was not a clean face ~ them* (all were dirty).

am·o·rous ['æmərəs] *adj.* easily moved to love; showing love: *~ looks.* ~·ly *adv.*

a·mor·phous [ə'mɔ:fəs] *adj.* having no definite shape or form.

a·mount [ə'maunt] *v.i.* add up (to); be equal (to): *What he said ~ed to little* (i.e. was not important, had not much meaning). *n.* 1. the whole; the total. 2. quantity: *large in ~ but poor in quality.*

am·pere ['æmpɛə*] *n.* unit of measurement of electric current.

am·phib·i·an [æm'fibiən] *n.* animal able to live on land and in water (e.g. a frog). **am·phib·i·ous** *adj.*

am·phi·the·a·tre ['æmfi,θiətə*] *n.* 1. round or oval building with rows of seats rising behind and above one another around an open space used for public games and amusements. 2. part of a theatre with rows of seats similarly arranged in a half-circle.

am·ple ['æmpl] *adj.* **1.** roomy; large-sized; with plenty of space. **2.** more than enough: £10 *will be* ~ *for my needs.* **am·ply** *adv.*

am·pli·fy ['æmplifai] *v.t.* give fuller information, more details, etc., about; increase the strength of (radio signals, etc.). **am·pli·fi·er** *n.* (esp.) apparatus for ~ing sound, esp. in radio. **am·pli·fi·ca·tion** [,æmplifi'keiʃən] *n.*

am·pu·tate ['æmpjuteit] *v.t.* cut off (e.g. an arm or leg). **am·pu·ta·tion** [,æmpju'teiʃən] *n.*

a·muck [ə'mʌk] *adv.* *run* ~, run about wildly with a desire to kill people.

am·u·let ['æmjulet] *n.* sth. worn on the body in the belief or hope that it will protect against harm, disease, or evil powers.

a·muse [ə'mju:z] *v.t.* cause the mind to be pleasantly occupied; make time pass happily; cause smiles or laughter. ~**ment** *n.* being ~d; sth. that ~s.

an, see *a.*

a·nach·ron·ism [ə'nækrənizm] *n.* mistake in dating sth.; sth. out of date now or in a description of past times. **a·nach·ro·nis·tic** [ə,nækrə'nistik] *adj.*

a·nae·mia [ə'ni:mjə] *n.* lack of enough blood; poor condition of the blood, causing paleness. **a·nae·mic** *adj.*

an·aes·the·sia [,ænis'θi:zjə] *n.* the state of being unable to feel (pain, cold, etc.). **an·aes·thet·ic** [,ænis'θetik] *n.* substance causing ~.

an·a·gram ['ænəgræm] *n.* word made by changing the order of the letters in another word (e.g. plum, lump).

a·nal·o·gy [ə'nælədʒi] *n.* **1.** partial likeness to, or agreement with, another thing or between two things: *the* ~ *between the heart and a pump.* **2.** process of reasoning from such partial likeness or agreement. **a·nal·o·gous** [ə'næləgəs] *adj.* that may be compared; similar in use, quality, or relations.

an·a·lyse ['ænəlaiz] *v.t.* examine (sth.) in order to learn what the parts are; separate (sth.) into its parts: *to* ~ *a chemical compound (a sentence, the soil).* **a·na·ly·sis** [ə'nælisis] *n.* process of analysing; statement of the result of this. **an·a·lyst** ['ænəlist] *n.* **an·a·lyt·i·cal** [,ænə'litikl] *adj.*

an·arch·ism ['ænəkizm] *n.* political theory that government is undesirable. **an·arch·ist** *n.* one who favours anarchism. **an·archy** ['ænəki] *n.* absence of government or control; disorder.

a·nath·e·ma [ə'næθimə] *n.* **1.** curse. **2.** sth. that is under a curse; sth. that is detested.

a·nat·o·my [ə'nætəmi] *n.* science of the structure of the animal body; the study of this structure by the cutting up of animal bodies and separation into parts. **an·a·tom·i·cal** [,ænə'tomikl] *adj.* **a·nat·o·mist** [ə'nætəmist] *n.*

an·ces·tor ['ænsistə*] *n.* any one of those persons from whom one's father or mother is descended. **an·ces·tral** [æn'sestrəl] *adj.* **an·ces·try** ['ænsistri] *n.* all one's ~s.

an·chor ['æŋkə*] *n.* iron hook lowered to the sea bottom to keep a ship at rest: *come to* ~, stop sailing and lower the ~; *weigh* ~, pull up the ~; *lie (be, ride) at* ~, be held fast by an ~. *v.t. & i.* lower an ~. ~**age** ['æŋkəridʒ] *n.* place where ships ~.

an·cient ['einʃənt] *adj.* **1.** belonging to times long past; not modern: *the* ~ *Greeks.* **2.** very old: *an* ~*-looking hat.*

an·cil·la·ry [æn'siləri] *adj.* serving or supporting sth. of greater importance: ~ *roads.*

and [ænd, ənd, ən] *conj.* **1.** *Jack* ~ *Jill went up the hill.* **2.** (colloq.) in order to: *If you want it, come and get it.*

an·ec·dote ['ænikdout] *n.* short, usu. amusing, story about some real person or event.

an·e·roid ['ænəroid] *n. & adj.* ~ *barometer,* one that measures air-pressure by the action of air on the lid of a sealed box from which air has been removed.

a·new [ə'nju:] *adv.* again; in a new way.

an·gel ['eindʒəl] *n.* (in Christian belief) messenger from God (usu. shown in pictures as a man in white with wings). ~**·ic** [æn-'dʒelik] *adj.* of ~s; good, pure, and beautiful.

an·ger ['æŋgə*] *n. & v.* (cause) the strong feeling that comes when one is being wronged or treated badly, or sees cruelty or injustice; the feeling that makes people want to fight.

¹an·gle ['æŋgl] *n.* 1. space between two lines or surfaces that meet. 2. (fig.) point of view.

²an·gle ['æŋgl] *v.i.* try to catch fish with a rod, line, hook, and bait. ~ *for*, (fig.) try by roundabout ways to get. **an·gler** *n.*

An·gli·can ['æŋglikən] *n. & adj.* (member) of the Church of England.

an·gli·cize ['æŋglisaiz] *v.t.* make (a word, etc.) English or similar to English.

An·glo- ['æŋglou-] *prefix.* English: ~-*American*, of England and America.

an·gry ['æŋgri] *adj.* (-ier, -iest). 1. filled with anger (*with* sb., *about* sth.). 2. (of the sea) rough; (of a wound) red, inflamed. **an·gri·ly** *adv.*

an·guish ['æŋgwiʃ] *n.* severe suffering (esp. of mind).

an·gu·lar ['æŋgjulə*] *adj.* 1. having angles or sharp corners. 2. (of a person) thin; with bones showing under the skin.

an·i·mal ['æniml] *n.* 1. living thing that can move about and feel, including men, dogs, birds, insects, fish, snakes. 2. ~ other than man. 4. four-footed ~. 4. (attrib.) of the physical, not spiritual, side of man: ~ *needs* (e.g. food); ~ *spirits*, natural light-heartedness.

an·i·mate ['ænimeit] *v.t.* make bright and full of life: *A smile* ~*d her face.* **an·i·ma·ted** *adj.* lively: *an* ~*d discussion.* **an·i·ma·tion** [ˌæni'meiʃən] *n.*

an·i·mos·i·ty [ˌæni'mositi] *n.* active and bitter hate.

an·kle ['æŋkl] *n.* joint and thin part of the human leg just above the foot.

an·nals ['ænlz] *n. pl.* historical records; accounts, year by year, of new knowledge; yearly records of the work of a society.

an·neal [ə'ni:l] *v.t.* cool (metals, glass, etc.) very slowly after heating, in order to toughen.

an·nex [ə'neks] *v.t.* add or join to (a larger thing); take possession of (a country or territory). (also *annexe* ['æneks]) *n.* smaller building added to or built close to an older one: *an* ~ *to a hotel.* ~·**a·tion** [ˌænek'seiʃən] *n.*

an·ni·hi·late [ə'naiəleit] *v.t.* destroy completely. **an·ni·hi·la·tion** [əˌnaiə'leiʃən] *n.*

an·ni·ver·sa·ry [ˌæni'və:səri] *n.* yearly return of the date on which sth. happened: *celebrate a wedding* ~.

an·no·tate ['ænəteit] *v.t.* add notes (explaining difficulties, giving opinions, etc.). **an·no·ta·tion** [ˌænou'teiʃən] *n.*

an·nounce [ə'nauns] *v.t.* make known (news, the name of a guest, speaker); give or be a sign of. **an·noun·cer** *n.* (esp.) one who ~s radio talks, speakers, etc. ~·**ment** *n.*

an·noy [ə'nɔi] *v.t.* give trouble to; make rather angry. ~·**ance** *n.*

an·nu·al ['ænjuəl] *adj.* 1. coming or happening every year. 2. lasting for one year. *n.* 1. plant that lives for one year or less and then dies. 2. book, etc., that appears under the same title but with new contents every year. ~·**ly** *adv.*

an·nu·i·ty [ə'njuiti] *n.* fixed sum of money paid to sb. yearly as income during his lifetime; form of insurance to provide such a regular, annual income.

an·nul [ə'nʌl] *v.t.* (-*ll*-). put an end to (a law, agreement, etc.); (in law) make of no effect.

an·ode ['ænoud] *n.* positive electrode, from which current enters.

a·noint [ə'nɔint] *v.t.* pour or rub oil on (the head or body), esp. at a religious ceremony.

a·nom·a·lous [ə'nɔmələs] *adj.* not normal or regular: '*Be*', '*have*', '*do*' are ~ *verbs.* **a·nom·a·ly** [ə'nɔməli] *n.* ~ thing.

a·non·y·mous [ə'nɔniməs] *adj.* without a name, or with a name which is not made known: *an ~ gift*; *an ~ letter* (i.e. unsigned); (abbreviated *anon.*) *by an ~ author.* **~·ly** *adv.*

an·o·rak ['ænəræk] *n.* waterproof and windproof jacket with hood.

an·oth·er [ə'nʌðə*] *adj. & pron.* different (one), one more of the same kind. *one ~*, each to each: *Tom and Mary give one ~ presents at Christmas.*

an·swer ['ɑ:nsə*] *v.t. & i. & n.* say, write, or do sth. (sth. said, etc.) in return (to): ~ *a question*, *a letter.* ~ *back*, give an impolite ~, esp. when being corrected; ~ *a purpose*, be suitable or sufficient; ~ *for*, (a) be responsible for: *to ~ for a person's honesty*; (b) atone for: ~ *for wrongdoing*; ~ *to*, correspond to: *to ~ to a description.* **~·a·ble** *pred. adj.* responsible.

ant [ænt] *n.* see the picture. **'ant-hill** *n.* pile of earth over an ants' nest; nest of termites.

an·tag·o·nize [æn'tægənaiz] *v.t.* make an enemy of. **an·tag·o·nist** *n.* enemy. **an·tag·o·nis·tic** [æn,tægə'nistik] *adj.* **an·tag·o·nism** [æn'tægənizəm] *n.* feeling of hatred; active opposition.

ant·arc·tic [ænt'ɑ:ktik] *adj.* of or near the South Pole. *n. the A~*, the area round the South Pole; the A~ Ocean.

an·te- ['ænti-] *prefix.* before. **~·date** *v.t.* **1.** put a date on (e.g. a letter, a cheque) earlier than the true one. **2.** come before in time. **~·'na·tal** *adj.* before birth. **~·room** *n.* small room leading to a larger one.

an·te·ced·ent [,ænti'si:dənt] *n.* **1.** (grammar) noun or noun-clause to which a pronoun refers ('*man*' in *the man who came yesterday*). **2.** (pl.) past history (of a person or persons).

an·te·lope ['æntiloup] *n.* deer-like animal.

an·ten·na [æn'tenə] *n.*(pl. *-ae*[-i:]). **1.** one of the two feelers on the head of an insect, etc. **2.** aerial for radio.

an·te·ri·or [æn'tiəriə*] *adj.* coming before in time or position.

An ant   An antelope

an·them ['ænθəm] *n.* piece of sacred music (usu. for choir and organ) sung in churches. *national ~*, the national song or hymn of a country (e.g. 'God Save the Queen').

an·ther ['ænθə*] *n.* part of the stamen containing pollen.

an·thol·o·gy [æn'θɔlədʒi] *n.* collection of poems or pieces of prose by different writers, or a selection from one writer's works.

an·thra·cite ['ænθrəsait] *n.* kind of hard, slow-burning coal.

an·thrax ['ænθræks] *n.* serious disease of sheep and cattle that can be transmitted to man.

an·thro·pol·o·gy [,ænθrə'pɔlədʒi] *n.* science of man, esp. of the beginnings, development, beliefs, and customs of mankind. **an·thro·pol·o·gist** *n.*

an·ti- ['ænti-] *prefix.* against: ~*-aircraft guns.* **an·ti·bi·ot·ic** [,æntibai'ɔtik] *n.* substance (like penicillin), produced by bacteria, that destroys disease germs. **an·ti·cy·clone** [,ænti'saikloun] *n.* area in which atmospheric pressure is high. **an·ti-Se·mite** [,ænti'si:mait] *n.* one who regards the Jews as enemies. **an·ti-Se·mit·ic** [,æntisi'mitik] *adj.* **an·ti·sep·tic** [,ænti'septik] *n. & adj.* (substance for) destroying germs and preventing their growth. **an·ti·so·cial** [,æntisouʃl **adj.** against the principles on which society is based : ∼social behaviour.

an·ti·tox·in [ˌænti'tɔksin] **n.** substance (usu. a serum) able to counteract a disease.

an·ti·ci·pate [æn'tisipeit] **v.t. 1.** do or make use of before the right or natural time : to ∼ one's next month's pay. **2.** do sth. before sb. else does it. **3.** see what needs doing and do it in advance : to ∼ a person's needs. **4.** look forward to. **5.** expect. **an·ti·ci·pa·tion** [ænˌtisi'peiʃən] **n.**

an·ti·cli·max [ˌænti'klaimæks] **n.** sudden fall or change from sth. noble, serious, or important.

an·tics ['æntiks] **n. pl.** playful, jumping movements, often amusing ; light-hearted or care-free behaviour.

an·ti·dote ['æntidout] **n.** medicine to prevent poison or disease from having an effect.

an·ti·pa·thy [æn'tipəθi] **n.** fixed, lasting feeling of dislike.

an·tip·o·des [æn'tipədi:z] **n. pl.** those parts of the world which are on the opposite side ; e.g. in England, New Zealand is in the ∼.

an·ti·qua·ry ['æntikwəri] **n.** one who studies, collects, or sells antiquities. **an·ti·qua·ri·an** [ˌænti'kwɛəriən] **adj.** (of the study) of antiquities. **n.** ∼.

an·ti·quat·ed ['æntikweitid] **adj.** out of date ; no longer in use ; (of a person) having old-fashioned ways and ideas.

an·tique [æn'ti:k] **adj.** belonging to the distant past ; in the style of past times. **n.** furniture, jewellery, etc., of a past period.

an·ti·qui·ty [æn'tikwiti] **n. 1.** the distant past ; early times in history, esp. the times of the Greeks and Romans : Athens was a great city of ∼. **2.** (pl.) buildings, ruins, works of art remaining from very early times : Greek and Roman antiquities.

an·tith·e·sis [æn'tiθisis] **n.** (pl. -es [-i:z]). direct opposite ; the putting together of opposite ideas.

ant·ler ['æntlə*] **n.** branched horn of a stag or other deer ; one of the branches.

Antlers   An anvil

an·to·nym ['æntənim] **n.** word opposite in meaning to another : Hot is the ∼ of cold. (Cf. synonym.)

an·vil ['ænvil] **n.** block of iron on which heated metal is hammered into shape.

an·xi·e·ty [æŋ'zaiəti] **n. 1.** feeling of uncertainty and fear about sth. **2.** eager desire : ∼ for knowledge. **anx·ious** ['æŋk-ʃəs] **adj.** feeling ∼ ; causing ∼ ; strongly wishing (to do or get sth.).

an·y ['eni] **adj., pron. & adv. I. adj. 1.** (in neg. and interr. sentences, clauses of condition, etc., see some, **I.** definition (1)). **2.** We did the work without any difficulty (easily). I have hardly any food in the larder (very little food). See that you do not do any damage (do no damage). Try to prevent any (even one) person from entering. **3.** Come any day (it does not matter which day) you like. **4.** in any case, whatever happens. **II. pron.** see some, **II. III. adv.** (Cf. no, none.) at all ; in any degree. Is your father any better? This pen isn't any use (i.e. it won't write). **an·y·bod·y** ['enibɔdi] **n. 1.** (Cf. somebody, someone.) a person (it does not matter who it is): Anybody who saw the accident is asked to get in touch with the police. **an·y·bod·y else**, see else. **2.** person of importance : Is he anybody, or just a nobody (unknown person)? **an·y·how** ['enihau] **adv. 1.** by one means or another : The door was shut and I could not open it anyhow. **2.** carelessly ; without order : The work was done all anyhow.

The room was left just anyhow (untidy). **an·y·one** ['eniwʌn] *n. & pron.* anybody. **an·y·thing** ['eniθiŋ] *n.* (Cf. *something.*) **1.** *I don't want anything to eat* (I don't want food) *but I should like something to drink.* **2.** *Has anything* (it does not matter what) *happened since I was last here?* **an·y·way** ['eniwei] *adv.* anyhow. **an·y·where** ['eniweə*] *adv.* (Cf. *somewhere.*) **1.** to some place, in a place: *Do you want to go anywhere special* (to one particular place)? *I don't want to live anywhere* (in a place that is) *damp or cold.* **2.** *Put the box down anywhere* (it does not matter where).

a·pace [ə'peis] *adv.* quickly.

a·part [ə'pɑːt] *adv.* **1.** distant: *The two houses are a mile ~.* **2.** to or on one side: *He took me ~ and whispered the secret.* **3.** separate: *I can't get these two pieces ~.* **4.** to pieces.

a·part·heid [ə'pɑːteit] *n.* (South African) policy of separate development of Europeans and non-Europeans.

a·part·ment [ə'pɑːtmənt] *n.* **1.** (pl.) number of rooms, with furniture, rented by the week or month: *to take ~s at the seaside for the summer holidays.* **2.** single room in a house.

ap·a·thy ['æpəθi] *n.* lack of feeling, sympathy, or interest. **ap·a·thet·ic** [ˌæpə'θetik] *adj.* showing ~.

ape [eip] *n.* large, tailless monkey able to walk on two feet (e.g. a gorilla or chimpanzee). *v.t.* imitate foolishly.

ap·er·ture ['æpətjuə*] *n.* opening (usu. small or narrow), esp. one that admits light into a scientific instrument.

a·pex ['eipeks] *n.* top or highest point: *the ~ of a triangle; at the ~ of one's fortunes.*

aph·o·rism ['æfərizm] *n.* short, wise saying; proverb.

a·piece [ə'piːs] *adv.* to, for, or by each one of a group.

a·poc·ry·pha [ə'pɒkrifə] *n.* writings of doubtful authorship, esp. certain books not generally included in the Old Testament. **a·poc·ry·phal** *adj.* false.

a·pol·o·gy [ə'pɒlədʒi] *n.* **1.** statement of regret for doing wrong, making a mistake, or hurting a person's feelings. **2.** explanation or defence (of beliefs, etc.). **a·pol·o·gize** *v.i.* make an ~ (*for*). **a·pol·o·get·ic** [əˌpɒlə'dʒetik] *adj.* offering an ~.

ap·o·plex·y ['æpəpleksi] *n.* loss of power to feel, move, or think, usu. caused by injury to the brain. **ap·o·plec·tic** [ˌæpə'plektik] *adj.* suffering from ~; easily made angry.

a·pos·tle [ə'pɒsl] *n.* **1.** one of the twelve men sent out by Jesus to spread his teaching, also Barnabas and Paul. **2.** leader or teacher of a faith or movement: *an ~ of temperance.* **a·pos·tol·ic** [ˌæpəs'tɒlik] *adj.*

a·pos·tro·phe [ə'pɒstrəfi] *n.* the sign ', as in *can't, John's,* etc.

a·poth·e·ca·ry [ə'pɒθikəri] *n.* (old use) person who prepared and sold medicines and medical goods; chemist.

ap·pal [ə'pɔːl] *v.t.* (-*ll*-). fill with fear or terror; shock.

ap·pa·ra·tus [ˌæpə'reitəs] *n.* (pl. ~*es*). set of tools, instruments, etc., or a machine, assembled for a special purpose; parts of the body with a special function: *the digestive ~.*

ap·par·el [ə'pærəl] *n.* (old use or liter.) dress; clothing.

ap·par·ent [ə'pærənt] *adj.* **1.** clearly seen or understood. **2.** seeming: *The ~ cause, but not the real cause, was. . . . ~ly adv.*

ap·pa·ri·tion [ˌæpə'riʃən] *n.* the coming into view, esp. of a ghost or spirit; ghost.

ap·peal [ə'piːl] *v.i.* **1.** ask earnestly (*for*). **2.** refer a question or decision (*to* a higher authority). **3.** ~ *to*, attract, interest, catch the attention of: *Bright colours ~ to small children.* *n.* **1.** act of ~ing: *an ~ for help.* **2.** interest; attraction; power of attraction.

ap·pear [ə'piə*] *v.i.* **1.** come into view; arrive. **2.** seem. **3.** (of an actor, lecturer, etc.) come before the public. ~**ance** *n.* **1.** the act of ~ing: *put in* (*make*) *an* ~*ance*, show oneself; attend. **2.** that which shows or can be seen; what sth. or sb. seems to be. *judge by* ~*ances*, form an opinion only from the look of things.

ap·pease [ə'pi:z] *v.t.* make calm or quiet: *to* ~ *sb.'s anger*; satisfy (usu. by giving what is wanted): *to* ~ *sb.'s hunger* (*curiosity*). ~**ment** *n.*

ap·pel·la·tion [ˌæpə'leiʃən] *n.* name or title; system of names.

ap·pend [ə'pend] *v.t.* add sth. (to sth.) at the end. ~**age** [ə'pend-idʒ] *n.* sth. added to, fastened to, or forming a natural part of, a larger thing. **ap·pen·dix** [ə'pendiks] *n.* **1.** (pl. *-dices* [-disi:z]) sth. added at the end of a book. **2.** (pl. also *-dixes*) small, narrow tube attached to the large intestine. **ap·pen·di·ci·tis** [əˌpendi'saitis] *n.* disease of the ~*ix*.

ap·per·tain [ˌæpə'tein] *v.i.* ~ *to*, belong to as a right; be part of; be concerned with.

ap·pe·tite ['æpitait] *n.* desire (esp. for food): *to lose one's* ~.

ap·pe·tiz·ing ['æpitaiziŋ] *adj.* pleasing to, exciting, the ~: *an appetizing smell.*

ap·plaud [ə'plɔ:d] *v.t. & i.* **1.** show approval (of) by clapping the hands, cheering, etc. **2.** express approval of. **ap·plause** [ə'plɔ:z] *n.*

ap·ple ['æpl] *n.* (tree having) round fruit as shown here.

Apples

ap·pli·ance [ə'plaiəns] *n.* instrument, tool, or apparatus: *an* ~ *for rescuing sailors from a wrecked ship* (e.g. by firing a rope to them).

ap·pli·ca·ble ['æplikəbl, ə'pli-kəbl] *adj.* fitting; suitable to be applied: *Rule number five is not* ~ *to this case.*

ap·pli·cant ['æplikənt] *n.* person who applies (*for* sth.).

ap·pli·ca·tion [ˌæpli'keiʃən] *n.* **1.** act of applying; request: *an* ~ *for a position*; *on* ~ *to*, by asking for or writing to. **2.** applying (2) of one thing to another: ~*s of ice to the forehead*; the substance so applied. **3.** industry; effort or attention: *to show* ~ *in one's studies.*

ap·plied, see apply.

ap·ply [ə'plai] *v.t. & i.* **1.** ask to be given: *to* ~ (*to sb.*) *for a position.* **2.** put (sth.) into position to serve its purpose: *to* ~ *the brake* (*a bandage*). **3.** put into use: *to* ~ *a rule*; *money to be applied for the benefit of the poor.* **4.** ~ *oneself to*, give one's efforts and attention to. **5.** ~ *to*, concern; have reference to: *What I have said does not* ~ *to you. The rule does not* ~ *to all cases.*

ap·plied *ppl. adj.* put to practical use: *applied art* (e.g. in industry).

ap·point [ə'point] *v.t.* **1.** fix or decide (a time or place *for*): *The time* ~*ed for the meeting was 6 p.m.* **2.** choose and name (sb. to fill a position): ~ *a secretary. A~ Miss Smith as secretary* (*to be secretary*) *of the company.* ~**ment** *n.* **1.** ~ing. **2.** position or office: *to get a good* ~*ment in a business firm.* **3.** arrangement to meet sb.: *to keep* (*break*) *an* ~*ment*, meet (fail to meet) sb. as arranged.

ap·por·tion [ə'pɔ:ʃən] *v.t.* divide (*among*); distribute (*among*); give a share (*to*).

ap·po·si·tion [ˌæpə'ziʃən] *n.* (grammar) the placing of a word or group of words to give additional information. In the sentence: 'Mr Green, our new teacher, has red hair', the words 'our new teacher' are in ~ to 'Mr Green'.

ap·pre·cia·ble [ə'pri:ʃəbl] *adj.* enough to be seen or felt; noticeable: *an* ~ *difference.*

ap·pre·ci·ate [ə'pri:ʃieit] *v.t. & i.* **1.** understand, judge, or enjoy rightly: *to* ~ *poetry.* **2.** put a high value on; be grateful for:

to ~ sb.'s help. **3.** become higher in value: *This land has ~d greatly since 1940.* **ap·pre·ci·a·tion** [əˌpriːʃiˈeiʃən] *n.* **ap·pre·cia·tive** [əˈpriːʃjətiv] *adj.*

ap·pre·hend [ˌæpriˈhend] *v.t.* **1.** understand. **2.** be anxious about; fear. **3.** arrest; seize (a thief, etc.). **ap·pre·hen·sion** [ˌæpriˈhenʃən] *n.* **ap·pre·hen·sive** [ˌæpriˈhensiv] *adj.* feeling afraid: *apprehensive for sb.'s safety (of danger, that sb. will be hurt).*

ap·pren·tice [əˈprentis] *n.* learner of a trade who has agreed to work for a number of years in return for being taught. *v.t.* bind as an ~ : *The boy was ~d to a tailor.*

ap·proach [əˈproutʃ] *v.t. & i.* **1.** come near or nearer to: *The rainy season is ~ing. He is ~ing manhood.* **2.** go to (sb.) with a request or offer: *to ~ one's employer for higher pay.* *n.* **1.** act of ~ing. **2.** way to a place, person, or thing: *The ~es to the palace were all guarded by soldiers.* **3.** thing or state which comes near: *an ~ to comfort and security.*

ap·pro·ba·tion [ˌæprəˈbeiʃən] *n.* approval.

ap·pro·pri·ate [əˈproupriit] *adj.* right or suitable (*for a purpose, to* an occasion). [əˈprouprieit] *v.t.* **1.** take and use (as one's own). **2.** put on one side (*for a special purpose*). **~·ly** *adv.* **ap·pro·pri·a·tion** [əˌprouprieiʃən] *n.*

ap·prov·al [əˈpruːvl] *n.* feeling, showing, or saying, that one is satisfied: *Your plans have my ~. goods on ~,* goods which may be sent back if they are not satisfactory. **ap·prove** [əˈpruːv] *v.t. & i.* give ~ (to).

ap·prox·i·mate [əˈprɔksimit] *adj.* very near (*to*), about right, in quantity, etc. [əˈprɔksimeit] *v.t. & i.* bring or come near (*to*) in value, etc. **ap·prox·i·ma·tion** [əˌprɔksiˈmeiʃən] *n.*

a·pri·cot [ˈeiprikɔt] *n.* (tree with) round, soft orange-yellow fruit with a large seed like a stone; the colour of this fruit when ripe.

A·pril [ˈeiprəl] *n.* the fourth month of the year.

a·pron [ˈeiprən] *n.* **1.** loose garment tied over the front of the body to keep clothes clean; any similar covering. **2.** hard-surfaced ground used for loading and unloading aircraft at an airfield.

a·pro·pos [ˌæprəˈpou] *adv. & pred. adj.* **1.** to the purpose; well suited. **2.** ~ *of,* in connexion with; with reference to.

apt [æpt] *adj.* (*-er, -est*). **1.** quick at learning: *one of my aptest pupils.* **2.** suitable; to the point: *an apt remark.* **3.** apt to, having a tendency to; likely to: *a clever boy but apt to get into mischief.* **apt·ly** *adv.* suitably.

ap·ti·tude [ˈæptitjuːd] *n.* natural tendency; fitness or suitability.

aq·ua·lung [ˈækwəlʌŋ] *n.* cylinder(s) of compressed air strapped to a person's back for use in swimming under water.

An aqualung

a·quar·i·um [əˈkwɛəriəm] *n.* pond or tank for keeping and showing living fish and water plants.

a·quat·ic [əˈkwætik] *adj.* **1.** (of plants, animals, etc.) growing or living in or near water. **2.** (of sports, etc.) taking place in or on water.

aq·ue·duct [ˈækwidʌkt] *n.* artificial channel for supplying water, esp. one made of brick or stone and higher than the surrounding land.

ar·a·ble [ˈærəbl] *adj.* (of land) suitable for ploughing.

ar·bit·er [ˈɑːbitə*] *n.* **1.** = arbitrator. **2.** person with complete control (*of*).

ar·bi·tra·ry [ˈɑːbitrəri] *adj.* based on opinion rather than reason: *an ~ decision;* overbearing or dictatorial.

ar·bi·trate [ˈɑːbitreit] *v.t. & i.* judge between one party and another (usu. at the request of the two parties). **ar·bi·tra·tor**

n. person who ~s. **ar·bi·tra·tion** [ˌɑːbiˈtreiʃən] *n.*

ar·bour [ˈɑːbə*] *n.* shady place among trees, often with a seat.

arc [ɑːk]*n.* part of a circle ; curved line. **'arc-light** *n.* light made by electric current passing across a space between two points (usu. of carbon).

ar·cade [ɑːˈkeid] *n.* covered passage, usu. with arches, esp. one with shops along one or both sides.

An arch

'arch [ɑːtʃ]*n.* **1.** curved structure supporting the weight of what is above it : *a bridge with three ~es.* **2.** curved structure built as an ornament or gateway. **3.** curve like an ~, e.g. the curved underpart of the foot. *v.t. & i.* **1.** form into an ~ : *The cat ~ed its back when it saw the dog.* **2.** be like an ~ : *The rocky cliffs ~ over the river.* **'~·way** *n.* = arch (2).

²arch [ɑːtʃ] *adj.* playfully mischievous : *an ~ smile.*

arch- [ɑːtʃ-] *prefix.* chief. **~·'bi·shop** *n.* chief bishop. **~·'dea·con** *n.* priest (in the Church of England) next below a bishop.

ar·chae·ol·o·gy [ˌɑːkiˈɔlədʒi] *n.* study of (often after digging up) ancient things, esp. of very early times (e.g. ancient cities, buildings, and monuments). **ar·chae·o·log·i·cal** [ˌɑːkiəˈlɔdʒikl] *adj.*

ar·cha·ic [ɑːˈkeiik]*adj.* of ancient times ; (of language) not now used. **ar·cha·ism** [ˈɑːkeiizəm] *n.* (the use of) ~ word(s) or phrase(s).

arch·er [ˈɑːtʃə*] *n.* one who shoots with a bow and arrows. **~·y** *n.* (art of) shooting with bows and arrows.

ar·chi·pel·a·go [ˌɑːkiˈpeləgou] *n.* sea with many islands ; group of small islands.

ar·chi·tect [ˈɑːkitekt] *n.* one who designs buildings and looks after the work of building. **ar·chi·tec·ture** *n.* art and science of building ; design or style of building(s). **ar·chi·tec·tu·ral** [ˌɑːkiˈtektʃərəl] *adj.*

ar·chives [ˈɑːkaivz] *n. pl.* (place for keeping) government or public records ; other historical records.

arc·tic [ˈɑːktik] *adj.* of or near the North Pole : *the A~ Ocean* ; *~ weather.*

ar·dour [ˈɑːdə*] *n.* enthusiasm ; warmth of feeling ; earnestness. **ar·dent** [ˈɑːdənt] *adj.* full of ~.

ar·du·ous [ˈɑːdjuəs] *adj.* (of work) needing and using up much energy.

are, aren't, see *be.*

a·re·a [ˈɛəriə] *n.* **1.** surface measure ; extent of surface : *an ~ of 200 square miles ; a field ten acres in ~.* **2.** part of the earth's surface ; region : *desert ~s of N. Africa.*

a·re·na [əˈriːnə] *n.* central part, for games and fights, of a Roman amphitheatre ; (fig.) any scene of struggle : *the ~ of politics.*

ar·gue [ˈɑːgjuː]*v.i. & t.* **1.** give reasons (for and against plans, opinions, etc.): *~ sb. into (out of) sth.,* urge him to do it (not to do it) by giving reasons. **2.** show ; be a sign of. **3.** maintain one's views in discussion. **ar·gu·ment** [ˈɑːgjumənt] *n.* **ar·gu·men·ta·tive** [ˌɑːgjuˈmentə·tiv] *adj.* fond of arguing ; full of arguments.

ar·id [ˈærid] *adj.* (of soil, land) dry ; barren. **a·rid·i·ty** [əˈridi·ti] *n.*

a·right [əˈrait] *adv.* rightly.

a·rise [əˈraiz] *v.i.* (p.t. *arose* [əˈrouz], p.p. *arisen* [əˈrizn]). **1.** come into existence ; come to notice : *A new difficulty has arisen.* **2.** result *(from)*: *conditions arising from (out of) the war.* **3.** (old use) get up ; stand up.

ar·is·toc·ra·cy [ˌærisˈtɔkrəsi] *n.* **1.** (country or state with) government by persons of the highest rank. **2.** the nobles and other persons of high rank. **3.** any group of the most distinguished persons : *an ~ of intellect.* **ar·is·to·crat** [ˈæristəkræt] *n.* person of high birth or rank; nobleman. **ar·is·to·crat·ic** [ˌærɪstəˈkrætik] *adj.*

a·rith·me·tic [əˈriθmətik] *n.* science of, working with, numbers. **ar·ith·met·i·cal** [ˌæriθˈmetikl] *adj.* of ~. **~al·ly** *adv.* **a·rith·me·ti·cian** [əˌriθməˈtiʃən] *n.*

ark [ɑːk] *n.* (in the Bible) covered ship in which Noah and his family were saved from the flood; *Ark of the Covenant*, box containing the law of Moses.

arm [ɑːm] *n.* **1.** one of the two upper limbs, from the shoulder to the hand. **'arm·pit** *n.* hollow under the arm where it joins the shoulder. **2.** (pl.) weapons. *in arms*, having weapons; ready to fight. *bear arms*, serve in the army. **3.** division of a country's military forces: *the air arm; the infantry arm.* **4.** (pl.) pictorial design used by a noble family, town, etc. *coat of arms*, such a design on a shield, etc. *v.t. & i.* **1.** supply with arms (2) or armour; prepare for war. **2.** supply with anything protective or useful: *armed with patience; armed with answers to all likely questions.* **'arm·chair** *n.* chair with supports for one's arms.

ar·ma·da [ɑːˈmɑːdə] *n.* fleet of warships, esp. the Spanish fleet sent against England in 1588.

ar·ma·ment [ˈɑːməmənt] *n.* **1.** forces (esp. armies, navies, and air forces) made ready for war; preparation for war. **2.** (also pl.) weapons, esp. guns on a warship, tank, etc.

ar·mi·stice [ˈɑːmistis] *n.* agreement during a war or battle to stop fighting for a time.

ar·mour [ˈɑːmə*] *n.* **1.** metal covering for the body, for ships, tanks, etc. **2.** fighting vehicles (esp. tanks) protected with ~. **~·er** *n.* maker of arms (2); man in control of arms (2). **'ar·moured** *ppl. adj.* provided with ~: *~ed cruisers; ~ed divisions.*

ar·my [ˈɑːmi] *n.* **1.** military forces of a country; large body of men trained for fighting on

land. **2.** any large body of organized persons: *the Salvation Army; an ~ of officials.*

a·ro·ma [əˈroumə] *n.* sweet smell. **ar·o·mat·ic** [ˌærəˈmætik] *adj.*

a·rose, see *arise*.

a·round [əˈraund] *adv. & prep.* **1.** on every side; in every direction. **2.** about; round; here and there.

a·rouse [əˈrauz] *v.t.* awaken; stir to activity: *Her jealousy is easily ~d.*

ar·raign [əˈrein] *v.t.* accuse; bring to trial. **~·ment** *n.*

ar·range [əˈreindʒ] *v.t. & i.* **1.** put in order. **2.** make plans (for): *to ~ a marriage; to ~ a date for a meeting.* **3.** come to an agreement about; settle: *to ~ differences.* **~·ment** *n.*

A suit of armour   A coat of arms

ar·rant [ˈærənt] *adj.* in the worst degree: *He's an ~ coward. What ~ nonsense!*

ar·ray [əˈrei] *v.t.* **1.** place (soldiers) in order for battle. **2.** (liter.) dress. *n.* **1.** (liter.) order or arrangement (for fighting): *in battle ~.* **2.** display: *a fine ~ of tools.* **3.** (liter.) dress: *in rich ~.*

ar·rears [əˈriəz] *n. pl.* **1.** overdue payments: *~ of rent (wages).* **2.** work, etc., waiting for attention: *~ of correspondence* (letters waiting to be answered). *in ~ (with)*, behindhand (with).

ar·rest [əˈrest] *v.t.* **1.** put a stop to (a process, etc.): *to ~ the decay of the teeth.* **2.** catch (sb.'s attention). **3.** make (sb.) a prisoner; seize (a thief, etc.) by the authority of the law. *n.* act of ~ing: *to make an ~. under ~*, held as a prisoner. **~·ing** *adj.* likely to catch the attention.

ar·rive [ə'raiv] *v.i.* **1.** reach the end of a journey; come to a place: *to ~ home*; *to ~ at a port*. **2.** *~ at*, agree on, fix, settle: *to ~ at a decision (a price)*. **3.** (of time) come: *The time for action has ~d*. **4.** establish one's reputation; become well known. **ar·ri·val** [ə'raivl] *n.* arriving; sth. or sb. that *~s*.

ar·ro·gant ['ærəgənt] *adj.* behaving in or showing a superior, proud manner. *~·ly adv.* **ar·ro·gance** *n.*

ar·row ['ærou] *n.* **1.** thin, pointed stick to be shot from a bow. **2.** the mark or sign →.

ar·row·root ['ærouru:t] *n.* (plant whose root provides a) starchy food.

ar·se·nal ['a:sənl] *n.* building(s) where weapons and ammunition are made or stored.

ar·se·nic ['a:sənik] *n.* (kind of) strong poison.

ar·son ['a:sn] *n.* act of setting sth. on fire unlawfully.

¹**art** [a:t] *n.* **1.** work of man, not of nature. **2.** study and creation of things which give pleasure to the mind through the senses of feelings: *a work of art* (e.g. a fine painting or piece of sculpture). *The Fine Arts* are drawing, painting, sculpture, and architecture. **3.** activity, esp. branch of learning in which skill and practice are needed as well as knowledge: *Grammar is a science but speaking a language is an art. Bachelor (Master) of Arts,* one who has reached fixed standards at a university in such branches of learning as history, languages, literature. (Cf. *the Sciences*.) **4.** cunning behaviour; tricks. **art·ful** *adj.* cunning. **art·less** *adj.* simple, innocent.

²**art** [a:t] old pres. t. form of *be,* used with *thou*: *Thou art* (= you are).

ar·ter·y ['a:təri] *n.* **1.** (cf. *vein*) one of the tubes carrying blood from the heart. **2.** main road or river; channel for supplies: *an ~ of traffic.* **ar·te·ri·al** [a:'tiəriəl] *adj.* of or like an *~*: *arterial roads.*

ar·te·sian [a:'ti:zjən] *adj. ~ well,* deep, narrow well producing a stream of water at the surface.

ar·ti·cle ['a:tikl] *n.* **1.** particular or separate thing: *~s of clothing*; *toilet ~s.* **2.** piece of writing, complete in itself, in a newspaper or other periodical. **3.** separate clause or item in an agreement. **4.** (grammar) *a, an,* and *the.*

ar·tic·u·late [a:'tikjulit] *adj.* **1.** (of speech) clear. **2.** (of persons) able to put thoughts and feelings into clear speech. [a:'tikjuleit] *v.t. & i.* say, speak, clearly and distinctly. **ar·tic·u·la·tion** [a:ˌtikju'leiʃən] *n.*

ar·ti·fice ['a:tifis] *n.* skill; skilful way of doing sth. **ar·tif·i·cer** [a:'tifisə*] *n.* clever workman, esp. one expert at handwork (usu. with metal).

ar·ti·fi·cial [ˌa:ti'fiʃl] *adj.* made by man in imitation of a natural object: *~ flowers (teeth, silk, light)*; forced, insincere: *~ smiles.*

ar·til·ler·y [a:'tiləri] *n.* big guns, usu. those mounted on wheels; branch of an army managing such guns.

ar·ti·san [ˌa:ti'zæn] *n.* skilled workman in industry or trade.

ar·tist ['a:tist] *n.* person who practises one of the arts, esp. painting; person of great skill. **ar·tis·tic** [a:'tistik] *adj.* of art; showing, done with, good taste; (of a person) fond of, able to enjoy, the arts. **ar·tis·try** *n.* *~*ic skill or quality.

ar·tiste [a:'ti:st] *n.* performer at a concert.

as [æz, əz] *adv. & conj.* **I.** *adv.* (followed by *as,* conj.): *I'm as tall as you* (i.e. we are the same height). **II.** *conj.* **1.** when; while: *I saw him as he fell (as he was falling).* **2.** (expressing reason) since; seeing that: *As he wasn't ready, we went without him.* **3.** (in comparisons): *It's as easy as ABC. This box is twice as heavy as that one.* **4.** in the way in which: *Do as I do.* **5.** like: *He escaped from prison dressed as a woman.* **6.** in the character of: *We think of Napoleon as a soldier and as a statesman.* **7.** (also *such as*): *I should like to visit the ancient cities of Europe, (such) as Athens and Rome.* **8.** *Such women as knew Tom (Those who did know him) admired him.* **9.** *as if, as though: She spoke to me as if (as though) she knew me, but I had never met her before.* **10.** *so as to,* in order to: *He stood up so as to see better.* **11.** *as (so) long as,* (a) on condition that, (b) while.

as·bes·tos [æz-, æs'bestɔs] *n.* soft, fibrous mineral substance which can be woven into a material which will not burn.

as·cend [ə'send] *v.t. & i.* go or come up (a river, mountain, etc.). ~ *the throne,* become king. ~**·an·cy**, ~**·en·cy** [ə'sendənsi] *n.* (position of) having power (*over*): *to gain an ~ancy over one's rivals.* ~**·ant,** ~**·ent** [ə'sendənt] *n. in the ~ant,* rising in importance and influence. **as·cen·sion** [ə'senʃən] *n. the Ascension,* the departure of Jesus from the earth. **as·cent** [ə'sent] *n.* act of ~ing: *the ascent of a mountain;* way up.

as·cer·tain [,æsə'tein] *v.t.* find out.

as·cet·ic [ə'setik] *n. & adj.* (person) leading a severely simple life without ordinary pleasures, usu. for religious reasons.

as·cribe [əs'kraib] *v.t.* **1.** consider as the cause, origin, reason, or author of: *He ~d his failure to bad luck.* **2.** consider as belonging to: *to ~ a wrong meaning to a word.* **as·crip·tion** [əs'kripʃən] *n.*

¹**ash** [æʃ] *n.* **1.** (sing. or pl.) powder left after sth. has burnt: *The village was burnt to ashes.* **2.** (pl.) the remains of burning or cremating.

²**ash** [æʃ] *n.* (wood of) forest-tree with silver-grey bark.

a·shamed [ə'ʃeimd] *pred. adj.* feeling shame.

a·shore [ə'ʃɔ:*] *adv.* to, on, on to, the shore: *to go ~;* (of a ship) *be driven ~ by the gale.*

a·side [ə'said] *adv.* on or to one side; away: *to lay one's book ~; to turn ~ from the main road.* *n.* words spoken ~, esp. (on the stage) words spoken which other persons on the stage are not supposed to hear.

ask [ɑ:sk] *v.t. & i.* **1.** seek an answer to (a question); make request (*for* help, information). **2.** *ask after,* make inquiry about the health, etc., of (sb.). **3.** invite: *We have been asked to dinner with the Joneses tomorrow.* **4.** request (permission): *I must ask to be excused.* **5.** demand (a price): *The owner is asking £10,000 for that house.*

a·skance [əs'kɑ:ns, əs'kæns] *adv. look ~ at,* look at with suspicion or doubt.

a·skew [əs'kju:] *adv. & pred. adj.* out of the straight or usual (level) position: *to hang a picture ~.*

a·slant [ə'slɑ:nt] *adv. & pred. adj.* in a slanting direction.

a·sleep [ə'sli:p] *adv. & pred. adj.* **1.** sleeping. **2.** (of the arms or legs) without feeling (as when under pressure).

as·par·a·gus [əs'pærəgəs] *n.* fern-like plant of which the young shoots are used as a vegetable.

as·pect ['æspekt] *n.* **1.** appearance: *a man of fierce ~.* **2.** direction in which a building, etc., faces: *a house with a southern ~;* (fig.) *to examine the different ~s of a subject* (i.e. from every direction).

as·per·i·ty [æs'periti] *n.* roughness; severity (of weather); harshness (of manner).

as·per·sion [əs'pə:ʃən] *n.* fault-finding or harmful report (about a person).

as·phalt ['æsfælt] *n.* black, sticky, waterproof substance; this substance mixed with gravel or crushed rock to give a smooth surface to roads.

as·phyx·i·ate [əs'fiksieit] *v.t.* make ill or cause death through lack of oxygen in the blood; suffocate. **as·phyx·i·a·tion** [əs-,fiksi'eiʃən] *n.*

as·pire [əs'paiə*] *v.i.* be filled with high ambition (for sth., to do or be sth.): *He ~d to lead his country to prosperity.* **as·pi·ra·tion** [ˌæspə'reiʃən] *n.*

as·pi·rin ['æspərin] *n.* medicine used for colds and to relieve pain; a tablet of this.

ass [æs] *n.* donkey; stupid person: *Don't make such an ass of yourself* (i.e. behave so stupidly).

as·sail [ə'seil] *v.t.* make an attack upon: *to be ~ed with doubts and fears.* ~·ant *n.* attacker.

as·sas·si·nate [ə'sæsineit] *v.t.* kill violently and treacherously, esp. for political reasons. **as·sas·sin** [ə'sæsin] *n.* person who ~s. **as·sas·si·na·tion** [əˌsæsi·'neiʃən] *n.*

as·sault [ə'sɔːlt] *v.t. & n.* (make a) violent and sudden attack (on): *The enemy's positions were taken by ~.*

as·say [ə'sei] *v.t. & n.* (make a) test of the quality or purity of (an ore, metal, etc.).

as·sem·ble [ə'sembl] *v.t. & i.* 1. gather together. 2. put (parts) together. **as·sem·blage** [ə'semblidʒ] *n.* assembling (of things or persons); things or persons which are, or which have been, ~d. **as·sem·bly** [ə'sembli] *n.* number of persons ~d for a special purpose, e.g. a national law-making body. *assembly-line,* (in a factory) line along which parts of machines, motorcars, etc., are put together.

as·sent [ə'sent] *v.i. & n.* (give one's) agreement (to): ~ *to a proposal; to give one's ~ (to …).*

as·sert [ə'sɔːt] *v.t.* 1. declare: *to ~ one's innocence (that one is innocent).* 2. make a claim to: *to ~ one's rights.* ~ *oneself,* draw attention to oneself; insist on one's rights. **as·ser·tion** [ə'sɔːʃən] *n.* **as·ser·tive** [ə'sɔː·tiv] *adj.* declaring firmly; putting forward oneself or one's opinions.

as·sess [ə'ses] *v.t.* decide or fix (value or amount, esp. for payment). ~·ment, **as·ses·sor** *nn.*

as·set ['æset] *n.* 1. (usu. pl.) anything owned by a person, company, etc., which may be used or sold to pay debts. 2. valuable or useful quality or skill: *Is your knowledge of English an ~ to you?*

as·sid·u·ous [ə'sidjuəs] *adj.* hard-working; persevering. **as·si·du·i·ty** [ˌæsi'djuiti] *n.*

as·sign [ə'sain] *v.t.* 1. give (to sb.) for use and enjoyment, or as a share or part in a distribution (of work, duty, etc.). 2. name, put forward (as a time, place, reason, purpose, etc.). ~·ment *n.*

as·sim·i·late [ə'simileit] *v.t. & i.* 1. (cause food to) become part of the body: *food that ~s easily; to ~ one's food.* 2. (cause people to) become part of another social group or state: *The U.S.A. has ~d people from many European countries.* 3. (of ideas, etc.) take into the mind. **as·sim·i·la·tion** [əˌsimi'leiʃən] *n.*

as·sist [ə'sist] *v.t. & i.* help. ~·ance *n.* ~·ant *n.*

as·siz·es [ə'saiziz] *n. pl.* (English law) meetings held regularly in each county for trying civil and criminal cases before the High Court judges.

as·so·ci·ate [ə'souʃieit] *v.t. & i.* 1. join (persons or things, one with another); connect (people, ideas) in one's mind: *to ~ oneself with others in business; to ~ Egypt with the Nile.* 2. (~ *with*) be often in the company of. [ə'souʃiit] *n. & adj.* (person) who ~s with another or others (in work or business). **as·so·ci·a·tion** [əˌsousi'eiʃən] *n.* associating; organized body of people with the same interests, e.g. Automobile Association, National Farmers' Association. *Association football,* played by teams of eleven with a round ball which must not be handled except by the goalkeeper.

as·sort·ed [ə'sɔːtid] *ppl. adj.* of various sorts; mixed. *ill-(well·) ~,* badly (well) suited to one another. **as·sort·ment** [ə'sɔːtmənt] *n.* (esp.) ~ collection of differing examples of one class or several classes.

as·suage [ə'sweidʒ] *v.t.* make (pain, suffering, grief) less.

as·sume [ə'sju:m] *v.t.* **1.** suppose; take as true: *to ~ the truth of a story (that a story is true)*. **2.** take up; undertake: *to ~ the direction of a business; to ~ office*. **3.** take to oneself: *to ~ a look of innocence; to ~ a new name*. **as·sum·ing** *ppl. adj.* claiming greater importance than one has the right to.

as·sump·tion [ə'sʌmpʃən] *n.* the act of assuming; sth. ~d.

as·sure [ə'ʃuə*] *v.t.* **1.** tell with confidence: *I ~ you there is no danger. He ~d me of his desire to help.* **2.** make certain: *Does hard work always ~ success? He has an ~d income.* **3.** make (sb.) feel safe or certain of sth.: *Nothing would ~ her that flying was safe.* **4.** insure (esp. one's life). **as·sured·ly** [ə'ʃuəridli] *adv.* without doubt. **as·sur·ance** [ə'ʃuərəns] *n.* **1.** assuring or being ~d. **2.** feeling of confidence about oneself, one's abilities, etc.; trust in one's own powers. **3.** (life) insurance.

as·ter·isk ['æstərisk] *n.* the mark *.

a·stern [ə'stə:n] *adv.* in, at, or towards the stern of a ship; behind; backwards: *fall ~, get behind other ships; full speed ~.*

asth·ma ['æsmə] *n.* chest disease causing difficulty in breathing. **asth·mat·ic** [æs'mætik] *adj.*

a·stig·ma·tism [ə'stigmətizəm] *n.* defect in the eye which prevents a person from seeing clearly.

a·stir [ə'stə:*] *adv. & pred. adj.* **1.** in motion; in an excited state: *The whole village was ~.* **2.** up; out of bed: *You're ~ early this morning.*

as·ton·ish [əs'tɔniʃ] *v.t.* surprise greatly. **~ment** *n.*

as·tound [əs'taund] *v.t.* overcome with surprise.

a·stray [ə'strei] *adv. & pred. adj.* away from, off, the right path, esp. as in wrongdoing: *to lead boys ~.*

a·stride [ə'straid] *adv. & prep.* with one leg on each side of: *sitting ~ his father's knee.*

as·trin·gent [əs'trindʒənt] *n.* (kind of) substance that shrinks the skin, etc., and checks bleeding. *adj.* of or like an ~.

as·trol·o·gy [əs'trɔlədʒi] *n.* art of observing the positions of the stars and telling how they influence human affairs. **as·trol·o·ger** *n.*

as·tro·naut ['æstrounɔ:t] *n.* traveller through space.

as·tron·o·my [əs'trɔnəmi] *n.* science of the sun, moon, planets, and stars. **as·tron·o·mer** *n.* **as·tro·nom·i·cal** [ˌæs-trə'nɔmikl] *adj.*

as·tute [əs'tju:t] *adj.* **1.** quick at seeing how to gain an advantage. **2.** shrewd. ~**ly** *adv.* ~**ness** *n.*

a·sun·der [ə'sʌndə*] *adv.* **1.** (of two or more things) apart. **2.** into pieces: *tear (sth.) ~.*

a·sy·lum [ə'sailəm] *n.* place of rest, peace, and safety; (formerly) place where mad people were cared for.

at [æt, ət] *prep.* **1.** (Place and Direction) (a) *She was educated at Oxford (but She lives in Spain, New York).* (b) *The child is looking at his mother. Aim at the target. Don't throw stones at the dog.* (c) *Try to guess at the meaning.* (d) *We saw the elephants at a distance (far off).* **2.** (Time and Order) (a) *at 2 o'clock; at sunset.* (b) *She left school at the age of 15. They couldn't see us at first. They're gone at last!* (c) *At times* (frequently) *she has violent headaches.* **3.** (Activity) *He must be disturbed at work (at his prayers). Are you good at games?* **4.** (State) *The country was at war then. Do it at leisure.* **5.** (Manner) *The horses went off at a gallop.* **6.** (Rate, Degree, Value) *The ship is steaming at full speed. Tomatoes are selling at four shillings per pound (at a loss). Tomatoes are at their best this month.* **7.** (Cause) *I was surprised at his knowledge of* *mathematics. They were impatient at the delay.*

ate, see *eat.*

a·the·ism ['eiθiizəm] *n.* belief that there is no God. **a·the·ist** *n.*

ath·let·ic [æθ'letik] *adj.* 1. of outdoor games and sports. 2. fond of these. **ath·let·ics** *n. pl.* outdoor sports, esp. competitions in running, jumping, etc. **ath·lete** ['æθli:t] *n.* person trained for and competing in races, etc.

at·las ['ætləs] *n.* book of maps.

at·mos·phere ['ætməsfiə*] *n.* 1. mixture of gases surrounding the earth. 2. the air in a particular place. 3. feeling (of good, evil, etc.) which the mind receives from a place, conditions, etc.: *an ~ of peace and calm.* **at·mos·pher·ic** [ˌætmos'ferik] *adj. atmospheric conditions* (i.e. the weather). **at·mos·pher·ics** *n. pl.* disturbances in radio reception caused by electrical effects in the ~.

at·oll ['ætol] *n.* island of coral, often with a belt of coral enclosing part of the sea.

at·om ['ætəm] *n.* 1. smallest unit of matter not divisible by chemical means: *Two ~s of hydrogen combine with one ~ of oxygen to form a molecule of water.* 2. small bit: *blow to ~s,* destroy completely (by explosion). *There's not an ~ of truth in what he said.* **a·tom·ic** [ə'tomik] *adj. ~ic bomb,* one which is exploded by releasing energy in ~s.

a·tone [ə'toun] *v.i.* give satisfaction, make repayment, *for* wrongdoing. **~ment** *n.*

a·tro·cious [ə'trouʃəs] *adj.* wicked; very bad. **a·troc·i·ty** [ə'trositi] *n.* cruel or wicked act.

at·ro·phy ['ætrəfi] *n.* wasting away (of a part of the body or a moral quality): *~ of the lungs (the conscience).* *v.t. & i.* suffer or cause ~.

at·tach [ə'tætʃ] *v.t.* 1. fasten or join (*to*): *to ~ a document to a letter.* 2. connect with; consider to have: *Do you ~ much importance to what he says?* 3.

belong to; go with: *the advantages ~ing to the position of President.* 4. *be ~ed to,* be fond of: *She is deeply ~ed to her young brother.* **~ment** *n.* ~ing or being ~ed; (esp.) sth. ~ed (to a larger thing). **at·ta·ché** [ə'tæʃei] *n.* person ~ed to the staff of an ambassador: *a naval (press) ~é.*

at·tack [ə'tæk] *n.* 1. violent attempt to hurt, overcome, or defeat. 2. adverse criticism in speech or writing. *v.t. & i.* make an ~ upon. **~er** *n.* person who ~s.

at·tain [ə'tein] *v.t. & i.* 1. reach; arrive at. 2. succeed in doing or getting: *to ~ knowledge (one's object).* **~a·ble** *adj.* **~ment** *n.* sth. ~ed, esp. skill in some branch of knowledge: *a man of great ~ments; easy of ~ment, easy to ~.*

at·tempt [ə'tempt] *n. & v.t.* try.

at·tend [ə'tend] *v.i. & t.* 1. give thought and care (*to*). 2. be present at; go to: *to ~ church (school).* 3. be waiting (on sb.); serve, look after (sb.): *Which doctor is ~ing you?* 4. accompany: *a method ~ed by great difficulties.* **~ance** *n.* ~ing or being ~ed upon; number of persons present: *a large ~ance at church.* **~ant** *n.* 1. servant: employee; companion. 2. one who ~s (a meeting, etc.). *adj.* accompanying: *old age and its ~ant evils* (e.g. deafness).

at·ten·tion [ə'tenʃən] *n.* 1. act of attending (1) to: *to pay ~ to sth. or sb.* 2. (often *pl.*) kind or polite acts. 3. drill position in which a man stands straight and still: *to come to (stand at) ~.* **at·ten·tive** [ə'tentiv] *adj.* giving, paying, ~.

at·test [ə'test] *v.t. & i.* 1. give a clear sign or proof of. 2. say that one is certain of the truth or reality of.

at·tic ['ætik] *n.* room within the roof of a house.

at·tire [ə'taiə*] *v.t. & n.* (liter. & poet.) dress.

at·ti·tude ['ætitju:d] *n.* 1. manner of placing or holding the body: *in a threatening* ~. **2.** way of feeling, thinking or behaving: *an ~ of hostility; to maintain a firm ~.*

at·tor·ney [ə'tə:ni] *n.* person with legal authority to act for another in business or law: *power of ~.*

at·tract [ə'trækt] *v.t.* **1.** pull towards (by unseen force): *A magnet ~s iron.* **2.** arouse interest and pleasure in; get the attention of: *Bright colours ~ babies. He shouted to ~ attention.* **at·trac·tion** [ə'trækʃən] *n.* (esp.) that which ~s. **at·trac·tive** *adj.* pleasing.

at·tri·bute ['ætribju:t] *n.* quality, sign, or mark which is characteristic of sth. or sb.: *Mercy is an ~ of God. Speech is an ~ of man but not of animals. The crown is an ~ of kingship.* [ə'tribju:t] *v.t.* ~ *to*, consider as belonging to, caused by or owing to (sth. or sb.): *to ~ one's failure to bad luck; to ~ wisdom to one's teachers.* **at·trib·u·ta·ble** [ə'tribjutəbl] *adj.* that can be ~d (*to*). **at·tri·bu·tion** [ˌætri'bju:ʃən] *n.* **at·trib·u·tive** [ə'tribjutiv] *adj.* (in grammar) naming an ~. In '*the old man*', *old* is an attributive adjective.

au·burn ['ɔ:bən] *adj.* reddish-brown (usu. of hair).

auc·tion ['ɔ:kʃən] *n.* public sale at which goods are sold to the person(s) offering the highest price. *v.t.* sell by ~. ~·**eer** [ˌɔ:kʃə'niə*] *n.* person who conducts an ~.

au·da·cious [ɔ:'deiʃəs] *adj.* bold; impudent. **au·dac·i·ty** [ɔ:'dæsiti] *n.*

au·di·ble ['ɔ:dibl] *adj.* loud enough to be heard. **au·di·bly** *adv.* **au·di·bil·i·ty** [ˌɔ:di'biliti] *n.* capacity for being heard.

au·di·ence ['ɔ:diəns] *n.* **1.** group of people listening. **2.** people within hearing (e.g. people all over the country listening to a radio talk). **3.** interview given by a ruler: *be granted an ~ by the King.*

au·dit ['ɔ:dit] *v.t.* examine (business accounts, etc.) to see that they are in order. *n.* ex-

amination of this kind. **au·di·tor** *n.* person who conducts ~s.

au·di·tion [ɔ:'diʃən] *n.* a hearing, esp. to test the voice of a speaker, singer, etc. **au·di·to·ri·um** [ˌɔ:di'tɔ:riəm] *n.* building, or part of a building, in which an audience sits.

aught [ɔ:t] *n.* (liter.) anything.

aug·ment [ɔ:g'ment] *v.t. & i.* make or become larger.

au·gur ['ɔ:gə*] *n.* (in ancient Rome) religious official who foretold the future from signs. *v.t. & i.* foretell; be a sign (of). **au·gu·ry** ['ɔ:gjuri] *n.* the art or practice of foretelling the future by reading signs; sign or omen.

au·gust [ɔ:'gʌst] *adj.* kinglike; causing feelings of respect or awe.

Au·gust ['ɔ:gəst] *n.* the eighth month of the year.

auld lang syne ['ɔ:ldlæŋ'sain] (Scot.; name of song). times long ago; the days of long ago.

aunt [ɑ:nt] *n.* sister of one's father or mother; wife of one's uncle.

au·ra ['ɔ:rə] *n.* mystic atmosphere (3) surrounding a holy person or object.

aus·pic·es ['ɔ:spisiz] *n. pl. under the ~ of,* helped and favoured by.

aus·pi·cious [ɔ:s'piʃəs] *adj.* showing signs, giving promise, of future success; favourable.

aus·tere [ɔ:s'tiə*] *adj.* **1.** (of a person, his behaviour) severely moral and strict. **2.** (of a way of living, of things) simple and plain; without ornament. **aus·ter·i·ty** [ɔ:s'teriti] *n.*

au·then·tic [ɔ:'θentik] *adj.* genuine; known to be true. **au·then·ti·cate** [ɔ:'θentikeit] *v.t.* prove to be ~.

au·thor ['ɔ:θə*] *n.* **1.** writer of a book, play, etc. **2.** one who begins or creates sth. ~·**ess** *n.* woman~. ~·**ship** *n.* being an ~; origin of a book, etc.: *a book of unknown ~ship.*

au·thor·i·ty [ɔ:'θɔriti] *n.* **1.** power or right to give orders. **2.** person(s) having such power or right. **3.** person with special knowledge; book, etc., supplying information, proof etc.: *He is an ~ on old coins.* **au·thor·i·ta·tive** [ɔ:'θɔritətiv] *adj.* having or showing ~. **au·thor·ize** ['ɔ:θəraiz] *v.t.* give ~ to (sb.) (*for sth., to do sth.*). **au·thor·i·za·tion** [ˌɔ:θərai'zeiʃən] *n.*

au·to·bi·og·ra·phy [ˌɔ:toubai-'ɔgrəfi] *n.* story of a person's life written by himself.

au·to·crat ['ɔ:təkræt] *n.* person who rules with unlimited power; person who does things (e.g. in the home) without considering the wishes of others. ~**ic** [ˌɔ:tə'krætik] *adj.* **au·toc·ra·cy** [ˌɔ:'tɔkrəsi] *n.* (country with a) government by an ~.

au·to·graph ['ɔ:təgrɑ:f] *n.* person's own handwriting, esp. his signature.

au·to·mat·ic [ˌɔ:tə'mætik] *adj.* **1.** self-acting; self-moving; (of a machine) able to work or be worked without attention. **2.** (of acts) done without thought: *Breathing is* ~. **au·to·mat·i·cal·ly** *adv.*

au·to·ma·tion [ˌɔ:tə'meiʃən] *n.* use of methods and machines to make industrial processes as automatic as possible.

au·to·mo·bile ['ɔ:təmə͵bi:l, ˌɔ:tə-'moubi:l] *n.* (esp. U.S.A.) motor-car.

au·ton·o·my [ɔ:'tɔnəmi] *n.* right of self-government; self-governing group or state. **au·ton·o·mous** [ɔ:'tɔnəməs] *adj.*

au·top·sy ['ɔ:tɔpsi] *n.* examination of a dead body (by cutting it open) to find the cause of death.

au·tumn ['ɔ:təm] *n.* season of the year between summer and winter. **au·tum·nal** [ɔ:'tʌmnəl] *adj.*

aux·il·ia·ry [ɔ:g'ziljəri] *adj.* supporting; helpful: ~ *troops; an* verb (e.g. *is* in *He is working* or *has* in *He has gone*). *n.* sth. or sb. that gives help.

a·vail [ə'veil] *v.t. & i. & n.* (be of) help or use (to). ~ *oneself of,* make use of; *of no* ~, useless. ~**·a·ble** *adj.* that may be used, obtained. **a·vail·a·bil·i·ty** [ə͵veilə'biliti] *n.*

av·a·lanche ['ævəlɑ:nʃ] *n.* loosened mass of snow, stones, etc., falling down a mountain-side; (fig.) *an* ~ *of letters.*

av·a·rice ['ævəris] *n.* greed (for possessions). **av·a·ri·cious** [ˌævə'riʃəs] *adj.* **av·a·ri·cious·ly** *adv.*

a·venge [ə'vendʒ] *v.t.* get or take vengeance for: *to* ~ *an insult; to* ~ *oneself; to be* ~*d.*

av·e·nue ['ævinju:] *n.* **1.** road with trees on each side. **2.** (esp. U.S.A.) wide street. **3.** (fig.) way of reaching: *the best* ~ *to success.*

a·ver [ə'və:*] *v.t.* (-*rr*-). state (that sth. is true).

av·er·age ['ævəridʒ] *n.* **1.** the result of adding several quantities together and dividing the total by the number of quantities. **2.** the standard or level usually found: *above* (*below, up to*) *the* ~, better than (not so good as, equal to) this level. *adj.* **1.** found by making an ~: *the* ~ *age of the class.* **2.** of the usual or ordinary standard: *men of* ~ *ability. v.t.* find the ~ of; come to as an ~.

a·verse [ə'və:s] *adj.* opposed, disinclined (*to, from*). **a·ver·sion** [ə'və:ʃən] *n.* strong dislike (*from, to*); sth. or sb. that is disliked strongly.

a·vert [ə'və:t] *v.t.* **1.** turn away (one's eyes, etc.) (*from*). **2.** avoid: *to* ~ *suspicion* (*an accident*).

a·vi·a·ry ['eivjəri] *n.* place for keeping birds.

a·vi·a·tion [ˌeivi'eiʃən] *n.* (art and science of) flying. **a·vi·a·tor** ['eivieitə*] *n.* airman.

av·id ['ævid] *adj.* eager; greedy: ~ *for fame.* ~**·i·ty** [ə'viditi] *n.*

av·o·ca·tion [ˌævou'keiʃən] *n.* person's ordinary business or occupation.

a·void [ə'void] *v.t.* keep away from; get or keep out of the way of: *to* ~ *danger; to* ~ *being seen.* ~**·a·ble** *adj.* ~**·ance** *n.*

av·oir·du·pois [ˌævədə'pɔiz] *n.* British system of weights in which 1 pound = 16 ounces; used for all goods except gold, silver, jewels, and medicines.

a·vow [ə'vau] v.t. confess; declare openly: to ~ one's faults. ~·al n. confession. ~·ed·ly [ə'vauidli] adv. by confession.

a·wait [ə'weit] v.t. be waiting for.

a·wake [ə'weik] v.t. & i. (p.t. & p.p. awoke [ə'wouk] or ~d [ə'weikt]) = wake. ~ to, become aware of, realize. pred. adj. Is he ~ or asleep? Is he ~ to (does he realize) the danger? a·wak·en v.t. & i. = awake. a·wak·en·ing n. becoming aware (esp. of sth. unpleasant): It was a sad awakening to find that his friend had deceived him.

a·ward [ə'wɔ:d] n. 1. decision made by a judge. 2. sth. given as the result of such a decision, esp. a prize in a competition. v.t. give as an ~: to be ~ed the first prize.

a·ware [ə'wɛə*] pred. adj. having knowledge or realization (of sth., that . . .). ~·ness n.

a·wash [ə'wɔʃ] pred. adj. washed over, flooded, by waves: The ship's deck was ~. rocks ~ at high tide.

a·way [ə'wei] adv. 1. to or at a distance: The sea is two miles ~. Keep the baby ~ from the fire. Take these books ~ (remove them). 2. continuously; vigorously: The children are working ~ at their lessons. 3. (indicating loss or disappearance): The water has all boiled ~. The sound of music died ~. 4. right ~, straight ~, at once. far and ~, very much: He is far and ~ the best runner.

awe [ɔ:] n. respect combined with fear and reverence. v.t. fill with awe. 'awe·some adj. causing awe.

aw·ful ['ɔ:ful] adj. 1. dreadful. 2. (colloq.) very bad; very great. ~·ly adv.

a·while [ə'wail] adv. for a short time.

awk·ward ['ɔ:kwəd] adj. 1. not well designed for use: an ~ tool to hold. 2. (of a person, animal, etc.) clumsy; having little skill: Sea-animals are usually ~ on land. 3. causing or experiencing trouble or inconvenience: an ~ question; an ~ time for a meeting; the ~ age (i.e. before young people become self-confident). ~·ly adv. ~·ness n.

awl [ɔ:l] n. pointed tool for making holes, esp. in leather.

An awl   An axe

awn·ing ['ɔ:niŋ] n. canvas overhead covering against sun or rain.

awoke, see awake.

a·wry [ə'rai] adv. & pred. adj. crooked(ly); wrong(ly): Our plans have gone ~.

axe [æks] n. see the picture.

ax·i·om ['æksiəm] n. statement accepted as true without proof or argument. ax·i·o·mat·ic [,æksiə'mætik] adj.

ax·is ['æksis] n. (pl. axes ['æksi:z]). 1. imaginary line around which a turning object spins: The world turns on its ~ once in twenty-four hours. 2. line that divides a regular figure symmetrically (e.g. the diameter of a circle).

ax·le ['æksl] n. rod around which a wheel turns; rod passing through the centres of a pair of wheels.

ay(e) [ai] int. yes. the ayes, the persons in favour (of a proposal).

az·ure ['eiʒə*, 'æʒə*] adj. & n. sky-blue.

B

baa [bɑ:] n. the cry of a sheep or a lamb.

bab·ble ['bæbl] v.i. & t. make sounds like a baby; talk foolishly; tell a secret.

babe [beib] n. (liter.) baby.

ba·bel ['beibl] n. noise, esp. of many voices.

ba·boon [bə'bu:n] n. large monkey with dog-like face, in Africa and S. Asia.

ba·by ['beibi] *n.* child during the first few years of its life; infant. '~·**hood** *n.* time when one is a ~. '~·**sit·ter** *n.* person looking after a baby while its parents are out of the house for a time.

bach·e·lor ['bætʃələ*] *n.* 1. unmarried man. 2. (attrib.) suitable for an unmarried person: ~ *flats.* 3. person who has taken a first university degree: *B~ of Arts.*

ba·cil·lus [bə'siləs] *n.* (pl. *bacilli* [bə'silai]). name given to many kinds of bacteria, harmful or harmless.

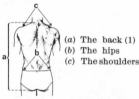

(a) The back (1)
(b) The hips
(c) The shoulders

back [bæk] *n.* 1. see the picture. 2. the part of sth. that is behind or farthest from the front of it, or less used or less important. '~·**bone** *n.* line of jointed bones in an animal's back; (fig.) stability. *adv.* to or at the rear: *The policemen held the crowd ~. Sit ~ in your chair and rest comfortably.* 2. in(to) an earlier position: *Put the book ~ on the shelf when you have finished with it.* 3. *If he hits you, don't hit him ~* (in return). *v.t. & i.* 1. go, cause to go, ~: *to ~ a car into a garage.* 2. support: *to ~ sb. up; to ~ a plan* (claim). ~ *down,* give up a claim, etc.; ~ *out of* (*a promise or undertaking*), escape or withdraw from; ~ *a horse,* bet money on its winning a race. ~·**er** *n.* supporter; person who bets. '~·**fire** *n.* (noise caused by) explosion of gas in an engine in the wrong place. *v.i.* explode in this way. '~·**ground** *n.* 1. that part of a view farthest away. *keep* (*stay*) *in the* ~*ground,* stay where one will not be noticed. 2. surface (e.g. of a

dress material) on which there is a design, etc. 3. past experiences or education or environment. ~·**ing** *n.* support; group of supporters; substance covering the ~ of sth. '~·**log** *n.* arrears of work to be done, orders to be executed, etc. '~·**slide** *v.i.* (of a person) fall away from goodness into bad old ways. '~·**ward** *adj.* (esp.) having made less than the usual or normal progress: *a* ~*ward child* (*country*). '~·**wards** *adv.* in the direction opposite to what is usual: *to look* (*walk*) ~*wards.* '~·**wash** *n.* movement of water going away in waves; rush of water behind a steamer. '~·**water** *n.* 1. part of a river not reached by its current. 2. place, condition of mind, untouched by events, progress, etc. '~·**woods** *n. pl.* wild forest land far from towns.

ba·con ['beikən] *n.* salted or smoked meat from the sides or back of a pig.

bac·te·ri·a [bæk'tiəriə] *n. pl.* simplest and smallest forms of plant life existing in air, water, soil and in living and dead creatures, necessary for making plant food, sometimes a cause of disease. **bac·te·ri·ol·o·gy** [,bæktiəri'ɔlədʒi] *n.*

bad [bæd] *adj.* (*worse, worst*). 1. wicked; evil; immoral. *bad language,* swearing. 2. unpleasant: *What bad weather we're having!* 3. severe; serious: *She has had a bad illness* (*accident*). 4. incorrect; of poor quality: *That is a bad translation.* 5. (of food, drink) unfit for use: *These eggs have gone bad.* 6. *bad for,* hurtful to: *Small print is bad for the eyes.* 7. painful; diseased: *I've got a bad leg* (*several bad teeth*). 8. too bad (colloq.), unfortunate: *It's too bad that she can't dance.* **n.** *go to the bad,* become completely immoral; become ruined. **bad·ly** *adv.* (*worse, worst*). 1. in a bad (4) manner. 2. severely; seriously. 3. by much: *We were badly beaten at tennis.* 4. (with *want, need*) very much. 5. *badly* *off*, without much money, poor. **~'ness** *n.*

bade, see *bid*.

badge [bædʒ] *n.* sth. worn (usu. a small design on cloth or made of metal) to show rank, position, etc.: *a policeman's* ~; (fig.) *Chains are the ~ of slavery.*

badg·er ['bædʒə*] *n.* small, grey animal living in holes in the ground. *v.t.* worry (sb.) with troublesome requests.

baf·fle ['bæfl] *v.t.* prevent (from doing sth.); cause to be uncertain: *a question that ~d everybody; a baffling problem.*

bag [bæg] *n.* see the picture. *v.t. & i.* (*-gg-*). put in a bag; hang loosely, or in folds: *trousers bagging at the knees.* **bag·gy** *adj.*

'bag·pipes *n. pl.* wind instrument supplied with air stored in a bag, held under the arm.

Bags

bag·gage ['bægidʒ] *n.* traveller's belongings; army supplies, e.g. tents and bedding. ~ *animals* (for carrying ~).

bah [bɑ:] *int.* used to show contempt.

¹bail [beil] *v.t.* ~ (*sb.*) *out*, secure freedom of (an accused person till called for trial, by lodging with a law court money which will not be given back if he does not attend). *n.* the money so demanded by the court: *go ~ for sb., ~ him out; out on ~,* free after payment of ~.

²bail [beil] *n.* (cricket) one of the two cross-pieces of wood placed on the stumps.

³bail [beil] *v.t. & i.* throw water out of a boat with buckets, etc.: *to ~ the boat out; to ~ water out.*

bail·iff ['beilif] *n.* **1.** law officer who helps a sheriff. **2.** agent or manager for a landowner.

bairn [bɛən] *n.* (Scot.) child.

bait [beit] *n.* food, or imitation of food, put on a hook or in a net, trap, etc., to catch fish,

birds, or animals. *v.t.* put ~ on (a hook, etc.); worry or annoy in order to make angry.

baize [beiz] *n.* thick (usu. coarse) woollen cloth used as a covering (e.g. green ~ on billiard-tables).

bake [beik] *v.t. & i.* **1.** cook, be cooked, by dry heat in an oven: *to ~ bread (cakes).* **2.** make or become hard by heating: *ground ~d hard by the sun.* **bak·er** *n.* **'bak·er·y** *n.* place where bread is ~d for many people.

bal·ance ['bæləns] *n.* **1.** apparatus for weighing. *in the ~,* (of a result or outcome) still uncertain. **2.** condition of being steady; condition existing when opposing amounts, forces, etc., are equal. *keep (lose) one's ~,* remain (fail to remain) upright; *~ of power,* condition in which no one country or group of countries is much stronger than another. **3.** difference between two columns of an account (money received and money paid out, etc.). *~-sheet,* statement of the details of an account, with the difference between credit and debts; *strike a ~,* find this difference; *~ of trade,* difference between values of exports and imports. **4.** apparatus in a watch, regulating the speed. **5.** *the balance* (colloq.), what is left. *v.t. & i.* **1.** keep, put, be, in a state of ~; *to ~ (oneself) on one foot.* **2.** weigh or compare two objects, plans, possibilities, etc. **3.** (accounts) compare debts and credit and record the sum needed to make them equal.

A balance (1)   A balcony (1)

bal·co·ny ['bælkəni] *n.* **1.** platform (with a wall or rail) built on an outside wall of a building, reached from upstairs room(s). **2.** rows of seats (in a hall, theatre, etc.) above floor level and (usu.) rising one above the other.

bald [bɔːld] *adj.* **1.** having no or not much hair, not many feathers, trees, leaves, etc. **2.** (fig.) plain; without ornament: *a ~ statement of facts*. **~'ly** *adv.* **~'ness** *n.*

bale [beil] *n.* **1.** bundle of goods packed (usu. in canvas) ready for transport. **2.** sometimes used for ³bail. *v.i.* ~ *out*, jump from an aircraft with a parachute.

balk [bɔːk] *v.t. & i.* **1.** prevent; hinder; purposely get in the way of: *~ed in one's plans*; *to ~ a person of his purpose.* **2.** (of a horse) refuse to go forward. *n.* beam (1).

¹ball [bɔːl] *n.* **1.** see the picture. **2.** see *bearing*. **'ball-point, 'ball-point 'pen** *n.* pen that writes with a tiny ball rotating at the end of a narrow tube of ink.

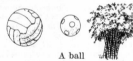

A ball

A football   Bamboo

²ball [bɔːl] *n.* social gathering for dancing.

bal·lad ['bæləd] *n.* kind of simple song or poem, esp. one that tells a story.

bal·last ['bæləst] *n.* heavy material (e.g. sand, stones) loaded into a ship to keep it steady: *in ~, carrying ~ only.* *v.t.* put ~ in.

bal·let ['bælei] *n.* **1.** musical play, without dialogue or singing, performed by a group of dancers in a theatre. **2.** the dancers. **3.** *the ~,* this kind of stage dancing as an art.

bal·loon [bə'luːn] *n.* bag filled with gas lighter than air, esp. one sent up into the sky.

bal·lot ['bælət] *n.* secret voting (by marking a paper); paper used in voting. *v.i.* give a secret vote.

balm [bɑːm] *n.* **1.** sweet-smelling oil or ointment. **2.** (fig.) that which gives peace of mind. **~'y** *adj.* sweet-smelling; (of air) soft and warm.

bal·sam ['bɔːlsəm] *n.* **1.** balm (1). **2.** flowering plant grown in gardens.

bal·us·ter ['bæləstə*] *n.* upright support for a handrail. **bal·us·trade** [,bæləs'treid] *n.* row of ~s.

Banisters

A balustrade

bam·boo [bæm'buː] *n.* tall plant with hard, hollow stems, of the grass family; its wood.

ban [bæn] *v.t.* (-nn-). order that sth. must not be done, said, etc. *n.* order which bans sth.: *under a ban.*

ba·nal [bə'nɑːl, 'beinl, 'bænl] *adj.* commonplace; uninteresting: *~ remarks.*

ba·na·na [bə'nɑːnə] *n.* long, yellow-skinned fruit; the tree (palm) on which it grows.

band [bænd] *n.* **1.** flat, thin strip of material, esp. for fastening things together or for fastening round an object to strengthen it: *~s of iron round a barrel.* **2.** flat, thin strip of material on an article of clothing: *A shirt has a neck~ and two wrist~s.* **3.** strip or line, different from the rest in colour or design, on sth.: *a white plate with a blue ~ round the rim.* **4.** group of persons acting together under a leader and with a common purpose: *a ~ of robbers;* (esp.) group of persons playing music together: *the regimental ~.* *v.t. & i.* (of people) join, bring, or come together: *to ~ together against a common enemy.* **ban·dage** ['bændidʒ] *n.* ~ or strip of material for tying round a wound or injury. *v.t.* put a ~age on: *a ~aged leg.* **'~stand**

n. outdoor stage or platform for a ~ of musicians.

ban·dit ['bændit] *n.* armed robber (e.g. one of a band (4) living in forests or mountains, or robbing banks, etc., in towns).

¹ban·dy ['bændi] *v.t.* pass or send backwards and forwards; exchange (words, blows): *have one's name bandied about*, be a subject for gossip.

²ban·dy ['bændi] *adj.* (of the legs) bending outwards at the knees.

bane [bein] *n.* (cause of) ruin, destruction, or trouble.

bang [bæŋ] *n.* violent blow; loud, sudden noise: *a ~ on the head*; *to shut the door with a ~*. *v.t. & i.* make a ~; give a ~ to: *~ one's fist on the table*; *~ a door. The door ~ed.*

ban·gle ['bæŋgl] *n.* ornamental metal band worn round the arm or ankle.

ban·ish ['bæniʃ] *v.t.* send (sb.) away, esp. out of the country, as a punishment; (fig.) put away from or out of (the mind): *to ~ cares (fear, etc.).* ~**'ment** *n.*

ban·is·ters ['bænistəz] *n. pl.* handrail and upright supports (balusters) at the side of stairs. See the picture at *baluster*.

ban·jo ['bændʒou] *n.* (pl. *-os, -oes*). musical instrument played by pulling at the strings with fingers.

A banjo

¹bank [bæŋk] *n.* **1.** sloping land or earth, strip of raised land, often a division between fields: *low ~s of earth between rice-fields.* **2.** land along each side of a river, canal, etc. **3.** large, usu. flat mass (of sand, snow, clouds, etc.), esp. one formed by wind or water. *v.t. & i.* **1.** make or form into a ~ or ~s: *The snow has ~ed up.* *to ~ up a fire* (i.e. make a ~ of coal for slow burning). **2.** (of an aircraft) go with one side higher than the other (e.g. when turning).

²bank [bæŋk] *n.* establishment for keeping money and valuables

safely, for lending and exchanging money. ~ *clerk*, one who works in a ~. ~ *holiday*, any weekday observed (by law) as a public holiday. ~*-note*, piece of paper money. *v.t.* place, keep (money, etc.) in a ~. ~**'er** *n.* person managing the business of a ~.

bank·rupt ['bæŋkrʌpt] *n.* person judged by a law court to be unable to pay his debts in full. *adj.* unable to pay debts in full. ~ *in (of)*, completely without: *~ of ideas.* ~**'cy** ['bæŋkrʌptsi] *n.*

ban·ner ['bænə*] *n.* flag or announcement carried on one or two poles.

banns [bænz] *n. pl.* public announcement in church that two persons are to be married: *call (put up) the ~; have one's ~ called.*

ban·quet ['bæŋkwit] *n.* feast, esp. official dinner for a special event.

ban·tam ['bæntəm] *n.* small-sized variety of hen or cock, esp. the cock (which is a fighter); boxer between 112 and 118 lb.

ban·ter ['bæntə*] *v.t. & i.* tease in a playful way (by joking talk). *n.* good-humoured teasing.

bap·tism ['bæptizəm] *n.* ceremony of sprinkling (a person) with, or bathing (him) in, water, in accepting (him) as a member of the Christian Church and giving (him) a Christian name; (fig.) first experience: *a soldier's ~ of fire.* **bap·tis·mal** [bæp'tizməl] *adj.* of ~. **bap·tize** [bæp'taiz] *v.t.* give ~ to.

bar [bɑ:*] *n.* **1.** long, stiff piece (of metal, wood, soap, etc.): *an iron bar.* **2.** rod or rail across a door, etc., to prevent its being opened or to stop passage: *to fasten a gate with a bar; behind prison bars.* **3.** sth. which stops or hinders progress: *Poor health may be a bar to success in life.* **4.** bank of mud or sand at the mouth of a river or entrance to a harbour. **5.** narrow band: *a bar of silver across the sky.* **6.** place in a law court where the prisoner stands before the judge. **7.** *the Bar*, the profession of barrister; all those lawyers who are barristers: *called to the Bar.* **8.** (room in a hotel, etc., with a) counter where drinks are sold and drunk. **9.** (music) upright line separating divisions equal in time-value; one such division with its notes. *v.t.* (p.t. & p.p. *barred*). **1.** put or have a bar or bars across; prevent by means of a bar: *to bar the doors and windows; to bar the way to success; a sky barred with clouds.* **2.** prohibit. *prep.* (also '**bar·ring**) except. '**bar·maid,** '**bar·man** *n.* woman, man, serving drinks at a bar (8).

barb [bɑːb] *n.* back-curving point of an arrow, spear, fishhook, etc. **barbed** *adj.* having ~s: *~ed wire.*

bar·ba·ri·an [bɑːˈbɛəriən] *n.* uncivilized person. **bar·bar·ic** [bɑːˈbærik] *adj.* in the manner of ~s; very cruel. **bar·ba·rism** [ˈbɑːbərizəm] *n.* state of being uncivilized. **bar·bar·i·ty** [bɑːˈbæriti] *n.* (esp.) savage cruelty. **bar·ba·rous** [ˈbɑːbərəs] *adj.* uncivilized; cruel and savage.

bar·be·cue [ˈbɑːbikjuː] *n.* framework for roasting meat (esp. a whole animal); open-air party at which this is done.

bar·ber [ˈbɑːbə*] *n.* one whose business is shaving and haircutting.

bard [bɑːd] *n.* (liter.) poet; singer of old songs.

bare [bɛə*] *adj.* **1.** not covered or clothed or decorated: *~-headed; riding a horse ~back* (i.e. without a saddle); *~ floors.* **2.** mere; minimum: *to earn a ~ living; a ~ possibility. v.t.* make ~; uncover. **~·ly** *adv.* **1.** in a ~ way: *a ~ly furnished room.* **2.** hardly; scarcely: *We have ~ly time to catch that train.*

bar·gain [ˈbɑːgin] *n.* **1.** agreement about buying and selling, or exchanging. **2.** sth. got as the result of a ~. *into the ~,* in addition. **3.** sth. bought, sold or offered, cheap. *v.i.* try to make a ~. *~ for,* expect; be

ready for: *That's more than I ~ed for.*

barge [bɑːdʒ] *n.* flat-bottomed boat for carrying goods on rivers, canals, etc. *v.i.* (colloq.) bump heavily (*into, against*). **bar·gee** [bɑːˈdʒiː] *n.* man in charge of a ~.

bar·i·tone [ˈbæritoun] *n.* male voice between tenor and bass.

¹bark [bɑːk] *n.* outer covering or skin on the trunk and branches of trees. *v.t.* take the ~ off.

²bark [bɑːk] *n. & v.i.* (make the) cry of a dog or fox.

³bark, barque [bɑːk] *n.* **1.** sailing-ship with three or four masts. **2.** (liter.) any kind of ship.

bar·ley [ˈbɑːli] *n.* grass-like plant; its grain, used as food and for making beer.

barn [bɑːn] *n.* farm building for storing grain, hay, etc.

bar·na·cle [ˈbɑːnəkl] *n.* small sea-animal or shell-fish which fastens itself to rocks, the bottoms of ships, etc.

ba·rom·e·ter [bəˈrɒmitə*] *n.* instrument for measuring the pressure of the atmosphere, used to get information about the weather, etc.

bar·on [ˈbærən] *n.* **1.** (in Gt. Brit.) nobleman of the lowest rank (called Lord X, not Baron X). **2.** (in other countries) nobleman (called Baron X). *~·ess n.* wife of a ~. **bar·o·ny** *n.* rank of a ~. **ba·ro·ni·al** [bəˈrouniəl] *adj.* of a ~.

bar·on·et [ˈbærənit] *n.* (in Gt. Brit.) person not a noble but higher in rank than a knight, with the title *Sir* (Sir J—— J——, Bart.), which is passed from father to son.

ba·roque [bəˈrouk, -ˈrɔk] *adj. & n.* florid and highly ornamented (style of art and architecture).

bar·rack [ˈbærək] *n.* large building for soldiers to live in (usu. pl., several such buildings); any building of plain or ugly appearance.

bar·rage [ˈbærɑːʒ, bæˈrɑːʒ] *n.* **1.** dam across a river. **2.** heavy continuous gunfire. **3.** balloon ~, anti-aircraft barrier of balloons, moored with steel cables; ~ balloon, one of these.

barred, see bar, v.

bar·rel ['bærəl] n. **1.** round container, as illustrated. **2.** metal tube of a gun, revolver, etc. '~-ˌor·gan n. instrument from which music may be produced by turning a handle which causes a cylinder to revolve.

A barrel (1)   A gun-barrel

bar·ren ['bærən] adj. **1.** (of land) not fertile enough to produce crops. **2.** (of plants, trees) not producing fruit or seeds. **3.** (of animals) unable to have young. **4.** (fig.) without value, result, or interest: an attempt ~ of results; a ~ subject.

bar·ri·cade [ˌbærɪ'keɪd] v.t. & n. (put up a) barrier of objects (e.g. carts, barrels) across or in front of sth. as a defence or obstruction.

bar·ri·er ['bærɪə*] n. sth. (e.g. a wall, rail, fence, etc.) which prevents, hinders, or controls progress and movement: Show your ticket at the ~ (in a railway station, etc.). (fig.) Poor health may be a ~ to success in life.

bar·ring prep. see bar, prep.

bar·ris·ter ['bærɪstə*] n. lawyer who has the right to speak and argue in higher courts; advocate.

¹**bar·row** ['bærou] n. small cart with one or two wheels, usu. pushed or pulled by hand.

²**bar·row** ['bærou] n. bank or heap of earth made in ancient times over a burial place.

bar·ter ['bɑːtə*] v.t. & n. (make an) exchange of goods or property without using money.

¹**base** [beɪs] n. **1.** lowest part of anything, esp. the part on which

sth. is supported: the ~ of a pillar (pyramid). **2.** place at which armed forces, expeditions, etc., keep stores: a naval ~. **3.** starting- (or finishing-) point for players in some games. **4.** substance into which other things are mixed. v.t. build or place (upon). ~·less adj. without cause or foundation. ~·ment n. part of a building partly or wholly below ground level.

²**base** [beɪs] adj. **1.** (of persons, their behaviour) selfish; dishonourable. **2.** (of thoughts and desires) mean; dishonourable. **3.** (of metals) low in value.

base·ball ['beɪsbɔːl] n. American game played with a bat and ball on a field with four ¹bases (3).

ba·ses, pl. of ¹base and basis.

bash [bæʃ] v.t. (colloq.) strike violently: to ~ the lid of a box in.

bash·ful ['bæʃful] adj. shy.

ba·sic ['beɪsɪk] adj. of, at, or forming a ¹base (1): ~ principles.

ba·sin ['beɪsn] n. **1.** round, open, wide bowl for holding liquids: Wash your hands in the ~. **2.** hollow place (e.g. below a waterfall) where water collects. **3.** deep harbour almost surrounded by land. **4.** area of land from which water is carried away by a river: the Thames ~.

ba·sis ['beɪsɪs] n. (pl. bases ['beɪsiːz]). **1.** = ¹base (1). **2.** facts, etc., on which an argument is built up.

bask [bɑːsk] v.i. enjoy warmth and light: ~ing in the sunshine.

bas·ket ['bɑːskɪt] n. container, usu. made of materials which have been twisted or woven. '~-ball n. game in which a ball is thrown into ~s or through ~-shaped nets which are the goals.

bass [beɪs] adj. low in tone; deep-sounding. n. singer, instrument, able to give out the lowest notes: ~-clarinet.

bas·soon [bə'suːn] n. musical instrument made of wood and giving low notes when blown.

bas·tard ['bɑːstəd] n. child whose parents were not married at the time it was born.

baste [beist] *v.t.* pour melted fat over (roasting meat, etc.).

bas·tion ['bæstiən] *n.* (often five-sided) part of a protecting wall or fortification which stands out from the rest.

¹**bat** [bæt] *n.* shaped wooden stick used for hitting the ball, esp. in cricket and baseball. *v.i.* use a bat. '**bats·man, bat·ter** *n.*

²**bat** [bæt] *n.* small, winged, four-footed, mouse-like animal that flies at night.

batch [bætʃ] *n.* number of loaves, cakes, etc., baked together; number of things or persons receiving attention as a group : *a ~ of recruits for the army (letters to be answered).*

ba·ted ['beitid] *ppl. adj. with ~ breath*, with the voice lowered to a whisper (in fear, anxiety, etc.).

bath [bɑːθ, pl. bɑːðz] *n.* **1.** see the picture; washing of the whole body. **2.** (pl.) building where ~s may be taken and where there may also be a large tank for swimming. (Cf. *pool*.) ~**·room** ['bɑːθrum] *n.* room in which to have a ~ (1). *v.t. & i.* have a ~; give a ~ to.

A bath (1)

bathe [beið] *v.t. & i.* **1.** go into the sea, a river, lake, etc., for swimming or pleasure. **2.** wash; apply water to (a wound, etc.). **3.** make wet, etc., all over : *~d in sweat (sunshine).* *n.* act of bathing, esp. to swim in the sea, etc. '**bath·er** *n.* bath·ing ['beiðiŋ] *n.* act or practice of swimming, etc. '**sun-,bath·ing** *n.* sitting or lying with the body exposed to sunlight.

ba·thos ['beiθɔs] *n.* sudden change (in writing or speech) from what is deeply moving to sth. foolish or unimportant.

bat·man ['bætmən] *n.* servant of an army officer.

bat·on ['bætən] *n.* **1.** policeman's thick stick (used as a weapon).

2. short, thin stick waved by the conductor of a band or orchestra to beat (3) time.

bat·tal·ion [bə'tæljən] *n.* army unit of about 1,000 soldiers.

bat·ten ['bætn] *n.* long, narrow piece of wood, esp. one used to keep others in place, or to which boards are nailed. *v.t.* make secure with ~s : *to ~ down the hatches.*

¹**bat·ter** ['bætə*] *v.t. & i.* strike violently (*at* or *on*) : *to ~ a door down; a ship ~ed to pieces by heavy waves.*

²**bat·ter** ['bætə*] *n.* beaten mixture of flour, eggs, milk, etc., for cooking.

bat·ter·y ['bætəri] *n.* **1.** army unit of big guns, with the men who work them. **2.** group of connected cells from which electric current will flow.

bat·tle ['bætl] *n.* fight between armies, etc.; any struggle. *v.i.* fight or struggle (*with, against*).

bat·tle·ment ['bætlmənt] *n.* (usu. pl.) wall round the flat roof of a tower or castle with openings for shooting through.

bau·ble ['bɔːbl] *n.* pretty and pleasing ornament of little value.

baulk = balk.

baux·ite ['bɔːksait] *n.* clay-like substance from which aluminium is obtained.

bawl [bɔːl] *v.t. & i.* shout; cry loudly : *to ~ out a curse.*

¹**bay** [bei] *n.* part of a sea within a deep curve of the coastline : *the Bay of Biscay.*

²**bay** [bei] *n.* division of a wall or building between columns or pillars; recess, sometimes with a window (called a *bay window*), built out beyond the line of an outside wall.

³**bay** [bei] *v.i. & n.* (give) the bark of large dogs, esp. when hunting. *at bay*, forced to turn and attack; *hold (keep) at bay*, keep (attackers) off.

bay·o·net ['beiənit] *v.t. & n.* (kill or wound with a) short stabbing knife fixed to the end of a rifle.

ba·zaar [bə'zɑː*] *n.* **1.** shopping centre (in Eastern countries). **2.**

shop selling cheap fancy goods.
3. sale to raise money for charity.

be [bi:, bi] I. *v.i.* (pres. t., *am* [æm], *is* [iz], *are* [ɑ:*]; p.t., *was* [wɔz, wəz], *were* [wə:*, wə*]; contracted forms, *I'm* [aim], *he's* [hi:z], *she's* [ʃi:z], *it's* [its], *we're* [wiə*], *you're* [juə*], *they're* [ˈðeiə*]; neg., *isn't* [ˈiznt], *aren't* [ɑ:nt], *wasn't* [ˈwɔznt], *weren't* [wə:nt]; *am I not* is contracted to *aren't I* [ɑ:nt ai]; pres. p., *being* [ˈbi:iŋ]; p.p., *been* [bi:n, bin]). **1.** (joining subject & predicate): *The world is round. This is a dictionary. Who is that? It is I.* (colloq.: *It's me* (*him, her.*).) *Aren't you ready yet? It's time you were* (i.e. were ready). **2.** (indicating time, measure, cost, etc.): *Today is Monday. When is your birthday? The station is a mile away. This book is five shillings. He is ten years old.* **3.** become: *What are you going to be when you grow up?* **4.** happen; take place: *When is the wedding to be?* II. *aux. v.* **1.** (used with a pres. p. to form the progressive or continuous tenses): *They are* (*were*) *reading. I shall be seeing him soon. What have you been doing this week?* **2.** (used with a p.p. to form the passive voice): *He was killed in the war. Where were they made? He is to be pitied.* **3.** (to indicate intention): *They are to be married in May.* III. *full v.* **1.** exist; occur; live (often with *there*): *God is. There is a God. There were six of us. He is the greatest man that ever was. For there to be life there must be air and water.* **2.** remain; continue: *Don't be long. Let them be* (i.e. don't move them, disturb them, etc.). **3.** (with adverbials): *The books are on the table. He is off to London.* **4.** go; come (esp. the p.p. *been*): *I have been to see* (have paid a visit to) *my uncle. Have you ever been to Cairo? Has the postman been* (i.e. called) *yet?* See also *being*, n.

be- *prefix.* all over: *beflagged*

(with flags out everywhere); *begrimed* (dirty all over).

beach [bi:tʃ] *n.* sandy or stony stretch at the edge of the sea covered at high tide. *v.t.* run (a boat) on to a ~.

bea·con [ˈbi:kən] *n.* **1.** warning light at sea, on the coast, on mountains (for aircraft). **2.** (formerly) fire lit on a hill-top as a signal. **3.** post, bearing a flashing lamp, erected at each end of a street-crossing for pedestrians.

bead [bi:d] *n.* **1.** small ball of wood, glass, etc., with a hole through, for threading it on a string or wire. **2.** small drop (of sweat, etc.). ~**y** *adj.* (of eyes) small and bright.

bea·dle [ˈbi:dl] *n.* (old use) parish officer who helped the priest.

beak [bi:k] *n.* hard, horny part of a bird's mouth.

beak·er [ˈbi:kə*] *n.* open glass vessel with a lip, esp. as used in chemical laboratories.

beam [bi:m] *n.* **1.** long, thick, and usu. heavy bar of wood, esp. one used in building (e.g. to support the roof) or in ships (to support decks). **2.** breadth, side, of a ship: *on the port* ~; *on her* ~-*ends* (i.e. on her side); *broad in the* ~. **3.** cross-bar of a balance (1). **4.** ray of light (*sun*~); directed radio wave; (fig.) smile. *v.t.* send out light and warmth; look happy: *a* ~*ing face*.

bean [bi:n] *n.* plant with seeds growing in pods, used as food; the seed; ~-like seeds of other plants (e.g. coffee ~s).

A bean-pod   A bear

¹bear [beə*] *v.t. & i.* (p.t. *bore* [bɔ:*], p.p. *borne* [bɔ:n]). **1.** carry, hold up (weight). **2.** produce; give birth to: *trees that* ~ *fruit.* (See also *born.*) **3.** provide; show (signs, evidence, likeness, love, etc.): to ~ *marks* (*traces, etc., of*); to ~ *sb. company* (i.e. go with him); to ~ *sb. out* (i.e. agree that he is right); to ~ *out what sb. says* (i.e. support his statement). **4.** stand up to; endure (suffering, etc.): *She can't ~ being laughed at.* **5.** turn; direct towards; press on: ~ *to the right*; *bring one's energies to ~ on*; *to ~ down on the enemy.* **6.** ~ *up*, be brave against (misfortune, etc.); ~ *on*, influence; refer to; ~ *in mind*, remember; ~ *oneself* (*well, etc.*), behave; ~ *arms*, have weapons and be able to use them; ~ *a hand*, help. ~'**a·ble** *adj.* that can be borne or endured. ~'**er** *n.* **1.** person who carries or brings sth. (e.g. a coffin, messages, news, a cheque to a bank for payment). **2.** house servant or porter (in the East).

²**bear** [bɛə*] *n.* large, heavy animal with rough hair. See the picture on page 42. *Great* (*Little*) *Bear*, two groups of stars in the northern sky.

beard [biəd] *n.* growth of hair on the cheeks and chin (not the lip). ~'**ed** ['biədid] *adj.* ~'**less** *adj.*

bear·ing ['bɛəriŋ] *n.* (in the senses of the verb, *bear*, esp.:) **1.** connexion, relationship, between one thing and others: *to examine a question in all its ~s.* **2.** direction of a place in relation to other places; position: *lose one's ~s*, be lost; *find* (*get*) *one's ~s.* **3.** part of a machine which supports a moving part. *ball-~*, device with small balls for reducing friction. **4.** way of behaving, walking, etc.: *a soldierly ~.*

beast [bi:st] *n.* **1.** animal. **2.** disgusting person. ~'**ly** *adj.* nasty; unpleasant.

beat [bi:t] *v.t. & i.* (p.t. *beat*, p.p. *beaten*). **1.** hit or strike (esp. with a stick); punish by hitting; (of the sun's rays, rain, etc.) bear down heavily (*upon*). **2.** win a victory over; do better than. **3.** (of the heart, a bird's wings, etc.) move regularly. ~ *time*, make regular movements to show the time in music. *n.* **1.** regularly repeated stroke, or

sound of this: *the ~ of a drum*; *heart-~s.* **2.** unit of time in music. **3.** path or course regularly used or taken: *on* (*off*) *his ~.* ~'**en** *ppl. adj.* shaped by ~*ing*: *~en silver*; *the ~en path*, made smooth by use. ~'**er** *n.* thing used for ~*ing*; man who ~s bushes, etc., to drive birds, etc., towards guns. ~'**ing** *n.* defeat; (punishment by) hitting with a stick, etc.

beat·nik ['bi:tnik] *n.* young person who (often with others) breaks away from convention, e.g. in dress and social behaviour.

beau [bou] *n.* (old use) man greatly interested in the fashion of his clothes; girl's admirer.

beau·ty ['bju:ti] *n.* quality that delights the eye, ear or mind: *the ~ of a picture* (*music, a mother's love*). **beau·ti·ful** *adj.* **beau·ti·ful·ly** *adv.* **beau·ti·fy** *v.t.* make beautiful.

bea·ver ['bi:və*] *n.* fur-covered animal living on land and in water; its soft brown fur.

be·calmed [bi'ka:md] *ppl. adj.* (of a sailing-ship) stopped because there is no wind.

be·came, see *become*.

be·cause [bi'kɔz] *conj.* **1.** for the reason that: *I did it ~ he told me to do it.* **2.** ~ *of*, by reason of; on account of: *We couldn't go out, ~ of the rain.*

beck·on ['bekən] *v.t. & i.* make a sign (to sb. asking him to come). **beck** *n.* ~*ing sign: be at sb.'s beck and call*, be under his orders, compelled to come and go all the time.

be·come [bi'kʌm] *v.i. & t.* (p.t. *became* [bi'keim], p.p. *become*). **1.** come, grow, or begin to be: *After passing his examinations he became a doctor. He has ~ accustomed to the climate. It is becoming expensive to travel.* **2.** ~ *of*, happen to: *Do you know what became of her after she married?* **3.** be suitable for; look well on: *a becoming hat. That hat ~s you.*

bed [bed] *n.* **1.** piece of furniture, etc., on which to sleep. *make the beds*, put the sheets, blankets,

etc., on them, ready for use.
'bed-clothes, sheets, blankets,
etc. 'bed·room *n.* room with
bed(s) for sleeping in. 'bed·,rid·
den ['bedridn] *adj.* obliged by
illness or old age to stay in bed.
2. base or foundation on which
sth. rests: *a bed of concrete.* **3.**
layer (of clay, rock, etc.). **4.**
ground underneath the sea, a
river, or lake: *a dry river-bed.*
5. piece of ground for plants:
flower-bed(s). v.t. (-dd-). provide
with, put into, a bed: *to bed out
plants; to bed down a horse with
straw; bedded in concrete.* **bed·
ding** *n.* mattress, bed-clothes,
pillows, etc.

bed·lam ['bedləm] *n.* state of
noisy confusion; (old use) asy-
lum for mad persons.

bed·ou·in ['beduin] *n.* (pl. un-
changed). Arab, esp. a nomad
Arab, living in the deserts of N.
Africa, Syria, or Arabia.

be·drag·gled [bi'drægəld] *ppl.
adj.* made wet and dirty by bad
weather, mud, etc.

bee [bi:] *n.* small flying insect
which gathers nectar from
flowers. *make a bee-line for,* go
by the shortest way to: *He.*
'bee·hive *n.* structure in which
~s are kept. 'bees·wax *n.* wax with
which bees make honeycombs.

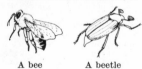

A bee   A beetle

beech [bi:tʃ] *n.* tree with smooth
grey bark, shiny leaves, and
nuts which may be eaten; its
wood.

beef [bi:f] *n.* meat from an ox,
cow, or bull.

been, see *be.*

beer [biə*] *n.* bitter drink made
from malted barley and hops.

beet [bi:t] *n.* plant with a large
sweet root. *red ~,* cooked and
eaten as a vegetable; *white ~,*
used for making ~-sugar.

¹**bee·tle** ['bi:tl] *n.* insect with hard,
shiny wing-covers.

²**bee·tle** ['bi:tl] *v.i.* overhang:
beetling cliffs (eyebrows).

be·fall [bi'fɔ:l] *v.t. & i.* happen
(to).

be·fit [bi'fit] *v.t.* (-tt-). be proper
for; be right or suitable for.

be·fore [bi'fɔ:*] *prep., adv. &
conj.* **I. prep. 1.** earlier than.
2. nearer the top (front, etc.):
*Your name comes ~ mine on the
list.* **3.** in the presence of: *He
was brought ~ a judge.* **4.** rather
than; in preference to: *Death
~ dishonour.* **II. adv. 1.** already; in the past: *I've seen
that film ~.* **2.** (of position) in
advance: *The children went on
~.* **III. conj. 1.** previously to
the time when: *Do it now, ~ you
forget.* **2.** rather than: *I'll die
~ I surrender!* ~**hand** [bi'fɔ:·
hænd] *adv. & pred. adj.* in
readiness; in advance; earlier
than necessary.

be·friend [bi'frend] *v.t.* act as a
friend to; be helpful to.

beg [beg] *v.t. & i.* (-gg-). ask for
(money, food, clothes, etc.); ask
earnestly for, or with deep feeling. *go begging,* (of things) be
unwanted. *beg to differ,* say that
one cannot agree. *beg off,* ask
to be excused from sth. *I beg
your pardon,* (a) I am sorry;
(b) Please excuse me; (c) Please
say that again.

be·gan, see *begin.*

be·get [bi'get] *v.t.* (p.t. *begot*
[bi'got], p.p. *begotten* [bi'gotn]).
1. (old use) give existence to (as
father). **2.** (liter.) be the cause
of: *War ~s misery and ruin.*

beg·gar ['begə*] *n.* person who
begs. *v.t.* make poor; ruin. ~
description, be so bad (good, etc.)
that description is inadequate.
~**ly** *adj.* fit for a ~. ~**y** *n.*
condition of being very poor.

be·gin [bi'gin] *v.t. & i* (-nn-; p.t.
began [bi'gæn], p.p. *begun* [bi-
'gʌn]). (Cf. *start.*) **1.** *It's time to
~ work. Sentences ~ with a
capital letter and end with a full
stop.* **2.** *When the sun came out,
the snow began to melt. I'm
beginning to understand.* **3.**
B~ to read (start reading) *at page
96.* ~**ner** *n.* person learning

sth. and without much knowledge of it yet. ~**ning** *n.* starting-point.

be·gone [bi'gɔn] *int. & v.* (imperative only) go away.

be·got(ten), see *beget*.

be·grudge [bi'grʌdʒ] *v.t.* = grudge.

be·guile [bi'gail] *v.t.* **1.** cause (sb. to do sth.) by guile (deceit, tricks). **2.** cause (time) to pass pleasantly.

be·gun, see *begin*.

be·half [bi'hɑːf] *n.* on (in) ~ of, for, in the interest of. on (in) his (her, etc.) ~, for him (her, etc.).

be·have [bi'heiv] *v.i.* act; conduct oneself. **be·hav·iour** [bi'heivjə*] *n.* way of behaving.

be·head [bi'hed] *v.t.* cut off the head of.

be·held, see *behold*.

be·hest [bi'hest] *n.* (old use, liter.) command: *at the ~ of; at his ~.*

be·hind [bi'haind] *prep., adv. & n.* **I. prep. 1.** in, at or to the rear of: *The boy was hiding ~ a bush.* **2.** having made less progress than: *John is ~ other boys of the same age.* **3.** after the departure of: *The storm left much damage ~ it.* **II. adv. 1.** in, at or to, the rear: *The rest of the runners are a long way ~.* **2.** *Stay ~* (after the others have gone home) *and help me clean up.* **3.** *You are ~ with* (late in paying) *your rent.* **III. n.** buttocks. ~**·hand** [bi'haindhænd] *adv. & pred. adj.* late; after others: *~hand with the rent; ~hand in one's work.*

be·hold [bi'hould] *v.t.* (p.t. and p.p. *beheld* [bi'held]). (old use, liter.) take notice; see (esp. sth. striking or unusual).

be·hold·en [bi'houldən] *pred. adj.* owing thanks; under an obligation: *much ~ to them for their help.*

beige [beiʒ] *n.* colour of sandstone (brown, brownish-grey, or greyish-yellow).

be·ing ['biːiŋ] *n.* **1.** state of existing. **2.** human creature. **3.** *the Supreme Being*, God.

be·la·bour [bi'leibə*] *v.t.* beat hard; give hard blows to.

be·la·ted [bi'leitid] *adj.* coming too or very late.

belch [beltʃ] *v.t. & i.* send out (air, wind, smoke, etc.) with force.

be·lea·guer [bi'liːgə*] *v.t.* besiege.

bel·fry ['belfri] *n.* tower, part of tower, esp. in a church, for bell(s).

be·lie [bi'lai] *v.t.* **1.** give a false idea of. **2.** fail to equal (sth. hoped for or promised).

be·lief [bi'liːf] *n.* the feeling that sth. is real and true; trust; confidence. *to the best of my belief,* so far as my knowledge goes.

be·lieve [bi'liːv] *v.t. & i.* **1.** have belief: *I ~ what he says* (i.e. that it is true). **2.** have trust (*in*): *I ~ in that man.* **3.** feel sure of the value of: *He ~s in getting plenty of exercise.* **4.** feel sure of the existence of: *to ~ in God.*

be·lit·tle [bi'litl] *v.t.* cause to seem unimportant or of small value.

bell [bel] *n.* see the picture. *one to eight ~s,* half-hour divisions of four-hour periods of duty in a ship, marked by strokes on the ship's bell: *eight ~s,* 4, 8, or 12 o'clock.

A bell   Belts

bel·li·cose ['belikous] *adj.* fond of fighting; anxious to fight.

bel·lig·er·ent [bi'lidʒərənt] *n.* country or party which is at war.

bel·low ['belou] *v.i. & n.* (make) the cry of a cow or bull; cry of pain or anger.

bel·lows ['belouz] *n.* (sing. or pl. v.) apparatus for blowing air into a fire or a church organ.

bel·ly ['beli] *n.* abdomen (1);

stomach. *v.i.* (often ~ *out*, usu. of sails) swell out; be curved.

be·long [bi'lɔŋ] *v.i.* **1.** ~ *to*, be the property of; be a member of. **2.** have as a right or proper place: *Do these books ~ here?* ~**·ings** *n. pl.* personal possessions (not land, a business, etc.).

be·loved [bi'lʌvd] *pred.adj.* much loved: *She is ~ by (of) all.* [bi-'lʌvid] *adj. & n.* (one who is) much loved: *his ~ wife; flowers for his ~.*

be·low [bi'lou] *prep. & adv.* **I. prep. 1.** lower than (cf. *under* and *over*): *When the sun sets, it sinks ~ the horizon. The temperature is ten degrees ~ zero. The Dead Sea is ~ sea level.* **2.** nearer the mouth of a river than: *ten yards ~ the bridge.* (Cf. *We stood under the bridge to shelter from the rain.*) **II. adv. 1.** at or to a lower level: *The people (in the room) ~ are very noisy. I feel seasick, I must go ~* (downstairs to my cabin). **2.** *Sign your name ~* (at the bottom of the sheet). *See ~* (refer to what is written later).

belt [belt] *n.* **1.** see the picture on page 45. **2.** endless (leather, etc.) band used to connect wheels and drive machinery; any wide strip: *a green ~ round a town* (i.e. strip of fields, woods, etc.). *v.t.* fasten on with a ~; beat with a ~.

be·moan [bi'moun] *v.t.* moan about (sth.).

bench [bentʃ] *n.* **1.** long, hard seat. **2.** work-table (for a shoemaker, etc.). **3.** *B~*, judge's or magistrate's seat; judge, group of judges, in a law court. *raised to the B~*, made a judge or bishop.

bend [bend] *v.t. & i.* (p.t. & p.p. *bent* [bent]). **1.** cause part of sth. straight or upright to be at an angle to the rest, or to curve: *If you ~ that stick too much it will break.* **2.** become curved; ²*bow; stoop: Her head was bent over her book. The branches were bent down with the weight of the fruit.* **3.** turn; cause (the mind, attention, etc.) to turn (towards): *to ~ one's mind to one's studies. bent on, having the mind set on; having a fixed purpose: bent on mastering English. n.* curve, turn, or angle.

be·neath [bi'ni:θ] *adv. & prep.* below; underneath.

ben·e·dic·tion [ˌbeni'dikʃən] *n.* blessing (esp. one given by a priest at the end of a church service).

ben·e·fac·tion [ˌbeni'fækʃən] *n.* good deed (esp. the giving of money for charity; the money so given). **ben·e·fac·tor** ['beni-fæktə*] *n.* person who does such a good deed.

be·nef·i·cent [bi'nefisənt] *adj.* good and kind. **be·nef·i·cence** *n.* **ben·e·fi·cial** [ˌbeni'fiʃl] *adj.* having good results. **ben·e·fi·ci·a·ry** [ˌbeni'fiʃəri] *n.* one who benefits under a will.

ben·e·fit ['benifit] *n.* help; advantage; improvement; good done or received. *death* (etc.) ~, compensation secured by life (etc.) insurance; *give sb. the ~ of the doubt*, free him from blame, etc., because there is doubt; ~ *performance*, one of which the profits are used for charity, etc. *v.t. & i.* do good to; be a ~ to.

be·nev·o·lent [bi'nevələnt] *adj.* kind and helpful; doing good. ~**·ly** *adv.* **be·nev·o·lence** *n.*

be·night·ed [bi'naitid] *adj.* without the light of knowledge; in moral darkness; overtaken by darkness.

be·nign [bi'nain] *adj.* **1.** (of persons) kind and gentle. **2.** (of diseases) not serious or dangerous. **3.** (of climate, etc.) favourable to growth.

bent [bent] *v.* see *bend.* *n.* inclination of the mind; natural skill in and liking (*for*); aptitude (*for*): *She has a ~ for sewing* (i.e. is fond of and clever at sewing).

be·numb [bi'nʌm] *v.t.* make numb.

be·queath [bi'kwi:ð] *v.t.* arrange (by making a will) to give (property, etc.) at death; hand down to those who come after. **be·quest** [bi'kwest] *n.* ~**ing**; sth. ~ed.

be·reaved [bi'ri:vd] *ppl. adj.*
having had (sb.) taken away by
death; made unhappy by the
loss of: ~ *of friends.* be·reave·
ment *n.* being ~; a great loss
(esp. by death).

be·reft [bi'reft] (old p.p. of
bereave) ~ *of*, having lost: ~ *of
reason* (i.e. insane).

be·ret ['beri, -rei] *n.* see the
picture.

A beret   Blackberries

ber·ry ['beri] *n.* small round
fruit containing seed(s): *straw~*;
black~; *holly berries.*

berth [bə:θ] *n.* 1. sleeping-place
in a train or ship. 2. place for
a ship in a river or harbour. *give
a wide ~ to*, keep at a safe distance from. 3. (colloq.) work;
position. *v.t. & i.* get (a ship)
into, go into, a ~.

be·seech [bi'si:tʃ] *v.t.* (p.t. & p.p.
besought [bi'sɔ:t]). ask earnestly
or urgently: *to ~ sb. to help (for
help).*

be·set [bi'set] *v.t.* (*-tt-*). attack
from all sides; have on all sides:
*a problem ~ with difficulties. His
~ting sin* (i.e. the sin of which he
is regularly guilty) *is laziness.*

be·side [bi'said] *prep.* 1. at the
side of; close to. 2. compared
with: *You're quite tall ~ your
sister.* ~ *oneself*, at the end of
one's self-control; ~ *the mark
(question, point)*, having nothing
to do with the question, etc.
be·sides *prep. & adv.* as well
(as); in addition (to).

be·siege [bi'si:dʒ] *v.t.* close in
upon, attack, from all sides. ~
(sb.) *with (requests, etc.)*, make a
large number of (requests, etc.).

be·sought, see *beseech.*

best [best] *adj. & adv.* I. *adj.*
(superl. of *good*). 1. of the most
excellent kind: *That was the ~
dinner I have ever eaten!* 2. the
most suitable, largest, most con-

venient, etc.: *Which is the ~
road to London? ~ man*, bridegroom's friend attending him
at his wedding. *at its (their)*
~, (of flowers, fruit, etc.) in the
~ condition. *do one's ~*, do as
well or as much as one can.
make the ~ of things, be cheerful
in spite of misfortune. II. *adv.*
(superl. of *well*). 1. in the most
excellent way: *He works ~ in
the morning. Do as you think ~.*
2. *had ~*, = had better.

bes·tial ['bestjəl] *adj.* of or like
a beast; nasty; brutal.

be·stir [bi'stə:*] *v.t.* (*-rr-*). (usu.)
~ *oneself*, move quickly; busy
oneself.

be·stow [bi'stou] *v.t.* 1. give:
*the advantages ~ed on us by
nature.* 2. put (in a place).

be·stride [bi'straid] *v.t.* (p.t.
bestrode [bi'stroud], p.p. *be-
stridden* [bi'stridn]). put, sit
with, stand with, one leg on each
side of: *to ~ a horse (ditch).*

bet [bet] *v.t. & i.* (*-tt-*; p.t. &
p.p. *bet*). risk money, etc., on the
result of a race or other event.
n. offer of this kind; the money,
etc., offered.

be·take [bi'teik] *v.t.* (p.t. *betook*
[bi'tuk], p.p. *betaken* [bi'teikn]). ~
oneself to, go to; apply oneself to.

be·tide [bi'taid] *v.i.* (old use)
Woe ~ you (if), may misfortune
come to you; *whatever may ~*
(i.e. happen).

be·times [bi'taimz] *adv.* (liter.)
early.

be·tray [bi'trei] *v.t.* 1. be false
or unfaithful to. 2. allow (a
secret) to become known (by
accident or on purpose). 3. be
or give a sign of; show. ~·al *n.*

be·troth [bi'trouð] *v.t.* (usu. in
p.p.) *be ~ed*, promised in
marriage. ~·al *n.* engagement
to be married. be·trothed *n.*
~ed person.

¹bet·ter ['betə*] *adj., adv., v.t.
& n.* I. *adj.* (comp. of *good*). 1.
*This is good but that is ~. He's
a ~ man than his brother. ~ off*,
richer, more comfortable. *no ~
than*, of the same value, merit,
etc. as: *He's no ~ than a lazy
dog* (i.e. a lazy dog would do as

much work as he does). get the ~ of. defeat. one's ~ half, (colloq.) wife. **2.** (of health) (a) less ill: She's ~ today but is still not well enough to get up; (b) fully recovered: She's (quite) ~ now and has gone back to work. **II. adv.** (comp. of well). **1.** You would write ~ if you used a good pen. You can do it ~ than I (can). You would like that picture ~ (more) if you studied it. **2.** had ~, would find it an advantage, wise, etc., to: I (You) had ~ take a raincoat. **III. v.t.** improve: The managers should ~ the conditions under which the staff work. He ~ed himself (earned more money, etc.) by changing his job. **IV. n. pl.** one's ~s, people who are of higher rank, etc.

'bet·ter ['betə*] **n.** person who bets.

be·tween [bi'twi:n] **prep. & adv. I. prep. 1.** (of place): The letter B comes ~ A and C. The Mediterranean Sea is ~ Europe and Africa. **2.** (of rank): A corporal ranks ~ a private soldier and a sergeant. **3.** (of time): ~ two and three o'clock; ~ Wednesday and Friday; ~ the two world wars. **4.** (of distance, amount, etc.): ~ five and six miles; ~ freezing- and boiling-points. **5.** to show sharing, combining: Share the money ~ (among) you. B~ the two of them, they did much to make the party a success. **6.** (showing relationship, comparison): We can usually distinguish ~ right and wrong. The relations ~ management and staff are excellent. **II. adv.** in(to) a place or time that is ~: I had appointments in the morning and afternoon and no time for lunch ~. There are bushes at each side of the garden and flowers in ~. The trees are few and far ~ (at wide intervals).

be·twixt [bi'twikst] **prep. & adv.** (old use) between.

bev·el ['bevəl] **n.** sloping surface at an edge. **v.t.** (-ll-). give a ~ to.

bev·er·age ['bevəridʒ] **n.** kind of drink (e.g. tea, coffee, milk, wine, beer).

bev·y ['bevi] **n.** group, company (of women).

be·wail [bi'weil] **v.t.** cry about; complain of.

be·ware [bi'wɛə*] **v.t. & i.** be on guard; be careful (of). In the imperative and infinitive only: B~ of the dog. You must ~ (how . . .; lest . . .; that . . . not).

be·wil·der [bi'wildə*] **v.t.** puzzle; confuse greatly. ~'ment **n.**

be·witch [bi'witʃ] **v.t. 1.** work magic on. **2.** attract or charm: her ~ing smile.

be·yond [bi'jɔnd] **prep. & adv. I. prep. 1.** at, on, or to, the far side of: The house is ~ the bridge. **2.** (of time) after: I cannot stay with you ~ Thursday. **3.** exceeding; out of reach of: Your work is ~ all praise (too good to describe adequately). He is living ~ his income (spending more than he earns). This lesson is ~ me (is too difficult for me to understand). **II. adv.** at or to a distance; further on: I can only see houses from the window—I don't know what lies ~.

bi- [bai-] **prefix.** twice; having two; coming once in every two.

bi·an·nu·al [bai'ænjuəl] **adj. & n.** (journal published) twice in a year.

bi·as ['baiəs] **n. 1.** have a ~ towards (against) sth., be in favour of (opposed to) sth., esp. without full knowledge or examination of all facts. **2.** cut on the ~, cut in a sloping direction across the material. **v.t.** (-s- or -ss-). give a ~ to.

bib [bib] **n. 1.** cloth tied under a child's chin for meals. **2.** upper part of an apron.

Bi·ble ['baibl] **n.** sacred writings of the Jews and the Christian church. **bib·li·cal** ['biblikl] **adj.**

bib·li·og·ra·phy [,bibli'ogrəfi] **n.** list of books and writings, usu. of one author or on one subject.

bi·car·bon·ate [bai'kɑ:bənit] **n.** salt of carbonic acid, a white powder used in cooking and medicine.

bi·cen·te·na·ry [,baisen'ti:nəri] **n.** (celebration of) the 200th anniversary of an event.

bi·ceps ['baiseps] *n.* large muscle at the front of the upper arm.

bick·er ['bikə*] *v.i.* quarrel (*with* sb. *over* or *about* sth. unimportant).

bi·cy·cle ['baisikl] *n.* (colloq. *bike*) two-wheeled machine for riding, driven along by the feet or (*motor-cycle*) by an engine. *v.i.* (usu. *cycle*) ride a ~, go (*to*) by ~.

Bicycles

bid [bid] *v.t. & i.* (-dd-). **1.** (p.t. & p.p. always *bid*). make an offer of money (*for*). **2.** (old use, p.t. *bade* [bæd, beid], p.p. *bidden* ['bidn]). command; say (good-bye, etc.). *n.* offer to pay a stated sum (*for* sth.). *make a bid for*, try to obtain. **bid·ding** *n. do sb.'s bidding*, obey him.

bide [baid] *v.t.* ~ *one's time*, wait for an opportunity.

bi·en·ni·al [bai'eniəl] *adj.* lasting for, happening once in, two years. *n.* plant which lives two years and has flowers and seed in the second year.

bier [biə*] *n.* movable wooden stand for a coffin or a corpse.

big [big] *adj.* (-ger, -gest). of great size or importance: *John's growing a big boy, isn't he? Charles is getting too big for his boots* (becoming conceited). *They are hunting big game* (lions, elephants, tigers, etc.).

big·a·my ['bigəmi] *n.* having two wives or two husbands living, a sin and crime in Christian countries. **'big·a·mous** *adj.: a bigamous marriage.* **'big·a·mist** *n.* person guilty of ~.

big·ot·ed ['bigətid] *ppl. adj.* strict and obstinate beyond reason in holding a belief or opinion. **'big·ot** *n.* ~ person. **'big·ot·ry** *n.*

bike [baik] *n.* (colloq.) bicycle.

bi·lat·er·al [bai'lætərəl] *adj.* of, on, with, two sides; (of an agreement, etc.) made between two (persons, governments, etc.).

bile [bail] *n.* bitter liquid produced by the liver to help in digesting food; (fig.) bad temper.

bil·ious ['biljəs] *adj.* caused by too much ~ : *a bilious attack*; (of a person) subject to sickness owing to trouble in the ~ or liver.

bilge [bildʒ] *n.* the widest part of a ship's bottom; (also ~-*water*) the dirty water which collects there.

bi·ling·ual [bai'liŋgwəl] *adj.* speaking two languages (esp. when these are learnt together in childhood); in two languages.

bil·ious, see *bile.*

¹bill [bil] *n.* horny part of a bird's mouth; beak. *v.i.* ~ *and coo*, put ~s together; behave like lovers.

²bill [bil] *n.* **1.** statement of money owing for goods or services. **2.** written or printed notice handed out or stuck on a wall, etc. **3.** proposed law, to be discussed by a parliament (and called an *Act* when passed). **4.** (commerce) *Bill of Exchange*, written order to a bank, etc., to pay money to sb. on a certain date. **5.** (U.S.A.) bank-note. *v.t.* make known by means of ~s (2); submit a ~ (1) to. **'~-,post·er, '~-,stick·er** *n.* person who sticks ~s (2) on walls, etc.

bil·let ['bilit] *n.* place (usu. a private house) where a soldier is lodged. *v.t.* ~ *on*, lodge (soldier(s), etc.) with.

bil·liards ['biljədz] *n.* indoor game played with balls and long sticks (cues) on an oblong, cloth-covered **'billiard-,table.**

bil·lion ['biljən] *n.* (Gt. Brit.) one million millions; (U.S.A.) one thousand millions.

bil·low ['bilou] *n.* (liter.) great wave; (pl.) the sea. *v.i.* rise or roll like great waves.

bin [bin] *n.* large container or enclosed place, usu. with a lid, for storing coal, grain, etc., or (*dustbin*) for rubbish.

bind [baind] *v.t. & i.* (p.t. & p.p. *bound* [baund]). **1.** tie or fasten together (with rope, etc.); put (one thing) round (another): *to ~ (up) a wound*; *to be bound hand and foot*; *to ~ the edge of a carpet.* **2.** fasten together, put (sheets of paper, etc.) into a cover: *a well-bound book.* **3.** become, cause to become, hard, solid, difficult to move: *Frost ~s the soil. The land is frost-bound.* **4.** hold sb. (by legal agreement, promise, or under penalty) to a certain course of action : ~ *oneself to*, promise or guarantee to (do sth.); ~ *sb. over*, ~ *sb. to keep the peace* (under the penalty of appearing before the judge again if he makes further trouble). (See *bound* for special uses of the p.p.) ~**er** *n.* person, thing, machine, that ~s. ~**ing** *n.* book cover.

bin·go ['biŋgou] *n.* gambling game in which numbered squares on cards are covered as the numbers are called at random.

bi·noc·u·lars [bi'nɔkjuləz] *n. pl.* instrument with lenses for both eyes, making distant objects seem nearer.

bi·og·ra·phy [bai'ɔgrəfi] *n.* person's life-history written by another; this branch of literature. **bi·o·graph·i·cal** [,baiə'græfikl] *adj.*

bi·ol·o·gy [bai'ɔlədʒi] *n.* science of life, of animals, and plants. **bi·ol·o·gist** *n.* **bi·o·log·i·cal** [,baiə'lɔdʒikl] *adj.*

bi·ped ['baiped] *n.* two-legged animal (e.g. a man or a bird).

bi·plane ['baiplein] *n.* aircraft with two pairs of wings, one above the other.

birch [bə:tʃ] *n.* tree with thin, smooth bark; its wood.

bird [bə:d] *n.* feathered animal with two legs and two wings.

birth [bə:θ] *n.* **1.** (process of) being born. **2.** descent (2): *He's an Englishman by ~. ~-rate*, number of ~s in one year for every 1,000 persons. ~*right*, the various rights, privileges, and property a person is entitled to as a member of his family, a citizen of his country, etc. '~*day n.* date of one's ~(1); each anniversary of it.

bis·cuit ['biskit] *n.* flat, thin, crisp cake of many kinds, sweetened or unsweetened.

bi·sect [bai'sekt] *v.t.* divide (an angle, etc.) into two (usu. equal) parts. **bi·sec·tion** [bai'sekʃən] *n.*

bish·op ['biʃəp] *n.* clergyman of high rank who organizes the work of the Church in a city or district. ~*ric n.* district under a ~.

bi·son ['baisn] *n.* wild ox; American buffalo.

¹bit [bit] *n.* very small piece. *bit by bit*, slowly, gradually. *a bit* (*better*, etc.), rather, somewhat (better, etc.). *not a bit*, not at all. *give sb. a bit of one's mind*, speak severely; show that one is annoyed. *threepenny bit*, coin worth threepence.

²bit [bit] *n.* **1.** steel bar placed in a horse's mouth to control it. **2.** the biting or cutting part of certain tools: *a brace and bit.*

³bit [bit], see *bite.*

bitch [bitʃ] *n.* female dog or wolf.

bite [bait] *v.t. & i.* (p.t. *bit* [bit], p.p. *bitten* ['bitn]). **1.** cut into with the teeth; (of insects, etc.) sting. **2.** (of acids, etc.) make holes in; damage. **3.** (of wheels, etc.) grip; take hold of. **4.** (of frost) cause smarting pain to (fingers, toes). *n.* **1.** act of biting. **2.** piece cut off by biting; food: *have a ~ to eat.* **3.** injury caused by the teeth or a sting.

bit·ten, see *bite.*

bit·ter ['bitə*] *adj.* **1.** tasting like beer or quinine. **2.** causing sorrow; hard to bear; filled with, showing, caused by, anger, envy, etc.: ~ *quarrels* (*words*). *n.* ~ beer. ~*ly adv.* ~*ness n.*

bi·tu·men ['bitjumin] *n.* asphalt. **bi·tu·mi·nous** [bi'tju·minəs] *adj.* containing ~ or tar.

biv·ou·ac ['bivuæk] *n.* soldiers' camp without tents or other cover. *v.i.* make, rest in, a ~.

bi·zarre [bi'za:*] *adj.* strange; queer.

black [blæk] *n. & adj.* the colour

of this printing ink. *give sb. a ~ look*, look ~ *at sb.*, look at with anger; *be in sb.'s ~ book(s)*, be quite out of his favour; ~ *sheep*, person of bad character; ~ *flag*, one used by sea-robbers; ~ *art*, evil magic; ~ *market*, unlawful buying and selling of goods, currencies, etc., which are officially controlled. **~·guard** ['blæga:d] *n.* person quite without honour; scoundrel. **'~·leg** *n.* person who offers to work for employer(s) whose men are on strike. **'~· list** *v.t. & n.* (put a person's name on a) list of persons who are considered dangerous or wrongdoers. **'~·mail** *v.t.* (try to) make (sb.) pay money by threatening to tell sth. against him. *n.* such a threat. **'~·out** *n.* 1. complete darkening of a room when lights are put out or windows, etc., covered for a cinema show, etc. 2. sudden attack of blindness, loss of memory, etc. **'~·smith** *n.* iron worker, esp. one who repairs farm machinery and makes horseshoes.

black·en ['blækən] *v.t. & i.* 1. make or become black. 2. speak evil of (sb.'s character).

blad·der ['blædə*] *n.* 1. skin bag in the body in which waste liquid collects. 2. rubber bag in a football.

blade [bleid] *n.* 1. sharpened part of a knife, sword, razor, etc. 2. flat, narrow leaf (e.g. of grass). 3. part of an oar which goes into the water.

blame [bleim] *v.t.* find fault with; say that (sb.' or sth.) is the cause of what is wrong: *Bad workmen ~ their tools. Who is to ~ (to be ~d) for this disaster?* *n.* blaming; responsibility for failure, etc. **~·less** *adj.*

blanch [blɑːntʃ] *v.t. & i.* (cause to) become white or pale: *to ~ celery.*

bland [blænd] *adj.* gentle or polite in manner; ironical.

blan·dish·ment ['blændiʃmənt] *n.* (often pl.) soft, gentle words or ways used in order to make sb. do sth.

blank [blæŋk] *adj.* 1. (of paper, etc.) with nothing drawn, written, or printed on it. 2. (of a person's face or look) without interest or expression; puzzled. 3. ~ *wall*, without doors or windows; ~ *verse*, without rhyme; ~ *cartridge*, with powder but not shot or bullet. *n.* 1. ~ space (in sth. printed or written). *telegraph ~*, form with ~ spaces for the message, etc. 2. emptiness: *His mind was a complete ~.* **~·ly** *adv.* **~·ness** *n.*

blan·ket ['blæŋkit] *n.* thick woollen cloth used as a bed-covering, etc.

blare [blɛə*] *n.* loud sound or noise (of trumpets, horns, etc.). *v.t.* make such a sound or sounds.

blas·pheme [blæs'fiːm] *v.t. & i.* cry out against God; speak in an irreverent way of sacred things. **blas·phe·mous** ['blæsfəməs] *adj.* **blas·phe·my** ['blæsfəmi] *n.*

blast [blɑːst] *n.* 1. strong, sudden rush of wind or air: *a ~ of hot air from a furnace*; *windows broken by ~* (e.g. after an explosion). 2. sound made by a wind-instrument such as a horn or trumpet. *v.t.* 1. break up or destroy by explosion (e.g. in a quarry or mine): *Danger! Blasting in progress!* 2. destroy; bring to nothing: *blossom ~ed by frost; a tree ~ed by lightning.* **'~-·fur·nace** *n.* one for melting iron-ore by forcing into it a current of heated air.

bla·tant ['bleitənt] *adj.* noisy; trying to attract attention in a vulgar and shameless way.

¹blaze [bleiz] *n.* 1. bright fire, flame, or light: *to burst into a ~; to put out a big ~* (extinguish a burning house, etc.). 2. violent outburst of feeling: *in a ~ of anger.* *v.i.* 1. burn with bright flames; burst into flames; shine brightly or with warmth: *The sun ~d down on us.* 2. burst out with strong feeling: *blazing with indignation.* 3. fire (guns) rapidly: *to ~ away at the enemy.*

²blaze [bleiz] *v.t.* make a cut or mark on a tree (e.g. to show a path through a forest): ~ a trail, (liter.) mark a path by doing this; (fig.) do sth. new and so be a leader.

³blaze [bleiz] *v.t.* ~ *(sth.) abroad*, make known far and wide.

bla·zer ['bleizə*] *n.* bright-coloured jacket worn for sports.

bla·zon ['bleizn] *v.t.* = ³blaze.

bleach [bli:tʃ] *v.t. & i.* make or become white (by chemical process or by sunlight).

bleak [bli:k] *adj.* (of weather) cold; dismal; (of a place, e.g. a hill-side) bare; windy; (of an outlook, etc.) comfortless; unhopeful.

blear [bliə*] *adj.* '~-'eyed, unable to see clearly.

bleat [bli:t] *v.i. & t. & n.* (make the) cry of a sheep, goat, or calf.

bled, see bleed.

bleed [bli:d] *v.i. & t.* (p.t. & p.p. *bled* [bled]). lose blood; cause blood to flow from.

blem·ish ['blemiʃ] *n.* mark, etc., which spoils the beauty or perfection of sth. or sb.: *a ~ on the skin (on sb.'s character).* *v.t.* spoil the beauty or perfection of.

blench [blenʃ] *v.i.* jump back or to one side quickly (in fear); close the eyes quickly to.

blend [blend] *v.t. & i.* **1.** (of tea, tobacco, etc.) mix together, become mixed (so as to make the mixture desired). **2.** (of colours) go well together; have no sharp contrasts: *colours that ~ well.* *n.* mixture made by ~ing: *an excellent ~ of tea.*

bless [bles] *v.t.* (p.t. & p.p. *blessed, blest* [blest]). **1.** ask God's favour for: *The priest ~ed the people (the crops).* **2.** wish good to; make happy: *Bless you, my boy!* **3.** *be ~ed with,* be fortunate in having: *be ~ed with good health; not greatly ~ed with worldly goods* (i.e. not rich). **4.** make sacred or holy: *relics ~ed by the Pope.* **5.** call (God) holy. **6.** (colloq. uses) *Bless me! Bless my soul! Well, I'm blest!* (all showing surprise). *~·ed* ['blesid] *ppl. adj.* holy; sacred; fortunate; bringing happiness.

'bles·sing *n.* the favour of God;

grace (before or after a meal): *to ask a ~ing;* sth. that brings happiness.

blew, see ¹blow.

blight [blait] *n.* **1.** plant disease. **2.** evil influence which spoils or interferes with hopes, pleasures, etc.: *a ~ upon my hopes (plans, etc.).* *v.t.* be a ~ to: *a life ~ed by constant illness.*

¹blind [blaind] *adj.* **1.** unable to see; (fig.) unable to judge well: *~ to the faults of her children.* **2.** not controlled by reason or purpose: *in ~ haste.* **3.** having no opening: *a ~ wall;* difficult or impossible to see past: *a ~ turning (corner)* (in a road). *v.t.* make ~. *~·ly adv.* *~·ness n.* '~·fold *v.t.* cover a person's eyes (with a band of cloth, etc.). *adj. & adv.* with the eyes so covered.

²blind [blaind] *n.* roll of cloth (usu. strong linen) fixed on a roller and pulled down to cover a window.

blink [bliŋk] *v.t. & i.* **1.** shut and open the eyes quickly; (fig.) *~ facts,* shut the mind to them. **2.** (of lights) come and go; shine in an unsteady way: *the lights of a steamer ~ing on the horizon.*

bliss [blis] *n.* perfect happiness. *~·ful adj.*

blis·ter ['blistə*] *n.* **1.** small, watery swelling under the skin. **2.** similar swelling, air-filled, under paint, etc. *v.t. & i.* cause, get, ~s on.

blitz [blits] *n.* rapid, violent attack (esp. from the air). **blitzed** *ppl. adj.* damaged or destroyed by such attacks.

bliz·zard ['blizəd] *n.* severe snow-storm with violent wind.

bloat·ed ['bloutid] *ppl. adj.* **1.** fat to an unhealthy extent. **2.** swollen; overgrown.

bloat·er ['bloutə*] *n.* salted and smoked herring.

bloc [blɔk] *n.* combination of States, etc., wishing to act together (politically or commercially).

block [blɔk] *n.* **1.** large, solid piece of stone, wood, etc.: *the ~s of stone in the Pyramids; a* *chip of(f) the old* ~, person who is like his father (in appearance or character); *go to the* ~, have one's head cut off (as a punishment). **2.** number of large buildings joined together, often with streets on all four sides; division of seats (in a theatre, etc.). **3.** piece of wood or metal with designs, etc., cut (engraved) on its surface for printing. **4.** sth. that stops movement, e.g. a number of cars, buses, etc., held up in a street. **5.** ~ *and tackle*, apparatus (pulley in a ~ of wood) for lifting and pulling. (See *tackle*.) **6.** ~ *letters,* ~ *writing,* with each letter separate and (usu.) in capitals. *v.t.* **1.** make movement difficult or impossible by putting sth., or getting, in the way of: *roads* ~*ed by snow*; *to* ~ *up the entrance to a cave.* **2.** ~ *in (a drawing),* draw the general arrangement without details. '~·**age** ['blok-idʒ] *n.* state of being ~ed; sth. ~ing. '~·**head** *n.* foolish, stupid person. '~·**house** *n.* military strong-point, fort.

block·ade [blɔ'keid] *n.* the enclosing or surrounding of a place, e.g. by armies or warships, to keep goods and people in or out. *raise a* ~, end it; *run a* ~, get through it. *v.t.* make a ~ of.

blond(e) [blɔnd] *n. & adj.* (person of European race) having light-coloured hair.

blood [blʌd] *n.* red liquid flowing throughout the body of man and higher animals in ~-*vessels* (veins and arteries). *in cold* ~, not in the heat of anger. *make bad* ~ (*between*), cause ill-feeling, anger. '~·**bank** *n.* store of blood kept available in hospitals, etc., for replacing blood lost during surgical operations, etc. (See *transfusion.*) '~·**hound** *n.* large dog able to trace a person by scent (3). ~·**less** *adj.* **1.** without killing: *a* ~*less revolution.* **2.** pale: ~*less lips.* '~·**shed** *n.* killing; putting to death. '~·**shot** *adj.* (of the whites of the eyes) red. '~·'**thirst·y** *adj.* cruel; eager to kill. ~·**y** *adj.*

covered with ~; with much ~*shed*: *a* ~*y fight.*

bloom [blu:m] *n.* any flower or blossom; (fig.) time of perfection: *in the* ~ *of youth. v.i.* be in flower.

blos·som ['blɔsəm] *n.* flower; mass of flowers, esp. on fruit-trees: *The apple-trees are in* ~. *v.i.* open into flower(s).

blot [blɔt] *n.* **1.** mark caused by ink spilt on paper. **2.** (fig.) sth. that takes away from the value, beauty, or goodness of; *a* ~ *on the landscape* (e.g. an ugly building); *a* ~ *on his character. v.t.* (*-tt-*). **1.** make a ~ or ~s on. **2.** dry wet ink-marks by pressing with special paper called ~*ting-paper.* **3.** ~ *out,* rub off; hide completely: *words* ~*ted out; a view* ~*ted out by mists.*

blotch [blɔtʃ] *n.* large, discoloured mark, usu. irregular in shape (e.g. one on the skin, or a dirty ink-mark). *v.t.* mark with ~es.

blouse [blauz] *n.* outer garment from neck to waist, usu. with sleeves.

Blouses

'**blow** [blou] *v.i. & t.* (p.t. *blew* [blu:], p.p. *blown* [bloun]). **1.** (of air) be moving or flowing: *It was* ~*ing hard* (i.e. there was a strong wind). ~ *over,* pass by; (fig.) be forgotten. **2.** (of things) be moved or carried by the wind or other air current; (of the wind, etc.) cause to move: *My hat blew off. The wind blew my hat off. I was almost* ~*n over by the wind.* **3.** force air upon, through, or into: *to* ~ (*on*) *one's tea* (to cool it); *to* ~ *one's nose* (to clear it); *to* ~ *up a tyre* (to fill it with air). ~ *up* (v.i. & t.), explode: *The barrel of gunpowder blew up. The soldiers blew up the bridge.* ~ *out one's* *brains,* kill oneself by shooting in the head. ~ *out,* (a) put out a flame by ~ing: *to ~ out a candle;* (b) (of wire) melt because electric current is too strong: *The fuse blew (out).* **4.** give out, cause to give out, sounds as the result of sending air through: *The whistle blew. I blew the whistle.* **5.** breathe hard and quickly. **6.** give shape to (glass) by ~ing. *n.* have (go for) a ~, go outdoors for fresh air. ~**·er** *n.* apparatus for forcing air into or through sth. (e.g. a fire); person who blows or pumps air; '*glass-*~*·er*, '*organ-*~*·er.* **blown** *ppl. adj.* (esp.) breathless. '~**·out** *n.* sudden (violent) escape of air, steam, etc.; (esp.) bursting of a tyre. '~**·pipe** *n.* pipe for sending air or gas into a flame to make it hotter.

²**blow** [blou] *n.* **1.** sudden stroke (given with the hand, etc.): *to kill three flies at one ~; come to* ~*s,* begin fighting; *strike a ~ for,* fight for (freedom, etc.). **2.** shock; misfortune; loss causing unhappiness.

blub·ber ['blʌbə*] *n.* fat of whales and other sea-animals from which oil is obtained.

blue [blu:] *n. & adj.* colour of the sky on a clear day or of deep sea when the sun is shining. ~ *ribbon* (*riband*), sign of great distinction; the leading position; *a bolt from the* ~, sth. sudden, unexpected, and greatly surprising. *Oxford* (*Cambridge*) *Blue,* sportsman who has played (football, etc.) or rowed for the University. '~**-book** *n.* government report. '~**·print** *n.* photographic print, with a white design on a blue background, usu. for building-plans. **blu·ish** *adj.* rather ~. *v.t.* make ~.

¹**bluff** [blʌf] *v.t. & i.* deceive (by pretending to be stronger, etc., than one really is). *n.* deception of this kind.

²**bluff** [blʌf] *n.* steep bank or cliff; headland. *adj.* (of a cliff, coast) having a wide, steep front.

³**bluff** [blʌf] *adj.* (of a person, his behaviour, etc.) rough but

honest and kindly; blunt (2) but hearty.

blun·der ['blʌndə*] *n.* foolish and careless mistake. *v.i.* make a ~; move about uncertainly, as if unable to see: *to ~ into a wall.*

blunt [blʌnt] *adj.* **1.** without a point or sharp edge. **2.** (of a person, his speech) not showing polite consideration. *v.t.* make ~. ~**·ly** *adv.* ~**·ness** *n.*

blur [blə:*] *v.t. & i.* (-rr-). (cause to) become unclear; (cause to) become confused in shape or appearance: *Tears* ~*red her eyes. Mists* ~*red the view. The writing was* ~*red.* *n.* dirty spot or mark; sth. seen only in indistinct outline: *If, when you look at this, the print is only a* ~, *you perhaps need glasses.*

blurt [blə:t] *v.t.* ~ *sth. out,* say or tell sth. (e.g. a secret) suddenly, often without thought.

blush [blʌʃ] *v.i.* become red in the face (from confusion or shame). *n.* redness spreading over the face.

blus·ter ['blʌstə*] *v.i.* be rough or violent. *n.* noise (of stormy weather); noisy threatening talk and behaviour. ~**·y** *adj.*

bo·a ['bouə] *n.* large snake which kills by crushing.

boar [bɔ:*] *n.* **1.** wild male pig. (Cf. *hog, sow.*) **2.** male domestic pig, not castrated.

board [bɔ:d] *n.* **1.** long, thin, flat piece of wood with squared edges, used in building walls, floors, boats, ship's decks, etc. *on* ~, in(to) a ship. *go by the* ~, (fig. of plans, hopes, etc.) be given up or abandoned; be lost. **2.** table; group of persons controlling a business or government department: *the Board of Governors; the Board of Trade.* **3.** (from the idea of *table*) *above-*~, openly; without deception; *sweep the* ~, win everything; be successful. **4.** the supply of meals by the week or month (e.g. at a lodging-house): *Board and lodging, £7 weekly. The servant has £5 a week and free* ~. **5.** flat piece of wood or other material used for a special purpose: *black-*

~ ; *notice-*~. **6.** thick, stiff paper, sometimes cloth-covered (also *card*~), used for book covers: *bound in cloth* ~s. *v.t. & i.* **1.** make or cover with ~s (1): *to* ~ *up a window.* **2.** get, supply with, ~ (4): *to make a living by* ~*ing students*; *to* ~ *with a butcher.* **3.** go on ~ (a ship, tram, etc.). ~**·er** *n.* person who gets ~ (4) at sb.'s house; child who lives at school. '~**·ing-house**, '~**·ing-school** *n.* one that provides ~ (4) and lodging.

boast [boust] *n.* **1.** proud words used in praise of oneself, one's acts, belongings, etc. **2.** cause for self-satisfaction. *v.i. & t.* **1.** make ~s. **2.** possess (sth.) with pride: *Our school* ~*s an excellent library.* ~**·er** *n.* ~**·ful** *adj.*

boat [bout] *n.* small open vessel for travelling on water, esp. '*rowing-*~, '*sailing-*~, '*fishing-*~. *be (all) in the same* ~, have the same dangers, problems, etc., to meet. *burn one's* ~*s*, do sth. which makes a change of plan impossible. ~**·er** *n.* kind of straw hat. '~**·man** *n.* man who rows or sails a small ~ for pay; man from whom rowing-~s may be hired. ~**·swain** ['bousn] *n.* senior seaman who controls the work of other seamen and is in charge of a ship's rigging, boats, anchors, etc. *v.i.* travel by ~, esp. for pleasure.

¹**bob** [bɔb] *v.i. & t.* (-bb-) *& n.* **1.** (make a) quick, short down-and-up movement (of the body, etc.): *The cork on his fishing-line was bobbing on the water. That question often bobs up* (i.e. is often asked). **2.** cut (a woman's or girl's hair) short and allow to hang loose: *to have one's hair bobbed.*

²**bob** [bɔb] *n.* (colloq.) shilling.

bob·bin ['bɔbin] *n.* small roller for thread or yarn (esp. in a machine).

bob·by ['bɔbi] *n.* (colloq.) policeman.

bode [boud] *v.t. & i.* tell, show, in advance; be a sign of: *It* ~*s ill (well) for his future. This* ~*s you no good.*

bod·ice ['bɔdis] *n.* close-fitting upper part of a woman's dress or undergarment.

bod·y ['bɔdi] *n.* **1.** the whole physical structure of a man or animal. **2.** the same without the head, arms, and legs. **3.** the main part of a structure: *the* ~ *of a motor-car*; *the* ~ *of a hall* (the central part where the seats are). **4.** group of persons: *the Governing Body of the school*; *in a* ~ (all together). **5.** collection (of facts, information, etc.). **6.** piece of matter: *the heavenly bodies*, the sun, stars, etc. **7.** (esp. in compounds) person: *any*~; *some*~; *no-*~. **bod·i·ly** *adj.* of or in the ~. *adv.* as a whole; completely. '~**·guard** *n.* man, group of men, guarding an important person.

bog [bɔg] *n.* (area of) wet, soft ground. **bog·gy** *adj.* **bogged** *ppl. adj.* *be (get) bogged down*, be unable to go forward; also fig.

bo·gus ['bougəs] *adj.* untrue; not genuine; sham.

bo·he·mian [bou'hi:mjən] *n. & adj.* (person) not living in the ways considered normal or conventional.

¹**boil** [bɔil] *v.i. & t.* **1.** (of water, etc.) reach, cause to reach, the temperature at which the change into gas occurs. **2.** cook, cause to be cooked, by ~ing. **3.** be excited or angry; ~*ing with indignation.* *n.* ~*ing-point: to bring sth. to the* ~; *to come to the* ~. ~**·er** *n.* metal container for heating or ~ing liquids.

²**boil** [bɔil] *n.* hard (usu. red, often painful) poisoned swelling under the skin which bursts when ripe.

bois·ter·ous ['bɔistərəs] *adj.* rough; violent; (of a person, his behaviour) noisy and cheerful.

bold [bould] *adj.* **1.** without fear. **2.** without feelings of shame. **3.** well marked: ~ *outlines.* ~**·ly** *adv.* ~**·ness** *n.*

bole [boul] *n.* trunk of a tree.

boll [boul] *n.* seed-vessel of cotton and flax.

bol·lard ['bɔləd] *n.* **1.** see the picture. **2.** cone, etc., erected to divert traffic away from road repairs, or on a traffic island.

Bollards

bol·ster ['boulstə*] *n.* long under-pillow for the head of a bed. *v.t.* (usu. ~ *up*) give greatly needed (often undeserved) support to.

¹bolt [boult] *n.* **1.** metal fastening for a door or window. **2.** metal pin for joining parts, usu. with a thread (3) at one end for a nut. **3.** (old use) short, strong arrow from a cross-bow: *a ~ from the blue*, see *blue*. *v.t. & i.* fasten or join with a ~ or ~s.

Bolts

²bolt [boult] *v.i. & t.* **1.** run away suddenly and unexpectedly: *The horse ~ed. The servant ~ed with all his master's money.* **2.** swallow (food) quickly. *n.* make a ~ *for it*, run away.

³bolt [boult] *adv.* ~ *upright*, quite upright.

bomb [bom] *n.* hollow metal ball or shell filled with explosive for causing destruction on bursting. *v.t.* drop ~s on; throw ~s at. **~·er** *n.* aircraft carrying ~s; soldier who throws ~s. **'~·shell** *n.* (fig.) great surprise.

bom·bard [bom'bɑːd] *v.t.* attack with gunfire; (fig.) worry (*with* questions, complaints, etc.) **~·ment** *n.*

bom·bas·tic [bom'bæstik] *adj.* (of a person, his talk, behaviour) promising much but not likely to do much; using fine high-sounding words.

bo·na fi·de ['bounə 'faidi] *adj. & adv.* (Latin) genuine(ly); sincere(ly).

bond [bond] *n.* **1.** binding (4)

written agreement or promise having force in law: *His word is as good as his ~* (i.e. he will keep his spoken promise as faithfully as if it were a legal agreement). **2.** printed paper (e.g. from a government) saying that money has been received and will be paid back with interest: *5% Development Bonds.* **3.** sth. that unites or joins: *the ~s of affection.* **4.** (commerce, of goods) *in ~*, in Customs warehouse (until duties are paid). **5.** (pl.) chains. *in ~s*, in prison or slavery; *burst one's ~s*, get free. **~·ed** *adj.* (of goods) placed or held in ~ (4): *~ed warehouse*, one where goods are stored until Customs duties are paid. **'~·age** *n.* slavery.

bone [boun] *n.* one of the parts that make up the hard framework of an animal's body (the skeleton). *to the ~*, completely; in a penetrating way: *frozen to the ~. have a ~ to pick with sb.*, have sth. to argue or complain about. *v.t.* take the ~s out of: *to ~ a chicken.* **bon·y** *adj.* (esp.) with little flesh.

bon·fire ['bonfaiə*] *n.* fire made in the open air (e.g. to burn garden rubbish).

bon·net ['bonit] *n.* **1.** small, round hat, usu. tied under the chin, worn by women and children, and by some soldiers. **2.** cover of a motor-car engine.

bon·ny, bon·nie ['boni] *adj.* healthy-looking: *a ~ baby.*

bo·nus ['bounəs] *n.* (pl. ~es) extra (usu. yearly) payment above the agreed amount.

boo(h) [buː] *v.t. & i., & n.* (make a) sound showing contempt or disapproval: *The speaker was ~ed by the crowd.*

boo·by ['buːbi] *n.* foolish person. ~ *trap*, one to catch an unwary person.

book [buk] *n.* **1.** number of sheets of paper, either blank or printed, fastened together in a cover; literary composition written or printed in a ~. **2.** division or part of the Bible or of a long poem. **3.** *bring sb. to ~*, require him to explain his conduct. *in sb.'s good (black, bad) ~s* having (not having) his favour and approval. *v.t.* 1. write down (orders, etc.) in a note~. 2. give, send, or record an order for seats at a theatre, tickets for a journey: *to ~ seats for a concert.* '~·**case** *n.* piece of furniture with shelves for ~s. '~·**ing-clerk** *n.* clerk who sells tickets (e.g. at a railway station). '~·**ing-office** *n.* office for the sale of tickets. '~·**ish** *adj.* of ~s or studies; fond of ~s. '~·**keeper** *n.* one who keeps business accounts. '~·**keeping** *n.* (system of) keeping business accounts. '~·**let** *n.* small ~, usu. in paper covers. '~·**maker** *n.* one whose business is the taking of bets (e.g. on horse-races).

¹**boom** [buːm] *n.* 1. long pole used to keep the bottom of a sail stretched. 2. pole fastened to a mast, used for (un)loading cargo. 3. heavy chain, mass of logs, etc., across a river or harbour mouth as a defence.

²**boom** [buːm] *v.i. & t. & n.* (of big guns, thunder, etc.) (give out a) deep, hollow sound.

³**boom** [buːm] *n.* sudden increase in trade activity, esp. a time when money is being made quickly. *v.i. & t.* have a ~; advertise in order to have a ~.

boom·e·rang ['buːməræŋ] *n.* curved throwing-stick of hard wood used in hunting by Australian aborigines—if it fails to hit anything it comes back to the thrower; (fig.) argument that recoils.

¹**boon** [buːn] *n.* advantage; blessing; favour; gift.

²**boon** [buːn] *adj.* ~ *companion*, merry, pleasant companion.

boor [buə*] *n.* rough, ill-mannered person. ~·**ish** ['buərif] *adj.*

boost [buːst] *v.t. & n.* (give a person, trade) encouragement by means of praise or advertisement; push (water, gas) along (a pipe) by means of a fan, etc.

boot [buːt] *n.* 1. see the picture. 2. compartment for luggage in a car or coach.

Boots   A motor-car boot

booth [buːð] *n.* 1. shelter (stall) made of boards, canvas, or other light materials, used as a shop. 2. place used for voting: *polling ~s.*

boo·ty ['buːti] *n.* things taken by robbers or captured from the enemy in war.

bo·rax ['bɔːræks] *n.* white powder used in glass-making and cleaning. **bo·ra·cic** [bə'ræsik] *adj.* of ~.

bor·der ['bɔːdə*] *n.* 1. edge; part near an edge. 2. (land near the) line dividing two countries. *v.t. & i.* put a ~ on; have a ~; be next to. '~·**land** *n.* land that forms a ~; (fig.) sth. between: *the ~land between sleeping and waking.*

¹**bore** [bɔː*] *v.t.* make (a narrow, round, deep hole in) by turning a pointed instrument or by digging, etc.: *to ~ a tunnel through a mountain; to ~ for oil.* *n.* 1. hole made by boring. 2. (width of) the hollow within a gun-barrel.

²**bore** [bɔː*] *v.t.* make (sb.) tired by dull or uninteresting talk or work: *This is a boring job. That man ~s me.* *n.* person or thing that ~s. '~·**dom** *n.* state of being ~d.

³**bore** [bɔː*] *n.* tidal wave in certain river mouths.

⁴**bore,** see ¹*bear.*

bor·ic ['bɔrik] *adj.* = boracic. ~ *acid*, a preservative.

born [bɔːn] a p.p. form of ¹*bear.* *be ~*, come into the world by birth. *adj.* by natural ability: *a ~ poet.*

borne, see ¹*bear.*

bor·ough ['bʌrə] *n.* (in England) town, part of town, sending one or more members to Parliament.

bor·row ['bɔrou] *v.t. & i.* get sth., or the use of sth., after promising to return it. (Cf. *lend*.)

bos·om ['buzəm] *n.* **1.** centre or inmost part, where one feels joy or sorrow. **2.** person's breast.

boss [bɔs] *n.* (colloq.) man who controls or gives orders to workmen; master. *v.t. & i.* give orders (to).

bot·a·ny ['bɔtəni] *n.* science of structure of plants. **bot·a·nist** *n.* **bo·tan·i·cal** [bə'tænikl] *adj. botanical gardens* (with specimens of plants for study).

botch [bɔtʃ] *v.t.* repair badly; spoil by poor work. *n.* piece of clumsy, badly-done work.

both [bouθ] *adj., pron. & adv.* **I. adj.** (of two things, persons, etc.) the two; the one and also the other: *I want ~ books (~ the books, ~ these books)*. **II. pron.** the two; not only the one: *B~ are good. B~ of them are good. We ~ want to go. They are ~ useful*. **III. adv.** *~ . . . and*, not only . . . but also: *He is ~ a soldier and a poet*.

both·er ['bɔðə*] *v.t. & i.* **1.** be or cause trouble to. **2.** take trouble. *n.* trouble; worry. *~'some adj.* causing ~.

bot·tle ['bɔtl] *n.* see the picture. *v.* put into, store in, ~s. ~ *up*, hold in (e.g. one's feelings). **¹~·neck** *n.* narrow part of a road, between wider parts; that part of a manufacturing process, etc., where production is slowed down (e.g. by shortage of materials).

Bottles

bot·tom ['bɔtəm] *n.* **1.** lowest part of anything, inside or outside; base. **2.** part farthest from the front or most important part: *at the ~ of my garden*. **3.** surface of land under a sea,

lake, river, etc. **4.** part of the body on which a person sits. *~·less adj.* very deep.

bou·doir ['bu:dwɑ:*] *n.* woman's private sitting-room or dressing-room.

bough [bau] *n.* large branch coming from a tree trunk.

bought, see *buy*.

boul·der ['bouldə*] *n.* large piece of rock, large stone, esp. one rounded by weather or water.

bou·le·vard ['bu:ləvɑ:d] *n.* wide street, often with trees on each side.

bounce [bauns] *v.i. & t.* **1.** (of a ball, etc.) (cause to) spring or jump back when sent against sth. hard. **2.** move, cause to move, violently; throw, be thrown, about: *to ~ into a room; to ~ on a bed (out of a chair). The car ~d along the bad road*.

¹bound [baund] *n.* (usu. pl.) limit: *no ~s to his ambition. in (out of) ~s*, within (outside) a limited or permitted area. *v.t.* form the ~s of; put ~s to. *~·a·ry n.* line marking the ~s or limits: *the ~ary between France and Italy. ~·less adj.*

²bound [baund] *v.i.* jump; move or run in jumps. *n.* jump up or forward: *by leaps and ~s*, very quickly.

³bound [baund] *ppl. adj.* about to start (*for*); on the way to: *The ship is outward (homeward) ~*.

⁴bound [baund] *p.p.* of *bind*. (special uses only) *~ to*, obliged or compelled to; certain to: *The plan is ~ to succeed. ~ up in*, much interested in; busy with; very fond of.

boun·der ['baundə*] *n.* (colloq.) cheerful and noisy, ill-bred, man.

boun·ty ['baunti] *n.* **1.** generosity. **2.** sth. given out of kindness (esp. to the poor). **3.** payment offered (usu. by government) to farmers, traders, to encourage production, etc. **boun·te·ous** ['bauntiəs], **boun·ti·ful** *adj.* generous.

bou·quet ['bukei, bu'kei] *n.* bunch of flowers for carrying in the hand.

bour·geois [ˈbuəʒwɑː] *n. & adj.* (person) of the middle class of society; of the habits and outlook of this class.

bout [baut] *n.* **1.** period of work or exercise. **2.** attack (of illness): *a ~ of coughing.*

¹bow [bou] *n.* **1.** curved piece of wood with string, used for shooting arrows. *draw the long bow*, exaggerate. **2.** rod of wood with hairs stretched from end to end, for playing the violin, etc. **3.** curve like a bow (1) (see *rainbow*). **4.** knot with a loop or loops: *a bow tie; shoelaces tied in a bow.* **'bow-legged** *adj.* with the legs curved outwards at the knees.

A bow and arrow

²bow [bau] *v.t. & i.* **1.** bend the head or body forward (as a greeting or in respect). **2.** bend: *bowed with age.* **3.** (fig.) give way (*to*); yield (*to*). *n.* act of bowing.

³bow [bau] *n.* front or forward end of a boat or ship.

bow·el [ˈbauəl] *n.* (usu. pl.) the long tube into which food passes from the stomach; the innermost part: *in the ~s of the earth* (i.e. deep underground).

¹bowl [boul] *n.* deep, round hollow dish: *a ~ of rice*; sth. shaped like a *~* : *the ~ of a tobacco-pipe.*

²bowl [boul] *v.i. & t.* **1.** (cricket) send a ball to the batsman; defeat the batsman by hitting the wicket with the ball. **2.** move quickly and smoothly (*along* a road) on wheels. **3.** knock (sb.) *over*; make sb. feel helpless. **~·er** *n.* **1.** one who ~s in cricket. **2.** hard, rounded **²felt** hat.

¹box [bɔks] *n.* **1.** container, usu. with a lid, made of wood, cardboard or metal, for holding solid articles. **2.** *Christmas box*, gratuity given at Christmas. *Boxing Day*, 26 Dec. **3.** separate compartment, with seats for several persons, in a theatre, or, in a court of law, for a witness to give his evidence. **'box-num·ber** *n.* reference number of an advertisement in a newspaper, to be used in addressing replies to be forwarded to the advertiser by the newspaper's staff. **'box-of·fice** *n.* place where tickets are sold in a theatre, concert hall, etc.

²box [bɔks] *v.t. & i.* **1.** *box sb.'s ear*, give him a blow there. **2.** fight with the fists, usu. with thick gloves, for sport. *n.* a blow with the open hand on the ear. **box·er** *n.* person who fights in this way. **box·ing** *n.* fighting with gloves: *a boxing-match.*

boy [bɔi] *n.* male child till about 17 years old. **boy·hood** *n.* period of being a boy. **boy·ish** *adj.* of, for, like, a boy.

boy·cott [ˈbɔikɔt] *v.t.* (join with others and) refuse to have anything to do with, to trade with, etc. *n.* refusal of this kind; ~ing.

¹brace [breis] *n.* **1.** piece of wood or iron used as a support or to hold things together. **2.** *~ and bit*, tool which is turned to make holes in wood, etc. **bra·ces** [ˈbreisiz] *n. pl.* straps passing over the shoulders, used to keep trousers up. *v.t.* support; give firmness or strength to: *to ~ oneself up; a bracing climate.*

²brace [breis] *n.* (pl. unchanged) pair or couple (of dogs, birds): *five ~ of pheasants.*

brace·let [ˈbreislit] *n.* band or chain (of metal, etc.) worn on the arm or wrist as an ornament.

brack·en [ˈbrækən] *n.* large fern; mass of such ferns.

brack·et [ˈbrækit] *n.* **1.** wood or metal support (e.g. for a shelf or lamp on a wall). **2.** marks ( ), [ ], { }, used in writing and printing. *v.t.* put inside, join with, ~s.

brack·ish [ˈbrækiʃ] *adj.* (of water) slightly salt.

brad·awl [ˈbrædɔːl] *n.* small tool for piercing holes for screws, etc.

brag [bræg] *v.i. & t. & n.* (-*gg*-). boast. **'~·gart** *n.* person who ~s.

braid [breid] *n.* **1.** band made by twisting together two or more strands of silk, thread, hair, etc. **2.** such bands used for binding edges of cloth or, if of silver or gold, for decoration (esp. on uniforms). *v.t.* make into ~s; put ~ on.

braille [breil] *n.* system of printing for the blind, to enable them to read by touch.

brain [brein] *n.* (often pl.) the mass of soft grey matter in the head, centre of the nervous system; the centre of thought: *to have a good* ~; *to use one's* ~*s*; *have sth. on the* ~, be thinking about sth. all the time. **Brains Trust** *n.* group of experts invited to answer questions asked by members of an audience. '~-ˌwashˑing *n.* process of forcing sb. (e.g. by persistent examination and instruction) to give up existing ideas or beliefs and accept new ones. *v.t.* kill by a hard blow on the head. ~ˑless *adj.* stupid. ~ˑy *adj.* clever.

braise [breiz] *v.t.* cook (meat, etc.) slowly in a covered pan.

brake [breik] *n.* apparatus which can be pressed or rubbed against a wheel to reduce the speed (of a motor-car, train, etc.). *v.i.* slow down, or stop, by using the ~(s).

bramˑble ['bræmbl] *n.* thorn-covered shrub.

bran [bræn] *n.* outer covering of grains (wheat, rye, etc.) separated from flour after grinding.

branch [brɑːntʃ] *n.* **1.** arm-like part of a tree growing out from the trunk or a bough. **2.** anything like a ~, going out from, or managed from, the central part; *a* ~ *railway* (*road, office*); *a* ~ *of knowledge.* *v.i.* send out, divide into, ~es. ~ *out*, become active in a new direction.

brand [brænd] *n.* **1.** piece of burning wood; red-hot iron used for marking (cattle, etc.). **2.** mark or design made in this way; trade-mark printed on boxes or packets of goods; named variety of goods: *the best* ~*s of coffee.* *v.t.* mark with a ~; (fig.) make a lasting mark on: ~*ed on my*

memory; *be* ~*ed as a coward.* '~-ˈnew *adj.* quite new.

branˑdish ['brændiʃ] *v.t.* wave about.

branˑdy ['brændi] *n.* strong alcoholic drink made from wine.

brass [brɑːs] *n.* **1.** bright yellow alloy made by mixing copper and zinc; things made of ~. *the* ~, ~ *musical instruments.* **2.** (colloq.) impudence. **brasˑsy** *adj.* impudent.

brasˑsiere ['bræsjɛə*] *n.* woman's close-fitting support for the breasts.

brat [bræt] *n.* (contemptuous) child.

braˑvaˑdo [brə'vɑːdou] *n.* display of (often foolish) daring or boldness.

brave [breiv] *adj. & v.t.* (ready to) face danger or pain without fear. ~ˑly *adv.* bravˑerˑy ['breivəri] *n.*

braˑvo [brɑː'vou] *int.* Well done!

brawl [brɔːl] *n.* noisy quarrel. *v.i.* take part in a ~.

brawn [brɔːn] *n.* **1.** strength; muscle. **2.** pickled pig-meat. ~ˑy *adj.* with strong muscles.

bray [brei] *v.i. & n.* (make the) cry of an ass; sound of a trumpet.

braˑzen ['breizn] *adj.* **1.** made of brass; like brass. **2.** shameless. *v.t.* ~ *it out*, behave, in spite of having done wrong, as if one has not.

braˑzier ['breizjə*] *n.* open metal framework (like a basket), usu. on legs, for holding burning coals.

breach [briːtʃ] *n.* **1.** act of breaking (a law, duty, promise, etc.). ~ *of the peace*, unlawful fighting in a public place. **2.** opening made in a defensive wall, etc., esp. one made by attacking forces. *stand in* (*throw oneself into*) *the* ~, be ready and eager to defend, give support, etc. *v.t.* make a ~ (**2**) in.

bread [bred] *n.* food (see *loaf*) made by baking flour with water and yeast.

breadth [bredθ] *n.* (see *broad*). **1.** distance from side to side. **2.** ~ *of mind*, quality of not being limited or narrow in one's opinions, views, etc., of being liberal or tolerant. (Cf. *broad-minded*.)

break [breik] *v.t. & i.* (p.t. **broke** [brouk], p.p. **broken** ['broukn]). **1.** (cause a whole thing to) divide into two or more pieces (as the result of a blow or other force, not by cutting, etc.): *The window broke. Who broke the window?* **2.** (with adv. & prep.) ~ *away*, (a) become separate; (b) (of members of a group) escape. ~ *down*, (a) (of machines, systems, plans, theories) fail to work; go wrong; prove to be useless; (b) (of a person, his health) become weak through overwork; (c) be overcome by emotion. ~ *sth.* (e.g. a door) *down*, use force to get it down. ~ *in(to)*, get in(to) by force. ~ *in on*, interrupt; burst suddenly into. ~ *(a horse, etc.) in*, tame; teach discipline to. ~ *in pieces, in two*, cause to come or go into two parts or several pieces. ~ *sth. off*, (a) separate: *to* ~ *a branch off*; (b) end: *to* ~ *off an engagement.* ~ *out*, (a) (of fires, war, disease) begin suddenly; (b) (of prisoners) escape. ~ *up*, (a) come or smash to pieces; (b) (of a meeting, school term, etc.) end; (c) (of a person) lose strength or health. **3.** (with nouns): ~ *a record*, create a new record. ~ *the back of*, finish the greater or more difficult part of (a piece of work, etc.). ~ *the ice* (fig.), overcome reserve (6) and get conversation started. **4.** fail to keep or obey (the law, a promise, etc.). **5.** stop, cause to stop, for a time; interrupt: *to* ~ *a silence (one's journey).* **6.** lessen the force of: *The bushes broke his fall.* ~ *the news*, be the first to give news (esp. of an unwelcome event). **7.** (of the voice) change because of strong feeling or when approaching manhood. *n.* **1.** ~ing; place of ~ing: *the* ~ *of day; day*~. **2.** space between (in place or time): *a* ~ *in the conversation; without a* ~ (i.e. continuously).

break·age ['breikidʒ] *n.* breaking; damage by breaking: *In this hotel* ~*s* (e.g. broken dishes, glasses, etc.) *cost £10 a month.*

break·down ['breikdaun] *n.* **1.** failure of a machine, system, etc.): *a* ~ *on the railway.* **2.** failure (of body or mind): *a nervous* ~.

break·er ['breikə*] *n.* large wave ready to break and fall (on the beach).

break·fast ['brekfəst] *n.* first meal of the day.

break·neck ['breiknek] *adj. at (a)* ~ *speed*, at a speed likely to cause an accident.

break·wa·ter ['breik,wɔːtə*] *n.* wall built (e.g. round a harbour) to break the force of the waves.

breast [brest] *n.* **1.** milk-producing part(s) of woman. *child at the* ~, one having its mother's milk. **2.** upper front part of the human body and part of a garment covering this: *a* ~ *pocket*; corresponding part of animal's body. **3.** the feelings: *a troubled* ~. *make a clean* ~ *of*, confess (wrongdoing, etc.). '~**work** *n.* wall (e.g. of earth or sandbags) built ~-high as a defence.

breath [breθ] *n.* air taken into or sent out of the lungs; single act of taking in air or sending it out. *catch one's* ~, stop taking in ~ for a moment (from excitement, etc.); *under one's* ~, in a whisper; *lose one's* ~, have difficulty in taking in ~ (e.g. when running); *out of* ~, needing to take in ~ more quickly than usual; *waste one's* ~, talk without result. ~**less** *adj.* **1.** out of ~. **2.** keeping one's ~ back (from excitement, etc.): *with* ~*less attention.*

breathe [briːð] *v.i. & t.* **1.** take air into the body and send it out. **2.** say in a whisper: *Don't* ~ *a word about it* (i.e. keep it secret).

bred, see **breed**.

breech [briːtʃ] *n.* back part of the barrel of a gun or other fire-arm, where a cartridge or shell is placed.

breech·es ['britʃiz] *n. pl.* short trousers fitting closely below the knees: *riding-~* (for wearing on horseback).

breed [bri:d] *v.t. & i.* (p.t. & p.p. **bred** [bred]). **1.** give birth to young; reproduce. **2.** keep (animals, etc.) for the purpose of having young: *to ~ horses.* **3.** train; educate: *an Englishman born and bred; a well-bred boy.* **4.** be the cause of: *War ~s misery and want.* *n.* kind or variety of animal, etc.; group of animals, etc., with the same qualities: *a good ~ of cattle.* **~'er** *n.* one who ~s (2) animals. **~'ing** *n.* (esp.) behaviour: *a man of good ~ing.*

breeze [bri:z] *n.* wind. **breez'y** *adj.* windy; (fig.) gay and cheerful.

breth'ren ['breðrin] *n. pl.* (old use) brothers.

bre·vi·a·ry ['bri:viəri] *n.* book with prayers to be said daily by priests of the Roman Catholic Church.

brev·i·ty ['breviti] *n.* shortness (e.g. in speaking and writing, and of human life).

brew [bru:] *v.t. & i.* **1.** prepare (drinks such as tea, beer) by soaking or boiling leaves, etc., in liquid. **2.** (fig.) (of storm, evil, etc.) be forming. **3.** set working (usu. for evil purposes): *They are ~ing mischief.* *n.* result of ~ing; liquid made by ~ing. **~'er** *n.* maker of beer. **~'er·y** *n.* place where beer is ~ed.

bri·ar ['braiə*] *n.* **1.** hard wood used for making tobacco-pipes. **2.** pipe made of this. **3.** see *brier.*

bribe [braib] *v.t. & n.* (give, offer) money, etc., tempting sb. to do sth. wrong, or sth. he does not want to do, usu. to the advantage of the giver. **'brib·er·y** *n.* giving or taking of ~s.

brick [brik] *n.* (rectangular block of) clay, baked by fire or sun, used for building houses, etc.

bride [braid] *n.* woman on her wedding-day; newly-married woman. **'~·groom** *n.* man on his wedding-day. **'brides'maid** *n.* girl or young unmarried woman attending a ~. **bri'dal** *adj.* of a ~ or wedding.

¹bridge [bridʒ] *n.* **1.** structure of wood, stone, bricks, etc., for carrying a road over a river, railway, etc. **2.** high platform over and across a ship's deck, from which the ship's officers give orders. **3.** upper, bony part of the nose. *v.t.* build a ~ (1) over.

²bridge [bridʒ] *n.* card game for four players.

bri'dle ['braidl] *n.* set of leather straps with a metal bit for the mouth, for controlling a horse. *v.t. & i.* **1.** put a ~ on (a horse). **2.** throw back the head in anger. **3.** (fig.) control (desires, etc.).

¹brief [bri:f] *adj.* (of time, events, writing, and speaking) short; lasting for only a short time. *in ~,* in a few words. **~'ly** *adv.*

²brief [bri:f] *n.* **1.** summary of the facts of a case, drawn up for a barrister. **2.** (also ~ing) instructions given to military officers before battle, etc. *v.t.* **1.** employ a barrister. **2.** instruct officers how to proceed.

briefs [bri:fs] *n. pl.* short undergarment held in place by an elastic waist-band.

bri'er ['braiə*] *n.* (see *briar*). bush covered with thorns, esp. the wild rose.

brig [brig] *n.* ship with two masts and square sails.

bri·gade [bri'geid] *n.* **1.** army unit of two, three, or four battalions. **2.** organized and uniformed body of persons with special duties: *the fire-~.* **brig·a·dier** [,brigə'diə*] *n.* officer commanding an army ~.

brig·and ['brigənd] *n.* robber, esp. one of a band attacking travellers in forests or mountains.

bright [brait] *adj.* **1.** giving out or reflecting strong light; shining. **2.** cheerful and happy. **3.** (fig.) clever. **~'ly** *adv.* **~'ness** *n.*

bright·en ['braitən] *v.t. & i.* make or become bright(er), more cheerful, etc.

bril·liant ['briljənt] *adj.* very bright; clever; splendid. **bril·liance** *n.*

brim [brim] **n. 1.** edge (of a cup, bowl, etc.): *full to the ~*. **2.** out-turned edge of a hat (giving shade). **v.i.** (-mm-). be full to the ~ (1). '**~ ful(l)** *pred. adj.* full to the ~ (1): *He's ~-full of new ideas.*

brim·stone ['brimstən] **n.** sul-phur.

brin·dle(d) ['brindl(d)] *adj.* brown with streaks of another colour: *a ~ cow (cat).*

brine [brain] **n.** salt water: *pickled in ~.* **bri·ny** *adj.*

bring [briŋ] **v.t.** (p.t. & p.p. *brought* [brɔːt]). **1.** cause to come, have, with oneself; carry, lead, drive, oneself towards the speaker; cause (sth. or sb.) to be (where the speaker is): *I will ~ you the book tomorrow. B~ that chair in from the garden.* **2.** cause; cause to become: *Can you ~ him to agree to the plan?* ~ *up (forward)*, cause (sth.) to be considered. ~ *sth. about*, ~ *sth. to pass*, cause to happen. ~ *back*, ~ *to mind*, cause to re-member. ~ *down*, cause to be lower (e.g. prices). ~ *off*, cause to be successful; succeed in an attempt. ~ *on*, lead to; help to produce. ~ *out*, cause to appear clearly. ~ *sb. round*, cause sb. to regain consciousness after fainting. ~ *sb. round to (one's opinion)*, cause, persuade, him to accept it or agree with it. ~ *sth. home to sb.*, cause him to realize it. **3.** ~ *up*, (a) look after during childhood; train; edu-cate: *well brought up children*; (b) vomit (1). ~ *out (a book, etc.)*, publish. ~ *forth*, produce (young, fruit). ~ *in*, introduce. ~ *to bear on*, bring towards: *to ~ pressure to bear on sb.*; *to ~ the big guns to bear on the enemy.*

brink [briŋk] **n. 1.** edge of sth. unknown, dangerous or excit-ing: *on the ~ of ruin (war).* **2.** upper end of a steep place.

brisk [brisk] *adj.* quick-moving: *a ~ walk(er). Trade is ~.*

bris·tle ['brisl] **n.** short, stiff hair. **v.i.** (of hair) stand up on end (with fear, etc.); (of an animal) have the hair on end. ~ *with*, have in large numbers: *a problem bristling with difficulties.*

Brit·ish ['britiʃ] *adj.* of Great Britain, the British Common-wealth of Nations or its in-habitants: *the ~, the ~ people.*

brit·tle ['britl] *adj.* hard but easily broken (e.g. glass, coal).

broach [broutʃ] **v.t.** open (a barrel); (fig.) begin to discuss.

broad [brɔːd] *adj.* **1.** wide; large across: *Rivers get ~er as they near the sea. His back is ~ enough to carry even that weight.* **2.** from side to side: *a table six feet ~.* (of the mind, ideas, etc.) liberal; not limited: *a man of ~ views; a ~-minded man.* **3.** full and complete: *~ daylight. in ~ outline*, giving the chief features or ideas. **4.** strongly marked: *a ~ hint; a ~ accent.* ~**·en** *v.t. & i.* make or become ~ (1). ~**·ly** *adv.* ~*ly speaking*, speaking in a general way with-out going into detail.

broad·cast ['brɔːdkɑːst] *v.t. & i.* (p.t. & p.p. *broadcast*). send out in all directions, esp. by radio: *to ~ the news; a ~ speech.* **n.** sth. ~ by radio: *the ~ of the Queen's speech.*

broad·side ['brɔːdsaid] **n.** (the firing of) all the guns on one side of a ship. ~ *(on) to*, with the side turned to.

bro·cade [brə'keid] **n.** fine cloth with raised designs (e.g. in silver thread) worked on it.

bro·chure [brou'ʃuə*] **n.** short, usu. descriptive, printed article in a paper cover.

brogue [broug] **n. 1.** strong, usu. ornamented, shoe for country wear. **2.** countrified speech.

broke, bro·ken, see *break*.

bro·ker ['broukə*] **n.** one who brings together buyers and sel-lers (esp. of 'shares (3), bonds (2), etc.). '~**·age** **n.** charge(s) made by a ~.

bro·mide ['broumaid] **n.** chemi-cal substance; medicine used to calm nerves and help a person to sleep.

bron·chi·tis [brɔŋ'kaitis] **n.** ill-ness (with coughing) caused by inflammation of the linings of the two main branches of the windpipe (the *bronchial tubes*).

bronze [brɒnz] *n.* **1.** mixture of copper and tin; its colour (reddish brown). **2.** work of art made of ~.

brooch [broutʃ] *n.* ornamental pin for fastening (on) a dress (esp. at the neck).

brood [bru:d] *n.* all the young birds hatched at one time in a nest. *v.i.* (of a bird) sit on eggs; (fig.) think about (troubles, etc.) for a long time. ~·**y** *adj.* (of hens) wanting to ~.

¹**brook** [bruk] *n.* small stream.

²**brook** [bruk] *v.t.* allow of; suffer.

broom [bru(:)m] *n.* **1.** brush on a long handle for sweeping floors. **2.** yellow-flowered shrub.

broth [brɒθ] *n.* meat soup.

broth·er [ˈbrʌðə*] *n.* **1.** another (male) child of the parents of sb. speaking or referred to. **2.** man in the same profession, religious society, etc., as another: *a* ~ *doctor*. '~-**in-law** *n.* ~ of one's husband or wife; husband of one's sister. '~·**hood** *n.* group of men with common interests and aims, esp. a religious society. ~·**ly** *adj.*

brought, see *bring*.

brow [brau] *n.* **1.** part of the face above the eyes. **2.** (also *eye*~) arch of hair above the eye(s): *to raise one's* ~s. **3.** top of a slope. '~·**beat** *v.t.* frighten by shouting or treating roughly.

brown [braun] *adj. & n.* colour of chocolate, toasted bread, and coffee mixed with milk.

browse [brauz] *v.i.* **1.** eat, ³crop (leaves, grass, etc.). **2.** (fig.) read here and there in a book, newspaper, etc. *n.* (act, period, of) browsing.

bruise [bru:z] *n.* injury to the body or a fruit, etc., so that the skin is discoloured but not broken. *v.t. & i.* cause ~(s) to; get ~(s): *to* ~ *one's leg*; *to* ~ *easily*.

brun·ette [bru(:)ˈnet] *n.* woman of European race with dark-brown or black hair and eyes.

brunt [brʌnt] *n.* bear the ~ of (an

attack), resist the weight or pressure of.

brush [brʌʃ] *n.* **1.** implement of hair, bristle, wire, etc., fastened into a handle, for cleaning, scrubbing, etc. (Cf. *broom*.) **2.** short, sharp fight. *v.t. & i.* **1.** use a ~ upon. **2.** ~ *up*, get back knowledge or skill which one has lost: *to* ~ *up one's French*. ~ *past* (*against*), touch when passing. '~·**wood** *n.* low bushes; undergrowth.

brusque [brusk] *adj.* rough (in or of speech, behaviour).

brute [bru:t] *n.* **1.** animal (except man). **2.** stupid and cruel man. **3.** (used attrib.) animal-like; unreasoning: ~ *strength* (i.e. strength without skill). **bru·tal** [ˈbru:tl] *adj.* savage; cruel. **bru·tal·ize** [ˈbru:təlaiz] *v.t.* make brutal. **bru·tal·i·ty** [bru:ˈtæliti] *n.* cruelty.

bub·ble [ˈbʌbl] *n.* **1.** (in air) floating ball formed of liquid and containing air or gas. **2.** (in water) ball of air or gas rising to the surface. *v.i.* send up ~s; rise in ~s.

buc·ca·neer [ˌbʌkəˈniə*] *n.* pirate.

¹**buck** [bʌk] *n.* **1.** male of deer, hare, or rabbit. (Cf. *doe*.) **2.** (slang, U.S.A.) dollar.

²**buck** [bʌk] *v.i.* (of a horse) jump high with the back arched (in order to throw the rider).

buck·et [ˈbʌkit] *n.* open vessel, cf. *pail*, of wood, metal, or plastic, for drawing and carrying liquids.

buck·le [ˈbʌkl] *n.* metal fastener for a belt or strap. *v.t. & i.* **1.** fasten with a ~. **2.** (of metal-work, etc.) bend, get twisted (from heat, because of strain).

buck·ler [ˈbʌklə*] *n.* small round shield.

buck·wheat [ˈbʌkwi:t] *n.* plant with small, triangular black seeds (used for feeding horses and hens, also made into flour).

bu·col·ic [bju:ˈkɒlik] *adj.* of country life and farming.

bud [bʌd] *n.* leaf, flower, or branch at the beginning of its growth; flower not fully open.

v.i. (*-dd-*). put out buds; begin to develop: *a budding lawyer.*

Bud·dhism ['budizəm] *n.* the religion founded by Buddha. **Bud·dhist** ['budist] *n.* follower of Buddha.

budge [bʌdʒ] *v.t. & i.* (usu. neg.) move sth. heavy or stiff (2): *I can't ~ it. It won't ~.*

bud·get ['bʌdʒit] *n.* **1.** estimate of probable future income and payments. **2.** collection of news, letters, etc. *v.i. ~ for,* make a ~ (1) for: *to ~ for the next year.*

buff [bʌf] *n.* thick, strong, soft leather; its colour, a brownish-yellow.

buf·falo ['bʌfəlou] *n.* (pl. *-oes*). kinds of ox (Asia, Africa, etc.).

buf·fer ['bʌfə*] *n.* apparatus (usu. with springs) for lessening the effect of a blow, esp. on or of a railway engine, etc. ~ *state,* small country between two larger countries.

¹**buf·fet** ['bʌfit] *n.* blow, esp. one given with the hand. *v.t.* hit; knock about: *~ed by the waves.*

²**buf·fet** ['bufei] *n.* **1.** counter where food and drink may be bought and eaten. **2.** sideboard, table, from which food and drink are served (e.g. in a hotel).

buf·foon [bʌ'fu:n] *n.* clown. ~'er·y *n.* clown-like behaviour.

bug [bʌg] *n.* small, flat, bad-smelling insect that sucks blood; (U.S.A.) any insect.

bug·bear ['bʌgbɛə*] *n.* sth. specially feared or disliked, often without good reason.

bu·gle ['bju:gl] *n.* musical wind instrument of brass or copper, used in the army. **bu·gler** *n.*

build [bild] *v.t. & i.* (p.t. & p.p. *built* [bilt]). make (a house, etc.) by putting the materials together. ~ *up,* make bigger or stronger (a business, one's health). ~ *upon,* use as a foundation; (fig.) allow to rest on. *built-up* (areas), covered with buildings. *n.* general shape: *a man of powerful ~*; *to recognize a man by his ~.* ~'**ing** *n.* **1.** constructing houses, etc. **2.** house or other thing that is built for living or working in.

bulb [bʌlb] *n.* **1.** thick, round part, in the ground, of such plants as onions and lilies, where plant food is stored. **2.** ~-shaped object (esp. electric lamp). ~'**ous** *adj.* ~-shaped.

Bulbs

bulge [bʌldʒ] *v.i. & t.* (cause to) swell beyond the usual size; curve outwards: *a sack bulging with cabbages; bulging pockets.* *n.* **1.** place where a swelling or curve shows. **2.** (statistics) temporary increase in numbers or volume.

bulk [bʌlk] *n.* **1.** quantity or volume, esp. when great. *in ~,* loose or in large amounts. **2.** the greater part or number (*of*). *v.i. ~ large,* seem large in respect of size, etc. ~'y *adj.* (*-ier, -iest*). taking up much space.

bulk·head ['bʌlkhed] *n.* watertight division or dividing wall in a ship.

¹**bull** [bul] *n.* **1.** uncastrated male of the ox family: *a prize ~.* **2.** male of elephant, whale, and some other large animals. *take the ~ by the horns,* attack a problem in a bold and straightforward way.* ~'**s-eye** *n.* centre of the target (for archers, etc.).

²**bull** [bul] *n.* formal order or announcement made by the Pope.

³**bull** [bul] *n.* foolish or amusing mistake in language, usu. because there is a contradiction in terms (e.g. 'If you do not get this letter, please write and tell me.').

bull·doz·er ['buldouzə*] *n.* machine for shifting large quantities of earth, levelling land, etc.

bul·let ['bulit] *n.* shaped piece of lead, often coated with another metal, fired from a rifle or revolver. (Cf. *shell* (3), *cartridge*.)

bul·le·tin ['bulitin] *n.* official statement of news.

bul·lion ['buljən] *n.* gold or silver in bulk, before manufacture.

bul·lock ['buləks] *n.* castrated bull.

bul·ly ['buli] *n.* person who uses his strength or power to frighten or hurt those who are weaker. *v.t.* use strength, etc., in this way: *to ~ sb. into doing sth.*

bul·wark ['bulwək] *n.* **1.** wall, esp. one built of earth, against attack; (fig.) defence. **2.** low wall round (esp. a sailing ship)'s deck.

bump [bʌmp] *n.* **1.** blow or knock (as when two things come together with force). **2.** swelling of, lump on, the flesh caused by this, or made on a road surface by traffic. *v.t. & i.* give or receive a ~ or ~s; *to ~ one's head against sth.*; *to ~ along a bad road.* ~·**y** *adj.* with many ~s.

bum·per ['bʌmpə*] *n.* **1.** (attrib., of crops) unusually large. **2.** bar on a motor-car to prevent damage from a slight collision.

bump·kin ['bʌmpkin] *n.* awkward person with unpolished manners, esp. from the country.

bump·tious ['bʌmpʃəs] *adj.* self-important; conceited.

bun [bʌn] *n.* **1.** small, round sweet cake. **2.** (of a woman's hair) *in a bun,* twisted into a knot behind and above the neck.

bunch [bʌntʃ] *n.* number of small, similar things naturally growing together (*a ~ of grapes*) or gathered together (*a ~ of flowers, keys*). *v.t. & i.* come or bring together into a ~.

bun·dle ['bʌndl] *n.* number of articles wrapped or tied together: *a ~ of books (sticks, old clothes).* *v.t. & i.* **1.** make into a ~. **2.** put away without order: *to ~ everything into a drawer.* **3.** go or send in a hurry: *to ~ the children off to school.*

bung [bʌŋ] *n.* large (usu. wooden) stopper for closing the hole in a barrel. *v.t.* put a ~ into. ~ed *up,* closed; stopped up.

bun·ga·low ['bʌŋgəlou] *n.* house with all rooms on one floor.

bun·gle ['bʌŋgl] *v.t. & i.* do (a piece of work) badly or clumsily. *n.* bungled piece of work. **bun·gler** *n.*

bunk [bʌŋk] *n.* sleeping-place fixed on the wall (e.g. in a ship or train).

bunk·er ['bʌŋkə*] *n.* **1.** part of a steamer where coal is stored. **2.** sandy hollow, made as an obstacle, on a golf-course. **3.** military underground stronghold.

bun·ny ['bʌni] *n.* (child's word for) rabbit.

bun·sen ['bʌnsən] *n.* ~ *burner,* device for burning coal-gas, for use in a laboratory.

bun·ting ['bʌntiŋ] *n.* (thin cloth used for making) flags and similar decorations.

buoy [bɔi] *v.t. & n.* (mark positions on the water with) floating, fixed object: *to ~ a wreck (channel).* ~ *up,* prevent from sinking; (fig.) keep up (hopes, etc.). ~·**ant** ['bɔiənt] *adj.* able to float or to keep things floating; (fig.) full of hope; light-hearted. ~·**an·cy** ['bɔiənsi] *n.*

bur·den ['bə:dn] *n.* load, esp. a heavy load carried on the back; anything difficult to bear: *a ~ of sorrow (taxation).* *v.t.* put a ~ on. ~·**some** *adj.*

bu·reau ['bjuərou, bjuə'rou] *n.* **1.** office, esp. for public information: *a travel ~.* **2.** writing-desk. ~·**crat** ['bjuəroukræt] *n.* government official, esp. one who does not lose his post when another political group comes into power. ~·**crat·ic** [,bjuərou'krætik] *adj.* ~·**cra·cy** [bjuə'rokrəsi] *n.* government by ~crats.

bur·glar ['bə:glə*] *n.* person who breaks into a house, shop, etc., by night to steal. ~·**y** *n.*

bur·i·al, see bury.

bur·lesque [bə:'lesk] *v.t. & n.* (make an) amusing imitation (of a book, speech, person's behaviour, etc.).

bur·ly ['bə:li] *adj.* (of a person) big and strong.

burn [bə:n] *v.i. & t.* (p.t. & p.p. *burned* or *burnt*). **1.** use for the purpose of driving, heating, or lighting: *Most large steamships ~ oil.* **2.** destroy by fire; damage or injure by fire or acid;

scorch; be hurt by fire or acid: *The house was burnt down. The boy was badly burnt about the face.* **3.** be in flames; be alight; be hot enough to hurt; give out heat or light. **4.** (fig.) be filled with strong feeling: *They are ~ing to defeat the enemy.* *n.* injury, mark made, by fire, acid, or the heat of the sun. *~ing adj. a ~ing question,* one causing heated argument.

bur·nish ['bə:niʃ] *v.t.* polish.

bur·row ['bʌrou] *v.t. & i. & n.* (make a) hole in the ground (esp. as dug by rabbits and foxes).

bur·sar ['bə:sə*] *n.* treasurer (esp. of a college).

burst [bə:st] *v.t. & i.* **1.** fly into pieces; (cause to) break open; explode. **2.** make a way *(out, through, into,* etc.). *to ~ out laughing, to ~ into laughter,* begin suddenly to laugh. *~ing with,* over-full of. *n.* **1.** a *~ing: the ~ of a shell; a ~ of laughter.* **2.** hole, etc., made by *~ing.* **3.** short, violent effort: *a ~ of speed (energy).*

bur·y ['beri] *v.t.* **1.** put (a dead body) in the ground, in a grave, in the sea, etc. **2.** cover with earth; hide from view, etc.: *half buried under dead leaves (snow,* etc.). *~ oneself in the country,* go and live where one will meet few people; *buried in thought (one's books,* etc.), paying no attention to anything else.

bur·i·al ['beriəl] *n.* act of *~ing.*

bus [bʌs] *n.* (pl. *buses* ['bʌsiz]). see the picture.

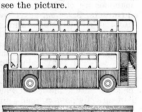

Buses

bush [buʃ] *n.* **1.** plant with many woody stems coming up from the root. (Cf. *tree,* with a trunk.) **2.** (sing. with *the*) wild uncultivated country (esp. in Africa and Australia). *~·y adj.*

bush·el ['buʃl] *n.* measure for grain and fruit; eight gallons.

busi·ness ['biznis] *n.* **1.** buying and selling; trade. **2.** shop; commercial firm. **3.** task; duty: *It is the ~ of a teacher to teach.* *~·like* ['biznislaik] *adj.*

bust [bʌst] *n.* **1.** head and shoulders of a person cut in stone or cast in bronze, etc. **2.** upper front part of a woman's body; measurement of this round the chest and back.

bus·tle ['bʌsl] *v.i. & t.* move about quickly and excitedly. *n.* such movement(s).

bus·y ['bizi] *adj.* *(-ier, -iest).* **1.** working; occupied; having much to do. **2.** filled with activity: *a ~ day.* **bus·i·ly** *adv.* *v.t. ~ oneself (with, about),* be or keep *~.* *~·bod·y n.* person who pushes himself into the affairs of others.

but [bʌt, bət] *conj., adv., prep. & rel. pron.* **I. conj.** *Tom was not there, but his brother was. He's hard-working, but not clever. Hardly a day passes but I think of her* (without my thinking of her). *I cannot but admire your courage* (I cannot help admiring). *I could not but go* (There was nothing else I could do except go). **II. adv.** only (which is the more usual word to use here): *We can but try. He's but a boy* (not old enough to know better). **III. prep.** except: *They're all wrong but me! Who but he would do this? We should have enjoyed the journey but for the rain. He would have helped us but for having no money himself* (except that he had . . .). **IV. rel. pron.** who ·or that not: *There is nobody but wishes you well* (nobody who does not wish you well).

but·cher ['butʃə*] *n.* person who kills, cuts up and sells animals for food. *v.t.* kill very violently, esp. with a knife.

but·ler ['bʌtlə*] *n.* head manservant (in charge of the winecellar, plate (5), etc.).

¹butt [bʌt] *n.* thicker (usu. wooden) end of a tool or weapon.

²butt [bʌt] *n.* **1.** (pl.) shootingrange (2). **2.** thing or person as a target for ridicule.

³butt [bʌt] *v.t. & i.* strike or hit (esp. with the head, as a goat does). ~ *in* (colloq.), force oneself (into company, conversation); interrupt.

but·ter ['bʌtə*] *n.* fatty food (usu. yellow or yellowish-white) made from cream. '~·**fly** *n.* insect with feelers and coloured wings. '~·**milk** *n.* sour milk remaining after butter has been made.

but·tock ['bʌtək] *n.* either side of that part of the body on which one sits.

but·ton ['bʌtn] *n.* **1.** small, usu. round bit of bone, metal, etc., for fastening articles of clothing. **2.** ~-like object, pushed or pressed (e.g. to ring an electric bell). *v.t. & i.* fasten, be fastened, with ~s. '~·**hole** *n.* **1.** slit through which a button is passed. **2.** flower(s) inserted in this or worn on a frock.

but·tress ['bʌtris] *v.t. & n.* (hold up, strengthen, with a) support built against a wall.

bux·om ['bʌksəm] *adj.* (of a woman) healthy-looking, goodlooking, and well covered with flesh.

buy [bai] *v.t. & i.* (p.t. & p.p. *bought* [bɔːt]). get by paying money or sth. else of value in return.

buzz [bʌz] *n.* sound made by bees when flying, by people talking, by machinery (at a distance). *v.i. & t.* **1.** make a ~; be filled with a ~ing sound. **2.** (of an aircraft) fly near (another aircraft) in a threatening way. ~·**er** *n.* instrument making a ~ing sound (as a signal or warning).

by [bai] *prep. & adv.* **I. prep.**

1. near; at or to the side of: *Come and sit by me (by my side) by oneself*, alone: *He did it (all, by himself* (without help). *stand by sb.*, support him. **2.** (in points of the compass): *East by North* (one point N. of E.). **3.** (showing direction of movement) through; along; across: *We came by the shortest route.* **4.** past: *As you go by the station* (pass it) *please get me an evening paper.* **5.** (of time) during: *The sun shines by day and the moon by night.* **6.** (of time) not later than: *Get the work finished by tomorrow.* **7.** (of time) indicating a period: *You can rent this house by the month.* **8.** through the agency of: *The house is lit by electricity. She was knocked down by a car.* **9.** (manner or method): *Will you travel by sea or by air? Learn this by heart. She took him by the hand. Send the letter by hand* (messenger), *not by post.* **10.** according to: *It's two o'clock by my watch.* **11.** to the extent of: *The car missed me by a few inches.* **II. adv. 1.** near: *When nobody was by, she felt lonely.* **2.** past: *We hurried by, hoping they wouldn't see us.* **3.** aside: *Lay the money by, for use later.* **4.** *by and by*, later on, eventually: *You will understand everything, by and by.*

by(e)- [bai] *prefix.* **1.** less important: '**by·road**; '**by·path**. **2.** made or obtained during the manufacture of sth. else: '**by·products. 3.** (= *by*, adv.) '**by·gone** *adj.* past; '**by·stand·er** *n.* person standing near and looking on. '**by(e)·law** *n.* rule made by a local authority (e.g. a town). '**by·e·lec·tion** *n.* election made necessary by the death or resignation of a member during the life of Parliament. '**by·pass** *n.* road joining two parts of an older road (usu. to avoid a town or village). '**by·word** *n.* person, place, etc., regarded and spoken of as a notable example (usu. bad).

byre ['baiə*] *n.* cow-house.

C

cab [kæb] *n.* **1.** horse-carriage or motor-car which may be hired for short journeys: *a taxicab.* **2.** part of a railway engine or lorry reserved for the driver.

cab·a·ret ['kæbərei] *n.* entertainment (songs and dancing) in a restaurant while guests are eating.

cab·bage ['kæbidʒ] *n.* plant with a round head of thick green leaves, used as a vegetable.

A cabbage

A cabinet

cab·by ['kæbi] *n.* cabman, driver of a (horse) cab.

cab·in ['kæbin] *n.* **1.** small, roughly-built house (e.g. of logs). **2.** small room (esp. for sleeping in) in a ship or aircraft. ~ *class,* (in liners) grade of accommodation between first class and tourist class. '~-**boy** *n.* boy servant in a ship.

cab·i·net ['kæbinit] *n.* **1.** piece of furniture with shelves or drawers for storing or displaying things. **2.** *the Cabinet,* group of men (chief ministers) chosen by a head of government to be responsible for state affairs. '~-,**mak·er** *n.* skilled workman who makes furniture.

ca·ble ['keibl] *n.* **1.** thick, strong rope of hemp, wire, etc. **2.** line containing insulated wires (laid underground or on the ocean bottom) for carrying messages by telegraph or telephone; message so carried. **3.** (as measure) 100 fathoms. *v.t. & i.* send a message) by ~ (2). '~·**car** *n.* railway up a steep hillside, worked by a cable and a station-

ary engine. '~·**gram** *n.* ~d telegram.

ca·ca·o [kə'ka:ou] *n.* tree with seeds from which cocoa and chocolate are made.

cache [kæʃ] *n.* (hiding-place for) food and stores left (e.g. by explorers) for later use.

cack·le ['kækl] *v.i. & n.* (make the) noise made by a hen after laying an egg; loud, shrill talk or laughter.

cac·tus ['kæktəs] *n.* (pl. sometimes *cacti* ['kæktai]). plant with thick, fleshy stem(s), (usu.) no leaves, often covered with sharp points.

cad [kæd] *n.* ill-mannered person; person who behaves dishonourably. **cad·dish** *adj.* of or like a ~.

ca·dav·er·ous [kə'dævərəs] *adj.* looking like a corpse.

cad·die, cad·dy ['kædi] *n.* person paid to carry a golfer's clubs for him round the course.

cad·dy ['kædi] *n.* small box for holding the dried leaves for making tea.

ca·dence ['keidəns] *n.* rise and fall of music or of the voice in speaking; rhythm.

ca·det [kə'det] *n.* student at a military or naval college. ~ *corps,* organization giving military training to older boys at school.

cadge [kædʒ] *v.t. & i.* (try to) get (from friends) by begging: *He's always cadging. He* ~d *a meal.*

ca·fé ['kæfei] *n.* small restaurant.

caf·e·te·ri·a [,kæfi'tiəriə] *n.* self-service restaurant.

cage [keidʒ] *n.* **1.** box, place, closed in with wires or bars in which birds or animals are kept. **2.** ~-like part of a lift used for lowering and raising workers in a mine. *v.t.* put, keep, in a ~: *a* ~d *bird.*

cairn [kɛən] *n.* pyramid of rough stones set up as a landmark or memorial.

ca·jole [kə'dʒoul] *v.t.* use flattery or deceit to persuade sb. to do sth. **ca·jol·er·y** [kə'dʒouləri] *n.*

cake [keik] *n.* **1.** sweet mixture of flour, butter, eggs, etc., baked in an oven; (usu. minced) portion of other kinds of food: *fish-~s*. **2.** shaped lump of a substance: *a ~ of soap*. *v.t. & i.* form into a thick, hard mass; coat thickly with sth. which dries hard: *shoes ~d with mud*.

cal·a·bash ['kæləbæʃ] *n.* (tree with) fruit of which the hard outer skin (or shell) is used for making bottles, bowls, etc.

ca·lam·i·ty [kə'læmiti] *n.* great and serious misfortune or disaster. **ca·lam·i·tous** *adj.*

cal·ci·um ['kælsiəm] *n.* soft metal forming part of limestone and chalk, present in milk and bones. *~ carbide* ['kɑ:baid], substance used to make acetylene gas.

cal·cu·late ['kælkjuleit] *v.i. & i.* **1.** find out by working with numbers: *to ~ the cost of a journey*. **2.** plan; arrange; intend: *an advertisement ~d to attract the attention of housewives*. **3.** *~ on*, rely on; be sure of. **cal·cu·la·ting** *adj.* careful; planning things from selfish motives. **cal·cu·la·tion** [ˌkælkju'leiʃn] *n.* **cal·cu·la·tor** *n.* person, machine, that *~s*.

cal·en·dar ['kælində*] *n.* **1.** list of the days, weeks, months, etc., of a particular year. **2.** system for fixing the beginning, length, and divisions of a year: *the Muslim ~*.

cal·en·der ['kælində*] *n.* roller-machine for pressing cloth and paper. *v.t.* put through a *~*.

¹**calf** [kɑ:f] *n.* (pl. *calves* [kɑ:vz]). the young of the cow and some other animals. '*~·skin* *n.* *~* leather.

²**calf** [kɑ:f] *n.* (pl. *calves* [kɑ:vz]). the fleshy part of the back of the leg, below the knee.

cal·i·bre ['kælibə*] *n.* **1.** inside measurement across (diameter of) a gun-barrel or any tube, or of a bullet. **2.** quality of mind or character: *a man of good ~*.

cal·i·brate ['kælibreit] *v.t.* find the *~* of a tube, etc.; mark or test the scale on a thermometer, etc.

cal·i·co ['kælikou] *n.* cheap cotton cloth.

cal·iph ['keilif, 'kælif] *n.* title once used by rulers who were descendants and successors of Muhammad. '*~·ate* *n.* *~*'s position.

call [kɔ:l] *v.t. & i.* **1.** give (a name) to. *~ sb. names*, insult him by giving him bad names. **2.** consider; think: *I ~ that a shame*. **3.** (often *~ out*) cry; shout: *Do you hear sb. ~ing? He ~ed (out) for help*. **4.** pay a short visit to: *to ~ on a friend*; (of, e.g., a ship) stop at: *to ~ at Cape Town*. *~ for*, visit a place to get sth. or to go with sb. to another place: *The grocer ~s each week for orders. I will ~ for you at six o'clock*. **5.** ask for the presence or attention of: *to ~ a doctor*; *to ~ sb. up by telephone*. **6.** (special uses) *~ for*, need, demand: *Your plan will ~ for a lot of money*. *~ off*, give orders to, decide to, stop sth.: *Please ~ your dog off. The football match was ~ed off*. *~ up*, *~ to mind*, (cause to) remember. *~ (sb.) to order*, ask (sb. at a meeting, etc.) to obey the rules. *~ sth. in question*, say that one is doubtful about its truth. *~ a meeting (a strike)*, announce that there will be one. *n.* **1.** cry or shout. *within ~*, near by; not far away. **2.** message: *telephone ~s*. **3.** short visit: *to pay a ~ on sb*. **4.** claim (for money, help, etc.): *~s on one's time and purse*. **5.** need: *no ~ for anxiety*. *~·er* *n.* *~·ing* *n.* (esp.) occupation; profession.

cal·lig·ra·phy [kə'ligrəfi] *n.* handwriting, esp. fine handwriting.

cal·(l)i·pers ['kælipəz] *n. pl.* instrument for measuring the calibre or diameter of tubes, cylinders, etc.

cal·lous ['kæləs] *adj.* **1.** (of the skin) hard; made hard by rough work. **2.** (of a person) disregarding the feelings and sufferings of others.

cal·low ['kælou] *adj.* (of a young person) without experience of life.

calm [kɑ:m] *adj.* quiet; untroubled. *n.* time when everything is ~. *v.t.* & *i.* make or become ~. ~·ly *adv.* ~·ness *n.*

cal·o·rie ['kæləri] *n.* unit of heat; unit of energy supplied by food.

cal·um·ny ['kæləmni] *n.* untrue and damaging statement about sb. ca·lum·ni·ate [kə'lʌmnieit] *v.t.*

calve [kɑːv] *v.t.* give birth to a calf.

calves, see *calf*.

cam·ber ['kæmbə*] *n.* slightly arched form (of road surface, etc.).

cam·bric ['keimbrik] *n.* fine, thin cloth of cotton or linen.

came, see *come*.

cam·el ['kæml] *n.* long-necked animal, with either one or two humps on its back, much used in desert countries for riding and carrying goods.

cam·e·o ['kæmiou] *n.* piece of hard stone, on which is a raised design often in a different colour, used as a jewel or ornament.

cam·er·a ['kæmərə] *n.* apparatus for taking photographs.

cam·ou·flage ['kæmuflɑːʒ] *v.t.* & *n.* (use a) system of hiding or disguising the real appearance of sth.; esp., in war, the use of paint, netting, etc., to deceive the enemy.

camp [kæmp] *n.* place where people (e.g. soldiers) live in tents or huts for a time. '~-'bed (-'chair, -'stool, etc.), that can be folded and carried easily. *v.i.* make, live in, a ~. go ~ing, spend a holiday living in tent(s).

cam·paign [kæm'pein] *n.* 1. group of military operations with a set purpose or objective, usu. in one area. 2. series of planned activities to gain a special object: *a political* ~. *v.i.* take part in, go on, a ~. ~·er *n.*

cam·phor ['kæmfə*] *n.* strong-smelling white substance used for medical purposes and to keep away insects. ~·a·ted ['kæmfəreitid] *adj.* containing ~: ~ated oil.

cam·pus ['kæmpəs] *n.* (U.S.A.) grounds of a college or university.

¹can [kæn, kən] *aux. v.* (cannot, can't [kɑːnt], p.t. could [kud, kəd], couldn't ['kudnt]). 1. be able to; know how to: *If you shut your eyes, you can't see.* 2. (indicating possibility): *That couldn't be true.* 3. (indicating wonder, doubt, etc.): *What 'can that strange thing be?* 4. (indicating a right): *You can't* (i.e. have no right to) *go into that private garden.* 5. (indicating permission): *The children asked if they could* (if I would let them) *go swimming.* 6. (could indicating condition): *Could you* (if it were necessary to ask you) *work late tomorrow? I could smack his face* (if I gave way to my feelings, but I don't intend to).

²can [kæn] *n.* metal container for liquids, etc.: 'oil-can; 'milk-can. (Cf. *tin.*) (-*nn-*). put into a can or cans: *canned food.* can·ner·y *n.* factory where food, etc., is canned.

ca·nal [kə'næl] *n.* 1. channel cut through land for the use of ships (e.g. the Suez Canal) or to carry water to irrigate fields. 2. tube in a plant or animal for food, liquid, etc.: *the alimentary* ~.

ca·na·ry [kə'nɛəri] *n.* small, yellow songbird, usu. kept in a cage; its colour, light yellow.

can·cel ['kænsl] *v.t.* (-*ll-*). 1. cross out; draw a line through (words or figures); make marks (on sth., e.g. postage stamps) to prevent re-use. 2. say that sth. already arranged or decided will not be done, will not take place, etc.: *to* ~ *an order* (*a meeting*). ~·la·tion [ˌkænsə'leiʃən] *n.*

can·cer ['kænsə*] *n.* diseased growth in the body, often causing death. ~·ous ['kænsərəs] *adj.*

can·did ['kændid] *adj.* frank; straightforward. ~·ly *adv.*

can·di·date ['kændideit] *n.* 1. person wishing, or put forward by sb., to take an office or position: *The Socialist* ~ *was elected.* 2. person entered for an examination. can·di·da·ture ['kændiditʃə*] *n.* being a ~.

can·dle ['kændl] *n.* see the picture. (*The game) is not worth the ~*, is more trouble (expense, etc.) than it is worth. **'~·stick** *n.* holder for a candle.

A candle in   A cane
a candlestick   chair

can·dour ['kændə*] *n.* quality of being candid, saying freely what one thinks; fairmindedness.

can·dy ['kændi] *n.* 1. sugar made hard by repeated boiling. 2. (U.S.A.) sweet things made with sugar (e.g. chocolate, toffee). *v.t.* preserve (e.g. fruit) by boiling in sugar.

cane [kein] *n.* 1. long, hollow, jointed stem of grass-like plants (e.g. bamboo, sugar-~), ~-*sugar*, made from sugar-~. 2. such stems used for making baskets, furniture, etc.: *a chair with a ~ seat*. 3. such a stem used as a walking-stick or as a stick for punishing children with. *v.t.* make or repair with ~(s)(2); punish with a ~(3).

ca·nine ['keinain] *adj.* of dogs.

can·is·ter ['kænistə*] *n.* small (usu. metal) box for tea, tobacco, etc.

can·ker ['kæŋkə*] *n.* disease which destroys the wood of trees; (fig.) evil influence or tendency causing decay.

canned, can·nery, see ²*can*.

can·ni·bal ['kænibl] *n.* person who eats human flesh; animal that eats its own kind.

can·non ['kænən] *n.* 1. large gun, fixed to the ground or to a gun-carriage, esp. the old kind firing a solid ball, called a ~-*ball*. 2. shell-firing gun used in aircraft. ~**ade** [,kænə'neid] *n.* continued firing of big guns.

can·not = can not.

can·ny ['kæni] *adj.* not prepared to take unknown risks; cautious (esp. about spending money).

ca·noe [kə'nu:] *n.* light boat moved by one or more paddles. *v.i.* travel by ~.

A canoe

can·on ['kænən] *n.* 1. church law. 2. general standard by which sth. is judged: ~*s of conduct* (*good taste, etc.*). 3. body of writings accepted as genuine, esp. those books of the Bible accepted by the Church. 4. priest (with the title *The Rev. Canon*) who is one of a group having duties in a cathedral. 5. list of saints. ~**i·cal** [kə'nonikl] *adj.* according to church laws; belonging to the ~(3). ~**ize** ['kænənaiz] *v.t.* place in the ~(5).

ca·ñon *n.* = canyon.

can·o·py ['kænəpi] *n.* covering over the head of a bed, a throne, etc.; any similarly placed covering.

cant [kænt] *n.* 1. insincere talk. 2. special talk, words, used by a particular class of people: *thieves' ~*.

can't [kɑ:nt] = cannot.

can·tan·ker·ous [kæn'tæŋkərəs] *adj.* bad-tempered; quarrelsome.

can·ta·ta [kæn'tɑ:tə] *n.* short musical work to be sung by soloists and a choir, usu. a dramatic story but not acted (Cf. *oratorio*.)

can·teen [kæn'ti:n] *n.* 1. place (esp. in factories, barracks, offices) where food, drink, and sometimes other articles are supplied. 2. box of table silver and cutlery. 3. soldier's eating and drinking utensils.

can·ter ['kæntə*] *v.t. & i. & n.* (cause a horse to go at a) slow or easy. gallop.

can·ti·lev·er [ˈkæntiˌliːvə*] *n.* long, large arm-like bracket extending from a wall or base (e.g. to support a balcony). ~ *bridge,* bridge of connected ~s.

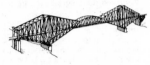

A cantilever bridge

can·to [ˈkæntou] *n.* one of the chief divisions in a long poem.

can·ton [ˈkæntən] *n.* subdivision of a country (esp. Switzerland).

can·vas [ˈkænvəs] *n.* strong, coarse cloth used for sails, bags, tents, etc., and by artists for oil-paintings. *under* ~, (a) sleeping in tents; (b) with sails spread.

can·vass [ˈkænvəs] *v.t. & i.* 1. ask (people) for support, orders for goods, votes, etc. 2. examine (a question) thoroughly by asking for opinions.

can·yon [ˈkænjən] *n.* deep gorge (usu. with a river flowing through it).

cap [kæp] *n.* 1. soft head-covering worn by boys and men, by some sailors and soldiers, without a brim but usu. with a peak. 2. sth. like a cap in use or shape (e.g. the cap of a milk-bottle, of a tube of toothpaste). *v.t.* (*-pp-*). put a cap on. *cap a story,* tell a better story; say sth. more amusing (than sb. else has said).

ca·pa·ble [ˈkeipəbl] *adj.* 1. able. 2. ~ *of,* (a) (of persons) having the power or inclination: *He's* ~ *of neglecting his duty.* (b) (of things) ready for; admitting of: *a situation* ~ *of improvement.*

ca·pa·bil·i·ty [ˌkeipəˈbiliti] *n.* power to do things; (pl.) qualities that await development.

ca·pac·i·ty [kəˈpæsiti] *n.* ability to hold, contain, get hold of, learn (things, ideas, knowledge, etc.): *a hall with a large, seating* ~, *a mind of great* ~; amount or number that can be held or contained: *filled to* ~ (i.e. quite full). *in the* ~ *of,* acting as, in the position of. **ca·pa·cious** [kəˈpeiʃəs] *adj.* able to hold much.

¹cape [keip] *n.* loose outer garment, without sleeves, worn over the shoulders.

²cape [keip] *n.* high point of land going out into the sea; headland.

ca·per [ˈkeipə*] *v.i.* jump about playfully. *n. cut* ~s, jump about merrily; behave foolishly.

ca·pil·lar·y [kəˈpiləri] *adj. & n.* thin, hair-like (pipe or tube) (e.g. joining veins or arteries). ~ *attraction,* force that causes oil to rise through the wick of an oil lamp, or ink to be absorbed by blotting-paper.

cap·i·tal [ˈkæpitl] *n. & adj.* 1. the chief city of a country. 2. (of letters) not small, e.g. A, P, Z. 3. wealth (money and property) used for producing more wealth. ~ *goods,* goods (to be) used in producing commodities. (Cf. *consumer goods.*) 4. ~ *punishment,* by death; ~ *crime,* punishable by death. 5. (colloq.) excellent. ~**ist** *n.* person owning and controlling much ~ (3). ~**ism** *n.* economic system in which a country's trade and industry are organized and controlled by the owners of ~ (3), the chief elements being competition, profit, supply and demand. (Cf. *socialism.*) ~**ize** *v.t.* change into, use as, ~ (3). ~**i·za·tion** [ˌkæpitəlaiˈzeiʃən] *n.*

ca·pit·u·late [kəˈpitjuleit] *v.i.* surrender (on stated conditions). **ca·pit·u·la·tion** [kəˌpitjuˈleiʃən] *n.*

ca·price [kəˈpriːs] *n.* (tendency towards a) sudden change of mind or behaviour without apparent cause. **ca·pri·cious** [kəˈpriʃəs] *adj.* full of ~; often changing: *a capricious breeze.*

cap·size [kæpˈsaiz] *v.t. & i.* (esp. of a boat) overturn.

cap·stan [ˈkæpstən] *n.* see the picture on page 74.

A capstan   A capsule (3)

cap·sule ['kæpsju:l] *n.* **1.** seed-case on a plant. **2.** tiny soluble container for medicine. **3.** part of a space-ship used for scientific instruments, an astronaut, etc.

cap·tain ['kæptin] *n.* **1.** leader or commander: *the ~ of a ship (football team)*. **2.** army officer below a Major and above a Lieutenant. **3.** naval officer below an Admiral and above a Commander. *v.t.* act as ~ of.

cap·tion ['kæpʃən] *n.* short title or heading of an article in a periodical, etc.; words printed with a picture, photograph, etc., or shown on a cinema screen to explain the story.

cap·tious ['kæpʃəs] *adj.* (fond of) finding fault, making protests, esp. about small matters.

cap·ti·vate ['kæptiveit] *v.t.* capture the fancy of; charm.

cap·tive ['kæptiv] *n.* prisoner; captured animal, etc. *be taken ~*, be captured. *~ balloon*, one moored to the ground (or a ship).

cap·tiv·i·ty [kæp'tiviti] *n.* state of being held ~. **cap·tor** ['kæptə*] *n.* person who takes a ~,

cap·ture ['kæptʃə*] *v.t.* make a prisoner of; take (by force, skill, trickery, etc.): *to ~ a thief (sb.'s attention)*. *n.* act of capturing; person or thing ~d.

car [kɑ:*] *n.* **1.** motor-car or tramcar. **2.** (on a railway-train) coach: *'sleeping-car; 'dining-car.* **3.** chariot: *the car of the sun-god.*

car·a·mel ['kærəmel] *n.* **1.** burnt sugar used for colouring and flavouring. **2.** sticky sweet.

car·at ['kærət] *n.* unit of weight for jewels: unit of quality for gold.

car·a·van ['kærəvæn] *n.* **1.** company of people (e.g. travellers, merchants) making a journey together (usu. across desert or dangerous country). **2.** covered vehicle used for living in (e.g. by holiday-makers, gipsies, etc.).

car·bide, see *calcium ~*.

car·bol·ic ac·id [kɑ:'bolik 'æsid] *n.* acid made from coal-tar, used as a disinfectant and germ-killer.

car·bon ['kɑ:bən] *n.* chemical substance, not a metal, present in coal, charcoal, diamonds. *~ paper*, thin paper coated with coloured matter, used between sheets of writing-paper for making copies. *~·ic ac·id* [kɑ:'bonik 'æsid] *n.* heavy, colourless, odourless, tasteless gas, soluble in water, formed when ~ burns.

car·bun·cle ['kɑ:bʌŋkl] *n.* **1.** bright-red jewel. **2.** red (usu. painful) swelling under the skin.

car·bu·ret·tor ['kɑ:bju,retə*] *n.* part of an engine in which petrol vapour and air are mixed.

car·cass, car·case ['kɑ:kəs] *n.* dead body of an animal (esp. one prepared for cutting up as meat).

card [kɑ:d] *n.* thick, stiff paper, esp. an oblong piece of this, as used for various purposes, e.g. *a post~ (see post); a visiting-~* (giving a person's name, etc.); *Christmas ~s; playing ~s* (in sets of 52, used for numerous games). *put one's ~s on the table*, make one's plans, intentions, etc., known. *play one's ~s well*, be clever at getting what one wants. *on the ~s*, possible or probable. *have a ~ up one's sleeve*, have a secret plan in reserve. *~·board* ['kɑ:d-bɔ:d] *n.* thick ~, used in making boxes, etc.

car·di·gan ['kɑ:digən] *n.* knitted woollen garment, with sleeves, which buttons up.

car·di·nal ['kɑ:dinl] *adj.* chief; most important: *~ numbers* (one, two, three, etc.**).** Cf. *ordinal. ~ points* (N., S., E., and W.). *n.* member of the Sacred College of the Roman Catholic Church which elects Popes.

care [kɛə*] *n.* **1.** serious attention; watchfulness. *take ~*, be on the watch; pay attention. **2.** protection; charge (5); responsibility: *take ~ of*, look after; see to the safety or welfare of. *in (under) the ~ of*, looked after by. *~ of* (usually written c/o): *John Smith, c/o William Brown, 2 Duke Street, Coventry* (indicating that J. S. is staying at W. B.'s house or that W. B. will forward the letter to J. S.'s address). **3.** troubled state of mind caused by doubt or fear; (cause of) sorrow or anxiety: *free from ~; the ~s of a large family.* *v.i.* **1.** feel interest, anxiety, or sorrow about: *We don't ~ what happens.* **2.** *~ for*, (a) have a liking for; (b) look after. *~ to* (inf.), be willing to: *Would you ~ to go for a walk?* **~ful** *adj.* **~less** *adj.* '**~',tak·er** *n.* person taking ~ of a building while its owners are away.

ca·reer [kəˈriə*] *n.* **1.** progress through life; (a person's) life history: *the ~s of great men.* **2.** way of earning a living; profession or occupation: *~s open to women.* **3.** quick or violent movement: *in full ~.* *v.i.* *~ along, ~ through (over)* (a place), rush wildly.

ca·ress [kəˈres] *v.t. & n.* (give a) loving touch (to); kiss.

car·et [ˈkærət] *n.* sign ∧ put below a line of writing to show where sth. is to be added.

car·go [ˈkɑːgou] *n.* (pl. *-oes*). goods carried in a ship or aircraft.

car·i·ca·ture [ˌkærikəˈtjuə*] *n.* picture of sb. or sth., imitation of a person's voice, behaviour, etc., stressing certain features in order to cause amusement or ridicule. *v.t.* make a ~ of.

car·il·lon [kəˈriljən] *n.* set of bells on which tunes may be played.

car·mine [ˈkɑːmain] *n. & adj.* deep red.

car·nage [ˈkɑːnidʒ] *n.* the killing of many people.

car·nal [ˈkɑːnəl] *adj.* of the body or flesh; sensual (opp. to spiritual): *~ desires.*

car·na·tion [kɑːˈneiʃən] *n.* **1.** garden plant with sweet-smelling flowers. **2.** rosy-pink colour.

car·ni·val [ˈkɑːnivl] *n.* public merry-making and feasting, esp. in Roman Catholic countries during the week before Lent.

car·niv·o·rous [kɑːˈnivərəs] *adj.* flesh-eating.

car·ol [ˈkærol] *n.* song of joy or praise, esp. a happy Christmas hymn. *v.i.* (*-ll-*). sing happily.

ca·rouse [kəˈrauz] *v.i.* drink heavily and have a merry time. **ca·rous·al** [kəˈrauzl] *n.* merry and noisy drinking-party.

¹**carp** [kɑːp] *v.i.* make unnecessary complaints about little things: *~ing at her husband; a ~ing tongue.*

²**carp** [kɑːp] *n.* freshwater fish.

car·pen·ter [ˈkɑːpintə*] *n.* workman who makes (esp.) the wooden parts of buildings. (Cf. *joiner*.) **car·pen·try** [ˈkɑːpintri] *n.* work of a ~.

car·pet [ˈkɑːpit] *n.* large, thick floor-covering of wool or hair, often with designs. *v.t.* cover (as) with a ~.

car·riage [ˈkæridʒ] *n.* **1.** vehicle, esp. one with four wheels, pulled by a horse, for carrying people. **2.** railway coach, or a division of it. **3.** (cost of) carrying goods from place to place: *~ forward, cost of ~ to be paid by the receiver.* **4.** manner of holding the head or body. **5.** moving part of a machine changing the position of other parts: *the ~ of a typewriter.*

car·ried, car·ri·er, see **carry.**

car·ri·on [ˈkæriən] *n.* dead and decaying flesh.

car·rot [ˈkærət] *n.* plant with yellow or orange-red root used as a vegetable.

car·ry [ˈkæri] *v.t. & i.* **1.** hold off the ground and move (sb. or sth.) from one place to another. **2.** have with one; take from place to place: *He always carries a walking-stick. He will ~ the news to everyone in the village.* **3.** support: *pillars which ~ the heavy roof.* **4.** keep (the head or body) in a certain way: *He carries himself like a soldier. How well she carries her head!* **5.** win, persuade, overcome (resistance): to ~ one's point (i.e. get people to agree that it is right); to ~ one's listeners with one (i.e. have their support); to ~ everything before one (i.e. succeed in everything); to ~ the enemy's positions (i.e. capture them). **6.** provide a path for, take along: pipes ~ing water to the town. **7.** make longer; continue: to ~ a fence round a field. **8.** (of sound) be heard: The sound of the guns carried many miles. **9.** (of guns) send (shells, etc.): Our guns do not ~ far enough. **10.** ~ away, take to another place; (fig.) cause to lose self-control; excite: He was carried away by his enthusiasm. ~ forward, take (figures) to the top of the next page or add to the next column. ~ off, take without permission or by force. ~ on, go forward (with); conduct; manage; continue. C~ on! (i.e. don't stop); ~ on business (as), employ oneself (as); ~ on a conversation with, talk to. ~ (sth.) through, bring to a successful end. ~ out, get done, give effect to: to ~ out orders (plans, threats). **car·ri·er** ['kæri·ə*] n. **1.** person or company ~ing goods for payment. **2.** support for parcels, boxes, etc., fixed to a bicycle, motor-car, etc. **3.** vehicle, ship, etc., built to ~ troops, aircraft, etc. **4.** person, etc., ~ing or transmitting a disease, although not himself suffering from it.

cart [kɑːt] n. strong (usu. two-wheeled) vehicle, pulled by an animal, for carrying goods: a coal-~. put the ~ before the horse, do or put things in the wrong order. v.t. carry in a ~. ~·age ['kɑːtidʒ] n. (price of) ~ing. ~·er n. man in charge of a ~.

car·tel ['kɑːtel] n. combination of traders, manufacturers, etc., to control output, fix prices, etc. (for their own advantage).

car·ti·lage ['kɑːtilidʒ] n. (structure of) firm elastic substance, esp. covering the joints, in animal bodies.

car·tog·ra·phy [kɑː'tɔgrəfi] n. map-drawing.

car·ton ['kɑːtən] n. cardboard box for holding goods.

car·toon [kɑː'tuːn] n. **1.** drawing dealing with current events (esp. politics) in an amusing way. **2.** cinema film made by photographing a series of drawings: a Walt Disney (Mickey Mouse) ~. ~·ist n. one who draws ~s.

car·tridge ['kɑːtridʒ] n. case containing explosive (for blasting), or bullet or shot and explosive (for a fire-arm).

carve [kɑːv] v.t. & i. **1.** make (a shape, design, etc.) by cutting: to ~ a statue out of wood; to ~ one's name on a tree trunk. **2.** cut up (cooked meat, etc.) into slices or pieces for eating at table: to ~ a chicken. **carv·er** n. one who ~s the meat at table; knife for carving. **carv·ing** n. piece of wood shaped by cutting or with a design cut on it.

cas·cade [kæs'keid] n. small waterfall; one part of a large broken waterfall.

¹**case** [keis] n. **1.** instance or example of the occurrence of sth.: There have been several accidents here, but only in one ~ was anybody killed. I have often excused you before, but in this ~ you must be punished. **2.** (medicine) person suffering from a disease; instance of diseased condition: five ~s of yellow fever; send the worst ~s to hospital. **3.** (law) question to be decided in a law court; the facts, arguments, etc., used on each side: When will the ~ come before the Court? He has a strong ~. State your ~ (i.e. give the facts and arguments in your favour).

²**case** [keis] n. box or container: ¹packing-~; ¸ciga'rette-~; ¹book-~; cloth covering: ¹pillow-~.

ca·se·in ['keisiin] n. body-building food present in milk and forming the basis of cheese.

case·ment ['keismənt] n. window that opens inwards or outwards. See the picture at window.

cash [kæʃ] *n.* money in coin or notes. ~ *down,* ~ *on delivery,* payment on delivery of goods. ~ *price,* price for immediate payment. ~ *register,* ~-*box* with device for recording ~ received. *v.t.* give or get ~ for (a cheque).

¹**cash·ier** [kæˈʃiə*] *n.* person receiving and paying out cash in a bank, office, or shop.

²**cash·ier** [kæˈʃiə*] *v.t.* dismiss (a commissioned officer) with dishonour and disgrace.

cash·mere [ˈkæʃmiə*] *n.* soft woollen material.

cas·ing [ˈkeisiŋ] *n.* covering: *copper wire with a ~ of rubber.*

ca·si·no [kəˈsiːnou] *n.* public building for music, dancing, etc., and in some places for gambling.

cask [kɑːsk] *n.* barrel for liquids.

cas·ket [ˈkɑːskit] *n.* small box, often ornamented, for jewels, letters, etc.

cas·sa·va [kəˈsɑːvə] *n.* tropical plant with starchy roots from which tapioca is obtained.

cas·se·role [ˈkæsəroul] *n.* covered dish in which food is cooked and served at table.

cas·sock [ˈkæsək] *n.* long close-fitting garment, usu. black, worn by some priests.

cast [kɑːst] *v.t. & i.* (p.t. & p.p. *cast*). **1.** throw; allow to fall: *to ~ a net or line for fish. Snakes ~ their skins.* ~ *a vote,* give a vote; ~*ing vote,* one given (e.g. by a chairman) to decide a question when votes on each side are equal. ~-*off clothes,* clothes which their owner does not want to wear again. ~ *anchor,* lower the anchor. ~ *lots,* choose by ²lot (1); let chance decide. **2.** send or turn in a particular direction: *to ~ a shadow on.* ~ *about for,* look round for. *be ~ down,* be unhappy. **3.** pour (liquid metal, etc.) into a ¹mould: *to ~ iron; to ~ a bronze statue.* **4.** add: *to ~ (up) a column of figures.* **5.** give (an actor) a part in a play. *n.* **1.** act of throwing (e.g. a net). **2.** sth. made by ~ing (3): *His leg was in a plaster ~.* **3.** sth. thrown off, esp. the skin of a snake. **4.** slight twist, esp. of the eye; squint. **5.** (all the) actors in a play for the theatre: *an all-star ~.* ˈ~·aˈway *n.* ship-wrecked person, esp. one reaching a strange country or lonely island. ~·ˈing *n.* sth. made by ~ing (3), esp. a metal part for a machine.

caste [kɑːst] *n.* one of the fixed social classes among the Hindus; the custom of dividing people into such classes; any exclusive social class.

cas·ti·gate [ˈkæstigeit] *v.t.* punish severely, esp. by scolding or criticizing. **cas·ti·ga·tion** [ˌkæstiˈgeiʃən] *n.*

cas·tle [ˈkɑːsl] *n.* large building or group of buildings fortified against attack in olden times. ~*s in the air* (*in Spain*), imagined adventures and hopes; day-dreams.

A castle   A cat

¹**cas·tor** [ˈkɑːstə*] *n.* small wheel for the foot of a piece of furniture, to make it easy to move.

²**cas·tor, -ter** [ˈkɑːstə*] *n.* small container with one or more holes in the top, for shaking salt, sugar, etc., on to food.

cas·tor oil [ˈkɑːstərˈɔil] *n.* thick, yellowish oil, used as a medicine to empty the bowels.

cas·trate [kæsˈtreit] *v.t.* remove the sex organs of (a male animal); take away the power (of a male animal) to breed.

cas·u·al [ˈkæʒjuəl] *adj.* **1.** happening by chance: *a ~ meeting.* **2.** careless; without special purpose. **3.** not regular (2): ~ *labour.* ~·ly *adv.* ~·ty [ˈkæʒ-juəlti] *n.* person injured, wounded, or killed (in war, an accident, etc.); accident.

cas·u·ist [ˈkæzjuist] *n.* expert in ~ry. **cas·u·ist·ry** *n.* judgement of right and wrong by reference to theories, social conventions, etc. (often with false but clever reasoning).

cat [kæt] *n.* **1.** see the picture on page 7 7. *let the cat out of the bag*, allow a secret to become known; *wait for the cat to jump*, wait to see what others think or do before giving an opinion, etc. **2.** any animal of the cat family (e.g. a lion or tiger). **3.** (short for) *cat-o'-nine-tails*, whip with many knotted cords, formerly used for punishing wrongdoers.

cat·a·clysm [ˈkætəklizəm] *n.* sudden and violent change, esp. in nature, e.g. a cloud-burst, earthquake, or flood.

cat·a·comb [ˈkætəkoum] *n.* (usu. pl.) underground gallery with openings along the sides for burial of the dead, esp. in ancient Rome.

cat·a·logue [ˈkætələg] *n.* list of names, places, books, goods, etc.) in a special order. *v.t.* make a ~ of; put in a ~.

cat·a·lyst [ˈkætəlist] *n.* substance that brings about a chemical change without itself undergoing any change.

cat·a·pult [ˈkætəpʌlt] *n.* **1.** Y-shaped stick with a piece of elastic, for shooting stones, etc. **2.** apparatus for helping an aircraft to get into the air quickly. **3.** (olden times) machine for throwing heavy stones in war.

cat·a·ract [ˈkætərækt] *n.* **1.** large waterfall. **2.** eye disease causing partial blindness.

ca·tarrh [kəˈtɑː*] *n.* disease of the nose and throat, causing a flow of liquid, as when one has a cold.

ca·tas·tro·phe [kəˈtæstrəfi] *n.* sudden happening causing great suffering (e.g. a flood, earthquake, or big fire). **cat·as·troph·ic** [ˌkætəˈstrɔfik] *adj.*

catch [kætʃ] *v.t. & i.* (p.t. & p.p. *caught* [kɔːt]). **1.** stop (sth. moving through the air, etc.), e.g. by grasping it, holding out sth. into which it falls, etc. **2.** be in time for; be able to use, meet, etc.: *to ~ a train (the post). I caught him as he was leaving the house.* **3.** ~ *sb. up*, ~

up with *sb.* or *sth.*, draw level with sb. in front; make up for lost time (by working quicker, etc.). **4.** come unexpectedly upon sb. doing sth.: *I caught him stealing vegetables from my garden.* **5.** get, receive: *to ~ cold (an illness); to ~ fire* (begin burning); *to ~ sb.'s words (his meaning)* (i.e. hear, understand); *to ~ sight of* (see for a moment); *to ~ sb.'s eye* (attract his attention). **6.** (cause to) become fixed or fastened: *The nail caught her dress. Her dress caught on a nail.* **7.** ~ *one's breath*, take a short, sudden breath. ~ *hold of*, seize. ~ *at*, try to seize. ~ (*sth.*) *up*, seize quickly. *n.* **1.** act of ~ing. **2.** sth. or sb. caught, or that one wants to ~: *a good ~ of fish.* **3.** part of a lock, fastener, etc., by which sth. is kept shut or secure. **4.** sth. intended to trick or deceive: *There's a ~ in it somewhere.* **5.** song for a number of voices starting one after another. ~·**y** *adj.* (of a tune) that often returns to the mind. ~·**ing** *adj.* (of a disease, etc.) that can be spread from person to person. ¹~·**word** *n.* word drawing attention to the subject of a paragraph, speech, etc.

cat·e·chism [ˈkætikizəm] *n.* set of questions and answers (esp. about religious teaching). **cat·e·chize** [ˈkætikaiz] *v.t.* teach or examine by asking a set of questions.

cat·e·gor·y [ˈkætigəri] *n.* one of the divisions or classes in a complete system of grouping. **cat·e·gor·i·cal** [ˌkætiˈgɔrikl] *adj.* (of a statement) unconditional; absolute. **cat·e·gor·i·cal·ly** *adv.*

ca·ter [ˈkeitə*] *v.i.* ~ *for*, undertake to provide (food, amusements, etc.). ~·**er** *n.* one who provides meals, etc., brought from outside, to clubs, homes, etc.; owner or manager of a hotel or restaurant.

cat·er·pil·lar [ˈkætəpilə*] *n.* **1.** moth or butterfly larva. **2.** endless belt passing over toothed wheels (to give tractors, tanks, etc., a grip on soft surfaces).

ca·the·dral [kə'θi:drəl] *n.* chief church of a diocese.

cath·ode ['kæθoud] *n.* negative pole of electric current. (See the diagram at *cell*.)

cath·o·lic ['kæθəlik] *adj.* 1. liberal(2); general; including everything: ~ *tastes and interests*. 2. (*Roman Catholic*) of the Church of Rome. *n.* member of the Church of Rome. **Ca·thol·i·cism** [kə'θɔlisizm] *n.* (*Roman Catholicism*) teaching, beliefs, etc., of the Church of Rome, ~**i·ty** [,kæθə'lisiti] *n.* quality of being ~ (1).

cat·kin ['kætkin] *n.* long, soft, downy hanging flower of certain trees (e.g. willow, birch).

cat·tle ['kætl] *n. pl.* oxen (bulls, bullocks, and cows).

caught, see *catch*.

caul·dron ['kɔ:ldrən] *n.* large hanging pot for cooking, etc.

caul·i·flow·er ['kɔliflauə*] *n.* (cabbage-like plant with) large white flower-head, used as a vegetable.

caulk [kɔ:k] *v.t.* make (joints between planks) watertight by filling with a sticky substance.

cause [kɔ:z] *n.* 1. that which produces an effect: *The ~ of the fire was carelessness.* 2. reason: *no ~ for anxiety.* 3. purpose for which efforts are being made: *to work in a good ~*; *to fight in the ~ of justice.* *v.t.* be the ~ of; make happen.

cause·way ['kɔ:zwei] *n.* raised path or road, esp. across wet land or a swamp.

caus·tic ['kɔ:stik] *adj.* 1. able to burn away by chemical action: ~ *soda.* 2. bitter; sarcastic: ~ *remarks*; *a ~ manner.* **caus·ti·cal·ly** *adv.*

cau·ter·ize ['kɔ:təraiz] *v.t.* burn (a wound, snake-bite, etc.) with a hot iron or a caustic substance (to destroy infection, etc.).

cau·tion ['kɔ:ʃən] *n.* 1. taking care; paying attention (to avoid danger or making mistakes). 2. warning words. *v.t.* give a ~ to. ~**·a·ry** *adj.* containing, giving, a ~. **cau·tious** ['kɔ:ʃəs] *adj.*

having or showing ~. **cau·tious·ly** *adv.*

cav·al·cade [,kævəl'keid] *n.* company or procession of persons on horseback or in carriages.

cav·a·lier [,kævə'liə*] *n.* 1. (old use) horseman or knight. 2. (in the Civil War, 17th-century England) supporter of Charles I.

cav·al·ry ['kævəlri] *n.* (collective) soldiers who fight on horseback.

cave [keiv] *n.* hollow place in the side of a cliff; large natural hollow under the ground. *v.t. & i.* ~ *in*, smash in, fall in, give way to pressure. '**~·man**, '**~·dwel·ler** *n.* person living in a ~. **cav·ern** ['kævən] *n.* ~. **cav·ern·ous** ['kævənəs] *adj.* full of ~s; shaped, etc., like a ~.

cav·il ['kævil] *v.i.* (-*ll*-). ~ *at*, make unnecessary protests against; find fault with.

cav·i·ty ['kæviti] *n.* hole; hollow space: *a ~ in a tooth.*

cay·enne [kei'en] *n.* red pepper.

cease [si:s] *v.t. & i.* come to a stop. *n.* end. ~**·less** *adj.* never ending.

ce·dar ['si:də*] *n.* (hard, red, sweet-smelling wood of) evergreen tree.

cede [si:d] *v.t.* give up (rights, land, etc.) to another (person, state, etc.).

ceil·ing ['si:liŋ] *n.* 1. under-surface of the top of a room. 2. highest (practicable) level (to be) reached: *price ~s*; *an aircraft with a ~ of 20,000 feet.*

cel·e·brate ['selibreit] *v.t.* 1. do sth. to show that a day or an event is important, or an occasion for rejoicing: *to ~ one's birthday (Christmas, a victory).* 2. praise and honour. **cel·e·brat·ed** *adj.* famous. **cel·e·bra·tion** [,seli'breiʃən] *n.* **ce·leb·ri·ty** [si'lebriti] *n.* being famous; famous person.

ce·ler·i·ty [si'leriti] *n.* quickness.

cel·er·y ['seləri] *n.* vegetable or salad plant.

ce·les·tial [si'lestjəl] *adj.* of the sky; heavenly; perfect.

cel·i·ba·cy ['selibəsi] *n.* state of living unmarried. **cel·i·bate** ['selibit] *adj. & n.* unmarried (person) (esp. of one who has taken a vow not to marry).

cell [sel] *n.* **1.** small room for one person (esp. in a prison or monastery). **2.** small division of a larger structure: ~*s in a honeycomb.* **3.** unit of living matter: *All animals and plants are made up of* ~*s.* **4.** unit of apparatus for producing electric current, part of a battery. ~**u·lar** ['seljulə*] *adj.* formed of ~s (2); (of material) loosely woven.

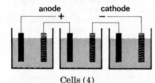

Cells (4)

cel·lar ['selə*] *n.* underground room for storing coal, wine, etc.
cel·lo ['tʃelou] *n.* **cel·list** ['tʃelist] *n.* see *violoncello.*
cel·lo·phane ['seləfein] *n.* transparent sheet used like paper for wrapping food and other goods.
cel·lu·loid ['seljuloid] *n.* plastic substance made from cellulose.
cel·lu·lose ['seljulous] *n.* substance forming the chief part of all plants and trees; used for making celluloid, artificial silk, printing-paper, etc.
ce·ment [si'ment] *n.* **1.** grey powder (made by burning lime and clay) which after being wetted becomes hard like stone and is used for building. (See *concrete.*) **2.** any similar soft, hard-setting substance, used for filling holes (e.g. in the teeth) or for joining things. *v.t.* put ~ on or in; join with ~; (fig.) strengthen; unite.
cem·e·tery ['semitri] *n.* area of ground, not a churchyard, for burying the dead.
cen·o·taph ['senətɑːf] *n.* monument put up in memory of a person or persons buried else where.
cen·ser ['sensə*] *n.* vessel in which incense is burnt (in churches).
cen·sor ['sensə*] *n.* official with

the power to examine letters, books, periodicals, plays, films, etc., and to cut out anything regarded as immoral or, in time of war, helpful to the enemy. *v.t.* examine, cut (parts) out, as a ~. ~**ship** *n.* office, duties, etc., of a ~. ~**i·ous** [sen'sɔːriəs] *adj.* fault-finding.
cen·sure ['senʃə*] *v.t. & n.* (express) blame or disapproval (of).
cen·sus ['sensəs] *n.* official counting of the population.
cent [sent] *n.* the 100th part of a dollar or other unit of currency. *per* ~ (%), in, by, or for every 100.
cen·taur ['sentɔː*] *n.* (in old Greek stories) creature, half man and half horse.
cen·te·na·ri·an [ˌsenti'nɛəriən] *n, & adj.* (person who is) (more than) 100 years old.
cen·te·na·ry [sen'tiːnəri] *adj. & n.* (having to do with a) period of 100 years; 100th anniversary.
cen·ten·ni·al [sen'teniəl] *adj. & n.* = ~.
cen·ti·grade ['sentigreid] *adj.* in, of, the temperature scale which has 100 degrees between the freezing-point and boiling-point of water: *the* ~ *thermometer.* (Cf. *Fahrenheit.*)
cen·ti·gramme ['sentigræm] *n.* the 100th part of a gramme.
cen·time ['sɔːntiːm] *n.* the 100th part of a franc.
cen·ti·me·tre ['sentiˌmiːtə*] *n.* the 100th part of a metre.
cen·ti·pede ['sentipiːd] *n.* small, wingless creature with a long, thin body, having numerous jointed sections, each bearing a pair of feet.
cen·tre ['sentə*] *n.* **1.** middle part or point: *the* ~ *of London*; *the* ~ *of a circle.* **2.** place of great activity, esp. one to which people are attracted from surrounding districts or from which they go out: *the shopping* ~ *of a town*; *a* ~ *of commerce.* **3.** person or thing attracting (attention, interest, etc.). *v.t. & i.* place in, bring to, the ~; have as ~: *to* ~ *one's hopes on sth.*; *hopes which* ~ *on sth.* **cen·tral**

['sentrəl] *adj.* of, at, or near the ~; chief; most important. **cen·tral·ize** ['sentrəlaiz] *v.t. & i.* bring to the ~; put, come, under central control. **cen·tral·i·za·tion** [,sentrəlai'zeiʃən] *n.* **cen·tri·fu·gal** [sen'trifjugəl] *adj.* tending to move away from the ~. **cen·trip·e·tal** [sen'tripitl] *adj.* tending to move towards the ~.

cen·tu·ri·on [sen'tjuəriən] *n.* (in ancient Rome) leader of a unit of 100 soldiers.

cen·tu·ry ['sentʃuri] *n.* **1.** 100 years. **2.** one of the periods of 100 years before or after the birth of Christ: *the 20th* ~, A.D. 1901–2000. **3.** (cricket) 100 runs.

ce·ram·ic [si'ræmik] *adj.* of the art of pottery.

ce·re·al ['siəriəl] *adj. & n.* (of) any kind of grain used for food. Rice, wheat, and maize are ~s.

cer·e·bral ['seribrəl] *adj.* of the brain.

cer·e·mo·ny ['serimɘni] *n.* **1.** special act(s), religious service, on an occasion such as a wedding, funeral, opening of a new public building, etc. **2.** behaviour required by social custom, esp. among officials, people of high class, etc. *stand on* ~, pay great attention to rules of behaviour. **cer·e·mo·ni·al** [,seri'mouniəl] *n.* special order of ceremony; formality. *adj.* formal; as used for ceremonies. **cer·e·mo·ni·ous** [,seri'mouniəs] *adj.* fond of, marked by, ~.

cer·tain ['sə:tn] *adj.* **1.** of which there is no doubt. *for* ~, without doubt; *make* ~, inquire in order to be ~. **2.** not named or described although known: *for a* ~ *reason*; *under* ~ *conditions*. **3.** some but not much: *There was a* ~ *coldness in her greeting*. ~·**ly** *adv.* without doubt. ~·**ty** *n.* being ~; sth. which is ~. **cer·tif·i·cate** [sə'tifikit] *n.* written or printed statement which may be used as proof, made by sb. in authority: *a marriage* ~; *a* ~ *of birth*. **cer·tif·i·cat·ed** *adj.* having the right to do sth. (e.g

teach) as the result of obtaining a ~.

cer·ti·fy ['sə:tifai] *v.t.* declare (usu. by giving a certificate) that sth. is true: *certified insane* (by a doctor).

cer·ti·tude ['sə:titju:d] *n.* condition of feeling certain.

ces·sa·tion [sə'seiʃən] *n.* ceasing; stop or pause.

ces·sion ['seʃən] *n.* act of ceding or giving up (land, rights, etc.); sth. ceded.

cess·pool ['sespu:l] *n.* underground tank for sewage.

chafe [tʃeif] *v.t. & i.* **1.** rub (the skin, etc.) for warmth. **2.** make or become rough or sore by rubbing: *The stiff collar* ~*d his neck*. **3.** become impatient or irritated: *to* ~ *under insults*.

¹**chaff** [tʃɑ:f] *n.* **1.** outer covering of grain, removed before the grain is used as food. **2.** hay or straw cut up as food for cattle.

²**chaff** [tʃɑ:f] *n.* good-humoured teasing or joking. *v.t.* make good-humoured fun of.

chaf·finch ['tʃæfintʃ] *n.* small, common European bird.

cha·grin ['ʃægrin] *n.* feeling of shame or annoyance (at having failed, made a mistake, etc.).

chain [tʃein] *n.* **1.** number of (usu. metal) rings or links going through one another to make a line. *in* ~s, kept as a prisoner. **2.** number of connected things, events, etc.: *a* ~ *of mountains* (*ideas, reasoning*). **3.** measure of length (66 feet). *v.t.* fasten with a ~: *The prisoner was* ~*ed to the wall. Don't keep your dog* ~*ed up all day*.

chair [tʃeə*] *n.* **1.** see the picture. **2.** post or position held by a professor at a university: *the Chair of French*. **3.** seat, authority, of sb. who presides at a meeting: *take the* ~, preside. ~·**man** ['tʃeəmən] *n.* person presiding at a meeting.

Chairs

chaise [ʃeiz] *n.* low, four-wheeled horse-carriage (formerly) used for pleasure.

chal·et [ˈʃælei] *n.* summer cottage; hut on a beach, etc., for holiday-makers.

chal·ice [ˈtʃælis] *n.* wine-cup (esp. one used for Holy Communion).

chalk [tʃɔːk] *n. & v.t.* (write or draw with a stick of) soft white mineral substance, a kind of limestone.

chal·lenge [ˈtʃælindʒ] *n.* **1.** invitation or call to play a game, run a race, have a fight, etc., to see which is better, stronger, etc. **2.** order given by a sentry to stop and explain who one is, what one is doing. *v.t.* give, send, be, a ~ to; ask for reasons (to support a statement, etc.).

cham·ber [ˈtʃeimbə*] *n.* **1.** (old use) room, esp. a bedroom. ~ *music*, music for a small number of players in a small hall or room. **2.** body of persons making laws; the place where they meet: *the Upper (Lower) Chamber*. **3.** *Chamber of Commerce*, group of persons organized to develop trade, etc. **4.** (pl.) set of rooms in a large building, esp. one occupied by lawyers. **5.** enclosed space in a gun (where a shell or cartridge is laid), or in a machine. ˈ~·maid *n.* woman servant who keeps bedrooms in order.

cham·ber·lain [ˈtʃeimbəlin] *n.* manager of the household of a king or queen or great noble.

cha·me·leon [kəˈmiːljən] *n.* small animal whose colour changes according to its background.

cham·ois [ˈʃæmwɑː] *n.* small, goat-like animal living in high mountains of Europe and S.W. Asia. ~·**leather** [ˈʃæmiˌleðə*] *n.* soft leather from the skin of sheep and goats.

champ [tʃæmp] *v.t. & i.* (of a horse) bite noisily (food or the bit); (fig.) show impatience.

cham·pagne [ʃæmˈpein] *n.* kind of effervescent French wine.

cham·pion [ˈtʃæmpjən] *n.* **1.** one who fights on behalf of another or for a cause, etc.: *a ~ of free speech (liberty, etc.)*. **2.** person, team, animal, etc., taking first place in a competition: *a boxing (swimming)* ~; *the ~ football team*. ~·**ship** [ˈtʃæmpjənʃip] *n.* act of ~ing; position held by a ~. *v.t.* support; defend.

chance [tʃɑːns] *n.* **1.** accident; luck; happening without known cause or planning: *to let ~ decide*; *to take one's ~* (trust to luck, take what comes); *game of ~* (one which luck, not skill, decides); *by ~* (by accident, not from design). **2.** possibility: *on the ~ that*, in view of the possibility that; *in the hope that*. **3.** opportunity; occasion when success seems certain: *the ~ of a lifetime*; *have (stand) a ~*, i.e. of being successful. **4.** (attrib.) coming or happening by ~: *a ~ meeting*. *v.t. & i.* **1.** happen by ~. **2.** ~ *upon*, find or meet by ~. **3.** take a risk.

chan·cel [ˈtʃɑːnsəl] *n.* eastern part of a church, used by priests and the choir.

chan·cel·lor [ˈtʃɑːnsələ*] *n.* (in some countries) chief minister of state; (of some universities) head or president; *C~ of the Exchequer*, chief finance minister in Great Britain; *The Lord C~ of England*, highest judge.

chan·cer·y [ˈtʃɑːnsəri] *n.* Lord Chancellor's division of the High Court of Justice.

chan·de·lier [ˌʃændəˈliə*] *n.* branched support hanging from the ceiling for two or more lights.

chand·ler [ˈtʃɑːndlə*] *n.* one who sells candles, oil, soap, paint, etc. *ship's* ~, dealer in ropes, canvas, and other supplies for ships.

change [tʃeindʒ] *v.t. & i.* **1.** take or put one thing in place of another: *to ~ one's clothes (address)*; *to ~ seats (places) with sb.* *to ~ trains*, get out of one train into another. ~ *one's mind*, come to a different opinion, make different plans. ~ *hands*, pass to another owner. **2.** (= exchange) give sth. to sb. and receive sth. else of equal value in return: *to ~ a £5 note* (i.e. give or get smaller notes, coins, etc., for it). **3.** make or become different. **n. 1.** changing; becoming different; difference. **2.** sth. needed in order to ~; sth. to be exchanged: *Take a ~ of clothes with you.* **3.** money in small units or in coin: *~ for a £1 note*; the difference between the cost of sth. and any higher amount handed to the seller in payment for it. ~'**a·ble** *adj.* likely to ~; able to be ~d; often changing.

chan·nel ['tʃænl] *n.* **1.** stretch of water joining two seas: *the English C~.* **2.** bed of a river; the deeper part of a waterway: *The ~ is marked by buoys.* **3.** passage along which a liquid may flow; (fig.) way by which news, ideas, etc., may travel.

chant [tʃɑ:nt] *n.* often-repeated tune, to which, e.g. the Psalms, are fitted, several words to one note. (Cf. *hymn.*) *v.i. & t.* sing a ~; use a singing note (e.g. for a prayer in church).

chan·ty ['tʃɑ:nti] *n.* sailors' song. (Cf. *shanty.*)

cha·os ['keiɔs] *n.* complete absence of order; confusion. **cha·ot·ic** [kei'ɔtik] *adj.*

¹**chap** [tʃæp] *v.t. & i.* (-*pp*-). (of the skin) become rough, sore, cracked; (of the wind, etc.) cause (the skin) to ~.

²**chap** [tʃæp] *n.* (colloq.) boy; man.

chap·el ['tʃæpl] *n.* **1.** place (not a parish church) used for Christian worship, e.g. in a school, prison, private house, etc. **2.** small place within a church for private prayer. **3.** the service held there.

chap·er·on ['ʃæpəroun] *n.* married or elderly woman in charge of a girl or young unmarried woman on social occasions. *v.t.* act as ~ to.

chap·lain ['tʃæplin] *n.* priest or clergyman, esp. in the navy or army, or in charge of a chapel (1).

chap·let ['tʃæplit] *n.* wreath (of leaves, flowers, etc.) for the head; string of prayer beads.

chap·ter ['tʃæptə*] *n.* **1.** division of a book. **2.** (general meeting of) the whole number of canons of a cathedral church, or members of a monastic order.

¹**char** [tʃɑ:*] *v.t. & i.* (-*rr*-). make or become black by burning: *~red wood.*

²**char** [tʃɑ:*] *v.i.* (-*rr*-). do odd job(s) (e.g. cleaning offices, houses, etc.) with payment by the hour or day. '~·,**wom·an** *n.* woman who ~s.

char·a·banc ['ʃærəbæŋ] *n.* (old-fashioned, usu. unroofed) motor-coach with all seats facing forward, used for touring.

char·ac·ter ['kæriktə*] *n.* **1.** (of a person, group of persons, etc.) mental or moral nature; mental and moral qualities which make one person or race different: *a man of weak (fine, etc.) ~*; *the ~ of the French.* **2.** moral strength: *Should ~-building be the chief aim of education?* **3.** person who is well known: *a public ~*; person in a play or book: *the ~s in the novels of Dickens*; person whose is unusual in his ways: *quite a ~* (e.g. of an amusing man). **4.** description of a person's qualities and abilities, esp. in a letter by an employer, that may be used when applying for a position. **5.** all those special qualities which make a thing, place, etc., what it is and different from other things, places, etc.: *the ~ of the desert areas of N. Africa.* **6.** letter, sign, mark, etc., used in a system of writing or printing: *Chinese (Greek, etc.) ~s.* ~·**is·tic** [,kærəktə'ristik] *adj.* forming part of, showing, the ~ of a person, thing, place, etc.: *with his ~istic enthusiasm.* **n.** special mark or quality. ~·**ize** ['kærəktəraiz] *v.t.* show the ~ of; be ~istic of.

cha·rade [ʃə'rɑ:d] *n.* game in which a word is guessed by the onlookers after the word itself, and each syllable in turn, have been spoken or suggested by actors in a little play.

char·coal ['tʃɑ:koul] *n.* black

substance, used as fuel, made by burning wood slowly in an oven.

charge [tʃɑːdʒ] *n.* **1.** accusation; statement that a person has done wrong, esp. that he has broken a law: *bring a ~ of murder against sb.* **2.** sudden and violent attack at high speed: *to capture a position after a bayonet ~.* **3.** price asked for goods or services: *hotel ~s.* **4.** amount of powder, etc., used in firing a gun or causing an explosion, or of electricity put into an accumulator. **5.** work given to sb. as a duty; thing or person given to sb. to be taken care of. *in ~ of,* taking care of; being taken care of by: *Mary was in ~ of the baby. The baby was in Mary's ~. take ~ of,* be responsible for. *give sb. in ~,* give him up to the police. *v.t. & i.* **1.** *~ sb. (with sth.),* bring a *~* (1) against; accuse. **2.** make a *~* (2) against: *to ~ the enemy.* **3.** ask as a price; ask in payment. **4.** load *(a gun)*; fill; put a *~* (4) into: *~ an accumulator.* **5.** give *(sb.)* orders or instructions; give as a task or duty. **~·a·ble** [ˈtʃɑːdʒəbl] *adj.* liable to be *~*d (with wrongdoing).

charg·er *n.* army officer's horse.

char·gé d'af·faires [ˈʃɑːʒeidæˈfeə*] *n.* person who is in charge of business when an ambassador is absent from his post.

char·i·ot [ˈtʃæriət] *n.* two-wheeled car, pulled by a horse, used in olden times in races and in war. **char·i·o·teer** [ˌtʃæriəˈtiə*] *n.* ~-driver.

char·i·ty [ˈtʃæriti] *n.* **1.** kindness in giving help to the poor; neighbourly love; willingness to judge other persons with kindness. **2.** society or organization for helping poor or suffering people. **char·it·a·ble** [ˈtʃærit-əbl] *adj.* showing, having, for, ~.

char·la·tan [ˈʃɑːlətən] *n.* person who pretends to have more skill, knowledge, or ability than he really has, esp. one who pretends to have medical knowledge.

charm [tʃɑːm] *n.* **1.** quality or power of attracting, giving pleasure. **2.** sth. believed to have magic power, good or bad: *~s against evil spirits; a ~ to bring good luck; under a ~* (influenced or affected by magic). *v.t. & i.* **1.** attract; give pleasure to. **2.** use magic on; influence or protect as if by magic: *He bears a ~ed life.* **~·ing** *adj.* full of ~ (1); giving pleasure (e.g. by personal appearance or actions).

chart [tʃɑːt] *n.* **1.** map of the sea, for sailors. **2.** sheet of paper with information, in the form of curves, diagrams, etc. (about such facts as the weather, prices, business conditions, etc.). *v.t.* make a ~ of; show on a ~.

char·ter [ˈtʃɑːtə*] *n.* (written or printed statement of) rights, permission to do sth., esp. from a ruler or government. *v.t.* **1.** give a ~ to. **2.** hire or engage (a ship, aircraft, etc.) for an agreed time, purpose and payment.

char·y [ˈtʃɛəri] *adj.* ~ *of,* shy, cautious, or careful about.

¹chase [tʃeis] *v.t.* run after in order to capture, kill, or drive away: *to ~ rabbits (a thief, a dog out of a garden). n.* the act of chasing: *give ~,* run after; try to catch. *the ~,* esp. the chasing of animals for sport.

²chase [tʃeis] *v.t.* cut patterns or designs on (metal or other hard material).

chasm [ˈkæzəm] *n.* deep opening or crack in the ground; (fig.) wide difference (of feeling or interests, between persons, nations, etc.).

chas·sis [ˈʃæsi] *n.* (pl. *chassis* [ˈʃæsiz]). framework of a motor-car or carriage upon which the body is fastened or built.

chaste [tʃeist] *adj.* pure in thought, word, and deed, esp. sexually pure. **chas·ti·ty** [ˈtʃæs-titi] *n.*

chas·ten [ˈtʃeisn] *v.t.* correct (sb.) by giving punishment or pain.

chas·tise [tʃæsˈtaiz] *v.t.* punish severely. **~·ment** [ˈtʃæstiz-mənt] *n.*

chas·ti·ty, see *chaste.*

chat [tʃæt] *v.i. & n.* (-*tt*-). (have a) friendly talk about (usu.) unimportant things. ~·ty *adj.* fond of ~ting.

châ·teau [ˈʃætou] *n.* (pl. *châteaux* [ˈʃætouz]). large country house in France.

chat·tel [ˈtʃætl] *n.* piece of movable property (e.g. a chair, motor-car, horse): *a person's goods and* ~s.

chat·ter [ˈtʃætə*] *v.i.* **1.** talk quickly or foolishly or without stopping. **2.** make quick, indistinct sounds (e.g. the cries of monkeys, of some birds, the noise of typewriter keys, of a person's upper and lower teeth striking together from cold or fear). *n.* sounds of the kinds noted above. '~·**box** *n.* person who ~s (1).

chauf·feur [ˈʃoufə*, ʃouˈfə:*] *n.* man paid to drive a privately owned motor-car.

cheap [tʃi:p] *adj.* **1.** low in price; costing little money. **2.** worth more than the price. **3.** of low quality. ~·ly *adv.* ~·en *v.t.* make ~(er). ~·ness *n.*

cheat [tʃi:t] *v.t. & i.* try to obtain an advantage by doing sth. dishonest: *to ~ at an examination. to ~ sb. out of sth.*, get sth. from him by ~ing. *n.* person who ~s; dishonest trick.

check [tʃek] *v.t.* **1.** examine in order to learn if sth. is correct: *to ~ a bill (sb.'s statements).* **2.** hold back; cause to go slow or stop: *to ~ sb.'s anger (the enemy's advance). n.* **1.** ~ing; person or thing that ~s. *keep a ~ on, keep sth. in ~*, control. **2.** receipt (piece of paper, bit of wood or metal with a number on it, etc.) showing that a person has a right to sth. (e.g. luggage sent by train or left in a railway station office to be collected later). **3.** pattern of crossed lines forming squares (often of different shades or colours); cloth with such a pattern. '~·**mate** *v.t.* obstruct or defeat (a person or his plans), as in winning the game of *chess*.

cheek [tʃi:k] *n.* **1.** each side of the face below the eye. **2.** saucy talk or behaviour; impudence. *v.t.* be impudent to. ~·y *adj.* impudent; saucy. ~·i·ly *adv.*

cheer [tʃiə*] *v.t. & i.* **1.** make sb. feel happy. ~ *up*, become happier; ~ *sb. up*, make him happier. **2.** give shouts of joy, approval, or encouragement. *n.* **1.** state of hope, gladness: *men of good* ~. **2.** shout of joy, encouragement, etc.: *give three* ~*s for*, shout 'hurray' three times. ~·**ful** *adj.* bringing or suggesting happiness. ~·**less** *adj.* without joy or comfort; dull and miserable: *wet and* ~*less weather.* ~·**i·ly** *adv.* in a ~ful manner. ~·**y** *adj.* lively; merry: *a* ~*y smile (greeting).*

cheese [tʃi:z] *n.* solid food made from milk curds.

chef [ʃef] *n.* head male cook in a restaurant, hotel, etc.

chem·ist·ry [ˈkemistri] *n.* branch of science dealing with the elements(1) and how they combine, etc. **chem·i·cal** [ˈkemikl] *adj.* of, made by, ~. *n.* substance used in, obtained by, ~. **chem·ist** [ˈkemist] *n.* person with a knowledge of ~; person who prepares and sells medical goods. *chemist's shop*, one selling medical goods, toilet articles, etc. (See *pharmacy*.)

cheque [tʃek] *n.* written order (usu. on a printed form) to a bank to pay money. '~-**book** *n.* number of cheque forms fastened together.

chequ·ered [ˈtʃekəd] *ppl. adj.* having checks(3); (fig.) *a* ~ *career*, one of great variety, esp. with frequent changes of fortune.

cher·ish [ˈtʃeriʃ] *v.t.* care for (sb.) tenderly; keep alive (hope, ambition) in one's heart.

cher·ry [ˈtʃeri] *n.* (tree with) soft, small, round, red, yellow, or black fruit with a stone-like seed. *adj.* of the colour of ripe red cherries.

cher·ub [ˈtʃerəb] *n.* small, beautiful, and innocent child.

chess [tʃes] *n.* game for two players with 16 pieces (called

~*men*) each, on a board with 64 squares (called a ~*board*).

chest [tʃest] *n.* **1.** large, strong wooden box for storing, e.g. clothes, tools, money, medicine, tea. *a ~ of drawers*, one with drawers for clothes. **2.** upper front part of the body, enclosed by the ribs, containing the heart and lungs.

chest·nut ['tʃestnʌt] *n.* (wood of) tree with shiny nuts ; the colour of these nuts, reddish-brown.

chev·ron ['ʃevrən] *n.* bent stripe (V or ∧) worn by soldiers, policemen, etc., on sleeves to show rank.

chew [tʃu:] *v.t. & i.* work (food, etc.) about between the teeth in order to crush it. *n.* act of ~*ing* ; sth. that is ~*ed*. '~·**ing-gum** *n.* sweetened and flavoured gum for ~*ing*.

chic [ʃi(:)k] *adj.* (of a woman or her clothes) in the latest fashion ; stylish. *n.* superior style.

chi·can·e·ry [ʃi'keinəri] *n.* use of unfair arguments or trickery, esp. in law and politics.

chick [tʃik] *n.* newly-hatched chicken or other young bird.

chick·en ['tʃikin] *n.* young bird, esp. young hen ; meat of a ~ as food. '~·**,heart·ed** *adj.* easily frightened. '~·**pox** *n.* disease (esp. of children) causing red spots on the skin.

chic·o·ry ['tʃikəri] *n.* plant with root which is roasted and made into a powder (mixed with or used instead of coffee).

chide [tʃaid] *v.t. & i.* (p.t. & p.p. *chid* [tʃid], or *chided* ['tʃaidid]). scold ; speak angrily to (because of wrongdoing).

chief [tʃi:f] *n.* leader or ruler ; head of a group. *adj.* principal ; most important : *the ~ thing to remember* ; *the ~ priest*. ~·**ly** *adv.* ~·**tain** ['tʃi:ftən] *n.* ~ of a tribe.

chif·fon ['ʃifən] *n.* thin transparent silk material used for dresses, etc.

chil·blain ['tʃilblein] *n.* painful swelling, esp. on a hand or foot, occurring in cold weather.

child [tʃaild] *n.* (pl. *children* ['tʃildrən]). not yet born or newly

born human being ; young boy or girl ; son or daughter (of any age). *be with ~*, be pregnant. '~·**birth** *n.* giving birth to a ~ : *Mrs Smith died in ~birth*. ~·**like** *adj.* simple ; innocent. ~·**hood** *n.* time during which one is a ~. ~·**ish** *adj.* of, behaving like, suitable for, a ~.

chill [tʃil] *n.* **1.** unpleasant cold feeling : *There's a ~ in the air this morning. Take the ~ off the water* (i.e. warm it a little). **2.** illness caused by cold or damp, often with shivering of the body : *to catch a ~*. *adj.* unpleasantly cold : *a ~ breeze* ; (fig.) cold ; unemotional : *a ~ greeting*. *v.t. & i.* make or become cold or cool : *~ed meat* (slightly frozen to keep it in good condition). **chil·ly** *adj.* rather cold.

chime [tʃaim] *n.* (series of notes sounded by a) tuned set of (church) bells. *v.i. & t.* (of bells or a clock) make bell or gong sounds ; give out bell tones ; (of a person) ring ~*s* on (bells) : *The church clock ~d twelve*. *~ in*, break in excitedly on the talk of others (usu. to express agreement).

chim·ney ['tʃimni] *n.* **1.** structure through which smoke, etc., is carried away from a fire. **2.** glass tube protecting the flame of an oil-lamp from draughts. '~·'**cor·ner** *n.* seat in an old-fashioned fire-place. '~·**pot** *n.* tube-shaped pot at the top of a ~ above a roof. '~·**stack** *n.* brickwork, etc. enclosing ~(s) above a roof. '~·**sweep** *n.* man who sweeps soot from ~*s*.

Chimney-pots in a chimney-stack

chim·pan·zee [,tʃimpæn'zi:] *n.* African ape, smaller than a gorilla.

chin [tʃin] *n.* part of the face under the mouth.

chi·na ['tʃainə] *n.* baked and glazed fine white clay; porcelain; articles (cups, plates, etc.) made of this.

¹chink [tʃiŋk] *n.* narrow crack or opening (through which the wind blows or through which one may peep).

²chink [tʃiŋk] *v.t. & i. & n.* (make the) sound of coins, pieces of glass, etc., striking together.

chintz [tʃints] *n.* kind of cotton cloth (usu. glazed) with printed designs in colours; used for curtains, covering furniture, etc.

chip [tʃip] *n.* **1.** small piece cut or broken off (from wood, stone, china, etc.). ~ *of(f) the old block*, son very like his father. **2.** thin slice cut from an apple, potato, etc. **3.** place (e.g. in a cup or plate) from which a ~ has come. *v.t. & i.* (*-pp-*). **1.** cut or knock ~s from; make into ~s: *to* ~ *the edge of a plate*; *to* ~ *potatoes*. **2.** become ~ped: *things which* ~ *easily*.

chi·rop·o·dy [ki'rɔpədi] *n.* expert treatment of troubles of the feet and toe-nails. **chi·rop·o·dist** *n.*

chirp [tʃə:p] *v.i. & t. & n.* (make) short, sharp sound(s) or note(s) of some birds (e.g. sparrows) and insects (e.g. crickets). ~**y** *adj.* lively.

chir·rup ['tʃirəp] *v.i. & t. & n.* (make) series of chirps.

chis·el ['tʃizl] *n.* steel tool with a squared, sharpened end for cutting and shaping wood, stone, or metal. *v.t.* (*-ll-*). use a ~ on.

chiv·al·ry ['ʃivəlri] *n.* **1.** laws and customs of knights in the Middle Ages. **2.** the ideal characteristics of a knight (e.g. the qualities of courage, honour, loyalty, readiness to help the weak, devotion to women and children). **3.** (old use) all the knights of a country. **chiv·al·rous** ['ʃivəlrəs] *adj.* having ~ (2).

chlo·rine ['klɔ:ri:n] *n.* greenish-yellow bad-smelling, irritating gas. **chlo·ri·nate** ['klɔ:rineit] *v.t.* treat (e.g. water-supplies) with ~ in order to purify. **chlo·ride** ['klɔ:raid] *n.* compound of ~:

chloride of lime (for bleaching and to disinfect).

chlo·ro·form ['klɔrəfɔ:m] *n.* vapour used by doctors to make a person unconscious. *v.t.* make unconscious by giving ~ to.

chock [tʃɔk] *n.* block of wood used to prevent sth. (e.g. a barrel or a door) from moving. '~-'**full** *adj.* quite full.

choc·o·late ['tʃɔkəlit] *n.* food substance made from crushed seeds of the cacao tree, usu. sweetened and flavoured; drink made by mixing this with hot water or milk; the colour of ~, dark brown. (Cf. *cocoa*.)

choice [tʃɔis] *n.* **1.** act of choosing; right or possibility of choosing: *to make a wise* ~; *to take one's* ~. *for* ~, (a) by preference; (b) if one must choose. **2.** person or thing chosen; number from which to choose: *a large* ~ *of books*. *adj.* specially or carefully chosen; exceptional; rare; *uncommonly good.*

choir ['kwaiə*] *n.* company of persons trained to sing together, esp. to lead the singing in church; part of a church for the ~.

choke [tʃouk] *v.i. & t.* **1.** be unable to breathe because of sth. in the windpipe, or because of emotion: *to* ~ *over one's food*; *to* ~ *with anger*. **2.** stop the breathing of, by pressing the windpipe from outside or by filling it: ~*d by smoke*; *to* ~ *the life out of sb.* **3.** (often ~ *up*) fill, partly or completely, a passage, etc., which is usually clear: *a chimney* (*pipe*, etc.) ~*d up with rubbish.* *n.* valve in a petrol engine which controls the intake of air.

chol·er·a ['kɔlərə] *n.* summer disease, common in hot countries, which attacks the bowels and may cause death.

choose [tʃu:z] *v.t. & i.* (p.t. *chose* [tʃouz], p.p. *chosen* ['tʃouzn]). **1.** pick out from two or more: *to* ~ *a wife* (*one's friends, a new hat*). **2.** decide (between one and another); be determined (to do sth.): *Do whatever you* ~.

¹chop [tʃɔp] *v.t.* (-*pp*-). cut by giving blows to : to ~ *wood* (*into sticks*); *to* ~ *a tree down.* *n.* ~ping blow; sth. ~ped off, esp. a thick piece of meat with a bone in it, cut off before cooking. ~**·per** *n.* heavy tool with a sharp edge for ~ping meat, wood, etc. ~**·py** *adj.* (of the sea) covered with short, rough waves.

²chop [tʃɔp] *n.* (in China and India) official seal or stamp.

chop·sticks ['tʃɔpstiks] *n. pl.* sticks used (two in one hand) by Chinese and Japanese for carrying food from a dish, etc., to the mouth.

chor·al ['kɔːrəl] *adj.* of, for, sung by or together with, a choir : *a* ~ *service.*

chord [kɔːd] *n.* **1.** straight line joining two points on a circle or part of a circle. **2.** (music) combination of usually three or more notes sounded together. **3.** string of a harp, etc. **4.** (in the body) string-like part (e.g. vocal ~s; spinal ~). (Also *cord.*)

chore [tʃɔː*, tʃɔə*] *n.* small duty or piece of work; esp. an ordinary daily task (in the home or on a farm).

cho·re·og·ra·phy [ˌkɔriˈɔgrəfi] *n.* art of designing ballet.

chor·is·ter ['kɔristə*] *n.* member of a choir, esp. a choir-boy.

chor·us ['kɔːrəs] *n.* **1.** (music for a) group of singers, esp. on the stage. **2.** (part of a) song for all to sing (after solo verses). **3.** sth. said or cried by many people together : *a* ~ *of praise*; *in* ~ (all together). **4.** (ancient Greece) group of dancers and singers taking part in religious ceremonies and dramas.

chose, chos·en, see *choose.*

chris·ten ['krisn] *v.t.* receive (an infant) into the Christian church by baptizing; give names to, at baptism; apply a nickname to. **Chris·ten·dom** *n.* all Christian people and Christian countries.

Chris·tian ['kristjən] *adj.* of Jesus Christ and his teaching; of the religion, beliefs, church, etc., based on this teaching. ~ *name*, first name, given when sb. is christened. *n.* ~ person.

Chris·ti·an·i·ty [ˌkristiˈæniti] *n.* the ~ religion.

Christ·mas (Day) ['krisməs] *n.* yearly celebration of the birth of Jesus Christ, 25 Dec.

chro·mium ['kroumjəm] *n.* metallic element. **chrome** [kroum] *n.* colouring substance obtained from compounds of ~; *chrome yellow* (*orange, etc.*); *chrome steel,* hard kind containing ~.

chron·ic ['krɔnik] *adj.* (of a disease, pain, etc.) continual, going on for a long time : ~ *invalid,* person with a ~ illness.

chron·i·cle ['krɔnikl] *n.* record of events in the order of their happening. *v.t.* enter in a ~.

chro·nol·o·gy [krəˈnɔlədʒi] *n.* science of fixing dates; arrangement of events with dates; list showing this. **chron·o·log·i·cal** [ˌkrɔnəˈlɔdʒikl] *adj. in chronological order* (in order of time).

chro·nom·e·ter [krəˈnɔmitə*] *n.* kind of watch or clock keeping very exact time, used on a ship in fixing longitude.

chrys·a·lis ['krisəlis] *n.* form taken by an insect in the second stage of its life (i.e. between the stage when it creeps or crawls as a larva, caterpillar, etc., and the time when it flies, as a butterfly, moth, etc.); the case covering it during this stage.

chrys·an·the·mum [kriˈsænθəməm] *n.* (flower of) garden plant from Japan, blooming in autumn and early winter.

chub·by ['tʃʌbi] *adj.* round-faced; plump.

chuck [tʃʌk] *v.t.* (colloq.) **1.** throw : *to* ~ *away rubbish.* **2.** ~ *sth. up,* give up : *to* ~ *up one's job.*

chuck·le ['tʃʌkl] *v.i. & n.* (give a) low, quiet laugh with closed mouth (indicating satisfaction or amusement).

chug [tʃʌg] *v.i. & n.* (-*gg*-). (make the) sound of an engine : *The boat* ~*ged down the river.*

chum [tʃʌm] *n.* close friend. *v.i.* (-*mm*-). ~ *up* (*with*), become friendly (with). ~**·my** *adj.*

chunk [tʃʌŋk] *n.* thick lump cut off (a loaf, a piece of meat, cheese, etc.).

church [tʃəːtʃ] *n.* **1.** building for public Christian worship. (Cf. *chapel*.) **2.** service in such a building: *What time does ~ begin?* **3.** *the C~ of Christ*, the whole body of Christians; one of the branches of the Christian religion: *the Church of England*; *the Methodist Church*; *enter the Church* (become a minister of religion). **~·yard** [ˈtʃəːtʃjɑːd] *n.* walled ground round a ~, often used as a burial-place.

churl·ish [ˈtʃəːliʃ] *adj.* bad tempered; ill bred.

churn [tʃəːn] *n.* **1.** container in which cream is shaken or beaten to make butter. **2.** large can for transporting milk. *v.t. & i.* **1.** make (butter) in a ~. **2.** (of the sea, etc.) (cause to) move about violently.

chute [ʃuːt] *n.* **1.** sloping channel along which, e.g. coal, postal packets, luggage, may slide to a lower level. **2.** smooth, rapid fall of water over a slope.

chut·ney [ˈtʃʌtni] *n.* hot-tasting mixture of fruit, peppers, etc., eaten with cold meat or curry.

ci·ca·da [siˈkɑːdə] *n.* winged insect which makes a loud, shrill noise.

ci·der [ˈsaidə*] *n.* fermented drink made from apples.

ci·gar [siˈgɑː*] *n.* roll of tobacco leaves for smoking. **cig·a·rette** [ˌsigəˈret] *n.* shredded tobacco rolled in thin paper for smoking.

cin·der [ˈsində*] *n.* small piece of coal or wood partly burned, not yet ash.

cin·e·ma [ˈsinəmə] *n.* theatre for showing films. **ci·ne·cam·e·ra** [ˌsiniˈkæmərə] *n.* camera for taking moving pictures. **ci·ne·pro·jec·tor** [ˈsiniprəˈdʒektə*] *n.* apparatus for showing films.

cin·na·mon [ˈsinəmən] *n.* spice from the inner bark of an E. Indian tree; its colour, reddish or yellowish-brown.

ci·pher [ˈsaifə*] *n.* **1.** the figure 0, representing nought or zero. **2.** person or thing of no importance. **3.** (method of, key to) secret writing. *v.t. & i.* **1.** do arithmetic. **2.** put (sth.) into secret writing.

cir·ca [ˈsəːkə] *prep.* about: *born ~ 150 B.C.*

cir·cle [ˈsəːkl] *n.* **1.** space enclosed by a curved line, every point of which is the same distance from the centre; the line enclosing this space. **2.** sth. round, like a ~: *a ~ of trees.* **3.** block of seats in curved rows, one above the other, between the highest part (or *gallery*) and the floor of a theatre or hall. **4.** body of persons bound together by having the same or similar interests, occupations, etc.: *He has a large ~ of friends. Business ~s expect prices to fall.* **5.** complete series: *the ~ of the seasons* (i.e. the four seasons in succession). *vicious ~*, series of events following and reacting upon one another. *v.t. & i.* move in a ~; go round: *The aircraft ~d over the landing-field.*

circ·let [ˈsəːklit] *n.* small round band (1) (e.g. of gold or flowers) worn on the head as an ornament.

cir·cuit [ˈsəːkit] *n.* **1.** journey round, from place to place, esp. a regular journey made by a judge from town to town to try cases; a district (one of eight in England and Wales) visited by such a judge. **2.** continuous path of an electric current. *short ~*, faulty shortening of such a path. **3.** regional group of Methodist churches sharing preachers. **cir·cu·i·tous** [səːˈkjuitəs] *adj.* indirect; roundabout; going a long way round.

cir·cu·lar [ˈsəːkjulə*] *adj.* in the shape of a circle: *~ tour* (journey ending at the starting-point without a place being visited more than once). *n.* printed announcement, letter, etc., sent to a number of people. **~·ize**

['sə:kjuləraiz] *v.t.* send ~s to.

cir·cu·late ['sə:kjuleit] *v.i. & t.* **1.** go round continuously; move or be sent freely from place to place, person to person: *Blood ~s through the body. The news (was) soon ~d.* **cir·cu·la·tion** [ˌsə:kju'leiʃən] *n.* **1.** circulating or being ~d (esp. of the blood): *He has a good (bad) circulation.* **2.** total number of each issue of a newspaper or other periodical sold to the public.

cir·cum·cise ['sə:kəmsaiz] *v.t.* cut off the loose skin covering the end of the male sex organ. **cir·cum·ci·sion** [ˌsə:kəm'siʒn] *n.*

cir·cum·fer·ence [sə(:)'kʌmfərəns] *n.* the line that marks out a circle or other curved figure; its length.

cir·cum·flex ['sə:kəmfleks] *n.* mark ʌ placed over a vowel in French, etc., to indicate a certain pronunciation.

cir·cum·lo·cu·tion [ˌsə:kəmlə'kju:ʃən] *n.* roundabout way of expressing sth.

cir·cum·nav·i·gate [ˌsə:kəm'nævigeit] *v.t.* sail round (esp. the world). **cir·cum·nav·i·ga·tion** ['sə:kəmˌnævi'geiʃən] *n.*

cir·cum·scribe ['sə:kəmskraib] *v.t.* draw a line round; mark the limit(s) of; narrow down; restrict. **cir·cum·scrip·tion** [ˌsə:kəm'skripʃən] *n.* (esp.) words inscribed round a coin.

cir·cum·spect ['sə:kəmspekt] *adj.* paying careful attention to everything before deciding on action; cautious. **cir·cum·spec·tion** [ˌsə:kəm'spekʃən] *n.*

cir·cum·stance ['sə:kəmstəns] *n.* **1.** (usu. pl.) conditions, facts, etc., connected with an event or person: *Don't judge the crime until you know the ~s. under (in) the ~s, the ~s being so; such being the state of affairs. under (in) no ~s,* never; not at all; whatever may happen. **2.** fact or detail: *There is one important ~ you have not mentioned.* **cir·cum·stan·tial** [ˌsə:kəm'stænʃl] *adj.* (of a description) giving full details; (of evidence) based on

details which strongly suggest sth. but do not give direct proof.

cir·cum·vent [ˌsə:kəm'vent] *v.t.* get the better of (a person), defeat (his plans).

cir·cus ['sə:kəs] *n.* **1.** (round or oval space with seats around it, for a) show of performing animals, clever horse-riding, etc.; the persons and animals giving such a show. **2.** place where a number of streets meet.

cir·rus ['sirəs] *n.* light, feathery cloud, high in the sky. (Cf. *cumulus.*)

cis·tern ['sistən] *n.* water-tank, esp. for storing water in a building.

cit·a·del ['sitədl] *n.* fortress for protecting a city; (fig.) place of refuge or safety.

cite [sait] *v.t.* **1.** give as an example (esp. by quoting from a book, in order to support an argument, etc.). **2.** mention (a soldier, etc.) for bravery: *~ in dispatches.* **ci·ta·tion** [sai'teiʃən] *n.* citing; sth. ~d.

cit·i·zen ['sitizn] *n.* **1.** person who lives in a town, not in the country: *the ~s of London.* **2.** person having full rights in a country, either by birth or by gaining such rights: *to become an American ~.* (Cf. *British subject* (1).) **~·ship** *n.* being a ~ (2); rights and duties of a ~.

cit·ron ['sitrən] *n.* (tree with) pale-yellow fruit similar to a lemon.

cit·rus ['sitrəs] *adj.* of such fruits as citrons, lemons, oranges, etc.: *citrus crops.* **cit·ric** ['sitrik] *adj. citric acid,* acid from citrus fruits.

cit·y ['siti] *n.* large and important town. *the City,* oldest part of central London, the banking and civic centre.

civ·ic ['sivik] *adj.* of the official life and affairs of a town: *~ duties (virtues); a ~ centre* (where the official buildings are situated). **civ·ics** *n.pl.* study of city government, the rights and duties of citizens, etc.

civ·il ['sivl] *adj.* **1.** of human society; of persons living together: ~ *law* (dealing with the private rights of citizens, not with crime); ~ *war* (between two parties of the same nation or state); ~ *marriage* (without a religious ceremony); ~ *engineering* (building of roads, railways, canals, docks, etc.). **2.** not of the armed forces: *the Civil Service* (all government departments except the Navy, Army, and Air Force); ~ *servant*, official in the Civil Service; ~ *life* (= civilian life). **3.** politely helpful: *to give a ~ answer.* **ci·vil·i·ty** [si'viliti] *n.* politeness; polite act. **~·ly** *adv.* **ci·vil·ian** [si'viljən] *n. & adj.* (person) not serving with the armed forces : *to get back to ~ian life* (e.g. after being in the army).

civ·i·lize ['sivilaiz] *v.t.* bring from a savage or ignorant condition to a higher one (by giving teaching in methods of government, morals, art, science, etc.). **civ·i·li·za·tion** [ˌsivilai'zeiʃən] *n.* **1.** making, becoming, ~d. **2.** system, stage of, civilization: *the civilization of ancient Egypt.* **3.** all ~d states: *an act that horrified civilization.*

clack [klæk] *v.i. & t. & n.* (make the) sound of objects struck together (e.g. wooden shoes on stone, typewriter keys).

clad [klæd] old p.p. of *clothe*: *poorly ~,* poorly dressed.

claim [kleim] *v.t.* **1.** demand recognition of the fact that one is, or owns or has a right to (sth.): *to ~ the throne. He ~ed to be the owner of the land* (that he owned the land). **2.** say that sth. is a fact: *He ~ed to have (that he had) done the work without help.* **3.** (of things) need; deserve: *matters ~ing my attention. n.* **1.** act of ~ing: *to lay ~ to sth.* **2.** right to ask for: *You have no ~ on my sympathies.* **3.** sth. which is ~ed. **4.** piece of land (e.g. in a gold-bearing region) allotted to a miner. **~·ant** *n.* person who makes a ~.

clair·voy·ant [klɛə'vɔiənt] *n.*

person with power to see in his mind what is happening or what exists at a distance. **clair·voy·ance** *n.* that power.

clam [klæm] *n.* large shell-fish used as food.

clam·ber ['klæmbə*] *v.i.* climb with some difficulty, esp. using the hands: *to ~ over a wall.*

clam·my ['klæmi] *adj.* damp, moist, usu. cold and sticky to the touch: *a face ~ with sweat.*

clam·our ['klæmə*] *n.* loud, confused noise, esp. of people complaining angrily or making demands. *v.i.* make a ~: *newspapers ~ing against the high taxes.* **clam·or·ous** *adj.*

clamp [klæmp] *n.* **1.** appliance for holding things together tightly by means of a screw. **2.** iron band for strengthening or making tight. *v.t.* put in a ~ (1); put ~s (2) on.

clan [klæn] *n.* large family-group, as found in tribal communities. **~·nish** *adj.* showing ~ feeling; in the habit of supporting one another. **clans·man** *n.* member of a ~.

clan·des·tine [klæn'destin] *adj.* secret; done secretly.

clang [klæŋ] *v.t. & i. & n.* (make a) loud ringing sound (like that of a heavy bell or a hammer striking an anvil). **~·our** ['klæŋgə*] *n.* ~ing sound(s).

clank [klæŋk] *v.t. & i. & n.* (make a) ringing sound (like that heard when swords or heavy chains strike together).

clap [klæp] *v.t. & i.* (-*pp*-). **1.** strike the hands together, esp. to show approval: ~ *one's hands. The audience ~ped for five minutes.* **2.** strike or slap lightly with the open hand, usu. in a friendly way: *to ~ sb. on the back.* **3.** set, place, quickly: ~ *sb. into prison; never to have ~ped eyes on sb. n.* sharp, loud noise: *a ~ of thunder.*

clar·et ['klærət] *n.* kind of red wine; dark-red colour.

clar·i·fy ['klærifai] *v.t. & i.* make or become clear; make (a liquid, etc.) free from impurities.

clar·i·net ['klærinet, klæri'net]
n. musical instrument, wood-wind, with holes and keys.

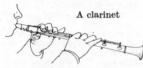

A clarinet

clar·i·on ['klæriən] *n.* loud, shrill
call; loud sound to rouse and
excite; (attrib.) clear and loud:
a ~ call (*voice*).

clar·i·ty ['klæriti] *n.* clearness.

clash [klæʃ] *v.i. & t. & n.* **1.**
(make a) loud, broken, confused
sound (as when metal objects,
e.g. swords, pans, strike to-gether). **2.** (be in) disagreement
or conflict: *colours that ~; a ~
of colours; ideas (plans) that ~;
a ~ of views.*

clasp [klɑːsp] *n.* **1.** device with
two parts which fasten together,
used for keeping together two
things or two parts of one thing
(e.g. a necklace or belt). **2.** firm
hold (with the fingers or arm);
handshake or embrace. *v.t. & i.*
1. fasten with a ~ (1). **2.** hold
tightly or closely: *to ~ sb.'s
hand; ~ing a knife; ~ed in
each other's arms.* **'~-knife** *n.*
folding knife.

class [klɑːs] *n.* **1.** group having
common qualities; kind, sort, or
division: *A ~ is the highest
division of the animal or vegetable
kingdom.* (Cf. *family, species.*)
*Society is divided into upper,
middle, and lower ~es. There
used to be first-~, second-~, and
third-~ carriages on the railways.*
2. group of persons taught to-gether; their course of teaching.
3. year's enrolment of con-scripts. *v.t.* put in the correct
group. **'~-'con·scious** *adj.*
realizing one's ~ in society and
the differences between social
~es.

clas·sic ['klæsik] *adj.* **1.** of the
highest quality; excellent; hav-ing a value or position recog-nized and unquestioned. **2.** of
the standard of ancient Greek

and Latin writers, art, and cul-ture. **3.** with qualities like those
of ~ art, i.e. simple, harmonious,
and restrained. **4.** famous be-cause of a long history: *a ~
event* (e.g. a race such as the
Marathon or the Oxford and
Cambridge boat-race). *n.* writer,
artist, book, work of art, etc., of
the highest class, esp. of ancient
Rome and Greece. *the Classics,*
works of famous Greek and
Latin writers. **clas·si·cal** ['klæ-sikl] *adj.* **1.** in, of, the best (esp.
ancient Greek and Roman) art
and literature: *~al studies
(scholars, education); of the
highest class.* **2.** of proved value
because of having passed the
test of time: *~al music* (con-trasted with modern music).
3. = ~ (2).

clas·si·fy ['klæsifai] *v.t.* arrange
in classes (1); put into a class
or classes (1). **clas·si·fi·ca·tion**
[,klæsifi'keiʃən] *n.*

clat·ter ['klætə*] *v.i. & t. & n.*
1. (make a) loud, confused noise
(as of hard things falling or
knocking together): *the ~ of
machinery (of plates and dishes
on a hard surface); horses ~ing
along a stony road.* **2.** (be full of,
echo with) noisy talk.

clause [klɔːz] *n.* **1.** (grammar)
component part of a sentence,
with its own subject and predi-cate, especially one doing the
work of a noun, adjective, or
adverb. **2.** complete paragraph
in an agreement, a law, etc.

claw [klɔː] *n.* **1.** one of the long,
pointed nails on the feet of some
animals and birds; foot with ~s.
2. instrument like a ~; sth.
shaped like a ~ (e.g. on a lobster
or crab). *v.t.* get hold of with
the ~s or fingers; scratch with
the ~s or finger-nails; pull
roughly with the ~s.

clay [klei] *n.* stiff, sticky earth
which becomes hard when
baked; material from which
bricks, pots, earthenware, etc.,
are made. **'~·ey** ['kleii] *adj.* like,
containing, ~: *a ~ey soil.*

clean [kliːn] *adj.* (*-er, -est*). **1.**
free from dirt or smoke; freshly

washed; unused. make a ~ breast of, confess fully (to wrong-doing, etc.). 2. not having rough or irregular lines; well formed; of good shape: a ~ cut (made by a sharp knife); ~-cut features (clear and well defined). 3. pure; innocent. v.t. & i. make ~. ~ up, make tidy; put in order. ~ out, get dirt, rubbish, unwanted articles, etc., from the inside of: to ~ out a desk. adv. completely: We ~ forgot you were coming. n. (= ~ing) Give your dirty boots a good ~. ~·ly ['klenli] adj. having ~ habits. ~·li·ness n. habit or condition of being ~.

cleanse [klenz] v.t. make thoroughly clean; (esp.) purify of sin.

clear [kliə*] adj. (-er, -est). 1. easy to see through: ~ glass; (of the sky) free from cloud; bright and pure: a ~ fire; distinct, easily seen or understood: a ~ photograph; a line of hills ~ in the morning sky. 2. (of sounds) easily heard; pure; distinct: a ~ voice (note). 3. (of and to the mind) easily understood; free from doubt or difficulty: a ~ thinker (statement); to make one's meaning ~. 4. easy or safe to pass along; free from dangers or obstacles. keep ~ of, keep out of the way of. 5. free: ~ of debt (suspicion). 6. complete: two ~ days; a ~ profit of £5. adv. completely: to get ~ away. v.t. & i. 1. get or make ~: to ~ the streets of snow; to ~ a desk (i.e. put all the papers, books, etc., away); The sky is ~ing. to ~ the table (esp. take away dishes, etc., after a meal); to ~ up (put things in order, or, of the weather, become bright); to ~ out (colloq., go away, leave). 2. get past or over without touching. 3. make a profit of. 4. ~ a ship (its cargo), do what is necessary (signing papers, etc.) before sailing. '~-·cut adj. having ~ outlines. ~·ly adv. ~·ance n. making ~; space left between two things. ~·ing n. (esp.) land made ~ of trees. ~·ness n.

¹cleave [kliːv] v.t. & i. (p.t. clove [klouv] or cleft [kleft], p.p. cleft or cloven). cut in two with a blow from a heavy axe, etc.; split; come apart (esp. along the line where there is a natural tendency, e.g. the grain of wood). cloven hoof, divided hoof of cow, ox, the Devil. cleft palate, malformation in the roof of the mouth. cleav·age ['kliːvidʒ] n. act of cleaving; state of being cleft; place where cleaving occurs easily or has occurred. cleav·er n. heavy tool for chopping up carcasses.

²cleave [kliːv] v.i. (old use) be faithful (to).

clef [klef] n. one of three signs, e.g. 𝄞, C, used in music to show pitch (5).

¹cleft, see ¹cleave.

²cleft [kleft] n. crack or split (esp. in the ground or in rock).

clem·a·tis ['klematis] n. (kinds of) climbing plant with flowers.

clem·ent ['klemənt] adj. (of the weather) mild; (of a person) showing mercy. 'clem·en·cy n.

clench [klentʃ] v.t. & i. 1. (of teeth, fingers, or fist) close, hold, tightly. 2. (usu. clinch) (of an argument or bargain) settle finally. 3. grip.

cler·gy ['kləːdʒi] n. the ~, (with pl. v.) ministers of the Christian Church. ~·man n. one of these.

cler·ic ['klerik] n. clergyman. cler·i·cal ['klerikl] adj. 1. of the clergy: ~al dress. 2. of the work of a clerk; of writing and copying.

clerk [klɑːk] n. office worker who keeps accounts, writes letters, etc. Town C~, C~ to the Council, (usu. lawyer) in charge of official business; ~ of the works, having charge of materials, etc., for building contract(s).

clev·er ['klevə*] adj. (-er, -est). (of people) quick in learning and understanding things; skilful; smart (2); (of things) done with skill: a ~ book. ~·ly adv. ~·ness n.

click [klik] v.i. & n. (make a) short sharp sound (like that of a lock closing).

cli·ent ['klaiənt] n. person who

gets help or advice from a lawyer or other professional man; customer (at a shop). **cli·en·tele** [ˌkliːɔnˈtel] *n.* customers.

cliff [klif] *n.* steep face of rock, esp. at the edge of the sea.

cli·mate [ˈklaimit] *n.* weather conditions of (a place). (fig.) *climate of opinion*, general attitude of people to a policy, etc. **cli·mat·ic** [klaiˈmætik] *adj.*

cli·max [ˈklaimæks] *n.* event, point, of greatest interest or importance.

climb [klaim] *v.t. & i.* go up (stairs, a tree, rope, mountain, etc.); go higher. ~ *down*, get down (with some difficulty or effort) from a tree or other high place; (fig.) admit fault of pride, etc. *n.* act of ~ing; place to be ~ed: *a difficult* ~. ~**er** *n.*

clime [klaim] *n.* (poet.) country.

clinch [klintʃ] *v.t. & i.* = *clench* (2).

cling [kliŋ] *v.i.* (p.t. & p.p. *clung* [klʌŋ]). hold tight (*to*); (of clothes) fit close to the skin.

clin·ic [ˈklinik] *n.* institution, hospital, etc., where advice and treatment are given; hospital ward where medical students are taught through observation of cases. **'clin·i·cal** *adj.*

clink [kliŋk] *v.i. & t. & n.* (make the) sound of small bits of metal (e.g. coins or keys), glass, etc., knocking together.

clink·er [ˈkliŋkə*] *n.* mass of material which forms in a coal fire and does not burn; kind of hard brick made by burning.

¹**clip** [klip] *n.* wire or metal device for holding papers, etc., together. *v.t.* (-*pp*-). put or keep together with a ~.

²**clip** [klip] *v.t.* (-*pp*-). cut with scissors, shears, etc.; make short or neat: *to* ~ *a hedge* (*the wool from a sheep's back*). ~**pers** [ˈklipəz] *n. pl.* instrument for ~ping hair. ~**ping** *n.* sth. ~ped out (esp. from a newspaper).

clip·per [ˈklipə*] *n.* sailing-ship formerly used in the tea trade.

clique [kliːk] *n.* group of persons united by common interests and

tastes (e.g. in literature or art), members of which support each other and shut out others from their company.

cloak [klouk] *n.* loose outer garment without sleeves; (fig.) anything that hides or covers. *v.t.* (fig.) hide or cover; keep secret. '~**-room** *n.* place where coats, parcels, etc., may be left for a short time.

clock [klɔk] *n.* instrument (other than a watch) for showing the time. '~·**wise** *adj. & adv.* moving in a curve in the direction taken by the hands of a ~. '~·**work** *n. & adj.* (machinery) with wheels driven by a spring. *like* ~*work*, regularly; without trouble. *v.i.* ~ *in* (*on, out, off*), (of workers) record the time of arrival and departure.

clod [klɔd] *n.* lump of earth.

¹**clog** [klɔg] *n.* shoe with a heavy wooden sole, or carved out of a block of wood.

²**clog** [klɔg] *v.t. & i.* (-*gg*-). be, cause to be, become, blocked with waste matter, dirt, grease, etc., so that movement or the flow of liquid is made difficult: *machinery* ~*ged with grease*; *pipes* ~*ged with dirt.*

clois·ter [ˈklɔistə*] *n.* 1. covered walk, usu. on the sides of an open square, esp. within a convent, cathedral, or college building. 2. convent or monastery. *v.t.* put in, live in, a convent or monastery.

¹**close** [klouz] *v.t. & i.* 1. shut. 2. (often ~ *up*) come near or together; make less space or fewer spaces between. ~ *in* (*upon*), come nearer, surround (esp. in order to attack). 3. end. ~ *with an offer*, accept it. *n.* end(ing): *draw* (*bring*) *to a* ~.

²**close** [klous] *adj.* (*closer, closest*). 1. near: *a* ~ *friend*, a very dear friend. 2. (of the air, the weather) not fresh; uncomfortably warm. 3. receiving care; thorough: ~ *attention*; *a* ~ *translation*; *with every step clearly shown*: *a* ~ *argument*. 4. secret; keeping things secret: *to keep sth.* ~, say nothing about

it; *to lie* ~, hide. **5.** with very little space for movement: *at* ~ *quarters*; *in* ~ *confinement*, strictly guarded; *a* ~ *prisoner*. **6.** ~ *season*, period of the year when certain wild birds, animals, etc., must not be killed. **7.** not giving help (esp. money) willingly: *He's very* ~(*-fisted*). **8.** (of competitions, games, their results) in which two or more competitors are almost equal: *a* ~ *game (finish)*. *adv.* near: *to stand or sit* ~ *to sb.* *n.* (esp. of a school or cathedral) space with buildings all round. ~'ly *adv.* ~'ness *n.* '~-up *n.* picture taken with the camera ~ to the person or object.

clos·et ['klɔzit] *n.* **1.** small room; cupboard. **2.** (U.S.A.) store-room. **3.** water-closet (q.v.). *v.* be ~ed *together*, be ~ed *with* (*sb.*), be having a private talk.

clot [klɔt] *n.* half-solid lump formed from liquid, esp. blood. *v.i. & t.* (-*tt*-). form into ~s.

cloth [klɔθ] *n.* **1.** material made by weaving (cotton, wool, silk, linen, etc., yarn). **2.** piece of ~ for a special purpose: *a table-~*.

clothe [kloud] *v.t.* (p.t. & p.p. *clothed*, old form *clad*). **1.** put ~s on; give ~s to: *to* ~ *one's family*. **2.** (fig.) cover: *to* ~ *thoughts in words*. **clothes** [klouðz] *n. pl.* garments; what one wears on one's body. '~s-line, rope on which washed garments are hung to dry. '~s-peg, for fastening garments to a ~s-line. **cloth·ing** ['klouðiŋ] *n.* = clothes.

cloud [klaud] *n.* **1.** see the picture. **2.** mass of things like a ~: *a* ~ *of arrows (mosquitoes)*. **3.** (fig.) state of unhappiness or fear: *a* ~ *of grief; the* ~*s of war*; *under a* ~ *(of suspicion)*. *v.t. & i.* make or become dark with ~s. ~ *over*, (of the sky) become covered with ~s. ~'less, ~'y *adj.*

clout [klaut] *n.* blow or knock. *v.t.* strike; hit.

¹**clove** [klouv] *n.* dried, unopened flower-bud of a tropical tree, used to flavour food, etc.

²**clove, clo·ven**, see *cleave*.

clo·ver ['klouvə*] *n.* low-growing plant with (usu.) three leaves on each stalk, grown as food for cattle. *in* ~, in great comfort.

clown [klaun] *n.* man (esp. in a circus) who makes a living by performing foolish tricks and antics; person who behaves like a ~; rude, clumsy man. *v.i.* behave like a ~. ~'ish *adj.*

Clouds   A clown

cloy [klɔi] *v.t. & i.* make distasteful; become weary of sth. (through excess): ~ed *with sweet food (foolish pleasures, etc.)*.

¹**club** [klʌb] *n.* heavy stick with a thick end used as a weapon, or for hitting the ball in some games (e.g. golf). *v.t.* (-*bb*-). hit with a ~: *He had been* ~bed *to death*.

²**club** [klʌb] *n.* society of persons who subscribe money to provide themselves with sport (e.g. football, golf), social entertainment, etc., sometimes in their own grounds or buildings where meals and bedrooms are available; the rooms or building(s) used by such a society. *v.i.* (-*bb*-). join together for a common cause: *to* ~ *together (with others) to raise a sum of money*.

³**club** [klʌb] *n.* black design like a clover-leaf printed on some playing-cards.

cluck [klʌk] *v.i. & n.* (make the) noise of a hen (e.g. when calling her chickens).

clue [klu:] *n.* fact, idea, etc., which suggests a possible answer to a problem, esp. a crime mystery or a crossword puzzle.

clump [klʌmp] *n.* group of trees, shrubs, plants, etc.).

clum·sy ['klʌmzi] *adj.* (-*ier*, *iest*). heavy and ungraceful in movement or construction; not

well designed for a purpose.
clum·si·ly *adv.* **clum·si·ness** *n.*

clung, see **cling.**

clus·ter ['klʌstə*] *n.* **1.** number of things of the same kind growing closely together: *a ~ of curls (flowers, berries).* **2.** number of persons, animals, objects, etc., in a small, close group: *a ~ of bees (houses, spectators).* *v.i.* be, grow, come together, in a ~.

¹**clutch** [klʌtʃ] *v.t. & i.* seize in fear or anger: *to ~ (at) a rope.* *n.* **1.** the act of ~ing; strong hold. *in the ~es of,* in the cruel power of. **2.** device in a machine for connecting and disconnecting working parts: *to let in the ~ of a motor-car engine.*

²**clutch** [klʌtʃ] *n.* set of eggs put under a hen to hatch at one time; number of young chickens hatched from these.

clut·ter ['klʌtə*] *v.t.* (often ~ *up*) make untidy or disordered: *a desk ~ed up with papers.*

co- [kou-] *prefix.* together with (another or others): *co-author*; *co-education* (of boys and girls).

Co. [kou] *abbr.* Company (2).

¹**coach** [koutʃ] *n.* **1.** four-wheeled carriage pulled by four or more horses. **2.** railway carriage. **3.** long-distance motor-bus; chara-banc. **~·man** *n.* driver of a ~ (1).

A ¹coach (1)

²**coach** [koutʃ] *n.* teacher, esp. one who gives private lessons to prepare students for public examinations; person who trains athletes for games. *v.t. & i.* teach, train.

co·ag·u·late [kou'ægjuleit] *v.t. & i.* (of liquids) change to a more solid state, as blood does in air. **co·ag·u·la·tion** [ˌkouægju'leiʃən] *n.*

coal [koul] *n.* black mineral that is burnt to supply heat, raise steam, generate electricity, make coal-gas, tar, etc. *v.t. & i.* put ~ into (a ship); take in ~. '~-'tar *n.* thick, black sticky substance obtained when gas is made from ~.

co·a·lesce [ˌkouə'les] *v.i.* come together and unite.

co·a·li·tion [ˌkouə'liʃən] *n.* uniting; union of (esp. political) groups or parties for a special purpose.

coarse [kɔːs, kɔəs] *adj.* (-r, -st). **1.** rough; of poor quality: ~ *food; clothes made of ~ material.* **2.** not fine and small; rough and lumpy: ~ *sand.* **3.** rude (1); uncultured: ~ *language (manners).* **~·ly** *adv.,* **~·ness** *n.*

coast [koust] *n.* land near or by the edge of the sea. *v.i. & t.* **1.** go in, sail, a ship along the ~. **2.** go downhill on a bicycle without working the pedals. '~·**guard** *n.* officer on police duty on the ~ (to prevent smuggling, report passing ships, etc.). **~·al** *adj.* of the ~. '~·**wise** *adj. & adv.* along the ~.

coat [kout] *n.* **1.** outer garment with sleeves, buttoned in front. **2.** animal's covering of hair, etc. **3.** covering of paint, etc. *v.t.* put a ~ (3) on. ~ **of arms** *n.* see *arm* (4). **~·ing** *n.* layer or covering: *a ~ing of soot*; material for making ~s (1).

coax [kouks] *v.t. & i.* get sb. or sth. to do sth. by kindness or patience: *to ~ a child to go to bed early; to ~ a fire to burn.*

cob [kɔb] *n.* **1.** strong, short-legged horse for riding. **2.** (also *corn-~*) that part of a head of maize on which the grain grows.

co·balt ['koubɔːlt] *n.* metal similar to nickel; deep-blue colouring matter made from it.

¹**cob·ble** ['kɔbl] *n.* (also ~*-stone*) stone worn round and smooth by water (formerly used for paving).

²**cob·ble** ['kɔbl] *v.t. & i.* mend, patch (esp. shoes), or put together roughly. **cob·bler** *n.* mender of shoes.

co·bra ['koubrə] *n.* poisonous snake of India.

cob·web ['kɔbweb] *n.* fine network or single thread made by a spider.

co·caine [kou'kein] *n.* drug used by doctors to deaden pain.

¹**cock** [kɔk] *n.* male bird of the farmyard fowl; the male of any other kind of bird named : *turkey-~*; *~sparrow*. '**~-crow** *n.* daybreak. '**~·pit** *n.* **1.** place for fights between *~s*. **2.** (formerly) hospital in a warship. **3.** place where the pilot sits in an aircraft. '**~s·comb** *n.* **~'s** red crest. '**~·sure** *adj.* quite sure; too confident.

²**cock** [kɔk] *n.* **1.** tap and spout for controlling the flow of liquid (from a pipe, barrel, etc.). **2.** lever in a gun: *at half (full) ~*, half-ready (ready) to be fired. *v.t.* turn upwards (showing attention, defiance, etc.): *to ~ the ears (an eye) at. . . .* **3.** raise the *~(2)* (of a gun) ready for firing. **cocked hat** *n.* triangular hat, pointed front and back, worn by some senior British officers and officials.

cock·ade [kɔ'keid] *n.* knot of ribbon worn in the hat as a badge.

cock·a·too [ˌkɔkə'tu:] *n.* crested parrot.

cock·er·el ['kɔkərəl] *n.* young cock.

cock·ney ['kɔkni] *adj. & n.* (of a) native of London.

cock·roach ['kɔkroutʃ] *n.* large dark-brown or black insect which comes out at night in kitchens and places where food is kept.

cock·tail ['kɔkteil] *n.* mixed alcoholic drink, usu. taken before meals; mixture of fruits or fruit juices served in a glass.

co·coa ['koukou] *n.* powder of crushed cacao seeds; drink made from this with hot water or milk.

co·co(nut) ['koukənʌt] *n.* large, hard, rough brown nut on the *~*-palm, filled with milky white juice and hard white substance (see *copra*). *~ matting*, made from rough fibre covering the nut.

co·coon [kə'ku:n] *n.* silky covering made by a caterpillar for protection while it is a chrysalis.

cod [kɔd] *n.* large sea-fish.

cod·dle ['kɔdl] *v.t.* treat very tenderly, or with unnecessary care.

code [koud] *n.* **1.** collection of laws arranged in a system. **2.** system of rules, principles, morals, etc. **3.** system of signs, secret writing, etc. **4.** system of sending messages: *the Morse ~*; *a telegraphic ~*. *v.t.* put into *~ signs*. **cod·i·fy** ['koudifai, 'kɔd-] *v.t.* put into the form of a *~*.

cod·i·cil ['kɔdisil] *n.* sth. added to a will.

co·erce [kou'ə:s] *v.t.* force (sb. into doing sth.). **co·er·cion** [kou'ə:ʃən] *n.* **co·er·cive** [kou'ə:siv] *adj.*

co·e·val [kou'i:vl] *n. & adj.* (person) of the same age; (person) existing at, lasting for, the same period of time.

cof·fee ['kɔfi] *n.* bush or shrub with seeds which, when roasted and powdered, are used for making a drink; the seeds; the powder; the drink. *~ bean (berry)*, *~ seed*.

cof·fer ['kɔfə*] *n.* large, strong box, esp. for holding money or valuables.

cof·fin ['kɔfin] *n.* box for a dead person to be buried in.

cog [kɔg] *n.* one of a number of teeth on a wheel or rod. '**~-wheel** *n.* toothed wheel to transfer motion from one part of a machine to another.

Cog-wheels

co·gent ['koudʒənt] *adj.* (of arguments) powerful. **co·gen·cy** ['koudʒənsi] *n.*

cog·i·tate ['kɔdʒiteit] *v.i. & t.* think (over) carefully. **cog·i·ta·tion** [ˌkɔdʒi'teiʃən] *n.*

cog·nac ['kounjæk] *n.* French brandy.

cog·nate ['kɔgneit] *n. & adj.* (word) coming from the same source or starting-point; having much in common: *The English word 'father' is ~ with the Latin 'pater'.*

cog·ni·zance ['kɔgnizəns] *n.* being aware; having knowledge (of).

co·here [kou'hiə*] *v.i.* stick together; remain united. **co·her·ence, co·her·en·cy** *n.* **co·her·ent** *adj.* (esp. of speech, thought, ideas) clear; easy to understand. **co·he·sion** [kou'hi:ʒən] *n.* cohering. **co·he·sive** [kou'hi:siv] *adj.*

coil [koil] *v.t. & i.* wind or twist (rope, etc.) into rings one above the other; curl (sth.) round and round. *n.* sth. ~ed; a single turn of sth. ~ed: *a ~ of rope;* ~ed wire for electric current.

A coiled snake

coin [koin] *n.* piece of metal money. *v.t.* make (metal) into ~s. *be ~ing money,* be making large profits; *~ a word (a phrase),* invent it. **co·'age** ['koinidʒ] *n.* making ~s; ~s so made; system of ~s: *a decimal ~age.*

co·in·cide [,kouin'said] *v.i.* 1. (of two or more objects) correspond in area or outline. 2. (of events) happen at the same time. 3. (of ideas, etc.) be in agreement (*with*). **co·in·ci·dence** [kou'insidəns] *n.* (esp.) chance coinciding of events, circumstances, etc.

coke [kouk] *n.* substance remaining when gas has been taken out of coal by heating in an oven. *v.t.* turn (coal) into ~.

col·an·der ['kʌləndə*] *n.* vessel with many small holes, used to drain off water when preparing or cooking vegetables.

cold [kould] *adj.* (-*er*, -*est*). 1. of low temperature, esp. when compared with that of the human body. 2. (fig.) not easily excited; unfriendly: *a ~ greeting (manner)*; *~hearted, ~blooded* (fig., pitiless). *in ~ blood,* when not excited or angry. *throw ~ water on,* (try) to discourage (enthusiasm, etc.). *give the ~ shoulder to,* treat in an unfriendly way. *n.* 1. low temperature: *He was shivering with (the) ~.* 2. illness with discharge from the nose, sneezing, etc. *~·ly adv. ~ness n.*

col·ic ['kɔlik] *n.* severe pain in the (stomach and) bowels.

col·lab·o·rate [kə'læbəreit] *v.i.* work together *with* another or others (esp. *in* writing a book or in art). **col·lab·o·ra·tion** [kə,læbə'reiʃən] *n.*

col·lapse [kə'læps] *v.i.* 1. fall down or in; come or break to pieces. 2. lose physical strength, courage, mental powers, etc., completely. *n.* complete breakdown, failure, or loss of these kinds. **col·laps·i·ble, -a·ble** *adj.* made so as to fold up for packing, storing, or transport: *a collapsible boat (table).*

col·lar ['kɔlə*] *n.* 1. part of a garment that fits round the neck. 2. separate article of clothing (linen, lace, etc.) worn round the neck and fastened to a shirt or blouse. 3. band of leather, etc., put round the neck of a horse, dog, or other animal. 4. metal band joining two pipes or rods. *v.t.* seize by the ~; take hold of roughly.

col·late [kɔ'leit] *v.t.* make a careful comparison between (two or more books, etc.) to learn the differences between them.

col·league ['kɔli:g] *n.* one of two or more persons working together and (usu.) having similar rank and duties.

¹col·lect ['kɔlekt] *n.* short prayer of the Church of Rome or the Church of England to be read on certain appointed days.

²col·lect [kə'lekt] *v.t. & i.* bring or come together; get from a number of people or places : *to ~ money (taxes, stamps, one's thoughts)*. *A crowd soon ~ed.* **col'lec·ted** *adj.* (esp. of a person) with feelings under control; cool and calm. **col'lec·tion** [kə-'lekʃən] *n.* ~ing; number of things which have been ~ed or which have come together; money ~ed at a meeting (e.g. at church). **col·lec·tive** *adj.* of a group or society as a whole : *~ive farms; ~ive ownership.* **col·lec·tor** *n.* person who ~s: *a tax-~or.*

col·lege ['kɔlidʒ] *n.* 1. school for higher or professional education; body of teachers and students forming part of a university; their building(s). 2. body of colleagues with common privileges: *the College of Surgeons; the College of Cardinals.* **col'le·gi·ate** [kə'liːdʒiit] *adj.*

col·lide [kə'laid] *v.i.* come together violently; be opposed. **col·li·sion** [kə'liʒən] *n.*

col·lier ['kɔliə*] *n.* coal-miner; ship carrying a cargo of coal. **~·y** *n.* coal-mine.

col·lo·qui·al [kə'loukwiəl] *adj.* (of words, phrases, style) belonging to, suitable for, ordinary conversation; not formal or literary.

col·lo·quy ['kɔləkwi] *n.* conversation.

col·lu·sion [kə'luːʒən] *n.* secret agreement or understanding for a wrong purpose.

¹co·lon ['koulən] *n.* the mark : in writing and printing.

²co·lon ['koulən] *n.* lower and greater part of the large intestine.

colo·nel ['kəːnl] *n.* army officer, above a major, commanding a regiment.

co·lo·ni·al, colo·nize, see *colony.*

col·on·nade [ˌkɔlə'neid] *n.* row of columns (1).

col·o·ny ['kɔləni] *n.* 1. land which has been developed by people from another country and which is still, fully or partly, controlled from the mother country. 2. group of people from another country,

or of people with the same trade or occupation, living together: *the American ~ in Paris; a ~ of artists.* **co·lo·ni·al** [kə'louniəl] *adj.* of a ~. *n.* person from overseas who has become resident in a ~. **co·lo·ni·al·ism** [kə'louniəlizm] *n.* policy of having and retaining colonies. **co·lo·nize** ['kɔlənaiz] *v.t.* form a ~ in; send colonists to. **co·lo·nist** ['kɔlənist] *n.* person who settles in a new ~. **col·o·ni·za·tion** [ˌkɔlənai'zeiʃən] *n.*

co·los·sal [kə'lɔsəl] *adj.* immense.

co·los·sus [kə'lɔsəs] *n.* immense statue (esp. of a man, much greater than life size); gigantic person or personification of sth.

col·our ['kʌlə*] *n.* 1. *The simple (or primary) ~s, red, blue and yellow, can be mixed together by painters to give all the other ~s. The ~ of blood is red. Your cheeks are (have) a healthy ~.* 2. materials used by artists: *water-~s.* 3. (of events, descriptions) appearance of truth or reality : *give (lend) ~ to,* make (sth.) seem reasonable or probable; *local ~,* (in writing) details which make a description more real. 4. (pl.) flag: *stick to one's ~s,* refuse to give up one's beliefs, party, etc.; *lower one's ~s,* give up one's demands, etc.; *show one's true ~s,* show what one really is; *come off with flying ~s,* be very successful. *v.t. & i.* put ~ on; become ~ed. **'~-blind** *adj.* unable to see the difference between certain ~s, esp. red and green. **col·oured** *adj.* (of persons) other than white-skinned. **~ing** *n.* (esp.) the style in which sth. is ~ed, or the way in which an artist uses ~.

colt [koult] *n.* young male horse (up to 4 or 5 years).

col·umn ['kɔləm] *n.* 1. tall, upright pillar, either supporting or decorating part of a building, or standing alone as a monument. 2. sth. shaped like a ~: *a ~ of smoke (figures).* 3. narrow upright division of the printed page of a newspaper or book; part of a newspaper occupied regularly by a special subject.

co·ma ['koumə] *n.* unnatural deep sleep. **com·a·tose** ['koumətous] *adj.* affected with ~; drowsy.

comb [koum] *n.* **1.** instrument with teeth for making the hair tidy, keeping it in place, etc. **2.** similar instrument in some machines for preparing wool, cotton, etc., for manufacture. **3.** see *honey*. *v.t.* **1.** use a ~ on (the hair). **2.** search thoroughly. ~ *out*, take out (unwanted things, persons) from a group.

com·bat ['kʌmbət, 'kɔmbæt] *n. & v.t. & i.* fight; struggle: *single* ~, one between two persons only; *mortal* ~, till one fighter is killed. **~·ant** ['kʌmbətənt] *adj. & n.* fighting (man).

com·bine [kəm'bain] *v.t. & i.* (cause to) join together; possess at the same time. ['kɔmbain] *n.* group of persons or parties, esp. for trade, controlling prices, etc. **com·bi·na·tion** [,kɔmbi'neiʃən] *n.* **1.** joining or putting together; number of persons or parties ~d for a purpose. **2.** (pl.) suit of underwear in one piece covering body and legs.

com·bus·ti·ble [kəm'bʌstibl] *n. & adj.* (substance) catching fire and burning easily.

com·bus·tion [kəm'bʌstʃən] *n.* process of burning; destruction by fire.

come [kʌm] *v.i.* (p.t. *came* [keim], p.p. *come*). **1.** move nearer to the position of the speaker or a point (in space or time) or a result: *C~ here. C~ to me. They came at six o'clock. They came towards the house. We argued till we came to blows* (began to fight). **2.** arrive: *The visitors haven't* ~ *yet.* **3.** occur: *The 2nd May* ~*s on a Friday.* **4.** amount to: *Our expenses came to £5.* **5.** prove to be: *I hope my dream will* ~ *true.* **6.** become: *My shoe has* ~ *undone.* **7.** (special combinations only): ~ *to* (*sth.*), get possession of; ~ *round*, ~ *to one's senses*, become conscious

(after fainting); become sensible (after being foolish); ~ *into* (*a fortune*), inherit (when sb. dies); ~ *out*, (of a book) be published, (of facts) become known, (of stains) be removed; ~ *of age*, reach the age of 21; ~ *about*, happen; ~ *across*, ~ *upon*, find by accident; ~ *true*, become real, become a fact; ~ *of*, have as a result: *What came of the discussion?* (What happened afterwards?) *What was the result?*); ~ *off*, (of an experiment) be successful, (of an expected event) happen; ~ *to* (inf.), happen to: *How did you* ~ *to hear of it? in years to* ~, in future years. *a coming man*, one who is thought likely to become important. **'~-back** *n.* return to one's earlier powers or status (1). **'~-down** *n.* change for the worse in one's circumstances.

com·e·dy ['kɔmidi] *n.* play for the theatre, usu. dealing with everyday life and intended to amuse; this branch of literature; amusing incident in real life. **co·me·di·an** [kə'mi:diən] *n.* actor in comedies; actor whose aim is to make people laugh.

come·ly ['kʌmli] *adj.* (-*ier*, -*iest*). (usu. of a person) pleasant to look at. **come·li·ness** *n.*

com·et ['kɔmit] *n.* heavenly body, looking like a star with a tail of light (moving round the sun).

com·fort ['kʌmfət] *n.* **1.** help or kindness to sb. who is suffering; relief from pain, trouble, or anxiety; sth. that brings such relief. **2.** the state of being free from worry; contentment: *to live in* ~. *v.t.* give ~ to; say kind words to (sb. who is sad, in trouble, etc.). **~·a·ble** ['kʌmfətəbl] *adj.* giving ~ to the body: *a* ~*able chair*; free from pain or trouble: *to be* (*feel*) ~*able.* **~·a·bly** *adv.* **~·less** ['kʌmfətlis] *adj.* without ~. **~·er** *n.* person who ~s; warm woollen scarf to be worn round the neck. **com·fy** ['kʌmfi] *adj.* (colloq.) ~able; snug.

com·ic ['komik] *adj.* **1.** causing people to laugh: *a ~ song.* **2.** of comedy: *~ opera.* *n.* **1.** ~ person. **2.** *~ paper; ~ cartoon.*

com·i·cal ['komikl] *adj.* amusing.

com·i·ty ['komiti] *n.* courtesy. *~ of nations*, courtesy shown by nations to each other's laws, customs, etc.

com·ma ['komə] *n.* the mark , used in writing and printing. *inverted ~s*, the marks " ".

com·mand [kə'maːnd] *v.t. & i.* **1.** give an order to; have authority over. **2.** control (the feelings, oneself): *to ~ one's temper.* **3.** be in a position to use; have at one's service; deserve to have: *to ~ respect and sympathy.* **4.** (of a place) be in a position that overlooks (and controls): *The fort ~ed the entrance to the valley.* *n.* order; authority; (power to) control; part of an army under sb.'s ~.

com·man·dant [,komən'dænt] *n.* officer in ~ of a fort or other military establishment. **com·man·deer** [,komən'diə*] *v.t.* take (horses, stores, buildings, etc.) for military purposes, usu. without asking for the owner's permission. **com·man·der** [kə'maːndə*] *n.* person in ~ ; (navy) officer above a lieutenant and below a captain. *~ment* [kə'maːndmənt] *n. the C~ments*, the ten laws given to Moses.

com·man·do [kə'maːndou] *n.* (member of a) specially picked and trained attacking force.

com·mem·o·rate [kə'meməreit] *v.t.* keep or honour the memory of (a person or event); (of things) be in memory of. **com·mem·o·ra·tion** [kə,memə'reifən] *n.*

com·mence [kə'mens] *v.t. & i.* begin. *~ment n.* beginning.

com·mend [kə'mend] *v.t.* **1.** praise. **2.** entrust for safe keeping: *~ one's soul to God.* *~·a·ble adj.* deserving praise. **com·men·da·tion** [,komen'deiʃən] *n.* praise; approval.

com·men·su·rate [kə'menʃərit] *adj.* in the right proportion (*to* or *with*).

com·ment ['koment] *n.* sth. said or written about an event, or in explanation or criticism of sth. *v.i.* make ~s (*on*); give opinions (*on*). **com·men·ta·ry** ['koməntəri] *n.* **1.** number of ~s (e.g. on a book): *a Bible ~ary.* **2.** continuous ~s on an event: *a broadcast ~ary on a race (football match)*; *running* (i.e. continuous) *~ary.* **com·men·ta·tor** ['komenteitə*] *n.*

com·merce ['komə:s] *n.* trade (esp. between countries); the exchange and distribution of goods. **com·mer·cial** [kə'mə:ʃl] *adj.* of ~. *commercial traveller*, person who travels with samples of goods to obtain orders. **com·mer·cial·ize** [kə'mə:ʃəlaiz] *v.t.* (try to) make money out of: *to commercialize sport.*

com·mis·er·ate [kə'mizəreit] *v.t. & i.* feel, say that one feels, pity for sb. and his troubles or misfortunes: *to ~ (with) sb. on his losses.* **com·mis·er·a·tion** [kə,mizə'reiʃən] *n.*

com·mis·sar [,komi'saː*] *n.* Soviet state official.

com·mis·sar·i·at [,komi'sɛəriət] *n.* department (esp. in an army) which supplies food, etc.

com·mis·sion [kə'miʃən] *n.* **1.** the giving of authority to sb. to act for another; the work, business, etc., done. **2.** performance (of wrongdoing): *the ~ of crime.* **3.** payment made to sb. for selling goods, etc., rising in proportion to the results gained: *to sell goods on ~* (i.e. draw a percentage of the receipts). **4.** official paper (warrant) giving a person authority; (esp.) (in Gt. Brit.) a royal warrant appointing a naval, air force, or military officer. **5.** body of persons given the duty of making an inquiry and writing a report: *a Royal Commission to report on local government.* **6.** *in ~*, (of a warship) ready to go to sea; with crew and supplies complete. *v.t.* give a ~ to. *~er n.* **1.** member of a ~ (5). **2.** high official in a department of government: *the Commissioners of Customs*; *the High Commissioner for Canada* (e.g. representing the Canadian government in London).

com·mis·sion·aire [kə₁miʃ-ə'neə*] *n.* uniformed door-porter at a cinema, theatre, hotel.

com·mit [kə'mit] *v.t.* (*-tt-*). **1.** perform (a crime, foolish act): *to ~ murder* (*a blunder*). **2.** entrust, send, hand over, for safe keeping or treatment: *~ a prisoner for trial*; *~ sb. to prison*; *~ to memory* (learn by heart); *~ to writing* (put into writing). **3.** *~ oneself*, make oneself responsible; promise; undertake. **~·ment** *n.* sth. to which one has ~ted oneself; promise or undertaking.

com·mit·tee [kə'miti] *n.* group of persons appointed (usu. by a larger group) to attend to special business: *to attend a ~ meeting*; *to sit on a ~*.

com·mo·di·ous [kə'moudiəs] *adj.* having plenty of space for what is needed: *a ~ house* (*cupboard*).

com·mod·i·ty [kə'mɔditi] *n.* useful thing, esp. an article of trade: *household commodities*.

com·mo·dore ['kɔmədɔ:*] *n.* naval officer having rank above a captain and below a rear-admiral.

com·mon ['kɔmən] *adj.* (*-er, -est*). **1.** belonging to, used by, coming from, done by, all members of a group: *a ~ language*; *~ law* (in England, unwritten law derived from customs and past decisions made by judges); *~ knowledge* (what is known to most persons, esp. in a group). **2.** usual and ordinary; happening or found often and in many places: *a ~ flower*; *the ~ man* (i.e. the ordinary or average man); *~ sense* (i.e. practical good sense gained by experience of life). **3.** (of persons and their behaviour) vulgar; rude. *n.* **1.** (usu. in or near a village) area of grassland for all to use. **2.** *House of Commons*, assembly (lower house of Parliament) of those who are elected by the ~ people. **3.** *in ~*, used by all (of a group); *have in ~ with*, share with; *out of the ~*, unusual. (*be on*) *short ~s*, (have) not enough food. **~·ly** *adv.* **~·er** *n.* one of the ~ (2) people, not a member of the nobility. **'~·place** *n. & adj.* (remark, happening, etc., which is) ordinary or usual. **'~·room** *n.* room in a college, etc. set aside for the use of teachers, students. **'~·wealth** *n.* State; group of States (esp. *the C~wealth of Australia*) associating politically, etc., for their ~ (1) good. *The C~wealth*, the C~wealth of Nations, consisting of Great Britain and some of the former British Dominions, Colonies, etc.

com·mo·tion [kə'mouʃən] *n.* noisy confusion; excitement; violent uprising.

com·mu·nal ['kɔmjunl] *adj.* **1.** of or for a community: *~ disturbances.* **2.** for the common use: *~ land* (*kitchens*).

com·mune [kɔm'ju:n, 'kɔmju:n] *v.i.* feel at one with; feel in close touch with; talk with in an intimate way: *to ~ with nature* (*one's friends*).

com·mu·ni·cant [kə'mju:nikənt] *n.* person who communicates; (esp.) one who receives Holy Communion.

com·mu·ni·cate [kə'mju:nikeit] *v.i. & t.* **1.** pass on (news, opinions, feelings, heat, motion, a disease, etc.) (*to sb.*). **2.** share or exchange (news, etc.) (*with sb.*). **3.** (of rooms, gardens, roads, etc.) be connected (by means of doors, gates, etc.). **4.** take Holy Communion. **com·mu·ni·ca·ble** [kə'mju:nikəbl] *adj.* that can be ~d (e.g. ideas, disease). **com·mu·ni·ca·tion** [kə₁mju:ni'keiʃən] *n.* the act of communicating; that which is ~d (esp. news); means of communicating; road, railway, telegraph, etc., which connects places: *communications with the north*; *telegraphic communications.* **com·mu·ni·ca·tive** [kə'mju:nikətiv] *adj.* ready and willing to talk and give information.

com·mu·nion [kə'mju:njən] *n.*
1. sharing. **2.** group of persons with the same religious beliefs. **3.** exchange of thoughts, feelings, etc. **4.** *Holy Communion,* (in the Christian Church) celebration of the Lord's Supper.

com·mu·ni·qué [kə'mju:nikei] *n.* official statement or announcement.

com·mu·nism ['kɔmjunizəm] *n.* **1.** (belief in the) social system in which property is owned by the community and used for the good of all its members. **2.** political system (as in U.S.S.R.) in which all power is held by the highest members of the Communist Party, which controls the land and its resources, the means of production, transport, etc., and directs the activities of the people. **com·mu·nist** ['kɔmjunist] *n.* believer in, supporter of ~. *adj.* of ~.

com·mu·ni·ty [kə'mju:niti] *n.* **1.** *the ~,* the people living in one place, district: *to work for the good of the ~.* **2.** group of persons with the same religion, race, occupation, interests, etc.: *the Polish ~ in London.* **3.** condition of sharing, having things in common, being alike in some way: *~ of views (religion, etc.);* *~ singing* (in which all those present join).

com·mute [kə'mju:t] *v.t. & i.* **1.** exchange (one thing for another, esp. as a method of payment). **2.** change (one punishment for another, less severe): *to ~ the death penalty* (e.g. by substituting 20 years' imprisonment). **3.** travel daily, esp. to and from a town to earn one's living. **com·mu·ta·tion** [ˌkɔmju'teiʃən] *n.* commuting; sth. paid in this way; reduced punishment. **com·mu·ter** *n.* person who ~s (3).

¹**com·pact** ['kɔmpækt] *n.* agreement.

²**com·pact** [kəm'pækt] *adj.* neatly fitted; closely packed together. ~·ly *adv.*

³**com·pact** ['kɔmpækt] *n.* small, flat box of face-powder, carried in a handbag.

¹**com·pan·ion** [kəm'pænjən] *n.* **1.** person who goes with, or is often or always with, another: *~s on a journey.* **2.** friendly, likable person, esp. one with similar interests. **3.** one of two things that go together; one thing that matches another: *the ~ to a glove or sock.* **4.** person (usu. a woman) paid to live with an old or sick person. **5.** handbook or reference book: *the Gardener's Companion.* ~·a·ble *adj.* friendly; sociable. ~·ship *n.*

²**com·pan·ion** [kəm'pænjən] *n.* (usu. ~*way*) staircase from the deck to cabins in a ship.

com·pa·ny ['kʌmpəni] *n.* **1.** being together with another or others: *to have the pleasure of sb.'s ~ on a journey; to keep (bear) sb. ~,* be or go with him; *to part ~,* to separate; *in ~ (with),* together (with); *be good (poor, etc.) ~,* be entertaining (boring). **2.** number of persons united for business or commerce: *a steamship ~; John Smith & Co.* **3.** a number of persons working together: *the ship's ~* (i.e. the crew); *a theatrical ~; a ~ of actors.* **4.** subdivision of an infantry battalion commanded by a captain or major.

com·par·a·tive [kəm'pærətiv] *adj.* **1.** of comparison or comparing: *the ~ method of science (studying, etc.).* **2.** measured by comparing: *living in ~ comfort* (i.e. as compared with other persons or with previous times). **3.** (grammar) form of adjectives and adverbs expressing 'more', as in *worse, better, more prettily.* ~·ly *adv.*

com·pare [kəm'pɛə*] *v.t.* **1.** examine, judge, say, how far persons or things are similar or not similar: *to ~ two translations. This cannot ~ with that* (is far different from that). **2.** *~ to,* point out the likeness or relation between: *to ~ death to sleep. Yours is not to be ~d to* *mine* (i.e. is quite different). **3.** (grammar) form the comparative and superlative degrees of adjectives and adverbs (usu. by adding *-er, -est,* or *more, most*). *n.* comparison (see below): chiefly in *beyond* (*without, past*) ~. **com·par·a·ble** ['kɔmpərəbl] *adj.* that can be ~d (*to*).

com·par·i·son [kəm'pærisən] *n.* **1.** the act of comparing; statement which compares: *the ~ of the heart to a pump; in ~ with* (when compared with); *by ~* (when compared); *can bear* (*stand*) ~ *with,* can be compared favourably with. **2.** *degrees of ~* (for adjectives and adverbs), positive, comparative, superlative (e.g. *bad, worse, worst*).

com·part·ment [kəm'pɑːtmənt] *n.* one of several separate divisions of a structure, esp. a railway coach: *the second-class* ~*s; a water-tight ~* (in a ship).

com·pass ['kʌmpəs] *n.* **1.** instrument with a needle that points north. **2.** (pl.) instrument for drawing circles. **3.** range; extent.

A compass

(A pair of)
compasses

com·pas·sion [kəm'pæʃən] *n.* pity; feeling for the suffering of others, prompting one to give help: *filled with ~ for; take ~ on.* ~**ate** *adj.* having ~.

com·pat·i·ble [kəm'pætəbl] *adj.* (of ideas, arguments, persons) in accord with, suited to, agreeing with, each other: *pleasure ~ with duty.* **com·pat·i·bil·i·ty** [kəm,pæti'biliti] *n.*

com·pat·ri·ot [kəm'pætriət] *n.* person born in or citizen of the same country as another person.

com·pel [kəm'pel] *v.t.* (*-ll-*) force (sb. to do sth.); get a result by force.

com·pen·di·ous [kəm'pendiəs]

adj. giving much information briefly.

com·pen·sate ['kɔmpenseit] *v.t. & i.* make suitable payment, give sth., to make up (*for* loss, injury, etc.). **com·pen·sa·tion** [,kɔmpen'seifən] *n.* compensating; sth. given to ~.

com·pete [kəm'piːt] *v.i.* take part in a race, an examination, etc.: *to ~ in a race* (*for a prize, with* or *against others*). **com·pe·ti·tion** [,kɔmpi'tiʃən] *n.* competing; any activity in which persons ~: *trade competition between countries; in competition with the world's best athletes; swimming competitions.* **com·pet·i·tive** [kəm'petitiv] *adj.* in or for which there is competition: *competitive examinations for government posts.* **com·pet·i·tor** [kəm'petitə*] *n.* one who ~s.

com·pe·tent ['kɔmpitənt] *adj.* having power, authority, skill, knowledge, etc., to do what is needed: *The magistrate is ~ to try this case. The teacher is ~ for* (*in*) *her work.* **com·pe·tence** ['kɔmpitəns] *n.* **1.** being ~; ability. **2.** income large enough for a person to live on in comfort.

com·pile [kəm'pail] *v.t.* collect (information) and arrange (in a book, etc.): *to ~ a guide-book* (*dictionary, index*). **com·pi·la·tion** [,kɔmpi'leiʃən] *n.* thing ~d; act of compiling.

com·pla·cent [kəm'pleisənt] *adj.* satisfied with oneself. **com·pla·cence, -cen·cy** [kəm'plei·səns, -si] *n.* self-satisfaction.

com·plain [kəm'plein] *v.i.* say that one is not satisfied, that sth. is wrong, that one is suffering in some way: *He ~ed of having* (*that he had*) *too much work.* ~**ant** *n.* plaintiff (q.v.). **com·plaint** *n.* **1.** ~ing; statement of, grounds for, dissatisfaction: *to make* (*lodge*) *a ~t against sb.* **2.** illness or disease: *a heart ~t.*

com·plai·sant [kəm'pleizənt] *adj.* ready and willing to do what is pleasing to others; obliging. **com·plai·sance** *n.*

com·ple·ment ['kɔmplimənt] *n.* that which makes sth. complete;

the full number or quantity needed; word(s) completing the predicate. **com·ple·men·ta·ry** [ˌkɔmpliˈmentəri] *adj.* serving to complete: *~ary colours* (giving white when mixed).

com·plete [kəmˈpliːt] *adj.* **1.** having all its parts; whole. **2.** finished; ended. **3.** thorough; in every way: *a ~ surprise*; *a ~ stranger*. *v.t.* finish; bring to an end; make perfect. **~·ly** *adv.* **com·ple·tion** [kəmˈpliːʃən] *n.* act of completing; state of being ~.

com·plex [ˈkɔmpleks] *adj.* made up of many parts; difficult to explain: *a ~ argument (situation)*. *n.* (pl. *-es*). ~ *thing*; (abnormal) mental state caused by past experiences, etc. **~·i·ty** *n.* [kəmˈpleksiti] state of being ~; sth. that is ~.

com·plex·ion [kəmˈplekʃən] *n.* **1.** natural colour, appearance, etc., of the skin, esp. the face. **2.** general character or aspect (of conduct, events, etc.).

com·pli·ance [kəmˈplaiəns] *n.* action of complying. *in ~ with*, complying with. **com·pli·ant** *adj.* ready to comply.

com·pli·cate [ˈkɔmplikeit] *v.t.* make complex; make (sth.) difficult to do or understand. **com·pli·cat·ed** *adj.* made up of many parts; complex: *a ~d machine*. **com·pli·ca·tion** [ˌkɔmpliˈkeiʃən] *n.* **1.** state of being complex, confused, difficult. **2.** that which makes an illness or other trouble more difficult or serious.

com·plic·i·ty [kəmˈplisiti] *n.* taking part with another person (in crime or other wrongdoing).

com·pli·ment [ˈkɔmplimənt] *n.* **1.** expression of admiration, approval, etc., either in words or by action (e.g. by asking for sb.'s opinion or advice). **2.** (pl.) greetings: *'My ~s to your husband.'* [ˈkɔmpliment] *v.t.* pay a ~ to. **com·pli·men·ta·ry** [ˌkɔmpliˈmentəri] *adj.* **1.** expressing admiration, etc. **2.** *~ary ticket*, one given free.

com·ply [kəmˈplai] *v.i.* ~ *with*, do (what is asked or needed).

com·po·nent [kəmˈpounənt] *adj.* helping to form (a complete thing). *n.* ~ part.

com·port [kəmˈpɔːt] *v.t. & i.* ~ *oneself*, behave; ~ *with*, be in harmony with.

com·pose [kəmˈpouz] *v.t. & i.* **1.** (usu. in the passive) *be ~d of*, be made up of (parts). **2.** put together (words, ideas, musical notes, etc.) in literary, musical, etc., form: *to ~ a letter (speech, poem, sentence, song, symphony)*. **3.** (printing) set up (type) to form words, paragraphs, pages, etc. **4.** get under control; make calm: *to ~ oneself (one's thoughts, passions)*; settle: *to ~ a quarrel (difference of opinion)*. **com·posed** *adj.* with feelings under control. **com·pos·ed·ly** [kəmˈpouzidli] *adv.* **com·pos·er** (esp.) one who ~s music. **com·pos·i·tor** [kəmˈpozitə*] *n.* one who ~s type.

com·po·site [ˈkɔmpəzit] *adj.* made up of different parts or materials.

com·po·si·tion [ˌkɔmpəˈziʃən] *n.* **1.** act of composing. **2.** that which is written (e.g. a poem, book, or music); arrangement of objects. **3.** nature of, way of arranging, the parts of which sth. is composed: *the ~ of the soil (a picture)*. **4.** substance composed of more than one material, esp. an artificial substance.

com·post [ˈkɔmpost] *n.* manure made from decayed vegetable stuff, dead leaves, etc. *v.t.* make into ~; treat with ~.

com·po·sure [kəmˈpouʒə*] *n.* condition of being composed in mind; calmness (of mind or behaviour).

com·pote [ˈkɔmpout] *n.* fruit cooked with sugar in water.

¹**com·pound** [ˈkɔmpaund] *n. & adj.* (sth.) made up of two or more parts. The word *bus-driver* is a ~. *chemical ~*, a combination of elements. ~ *interest*, interest reckoned on the capital and on interest already accumulated. [kəmˈpaund] *v.t. & i.* mix together (to make sth.

different): to ~ *a medicine*; settle (a debt, etc.) by part payment.

'com·pound ['kɒmpaund] *n.* (in India, China, etc.) enclosed area with buildings, etc., esp. one used as a trading or commercial centre.

com·pre·hend [,kɒmpri'hend] *v.t.* 1. understand fully. 2. include. **com·pre·hen·si·ble** [,kɒmpri'hensibl] *adj.* that can be ~ed. **com·pre·hen·sion** [,kɒmpri'henʃən] *n.* the mind's act or power of understanding. **com·pre·hen·sive** [,kɒmpri'hensiv] *adj.* that ~s (2) much.

com·press [kəm'pres] *v.t.* 1. press together; get into a small(er) space: ~ed air. 2. (of writings, ideas) condense; get into fewer words. ['kɒmpres] *n.* pad of cloth pressed on to a part of the body (to stop bleeding, reduce fever, etc.). **com·pres·sion** [kəm'preʃən] *n.*

com·prise [kəm'praiz] *v.t.* include; have as parts.

com·pro·mise ['kɒmprəmaiz] *n.* settlement of a disagreement by which each side gives up sth. it has asked for and neither side gets all it has asked for. *v.t. & i.* 1. settle a disagreement, quarrel, etc., by making a ~. 2. bring (sb.) under suspicion by unwise behaviour, etc.

comp·trol·ler [kən'troulə*] *n.* controller: ~ *of accounts.*

com·pul·sion [kəm'pʌlʃən] *n.* compelling or being compelled: *under (upon)* ~, because one is forced or compelled. **com·pul·so·ry** [kəm'pʌlsəri] *adj.* that must be done.

com·punc·tion [kəm'pʌŋkʃən] *n.* uneasiness of conscience; feeling of doubt about, or regret for, one's action: *to disobey one's superior without the slightest* ~.

com·pute [kəm'pju:t] *v.t.* reckon; calculate. **com·pu·ta·tion** [,kɒmpju'teiʃən] *n.* **com·put·er** [kəm'pju:tə*] *n.* machine that stores information on discs or magnetic tapes, analyses it, and produces information as required.

com·rade ['kɒmrid, 'kʌm-] *n.* trusted companion; loyal friend;

fellow member of a trade union, etc. ~**·ship** *n.*

'con [kɒn] *v.t.* (-nn-). (often con over) learn by heart; study: con one's lessons.

'con [kɒn] *adv.* pro and con, for and against. *pros and cons,* arguments for and against.

con·cave ['kɒn'keiv] *adj.* (of an outline or surface) curved inwards like the inside of a circle or ball. (See diagram at *convex.*)

con·cav·i·ty [kɒn'kæviti] *n.*

con·ceal [kən'si:l] *v.t.* hide; keep secret. ~**·ment** *n.* act of, state of, hiding: to stay in ~ment.

con·cede [kən'si:d] *v.t.* 1. admit or allow (a point in an argument, that sth. is true). 2. allow (a person, country, etc.) to have (a right, privilege, etc.). **con·ces·sion** [kən'seʃən] *n.* conceding; right ~d by an owner of ground (e.g. to take minerals from it); sth. ~d.

con·ceit [kən'si:t] *n.* over-high opinion of, too much pride in, oneself or one's powers. ~**·ed** *adj.* full of ~.

con·ceive [kən'si:v] *v.t. & i.* 1. (of a woman) become pregnant. 2. form (an idea, plan, etc.) in the mind: a well-~d scheme. **con·ceiv·a·ble** *adj.* that can be ~d (2) or believed.

con·cen·trate ['kɒnsentreit] *v.t. & i.* 1. bring or come together to one point: to ~ soldiers in a town (one's attention on one's work). 2. increase the strength of (a solution) by reducing its volume (e.g. by boiling). **con·cen·tra·tion** [,kɒnsen'treiʃən] *n.* concentrating or being ~d; power of concentrating; that which is ~d. concentration camp, place where civilian political prisoners are confined.

con·cen·tric [kɒn'sentrik] *adj.* having a common centre (*with* another circle, etc.).

con·cept ['kɒnsept] *n.* idea underlying a class of things; general notion. **con·cep·tion** [kən'sep·ʃən] *n.* 1. (act of forming an) idea or plan: to have a clear ~ion of what must be done; great powers of ~ion. 2. conceiving (1).

con·cern [kən'sə:n] *v.t.* **1.** have relation to; be about; be of importance to: *Does this ~ me? So far as I'm ~ed* ... (i.e. so far as the matter affects me, or is important to me); *to be ~ed in a crime*, etc., to have some part in it. **2.** *~ oneself with*, take an interest in; be busy with. **3.** *~ed at* or *about*, made unhappy or troubled: *to be ~ed about the future* (*at the news*, etc.). *n.* **1.** relation (with); connexion (with); reference (with); sth. in which one is interested or which is important to one: *It's no ~ of yours.* **2.** business or undertaking. **3.** share: *to have a ~ in a business.* **4.** anxiety: *filled with ~; to ask with deep ~.* *~·ing prep.* about.

con·cert ['kɔnsət] *n.* **1.** musical entertainment, esp. one given in public by players or singers. **2.** *in ~* (*with*), in agreement or harmony; together. *~·ed* [kən'sə:tid] *adj.* planned, designed, performed, by two or more together: *~ed action*; *a ~ed attack.*

con·cer·ti·na [,kɔnsə'ti:nə] *n.* musical wind-instrument with keys at each end.

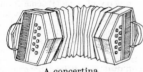

A concertina

con·cer·to [kən'tʃə:tou] *n.* (pl. *-os*). composition for one or more solo instruments supported by an orchestra: *a piano ~.*

con·ces·sion, see *concede*.

con·cil·i·ate [kən'silieit] *v.t.* win the support, goodwill, or friendly feelings of; calm sb.'s anger; soothe. **con·cil·i·a·tion** [kən,sili'eiʃən] *n.* **con·cil·i·a·to·ry** [kən'siliətəri] *adj.*

con·cise [kən'sais] *adj.* (of a person, his speech or style of writing, etc.) brief; giving much information in few words. *~·ly adv.* *~·ness n.*

con·clave ['kɔnkleiv] *n.* private or secret meeting: *sitting in ~.*

con·clude [kən'klu:d] *v.t. & i.* **1.** come or bring to an end: *to ~ a concert with the National Anthem. The meeting ~d at eight o'clock.* **2.** bring about; arrange: *to ~ a treaty of peace.* **3.** arrive at a belief or opinion: *to ~, from the evidence, that.* .... **con·clu·sion** [kən'klu:ʒən] *n.* **1.** end. *in conclusion*, lastly. **2.** belief or opinion that is the result of reasoning. **3.** decision; settling (of sth.). **con·clu·sive** [kən'klu:siv] *adj.* (of facts, evidence, etc.) convincing; ending doubt. **con·clu·sive·ly adv.**

con·coct [kən'kɔkt] *v.t.* **1.** prepare by mixing together: *to ~ a new kind of soup.* **2.** invent (a story, excuse, etc.). **con·coc·tion** [kən'kɔkʃən] *n.*

con·cord ['kɔnkɔ:d] *n.* agreement or harmony (between persons or things). *~·ance* [kən'kɔ:dəns] *n.* **1.** agreement. **2.** arrangement in ABC order of the important words used by an author or in a book: *a Bible ~ance; a Shakespeare ~ance.* *~·ant* [kən'kɔ:dənt] *adj.* agreeing.

con·course ['kɔnkɔ:s] *n.* coming or moving together of things or persons; a crowd of people.

con·crete ['kɔnkri:t, 'kɔn-] *adj.* of material things; existing in material form. *~ noun*, name of a thing, not of a quality. *n.* building substance made by mixing cement with sand, gravel, etc.: *~ walls* (*roads*, etc.). *v.t.* cover with ~.

con·cu·bine ['kɔnkjubain] *n.* woman who lives with a man as his wife although not lawfully married to him; (in some countries, where polygamy is allowed) lesser wife.

con·cur [kən'kə:*] *v.i.* (*-rr-*). **1.** agree in opinion (*with* sb., *in* sth.) **2.** happen together. *~·rence* [kən'kʌrəns] *n.* agreement. *~·rent* [kən'kʌrənt] *adj.* ~·ring.

con·cus·sion [kən'kʌʃən] *n.* violent shaking or shock; injury (to the brain) caused by a blow, knock, or fall.

con·demn [kən'dem] *v.t.* **1.** say

that sb. is, or has done, wrong or that sth. is faulty or unfit for use. **2.** (law) give judgement against: *to ~ a murderer to imprisonment for life.* **3.** doom; send, appoint (to sth. unhappy or painful): *~ed to suffer a life of pain.* **con·dem·na·tion** [ˌkɔndem'neiʃən] *n.*

con·dense [kən'dens] *v.t. & i.* **1.** (cause to) increase in density or strength; (of a gas or vapour) (cause to) become liquid; (of a liquid)(cause to) become thicker: *~d milk.* **2.** put into fewer words: *a ~d account of an event.* **con·den·ser** *n.* apparatus for condensing (e.g. steam into water, or electricity until it has the power needed). **con·den·sa·tion** [ˌkɔnden'seiʃən] *n.* condensing; drops of liquid (e.g. dew) formed when vapour ~s.

con·de·scend [ˌkɔndi'send] *v.i.* **1.** (genuinely or falsely) behave to sb. of inferior position, ability, etc., as if he were one's equal. **2.** lower oneself to do sth. unworthy. **3.** act in a patronizing (2) manner. **con·de·scen·sion** [ˌkɔndi'senʃən] *n.*

con·di·ment ['kɔndimənt] *n.* sth. (e.g. pepper) tasting hot or salty added to food to flavour it.

con·di·tion [kən'diʃən] *n.* **1.** sth. needed before sth. else is possible; sth. on which another thing depends: *on ~ that,* only if, provided that; *on this (that) ~.* **2.** the present state of being; nature, state, quality of sth. or sb.: *The ~ of my health prevents me from working. Everything arrived in good ~* (i.e. unbroken, undamaged, fit for use). *in (out of) ~,* in good (bad) ~. **3.** (pl.) circumstances: *under existing ~s* (i.e. while things are as they are now); *under favourable ~s.* **4.** position in society: *persons of every ~* (i.e. of all ranks). *v.t.* determine; place ~s upon; govern, control: *Your expenditure is ~ed by your income.* **~·al** [kən'diʃənl] *adj.* depending on, containing, a ~: *a ~al clause* (beginning with 'if' or 'unless').

con·dole [kən'doul] *v.i.* express sympathy (*with* sb., *on* or *upon* a loss, misfortune, etc.). **con·dol·ence** [kən'douləns] *n.* (often pl.) expression of sympathy.

con·done [kən'doun] *v.t.* (of a person) overlook or forgive (an offence); (of an act) make up for: atone for: *a fact that ~s his failure to help.*

con·dor ['kɔndɔː*] *n.* large kind of vulture (in S. America).

con·duce [kən'djuːs] *v.i.* ~ *to,* help to produce; contribute to (a result): *Does wealth ~ to happiness?* **con·du·cive** [kən'djuːsiv] *adj.*

con·duct ['kɔndʌkt] *n.* **1.** behaviour (esp. moral): *good and bad ~.* **2.** manner of directing or managing affairs, business, etc. [kən'dʌkt] *v.t. & i.* **1.** lead, guide: *to ~ visitors round a museum.* **2.** control; manage; direct: *to ~ an orchestra* (i.e. guide and control the players). **3.** ~ *oneself (well,* etc.), behave. **4.** (of substances) transmit; allow (heat, electric current) to pass along or through. **con·duc·tion** [kən'dʌkʃən] *n.* the ~ing (4) of heat, etc. **con·duc·tiv·i·ty** *n.* property of ~ing (4) some form of energy, e.g. electricity. **con·duc·tor** *n.* **1.** person who ~s (1), (2), esp. the man on a bus, tram, etc., who collects fares. **2.** substance that ~s (4) heat or electric current.

con·duit ['kʌndit] *n.* large pipe or waterway.

cone [koun] *n.* **1.** solid figure which narrows to a point from a round, flat base. **2.** sth. of this shape, whether solid or hollow. **3.** fruit of certain evergreen trees (fir, pine, cedar). **con·ic** ['kɔnik] *adj.* of a ~ (1). **con·i·cal** ['kɔnikl] *adj.* ~-shaped.

A cone (1)   A cone (3)

con·fec·tion [kənˈfekʃən] *n.* mixture of sweet things; sweet cake. **~·er** *n.* person who makes and sells cakes, etc. **~·er·y** *n.* cakes, pastries, pies, sweets.

con·fed·er·ate [kənˈfedərit] *adj.* joined together by an agreement or treaty. *n.* person who joins with another or others (esp. in wrongdoing). **con·fed·er·a·cy** [kənˈfedərəsi] *n.* group of ~ States, esp. the eleven States which separated from the Union (U.S.A.) during the Civil War of 1861–5. **con·fed·er·a·tion** [kən͵fedəˈreiʃən] *n.* uniting or being united; alliance.

con·fer [kənˈfə:*] *v.t. & i.* (*-rr-*). **1.** give or grant (a right, title, favour): *to ~ a knighthood on sb.* **2.** consult or discuss (*with*): *to ~ with a lawyer.* **~·ence** [ˈkɒnfərəns] *n.* (meeting for) discussion, consultation.

con·fess [kənˈfes] *v.t. & i.* **1.** acknowledge; admit (that one has done wrong). **2.** tell one's sins or faults to a priest (esp. in the Roman Catholic Church); (of a priest) listen to sb. doing this: *John ~ed to the priest. The priest ~ed John.* **con·fess·ed·ly** [kənˈfesidli] *adv.* as ~ed. **con·fes·sion** [kənˈfeʃən] *n.* ~ing; what is ~ed: *a ~ion of guilt; to go to ~ion* (i.e. to ~ (2) one's sins); *a ~ion of faith* (a declaration of religious or similar beliefs). **con·fes·sion·al** *n.* private place in a church where a priest sits to hear ~ions. **con·fes·sor** *n.* priest who hears ~ions.

con·fet·ti [kənˈfeti] *n.* small bits of coloured paper showered on e.g. the bride and bridegroom at a wedding.

con·fide [kənˈfaid] *v.t. & i.* **1.** tell (a secret *to*); give (sth. or sb. to sb.) to be looked after; give (a task or duty to sb.) to be carried out. **2.** have trust or faith (*in*): *I feel that I can ~ in that man.* **con·fi·dant(e)** [͵kɒnfiˈdænt] *n.* man (woman) who is trusted with private affairs or secrets (esp. love affairs). **con·fi·dence** [ˈkɒnfidəns] *n.* **1.** (act of) confiding in,

to: *to take sb. into one's ~nce* in *~nce* (i.e. as a secret). **2.** secret which is ~d to sb.: *to exchange ~nces.* **3.** belief in oneself or others; belief that one is right: *to answer questions with ~nce.* **con·fi·dent** [ˈkɒnfidənt] *adj.* feeling or showing ~nce; certain: *to be ~nt of success; a ~nt manner.* **con·fi·den·tial** [͵kɒnfiˈdenʃl] *adj.* **1.** (to be kept) secret; given in ~nce: *~ntial information.* **2.** having the ~nce of another: *my ~ntial secretary.* **con·fig·u·ra·tion** [kən͵figjuˈreiʃən] *n.* shape or outline; method of arrangement.

con·fine [kənˈfain] *v.t.* **1.** restrict within limits: *to ~ oneself to saying* (say only); *to ~ one's remarks to* (speak only about). **2.** keep shut up: *to be ~d to the house by illness.* [ˈkɒnfain] *n.* (usu. pl.) limit; edge. **con·fined** *ppl. adj.* (esp.) in bed giving birth to a baby: *She expects to be ~d next month.* **~·ment** [kənˈfainmənt] *n.* being ~d, esp. in giving birth; imprisonment.

con·firm [kənˈfə:m] *v.t.* **1.** make (power, ownership, opinions, feelings, rights, etc.) firmer or stronger: *to ~ sb. in sth.* **2.** ratify; agree definitely to (a treaty, appointment, etc.). **3.** admit to full membership of the Christian Church. **con·firmed** *ppl. adj.* (esp.) unlikely to change or be changed. **con·fir·ma·tion** [͵kɒnfəˈmeiʃən] *n.* ~ing or being ~ed (all senses).

con·fis·cate [ˈkɒnfiskeit] *v.t.* (as punishment or in enforcing authority) take possession of the private property of sb.: *houses ~d by the government.* **con·fis·ca·tion** [͵kɒnfisˈkeiʃən] *n.*

con·fla·gra·tion [͵kɒnfləˈgreiʃən] *n.* great fire, esp. one that destroys buildings, forests, etc.

con·flict [ˈkɒnflikt] *n.* **1.** fight; fighting; struggle; quarrel. **2.** (of opinions, desires, etc.) disagreement; difference: *a statement that is in ~ with other evidence.* [kənˈflikt] *v.i.* be in opposition or disagreement:

wishes that ~ with one's duty;
~ing emotions.

con·flu·ence ['kɒnfluəns] *n.* a flowing together, esp. a place where rivers unite.

con·form [kən'fɔːm] *v.i. & t.* make or be in agreement with; comply; adapt: *to ~ to the rules (to the wishes of others).* **~·a·ble** [kən'fɔːməbl] *adj.* similar; obedient: *~able to your wishes.* **con·for·ma·tion** [ˌkɒnfɔː'meiʃən] *n.* way in which sth. is formed or constructed. **~·i·ty** [kən'fɔːmiti] *n.* agreement; doing what is asked, required, or expected: *in ~ity with your request.*

con·found [kən'faund] *v.t.* **1.** fill with, throw into, perplexity or confusion. **2.** mix up; confuse (ideas, etc.). **3.** defeat or overthrow (enemies, plans, etc.).

con·front [kən'frʌnt] *v.t.* be, come, bring, face to face with; be opposite to: *to be ~ed with evidence of one's wrongdoing.* **con·fron·ta·tion** [ˌkɒnfrʌn'teiʃən] *n.* state of hostility between two States, esp. when likely to lead to war).

con·fuse [kən'fjuːz] *v.t.* put into disorder; mix up in the mind; mistake one thing for another. **con·fu·sion** [kən'fjuːʒn] *n.* disorder; being ~d.

con·fute [kən'fjuːt] *v.t.* prove (a person) to be wrong; show (an argument, etc.) to be false. **con·fu·ta·tion** [ˌkɒnfjuː'teiʃən] *n.*

con·geal [kən'dʒiːl] *v.t. & i.* make or become stiff or solid (esp. as the effect of cold or of the air, e.g. on blood).

con·ge·nial [kən'dʒiːnjəl] *adj.* **1.** (of persons) having the same or a similar nature, common interests, etc. **2.** (of things, occupations, etc.) in agreement with one's nature, tastes, etc.: *a ~ climate.*

con·gen·i·tal [kən'dʒenitl] *adj.* (of diseases, etc.) present since birth.

con·gest·ed [kən'dʒestid] *ppl. adj.* **1.** overcrowded; too full: *streets ~ with traffic.* **2.** (of parts of the body, e.g. the brain, lungs) having too much blood. **con·ges·tion** [kən'dʒestʃən] *n.*

con·glom·er·ate [kən'glɒmərit] *adj. & n.* (made up of a) number of things or parts stuck together in a mass or ball. [kən'glɒməreit] *v.t. & i.* collect into a ball or rounded mass. **con·glom·er·a·tion** [kənˌglɒmə'reiʃən] *n.* conglomerating; being ~; mass of ~ things.

con·grat·u·late [kən'grætjuleit] *v.t.* tell (sb.) that one is pleased about sth. happy or fortunate that has come (to him): *to ~ sb. on his marriage*; *~ oneself*, consider oneself fortunate. **con·grat·u·la·tion** [kənˌgrætju'leiʃən] *n.* (often pl.) words which ~ sb.

con·gre·gate ['kɒngrigeit] *v.t. & i.* come or bring together. **con·gre·ga·tion** [ˌkɒngri'geiʃən] *n.* (esp.) body of people (usu. except the minister and choir) taking part in a religious service. **con·gre·ga·tion·al** *adj.* of a ~; *C~al*, of the system in which separate churches manage their own affairs.

con·gress ['kɒngres] *n.* **1.** meeting, series of meetings, of representatives (of societies, etc.) for discussions: *a medical ~*; *the Church C~.* **2.** *C~*, law-making body of U.S.A. and some other republics in America; political party in India. **con·gres·sion·al** [kɒn'greʃənl] *adj.* of a ~: *~ional debates.*

conic, conical, see *cone*.

co·ni·fer ['kouniʃə*] *n.* tree of the kind (e.g. pine, fir) which bears cones (3). **~·ous** [kou'niʃərəs] *adj.* (of trees) bearing cones.

con·jec·ture [kən'dʒektʃə*] *v.i. & t. & n.* (make a) guess; (put forward an) opinion formed without facts as proof. **con·jec·tur·al** [kən'dʒektʃərəl] *adj.*

con·ju·gal ['kɒndʒugl] *adj.* of marriage and of wedded life; of husband and wife: *~ happiness.*

con·ju·gate ['kɒndʒugeit] *v.t. & i.* **1.** give the forms of a verb (for number, tense, etc.). **2.** (of a verb) have these forms. **con·ju·ga·tion** [ˌkɒndʒu'geiʃən] *n.* scheme or system of verb forms; class of verbs.

con·junc·tion [kən'dʒʌŋkʃən] *n.*
1. (grammar) word that joins
other words, clauses, etc., e.g.
and, *but*. **2.** state of being
joined: *in* ~ *with*, together with.
3. combination of events, etc.
con·junc·tive [kən'dʒʌŋktiv]
adj. serving to join.
con·jure ['kʌndʒə*] *v.t. & i.* **1.**
do clever tricks which appear
magical, esp. by quick movements of the hands: *to* ~ *a
rabbit out of a hat.* **2.** ~ *up*,
cause to appear as a picture in
the mind: *to* ~ *up scenes from
one's childhood days.* **con·jur·
er, con·jur·or** ['kʌndʒərə*] *n.*
person who ~s (1).
con·nect [kə'nekt] *v.t. & i.* **1.**
join, be joined: *towns* ~*ed by a
railway*; *the place where the gas-
stove and the gas-pipe* ~ ; ~*ed
with a family by marriage.* **2.**
think of (different things) as
being related to each other: *to*
~ *Malaya with rubber.* **con·
nec·tion, con·nex·ion** [kə-
'nekʃən] *n.* **1.** ~ing or being
~ed ; part which ~s two things:
a bicycle pump ~*ion*; *in this (that)*
~*ion*, with reference to this
(that); *in* ~*ion with*, with reference to. **2.** train, boat, etc.,
timed to leave a station, port,
etc., soon after the arrival of
another, enabling passengers to
change from one to the other.
3. number of persons who are
regular customers, patients,
clients, etc.: *a shop (dressmaker)
with a good* ~*ion among the well-
to-do.* **4.** number of people
united in a religious organization: *the Methodist* ~*ion.* **5.**
relative (esp. by marriage). **con·
nec·tive** *n. & adj.* (word) that
~s (e.g. a conjunction).
con·ning-tow·er ['kɔniŋtauə*]
n. raised structure from which
a warship (esp. a submarine) is
controlled.
con·nive [kə'naiv] *v.i.* ~ *at*,
pretend not to know about
(what is wrong, what ought to
be stopped). **con·ni·vance** [kə-
'naivəns] *n.*
con·nois·seur [,kɔni'sə:*] *n.* person with reliable judgement in

matters of taste (5): *a* ~ *of
painting* (*old porcelain, wine,
etc.*).
con·note [kə'nout] *v.t.* (of words)
suggest in addition to the
fundamental meaning: *The word
'Tropics'* ~*s heat.* **con·no·ta·
tion** [,kɔnou'teiʃən] *n.*
con·quer ['kɔŋkə*] *v.t.* **1.** defeat
or overcome (enemies, bad
habits, etc.). **2.** take possession
of by force, esp. in war. ~·**or**
n. **con·quest** ['kɔŋkwest] *n.*
~ing; sth. got by ~ing: *the
Roman conquests in Africa.*
con·san·guin·i·ty [,kɔnsæŋ'gwin-
iti] *n.* relationship by blood or
birth.
con·science ['kɔnʃəns] *n.* the
awareness within oneself of the
choice one ought to make between right and wrong: *to have
a clear (guilty)* ~ ; *to have sth.
on one's* ~ (i.e. feel troubled in
one's ~ about sth.); ~ *money*
(paid because one has a troubled
~). **con·sci·en·tious** [,kɔnʃi-
'enʃəs] *adj.* guided by one's
sense of duty: *a conscientious
worker*; done as one's sense of
duty directs; done carefully and
honestly: *conscientious work.*
con·scious ['kɔnʃəs] *adj.* **1.**
(predic. use) awake; aware;
knowing things because one is
using the bodily senses and
mental powers: *to be* ~ *of one's
guilt* (*that one is guilty*). *The
man was knocked down by a bus
and was not* ~ *when we picked
him up.* *A healthy man is not
~ of his breathing.* **2.** (of actions,
feelings, etc.) realized by oneself: *to act with* ~ *superiority*
(i.e. knowing that one is superior). **3.** = self-~ (q.v.). ~·**ly**
adv. ~·**ness** *n.* **1.** being ~. **2.**
all the ideas, thoughts, feelings,
etc., of a person.
con·script [kən'skript] *v.t.* compel (sb.) by law to serve in the
armed forces; summon (call
up for) such service. ['kɔn-
skript] *n.* person compelled to
serve in this way. **con·scrip·tion**
[kən'skripʃən] *n.*
con·se·crate ['kɔnsikreit] *v.t.* set
apart as sacred or for a special

purpose (*to*); make sacred. **con·se·cra·tion** [ˌkɔnsiˈkreiʃən] *n.*

con·sec·u·tive [kənˈsekjutiv] *adj.* following continuously; coming one after another in regular order. ~·**ly** *adv.*

con·sen·sus [kənˈsensəs] *n.* common agreement (of opinion, etc.).

con·sent [kənˈsent] *v.i. & n.* (give) agreement or permission: *to ~ to a proposal.*

con·se·quence [ˈkɔnsikwəns] *n.* 1. that which follows or is brought about as the result or effect of sth. *in ~ (of)*, as a result (of). 2. importance: *It's of no ~* (i.e. it is unimportant). **con·se·quent** [ˈkɔnsikwənt] *adj.* following as a ~. **con·se·quen·tial** [ˌkɔnsiˈkwenʃl] *adj.* following as a ~; (of a person) full of self-importance.

con·ser·va·tion [ˌkɔnsəˈveiʃən] *n.* preservation; prevention of loss, waste, damage, etc.

con·ser·va·tism [kənˈsəːvətizəm] *n.* tendency to maintain a state of affairs (esp. in politics) without great or sudden changes. **con·ser·va·tive** [kənˈsəːvətiv] *n. & adj.* 1. (person) opposed to great or sudden change; *the C~ Party*, British political party (cf. Labour Party, Liberal Party. 2. (colloq. use of adj.) cautious; moderate: *a conservative estimate.*

con·ser·va·to·ry [kənˈsəːvətri] *n.* building or part of a building with glass walls and roof in which plants are protected from cold.

con·serve [kənˈsəːv] *v.t.* keep from change, loss, or destruction.

con·sid·er [kənˈsidə*] *v.t. & i.* 1. think about. 2. take into account; make allowances for: *to ~ the feelings of others.* 3. be of the opinion; regard as. ~·**a·ble** [kənˈsidərəbl] *adj.* deserving to be ~ed; great; much. ~·**a·bly** *adv.* much. ~·**ate** [kənˈsidərit] *adj.* thoughtful (of the needs, etc., of others). ~·**a·tion** [kənˌsidəˈreiʃən] *n.* 1. quality of being ~ate: *in ~ation of his youth.* 2. act of ~ing: *proposals still under ~ation* (i.e. still being thought about). 3. sth. which

must be ~ed: *~ations which influenced him in making his plans.* 4. reward or payment. ~·**ing** *prep.* in view of; having regard to.

con·sign [kənˈsain] *v.t.* 1. send (goods, etc., by rail, etc. *to* sb.). 2. hand over, give up (*to*). ~·**ee** [ˌkɔnsaiˈniː] *n.* person to whom sth. is ~ed. ~·**ment** [kənˈsainmənt] *n.* ~ing; goods ~ed. ~·**or** *n.* person ~ing goods.

con·sist [kənˈsist] *v.i.* 1. ~ *of*, be made up of. 2. ~ *in*, have as the chief (or only) element: *Does happiness ~ in wanting little?* **con·sis·tence** (·**cy**) [kənˈsistəns(i)] *n.* 1. (always ~ency) the state of being always the same in thought, behaviour, etc. 2. degree of thickness, firmness, or solidity (esp. of a thick liquid or of sth. made by mixing with a liquid): *to mix flour and milk to the right ~ency.* **con·sis·tent** *adj.* 1. (of a person, his behaviour, opinions, etc.) constant to the same principles; regular; conforming to a regular pattern or style. 2. in agreement (*with*): *theories not ~ent with the facts.*

con·sole [kənˈsoul] *v.t.* give comfort or sympathy to (sb. who is unhappy, disappointed, etc.). **con·so·la·tion** [ˌkɔnsəˈleiʃən] *n.* consoling; sth. which ~s.

con·sol·i·date [kənˈsɔlideit] *v.t. & i.* 1. make or become solid or strong. 2. unite or combine into one: *to ~ debts (business companies).* **con·sol·i·da·tion** [kənˌsɔliˈdeiʃən] *n.* **con·sols** [kənˈsɔlz] *n. pl.* British Government securities ~d (2) in 1751.

con·so·nant [ˈkɔnsənənt] *n.* speech sound which is not a vowel sound; letter or symbol representing such a sound.

¹**con·sort** [ˈkɔnsɔːt] *n.* husband or wife, esp. of a ruler. *prince ~*, reigning queen's husband.

²**con·sort** [kənˈsɔːt] *v.i.* ~ *with*, pass much time in the company of; be in harmony with.

con·spic·u·ous [kənˈspikjuəs] *adj.* easily seen; attracting attention; remarkable.

con·spire [kən'spaiə*] *v.i.* **1.** make secret plans with others (esp. to do wrong). **2.** combine; unite: *events that ~d to bring about his failure.* **con·spir·a·cy** [kən'spirəsi] *n.* act of conspiring; plan made by conspiring. **con·spir·a·tor** [kən'spirətə*] *n.* person who ~s (1).

con·sta·ble ['kʌnstəbl] *n.* policeman. **con·stab·u·lary** [kən'stæbjuləri] *n.* police force.

con·stan·cy ['kɔnstənsi] *n.* quality of being firm or unchanging: *~ of purpose.*

con·stant ['kɔnstənt] *adj.* **1.** going on all the time; never-ending: *~ complaints.* **2.** firm; faithful; unchanging. **~·ly** *adv.* often; always.

con·stel·la·tion [ˌkɔnstə'leiʃən] *n.* group of fixed stars.

con·ster·na·tion [ˌkɔnstə'neiʃən] *n.* surprise and fear; dismay.

con·sti·pa·tion [ˌkɔnsti'peiʃən] *n.* difficulty in emptying the bowels. **con·sti·pate** ['kɔnstipeit] *v.t.* cause ~.

con·stit·u·en·cy [kən'stitjuənsi] *n.* (persons living in a) town or district sending a representative to Parliament.

con·stit·u·ent [kən'stitjuənt] *adj.* **1.** having the power to make or alter a political constitution. **2.** forming or helping to make a whole: *a ~ part.* *n.* member of a constituency.

con·sti·tute ['kɔnstitju:t] *v.t.* **1.** give (sb.) authority to hold (a position, etc.); appoint. **2.** establish; give (a committee, etc.) legal authority. **3.** make up (a whole); amount to: *This ~s an infringement of the law.*

con·sti·tu·tion [ˌkɔnsti'tju:ʃən] *n.* **1.** system of government; laws and principles according to which a State is governed. **2.** general physical structure and condition of a person's body. **3.** general structure of a thing. **4.** person's mental qualities and nature. **~·al** [ˌkɔnsti'tju:ʃənl] *adj.* of a ~: *~ government;* a *~al ruler* (i.e. controlled or limited by a ~ (1)); *a ~al weakness* (i.e. of the ~ (2)). **~·al·ism**

[ˌkɔnsti'tju:ʃənəlizəm] *n.* (belief in) ~al government.

con·strain [kən'strein] *v.t.* make (sb.) do sth. by using force or strong persuasion. **con·strained** *ppl. adj.* (of voice, manner, etc.) forced; unnatural; uneasy. **con·straint** *n.* ~ing or being ~ed: *to act under ~t.*

con·strict [kən'strikt] *v.t.* make tight or smaller; cause (a vein or muscle) to become tight or narrow. **con·stric·tion** [kən'strikʃən] *n.*

con·struct [kən'strʌkt] *v.t.* build; put or fit together: *to ~ a factory (aircraft, sentence).* **con·struc·tor** *n.* **con·struc·tion** [kən'strʌkʃən] *n.* **1.** act or manner of ~ing; being ~ed: *a railway that is under (in the course of) ~ion.* **2.** sth. ~ed. **3.** meaning; sense in which words, acts, etc., are taken: *to put a wrong ~ion on what sb. says or does.* **con·struc·tive** *adj.* helping to ~; giving suggestions that help.

con·strue [kən'stru:] *v.t. & i.* **1.** translate or explain the meaning of (words, sentences, acts). **2.** (grammar) analyse (a sentence); combine (words with words) grammatically.

con·sul ['kɔnsl] *n.* **1.** State's agent living in a foreign town to help and protect his countrymen there. **2.** (in ancient Rome) one of the two heads of the State before Rome became an empire. **con·su·lar** ['kɔnsjulə*] *adj.* of a ~ or his work. **con·su·late** ['kɔnsjulit] *n.* ~'s position; ~'s office(s).

con·sult [kən'sʌlt] *v.t.* **1.** go to (a person, book) for information, advice, opinion, etc.: *to ~ one's lawyer (a map, etc.).* **2.** consider; take into account: *to ~ sb.'s convenience.* **con·sul·tant** [kən'sʌltənt] *n.* expert (e.g. a physician) ~ed for special advice. **con·sul·ta·tion** [ˌkɔnsʌl'teiʃən] *n.* ~ing; meeting for ~ing.

con·sume [kən'sju:m] *v.t. & i.* **1.** eat or drink. **2.** use up; get to the end of. **3.** destroy (by fire, wasting). **4.** *be ~d with,* be filled

with (desire, envy, grief, etc.).
5. ~ *away,* waste away. **con·sum·er** *n.* (opp. to *producer*) person who uses goods: ~*r goods,* (opp. to capital (3) goods) commodities such as food and clothing which directly satisfy one's needs.

con·sum·mate [kən'sʌmit] *adj.* complete; perfect: ~ *skill* (*taste*). ['kɔnsəmeit] *v.t.* make perfect or complete; bring to a perfect finish. **con·sum·ma·tion** [ˌkɔnsʌ'meiʃən] *n.*

con·sump·tion [kən'sʌmpʃən] *n.* **1.** using up, consuming (of food, energy, materials, etc.); the amount consumed. **2.** disease in which there is a wasting away of part of the body, esp. of the lungs; tuberculosis. **con·sump·tive** [kən'sʌmptiv] *adj.* suffering from, having a tendency to, ~ (2). *n.* sufferer from ~ (2).

con·tact ['kɔntækt] *n.* (state of) touching or coming together: *to be in ~ with sb.* (i.e. in communication, exchanging news, views, etc.). [kən'tækt] *v.t.* get into touch with: *You ought to ~ the police at once.*

con·ta·gion [kən'teidʒən] *n.* the spreading of disease by touch; (fig.) the spreading of evil ideas, false rumours, feelings, etc. **con·ta·gious** [kən'teidʒəs] *adj.* (of disease) spreading by touch; (fig.) spreading easily by example: *contagious laughter* (*gloom*).

con·tain [kən'tein] *v.t.* **1.** have or hold within itself: *The bag ~s 14 lb. of potatoes. Whisky ~s alcohol.* **2.** keep (feelings, enemy force, etc.) under control, within limits. **3.** (geometry) form the boundary of. ~**er** *n.* box, bottle, etc., made to ~ sth.

con·tam·i·nate [kən'tæmineit] *v.t.* make dirty, impure, or diseased. **con·tam·i·na·tion** [kən,tæmi'neiʃən] *n.*

con·tem·plate ['kɔntempleit] *v.t.* look at (with the eyes or in the mind); have in view as a purpose, intention, or possibility. **con·tem·pla·tion** [ˌkɔntem'pleiʃən] *n.* **con·tem·pla·tive** [kən-

'templətiv] *adj.* thoughtful; fond of contemplation.

con·tem·po·ra·ry [kən'tempərəri] *adj.* **1.** of the period to which reference is being made: *a ~ record of events* (i.e. one made by persons then living). **2.** of the times in which we live. *n.* person ~ with another: *John and I were contemporaries at college.* **con·tem·po·ra·neous** [kən,tempə'reinjəs] *adj.* existing, happening, at the same time.

con·tempt [kən'tempt] *n.* **1.** condition of being looked down upon or despised: *to fall into ~ by foolish or bad behaviour.* **2.** mental attitude of scorn towards things which should not be feared or respected: *to feel ~ for a liar; to show one's ~ of danger or death in battle.* **3.** ~ *of court,* act disobeying an order made by a court of law; disrespect shown to a judge. ~**i·ble** *adj.* rightly deserving ~. ~**u·ous** *adj.* showing ~. ~**u·ous·ly** *adv.*

con·tend [kən'tend] *v.i.* **1.** struggle, be in rivalry or competition (*with* sb. or sth., *for* a purpose). **2.** argue (*that*). **con·ten·tion** [kən'tenʃən] *n.* ~ing; argument used in ~ing. **con·ten·tious** [kən'tenʃəs] *adj.* fond of ~ing; likely to cause contention.

¹**con·tent** [kən'tent] *adj.* **1.** not wanting more; satisfied with what one has. **2.** ~ *to,* willing or ready to. *n.* condition of being ~. *v.t.* make ~; satisfy. ~**ed** *ppl. adj.* satisfied; showing or feeling ~. ~**ment** *n.* state of being ~.

²**con·tent** ['kɔntent] *n.* **1.** (usu. pl.) that which is contained in sth.: *the ~s of a room* (*a book,* etc.). **2.** the amount which a vessel will contain: *the ~ of a cask.*

con·test [kən'test] *v.t. & i.* **1.** take part in a struggle or competition (*for*). **2.** argue against: *to ~ a statement.* ['kɔntest] *n.* struggle; fight; competition. ~**ant** [kən'testənt] *n.* person taking part in a ~.

con·text ['kɔntekst] *n.* what comes before and after (a word, phrase, statement, etc.), helping to fix the meaning. ~**u·al** [kən·'tekstjuəl] *adj.*

con·tig·u·ous [kən'tigjuəs] *adj.* touching; neighbouring; next (*to*). **con·ti·gu·i·ty** [ˌkɔnti'gjuiti] *n.* being ~.

¹**con·tin·ent** ['kɔntinənt] *adj.* self-controlled; having control of one's feelings and desires. **con·ti·nence** ['kɔntinəns] *n.*

²**con·tin·ent** ['kɔntinənt] *n.* one of the main land masses (Europe, Asia, Africa, etc.): *the C~*, (usu.) Europe without the British Isles. **con·ti·nen·tal** [ˌkɔnti'nentl] *adj.* belonging to, typical of, a ~; (esp.) of Europe.

con·tin·gent [kən'tindʒənt] *adj.* 1. uncertain; accidental. 2. dependent (on sth. that may or may not happen). *n.* body of troops, number of ships, sent to form part of a larger force. **con·tin·gen·cy** [kən'tindʒənsi] *n.* ~ event.

con·tin·ue [kən'tinju:] *v.i. & t.* 1. go further; go on (being); go on (doing); go on (to do); stay (in, at); remain (in). 2. start again after stopping. **con·tin·u·al** [kən'tinjuəl] *adj.* going on all the time without stopping or with only short breaks. **con·tin·u·ance** [kən'tinjuəns] *n.* (esp.) time for which sth. is ~s: *during the continuance of the war.* **con·tin·u·a·tion** [kənˌtinju'eiʃən] *n.* continuing; part, etc., by which sth. is ~d: *The continuation of the story is on page 17.* **con·ti·nu·i·ty** [ˌkɔnti'njuiti] *n.* 1. the state of being continuous. 2. arrangement of the parts of a film story. 3. connecting comments, etc., between parts of a broadcast. **con·tin·u·ous** [kən'tinjuəs] *adj.* going on without a break.

con·tort [kən'tɔ:t] *v.t.* force or twist out of the usual shape or appearance. **con·tor·tion** [kən'tɔ:ʃən] *n.* **con·tor·tion·ist** *n.* person clever at ~ing his body.

con·tour ['kɔntuə*] *n.* outline (of a coast, mountain, etc.); (on a map, design, etc.) line separating differently coloured parts. ~ *line*, line (on a map) joining all points at the same height above sea level; ~ *map*, one with ~ lines at fixed intervals (e.g. of 100 metres).

con·tra- ['kɔntrə-] *prefix.* against.

con·tra·band ['kɔntrəbænd] *n.* bringing into or taking out of a country goods contrary to the law; (trade in) goods so brought in or taken out.

¹**con·tract** ['kɔntrækt] *n.* agreement (between persons, groups, or states); business agreement to supply goods, do work, etc., at a fixed price. [kən'trækt] *v.t. & i.* 1. make a ~: *to ~ to build a railway*; *to ~ a marriage.* 2. become liable for: *to ~ debts.* 3. catch; form; acquire: *to ~ a disease (bad habits, a friendship).* **con·trac·tor** *n.*

²**con·tract** [kən'trækt] *v.t. & i.* 1. make or become smaller or shorter: *to ~ 'I will' to 'I'll'. Metals ~ when they become cool.* 2. make or become tighter or narrower: *to ~ a muscle*; *a valley which ~s as one goes up it.* **con·trac·tion** [kən'trækʃən] *n.* ¹~ing or ²~ed; sth. ²~ed.

con·tra·dict [ˌkɔntrə'dikt] *v.t.* 1. say (that sth. said or written) is not true. 2. (of facts, statements, etc.) be contrary to. **con·tra·dic·tion** [ˌkɔntrə'dikʃən] *n.* **con·tra·dic·to·ry** [ˌkontrə'diktəri] *adj.*

con·tral·to [kən'træltou] *n.* lowest female voice; woman with such a voice; musical part to be sung by her.

con·trap·tion [kən'træpʃən] *n.* (colloq.) strange-looking apparatus or device.

con·tra·ry ['kɔntrəri] *adj.* 1. opposite (in nature or tendency). 2. (of the wind) unfavourable (for sailing). 3. (colloq. [kən'treəri]) obstinate; self-willed. *adv.* in opposition to; against. *n. the ~*, the opposite (of sth.). *on the ~*, used to make a denial or contradiction more emphatic: '*Have you nearly done it?' 'On*

the ~, *I have only just begun.'*
to the ~, to the opposite effect.
con·tra·ri·ly [kən'trɛərili] *adv.*
con·tra·ri·ness [kən'trɛərinis]
n. being ~ (3).

con·trast [kən'trɑːst] *v.t. & i.*
1. compare (one thing *with* another) so that their difference is made clear. **2.** show a difference when compared: *actions which* ~ *with his promises.*
['kɒntrɑːst] *n.* **1.** the act of ~ing.
2. difference which is clearly seen when unlike things or persons are put together; sth. showing such difference (*to*).

con·tra·vene [ˌkɒntrə'viːn] *v.t.*
1. act in opposition to; go against (a law, custom). **2.** dispute (a statement, etc.). **3.** (of things) be out of harmony with.
con·tra·ven·tion [ˌkɒntrə'venʃən] *n.*

con·tre·temps ['kɒntrətɒŋ] *n.*
set-back; unfortunate happening.

con·trib·ute [kən'tribjuːt] *v.t. & i.* **1.** join with others in giving (help, money, etc., *to* a common cause); give (ideas, suggestions, etc.). **2.** have a share in; help to bring about: *His hard work* ~*d to the success of the exhibition.* **3.** write (articles, etc.) and send in (*to* a newspaper). con·tri·bu·tion [ˌkɒntri'bjuːʃən] *n.* act of contributing; sth. ~d. con·trib·u·tor *n.*

con·trite ['kɒntrait] *adj.* filled with, showing, deep sorrow for wrongdoing. con·tri·tion [kən'triʃən] *n.*

con·trive [kən'traiv] *v.t. & i.* invent; design; find a way of doing (sth.), of causing (sth. to happen): *to* ~ *an escape from prison; to* ~ *to live on one's income.* con·tri·vance [kən'traivəns] *n.* sth. ~d, esp. an invention or apparatus.

con·trol [kən'troul] *n.* **1.** power or authority to rule, order, or direct: *to have* ~ *over one's children; to lose (get)* ~ *over (of) one's horse; to get flood waters under* ~. **2.** means of regulating, directing, or keeping in order: ~ *of traffic (foreign exchange);*

government ~*s on trade and industry.* **3.** (often pl.) means by which machines are operated: *at the* ~*s of an aircraft. v.t.* (*-ll-*). have ~ of: *to* ~ *one's temper (a horse, oneself).* ~**ler** *n.* person who ~s: *the Food Controller.*

con·tro·ver·sy ['kɒntrəvəsi] *n.* prolonged argument, esp. over social, moral, or political matters. con·tro·ver·sial [ˌkɒntrə'vəːʃl] *adj.* likely to cause ~; (of a person) fond of ~.

con·tume·ly ['kɒntjumli] *n.* abusive language or treatment.

con·tu·sion [kən'tjuːʒn] *n.* bruise.

co·nun·drum [kə'nʌndrəm] *n.* puzzling question, esp. one asked for fun.

con·va·les·cent [ˌkɒnvə'lesnt] *n. & adj.* (person who is) recovering from illness. con·va·les·cence *n.*

con·vec·tion [kən'vekʃən] *n.* conveying of heat through liquid or gas in contact with a hot surface.

con·vec·tor [kən'vektə*] *n.* apparatus for warming a room by ~. (Cf. *radiation, conduction.*)

con·vene [kən'viːn] *v.t. & i.* call (persons) to come together (for a meeting, etc.); come together (for a meeting, council, etc.).

con·ve·nient [kən'viːnjənt] *adj.* suitable; not causing trouble or difficulty: *a* ~ *time and place for a meeting.* con·ve·nience *n.* the quality of being ~; sth. which is ~; useful appliance. *public conveniences,* lavatories. *make a convenience of sb.,* use his services unreasonably. *at your convenience,* whenever you wish.

con·vent ['kɒnvənt] *n.* **1.** society of women (called *nuns*) living apart from others in the service of God. **2.** building(s) in which they live.

con·ven·tion [kən'venʃən] *n.* **1.** general conference of members of societies, etc., devoted to a special object. **2.** agreement between States, etc. (less formal than a treaty). **3.** general consent (esp. about forms of behaviour); practice or custom based on such general consent.

~**al** *adj.* **1.** based on ~ (3): *~al remarks* (*greetings*). **2.** using ~s (3); (of art) traditional.

con·verge [kən'və:dʒ] *v.i. & t.* (of lines, moving objects, opinions) come, cause to come, towards each other and meet at a point; tend to do this.

con·ver·sant [kən'və:sənt] *adj.* ~ *with*, having a knowledge of.

con·ver·sa·tion [ˌkɔnvə'seiʃən] *n.* talking. ~**·al** *adj.* fond of ~; (of words, etc.) used in ~.

¹**con·verse** *v.i.* [kən'və:s] talk (*with* sb. *about*, *on*, sth.).

²**con·verse** ['kɔnvə:s] *n. & adj.* (idea, statement which is) opposite (to another): '*Hot*' is the ~ of '*cold*'. ~**·ly** *adv.*

con·vert [kən'və:t] *v.t.* **1.** change (from one form, use, etc., into another): *to* ~ *rags into paper* (*cream into butter*). **2.** cause (a person) to change beliefs, etc.: *to* ~ *a man to Christianity*. ['kɔnvə:t] *n.* person ~ed to a religious belief. **con·ver·sion** [kən'və:ʃən] *n.* ~ing or being ~ed.

con·ver·ti·ble [kən'və:tibl] *adj.* that can be ~ed (1): *These banknotes are not* ~*ible into gold*.

con·vex ['kɔnveks] *adj.* with the surface curved like the outside of a ball. (Cf. *concave*.)

Concave   Convex

con·vey [kən'vei] *v.t.* **1.** carry, take, from one place to another. **2.** make known (ideas, news, feelings, etc.) to another person. **3.** (law) give (to sb.) full legal rights (in land or property). ~**·ance** [kən'veiəns] *n.* **1.** ~ing; sth. which ~s; carriage or other vehicle. **2.** (law) form of agreement ~ing property. ~**·er** *n.* person or thing that ~s, esp. (~*er belt*) an endless belt for moving goods.

con·vict [kən'vikt] *v.t.* make (sb.) feel sure that he has done wrong: *to* ~ *sb. of error*; (of a jury or judge) declare in a law court that (sb.) is guilty of crime. ['kɔnvikt] *n.* sb. ~ed of crime and undergoing punishment. **con·vic·tion** [kən'vikʃən] *n.* **1.** the ~ing of a person of crime. **2.** the act of convincing. **3.** firm belief.

con·vince [kən'vins] *v.t.* make (sb.) feel certain (*of* sth., *that* . . .); cause (sb.) to realize. **con·vinc·ing** *adj.*

con·viv·i·al [kən'viviəl] *adj.* **1.** gay; fond of drinking and merry-making: ~ *companions*. **2.** marked by drinking and merry-making: *a* ~ *evening*.

con·voke [kən'vouk] *v.t.* call together, summon (a meeting). **con·vo·ca·tion** [ˌkɔnvə'keiʃən] *n.* convoking; meeting or assembly, esp. to discuss affairs of the Church or of a University.

con·voy [kɔn'vɔi, 'kɔnvɔi] *v.t.* (esp. of a warship) go with (other ships) to protect (them). ['kɔnvɔi] *n.* ~ing; protecting force (of ships, etc.); number of ships sailing together for self-protection or accompanied by warship(s).

con·vulse [kən'vʌls] *v.t.* cause violent movements or disturbances: ~*d by an earthquake* (*civil war*); ~*d with laughter*. **con·vul·sion** [kən'vʌlʃən] *n.* **con·vul·sive** [kən'vʌlsiv] *adj.*

coo [ku:] *v.i. & n.* (make a) soft, murmuring sound (as of doves).

cook [kuk] *v.t. & i.* prepare (raw food) for use, by heating (eg. boiling, baking, frying). *n.* person who does this. ~**·er** *n.* sth., esp. a stove, for ~ing food: *a gas-~er*. ~**·er·y** ['kukəri] *n.* art or practice of ~ing.

cool [ku:l] *adj.* (-*er*, -*est*). **1.** between warm and cold; enabling a person to feel thus: *a* ~ *day*, *a* ~ *room*. **2.** calm; unexcited: ~ *in the face of danger*. **3.** impudent in a calm way; without shame. **4.** (of behaviour) not showing interest or enthusiasm. *v.t. & i.* make or become ~. ~**·ly** *adv.*

cool·ie ['ku:li] *n.* unskilled workman or porter (in the Far East).

coop [ku:p] *n.* small cage, esp. for hens with small chickens. *v.t.*

put or keep in a ~; ~ *up* (*in*), keep in a small room or space.

coop·er ['ku:pə*] *n.* maker of tubs, casks, barrels, etc.

co-op·er·ate [kou'ɔpəreit] *v.i.* work or act together to bring about a result. **co-op·er·a·tion** [kou,ɔpə'reiʃən] *n.* **co-op·er·a·tive** [kou'ɔpərətiv] *adj.* of co-operation; willing to ~. *Co-operative Society*, group of persons who ~, e.g. to buy machines and services for all members to share; produce, buy, and sell goods amongst themselves for mutual benefit; save and lend money. *n.* (shop of) Co-operative Society.

co-opt [kou'ɔpt] *v.t.* (of a committee) add (a person) as a member by the votes of those who are already members.

co-or·di·nate [kou'ɔ:dinit] *adj.* equal in importance. *n.* ~ thing. [kou'ɔ:dineit] *v.t.* make ~; bring, put, into proper relation. **co-or·di·na·tion** [kou,ɔ:di'neiʃən] *n.* the act of co-ordinating; the state of being co-ordinate.

¹cope [koup] *n.* long, loose cloak worn by the clergy on some special occasions.

²cope [koup] *v.i.* ~ *with*, manage successfully; be equal to: *to* ~ *with difficulties.*

cop·ing ['koupiŋ] *n.* line of (sometimes overhanging) stonework or brickwork on top of a wall.

co·pious ['koupjəs] *adj.* plentiful; (of a writer) writing much. ~**·ly** *adv.*

cop·per ['kɔpə*] *n.* 1. common reddish-brown metal. 2. coin made of ~ or bronze (e.g. an English penny). 3. large vessel made of metal, used for boiling clothes, etc. *v.t.* cover with a coating of ~.

cop·pice ['kɔpis] *n.* small area of small trees and undergrowth.

cop·ra ['kɔprə] *n.* dried kernel of coconut, used in soap-making.

copse [kɔps] *n.* coppice.

cop·y ['kɔpi] *n.* 1. thing made to be like another; reproduction of a letter, picture, etc. 2. one

example of a book, newspaper, etc., of which many have been made. 3. handwritten or typed matter (to be) sent to a printer. *v.t. & i.* 1. make a ~ of. 2. do, try to do, the same as; imitate. ~**·right** ['kɔpirait] *n.* legal right, held for a certain period of years only, by the author or composer of a work or someone allowed by him, to print, publish, sell, broadcast, perform, film, or record his work or any part of it. *adj.* protected by ~right. *v.t.* secure ~right for (a book, etc.).

cor·al ['kɔrəl] *n.* hard red, pink, or white substance built on the sea-bed by small sea-creatures (till it reaches the surface, forming reefs and islands). *adj.* pink or red like ~.

cord [kɔ:d] *n.* 1. length of twisted threads, thicker than string, thinner than rope. 2. part of the body like a ~: *the spinal* ~; *the vocal* ~s. *v.t.* put a ~ or ~s round. ~**·age** ['kɔ:didʒ] *n.* ~s, ropes, etc., esp. of a ship.

cor·dial ['kɔ:djəl] *adj.* warm and sincere (in feeling, behaviour). *n.* drink that gives a feeling of warmth; sweetened and concentrated fruit juice. ~**·ly** *adv.* **cor·di·al·i·ty** [,kɔ:di'æliti] *n.*

cor·dite ['kɔ:dait] *n.* smokeless explosive.

cor·don ['kɔ:dn] *n.* line, ring, of police, etc., acting as guards.

cor·du·roy ['kɔ:djurɔi] *n.* thick, coarse, strong cotton cloth with raised lines on it; (pl.) trousers made of this cloth.

core [kɔ:*, kɔə*] *n.* 1. hard middle part, with seeds, of such fruits as the apple and pear. 2. central or most important part of anything: *the* ~ *of a subject*; *true to the* ~ (i.e. thoroughly faithful). *v.t.* take out the ~(1) of.

cork [kɔ:k] *n.* light, tough material forming the thick outer bark of the tree called ~-oak; round piece of this used as a stopper for a bottle. *v.t.* put a ~ in. '~**·screw** *n.* tool for pulling out ~s.

¹**corn** [kɔːn] *n.* seed of various cereal plants, chiefly wheat, barley, oats, rye, and (in U.S.A.) maize; such plants while growing. **'~flour** *n.* flour made from maize or rice.

²**corn** [kɔːn] *n.* small area of hardened skin on a toe, etc.

³**corn** [kɔːn] *v.t.* preserve (meat) in salt: *~ed beef.*

cor·ner ['kɔːnə*] *n.* **1.** place where two lines, sides, edges, or surfaces meet; angle enclosed by two walls, sides, etc., that meet. *turn the ~,* (fig.) pass safely from a crisis, e.g. in a serious illness. *a tight ~,* a difficult situation. **2.** (commerce) *make a ~ in* (e.g. wheat), buy up all available supplies in order to control the price. *v.t.* **1.** drive into a ~; put in a difficult position. **2.** make a ~ (2) in (goods, etc.). **'~-stone** *n.* (fig.) foundation; that on which sth. is based: *Hard work was the ~-stone of his success.*

cor·net ['kɔːnit] *n.* small musical instrument of brass, like a trumpet.

co·rol·la·ry [kə'rɔləri] *n.* natural consequence or outcome of sth.

co·ro·na [kə'rounə] *n.* ring of light seen round the sun or moon, esp. during an eclipse.

cor·o·na·tion [ˌkɔrə'neiʃən] *n.* ceremony of crowning a king, queen, or other sovereign ruler.

cor·o·ner ['kɔrənə*] *n.* official who inquires into the cause of any violent or unnatural death. *~'s inquest,* such an inquiry.

cor·o·net ['kɔrənit] *n.* small crown worn by a noble; ornament designed like a ~.

¹**cor·por·al** ['kɔːpərəl] *adj.* of the body: *~ punishment* (whipping, beating).

²**cor·por·al** ['kɔːpərəl] *n.* (army) non-commissioned officer (below a sergeant).

cor·po·ra·tion [ˌkɔːpə'reiʃən] *n.* **1.** group of persons elected to govern a town: *the mayor and ~.* **2.** group of persons allowed by law to act, for business purposes, as one person. **cor·por·ate** ['kɔːpərit] *adj.* **1.** of a ~: *corporate property.* **2.** of or belonging to a body (4): *corporate responsibility.*

corps [kɔː*] *n.* (pl. [kɔːz]). **1.** one of the technical branches of an army: *the Royal Army Medical Corps.* **2.** military force made up of two or more Divisions.

corpse [kɔːps] *n.* dead body (usu. of a human being). (Cf. *carcass.*)

cor·pu·lent ['kɔːpjulənt] *n.* (of a person's body) fat and heavy. **cor·pu·lence,** **cor·pu·len·cy** ['kɔːpjuləns(i)] *n.*

cor·pus·cle ['kɔːpʌsl] *n.* one of the red or white cells in blood.

cor·ral [kɔ'rɑːl] *n.* enclosure for horses and cattle.

cor·rect [kə'rekt] *adj.* true; right. *v.t.* make ~; take out mistakes from; point out faults; punish. **cor·rec·tion** [kə'rekʃən] *n.* ~ing; sth. ~ put in place of an error: *a schoolboy's essay covered with ~ions.* **cor·rec·tive** [kə'rektiv] *n. & adj.* (sth.) serving to ~.

cor·re·late ['kɔrileit] *v.t. & i.* bring (one thing) into relation (*with* another); have a mutual relationship (*with, to*). **cor·re·la·tion** [ˌkɔri'leiʃən] *n.*

cor·re·spond [ˌkɔris'pɔnd] *v.i.* **1.** be in harmony (*with*). **2.** be equal (*to*); be similar (*to*). **3.** exchange letters (*with* sb.). **cor·re·spon·dence** *n.* **1.** agreement; similarity. **2.** letter-writing; letters. **cor·re·spon·dent** *n.* **1.** person with whom one exchanges letters. **2.** *newspaper ~ent,* person regularly contributing local news or special articles to a newspaper.

cor·ri·dor ['kɔridɔː*] *n.* long, narrow passage from which doors open into rooms or compartments.

cor·rob·o·rate [kə'rɔbəreit] *v.t.* give support or certainty to (a statement, theory, etc.). **cor·rob·o·ra·tion** [kəˌrɔbə'reiʃən] *n.*

cor·rode [kə'roud] *v.t. & i.* wear away, destroy slowly by chemical action or disease; be worn away thus. **cor·ro·sion** [kə'rou-ʒən] *n.* **cor·ro·sive** [kə'rousiv] *n. & adj.* (substance) corroding.

cor·ru·ga·ted ['kɔrugeitid] **ppl. adj.** shaped into narrow folds or wave-like furrows : ~ *iron* (*cardboard*) ; ~ *roads in tropical countries*.

Corrugated

cor·rupt [kə'rʌpt] **adj. 1.** (of persons, their actions) bad ; dishonest (esp. through taking bribes). **2.** impure : ~ *air*. **v.t.** make ~. **cor·rup·ti·ble** [kə'rʌptibl] **adj.** (esp.) that can be ~ed by bribes. **cor·rup·tion** [kə'rʌpʃən] **n.** ~ing ; being ~.

cor·set ['kɔːsit] **n.** tight-fitting undergarment confining the waist and hips.

cos·met·ic [kɔz'metik] **n.** substance used to make the skin or hair beautiful.

cos·mo·naut ['kɔzmounɔːt] **n.** = astronaut.

cos·mo·pol·i·tan [,kɔzmə'pɔlitən] **adj.** of or from all, or many different, parts of the world ; free from national prejudices because of wide experience of the world : *a* ~ *outlook*. **n.** ~ person.

cos·mos ['kɔzmɔs] **n.** the universe, all space, considered as a well-ordered system (contrasted with *chaos*). **cos·mic** ['kɔzmik] **adj.** of the ~.

cost [kɔst] **v.i. & t.** (p.t. & p.p. *cost*). **1.** be obtainable at the price of ; require the payment of ; result in the loss or disadvantage of. **2.** (p.t. & p.p. *costed* ['kɔstid]). (commerce) estimate the price to be charged for an article based on the expense of producing it. **n. 1.** price (to be) paid ; that which is needed in order to obtain. **2.** (law, pl.) expenses of having sth. decided in a law court. **3.** *at all* ~*s*, however much expense, trouble, etc., may be needed ; *to one's* ~, to one's loss or disadvantage. ~**ly adj.** of great value ; ~ing much.

cos·ter, cos·ter·mon·ger ['kɔstə-ˌmʌŋgə*] **n.** person selling fruit, vegetables, etc., from a barrow in the street.

cos·tume ['kɔstjuːm] **n. 1.** style of dress : *actors wearing historical* ~ (i.e. clothes in the fashion of a period of past time). **2.** woman's suit (short coat and skirt).

co·sy ['kouzi] **adj.** (-*ier*, -*iest*). warm and comfortable. **co·si·ly adv.**

cot [kɔt] **n.** easily-moved bed, esp. for a small child.

cote [kout] **n.** shelter for animals or birds : *dove*~.

cot·tage ['kɔtidʒ] **n.** small house, esp. in the country : *farm-labourers'* ~*s*.

cot·ton ['kɔtn] **n. 1.** see picture (i). ~ *wool*, cleaned raw or natural ~ as used for padding, bandaging. **2.** see picture (ii).

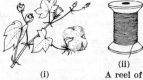

(i)
A cotton-plant

(ii)
A reel of cotton

couch [kautʃ] **n. 1.** (liter.) bed. **2.** long bed-like seat for sitting or lying on during the day. **v.t. & i. 1.** put (a thought) (*in* words). **2.** (of animals) lie flat either to hide or in readiness for a jump forward.

cough [kɔf] **v.i.** send out air from the lungs violently and noisily. ~ *sth. up* (*out*), get sth. out of the throat by ~ing. **n. 1.** act or sound of ~ing. **2.** condition, illness, causing a person to ~ often.

could, see *can*.

coun·cil ['kaunsil] **n.** group of persons appointed or chosen to give advice, make rules, carry out plans, manage affairs, etc., esp. of government : *the legislative* ~. ~**lor n.** member of a ~.

coun·sel ['kaunsəl] **n. 1.** advice ; opinions ; suggestions : *keep one's* own ~, keep one's views, plans, etc., secret; *hold* ~ *with* (*sb.*), take ~ together, consult in order to get suggestions, etc. **2.** (pl. unchanged) barrister(s) giving advice, etc., in a law case. *Queen's Counsel*, barrister appointed to act for the British Government, higher in authority than other barristers. *v.t.* (-*ll*-). give ~ to. ~**lor** *n.* adviser.

¹**count** [kaunt] *v.t. & i.* **1.** say or name (the numerals) in order. *be* ~*ed out*, (of a boxer) fail to rise to his feet before the ~*ing* of ten seconds after being knocked down. ~ *down* (also '~*-down*, *n.*), ~ backwards, e.g. 10, 9, 8, etc., in preparing to launch a space-rocket. **2.** include; take into account; be included: *fifty people, not* ~*ing the children. That doesn't* ~ (i.e. need not be taken into account or considered). ~ *on* (*upon*), rely upon; consider as certain: *You mustn't* ~ *upon any help from me.* ~ *for much* (*little, nothing*), be of much (little, no) importance. **3.** consider; look upon (as): *to* ~ *oneself fortunate; to* ~ *sb. as lost.* *n.* **1.** act of ~*ing*; number got by ~*ing. take the* ~, (boxing) *be* ~*ed out* (see above). **2.** account; notice: *to take no* ~ *of what people say.* **3.** (law) one of several things of which a person has been accused: *guilty on all* ~*s.* '~*-ing-house n.* building or room for book-keeping (e.g. in a bank). ~**less** *adj.* too many to be ~ed.

²**count** [kaunt] *n.* title of nobility in some countries (but not Gt. Brit.). ~**ess** ['kauntis] *n.* wife or widow of an earl or count; woman with rank equal to that of an earl.

coun·te·nance ['kauntinəns] *n.* **1.** face, including its appearance and expression: *a fierce* ~. *keep one's* ~, control one's expression, esp. in hiding amusement. *put sb. out of* ~, cause him to feel troubled or at fault. **2.** support; approval: *to give* ~ *to a proposal. v.t.* give ~ (2) to.

¹**coun·ter** ['kauntə*] *n.* table

on which goods are shown, customers are served, in a shop or bank.

²**coun·ter** ['kauntə*] *n.* small, round, flat piece of metal, plastic, etc., used for keeping count in games, etc.

³**coun·ter** ['kauntə*] *adv.* against; in the opposite direction: *acting* ~ *to my wishes. v.t. & i.* act ~ to; oppose.

coun·ter- ['kauntə*] *prefix.* **1.** opposite in direction: ~*march*; ~*-attraction.* **2.** made in answer to: ~*-attack*; ~*-claim.*

coun·ter·act [,kauntə'rækt] *v.t.* act against and make (action, force) of less or no effect: *to* ~ *a poison.* **coun·ter·ac·tion** *n.*

coun·ter·bal·ance [,kauntə-'bæləns] *n.* weight, force, etc., equal to another and balancing it. *v.t.* act as a ~ to.

coun·ter·feit ['kauntəfi:t] *n. & adj.* (sth.) false; (sth.) made in imitation of another thing in order to deceive: ~ *money* (*virtue*). *v.t.* copy or imitate (coin, handwriting) in order to deceive.

coun·ter·foil ['kauntəfoil] *n.* section of a cheque, receipt, etc., kept by the sender as a record.

coun·ter·mand [,kauntə'mɑ:nd] *v.t.* take back, cancel, a command already given.

coun·ter·part ['kauntəpɑ:t] *n.* person or thing exactly like, or corresponding closely to, another.

coun·ter·sign ['kauntəsain] *n.* password; secret word to be given, on demand, to a sentry to prove that one is not an enemy: '*Advance and give the* ~.' *v.t.* add another signature to a document to give it more authority.

coun·try ['kʌntri] *n.* **1.** land occupied by a nation. **2.** land in which a person was born. **3.** the people of a ~ (1); the nation as a whole. **4.** region of open spaces, of land used for farming: *Do you like living in the* ~? *We passed through miles of densely wooded* ~. (Cf. *town.*) **coun·tri·fied** ['kʌntrifaid] *adj.* with the ways and habits of the ~, not of towns. ~**man** ['kʌntrimən] *n.* man of the ~, not of a town; (also *fellow* ~*man*) man of the same nation as another. '**coun·try·side** *n.* district in the ~.

coun·ty ['kaunti] *n.* division of Great Britain, the largest unit of local government. ~ *town*, chief town in a ~.

coup [ku:] *n.* sudden action taken to get power, obtain a desired result, etc.

coup·le ['kʌpl] *n.* 1. two persons, or things, seen or associated together. 2. two persons (to be) married to one another. *v.t.* 1. join (two things) together. 2. associate (two things) in thought. **coup·let** ['kʌplit] *n.* two lines of verse, equal in length and with a rhyme. **coup·ling** ['kʌpliŋ] *n.* (esp.) link, etc., that joins two parts of a machine, two railway coaches or other vehicles.

cou·pon ['ku:pɒn] *n.* ticket, part of a document, paper, bond, etc., which gives the holder the right to receive sth. or do sth.

cour·age ['kʌridʒ] *n.* bravery; quality that enables a person to control fear in face of danger or pain. **cou·ra·geous** [kə'reidʒəs] *adj.* brave.

cou·ri·er ['kuriə*] *n.* 1. person who is paid to conduct parties of tourists, esp. abroad. 2. messenger carrying news or important government papers.

¹**course** [kɔ:s, kɔəs] *n.* 1. forward movement in space or time: *the* ~ *of events. in* ~ *of*, in process of: *a railway in* ~ *of construction* (i.e. being built). *in the* ~ *of*, during. *in due* ~, in the proper or natural order. 2. direction taken by sth.; line along which sth. moves; line of action: *The ship is on her right* ~. *The disease ran its* ~ (i.e. developed in the usual way). *the* ~*s open to us* (i.e. the ways in which we may proceed to act). *a matter of* ~, that which one would expect (to do, happen, etc.). *of* ~, naturally; certainly. 3. ground for golf: *a golf-*~; place for races:

a race-~. 4. series (of talks, treatments, etc.): *a* ~ *of lectures* (*mud baths*). 5. continuous line of stone or brick in a wall. 6. one of the separate parts of a meal (e.g. soup, meat, dessert).

²**course** [kɔ:s, kɔəs] *v.t. & i.* 1. chase (esp. hares) with dogs. 2. move quickly; run (esp. of liquids). **cours·ing** *n.* the sport of chasing hares.

court [kɔ:t] *n.* 1. place where law cases are heard; those persons (judges and other officers) who hear law cases. 2. great ruler (king, emperor, etc.), his family and officials, councillors, etc.; State gathering or reception given by a ruler. 3. space marked out for certain games: *a tennis* ~. 4. (also ~*yard*) space with walls or buildings round it; the houses round such a space. (Cf. ²*close*.) 5. special service or politeness offered in order to please sb.: *pay* ~ *to a woman*, try to win her affections. *v.t.* 1. pay one's ~ (5) to; try to win or obtain (support, approval, etc.). 2. take action that may lead to (defeat, danger). **cour·teous** ['kə:tjəs] *adj.* having, showing, good manners; polite and kind. **cour·te·sy** ['kə:təsi] *n.* ~eous behaviour; ~eous act. **cour·tier** ['kɔ:tjə*] *n.* person belonging to the ~ (2) of a ruler. ~**·ly** ['kɔ:tli] *adj.* polite and dignified. ~ **mar·tial**, ~**-mar·tial** *v.* ['kɔ:t'mɑ:ʃl] (~ (1) for) trying(ing) offences against military law. ~**·ship** ['kɔ:tʃip] *n.* (time of) paying ~ (5) to a woman. ~**·yard** ['kɔ:tjɑ:d] *n.* = court (4).

cous·in ['kʌzn] *n.* (*first* ~) child of one's uncle or aunt; (*second* ~) child of one's parent's first ~.

cove [kouv] *n.* small ¹bay.

cov·e·nant ['kʌvənənt] *v.i. & t. & n.* (make a) solemn agreement.

cov·er ['kʌvə*] *v.t.* 1. place one substance or thing over or in front of (another); hide or protect (sth.) in this way; lie or extend over; occupy the surface of. 2. travel (a distance): *to* ~ *ten miles in an hour.* 3. aim at (with a gun or pistol). **4.** protect; provide with an insurance (*against*): *to have one's property ~ed (by insurance) against loss.* **5.** (of money) be enough for: *£5 will ~ my needs for the journey.* *n.* **1.** thing that ~s, hides, protects or encloses. **2.** place giving shelter: *to take ~ from the enemy's fire; to get under ~* (e.g. when it rains). **~·let** *n.* bed-~.

¹**cov·ert** ['kʌvət] *adj.* (of glances, threats, etc.) half-hidden, disguised. **~·ly** *adv.*

²**cov·ert** ['kʌvət] *n.* area of thick undergrowth in which animals hide.

cov·et ['kʌvit] *v.t.* desire eagerly (usu. sth. belonging to sb. else). **~·ous** ['kʌvitəs] *adj.*

¹**cow** [kau] *n.* see the picture. **'cow·boy** *n.* man looking after cattle on a ranch, etc. **'cow·,catch·er** *n.* metal frame fastened to the front of a railway engine to push obstacles off the track. **'cow·herd** *n.* person looking after cows in the fields. **'cow·hide** *n.* leather from the skin of cows.

A cow   A cow-boy

²**cow** [kau] *v.t.* frighten (sb.) into submission.

cow·ard ['kauəd] *n.* person unable to control his fear; one who runs away from danger. **~·ly** *adj.* not brave; contemptible: *a ~ly act (lie).* **~·ice** ['kauədis] *n.* feeling, way of behaving, of a ~.

cow·er ['kauə*] *v.i.* lower the body as when frightened; crouch; droop; shrink (from cold, misery, fear, or shame).

cowl [kaul] *n.* **1.** long, loose gown with a hood that can be pulled up over the head. **2.** the hood alone. **3.** metal, etc., cap for a chimney.

cow·rie ['kauri] *n.* small shell formerly used as money in parts of Africa and Asia.

cow·slip ['kauslip] *n.* yellow flower growing wild in temperate countries.

cox [kɔks], **cox·swain** ['kɔksn] *n.* person who steers a rowing-boat; person in charge of a ship's boat and crew.

cox·comb ['kɔkskoum] *n.* vain, foolish person, esp. one who pays too much attention to his clothes.

coy [kɔi] *adj.* (esp. of a girl) shy; modest. **coy·ly** *adv.* **coy·ness** *n.*

¹**crab** [kræb] *n.* shellfish as shown here; its meat as food.

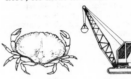

A ¹crab   A crane (2)

²**crab** [kræb] *n.* (also ~-*apple*) wild apple-tree; its hard, sour fruit.

crab·bed ['kræbid] *adj.* bad-tempered; (of handwriting) difficult to read.

crack [kræk] *n.* **1.** line of division where sth. is broken, but not into separate parts: *~s in a cup; ~s in the ground during dry weather.* **2.** sudden, sharp noise (of a gun, whip, etc.). **3.** sharp blow which can be heard: *a ~ on the head.* *v.t. & i.* **1.** get or make a ~ or ~s (1) in. **2.** make, cause to make, a ~ or ~s (2). **3.** (of the voice) become harsh; undergo a change (esp. of a boy's voice when he is reaching manhood). **4.** (colloq.) *~ up,* lose strength (e.g. in old age). *~ sb. or sth. up,* praise highly. *~ a joke,* make a joke. *adj.* first-rate; very clever: *a ~ polo-player.* **~·er** *n.* **1.** thin, hard, dry biscuit. **2.** firework that makes a ~ or ~s (2) when set off or pulled apart. **3.** (pl., also *nut-~ers*) instrument for ~ing nuts. **crack·le** ['krækl] *v.i. & n.* (make) small ~ing sounds: *the ~le of machine-gun fire.*

cra·dle ['kreidl] *n.* small bed or cot, mounted on rockers, for a baby; (fig.) place where sth. is born or begins. *v.t.* place, hold, in or as in a ~.

craft [krɑːft] *n.* **1.** occupation, esp. one in which skill in the use of the hands is needed: *the ~ of the wood-carver; a school for arts and ~s.* **2.** cunning; trickery; skill in deceiving. **3.** (pl. unchanged) boat(s); ship(s): *a harbour full of all kinds of ~.* **'crafts·man** *n.* skilled workman. **~·y** *adj.* cunning; full of ~ (2). **~·i·ly** *adv.* **~·i·ness** *n.*

crag [kræg] *n.* high, sharp rock. **~·gy** *adj.* with many ~s.

cram [kræm] *v.t. & i.* (*-mm-*). **1.** make too full; put, push, too much into. **2.** fill the head with facts in preparation (*for an examination*). **~·mer** *n.* one who ~s (2) pupils for examinations by special lessons.

cramp [kræmp] *n.* painful tightening of muscles, usu. caused by cold or overwork, making movement difficult: *a swimmer seized with ~.* *v.t.* keep in a narrow space; hinder or prevent movement or growth (lit. and fig.). **cramped** *adj.* (of space) ~ing; (of handwriting) with small letters close together and for this reason difficult to read.

crane [krein] *n.* **1.** large waterbird with long legs and neck. **2.** machine for lifting heavy loads. See the picture on page 123. *v.t. & i.* stretch out (the neck) so to see: *to ~ one's neck.*

cra·nium ['kreinjəm] *n.* bony part of the head enclosing the brain.

¹crank [kræŋk] *n.* person with fixed (often strange) ideas, esp. on one matter (e.g. a man who refuses to sleep indoors). **~·y** *adj.* (*-ier, -iest*). (of people) odd; rather mad; (of buildings, etc.) unsteady; shaky.

²crank [kræŋk] *n.* L-shaped arm and handle used to turn a machine. *v.t.* move, cause to move, by turning a ~-handle: *to ~ up an engine* (to make it start.)

cran·ny ['kræni] *n.* small crack or hole (e.g. in a wall).

crape [kreip] *n.* black silk or cotton material with a wrinkled surface.

crash [kræʃ] *v.t. & i.* **1.** fall or strike suddenly and noisily (esp. of things that break): *The bus ~ed into a house. The aircraft ~ed.* **2.** (of a business, government, etc.) come to ruin; meet disaster. **3.** cause to ~. *n.* **1.** (noise made by a) violent fall, blow, or breaking. **2.** ruin, downfall (of a government, business). **'~·,hel·met** *n.* helmet worn by a motor-cyclist to protect his head in a ~.

crass [kræs] *adj.* (of a quality such as ignorance, stupidity) complete; very great.

crate [kreit] *n.* large framework of light boards or basketwork for goods in transport. *v.t.* put in a ~.

cra·ter ['kreitə*] *n.* mouth of a volcano; hole in the ground made by a bomb or shell, etc.

cra·vat [krə'væt] *n.* an old-fashioned kind of necktie.

crave [kreiv] *v.t. & i.* ask earnestly for; have a strong desire for. **crav·ing** *n.* desire.

cra·ven ['kreivn] *n. & adj.* (person who is) cowardly.

crawl [krɔːl] *v.i.* **1.** move on hands and knees with the body close to the ground. **2.** go very slowly. **3.** be full of ~ing things: *a garden ~ing with ants.* **4.** (of the flesh) feel as if covered with ~ing things. *n.* **1.** ~ing movement: *to go at a ~* (i.e. slowly). **2.** *the ~,* fast swimming-stroke.

cray·fish ['kreifiʃ] *n.* lobster-like shell-fish living in rivers.

cray·on ['kreiən] *n.* stick or pencil of soft coloured chalk or other material for drawing, etc.

cra·zy ['kreizi] *adj.* (*-ier, -iest*). **1.** mad. **2.** distraught; excited: *~ with pain; ~ on the cinema.* **3.** foolish: *a ~ idea.* **4.** (of buildings, etc.) unsafe; likely to collapse. **craze** [kreiz] *v.t.* make ~ (1). *n.* **1.** strong enthusiasm, esp. for sth. which is popular for a short time: *a boyish craze for* stamp-collecting. 2. the object of such enthusiasm. **cra·zi·ly** adv. **cra·zi·ness** n.

creak [kri:k] v.i. & n. (make a) sound like that of new leather boots, a dry or rusty door-hinge, or badly fitting floorboards when trodden on. ~·y adj. ~y stairs.

cream [kri:m] n. 1. fatty or oily part of milk which rises to the surface and can be made into butter. 2. substance containing ~ or like ~ in appearance; ~-like paste, etc.: ~ cheese; face-~. 3. best part of anything: the ~ of society (the 'best' people). 4. the colour of ~. ~·er·y ['kri:məri] n. place where ~, milk, butter, etc., are sold. ~·y adj.

crease [kri:s] n. 1. line made (on cloth, paper, etc.) by crushing, folding, or pressing. 2. (cricket) chalk line on the ground marking certain players' positions by the wicket. v.t. & i. make, get, ~s in.

create [kri(:)'eit] v.t. cause sth. to exist; make (sth. new or original); produce. **cre·a·tion** [kri(:)'eiʃən] n. act of creating; sth. ~d, esp. the Creation, the world or universe as ~d by God. **cre·a·tive** [kri(:)'eitiv] adj. having power to ~; of creation. **cre·a·tor** [kri(:)'eitə*] n. one who ~s. the Creator, God. **crea·ture** ['kri:tʃə*] n. 1. living being; (of persons): a lovely (poor, sickly) ~; (of animals): dumb ~s. 2. person who is merely a tool of another person, carrying out his orders without question. 3. ~ comforts, material or physical comforts.

crèche [kreiʃ] n. public nursery where babies are looked after while their mothers are at work.

cre·dence ['kri:dəns] n. give ~ to, believe (what is said, etc.).

cre·den·tials [kri'denʃəlz] n. pl. letters or papers showing that a person is what he claims to be.

cred·i·ble ['kredibl] adj. that can be believed. **cred·i·bly** adv. **cred·i·bil·i·ty** [ˌkredi'biliti] n.

cred·it ['kredit] n. 1. belief; trust. 2. good name; reputation. 3. honour, approval, coming to a person because of what he is or does: The work does you ~. He is cleverer than I gave him ~ for. 4. person, thing, act, etc., which adds to the reputation or good name of someone responsible for him (it): pupils who are a ~ to their teacher. 5. belief of others that a person can pay his debts or will keep a promise to pay: His ~ is good only for £10. No ~ given at this shop (i.e. all goods must be paid for in cash). letter of ~ (from one bank to another giving authority for a stated payment). 6. money shown as owned by a person in his account with a bank. 7. (book-keeping) record of money, etc., possessed by, or due to (sb., a business) (opp. debit). v.t. 1. believe; put trust in: ~ sb. with, believe that he has. 2. enter on the ~ (7) side of an account. ~·a·ble ['kreditəbl] adj. bringing ~ (2), (3). **cred·i·tor** n. person to whom one owes money.

cred·u·lous ['kredjuləs] adj. (too) ready to believe things. **cre·du·li·ty** [kri'dju:liti] n.

creed [kri:d] n. (system of) beliefs or opinions. the Creed, summary of the essential Christian beliefs.

creek [kri:k] n. narrow inlet of water on the sea-shore or in a river-bank; small river.

creel [kri:l] n. wicker basket for carrying fish.

creep [kri:p] v.i. (p.t. & p.p. crept [krept]). move along with the body close to the ground or floor; move slowly, quietly, or secretly. n. pl. the ~s, feeling of horror or disgust as if insects were ~ing over one's flesh. ~·er n. insect, bird, etc., that ~s; (esp.) plant that ~s along the ground, over walls, etc. ~·y adj. having or causing the ~s.

cre·mate [kri'meit] v.t. burn (a dead body) to ashes. **cre·ma·tion** [kri'meiʃən] n. **cre·ma·tori·um** [ˌkremə'tɔ:riəm] n. furnace, place, for cremation.

cre·o·sote ['kri:əsout] *n.* oily liquid made from wood-tar.

crêpe [kreip] *n.* name for crape-like materials, usu. white or coloured. ~ *rubber*, raw rubber with a wrinkled surface used for soles of shoes. ~ *paper*, paper with a wavy or wrinkled surface.

crept, see *creep.*

cre·scen·do [kri'ʃendou] *n. & adv.* (passage of music to be played, sth. heard) with, of, increasing loudness.

cres·cent ['kresənt] *n.* (sth. shaped like) the curve of the moon in the first or last quarter. *adj.* (of the moon) increasing; growing.

cress [kres] *n.* name of various green plants with small, hot-tasting leaves, used in salads.

crest [krest] *n.* 1. tuft of feathers on a bird's head or of hair on an animal's head; cock's comb. 2. ~-like decoration formerly worn on top of a helmet. 3. design over the shield of a coat of arms, or used on notepaper, etc. 4. top of a slope, hill, etc.; white top of a large wave. *v.t.* supply with, decorate with, a ~; get to the top of: *to* ~ *a wave.* '~·**fal·len** *adj.* dejected; disappointed (at failure, etc.).

cre·tonne ['kreton, kre'ton] *n.* cotton cloth with printed designs, used for curtains, etc.

cre·vasse [kri'væs] *n.* deep open crack, esp. in ice on a glacier.

crev·ice ['krevis] *n.* narrow opening or crack (in a rock, etc.).

¹crew [kru:] *n.* 1. all the persons working a ship, aircraft, rowing a boat, etc. 2. all these persons but the officers: *officers and* ~.

²crew, see **²crow.**

¹crib [krib] *n.* 1. baby's or child's bed with sides of rails or bars. 2. rack (framework) from which animals eat hay, etc. *v.t.* (-*bb*-). shut up in a small space.

²crib [krib] *n.* sth. copied dishonestly from the work of sb. else; word-for-word translation of a foreign text used by students of the language. *v.t. & i.* (-*bb*-). use a ~; copy (another's written work) dishonestly.

crick [krik] *n.* stiff condition of neck or back muscles causing sharp, sudden pain.

¹crick·et ['krikit] *n.* small brown jumping insect which makes a shrill noise by rubbing its wings together.

²crick·et ['krikit] *n.* ball game played on a grass field with bats and wickets by two teams of eleven players. *not* ~, (colloq.) unfair; unsportsman-like. ~·**er** *n.*

cried, cri·er, see *cry.*

crime [kraim] *n.* 1. offence(s) for which there is severe punishment by law; serious law-breaking; (in the army) serious breaking of rules, not necessarily an offence against the civil law. 2. foolish or wrong act (not necessarily an offence against the law). **crim·i·nal** ['kriminl] *adj.* of ~; guilty of ~. *n.* person who commits a ~ or ~s. **crim·i·nol·o·gy** [ˌkrimi'nolədʒi] *n.* science of ~; study of ~ and criminals.

crimp [krimp] *v.t.* make (e.g. hair) wavy or curly (as with a hot iron).

crim·son ['krimzən] *adj. & n.* deep red.

cringe [krindʒ] *v.i.* 1. move (the body) back or down in fear. 2. behave (towards a superior) in a way that shows lack of self-respect; be too humble.

crin·kle ['kriŋkl] *n.* small narrow wave or fold (in material such as cloth or paper). *v.t. & i.* make or get a ~ or ~s in.

crin·o·line ['krinəli:n] *n.* light framework covered with stiff material, formerly worn to make a skirt swell out; skirt with this.

crip·ple ['kripl] *n.* person unable to walk properly, through injury or disease in the spine or limbs. *v.t.* make a ~ of; damage or weaken seriously.

cri·sis ['kraisis] *n.* (pl. *crises* ['kraisi:z]). turning-point (in illness, life, history, etc.); time of danger or difficulty or anxiety about the future.

crisp [krisp] *adj.* (-*er*, -*est*). 1. hard, dry, and easily broken (esp. of food). 2. (of the weather, air) frosty, cold. **3.** with small tight curls or wrinkles: ~ *hair*. **4.** (of style, manners) quick, precise and decided. ~**ly** *adv*. ~**ness** *n*.

cri·te·ri·on [krai'tiəriən] *n.* (pl. -*ria* [-riə]). standard of judgement; principle by which sth. is measured for value.

crit·ic ['kritik] *n.* **1.** person who judges and writes about literature, art, music, etc. **2.** person who finds fault, points out mistakes, etc. **crit·i·cism** ['kritisizm] *n.* **1.** the work of a ~; judgement(s) given by a ~. **2.** fault-finding. **crit·i·cize** ['kritisaiz] *v.t. & i.* give a ~ism of; find fault (with).

crit·i·cal ['kritikl] *adj.* **1.** of or at a crisis: *a ~ moment in our history*; *a patient who is in a ~ condition*. **2.** of the work of a critic: ~ *opinions on literature*. **3.** fault-finding: ~ *remarks*. ~**ly** *adv*.

croak [krouk] *n.* hoarse sound (as) made by frogs and ravens. *v.t. & i.* **1.** make this sound; say or speak in a ~ing voice. **2.** express dismal views about the future; foretell evil.

cro·chet ['krouʃi, -ʃei] *v.t. & i.* make (needlework) with threads looped over others with the help of a small hook. *n.* needlework of this kind.

¹**crock** [krɔk] *n.* pot or jar made of baked earth, e.g. for containing water; broken piece of such a pot. ~**·er·y** ['krɔkəri] *n.* pots, plates, cups, and other dishes made of baked clay.

²**crock** [krɔk] *n.* (colloq.) broken-down animal (esp. horse); person who cannot work well because of bad health, lameness, etc. *v.i.* ~ *up*, become a ~.

croc·o·dile ['krɔkədail] *n.* river reptile with a long body and tail, covered with hard skin. ~ *tears*, insincere sorrow.

A crocodile

cro·cus ['kroukəs] *n.* early spring flower growing from a bulb.

cro·ny ['krouni] *n.* close friend.

crook [kruk] *n.* **1.** stick with a rounded hook at one end, esp. such a stick used by a shepherd. **2.** bend or curve. **3.** person who makes a living by dishonest or criminal means. *v.t. & i.* bend, curve, like a ~. ~**ed** ['krukid] *adj.* bent, not straight; (of a person, his actions) dishonest; not straightforward.

croon [kru:n] *v.t. & i.* hum or sing gently in a narrow range of notes: ~ *to oneself*; ~ *a lullaby*. ~**er** *n.* kind of entertainer.

¹**crop** [krɔp] *n.* **1.** yearly (or season's) produce of grain, grass, fruit, etc.: *the potato ~*; *a good ~ of wheat*; (pl.) agricultural plants in the fields: *to get the ~s in*. **2.** group of persons or things, amount of anything, appearing or produced together: *a ~ of questions put to the Minister of Defence*.

²**crop** [krɔp] *n.* **1.** bag-like part in a bird's throat where food is broken up for digestion before going into the stomach. **2.** handle of a whip. **3.** very short hair-cut.

³**crop** [krɔp] *v.t. & i.* (-*pp*-). **1.** (of animals) bite off the tops of (grass, plants, etc.). **2.** cut short (hair, a horse's tail or ears). **3.** ~ *up*, appear or arise unexpectedly: *difficulties that ~ped up*; ~ *up* (*out*), (of rock, minerals) show above the surface of the earth.

crop·per ['krɔpə*] *n.* come a ~, (colloq.) have a bad fall; meet with failure (e.g. in an examination).

cro·quet ['krouki] *n.* game played on short grass with wooden balls which are knocked with wooden mallets through hoops.

cro·sier, cro·zier ['krouʒə*] *n.* bishop's staff, usu. shaped like a shepherd's crook.

cross [krɔs] *n.* **1.** mark like this X: *at the place marked with a X*. **2.** see the picture on page 128. *the C~*, structure on which Jesus was crucified; (fig.) *sb.'s ~*, his burden of sorrow. **3.** offspring of two animals or plants of different sorts: *A mule is a ~ between a*

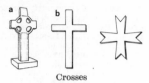

Crosses

horse and an ass. **adj. 1.** bad-tempered; irritable. **2.** passing or lying across; (of winds) contrary. **3.** be at ~ purposes, (of two persons) be talking of different things, having different purposes, etc., without realizing it. **v.t. & i. 1.** pass from one side to the other of: ~ the road; go across: ~ from Dover to Calais. **2.** ~ (sth.) out, cancel (sth. written) by drawing a line, etc., through it. ~ a cheque, draw two lines across it so that payment can be made only through a bank. ~ oneself, make the sign of the Cross with the hand as a religious act. **3.** produce a ~ (3) by mixing breeds, etc. **4.** oppose; obstruct (sb. or his plans or wishes). **5.** ~ one's mind, (of an idea) occur to, come into, the mind. **'~-bow n.** old kind of bow placed across a grooved wooden support. **'~-ex·'am·ine v.t.** question closely, esp. to test answers already given in answer to sb. else. **'~-eyed adj.** with one or both eyes turned towards the nose. **'~-'head·ing n.** (in a book, newspaper, etc.) short announcement printed across the column to point out the contents of what is beneath. **cros·sing n.** (level-~ing) place where a road and a railway ~; (street-~ing) place marked for ~ing a street. **'~-'ref·er·ence n.** reference from one part of a book to sth. in another book or another part of the same book. **'~-roads n.** (sing.) place where two roads ~; (fig.) time when one must make an important choice (of action, etc.). **'~-'sec·tion n.** (drawing of) what is seen when sth. is cut through vertically; (fig.) typical selection (of people or things).

'~-'wise adv. across; diagonally. **'~-word (puz·zle) n.** square with spaces in which letters forming words (indicated by clues) are to be written across and downwards. **~·ly adv.** irritably.

crotch·et ['krɔtʃit] **n. 1.** black-headed note (♩) in music. **2.** strange, unreasonable idea. **~·y adj.** full of ~s (2).

crouch [krautʃ] **v.i.** stoop with the limbs together (in fear, or to hide, or, of animals, ready to jump). **n.** ~ing position.

¹crow [krou] **n.** large, black bird with a harsh cry. as the ~ flies, in a straight line.

²crow [krou] **v.i.** (p.t. crowed or (only of birds) crew [kru:], p.p. crowed). **1.** (of a cock) cry. **2.** (of a baby) make sounds showing happiness. **3.** (of persons) express triumph at having succeeded: to ~ over a defeated enemy. **n.** ~ing sound.

crow-bar ['krouba:*] **n.** long iron bar or rod useful as a lever for moving heavy objects.

crowd [kraud] **n.** large number of people in one place, esp. out of doors: A ~ (C~s) of people watched the procession. **v.i. & t.** form, come together in, a ~; (cause to) fill a space: ~ a hall with people; ~ing into the buses.

crown [kraun] **n. 1.** ornamental head-dress of gold, jewels, etc., worn by a king or queen on special occasions. **2.** symbol, sign, of royal power or victory: the C~, royal authority; officer of the C~ (state official). **3.** top of the head or of a hat; part of a tooth that shows. **4.** half-crown, (formerly) British coin, value 2s. 6d. (= 12½p). **v.t. 1.** put a ~ (1) on (a king, etc.); reward as with a ~ (2). **2.** be or have at the top of: a hill ~ed with a wood.

cro·zier, see crosier.

cru·cial ['kru:ʃl, 'kru:ʃjəl] **adj.** critical (1).

cru·ci·ble ['kru:sibl] **n.** pot in which metals are melted.

cru·ci·fix ['kru:sifiks] **n.** small model of the Cross with the

figure of Jesus on it. **~ion**
[ˌkruːsiˈfikʃən] *n.* crucifying. *the
Crucifixion,* that of Jesus. **cru·
ci·fy** [ˈkruːsifai] *v.t.* put to death
by nailing or binding to a cross.
crude [kruːd] *adj.* **1.** (of materials) in a natural state; not
refined or manufactured: *~ oil
(sugar).* **2.** (of persons, their
behaviour) rough; not polite or
refined. **3.** of unskilled workmanship: *a ~ hut.* **~·ly** *adv.*
~·ness *n.* **cru·di·ty** [ˈkruːditi] *n.*
cruel [kruəl] *adj.* taking pleasure
in, causing or ready to cause,
pain or suffering. **~·ly** *adv.*
cru·el·ty *n.*
cru·et [ˈkruit] *n.* container(s) for
condiment(s) to be used at table.
cruise [kruːz] *v.i.* sail about,
either for pleasure, or (in war)
looking for enemy ships. *n.*
cruising voyage. **cruis·er** *n.*
large warship; *cabin-cruiser,*
motor-boat with a cabin, for
pleasure *~s.*
crumb [krʌm] *n.* very small
piece of dry food, esp. bit of
bread or cake rubbed off or
dropped from a large piece;
(fig.) small amount: *a few ~s
of comfort (information).*
crum·ble [ˈkrʌmbl] *v.t. & i.*
break or rub into crumbs or
small pieces: *crumbling cliffs.*
crum·ple [ˈkrʌmpl] *v.t. & i.*
press or crush into folds or
creases; become full of folds or
creases. *~ up,* crush (lit. & fig.)
collapse.
crunch [krʌntʃ] *v.t. & i.* crush
noisily with the teeth when eating; crush noisily under foot,
under wheels, etc. *n.* noise
made by *~ing.*
cru·sade [kruːˈseid] *n.* **1.** any
one of the wars made by the
Christian rulers and people of
Europe during the Middle Ages
to get the Holy Land back from
the Muslims. **2.** any struggle or
movement in support of sth.
believed to be good or against
sth. believed to be bad. *v.i.* take
part in a *~.* **cru·sad·er** *n.*
crush [krʌʃ] *v.t. & i.* press, be
pressed, so that there is breaking
or harming: *to ~ sth. to powder.*

n. crowd of people pressed together. **~·ing** *adj.* over-
whelming.
crust [krʌst] *n.* hard outer part
of bread; piece of this; hard
outer covering of a pie; hard
surface: *a ~ of ice; the earth's
~. v.t. & i.* cover with, form
into, a *~.* **~ed** *adj.* **1.** (of bread)
having much *~* or a hard *~.* **2.**
(of persons) easily made cross (1).
crutch [krʌtʃ] *n.* support put
under the arm to help a lame
person to walk: *a pair of ~es.*
crux [krʌks] *n.* part of a problem which is the most difficult
to solve.
cry [krai] *v.i. & t.* **1.** make (loud)
sounds of pain, grief, fear; weep,
shed tears. **2.** shout; announce;
advertise. *~ sth. down,* suggest
that it is worth little. *n.* **1.**
loud sound made in *~ing*; fit
of weeping. **2.** *in full ~,* (of a
pack of dogs) barking together
as they hunt or pursue (an
animal). **~·ing** *adj.* demanding
attention: *a ~ing evil (need).*
cri·er *n.* (esp. *town crier*) person
making public announcements.
crypt [kript] *n.* underground
room, esp. of a church, used for
burials.
cryp·tic [ˈkriptik] *adj.* secret;
with a hidden meaning or a
meaning not easily seen.
crys·tal [ˈkristl] *n.* **1.** clear,
natural substance like quartz;
piece of this cut as an ornament.
2. glassware of best quality
made into bowls, vessels, etc.
3. (science) one of the fragments,
regular and clearly defined in
shape, into which certain minerals separate naturally: *sugar
and salt ~s.* **'~-·gaz·ing** *n.*
looking into a *~* ball in an
attempt to see future events
pictured there. **~·line** [ˈkris-
təlain] *adj.* of or like *~.* **~·lize**
[ˈkristəlaiz] *v.t. & i.* form, cause
to form, into *~s*; cover (fruit,
sweets, etc.) with sugar *~s*;
(fig., of ideas, plans) become,
cause to be, clear and definite.
cub [kʌb] *n.* young lion, bear,
fox, tiger; badly-behaved young
man.

cube [kju:b] *n.* solid body having six equal square sides. **cu·bic** ['kju:bik] *adj.* ~-shaped; of a ~; *cubic foot*, volume of a ~ whose edge is twelve inches; *cubic content*, volume expressed in cubic feet (metres, etc.).

cu·bi·cle ['kju:bikl] *n.* small division of a larger room, walled or curtained to make a separate compartment, esp. for sleeping in.

cuck·oo ['kuku:] *n.* bird whose call sounds like its name; it lays its eggs in the nests of other birds.

cu·cum·ber ['kju:kʌmbə*] *n.* plant with long, green fleshy fruit used for salads, etc.

cud [kʌd] *n.* food which oxen and some other animals bring back from the first stomach and chew again.

cud·dle ['kʌdl] *v.t. & i.* hold close and lovingly in one's arms: *to ~ a doll.*

cud·gel ['kʌdʒəl] *v.t. & n.* (-*ll*-). (beat with a) short, thick stick.

¹**cue** [kju:] *n.* sth. (e.g. the last words of an actor's speech) which shows when sb. else is to do or say sth.

²**cue** [kju:] *n.* billiard-player's long stick.

¹**cuff** [kʌf] *n.* end of a shirt or coat sleeve at the wrist.

²**cuff** [kʌf] *v.t. & n.* (give sb. a) light blow with the fist or open hand.

cul-de-sac ['kuldə'sæk] *n.* street with an opening at one end only.

cu·li·na·ry ['kʌlinəri] *adj.* of cooking.

cul·mi·nate ['kʌlmineit] *v.i.* (of a career, efforts, hopes, etc.) reach the highest point. **cul·mi·na·tion** [ˌkʌlmi'neiʃən] *n.*

cul·pa·ble ['kʌlpəbl] *adj.* blameworthy; deserving punishment.

cul·prit ['kʌlprit] *n.* person who has done wrong; offender.

cult [kʌlt] *n.* system of religious belief and worship; devotion to a person, thing, or practice: *the ~ of archery.*

cul·ti·vate ['kʌltiveit] *v.t.* **1.** prepare (land) for crops by ploughing, etc.; help (crops) to grow. **2.** give care, thought, time, in order to develop sth.: *to ~ the mind* (one's manners, *sb.'s friendship*). **cul·ti·vat·ed** *adj.* (of a person) having good manners and education. **cul·ti·va·tion** [ˌkʌlti'veiʃən] *n.* **cul·ti·va·tor** ['kʌltiveitə*] *n.* (esp.) machine for breaking up ground, destroying weeds, etc.

cul·ture ['kʌltʃə*] *n.* **1.** advanced development of the human powers; development of the body, mind, and spirit by training and experience. **2.** evidence of intellectual development (of arts, science, etc.) in human society or of a particular nation: *Greek ~.* **3.** cultivating; the rearing of bees, silkworms, etc. **4.** growth of bacteria. **cul·tured** *adj.* (of a person) having ~ of the mind.

cul·vert ['kʌlvət] *n.* channel built to carry water or electric cables under the ground.

cum·ber·some ['kʌmbəsəm], **cum·brous** ['kʌmbrəs] *adj.* burdensome; heavy and awkward to move or carry.

cu·mu·la·tive ['kju:mjulətiv] *adj.* increasing in amount by one addition after another.

cu·mu·lus ['kju:mjuləs] *n.* rounded masses of cloud, flat on the under side. (Cf. *cirrus*.)

cu·ne·i·form ['kju:ni(i)fɔ:m] *adj.* wedge-shaped: *~ characters* (as used in Assyrian writing).

cun·ning ['kʌniŋ] *adj.* **1.** clever at deceiving; showing such cleverness: *a ~ old fox; a ~ trick.* **2.** (old use) skilful. *n.* quality of being ~. **~·ly** *adj.*

cup [kʌp] *n.* **1.** see the picture on page 131. **2.** vessel (usu. gold or silver) given as a prize in competitions. *v.t.* (-*pp*-). put into the shape of a cup: *to cup one's hands.*

cup·board ['kʌbəd] *n.* set of shelves enclosed by a door, either a separate piece of furniture or built into a room, used for stores(3), dishes, clothes, etc.

cu·pid·i·ty [kju:'piditi] *n.* greed, esp. for money or property.

A cup (1)
and saucer

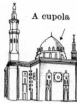

A cupola

cu·po·la ['kjuːpələ] *n.* small dome.

cur [kəː*] *n.* bad-tempered or worthless dog; cowardly or badly-behaved man.

cur·a·ble, cur·a·tive, see cure.

cu·rate ['kjuərit] *n.* clergyman who helps a rector or vicar.

cu·ra·cy ['kjuərəsi] *n.* ~'s office (3) and work.

cu·ra·tor [kjuə'reitə*] *n.* official in charge, esp. of a museum.

¹curb [kəːb] *n.* chain or leather strap under a horse's lower jaw, used to control it; sth. that restrains: *to keep a ~ on one's temper. v.t.* control (a horse) by means of a ~; keep (feelings, etc.) under control.

²curb = kerb.

curd [kəːd] *n.* thick, soft substance formed when milk turns sour, used to make cheese. **~le** ['kəːdl] *v.t. & i.* form, cause to form, into ~s; become ~-like.

cure [kjuə*] *v.t.* **1.** bring back to health; make well again. **2.** take away, get rid of, sth. wrong or evil: *to ~ poverty*. **3.** treat (meat, fish, skins, tobacco, etc.) in order to keep in good condition. *n.* curing or being ~d; substance or treatment which ~s. **cur·a·ble** ['kjuərəbl] *adj.* that can be ~d. **cur·a·tive** ['kjuərətiv] *adj.* helping to, able to, ~ ill health.

cur·few ['kəːfjuː] *n.* **1.** (old use) ringing of a bell as a signal for lights to be put out and fires covered; bell for this; hour at which the bell was rung. **2.** time or signal (under martial law) for people to remain indoors.

cu·ri·o ['kjuəriou] *n.* work of art of a strange or unusual character and therefore valued.

cu·ri·ous ['kjuəriəs] *adj.* **1.** eager to learn or know. **2.** having or showing too much interest in the affairs of others: ~ *neighbours.* **3.** strange; unusual; difficult to understand. **cu·ri·os·i·ty** [ˌkjuəri'ositi] *n.* **1.** being ~. **2.** ~(3) thing. **~·ly** *adv.*

curl [kəːl] *n.* sth. shaped like or twisted into a shape like the thread of a screw: ~*s of hair falling over a girl's shoulders; to keep one's hair in ~ with pins. v.t. & i.* make into ~s; grow or be in ~s: *to ~ up in a big chair; smoke ~ing upwards.* **~·y** *adj.* full of ~s; arranged in ~s: ~*y hair.*

cur·rant ['kʌrənt] *n.* **1.** small, sweet dried grape used in cooking. **2.** (bush with) small black, white, or red juicy fruit growing in clusters.

cur·ren·cy ['kʌrənsi] *n.* **1.** being current (1): *words in common ~.* **2.** the money at present in use in a country.

¹cur·rent ['kʌrənt] *adj.* **1.** in common or general use: ~ *words (coin).* **2.** now passing; of the present time: *the ~ year* (this year); *the ~ issue of a magazine.*

²cur·rent ['kʌrənt] *n.* **1.** stream of water, air, or gas, esp. one flowing through slower-moving or still water, etc. **2.** flow of electricity through sth. or along a wire, etc. **3.** course or movement (of events, thought, opinions, life).

cur·ric·u·lum [kə'rikjuləm] *n.* course of study in a school, college, etc.

¹cur·ry ['kʌri] *n.* dish of food (meat, eggs, etc.) cooked with ~-powder (made from hot-tasting spices). *v.t.* prepare (food) with ~-powder.

²cur·ry ['kʌri] *v.t.* rub down or clean (a horse) with a special comb. ~ *favour with*, try to win the favour or approval of (by using flattery, etc.).

curse [kəːs] *n.* **1.** words or phrases calling for the punishment, injury, or destruction of sb. or sth. **2.** word or words used in violent language expressing anger. **3.** cause of misfortune, ruin, etc.: *Gambling is often a ~. v.t. & i.* **1.** use a ~ against; use violent language. **2.** be ~d with, suffer misfortune, trouble, etc., because of: *to be ~d with idle daughters.* **cur·sed** ['kə:sid] *adj.* hateful; deserving to be ~d: *This work is a ~d nuisance.*

cur·so·ry ['kə:səri] *adj.* (of work, reading, etc.) quick; hurried; done without attention to details: *a ~ glance (inspection).*

curt [kə:t] *adj.* (of a speaker or what he says) short-spoken; hardly polite. **~·ly** *adv.*

cur·tail [kə:'teil] *v.t.* make shorter than was at first planned: *to ~ a speech (one's holidays).* **~·ment** *n.*

cur·tain ['kə:tn] *n.* **1.** piece of cloth or lace hung in front of a window, door, etc. **2.** sheet of heavy material separating the stage of a theatre from the part where the audience sits. **3.** sth. that hides or covers like a ~. *v.t.* furnish with ~s.

curt·sey ['kə:tsi] *n.* movement of respect (bending the knees) made by women and girls (e.g. to a queen). *v.i.* make a ~.

curve [kə:v] *n.* line of which no part is straight, thus: ∩. *v.t. & i.* have, cause to have, the form of a curve. **cur·va·ture** ['kə:vətʃə*] *n.* curving; state of being ~d: *the curvature of the earth's surface.*

cush·ion ['kuʃən] *n.* small bag filled with feathers, etc. (to make a seat more comfortable).

cus·tard ['kʌstəd] *n.* mixture of eggs and milk, sweetened and flavoured, baked or boiled.

cus·to·dy ['kʌstədi] *n.* (duty of) keeping safe, under one's control, caring for. **cus·to·di·an** [kʌs'toudiən] *n.* person who has ~ of sb. or sth.; caretaker of a public building.

cus·tom ['kʌstəm] *n.* **1.** generally accepted behaviour among members of a social group. (Cf. *habit* (1) for sth. done regularly

by an individual.) **2.** regular support given to a tradesman by those who buy his goods: *to take away one's ~ from a shop because prices are too high.* **3.** (pl.) tax due to the government on goods imported into a country; import duties; department of government collecting such taxes. (Cf. ¹*excise.*) **~·a·ry** ['kʌstəməri] *adj.* in agreement with, according to, ~. **~·er** *n.* **1.** person who gives his ~ (2) to a tradesman; person buying things in a shop. **2.** (colloq.) person or fellow, esp.: *a queer (awkward) ~er.* '**~(s)-house** *n.* office at a port or station where ~s (3) are collected.

cut [kʌt] *v.t. & i.* (present part. *cutting,* p.t. & p.p. *cut*). **1.** divide or separate; make an opening, tear, or wound in (using a knife, razor, pair of scissors, etc.). **2.** (with adv., prep. or adj.) cut sth. *down,* make smaller in size or amount. cut sth. *or sb. off,* stop, separate, or interrupt: *to cut off the enemy's retreat; to be cut off while telephoning.* to cut sth. *out,* remove, make, or shape by cutting: *to cut out a picture from a magazine; to cut out a dress (from cloth).* be cut *out for,* be suited to; have the necessary qualities for: *He's not cut out for that sort of work.* cut sth. *up,* cut to pieces; destroy. be cut *up by,* be made very unhappy by. cut sth. *short,* make short(er): *to cut a long story short.* cut at sth., aim a sharp blow at (e.g. with a stick). cut *in(to),* interrupt. **3.** pass (a person) and pretend not to know (him): *to cut a man in the street.* **4.** stay away from (a class or lecture at school, etc.). **5.** cut *a tooth,* have a new tooth showing through the gums. cut *cards,* (in card games) divide the pack into two parts. cut *both ways,* (of an argument, etc.) have advantages and disadvantages. cut *a loss,* accept it and make a fresh start. cut *and dried,* (of opinions, plans, etc.) all decided and ready. *n.* **1.** act of cutting; stroke, blow, with a knife, razor, sword, or whip. **2.** sth. obtained

by cutting: *a nice cut of beef.* **3.**
style in which clothes, etc., are
made by cutting: *the cut of a
coat.* **4.** sharp, quick stroke: *a
cut to the boundary* (in cricket).
cut·ter *n.* **1.** person or thing that
cuts: *a tailor's cutter*; *wire-
cutters.* **2.** sailing-vessel with
one mast. **3.** warship's boat
for rowing or sailing to or from
it.   '**cut-throat** *n.* murderer
who uses violent methods. *adj.*
(fig.) deadly: *cut-throat competition.* **cut·ting** *n.* **1.** unroofed passage dug through
ground (for a road, railway,
canal, etc.). **2.** sth. cut from a
newspaper, etc. **3.** short piece
of stem, etc., cut from a plant,
to be used for growing a new
plant. *adj.* (of words, etc.) unkind; wounding the feelings.
cute [kju:t] *adj.* sharp-witted,
quick-thinking.
cu·ti·cle ['kju:tikl] *n.* outer layer
of skin (esp. at the base of the
finger-nails).
cut·lass ['kʌtləs] *n.* sailor's short
sword; cacao-grower's, copra-
grower's, cutting tool.
cut·ler ['kʌtlə*] *n.* man who
makes or repairs knives and
other cutting instruments. ~'**y**
n. cutting instruments (knives,
scissors, etc.).
cut·let ['kʌtlit] *n.* thick slice of
meat or fish cut off before cooking.
cy·cle ['saikl] *n.* **1.** series of
events taking place in a regularly
repeated group: *the ~ of the
seasons*; complete set or series.
2. (short for) bicycle. *v.i.* ride
a bicycle. **cy·clist** ['saiklist]
n. person who rides a bicycle.
cy·clone ['saikloun] *n.* violent
wind moving round a calm central area.
cy·clo·pae·dia *n.* = encyclopaedia.
cyl·in·der ['silində*] *n.* **1.** solid
or hollow body shaped as in this
diagram. **2.** ~-shaped chamber
(in an engine) in which gas or
steam works a piston: *a six-~
motor-car.* **cy·lin·dri·cal** [si'lin-
drikl] *adj.*

Cylinders

cym·bal ['simbl] *n.* one of a pair
of round metal plates struck
together to make clanging
sounds.
cyn·ic ['sinik] *n.* person who
finds pleasure in detecting and
sneering at human weaknesses.
cyn·i·cal ['sinikl] *adj.* of or like
a ~;   contemptuous. **cyn·i·
cism** ['sinisizm] *n.*
cy·no·sure ['sinəзjuə*] *n.* sth. or
sb. that draws everyone's attention.
cy·pher *n.* = cipher.
cy·press ['saiprəs] *n.* evergreen
tree with dark leaves and hard
wood.

D

dab [dæb] *v.t. & i.* (-*bb*-). touch,
put on, lightly and gently. *n.*
quick, light touch; small quantity (of paint, etc.) dabbed on
sth.
dab·ble ['dæbl] *v.t. & i.* **1.** splash
(the hands, feet, etc.) about in
water. **2.** ~ *in* (politics, art,
etc.), take an interest in, study,
but not seriously.
dad(dy) ['dæd(i)] *n.* child's word
for 'father'. **dad·dy-long-legs**
['dædi'loŋlegz] *n.* long-legged
flying insect.
daf·fo·dil ['dæfədil] *n.* yellow
flower with long narrow leaves
growing from a bulb.
dag·ger ['dægə*] *n.* short, pointed, two-edged knife used as a
weapon.
dah·lia ['deiljə] *n.* garden plant
with bright-coloured flowers.
dai·ly ['deili] *adj. & adv.* happening, done, appearing, every

day (or every weekday). **n.** newspaper published every weekday.

dain·ty ['deinti] **adj.** (-*ier*, -*iest*). **1.** delicate (1), (7), in appearance or to the taste: ~ *china* (*food*). **2.** (of a person) having delicate(5) tastes; difficult to please. **n.** choice and delicate (1), (7), food. **dain·ti·ly** **adv.** **dain·ti·ness n.**

dair·y ['dɛəri] **n.** **1.** building or part of building where milk is kept and butter made. **2.** shop selling milk, butter, eggs, etc. ~-*farm*, one producing milk, etc.; ~*maid*, girl or woman working in a farm ~.

da·is ['deiis] **n.** low platform for a lecturer, a throne, etc., facing an audience.

dai·sy ['deizi] **n.** small white flower with a yellow centre, commonly growing wild; similar garden flower.

dale [deil] **n.** valley.

dal·li·ance ['dæliəns] **n.** trifling behaviour; love-making for amusement.

dal·ly ['dæli] **v.i.** **1.** waste time. **2.** ~ *with*, trifle with; think idly about.

¹dam [dæm] **n.** wall to hold back water. **v.t.** make a ~ across; hold back by means of a ~.

²dam [dæm] **n.** mother (of an animal).

dam·age ['dæmidʒ] **n.** **1.** harm, injury, causing loss of value. **2.** (pl.) (law) money asked from or paid by a person causing loss or injury. **v.t.** cause ~ (1) to.

dam·ask ['dæməsk] **n.** silk or linen material with designs shown by reflection of light.

dame [deim] **n.** **1.** (old use) woman, esp. married woman. **2.** (title of) woman who has received an honour corresponding to that of knighthood: *D~ of the Order of the British Empire*.

damn [dæm] **v.t.** **1.** condemn to everlasting punishment. **2.** say that sth. is worthless, bad, etc.: *a book* ~*ed by the critics*. **3.** (esp. as int.) used to express anger, annoyance, etc. *I'll be* ~*ed if I'll* . . ., I refuse to. . . . **dam·na·ble** ['dæmnəbl]

adj. deserving ~*ation*; hateful. **dam·na·bly** **adv.** **dam·na·tion** [dæm'neiʃən] **n.** being ~*ed*; ruin.

damp [dæmp] **adj.** (-*er*, -*est*). not quite dry; having some moisture (in or on): ~ *clothes*; *to wipe a window with a* ~ *cloth*. **n.** **1.** state of being ~. **2.** (also *fire-*~) dangerous gas which may collect in coal-mines. **v.t.** **1.** make ~. **2.** (also ~*en*) make sad or dull. **3.** ~ *down* (*a fire*), cause to burn slowly. ~·*er* **n.** **1.** metal plate which regulates the flow of air through a fire in a stove or furnace. **2.** person or thing that ~*s* (1), (2). ~·*ness* **n.**

dam·sel ['dæmzl] **n.** (old use) girl; young unmarried woman.

dam·son ['dæmzən] **n.** (tree producing) small dark purple plum.

dance [dɑ:ns] **v.i. & t. & n.** see the picture.

Dancing

dan·de·li·on ['dændilaiən] **n.** common wild plant with bright yellow flowers.

dan·dle ['dændl] **v.t.** move (e.g. a child) up and down on one's knee(s) or in the arms.

dan·dy ['dændi] **n.** person who pays great attention to his clothes and personal appearance.

dan·ger ['deindʒə*] **n.** chance of suffering, receiving injury, or being killed. ~·*ous* **adj.** likely to be a ~ or cause ~ to. ~·*ous·ly* **adv.**

dan·gle ['dæŋgl] **v.i. & t.** **1.** hang or swing loosely; hang or carry (sth.) so that it swings loosely. **2.** ~ *round* (*about, after, sb.*), stay near (sb.) as a follower, lover, etc.

dank [dæŋk] **adj.** **1.** wet: ~ *undergrowth in a forest*. **2.** unpleasantly damp: ~ *weather* (*climate, air*).

dap·per ['dæpə*] *adj.* well and smartly dressed; neat.

dap·ple ['dæpl] *v.t. & i.* mark with patches of different colours or shades of colour, esp. of an animal, of sunlight and shadow.

dare [deə*] *v.t.* (p.t. **dared** or, less often, **durst** [də:st]). **1.** be brave enough to; be bold or impudent enough to: *How ~ you say that I am a liar? I ~ say*, I think it likely, it seems to me probable: *He's not here yet, but I ~ say he will come later.* **2.** attempt; face the risks of (sth.): *to ~ any danger; to ~ sb.'s anger.* **3.** suggest that a person is unwilling to do sth.; challenge: *to ~ sb. to jump across a stream.* '**~·,dev'il** *adj. & n.* foolishly bold (person). **dar·ing** *n. & adj.* (quality of being) bold and adventurous.

dark [dɑ:k] *adj.* (-er, -est). **1.** with no or very little light. **2.** (of colour) deep (3) ~ *keep sth. ~*, keep it secret. *look on the ~ side of things*, see only what is sad or cheerless. *n.* absence of light: *We came home in the ~. keep sb. in the ~*, keep things secret from him. *be in the ~ about*, have no knowledge of. **~·en** *v.t. & i.* make or become ~. **~·ly** *adv.* **~·ness** *n.*

dar·ling ['dɑ:liŋ] *n. & adj.* (person or object) much loved.

darn [dɑ:n] *v.t. & i.* mend (esp. a hole in sth. knitted, e.g. a sock) by passing thread in and out and across in two directions. *n.* place mended by ~ing. **~·ing** *n.* (esp.) things needing to be ~ed.

dart [dɑ:t] *v.i. & t.* (cause to) move forward suddenly and quickly: *to ~ out of a shop; a snake ~ing out its tongue. n.* **1.** small, sharp-pointed object, esp. one thrown at a ~board in the indoor game called ~s. **2.** quick, sudden movement.

dash [dæʃ] *v.t. & i.* **1.** send or throw violently; move, be moved, quickly and violently. **2.** (fig.) destroy; discourage: *to ~ a person's hopes.* **3.** splash (with water, mud, etc.). *n.* **1.** sudden and violent forward movement: *to make a ~ for shelter (freedom).* **2.** sound made by water, etc., when striking sth. or when being struck: *the ~ of the waves (of oars on the water).* **3.** small amount of sth. added or mixed: *a ~ of pepper in the soup.* **4.** stroke of the pen or a mark — used in printing. **5.** (capacity for) vigorous action; energy: *a soldier with plenty of ~.* **6.** *cut a ~*, appear to be rich (e.g. by spending money freely). **~·ing** ['dæʃiŋ] *adj.* showing energy, full of life(7) and gallantry(1): *a ~ing young officer.*

das·tard ['dæstəd] *n.* brutal coward; bully. **~·ly** *adj.*

da·ta ['deitə] *n. pl.* facts; things certainly known (from which conclusions may be drawn).

¹date [deit] *n.* **1.** statement of the day, month, year, when something happened or is due to happen. *out of ~*, no longer used; old-fashioned. *up to ~*, in line with, according to, what is now known, used, etc.: *up-to-~ ideas (methods, etc.).* **2.** (colloq.) meeting fixed with sb. at a certain time and place. *v.t. & i.* have, put, a ~ on; give a ~ to. *~ from, ~ back to*, have existed since: *a house dating from the 17th century.*

²date [deit] *n.* small, brown, sweet fruit of the ~-palm, common in N. Africa and W. Asia.

da·tive ['deitiv] *n.* form of a word (in Latin and other languages, but not English) showing that it is an indirect object of the verb.

daub [dɔ:b] *v.t. & i.* **1.** put (paint, clay, plaster, etc.) roughly on a surface. **2.** make dirty marks on. **3.** paint (pictures) without skill. *n.* material used for ~ing (e.g. clay); badly painted picture. **~·er** *n.*

daugh·ter ['dɔ:tə*] *n.* one's female child. '**~-in-law** *n.* one's son's wife.

daunt [dɔ:nt] *v.t.* discourage. **~·less** ['dɔ:ntlis] *adj.* not ~ed; persevering.

dav·it ['dævit] *n.* one of a pair of metal arms supporting a ship's boat. See the picture at *derrick*.

daw·dle ['dɔːdl] *v.i.* be slow; waste time. **daw·dler** *n.*

dawn [dɔːn] *n.* first light of day; (fig.) beginning: *the ~ of intelligence.* *v.i.* begin to grow light; (fig.) begin to appear: ~ *on sb.,* grow clear to his mind.

day [dei] *n.* **1.** time between sunrise and sunset; period of twenty-four hours, from midnight. *pass the time of day (with sb.),* exchange greetings, etc. (with). *the other day,* a few days ago. *one day,* on a day (past or future). *some day,* on some day in the future. *have one's day,* have a period of power, success, etc. **2.** event; contest. *The day is ours. We've won the day* (i.e. we have won). **'day·break** *n.* dawn. **'day·dream** *v.i. & n.* (have) idle, pleasant thoughts. **'day·light** *n.* light of day, from dawn to darkness. **'day·light-ˌsav·ing** *n.* putting the hands of the clock forward so that darkness falls at a later hour.

daze [deiz] *v.t.* make (sb.) feel stupid or unable to think clearly. *n. in a ~,* in a ~d state.

daz·zle ['dæzl] *v.t.* make (sb.) unable to see clearly or act naturally because of too much light, brilliance, splendour, etc.: ~*d by bright lights; dazzling sunshine* (*diamonds, beauty*).

dea·con ['diːkən] *n.* minister or officer who has various duties in certain Christian churches. ~**·ess** *n.*

dead [ded] *adj.* **1.** (of plants, animals, persons) no longer living; (of matter) never having had life. **2.** without movement or activity: *the ~ hours of the night.* **3.** complete: *in ~ earnest; to come to a ~ stop.* **4.** used up; not working: *a ~ match* (one that has already been used). *The telephone is ~.* ~ *letter,* rule, law, etc., to which attention is no longer paid; letter kept by the post office because the person to whom it is addressed cannot be found. **5.** exact: ~ *heat,* race,

etc., in which two or more persons, horses, etc., reach the winning-post together. ~ *shot,* one going to the exact point aimed at. *in the ~ centre,* exactly in the centre. *adv.* absolutely: ~ *beat* (*tired*) (i.e. tired out, exhausted). *n. the ~ of night,* the darkest and quietest part. ~**·en** ['dedn] *v.t.* take away force or feeling: *drugs to ~en pain.* ~**·ly** *adj.* causing, likely to cause, death. *adv.* deathly. '~**·line** *n.* fixed limit of time for completion, etc. '~**·lock** *n.* complete failure to settle a grievance or quarrel.

deaf [def] *adj.* (*-er, -est*). unable to hear; (fig.) unwilling to listen. ~**·en** ['defn] *v.t.* make so much noise that hearing is difficult or impossible: ~*ening cheers.* ~**·ness** *n.*

¹deal [diːl] *n.* (board of) fir or pinewood: *a ~ table.*

²deal [diːl] *n. a good* (*great*) ~ (*of*), very much, a lot (of). *a good ~ better,* (very) much better.

³deal [diːl] *v.t. & i.* (*p.t. & p.p. dealt* [delt]). **1.** give out to several persons: *to ~ out money; to ~ cards.* **2.** ~ *a blow* (*at*), hit; strike. **3.** do business; buy from: *shops which ~ in goods of all kinds; to ~ with Smith, the butcher; to ~ at a small shop.* **4.** ~ *with,* (a) be about: *a book ~ing with E. Africa.* (b) behave towards; have relations with: *to ~ fairly with one's neighbours; people who are difficult to ~ with.* (c) attend to; manage: *a difficult problem to ~ with.* *n.* **1.** (in games, etc.) the act of ~ing cards. *a new ~,* a new plan or system, esp. one that is thought to be just or fair. *a square ~,* fair treatment. **2.** business agreement, esp. (colloq.) a bargain: *It's a ~* (i.e. I agree to the terms proposed). ~**·er** *n.* **1.** trader. **2.** person who ~s cards. ~**·ings** *n. pl.* business relations: *to have no ~ings with a dishonest man.*

dealt, see *³deal.*

dean [diːn] *n.* **1.** church officer at the head of a cathedral chapter. **2.** (in some universities) person with authority to maintain discipline; head of a department of studies. ~·er·y **n.** position or house of a ~ (1).

dear [diə*] **adj.** (-er, -est) & **n.** **1.** loved (person); lovable (person). **2.** polite form of address: *Dear Sir (Madam), Dear Miss Smith, My dear Jack.* **3.** high-priced in relation to value: *Potatoes are ~ this week.* **4.** precious: *Her house and garden are very ~ to her.* **adv.** *He got rich by buying cheap and selling ~.* **int.** (often with some other word: *Oh dear! Dear me!*) to express surprise, impatience, wonder, dismay, etc. ~·ly **adv.** **1.** very much: *He would ~ly love to see his mother again. He loved his mother ~ly.* **2.** at great cost: *Victory was ~ly won* (at the cost of many lives).

dearth [də:θ] **n.** scarcity; small supply (esp. of food).

death [deθ] **n.** ending of life; dying; killing or being killed: *The murderer was put to ~,* executed. '~-,du·ties **n.** **pl.** taxes to be paid on the property of a person who dies. ~·less **adj.** never dying; ~less *glory (fame).* ~·ly **adj.** like ~. '~-rate **n.** average number of persons who die each year among every 1,000 people. '~-trap **n.** dangerous place, esp. on a road.

de·bar [di'ba:*] **v.t.** (-rr-). shut out *(from)*; prevent (sb.) by a regulation *(from* doing or having sth.).

de·base [di'beis] **v.t.** make lower in value, poorer in quality, character, etc. ~·ment **n.**

de·bate [di'beit] **n.** discussion (esp. at a public meeting or in Parliament). **v.t. & i.** have a ~ about: take part in a ~; think over in order to decide. **de·bat·er n. de·bat·a·ble adj.** that can be ~d; open to question.

de·bauch [di'bɔ:tʃ] **v.t.** cause sb. to lose virtue, to turn away from good taste or judgement or to act immorally. **n.** occasion of over-drinking, immoral behav-

iour, usu. in company. ~·er·y [di'bɔ:tʃəri] **n.** act or practice of debauching.

de·ben·ture [di'bentʃə*] **n.** certificate given by a business corporation, etc., as a receipt for money lent at a fixed rate of interest till the loan is repaid.

de·bil·i·tate [di'biliteit] **v.t.** make (a person, his constitution) feeble. **de·bil·i·ty** [di'biliti] **n.** weakness (of health, purpose).

deb·it ['debit] **n.** entry (in an account) of a sum owing; left-hand side of an account, on which such entries are made. (Cf. *credit.*) **v.t.** put on the ~ side of an account.

deb·o·nair [,debə'nɛə*] **adj.** cheerful; bright and light-hearted.

de·bris, dé·bris ['deibri:] **n.** scattered broken pieces.

debt [det] **n.** payment that must be, but has not yet been, made to sb. *in, out of, ~,* owing, not owing, money. *National Debt,* money owed by the State to those who have lent it money. ~·or **n.** person in ~ to another.

dé·but ['deibu:] **n.** (esp. of a young woman) first appearance at adult parties and other social events; (of an actor, musician, etc.) first appearance on a public stage. **dé·bu·tante** [,deibu:-'tɔnt] **n.** young woman making her ~.

dec·ade ['dekeid, -əd] **n.** period of ten years.

dec·a·dent ['dekədənt] **adj.** (of a person, art, literature, community, society) becoming less worthy, honourable or moral (2). **dec·a·dence** ['dekədəns] **n.**

dec·a·logue ['dekələg] **n.** the Ten Commandments of Moses.

de·camp [di'kæmp] **v.i.** leave suddenly and often secretly.

de·cant [di'kænt] **v.t.** pour (wine) from a bottle into another vessel slowly and carefully so as not to disturb any sediment. ~·er **n.** vessel into which wine is ~ed before being brought to the table.

de·cap·i·tate [di'kæpiteit] **v.t.** cut off the head of.

de·car·bon·ize [di:'kɑ:bənaiz] *v.t.* remove carbon from (esp. the engine of a motor-car, etc.).

de·cay [di'kei] *v.i.* go bad; lose power, health : ~*ing teeth* (*fruit, empires*). *n.* ~*ing.*

de·cease [di'si:s] *n.* (esp. legal) (a person's) death. *the* ~*d,* (legal) person(s) who has (have) recently died.

de·ceit [di'si:t] *n.* deceiving. ~*·ful adj.* in the habit of deceiving; intended to deceive. ~*·ful·ly adv.* ~*·ful·ness n.*

de·ceive [di'si:v] *v.t.* cause (sb.) to believe sth. false; play a trick on; mislead, esp. on purpose. **de·ceiv·er** *n.* person who ~s.

de·cep·tion [di'sepʃən] *n.* deceiving; being ~d; trick intended to ~ sb. **de·cep·tive** [di'septiv] *adj.* deceiving; easily causing a person to be ~d. **de·cep·tive·ly** *adv.*

De·cem·ber [di'sembə*] *n.* the twelfth month of the year.

de·cent ['di:sənt] *adj.* 1. right and suitable; respectable. 2. modest; not likely to cause others to feel shame : ~ *language and behaviour.* 3. (colloq.) good; satisfactory : ~ *weather;* *a* ~ *meal.* ~*·ly adv.* **de·cen·cy** *n.* being ~; general opinion as to what is ~ : *an offence against decency.*

de·cen·tra·lize [di:'sentrəlaiz] *v.t.* give greater powers (for self-government, etc.) to (places, branches, etc., away from the centre). **de·cen·tra·li·za·tion** [di:ˌsentrəlai'zeiʃən] *n.*

de·cep·tion, de·cep·tive, see *deceive.*

dec·i- ['desi-] *prefix.* one-tenth : ~*metre,* ~*litre.*

de·cide [di'said] *v.t. & i.* 1. settle (a question, doubt); give judgement (*between, for, in favour of, against*). 2. think about and come to a conclusion; resolve. 3. cause to ~ (2). **de·cid·ed** *adj.* clear; definite; (of a person) having definite opinions. **de·cid·ed·ly** *adv.*

de·cid·u·ous [di'sidjuəs] *adj.* (of trees) losing their leaves regularly, esp. in autumn.

dec·i·mal ['desiml] *adj.* of tens or one-tenths : *the* ~ *system* (for money, weights and measures); *the* ~ *point* (e.g. the point in 15·61).

dec·i·mate ['desimeit] *v.t.* kill or destroy at least one-tenth of : *a population* ~*d by disease.*

de·ci·pher [di'saifə*] *v.t.* find the meaning of (sth. written in cipher, bad handwriting, sth. puzzling or difficult to understand).

de·ci·sion [di'siʒn] *n.* 1. deciding; making up one's mind; result of this; settlement (of a question) : *to come to a* ~. 2. ability to decide and act accordingly : *a man of* ~.

de·ci·sive [di'saisiv] *adj.* 1. causing the result of sth. to be decided or certain : *a* ~ *battle.* 2. (= decided) showing decision; definite. ~*·ly adv.*

¹deck [dek] *n.* floor in a ship, usu. of wooden planks, in or above the hull. *clear the* ~*s,* make ready for a fight; (fig.) make ready for activity of any kind.

²deck [dek] *v.t.* decorate (sth.).

de·claim [di'kleim] *v.t. & i.* speak with strong feeling (*against*); speak in the manner of addressing an audience or reciting a poem. **dec·la·ma·tion** [ˌdeklə'meiʃən] *n.*

de·clare [di'kleə*] *v.t. & i.* 1. make known publicly and clearly : *to* ~ *war* (*the result of an election*). 2. say solemnly or to show that one has no doubt or hesitation : *The accused man* ~*d that he was not guilty.* ~ *for* (*against*), say that one is in favour of (against) (sth.). 3. make a statement (to customs officials) of dutiable goods brought into a country. 4. (int.) *Well, I* ~! (expressing surprise). **dec·la·ra·tion** [ˌdeklə'reiʃən] *n.* declaring; that which is ~d : *a declaration of war.*

de·cline [di'klain] *v.t. & i.* 1. say 'no' to; refuse (sth. offered, sth. one is asked to do). 2. (of the sun) go down. 3. continue to become smaller, weaker, lower :

a declining birth-rate; prices beginning to ~; an empire that has ~d; a man's declining years (when, because of age, he is losing strength). **n.** declining; gradual and continued loss of strength. *fall into a ~*, lose strength; (esp.) suffer from tuberculosis.

de·cliv·i·ty [di'kliviti] **n.** downward slope.

de·clutch ['di:'klʌtʃ] **v.i.** disconnect the clutch (of a motorcar, etc.) so as to be ready to change gear.

de·code ['di:'koud] **v.t.** put in plain language (sth. written in code).

de·com·pose [ˌdi:kəm'pouz] **v.t. & i.** 1. separate (a substance) into its parts. 2. (cause to) become bad or rotten; decay. **de·com·po·si·tion** [ˌdi:kɔmpə'ziʃən] **n.**

de·con·tam·i·nate [ˌdi:kən'tæmineit] **v.t. & i.** remove that which poisons or spreads disease.

dec·o·rate ['dekəreit] **v.t.** 1. put ornaments on; make more beautiful by placing adornments on or in: *to ~ streets with flags (a church with flowers)*. 2. paint (a house); put new paper, etc., on (walls of rooms). 3. give (sb.) a mark of distinction or honour (e.g. a rank, medal, etc.): *~d for bravery in battle.* **dec·o·ra·tion** [ˌdekə'reiʃən] **n.** decorating; sth. used for decorating; medal, ribbon, etc., given and worn as an honour or reward. **dec·o·ra·tive** ['dekərətiv] **adj.** suitable for decorating(1); ornamental. **dec·o·ra·tor** ['dekəreitə*] **n.** (esp.) workman who ~s(2) houses.

de·co·rum [di'kɔ:rəm] **n.** right and proper behaviour, as required by good manners. **dec·or·ous** ['dekərəs] **adj.**

de·coy [di'kɔi] **n.** (real or imitation) bird or animal used to attract others so that they may be caught; person or thing used to tempt sb. into a position of danger. **v.t.** trick into a place of danger by means of a ~.

de·crease [di'kri:s] **v.i. & t.** (cause to) become shorter, smaller, less. ['di:kri:s] **n.** decreasing; amount by which sth. ~s: *Is crime on the ~?*

de·cree [di'kri:] **n.** 1. order given by a ruler or authority and having the force of a law. 2. judgement or decision by some law courts. **v.t. & i.** make a ~ *(that).*

de·crep·it [di'krepit] **adj.** made weak by old age. **de·crep·i·tude** [di'krepitju:d] **n.** being ~.

de·cry [di'krai] **v.t.** try, by speaking against sth., to make it seem less valuable or useful.

ded·i·cate ['dedikeit] **v.t.** 1. give up (*to a noble cause or purpose*): *to ~ one's life to missionary work.* 2. devote with solemn ceremonies (to God, to a sacred use): *to ~ a new church building.* 3. (of an author) write (or print) a person's name at the beginning of a book (to show gratitude or friendship). **ded·i·ca·tion** [ˌdedi'keiʃən] **n.** dedicating; (esp.) words used in dedicating a book.

de·duce [di'dju:s] **v.t.** arrive at (knowledge, a theory, etc.) by reasoning (*from* facts); reach a conclusion (*from*).

de·duct [di'dʌkt] **v.t.** take away (an amount or part). (Cf. *subtract* for numbers.)

de·duc·tion [di'dʌkʃən] **n.** 1. the act of deducting; amount deducted. 2. deducing; conclusion reached by reasoning from general laws to a particular case. **de·duc·tive adj.** of, reasoning by, ~ (2).

deed [di:d] **n.** 1. sth. done; act: *to be rewarded for one's good ~s.* 2. (legal) written (or printed) and signed agreement, esp. about ownership or rights.

deem [di:m] **v.t.** believe; consider.

deep [di:p] **adj.** (-er, -est). 1. going far down from the surface or top. 2. going far in from the front: *a ~ shelf.* 3. (of colour) dark; strong (cf. *pale*). 4. (of sounds) low. 5. (of persons) inclined to secrecy; having ways of thinking and behaving that are difficult to understand. 6.

(of feelings) keen, intense: ~ *sorrow*. **7.** ~ *in* (*thought, study, etc.*), having all one's attention centred on. *adv.* far down or in. *n. the* ~, (in poetry) the sea. ~**·en** ['diːpn] *v.t. & i.* make or become ~(er). ~**·ly** *adv.*

deer [diə*] *n.* graceful, quick-running animal, the male of which has horns.

de·face [di'feis] *v.t.* spoil the appearance of (by marking, damaging, the surface of).

de·fame [di'feim] *v.t.* attack the good reputation of; say evil things about. **def·a·ma·tion** [ˌdefə'meiʃən] *n.* **de·fam·a·to·ry** [di'fæmətəri] *adj.* intended to ~.

de·fault [di'fɔːlt] *v.i.* fail to perform a duty, or to appear (e.g. in a court of law) when required to do so, or to pay a debt. *n.* act of ~ing. *by* ~, because the other person (or side) did not appear: *to win a case* (*a game*) *by* ~. *in* ~ *of*, in the absence of; if (sth.) is not to be obtained, does not take place, etc. ~**·er** *n.* person (esp. a soldier) who fails to perform a duty.

de·feat [di'fiːt] *v.t.* **1.** overcome; beat; win a victory over. **2.** bring to nothing; make useless: *Our hopes were ~ed. n.* ~ing or being ~ed. ~**·ism** [di'fiːtizm] *n.* attitude, argument, conduct, based on expectation of ~.

de·fect [di'fekt] *n.* fault; imperfection; shortcoming; sth. lacking in completeness or perfection: ~*s in a system of education. v.i.* ¹*desert* (2) (from the army, allegiance, etc.). **de·fec·tion** [di'fekʃən] *n.* (instance of) falling away from loyalty to a cause (3). **de·fec·tive** [di'fektiv] *adj.* having a ~ or ~s. *mentally ~ive*, not quite sane.

de·fence [di'fens] *n.* **1.** defending from attack; fighting against attack. **2.** sth. that protects or guards against attack. **3.** (law) argument(s) used in favour of an accused person; the lawyer(s) acting for such a person. ~**·less** *adj.* having no ~; unable to defend oneself.

de·fend [di'fend] *v.t.* **1.** guard;

protect; make safe. **2.** speak or write in support of (an accused person, etc.) **de·fen·dant** *n.* person against whom a legal action is brought. **de·fen·der** [di'fendə*] *n.* (football) player who guards the goal area. **de·fen·si·ble** [di'fensibl] *adj.* able to be ~ed. **de·fen·sive** [di'fensiv] *adj.* used for, intended for, ~ing. *n. on the defensive*, ready to ~; resisting, expecting, attack.

¹**de·fer** [di'fə:*] *v.t.* (-*rr*-). put off to a later time; postpone: *a* ~*red telegram* (sent later at a cheaper rate). ~**·ment** *n.*

²**de·fer** [di'fə:*] *v.t.* (-*rr*-). ~ *to*, give way to; yield to (often to show respect): *to* ~ *to one's elders* (*to sb.'s opinions*). **def·er·ence** ['defərəns] *n.* ~ring; respect: *in* ~ *ence to the opinion of the court.* **def·er·en·tial** [ˌdefə'renʃl] *adj.* showing great respect.

de·fi·ance, de·fi·ant, see *defy.*

de·fi·cient [di'fiʃənt] *adj.* wanting (*in*); not having enough of: ~ *in courage*; *mentally* ~ (weak-minded; half-witted). **de·fi·cien·cy** [di'fiʃənsi] *n.* being ~; amount by which sth. is ~.

def·i·cit ['de-, 'di:fisit] *n.* amount by which sth. (esp. a sum of money) is too small; amount by which payments exceed receipts. (Cf. *surplus.*)

¹**de·file** [di'fail] *v.t.* make unclean or impure. ~**ment** *n.*

²**de·file** ['di:fail, di'fail] *n.* narrow way, gorge, between mountains.

de·fine [di'fain] *v.t.* **1.** explain the meaning of (e.g. words). **2.** state or show clearly: *to* ~ *sb.'s duties* (*powers*); *hills clearly* ~*d* (= outlined) *against the sky.* **3.** lay down, decide the shape, outlines, or limits of sth.: *to* ~ *a country's boundaries.* **def·i·nite** ['definit] *adj.* clear; not doubtful or uncertain. *definite article*, the word 'the'. **def·i·ni·tion** [ˌdefi'niʃən] *n.* **1.** defining; statement that ~s. **2.** clearness of outline; making or being distinct in outline. **de·fin·i·tive** [di'finitiv] *adj.* final; to be looked upon as decisive and without need for, possibility of, change or addition.

de·flate [di:'fleit] *v.t.* **1.** make (a tyre, balloon, etc.) smaller by letting out air or gas. **2.** take action to reduce the amount of money in circulation, in order to lower prices of salable goods. (Cf. *inflate*.) **de·fla·tion** [di:'fleiʃən] *n.*

de·flect [di'flekt] *v.t. & i.* (cause to) turn aside (*from*). **de·flec·tion** [di'flekʃən] *n.*

de·form [di'fɔ:m] *v.t.* spoil the form or appearance of; put out of shape. **de·formed** *adj.* (esp. of the body, or part of the body; fig. of the mind) badly shaped; unnaturally formed. ~·i·ty [di'fɔ:miti] *n.* being ~ed ; ~ed part of the body.

de·fraud [di'frɔ:d] *v.t.* trick (sb.) out of what is rightly his: *to ~ an author of his royalties by ignoring copyright.*

de·fray [di'frei] *v.t.* supply the money needed for sth.; pay (the cost or expenses of sth.).

de·frost [di:'frɔst] *v.t.* remove frost (from a refrigerator, the windscreen of a motor-car, etc.).

deft [deft] *adj.* quick and clever (esp. at doing things with the fingers); (of work) showing such skill. ~·ly *adv.* ~·ness *n.*

de·funct [di'fʌŋkt] *adj.* dead; no longer existing or in use.

de·fy [di'fai] *v.t.* **1.** resist openly; say that one is ready to fight. **2.** refuse to obey or show respect to: *to ~ the law (one's superiors).* **3.** ~ *sb. to do sth.,* call on sb. to do sth. one believes he cannot or will not do. **4.** offer difficulties that cannot be overcome. **de·fi·ance** [di'faiəns] *n.* ~ing; refusal to obey, to show respect to: *to act in defiance of orders; to set the law at defiance.* **de·fi·ant** [di'faiənt] *adj.* showing defiance; openly disobedient.

de·gen·er·ate [di'dʒenəreit] *v.i.* pass from a state of goodness to a lower state by losing qualities which are considered desirable. [di'dʒenərit] *adj.* having ~d. *n.* ~ person. **de·gen·er·a·tion** [di-ˌdʒenə'reiʃən] *n.* degenerating; being ~.

de·grade [di'greid] *v.t.* **1.** move (e.g. a soldier) down to a lower rank or position, usu. as a punishment. **2.** cause (sb.) to be less moral or less deserving of respect: *to ~ oneself by cheating (living an idle life).* **deg·ra·da·tion** [ˌdegrə'deiʃən] *n.*

de·gree [di'gri:] *n.* **1.** unit of measurement for angles: *an angle of ninety ~s* (90°). **2.** unit of measurement for temperature *Water freezes at 32 ~s* (32°) *Fahrenheit or zero Centigrade.* **3.** step or stage in a scale or process showing extent, quantity, or progress: *various ~s of skill; a high ~ of excellence. by ~s,* gradually; step by step; slowly. *to a high (to the last) ~,* intensely ; exceedingly. *to what ~,* to what extent. **4.** position in society: *people of high ~.* **5.** rank or grade given by a university to one who has passed an examination: *the ~ of Master of Arts.* **6.** (grammar) one of the three forms of comparison of an adjective or adverb: *'Good', 'better', and 'best' are the positive, comparative, and superlative ~s of 'good'.*

de·hy·drate [di:'haidreit] *v.t.* deprive (a substance) of water or moisture: *~d vegetables.*

de-ice ['di:'ais] *v.t.* remove ice (e.g. from the wings of an aeroplane).

de·i·fy ['di:ifai] *v.t.* make a god of; worship as a god.

deign [dein] *v.t.* condescend; be kind and gracious enough (*to do* sth.).

de·i·ty ['di:iti] *n.* **1.** divine quality or nature; state of being a god(dess). **2.** god(dess): *the Greek deities. the Deity,* God.

de·ject·ed [di'dʒektid] *adj.* sad; gloomy; in low spirits; hopeless. **de·jec·tion** [di'dʒekʃən] *n.* ~ state.

de·lay [di'lei] *v.t. & i.* **1.** make or be slow or late. **2.** put off until later. *n.* ~ing or being ~ed: *to start without ~.*

de·lec·ta·ble [di'lektəbl] *adj.* pleasant; delightful.

del·e·gate ['deligeit] *v.t.* 1. appoint and send as a representative to a meeting. 2. entrust (one's duties, rights, etc.) *to* sb. ['deligit] *n.* person to whom sth. is ~d. **del·e·ga·tion** [ˌdeli-'geifən] *n.* delegating; group of persons to whom sth. is ~d.

de·lete [di(:)'li:t] *v.t.* strike or take out (sth. written or printed). **de·le·tion** [di(:)'li:fən] *n.* deleting; sth. ~d.

de·lib·er·ate [di'libəreit] *v.t. & i.* consider, talk about, carefully. [di'libərit] *adj.* 1. done on purpose; intentional: *a ~ insult.* 2. slow and cautious (in action, speech, etc.). ~·ly *adv.* **de·lib·er·a·tion** [diˌlibə'reifən] *n.* deliberating; being ~; discussion, esp. with arguments for and against.

del·i·cate ['delikit] *adj.* 1. soft; tender; of fine or thin material: *as ~ as silk.* 2. easily injured; becoming ill easily; needing great care: *~ china (plants); a ~-looking child.* 3. requiring careful treatment or skilful handling: *a ~ surgical operation.* 4. (of colours) soft; not strong. 5. (of the senses, instruments) able to appreciate or indicate very small changes or differences: *a ~ sense of smell; the ~ instruments used by scientists* (e.g. in weighing things, measuring, etc.). 6. taking or showing care not to be immodest or to hurt the feelings of others. 7. (of food) dainty (1); pleasing to the taste: *fish with a ~ flavour.* **del·i·ca·cy** ['delikəsi] *n.* quality of being ~; ~ kind of food.

de·li·cious [di'lifəs] *adj.* giving delight (esp. to the senses of taste and smell, and to the sense of humour).

de·light [di'lait] *v.t. & i.* 1. give great pleasure to. 2. find great pleasure (*in* sth., *in* doing sth.). *n.* great pleasure; sth. that gives great pleasure. ~·ed *adj.* filled with ~. ~·ful *adj.* giving great ~; charming.

de·lin·e·ate [di'linieit] *v.t.* show by drawing or describing.

de·lin·quent [di'linkwənt] *n. &*

adj. (person) doing wrong, failing to perform a duty. **de·lin·quen·cy** [di'linkwənsi] *n.* wrongdoing; failure to perform a duty.

de·li·ri·um [di'liriəm] *n.* violent mental disturbance during feverish illness, often accompanied by wild talk. **de·li·ri·ous** [di'liriəs] *adj.* suffering from ~; wild (*with* excitement, etc.).

de·liv·er [di'livə*] *v.t.* 1. take (letters, parcels, goods, etc.) to houses, to the person(s) to whom they are addressed, to the buyer(s). 2. rescue, save, set free (*from* danger, temptation, etc.). 3. give or recite (a speech, sermon, course of lectures). 4. aim, send against: *to ~ a blow in the cause of freedom.* 5. *be ~ed of* (a child), give birth to. ~·ance [di'livərəns] *n.* rescue; being set free. **de·liv·er·y** *n.* ~ing (1) to; manner of making a speech, sermon, etc.; childbirth.

dell [del] *n.* small valley with trees.

del·ta ['deltə] *n.* Greek letter *d* (Δ, δ); land in the shape of a capital delta (Δ) at the mouth of a river between two or more branches, e.g. the Niger Delta.

de·lude [di'lu:d] *v.t.* deceive; mislead (on purpose). **de·lu·sion** [di'lu:ʒən] *n.* deluding or being ~d; false opinion or belief, esp. as a form of madness. **de·lu·sive** *adj.*

del·uge ['delju:dʒ] *n.* great flood; heavy rush of water or violent rainfall; anything coming in a heavy rush: *a ~ of words (questions).* *v.t.* flood; come down on (sb. or sth.) like a ~.

delve [delv] *v.t. & i.* (old use) dig; (fig.) ~ *into*, make researches into (e.g. old books or manuscripts).

dem·a·gogue ['deməgog] *n.* political leader who tries, by speeches appealing to the feelings instead of the reason, to stir up the people. **dem·a·gog·y** ['deməgogi] *n.*

de·mand [di'mɑ:nd] *v.t.* 1. ask for (sth.) as if ordering, or as if one has a right. 2. require; need. *n.* 1. act of ~ing(1);

sth. ~ed (1). on ~, when ~ed; when asked for. **2.** desire (by people ready to buy, pay for) for goods, services, etc.: *a great ~ for good typists* ; *goods in great ~*.

de·mar·cate ['di:mɑ:keit] *v.t.* mark or fix the limits of. **de·mar·ca·tion** [,di:mɑ:'keiʃən] *n.*

de·mean [di'mi:n] *v.t.* ~ *oneself*, lower oneself in dignity. ~**our** *n.* behaviour; manner.

de·men·ted [di'mentid] *adj.* mad; (colloq.) wild with worry. ~**ly** *adv.*

dem·i- ['demi-] *prefix.* half.

de·mise [di'maiz] *n.* (legal) death.

de·mist [di:'mist] *v.t.* wipe condensation from (the windscreen of a motor-car, etc.).

de·mo·bi·lize [di:'moubilaiz] *v.t.* release after military service. **de·mo·bi·li·za·tion** [di:,moubilai'zeiʃən] *n.*

de·moc·ra·cy [di'mɔkrəsi] *n.* of) (country with the principle **1.** government in which all adult citizens share through their elected representatives. **2.** (country with) government which encourages and allows free discussion of policy, majority rule, accompanied by respect for the rights of minorities, freedom of religion, opinions, speech, and association. **3.** society in which citizens treat each other as equals. **dem·o·crat** ['deməkræt] *n.* person who favours or supports ~. **dem·o·crat·ic** [,demə'krætik] *adj.* of, like, supporting, ~; (esp.) paying no attention to class divisions based on birth or wealth.

de·mol·ish [di'mɔliʃ] *v.t.* pull down; destroy; overthrow. **dem·o·li·tion** [,demə'liʃən] *n.*

de·mon ['di:mən] *n.* evil, wicked, or cruel supernatural being or spirit.

dem·on·strate ['demənstreit] *v.t. & i.* **1.** show clearly by giving proof(s) or example(s). **2.** make known (one's feelings, sympathies) ; (of workmen, students, etc.) support, protest, by means of processions, public meetings, etc. **dem·on·stra·tion** [,demən'streiʃən] *n.* demon-strating (all senses). **de·mon·stra·tive** [di'mɔnstrətiv] *adj.* **1.** showing the feelings. **2.** (grammar) pointing out: *'This'*, *'that'*, *'these'*, and *'those'* are *demonstrative pronouns.* **dem·on·stra·tor** ['demənstreitə*] *n.* person who ~s (2) at a public meeting; person who teaches by demonstrating (1).

de·mor·al·ize [di'mɔrəlaiz] *v.t.* **1.** hurt or weaken the morals of. **2.** weaken the courage, confidence, self-discipline, etc., of (e.g. an army). **de·mor·al·i·za·tion** [di,mɔrəlai'zeiʃən] *n.*

de·mur [di'mə:*] *v.i.* (*-rr-*). raise an objection to; protest or hesitate about: *to ~ at working on Sundays.* *n.* hesitation or protest: *to obey without ~.*

de·mure [di'mjuə*] *adj.* quiet and serious; pretending to be shy.

den [den] *n.* **1.** animal's hidden lying-place (e.g. a cave). **2.** secret place for ill-doers: *opium den.* **3.** (colloq.) room in which a person works or studies without being disturbed.

de·na·tion·al·ize [di:'næʃənəlaiz] *v.t.* transfer to private ownership (an industry acquired by the State).

de·ni·al, see *deny.*

den·i·zen ['denizn] *n.* person, kind of animal or plant, having a permanent home in the district mentioned.

de·nom·i·na·tion [di,nɔmi'neiʃən] *n.* **1.** name, esp. one given to a class or religious party. **2.** class of units (of weight, length, money, etc.).

de·nom·i·na·tor [di'nɔmineitə*] *n.* number below the line in a fraction (e.g. 4 in ⅘).

de·note [di'nout] *v.t.* be the sign of; stand as, be, a name for.

de·nounce [di'nauns] *v.t.* speak publicly against; betray; give notice that one intends to end (a treaty or agreement).

dense [dens] *adj.* (*-r, -st*). **1.** (of liquids, vapour) thick, not easily seen through. **2.** (of things, people) packed close together and in great numbers: *a ~ crowᵈ*

3. (of a person) stupid. ~·ly *adv.* den·si·ty ['densiti] *n.* being ~; (physics) relation of weight to volume.

dent [dent] *n.* hollow in a hard surface made by a blow or by pressure. *v.t.* make a ~ in.

den·tal ['dentl] *adj.* of or for the teeth. den·tist ['dentist] *n.* person who fills or removes decayed teeth and fits artificial ones. den·tis·try *n.* work of a dentist. den·ture ['dentʃə*] *n.* plate (6) of artificial teeth.

de·nude [di'njuːd] *v.t.* make bare; take away clothing, covering, possessions: *hillsides ~d of trees.*

de·nun·ci·a·tion [di‚nʌnsi'eiʃən] *n.* denouncing.

de·ny [di'nai] *v.t.* **1.** say that (sth.) is not true. **2.** say 'no' to (a request); refuse to give (sth. asked for or needed). **3.** say that one knows nothing about: *He denied the signature* (said that it was not his). de·ni·al [di'naiəl] *n.* ~ing.

de·o·dor·ize [diː'oudəraiz] *v.t.* remove a (bad) smell from.

de·part [di'paːt] *v.i.* go away (*from*); leave; do or be sth. different: *to ~ from old customs.* de·par·ture [di'paːtʃə*] *n.* ~ing.

de·part·ment [di'paːtmənt] *n.* one of several divisions of a government, business, shop, university, etc.

de·pend [di'pend] *v.i.* ~ (*up*)*on.* **1.** need, rely on (the support, etc., of) in order to exist or to be true or to succeed: *The old woman still ~s on her own earnings* (i.e. she has no one else to provide for her). *Good health ~s on good food, sleep, and exercise. That ~s. It all ~s* (i.e. the result ~s on something else). **2.** trust; be certain about: *You can always ~ on John to be there when needed. Depend upon it!* (i.e. you can be quite certain about the result). ~·a·ble *adj.* that can be ~ed (2) upon. de·pen·dant *n.* sb. who ~s(1) upon another for a home, food, etc.; servant. de·

pen·dence *n.* the state of ~ing (1), (2), on sb. or sth. de·pen·den·cy *n.* country governed by another country. de·pen·dent *adj.* ~ing (1), (2), (*on*). *n.* = ~ant.

de·pict [di'pikt] *v.t.* draw or paint; describe in words.

de·plete [di'pliːt] *v.t.* use up, empty out until little or none remains. de·ple·tion [di'pliːʃən] *n.*

de·plore [di'ploː*] *v.t.* show that one is filled with sorrow or regret for. de·plor·a·ble [di'ploːrəbl] *adj.* that is, or should be, ~d.

de·ploy [di'ploi] *v.t. & i.* (of troops, warships) spread out in line of battle; (fig. of resources) put to practical use.

de·pop·u·late [diː'pɔpjuleit] *v.t.* lessen the number of people living in (a country): *a country ~d by war.* de·pop·u·la·tion [diː‚pɔpju'leiʃən] *n.*

¹de·port [di'pɔːt] *v.t.* send (an unwanted person) out of the country. de·por·ta·tion [‚diːpɔː'teiʃən] *n.* ~ing or being ~ed.

²de·port [di'pɔːt] *v.t.* ~ *oneself,* behave: *to ~ oneself with dignity.* ~·ment *n.* behaviour; way of bearing oneself.

de·pose [di'pouz] *v.t.* **1.** remove (sb., esp. a ruler such as a king) from a position of authority; dethrone. **2.** give evidence (esp. on oath in a law court). dep·o·si·tion [‚depə'ziʃən] *n.* deposing or being ~d (1); evidence given on oath.

de·pos·it [di'pozit] *v.t.* **1.** put (e.g. money, valuables) in a place, or in sb.'s care, for safe-keeping. **2.** (esp. of a liquid, a river) leave a layer of matter on: *rivers that ~ mud and sand on the fields during a flood.* **3.** make part payment of money that is or will be owed. *n.* **1.** money that is ~ed (1), (3); valuables ~ed (1). **2.** layer of matter ~ed (2): *a ~ of gravel (tin, volcanic ash).* de·pos·i·tor *n.* person who makes a ~ in a bank. de·pos·i·to·ry [di'pozitəri] *n.* place where goods are ~ed; storehouse.

dep·ot ['depou] *n.* storehouse, esp. for military supplies; warehouse.

de·praved [di'preivd] *adj.* morally bad; (of tastes, habits) corrupt; evil; low. **de·prav·i·ty** [di'præviti] *n.* ~ state.

dep·re·cate ['deprikeit] *v.t.* feel and express disapproval of.

de·pre·ci·ate [di'pri:ʃieit] *v.t. & i.* make or become less in value; say sth. has little value. **de·pre·ci·a·tion** [di,pri:ʃi'eiʃən] *n.* lessening of value.

dep·re·da·tion [,deprə'deiʃən] *n.* (usu. pl.) destruction or robbery of property.

de·press [di'pres] *v.t.* 1. press, push, or pull down: *to ~ a lever (the keys of a piano).* 2. make sad. 3. make less active; cause (prices) to be lower. **de·pres·sing** *adj.* making sad or unhappy: *~ing news (weather).* **de·pres·sion** *n.* 1. being ~ed (2) 2. hollow place in the surface of the ground. 3. time when business is ~ed (3). 4. lowering of atmospheric pressure: (esp.) centre where this pressure is lowest.

de·prive [di'praiv] *v.t.* ~ *sb. or sth. of,* take away from, prevent from using or enjoying: *trees that ~ a house of light and air.*

depth [depθ] *n.* 1. being deep: *the ~ of the ocean.* 2. measure from top to bottom, or from front to back: *snow three feet in ~. out of one's ~,* in water too deep to stand in; (fig.) considering sth. beyond one's understanding.

de·pute [di'pju:t] *v.t.* give (one's work, authority, etc.) to a substitute; give (another person) authority (to do sth.) as one's representative. **dep·u·ty** ['depjuti] *n.* person to whom work, authority, is ~d. **dep·u·ta·tion** [,depju'teiʃən] *n.* group of representatives. **dep·u·tize** ['depjutaiz] *v.i.* act as deputy *(for).*

de·rail [di'reil] *v.t.* cause (a train, tram) to go off the rails. **~·ment** *n.*

de·range [di'reindʒ] *v.t.* put into confusion or out of working order. *mentally ~d,* mad.

der·e·lict ['derilikt] *adj.* (esp. of a ship at sea) deserted (usu. because dangerous or useless).

de·ride [di'raid] *v.t.* laugh scornfully at; mock. **de·ri·sion** [di'riʒən] *n.* **de·ri·sive** [di'raisiv] *adj.* showing or deserving scorn: *derisive laughter; a derisive offer.* **de·ri·so·ry** [di'raisəri] *adj.* not to be taken seriously.

de·rive [di'raiv] *v.t. & i.* 1. get: *to ~ great pleasure from one's studies.* 2. have as a starting-point or origin: *English words ~d from Latin.* **de·riv·a·tion** [,deri'veiʃən] *n.* (esp.) first form and meaning of a word; statement of how a word was formed and how it changed. **der·i·va·tive** [di'rivətiv] *adj. & n.* (thing, word, substance) ~d from another; sth. not original.

de·rog·a·to·ry [di'rogətəri] *adj.* tending to damage one's credit, etc.: *remarks ~ to one's reputation.*

der·rick ['derik] *n.* machine for moving or lifting heavy weights, esp. a ship's cargo.

A derrick   Davits

der·vish ['də:viʃ] *n.* Muslim monk who has vowed to live a life of poverty.

des·cend [di'send] *v.i. & t.* 1. come or go down. 2. *be ~ed from,* have as ancestors. 3. (of property, qualities, rights) pass (from father to son) by inheritance; come from earlier times. 4. ~ *upon,* attack suddenly. **de·scen·dant** *n.* person ~ed from person(s) named. **des·cent** [di'sent] *n.* 1. ~ing; downward slope. 2. ancestry: *of French descent.* 3. sudden attack.

des·cribe [dis'kraib] *v.t.* 1. say what a person or thing is like; give a picture of in words. 2. draw (a geometrical figure).

des·crip·tion [dis'kripʃən] *n.*
1. describing; picture in words.
2. *of any (every) description*, of
any kind at all (of all kinds).

de·scrip·tive [dis'kriptiv] *adj.*

des·cry [dis'krai] *v.t.* catch sight
of; see (esp. sth. a long way off).

des·e·crate ['desikreit] *v.t.* use
(a sacred place or thing) in an
unworthy or wicked way. **des·
e·cra·tion** [ˌdesi'kreiʃən] *n.*

¹de·sert [di'zəːt] *v.t. & i.* **1.** go
away from, leave without help
or support, esp. in a wrong or
cruel way. **2.** run away from;
leave (esp. service in a ship, the
armed forces) without authority
or permission: *soldiers who ~.*
3. fail: *His courage ~ed him.*
~·er *n.* person (esp. a soldier or
sailor) who ~s (2). **de·ser·tion**
n. [di'zəːʃən] ~ing or being ~ed.

²des·ert ['dezət] *n.* large area of
dry waste land, esp. sand-
covered. *adj.* uninhabited; barren: *a ~ island.*

³de·sert [di'zəːt] *n.* (usu. pl.) what
sb. deserves: *get one's ~s.*

de·serve [di'zəːv] *v.t.* be worthy
of (reward, etc.) because of one's
qualities, actions: *to ~ praise
(punishment) for good (careless)
work.* **de·serv·ing** *adj.* worthy
(*of*). **de·serv·ed·ly** [di'zəːvidli]
adv. justly; as ~d.

des·ic·cate ['desikeit] *v.t.* dry
out all the moisture from (esp.
solid food): *~d apples.*

de·sign [di'zain] *n.* **1.** drawing
or outline from which sth. may
be made: *~s for a dress (garden).*
2. general arrangement or plan
(of a picture, book, building,
machine, etc.). **3.** pattern,
arrangement of lines, shapes, details, as ornament (e.g. on a bowl
or a carpet). **4.** purpose; intention. *have ~s on (against)*, intend to harm, take, or steal.
v.t. & i. **1.** make ~s (1) for: *to
~ wall-paper (carpets).* **2.** intend; plan; have in mind: *a
room ~ed for a workshop.* **~·
ed·ly** [di'zainidli] *adv.* on purpose. **~·er** *n.* person who ~s
(1). **~·ing** *adj.* (esp.) cunning;
having ~s (4) on sth. or sb.

des·ig·nate ['dezigneit] *v.t.* **1.**
point out or mark: *to ~ boundaries.* **2.** serve as a distinguishing name or mark for. **3.** appoint (sb.) to a position: *He ~d
Smith as (for) his successor.*
['dezignit] *adj.* (after a noun) appointed but not yet in office.

des·ig·na·tion [ˌdezig'neiʃən] *n.*

de·sire [di'zaiə*] *n.* **1.** strong
wish or longing (*for*). **2.** request:
at the ~ of the manager. **3.** thing
that is wished for: *to get one's
~.* *v.t.* **1.** have a ~ (1) for. **2.**
request. **de·sir·a·ble** [di'zaiər-
əbl] *adj.* to be ~d (1), causing
~ (1). **de·sir·a·bil·i·ty** [diˌzaiər-
ə'biliti] *n.* **de·sir·ous** [di'zaiər-
əs] *adj.* feeling ~ (1); *desirous
of success.*

de·sist [di'zist] *v.i. ~ from*, cease.

desk [desk] *n.* piece of furniture
with a level or sloping top for
reading, writing, or office work.

des·o·late ['desəlit] *adj.* **1.** (of a
place) in a ruined, neglected condition; (of land, a house, a
country) unoccupied; unfit to
live in. **2.** friendless; wretched;
hopeless. ['desəleit] *v.t.* make ~
(1), (2). **des·o·la·tion** [ˌdesə-
'leiʃən] *n.* making or being ~.

des·pair [dis'pɛə*] *v.i. & n.* (be
in) the state of having lost all
hope. **~·ing** *adj.* feeling or
showing ~.

des·patch, see *dispatch.*

des·per·ate ['despərit] *adj.* **1.** (of
a person) filled with despair and
ready to do anything, regard-
less of danger; lawless; violent:
~ criminals. **2.** extremely serious or dangerous: *a ~ state of
affairs.* **~·ly** *adv.* **des·per·a·
tion** [ˌdespə'reiʃən] *n.* **des·per·
a·do** [ˌdespə'rɑːdou] *n.* person
ready to do any dangerous or
criminal act.

des·pise [dis'paiz] *v.t.* feel contempt for; consider worthless.
des·pic·a·ble ['despikəbl] *adj.*
deserving to be ~d.

des·pite [dis'pait] *prep.* in spite
of. *n. in ~ of*, in spite of.

des·poil [dis'pɔil] *v.t.* (with *of*)
rob, plunder.

des·pond [dis'pɔnd] *v.i.* lose
hope. **des·pon·den·cy** *n.* **des·
pon·dent** *adj.*

des·pot ['despɔt] *n.* ruler with unlimited powers, esp. one using these powers wrongly, cruelly. ~**ic** [des'pɔtik] *adj.* ~**ism** ['despɔtizəm] *n.* rule of a ~; ~ic government.

des·sert [di'zə:t] *n.* course of fresh fruit, etc., at the end of dinner.

des·ti·na·tion [,desti'neiʃən] *n.* place to which a person or thing is going or is being sent.

des·tined ['destind] *p.p.* intended, designed (by God, fate, or a person) *to be* or *do* sth., or *for* sth. **des·ti·ny** ['destini] *n.* 1. power believed to control events. 2. that which happens to sb., thought of as determined in advance by that power.

des·ti·tute ['destitju:t] *adj.* 1. without food, clothes, and other things necessary for life. 2. ~ *of*, lacking; without: *entirely ~ of sympathy.* **des·ti·tu·tion** [,desti'tju:ʃən] *n.*

de·stroy [dis'trɔi] *v.t.* break to pieces; make useless; put an end to. ~**er** *n.* (esp.) small, fast warship armed with missiles.

de·struc·ti·ble [dis'trʌktəbl] *adj.* that can be destroyed. **de·struc·tion** [dis'trʌkʃən] *n.* **de·struc·tive** [dis'trʌktiv] *adj.* causing destruction; fond of, in the habit of, ~ing.

des·ul·to·ry ['desəltəri] *adj.* without system, purpose, or regularity: ~ *reading.*

de·tach [di'tætʃ] *v.t.* 1. unfasten and take apart from; separate. 2. (armed forces) send (a party) away from the main body. **de·tached** *adj.* (of the mind, opinions, etc.) impartial; not influenced by others; (of a house) not joined to another on either side. ~**·a·ble** *adj.* that can be ~ed. ~**·ment** *n.* 1. ~ing or being ~ed. 2. ~ed state of mind; being uninfluenced by surroundings, the opinions of others. 3. (armed forces) party of men, number of ships, etc., acting separately.

de·tail ['di:teil] *n.* 1. small, particular fact or item. 2. a collection of such small facts: *to go*

into ~s; to explain sth. in ~ (i.e. give all the small points of fact). [di'teil] *v.t.* 1. give full ~s of; describe fully. 2. appoint for special duty: *Three soldiers were ~ed to guard the bridge.*

de·tain [di'tein] *v.t.* keep waiting; keep back; prevent from leaving: *to be ~ed at the office.* **de·ten·tion** [di'tenʃən] *n.* ~ing or being ~ed.

de·tect [di'tekt] *v.t.* discover (the existence or presence of sb. or sth.; the identity of sb. guilty of wrongdoing). **de·tec·tion** [di'tekʃən] *n.* ~ing: *the ~ion of crime.* **de·tec·tive** *n.* person whose business is to ~ criminals.

de·ter [di'tə:*] *v.t.* (-rr-). discourage, hinder (sb. *from* doing sth.): *Let nothing ~ you from trying to succeed in life.* ~**rent** [di'terənt] *n. & adj.* (thing) tending to ~ or discourage.

de·ter·gent [di'tə:dʒənt] *n.* substance used for removing dirt, esp. from the surface of things.

de·te·ri·o·rate [di'tiəriəreit] *v.t. & i.* make or become worse, of less value. **de·te·ri·o·ra·tion** [di,tiəriə'reiʃən] *n.*

de·ter·mine [di'tə:min] *v.t. & i.* 1. be the fact that decides (sth.): *The size of your feet ~s the size of your shoes.* 2. decide (sb.'s future); make up one's mind (to do sth.); settle. 3. cause to decide. 4. learn, find out, exactly: *to ~ the meaning of a word.* **de·ter·mined** *adj.* strong-willed; of fixed purpose. **de·ter·mi·na·tion** [di,tə:mi'neiʃən] *n.* determining; sth. ~d; firmness of purpose. **de·ter·mi·nate** [di'tə:minit] *adj.* limited; definite.

de·ter·rent, see *deter.*

de·test [di'test] *v.t.* hate. ~**·a·ble** *adj.* deserving to be hated. **de·tes·ta·tion** [,di:tes'teiʃən] *n.* hatred; sth. ~ed.

de·throne [di'θroun] *v.t.* remove (a ruler) from his position of authority.

det·o·nate ['detouneit] *v.t. & i.* (cause to) explode with a loud noise. **det·o·na·tor** *n.* (esp.) part of a bomb, shell, etc., that sets off the explosion. **det·o·na·tion** [ˌdetou'neiʃən] *n.*

de·tour [di'tuə*], **dé·tour** ['deituə*] *n.* turning aside; roundabout way : *to make a ~.*

de·tract [di'trækt] *v.i.* ~ *from*, take away from (the credit or value of). **de·trac·tion** [di'trækʃən] *n.* **de·trac·tor** *n.* person who says things to lessen sb.'s credit or reputation.

det·ri·ment ['detrimənt] *n.* damage; harm : *A child cannot smoke without ~ to its health.* **det·ri·men·tal** [ˌdetri'mentl] *adj.*

dev·as·tate ['devəsteit] *v.t.* ruin; make desolate. **dev·as·ta·tion** [ˌdevəs'teiʃən] *n.*

de·vel·op [di'veləp] *v.t. & i.* **1.** (cause to) grow larger, fuller, or mature; (cause to) unfold. **2.** (of sth. not at first active or seen) come or bring it into a form in which it is active or can be seen; (esp.) treat (an exposed film) with chemicals so that the picture shows. **~·ment** *n.* ~ing or being ~ed; growth; new stage which is the result of ~ing : *the latest ~ments in foreign affairs.*

de·vi·ate ['di:vieit] *v.i.* turn away (*from* the right or usual way, a rule, custom, etc.). **de·vi·a·tion** [ˌdi:vi'eiʃən] *n.*

de·vice [di'vais] *n.* **1.** plan; scheme; trick. *leave sb. to his own ~s*, let him do as he wishes, get over his own difficulties. **2.** sth. thought out, invented or adapted for a special purpose. **3.** sign, symbol, or crest (3).

dev·il ['devl] *n.* **1.** the spirit of evil; wicked spirit; cruel or mischievous person. **2.** (in exclamations) *How the ~ . . ., how ever; the ~ of a time*, a time of difficulty, excitement, etc. (according to context). **dev·il·ish** ['devliʃ] *adj.* wicked; cruel.

de·vi·ous ['di:viəs] *adj.* winding; not straightforward; roundabout.

de·vise [di'vaiz] *v.t.* plan; invent.

de·vi·tal·ize [di:'vaitəlaiz] *v.t.* take away strength and vigour from.

de·void [di'vɔid] *adj.* ~ *of*, empty of; without : ~ *of sense.*

de·volve [di'vɔlv] *v.t. & i.* (of work, duties) ~ (*up*)*on*, be passed on to (another person, a deputy) : *When Smith is ill, his work ~s upon me.*

de·vote [di'vout] *v.t.* give up (oneself, one's time, energy, etc.) (*to* sth. or sb.) : *to ~ all one's spare time to sport.* **de·vot·ed** *adj.* very loving or loyal. **dev·o·tee** [ˌdevou'ti:] *n.* person ~d to (e.g. some form of religion). **de·vo·tion** [di'vouʃən] *n.* being ~d; strong deep love; (pl.) prayers.

de·vour [di'vauə*] *v.t.* eat (fig. look at, hear) hungrily (and anxiously); (of flames) destroy. (fig.) ~ed by (anxiety, etc.), having one's whole attention taken up by.

de·vout [di'vaut] *adj.* paying serious attention to religious duties; (of prayers, wishes) deep-felt; sincere. ~·ly *adv.*

dew [dju:] *n.* tiny drops of moisture formed between evening and morning on cool surfaces from water vapour in the air. **dew·y** ['dju:i] *adj.* wet with ~.

dex·ter·ous ['dekstərəs] *adj.* clever and quick, esp. in using the hands. **dex·ter·i·ty** [deks'teriti] *n.*

dhow [dau] *n.* single-masted ship as used by Arab sailors.

di·a·bol·ic(al) [ˌdaiə'bolik(l)] *adj.* of or like the Devil; very wicked.

di·ag·nose ['daiəgnouz] *v.t.* determine (1) the nature of (esp. a disease). **di·ag·no·sis** [ˌdaiəg'nousis] *n.* (pl. *-es* [-i:z]). diagnosing; statement about this.

di·ag·o·nal [dai'ægənl] *n. & adj.* (straight line) going across a straight-sided figure (e.g. an oblong) from corner to corner. ~·ly *adv.* in the slanting direction of a ~. See the picture on page 149.

di·a·gram ['daiəgræm] *n.* drawing, design, or plan to explain or illustrate sth. ~·ma·tic [ˌdaiəgrə'mætik] *adj.*

(1)   (2)

A diagonal   A diamond

di·al ['daiəl] *n.* **1.** face (of a clock); marked face or flat plate with a pointer for measuring (weight, pressure, etc.). **2.** part of an automatic telephone used when calling a number. *v.t. & i.* (-ll-). call by means of a telephone ~ : to ~ *6652.*

Dials

di·a·lect ['daiəlekt] *n.* form of a spoken language, way of speaking, used in a part of a country or by a class of people: *the Yorkshire* ~; *the Negro ~ in America*; ~ *words (pronunciations).*

di·a·logue ['daiəlog] *n.* (writing in the form of a) conversation or talk; talk between two persons.

di·am·e·ter [dai'æmitə*] *n.* (length of) straight line passing from side to side of a circle or sphere through the centre; measurement across any other geometrical figure; width; thickness. **di·a·met·ri·cal·ly** [,daiə-'metrikəli] *adv.* completely; directly.

di·a·mond ['daiəmənd] *n.* **1.** brilliant precious stone or jewel, the hardest substance known. ~ *wedding*, sixtieth anniversary of a wedding. **2.** figure with four equal sides whose angles are not right angles; this figure printed in red on some playing-cards.

di·aph·a·nous [dai'æfənəs] *adj.* (of dress materials) transparent.

di·a·phragm ['daiəfræm] *n.* **1.** wall of muscle between chest and abdomen. **2.** thin round plate in some instruments (e.g. a microphone).

di·ar·rhoe·a [daiə'riə] *n.* too frequent emptying of the bowels.

di·a·ry ['daiəri] *n.* daily record of events, thoughts; book for this.

di·a·tribe ['daiətraib] *n.* angry or violent attack in words.

dice [dais] *pl. n.* (sing. *die* [dai]). small pieces of wood, bone, etc., with six square sides marked with numbers, used in the game of ~, etc. *v.i. & t.* **1.** play with ~. **2.** cut (food, e.g. carrots) into pieces shaped like ~.

dic·tate [dik'teit] *v.t. & i.* **1.** say (words) for another person to write down: *to ~ a letter.* **2.** ~ *to,* give authoritative orders to. *n. pl.* ['dikteits] directions or orders (given by one's reason, conscience, common sense). **dic·ta·tion** [dik'teifən] *n.* dictating; sth. ~d. **dic·ta·tor** [dik'teitə*] *n.* ruler with absolute power, esp. one who has obtained such power by force or in an irregular way. **dic·ta·tor·ship** *n.* government by a dictator. **dic·ta·tor·i·al** [,diktə'tɔːriəl] *adj.* of or like a dictator.

dic·tion ['dikfən] *n.* choice and use of words; style or manner of speaking and writing.

dic·tion·a·ry ['dikfənəri] *n.* book dealing with the words of a language or of some special subject (e.g. the Bible, architecture), and arranged in ABC order.

did, see *do.*

di·dac·tic [di'dæktik] *adj.* **1.** intended to teach: ~ *poetry.* **2.** having the manner of a teacher.

¹die [dai] *v.i.* (p.t. & p.p. *died* [daid], pres. p. *dying* ['daiiŋ]). come to the end of life; cease to live. *be dying (for* sth., *to do* sth.), have a strong wish.

²die, see *dice.*

³die [dai] *n.* metal block with a

design, etc., cut in it, used for shaping coins, medals, etc., or stamping(2) (words, etc.) on paper, leather, etc.

dies·el en·gine ['di:zl 'endʒin] *n.* one burning heavy oil (not motor spirit).

¹**di·et** ['daiət] *n.* 1. sort of food a person usually eats. 2. sort of food to which a person is limited (e.g. for medical reasons): *The doctor put her on a* ~. *v.t. & i.* restrict oneself, be restricted, to a ~ (2).

²**di·et** ['daiət] *n.* series of meetings for discussion of national or international or church affairs.

dif·fer ['difə*] *v.i.* be unlike. ~·ence ['difrəns] *n.* ~·ent ['difrənt] *adj.* ~·en·ti·ate [ˌdifər-'enʃieit] *v.t. & i.* see or be the ~ence between; (cause to) become ~ent.

dif·fi·cult(y) ['difikəlt(i)] *adj. & n.* (the state or quality of) requiring much effort, skill, thought, etc.

dif·fi·dent ['difidənt] *adj.* not having, not showing, much belief in one's own abilities. **dif·fi·dence** *n.*

dif·fract [di'frækt] *v.t.* break up (a beam of light) into dark and light bands or the spectrum.

dif·fuse [di'fju:z] *v.t. & i.* 1. spread, cause to spread, in every direction. 2. (of gases, fluids) mix slowly with one another. [di'fju:s] *adj.* 1. using too many words. 2. spread about; scattered. **dif·fu·sion** [di'fju:ʒən] *n.*

dig [dig] *v.t. & i.* (-*gg*-, p.t. & p.p. *dug* [dʌg]). 1. use a spade, etc., to break up and move earth; make (a hole, etc.) by doing this; get (potatoes, etc.) from the ground in this way. 2. (colloq.) push a (pointed thing into): *to dig a person in the ribs* (with one's fingers). *n.* push or poke with sth. pointed; (pl. colloq.) lodgings. **dig·ger** *n.* person who digs. **dig·gings** ['digiŋz] *n. pl.* gold-field; (colloq.) lodgings.

di·gest [di'dʒest] *v.t. & i.* 1. (of food) change, be changed, in the stomach and bowels so that it can be used in the body. 2.

take in to the mind; reduce (a mass of facts, etc.) to order. ['daidʒest] *n.* short, condensed account; summary: *a* ~ *of the week's news.* ~·i·ble [di'dʒestibl] *adj.* that can be ~ed (1) easily. **di·ges·tion** [di'dʒestʃən] *n.* (esp.) person's power of ~ing food. **di·ges·tive** [di'dʒestiv] *adj.* of ~ion.

dig·it ['didʒit] *n.* any one of the numbers 0 to 9; finger or toe.

dig·ni·fy ['dignifai] *v.t.* give dignity to; make worthy or honourable. **dig·ni·fied** *adj.* having, showing, dignity.

dig·ni·ta·ry ['dignitəri] *n.* person holding high position, esp. in the church (e.g. a bishop).

dig·ni·ty ['digniti] *n.* 1. true worth; the quality that wins or deserves respect. 2. calm and serious behaviour: *to lose one's* ~ (e.g. by making a foolish mistake); *beneath one's* ~, not worthy of a person's position or powers. 3. high or honourable rank, post, or title.

di·gress [dai'gres] *v.i.* (esp. in speaking or writing) turn aside (from the main subject). **di·gres·sion** [dai'greʃən] *n.*

dike, dyke [daik] *n.* 1. ditch (for carrying away water from land). 2. long wall of earth, etc. (to keep back water and prevent flooding).

di·lap·i·dat·ed [di'læpideitid] *adj.* (of buildings, furniture, etc.) falling to pieces; in a state of disrepair. **di·lap·i·da·tion** [di-ˌlæpi'deiʃən] *n.* being or becoming ~.

di·late [dai'leit] *v.i. & t.* 1. (cause to) become wider, larger, further open: *with* ~*d eyes* (*nostrils*). 2. ~ *upon*, speak or write at great length about.

di·la·to·ry ['dilətəri] *adj.* slow in doing things; causing delay.

di·lem·ma [di'lemə] *n.* situation in which one has to choose between two things, courses of action, etc., that are either unfavourable or undesirable.

dil·et·tan·te [ˌdili'tænti] *n.* (pl. -*ti* [-ti:]). lover of the fine arts; one who studies the arts but not seriously and not with real understanding.

dil·i·gent ['dilidʒənt] *adj.* hardworking; showing care and effort. **dil·i·gence** ['dilidʒəns] *n.*

dil·ly-dal·ly ['dili'dæli] *v.i.* waste time (by not making up one's mind).

di·lute [dai'lju:t] *v.t.* make (a liquid or colour) weaker or thinner (by adding water or other liquid); (fig.) weaken the force of (by mixing). *adj.* thus weakened. **di·lu·tion** [dai'lju:ʃən] *n.*

dim [dim] *adj.* (*dimmer*, *-est*). not bright; not clearly to be seen; (of the eyes) not able to see clearly: *eyes dim with tears.* *v.t. & i.* (*-mm-*). make or become dim. **dim·ly** *adv.*

dime [daim] *n.* (U.S.A.) coin worth ten cents.

di·men·sion [di-, dai'menʃən] *n.* measurement of any sort (breadth, length, thickness, area, etc.); (pl.) size: *of great ~s.*

di·min·ish [di'miniʃ] *v.t. & i.* make or become less. **dim·i·nu·tion** [,dimi'nju:ʃən] *n.*

di·min·u·tive [di'minjutiv] *adj.* very small. *n.* word which indicates a small size of sth., often a word with a suffix such as *-kin* or *-let*. *Streamlet* is a ~ of *stream.*

dim·ple ['dimpl] *n.* small hollow which appears in the chin or in the cheeks when sb. smiles. *v.t. & i.* form or make ~s.

din [din] *n.* loud, confused noise that continues. *v.i. & t.* (*-nn-*). 1. make a ~. 2. ~ *sth. into sb.*, tell him again and again.

dine [dain] *v.i.* have dinner. **din·er** ['dainə*] *n.* dining-car on a train.

ding-dong ['diŋ'dɒŋ] *n. & adv.* (with the) sound of two bells striking alternately.

din·ghy ['diŋgi] *n.* small open boat.

din·gy ['dindʒi] *adj.* dirty-looking.

din·ner ['dinə*] *n.* main meal of the day: *Have you had ~ yet? We enjoyed the ~ they served.*

dint [dint] *n.* 1. = dent. 2. *by ~ of*, by force or means of.

di·o·cese ['daiəsis] *n.* bishop's district. **di·o·ce·san** [dai'ɒsisn] *adj.* of a ~.

dip [dip] *v.t. & i.* (*-pp-*). 1. put, lower, (sth.) into a liquid and take it out again: *to dip one's pen in the ink.* 2. put (one's hand, a spoon, etc., *into* sth.) and take out (liquid, grain, etc.); get (liquid, grain, etc.) by doing this: *to dip a bucket into a lake; to dip up a bucket of water.* 3. go below a surface or level; (of land) slope downwards: *The sun dipped below the horizon. The birds rose and dipped in their flight.* 4. (cause to) go down and up again: *to dip a flag* (as a salute). 5. *dip into* (a book, subject), examine or study but not thoroughly. *n.* 1. act of dipping; being dipped; (esp.) a short swim or bathe. 2. cleansing liquid in which sheep are dipped. 3. downward slope: *a dip in the road.*

diph·the·ri·a [dif'θiəriə] *n.* serious infectious disease of the throat.

diph·thong ['difθɒŋ] *n.* union of two vowel sounds or vowel letters (e.g. the sounds [ai] in *pipe* [paip], the letters *ou* in *doubt*).

di·plo·ma [di'ploumə] *n.* educational certificate.

di·plo·ma·cy [di'plouməsi] *n.* 1. management of international relations; skill in this. 2. art of, skill in, dealing with people so that business is done smoothly.

dip·lo·mat ['dipləmæt], **di·plom·a·tist** [di'ploumətist] *n.* 1. person engaged in ~ for his government (e.g. an ambassador). 2. person clever in dealing with people. **dip·lo·mat·ic** [,diplə'mætik] *adj.* of ~; tactful.

dip·per ['dipə*] *n.* cup-shaped vessel on a long handle for dipping out liquids.

dire ['daiə*] *adj.* dreadful; terrible.

di·rect [di'rekt, dai-] *adj. & adv.* 1. (going) straight; not curved or crooked; not turned aside: *in a ~ line with; a ~ hit.* 2. with nothing or no one in between; in an unbroken line. 3. straightforward; going straight to the point: *a ~ answer*; *a ~ way of speaking (doing things)*. **4.** *~ action*, use of strike action by workers to get their demands. *~ current*, electric current flowing continuously (cf. *alternating*). *~ speech*, speaker's actual words. *v.t. & i.* **1.** tell or show (sb.) how to do sth., get somewhere; manage; control: *to ~ sb. to the post office*; *to ~ workmen.* **2.** address (a letter, etc.); speak or write (remarks, etc., *to*). **3.** guide (*to*); cause to turn (the eyes, one's attention) straight (*to* sth.): *to ~ one's attention to what is being done*. **di·rec·tion** [di'rekʃən] *n.* **1.** course taken by a moving person or thing; point towards which a person looks, moves, etc.: *people running in every ~ion*. **2.** (often pl.) information about what to do, where to go, how to do sth., etc.; command. **3.** (usu. pl.) address on a letter, parcel, etc. **4.** act of ~ing, managing, giving orders: *to work under the ~ion of an expert*. **di·rec·tive** [di'rektiv] *n.* detailed instructions given to staff (3) to guide them in their work. **~·ly** *adv.* **1.** in a ~ manner. **2.** at once; now. **3.** (colloq., as conj.) as soon as. **~·ness** *n.* **di·rec·tor** *n.* person who ~s, esp. one of a group (called the Board) ~ing the affairs of a business company. **di·rec·tor·ate** [di'rektərit] *n.* Board of Directors. **di·rec·to·ry** [di'rektəri] *n.* list of names (and usu. addresses) in ABC order: *a telephone ~ory*.

dirge [də:dʒ] *n.* song sung at a burial or for a dead person.

dirk [də:k] *n.* kind of dagger.

dirt [də:t] *n.* unclean matter (e.g. dust, mud) esp. where not wanted, e.g. on the body, clothing, buildings; (fig.) unclean thought or talk. **~·y** *adj.* not clean; covered with ~; (of the weather) rough; stormy; rainy. *v.t.* make ~y. **~·i·ly** *adv.* **~·i·ness** *n.*

dis- [dis] *prefix* indicating the opposite of. **dis·ad·van·tage, dis·ad·van·ta·geous, dis·ap·** pro·ba·tion, dis·ap·prove, dis·ap·prov·al, dis·ar·range, dis·be·lieve, dis·be·lief, dis·cour·teous, dis·cour·te·sy, dis·em·bark, dis·en·gaged, dis·en·tan·gle, dis·es·tab·lish, dis·fa·vour, dis·en·fran·chise, dis·heart·en, dis·hon·est, dis·like, dis·loy·al(ty), dis·mount, dis·o·bey, dis·o·be·dient, dis·please, dis·pleas·ure, dis·prove, dis·qual·i·fy, dis·re·spect, dis·sat·is·fy, dis·sim·i·lar.

dis·a·ble [dis'eibl] *v.t.* make unable to do sth.; esp. take away power of using the limbs: *soldiers ~d in the war* (i.e. crippled). **dis·a·bil·i·ty** [ˌdisə'biliti] *n.* being ~d; sth. that ~s.

dis·a·buse [ˌdisə'bju:z] *v.t.* free (sb., his mind) from false ideas; put (a person) right (in his ideas).

dis·af·fec·ted [ˌdisə'fektid] *adj.* unfriendly; discontented; disloyal. **dis·af·fec·tion** [ˌdisə'fekʃən] *n.*

dis·a·gree [ˌdisə'gri:] *v.i.* **1.** take a different view; not agree (*with* sb.). **2.** ~ *with*, (of food, climate, etc.) be unsuited to; have bad effects on. **~·a·ble** [ˌdisə'griəbl] *adj.* unpleasant; bad-tempered. **dis·a·gree·ment** *n.*

dis·al·low [ˌdisə'lau] *v.t.* refuse to allow or accept as correct.

dis·ap·pear [ˌdisə'piə*] *v.i.* go out of sight; be seen no more. **~·ance** *n.*

dis·ap·point [ˌdisə'point] *v.t.* fail to do or be equal to what is hoped or expected; prevent (a plan, hope, etc.) from being realized. **~·ed** *adj.* sad at not getting what was hoped for, etc. **~·ment** *n.* being ~ed; person or thing that ~s.

dis·arm [dis'a:m] *v.t. & i.* **1.** take away weapons, etc., from. **2.** (of a country) reduce the size of, give up the use of, armed forces. **3.** make it hard for sb. to feel anger, suspicion, doubt. **~·a·ment** [dis'a:məmənt] *n.* ~ing (2) or being ~ed (2).

dis·as·ter [di'za:stə*] *n.* great

or sudden misfortune. **dis·as·trous** *adj.* causing ~.

dis·a·vow [ˌdisəˈvau] *v.t.* say that one does not know; refuse to approve of. ~**al** *n.*

dis·band [disˈbænd] *v.t. & i.* (of a force of soldiers, etc.) break up (as an organized body).

dis·burse [disˈbəːs] *v.t. & i.* pay out (money). ~**ment** *n.*

disc, disk [disk] *n.* thin, flat, round plate (e.g. a coin, gramophone record); round surface appearing to be flat: *the sun's ~.*

dis·card [disˈkɑːd] *v.t.* throw out or away, put aside, give up (sth. useless, sth. not wanted).

dis·cern [diˈsəːn] *v.t. & i.* see clearly (with the senses or with the mind); (esp.) see with an effort. ~**ing** *adj.* able to understand and judge well. ~**ment** *n.*

dis·charge [disˈtʃɑːdʒ] *v.t. & i.* **1.** unload (cargo from a ship). **2.** fire (a gun); shoot (an arrow, etc.). **3.** give or send out (liquid, gas, electric current, etc., which is inside sth.): *chimneys discharging smoke; rivers that ~ (themselves) into the ocean.* **4.** (of persons) send away (from); allow to leave: *men ~d from prison; patients ~d from hospital; a servant ~d for laziness* (i.e. dismissed). **5.** pay (a debt); perform (a duty). *n.* discharging or being ~d; sth. (esp. a liquid) which is ~d: *the ~ of water from a reservoir.*

dis·ci·ple [diˈsaipl] *n.* follower of any leader of religious thought, art, learning, etc.; one of the twelve personal followers of Jesus Christ.

dis·ci·pline [ˈdisiplin] *n.* **1.** training, esp. of the mind and character, to produce self-control, habits of obedience, etc. **2.** the result of such training; order kept (e.g. among school-children, soldiers). **3.** set of rules for conduct. **4.** branch of knowledge; subject of instruction. *v.t.* apply ~ to. **dis·ci·plin·ar·i·an** [ˌdisipliˈnɛəriən] *n.* person good at maintaining ~ (2). **dis·ci·plin·a·ry** [ˈdisiplinəri]

adj. of ~: *disciplinary measures* (intended to maintain ~).

dis·claim [disˈkleim] *v.t.* say that one does not own, that one has not said or done, that one has no connexion with.

dis·close [disˈklouz] *v.t.* uncover; allow to be seen; make known. **dis·clo·sure** [disˈklouʒə*] *n.* sth. ~d; disclosing.

dis·col·our [disˈkʌlə*] *v.t. & i.* change, spoil, the colour of; become changed or spoilt in colour. **dis·col·or·a·tion** [disˌkʌləˈreiʃən] *n.*

dis·com·fit [disˈkʌmfit] *v.t.* upset the plans of; embarrass. ~**ure** [disˈkʌmfitʃə*] *n.*

dis·com·fort [disˈkʌmfət] *n.* uneasiness; absence of comfort; sth. that causes uneasiness; hardship.

dis·com·pose [ˌdiskəmˈpouz] *v.t.* disturb the composure or calmness of. **dis·com·po·sure** [ˌdiskəmˈpouʒə*] *n.*

dis·con·cert [ˌdiskənˈsəːt] *v.t.* spoil or upset (sb.'s plans, etc.); upset the calmness or self-possession of.

dis·con·nect [ˌdiskəˈnekt] *v.t.* detach from; take (two things) apart. ~**ed** *adj.* (of talk or writing) having the ideas, etc., badly connected.

dis·con·so·late [disˈkɔnsəlit] *adj.* unhappy; without hope or comfort.

dis·con·tent [ˌdiskənˈtent] *n.* cause of, feeling of, dissatisfaction or restlessness. ~**ed** *adj.* dissatisfied; not contented. ~**ed·ly** *adv.*

dis·con·tin·ue [ˌdiskənˈtinjuː] *v.t. & i.* put an end to; come to an end.

dis·cord [ˈdiskɔːd] *n.* **1.** disagreement; quarrelling. **2.** lack of harmony; chord (2) that jars. ~**ant** [disˈkɔːdənt] *adj.* not in agreement or harmony; unpleasing to the ear.

dis·count [ˈdiskaunt] *n.* amount that may be taken off the full price, e.g. of (a) goods bought by shopkeepers for resale, (b) an account if paid promptly, (c) a bill of exchange not yet due for

F

payment. **at a ~**, (of goods) not in demand; easily obtained. [dis'kaunt] *v.t.* 1. give or receive the present value of a bill of exchange not yet due. 2. refuse complete belief to (a story, piece of news, etc.).

dis·cour·age [dis'kʌridʒ] *v.t.* 1. lessen, take away, the courage or confidence of. 2. ~ *from*, try to persuade (sb.) not to do sth. ~**·ment** *n.*

dis·course ['disko:s] *n.* speech; lecture; sermon; treatise. [dis-'ko:s] *v.i.* lecture; speak or write at length (*on* sth.).

dis·cov·er [dis'kʌvə*] *v.t.* find out, bring to view (sth. existing but not known); realize (sth. new or unexpected). ~**er** *n.* ~**·y** *n.* ~**ing**; sth. ~ed.

dis·cred·it [dis'kredit] *v.t.* cause the truth, value, or credit, of sth. or sb. to seem doubtful. *n.* loss of credit or reputation; person, thing, causing such loss; doubt; disbelief. ~**·a·ble** [dis-'kreditəbl] *adj.* bringing ~.

dis·creet [dis'kri:t] *adj.* careful, tactful, in what one does and says; prudent. **dis·cre·tion** [dis'kreʃən] *n.* 1. being ~; prudence. 2. freedom to act according to one's own judgement, to do what seems best.

dis·crep·an·cy [dis'krepənsi] *n.* (in statements, accounts) difference; absence of agreement.

dis·crim·i·nate [dis'krimineit] *v.t. & i.* 1. see, make, a difference between: *to* ~ *good books from bad* (*between good and bad books*). 2. make distinctions; treat differently: *laws which do not* ~ *against anyone.* **dis·crim·i·na·ting** *adj.* able to see or make small differences; giving special or different treatment: *discriminating duties* (*tariffs*). **dis·crim·i·na·tion** [dis,krimi'neiʃən] *n.*

dis·cur·sive [dis'kə:siv] *adj.* (of a person, what he says or writes) wandering from one point or subject to another.

dis·cuss [dis'kʌs] *v.t.* examine and argue about (a subject). **dis·cus·sion** [dis'kʌʃən] *n.*

dis·dain [dis'dein] *v.t.* look at with contempt; be too proud (to do sth.). *n.* contempt, scorn. ~**·ful** *adj.*

dis·ease [di'zi:z] *n.* illness of body, mind, a plant; particular sort of such disorder with its own name. **dis·eased** *adj.* suffering from, injured by, ~.

dis·em·bod·ied [,disim'bodid] *adj.* (of the soul, spirit) apart from the body.

dis·en·chant [,disin'tʃɑ:nt] *v.t.* free from enchantment or illusion.

dis·fig·ure [dis'figə*] *v.t.* spoil the appearance or shape of. ~**·ment** *n.* disfiguring or being ~d; sth. that ~s.

dis·gorge [dis'gɔ:dʒ] *v.t.* throw up and out from, or as from, the throat; (fig.) give up unwillingly (esp. sth. taken wrongfully).

dis·grace [dis'greis] *n.* 1. loss of respect, favour, reputation; fall from an honourable position; public shame. 2. person or thing causing ~. *v.t.* bring ~ upon; be a ~ to; remove (sb.) from his position with ~. ~**·ful** *adj.*

dis·grun·tled [dis'grʌntld] *adj.* discontented; in a bad temper (*with* sb., *at* sth.).

dis·guise [dis'gaiz] *v.t.* change the appearance of, in order to deceive or hide the identity of: *He* ~*d his looks but could not* ~ *his voice. n.* disguising; ~d condition; dress, actions, manner, etc., used to ~.

dis·gust [dis'gʌst] *n.* strong feeling of distaste; violent turning away: ~ *at* (*for, against, towards*) sth. *dirty* (*bad-tempering, etc.*). *v.t.* cause ~ in: ~ed *at his laziness.* ~**·ing** *adj.*

dish [diʃ] *n.* (often oval) plate, bowl, etc., from which food is served at table; the food brought to table in or on a ~. *wash up the* ~es, clean them after a meal. *v.t.* put into or on a ~ or ~es: *to* ~ *up the dinner.*

di·shev·elled [di'ʃevld] *adj.* with the hair uncombed; (of the hair and clothes) in disorder; untidy.

dis·hon·our [dis'onə*] *n.* 1. disgrace or shame; loss, absence of, honour and self-respect. **2.** person or thing bringing ~. **v.t.** bring shame, disgrace, loss of honour, on. ~ *a cheque*, (by a bank) refuse to make payment. ~**·a·ble** *adj.*

dis·il·lu·sion [ˌdisi'luːʒn] **v.t.** set (sb.) free from mistaken beliefs. **n.** the state of being ~ed. ~**·ment** *n.*

dis·in·cline [ˌdisin'klain] **v.t.** be ~d to, be unready or unwilling to. **dis·in·cli·na·tion** [ˌdisinkli-'neiʃən] **n.** unwillingness: *a disinclination to work (for hard work).*

dis·in·fect [ˌdisin'fekt] **v.t.** make free from infection by disease germs. ~**ant** *n. & adj.* ~**ing** (substance).

dis·in·gen·u·ous [ˌdisin'dʒenjuəs] *adj.* insincere.

dis·in·her·it [ˌdisin'herit] **v.t.** take away the right (of sb.) to inherit. ~**ance** *n.*

dis·in·te·grate [dis'intigreit] **v.t. & i.** (cause to) break up into small pieces: *rocks ~d by frost and rain.* **dis·in·te·gra·tion** [disˌinti'greiʃən] **n.**

dis·in·ter·est·ed [dis'intəristid] *adj.* not influenced by personal feelings or interests.

dis·joint·ed [dis'dʒɔintid] *adj.* (of speech and writing) not connected; broken.

disk, see *disc.*

dis·lo·cate ['disləkeit] **v.t. 1.** put (esp. a bone in the body) out of position: *to ~ one's shoulder.* **2.** put (traffic, machinery, etc.) out of order. **dis·lo·ca·tion** [ˌdislə'keiʃən] **n.**

dis·lodge [dis'lɔdʒ] **v.t.** force (sb. or sth.) from the place occupied.

dis·mal ['dizml] *adj.* gloomy; sad; miserable; comfortless.

dis·man·tle [dis'mæntl] **v.t. 1.** take away fittings, furnishings, etc., from: *to ~ an old warship (a fort).* **2.** take to pieces: *to ~ a machine.*

dis·may [dis'mei] **n.** feeling of fear and discouragement. **v.t.** fill with ~.

dis·mem·ber [dis'membə*] **v.t.** tear or cut the limbs from;

divide up (a country, etc.). ~**·ment** *n.* the ~*ment of the old Austrian Empire.*

dis·miss [dis'mis] **v.t. 1.** send away (esp. from one's employment): *to ~ workmen.* **2.** put away from the mind: *to ~ thoughts of revenge.* **dis·mis·sal** [dis'misl] **n.**

dis·o·blige [ˌdisə'blaidʒ] **v.t.** refuse to be helpful or to think about another person's wishes or needs.

dis·or·der [dis'ɔːdə*] **n. 1.** absence of order; confusion. **2.** political trouble marked by angry outbursts or rioting. **3.** disease; disturbance of the body's normal working: *a digestive ~.* **v.t.** put into ~. ~**·ly** *adj.* in ~; lawless: ~*ly behaviour*; ~*ly crowds.*

dis·or·gan·ize [dis'ɔːgənaiz] **v.t.** throw into confusion; upset the system or order of. **dis·or·gan·i·za·tion** [disˌɔːgənai'zeiʃən] **n.**

dis·own [dis'oun] **v.t.** say that one does not know (sb. or sth.), that one has not, or no longer wishes to have, any connexion with (sb. or sth.).

dis·par·age [dis'pæridʒ] **v.t.** say things to suggest that (sb. or sth.) is of small value or importance. ~**·ment** *n.* **dis·par·ag·ing·ly** *adv.*

dis·par·i·ty [dis'pæriti] **n.** inequality; difference: ~ *in age (intelligence).*

dis·pas·sion·ate [dis'pæʃənit] *adj.* free from passion, not taking sides, not showing favour (in a quarrel, etc., between others).

dis·patch, des- [dis'pætʃ] **v.t. 1.** send off (to a destination, on a journey, for a special purpose): *to ~ letters (telegrams, messengers).* **2.** finish, get through (business, a meal) quickly. **3.** kill: *to ~ a murderer.* **n. 1.** ~*ing or being ~ed.* **2.** sth. ~*ed (1), esp. government, military, or newspaper message or report.* **3.** promptness; speed: *to act with ~.*

dis·pel [dis'pel] **v.t.** (-ll-). drive away; scatter (clouds, fears, doubts).

dis·pense [dis'pens] *v.t. & i.* **1.** ~ *with*, do without: *to* ~ *with the cook's services.* **2.** distribute; administer: *to* ~ *justice.* **3.** mix, prepare, give out (medicine). **dis·pens·er** *n.* person who makes up medicines from a doctor's prescriptions. **dis·pen·sa·ry** [dis'pensəri] *n.* place where medicines are ~d. **dis·pen·sa·tion** [ˌdispen'seiʃən] *n.* **1.** act of dispensing (2); sth. looked upon as ~d (2) or ordered by God. **2.** authority given by the Church to do sth. usually forbidden, or not to do sth. which must usually be done.

dis·perse [dis'pə:s] *v.t. & i.* (cause to) go in different directions; scatter; send out, space out, go out (esp. troops under attack), to separate positions. **dis·per·sal** *n.*

dis·pir·it·ed [dis'piritid] *adj.* discouraged; depressed.

dis·place [dis'pleis] *v.t.* put out of the right or usual position; take or put sb. or sth. in the place of. ~*d person*, stateless refugee in exile. ~·**ment** *n.* (esp.) amount of water ~d by a solid body in it, or floating in it: *a ship of 10,000 tons* ~*ment.*

dis·play [dis'plei] *v.t.* **1.** show; place or arrange so that things may be seen easily. **2.** allow to be seen: *to* ~ *one's ignorance.* *n.* ~ing; sth. ~ed: *a fashion* ~; *a* ~ *of one's knowledge.*

dis·port [dis'pɔ:t] *v.t.* ~ *oneself*, enjoy or amuse oneself (e.g. in the sea, or in the sunshine).

dis·pose [dis'pouz] *v.i. & t.* **1.** ~ *of*, finish with; get rid of; deal with: *to* ~ *of rubbish* (*business, sb.'s arguments*). **2.** place (persons, objects) in good order or in suitable positions. **3.** *be, feel,* ~*d*, be willing or ready: *to feel* ~*d for a walk*; *to be not at all* ~*d to help.* *well-*~*d* (i.e. friendly and helpful) *toward.* . . . **dis·po·sal** [dis'pouzl] *n.* the act of disposing (1), (2): *the disposal of property* (*business affairs, troops*). *at one's disposal*, to be used as one wishes: *to place one's time, etc., at sb. else's disposal.*

dis·po·si·tion [ˌdispə'ziʃən] *n.* **1.** arrangement; disposing (2). **2.** person's natural qualities of mind and character: *a man with a cheerful disposition*; *a woman with a disposition to jealousy.*

dis·pos·sess [ˌdispə'zes] *v.t.* ~ (*sb.*) *of*, take away property (esp. land) from; compel (sb.) to give up (the house he occupies). **dis·pos·ses·sion** [ˌdispə'zeʃən] *n.*

dis·pro·por·tion [ˌdisprə'pɔ:ʃən] *n.* state of being out of proportion. ~·**ate** *adj.*

dis·pute [dis'pju:t] *v.t. & i.* **1.** argue, quarrel (*with, against,* sb.) (*on, about,* sth.); question the truth or justice of (sth.). **2.** oppose; try to prevent: *to* ~ *the enemy's advance.* *n.* disputing; argument. *beyond* ~, undoubtedly. **dis·pu·ta·ble** [dis'pju:təbl] *adj.* that may be ~d; questionable. **dis·pu·tant** ['dispjutənt] *n.* person taking part in a ~.

dis·qui·et [dis'kwaiət] *v.t.* make troubled, anxious, uneasy. *n.* anxiety; troubled condition. **dis·qui·e·tude** [dis'kwaiitju:d] *n.* state of ~.

dis·qui·si·tion [ˌdiskwi'ziʃən] *n.* long, elaborate speech or piece of writing on a subject.

dis·re·gard [ˌdisri'gɑ:d] *v.t.* pay no attention to; show no respect for. *n.* inattention; indifference; neglect.

dis·re·pair [ˌdisri'peə*] *n.* state of needing repair: *old buildings in* ~.

dis·rep·u·ta·ble [dis'repjutəbl] *adj.* having a bad reputation; not respectable. **dis·re·pute** [ˌdisri'pju:t] *n.* discredit; condition of being ~: *to fall into disrepute.*

dis·robe [dis'roub] *v.i. & t.* (esp.) take off official or ceremonial robes.

dis·rupt [dis'rʌpt] *v.t.* break up, separate by force (a State, communications, other non-physical things). **dis·rup·tion** [dis'rʌpʃən] *n.* **dis·rup·tive** [dis'rʌptiv] *adj.*

dis·sect [di'sekt] *v.t.* cut up

(parts of an animal, plant, etc.) in order to study its structure; examine (a theory, argument, etc.), part by part to judge its value. **dis·sec·tion** [di'sekʃən] *n.*

dis·sem·ble [di'sembl] *v.t. & i.* speak, behave, so as to hide one's real feelings, thoughts, plans, etc., or give a wrong idea of them. **dis·sem·bler** *n.*

dis·sem·i·nate [di'semineit] *v.t.* distribute or spread widely (ideas, doctrines, etc.). **dis·sem·i·na·tion** [di,semi'neiʃən] *n.*

dis·sent [di'sent] *v.i.* 1. ~ *from*, have a different opinion from; refuse to assent to. 2. (esp.) refuse to accept the religious doctrine of the Church of England. *n.* ~ing. **dis·sen·sion** [di'senʃən] *n.* angry disagreement; quarrel(ling). ~·er *n.* Protestant nonconformist.

dis·ser·ta·tion [,disə'teiʃən] *n.* long spoken or written account of sth.

dis·ser·vice [dis'sə:vis] *n.* harmful or unhelpful action; ill turn.

dis·sim·u·late [di'simjuleit] *v.t. & i.* = dissemble. **dis·sim·u·la·tion** [di,simju'leiʃən] *n.*

dis·si·pate ['disipeit] *v.t. & i.* 1. drive away (clouds, fear, ignorance, etc.); disperse. 2. waste (time, money) foolishly. **dis·si·pat·ed** *adj.* given up to foolish and often harmful pleasures. **dis·si·pa·tion** [,disi'peiʃən] *n.* (esp.) foolish wasting of energy, money, etc., on harmful pleasures.

dis·so·ci·ate [di'souʃieit] *v.t.* separate (in thought, feeling) (*from*); not associate.

dis·so·lute ['disəlu:t] *adj.* given up to immoral conduct; immoral.

dis·so·lu·tion [,disə'lu:ʃən] *n.* breaking up; undoing or ending (of a marriage, partnership, etc.); (esp.) ending of Parliament before a general election.

dis·solve [di'zɔlv] *v.t. & i.* 1. (of a liquid) soak into a solid so that the solid itself becomes liquid: *Water ~s salt.* 2. (of a solid) become liquid as the result of being taken into a liquid:

Salt ~s in water. 3. cause (a solid) to ~: *He ~d the salt in water.* 4. disappear; vanish: *The view ~d in mist.* 5. bring to, come to, an end: *to ~ a marriage (Parliament).*

dis·so·nant ['disənənt] *adj.* discordant; not harmonious. **dis·so·nance** *n.* discord.

dis·suade [di'sweid] *v.t.* advise against; (try to) turn (sb.) away (*from* sth., *from* doing sth.): *to ~ a friend from marrying a fool.* **dis·sua·sion** [di'sweiʒn] *n.*

dis·taff ['distɑ:f] *n.* stick round which wool, flax, etc., is wound for spinning by hand. *the ~ side*, the mother's side of the family.

dis·tance ['distəns] *n.* 1. measure of space between two points, places, etc.; being far off; that part of a view, etc., which is a long way off: *to (from) a ~; in the ~.* 2. space of time: *to look back over a ~ of fifty years.* **dis·tant** ['distənt] *adj.* 1. far away in space or time; far off in family relationship: *a ~ cousin.* 2. (of behaviour) unfriendly; cool.

dis·taste [dis'teist] *n.* dislike: *a ~ for hard work.* ~·ful *adj.* disagreeable; causing ~.

dis·tem·per [dis'tempə*] *n.* colouring matter (to be) mixed with water and brushed on ceilings, etc. *v.t.* put ~ on.

dis·tend [dis'tend] *v.t. & i.* (cause to) swell out (by pressure from inside): *a ~ed stomach.*

dis·til [dis'til] *v.i. & t.* (-*ll*-). 1. turn (a liquid) to vapour by heating, cool the vapour and collect the drops of liquid that condense from the vapour; purify (a liquid) thus; drive *off* or *out* impurities thus; make whisky, essences, thus. 2. fall, let fall, in drops. ~·la·tion [,disti'leiʃən] *n.* ~ling or being ~led. ~·ler·y *n.* place where spirits such as whisky and gin are ~led.

dis·tinct [dis'tiŋkt] *adj.* 1. easily heard, seen, understood; plain; clearly marked. 2. separate; different in kind. ~·ly *adv. to speak ~ly.* **dis·tinc·tive**

adj. serving to make or mark a ~ difference. ~**ness** *n.*

dis·tinc·tion [dis'tiŋkʃən] *n.* **1.** being, keeping things, different or distinct; distinguishing, being distinguished, as different. **2.** that which makes one thing different from another. **3.** quality of being superior, excellent, distinguished : *a writer (novel) of* ~. **4.** decoration, reward; mark of honour, title, etc.

dis·tin·guish [dis'tiŋgwiʃ] *v.t. & i.* **1.** see, hear, recognize, understand well, the difference (*between* two things) (of one thing *from* another). **2.** be a mark of character, difference. **3.** make (oneself) well known; do credit to : *to* ~ *oneself in an examination.* **dis·tin·guished** *adj.* famous; remarkable; showing distinction (3).

dis·tort [dis'tɔ:t] *v.t.* **1.** pull, twist, out of the usual shape: *a face* ~*ed by pain.* **2.** give a false account of; twist away from the truth : ~*ed accounts of what happened.* **dis·tor·tion** [dis'tɔ:ʃən] *n.*

dis·tract [dis'trækt] *v.t.* draw away (a person's attention *from* sth.): *to have one's mind* ~*ed from one's work.* ~**ed** *adj.* with the mind confused or bewildered; with the attention drawn in different directions: ~*ed between love and duty.* **dis·trac·tion** [dis'trækʃən] *n.* ~*ing or being* ~*ed;* sth. (either a pleasure or amusement or an annoyance) that ~*s.*

dis·traught [dis'trɔ:t] *adj.* distracted; violently upset in mind.

dis·tress [dis'tres] *n.* **1.** (cause of) great pain, sorrow, or discomfort; (suffering caused by) want of money or other necessary things. **2.** serious danger or difficulty : *a ship in* ~. *v.t.* cause ~ to.

dis·trib·ute [dis'tribju:t] *v.t.* **1.** give or send out (*to, among,* a number of persons or places). **2.** spread out (over a larger area). **3.** put into groups or classes. **dis·tri·bu·tion** [ˌdistri'bju:ʃən] *n.* **dis·trib·u·tive**

[dis'tribjutiv] *adj.* of distribution : *the distributive trades* (e.g. shipping, shopkeeping). **dis·trib·u·tor** *n.* person or thing that ~*s.*

dis·trict ['distrikt] *n.* part of a country : *mountainous* ~*s of Scotland;* part of a country or town marked out for a special purpose : *postal* ~*s of London.*

dis·trust [dis'trʌst] *v.t. & n.* (have) doubt or suspicion (about): *look at sb. with* ~; ~ *what one reads in a newspaper.* ~**ful** *adj.* ~**ful·ly** *adv.*

dis·turb [dis'tə:b] *v.t.* break the quiet, calm, peace, or order of; put out of the right or usual position : *to* ~ *sb.'s sleep (papers, desk, plans).* ~**·ance** *n.* ~*ing or being* ~*ed;* (esp.) social or political disorder.

dis·use [dis'ju:s] *n.* state of being no longer used : *rusty from* ~. **dis·used** [dis'ju:zd] *p.p.* no longer used.

ditch [ditʃ] *n.* narrow channel dug in or between fields, etc., to hold or carry off water.

dit·to, *abbr.* **do.** ['ditou] *n.* the same. (Used in lists to avoid writing words again.)

dit·ty ['diti] *n.* short, simple song.

di·van [di'væn] *n.* long, low, soft, backless seat, used also as a bed.

dive [daiv] *v.i.* **1.** go head first (*into* water). **2.** go quickly to a lower level; move the hand (*into* sth.) quickly and suddenly : *to* ~ *into one's pocket.* *n.* act of diving. **div·er** *n.* (esp.) person who works under water in a special dress (*diving-dress*).

di·verge [dai'və:dʒ, di-] *v.i.* (of paths, opinions, etc.) get farther apart from each other or from a point as they progress; turn or branch away (*from*). **di·ver·gence, di·ver·gen·cy** *n.* **di·ver·gent** *adj.*

di·vers ['daivəz] *adj.* (old use) several; more than one.

di·verse [dai'və:s] *adj.* quite unlike in quality or character; of different kinds. **di·ver·si·fy** [dai'və:sifai] *v.t.* make ~. **di·ver·si·ty** [dai'və:siti] *n.*

di·vert [dai'və:t, di-] **v.t. 1.** turn in another direction: *to ~ the course of a river.* **2.** turn the attention away (*from* sth.); amuse; entertain: *an easily ~ed child.* **~·ing** *adj.* amusing. **di·ver·sion** [dai'və:ʃən,di-] *n.* **~·ing;** (esp.) sth. which turns the attention from serious things; sth. giving rest or amusement. *traffic diversion,* (instance of) directing traffic away from a road (e.g. when under repair or blocked by an accident).

di·vest [dai'vest] **v.t. 1.** take off (clothes): *to ~ a king of his robes.* **2.** take away from: *to ~ a man of his rank and honours.* **3.** *~ oneself of,* give up; get rid of. **di·vide** [di'vaid] **v.t. & i. 1.** separate, be separated (into); split or break up. **2.** find out how often one number is contained in another. **div·i·dend** ['dividend] *n.* **1.** number to be ~d by another. **2.** periodical payment of a share of a limited company's profits to shareholders: *to pay a 10% ~nd.* **di·vi·ders** [di'vaidəz] *n. pl.* see the picture. **di·vis·i·ble** [di'vizibl] *adj.* that can be ~d. **di·vi·sion** [di'viʒən] *n.* dividing or being ~d; the effect of dividing; a line that ~s; divided part. **2.** (army) unit of two or more brigades. **di·vi·sor** [di'vaizə*] *n.* number by which another number is ~d.

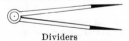

Dividers

¹**di·vine** [di'vain] *adj.* **1.** of, from, or like God or a god: *Divine Service,* the public worship of God. **2.** (colloq.) excellent; very beautiful: *~ weather.* *n.* priest trained in theology. **di·vin·i·ty** [di'viniti] *n.* **1.** quality of being ~: *the divinity of Christ;* a ~ being. **2.** (study of) theology: *a doctor of divinity (D.D.).* ²**di·vine** [di'vain] **v.t. & i.** discover or learn sth. about future events, hidden things, etc., by means not based on reason: *to ~*

sb.'s intentions. **di·vin·er** *n.* person who ~s, esp. one who claims to have the power to find out where water, metals, etc., lie under the earth by using a Y-shaped stick (called a *divining-rod*). **div·i·na·tion** [ˌdivi'neiʃən] *n.*

di·vis·i·ble, di·vi·sion, di·vi·sor, see *divide.*

di·vorce [di'vɔ:s] *n.* **1.** legal ending of a marriage. **2.** ending of a connexion or relationship between two things. **v.t. 1.** put an end to a marriage by law. **2.** separate (things usually together).

di·vulge [dai'vʌldʒ] **v.t.** make known (sth. secret).

diz·zy ['dizi] *adj.* (*dizzier, dizziest*). (of a person) feeling as if everything were turning round, as if unable to balance; (of places) causing such a feeling. **diz·zi·ly** *adv.* **diz·zi·ness** *n.*

¹**do** [du:, du] **v.** (1st person sing. pres. t. neg. *don't* [dount], 3rd person sing. pres. t. *does* [dʌz, dəz], neg. *doesn't* ['dʌznt], p.t. *did* [did], neg. *didn't* ['didnt], p.p. *done* [dʌn]). **I.** *aux. v.* **1.** used to form the expanded present and past tenses: (a) *Does (Did) he want it?* (b) *He did not go. Do not go yet.* **2.** used for emphasis: *'Do stop that noise! I 'do want you to know how sorry I am.* **II.** *verb substitute* in a question phrase, answer, or comment, replacing the verb in a preceding statement: *He lives in London, doesn't he? You don't blame me, do you? Who broke the window? I did.* **III.** **v.t. & i. 1.** perform, carry out (an action); busy oneself with: *When are you going to do the housework? I've nothing to do.* **2.** serve, be convenient, suitable, or satisfactory (*for*); be good enough: *These shoes won't do for mountain-climbing.* **3.** cook (thoroughly): *The meat isn't done yet.* **4.** (colloq.) cheat; get the better of: *do sb. out of sth.,* get sth. from him by trickery. **5.** (colloq.) ruin; spoil: *do for (sb.),* kill or

injure; *be done for*, be ruined, made worthless, etc. *done up*, tired out. **6.** *do sth. up*, (a) clean; make like new again; (b) tie up (into a parcel); (c) fasten up (clothing, etc.). **7.** *(can, could) do with*, be ready for; welcome; need; be satisfied with: *I could do with a drink. He could do with a new hat. do without*, manage without; deny oneself: *to do without tobacco in prison. do away with*, put an end to. *have to do with*, be concerned with. *have (something, nothing, etc.) to do with*, have relations, business, etc., with. *do for (sb.)*, (colloq.) look after (a person's) rooms, etc.; cook and clean for. *have done with*, make an end of; finish with: *Let's be quick and have done with it.*

²**do.**, see *ditto*.

do·cile ['dousail] *adj.* easily trained or controlled. **do·cil·i·ty** [dou'siliti] *n.*

¹**dock** [dɔk] *n.* **1.** place in a harbour or river, with gates through which water may be let in and out, where ships are (un)loaded or repaired. *dry ~*, one from which water may be pumped out. **2.** (pl.; also *dockyard*) row of ~s (1) with wharves, sheds, offices, etc. *v.t. & i.* (of ships) come, go, bring into, a ~. **~·er** *n.* ~yard labourer.

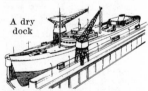

A dry dock

²**dock** [dɔk] *n.* place in a criminal court where the prisoner stands.

³**dock** [dɔk] *v.t.* cut short (an animal's tail); (colloq.) make (wages, allowances, supplies) less.

doc·tor ['dɔktə'] *n.* **1.** person who has received the highest university degree in any faculty, e.g., *Doctor of Laws.* **2.** person who has been trained in medical science. *v.t.* **1.** (colloq.) give

medical treatment to or for. **2.** make (esp. food and drink) inferior by adding sth.; add drugs to. **3.** make false: *to ~ accounts (evidence).* **~·ate** ['dɔktərit] *n.* ~'s degree.

doc·trine ['dɔktrin] *n.* body of teaching; beliefs and teachings (of a church, political party, school of scientists, etc.).

doc·u·ment ['dɔkjumənt] *n.* sth. written or printed, to be used as a record or in evidence. **~·a·ry** [ˌdɔkju'mentəri] *adj.* in the form of a ~: *~ary proof.* *n.* factual film, e.g. on a scientific or historical subject.

dodge [dɔdʒ] *v.t. & i.* move quickly to one side, change position or direction, in order to escape or avoid sth.; get round (difficulties, etc.) by cunning or trickery. *n.* act of dodging; trick; clever little invention.

doe [dou] *n.* female deer or rabbit.

does, see *do*.

dog [dɔg] *n.* see the picture. *v.t.* (-*gg*-). keep close behind, in the footsteps of. **'~-'tired** *adj.* very tired.

A dog	A dome

dog·ged ['dɔgid] *adj.* obstinate.

dog·ger·el ['dɔgərəl] *n.* irregular, inexpert verse.

dog·ma ['dɔgmə] *n.* belief, system of beliefs, put forward by some authority (esp. the Church), to be accepted as true without question. **dog·mat·ic** [dɔg-'mætik] *adj.* put forward as ~s; (of a person) making purely personal statements as if they were ~s. **~·tize** ['dɔgmətaiz] *v.t.* make ~tic statements.

dol·drums ['dɔldrəmz] *n. pl.* *in the ~*, (fig.) in low spirits.

dole [doul] *v.t.* ~ *out*, give out (food, money, etc.) in small amounts (e.g. to poor people). **n**. sth. ~d out.

dole·ful ['doulful] **adj.** sad; mournful; dismal. ~·ly **adv.**

doll [dɔl] **n**. model of a baby or person, usu. for a child to play with.

dol·lar ['dɔlə*] **n**. ($) unit of money in U.S.A., Canada, etc.

dol·or·ous ['dɔlərəs] **adj.** sorrowful; distressing, distressing.

dol·phin ['dɔlfin] **n**. sea-animal like a porpoise.

dolt [doult] **n**. stupid person.

do·main [də'mein] **n**. lands under the rule of a king, government, etc.; (fig.) field or province (of thought, knowledge, activity).

dome [doum] **n**. rounded roof with a circular base. See the picture on page 160.

do·mes·tic [də'mestik] **adj. 1.** of the home, family, household: ~ *servants*. **2.** not foreign; native; of one's own country: ~ *news (loans)*. **3.** (of animals) kept by, living with, man. (Cf. *wild*.) **do·mes·ti·cate** [də'mestikeit] **v.t. 1.** (chiefly in p.p., ~ated) make fond of, interested in, household work. **2.** (of animals) tame. **do·mes·ti·ci·ty** [ˌdoumes'tisiti] **n**. home or family life.

dom·i·cile ['dɔmisail, -sil] **n**. dwelling-place; (legal) place where sb. lives permanently.

dom·i·nate ['dɔmineit] **v.t. & i.** have control, authority, commanding influence, over; (of a place, esp. a height) overlook. **dom·i·nant** ['dɔminənt] **adj.** dominating. **dom·i·nance n**. state of being dominant; control. **dom·i·na·tion** [ˌdɔmi'neiʃən] **n**. dominating or being ~d. **dom·i·neer** [ˌdɔmi'niə*] **v.i.** act, speak, in a dominating manner.

do·min·ion [də'minjən] **n̈. 1.** authority to rule. **2.** (often pl.) territory of a sovereign (2) government; used formerly to describe certain self-governing territories of the British Commonwealth of Nations.

dom·i·noes ['dɔminouz] **n. pl.** table game played with 28 small, flat, oblong pieces of wood, etc.

don [dɔn] **n. 1.** university teacher. **2.** Spanish gentleman; Spanish title (used before a man's name): *Don Juan*.

do·nate [dou'neit] **v.t.** give (money, etc., to a cause, charity). **do·na·tion** [dou'neiʃən] **n**. giving; sth. given.

done, see *do*.

don·key ['dɔŋki] **n**. see the picture. '~·ˌen·gine **n**. small steam-engine on a ship's deck.

A donkey A door

do·nor ['dounə*] **n**. giver.

doom [du:m] **n. 1.** ruin; death; sth. evil that is to come. **2.** (also ~s-day) the Day of Judgement. **doomed p.p.** condemned (*to* sth., *to do* sth.); facing certain death.

door [dɔ:*, dɔə*] **n**. see the picture. *next* ~, (in, to) the next house. *out of* ~s, outside; in the open air. ~·**way n**. cf. *gateway*.

dope [doup] **n. 1.** thick, heavy liquid used as varnish. **2.** (colloq.) harmful drug (e.g. opium). **v.t.** give ~ (2) to; make unconscious with ~ (2).

dor·mant ['dɔ:mənt] **adj.** in a state of inactivity but awaiting development or activity: *a ~ volcano*; ~ *faculties*; *plants which are ~ during the winter*.

dor·mi·to·ry ['dɔ:mitəri] **n**. sleeping-room with several or many beds, esp. in a boarding-school. (Cf. *ward* (4).)

dor·mouse ['dɔ:maus] **n**. (pl. *-mice* [-mais]). small animal (like a mouse) which sleeps through the winter.

dor·sal ['dɔ:sl] **adj.** of, on, or near the back: *the ~ fin*.

dose [dous] **n**. amount (of medicine) to be taken at one time. **v.t.** give ~(s) to.

dos·si·er ['dɔsiei] **n**. set of papers giving information about a person or event, esp. a person's record.

dot [dot] *n.* small round (pen) mark (as over the letter i). *v.t.* (*-tt-*). mark with a dot; make with, cover with, dots: *to dot one's i's; a dotted line. dotted about*, scattered here and there.

do·tage ['doutidʒ] *n.* weakness of mind caused by old age: *in his ~.*

dote [dout] *v.i. ~ on*, show much, or too much, fondness for.

dou·ble ['dʌbl] *adj.* **1.** twice as much (large, good, etc.): *~ width; a ~ share.* **2.** having two like things or parts: *a gun with a ~ barrel; ~ doors.* **3.** made for two persons or things: *a ~ bed;* serving two purposes. **4.** (of flowers) having more than one set or circle of petals. *adv.* **1.** twice (as much): *to cost ~.* **2.** *to see ~*, to see two things when there is only one. *n.* **1.** *~* quantity. **2.** person or thing very or exactly like another. **3.** *at the ~*, at a slow run. **4.** sharp turn or twist. *v.t. & i.* **1.** make or become twice as great. **2.** bend or fold in two. *~ up*, fold up; (of a person) bend the body with pain. **3.** (military) run at *~* the speed of marching. *~ back*, turn back quickly to avoid capture, etc. '*~*-'**deal·er** *n.* person who deceives (esp. in business). '*~*-'**en·try** *n.* system of book-keeping in which everything is written in two places.

dou·blet ['dʌblit] *n.* close-fitting garment for the upper part of the body, worn by men (about A.D. 1400-1600).

doubt [daut] *n.* uncertainty of mind; feeling of uncertainty: *in ~*, uncertain; *without (a) ~*, certainly; *no ~*, very probably. *v.t. & i.* feel ~ (about). *~*·**ful** *adj.* feeling, full of, ~; causing ~. *~*·**ful·ly** *adv. ~*·**less** *adv.* (colloq.) very probably.

dough [dou] *n.* mixture of flour, water, etc., in a paste (for making bread, etc.).

dough·ty ['dauti] *adj.* (old use) brave; strong; valiant.

dour [duə*] *adj.* (of a person) stern; severe.

dove [dʌv] *n.* **1.** kind of pigeon. **2.** symbol of peace. '*~*-'**col·our(ed)** *adj.* soft grey. '*~*-'**tail** *v.t. & i.* join together, interlock (pieces of wood, (fig.), plans, etc.).

dow·a·ger ['dauədʒə*] *n.* woman with title or property from her late husband: *the queen ~; the ~ duchess.*

dow·dy ['daudi] *adj.* (of clothes, etc.) shabby or unfashionable; (of a person) dressed in *~*-clothes.

dow·di·ly ['daudili] *adv.*

¹**down** [daun] *adv.* **1.** from a high(er) to a low(er) level: *The sun went ~.* **2.** from an upright to a lying position: *She was knocked ~ by a bus.* **3.** to or in a less erect attitude or less important place or position: *Sit ~. He has gone ~ three places in class. They have gone ~ to the country for a holiday.* **4.** to a lower degree: *The temperature has gone ~. The clock has run ~.* **5.** firmly; permanently; on paper: *Put your name ~ for a ticket. She put her foot ~* (insisted). **6.** from an earlier to a later time: *the history of Europe ~ to 1914.* **7.** *walk up and ~*, backwards and forwards. *be ~ and out*, exhausted; beaten. *prep.* **1.** from a high(er) to a low(er) level: *to run ~ a hill.* **2.** at a lower part of: *They live ~ the road.* **3.** along: *Pass ~ the bus and make room for more passengers.* **4.** from an earlier to a more recent time: *Has mankind improved ~ the centuries? v.t.* put *~: to ~ tools* (refuse to work); *to ~ an enemy* (knock him ~). *~*·**cast** ['daunkɑːst] *adj.* (of a person) sad; (of eyes) looking *~*wards. *~*·**fall** ['daunfɔːl] *n.* heavy fall (e.g. of rain); (fig.) ruin; sudden fall from fortune or power. *~*·**heart·ed** ['daun'hɑːtid] *adj.* sad. *~*·**pour** ['daunpɔː*] *n.* heavy fall (esp. of rain). *~*·**right** ['daunrait] *adj.* honest; straightforward; thorough. *adv.* thoroughly; completely. *~*·**stairs** ['daun'stɛəz] *adv.* to,

at or on a lower floor. **~·town** ['dauntaun] *adv.* (U.S.A.) to or in the main or business part of town. **~·trod·den** ['daun,trɒdn] *adj.* oppressed; kept ~ and treated badly. **~·ward** ['daun-wəd] *adj.* moving, leading, to what is lower. **~·wards** *adv.* towards what is lower.

²**down** [daun] *n.* stretch of bare, open highland.

³**down** [daun] *n.* soft hair or feathers, esp. the first soft under-feathers of young birds. **~·y** *adj.* made of, covered with, ~ ; soft like ~.

dow·ry ['dauəri] *n.* property, money, given to or with a daughter when she marries.

dox·ol·o·gy [dɒk'sɒlədʒi] *n.* words of praise to God, used in church services (e.g. 'Glory be to God . . .').

doz. short for *dozen*.

doze [douz] *v.i.* sleep lightly; be half asleep. ~ *off*, fall lightly asleep. *n.* short, light sleep.

doz·en ['dʌzn] *n.* twelve.

drab [dræb] *adj.* (-*bb*-) *&* *n.* muddy brown; (fig.) dull; un-interesting; monotonous.

draft [drɑːft] *n.* **1.** outline (in the form of rough notes) of sth. to be done: *a ~ for a speech* (*a letter*). Cf. *draught*(8), draw-ing for a machine. **2.** written order for payment of money by a bank; drawing of money by means of such an order. **3.** party of men chosen from a larger group for a special pur-pose, esp. of soldiers. *v.t.* make a ~ (1) of; choose men for a ~ (3). **'drafts·man** *n.* man who prepares ~ s (1) . Cf. *draughtsman* (in engineering, etc.).

drag [dræg] *v.t.* & *i.* (-*gg*-). **1.** pull along (esp. with effort and difficulty): *to ~ a box out of a cupboard.* **2.** (allow to) move slowly and with effort: *to walk with ~ging feet.* **3.** (of time, work, an entertainment) go on slowly in a dull manner. **4.** use nets, etc., to search the bottom of a river, lake, etc. (usu. for something lost or missing). *n.* sth. which is ~ged, e.g. a net

(~-*net*) pulled over the bottom of a river to catch fish ; (fig.) sth. that slows down progress.

drag·gled ['drægld] *adj.* wet, dirty, or muddy (as if dragged through mud, etc.).

drag·o·man ['drægoumən] *n.* (pl. ~ s). guide and interpreter (esp. for travellers in Arabic-speaking countries).

drag·on ['drægən] *n.* (in old stories) winged, fire-breathing creature. **'~-fly** *n.* insect with a stick-like body and two pairs of wings.

dra·goon [drə'guːn] *n.* horse-soldier; cavalryman. *v.t.* force (sb. *into* doing sth.).

drain [drein] *n.* **1.** pipe, channel, trench, etc., for carrying away water and other unwanted liquids. **2.** sth. that continually uses up force, time, wealth, etc. *v.t.* & *i.* **1.** lead off (liquid) by means of ~ s (1): *to ~ swamps* ; (of liquid) flow away. **2.** (cause to) lose (strength, wealth, etc.) by degrees: *a country ~ ed of its manpower and wealth by war.* **3.** drink; empty (a cup, etc.). **~·age** ['dreinidʒ] *n.* ~ing or being ~ed; system of ~ s (1).

drake [dreik] *n.* male duck.

dram [dræm] *n.* ¹⁄₁₆ ounce (avoir-dupois); ⅛ ounce for medical substances.

dra·ma ['drɑːmə] *n.* **1.** play for the theatre; art of writing and performing plays. **2.** series of exciting events. **dra·mat·ic** [drə'mætik] *adj.* of ~ ; sudden or exciting, like an event in a ~. **dra·mat·ics** *n. pl.* ~ tic per-formances. **dram·a·tist** ['dræm-ətist] *n.* writer of plays. **dram·a·tize** ['dræmətaiz] *v.t.* make (a story, etc.) into a ~.

drank, see *drink*.

drape [dreip] *v.t.* **1.** hang (cur-tains, cloth, clothes, etc.) in folds round or over sth: *to ~ curtains over a window* (*a cloak round one's shoulders*). **2.** cover or decorate with cloth, etc.: *walls ~ d with flags.* **drap·er** ['dreipə*] *n.* dealer in cloth, articles of clothing, esp. a shop-keeper selling such things.

drap·er·y *n.* **1.** goods sold by a ~r. **2.** clothing, curtains, etc., ~d round sth.

dras·tic ['dræstik] *adj.* (of actions, methods, medicines) having a strong or violent effect. **dras·ti·cal·ly** *adv.*

draught [drɑːft] *n.* **1.** current of air in a room, chimney, or other shut-in place. **2.** the pulling in of a net for fish; the fish caught in it. **3.** depth of water needed to float a ship. **4.** drawing of liquid from a container (e.g. a barrel): *beer on ~; ~ beer.* **5.** (amount drunk during) one continuous act of swallowing: *a long ~ of water.* **6.** (of animals) used for pulling: *a ~-horse.* **7.** (pl.) board game for two players using 24 flat, round pieces (called ~*smen*). **8.** rough drawing, sketch, or plan (engineering, etc.). ~'**y** *adj.* with ~s(1) blowing through. '**draughts·man** *n.* **1.** see 7. **2.** man who makes ~s(8).

draw [drɔː] *v.t. & i.* (p.t. *drew* [druː], p.p. *drawn* [drɔːn]). **1.** move by pulling: *to ~ a boat up out of the water; to ~ sb. aside.* **2.** cause to move after or behind by pulling: *a train drawn by two engines.* **3.** take out by pulling: *to ~ a cork from a bottle.* **4.** obtain from a source: *to ~ rations from a store (money from a bank).* **5.** take in: *to ~ a deep breath;* (of a chimney) allow air to flow through: *The chimney ~s well.* **6.** make longer by pulling; become longer: *to ~ wire;* (fig.) *long-drawn-out discussions.* **7.** attract; cause to come or be directed towards: *a film that drew large audiences.* **8.** (of a ship) need (a certain depth of water) in order to float. **9.** cause (a person) to say what he knows, to show his feelings, etc.: *to ~ sb. out; to ~ information from a witness; to ~ tears (sb.'s wrath).* **10.** move or come (towards, near, forward, away from, level with, to an end, etc.): *The ships drew level. The day drew to its close.* **11.** (of two teams, etc.) end (a game, competition, etc.) without a result, neither side winning: *a ~n game; to ~ 2–2.* **12.** make (lines, designs, pictures, etc.) with a pen, pencil, chalk, etc.; use a pencil, etc., for doing this: *to ~ a tree; to ~ a pen through a word. ~ the line at,* refuse to go as far as. **13.** write out (a cheque, etc.); compose, put into writing: *~ up a document, agreement, etc.* **14.** (with adverbs): *~ in,* (of days) get shorter, as in autumn; *~ out,* (of days) get longer (as in spring). *~ oneself up,* stand up straight. *~ up,* (of a carriage, etc.) stop; (of troops, etc.) get into formation or order. *n.* act of ~ing; (esp.) sb. or sth. that ~s attention or attracts; the ~ing of lots (see *lot*); a game or competition that is ~n(11). **drawn** *ppl. adj.* (of the face, eyes) haggard through strain or worry. '~·**back** *n.* disadvantage; sth. that lessens one's satisfaction. '~·**bridge** *n.* bridge that can be pulled up at the end(s) by chains. ~**er** [drɔː*] *n.* container that slides in and out of a piece of furniture, etc., used for clothes, etc. ~**ers** [drɔːz] *n. pl.* two-legged undergarment fastened at the waist. ~**ing** *n.* art of ~ing(12); sth. ~n(12) with a pencil or crayon. '~·**ing-pin** *n.* pin with a flat head, used e.g. for fastening papers to a notice-board, etc. '~·**ing-room** *n.* room in which guests are received.

drawl [drɔːl] *v.i. & t.* speak so that the sounds of the vowels are longer than usual. *n.* slow way of speaking.

dray [drei] *n.* low, flat, four-wheeled cart for heavy loads.

dread [dred] *n.* great fear and anxiety. *v.t. & i.* feel great fear of. ~**ful** *adj.* causing ~; (colloq.) unpleasant. ~**ful·ly** *adv.*

dream [driːm] *n.* **1.** sth. which one seems to see or experience during sleep. **2.** state of mind in which what is happening seems like a ~(1). **3.** mental picture(s) of the future: *to have ~s of wealth and happiness.*

4. beautiful or pleasing person or thing. *v.t. & i.* (p.t. and p.p. *dreamed* or *dreamt* [dremt]). have ~s; see, etc., in a ~; imagine, think possible. **~·y** *adj.* (of a person) with thoughts far away from his surroundings; (of things) vague; unreal. **~·i·ly** *adv.*

drear·y [ˈdriəri] *adj.* (*-ier*, *-iest*). dull; gloomy; causing low spirits: ~ *weather* (*work*, *surroundings*). **drear·i·ly** *adv.*

¹dredge [dredʒ] *n.* apparatus for bringing up mud, etc., from the bed of the sea, rivers, etc. *v.t. & i.* bring up with a ~; clean, make a channel, etc., with a ~. **dredg·er** *n.* boat carrying a ~.

²dredge [dredʒ] *v.t.* scatter (flour, sugar, etc.) on.

dregs [dregz] *n. pl.* **1.** bits of worthless matter which sink to the bottom of a glass, bottle, barrel, etc., of liquid. **2.** (fig.) worst and useless part (e.g. of society). (Cf. *scum*.)

drench [drentʃ] *v.t.* make wet all over, right through.

dress [dres] *n.* **1.** long outer garment worn by a woman or girl; frock. **2.** clothing: *to pay too much attention to ~*. *full ~*, clothes for special occasions (esp. uniform); *evening ~*, as worn on formal social occasions (e.g. dinner-parties, dances); ~ *suit*, evening ~ for a man. *v.t. & i.* **1.** put on clothes. **2.** (in passive) *be ~ed in*, be wearing. **3.** make ready for use; prepare: *to ~ leather* (make it smooth); *to ~ a salad* (add ~ing to). **4.** clean and bandage (a wound, etc.). **5.** brush and comb (one's hair). **6.** make cheerful or attractive: *to ~ a ship* (*street*) *with flags*; *to ~ a shop-window* (with attractive goods). **dres·ser** *n.* **1.** (esp.) person employed to help a doctor to ~ wounds. **2.** piece of furniture with shelves for dishes, etc. **dres·sing** *n.* (esp.) **1.** covering used in ~ing (4) wounds. **2.** mixture of oil and other things as a sauce for salads. **ˈdres·sing-gown** *n.* loose gown worn over nightclothes.

drew, see *draw*.

drib·ble [ˈdribl] *v.t. & i.* **1.** (of liquids) fall, allow to fall, drop by drop (esp. a trickling flow from the side of the mouth). **2.** (football) take (the ball) forward between the feet. **drib·let** *n.* small amount: *in ~s*.

drier, see *dry*.

drift [drift] *v.i. & t.* (cause to) be carried along by, or as by, a current of air or water; (fig., of persons) go through life without aim, purpose, or self-control. *n.* ~*ing* movement: *the ~ of the tide*; sth. caused by ~ing: ~*s of snow*; (fig.) general tendency or meaning; the way in which events, etc., tend to move. ~*ing* train, fishing-boat. **ˈ~-wood** *n.* wood carried and left on beaches by tides.

¹drill [dril] *n.* pointed instrument for making holes in or through hard substances. *v.t. & i.* make (a hole) with a ~; use a ~.

²drill [dril] *n.* army training or exercises in the handling of weapons, marching, etc.; physical training (in groups); training (e.g. in grammar) by practical exercises. *v.t. & i.* train, be trained, by means of ~s: *to ~ troops on the parade ground*.

³drill [dril] *n.* furrow (long channel where seeds are to be sown); machine for sowing seeds in a ~; row of seeds sown in this way.

⁴drill [dril] *n.* heavy, strong linen or cotton cloth.

drink [driŋk] *v.t. & i.* (p.t. *drank* [dræŋk], p.p. *drunk* [drʌŋk]). **1.** take into the mouth and swallow (liquid). **2.** take alcoholic liquors (beer, wine, etc.), esp. in excess. **3.** ~ *sth. in*, take into the mind eagerly or with pleasure. *n.* **1.** (kind of) liquid for ~ing: *soft ~s* (without alcohol). **2.** alcoholic liquors: *He's too fond of ~*. ~*·a·ble* *adj.* suitable or fit for ~ing.

drip [drip] *v.t. & i.* (*-pp-*). (of a liquid) fall, allow to fall, in drops: *a ~ping tap*; *sweat ~ping from his face*. *n.* the drop-by-drop fall of a liquid.

~·**ping** *n.* fat melted out of roasting meat.

drive [draiv] *v.t. & i.* (p.t. *drove* [drouv], p.p. *driven* ['drivn]). **1.** operate, cause to work or move (an engine, tram, motor-car, etc.) as required; cause to move in a certain direction: *to ~ a car* (*cattle to market, the enemy away*); *a ship ~n on the rocks by a gale.* **2.** (usu. passive) be the power to operate: *~n by steam* (*water-power, etc.*). **3.** go, take, be taken, in a carriage, motor-car, etc.: *to ~ (a friend) to the station.* **4.** force: *~n by hunger to steal.* **5.** ~ *at,* mean: *What's he driving at?* (i.e. What's the purpose behind what he is saying?) **6.** ~ *a bargain,* make one. **7.** (of clouds, rain) be carried along violently by the wind: *clouds driving across the sky; rain driving into our faces.* **8.** force (a post, nail, screw, etc.) (*into*) sth.; strike (a ball, e.g. in golf) hard; *let ~ at,* aim a blow at. *n.* **1.** driving or being driven in a car, etc.: *to go for a ~.* **2.** private road through a garden or park to a house. **3.** stroke (given to a ball); force with which a ball is struck; (fig.) energy; capacity to get things done. **driv·er** *n.* person who ~s (animals, a car, etc.); tool for driving (8): *screw~r.*

driv·el ['drivl] *v.i. & n.* (*-ll-*). (talk) nonsense. ~**ler** *n.*

driz·zle ['drizl] *v.i. & n.* rain (in very small fine drops).

droll [droul] *adj.* causing amusement (because strange or peculiar).

drom·e·da·ry ['drʌm-, 'drɔmə-dəri] *n.* fast, one-humped riding-camel.

drone [droun] *n.* **1.** male bee; person who does no work and lives on others. **2.** low humming sound (as) made by bees. *v.i. & t.* make a ~ (2); talk or sing in a low, monotonous tone: *to ~ out a song or poem.*

droop [dru:p] *v.i. & t.* bend or hang down (through tiredness or weakness): *~ing flowers* (*spirits*).

drop [drɔp] *n.* **1.** tiny ball of liquid: *rain~s.* **2.** movement from higher to lower level, esp. the distance of a fall: *a ~ in temperature* (*in prices*). *v.i. & t.* (*-pp-*). **1.** (allow to) fall. **2.** (allow to) become weaker or lower: *The wind* (*temperature*) *has ~ped. He ~ped his voice to a whisper.* **3.** give up: *to ~ a bad habit; to ~ a subject* (stop talking about it). **4.** ~ *behind,* fail to keep up (with). ~ *in* (*on sb.*), pay a casual visit (to). ~ *off,* (a) become fewer or less: *His friends* (*customers*) *are ~ping off.* (b) fall asleep. ~ (*sb.*) *at,* allow (him) to get out of a car, etc.: *D~ me at the post office.* ~ *sb. a hint,* give him a hint or warning.

dross [drɔs] *n.* waste material rising to the surface of melted metals; anything considered worthless, mixed with something else.

drought [draut] *n.* continuous dry weather causing distress.

¹**drove,** see *drive.*

²**drove** [drouv] *n.* large number of animals driven along. **drov·er** *n.* man who drives cattle, sheep, etc., to market.

drown [draun] *v.t. & i.* **1.** (cause sb. to) die in water because unable to breathe: *a ~ing man; to be ~ed.* **2.** (of sound) be strong enough to prevent another sound from being heard. **3.** *be ~ed out,* be forced to leave a place by floods, etc.

drowse [drauz] *v.i. & t.* be half asleep. **drow·sy** *adj.* (*-ier, -iest*). feeling sleepy; making one feel sleepy. **drow·si·ness** *n.*

drudge [drʌdʒ] *n. & v.i.* (person who must) work hard and long at unpleasant tasks. **drudg·er·y** *n.* work that seems tiresome to the worker.

drug [drʌg] *n.* **1.** substance used for a medical purpose, either alone or in a mixture, esp. one causing unconsciousness or having an effect on the senses (e.g. opium). **2.** unsalable article: (usu.) *a ~ on the market.* *v.t. & i.* **1.** add harmful ~s to (food or drink). **2.** give ~s to, esp. in order to make unconscious. ~·gist *n.* tradesman in ~s, etc.

drum [drʌm] *n.* **1.** see the picture. **2.** sth. shaped like a ~ (e.g. a container for oil, a cylinder on which thick wire is wound). *v.t. & i.* (*-mm-*). **1.** play the ~ ; make ~-like sounds : *to ~ on the table with one's fingers.* **2.** ~ *sth. into sb.* (*into his head*), make him remember sth. by repeating it to him many times. ~·**mer** *n.* ~-player.

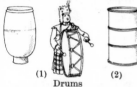

(1)   Drums   (2)

drunk [drʌŋk] *p.p.* of *drink.* be ~, be overcome by drinking alcoholic drinks. ~·**ard** [ˈdrʌŋkəd] *n.* person who is often ~. ~·**en** *adj.* associated with, showing the effect of, drinking too much : *~en revels.* '~·**en·ness** *n.*

dry [drai] *adj.* **1.** (*-ier, -iest*). free from moisture. **2.** *dry bread,* without butter ; *dry goods, corn,* (U.S.A.) cloth, etc. ; *dry wines* (etc.), not sweet ; *dry humour,* presented in a serious way ; *dry books* (*subjects, etc.*), uninteresting. *v.t. & i.* make dry. **dri·ly** *adv.* **dry·ness** *n.* **dri·er** *n.* apparatus for drying wet clothing, etc.

dry·ad [ˈdraiæd] *n.* tree nymph.

du·al [ˈdjuːəl] *adj.* of two ; double ; divided in two: ~ *control car,* etc. ~ *carriageway,* road divided along the centre so that the two streams (2) of traffic are separated.

dub [dʌb] *v.t.* (*-bb-*). give a nickname to ; make (sb.) a knight by touching him on the shoulder with a sword.

du·bious [ˈdjuːbjəs] *adj.* doubtful ; causing doubt.

du·cal [ˈdjuːkl] *adj.* of a duke.

duch·ess [ˈdʌtʃis] *n.* wife or widow of a duke. **duch·y**

[ˈdʌtʃi] *n.* land ruled by a royal duke or ~.

¹**duck** [dʌk] *n.* common waterbird ; its flesh as food. *make a ~,* score 0 at cricket.

²**duck** [dʌk] *v.t. & i.* move quickly down or to one side (to avoid being seen or hit) ; go, push sb., quickly under water. *n.* quick, downward or sideways movement of the head or body. ~·**ing** *n.* thorough wetting.

duct [dʌkt] *n.* tube for carrying liquid, esp. in the body : *tear-~s.* ¹**air-~,** channel through which air is forced for ventilating or warming (rooms, cabins, etc.).

dud [dʌd] *n. & adj.* (colloq.) (thing or person) of no use.

dudg·eon [ˈdʌdʒən] *n. in high ~,* feeling very indignant.

due [djuː] *adj.* **1.** owing ; to be paid. **2.** suitable ; right: *after due consideration.* **3.** (to be) expected: *When is the train due* (*in*)? **4.** *due to,* caused by. *adv.* *due* (*north, east, etc.*), exactly ; directly. *n.* **1.** (sing.) that which sb. deserves. **2.** (pl.) sums of money to be paid (e.g. for use of a harbour, membership of a club).

du·el [ˈdjuəl] *n.* unlawful fight between two persons who have quarrelled, usu. with swords or pistols, at a meeting arranged and conducted according to rules ; any two-sided contest. *v.i.* (*-ll-*). fight a ~. ~·**list** *n.*

du·et [djuːˈet] *n.* piece of music for two voices or instruments.

duf·fel [ˈdʌfl] *n.* ~ *coat,* see the picture.

A duffel coat   Dungarees

duf·fer [ˈdʌfə*] *n.* stupid or inefficient person.

dug, see *dig.*

dug·out [ˈdʌgaut] *n.* rough

covered shelter made by digging, esp. by soldiers for protection in war; canoe made by hollowing a tree trunk.

duke [dju:k] *n.* nobleman of high rank (next below a prince), ~**·dom** *n.* position and duties, rank, land, of a ~.

dull [dʌl] *adj.* (-*er*, -*est*). **1.** opposite of clear or bright; not sharp. **2.** slow in understanding; (of trade) inactive. *v.t. & i.* make or become ~. **dul·ly** *adv.* ~**·ness** *n.* **dul·lard** ['dʌləd] *n.* person with a ~ mind.

du·ly ['dju:li] *adv.* in a right or suitable manner; at the right time.

dumb [dʌm] *adj.* unable to speak; not saying anything. ~ *show,* giving ideas by actions without words. ~**·'found** *v.t.* make ~ with surprise.

dum·my ['dʌmi] *n.* object made to look like and serve the purpose of the real person or thing: *a tailor's* ~ (for clothes); (attrib.) *a* ~ *gun* (to deceive the enemy).

dump [dʌmp] *n.* **1.** place where rubbish, etc., may be unloaded and left. **2.** place for military stores. *v.t.* **1.** put on a ~(1); put or throw down carelessly. **2.** (commerce) sell abroad at low prices goods which are unwanted in the home country.

dun [dʌn] *adj.* dull greyish-brown.

dunce [dʌns] *n.* slow learner.

dune [dju:n] *n.* low ridge of loose, dry sand formed by the wind, esp. near the sea-shore.

dung [dʌŋ] *n.* waste matter dropped by domestic animals; manure.

dun·ga·rees [ˌdʌŋgəˈriːz] *n. pl.* worker's overalls (trousers and blouse, combined). See the picture on page 167.

dun·geon ['dʌndʒən] *n.* (formerly) dark underground room used as a prison.

dupe [dju:p] *v.t.* cheat; deceive. *n.* person who is ~d.

du·pli·cate ['dju:plikeit] *v.t. &* [-kit] *n.* (make an) exact copy (of a letter, etc.); (make) a thing exactly like another. *in* ~, (of

documents, etc.) with a ~. *adj.* exactly like. **du·pli·ca·tor** *n.* machine that ~s sth. written or typed.

du·pli·ci·ty [dju:ˈplisiti] *n.* deceit.

du·ra·ble ['djuərəbl] *adj.* likely to last for a long time. **du·ra·bil·i·ty** [ˌdjuərəˈbiliti] *n.*

du·ra·tion [djuəˈreiʃən] *n.* time during which sth. lasts or exists.

du·ress [djuəˈres] *n. under* ~, compelled (by use of force).

dur·ing ['djuəriŋ] *prep.* **1.** throughout; for as long as sth. lasts: *The band played* ~ *the afternoon.* **2.** at a moment within a period of time: *He called to see me* ~ *my stay in hospital.*

dusk [dʌsk] *n.* time just before it gets quite dark.

dust [dʌst] *n.* dried earth, etc., in the form of powder that settles on a surface or is blown about by the wind. *throw* ~ *in sb.'s eyes,* mislead him; keep him from seeing the truth. *shake the* ~ *off one's feet,* go away in anger or scorn. *v.t. & i.* **1.** remove ~ from (e.g. books, furniture). **2.** cover with powder: *to* ~ *a cake with sugar.* '~**·bin** *n.* metal container for household waste and rubbish. '~**·man** *n.* man who empties ~bins and takes rubbish, etc., away. ~**·er** *n.* cloth for taking ~ off things. ~**·y** *adj.* (-*ier*, -*iest*) covered with ~; like ~. '~**·pan** *n.* pan into which ~, etc. is swept from the floor.

du·ty ['dju:ti] *n.* **1.** what one is obliged to do (by morality, law, conscience, etc.); inner force urging one to behave in a certain way: *one's* ~ *to one's parents; a postman's duties.* *be on (off)* ~, be actually engaged (not engaged) in one's ~ or usual work. *do* ~ *for,* be used instead of. **2.** payment demanded by the government on certain goods imported or exported (customs duties), or manufactured in the country (excise duties), or when property, etc., is transferred to a new owner by sale or death

(stamp ~, death duties). **'~-'free
adj.** (of goods) allowed to enter
without payment of customs
duties. **du·ti·a·ble** ['dju:tiəbl]
adj. on which such payments
must be made. **du·ti·ful** ['dju:ti-
ful] **adj.** doing one's ~ (1) well;
showing respect and obedience.

dwarf [dwɔ:f] **n.** (pl. ~s). person,
animal, or plant much below
the usual size; (attrib.) under-
sized. **v.t.** prevent from growing
to full size; cause to appear
small by contrast or distance.

dwell [dwel] **v.i.** (p.t. dwelt).
1. live (in, at, etc.). **2.** ~
(up)on, think, speak, or write
at length about. **dwel·ling n.**
house, etc., to live in.

dwin·dle ['dwindl] **v.i.** become
less or smaller by degrees.

dye [dai] **v.t. & i.** (3rd pers. sing.
pres. t. dyes [daiz], p.t. & p.p.
dyed, pres. p. dyeing ['daiiŋ]). **1.**
colour, usu. by dipping in a
liquid : to dye a white dress blue.
2. take colour from dyeing: cloth
that dyes well. **n.** substance used
for dyeing cloth; the colour
given by dyeing. **dy·er n.**
tradesman who dyes clothes.

dy·ing, see die.

dyke = dike.

dy·nam·ic [dai'næmik] **adj.** of
physical power and forces producing motion; (of a person)
having energy, force of character. **dy·nam·ics n.** (with sing.
v.) branch of physics dealing
with matter in motion.

dy·na·mite ['dainəmait] **n.**
powerful explosive (used in
mining and quarrying). **v.t.**
blow up with ~.

dy·na·mo ['dainəmou] **n.** machine for changing steam-power,
water-power, etc., into electrical
energy.

dyn·as·ty ['di-, 'dainəsti] **n.**
succession of rulers belonging to
one family. **dy·nas·tic** [di'næs-
tik] **adj.**

dys·en·tery ['disəntri] **n.** painful
disease of the bowels.

dys·pep·si·a [dis'pepsiə] **n.** indigestion. **dys·pep·tic adj.** of
~. **n.** person suffering from
~.

E

each [i:tʃ] **adj. & pron. I. adj.**
(of two or more) every one
(thing, group, person, etc.) taken
separately or individually. **II.
pron. 1.** ~ thing, person,
group, etc.: They gave ~ of their
four sons a watch. The four boys
~ received a watch. **2.** ~ other
(cf. one another): We see ~ other
(i.e. each of us sees the other)
every day.

ea·ger ['i:gə*] **adj.** full of, showing, strong desire (for, after,
about, to do, sth.). **~·ly adv.
~·ness n.**

ea·gle ['i:gl] **n.** large, strong bird
of prey with keen sight.

¹ear [iə*] **n. 1.** organ of hearing.
2. ability to distinguish between
sounds : to have a good ear for
music; play by ear, play sth.
from memory, without having
read the printed music. **'ear-
drum n.** hollow part of the
middle ear. **'ear·mark v.t.** put
(money, etc.) on one side (for
a special purpose). **'ear·shot n.**
within (out of) earshot, near
enough (too far away) to hear.

²ear [iə*] **n.** part of a grain plant
on which the seeds appear.

earl [ə:l] **n.** title of British nobleman of high rank. **'~·dom n.**
rank, lands, of an ~.

ear·ly ['ə:li] **adj. & adv.** (-ier,
-iest). near to the beginning of
a period of time; sooner than
usual; sooner than others.

earn [ə:n] **v.t.** get in return for
work or as a reward for one's
qualities. **~·ings n. pl.** money
~ed.

¹ear·nest ['ə:nist] **adj.** serious;
determined. in ~, serious(ly);
in a determined, not in a joking,
manner. **~·ly adv. ~·ness n.**

²ear·nest ['ə:nist] **n.** part payment made as a pledge that full
payment will follow; sth. coming
in advance as a sign of what is to
come after.

earth [ə:θ] **n. 1.** this world. why
(where, what, who) on ~?, why
(etc.) ever? (used for emphasis).

2. dry land. **3.** soil: *to fill a hole with* ~. **4.** hole of a fox or badger. *run to* ~, chase (a fox) to its hole; find sth. hidden. **5.** ~-connexion for electrical apparatus. ~'**en** ['ə:θən] *adj.* made of ~ or baked clay. ~'**en·ware** ['ə:θənwɛə*] *n.* dishes, pots, etc., made of baked clay. ~'**ly** *adj.* **1.** of this world, not of heaven: ~*ly joys* (*possessions*). **2.** (colloq.) possible: *not an* ~*ly chance* (no chance at all). '~-**clos·et** *n.* latrine. ~'**quake** ['ə:θkweik] *n.* sudden, violent shaking of the ~'s surface. '~-**work** *n.* bank or wall of ~ built for defence.

ear·wig ['iəwig] *n.* small insect.

ease [i:z] *n.* freedom from work, discomfort, trouble, anxiety: *a life of* ~; *to stand at* ~, with the legs apart in a restful position; *ill at* ~, uncomfortable, feeling anxious or embarrassed; *with* ~, without difficulty. *v.t. & i.* **1.** give ~ to (the body or mind). **2.** make looser, less tight; lessen (speed, efforts). ~ *off*, (cause to) become less intense.

ea·sel ['i:zl] *n.* wooden frame to support a picture or blackboard.

east [i:st] *n. & adj. & adv.* point of the horizon where the sun rises. *the E*~, Asia, from India eastwards; *the Far E*~, Eastern Asia; *the Middle E*~, Egypt, Arabia, Syria, Iraq, etc. '~·**er·ly** *adj. & adv.* in an ~ern position or direction; (of the wind) from the ~. '~·**ern** *adj.* lying towards the ~; of, from, or in, the ~. '~·**wards** *adv.*

East·er ['i:stə*] *n.* anniversary of the Resurrection: ~ *Day* (*Sunday*); ~ *week* (beginning on ~ Sunday).

eas·y ['i:zi] *adj.* (-*ier*, -*iest*). **1.** within one's strength, ability, etc.; not requiring much effort: *Everybody can do this exercise, it is quite* ~. **2.** free from pain or anxiety: *to feel* ~ *about one's future*. **3.** comfortable in or for body or mind. ~ *chair*, soft, restful one. *adv.* go ~, *take things* ~, not work hard; go

slowly. '~·**go·ing** *adj.* (of a person) not causing or taking trouble. **eas·i·ly** *adv.*

eat [i:t] *v.t. & i.* (p.t. *ate* [et], p.p. *eaten* ['i:tn]). **1.** take (solid food, also soup) into the mouth and swallow (it). **2.** destroy as if by ~*ing*: ~*en into by acids*. '~·**a·ble** *adj.* fit to be ~en. *n. pl.* (colloq.) food.

eaves [i:vz] *n. pl.* overhanging edges of a roof. '~·**drop** *v.i.* (-*pp*-). listen secretly to private conversation.

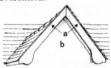

The eaves (*a*)
in a gable roof (*b*)

ebb [eb] *v.i.* (of the tide) flow back from the land; (fig.) grow less; become weak or faint. *n.* the flowing out of the tide: *the ebb and flow of the sea*; (fig.) low state; decay. '**ebb-'tide** *n.* ebbing of the sea.

eb·on·y ['ebəni] *n.* hard, black wood. *adj.* black like ~; made of ~.

ec·cen·tric [ek'sentrik] *adj.* (of a person, his behaviour) peculiar; not normal. *n.* ~ person. **ec·cen·tri·ci·ty** [,eksen'trisiti] *n.* strangeness of behaviour; strange or unusual act or habit.

ec·cle·si·as·tic [i,kli:zi'æstik] *n.* clergyman. **ec·cle·si·as·ti·cal** *adj.* of the Christian Church; of clergymen.

ech·o ['ekou] *n.* sound reflected or sent back (e.g. from a wall of rock); (fig.) person who, statement, thing, etc. which, is a copy or repetition of another. *v.i. & t.* send back an ~; be sent back as an ~; be an ~ of; repeat the words, etc., of.

e·clipse [i'klips] *n.* total or partial cutting off of the light of the sun (when the moon is between it and the earth), or of the reflected light of the moon (when the earth's shadow falls on it); (fig.) loss of brilliance, power, reputation, etc. **v.t.** (of a planet, etc.) cause an ~; cut off the light from; (fig.) make (sth. or sb.) appear dull by comparison; outshine.

e·con·o·my [i(:)'kɔnəmi] **n. 1.** (instance of) avoidance of waste of money, strength, or anything else of value. **2.** control and management of the money, goods, and other resources of a community, society, or household. **e·co·nom·ic** [ˌi:kə'nɔmik] **adj.** of economics (see below); designed to give a profit. **e·co·nom·ics n.** (sing. v.) science of production and distribution of money and goods. **e·co·nom·i·cal adj.** careful in the spending of money, time, etc., and in the use of goods; not wasteful. **e·con·o·mist** [i'kɔnəmist] **n. 1.** expert in economics. **2.** person who is economical. **e·con·o·mize** [i(:)'kɔnəmaiz] **v.t. & i.** be economical; use or spend less than before.

ec·sta·sy ['ekstəsi] **n.** feeling of great joy and spiritual uplift: *in an ~ of delight.* **ec·stat·ic** [ek'stætik] **adj.** of, in, causing, ~.

e·cu·men·i·cal [ˌi:kju'menikəl] **adj.** of or representing the whole Christian world: *the ~ movement,* i.e. towards Christian unity.

ec·ze·ma ['eksimə] **n.** a skin disease.

ed·dy ['edi] **n.** circular or spiral movement (of wind, smoke, fog, dust, water). **v.i.** move in small circles; move in eddies.

E·den ['i:dn] **n.** (Bible) garden where Adam and Eve lived; place of delight.

edge [edʒ] **n. 1.** sharp, cutting part of a knife, sword, or other tool or weapon. *take the ~ off sth.,* make blunt or dull; (of the appetite) satisfy partly; make less troublesome or painful. *put an ~ on,* sharpen. *on ~,* (fig.) with the nerves upset or jarred. **2.** (line marking the) outer limit or boundary of a (flat) surface: *to sit on the ~ of a table; the ~*

of a lake. **v.t. & i.** (cause to) move slowly forward or along: *to ~ oneself (one's way) through a crowd; to ~ along a cliff.* **~·ways, ~·wise** ['edʒweiz, -waiz] **adv.** with the ~ outwards or forwards. *be unable to get a word in ~ways,* be unable to speak because others never stop talking. **edg·ing** ['edʒiŋ] **n.** narrow border.

ed·i·ble ['edibl] **adj. & n.** (usu. pl.) (thing that is) fit to be eaten.

e·dict ['i:dikt] **n.** order sent out by authority (e.g. the Pope).

ed·i·fice ['edifis] **n.** large building.

ed·i·fy ['edifai] **v.t.** improve in morals or mind. **ed·i·fi·ca·tion** [ˌedifi'keiʃən] **n.**

ed·it ['edit] **v.t. 1.** prepare (another person's writing) for publication (esp. in a newspaper or other periodical). **2.** plan and direct the publication of a journal, etc. **3.** put together the various sections of a cinema film, tape recording, etc., in suitable order. **e·di·tion** [i'diʃən] **n.** form in which a book is published; number of copies printed from the same type. **ed·i·tor n. ed·i·tor·i·al** [ˌedi'tɔ:riəl] **adj.** of an ~or. **n.** special article or discussion of news in a newspaper, etc., usu. written by the ~or.

ed·u·cate ['edjukeit] **v.t.** give intellectual and moral training to. **ed·u·ca·tion** [ˌedju'keiʃən] **n. ed·u·ca·tion·al adj. ed·u·ca·tion(al)ist n.** expert in education.

eel [i:l] **n.** long, snake-like fish.

ee·rie, ee·ry ['iəri] **adj.** causing a feeling of fear or mystery.

ef·face [i'feis] **v.t.** rub or wipe out. ~ *oneself,* keep oneself in the background in order to escape notice.

ef·fect [i'fekt] **n. 1.** result; outcome. *of no ~,* useless. *take ~,* produce the result expected or required, come into use. *give ~ to,* cause to become active or to have a result. *bring into ~,* cause to operate. **2.** impression made on the mind; general appearance: *cloud ~s*; *to talk for ~*; *calculated for ~* (i.e. to impress people); *to the ~ that* (*to this ~, etc.*) (i.e. with the general meaning of). **3.** (pl.) goods; property: *personal ~s.* *v.t.* bring about; cause to happen. **ef·fec'tive** *adj.* having an ~; making a striking impression; (military) ready for service. **ef·fec'tu·al** [i'fektjuəl] *adj.* bringing about the result required.

ef·fem'i·nate [i'feminit] *adj.* womanish; unmanly. **ef·fem'i·na·cy** *n.*

ef·fer·vesce [,efə'ves] *v.i.* give off bubbles of gas. **ef·fer·ves'cence** *n.* **ef·fer·ves'cent** *adj.*

ef·fete [e'fi:t] *adj.* exhausted; weak and worn-out.

ef·fi·ca'cious [,efi'keiʃəs] *adj.* (of things) producing the desired result. **ef·fi·ca·cy** ['efikəsi] *n.*

ef·fi'cient [i'fiʃənt] *adj.* producing an effect; (of persons) capable; able to perform duties well. **ef·fi'cien·cy** [i'fiʃənsi] *n.*

ef·fi'gy ['efidʒi] *n.* person's portrait or image (in wood, stone, etc.).

ef·fort ['efət] *n.* trying hard; use of mental powers or bodily strength.

ef·fron'ter·y [e'frʌntəri] *n.* shameless boldness; impudence.

ef·fu'sion [i'fju:ʒən] *n.* sending or pouring out (of liquid, e.g. blood); outpouring of thoughts.

ef·fu'sive [i'fju:siv] *adj.* (of the feelings, signs of pleasure, gratitude) pouring out too freely.

¹egg [eg] *n.* oval or round protective covering produced by a female creature, containing the germ of a new creature: *The hen has laid an egg. Have chickens hatched (out) from those eggs yet? Have those eggs hatched?*

²egg [eg] *v.t.* *egg sb. on*, urge (to do sth.).

eg·o·ism ['egouizm] *n.* continual selfishness. **eg·o·ist** *n.* selfish person.

eg·o·tism ['egoutizm] *n.* practice of talking about oneself.

e·gress ['i:gres] *n.* (right of) going out; way out.

ei·der-down ['aidədaun] *n.* (bed-covering filled with) soft breast feathers of large, wild duck.

eight [eit] *n. & adj.* 8. **~·een** ['ei'ti:n] *n. & adj.* 18. **eighth** [eitθ] *n. & adj.* 8th; ⅛. **~·y** ['eiti] *n. & adj.* 80. **~·i·eth** ['eitiiθ] *n. & adj.* 1/80 ; the next after the 79th.

ei·ther ['aiðə*, 'i:ðə*] **I.** *adj. & pron.* **1.** one or the other of two. (Cf. *any*, for numbers greater than two.) **2.** (Cf. *each.*) *There was a chair on ~ side of the fire-place.* **II.** *adv. & conj.* **1.** after *not*: *I don't like this one, and I don't like that one, ~* (i.e. I dislike both of them). (Cf. *neither.*) **2.** used to introduce the first of two alternatives: *He must be ~ mad or drunk. We must ~ go now or stay till the end.* (Cf. *neither . . . nor.*)

e·jac·u·late [i'dʒækjuleit] *v.t. & i.* say suddenly. **e·jac·u·la'tion** *n.*

e·ject [i'dʒekt] *v.t.* expel (*sb. from* a place); send out (liquid, etc.).

eke [i:k] *v.t.* *~ out*, make (small supplies of sth.) enough for one's needs by adding sth. extra; make (a living) by doing this.

e·lab·o·rate [i'læbərit] *adj.* worked out with much care and in detail. [i'læbəreit] *v.t.* work out, describe, in (greater) detail. **e·lab·o·ra'tion** [i,læbə'reiʃən] *n.*

e·lapse [i'læps] *v.i.* (of time) pass.

e·las'tic [i'læstik] *adj.* **1.** having the tendency to go back to the normal size or shape after being pulled or pressed. **2.** (fig.) not firm or fixed; able to be adapted. *n.* cord or material made ~ by weaving rubber into it.

e·late [i'leit] *v.t. be ~d*, be in high spirits (because of success). **e·la'tion** [i'leiʃən] *n.*

el·bow ['elbou] *n.* **1.** (outer part of) joint between the two parts of the arm. *out at ~s*, (of dress) worn-out; (of sb.) in worn-out clothes. **2.** sharp bend or angle in a pipe, etc. *v.t.* push or force (one's) way through, forward, etc.).

el·der ['eldə*] *adj.* (of two per-

sons, esp. relations) older. **n.**
1. (pl.) persons deserving respect,
possessing authority, because of
age. **2.** member of the governing
body (session) in a Presbyterian
church. **~·ly** *adj.* rather old.
el·dest *adj.* (of persons) oldest;
first-born.
e·lect [i'lekt] *v.t.* **1.** choose (sb.)
by vote. **2.** choose (sth., to do
sth.) *adj.* **1.** chosen: *the bishop*
~ (chosen, but not yet in office).
2. *the ~*, those persons specially
chosen or considered to be the
best. **e·lec·tion** [i'lekʃən] *n.*
choosing or selection (by vote)
of candidates for an office, for
Parliament, etc. **e·lec·tion·**
eer·ing [i,lekʃə'niəriŋ] *n.* working at an ~ion. **e·lec·tor** *n.*
person having the right to ~
by voting. **e·lec·tor·ate** [i'lek-
tərit] *n.* the whole body of ~ors.
e·lec·tri·ci·ty [i,lek'trisiti] *n.*
property or condition, developed
in and around substances, by
rubbing, chemical change, etc.,
which can be used to produce
heat, light, and sound and to
drive machines; science of
this. **e·lec·tric** [i'lektrik] *adj.*
of, producing, worked by, ~.
e·lec·tri·cal *adj.* having to do
with ~: *electrical engineering.*
e·lec·tri·cian [,elek'triʃən] *n.*
expert in setting up and servic-
ing electrical apparatus. **e·lec·**
tri·fy [i'lektrifai] *v.t.* **1.** fill (sth.)
with ~; alter (railway, etc.) for
working by ~. **2.** excite, shock
sb., as by ~: *to electrify an*
audience. **e·lec·tri·fi·ca·tion**
[i,lektrifi'keiʃən] *n.* **e·lec·tro·**
cute [i'lektrəkju:t] *v.t.* put to
death, kill accidentally, by means
of an electric current. **e·lec·tro·**
cu·tion [i,lektrə'kju:ʃən] *n.*
e·lec·trol·y·sis [ilek'trolisis] *n.*
separation of a substance into
its chemical parts by electric
current. **e·lec·tro·plate** *v.t.*
coat (dishes, spoons, etc.) with
silver by electrolysis. *n.* articles
coated with silver thus.
e·lec·trode [i'lektroud] *n.* either
pole (*anode, cathode*) of an electric battery.
e·lec·tron [i'lektron] *n.* negative

electric charge forming part of
an atom. **~·ic** [ilek'tronik] *adj.*
~·ics *n.* (sing. v.) study and
application of the phenomena of
~s (as in transistors, television
tubes, computers, etc.).
el·e·gant ['eligənt] *adj.* showing,
having, good taste; beautiful;
graceful. **el·e·gance** *n.*
el·e·gy ['elidʒi] *n.* poem or song of
sorrow, esp. for the dead. **e·le·**
gi·ac [,eli'dʒaiæk] *adj.*
el·e·ment ['elimənt] *n.* **1.**
(science) substance which has
not so far been separated into
simpler substances. **2.** one of
the parts of which something is
composed; necessary feature or
part: *the ~s of geometry*, the
simplest parts which are learnt
first. **3.** *the ~s*, the weather;
storms, etc. *in (out of) one's*
~, in (not in) one's natural or
satisfying surroundings. **4.** *an*
~ (of doubt, etc.), suggestion, indication, trace. **el·e·men·tal**
[,eli'mentl] *adj.* of the forces of
nature; uncontrolled. **el·e·men·**
ta·ry [,eli'mentəri] *adj.* of or
in the beginning stages; not
developed; simple.
el·e·phant ['elifənt] *n.* the largest
four-footed animal on earth,
with tusks and a trunk. *white*
~, costly or troublesome possession useless to its owner.
el·e·vate ['eliveit] *v.t.* lift up;
make (the mind, morals) higher
and better. **el·e·va·tion** [,eli-
'veiʃən] *n.* **1.** elevating or being
~d. **2.** height (esp. above sea
level); hill or high place. **3.**
flat drawing of one side of a
building. **el·e·va·tor** *n.* **1.** =
lift (2). **2.** machine for hoisting
hay, etc.
e·lev·en [i'levn] *n. & adj.* 11.
e·lev·enth *n. & adj.* 11th; $\frac{1}{11}$.
elf [elf] *n.* (pl. *elves* [elvz]). small
fairy. **elf·in** *adj.* of elves.
e·lic·it [i'lisit] *v.t.* draw out (a
quality *from* sb.); get (an
answer, the truth, applause)
(*from* sb.).
e·lide [i'laid] *v.t.* drop (a vowel
or syllable from a word) in
speech. **e·li·sion** [i'liʒən] *n.*
e·li·gi·ble ['elidʒibl] *adj.* fit,

el·i·gi·bil·i·ty [ˌelidʒi'biliti] *n.*

e·lim·i·nate [i'limineit] *v.t.* remove, take or put away, get rid of (because unwanted).

e·lix·ir [i'liksə*] *n.* preparation by means of which medieval scientists hoped to change metals into gold and to lengthen life for ever.

el·lipse [i'lips] *n.* regular oval.

el·lip·ti·cal [i'liptikl] *adj.* shaped like an ~.

elm [elm] *n.* common European tree; its hard, heavy wood.

el·o·cu·tion [ˌelə'kjuːʃən] *n.* art or style of speaking well, esp. in public.

e·lon·gate ['iːlɔŋgeit] *v.t.* make longer.

e·lope [i'loup] *v.i.* (of a woman) run away (from home) with a lover. ~**ment** *n.*

el·o·quence ['eləkwəns] *n.* skilful use of language to persuade or to appeal to the feelings; fluent speaking. **el·o·quent** *adj.*

else [els] *adv.* 1. besides; in addition: *What — have you to do?* 2. *or ~*, otherwise; if not: *Run, or ~ you will miss the bus.* ~**where** ['els'wɛə*] *adv.* in, at or to some other place.

e·lu·ci·date [i'luːsideit] *v.t.* explain; make clear.

e·lude [i'luːd] *v.t.* escape from (esp. by means of a trick); avoid. **e·lu·sive** [i'luːsiv] *adj.* not easy to find.

elves, see *elf.*

e·ma·ci·at·ed [i'meiʃieitid] *ppl. adj.* lean; wasted away; skinny.

e·ma·ci·a·tion [iˌmeisi'eiʃən] *n.*

em·a·nate ['eməneit] *v.i.* come out (*from* a source). **em·a·na·tion** [ˌemə'neiʃən] *n.* sth. coming from a source.

e·man·ci·pate [i'mænsipeit] *v.t.* set free (esp. from legal, political, or moral restraint). **e·man·ci·pa·tion** [iˌmænsi'peiʃən] *n.*

e·mas·cu·late [i'mæskjuleit] *v.t.* make weak or effeminate.

em·balm [im'bɑːm] *v.t.* prevent (a dead body) from decaying by using spices or chemicals.

em·bank·ment [im'bæŋkmənt] *n.* wall of earth, stone, etc., to hold back water or support a raised road or railway.

em·bar·go [em'bɑːgou] *n.* (pl. *-goes*). order forbidding (trade, movement of ships, etc.): *lay an ~ on ; be under an ~.*

em·bark [im'bɑːk] *v.i. & t.* 1. go, put, or take on board a ship. 2. ~ (*up)on*, start; take part in. ~**a·tion** [ˌembaː'keiʃən] *n.*

em·bar·rass [im'bærəs] *v.t.* 1. cause perplexity, mental discomfort or anxiety to: *~ing questions.* 2. hinder movement of. ~**ment** *n.*

em·bas·sy ['embəsi] *n.* duty, mission, residence, of an ambassador; ambassador and his staff.

em·bed [em'bed] *v.t.* (*-dd-*). fix firmly (in a surrounding mass).

em·bel·lish [im'beliʃ] *v.t.* make beautiful; add ornaments to; add untrue details to. ~**ment** *n.*

em·ber ['embə*] *n.* (usu. pl.) small piece of burning coal or wood in a dying fire.

em·bez·zle [im'bezl] *v.t.* use (money placed in one's care) in a wrong way for one's own benefit. ~**ment** *n.*

em·bit·ter [im'bitə*] *v.t.* arouse bitter feelings in.

em·blem ['embləm] *n.* symbol; device(s) representing an idea. **em·ble·mat·ic** [ˌemblə'mætik] *adj.* serving as an ~.

em·bod·y [im'bɔdi] *v.t.* give form to (ideas, feelings); include; comprise. **em·bod·i·ment** [im'bɔdimənt] *n.* (esp.) that which gives form to sth.

em·bold·en [im'bouldən] *v.t.* give courage or confidence to.

em·brace [im'breis] *v.t.* 1. put one's arms round (lovingly). 2. accept (an offer, belief, etc.). 3. (of things) include. *n.* act of embracing (1).

em·bra·sure [im'breiʒə*] *n.* opening in a (castle) wall suitably shaped for shooting through.

em·bro·ca·tion [ˌembrə'keiʃən] *n.* liquid rubbed into a bruised or aching part of the body.

em·broi·der [im'brɔidə*] *v.t.* ornament (cloth) with needlework; (fig.) add untrue details to a story. ~·y n. ornamental needlework.

em·broil [im'brɔil] v.t. cause (sb., oneself) to be mixed up (in a quarrel, etc.).

em·bry·o ['embriou] n. offspring of an animal before birth or of a bird, etc., before coming out of the egg; thing in an early stage of development. em·bry·on·ic [,embri'ɔnik] adj.

e·mend [i'mend] v.t. take out errors from. e·men·da·tion [,i:men'deiʃən] n. improvement by ~ing.

em·er·ald ['emərəld] n. bright green precious stone.

e·merge [i'mə:dʒ] v.i. 1. come into view; (esp.) come out (from water, etc.). 2. (of facts, ideas) appear; become known. e·mer·gen·cy [i'mə:dʒənsi] n. sudden happening which makes quick action necessary : emergency exit, for use in an emergency.

em·er·y ['eməri] n. hard metal used (esp. in powdered form) for polishing metal, etc.

e·met·ic [i'metik] n. medicine causing a person to throw up food from the stomach.

em·i·grate ['emigreit] v.i. go away from one's country to another to settle there. em·i·grant n. person who does this. em·i·gra·tion [,emi'greiʃən] n.

em·i·nent ['eminənt] adj. (of a person) distinguished; (of qualities) remarkable in degree. ~·ly adv. in an unusually high degree. em·i·nence ['eminəns] n. 1. being ~. 2. high or rising ground. 3. His (Your) E~, title used of, to, a cardinal.

e·mir [e'miə*] n. Arab prince or governor.

em·is·sa·ry ['emisəri] n. person sent out on (usu. an unpleasant) errand.

e·mit [i'mit] v.t. (-tt-). give or send out (light, liquid, sound, etc.). e·mis·sion [i'miʃən] n. ~ting; sth. ~ted.

e·mol·u·ment [i'mɔljumənt] n. profit from employment or office; fee.

e·mo·tion [i'mouʃən] n. stirring-up, excitement, of the mind or the feelings; excited state of mind or the feelings. ~·al [i'mouʃənl] adj. 1. of the ~s. 2. having ~s easily roused.

em·per·or ['empərə*] n. ruler of an empire.

em·pha·sis ['emfəsis] n. force or stress laid on word(s) in order to show their importance; the placing of special value or importance on sth. em·pha·size ['emfəsaiz] v.t. give ~ to. em·phat·ic [im'fætik] adj. having, showing, using, ~. em·phat·i·cal·ly adv.

em·pire ['empaiə*] n. 1. group of countries under one ruler, called emperor. 2. supreme and wide political power.

em·pir·i·cal [em'pirikl] adj. based on observation and experiment, not on theory.

em·place·ment [im'pleismənt] n. prepared position for artillery.

em·ploy [im'plɔi] v.t. 1. give work to, usu. for payment. 2. make use of. n. in the ~ of, working for. ~·ment n. being ~ed; one's regular work. ~·ee [,emplɔi'i:] n. person ~ed for wages.

em·pow·er [im'pauə*] v.t. give power or authority (to do sth.).

em·press ['empris] n. wife of an emperor; woman governing an empire.

emp·ty ['empti] adj. (-ier, -iest). having nothing inside; containing nothing. v.t. & i. make or become ~; remove what is inside (sth.). emp·ti·ness n.

em·u·late ['emjuleit] v.t. try to do as well as or better than. em·u·la·tion [,emju'leiʃən] n.

e·mul·sion [i'mʌlʃən] n. creamy liquid holding oil or fat.

en·a·ble [i'neibl] v.t. make able, give authority or means (to do sth.).

en·act [i'nækt] v.t. 1. make (a law); ordain (1). 2. play (a scene or part in a play or in real life). ~·ment n. ~ing or being ~ed : (a) law.

e·nam·el [i'næml] n. 1. glass-like coating on metal, etc. 2. (~ paint) paint which hardens to make such a coating. **3.** hard outer covering of teeth. *v.t.* (-*ll*-). cover, decorate, with ~.

e·nam·oured [i'næməd] *ppl. adj.* ~ *of*, in love with; delighted with.

en·camp·ment [in'kæmpmənt] *n.* camp (esp. military).

en·case [in'keis] *v.t.* put into a case; cover as with a case.

en·chant [in'tʃɑːnt] *v.t.* **1.** charm; delight. **2.** work magic on. ~·**er**, ~·**ress** *n.* man, woman, who ~s. ~·**ment** *n.* being ~ed; thing which ~s; charm; delight.

en·cir·cle [in'səːkl] *v.t.* surround.

en·close [in'klouz] *v.t.* **1.** put a wall, fence, etc., round; shut in on all sides. **2.** put (sth.) in (an envelope, parcel, etc.), esp. with a letter. **en·clo·sure** [in-'klouʒə*] *n.* enclosing; sth. ~d (e.g. a fenced playground); article sent (in the same envelope) with a letter.

en·core [oŋ'kɔː*] *int.* Repeat! Again! *v.t. & n.* (call for a) repetition of a song, etc.) or further performance by the same person(s).

en·coun·ter [in'kauntə*] *v.t. & n.* (have a) sudden or unexpected meeting (e.g. with a friend, or with danger).

en·cour·age [in'kʌridʒ] *v.t.* give hope, courage, or confidence to. ~·**ment** *n.* encouraging; sth. that ~s.

en·croach [in'kroutʃ] *v.i.* go beyond what is right or natural (*on* or *upon* what belongs to sb. else).

en·crust·ed [in'krʌstid] *ppl. adj.* covered as with a crust: *a crown ~ with jewels.*

en·cum·ber [in'kʌmbə*] *v.t.* get in the way of; be a burden to; weigh down. **en·cum·brance** *n.*

en·cy·clo·pae·dia [en,saiklou-'piːdjə] *n.* book, or set of books, giving information about every branch of knowledge, or on one subject, with articles in ABC order.

end [end] *n.* **1.** farthest or last part: *the end of a journey. on end,* (of a barrel, etc.) upright. *for*

(*five, etc.*) *hours (days, etc.) on end,* consecutively; without an interval. *make both ends meet,* manage to earn as much as one needs to spend. *put an end to, make an end of,* destroy, abolish, stop. **2.** small piece that remains: *a candle end.* **3.** finish; conclusion: *I've come to the end of my book.* **4.** death: *He's nearing his end* (is dying). **5.** purpose, aim: *I hope she will gain (achieve) her end(s). v.i. & t.* (cause to) come to an end; reach an end. *end up,* finish. **end·ing** *n.* end of a story; end of a word. **end·less(ly)** *adj. & adv.* '**end·ways**, '**end·wise** *adv.* with the end forward or up.

en·dan·ger [in'deindʒə*] *v.t.* put in danger; cause danger to.

en·dear [in'diə*] *v.t.* make dear or precious. ~·**ment** *n.* (act, word, expression, of) affection.

en·deav·our [in'devə*] *n. & v.i.* attempt.

en·dem·ic [en'demik] *n. & adj.* (disease) regularly present in a country or among a class of people.

en·dorse [in'dɔːs] *v.t.* **1.** write one's name or comments on (a document). **2.** approve, support (a claim, statement, etc.). ~·**ment** *n.*

en·dow [in'dau] *v.t.* **1.** give (money, property, etc.) to provide a regular income for (e.g. a college). **2.** *be ~ed with,* possess naturally; be born with (a quality). ~·**ment** *n.*

en·dure [in'djuə*] *v.t. & i.* **1.** suffer, undergo (pain, hardship, etc.). **2.** bear; put up with: *She can't ~ seeing animals cruelly treated.* **3.** last; continue in existence. **en·dur·ance** *n.* **1.** ability to ~: *past (beyond) endurance,* to an extent that cannot be ~d. **2.** act, instance of, enduring.

en·e·my ['enimi] *n.* one who hates, wishes to harm, or attacks, another; anything that harms or injures; the armed forces of a country with which one's own country is at war.

en·er·gy ['enədʒi] *n.* **1.** force; vigour; (person's) powers available for or used in working. **2.** capacity for, power of, doing work. **en·er·get·ic** [ˌenəd'ʒetik] *adj.* full of, done with, ~.

en·er·vate ['enəveit] *v.t.* cause to lose (physical, moral) strength.

en·fee·ble [in'fi:bl] *v.t.* make (sb. or his efforts) feeble.

en·fold [in'fould] *v.t.* put one's arms round; cover or wrap up.

en·force [in'fɔ:s] *v.t.* **1.** compel obedience to (a law, etc.). **2.** get (sb.) by force (to do sth.). **3.** urge (an argument, demand). ~·ment *n.*

en·fran·chise [in'fræntʃaiz] *v.t.* **1.** give political rights to (esp. the right to vote at parliamentary electionś). **2.** set free (slaves).

en·gage [in'geidʒ] *v.t. & i.* **1.** get the right to occupy (a seat, taxi, etc.) or to employ (e.g. a workman, guide). **2.** promise; undertake. **3.** *be ~d in*, be occupied with; have one's time or attention taken up with : *~d in conversation.* **4.** begin fighting (*with* the enemy); attack. **5.** (of parts of a machine) lock together; (cause to) fit into. **en·gaged** *ppl. adj.* (esp.) having given a promise of marriage (*to*). ~·ment *n.* **1.** promise or undertaking, esp. (a) to marry or (b) to go or be somewhere, meet sb., at a fixed time. **2.** battle. **en·gag·ing** *adj.* attractive; pleasing.

en·gen·der [in'dʒendə*] *v.t.* be the cause of (a situation or condition).

en·gine ['endʒin] *n.* machine producing power or motion. '~-,driv·er *n.* man who drives a railway-~. **en·gi·neer** [ˌendʒi'niə*] *n.* **1.** person who designs machines, bridges, railways, ships, docks, etc. **2.** person in control of a ship's ~s. *v.t.* construct as an ~er; (fig.) arrange or bring about skilfully : *to ~er a scheme.*

Eng·lish ['ingliʃ] *n. & adj.* (people) of England; language of ~ people.

en·grave [in'greiv] *v.t.* cut (lines, words, designs, etc.) into stone, metal plates or other hard material. **en·grav·ing** *n.* picture, etc., printed from an ~d plate.

en·gross [in'grous] *v.t.* **1.** take up all the time or attention of : *~ed in one's work*; *an ~ing story.* **2.** write (a legal document) in large letters.

en·gulf [in'gʌlf] *v.t.* swallow up.

en·hance [in'ha:ns] *v.t.* add to (the value, attraction).

e·nig·ma [i'nigmə] *n.* question, person, thing, circumstance, that is puzzling. **e·nig·mat·ic** [ˌenig'mætik] *adj.*

en·join [in'dʒɔin] *v.t.* give an order for (silence, action); command (sb. to do sth.).

en·joy [in'dʒɔi] *v.t.* get pleasure from. ~·a·ble *adj.* ~·ment *n.*

en·large [in'la:dʒ] *v.t. & i.* make or become larger. ~ (*up*)*on*, say or write more about. ~·ment *n.* sth. ~d (esp. a photograph); sth. added to.

en·light·en [in'laitn] *v.t.* give more knowledge to; free from ignorance, misunderstanding or false beliefs. ~·ment *n.*

en·list [in'list] *v.t. & i.* **1.** obtain (sb.'s help, support, etc.). **2.** enter, take into, the armed forces.

en·liv·en [in'laivn] *v.t.* make lively.

en·mesh [in'meʃ] *v.t.* take (as) in a net.

en·mi·ty ['enmiti] *n.* hatred.

en·no·ble [i'noubl] *v.t.* **1.** make (sb.) a noble. **2.** make morally noble; make dignified.

en·nui [on'wi:] *n.* weariness of mind caused by lack of interesting occupation.

e·nor·mi·ty [i'nɔ:miti] *n.* great wickedness; serious crime.

e·nor·mous [i'nɔ:məs] *adj.* very great; immense. ~·ly *adv.*

e·nough [i'nʌf] *n. & adj.* (quantity or number) as great as is needed; as much or as many as necessary. *adv.* **1.** sufficiently : *Are you warm ~?* **2.** *oddly* (*curiously, etc.*) ~, sufficiently odd, etc., to be mentioned.

en·quire [in'kwaiə*] *v.i. & t* = inquire.

en·rage [in'reidʒ] *v.t.* fill with rage.

en·rap·ture [in'ræptʃə*] *v.t.* fill with great delight or joy.

en·rich [in'ritʃ] *v.t.* make rich; improve (the mind, the soil) by adding sth.: *soil ~ed with manure.*

en·roll [in'roul] *v.t.* put (sb.'s name) *on* a list or register.

en route [ɒn'ru:t] (Fr.) *adv.* on the way (*to, for*).

en·sign ['ensain] (in the navy ['ensn]) *n.* flag, esp. as used on ships: *white ~* (used by the Royal Navy); *red ~* (used by British merchant ships).

en·slave [in'sleiv] *v.t.* make a slave of.

en·sue [in'sju:] *v.i.* happen later; take place as a result.

en·sure [in'ʃuə*] *v.t.* make certain; make safe (*against* risks, etc.).

en·tail [in'teil] *v.t.* make necessary.

en·tan·gle [in'tæŋgl] *v.t.* catch in a net or among obstacles; (fig.) cause (sb.) to be in difficulty: *~d with money-lenders.* *~·ment n.*

en·ter ['entə*] *v.t. & i.* 1. come or go into; become a member of. 2. put (notes, names, records, etc.) down in writing: *to ~ for an examination; to ~ figures in an account.* 3. *~ into*, take part in; begin to deal with or talk about; *~ upon*, make a start upon (new work, duties, etc.).

en·ter·prise ['entəpraiz] *n.* 1. undertaking, esp. one that needs courage or that offers difficulty. 2. courage, eagerness, to start new *~s.* **en·ter·pris·ing** *adj.* having, showing, *~* (2).

en·ter·tain [,entə'tein] *v.t. & i.* 1. receive (people) as guests; give food or drink to. 2. amuse; interest. 3. be ready to consider: *to ~ a proposal;* have in the mind: *to ~ ideas (feelings).* *~·ing adj.* amusing. *~·ment n.*

en·thral(l) [in'θrɔ:l] *v.t.* (*-ll-*). take the whole attention of; please greatly.

en·throne [in'θroun] *v.t.* place (e.g. a bishop) on a throne. *~·ment n.*

en·thu·si·asm [in'θju:ziæzəm] *n.* strong feeling of, interest in, admiration for. **en·thu·si·ast** [in'θju:ziæst] *n.* person filled with *~.* **en·thu·si·as·tic** [in,θju:zi'æstik] *adj.* showing, having, *~.* **en·thu·si·as·ti·cal·ly** *adv.*

en·tice [in'tais] *v.t.* tempt or persuade (a person, etc.) (*away from* sth., *to do* sth.). *~·ment n.*

en·tire [in'taiə*] *adj.* whole; complete; not broken. *~·ly adv.* *~·ty* [in'taiəti] *n.* being *~: in its ~ty* (as a whole).

en·ti·tle [in'taitl] *v.t.* give a title to (a book, etc.); (of conditions, qualities, etc.) give (sb.) a right (*to*).

en·ti·ty ['entiti] *n.* 1. something that has existence. 2. being; existence.

en·to·mol·o·gy [,entə'mɒlədʒi] *n.* the study of insects.

en·trails ['entreilz] *n. pl.* bowels; intestines.

¹en·trance ['entrəns] *n.* 1. opening, gate, way into. 2. act of coming or going in, of entering (*into* or *upon* an office or position). 3. right of entering: *~ fees (examinations).*

²en·trance [in'trɑ:ns] *v.t.* (usu. passive) overcome, carry away as in a dream, with pleasure.

en·trant ['entrənt] *n.* person entering (a profession, *for* a competition, etc.).

en·treat [in'tri:t] *v.t.* beg (sb.) earnestly (*to do* sth.). *~·y n.* earnest request.

en·trench [in'trentʃ] *v.t.* surround with trenches. *~ oneself,* dig oneself into the ground; (fig., of legal clauses, customs) establish firmly. *~·ment n.*

en·trust [in'trʌst] *v.t.* give (sth. *to* sb.) as a responsibility, task, or duty; trust (sb. *with* a task).

en·try ['entri] *n.* entering; (place of) entrance; item noted in an account book, etc.; list, number, of persons, etc., entering for a competition, etc.

en·twine [in'twain] *v.t.* make by

twining; curl (one thing) (*with* or *round* another).

e·nu·mer·ate [i'nju:məreit] *v.t.* count, go through (a list of articles) naming them one by one. **e·nu·mer·a·tion** [i,nju:-mə'reiʃən] *n.*

e·nun·ci·ate [i'nʌnsieit] *v.t. & i.* 1. say, pronounce (words). 2. express (a theory, etc.) clearly or definitely. **e·nun·ci·a·tion** [i,nʌnsi'eiʃən] *n.*

en·vel·op [in'veləp] *v.t.* wrap up, cover, on all sides: ~*ed in mist* (*a shawl*).

en·ve·lope ['envəloup, 'on-] *n.* wrapper or covering, esp. one made of paper for a letter.

en·vi·a·ble, en·vi·ous, see *envy*.

en·vi·ron·ment [in'vaiərənmənt] *n.* surroundings, conditions, and influences (of a person, etc.).

en·vis·age [in'vizidʒ] *v.t.* see; face; picture in the mind.

en·voy ['envɔi] *n.* messenger, esp. one sent on a special mission by one government to another.

An envelope

An epaulette

en·vy ['envi] *v.t. & n.* (be filled with) feeling of disappointment or ill will at another's better fortune; object of such feeling. **en·vi·a·ble** ['enviəbl] *adj.* causing ~; likely to be envied. **en·vi·ous** ['enviəs] *adj.* having, feeling, or showing ~.

ep·au·lette ['epɔulet] *n.* shoulder ornament on a naval or military officer's uniform.

e·phem·er·al [i'femərəl, -'fi:m-] *adj.* living, lasting, for a very short time.

ep·ic ['epik] *n. & adj.* (poetic account) of the deeds of one or more great heroes or of a nation's past history.

ep·i·cure ['epikjuə*] *n.* person who understands the pleasures to be had from delicate(7) eating and drinking.

ep·i·dem·ic [,epi'demik] *n. & adj.* (disease) widespread among many people in the same place for a time. (Cf. *endemic*.)

ep·i·gram ['epigræm] *n.* short saying that expresses an idea in a clever and amusing way. ~·**mat·ic** [,epigrə'mætik] *adj.*

ep·i·lep·sy ['epilepsi] *n.* nervous disease causing a person to fall unconscious (often with violent, involuntary movements). **ep·i·lep·tic** [,epi'leptik] *adj.* of ~. *n.* person suffering from ~.

ep·i·logue ['epilɔg] *n.* last part of a literary work, esp. a poem spoken at the end of a play.

e·pis·co·pal [i'piskəpl] *adj.* of, governed by, bishops. **e·pis·co·pa·lian** [i,piskə'peiljən] *n. & adj.* (member) of an ~ church.

ep·i·sode ['episoud] *n.* (description of) one event in a chain of events.

e·pis·tle [i'pisl] *n.* (old word for) letter. *the Epistles,* (Bible) those written by the apostles. **e·pis·to·la·ry** [i'pistələri] *adj.* of ~s.

ep·i·taph ['epita:f] *n.* words (e.g. on a tombstone) describing a dead person. (Cf. *obituary*.)

ep·i·thet ['epiθet] *n.* adjective expressing a quality; word added to a name, as in 'Alfred the *Great*'.

e·pit·o·me [i'pitəmi] *n.* short summary of a book, speech, etc.; sth. which shows, on a small scale, the characteristics of sth. much larger.

e·poch ['i:pɔk] *n.* (beginning of a) period of time (in history, life, etc.) marked by special events or characteristics.

e·qua·ble ['ekwəbl] *adj.* steady; regular; not changing much: *an ~ climate* (*temper*).

e·qual ['i:kwəl] *adj.* the same in size, amount, number, degree, etc. ~ *to* (a task, etc.), strong enough for, capable of. *n.* person or thing ~ to another. *v.t.* (*-ll-*). be ~ to. ~·**ly** *adv.* ~·**i·ty** [i:'kwɔliti] *n.* state of being ~. ~·**ize** ['i:kwəlaiz] *v.t.* make ~.

e·qua·nim·i·ty [,i:kwə'nimiti] *n.* calmness of mind or temper.

e·quate [i'kweit] *v.t.* consider, treat, one thing as being equal (*to, with*) another. **e·qua·tion** [i'kweiʃən] *n.* making or being equal; (maths.) expression of equality between two quantities by the sign =.

e·qua·tor [i'kweitə*] *n.* imaginary line round the earth, real line drawn on maps, to represent points at an equal distance from the north and south poles. **~·i·al** [,ekwə'tɔ:riəl] *adj.* of or near the ~.

e·ques·tri·an [i'kwestriən] *n. & adj.* 1. (person) on horseback: *an ~ statue.* 2. of horse-riding: *~ skill.*

e·qui·dis·tant [,i:kwi'distənt] *adj.* separated by equal distance(s).

e·qui·lat·er·al [,i:kwi'lætərəl] *adj.* having all sides equal.

e·qui·lib·ri·um [,i:kwi'libriəm] *n.* state of being balanced.

e·quine ['i:kwain] *adj.* of, like, horses.

e·qui·nox ['i:kwinɔks] *n.* time of the year at which the sun crosses the equator and when day and night are of equal length. **e·qui·noc·tial** [,i:kwi'nɔkʃl] *adj.* of, at, near, the ~.

e·quip [i'kwip] *v.t.* (-*pp*-). supply (a person, oneself, a ship, etc.) (*with*) what is needed, *for* a purpose). **~·ment** *n.* things needed for a purpose.

eq·ui·ty ['ekwiti] *n.* fairness; right judgement; esp. (English law) principles of justice used to correct laws when these would apply unfairly in special circumstances. **eq·ui·ta·ble** ['ekwitəbl] *adj.* fair; just; reasonable.

e·quiv·a·lent [i'kwivələnt] *n. & adj.* (sth.) equal in value, amount, meaning (*to*).

e·quiv·o·cal [i'kwivəkl] *adj.* having a double or doubtful meaning; open to doubt.

e·ra ['iərə] *n.* period in history, starting from a particular time or event: *the Christian era.*

e·rad·i·cate [i'rædikeit] *v.t.* pull up by the roots; destroy or put an end to: *to ~ crime.*

e·rase [i'reiz] *v.t.* rub out. **e·ras·er** [i'reizə*] *n.* sth. with which to ~. **e·ra·sure** [i'reiʒə*] *n.* rubbing out; thing rubbed out.

ere [ɛə*] *conj. & prep.* (poet.) before.

e·rect [i'rekt] *adj.* upright; standing on end. *v.t.* 1. set ~ : *to ~ a pole.* 2. build; establish; set up: *to ~ a new school (a flagstaff).* **e·rec·tion** [i'rekʃən] *n.*

er·mine ['ə:min] *n.* small animal with (in winter) white fur and black-pointed tail; (pl.) garment made of its fur.

e·rode [i'roud] *v.t.* (of acids, rain, currents, etc.) wear away; eat into. **e·ro·sion** [i'rouʒən] *n.* eroding; being ~d: *soil erosion* (by wind and rain).

e·rot·ic [i'rɔtik] *adj.* of sexual love.

err [ə:*] *v.i.* do or be wrong.

er·rand ['erənd] *n.* short journey to take or get sth. (e.g. a message, goods from a shop); object or purpose of such a journey. **'~·boy** *n.* boy paid to run ~s.

er·rat·ic [i'rætik] *adj.* (of a person, a clock, etc.) irregular in behaviour or opinion; uncertain in movement.

er·ra·tum [e'reitəm] *n.* (pl. -ta [-ə]). mistake in printing or writing.

er·ro·neous [i'rouniəs] *adj.* incorrect; mistaken.

er·ror ['erə*] *n.* 1. sth. done wrong; mistake: *spelling ~s; an ~ of judgement.* 2. condition of being wrong in belief or conduct: *to lead sb. into ~.*

er·u·dite ['eru:dait] *adj.* having, showing, great learning; scholarly. **er·u·di·tion** [,eru:'diʃən] *n.*

e·rupt [i'rʌpt] *v.i.* (esp. of a volcano) burst out. **e·rup·tion** [i'rʌpʃən] *n.* outbreak (of a volcano: fig. of war, disease, etc.).

es·ca·late ['eskəleit] *v.t. & i.* increase by stages; (of warfare) (cause) become more violent and extensive. **,es·ca·'la·tion** *n.*

es·ca·la·tor ['eskəleitə*] *n.* moving stairs carrying people up or down.

es·ca·pade [,eskə'peid] *n.* daring,

mischievous, or adventurous act, often one causing gossip or trouble.

es·cape [is'keip] *v.i. & t.* **1.** get free; get away from; avoid. **2.** (of gas) flow out. **3.** be forgotten or unnoticed by. *n.* escaping; a means of escaping: *a fire-~.*

es·cape·ment [is'keipmənt] *n.* device in a clock or watch to regulate the movement.

es·chew [is'tʃu:] *v.t.* avoid; keep oneself away from (bad conduct).

es·cort ['eskɔ:t] *n.* person(s), ship(s), going with another or others to give protection or as a sign of honour: *under police ~.* *v.t.* [es'kɔ:t] go with as an ~: *a convoy ~ed by destroyers; to ~ the King to the Palace.*

es·cutch·eon [is'kʌtʃən] *n.* shield with a coat of arms on it. *a blot on one's ~,* a stain on one's reputation.

es·pec·ial [is'peʃl] *adj.* particular; exceptional. *~·ly adv.* to an exceptional degree; in particular.

es·pi·o·nage ['espiənɑ:ʒ] *n.* spying (1).

es·pouse [is'pauz] *v.t.* **1.** give one's support to (a cause, theory, etc.). **2.** (old use, of a man) marry.

es·prit de corps [espri:də'kɔ:*] (Fr.) *n.* spirit of loyalty and devotion which unites the members of a group or society.

es·py [is'pai] *v.t.* catch sight of.

es·quire [is'kwaiə*] *n.* title (written as *Esq.*), used (esp. in an address on a letter) *after* a man's name instead of Mr *before* it.

¹**es·say** ['esei] *n.* piece of writing (not poetry), usu. short, on any one subject. *~·ist n.*

²**es·say** [e'sei] *v.t.* try; attempt.

es·sence ['esns] *n.* **1.** that which makes a thing what it is; the inner nature or most important quality of a thing. **2.** extract (1) (usu. a liquid, obtained from a substance by removing, e.g. by boiling away, everything except the most important or valuable part): *meat ~; ~ of peppermint.*

es·sen·tial [i'senʃl] *adj.* **1.** neces-

sary; most important; indispensable: *conditions ~ to good health.* **2.** of an essence (2): *~ oils.* *~·ly adv.*

es·tab·lish [is'tæbliʃ] *v.t.* **1.** set up, put on a firm foundation (a state, business, etc.). **2.** settle, place (a person, oneself) in a position, office, place: *to ~ sb. as governor.* **3.** cause people to accept (a belief, claim, custom, etc.). **4.** make (a church) national by law. *~·ment n.* ~ing or being ~ed; that which is ~ed, e.g. a large organized body of persons (an army or navy, a civil service, a household and the servants in it).

es·tate [is'teit] *n.* **1.** piece of property in the form of land, esp. in the country: *~ agent,* person managing an ~; person who buys and sells buildings and land for others. **2.** all a person's property: *real ~* (land and buildings); *personal ~* (money and other kinds of property). **3.** (old use) condition: *to reach man's ~; the holy ~ of matrimony.*

es·teem [is'ti:m] *v.t.* **1.** have a high opinion of; respect greatly. **2.** consider: *I shall ~ it a favour if. . . . n.* high regard.

es·tim·a·ble ['estiməbl] *adj.* worthy of ~.

es·ti·mate ['estimeit] *v.t.* form a judgement about; calculate (the cost, value, size, etc., of sth.). ['estimit] *n.* judgement; approximate calculation (about the cost, value, size, etc., of sth.).

es·ti·ma·tion [estiˈmeiʃən] *n.* judgement; regard: *in the ~ of his friends; to be held in high ~.*

es·trange [is'treindʒ] *v.t.* bring about a separation in feeling and sympathy; *foolish behaviour that ~d his friends. ~·ment n.*

es·tu·a·ry ['estjuəri] *n.* river mouth into which the tide flows.

et·cet·er·a [et'setrə] (usu. shortened to *etc.*) and other things; and so on.

etch [etʃ] *v.t. & i.* (by the use of acids) engrave (a picture, etc.) on a metal plate from which copies may be printed. *~·ing n.* print made in this way; the art

of making pictures in this way.
~·'er *n.*

e·ter·nal [i'tə:nl] *adj.* without beginning or end; lasting for ever. *the E~*, God. e·ter·ni·ty [i'tə:niti] *n.* time without end; the future life.

¹e·ther ['i:θə*] *n.* colourless liquid made from alcohol, used as an anaesthetic.

²e·ther ['i:θə*] *n.* 1. *(the ~)* elastic fluid once thought to fill all space providing a means for waves of light, etc., to pass across. 2. (poet.) the pure, upper air above the clouds. e·the·re·al [i'θiəriəl] *adj.* 1. of or like the ²~ (1). 2. of supernatural delicacy; seeming too light or spiritual for this world: ~*eal beauty (music).*

eth·ics ['eθiks] *n.* (pl. or sing. v.). science of morals; rules of conduct. eth·i·cal ['eθikl] *adj.* of morals or moral questions; moral.

eth·nog·ra·phy [eθ'nɔgrəfi] *n.* description of the world's peoples.

eth·nol·o·gy [eθ'nɔlədʒi] *n.* science of the races of mankind, their relations to one another, etc. eth·nol·o·gist *n.* eth·no·log·i·cal [,eθnə'lɔdʒikl] *adj.*

et·i·quette ['etiket, eti'ket] *n.* rules of behaviour among polite people, a class of society, or members of a profession.

et·y·mol·o·gy [,eti'mɔlədʒi] *n.* science of the origin and history of words; account of the origin and history of a word. et·y·mo·log·i·cal [,etimə'lɔdʒikl] *adj.*

eu·ca·lyp·tus [,ju:kə'liptəs] *n.* sorts of evergreen tree from which an oil, used for colds, is obtained.

Eu·char·ist ['ju:kərist] *n. the E~*, Holy Communion; the bread and wine taken at the ~.

eu·gen·ics [ju:'dʒeniks] *n.* science of producing healthy offspring and thus improving the human race.

eu·lo·gy ['ju:lədʒi] *n.* (speech or writing full of) high praise. eu·lo·gize ['ju:lədʒaiz] *v.t.* praise highly in speech or writing.

eun·uch ['ju:nək] *n.* castrated

man, esp. one employed in former times in the household of an Eastern ruler.

eu·phe·mism ['ju:fimizəm] *n.* (example of) use of other, usu. more pleasing or less exact, words or phrases in place of words required by truth or accuracy: '*Pass away*' *is a ~ for* '*die*'. eu·phe·mis·tic [,ju:fi-'mistik] *adj.*

eu·pho·ny ['ju:fəni] *n.* pleasantness of sound; pleasing sound.

e·vac·u·ate [i'vækjueit] *v.t.* 1. (esp. of soldiers) withdraw from; leave empty: *to ~ a fort.* 2. remove (people) from a place or district (e.g. during a war). e·vac·u·a·tion [i,vækju'eiʃən] *n.* e·vac·u·ee [i,vækju'i:] *n.* person who is ~d (2).

e·vade [i'veid] *v.t.* 1. get, keep, out of the way of: *to ~ one's enemies (a blow).* 2. find a way of not doing sth.: *to ~ paying one's debts.* e·va·sion [i'veiʒən] *n.* evading; statement, excuse, etc., made to ~ sth. e·va·sive [i'veisiv] *adj.* trying to, intended to, ~: *an evasive answer.*

e·val·u·ate [i'væljueit] *v.t.* find out, decide, the amount or value of.

e·va·nes·cent [,i:və'nesnt, ,ev-] *adj.* quickly fading; soon going from the memory.

e·van·gel·i·cal [,i:væn'dʒelikl] *adj.* 1. of, according to, the teachings of the Gospel. 2. of the beliefs and teachings of those who maintain that the soul can be saved only by faith in Jesus Christ. e·van·ge·list [i'vændʒilist] *n.* 1. one of the writers (Matthew, Mark, Luke, or John) of the Gospel. 2. journeying preacher of the Gospel.

e·vap·o·rate [i'væpəreit] *v.t. & i.* 1. (cause to) change into vapour. 2. remove water or other liquid from (a substance, e.g. by heating): ~*d milk.* 3. (fig.) disappear; come to nothing: *hopes that ~d.* e·vap·o·ra·tion [i,væpə'reiʃən] *n.*

e·va·sion, e·va·sive, see *evade.*

eve [i:v] *n.* 1. day or evening

before a special day: *New Year's Eve*, 31 Dec. **2.** *on the eve of* (*great events*), at the time just before.

¹e·ven ['i:vn] *n.* (poet.) evening. '~·**song** *n.* Evening Prayer in the Church of England. '~·**tide** *n.* evening.

²e·ven ['i:vn] *adj.* **1.** level; smooth. **2.** regular: *~ breathing*; *at an ~ pace*. **3.** having the same quality throughout; uniform: *~ work* (*writing*). **4.** (of amounts, distances, values) equal. *be* (*get*) *~ with* (*sb.*), have revenge on. **5.** (of numbers) that can be divided by two with no remainder. (Cf. *odd*.) *v.t.* make *~* or equal. *~·ly adv.* in an *~* manner: *~ly divided*.

³e·ven ['i:vn] *adv.* **1.** *It is warm there, ~ in winter* (and so you can be sure it will be very warm there in summer). *E~ a child can understand the book* (therefore you can be sure it is a simple one). *It puzzled ~ the experts* (and so it was a very difficult problem). **2.** *even if, even though*: *I'll go, ~ if* (*though*) *you forbid me to*. **3.** still, yet: *You know ~ less than I do about it* (suggesting that I know only a little about it). **4.** *even so*, in spite of that: *The book is expensive, but ~ so you ought to buy it*.

eve·ning ['i:vnɪŋ] *n.* that part of the day between about 6 p.m. and bedtime.

e·vent [i'vent] *n.* **1.** happening, usu. an important one: *the chief ~s of 1968. at all ~s,* whatever happens; *in that ~,* if that is the case. **2.** one of the races, etc., in a sports programme. *~·ful adj.* full of important *~s*. **e·ven·tu·al** [i'ventjuəl] *adj.* likely to happen under certain circumstances; coming at last (as a result). **e·ven·tu·al·ly** *adv.* in the end. **e·ven·tu·al·i·ty** [i,ventju'æliti] *n.* possible event.

ev·er ['evə*] *adv.* **1.** at any time: *Do you ~ wish you were rich?* **2.** at any time up to the present: *Have you ~ seen an iceberg?* **3.** at all times: *He has been unhappy ~ since he left home.*

I will love you for ~ (*and ~*). *Yours ~* (ending a letter to an intimate friend). '~·**green** *n.* & *adj.* (tree) having green leaves throughout the year. ,~·**last·ing** *adj.* going on for *~*. *the Everlasting,* God. ,~·**more** *adv.* for *~*.

ev·er·y ['evri] *adj.* **1.** all or each one of a group, without exception: *I've read ~ book on that shelf. E~ boy in the class passed the test. He enjoyed ~ minute of his holiday.* **2.** used to indicate regular intervals of space or time: *Buses run ~ ten minutes* (i.e. six per hour). *Plant trees ~ twenty yards.* **3.** *~ other one*, each alternate one. *~ now and then*, occasionally. '~·**bod·y**, '~·**one** *pron.* ~ person. ~·**day** ['evridei] *adj.* happening or used every day. ~·**thing** ['evriθɪŋ] *pron.* **1.** all things. **2.** thing of the greatest importance: *Money is ~thing to him.* ~·**where** ['evriwɛə*] *adv.* in, at, to *~* place.

e·vict [i'vikt] *v.t.* turn (sb.) out from, dispossess (sb.) of, house or land, by authority of the law: *~ed for not paying rent.* **e·vic·tion** [i'vikʃən] *n.*

ev·i·dence ['evidəns] *n.* anything that gives reason for believing sth.; facts, statements, etc., giving support for or proof of a belief: *to give ~ in a law court; to bear ~ of* (i.e. show signs of); *in ~,* clearly or easily seen. *v.t.* prove by *~*; be *~* of. **ev·i·dent** ['evidənt] *adj.* plain and clear (to the eyes or the mind). **ev·i·dent·ly** *adv.*

e·vil ['i:vl] *adj.* wicked; sinful. *the E~ One,* Satan. *n.* wickedness; sin; *~* thing; disaster. *adv.* in an *~* manner: *to think ~ of sb.*

e·vince [i'vins] *v.t.* show that one has (a feeling or quality).

e·voke [i'vouk] *v.t.* call up, bring out (memories, admiration, feelings).

e·vo·lu·tion [,i:və'lu:ʃən] *n.* **1.** process of opening out or developing: *the ~ of a plant from a seed.* **2.** *Theory of E~,* theory that living things have been developed from earlier, simpler forms and are not each the result of special creation. **3.** movement according to plan (of dancers, soldiers, warships, etc.). **~·a·ry** [ˌi:vəˈlu:ʃənri] *adj.*

e·volve [iˈvɔlv] *v.t. & i.* (cause to) unfold; develop, be developed, naturally and gradually: *to ~ a new theory.*

ewe [ju:] *n.* female sheep.

ew·er [juə*] *n.* large, wide-mouthed jug for holding water.

ex- [eks] *prefix.* former(ly): *the ex-king.*

¹ex·act [igˈzækt] *adj.* correct in every detail; free from error. **~·ly** *adv.* **~·ness**, **~·i·tude** [igˈzæktitju:d] *n.* (quality of) being ~.

²ex·act [igˈzækt] *v.t.* demand and get by force: *to ~ payment from a debtor*; insist on: *to ~ respect (obedience).* **~·ing** *adj.* making great demands; severe: *an ~ing master.* **ex·ac·tion** [igˈzækʃən] *n.* the ~ing (of money, etc.); sth. ~ed, esp. a tax which is considered too high.

ex·ag·ger·ate [igˈzædʒəreit] *v.t. & i.* stretch (description) beyond the truth; make sth. seem larger, better, worse, etc., than it really is. **ex·ag·ger·a·tion** [igˌzædʒəˈreiʃən] *n.*

ex·alt [igˈzɔ:lt] *v.t.* **1.** make high(er) in rank, great(er) in power or dignity. **2.** praise highly. **~·ed** *adj.* dignified; of high rank. **ex·al·ta·tion** [ˌegzɔlˈteiʃən] *n.* (esp.) state of spiritual delight or elation.

ex·am·ine [igˈzæmin] *v.t.* **1.** look at carefully in order to learn about or from. **2.** put questions to in order to test knowledge or to get information. **ex·am·i·na·tion** [igˌzæmiˈneiʃən] *n.* examining or being ~d.

ex·am·ple [igˈzɑ:mpl] *n.* **1.** fact, thing, etc., which illustrates or represents a general rule. **2.** specimen showing the quality of others in the same group or of the same kind: *a good ~ of his work.* **3.** person's conduct to be copied or imitated: *to follow*

sb.'s ~; to set sb. a good ~. **4.** warning: *Let this be an ~ to you.* *make an ~ of sb.,* punish him as a warning to others.

ex·as·per·ate [igˈzɑ:spəreit] *v.t.* irritate; make angry; make (ill feeling, anger, etc.) worse. **ex·as·per·a·tion** [igˌzɑ:spəˈreiʃən] *n.*

ex·ca·vate [ˈekskəveit] *v.t.* make, uncover, by digging: *to ~ a trench (a buried city).* **ex·ca·va·tor** *n.* person engaged in, machine used for, excavation. **ex·ca·va·tion** [ˌekskəˈveiʃən] *n.*

ex·ceed [ikˈsi:d] *v.t.* **1.** be greater than. **2.** go beyond what is necessary or allowed: *to ~ the speed limit.* **~·ing·ly** *adv.* extremely.

ex·cel [ikˈsel] *v.t. & i.* (-ll-). do better than; be very good (*at* sth.).

ex·cel·lent [ˈeksələnt] *adj.* very good; of high quality. **~·ly** *adv.* **ex·cel·lence** *n.* **Your** (**His**) **Ex·cel·len·cy** *n.* title used when speaking to, of, an ambassador or governor.

ex·cept [ikˈsept] *prep.* **1.** not including; but not: *They were all tired ~ John.* **2.** *That was a good essay, ~ for* (apart from) *a few spelling mistakes.* **3.** *She knows nothing about him ~ that* (apart from the fact that) *he is handsome and well dressed. v.t.* set apart (e.g. not include sth. in a list, statement, etc.). **ex·cep·tion** [ikˈsepʃən] *n.* sth. or sb. ~ed; sth. not following or covered by a general rule. *take ~ion to,* object to; disagree with; protest against. **ex·cep·tion·al** [ikˈsepʃənl] *adj.* uncommon; out of the ordinary. **ex·cep·tion·al·ly** *adv.* unusually.

ex·cerpt [ˈeksə:pt] *n.* passage from a book, speech, etc.

ex·cess [ikˈses] *n.* **1.** fact of being, amount by which sth. is, more than sth. else or more than is expected or proper. *in ~ of,* more than. **2.** (pl.) personal acts which go beyond the limits of good behaviour, morality, or humanity. **3.** (attrib. use): ~

luggage, weight above what is carried free; ~ *postage*, fee charged when a letter, etc., has been understamped. **ex·ces·sive** [ik'sesiv] *adj.* too much; too great; extreme.

ex·change [iks'tʃeindʒ] *v.t.* give (one thing) and receive (another) for it. ~ *blows*, fight; ~ *words*, quarrel. *n.* **1.** act of exchanging: *an ~ of views*; *to give English lessons in ~ for French lessons.* **2.** the giving and receiving of the money of one country for that of another; relation in value between kinds of money used in different countries. **3.** place where merchants or financiers meet for business: *the Cotton E~, the Stock E~.* **4.** *telephone ~*, central office where lines are connected; *labour ~*, (in Gt. Brit.) office where employers and unemployed workmen may be brought together.

ex·cheq·uer [iks'tʃekə*] *n.* **1.** *the E~*, government department in charge of public money. *Chancellor of the E~*, minister at the head of this department. **2.** supply of money (public or private).

¹**ex·cise** [ek'saiz, 'eksaiz] *n.* government tax on certain goods manufactured, sold, or used within a country: *the ~ duty on beer.* (Cf. *customs.*)

²**ex·cise** [ek'saiz] *v.t.* cut out (a part of the body, a passage from a book, etc.). **ex·ci·sion** [ek'siʒən] *n.* excising or being ~d; sth. ~d.

ex·cite [ik'sait] *v.t.* **1.** stir up the feelings of; cause (sb.) to feel strongly. **2.** set (a feeling) in motion: *to ~ envy (affection) in sb.* **3.** cause (a bodily organ) to be active: *to ~ the nerves.* **ex·ci·ta·ble** [ik'saitəbl] *adj.* easily ~d. **ex·ci·ta·bil·i·ty** [ik‚saitə'biliti] *n.* ~**ment** [ik'saitmənt] *n.* state of being ~d; exciting thing, event, etc.

ex·claim [iks'kleim] *v.t. & i.* cry out, say, suddenly and loudly (from pain, anger, surprise, etc.). **ex·cla·ma·tion**

[‚eksklə'meiʃən] *n.* sudden short cry, expressing pain, surprise, etc.; *exclamation mark*, the mark ! . **ex·clam·a·to·ry** [iks'klæmətəri] *adj.* containing or consisting of an exclamation.

ex·clude [iks'klu:d] *v.t.* **1.** prevent (sb. *from* getting in somewhere): *to ~ sb. from membership of a club.* **2.** prevent (the chance of doubt, etc., arising). **ex·clu·sion** [iks'klu:ʒn] *n.* excluding or being ~d. *to the exclusion of*, so as to ~. **ex·clu·sive** [iks'klu:siv] *adj.* **1.** (of a person) not willing to mix with others, esp. those considered to be inferior. **2.** (of a group or society) not readily admitting new members. **3.** (of a shop, things sold in it, etc.) above the ordinary sort: superior. **4.** reserved to the person(s) concerned: *exclusive rights (privileges)* (i.e. not shared with others). **5.** *exclusive of*, not including.

ex·com·mu·ni·cate [‚ekskə'mju:nikeit] *v.t.* exclude (as a punishment) from the privileges of a member of the Church (e.g. Christian burial). **ex·com·mu·ni·ca·tion** ['ekskə‚mju:ni'keiʃən] *n.*

ex·cre·ment ['ekskrimənt] *n.* solid waste matter discharged from the body.

ex·cres·cence [iks'kresns] *n.* unnatural (usu. ugly and useless) out-growth on an animal or vegetable body.

ex·crete [eks'kri:t] *v.t.* (of an animal or plant) discharge from the system (e.g. waste matter, sweat). **ex·cre·tion** [eks'kri:ʃən] *n.* excreting; sth. ~d.

ex·cru·ci·a·ting [iks'kru:ʃieitiŋ] *adj.* (of pain) very severe.

ex·cul·pate ['ekskʌlpeit] *v.t.* free from blame; say that (sb.) is not guilty of wrongdoing.

ex·cur·sion [iks'kə:ʃən] *n.* short journey, esp. one made by a party for pleasure.

ex·cuse [iks'kju:z] *v.t.* **1.** give reasons showing, or intended to show, that a person or his action is not to be blamed; overlook (a fault, etc.): *to ~ sb.'s rudeness;*

to ~ *sb. for being rude.* **2.** set (sb.) free from a duty or punishment. **3.** ~ *oneself (from* a duty, etc.), ask (take) leave to be set free from. **ex·cu·sa·ble** [iks'kju:s] *n.* reason (true or invented) given to explain or defend one's conduct. **ex·cu·sa·ble** [iks'kju:zəbl] *adj.* that may be ~d.

ex·e·cra·ble ['eksikrəbl] *adj.* very bad; deserving hate. **ex·e·crate** ['eksikreit] *v.t.* express or feel hatred for.

ex·e·cute ['eksikju:t] *v.t.* **1.** carry out, do: *to ~ a plan (sb.'s commands).* **2.** give effect to: *to ~ a will.* **3.** make legally binding: *to ~ a legal document* (by having it signed, witnessed, sealed, and delivered). **4.** carry out punishment by death on (sb.): *to ~ a murderer.* **5.** perform (on the stage, at a concert, etc.). **ex·ec·u·tant** [ig'sekjutənt, eg'zek-] *n.* person who ~s(1) a design, etc., or who performs (music, etc.). **ex·e·cu·tion** [ˌeksi'kju:ʃən] *n.* **1.** the carrying out or performance (of a piece of work, design, etc.). **2.** skill in performing music. **3.** legal putting to death. **ex·e·cu·tion·er** *n.* public official who ~s(4) criminals. **ex·ec·u·tive** [ig'zekjutiv] *adj.* having to do with managing or executing (1); having authority to carry out laws and decisions: *the executive branch of a government; executive ability.* *n.* **1.** the executive branch of a government. **2.** person who manages a business, etc. **ex·ec·u·tor** [ig'zekjutə*] *n.* person who is chosen to carry out the terms of a will. **ex·ec·u·trix** [ig'zekjutriks] *n.* woman executor.

ex·em·pla·ry [ig'zempləri] *adj.* serving as an example or warning : ~ *conduct (punishment).*

ex·em·pli·fy [ig'zemplifai] *v.t.* illustrate by example; be or serve as an example.

ex·empt [ig'zempt] *v.t. & adj.* (set) free *(from* taxes, work, etc.). **ex·emp·tion** [ig'zempʃən] *n.*

ex·er·cise ['eksəsaiz] *n.* **1.** use, practice (of mental or physical powers, rights): *the ~ of patience.* **2.** training (of mind or body); activity, drill, etc., designed for this purpose: *vocal (gymnastic)* ~s; ~*s in grammar.* **3.** series of movements for training troops, crews of warships, etc.: *military* ~s. *v.t. & i.* **1.** take ~; give ~ to. **2.** employ (2): *to ~ patience (one's rights).* **3.** trouble (the mind): ~*d about one's shortcomings.*

ex·ert [ig'zə:t] *v.t.* **1.** put forth; bring into use; use (one's strength, influence, etc., to do sth.). **2.** ~ *oneself,* make an effort; use one's powers. **ex·er·tion** [ig'zə:ʃən] *n.*

ex·e·unt ['eksiʌnt] (Latin) *v.i.* (stage direction in plays) 'they go out'. (Cf. *exit.*)

ex·hale [iks'heil] *v.t. & i.* breathe out; give off (gas, vapour); be given off (as gas or vapour). **ex·ha·la·tion** [ˌekshə-'leiʃən] *n.* act of exhaling; sth. ~d.

ex·haust [ig'zɔ:st] *v.t.* **1.** use up completely: *to ~ one's strength (patience); to feel* ~ed, to feel tired out. **2.** make empty. **3.** say, find out, all there is to say about (sth.). *n.* (outlet, in an engine or machine, for) steam, vapour, etc., which has done its work. **ex·haus·tion** [ig'zɔ:s-tʃən] *n.* **ex·haus·tive** [ig'zɔ:stiv] *adj.* (of writing, discussion) thorough; complete.

ex·hib·it [ig'zibit] *v.t.* **1.** show publicly (for sale, in a competition, etc.): *to ~ paintings in an art gallery.* **2.** give clear evidence of (a quality). *n.* sth. ~ed: *an ~ in a museum.* **ex·hi·bi·tion** [ˌeksi'biʃən] *n.* **1.** collection of things ~ed publicly (e.g. in a museum). **2.** display of goods, etc., for commercial advertisement. **3.** act of ~ing (a quality, etc.): *an ~ion of bad temper; to make an ~ion of oneself,* behave in public so that one suffers contempt. **4.** money allowance to a student from school or college funds.

ex·hil·a·rate [ig'ziləreit] *v.t.* make glad; fill with high spirits.

ex·hil·a·ra·tion [ig,zilə'reiʃən] *n.*

ex·hort [ig'zɔ:t] *v.t.* urge, advise, earnestly (to do good, to give up bad ways, etc.). **ex·hor·ta·tion** [,egzɔ:'teiʃən] *n.*

ex·hume [eks'hju:m] *v.t.* take out (a dead body) from the earth for examination.

ex·i·gen·cy ['eksidʒənsi, ek'si-] *n.* condition of great need.

ex·ile ['eksail] *v.t.* send (sb.) away from his country as a punishment. *n.* (condition of) being ~d; person who is ~d.

ex·ist [ig'zist] *v.i.* be; have being; live; continue living. ~**ence** *n.* ~ing; everything that ~s; way of living: *to lead a happy* ~*ence.*

ex·it ['eksit] *n.* (passage, etc. for) going out. *v.i.* (in a printed play) 'he (she) goes out' (i.e. off the stage). (Cf. *exeunt.*)

ex·o·dus ['eksədəs] *n.* a going out or away of many people.

ex·on·er·ate [ig'zɔnəreit] *v.t.* free (sb. *from* blame or responsibility); set free from obligation.

ex·or·bi·tant [ig'zɔ:bitənt] *adj.* (of a price, charge, or demand) much too high or great.

ex·or·cize ['eksɔ:saiz] *v.t.* drive out (an evil spirit *from* sb. or *from* a place) by prayers or magic.

ex·ot·ic [eg'zɔtik, ek's-] *adj.* (of plants, fashions, words, etc.) introduced from another country.

ex·pand [iks'pænd] *v.t. & i.* 1. make or become larger or wider. 2. unfold or spread out. 3. (of a person) become good-humoured or genial. **ex·panse** [iks'pæns] *n.* wide area: *the broad* ~ *of the sky.* **ex·pan·sion** [iks'pænʃən] *n.* ~ing or being ~ed. **ex·pan·sive** [iks'pænsiv] *adj.* able to ~; covering a large area; (of a person) ~ing(3) in company.

ex·pa·ti·ate [eks'peiʃieit] *v.i.* ~ (*up*)*on*, write or speak at great length, in detail, about.

ex·pat·ri·ate [eks'pætriət] *n. & adj.* (person) living away from his own country.

ex·pect [iks'pekt] *v.t.* regard as

likely; think that sth. or sb. will come, that sth. will happen; wish for and feel confident that one will receive. ~**an·cy** [iks-'pektənsi] *n.* state of ~ing. ~**ant** *adj.* expecting: ~*ant mother*, pregnant woman. **ex·pec·ta·tion** [,ekspek'teiʃən] *n.* 1. ~ing; probability: ~*ation of life* (i.e. years a person is ~ed to live). 2. (pl.) what one ~s to receive (esp. at sb.'s death).

ex·pe·di·ent [iks'pi:diənt] *n. & adj.* (plan, action, device) likely to be helpful or useful for a purpose.

ex·pe·dite ['ekspidait] *v.t.* help the progress of; speed up (business, etc.). **ex·pe·di·tious** [,ekspi'diʃəs] *adj.* acting, done, quickly.

ex·pe·di·tion [,ekspi'diʃən] *n.* 1. (men, ships, etc., making a) journey or voyage with a definite purpose: *hunting* (*exploring*) ~*s.* 2. promptness.

ex·pel [iks'pel] *v.t.* (*-ll-*). send out or away by force: *to* ~ *the enemy from a town*; send away (from a place) as a punishment. **ex·pul·sion** [iks'pʌlʃən] *n.*

ex·pend [iks'pend] *v.t.* spend. ~**i·ture** [iks'penditʃə*] *n.* ~ing; money ~ed.

ex·pense [iks'pens] *n.* spending (of money, energy, time, etc.); (usu. pl.) money used or needed for sth.: *travelling* ~*s.* **ex·pen·sive** *adj.* causing ~; high priced.

ex·pe·ri·ence [iks'piəriəns] *n.* 1. process of gaining knowledge or skill by doing and seeing things; knowledge or skill so gained. 2. event, activity, which has given one ~ (1). *v.t.* have ~ of; find by ~. **ex·pe·ri·enced** *adj.* having ~; having knowledge or skill as the result of ~.

ex·per·i·ment [iks'perimənt] *n.* test or trial carried out carefully in order to study what happens and gain new knowledge. *v.i.* make ~s (*on* or *with*). **ex·per·i·men·tal(ly)** [iks,peri'mentl, -təli] *adj.* (*adv.*)

ex·pert ['ekspə:t] *n.* person with special knowledge, skill, or training. *adj.* (also [eks'pə:t] when predic.). skilful; trained by practice. ~·ly *adv.* ~·ness *n.*

ex·pi·ate ['ekspieit] *v.t.* make amends, submit to punishment (for wrongdoing). **ex·pi·a·tion** [,ekspi'eiʃən] *n.*

ex·pire [iks'paiə*] *v.i.* **1.** (of a period of time) come to an end. **2.** breathe out; (liter.) die. **ex·pi·ra·tion** [,ekspi'reiʃən] *n.* **ex·pi·ry** [iks'paiəri] *n.* ending (of a period of time).

ex·plain [iks'plein] *v.t. & i.* **1.** make clear and understood; show the meaning of. **2.** account for: *Can you ~ your absence from work yesterday?* ~ *oneself,* make one's meaning clear; give reasons for one's conduct. ~ *sth. away,* show why one should not be blamed for a fault, mistake, etc. **ex·pla·na·tion** [,eksplə'neiʃən] *n.* **ex·plan·a·tory** [iks'plænətəri] *adj.*

ex·ple·tive [eks'pli:tiv] *n.* violent (often meaningless) exclamation.

ex·plic·it [iks'plisit] *adj.* (of a statement, etc.) clearly and fully expressed. ~·ly *adv.*

ex·plode [iks'ploud] *v.t. & i.* **1.** (cause to) burst with a loud noise. **2.** (of feelings) burst out; (of a person) show violent emotion: *His anger ~d. He ~d with rage.* **3.** show that (an idea, theory, etc.) is false. **ex·plo·sion** [iks'plouʒən] *n.* **ex·plo·sive** [iks'plousiv] *n. & adj.* (substance) tending to or likely to ~.

¹**ex·ploit** [iks'plɔit] *v.t.* **1.** use, work, or develop (mines, waterpower, and other natural resources). **2.** use selfishly, or for one's own profit. **ex·ploi·ta·tion** [,eksplɔi'teiʃən] *n.*

²**ex·ploit** ['eksplɔit] *n.* bold or adventurous act.

ex·plore [iks'plɔ:*, -'plɔə*] *v.t.* **1.** travel into or through (a country, etc.) for the purpose of discovery. **2.** examine thoroughly (problems, etc.) in order to test, learn about. **ex·plor·er** *n.* traveller in unknown lands. **ex·plo·ra·tion** [,eksplə'reiʃən] *n.* **ex·plor·a·to·ry** [iks'plɔ:rətəri] *adj.*

ex·plo·sion, ex·plo·sive, see *explode.*

ex·po·nent [eks'pounənt] *n.* person explaining or interpreting (a theory, etc.).

ex·port [eks'pɔ:t] *v.t.* send (goods) to another country. ['ekspɔ:t] *n.* (the business of) ~ing; sth. ~ed.

ex·pose [iks'pouz] *v.t.* **1.** uncover; leave unprotected; ~ *soldiers to the enemy's fire;* ~*d to the weather.* **2.** display (e.g. goods for sale). **3.** show up (sb. or his wrongdoing). **4.** allow light to reach (camera film, etc.). **ex·po·sure** [iks'pouʒə*] *n.* exposing or being ~d.

ex·po·si·tion [,ekspə'ziʃən] *n.* **1.** expounding or explaining. **2.** exhibition (2).

ex·pos·tu·late [iks'pɔstjuleit] *v.i.* make a friendly protest.

ex·po·sure, see *expose.*

ex·pound [iks'paund] *v.t.* explain, make clear, by giving details: *to ~ the Scriptures (a theory).*

ex·press [iks'pres] *v.t.* **1.** make known, show (by words, looks, actions): *to ~ one's feelings (meaning).* **2.** send (a letter, goods) fast by special messenger. *adj.* **1.** clearly said or indicated: *an ~ wish (command).* **2.** going, sent, quickly: *an ~ train (messenger, letter).* *n.* ~ train. *adv.* by special delivery; by ~ train. **ex·pres·sion** [iks'preʃən] *n.* **1.** process of ~ing (one's meaning, feeling, etc.): *to give ~ion to one's gratitude.* **2.** word or phrase: *a polite ~ion.* **3.** look (2) on sb's face ~ing his feelings. **ex·pres·sive** [iks'presiv] *adj.* serving to ~ the feelings: *looks that were ~ive of despair.*

ex·pul·sion, see *expel.*

ex·punge [eks'pʌndʒ] *v.t.* wipe or rub out (words *from*).

ex·pur·gate ['ekspə:geit] *v.t.* take out (what are considered) improper passages(4): *an ~d edition.*

ex·qui·site ['ekskwizit, eks'kwizit] *adj.* **1.** of great excellence; brought to a high state of perfection. **2.** (of pain, pleasure, etc.) keenly felt. **3.** (of power to feel) keen; delicate.

ex·tant [eks'tænt] *adj.* still in existence.

ex·tem·po·re [eks'tempəri] *adv. & adj.* (spoken or done) without preparation or previous thought.

ex·tend [iks'tend] *v.t. & i.* **1.** make longer (in space or time). **2.** offer; stretch out: *to ~ an invitation* (*one's hand*) *to* sb. **3.** stretch out (one's arms, legs) to full length. **4.** (of space, land, etc.) reach; stretch: *land ~ing for hundreds of miles.* **ex·ten·sion** [iks'tenʃən] *n.* ~ing or being ~ed; sth. ~ed; sth. added: *an extension to a hotel.* **ex·ten·sive** [iks'tensiv] *adj.* far-reaching; ~ing far.

ex·tent [iks'tent] *n.* **1.** length; area; range. **2.** degree: *to a certain ~* (i.e. partly).

ex·ten·u·ate [eks'tenjueit] *v.t.* make (wrongdoing) seem less serious (by finding an excuse). **ex·ten·u·a·tion** [eks‚tenju'eiʃən] *n.*

ex·te·ri·or [eks'tiəriə*] *adj. & n.* outside; outer.

ex·ter·mi·nate [eks'tə:mineit] *v.t.* make an end of (disease, ideas, beliefs); destroy completely. **ex·ter·mi·na·tion** [eks‚tə:mi'neiʃən] *n.*

ex·ter·nal [eks'tə:nl] *adj.* outside; situated outside; for use on the outside of the body. ~·ly *adv.*

ex·tinct [iks'tiŋkt] *adj.* **1.** no longer burning; no longer active: *an ~ volcano.* **2.** no longer in existence; having died out; *an ~ species.* **ex·tinc·tion** *n.*

ex·tin·guish [iks'tiŋgwiʃ] *v.t.* **1.** put out(a light, fire). **2.** destroy; end the existence of (hope, love, etc.). ~·er *n.* device for ~ing fire, etc.

ex·tir·pate ['ekstəpeit] *v.t.* pull up by the roots; destroy.

ex·tol [iks'tɔl] *v.t.* (*-ll-*). praise highly.

ex·tort [iks'tɔ:t] *v.t.* obtain (money, promises, etc.) by threats, violence, etc. **ex·tor·tion** [iks'tɔ:ʃən] *n.* **ex·tor·tion·**ate [iks'tɔ:ʃənit] *adj.* (of a demand, price) too high.

ex·tra ['ekstrə] *adj. & n.* additional; beyond what is usual, expected, or arranged for.

ex·tract [iks'trækt] *v.t.* **1.** take, pull, or get out (usu. with effort); get (money, information, etc. *from* sb. unwilling to give it.) **2.** obtain (juices, etc.) by crushing, boiling, etc.: *to ~ oil from cotton-seed.* **3.** select and copy out words, examples, passages, etc. (*from* a book). ['ekstrækt] *n.* **1.** liquid ~ed (2): *beef ~.* **2.** passage ~ed (3) *from* a book, etc. **ex·trac·tion** [iks'trækʃən] *n.* (esp. of persons) descent or origin: *of French ~ion.*

ex·tra·dite ['ekstrədait] *v.t.* give up, hand over (a person) from the territory of one State to that of another where he is (alleged to be) guilty of wrongdoing.

ex·tra·neous [eks'treinjəs] *adj.* not related (*to* the object to which it is attached); not belonging (*to* what is being dealt with).

ex·traor·di·nary [iks'trɔ:dinəri] *adj.* unusual; remarkable.

ex·trav·a·gant [iks'trævəgənt] *adj.* **1.** wasteful; (in the habit of) wasting money: *an ~ man; ~ habits.* **2.** (of ideas, speech, behaviour) going beyond what is reasonable; uncontrolled. **ex·trav·a·gance** *n.*

ex·treme [iks'tri:m] *adj.* **1.** at the end(s); farthest possible. **2.** reaching the highest degree: *~ patience* (*danger*); *in ~ pain.* **3.** (of persons, their ideas, etc.) far from moderate: *to hold ~ opinions; ~ measures. n.* **1.** ~ part or degree. **2.** (pl.) qualities, etc., which are as wide apart as possible: *the ~s of heat and cold. go to ~s, take ~ measures.* **ex·trem·ist** *n.* person with ~(3) views. **ex·trem·i·ty** [iks'tremiti] *n.* **1.** ~ point, end, or limit; (pl.) hands and feet. **2.** ~ degree (of joy, misery, esp. of misfortune): *to help friends in extremity.* **3.** (pl.) ~ measures (e.g. for punishing wrongdoers).

ex·tri·cate ['ekstrikeit] *v.t.* set free, get (sb., oneself) free (*from* sth. holding someone back, or *from* difficulties).

ex·trin·sic [eks'trinsik] *adj.* (of qualities, values, etc.) not a part of the real character; operating from the outside. (Cf. *intrinsic*.)

ex·u·ber·ant [ig'zju:bərənt] *adj.* 1. growing luxuriantly. 2. full of life and vigour; high-spirited. **ex·u·ber·ance** *n.*

ex·ude [ig'zju:d] *v.t. & i.* (of drops of liquid) come or pass out slowly: *Sweat ~s through the pores.*

ex·ult [ig'zʌlt] *v.i.* rejoice greatly (*at* or *in* sth., to learn that . . .). **ex·ul·tant** *adj.* **ex·ul·ta·tion** [ˌegzʌl'teiʃən] *n.*

eye [ai] *n.* 1. organ of sight. *see eye to eye (with sb.)*, have the same opinion. *have an (a good) eye for*, be a good judge of; be able to see quickly. *with an eye to*, hoping for. *keep an eye on*, watch carefully. *make eyes at*, look lovingly at. 2. thing like an eye, esp. the hole in a needle. *v.t.* look at. **'eye·brow** (see *brow*). **'eye·lash** *n.* one of the hairs on the edge of the eyelids. **'eye·let** *n.* (metal ring round a) small hole made in leather, etc., for a shoe-lace, etc., to go through. **'eye·lid** *n.* one of two movable fleshy coverings of the eye. **'eye·sore** *n.* ugly thing. **'eye·wit·ness** *n.* person who can describe an event because he saw it.

F

fa·ble ['feibl] *n.* 1. short tale, not based on fact, esp. one with animals in it (e.g. *Aesop's ~s*) and intended to give moral teaching. 2. lie; false account. **fab·u·lous** ['fæbjuləs] *adj.* of or in *~s*; such as exists only in tales; difficult to believe in: *fabulous wealth.*

fab·ric ['fæbrik] *n.* 1. material, esp. woven material. 2. frame-

work or structure. **fab·ri·cate** *v.t.* make up (sth. false). **fab·ri·ca·tion** [ˌfæbri'keiʃən] *n.* sth. ~ated.

fa·çade [fə'sɑ:d] *n.* front of a building.

face [feis] *n.* 1. front part of the head (forehead, eyes, nose, mouth, cheeks, and chin). *make (pull) a ~ (at)*, pull the ~ out of shape (e.g. as a sign of disgust). *save (lose) one's ~*, escape (suffer) loss of honour or reputation. *put a good ~ on (sth.)*, make it seem less bad than it is; ~ it boldly. *keep a straight ~*, hide one's amusement. 2. surface of one side, esp. the front, of a many-sided object: *the ~ of a clock.* ~ *value*, value marked on a coin, bank-note, etc. 3. outward appearance of a situation: *on the ~ of it*, from its appearance; from what it appears to be. *v.t. & i.* 1. have or turn the ~ to or in a certain direction; be opposite to. ~ *the music*, show no fear at a time of danger or trial. ~ *it out*, refuse to give way to opposition, etc. 2. cover with a layer of different material: *a wall ~d with concrete.* **fa·cial** ['feiʃl] *adj.* of the ~.

fac·et ['fæsit] *n.* one of the many sides of a cut stone or jewel.

fa·ce·tious [fə'si:ʃəs] *adj.* (intended to be) humorous; fun-making.

fa·cile ['fæsail] *adj.* 1. easily done or obtained. 2. (of a person) able to do things easily; (of speech, writing) done easily but without enough attention to quality. **fa·cil·i·tate** [fə'siliteit] *v.t.* make easy; lessen the difficulty of. **fa·cil·i·ty** [fə'siliti] *n.* 1. quality which makes learning and doing things easy or simple. 2. (pl.) things, circumstances, which facilitate (work, travel, etc.).

fac·sim·i·le [fæk'simili] *n.* exact copy (of writing, etc.).

fact [fækt] *n.* sth. that has happened or been done; sth. known to be true or accepted as true. *in (point of) ~*, the truth is that. . . . *as a matter of ~*, really. **fac·tu·al** ['fæktjuel] *adj.* concerned with ~.

fac·tion ['fækʃən] *n.* **1.** discontented, usu. selfish and troublesome, group of persons within a party (esp. political). **2.** quarrelling of ~s. **fac·tious** ['fækʃəs] *adj.*

fac·tor ['fæktə•] *n.* **1.** whole number (except 1) by which a larger number can be divided exactly: *The ~s of 12 are 2, 3, 4, 6.* **2.** fact, circumstance, etc., helping to bring about a result.

fac·to·ry ['fæktəri] *n.* building(s) where goods are made (esp. by machinery).

fac·ul·ty ['fækəlti] *n.* **1.** power of mind; power of doing things. **2.** sense (e.g. hearing, sight). **3.** branch of learning, esp. as studied in a university: *the F~ of Law*; all the teachers in one of these.

fad [fæd] *n.* fanciful fashion, interest, preference, enthusiasm, unlikely to last. **fad·dy** *adj.* having fads; having odd likes and dislikes (e.g. about food).

fade [feid] *v.t. & i.* **1.** (cause to) lose colour or freshness. **2.** go slowly out of view, out of the memory, etc.

fag [fæg] *v.i. & i.* (-gg-). do very tiring work; (of work) make very tired. *n.* (sing. only, colloq.) hard work.

fag·got ['fægət] *n.* bundle of sticks for burning as fuel.

Fahr·en·heit ['færənhait] *n.* name of a thermometer scale with freezing-point at 32° and boiling-point at 212°. (Cf. *centigrade.*)

fail [feil] *v.i. & t.* **1.** be unsuccessful (in doing sth. one tries to do): *to ~ to pass an examination*; *to ~ in an attempt.* **2.** (of examiners) decide that a candidate has ~ed. **3.** be too little or insufficient; come to an end while still needed: *crops (water-supplies) that ~ed because of the hot summer.* **4.** (of health, eyesight, etc.) become weak. **5.** neglect (to do sth.). **6.** become bankrupt. *n.* (only in) *without* ~, certainly. **~·ing** *n.* weakness

or fault (of character). **~·ure** ['feiljə•] *n.* act of ~ing; person, thing, that ~s.

faint [feint] *adj.* (-er, -est). **1.** weak; indistinct; not clear. **2.** *to feel (look)* ~, as if about to lose consciousness. *v.i.* become unconscious (because of loss of blood, the heat, etc.). *n.* act, state, of ~ing (2). **~·ly** *adv.* '~·'heart·ed *adj.* having little courage.

¹**fair** [fɛə•] *adj.* (-er, -est). **1.** just; acting in a just and honourable manner; in accordance with justice or the rules of a game: *a ~ share*; *~ play.* **2.** average; quite good: *a ~ chance of success.* **3.** (of the weather) good; dry and fine; (of winds) favourable. **4.** (of the skin, hair) pale; light in colour. **5.** (old use) beautiful. *the ~ sex,* women. **6.** ~ *copy,* clear and clean copy of a draft(1); ~ *name,* reputation. *adv.* in a ~ manner: *to play* ~. **~·ly** *adv.* **1.** justly. **2.** moderately: *to speak English ~ly well.* **~·ness** *n.*

²**fair** [fɛə•] *n.* **1.** market (esp. for farm products, cattle, etc.), often with entertainments, held regularly in a particular place. **2.** large-scale exhibition (2).

fair·y ['fɛəri] *n.* small imaginary being (usu. female) with magic powers, able to help people. '~·tale *n.* **1.** tale about fairies. **2.** untrue story.

faith [feiθ] *n.* **1.** trust; strong belief; unquestioning confidence: *to have (put one's)* ~ *in God.* **2.** system of religious belief. **3.** promise: *to keep (break)* ~ *(with sb.).* **4.** *in good (bad)* ~, with (without) sincerity. **~·ful** *adj.* **1.** keeping ~; loyal and true (*to* sb., *to* a cause). **2.** true to the facts; exact: *a ~ful copy (description).* **~·ful·ly** *adv.* **~·less** *adj.* false; disloyal.

fake [feik] *v.t. & n.* (make up a) story, work of art, etc., that looks genuine but is not.

fal·con ['fɔ:lkən] *n.* meat-eating bird trained to hunt and kill other birds and small animals.

fall [fɔːl] *v.i.* (p.t. *fell* [fel], p.p. *fallen* ['fɔːlən]). **1.** come or go downwards or to the ground by force of weight, loss of balance or support, etc.: ~ *flat on one's face.* **2.** (of a fort, town, etc.) be captured in war. **3.** give way to temptation. **4.** drop down, wounded or killed: *to ~ in battle.* **5.** become; occur: *Christmas Day ~s on a Saturday this year.* ~ *in love* (*with*), become filled with love (of). ~ *asleep,* begin to sleep. ~ *short* (*of*), be not enough; be unequal to (what is wanted). **6.** (with adv. and prep.) ~ *back,* move or turn back. ~ *back on,* make use of (when sth. else has failed). ~ *behind,* fail to keep level with. ~ *in,* (army) form a rank. ~ *in with,* agree to (sb.'s plans, etc.). ~ *off,* (esp.) become fewer or smaller. ~ *on* (the enemy), attack. ~ *out,* quarrel (*with*). *It fell out that,* it happened that. ~ *through,* come to nothing. ~ *to,* begin. *n.* **1.** act of ~ing. **2.** (U.S.A.) autumn. **3.** (often pl.) place where a river ~s suddenly to a lower level: *the Niagara Falls.* **4.** amount (of rain, snow) that ~s; extent to which sth. (a river, temperature) ~s.

fal·la·cy ['fæləsi] *n.* mistaken belief; false reasoning or argument. **fal·la·cious** [fə'leifəs] *adj.*

fal·li·ble ['fælibl] *adj.* liable to error.

fal·low ['fælou] *n. & adj.* (land) ploughed but not sown or planted.

false [fɔːls] *adj.* not true or genuine: ~ *ideas* (*alarms, teeth*). *adv. play sb.* ~, be ~ to him, betray him. ~**'ly** *adv.* ~**'hood** *n.* untrue statement; lie; telling lies. **fal·si·fy** ['fɔːlsifai] *v.t.* **1.** make (records, etc.) ~; tell (a story, etc.) ~ly. **2.** *falsify fears* (*hopes*), be the opposite of what was feared (hoped). **fal·si·fi·ca·tion** [,fɔːlsifi'keifən] *n.*

fal·set·to [fɔːl'setou] *n.* male voice forced to an unnaturally high pitch.

fal·ter ['fɔːltə*] *v.i. & t.* move,

walk, act, speak, in an uncertain or hesitating manner.

fame [feim] *n.* (condition of) being known or talked about by all; what people say about sb. (esp. good). **famed** [feimd] *adj.* famous: ~*d for their courage.*

fa·mil·iar [fə'miljə*] *adj.* **1.** ~ *with,* having a good knowledge of. **2.** common and well known; often seen, heard, etc.: ~ *scenes* (*voices*). **3.** close; intimate: ~ *friends.* **4.** showing or claiming closer friendship than there is: *too ~ with a stranger.* **fa·mil·i·ar·i·ty** [fə,mili'æriti] being ~. **fa·mil·iar·ize** [fə'miljəraiz] *v.t.* make (oneself, sb.) ~ with, used to.

fam·i·ly ['fæmili] *n.* **1.** parents and children. **2.** all descendants of a man and wife. **3.** all persons related by blood. **4.** group of living things (plants, animals, etc.) or of languages, with common characteristics and having a common source.

fam·ine ['fæmin] *n.* extreme scarcity (esp.) of food in a region.

fam·ish ['fæmiʃ] *v.i.* be ~ed, suffering from extreme hunger.

fa·mous ['feiməs] *adj.* known widely; having fame.

¹**fan** [fæn] *n.* object (waved in the hand or operated by electricity) for making a current of air. *v.t. & i.* (-*nn*-). send a current of air on to: *to fan oneself* (*a fire*).

²**fan** [fæn] *n.* (colloq.) fanatical supporter or admirer: *film fans.*

fa·nat·ic [fə'nætik] *n. & adj.* (person) having a too passionate enthusiasm for sth., esp. religion. **fa·nat·i·cal** *adj.* ~ *ly.* **fa·nat·i·cism** [fə'nætisizm] *n.* violent, unreasonable enthusiasm.

fan·cy ['fænsi] *n.* **1.** (power of creating a) mental picture; sth. imagined. **2.** idea, belief, without foundation. **3.** fondness; liking; desire (*for*). *take a ~ to sb.,* begin to like him. *adj.* **1.** (esp. of small things) decorated; brightly coloured; made to please the eye: ~ *cakes* (*goods*). **2.** ~ *dress,* dress of a fantastic or unusual kind, as worn at some parties. ~ *price,* unusually high

price. **v.t. 1.** picture in the
mind. **2.** have a ~ (3) for (sth.).
3. have a ~ (2) (*that* sth. will
happen). **4.** (as exclamation)
How surprising! **5.** ~ *oneself*,
have a high opinion of oneself.
fan·ci·ful *adj.* full of fancies
(2); unreal; curiously designed.
'~-work *n.* ornamented needlework.

fang [fæŋ] *n.* long, sharp tooth;
snake's poison-tooth.

fan·tas·tic [fæn'tæstik] *adj.* **1.**
wild and strange: ~ *dreams.* **2.**
(of ideas, plans) impossible to
carry out; absurd. **fan·tas·ti·**
cal·ly *adv.*

fan·ta·sy ['fæntəsi] *n.* **1.** fancy
(1). **2.** sth. highly imaginative
and dream-like.

far [fɑ:*] *adv.* (*farther* ['fɑ:ðə*] or
(now more usual) *further* ['fə:ðə*],
farthest ['fɑ:ðist] or (now less
usual) *furthest* ['fə:ðist]). **1.** indicating distance in space or time:
*Did you walk far? They talked far
into the night.* **2.** *in so far as, as
far as,* to the degree to which:
in so far as I am concerned. *far
and away,* very much (better,
etc.). *adj.* a long way off, distant: *the Far East. be a far cry,*
be a long way. **'far-a·way** *adj.*
distant; (of a person's look)
as if fixed on sth. far away in
space or time. **'far-'fetched** *adj.*
(of a comparison, etc.) forced;
unnatural. **'far-off** *adj.* =
far-away. **'far-'reach·ing** *adj.*
having wide effects. **'far-**
'see·ing, 'far-'sight·ed *adj.*
(fig.) wise; having good judgement of future needs, etc.

farce [fɑ:s] *n.* **1.** play for the
theatre, full of ridiculous situations designed to make people
laugh; this style of drama. **2.**
series of actual events like a ~.
far·ci·cal ['fɑ:sikl] *adj.*

fare [feə*] *n.* **1.** money charged
for a journey (by ship, taxi,
etc.). **2.** food and drink. *bill
of* ~, menu. *v.i.* travel; progress: *How did you* ~? (What
happened to you?). *He* ~*d well*
(was successful).

fare·well ['feə'wel] *int.* good-bye.
n. leave-taking.

farm [fɑ:m] *n.* **1.** area of land,
with barns, etc. for growing
crops, raising animals, etc.
2. (also ~*house*) farmer's house
on a ~. *v.t. & i.* **1.** use (land)
for growing crops, raising animals, etc. **2.** ~ *out* (*work*), send
out to be done by others. **~·er**
n. man who manages a ~.
'~·yard *n.* space enclosed by ~
buildings (sheds, barns, etc.).

far·ther, far·thest, see *far.*

far·thing ['fɑ:ðiŋ] *n.* (formerly)
coin worth one-quarter of a penny.

fas·ci·nate ['fæsineit] *v.t.* **1.**
charm or attract greatly. **2.**
take away the power of movement by a fixed look, as a snake
does. **fas·ci·na·tion** [,fæsi'nei-
ʃən] *n.* (esp.) thing that ~s.

fash·ion ['fæʃən] *n.* **1.** (of clothes,
behaviour, thought, speech, etc.)
that which is considered best
and most to be admired and
imitated during a period or at a
place: *the Paris* ~*s* ; *changes of*
~ ; *styles which are in* (*out of*)
~. **2.** manner of doing or making sth.: *to behave in a strange*
~. *in some* ~, *after a* ~, somehow or other, not well. *v.t.* form
or shape: *to* ~ *a canoe from a
tree-trunk.* **~·a·ble** *adj.* following the ~(1); used by, visited
by, many people, esp. of the
upper classes: *a* ~*able tailor*
(*hotel*). **~·a·bly** *adv.*

¹**fast** [fɑ:st] *adj.* **1.** firmly fixed:
to be ~ *in the ground.* **2.** (of
friends) close; loyal. **3.** (of
colours) unfading. *adv.* strongly; firmly: *to hold* ~ (*to sth.*). ~
asleep, in a deep sleep; *play* ~
and loose with, repeatedly change
one's attitude towards.

²**fast** [fɑ:st] *adj.* (*-er, -est*). **1.**
quick; rapid: *a* ~ *train.* **2.** (of
a person, his way of living)
immodest; intent on worldly
pleasures: *a* ~ *life* (*woman*). **3.**
This clock is ten minutes ~ (at 2
o'clock, for example, the hands
point to 2.10). *adv.* quickly: *to
speak* ~ ; *raining* ~ (i.e. heavily).

³**fast** [fɑ:st] *v.i.* go without (certain
kinds of) food, esp. as a religious
duty. *n.* act of, period of,
~ing.

fast·en ['fɑːsn] *v.t. & i.* **1.** make fast; fix firmly; tie or join together: *to ~ doors and windows (two things together)*. **2.** become ~ed: *Most jackets ~ with buttons.* **3.** ~ *upon*, take firm hold of. ~**er**, ~**ing** *n.* sth. that ~s things together.

fas·ti·di·ous [fæs'tidiəs] *adj.* not easily pleased; particular (3).

fat [fæt] *n.* **1.** oily substance in animal bodies; this substance purified for cooking purposes. **2.** oily substance obtained from certain seeds: *vegetable cooking fats. live on the fat of the land*, have the best of everything to eat. *adj.* (*fatter, fattest*). **1.** covered with, having, much fat (1): *fat men (meat)*. **2.** thick; well filled: *a fat pocket-book.* **3.** profitable; fertile: *a fat job; fat lands.* '**fat-head** *n.* foolish person. *v.t. & i.* (*-tt-*). (also **fat·ten**) (cause to) become fat: *fatted cattle.*

fa·tal ['feitl] *adj.* causing, ending in, death or disaster. ~**ly** *adv.* ~*ly wounded.* ~**ism** ['feitəlizəm] *n.* belief that events are determined by fate (1). ~**ist** *n.* person who has this belief. ~**is·tic** [,feitə'listik] *adj.* of ~ism. ~**i·ty** [fə'tæliti] *n.* (instance of) death in an accident, in war, etc.: *bathing fatalities.*

fate [feit] *n.* **1.** power looked upon as controlling all events. **2.** the future fixed by ~ for sb. or sth. **3.** death; ruin; destruction: *to meet (go to) one's ~.* **fa·ted** ['feitid] *adj.* fixed by ~. ~**ful** *adj.* deciding the future.

fath·er ['fɑːðə*] *n.* **1.** male parent. **2.** founder or first leader: *the Fathers of the Church.* **3.** priest (esp. in the Roman Catholic Church). *v.t.* **1.** be the originator of (an idea, plan, etc.). **2.** ~ *sth. on sb.*, cause him to seem responsible for. '~**-in-law** *n.* ~ of one's wife or husband. ~**ly** *adj.* of or like a ~.

fath·om ['fæðəm] *n.* measure (six feet) of depth of water. *v.t.* (fig.) understand; get to the bottom of. ~**less** *adj.* too deep to ~.

fa·tigue [fə'tiːg] *n.* **1.** condition of being very tired. **2.** (army) task such as cleaning, cooking, etc. *v.t.* cause ~ (1) to.

fat·ten, see *fat.*

fat·u·ous ['fætjuəs] *adj.* foolish; showing foolish self-satisfaction.

fau·cet ['fɔːsit] *n.* (U.S.A.) tap.

fault [fɔːlt] *n.* **1.** sth. making a thing or person imperfect. *find ~ with*, point out ~s in; complain about. *at ~*, in the wrong; at a loss. **2.** responsibility for being wrong: *It's your own ~ if you've hurt yourself.* **3.** error: ~*s of grammar.* **4.** place where a layer of rock, etc., is broken. ~**less** *adj.* without ~. ~**less·ly** *adv.* ~**y** *adj.* imperfect. ~**i·ly** *adv.*

faun [fɔːn] *n.* (ancient Rome) god of the woods and fields, with goat's horns and legs.

faun·a ['fɔːnə] *n.* all the animals of an area or epoch: *the ~ of E. Africa.*

fa·vour ['feivə*] *n.* **1.** friendly regard; willingness to help. *in ~ of*, (a) in sympathy with; willing to help; (b) on behalf of. *out of ~ (with)*, not popular or liked. **2.** sth. done from kindness: *to ask a ~ of sb.* (i.e. ask him to help). *v.t.* **1.** show ~ to; support. **2.** show more ~ to (one person) than to others. **3.** be like (sb.) in appearance. ~**a·ble** ['feivərəbl] *adj.* giving or showing approval; helpful. ~**a·bly** *adv.* ~**ite** ['feivərit] *n. & adj.* (person or thing) specially ~ed. ~**it·ism** *n.* practice of ~ing (2).

¹**fawn** [fɔːn] *n.* **1.** young deer. **2.** light yellowish-brown.

²**fawn** [fɔːn] *v.i.* **1.** (of dogs) show pleasure (by jumping up, tail-wagging, etc.). **2.** (fig.) try to win sb.'s favour by flattery: *to ~ on a rich relative.*

fear [fiə*] *n.* **1.** being afraid; uncomfortable feeling caused by danger, evil, threats; alarm. **2.** risk; likelihood. **3.** reverence and dread; awe: *the ~ of God. v.t. & i.* have ~; feel ~ of; be anxious. ~**ful** *adj.* causing ~;

terrible; (colloq.) annoying; very great. **~·ful·ly** *adv.* **~·less** *adj.* without ~.

feas·i·ble ['fi:zəbl] *adj.* that can be done.

feast [fi:st] *n.* **1.** day kept (2) in memory of an important event. **2.** meal (esp. a public one) with many good things to eat and drink. *v.t. & i.* give a ~ to; take part in a ~.

feat [fi:t] *n.* difficult action done well.

feath·er ['feðə*] *n.* see the picture. *birds of a* ~, people of the same sort. *show the white* ~, show fear. *in high* ~, in high spirits. ~ *bed*, one stuffed with ~s. *v.t.* put ~s on (e.g. an arrow). ~ *one's nest*, make things comfortable for oneself.

Feathers

fea·ture ['fi:tʃə*] *n.* **1.** one of the named parts of the face; (pl.) the face as a whole. **2.** characteristic or striking part: *geographical ~s of a district* (e.g. mountains, lakes); *unusual ~s* (points) *in a speech. v.t.* be a ~ (2) of; make (sb. or sth.) a ~ (2) of; have a prominent part for (e.g. an actor in a film). **~·less** *adj.* without ~s (2).

Feb·ru·a·ry ['februəri] *n.* the second month of the year.

fed, see **feed.** ~ *up,* (colloq.) discontented (*with*).

fed·er·al ['fedərəl] *adj.* of, based upon, federation. **~·ism** *n.* ~ union. **fed·er·ate** ['fedəreit] *v.t. & i.* (of states, societies) organize, combine, as a ~ group. **fed·er·a·tion** [,fedə'reiʃən] *n.* **1.** political system (e.g. in Australia) in which States govern themselves but leave foreign affairs, defence, etc., to the central (Federal) govern-

ment. **2.** such a union of States; similar union of societies, trade unions, etc. **3.** act of federating.

fee [fi:] *n.* charge, payment, for professional (e.g. teaching, examining, medical, legal, surveying) advice or services.

fee·ble ['fi:bl] *adj.* (-bler, -blest). weak. **fee·bly** *adv.*

feed [fi:d] *v.t. & i.* (p.t. & p.p. *fed*). **1.** give food to; supply (one's family, etc.) with food. **2.** (chiefly of animals) eat: *cows ~ing in the meadows.* ~ (*up*)*on,* take as food. *n.* food for animals; (of animals and babies) a meal. (See also *fed.*)

feel [fi:l] *v.t. & i.* (p.t. & p.p. *felt* [felt]). **1.** touch with the hand; be aware of by touching; learn about by touching. **2.** be aware through the senses; know that one is (cold, hungry, happy, etc.). ~ *like* (*doing sth.*), have a wish (to do sth.). **3.** seem, appear (smooth, rough, etc.) to the senses: *A baby's hand ~s smooth. Her skin ~s like silk.* **4.** have a vague idea (*that*). **5.** be moved by, sensitive to: *to ~ sorrow for sb.; to ~ the heat* (i.e. suffer from it). *n.* by the ~, by ~ing. **~·er** *n.* **1.** organ of touch in some insects. **2.** suggestion put forward to discover what others think. **~·ing** *n.* **1.** power to ~; awareness: *a ~ing of discomfort.* **2.** sth. felt in the mind: *~ings of joy.* **3.** (pl.) non-intellectual part of the character: *to rouse the ~ings* (i.e. make excited, angry, etc.); *to hurt sb.'s ~ings* (i.e. offend him). **4.** *~ing for* (art, beauty, etc.), appreciation, awareness, of. *adj.* having, showing, ~ing (2) or sympathy.

feet, see **foot.**

feign [fein] *v.t.* pretend.

fe·lic·i·tate [fi'lisiteit] *v.t.* congratulate.

fe·lic·i·tous [fi'lisitəs] *adj.* (of words, remarks) well chosen.

fe·lic·i·ty [fi'lisiti] *n.* great happiness or contentment.

fe·line ['fi:lain] *adj.* of or like a cat.

¹**fell**, see *fall*.

²**fell** [fel] *v.t.* cause to fall; knock (sb.) down; cut (a tree) down.

fel·low ['felou] *n.* **1.** (colloq.) man. **2.** (pl.) companions; those sharing experiences : ~*s in misfortune*. **3.** (attrib.) of the same class, kind, etc.: ~*-citizens*; ~*-passengers*. **4.** member of a learned society (*F~ of the British Academy*) or of the governing body of some university colleges. '~-'**feel·ing** *n.* sympathy; feeling which is shared. '~-'**ship** *n.* **1.** friendly association; companionship. **2.** (membership of a) group or society. **3.** position of a college ~.

fel·on ['felən] *n.* person who has committed a serious crime. ~**y** *n.* serious crime.

¹**felt**, see *feel*.

²**felt** [felt] *n.* wool, hair, etc., pressed and rolled flat : ~ *hats* (*slippers*).

fe·male ['fi:meil] *adj.* **1.** of the sex able to produce offspring or lay eggs; (of plants) producing fruit. **2.** of women. *n.* ~ animal or person.

fem·i·nine ['feminin] *adj.* **1.** of, like, suitable for, women: ~ *hobbies* (e.g. needlework). **2.** of female gender: '*Actress' is a ~ noun.* (Cf. *masculine.*) **fem·i·nism** ['feminizm] *n.* movement for giving women the same rights as men.

fen [fen] *n.* area of low, wet land.

¹**fence** [fens] *v.t. & n.* (surround, divide, with a) barrier made of wooden stakes, wire, etc.

²**fence** [fens] *v.i.* **1.** practise the art of fighting with swords. **2.** (fig.) avoid giving a direct answer to (a question). **fenc·er** *n.*

fend [fend] *v.t. & i.* **1.** ~ *off* (*a blow*), defend oneself from. **2.** ~ *for* (*oneself, young ones*), provide (food, etc.) for; care for.

fend·er ['fendə*] *n.* **1.** metal frame bordering an open fireplace. **2.** (on the sides of a ship, on machinery, on the front of a tram car, etc.) part or appliance which lessens shock or damage in a collision.

fer·ment [fə:'ment] *v.t. & i.* (cause to) undergo chemical change through the action of organic bodies (esp. yeast); (fig.) (cause to) become excited. ['fə:ment] *n.* substance (e.g. yeast) causing others to ~. *in a ~*, (fig.) in a state of (e.g. social, political) excitement. **fer·men·ta·tion** [,fə:men'teiʃən] *n.*

A fender (1), (2)   Fern(s)

fern [fə:n] *n.* sorts of feathery, green-leaved flowerless plant as illustrated above.

fe·ro·cious [fə'rouʃəs] *adj.* fierce; cruel; violent. **fe·roc·i·ty** [fə'rositi] *n.*

fer·ret ['ferit] *n.* small animal clever at killing rats and forcing rabbits from their burrows. *v.t. & i.* hunt (rabbits, etc.) with ~s. ~ (*sth. or sb.*) *out*, discover after a careful search.

fer·ro-con·crete ['ferou-'kɔn-kri:t] *n.* concrete with an iron or steel framework inside it.

fer·rous ['ferəs] *adj.* of iron.

fer·ry ['feri] *n.* (place where there is a) boat or aircraft that carries people and goods across a river, channel, etc. *v.t. & i.* take, go, across in a ~.

fer·tile ['fə:tail] *adj.* **1.** (of land, plants, etc.) producing much; (of a person, his mind, etc.) full of ideas, plans, etc. **2.** (opp. of *sterile*) able to produce fruit, young; capable of developing: ~ *seeds* (*eggs*). **fer·til·i·ty** [fə:'tiliti] *n.* being ~. **fer·ti·lize** ['fə:tilaiz] *v.t.* make ~. **fer·ti·li·za·tion** [,fə:tilai'zeiʃən] *n.* **fer·ti·liz·er** ['fə:tilaizə*] *n.* substance for making land or soil ~.

fer·vent ['fə:vənt] *adj.* **1.** hot; glowing. **2.** (fig.) passionate: ~ *love*; feeling deeply : *a ~ lover.* **fer·vour** ['fə:və*] *n.* deep feeling. **fer·vid** ['fə:vid] *adj.* = ~ (2).

fes·tal ['festl] *adj.* of a festival.

fes·ter ['festə*] *v.i. & t.* 1. (of a wound) fill with poisonous matter. 2. cause bitterness; act like poison on the mind.

fes·ti·val ['festəvəl] *n.* (day or season for) merry-making; public celebrations. **fes·tive** ['festiv] *adj.* of a ~: *festive scenes.* **fes·ti·vi·ty** [fes'tiviti] *n.* 1. = ~. 2. (pl.) joyful events: *wedding festivities.*

fes·toon [fes'tu:n] *n.* chain of flowers, leaves, etc., hanging between two points, as a decoration. *v.t.* make into, decorate with, ~s.

fetch [fetʃ] *v.t. & i.* 1. go for and bring back (sb. or sth.). 2. cause (a sigh, blood, tears) to come out; (of goods) bring in; sell at (a price).

fête [feit] *n.* (usu. outdoor) festival.

fe·tid ['fet-, 'fi:tid] *adj.* bad-smelling.

fe·tish, fe·tich ['fi:t-, 'fetiʃ] *n.* object worshipped by pagan people because they believe a spirit lives in it; anything to which foolishly excessive respect is paid.

fet·ter ['fetə*] *n.* chain for the ankle of a prisoner or the leg of a horse; (fig., usu. pl.) anything that hinders progress. *v.t.* put in ~s; hinder.

fet·tle ['fetl] *n. in fine ~,* in good health (spirits).

feud [fju:d] *n.* bitter quarrel between two persons, families, or groups, over a long period of time.

feu·dal ['fju:dl] *adj.* of the method of holding land (by giving services to the owner) during the Middle Ages in Europe. ~·**ism** *n.* the ~ system.

fe·ver ['fi:və*] *n.* 1. condition of the human body with temperature higher than normal, esp. as a sign of illness. 2. one of a number of diseases in which there is high ~. 3. excited state: *in a ~ of impatience.* ~·**ish** *adj.* of, having, caused by, ~: *~ish dreams.*

few [fju:] *adj.* (*-er, -est*) *& n.* 1. (with pl. noun) not many: *Few*

people live to be ninety, even fewer live to be 100. Who made the fewest (smallest number of) *mistakes? no fewer than,* as many as. 2. (with *a*) a small number (of): *Would you like to have a few friends to supper?*

fez [fez] *n.* red felt head-dress worn by some Muslim men.

fi·an·cé(e) [fi'ɑ:nsei] *n.* man (woman) to whom one is engaged to be married.

fi·as·co [fi'æskou] *n.* complete failure, breakdown, in sth. attempted.

fi·at ['faiæt] *n.* order made by a ruler.

fib [fib] *n.* (colloq.) untrue statement (esp. about sth. unimportant). *v.i.* (*-bb-*). tell a fib.

fi·bre ['faibə*] *n.* 1. one of the slender threads of which many animal and vegetable growths are formed (e.g. cotton, wood, nerves). 2. substance formed of a mass of ~s (e.g. cotton ~) for manufacture into cloth, etc. **fi·brous** ['faibrəs] *adj.* made of, like, ~s.

fick·le ['fikl] *adj.* (of moods, weather, etc.) often changing.

fic·tion ['fikʃən] *n.* 1. sth. invented or imagined (contrasted with truth). 2. (branch of literature concerned with) stories, novels, and romances: *works of ~.* **fic·ti·tious** [fik'tiʃəs] *adj.* not real; imagined or invented.

fid·dle ['fidl] *n.* violin; any instrument of the violin family. *fit as a ~,* very well; in good health; *play second ~ to,* take a less important place than. *v.t. & i.* 1. play the ~. 2. play aimlessly (*with* sth. in one's fingers). **'F~·sticks** *int.* Nonsense!

fi·del·i·ty [fi'deliti] *n.* 1. loyalty; faithfulness (*to* sb. or sth.). 2. accuracy, exactness.

fid·get ['fidʒit] *v.i. & t.* (cause sb. to) move the body (or part of it) about restlessly; make (sb) nervous. *n.* (pl.) ~ing movements; (sing.) person who ~s. ~·**y** *adj.*

field [fi:ld] *n.* 1. area of land (usu. enclosed by a fence or hedge) for pasture or growing crops. **2.** (usu. in compound words)land from which minerals, etc., are obtained: *gold-*(*oil-*, *coal-*)~. **3.** expanse; open space: *ice-*~; *flying-*~. ~*-sports*, (b) hunting, shooting, fishing; (b) certain athletic contests. **4.** branch of study; range of activity or use: *the* ~ *of medical research*; *the* ~ *of a telescope*; ~ *of vision.* **5.** place, area, where a battle or war is fought: *take the* ~, begin a war. ~*-artillery* (*-gun*, *-hospital*, etc.), light and movable. **v.i. & t.** (stand on the cricket field ready to) catch or stop (the ball). '~-**glas·ses** *n. pl.* long-distance glasses for outdoor use with both eyes. 'F~ 'Mar·shal *n.* army officer of highest rank.

fiend [fi:nd] *n.* devil; very wicked or cruel person. ~·ish *adj.*

fierce [fiəs] *adj.* (*-r*, *-st*). **1.** violent; cruel; angry: ~ *dogs* (*looks*, *winds*). **2.** (of heat, desire, etc.) intense. ~·ly *adv.* ~·ness *n.*

fi·er·y ['faiəri] *adj.* flaming; looking like, hot as, fire; (of a person) quickly or easily made angry.

fife [faif] *n.* small musical wind instrument.

fif·teen ['fif'ti:n] *n. & adj.* 15. **fifth** *n. & adj.* 5th; ⅕. **fif·ty** ['fifti] *n. & adj.* 50. **fif·ti·eth** ['fiftiiθ] *n. & adj.* ¹⁄₅₀; next in order after 49th.

fig [fig] *n.* (tree having) soft, sweet fruit full of small seeds.

fight [fait] **v.t. & i.** (p.t. & p.p. **fought** [fɔ:t]). **1.** struggle (with hands, weapons) against (sb. or sth.). **2.** engage in (a battle *against* or *with* sb.). ~ *shy of*, keep away from. ~ *it out*, settle by ~ing. *n.* struggle; battle. ~·er *n.* (esp.) aircraft for ~ing.

fig·ment ['figmənt] *n.* sth. unreal and imagined.

fig·u·ra·tive ['figjurətiv] *adj.* (of words) used not in the literal sense but in an imaginative way (as when *fiery* is used of a man who is easily made very angry).

fig·ure ['figə*] *n.* **1.** sign for a number, esp. 0 to 9. **2.** price: *to buy sth. at a low* ~. **3.** human form, esp. the appearance and what it suggests: *a fine* ~ *of a man*; *a* ~ *of distress.* **4.** person, esp. his influence: *Churchill, the greatest* ~ *of his time.* **5.** person's ~ drawn or painted, cut in stone, etc.; drawing, painting, image, of the body of a bird, animal, etc.; diagram or illustration. **6.** ~ *of speech*, word(s) used figuratively. **v.t. & i. 1.** have a part; appear: *to* ~ (*as* sb., *in* a play; *in* history). **2.** ~ *sth. out*, reach a result (esp. by using ~s(1)); think about until one understands. **3.** represent (in art); form a mental picture of. **fig·ured** ['figəd] *adj.* marked with designs or patterns. '~-**head** *n.* person with high position but no power.

fil·a·ment ['filəmənt] *n.* slender thread, esp. of wire in an electric lamp bulb.

filch [filtʃ] **v.t.** steal (things of small value).

¹**file** [fail] *n.* holder for keeping papers, etc., together and in order; (set of) letters, documents, newspapers, etc., kept together on or in a ~. **v.t.** put on or in a ~.

²**file** [fail]*n.* metal tool with a rough face for cutting or smoothing hard surfaces. **v.t.** use a ~ on. **fil·ings** *n. pl.* bits ~d off.

³**file** [fail] *n. in* (*single*) ~, (of persons) in one line, one behind the other. **v.i.** ~ *in* (*out*), go in (out) in ~(s).

fil·ial ['filjəl] *adj.* of a son or daughter: ~ *duty.*

fil·i·gree ['filigri:] *n.* ornamental lace-like work of gold or silver wire.

fill [fil] **v.t. & i. 1.** make or become full; occupy all the space in. **2.** ~ *in*, (esp.) write what is needed to complete (a form, etc.); ~ *out*, make or become larger, rounder, or fatter. **3.** execute (an order for goods, a prescription). **fil·ling** *n.* sth. put in to ~ (a hole in) sth. *n.* eat (*have*) one's ~, as much as one wants or can take.

fil·let ['filit] *n.* **1.** band worn to keep the hair in place. **2.** slice of fish or meat without bones. *v.t.* cut (fish) into ~s.

film [film] *n.* **1.** thin coating or covering: *a ~ of dust* (*mist*). **2.** roll or sheet of thin flexible material prepared for use in photography. **3.** cinema picture: *travel ~s*; *~ actors.* *v.t. & i.* **1.** cover, become covered, with a ~ (1). **2.** make a ~ (3) of. ~·**y** *adj.* like a ~ (1): *~y clouds.*

fil·ter ['filtə*] *n.* apparatus (containing, e.g., sand, charcoal, paper, or cloth) for holding back solid substances in impure liquid poured through it. *v.t. & i.* (cause to) flow through a ~; (fig. of a crowd, news, etc.) make its way (*out, through,* etc.)

filth [filθ] *n.* disgusting dirt. ~·**y** *adj.* ~·**i·ly** *adv.*

fin [fin] *n.* one of those parts of a fish (other than the tail) used in swimming.

fi·nal ['fainl] *adj.* **1.** at the end. **2.** putting an end to doubt or argument: *~ judgements.* *n.* (often pl.) ~ examinations or contests. **fi·na·le** [fi'nɑːli] *n.* ~ part of a piece of music; closing scene of an opera or play; end. ~·**ly** *adv.* lastly.

fi·nance [fi-, fai'næns] *n.* **1.** (science of) the management of (esp. public) money. **2.** (pl.) money (esp. of a government or business company). *v.t.* provide money for (a scheme, etc.). **fi·nan·cial** [fi-, fai'nænʃl] *adj.* **fi·nan·cier** [fi-, fai'nænsiə*] *n.* person skilled in ~.

find [faind] *v.t.* (p.t. & p.p. *found* [faund]). **1.** look for and get back (sth. or sb. lost, etc.); discover (sth. or sb. not lost) as a result of searching; discover by chance. **2.** ~ *one's feet,* discover one's powers and begin to do well. **3.** learn by experience: *to ~ that one is mistaken.* **4.** (often ~ *out*) learn by inquiry; discover: *to ~* (*out*) *when the train starts* (*how to do sth.,* etc.). ~ *sb. out,* learn that he has

done sth. wrong, is at fault, etc. **5.** get, supply (money, other needs): *to ~ one's daughter in clothes.* *~ favour with,* win the favour or approval of. **6.** (legal) reach a decision: *to ~ a prisoner guilty.* *n.* sth. found, esp. sth. valuable or pleasing. ~·**ing** *n.* (often pl.) legal decision(s); sth. discovered after inquiries.

¹**fine** [fain] *adj.* **1.** (of weather) bright; not raining. **2.** enjoyable; pleasing; splendid: *a ~ view*; *~ clothes*; *to have a ~ time.* **3.** delicate: *~ workmanship.* **4.** of very small particles: *~ dust.* **5.** very thin; sharp: *~ thread*; *a ~ point.* **6.** (of metals) refined; pure. **fin·er·y** ['fainəri] *n.* splendid clothes, ornaments, etc.

²**fine** [fain] *adv.* cut (run) it ~, leave oneself hardly enough time.

³**fine** [fain] *n.* sum of money (to be) paid as a penalty for breaking a law or rule. *v.t.* make (sb.) pay a ~.

⁴**fine** [fain] *n.* **in** ~, in short; finally.

fi·nesse [fi'nes] *n.* artful or delicate way of dealing with a situation.

fin·ger ['fiŋgə*] *n.* see the picture. (Cf. *thumb.*) *v.t.* touch with the ~s. **'~-post** *n.* sign-post at a cross-roads. **'~-print** *n.* mark made by the ~-tip(s), esp. as used to detect criminals.

The fingers   A finger-print

fin·i·cal ['finikl], **fin·ick·ing** ['finikiŋ], **fin·ick·y** ['finiki] *adjs.* too fussy or fastidious (about food, details).

fin·ish ['finiʃ] *v.t. & i.* **1.** bring or come to an end. **2.** make complete or perfect; polish. *n.* **1.** the last part. **2.** ~ed (2) state.

fi·nite ['fainait] *adj.* **1.** limited. **2.** (grammar) limited by number and person: '*Am' is a ~ form of 'be'.

fiord [fjɔːd] *n.* (as in Norway) narrow arm of the sea, between high cliffs.

fir [fəː*] *n.* (wood of) evergreen tree with needle-like leaves.

fire ['faiə*] *n.* **1.** (condition of) burning: *to set the house on fire*; instance of burning: *to light a ~ in the sitting-room*; *a forest ~*. **2.** shooting (from guns): *under ~*, being shot at. **3.** angry or excited feeling. *v.t. & i.* **1.** cause to begin burning: *to ~ a haystack*. **2.** harden in an oven: *to ~ bricks*. **3.** supply (a furnace, etc.) with fuel. **4.** shoot (5) with, pull the trigger of, discharge (2) (a rifle, etc.); send (a bullet, shell) from a gun; (of a gun) go off. **5.** excite (the imagination, etc.). *~ up*, become excited or angry. **6.** (colloq.) dismiss (a servant). '**~-a¸larm** *n.* bell, etc., which is sounded as a signal of an outbreak of ~. '**~-arm** *n.* rifle or revolver. '**~-brand** *n.* person who stirs up social or political discontent. '**~-bri¸gade** *n.* company of men who put out ~s. '**~-¸crack·er** *n.* ~work which explodes with a cracking sound. '**~-damp** *n.* explosive gas in coal-mines. '**~-¸en·gine** *n.* motor pump manned by ~men. '**~-es¸cape** *n.* kind of extending ladder, or outside stairs, for escaping from a burning building. '**~-fly** *n.* flying insect giving out light in the dark. '**~-guard** *n.* wire protection round a ~ in a room. '**~-¸irons** *n. pl.* poker, tongs, etc., for keeping a ~ burning in a ~-place. '**~-man** *n.* member of a ~-brigade; stoker on a steam-engine. '**~-place** *n.* place where a ~ may be made in a room. '**~-proof** *adj.* that does not burn; that does not break if heated. '**~-'side** *n.* part of a room round the ~-place. '**~-work** *n.* device containing gunpowder, etc., used for display or signals.

¹**firm** [fəːm] *adj.* (*-er*, *-est*). **1.** solid; hard. **2.** not easily

changed or influenced; having or showing strength of character, etc. *adv.* (= ~ly): *to stand ~*. **~ly** *adv.* **~ness** *n.*

²**firm** [fəːm] *n.* (two or more) persons carrying on a business.

firm·a·ment ['fəːməmənt] *n.* sky.

first [fəːst] *adv.* **1.** before anyone or anything else. **2.** for the ~ time. **3.** before some other time. **4.** in preference: *She said she would starve ~* (rather than steal, for example). *adj.* coming before all others in time, order, importance, merit, etc. '**~-'class** *adj.* of the best quality. '**~-'hand** *adj. & adv.* obtained through practice, observation of facts, etc., not from books, etc. '**~-'rate** *adj.* excellent. **~ly** *adv.* in the ~ place.

firth [fəːθ] *n.* narrow arm of the sea, esp. (Scotland) river estuary.

fis·cal ['fiskl] *adj.* of public money.

fish [fiʃ] *v.i. & t. & n.* (try to catch a) cold-blooded animal living wholly in water, breathing through gills and having fins and tail for swimming. *~ for (information, compliments)*, try to get (by indirect methods). *~ sth. up (out of . . .)*, pull up (e.g. from one's pocket); '**~-ing-rod**, '**~-ing-line**, for catching fish. '**~-er·man** *n.* man who catches ~, esp. for a living. (Cf. *angler*.) **~-mon·ger** ['fiʃ¸mʌŋgə*] *n.* person who sells ~. **~y** *adj.* (colloq.) causing a feeling of doubt: *a ~y story.*

fis·sion ['fiʃən] *n.* splitting, esp. of the nucleus of an atom.

fis·sure ['fiʃə*] *n.* deep crack (in rocks, etc.).

fist [fist] *n.* hand when tightly closed (as in fighting).

¹**fit** [fit] *adj.* (*-ter*, *-test*). **1.** suitable, right (*for*), good enough (*for sth., to do, to be . . .*). **2.** right or proper. *think (see) fit to*, decide or choose to. **3.** in good health or condition: *to feel quite fit*; *not fit to travel*. *v.t & i.* (*-tt-*). **1.** be the right size and shape: *shoes that fit well*; *a badly-fitting door*. **2.** put on (esp. clothing) to see that it is the right size,

shape, etc.: *to have a new coat fitted* (*on*). **fit**(1) (*for, to do, to be*): *to fit oneself for new duties.* **4.** put into place: *to fit a new tap.* **fit in**, be in harmony with. **fit sth. or sb. in**, find the right or a suitable place or time for. **fit sb. or sth. out** (*up*), equip: *to fit out a ship* (*a boy for school*). *n.* the way sth. fits; the result of fitting: *a good* (*bad, exact*) *fit.* **fit·ter** *n.* person whose work is fitting clothing; mechanic who fits parts of machinery, etc., together. **fit·ting** *adj.* suitable; right (for the purpose). *n.* (pl.) things fixed in a building: *electric light fittings.*

²**fit** [fit] *n.* **1.** sudden attack of illness: *a fit of coughing*; esp. one with violent movements or unconsciousness: *to fall down in a fit.* **2.** sudden outburst (of laughter, anger, etc.). *by fits and starts*, in efforts that start and stop irregularly. **fit·ful** *adj.* irregular.

five [faiv] *n. & adj.* 5.

fix [fiks] *v.t. & i.* **1.** make (sth.) fast so that it cannot be moved: *to fix a post in the ground.* **2.** determine or decide: *to fix prices* (*a date for a meeting*). **3.** direct (the eyes, one's attention) steadily (*on*). **4.** treat (photographic films, colours used in dyeing, etc.) so that light does not affect them. **5.** (often *fix up*) arrange or provide for: *to fix sb. up with a job*; *to fix up a friend for the night* (i.e. give him a bed); *to fix up a quarrel* (i.e. settle it). **6.** repair; mend: *to fix a motor-car.* *n. in a fix*, in a difficult or awkward state of affairs. **fixed** [fikst] *adj.* immovable, ¹*fast*(1), unchanging. **fix·ed·ly** [ˈfiksidli] *adv.* to look fixedly at, to look at with a fixed stare. **fix·ture** [ˈfikstʃə*] *n.* **1.** sth. fixed in place, esp. (pl.) built-in cupboards, fire-grates, electric light fittings, etc., which are bought with a building. **2.** (day fixed (2) for a) sporting event.

fizz [fiz] *v.i. & n.* (make a) hissing sound (as when gas escapes from a liquid). **fiz·zle** [ˈfizl] *v.i.* make a slight fizzing sound. *fizzle out*, end feebly; end in failure.

fjord [fjɔːd] *n.* = fiord.

flab·ber·gast [ˈflæbəgɑːst] *v.t.* overcome with amazement.

flab·by [ˈflæbi] *adj.* (-ier, -iest). **1.** (of the muscles, flesh) soft; not firm. **2.** (fig.) weak; without moral force. **flab·bi·ness** *n.*

¹**flag** [flæg] *n.* see the picture. *v.t.* (-gg-). make signals with a ~ or ~s; decorate with ~s. **'~·ship** *n.* admiral's ship. **'~·staff** *n.* pole from which a ~ is flown.

A ¹flag   Flagons

²**flag** [flæg] *n.* (also ~-*stone*) flat, square or oblong piece of stone for a floor, path, or pavement.

³**flag** [flæg] *v.i.* (-gg-). **1.** (of plants, etc.) droop. **2.** become tired or weak.

flag·on [ˈflægən] *n.* large, rounded container for wine.

fla·grant [ˈfleigrənt] *adj.* (of crime) openly and obviously wicked: ~ *offences.*

flail [fleil] *n.* strong stick hinged on a long handle, used to beat corn, etc., in order to separate grain from straw.

flair [flɛə*] *n.* natural ability (to see or do what is best, most advantageous, etc.): *to have a ~ for good art.*

flake [fleik] *n.* small, light, leaf-like piece: *snow-~s*; *~s of rust.* *v.i.* fall (*off*) in ~s. **flak·y** *adj.* made up of ~s.

flam·boy·ant [flæmˈbɔiənt] *adj.* brightly coloured or decorated.

flame [fleim] *n.* **1.** burning gas. *in ~s*, burning; on fire. **2.** blaze of colour. *v.i.* **1.** send out ~s; be like ~s in colour. **2.** (fig.) blaze with anger.

fla·min·go [fləˈmiŋgou] *n.* water-bird with long legs and light-red wing feathers.

flange [flænd3] *n.* projecting edge or rim of, e.g. an engine wheel, which keeps it on the rail.

Flanges

flank [flæŋk] *n.* **1.** side of a human being or animal, between ribs and hip. **2.** side of a mountain, building, or (esp.) an army or fleet: *to attack the left ~; a ~ attack.* *v.t.* **1.** be at or on the ~ of. **2.** (military) go round the ~ of (the enemy).

flan·nel ['flænl] *n.* **1.** soft, smooth woollen material: ~ *trousers.* **2.** piece of ~ (for cleaning, etc.). **3.** (pl.) clothes, esp. for sports wear in summer. **~·ette** [ˌflænə'let] *n.* cotton material made to look like ~.

flap [flæp] *v.t. & i.* (*-pp-*). **1.** (of wings, flags, other soft and flat things) move, cause to move, up and down or from side to side. **2.** hit lightly, with sth. soft and wide. **3.** (colloq.) get into a ~ (see below). *n.* **1.** (sound of a) flapping blow or movement. **2.** bit of material that hangs down or covers an opening; *the ~ of an envelope (a pocket).* **3.** (colloq.) *be in (get into) a ~,* be(come) nervous or confused.

¹flare [fleə*] *v.i.* burn with a bright, unsteady flame; burst into bright flame. ~ *up,* (fig.) burst into anger. *n.* flaring flame; device for giving such a light, used as a signal.

²flare [fleə*] *v.i.* (of a skirt) become, make, wider at the bottom.

flash [flæʃ] *n.* sudden burst of flame or light: ~*es of gun-fire;* (fig.) *a ~ of hope.* *in a ~,* in an instant. *v.t. & i.* **1.** send, give out a ~ or ~es. **2.** come suddenly (into view or into the mind). **3.** send instantly: *to ~ news across the world.* **¹~·light**

n. light that ~es (e.g. in a lighthouse); small electric torch; brilliant light used for taking photographs. **~·y** *adj.* looking smart and brilliant but not in good taste.

flask [flɑːsk] *n.* **1.** narrow-necked bottle used in laboratories, or for oil, wine, etc. **2.** flat bottle for carrying drink in the pocket.

flat [flæt] *adj.* (*-ter, -test*). **1.** smooth; level; spread out on the ground; with a broad level surface: *a ~ dish.* **2.** dull; uninteresting; (of beer, etc.) tasteless because the gas has gone. **3.** (music) below the true pitch: *to sing ~; B ~,* note half a tone lower than B. **4.** (colloq.) absolute; downright: *a ~ denial.* **5.** ~ *rate,* common price paid for each of different things or services bought in quantity. *adv.* in a ~ manner. *n.* **1.** ~ part of sth. (e.g. a sword). **2.** stretch of ~ land, esp. near water: *river ~s; a mud ~.* **3.** (music) ~ note; the sign ♭. **4.** set of living rooms, kitchen, etc., on one floor. **~·ly** *adv.* (deny) in a ~ (4) manner. **~·ten** *v.t. & i.* make, become, ~.

flat·ter ['flætə*] *v.t.* **1.** praise too much; praise insincerely. **2.** give a feeling of pleasure to: *to be ~ed by an invitation to address a meeting.* **3.** (of a picture, artist, etc.) show (sb.) as better-looking than he is. **4.** ~ *oneself (that),* be pleased with one's belief (that). **~·er** *n.* **~·y** *n.*

flat·u·lence ['flætjuləns] *n.* (having) gas in the stomach or bowels.

flaunt [flɔːnt] *v.t. & i.* display proudly, esp. by waving about; shamelessly try to attract attention to: *to ~ one's riches.*

fla·vour ['fleivə*] *n.* quality giving taste and (or) smell: *food with little ~; a ~ of onion.* *v.t.* give a ~ to. **~·ing** *n.* sth. used to give ~.

flaw [flɔː] *n.* crack; sth. that lessens the value, beauty, or perfection of a thing. **~·less** *adj.* perfect.

flax [flæks] *n.* plant cultivated

for the fibres obtained from its stems; ~ fibres (for making linen). ~·'en *adj.* (of hair) pale yellow.

flay [flei] *v.t.* take the skin or hide off (an animal); whip; (fig.) attack violently in words.

flea [fli:] *n.* small jumping insect that feeds on blood.

fleck [flek] *n.* 1. small spot or patch; ~s of colour on a bird's breast. 2. particle (of dust, etc.). *v.t.* mark with ~s.

fled, see *flee*.

fledged [fledʒd] *adj.* (of birds) with fully grown wing feathers; able to fly. **'fledg(e)'ling** *n.* young bird just able to fly; (fig.) inexperienced person.

flee [fli:] *v.i. & t.* (p.t. & p.p. *fled* [fled]). run or hurry away (from).

fleece [fli:s] *n.* sheep's woolly coat; ~-like mass or covering. *v.t.* rob (sb.) of money, property, etc., by trickery. **flee·cy** *adj.* looking like ~: *fleecy clouds.*

¹**fleet** [fli:t] *n.* 1. number of warships under one commander; all the warships of a country. 2. number of ships, aircraft, buses, etc., moving or working under one command or ownership.

²**fleet** [fli:t] *adj.* quick-moving. ~'ing *adj.* (of a visit, thoughts) passing quickly.

flesh [fleʃ] *n.* 1. soft substance, esp. muscle, between skin and bone of animal bodies. *one's own ~ and blood*, one's near relations. *in the ~*, in bodily form. 2. physical or bodily desires: *the sins of the ~.* ~'y *adj.*

flew, see ¹*fly*.

flex [fleks] *n.* (length of) flexible insulated wire for electric current.

flex·i·ble ['fleksəbl] *adj.* easily bent without breaking; (fig.) easily changed to suit new conditions, etc. **flex·i·bil·i·ty** [,fleksi'biliti] *n.*

flick [flik] *v.t. & n.* (give a) quick tap or light blow to (e.g. with a whip or the end of one's finger).

flick·er ['flikə*] *v.i.* 1. (of a light; fig. of hopes, etc.) burn or shine unsteadily; flash and die

away by turns. 2. move back and forth: ~ing *shadows.* *n.* ~ing light or movement.

fli·er *n.* = flyer. See ¹*fly.*

¹**flight** [flait] *n.* 1. flying; movement through the air. 2. journey made by flying. 3. number of birds or objects in ~: *a ~ of swallows (arrows).* 4. group of aircraft as a unit: *the Queen's ~; F~ Commander of the Royal Air Force.* 5. set of stairs between two landings. ~'y *adj.* fickle; frivolous.

²**flight** [flait] *n.* act of fleeing or running away (from danger, etc.). *put (the enemy) to ~*, cause (them) to run away.

flim·sy ['flimzi] *adj.* (*flimsier, -iest*). (of material) light and thin; (of objects, etc.) easily injured or destroyed.

flinch [flintʃ] *v.i.* start (3) back or away (*from*) (in fear or pain).

fling [fliŋ] *v.t. & i.* (p.t. & p.p. *flung* [flʌŋ]). 1. throw violently. 2. put (*out*) or move (hands, etc., *about*) violently; move (oneself) hurriedly and carelessly or angrily: *to ~ oneself into a chair; to ~ up one's hands.* *n.* 1. act of ~ing; ~ing movement. *have a ~ at*, make an attempt at; *have one's ~*, have a time of unrestricted pleasure. 2. kind of dance with quick movements.

flint [flint] *n.* very hard stone, esp. a chip of this struck against steel to produce sparks.

flip [flip] *v.t. & i. & n.* (*-pp-*). (give a) sudden tap to (e.g. with the finger or a whip).

flip·pant ['flipənt] *adj.* not showing due respect. **flip·pan·cy** *n.*

flirt [flə:t] *v.i.* 1. make love without serious intentions: ~ing *with the girls.* 2. consider (a scheme, etc.) but not seriously. *n.* person who ~s (1). **flir·ta·tion** [flə:'teiʃən] *n.* **flir·ta·tious** [flə:'teiʃəs] *adj.* fond of, given to, ~ing.

flit [flit] *v.i.* (*-tt-*). fly or move lightly and quickly (from place to place).

float [flout] *v.i. & t.* 1. be held up in air, gas, or (esp.) on the surface of liquid: *dust ~ing in*

the air; boats ~ing down the river.
2. cause to ~; keep ~ing. **3.** ~ *a business company,* get financial support in order to start it. *n.* **1.** piece of cork, etc., used to keep a net, etc., from sinking. **2.** cart with a low floor: *a milk ~.*

¹**flock** [flok] *n.* **1.** number of birds or animals (usu. sheep, goats) of one kind, either kept together or feeding and travelling together: *a ~ of wild geese.* **2.** (of people) *in ~s,* in great numbers. **3.** a Christian congregation; large family of children. *v.i.* gather, come, or go together, in great numbers.

²**flock** [flok] *n.* tuft of wool; (pl.) wool waste for mattresses, etc.

floe [flou] *n.* sheet of ice moving on the sea.

flog [flog] *v.t.* (-*gg*-). beat with a rod or whip. ~**·ging** *n.* beating or whipping.

flood [flʌd] *n.* **1.** (coming of a) great quantity of water in a place usually dry. *in ~,* (of a river) overflowing its banks. **2.** outburst (of rain, anger, words, tears, etc.). *v.t. & i.* **1.** cover with water; fill with water. **2.** come, send, in large numbers or amounts: *to be ~ed with requests for help.* '~**-light** *n.* (usu. pl.) strong lamp(s) for lighting up the outside of buildings. *v.t.* (p.t. & p.p. ~-*lit*). light up with such lamps. '~**-tide** *n.* incoming tide.

floor [flɔ:*] *n.* **1.** lower surface of a room; part of a building on which one walks. (Cf. ¹*ground*(1).) **2.** rooms on one level of a building: *ground ~* (level with the street); *first ~* (above the ground ~; in U.S.A. = ground ~). **3.** *take, have, the ~,* take, have, one's turn in speaking during a public debate. *v.t.* **1.** put a ~ in a building. **2.** knock down; (of a problem, arguments, etc.) defeat; puzzle. ~**·ing** *n.* material for ~s.

flop [flop] *v.i. & t.* (-*pp*-). **1.** move, fall, clumsily or helplessly. **2.** put or throw down clumsily or roughly. *n.* act or sound of ~ping. *adv.* with a

~ : *to fall ~ into the water.* ~**·py** *adj.* hanging down loosely; not stiff: *a ~py hat.*

flo·ra ['flɔ:rə] *n.* all the plants of a particular area or period.

flo·ral ['flɔ:rəl] *adj.* of flowers.

flor·id ['florid] *adj.* **1.** (of the face) naturally red. **2.** very much ornamented; too rich in ornament and colour.

flor·in ['florin] *n.* (formerly) British coin, value 2s. (= 10p).

flor·ist ['florist] *n.* shopkeeper selling (and sometimes growing) flowers.

floss [flos] *n.* rough silk threads on a silkworm's cocoon; silk spun from these for needlework.

flo·til·la [flou'tilə] *n.* fleet of small warships (e.g. destroyers).

flot·sam ['flotsəm] *n.* parts of a wrecked ship or its cargo floating in the sea. (Cf. *jetsam.*)

¹**flounce** [flauns] *n.* strip of cloth or lace sewn by the upper edge to a woman's skirt as an ornament.

²**flounce** [flauns] *v.i. & n.* (make a) quick, angry or impatient movement of the body: *to ~ out of a room.*

floun·der ['flaundə*] *v.i.* **1.** make violent and usu. vain efforts (as when trying to get out of deep snow or mud or when one is in deep water and unable to swim). **2.** (fig.) hesitate, make mistakes, when trying to do sth. (e.g. make a speech in a foreign language).

flour ['flauə*] *n.* fine meal, powder, made from grain, used for bread, cakes, etc.

flour·ish ['flʌriʃ] *v.i. & t.* **1.** grow in a healthy manner; be well and active; prosper. **2.** wave about and show: *to ~ a sword.* *n.* ~ing movement; curve or decoration in handwriting; loud, exciting passage of music (esp. for trumpets).

flout [flaut] *v.t.* oppose; treat with contempt: *to ~ advice.*

flow [flou] *v.i.* **1.** move along or over as a river does; move smoothly. **2.** (of hair, articles of dress, etc.) hang down loosely. **3.** (of the tide) come in; rise.

n. ~ing movement; quantity that ~s: *a good ~ of water; a ~ of angry words.*

flow·er ['flauə*] *n. & v.i.* **1.** (usu. colourful) part of a plant from which fruit or seed is later developed; blossom. *in ~,* with the ~s open. **2.** (fig.) finest part: *the ~ of the nation's youth.* **3.** ~*s of speech,* ornamented phrases. ~·**y** *adj.* (fig.) full of ~s of speech.

flown, see *fly.*

flu [fluː] *n.* = influenza.

fluc·tu·ate ['flʌktjueit] *v.i.* (of prices, levels, etc.) move up and down; be irregular. **fluc·tu·a·tion** [,flʌktju'eiʃən] *n.*

flue [fluː] *n.* pipe in chimney, etc., for carrying away smoke; passage for taking hot air through a boiler, round an oven, etc.

flu·ent ['fluənt] *adj.* (of a person) able to speak smoothly and readily; (of speech) coming easily: *to speak ~ English.* ~·**ly** *adv.* **flu·en·cy** *n.*

fluff [flʌf] *n.* soft feathery stuff that comes from blankets or other soft woolly material; soft woolly fur, feathers, hair, etc. *v.t.* make like ~ by shaking, spreading out: *to ~ out a pillow.* **fluf·fy** *adj.* like ~; covered with ~.

flu·id ['fluːid] *n. & adj.* (substance) able to flow (as gases and liquids do); (of ideas, etc.) not fixed. ~·**i·ty** [fluː'iditi] *n.*

fluke [fluːk] *n.* sth. resulting from a fortunate accident; lucky stroke.

flum·mox ['flʌməks] *v.t.* (colloq.) disconcert.

flung, see *fling.*

flun·key ['flʌŋki] *n.* (in contempt) manservant in uniform.

flu·or·es·cent [fluː'resənt] *adj.* (esp.) ~ *lighting,* type of electric lighting with a lamp giving violet, etc., light.

flur·ry ['flʌri] *n.* **1.** short, sudden rush of wind or fall of rain or snow. **2.** (fig.) nervous hurry. *v.t.* cause (sb.) to be in a ~ (2).

¹**flush** [flʌʃ] *v.i. & t.* **1.** (of a person, his face) become red through a rush of blood to the skin. **2.** (of health, heat, emotions, etc.) cause the face to become red in this way: *~ed with happiness (wine, etc.);* (of blood) make (the skin) red. **3.** clear or wash (e.g. drains) with a flood of water; (of water) rush out in a flood. *n.* **1.** sudden rush of water. **2.** ~ing (1) of the face. **3.** rush of strong feeling (e.g. pleasure); high point (of growth, powers, etc.).

²**flush** [flʌʃ] *adj.* **1.** level; in a line: *a door ~ with the wall.* **2.** well supplied (*with* money).

flus·ter ['flʌstə*] *v.t.* make nervous or confused. *n.* ~ed condition.

flute [fluːt] *n.* (musical instrument) long wooden pipe with holes to be stopped by the fingers. *v.i.* play the ~. **flu·tist** *n.* ~-player.

A flute   A house-fly

flut·ter ['flʌtə*] *v.t. & i.* **1.** (of birds) move the wings hurriedly and irregularly but without flying, or in short flights only. **2.** (cause to) move about in a quick, irregular way; (of the heart) beat irregularly. *n.* ~ing movement; nervous condition; excitement: *in a ~; to cause a ~.*

flux [flʌks] *n.* constant change of movement or conditions: *in a state of ~.*

¹**fly** [flai] *v.t. & i.* (p.t. *flew* [fluː], p.p. *flown* [floun]). **1.** move through the air as a bird does, or in an aircraft; direct or control the flight of (aircraft); transport (passengers, goods) in aircraft. **2.** (of flags, kites, etc.) float in the air; cause to do this. **3.** go or run quickly; move quickly: *to fly to the rescue; a flying visit* (i.e. a short one); *to fly open* (*to bits, into pieces*), come open, break to bits, etc., suddenly. *let fly at,* shoot at; attack

angrily. *fly into a rage*, become angry suddenly. **fli·er, fly·er** *n.* airman. **'fly-leaf** *n.* loose half of an end-paper joining a book to its cover. **'fly-wheel** *n.* heavy wheel in a machine, to keep its speed regular.

²**fly** [flai] *n.* two-winged insect, esp. the common house-fly. See the picture on page 205. **'fly-blown** *adj.* (of meat, etc.) (going bad because) containing flies' eggs.

foal [foul] *n.* young horse or ass. *in* (*with*) ~, (of a mare) going to give birth to a ~. *v.i.* give birth to a ~.

foam [foum] *n.* **1.** white mass of small air bubbles formed in or on liquid by motion, or on an animal's lips (e.g. after exertion). **2.** (also ~ *rubber*) spongy rubber used as filling for mattresses, cushions, etc. *v.i.* form ~; break into ~; send out ~.

fob [fob] *v.t.* (-bb-). *fob sth. off on sb., fob sb. off with sth.*, get a person to accept sth. of little or no value by deceit or trickery.

fo'c's'le ['fouksl] *n.* forecastle.

fo·cus ['foukəs] *n.* **1.** meeting-point of rays of light (heat, etc.); point, distance, at which the sharpest outline is given (to the eye, through a telescope, on a camera plate, etc.): *in* (*out of*) ~. **2.** point at which interests, tendencies, etc., meet. *v.t. & i.* (cause to) come together at a ~; adjust (an instrument, etc.) so that it is in ~: *to ~ a lens* (*one's attention*) *on sth.* **fo·cal** ['foukl] *adj.* of or at a ~.

fod·der ['fodə*] *n.* dried food, hay, etc., for cattle, horses, etc.

foe [fou] *n.* enemy.

fog [fog] *n.* thick mist (on land or sea surface). *v.t.* (-gg-). cover as with a fog. **'fog-horn** *n.* horn used to warn ships during fog. **fog·gy** *adj.* (-ier, -iest).

fo·gey ['fougi] *n.* (usu. *old* ~) person with old-fashioned ideas which he is unwilling to change.

foi·ble ['foibl] *n.* a certain slight peculiarity of character, often one of which a person is wrongly proud.

¹**foil** [foil] *n.* **1.** metal rolled or hammered very thin like paper. **2.** person or thing that contrasts with, and thus shows up, the qualities of another.

²**foil** [foil] *n.* light sword without a sharp point or edge, for fencing.

³**foil** [foil] *v.t.* baffle; prevent (sb.) from carrying out a plan; make (purposes) ineffective.

foist [foist] *v.t.* ~ *sth.* (*off*) *on sb.*, trick him into accepting a useless or valueless article.

¹**fold** [fould] *v.t. & i.* **1.** bend one part of a thing over on itself; become ~ed or be able to be ~ed. **2.** ~ *one's arms*, cross them over the chest. ~ (*a child*) *in one's arms*, hold to one's breast. *n.* part that is ~ed; line made by ~ing. ~**er** *n.* **1.** ~ holder for loose papers. **2.** ~ing card with advertisements, railway time-tables, etc., on it.

²**fold** [fould] *n.* enclosure for sheep. *v.t.* put (sheep) in a ~.

fol·i·age ['fouliidʒ] *n.* leaves (on trees and plants).

folk [fouk] *n. pl.* **1.** people in general. **2.** (colloq.) *one's* ~, one's relations. **'~-dance** (-song) *n.* old-time dance (song) handed down, esp. among country ~. **'~-lore** *n.* (study of) old beliefs, tales, customs, etc., of a people.

fol·low ['folou] *v.t. & i.* **1.** come, go, have a place, after (in space, time or order). **2.** go along, keep to (a road, etc.); understand (an argument, sth. said, studied, etc.). **3.** engage in (as a business, trade, etc.): *to ~ the sea* (*the plough, the law, the trade of a hatter*). **4.** take or accept (as a guide, example, etc.): *to ~ sb.'s advice* (*the fashion*). **5.** be necessarily true: *It ~s from what you say that. . . . That does not ~ at all.* ~ *sth. up*, pursue, work at, further. *as ~s*, as now to be given. ~**er** *n.* supporter. ~**ing** *n.* body of supporters or ~ers.

fol·ly ['foli] *n.* foolishness; foolish act, etc.

fo·ment [fou'ment] *v.t.* put warm water or cloths, lotions, etc., on (a part of the body, to lessen pain, etc.); (fig.) cause or increase (trouble, ill feeling, discontent). **fo·men·ta·tion** [ˌfoumenˈteiʃən] **n.** ~ing; sth. used for ~ing.

fond [fond] **adj.** (-er, -est). **1.** be ~ of, like; enjoy. **2.** loving and kind. **3.** foolishly loving: a young wife with a ~ old husband. **4.** (of hopes, ambitions) held but unlikely to be realized. **~·ly adv.** in a ~ (1), (4), manner.

fon·dle [ˈfondl] **v.t.** touch lovingly.

font [font] **n.** basin to hold water for baptism, in a church.

food [fuːd] **n.** that which can be eaten by people or animals or used by plants to nourish them. **~·less adj.** without ~. **~·stuffs n. pl.** materials used as ~.

fool [fuːl] **n. 1.** person without much sense; stupid or rash person. make a ~, trick; cause to seem like a ~. ~'s errand, one that in the end is seen to be useless. ~'s paradise, unthinking happiness that is unlikely to last. **2.** (in the Middle Ages) person employed by a ruler to make jokes, etc.; jester. play the ~, make silly jokes; act like a ~. **v.i. & t. 1.** behave like a ~. **2.** trick (sb.) so that he looks silly. ~ away (one's time, money, etc.), waste it. **~·er·y n.** ~ing; ~ish act. **~·har·dy adj.** ~ishly bold. **~·ish adj.** silly; without sense. **~·ish·ly adv.** **~·proof adj.** so simple or easy that even a ~ cannot make a mistake. **~·scap** [ˈfuːlskæp] **n.** size of writing paper (17″ × 13½″ unfolded).

foot [fut] **n.** (pl. feet [fiːt]). **1.** bottom part of the leg, below the ankle, on which one walks; corresponding part of an animal's leg (cf. paw). on ~, walking. set sth. on ~, set it going. set (sb.) on his feet, (esp.) make him able to support himself (in trade, etc.). put one's ~ down, object; protest; be firm. sweep (carry) sb. off his feet, fill him with enthusiasm. put one's ~ in it, say or do sth. unsuitable; blunder. **2.** bottom: the ~ of a page (mountain). **3.** measure of length, 12 inches: a

pole ten feet long; a ten-~ pole. **4.** division or unit of verse, each with one strong stress and one or more weak stresses. **v.t. & i. 1.** make a ~ for (e.g. a sock). **2.** ~ the bill, (agree to) pay it. **~·ball n.** (air-filled leather ball kicked in the) field-game. **~·fall n.** sound of a ~step. **~·hills n. pl.** low hills at the ~ of a mountain range. **~·hold n.** safe place for the ~ (when climbing rocks, etc.). **~·ing n. 1.** = ~hold. **2.** position (e.g. in society); relationships (with people). **3.** foundation. **~·lights n. pl.** lights along the front of the stage in a theatre. **~·man n.** manservant who admits visitors, waits at table, etc. **~·note n.** note at the ~ of a printed page. **~·path n.** narrow path, esp. across fields or open country, or at the side of a country road. **~·print n.** mark left by a ~ on the ground. **~·step n.** tread.

fop [fop] **n.** man who pays too much attention to his clothes.

for [fɔː*, fə*] **prep. 1.** indicating destination: sailing for home; the train for London. **2.** indicating progress: The time is getting on for two o'clock (advancing towards two o'clock). **3.** indicating what is intended: Reserve a seat for me. He is studying for the law. **4.** indicating preparation: Buy some coal for the winter. **5.** indicating purpose: Let us go for a walk. What is this tool for? They chose him for their leader. **6.** indicating liking, suitability, skill, etc.: have a liking for sb.; have a good ear for music; bad for the health. **7.** with too: She is too good for such a man (to be his wife). with enough: This coat is good enough for gardening. **8.** in view of: That's good work for (in view of the fact that it was done by) a beginner. **9.** instead of; representing: Please act for me in this matter. Who is the Member of Parliament for Oxford? **10.** in favour of: Are you for or against the proposal? **11.** with regard to : *We are anxious for news.* **12.** because of : *I went for her sake (for a good reason).* **13.** as the result of : *My shoes are the worse for wear.* **14.** in spite of : *For all the care I took, I lost my way.* **15.** as penalty, reward, or in exchange : *suffer for one's sins; payment for work done; a medal for bravery; pay 10s. for a book.* **16.** indicating extent in time or space: *go away for a week; walk for miles without seeing a house.* **conj.** because.

for·age ['fɔridʒ] **n.** food for horses and cattle. **v.i.** search (for food).

for·ay ['fɔrei] **v.i. & n.** (make a) sudden attack (esp. to get food, etc.).

¹for·bear [fɔ:'bɛə*] **v.i.** (p.t. *forbore* [fɔ:'bɔ:*], p.p. *forborne* [fɔ:'bɔ:n]). refrain, keep oneself back (from doing sth. one wishes to do): ∼ *from asking (to ask) questions.* ∼**·ance** [fɔ:'bɛərəns] **n.** patience.

²for·bear ['fɔ:bɛə*] **n.** ancestor.

for·bid [fə'bid] **v.t.** (p.t. *forbade* [fə'beid, -'bæd], p.p. *forbidden* [fə'bidn]). order (sb.) not to do sth.; order that sth. must not be done : *to* ∼ *a girl to marry; to* ∼ *a marriage.* ∼**·ding adj.** stern; threatening.

force [fɔ:s] **n.** **1.** strength; power of body or mind; physical power: *the* ∼ *of a blow (explosion, argument); the* ∼*s of nature (e.g. storms).* **2.** sth. tending to cause change (e.g. in society): *Fascism and Communism have been powerful* ∼*s in world affairs.* **3.** (intensity of, measurement of) pressure or influence exerted at a point, tending to cause movement : *the law of* ∼*s.* **4.** body of armed men: *the Air F*∼; *to join the Forces* (Navy, Army, Air Force). *in* ∼, in great numbers. **5.** (law) authority; power of binding (4). *put (a law) into* ∼, make it binding. **v.t.** **1.** use ∼ to get or do sth., to make sb. do sth.; break open by using ∼. ∼ *a person's hand*, make him do sth. ∼*d march*, rapid one made by soldiers for a special purpose.

2. cause (plants, etc.) to mature earlier than usual (e.g. by giving warmth in winter). ∼**·ful adj.** (of a person, his character, of an argument, etc.) full of ∼. **for·ci·ble** ['fɔ:sibl] **adj.** done by the use of ∼; showing ∼. **for·ci·bly adv.**

for·ceps ['fɔ:seps] **n.** instrument used by doctors and dentists for gripping things.

ford [fɔ:d] **n.** shallow place in a river where it is possible to walk across. **v.t.** cross (a river) at a ∼.

fore [fɔ:*] **n.** front part: *come to the* ∼, become prominent. **adj. & adv.** in front.

fore- *prefix.* **1.** front : '∼-*foot* **n.** '∼-*leg* **n.** '∼-*mast* **n.** '∼-*part* **n.** **2.** in advance; before in time: ∼'*see* **v.** '∼'*taste* **n.** ∼'*warn* **v.**

fore·arm ['fɔ:rɑ:m] **n.** arm from elbow to wrist or finger-tips.

fore·bode [fɔ:'boud] **v.t.** be a warning of (*trouble*); have a feeling *that* (trouble is coming). **fore·bod·ing n.** feeling that trouble is coming.

fore·cast [fɔ:'kɑ:st] **v.t.** say in advance what is likely to happen. ['fɔ:kɑ:st] **n.** *the weather* ∼.

fore·cas·tle ['fouksl] **n.** (in some ships) part in the bows where sailors eat and sleep; deck above this.

fore·fa·thers ['fɔ:fɑ:ðəz] **n. pl.** ancestors.

fore·fin·ger ['fɔ:fiŋgə*] **n.** first finger, next to the thumb.

fore·front ['fɔ:frʌnt] **n.** most forward part; centre of activity.

fore·go·ing [fɔ:'gouiŋ] **adj.** preceding; which goes before (in time, etc.).

fore·gone ['fɔ:gɔn] **adj.** ∼ *conclusion*, ending that can be or could have been seen from the start.

fore·ground ['fɔ:graund] **n.** part of a view nearest the person looking.

fore·head ['fɔrid] **n.** part of the face above the eyes.

for·eign ['fɔrin] **adj.** **1.** of or from another country, not one's own; of relations with other countries. **2.** ∼ *to*, not natural to; unconnected with. **3.** coming from outside: *a ~ body in the eye* (a bit of dirt, etc.). **~'er** *n.* person from a ~ country.

fore·man ['fɔːmən] *n.* workman in authority over others; chief member of a jury.

fore·most ['fɔːmoust] *adj. & adv.* first(ly); most important.

fore·noon ['fɔːnuːn] *n.* part of day between sunrise and noon.

fore·run·ner ['fɔːrʌnə*] *n.* sign of what is to follow; person who foretells and prepares for the coming of another in history.

fore·see [fɔː'siː] *v.t.* (p.t. *-saw*, p.p. *seen*). see in advance: ~ *trouble*; ~ *what will happen*.

fore·shad·ow [fɔː'ʃædou] *v.t.* be a sign or warning of (sth. to come).

fore·shore ['fɔːʃɔː*] *n.* part of the shore between the sea and land that is cultivated, built on, etc.

fore·short·en [fɔː'ʃɔːtn] *v.t.* (in drawing pictures) show (an object) with shortening of lines (to give perspective).

fore·sight ['fɔːsait] *n.* ability to see future needs; care in preparing for these.

for·est ['fɔrist] *n.* large area of tree-covered land. **~'er** *n.* man in charge of a ~. **~'ry** *n.* (science of) planting and caring for ~s.

fore·stall [fɔː'stɔːl] *v.t.* do sth. before sb. else and so prevent him from doing it: *to ~ a rival*.

fore·tell [fɔː'tel] *v.t.* forecast.

fore·thought ['fɔːθɔːt] *n.* careful thought or planning for the future.

fore·word ['fɔːwəːd] *n.* introductory comments on a book, printed in it, esp. by someone not the author. (Cf. *preface*.)

for·feit ['fɔːfit] *v.t.* (have to) suffer the loss of sth. as a punishment or consequence or because of rules. *n.* sth. (to be) ~ed. *adj.* (to be) ~ed. **~'ure** ['fɔːfitʃə*] *n.* ~ing.

for·gath·er [fɔː'gæðə*] *v.i.* come together; meet (*with*).

for·gave, see *forgive*.

¹**forge** [fɔːdʒ] *v.i.* ~ *ahead*, go forward, get in front, through hard work, by making efforts.

²**forge** [fɔːdʒ] *n.* workshop with fire and anvil where metal is heated and shaped, esp. one used by a smith for making shoes for horses, repairing farm machinery, etc. *v.t. & i.* shape (metal) by heating, hammering, etc.

³**forge** [fɔːdʒ] *v.t. & i.* make a copy of sth. (e.g. a signature, bank-note) in order to deceive. **for·ger** *n.* person who does this. **for·ger·y** *n.* forging; sth. ~d, esp. a person's signature.

for·get [fə'get] *v.t. & i.* (p.t. *forgot* [fə'got], p.p. *forgotten* [fə'gotn]). fail to remember or recall. ~ *oneself*, behave thoughtlessly in a way not suited to one's dignity, or to the circumstances. **~·ful** *adj.* in the habit of ~ting.

for·give [fə'giv] *v.t. & i.* (p.t. *forgave* [fə'geiv], p.p. *forgiven* [fə'givn]). pardon (wrongdoing, a person); show mercy to (sb.); (say that one does) not wish to punish (sb. *for* wrongdoing); give up hard feelings towards (sb.) **~·ness** *n.* forgiving; willingness to ~; being ~n.

for·go [fɔː'gou] *v.t.* (p.t. *forwent*, p.p. *forgone*). do without; give up.

for·got(·ten), see *forget*.

fork [fɔːk] *n.* **1.** handle with two or more points (prongs), used for lifting food. **2.** farm tool for breaking up ground, lifting hay, straw, etc. **3.** place where a road, tree trunk, etc., divides into branches. *v.t. & i.* **1.** lift, move, carry, with a ~ (2). **2.** (of a road, etc.) divide in two directions.

for·lorn [fə'lɔːn] *adj.* unhappy; uncared for; forsaken.

form [fɔːm] *n.* **1.** shape or outward appearance. **2.** general arrangement or structure; sort or variety: ~*s of government*. **3.** (grammar) shape taken by a word (in sound or spelling) to show its use, etc.: *The past tense ~ of 'run' is 'ran'*. **4.** fixed order: ~*s of worship*; manner of behaving or speaking: *good* (*bad*) ~, behaviour according to (not according to) custom or etiquette. **5.** printed paper with spaces to be filled in : *income-tax* (*telegraph*) ~s. **6.** physical condition (esp. of horses, athletes): *in good* ~ ; *out of* ~. **7.** long wooden bench, usu. without a back, for several persons to sit on. **8.** class in a secondary school. *v.t. & i.* **1.** give ~ or shape to ; make: *to* ~ *words and sentences*. **2.** (of ideas, etc.) give shape to ; take shape. **3.** be ; become ; come into existence : *Ice began to* ~. **4.** move, cause to move, into a particular order : *to* ~ *a regiment into columns.* **for·mal** ['fɔ:ml] *adj.* **1.** in accordance with rules and customs. **2.** of the outward shape (not the reality or substance): *a* ~*al resemblance.* **3.** regular or geometric in design : ~*al gardens.* **4.** (of behaviour) stiff or ceremonious. **for·mal·i·ty** [fɔ:'mæli-ti] *n.* ~al behaviour ; observance required by custom or rules : *legal* ~*alities.* **for·ma·tion** [fɔ:'meifən] *n.* ~ing ; sth. ~ed ; (esp.) structure or arrangement. ~**less** *adj.* without ~.

for·mer ['fɔ:mə*] *adj.* **1.** of an earlier period : *her* ~ *husband.* **2.** (also as *n.*) the first-named of the two. (Cf. *the latter.*) ~**ly** *adv.* in ~ times.

for·mid·a·ble ['fɔ:midəbl] *adj.* **1.** causing fear. **2.** requiring great effort to deal with or overcome : ~ *opposition* (*enemies*).

for·mu·la ['fɔ:mjulə] *n.* **1.** form of words (e.g. ' How d'you do ?'). **2.** statement of a rule, fact, etc., esp. one in signs or numbers (e.g. for chemistry, mathematics). **3.** set of directions (usu. in symbols) for a medical preparation. **for·mu·late** ['fɔ:mjuleit] *v.t.* express clearly and exactly.

for·sake [fə'seik] *v.t.* (p.t. *forsook* [fə'suk], p.p. *forsaken* [fə'seikn]). go away from ; give up ; desert.

for·swear [fɔ:'swɛə*] *v.t.* (p.t. *forswore* [fɔ:'swɔ:*], p.p. *forsworn* [fɔ:'swɔ:n]). **1.** give up doing or using (sth.). **2.** ~ *oneself*, after taking an oath to tell the truth, say sth. that is untrue.

fort [fɔ:t] *n.* building(s) specially erected or strengthened for military defence.

forth [fɔ:θ] *adv.* **1.** out. **2.** onwards ; forwards : *from this day* ~ ; *back and* ~, to and fro. *and so* ~, and so on. ~''**com·ing** *adj.* **1.** about to come out : ~*coming books.* **2.** *be* ~*coming,* (of help, money, etc.) be ready when needed. '~''**right** *adj.* outspoken ; straightforward. ~'**with** *adv.* at once ; without losing time.

for·ti·eth, see *forty.*

for·ti·fy ['fɔ:tifai] *v.t.* strengthen (a place) against attack (with walls, trenches, guns, etc.) ; support or strengthen (oneself, one's courage, etc.). **for·ti·fi·ca·tion** [,fɔ:tifi'keifən] *n.* ~ing ; fort.

for·ti·tude ['fɔ:titju:d] *n.* calm courage, self-control, in the face of pain, danger, or difficulty.

fort·night ['fɔ:tnait] *n.* period of two weeks. ~**ly** *adj. & adv.* occurring every ~.

for·tress ['fɔ:tris] *n.* fortified town ; fort.

for·tu·i·tous [fɔ:'tju:itəs] *adj.* happening by chance.

for·tune ['fɔ:tfən] *n.* **1.** chance ; chance looked upon as a power deciding or influencing the future of sb. or sth. ; fate ; (good or bad) luck coming to a person or undertaking : *to have* ~ *on one's side* ; *to tell sb. his* ~, say, e.g. by means of cards, what will happen to him. *a* ~*-teller,* one who claims to be able to tell ~s. **2.** prosperity ; success. **3.** great sum of money. **for·tu·nate** ['fɔ:tfənit] *adj.* having, bringing, brought by, good ~.

for·ty ['fɔ:ti] *n. & adj.* 40. **for·ti·eth** *n. & adj.* $\frac{1}{40}$; next in order after the 39th.

fo·rum ['fɔ:rəm] *n.* (ancient Rome) public place for meetings, etc. ; any place for public discussion.

for·ward ['fɔ:wəd] *adj.* **1.** directed towards, situated in, the front. **2.** well advanced or early. **3.** ready and willing (to help, etc.). **4.** too eager; presumptuous. **n.** front-line player (in football, etc.). **v.t.** help or send ~; send (letters, etc.) after a person to a new address. **adv.** (also ~s) in a ~ direction: *to bring sth.* ~; *to come* ~; *to look* ~ *to*, think, usu. with pleasure, about sth. coming in the future; *carriage* ~, see *carriage*.

fos·sil ['fɒsl] **n. 1.** recognizable (part of a) prehistoric animal or plant once buried in earth, now changed to rock. **2.** person who is out of date and unable to accept new ideas. **3.** (attrib.) of or like a ~: ~ *shells.* ~**·ize** **v.t. & i.** (cause to) become a ~.

fos·ter ['fɒstə*] **v.t.** care for; help the growth or development of. '~-ˌpar·ent (-ˌmoth·er, -ˌfath·er) **n.** one who acts as a parent in place of a real parent. '~-ˌbroth·er (-ˌsis·ter) **n.** boy or girl adopted by one's parent(s) and brought up as a member of the family.

fought, see *fight*.

foul [faul] **adj.** (-*er*, -*est*). **1.** causing disgust; having a bad smell or taste; filthy. **2.** wicked; (of language) full of oaths; (of the weather) stormy; rough. **3.** ~ *play*, (a) (in sport) sth. contrary to the rules; (b) violent crime, esp. murder. **n.** (sport) action contrary to the rules. **adv.** *fall (run)* ~ *of*, (of ships) collide with; become entangled with; (fig.) get into trouble with. **v.t. & i. 1.** make or become dirty. **2.** (of ships) collide with; (of anchors, chains, nets, etc.) become entangled with. **3.** (sport) break a rule.

¹found, see *find*.

²found [faund] **v.t. 1.** begin the building of; lay the base of: *to* ~ *a new city.* **2.** get sth. started (by providing money, etc.): *to* ~ *a new school.* **foun·da·tion** [faun'deɪʃən] **n. 1.** ~ing; sth. ~ed, esp. an organization or institution such as a school or hospital; fund of money to be used for such an organization, etc. **2.** (often pl.) strong base of a building, usu. below ground

level, on which it is built up. **found·er** **n.** person who ~s (2) a school, etc.

found·er ['faundə*] **v.i. & t. 1.** (of a ship) (cause to) fill with water and sink. **2.** (of a horse) fall; stumble (esp. in mud); cause to break down from overwork.

found·ling ['faundlɪŋ] **n.** deserted child of unknown parents.

found·ry ['faundrɪ] **n.** place where metal or glass is melted and moulded.

fount [faunt] **n. 1.** (poet.) spring of water. **2.** set of printer's type of the same size and style.

foun·tain ['fauntɪn] **n.** spring of water; water forced through small holes in a pipe for ornamental purposes, or to provide drinking-water in a public place. '~-pen **n.** pen with a supply of ink in the holder.

four [fɔ:*] **n. & adj. 4.** *on all* ~*s*, on the hands and knees. '~-ˌpost·er **n.** old-fashioned bed with four posts supporting curtains. '~-'score **adj.** 80. ~'teen ['fɔ:'ti:n] **n. & adj. 14.** ~·teenth **n. & adj.** 14th; $\frac{1}{14}$. ~th [fɔ:θ] **n. & adj.** 4th; $\frac{1}{4}$.

fowl [faul] **n. 1.** (old use) any bird. **2.** domestic cock or hen.

fox [fɒks] **n.** wild animal of the dog family, with (usu.) red fur and a bushy tail. '**fox-hound** **n.** dog used in fox-hunting.

frac·tion ['frækʃən] **n. 1.** small part or bit. **2.** number that is not a whole number (e.g. $\frac{1}{2}$, $\frac{2}{3}$, 0·76).

frac·tious ['frækʃəs] **adj.** irritable.

frac·ture ['fræktʃə*] **n.** (esp. of a bone) breaking; breakage. **v.t. & i.** break; crack.

frag·ile ['frædʒaɪl] **adj.** easily injured, broken, or destroyed. **fra·gil·i·ty** [frə'dʒɪlɪtɪ] **n.**

frag·ment ['frægmənt] **n.** part broken off; (of a book, etc.) incomplete part. '**frag·men·ta·ry** **adj.** incomplete.

fra·grant ['freɪgrənt] **adj.** sweet-smelling. '**fra·grance** **n.**

frail [freil] **adj.** (-*er*, -*est*). physically or morally weak; fragile.

~·ty *n.* tendency to do wrong; weakness.

frame [freim] *n.* **1.** skeleton or main structure (e.g. steel girders, brick walls, wooden struts) of a ship, building, aircraft, e.g. which makes its shape. **2.** human or animal body. **3.** border of wood, etc., round a picture, window, or door; part of spectacles (4) that holds the lenses. **4.** structure of wood and glass for protecting plants from cold. **5.** ~ *of mind*, state or condition of mind. *v.t. & i.* **1.** put together; build up: *to ~ a plan (a theory, a sentence).* **2.** put a ~ (3) on or round. **3.** take shape: *plans that ~ well (badly).* '**~·work** *n.* part of a structure giving shape and support: *a bridge with a steel ~work.*

fran·chise [ˈfræntʃaiz] *n.* full rights of citizenship given by a country or town, esp. the right to vote at elections; special right given by public authorities to a person or company.

frank [fræŋk] *adj.* (**-er, -est**). showing clearly the thoughts, etc.; open: *to be quite ~ with sb.; a ~ confession.* **~·ness** *n.*

frank·in·cense [ˈfræŋkinsens] *n.* kind of resin from trees, giving a sweet smell when burnt.

fran·tic [ˈfræntik] *adj.* wildly excited (with pain, anxiety, etc.): *to drive sb. ~.* **fran·ti·cal·ly** *adv.*

fra·ter·nal [frəˈtə:nl] *adj.* brotherly. **fra·ter·ni·ty** [frəˈtə:niti] *n.* **1.** brotherly feeling. **2.** society of men (e.g. monks) who treat each other as brothers; men with the same interests: *the fraternity of the Press (5).* **frat·er·nize** [ˈfrætənaiz] *v.i.* make friends (*with*).

fraud [frɔ:d] *n.* **1.** criminal (act of) deception. **2.** person or thing that deceives. **~·u·lent** [ˈfrɔ:djulənt] *adj.*

fraught [frɔ:t] *adj.* (only) ~ *with*, filled with, having (meaning); involving, threatening (unpleasant consequences): *~ with risks.*

¹**fray** [frei] *n.* fight; contest.

²**fray** [frei] *v.t. & i.* (of cloth, rope, etc.) become worn, make worn, by rubbing so that there are loose threads: *~ed cuffs (ropes).*

freak [fri:k] *n.* **1.** absurd or most unusual idea, act or occurrence; person full of absurd ideas, etc. **2.** person, animal, or plant that is abnormal in form (e.g. a five-legged sheep). **~·ish** *adj.* abnormal: *~ish behaviour.*

freck·le [ˈfrekl] *n.* one of the small, light-brown spots sometimes caused by sunlight on a fair skin. *v.t. & i.* (cause to) become covered with ~s.

free [fri:] *adj.* (*freer* [ˈfri:ə*], *freest* [ˈfri:ist]). **1.** (of a country) self-governing; having a system of government that allows private rights. **2.** (of a person) not a slave; not in prison; not prevented from doing what one wants to do. *have (give sb.) a ~ hand*, permission to do what seems best without consulting others. **3.** (of things) not fixed, controlled, or held back: *the Free Churches*, nonconformists. **4.** without payment: *~ trade*, the admission of goods into a country without payment of import duties. **5.** (of place or time) not occupied or engaged; (of a person) having ~ time. **6.** (of a translation) not word-for-word but giving the general meaning. **7.** *be ~ with (of)* (one's money, etc.), give readily. *make ~ with*, use (another person's things) as if they were one's own. *be ~ from (error, etc.)*, be without. **8.** ~ *fight*, one in which anyone may join. ~ *will*, power of guiding one's actions without being controlled by events or necessity. *v.t.* (p.t. & p.p. *freed*). make ~. **~·dom** *n.* condition of being ~ (all senses). '**~·hand** *adj.* (of drawing) done without the help of a ruler, compasses, etc. '**~·hand·ed** *adj.* generous; giving readily. '**~·hold** *n. & adj.* (land)(to be) held as absolute property. **~·ly** *adv.* in a ~ manner; readily. **~·man** *n.* person not a slave; person given all the privileges of a city.

'~·ˌma·son *n.* member of a secret society that has branches throughout the world. '~· 'think·er *n.* person not accepting traditional religious teaching but basing his ideas on reason. (Hence ~ *thought.*)

freeze [fri:z] *v.i. & t.* (p.t. *froze* [frouz], p.p. *frozen*). 1. *be freezing,* be so cold that water becomes ice. 2. (of water) become ice; (of other substances) become hard or stiff from cold. 3. make cold; make hard: *frozen roads;* ~ *one's blood,* fill with terror. 'freez·ing-point *n.* temperature at which a liquid (esp. water) ~s.

freight [freit] *n.* (money charged for) the carriage of goods from place to place; the goods carried. *v.t.* load (a ship) with cargo. ~·er *n.* cargo ship.

french [frentʃ] *adj.* ~ *window,* one that serves as both window and door. *take* ~ *leave,* go away, do sth., without asking permission.

fren·zy ['frenzi] *n.* violent excitement. fren·zied *adj.* filled with, showing, ~.

fre·quent ['fri:kwənt] *adj.* often happening; numerous; common; habitual. [fri'kwent] *v.t.* go ~ly to; be often found in or at. ~·ly *adv.* often. fre·quen·cy ['fri:kwənsi] *n.* being ~; rate of occurrence.

fres·co ['freskou] *n.* (method of) painting on plaster (of walls or ceilings).

fresh [freʃ] *adj.* (-*er,* -*est*). 1. newly made, produced, gathered, grown, arrived, etc. 2. new or different. 3. (of food) not salted or tinned; (of water) not salt; (of a person's complexion) healthy-looking; (of weather, the wind) cool. ~ *air,* clean out-of-doors air. ~·ly *adv.* ~·ness *n.*

¹fret [fret] *v.t. & i.* (-*tt*-). 1. worry; (cause to) be discontented or bad-tempered. 2. wear away by rubbing or biting at. ~·ful *adj.* discontented; irritable.

²fret [fret] *v.t.* ornament (wood,

etc.) with designs made by cutting. '~-saw *n.* narrow saw for cutting (designs in) thin wood. '~·work *n.* wood cut in this way.

fri·ar ['fraiə*] *n.* man who is a member of one of certain religious orders, esp. one who has vowed to live in poverty.

fric·tion ['frikʃən] *n.* 1. the rubbing of one thing against another, esp. when this wastes energy. 2. difference of opinion leading to arguments, etc.

Fri·day ['fraidi] *n.* the sixth day of the week. *Good F*~, the F~ before Easter.

fridge [fridʒ] *n.* colloq. abbr. for *refrigerator.*

friend [frend] *n.* 1. person, other than a relative, whom one likes and knows well; helpful person or thing. *make* ~*s with,* become the ~(s) of. 2. (F~) member of the *Society of Friends* (Quakers). ~·ly *adj.* (-*ier,* -*iest*). acting, ready to act, as a ~. ~·li·ness *n.* ~ly feeling or behaviour. ~·ship *n.*

frieze [fri:z] *n.* ornamental band or strip along a wall (usu. at the top).

frig·ate ['frigit] *n.* fast sailing-ship formerly used in war; (modern use) fast escort vessel.

fright [frait] *n.* 1. great and sudden fear: *filled with* ~; *give sb. a* ~. 2. (colloq.) ridiculous-looking person or thing. ~·en *v.t.* fill with ~; give a ~ to. ~·ful *adj.* 1. causing fear; horrible. 2. (colloq.) unpleasant; unsatisfactory. ~·ful·ly *adv.* (colloq.) very.

frig·id ['fridʒid] *adj.* 1. cold: *the* ~ *zones* (within the polar circles). 2. unfriendly; without warmth of feeling. fri·gid·i·ty [fri'dʒiditi] *n.*

frill [fril] *n.* 1. ornamental edging. 2. (usu. pl.) unnecessary adornment (e.g. of speech or writing). frilled *adj.* having ~s.

fringe [frindʒ] *n.* 1. ornamental border of loose threads (e.g. on a shawl or rug). 2. edge (of a crowd, forest, etc.). 3. part of (usu. woman's) hair allowed to cover the forehead. *v.t.* put a ~ on; serve as a ~ to.

frisk [frisk] *v.i.* jump and run about playfully. ~·**y** *adj.* ready to ~; lively: *a ~y kitten.*

¹**frit·ter** ['fritə*] *v.t.* ~ *away*, waste (time, energy, etc.) bit by bit.

²**frit·ter** ['fritə*] *n.* ²batter, cooked in fat, usu. with a slice of apple or other fruit in it.

friv·o·lous ['frivələs] *adj.* not serious or important; (of persons) lacking in seriousness. **fri·vol·i·ty** [fri'vɔliti] *n.*

fro [frou] *adv.* to and fro, backwards and forwards.

frock [frɔk] *n.* 1. woman's dress (1) or gown; child's dress. 2. long robe worn by a monk.

frog [frɔg] *n.* small, cold-blooded, tail-less jumping animal living in water and on land.

frol·ic ['frɔlik] *v.i.* (p.t. & p.p. *frolicked*). play about in a gay, lively way. *n.* happy, lively play; outburst of merry-making. ~·**some** *adj.*

from [frɔm, frəm] *prep.* (indicating): 1. a starting-point in space: *travelling ~ London to Rome.* 2. the beginning of a period: ~ *the first of May to the third of June. ~ time to time*, occasionally. 3. place concerned with distance, absence, etc.: *ten miles ~ the coast; stay away ~ school; be away ~ home.* 4. giver, sender, etc.: *I've received a letter (a present from) my brother.* 5. source, origin: *a passage ~ Shakespeare; a painting ~ nature* (sth. which the artist was looking at). *Wine is made ~ grapes.* 6. escape, separation, release: *flee ~ the enemy; released ~ prison. Take the knife away ~ the baby.* 7. cause, motive: *collapse ~ weakness; do sth. ~ a sense of duty.* 8. distinction, difference: *You can't distinguish the one ~ the other. This is different ~ that.*

frond [frɔnd] *n.* leaf-like part of a fern or a palm-tree.

front [frʌnt] *n.* 1. the best-looking or most important side: *Visitors go to the ~ door. a ~ seat at the theatre*, in the first few rows nearest the stage. 2. (war) part where fighting is taking place. 3. road bordering part of a town facing the sea; road or path bordering a lake. 4. *put on* (*show*) *a bold ~*, show, pretend to have, no fear. **in front** *adv.* **in front of** *prep. v.t. & i.* be opposite; have the ~ facing: *hotels ~ing the sea.* ~·**age** ['frʌntidʒ] *n.* extent of land or building along its ~, esp. bordering a road or river. ~·**al** ['frʌntl] *adj.* of, on, or to, the ~.

fron·tier ['frʌntjə*] *n.* part of a country bordering on another country; boundary.

fron·tis·piece ['frʌntispi:s] *n.* picture coming before the text of a book.

frost [frɔst] *n.* 1. weather condition with temperature below the freezing-point of water. 2. white powder-like coating of frozen vapour on ground, roofs, plants, etc. 3. (colloq.) event that fails to come up to expectations; failure. *v.t.* 1. cover with ~ (2). 2. kill or damage by ~: *~ed plants.* 3. *~ed glass*, made opaque. '~-**bite** *n.* injury to a part of the body from ~ (1). '~-,**bit·ten** *adj.* having ~-bite. ~·**y** *adj.* freezing; covered with ~.

froth [frɔθ] *n.* 1. creamy mass of small bubbles; foam. 2. light, worthless talk or ideas. *v.i.* give off ~. ~·**y** *adj.* of, like, covered with, ~.

frown [fraun] *v.i.* (in anger, puzzlement) draw the eyebrows together causing lines on the forehead. ~ *on*, show disapproval of. *n.* ~ing look.

frow·zy ['frauzi] *adj.* dirty; untidy.

froze(n), see *freeze*.

fru·gal ['fru:gl] *adj.* 1. economical (esp. of food). 2. costing little. ~·**ly** *adv.* ~·**i·ty** [fru:'gæliti] *n.*

fruit [fru:t] *n.* 1. part of a plant containing the seed(s); (esp.) sweet ~ that can be used as food (e.g. apples, bananas). 2. (fig.) profit, result or outcome (of industry, labour, study, etc.).

v.i. (of trees and plants) bear ~. ~·er·er ['fru:tərə*] *n.* person who sells ~. ~·ful *adj.* producing ~ or (fig.) good results.

fru·i·tion [fru:'iʃən] *n.* realization of hopes; getting what was wanted: *aims brought to fruition.* ~·less *adj.* without ~ or (fig.) success. ~·y *adj.* of or like ~ in taste or smell.

frus·trate [frʌs'treit] *v.t.* prevent (sb.) from doing sth.; prevent (sb.'s plans, etc.) from being carried out. frus·tra·tion [frʌs'treiʃən] *n.*

¹fry [frai] *v.t. & i.* cook, be cooked, in boiling fat.

²fry [frai] *n.* newly-hatched fishes. *small fry,* (contemptuous) unimportant persons.

fud·dle ['fʌdl] *v.t.* make stupid, esp. with alcoholic drink.

fu·el [fjuəl] *n.* material for burning (e.g. wood, coal, oil, petrol). *v.t. & i.* (-*ll*-). supply with ~; take in ~.

fu·gi·tive ['fju:dʒitiv] *n. & adj.* (person) running away (from justice, danger, etc.).

ful·crum ['fʌlkrəm] *n.* point on which a lever is supported when pressed down to lift or move sth.

ful·fil [ful'fil] *v.t.* (-*ll*-). perform or carry out (a task, duty, promise, etc.); complete (an undertaking, etc.); do what is required (by conditions, etc.). ~·ment *n.*

full [ful] *adj.* (-*er*, -*est*). 1. holding as much or as many as possible; filled completely. 2. ~ *of,* having or holding plenty of; crowded: *a dictionary ~ of examples; a train ~ of passengers.* 3. complete: *drive at ~* (top) *speed. Write in ~,* with all particulars. *a ~ stop,* punctuation mark ending a sentence. 4. completely occupied with: *He was ~ of his own importance.* 5. (of clothing) allowing plenty of room for the body or limbs; (of people) plump: *be rather ~ in the face.* (But note: *~ dress,* ceremonial uniform; *~ face* (portrait), looking directly at the camera.) *adv.* completely: *~-grown; ~-blown,* (of flowers)

quite open. ful·ly *adv.* ~·ness *n.*

ful·mi·nate ['fʌlmineit] *v.i.* protest loudly and bitterly (*against*).

ful·some ['fulsəm] *adj.* (of praise, flattery, etc.) excessive and insincere; sickening.

fum·ble ['fʌmbl] *v.i. & t.* feel about uncertainly with the hands; use the hands awkwardly.

fume [fju:m] *n.* (usu. pl.) strong-smelling smoke, gas, or vapour. *v.i. & t.* 1. give off ~s. 2. show signs of anger or discontent. 3. darken the surface of wood with ~s. fu·mi·gate ['fju:migeit] *v.t.* disinfect by means of ~s. fu·mi·ga·tion [ˌfju:mi'geiʃən] *n.*

fun [fʌn] *n.* amusement; playfulness; sport(4). *in fun,* not seriously; *make fun of, poke fun at,* tease; cause others to laugh at.

func·tion ['fʌŋkʃən] *n.* 1. special activity or purpose of a person or thing: *the ~s of a judge (of the nerves, of education).* 2. public ceremony or event. *v.i.* fulfil a ~(1); operate. *~ as,* do the duty of. ~·al *adj.* ~·a·ry *n.* person with official ~s; official.

fund [fʌnd] *n.* 1. store or supply (of non-material things): *a ~ of common sense (funny stories).* 2. (also pl.) sum of money available for a purpose: *a relief ~; mission ~s.*

fun·da·men·tal [ˌfʌndə'mentl] *adj.* of or forming a foundation; of great importance. *n.* (usu. pl.) ~ rule or principle; essential part. ~·ly *adv.*

fu·ner·al ['fju:nərəl] *n.* burial or burning of a dead person with religious ceremonies. fu·ne·re·al [fju:'niəriəl] *adj.* of or like a ~; dark, sad, or gloomy.

fun·gus ['fʌŋgəs] *n.* (pl. fungi ['fʌŋgai]). plant, without green leaves, which usu. grows on other plants or on decaying matter (e.g. old wood).

funk [fʌŋk] *n.* (colloq.). 1. great fear: *in a ~.* 2. coward. *v.i. & t.* show fear; (try to) escape doing sth.

fun·nel ['fʌnl] *n.* **1.** tube or pipe, wide at the top and narrowing at the bottom. for pouring liquids or powder into small openings. **2.** outlet for smoke from a steamer, railway engine, etc.

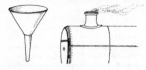

Funnels

fun·ny ['fʌni] *adj.* (*-ier*, *-iest*). **1.** causing fun or amusement. **2.** strange; surprising; difficult to understand. '**~-bone** *n.* sensitive part of the elbow. **fun·ni·ly** *adv.*

fur [fə:*] *n.* **1.** soft thick hair covering certain animals (e.g. cats, rabbits). **2.** animal skin with the fur on it, used as clothing: *a fox fur*; *a fur coat*. **3.** rough coating on a person's tongue when ill, or on the inside of a kettle or boiler when water is chalky. **furred** *adj.* covered with ~ (3). **fur·ry** *adj.* of or like ~.

fur·bish ['fə:biʃ] *v.t.* ~ (*sth.*) *up*, make like new; polish up.

fu·ri·ous ['fjuəriəs] *adj.* violent; uncontrolled; full of fury.

furl [fə:l] *v.t. & i.* (of sails, flags, umbrellas) roll up.

fur·long ['fə:lɔŋ] *n.* 220 yards.

fur·lough ['fə:lou] *n.* (permission for) absence from duty (esp. missionaries, civil officials, members of the armed forces, living abroad) for a holiday: *going home on* ~; *six months'* ~.

fur·nace ['fə:nis] *n.* **1.** shut-in fire-place for heating water. **2.** enclosed space for heating metals, making glass, etc.

fur·nish ['fə:niʃ] *v.t.* supply or provide (*with*); put furniture in.

fur·ni·ture ['fə:nitʃə*] *n.* such things as tables, chairs, beds, etc., needed for a room, house, or office.

fur·row ['fʌrou] *n.* long deep cut made in the ground by a plough; line on the forehead. *v.t.* make ~s in.

fur·ther ['fə:ðə*] *adv.* **1.** at a greater distance in time or space (see under *far*). **2.** besides; in addition. *adj.* beyond what exists; additional. *v.t.* help forward (plans, undertakings, etc.). **fur·thest** *adj. & adv.* see under *far*. '**~·more** *adv.* in addition; moreover. '**~·most** *adj.* farthest.

fur·tive ['fə:tiv] *adj.* (of actions) done secretly or without wishing to attract attention; (of a person) having a wish to escape notice.

fu·ry ['fjuəri] *n.* **1.** violent excitement, esp. anger; outburst of wild feeling. **2.** violently furious woman.

furze [fə:z] *n.* shrub with thorns and yellow flowers.

fuse [fju:z] *v.t. & i.* melt with great heat; (of an electric circuit) be broken through melting of the ~; join or become one whole as the result of fusing. *n.* **1.** (in an electric circuit) short piece of wire which melts and breaks the circuit if a fault develops. **2.** device for carrying a spark to explode powder, etc.

fu·se·lage ['fju:zila:ʒ] *n.* body of an aircraft.

fu·sion ['fju:ʒən] *n.* mixing or blending of different things into one: *the* ~ *of copper and tin*; *a* ~ *of races.*

fuss [fʌs] *n.* unnecessary excitement, esp. about unimportant things. *v.i. & t.* get into a ~; make nervous or excited. **fus·sy** *adj.* full of, showing, nervous excitement; worrying about little things.

fus·ty ['fʌsti] *adj.* (*-ier*, *-iest*). smelling of dust and mould; stale.

fu·tile ['fju:tail] *adj.* of no use; unlikely to do much. **fu·til·i·ty** [fju:'tiliti] *n.*

fu·ture ['fju:tʃə*] *n. & adj.* (time, events) coming after the present. *for the* ~, *in* ~, from this time onwards. **fu·tu·ri·ty** [fju:'tjuəriti] *n.* ~ time; ~ event.

fuz·zy ['fʌzi] *adj.* blurred; indistinct (in shape or outline).

G

gab·ble ['gæbl] *v.t. & i.* say things quickly and indistinctly. *n.* fast, indistinct talk.

ga·ble ['geibl] *n.* three-cornered part of an outside wall between sloping roofs. (See *eaves*.)

gad [gæd] *v.i.* (*-dd-*). *gad about*, go from place to place looking for excitement or pleasure.

gad·get ['gædʒit] *n.* small convenient contrivance or apparatus.

gaff [gæf] *n.* hook for landing fish caught with rod and line.

gag [gæg] *n.* **1.** sth. put in a person's mouth to keep it open, or over it to keep him quiet. **2.** words or actions added to his part by an actor; stage joke. *v.t. & i.* (*-gg-*). **1.** put a gag (1) in or over the mouth of. **2.** (of an actor) use gags (2).

gage [geidʒ] *n.* **1.** sth. given as security or guarantee. **2.** = ¹gauntlet (1).

gai·ety [gei·ty], **gai·ly**, see *gay*.

gain [gein] *v.t. & i.* **1.** obtain (sth. wanted or needed): *to ~ one's living*; *to ~ experience*; *to ~ time* (i.e. improve one's chances by postponing sth., etc.). **2.** make progress: *to ~ in strength* (*weight*). **3.** ~ (*up*)*on*, (a) get nearer to (other runners who are ahead in a race); (b) get further ahead of (others who are behind). *n.* sth. ~ed; profit: *a ~ in health*; *the love of ~*. **~·ful** *adj.* yielding profit or pay: *~ful occupations*.

gain·say [gein'sei] *v.t.* deny; contradict: *There is no ~ing his honesty.*

gait [geit] *n.* manner of walking.

gai·ter ['geitə*] *n.* cloth or leather covering for the leg from knee to ankle.

ga·la ['gɑːlə] *n.* occasion of public merry-making; (attrib.) ~ *night*, one with special features (e.g. at a theatre).

gal·ax·y ['gæləksi] *n.* **1.** irregular band of stars not seen separately

but making the sky bright. **2.** group (of brilliant, famous, etc., persons).

gale [geil] *n.* strong wind.

¹gall [gɔːl] *n.* **1.** bitter liquid (bile) made by the liver. **2.** (fig.) bitter feeling.

²gall [gɔːl] *n.* painful swelling on an animal (esp. a horse) caused by rubbing; place rubbed bare. *v.t. & i.* **1.** rub sore. **2.** (fig.) hurt the feelings of (sb); vex.

gal·lant ['gælənt] *adj.* **1.** brave. **2.** fine; beautiful; stately: *a ~ ship*. [gə'lænt] *n.* young man of fashion, esp. one fond of and attentive to women. **~·ry** ['gæləntri] *n.* **1.** bravery. **2.** words, acts, etc., of a ~; devotion, polite attention, to women.

gal·leon ['gæljən] *n.* Spanish sailing-ship (15th to 17th centuries).

gal·ler·y ['gæləri] *n.* **1.** room or building for the display of works of art. **2.** (people in the) highest and cheapest seats in a theatre. *play to the ~*, try to win approval by appealing to popular taste. **3.** raised floor or platform extending from an inner wall of a hall, church, etc. **4.** covered walk or corridor, partly open at one side. **5.** horizontal underground passage in a mine. (Cf. *shaft* (1).)

gal·ley ['gæli] *n.* **1.** (ancient) low flat ship with one deck, rowed by slaves or criminals; ancient Greek or Roman warship. **2.** ship's kitchen.

gal·li·vant [ˌgæli'vænt] *v.i.* gad about.

gal·lon ['gælən] *n.* measure for liquids; four quarts.

gal·lop ['gæləp] *n.* (of a horse, etc.) fastest pace with all four feet off the ground at each stride; a ride at this pace. *v.i. & t.* (cause to) go at a ~; (fig.) hurry (*through* work, etc.).

gal·lows ['gæləuz] *n. pl.* (usu. with sing. vb.) wooden framework for putting criminals to death by hanging. **'~-bird** *n.* person likely to suffer the death penalty.

ga·lore [gə'lɔː*] *adv.* in plenty.

ga·losh [gə'lɒʃ] *n.* rubber over-shoe: *a pair of ~es.*

gal·van·ic [gæl'vænik] *adj.* of galvanism.

gal·van·ism ['gælvənizm] *n.* (science of, medical use of) electricity produced by chemical action.

gal·van·ize ['gælvənaiz] *v.t.* coat (sheet iron, etc.) with metal (e.g. zinc) by galvanism; (fig.) shock or rouse (a person into doing sth.).

gam·bit ['gæmbit] *n.* opening move in chess.

gam·ble ['gæmbl] *v.i. & t.* play games of chance for money; take great risks on the chance of making a profit or winning sth. *n.* undertaking or attempt with risk of loss and chance of profit or advantage. **gam·bler** *n.* **gam·bling** *n.* playing games to win money; taking serious risks in business, etc.

gam·bol ['gæmbl] *n.* (usu. pl.) *& v.i.* (-ll-). (make) quick, playful, jumping or skipping movements.

¹game [geim] *n.* 1. form of play, esp. with rules (e.g. tennis, football). *play the ~*, keep the rules; (fig.) be honest. 2. (pl.) athletic contests: *the Olympic Games.* 3. points, score, needed by a player to win. 4. scheme, plan, or undertaking; dodge or trick: *having a ~ with them*, playing a trick on them; *making ~ of me*, ridiculing me. *The ~ is up*, everything has failed. 5. (collective) (flesh of) animals and birds hunted for sport and food. *big ~*, elephants, lions, tigers, etc. '~·keep·er *n.* man employed to breed and protect ~(5). '~-laws *n. pl.* laws on the killing and selling of ~(5).

²game [geim] *adj.* 1. brave; ready to go on fighting. 2. having the spirit or energy (*for* sth., *to do* sth.).

³game [geim] *adj.* (of a leg, arm, etc.) crippled; that cannot be used.

gamp [gæmp] *n.* (humor.) umbrella.

gam·ut ['gæmət] *n.* whole range of musical notes, (fig.) of feeling, etc.

gan·der ['gændə*] *n.* male goose.

gang [gæŋ] *n.* number of labourers, slaves, prisoners, criminals, working together. **~·ster** *n.* member of a ~ of criminals.

gang-plank ['gæŋplæŋk] *n.* movable plank placed between a ship and land.

gan·grene ['gæŋgri:n] *n.* decay of a part of the body.

gang·way ['gæŋwei] *n.* 1. opening in a ship's side; movable bridge from this to the land. 2. passage between rows of seats or persons.

gan·try ['gæntri] *n.* structure supporting a travelling crane, railway signals, etc.

gaol [dʒeil] *n.* (also *jail*). public prison. *v.t.* put in ~. '~-bird *n.* person often in ~. ~·er *n.* person in charge of prisoners in ~.

gap [gæp] *n.* 1. break or opening (in a wall, hedge, etc.). 2. unfilled space; interval; wide separation (of ideas, etc.).

gape [geip] *v.i.* open the mouth wide; yawn; stare with open mouth and in surprise (*at* sth.). *n.* yawn.

ga·rage ['gæra:ʒ, 'gæridʒ] *n.* building or shed where motorcars are stored; roadside (petrol and) service station.

garb [ga:b] *n.* (style of) dress (esp. as worn by a particular kind of person): *in clerical ~. v.t.* (usu. passive) dress (*in* or *as*): *~ed as a sailor.*

gar·bage ['ga:bidʒ] *n.* waste food put out as worthless, or for pigs, etc.

gar·ble ['ga:bl] *v.t.* make an unfair selection from (statements, facts, etc.) in order to give false ideas.

gar·den ['ga:dn] *n.* 1. (piece of) ground used for growing flowers, vegetables, lawns, etc. 2. (often pl.) public park. ~·er *n.*

gar·gle ['ga:gl] *v.t. & i.* wash the throat with liquid kept in motion by a stream of breath. *n.* liquid used for this purpose.

gar·goyle ['ga:goil] *n.* stone or metal spout, usu. in the form of a grotesque human or animal creature, to carry off rain-water

gar·ish ['gɛəriʃ] *adj.* too bright; over-coloured or over-decorated.

gar·land ['gɑːlənd] *n.* circle of flowers or leaves as ornament or decoration.

gar·lic ['gɑːlik] *n.* onion-like plant with a strong taste and smell, used in cooking.

gar·ment ['gɑːmənt] *n.* article of clothing.

gar·ner ['gɑːnə*] *v.t.* store up.

gar·nish ['gɑːniʃ] *v.t.* decorate (esp. a dish of food).

gar·ret ['gærit] *n.* room on the top floor, esp. in the roof.

gar·ri·son ['gærisən] *n.* military force stationed in a town or fort. *v.t.* supply with a ~.

gar·ru·lous ['gæruləs] *adj.* talkative. **gar·ru·li·ty** [gæ'ruːliti] *n.*

gar·ter ['gɑːtə*] *n.* (elastic) band worn round the leg to keep a stocking in place.

gas [gæs] *n.* (pl. *gases* ['gæsiz]). **1.** any air-like substance that is not solid or liquid at ordinary temperatures. **2.** the kinds of gas, natural or manufactured from coal, used for heating, etc. **3.** (colloq., U.S.A.) = gasolene (petrol). *v.t. & i.* (-ss-). **1.** poison or overcome by gas. **2.** (slang) talk for a long time without saying much that is useful. **'gas-bag** *n.* (colloq.) person who talks too much. **gas·e·ous** ['geisiəs] *adj.* of or like gas. **gas-hold·er** ['gæs,houldə*], **gas·om·e·ter** [gæ'sɔmitə*] *n.* large, round tank in which gas is stored for distribution. **'gas-ring** *n.* ring pierced with small holes for gas(2), used for cooking. **'~ station** *n.* (U.S.A.) roadside petrol station.

gash [gæʃ] *n.* long deep cut or wound. *v.t.* make a ~ in.

gas·o·lene ['gæsəliːn] *n.* (U.S.A.) petrol.

gasp [gɑːsp] *v.i. & t.* take short quick breaths as a fish does out of water; struggle for breath. *n.* catching of the breath through pain, surprise, etc. *at one's last* ~, exhausted; at the point of death.

gas·tric ['gæstrik] *adj.* of the stomach.

gate [geit] *n.* **1.** opening in a wall, fence, etc., that can be closed by a barrier; barrier, usu. on hinges, that closes such an opening. **2.** (total sum paid by) number of people attending a football match, etc. **'~way** *n.* way in or out, closed by ~(s).

gath·er ['gæðə*] *v.t. & i.* **1.** get, come, or bring together. **2.** pick (flowers, etc.); collect (one's papers, books, etc.). **3.** understand; conclude : *I — he was in a hurry. What did you ~ from his statement?* **4.** draw (cloth, the brows) together into small folds. **5.** (of an abscess) fester; form pus. **~ing** *n.* coming together of people; meeting.

gaud·y ['gɔːdi] *adj.* (-ier, -iest). too bright and showy: ~ *decorations.* **gaud·i·ly** *adv.*

gauge [geidʒ] *n.* **1.** standard measure; size or extent: *take the ~ of sb.'s character,* estimate it. **2.** distance between rails or a pair of wheels; thickness of wire, sheet-metal; diameter of a bullet, etc. **3.** instrument for measuring (e.g. rainfall, the strength of wind, the size of tools, the thickness of wire, etc.). *v.t.* measure accurately; (fig.) form an opinion or estimate of.

gaunt [gɔːnt] *adj.* lean; thin; grim.

¹gaunt·let ['gɔːntlit] *n.* **1.** glove with metal plates formerly worn by soldiers. *throw down (pick up) the ~,* give (accept) a challenge to fight. **2.** strong glove covering the wrist.

²gaunt·let ['gɔːntlit] *n. run the ~,* run between two rows of men who strike the runner with sticks, etc., as punishment.

gauze [gɔːz] *n.* thin, transparent net-like material of silk, cotton, etc., or of wire (for screening windows, etc.).

gave, see *give.*

gay [gei] *adj.* (-er, -est). light-hearted; cheerful; full of fun. **gai·ly** *adv.* **gai·e·ty** ['geiəti] *n.* cheerfulness.

gaze [geiz] *v.i. & n.* (take a)

long and steady look (*at* sth. or sb.).

ga·zelle [gə'zel] *n.* small antelope.

ga·zette [gə'zet] *n.* (government) periodical with news (of appointments, promotions, etc., of officers and officials).

gaz·et·teer [,gæzi'tiə*] *n.* dictionary of geographical names.

gear [giə*] *n.* **1.** equipment or apparatus for a special purpose: *hunting* ~ ; *steering* ~ ; *the landing* ~ *of an aircraft.* **2.** set of toothed wheels working together in a machine, esp. such a set to connect a motor-car engine with the road wheels. *in* (*out of*) ~, with the ~ wheels connected with (disconnected from) the engine. *high* (*low*) ~, that which causes high (low) speed. The lower ~s are used when starting or when going uphill. *v.t. & i.* put in ~. ~ *up* (*down*), put into high (low) ~.

geese, see **goose.**

gel·a·tin(e) ['dʒelətin] *n.* clear, tasteless substance, made by boiling bones and waste parts of animals, dissolved in water to make jelly.

gem [dʒem] *n.* **1.** precious stone or jewel, esp. when cut and polished. **2.** sth. or sb. valued because of great beauty or usefulness.

gen·der ['dʒendə*] *n.* any of the three classes, *masculine*, *feminine*, and *neuter*, used of nouns and pronouns.

gen·e·al·o·gy [,dʒi:ni'ælədʒi] *n.* **1.** science of development of plants and animals from earlier forms. **2.** descent of persons from ancestors; diagram (called a *family tree*) illustrating this. **gen·e·al·o·gist** *n.* **gen·e·a·log·i·cal** [,dʒi:niə'lɒdʒikl] *adj.*

gen·er·a, see *genus.*

gen·er·al ['dʒenərəl] *adj.* **1.** of, affecting, all or nearly all; not special or particular: *a matter of* ~ *interest.* *a* ~ *election,* one for parliamentary representatives over the whole country. ~ *knowledge,* of a variety of subjects. *a* ~ *practitioner,* a doctor who is not a specialist. *as a* ~

rule, in ~, usually. **2.** not in detail: *a* ~ *outline of a scheme.* **3.** (after an official title) chief: *inspector-*~. *n.* army officer with highest rank below Field Marshal. ~·**is·si·mo** [,dʒenərə-'lisimou] *n.* supreme commander of land and sea forces or of combined armies. ~·**i·ty** [,dʒenə-'ræliti] *n.* **1.** ~ rule or statement. **2.** quality of being ~ (1). ~·**ize** ['dʒenərəlaiz] *v.i. & t.* **1.** draw a ~ conclusion (*from*); make a ~ statement. **2.** bring into ~ use. ~·**i·za·tion** [,dʒenərəlai'zeiʃən] *n.* ~·**ly** ['dʒenərəli] *adv.* usually; widely; in a ~ sense.

gen·er·ate ['dʒenəreit] *v.t.* cause to exist or occur; produce: *to* ~ *heat* (*electricity, bitter feelings*). **gen·er·a·tion** [,dʒenə'reiʃən] *n.* **1.** generating. **2.** single stage or step in family descent: *three generations* (children, parents, grandparents). **3.** all persons born about the same time: *the rising generation.* **4.** average period (regarded as 30 years) in which children grow up, marry, and have children. **gen·er·a·tor** ['dʒenəreitə*] *n.* machine, apparatus, for generating steam, electric current, etc.

ge·ner·ic [dʒi'nerik] *adj.* of a genus; common to a whole group or class; not special.

gen·er·ous ['dʒenərəs] *adj.* **1.** ready to give freely; given freely; noble-minded. **2.** plentiful: *a* ~ *harvest.* **gen·er·os·i·ty** [,dʒenə'rɒsiti] *n.*

gen·e·sis ['dʒenisis] *n.* beginning; starting-point.

ge·net·ics [dʒi'netiks] *n.* science (branch of biology) dealing with breeding, principles of heredity. **ge·ni·al** ['dʒi:njəl] *adj.* **1.** kindly; sympathetic; sociable. **2.** (of climate, etc.) warm; favourable to growth. ~·**ly** *adv.* **ge·ni·al·i·ty** [,dʒi:ni'æliti] *n.* quality of being ~.

ge·nie ['dʒi:ni] *n.* (pl. *genii* [-iai]). supernatural being (in Arabian stories) with strange powers.

gen·i·tive ['dʒenitiv] *n. & adj.* (grammar) possessive: ~ *case,* showing source or possession.

ge·nius ['dʒi:njəs] *n.* **1.** (person with) unusually great powers of mind or imagination. **2.** special character or spirit of a nation, period, institution, language, etc. **3.** (*sb.'s*) good ~, other person or spirit with good (evil) influence upon him.

gen·teel [dʒen'ti:l] *adj.* **1.** (formerly) polite and well bred. **2.** (modern use, usu. ironical) imitating the speech, ways of living, of the upper classes. **gen·til·i·ty** [dʒen'tiliti] *n.*

Gen·tile ['dʒentail] *n. & adj.* (person) not of the Jewish race.

gen·tle ['dʒentl] *adj.* (*-r, -st*). **1.** kind; friendly; not rough or violent. **2.** (of a slope) not steep. **3.** (of a family) with good social position. '~·folk *n. pl.* persons of good social position. '~·man *n.* man of honourable and kindly behaviour; (genteel name for) man; (formerly) man who did not have to earn his living. ~·ly *adv.* well-behaved. '~·,wom·an *n.* lady. **gen·tly** *adv.* in a ~ manner.

gen·try ['dʒentri] *n.* persons of good social position but without titles of nobility.

gen·u·ine ['dʒenjuin] *adj.* true; really what it is said to be. ~·ly *adv.* ~·ness *n.*

ge·nus ['dʒi:nəs] *n.* (pl. *genera* ['dʒenərə]). **1.** (science) division of animals or plants within a family: *genus Homo*, mankind. **2.** sort; class.

ge·og·ra·phy [dʒi'ɔgrəfi] *n.* science of the earth's surface, climate, vegetation, products, population, etc. **ge·o·graph·i·cal** [dʒiə'græfikl] *adj.*

ge·ol·o·gy [dʒi'ɔlədʒi] *n.* science of the earth's history as shown by its crust, rocks, etc. **ge·ol·o·gist** *n.* expert in ~. **ge·o·log·i·cal** [dʒiə'lɔdʒikl] *adj.*

ge·om·e·try [dʒi'ɔmətri] *n.* science of the properties and relations of lines, angles, surfaces, and solids. **ge·o·met·ri·cal** [,dʒiə'metrikl] *adj.*

ge·ra·ni·um [dʒi'reinjəm] *n.* kind of garden plant with red, pink, or white flowers.

germ [dʒə:m] *n.* **1.** portion of living organism capable of becoming a new organism; (fig.) beginning or starting-point (of an idea, etc.). **2.** microbe or bacillus, esp. one causing disease. **ger·mi·cide** ['dʒə:misaid] *n.* ~-destroying substance. **ger·mi·nate** ['dʒə:mineit] *v.t. & i.* (of seeds) (cause to) start growth. **ger·mi·na·tion** [,dʒə:mi'neiʃən] *n.*

ge·rund ['dʒerənd] *n.* the *-ing* form of an English verb when used as a noun (as in 'fond of *swimming*').

ges·tic·u·late [dʒes'tikjuleit] *v.i.* make movements of the hands, arms, or head while, or instead of, speaking. **ges·tic·u·la·tion** [dʒes,tikju'leiʃən] *n.*

ges·ture ['dʒestʃə*] *n.* movement of the hand or head to indicate or illustrate an idea, feeling, etc.; sth. done to convey an attitude.

get [get] *v.t. & i.* (p.t. & p.p. *got* [gɔt]). **1.** obtain; buy; earn; win; fetch; be given; receive; understand or see (the point or meaning of sth. said or written). **2.** (cause to) become: *to get tired*; *to get a door open*; *to get sb. elected*. **3.** (cause to) arrive, come, or go, somewhere: *to get home*; *to get the children to bed*. **4.** catch (disease); suffer; experience: *to get a shock*. **5.** cause sth. to be done: *to get one's hair cut*. **6.** engage, persuade, (sb.) to do sth.: *get the doctor to call tomorrow*. **7.** (with adv. & prep.): *get about*, (of news, etc.) spread; (of people) travel. *get sth. across*, (colloq.) cause people to understand or accept it: *get a joke* (*a new idea*) *across*. *get along*, make progress; manage; live sociably (*with sb.*). *get at*, reach; find out; (colloq.) bribe. *get away* (*with*), leave; escape; avoid the penalty of: *get away with murder*. *get by heart*, learn. *get in*, arrive; be elected. *get sth. in*, collect (e.g. debts, crops). *get off*, start; escape (punishment). *get on*, proceed (*with sth.*). *get on with sb.*, be friendly together; approach: *getting on for tea-time*. *get out of*, escape (doing sth.); give up (a habit). *get over*, overcome (difficulties); recover from (an illness, etc.); finish (a task). *get round (a rule, etc.)*, evade it; *get round sb.*, persuade to do what is desired: *A pretty young wife easily gets round an old husband*. *get through*, pass (an examination); reach the end of (work, money, etc.). *get (down) to (work, business, etc.)*, start. *get to know (like, etc.)*, reach the stage of knowing (liking, etc.). *get up*, stand; get out of bed; (of wind) become strong. *get up to*, reach; overtake. *get up to mischief*, engage in it. *get sth. up*, prepare (clothes, goods, etc.) for use or display; organize (an entertainment); produce (steam). 8. (in the perfect tenses) *have got* = have. *have got to* = must. **get-at-a·ble** [get-'ætəbl] *adj.* able to be reached. **get-up** *n.* style in which sth. appears; (colloq.) costume: *Mrs S. appeared in a new get-up.*

gey·ser *n.* 1. ['gaizə*] natural spring sending up at intervals a column of hot water or steam. 2. ['gi:zə*] apparatus for heating water (e.g. by gas) in a kitchen, bathroom, etc.

ghast·ly ['gɑ:stli] *adj.* 1. death-like; pale and ill: *looking ~*. 2. causing horror or fear: *a ~ accident*.

ghet·to ['getou] *n.* (in some countries) Jewish quarter of a town.

ghost [goust] *n.* 1. spirit of a dead person appearing to sb. living. 2. (old use) spirit of life; *to give up the ~*, to die. *Holy G~*, third Being of the Trinity. 3. *not the ~ of a chance*, not even a small chance. *~·ly adj.* like, suggesting, a ~.

gi·ant ['dʒaiənt] *n.* 1. (in fairy-tales) man of very great height and size. 2. man, animal, or plant much larger than normal. 3. (attrib.) of great size.

gib·ber ['dʒibə*] *v.i.* talk fast or make meaningless sounds. *~·ish n.* ['gibərif] meaningless talk or sounds.

gib·bet ['dʒibit] *n.* wooden post on which corpses of criminals were formerly exposed as a warning.

gibe [dʒaib] *v.i.* jeer or mock (*at*); make fun of. *n.* mocking word(s).

gib·lets ['dʒiblits] *n. pl.* heart, liver, etc., taken from a fowl, goose, etc., before it is cooked.

gid·dy ['gidi] *adj.* (-*ier*, -*iest*). 1. causing, having, the feeling that everything is turning round: *feeling ~* ; *a ~ height*. 2. too fond of pleasure; not serious. **gid·di·ly** *adv.* **gid·di·ness** *n.*

gift [gift] *n.* 1. sth. given or received without payment. 2. natural ability or talent: *a boy with a ~ for languages*. 3. (law) right or power to give. *~·ed* ['giftid] *adj.* having great natural ability.

gig [gig] *n.* 1. small, light two-wheeled carriage pulled by one horse. 2. ship's small boat.

gi·gan·tic [dʒai'gæntik] *adj.* of immense size.

gig·gle ['gigl] *v.i. & n.* (give a) silly, often nervous, laugh.

gild [gild] *v.t.* cover with gold-leaf or gold-coloured paint; make bright. *~ the pill*, make sth. unpleasant seem attractive.

gilt [gilt] *adj.* = ~ed: *gilt-edged paper*. (fig.) *gilt-edged securities*(3), investments considered to be very safe. *n.* material for ~ing.

¹**gill** [gil] *n.* part of the body with which a fish breathes.

²**gill** [dʒil] *n.* one-quarter of a pint.

gilt, see *gild*.

gim·crack ['dʒimkræk] *adj.* cheap, badly-made (ornament, etc.).

gim·let ['gimlit] *n.* tool for making a small hole in wood.

gim·mick ['gimik] *n.* ingenious method of attracting attention or getting publicity.

¹**gin** [dʒin] *n.* colourless alcoholic drink made from grain.

²**gin** [dʒin] *n.* machine for separating cotton from its seeds. *v.t.* (-*nn*-). treat (cotton) in a gin.

²gin [dʒin] *n.* trap for catching animals.

gin·ger ['dʒindʒə*] *n.* **1.** plant with a hot-tasting root used in cooking and as a flavouring. **2.** light reddish-yellow. **3.** (colloq.) spirit; liveliness. *v.t.* ~ *up*, make more vigorous.

gin·ger·ly ['dʒindʒəli] *adj.* & *adv.* cautious(ly).

gip·sy, gyp·sy ['dʒipsi] *n.* member of an Asiatic race, wandering in parts of Europe, making a living by horse-dealing, fortune-telling, basket-making, etc.

gi·raffe [dʒi'rɑːf] *n.* African animal with dark spots on yellow skin, and a long neck and legs.

gird [gəːd] *v.t.* (p.t. & p.p. *girded* or *girt*). (liter.) put (*on*): *to ~ on one's sword*; fasten with a belt, etc.

gir·der ['gəːdə*] *n.* wood, iron or steel beam to support the joists of a floor, bridge, etc.

gir·dle ['gəːdl] *n.* **1.** cord or belt fastened round the waist. **2.** sth. that encircles: *a ~ of green fields round a town*. *v.t.* encircle.

girl [gəːl] *n.* female child; daughter; unmarried woman; female assistant in a shop, office, etc. ~**ish** *adj.* of, for, like, a ~.

girt, see *gird*.

girth [gəːθ] *n.* **1.** band fastened round the belly of a horse to keep a saddle in place. **2.** measurement round sth. (e.g. a tree): *30 ft. in ~*.

gist [dʒist] *n.* the ~ of (*sb.'s remarks*, *etc.*), the substance or general sense; the main points.

give [giv] *v.t.* & *i.* (p.t. *gave* [geiv], p.p. *given* ['givn]). **1.** hand over as a present; cause (sb.) to have without payment; cause (sb.) to have in exchange for sth. else or for payment; hand over to sb. to use or keep; furnish, supply, provide. **2.** (with adv. & prep., special senses only): ~ *sth. away*, allow (a secret) to become known; ~ *sb. away*, betray, be false to, him; ~ (*the bride*) *away*, hand her over to the bridegroom. ~ *in*, stop struggling, trying to do

or get sth. ~ *out*, (of supplies, etc.) come to an end, be used up; ~ (*sth.*) *out*, distribute, announce. ~ *over*, stop (doing sth.); ~ *up*, stop (doing sth.); discontinue (a habit); surrender: *to ~ up one's seat to sb.* **3.** (with nouns): ~ *a laugh* (*a groan*, *etc.*) = laugh, groan, etc.; ~ *a hand*, help; ~ *evidence of*, show that one has; ~ *ground*, (of an army) retire; ~ *rise to*, cause, produce; ~ *way*, (of a rope, ice, structure) break; (of an army) be forced back; surrender oneself (to despair, etc.); ~ *place* (to). **4.** ~ *sb. to understand that* . . ., assure him, cause him to think, that. . . . **5.** (be able to) be forced out of the natural or usual shape; be elastic. *The foundations are giving. The branch gave but didn't break. The marshy ground gave under our feet.* **6.** ~ (*up*)*on*, (of doors, windows) open on to; overlook. *n.* quality of being elastic or yielding to pressure. ~ *and take*, willingness to compromise.

giv·en *p.p.* (special uses): **1.** agreed upon: *at a ~n time and place.* **2.** ~*n to*, addicted to (a habit, e.g. boasting). **3.** ~*n name*, name given to a child in addition to the family name.

giv·er *n.*

giz·zard ['gizəd] *n.* bird's second stomach, for grinding food.

gla·cial ['gleisjəl] *adj.* of ice: *the ~ era* (*epoch*), the time when the northern hemisphere was mostly covered with ice.

gla·cier ['glæsjə*] *n.* mass of ice, formed by snow on mountains, moving slowly along a valley.

glad [glæd] *adj.* (-dd-). pleased; joyful. ~**ly** *adv.* ~**ness** *n.* ~**den** *v.t.* make ~.

glade [gleid] *n.* clear, open space in a forest.

glad·i·a·tor ['glædieitə*] *n.* (Ancient Rome) man trained to fight with weapons at public entertainments.

glam·our ['glæmə*] *n.* charm or enchantment; power of beauty or romance to move the feelings. **glam·or·ous** *adj.* full of ~.

glance [glɑːns] *v.i. & t.* **1.** take a quick look (*at, over, through,* etc.). **2.** (of bright objects, light) flash. **3.** (of a weapon or blow) slip or slide (*off*). *n.* quick look.

gland [glænd] *n.* one of certain organs that separate from the blood the substances needed or not needed for the body's use: *a snake's poison ~s; sweat ~s.* **glan·du·lar** ['glændjulə*] *adj.* of or like a ~.

glare [gleə*] *v.i. & n.* (shine with) strong bright light; (give an) angry or fierce look (*at*). **glar·ing** *adj.* (esp. of errors) easily seen.

Glasses

glass [glɑːs] *n.* **1.** hard, easily broken substance of which window-panes are made. **2.** ~ drinking-vessel. **3.** looking-~; ~ mirror. **4.** telescope; (pl.) binoculars. **5.** barometer. **6.** (pl.) eye-~es; spectacles. **7.** vessels made of ~ (bowls, dishes, wine-~es, etc.): *plenty of ~ and china.* '~-ˌblow·er *n.* workman who blows molten ~ to shape it into bottles, etc. '~-house *n.* building with ~ sides and roof (for growing plants, etc.). ~·y *adj.* like ~; (of the eyes, a look) dull; fixed.

glaze [gleiz] *v.t. & i.* **1.** fit glass into. **2.** cover (pots, etc.) with a glass-like coating. **3.** (of eyes) become lifeless in appearance. *n.* (substance used for, surface obtained by giving, a) thin glassy coating on pots, etc. **gla·zier** ['gleizjə*] *n.* workman who ~s window-panes.

gleam [gliːm] *v.i. & n.* (give or send out a) ray of soft light, esp. one that comes and goes; (fig.) brief show of hope, humour, etc.

glean [gliːn] *v.t. & i.* pick up grain left in a (harvest) field by the workers; (fig.) gather in small quantities (news, facts, etc.). ~·ings *n. pl.* what is ~ed.

glee [gliː] *n.* **1.** delight given by triumph, etc. **2.** song for three or four voices singing different parts in harmony. ~·ful *adj.* ~·ful·ly *adv.*

glen [glen] *n.* narrow valley.

glib [glib] *adj.* (of a person, what he says) ready and smooth, but not sincere: *a ~ talker (excuse).*

glide [glaid] *v.i.* move along smoothly and continuously. *n.* such a movement. **glid·er** *n.* kind of aircraft without an engine. **glid·ing** *n.* sport of flying in gliders.

glim·mer ['glimə*] *v.i. & n.* (send out a) weak uncertain light. *not a ~ of hope,* none at all.

glimpse [glimps] *v.t. & n.* (catch a) short imperfect view (of sb. or sth.).

glint [glint] *v.i. & n.* gleam; glitter.

glis·ten ['glisn] *v.i.* (esp. of wet or polished surfaces, tear-filled eyes) shine: *~ing raindrops; pavements ~ing in the rain.*

glit·ter ['glitə*] *v.i. & n.* (shine brightly with) flashes of light: *clothes ~ing with jewels; the ~ of stars on a moonless night.*

gloam·ing ['gloumiŋ] *n.* evening twilight.

gloat [glout] *v.i. ~ over,* look on (one's possessions, successes) with selfish delight.

globe [gloub] *n.* object shaped like a ball, esp. one with a map of the earth on it; ~-shaped glass lamp-shade, etc. '~-ˌtrot·ter *n.* sight-seeing traveller visiting many countries. **glob·u·lar** ['globjulə*] *adj.* ~-shaped; made of globules. **glob·ule** ['globjuːl] *n.* tiny ~ (esp. of liquid); drop.

gloom [gluːm] *n.* **1.** semi-darkness; obscurity. **2.** feeling of sadness and hopelessness. ~·y *adj.* ~·i·ly *adv.*

glor·i·fy, see *glory.*

glory ['glɔːri] *n.* **1.** high fame and honour won by great achievements. **2.** adoration and thanksgiving offered to God. **3.** reason for pride; subject for boasting; sth. deserving respect and honour. **4.** quality of being beautiful or magnificent: *the ~ of a sunset. v.i. ~ in*, rejoice in, take great pride in. **glor·i·fy** ['glɔːrifai] *v.t.* give ~ (2), (3), to; worship. **glo·ri·ous** ['glɔːriəs] *adj.* having or causing ~; (colloq.) enjoyable.

¹**gloss** [glɔs] *v.t. & n.* (give a) smooth, bright surface (to). ~ *sth. over*, cover up or explain away (an error, etc.). **glos·sy** *adj.* shiny.

²**gloss** [glɔs] *n.* explanation (in a foot-note or list in a book) of a difficult word or term. *v.t. & i.* add ~(es) to; write ~(es). **glos·sa·ry** *n.* list of ~es.

glove [glʌv] *n.* covering of leather, wool, etc., for the hand, usu. with separated fingers. *be hand in ~ with*, be very intimate with.

glow [glou] *v.i. & n.* **1.** (send out) brightness and warmth without flame. **2.** (have a) warm or flushed look or feeling (as after exercise or when excited): *~ing with pride; in a ~ of enthusiasm.* '**~worm** *n.* insect of which the wingless female gives out a green light at its tail.

glow·er ['glauə*] *v.i.* look in an angry or threatening way (*at*).

glu·cose ['gluːkous] *n.* grape-sugar.

glue [gluː] *n.* sticky substance used for joining (esp. wooden) things. *v.t.* stick, make fast, with ~.

glum [glʌm] *adj.* (*-mm-*). gloomy.

glut [glʌt] *v.t.* (*-tt-*). **1.** supply too much to: *to ~ the markets.* **2.** over-eat: *to ~ oneself.* *n.* supply in excess of demand.

glu·ti·nous ['gluːtinəs] *adj.* sticky.

glut·ton ['glʌtn] *n.* person who eats too much; (fig.) *a ~ for work.* ~·**ous** *adj.* very greedy (for food). ~·**y** *n.*

glyc·er·in(e) ['glisəri(ː)n] *n.* thick, sweet, colourless liquid made from oils and used in medical and toilet preparations and explosives.

gnarled [naːld] *adj.* (of tree trunks) twisted and rough; covered with knobs.

gnash [næʃ] *v.i. & t.* (of teeth) strike together (e.g. in rage); (of a person) cause (the teeth) to do this.

gnat [næt] *n.* small two-winged blood-sucking fly. *strain at a ~*, hesitate about a trifle.

gnaw [nɔː] *v.t. & i.* **1.** bite steadily at (something hard): *a dog ~ing (at) a bone.* **2.** (of pain, anxiety, etc.) trouble or torment (sb.) steadily.

gnome [noum] *n.* (in tales) imp living under the ground.

go [gou] *v.i.* (p.t. *went*, p.p. *gone* [gɔn]). **1.** start; move; pass; continue moving; travel; proceed. **2.** extend; stretch: *How far does this road go?* **3.** become: *to go blind; to go bad* (e.g. food); *to go to sleep.* **4.** (of machines, etc.) work; be in working order: *Is your clock going? It goes by electricity.* **5.** be or live (esp. as a habit): *to go armed (naked); to go in fear of one's life.* **6.** be usually or normally kept or placed: *These books go on the top shelf.* **7.** give way; break: *The masts went in the storm.* **8.** (of money) be spent (*on*). **9.** (with adv. and prep.): *go about sth.*, set to work at it: *We're not going about it in the right way. go ahead*, start; make progress. *go after*, try to obtain or overtake. *go away*, leave home, move to a distance. *go back* (*up*)*on*, withdraw from (a promise, etc.). *go by*, pass; be guided by: *a good rule to go by. go by the name of*, be called. *go down*, (of a ship) sink; (of the sea, wind, etc.) become calm; (of a story, play, etc.) be accepted or approved by the reader, audience, etc. *go for*, attack; be sold for (sixpence); be expended: *All his work went for nothing. go in for*, take part in (a competition, examination); take up (as a hobby, pursuit, etc.): *to go in for golf (stamp-collecting). go into*, enter: *to go into business (society)*; examine:

to go into the evidence; occupy oneself with: *to go into details*; (of a number) be capable of being contained in another exactly: *3 goes into 9*; *9 into 5 won't go*. go off, (of a gun, explosives, etc.) be fired with a loud noise; (of food, etc.) lose quality: *This milk has gone off* (i.e. is bad). *The goods in this shop have gone off* (i.e. are now inferior). go off *well* (*badly*), (of an entertainment, plan, etc.) have (fail to have) the result hoped for. go on, continue; happen. be going on for, be getting near to. go out, (of a fire or light) stop burning. go over (*through*), examine or study thoroughly. go round, be enough for everyone: *not enough food to go round*. go through, suffer; undergo (hardships, etc.). go through with, complete (an undertaking, etc.). go together, be satisfactory when together. go with, (of colours) be in harmony with. go without, endure the lack of. **10.** go to sea, become a sailor; go halves, divide equally; go shares, share equally; go to law, start legal action (against sb.); go to pieces, break up (physically or in intellect); go to seed, (fig.) become less active intellectually. **n. 1.** energy; enthusiasm: *full of go*. **2.** have a go (*at sth.*), attempt; on the go, busy; active; all the go, in fashion. **'go-be·,tween** *n.* person making arrangements for others who have not yet met. **'go·ing** *n.* condition of a road, etc., for travelling; method or speed of working or travelling. **'go·ings-'on** *n. pl.* (colloq.) strange or surprising behaviour or happenings.

goad [goud] *n.* pointed stick for urging cattle on; sth. urging a person to action. *v.t.* urge (to do sth.): *~ed by hunger to steal*.

goal [goul] *n.* **1.** point marking the end of a race; (football, etc.) posts between which the ball is to be driven; point(s) made by doing this. **2.** (fig.) object of efforts; destination: *one's ~ in life*. **'~-·keep·er** *n.* player whose duty is to keep the ball out of the ~.

goat [gout] *n.* small, active horned animal kept for its flesh and hair, and for the milk of the female. **'~·herd** *n.* person looking after a flock of ~s.

gob·ble ['gɔbl] *v.t. & i.* eat fast, noisily, and greedily.

gob·let ['gɔblit] *n.* drinking-glass with a stem and base.

gob·lin ['gɔblin] *n.* = *hob~*.

god [gɔd] *n.* **1.** any being regarded as, worshipped as, having power over nature and control over human affairs (e.g. Jupiter, Neptune); image in wood, stone, etc., to represent such a being. **2.** *God*, creator and ruler of the universe. **'god·child, 'god·,daugh·ter, 'god·son** *n.* person for whom a godparent acts as sponsor at baptism. **'god·dess** ['gɔdis] *n.* female ~. **'god·,fath·er, 'god·,moth·er, 'god·,par·ent** *n.* person who undertakes, when a child is baptized, to see that it is trained as a Christian. **'god·,fear·ing** *adj.* reverent; living a good life. **'god·for·,sa·ken** *adj.* (of places) wretched. **god·less** *adj.* wicked; not having belief in God. **god·ly** *adj.* loving and obeying God; deeply religious. **'god·send** *n.* piece of good fortune coming unexpectedly; sth. welcome because it is a great help.

go·down ['goudaun] *n.* (in the East) warehouse.

gog·gle ['gɔgl] *v.i. & t.* roll the eyes about, or *at* sth.; (of the eyes) open widely; roll. **'gog·gles** *n. pl.* large round glasses with hoods to protect the eyes from the wind, dust, etc.

go·ing, see *go*.

gold [gould] *n.* **1.** precious yellow metal used for making, e.g., jewellery, prize medals, and (rarely) coins. **2.** coins made of ~, money in large sums, wealth. **3.** (fig.) precious, pure, or brilliant quality: *a heart* (*voice*) *of ~*. **4.** colour of the metal. **5.** **'~-leaf** *n.* sheet of ~ beaten extremely thin for use in gilding, in stamping titles on book covers, etc. '~·**smith** *n.* one who makes articles of ~. ~·**en** ['gouldn] *adj.* of ~ or like ~ in value or colour: ~*en hair; the* ~*en age,* (in Greek stories) earliest and happiest period in history; period in a nation's history when art and literature were most flourishing. ~*en mean,* moderation. ~*en wedding, 50th* anniversary of the wedding-day.

golf [golf] *n.* game played by two or four persons with a small hard ball, driven with ~-clubs into a series of 9 or 18 holes over a stretch of land called a ~-course or ~-links.

gol·li·wog ['goliwog] *n.* black-faced doll with thick, stiff hair on end like a brush.

go·losh [gə'lof] *n.* = galosh.

gon·do·la ['gondələ] *n.* long, light, flat-bottomed boat as used on canals in Venice. **gon·do·lier** [ˌgondə'liə*] *n.* man who propels a ~.

gone, see go.

gong [gon] *n.* round metal plate struck with a stick as a signal (e.g. for meals).

good [gud] *adj.* (*better, best*). **1.** having the right qualities; giving satisfaction; beneficial; wholesome; kind; able to do well what is required; complete; strong. ~ *for,* having a ~ effect upon: ~ *for the health.* **2.** thorough: *Give him a* ~ *beating.* **3.** rather more than: *He took a* ~ *half of the cake. It's a* ~ *five miles.* **4.** considerable in number or quantity: *a* ~ *many, a* ~ *few,* a considerable number; *a* ~ *way,* quite a long way. **5.** *as* ~ *as,* practically: *The battle was as* ~ *as lost.* **6.** *in* ~ *time (for),* early enough (for); *all in* ~ *time,* when the right time comes. **7.** eatable; untainted. **8.** *be* ~ *for,* have the necessary energy, money, etc., for; be in a condition to undertake, pay, etc.: ~ *for a ten-mile walk;* ~ *for £50.* **9.** *make sth.* ~, replace, restore, pay for (sth. lost or damaged); carry out (a promise); accomplish (a purpose). *n.* **1.** that which is ~. **2.** advantage; benefit: *do sb.* ~, make him healthier, happier, etc. **3.** use (3): *It's no* ~ *trying.* **4.** *for* ~ *(and all),* for ever. **5.** *ten pounds to the* ~, as a balance on the right side. **6.** (pl.) property; things bought and sold; things carried by road and rail: *a* ~*s train.* (Cf. *cargo* for ships.) ~·**bye** [gud'bai] *int.* word said at parting. '~·**for-·noth·ing** *n. & adj.* (person who is) useless. ~·**look·ing** *adj.* handsome. ~·**ly** *adj.* pleasant-looking; of considerable size. ~·**na·tured** *adj.* having, showing, kindness, willingness to help. ~·**ness** *n.* **1.** quality of being ~. **2.** strength or essence: *meat with the* ~*ness boiled out. int.* expressing surprise. ~·**will** *n.* **1.** friendly feeling. **2.** privilege of trading as successor to a well-established business.

goose [gu:s] *n.* (pl. *geese* [gi:s]). **1.** water-bird larger than a duck; its flesh as food. **2.** silly person.

goose·ber·ry ['guzbəri] *n.* (bush with) green, hairy, smooth berry (used for jam, tarts, etc.).

¹**gore** [gɔ:*] *n.* thickened blood from a cut or wound. **gor·y** ['gɔ:ri] *adj.*

²**gore** [gɔ:*] *v.t.* (of horned animals) pierce with the horns.

gorge [gɔ:dʒ] *n.* **1.** contents of the stomach. *make one's* ~ *rise,* cause a feeling of disgust. **2.** narrow opening between hills or mountains. *v.t. & i.* eat greedily; fill oneself (with).

gor·geous ['gɔ:dʒəs] *adj.* richly coloured; magnificent.

go·ril·la [gə'rilə] *n.* man-sized, tree-climbing African ape.

gorse [gɔ:s] *n.* furze.

gos·ling ['gozlin] *n.* young goose.

gos·pel ['gospəl] *n.* (the life and teaching of Jesus Christ as recorded in) the first four books of the New Testament; any one of these four books. ~ *truth,* sth. absolutely true.

gos·sa·mer ['gosəmə*] *n.* **1.** (thread of) fine silky substance of webs made by small spiders, floating in calm air or spread on grass, etc. **2.** soft, light, delicate material.

gos·sip ['gɔsip] *n.* (person fond of) idle talk about the affairs of other people. *v.i.* talk ~.

got, see *get.*

gouge [gaudʒ, gu:dʒ] *n.* tool with sharp semicircular edge for cutting grooves in wood. *v.t.* cut with a ~; ~ *sth. out,* shape with a ~; force out with, or as with, a ~.

gourd [guəd] *n.* (hard-skinned fleshy fruit of) kinds of climbing or trailing plant; bottle or bowl consisting of the dried skin of this fruit.

gour·mand ['guəmənd] *n.* lover of food; glutton.

gour·met ['guəmei] *n.* person expert in judging food and wine.

gout [gaut] *n.* disease causing painful swellings in joints, esp. of fingers, toes, and knees. ~·y *adj.*

gov·ern ['gʌvən] *v.t. & i.* **1.** rule (a city, country, etc.). **2.** control (e.g. one's temper). **3.** influence; determine: *to be ~ed by the opinions of others.* ~·ment *n.* (system of) ~ing; body of persons who ~; body of Ministers of State. **gov·er·nor** *n.* **1.** person who ~s a province or colony or (U.S.A.) a State. **2.** member of the ~ing body of an institution (e.g. a college). **3.** regulator. **4.** (colloq.) chief; employer.

gov·er·ness ['gʌvənis] *n.* woman who is paid to teach children at home.

gown [gaun] *n.* **1.** woman's dress. **2.** loose, flowing robe worn by members of a university, judges, etc.

grab [græb] *v.t. & i.* (-bb-). take roughly or selfishly; snatch (*at*). *n.* ~bing; a sudden snatch.

grace [greis] *n.* **1.** quality of being pleasing, attractive, or beautiful, esp. in structure or movement. **2.** (usu. pl.) pleasing accomplishment; elegance of manner. **3.** favour; goodwill: *an act of ~,* sth. freely given, not taken as a right. *days of ~,* time allowed after the day on

which a payment is due. *be in sb.'s good ~s,* enjoy his favour and approval. **4.** (do sth.) *with a good* (*bad*) ~, willingly (unwillingly). **5.** short prayer of thanks before or after a meal: *to say* (*a*) ~. **6.** God's mercy and favour towards mankind; influence and result of this: *in the year of ~ 1950,* = A.D. 1950, after the birth of Jesus. **7.** *His* (*Your*) *G~,* used in speaking of or to a duke or an archbishop. *v.t.* add ~ to; confer honour or dignity on; be an ornament to. ~·ful *adj.* having or showing ~ of looks or movement. ~·ful·ly *adv.* ~·less *adj.* without a sense of what is right and proper.

gra·cious ['greiʃəs] *adj.* **1.** pleasant; kind; agreeable. **2.** (of God) merciful. **3.** (in exclamations expressing surprise): *Good ~!* ~·ly *adv.*

gra·da·tion [grə'deiʃən] *n.* **1.** gradual change from one state or quality to another: *~s in shades of colour.* **2.** (step or stage in) development.

grade [greid] *n.* **1.** step or degree (in rank, quality, value, etc.); number or class of things of the same ~. **2.** (U.S.A.; cf. *gradient*) slope. *on the up* (*down*) ~, rising (falling). *v.t.* **1.** arrange in order of ~s. **2.** make land (esp. for roads) more nearly level by reducing slope.

gra·dient ['greidjənt] *n.* degree of slope: *a ~ of one in twenty.*

grad·u·al ['grædjuəl] *adj.* **1.** taking place by degrees. **2.** (of a slope) not steep. ~·ly *adv.*

grad·u·ate ['grædjueit] *v.t. & i.* **1.** mark with degrees for measuring: *a ruler ~d in both inches and centimetres.* **2.** arrange according to grade. **3.** take a university degree. ['grædjuit] *n.* person who has taken a degree.

¹graft [grɑ:ft] *n.* **1.** shoot from a branch of a living tree, fixed in a cut made in another tree, to form a new growth. **2.** piece of skin, bone, etc., from a living person or animal, applied to another body or another part of the same body to become part of it. *v.t. & i.* put a ~ (*in*, *on*, *into*).

²graft [grɑːft] *n.* profit-making, getting business advantages, etc., by dishonest methods (esp. using political influence). *v.i.* practise ~.

grain [grein] *n.* **1.** seed of food plants such as wheat and rice. **2.** tiny hard bit (of sand, salt, gold, etc.); (fig.) *without a ~ of sense.* **3.** smallest British unit of weight, 1/7000 of 1 pound (avoirdupois) or 0·065 grammes. **4.** natural arrangement of lines of fibre in wood, etc.: *against the ~*, (fig.) contrary to one's wishes or inclination.

gram·mar ['græmə*] *n.* study or science of, rules for, the words and structure of a language. ~ *school*, secondary school in which Latin was once the chief subject. ~·**i·an** [grə'mɛəriən] *n.* expert in ~. **gram·mat·i·cal** [grə'mætikl] *adj.* of, conforming to, the rules of, ~.

gram(me) [græm] *n.* metric unit of weight; weight of 1 cubic centimetre of water at maximum density.

gram·o·phone ['græməfoun] *n.* machine for reproducing music and speech recorded on discs.

gran·a·ry ['grænəri] *n.* storehouse for grain.

grand [grænd] *adj.* (*-er*, *-est*). **1.** chief; most important. **2.** complete: *the ~ total.* **3.** splendid; magnificent-looking: *a ~ view*; *living in ~ style.* **4.** self-important. **5.** (colloq.) very fine or enjoyable: *to have a ~ time.* **6.** ~ *piano*, large one with horizontal strings. '~*stand*, roofed rows of seats for spectators at races, sports-meetings, etc. **gran·deur** ['grænd͡ʒə*] *n.* greatness; magnificence.

grand- *prefix.* '~·**child**, '~·ˌ**daugh·ter**, '~·**son** *n.* daughter or son of one's son or daughter. '~·ˌ**par·ent**, '~·ˌ**fath·er**, '~·ˌ**moth·er** *n.* father or mother of one's father or mother. '~·**fath·er('s) clock**, clock in a tall wooden case.

gran·dee [græn'diː] *n.* Spanish or Portuguese nobleman of high rank.

gran·dil·o·quent [græn'diləkwənt] *adj.* using, full of, pompous words.

gran·di·ose ['grændious] *adj.* planned on a large scale; imposing.

grange [grein͡dʒ] *n.* country house with farm buildings.

gran·ite ['grænit] *n.* hard, usu. grey, stone used for building.

gran·ny ['græni] *n.* (child's name for) grandmother.

grant [grɑːnt] *v.t.* **1.** consent to give or allow (what is asked for). **2.** agree (that sth. is true). *take (sth.) for ~ed*, regard it as true or as certain to happen. *n.* sth. ~ed, e.g. money or land by a government.

gran·u·la·ted ['grænjuleitid] *adj.* in the form of grains. **gran·ule** ['grænjuːl] *n.* tiny grain.

grape [greip] *n.* green or purple berry growing in clusters on vines, used for making wine. '~·ˌ**sug·ar** *n.* form of sugar made from ripe ~s; glucose. **grape·fruit** ['greipfruːt] *n.* fruit like a large orange but with a sharp taste.

graph [græf, grɑːf] *n.* diagram consisting of a line showing the variation of two quantities, e.g. the temperature at each hour. **graph·ic** ['græfik] *adj.* **1.** of writing, drawing, and painting: *the ~ arts.* **2.** (of descriptions) causing one to have a clear picture in the mind. **graph·i·cal·ly** *adv.*

graph·ite ['græfait] *n.* form of carbon used as a lubricant and in making lead pencils.

grap·nel ['græpnəl] *n.* **1.** anchor with more than two hooks. **2.** instrument like this formerly used in sea battles for grappling with enemy ships.

grap·ple ['græpl] *v.t. & i.* seize firmly; struggle (*with*) at close quarters; (fig.) try to deal (*with* a problem). *n.* (also *grappling-iron*) = grapnel (2).

grasp [grɑːsp] *v.t. & i.* **1.** seize firmly with the hand(s) or arm(s);

understand with the mind. **2.** ~ *at*, try to seize; accept eagerly. **n.** (power of) ~*ing*: *in the ~ of one's enemies*; *to have a thorough ~ of a problem*. ~**ing** *adj.* greedy (for money, etc.).

grass [grɑːs] **n.** kinds of wild (usu. low-growing) plant, also sown to make lawns and pastures, grazed by animals and cut and dried to make hay. **gras·sy** *adj.* '~·ˌhop·per **n.** jumping insect which makes a shrill noise with its wings.

¹**grate** [greit] **v.t. & i. 1.** rub into small pieces, usu. against a rough surface; rub small bits off; make a harsh noise by rubbing. **2.** have an irritating effect (on a person, his nerves). **gra·ter n.** device with a rough surface for grating (food, etc.).

²**grate** [greit] **n.** metal frame for holding coal, etc., in a fire-place.

A ²grate in the fire-place or on the hearth

grate·ful ['greitful] *adj.* **1.** feeling or showing thanks (*to* sb., *for* help, kindness, etc.). **2.** agreeable; comforting.

grat·i·fy ['grætifai] *v.t.* give pleasure or satisfaction to: *to ~ sb.'s desire* (*thirst for knowledge*). **grat·i·fi·ca·tion** [ˌgrætifi'keiʃən] **n.**

grat·ing ['greitiŋ] **n.** framework of bars placed across an opening.

gra·tis ['greitis] *adv. & adj.* free of charge.

grat·i·tude ['grætitjuːd] **n.** thankfulness; being grateful.

gra·tu·i·tous [grə'tjuːitəs] *adj.* **1.** given, obtained, or done, without payment. **2.** unjustifiable: *a ~ insult.* ~**·ly** *adv.*

gra·tu·i·ty [grə'tjuːiti] **n. 1.** gift (of money) to an employee, etc., for services. **2.** money given to a soldier at the end of his period of service.

¹**grave** [greiv] **n.** hole dug in the ground for a dead person. '~·

stone **n.** stone over a ~, with particulars of the dead person. '~·ˌyard **n.** burial ground.

²**grave** [greiv] *adj.* (-*r*, -*st*). serious; requiring careful consideration. ~**·ly** *adv.*

grav·el ['grævl] **n.** small stones with coarse sand, as used for roads and paths. *v.t.* (-*ll-*). cover with ~: ~*led paths.*

grav·en ['greivn] *p.p.* carved. (only in) ~ *image*, idol.

grav·i·tate ['græviteit] *v.i.* move or be attracted (*to* or *towards*). **grav·i·ta·tion** [ˌgrævi'teiʃən] **n.**

grav·i·ty ['græviti] **n. 1.** degree of attraction between any two objects, esp. that force which attracts objects towards the centre of the earth. **2.** seriousness; serious or solemn appearance. **3.** weight. *specific ~*, relative weights of any kind of matter and the same volume of water or air.

gra·vy ['greivi] **n.** juice which comes from meat while cooking; sauce made from this.

gray [grei] *adj.* = *grey*.

¹**graze** [greiz] *v.i. & t.* **1.** (of animals) eat growing grass. **2.** put (cattle, etc.) in fields to ~.

²**graze** [greiz] *v.t.* touch or scrape lightly in passing; scrape the skin from: *The bullet ~d his cheek.* **n.** place where skin is ~d.

grease [griːs] **n. 1.** animal fat melted soft. **2.** any thick, semi-solid oily substance. [griːz] *v.t.* put or rub ~ on or in (esp. parts of a machine). ~ *sb.'s palm*, bribe him. **greas·y** ['griːzi] *adj.* covered with ~; slippery.

great [greit] *adj.* (-*er*, -*est*). **1.** above the average in size, quantity, or degree. **2.** important; noted. **3.** of great ability: ~ *poets and painters.* **4.** (colloq.) very satisfactory. **5.** *a ~ many*, very many. *a ~ deal*, (a) a large amount; (b) very much. '~·coat **n.** heavy overcoat. ~**·ly** *adv.* much. ~**·ness n.**

great- [greit] *prefix.* ~-*grandfather*, one's father's or mother's grandfather; ~-*grandson*, grandson of one's son or daughter.

greed [griːd] **n.** strong desire

for more (food, wealth, etc.), esp. for more than is right. ~·y adj. (-ier, -iest). ~·i·ly adv.

green [gri:n] adj. (-er, -est). 1. the colour of growing grass. 2. (of fruit) not yet ripe; (of wood) not yet dry enough for use. 3. (of a person) inexperienced or untrained. n. 1. ~ colour; what is ~. 2. (pl.) ~ leaf vegetables (e.g. cabbage). 3. area of grass-covered land, esp. one for public use in a village. ~·er·y ['gri:nəri] n. ~ plants, leaves, etc. '~·fly n. pl. small ~ insects that attack plants. '~·gro·cer n. shopkeeper selling fresh vegetables and fruit. '~·horn n. inexperienced person easily tricked. '~·house n. glass house for growing plants that need protection from weather.

greet [gri:t] v.t. 1. say words of welcome to; express one's feelings on receiving (news, etc.); write (in a letter) words expressing respect, friendship, etc.: to ~ a friend with a smile; to be ~ed with loud applause. 2. (of sights and sounds) meet the eyes (ears): the view that ~ed us at the hilltop. ~·ing n. first words used on seeing sb. or in writing to sb.: Good morning. Dear Sir.

gre·gar·i·ous [gri'gɛəriəs] adj. living in groups or societies; liking the company of others.

gre·nade [gri'neid] n. small bomb thrown by hand or fired from a rifle.

grew, see grow.

grey, gray [grei] adj. & n. between black and white, coloured like ashes or the sky on a cloudy day.

grey·hound ['greihaund] n. slender, long-legged dog, able to run fast.

grid [grid] n. 1. system of overhead cables for distributing electric current over a large area. 2. system of squares on maps, numbered for reference.

grief [gri:f] n. 1. deep or violent sorrow; sth. causing this. 2.

come (bring) to ~, (cause to) be injured or ruined or come to a bad end. grieve [gri:v] v.t. & i. cause ~ to; feel ~. griev·ance ['gri:vəns] n. real or imagined cause for complaint or protest. griev·ous ['gri:vəs] adj. causing ~; painful; severe.

grif·fin, grif·fon, gryph·on ['grifin] n. fabulous creature with the head and wings of an eagle and a lion's body.

grill [gril] n. 1. = grating, grille. 2. meat, etc., cooked over a fire. 3. (also '~-room) (part of) restaurant, room in a hotel, where ~s (2) are served. v.t. & i. cook, be cooked, over or under a fire or other direct heat.

grille [gril] n. screen of bars or rods across an opening (e.g. a window) or over a counter (e.g. in a bank or post office).

grim [grim] adj. (-mm-). stern; severe; merciless; cruel; gaunt. ~·ly adv.

gri·mace [gri'meis] n. ugly, twisted expression (on the face), expressing pain, disgust, etc., or intended to cause laughter. v.i. make ~s.

grime [graim] n. dirt, esp. a thick coating on the surface of sth. or on the body. grim·y adj. covered with ~.

grin [grin] v.i. (-nn-) & n. (give a) broad smile.

grind [graind] v.t. & i. (p.t. & p.p. ground [graund]). 1. crush to grains or powder: to ~ wheat. 2. produce in this way: to ~ flour. 3. (fig.) crush or oppress: ground down by taxation (cruel rulers). 4. polish or sharpen by rubbing on or with a rough, hard surface: to ~ a knife. 5. rub together, esp. with a circular motion: to ~ one's teeth; a ship ~ing on the rocks. 6. work hard: to ~ away at one's studies. n. (colloq.) long, monotonous work. '~·stone n. stone, esp. one shaped like a wheel and used for sharpening and polishing tools, etc.: keep sb.'s nose to the ~stone, force him to work hard without rest.

grip [grip] *v.t. & i.* (-pp-). take and keep a firm hold (of): *to ~ sb.'s hand*; *brakes that fail to ~*; (fig.) *to ~ the attention of an audience.* *n.* **1.** (power, manner, act of) ~ping: *to let go one's ~ of sth.*; *to have a good ~* (fig. = understanding) *of a problem*; *come to ~s with*, attack in earnest. **2.** (U.S.A.) traveller's suitcase. **3.** part of a machine that ~s or is to be ~ped.

gris·ly ['grizli] *adj.* causing horror.

grist [grist] *n.* grain to be ground. *It is all ~ to the mill*, yields a profit.

gris·tle ['grisl] *n.* tough, elastic substance in animal bodies, esp. in meat for cooking.

grit [grit] *n.* **1.** grains of stone, sand, etc.: *to get a bit of ~ in one's eye* (*shoe*). **2.** quality of courage and endurance. *v.t.* (-tt-). *~ the teeth*, keep the jaws tight together. *~·ty adj.* like, containing, ~ (1): *The sandstorm made the food ~ty*.

griz·zled ['grizld] *adj.* greyhaired.

griz·zly ['grizli] *n.* (also *~ bear*) large, fierce, N. American bear.

groan [groun] *v.i. & t. & n.* **1.** (make) deep sound(s) forced out by pain or expressing despair, etc. **2.** be weighted down: *tables ~ing with food.*

gro·cer ['grousə*] *n.* person who sells tea, sugar, butter, tinned and bottled food, etc. *~·y* ['grousəri] *n.* ~'s trade; (pl.) goods sold by a ~.

grog [grɔg] *n.* drink of rum (or whisky, etc.) mixed with water.

grog·gy ['grɔgi] *adj.* **1.** unsteady and likely to collapse: *a table with ~ legs.* **2.** weak and unsteady as the result of illness, shock, etc.: *to feel ~.*

groin [grɔin] *n.* curved part where the thighs and belly join.

groom [gru:m] *n.* **1.** servant in charge of horses. **2.** bride~. *v.t.* keep (horses) well brushed, etc. **'well-'groomed** *adj.* (of a person) neatly dressed, with the hair well brushed.

groove [gru:v] *n.* **1.** long, hollow cut in the surface of wood, etc., esp. one made to guide the motion of sth. that slides into it. **2.** way of living that has become a habit. *v.t.* make ~s in.

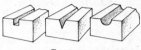

Grooves

grope [group] *v.i.* feel about (*for* or *after* sth.) as one does in the dark; search (*for*).

gross [grous] *adj.* **1.** vulgar; not refined: *~ jokes* (*manners*). **2.** (of error, injustice, etc.) obviously bad. **3.** (of a person) too fat; (of the senses) dull; heavy; (of food) coarse. **4.** total; whole (opposite of ²*net*): *the ~ income* (i.e. before any deductions are made). *n.* (pl. unchanged) 12 dozen (144). *~·ly adv.* obviously (*unfair*, etc.).

gro·tesque [grou'tesk] *adj.* absurd; fantastic; comically extravagant (2): *~ manners* (*mistakes*).

¹ground [graund] *n.* **1.** solid surface of the earth: *The runner fell to the ~, exhausted.* (fig.) *Our plans fell to the ~* (failed). *hold one's ~*, stand firm. *shift one's ~*, change one's arguments. *suit sb. down to the ~*, please him in every respect. *cover much ~*, (a) travel far; (b) (of a report, etc.) be far-reaching. **2.** sea bottom; *to touch ~.* **3.** piece of land for a special purpose: *cricket ~*; *fishing-~s*, parts of sea regularly fished. **4.** (pl.) gardens, lands round a building, usu. enclosed with walls, fences, or hedges. **5.** (pl.) particles of solid matter that sink to the bottom of a liquid, esp. *coffee-~s.* **6.** reason(s) for saying, doing, or believing sth.: *excused on the ~ of* (because of) *his youth.* **7.** surface on which a design is painted, printed, cut, etc.; the undecorated part. *v.t. & i.* **1.** (of a ship) (cause to) touch the sea bottom; (of aircraft) compel to stay on the ~ (e.g. because of bad weather). **2.** base (a belief, etc., *on*): *arguments* ~*ed on experience.* **3.** give (sb.) teaching or training (*in* a subject, etc.). **~ing** *n.* thorough teaching of the elements of a subject. **~·less** *adj.* without good reason: ~*less fears.* '**~(s)·man** *n.* man in charge of a sports ~. '**~·nut** *n.* (nut of) plant whose seed-pods bend to the ~ and develop and ripen in the soil: the seeds

Groundnuts

are used as food and for making oil. '**~-plan** *n.* plan of a building at ~ level. '**~-rent** *n.* rent paid to the owner of land used for building on. '**~-'swell** *n.* heavy slow-moving waves caused by a distant or recent storm. '**~-work** *n.* **1.** = ~ing. **2.** (usu. fig.) basis.

²**ground,** see *grind.*

group [gru:p] *n.* number of persons or things gathered or placed together or naturally associated: *a ~ of trees; people standing about in* ~*s.* *v.t. & i.* form into, gather in, a ~.

¹**grouse** [graus] *n.* (pl. unchanged) (sorts of) bird with feathered feet, shot for sport and food.

²**grouse** [graus] *v.i. & n.* (colloq.) grumble; (make a) complaint.

grove [grouv] *n.* group of trees; small wood.

grov·el ['grɔvl] *v.i.* (*-ll-*). lie down on one's face in front of sb. whom one fears, (as if) begging for mercy; (fig.) show that one has no respect for oneself.

grow [grou] *v.t. & i.* (p.t. *grew* [gru:], p.p. *grown* [groun]). **1.** develop; increase in size, height, length, etc. ~ *out of,* become too big for (e.g. one's clothes) or too old for (e.g. childish habits); ~ *up,* (of persons, animals) reach the stage of full development; become adult. **2.** cause or allow to ~: *to ~ vegetables (a beard).* **3.** become: *to ~ older;*

to ~ smaller. **4.** ~ (*up*)*on,* (a) become more deeply rooted: *a habit that* ~*s upon one*; (b) win the liking of: *a book (piece of music) that* ~*s upon one,* of which one gradually becomes fonder. **~·er** *n.* **1.** (in compounds) person who ~s things: *a fruit-* ~*er.* **2.** plant that ~s in a certain way: *a rapid* ~*er.* '**grown-up** *n. & adj.* adult (person). **growth** [grouθ] *n.* **1.** process of ~ing: *a period of quick* ~. **2.** increase. **3.** sth. that ~s or has ~n: *a week's* ~*th of beard.* **4.** diseased formation in the body (e.g. cancer).

growl [graul] *v.i. & n.* (make a) low threatening sound (esp. of dogs).

growth, see *grow.*

¹**grub** [grʌb] *v.t. & i.* (*-bb-*). turn over the soil, esp. to get sth. up: *to ~ up weeds.* **~·by** *adj.* (*-ier, -iest*). dirty.

²**grub** [grʌb] *n.* larva of an insect.

grudge [grʌdʒ] *v.t.* be unwilling to give or allow. *n.* to have a ~ *against sb.*; *to bear (owe) sb. a ~,* to feel ill will against him for causing oneself trouble, etc. **grudg·ing·ly** *adv.* unwillingly.

gruel [gruəl] *n.* liquid food of oatmeal boiled in milk or water. **~·ling** *adj.* tiring; strenuous: *a ~ling race.*

grue·some ['gru:səm] *adj.* filling one with horror and fear; frightful.

gruff [grʌf] *adj.* (of a person, his voice, behaviour) rough; surly.

grum·ble ['grʌmbl] *n.* (bad-tempered) complaint or protest; noise like distant thunder. *v.i. & t.* utter ~s; say with ~s. **grum·bler** *n.*

grump·y ['grʌmpi] *adj.* (*-ier, -iest*). bad-tempered.

grunt [grʌnt] *v.i. & t. & n.* (esp. of pigs) (make a) low rough sound.

gua·no ['gwɑːnou] *n.* waste matter dropped by sea-birds, used as a fertilizer.

guar·an·tee [,gærən'tiː] *n.* **1.** promise or undertaking (usu. in writing or print) that certain conditions agreed to in a transaction will be fulfilled: *a clock with a year's* ~. **2.** undertaking given by one person to another that he will be responsible for sth. to be done (e.g. payment of a debt) by a third person. **3.** person who gives such an undertaking: *to be* ~ *for a friend's good behaviour*. **4.** sth. offered (e.g. the deeds of a house) as security for the fulfilling of conditions in a ~ (1), (2). **5.** (colloq.) sth. that seems to make an occurrence likely: *Blue skies are not always a* ~ *of good weather.* **v.t. 1.** give a ~ (1), (2), for sth. or sb. **2.** (colloq.) promise. **guar·an·tor** [ˌgærənˈtɔː*] *n.* = ~ (3).

guard [gɑːd] *n.* **1.** state of watchfulness against attack, danger, or surprise: *to be on* ~; *to keep* ~. **2.** attitude of readiness (to defend oneself): *on* (*off*) *one's* ~. **3.** soldier(s) keeping ~; sentry. **4.** man in charge of a railway train. **5.** (esp. in compounds) (part of) apparatus designed to prevent injury or loss: *fire-*~ (in front of a fire-place); *mud-*~ (over the wheel of a bicycle, etc.). **v.t. & i. 1.** protect; keep from danger; control (an exit). **2.** ~ *against*, use care and caution to prevent: *to* ~ *against misunderstandings.* ~**·ed** *adj.* (esp. of statements) cautious; not promising or telling too much. **¹**~**·room** *n.* room for soldiers on ~ or for soldiers under arrest.

guard·ian [ˈgɑːdjən] *n.* (official or private) person who guards, esp. (law) one who is responsible for the care of a young or incapable person and his property. ~**·ship** *n.*

guer·(r)il·la [gəˈrilə] *n.* ~ *war*, war carried on by fighters not members of a regular army; person engaged in such a war.

guess [ges] *v.t. & i. & n.* (form an) opinion, (give an) answer, (make a) statement, based on supposition, not on careful thought, calculation, or definite knowledge.

guest [gest] *n.* **1.** person staying at or paying a visit to another's house, or being entertained at a meal. **2.** person staying at a hotel or having a meal at a restaurant.

guf·faw [gʌ-, gəˈfɔː*] *v.i. & n.* (give a) noisy laugh.

guide [gaid] *n.* **1.** person who shows others the way; person paid to point out interesting sights on a journey or visit. **2.** sth. that directs or influences (conduct, etc.): *Instinct is not always a good* ~. **3.** book with information about a place or subject. **4.** *G*~, member of an organization for girls, like the Scouts' Association for boys. **v.t.** act as ~ to. **guid·ance** *n.* guiding; being guided.

guild (old spelling **gild**) [gild] *n.* society of persons for helping one another, forwarding common interests, e.g. trade, social welfare.

guile [gail] *n.* deceit; cunning. ~**·less** *adj.* without ~; frank.

guil·lo·tine [ˈgilotiːn] *n.* machine for cutting off the heads (of criminals, in France) with a knife sliding between two posts. **v.t.** behead with a ~.

guilt [gilt] *n.* condition of having done wrong; responsibility for wrongdoing. ~**·y** *adj.* (*-ier, -iest*). having done wrong: ~*y of theft*; showing or feeling ~: *a* ~*y look* (*conscience*).

guin·ea [ˈgini] *n.* sum of 21*s.*; former gold coin worth 21*s.*

guin·ea-pig [ˈginipig] *n.* short-eared animal like a big rat, often used in experiments; sb. allowing himself to be used in medical or other experiments.

guise [gaiz] *n.* dress; outward appearance: *in the* ~ *of a monk*; *under the* ~ *of*, under pretence of being.

gui·tar [giˈtɑː*] *n.* six-stringed musical instrument plucked with the fingers.

gulf [gʌlf] *n.* **1.** part of the sea almost surrounded by land. **2.** deep hollow in the ground; (fig.) dividing line, division (*between* opinions, etc.).

¹gull [gʌl] *n.* large sea-bird.

²gull [gʌl] *v.t.* cheat; trick. *n.* sb.

easily ~ed.

gul·let ['gʌlit] *n.* food passage from mouth to stomach; throat.

gul·ly ['gʌli] *n.* narrow channel cut or formed by rain-water (on a hillside, etc.), or made for carrying away water from a building.

gulp [gʌlp] *v.t. & i.* swallow (*down*) food or drink quickly or greedily; work the throat as if swallowing sth. *n.* act of ~ing; amount ~ed.

¹**gum** [gʌm] *n.* firm pink flesh round the teeth. **'gum·boil** *n.* abscess on the gum.

²**gum** [gʌm] *n.* **1.** sticky substance obtained from some trees, used for sticking things together. **2.** = *chewing-gum. v.t.* (-*mm*-). put gum on; fasten (*down, together*) with gum. **'gum·boot** *n.* high rubber boot. ~**·my** *adj.* sticky.

gun [gʌn] *n.* general name for any kind of fire-arm that sends shot (3), bullets or shells from a metal tube. *stick to one's ~s,* defend one's opinions against attack. **'gun·boat** *n.* small warship with heavy guns. **'gun-ˌcar·riage** *n.* wheeled support for a heavy gun. **'gun-ˌcot·ton** *n.* explosive of acid-soaked cotton. **'gun-ˌmet·al** *n.* alloy of copper and tin or zinc. **gun·ner** *n.* man operating large guns. **'gun·pow·der** *n.* explosive powder used in fireworks and blasting. **'gun·shot** *n.* range of a gun: *within gunshot.* **'gun·smith** *n.* maker of small fire-arms.

gun·wale ['gʌnl] *n.* upper edge of a ship's or boat's side.

gur·gle ['gəːgl] *v.i. & n.* (make a) bubbling sound as of water flowing from a narrow-necked bottle.

gush [gʌʃ] *v.i. & n.* **1.** (come out with a) rushing outflow: *oil ~ing from a new well.* **2.** (talk with) excessive enthusiasm: *girls ~ing over film actors.* ~**·er** *n.* oil-well from which oil ~es.

gust [gʌst] *n.* sudden, violent rush of wind; burst of rain, fire, etc.; outburst (of strong feeling). ~**·y** *adj.*

gus·to ['gʌstou] *n.* enjoyment in doing sth.

gut [gʌt] *n.* **1.** (usu. pl.) intestines; bowels; (fig.) courage and determination. **2.** strong cord made from intestines of animals, used for the strings of a violin, etc. *v.t.* (-*tt*-). **1.** take the guts(1) out of (fish, etc.). **2.** destroy the inside of or contents of: *a building gutted by fire.*

gut·ter ['gʌtə*] *n.* channel fixed under the edge of a roof, channel at the side of a road, to carry off rain-water. *v.i.* (of a candle) burn unsteadily so that the wax flows down the sides.

gut·tur·al ['gʌtərəl] *n. & adj.* (sound) produced in the throat.

¹**guy** [gai] *n.* rope or chain used to keep sth. steady or secure.

²**guy** [gai] *n.* **1.** figure in the form of a man, dressed in old clothes; person dressed in a strange or queer-looking way. **2.** (U.S.A. colloq.) man.

guz·zle ['gʌzl] *v.i. & t.* eat or drink greedily. **guz·zler** *n.*

gym·kha·na [dʒim'kɑːnə] *n.* display of athletics; sports events.

gym·na·sium [dʒim'neizjəm] *n.* room with apparatus for physical training.

gym·nas·tic [dʒim'næstik] *adj.* of bodily training. **gym·nas·tics** *n. pl.* (forms of) exercises for physical training. **'gym·nast** *n.* person skilled in ~s.

gyp·sy *n.* = *gipsy.*

gy·rate [dʒaiə'reit] *v.i.* move round in circles or spirals. **gy·ra·tion** *n.*

gy·ro·scope ['dʒaiərəskoup] *n.* heavy wheel which, when turning fast, keeps steady the object in which it is fixed. **ˌgy·ro·'scop·ic** *adj.*

H

ha!, ha, ha! [hɑː, hɑː'hɑː] *int.* showing satisfaction, triumph.

hab·er·dash·er ['hæbədæʃə*] *n.* shopkeeper selling small articles of dress, pins, cotton, thread, etc. ~**·y** *n.*

hab·it ['hæbit] *n.* **1.** sb.'s settled practice, esp. sth. that cannot easily be given up: *the ~ of smoking*; *to be in the ~ of getting up late.* **2.** (old use) dress: *riding-~*, woman's coat and skirt for horse-riding. **ha·bit·u·al** [hə-'bitjuəl] *adj.* regular; usual; from ~. **ha·bit·u·al·ly** *adv.* as a usual practice. **ha·bit·u·ate** [hə'bitjueit] *v.t.* accustom; get (sb., oneself) used to.

hab·i·ta·ble ['hæbitəbl] *adj.* fit to be lived in. **hab·i·tat** ['hæbitæt] *n.* (of plants, animals) natural place of growth or home. **hab·i·ta·tion** [ˌhæbi'teiʃən] *n.* **1.** living in: *not fit for habitation.* **2.** place to live in.

ha·bit·u·al(ly), ha·bit·u·ate, see *habit.*

¹**hack** [hæk] *v.t. & i.* cut roughly; chop: *to ~ sth. to pieces*; *to ~ at a branch*; *a ~ing cough*, one that seems to tear the chest. **'~·saw** *n.* saw for cutting metal.

²**hack** [hæk] *n.* **1.** horse that may be hired. **2.** person paid to do undistinguished literary work. **hack·neyed** ['hæknid] *adj.* (esp. of sayings) too common; repeated too often.

had, see *have.*

had·dock ['hædək] *n.* sea-fish much used for food, esp. when smoked.

haem·or·rhage, hem- ['hem-əridʒ] *n.* escape of blood from blood-vessels.

hag [hæg] *n.* ugly old woman; witch.

hag·gard ['hægəd] *adj.* (of the face) looking tired and lined (esp. from worry, lack of sleep).

hag·gle ['hægl] *v.i.* argue, dispute (esp. *about* the price of sth.).

¹**hail** [heil] *n.* frozen rain-drops falling from the sky; sth. coming in great numbers and force: *a ~ of blows* (*curses*). *v.i. & t.* **1.** *It's ~ing*, ~ is falling. **2.** (fig., of blows, etc.) come down like ~. **'~·stone** *n.* small ball of ice.

²**hail** [heil] *v.t. & i.* **1.** greet; give a welcoming cry to; call out to (to attract attention): *to be ~ed by a friend*; *to ~ a taxi.* **2.** ~ *from*, have come from. *n. within*

~, near enough to be ~ed. *be ~-fellow-well-met with* (sb.), be very informal with.

hair [heə*] *n.* fine thread-like growth on the skin of animals; mass of such growths, esp. that which covers the human head. (describe sb.) *to a ~*, exactly; *not turn a ~*, give no sign of being troubled; *make one's ~ stand on end*, fill one with terror. **'~-do** *n.* (colloq.) style of ~dressing. **'~·dres·ser** *n.* person who dresses and cuts ~. **'~·pin** *n.* one for keeping the ~ in place. *~pin bend*, sharp bend in a road, esp. on a hillside. **'~·split·ting** *adj.* making or showing differences too small to be important. **~·spring** *n.* very delicate spring in a watch. **~·less** *adj.* bald. **~·y** *adj.* (*-ier, -iest*) of or like ~; covered with ~.

hal·cy·on ['hælsiən] *adj.* ~ *days*, ~ *weather*, calm and peaceful.

¹**hale** [heil] *adj.* (usu. of old persons) strong and healthy.

²**hale** [heil] *v.t.* haul (sb.) by force (*away, off, to prison*, etc.).

half [hɑːf] *n.* (pl. *halves* [hɑːvz]) *& adj.* one of two equal or corresponding parts into which a thing can be divided; ½. *go halves* (*with* sb., *in* sth.), share equally; *do sth. by halves*, do it incompletely or badly; *too clever by ~*, (usu. ironical) far too clever; *one's better ~*, (colloq., humor.) one's wife. *adv. not ~ bad*, (colloq.) good; *not ~!*, (colloq., humor.) certainly; *by all means.* **'~-blood** *n.* (relationship of) persons having the same father or mother but not both. **'~-breed, '~-caste** *n.* **1.** person with parents of different races, esp. differently coloured races. **2.** offspring of two animals or plants of different species. **'~-broth·er, '~-sis·ter** *n.* by one parent only. **'~-'crown** *n.* (formerly) British coin, value 2s. 6d. (= 12½p). (See p. 628.) **'~-'heart·ed** *adj.* done with, showing, little interest or enthusiasm. **'~-hol·i·day** *n.* day of which half (usu. the afternoon) is free from work or duty.

'~-'mast *n.* at ~-*mast*, position, near the middle of a mast, of a flag flown to indicate mourning. **~'pen·ny** ['heipni] *n.* British coin worth a ~ of one penny. (See p. 628.) **~'pen·ny·worth, ha'p'orth**: ['heipniwə:θ, 'heipəθ] *n.* '**~-'wit·ted** *adj.* weak-minded. '**~-wit** *n.* ~-witted person.

hall [hɔ:l] *n.* **1.** (building with a) large room for meetings, concerts, public business, etc. **2.** large room for meals (in colleges of some universities): *dine in* ~. **3.** space into which the main entrance of a building opens.

hal·le·lu·jah [,hæli'lu:jə] *n.* & *int.* song of, cry of, praise to God.

hall'mark ['hɔ:lma:k] *n.* mark stamped on gold or silver articles as a guarantee of quality. *v.t.* stamp the ~ on.

hal·lo [hə'lou, 'hɑ'lou] *int.* cry to attract attention; greeting.

hal·low ['hælou] *v.t.* make holy; regard as holy: ~ed *ground*.

hal·lu·ci·na·tion [hə,lu:si'neiʃən] *n.* seeming to see sth. not present; sth. so imagined.

ha·lo ['heilou] *n.* circle of light round the sun or moon or (in paintings, etc.) shown above the head of a sacred figure (5).

halt [hɔ:lt] *v.t.* & *i.* & *n.* **1.** (esp. of soldiers) (come to a) stop on a march or journey; (bring to a) stop. **2.** show hesitation: *to* ~ *between two opinions*; speak in a hesitating way. **3.** minor stopping-place for a railway train. **~·ing·ly** *adv.*

hal·ter ['hɔ:ltə*] *n.* rope or leather strap put round a horse's head; rope used for hanging (2) a person.

halve [ha:v] *v.t.* divide into two equal parts; lessen by one half.

hal·yard ['hæljəd] *n.* rope for raising or lowering a sail or flag.

ham [hæm] *n.* (salted and smoked) upper part of a pig's leg.

ham·let ['hæmlit] *n.* group of houses in the countryside.

ham·mer ['hæmə*] *n.* tool with a heavy metal head used for breaking things, driving in nails,

etc. *go at it* ~ *and tongs*, fight, argue, with great energy and noise. *come under the* ~, be sold by auction. *v.t.* & *i.* **1.** strike with, or as with, a ~: *to* ~ *a nail in*; *to* ~ *sth. flat*; *to* ~ *at a door.* **2.** (fig.) produce by hard work: *to* ~ *out a scheme*; work hard: *to* ~ *away at sth.*

A hammer

ham·mock ['hæmək] *n.* hanging bed of canvas or rope network.

¹ham·per ['hæmpə*] *v.t.* hinder; prevent free movement or activity.

²ham·per ['hæmpə*] *n.* basket with lid, esp. one for food.

ham·string ['hæmstriŋ] *v.t.* cripple (a person or animal).

A hammock — A hand

hand [hænd] *n.* **1.** see the picture. *at* ~, within reach; present. *live from* ~ *to mouth*, spend money as soon as it is earned, saving nothing. *give a (helping)* ~ *to sb.*, help him. *in* ~, (a) held in reserve, available, for use; (b) receiving attention. *out of* ~, (a) out of control; (b) at once; without preparation. *win* ~*s down*, win easily. *keep one's* ~ *in*, keep one's skill by practice. *with a heavy* ~, cruelly, severely. *with a high* ~, arrogantly. **2.** (pl.) care; keeping; possession: *The matter is in your* ~*s*. **3.** worker in a factory, dockyard, etc.; member of a ship's crew. **4.** pointer on a watch or clock: *the hour* ~. **5.** source of information: *to hear sth. at first (second)* ~, directly (indirectly, by hearsay). **6.** side; direction: *on all*

~*s*, to or from all sides; *on the one* ~, . . . *on the other* ~ (contrasting two sides of a question). **7.** ~writing; signature: *to set one's* ~ *to an agreement.* **8.** cards dealt to a player; one round in a game of cards. **9.** unit of measurement, four inches, for the height of a horse. *v.t.* give; pass; help with the ~: *to* ~ *sb. a book; to* ~ *in an essay; ~ed down from one generation to another; to* ~ *on the news,* tell it to others. '~**bag** *n.* woman's bag for carrying money, handkerchief, etc. '~**bill** *n.* printed advertisement distributed by ~. '~**book** *n.* small guide-book or book of information on a subject. '~**cart** *n.* one pushed or pulled by ~. '~**cuff** *n.* one of a pair of metal rings joined by a short chain placed round a prisoner's wrists. *v.t.* put ~cuffs on. ~**ful** *n.* (a) as much as a ~ holds; (b) a small number; (c) person or animal difficult to control. '~**i·craft** *n.* art or craft needing skill with the ~s, e.g. pottery. '~**i·work** *n.* sth. done or made by ~ or by a named person. '~**,writ·ing** *n.* (person's style of) writing with a pen or pencil. ~**y** *adj.* (*-ier, -iest*). **1.** clever with the ~s. **2.** available for use; not far away. **3.** (of tools, etc.) easily used; useful. ~**i·ly** *adv.*

hand·i·cap ['hændikæp] *n.* **1.** something that hinders or lessens one's chance of success. **2.** race, etc., in which the strongest competitors are ~ped, so that everyone may have a fair chance of winning. *v.t.* (*-pp-*). give or be a ~ to: *~ped by ill health.*

hand·ker·chief ['hæŋkətʃif] *n.* square piece of cotton, silk, linen, etc., carried in the pocket for blowing the nose on, wiping the face, or worn for ornament.

han·dle ['hændl] *n.* part of tool, cup, door, etc., by which it may be held in the hand. *v.t.* **1.** touch with, take in, the hands. **2.** control (men). '~**bar** *n.* bar for steering a bicycle.

hand·some ['hænsəm] *adj.* **1.** of fine appearance. **2.** (of gifts, etc.) generous.

hang [hæŋ] *v.t. & i.* (p.t. & p.p. *hung* [hʌŋ]). **1.** support, be supported, from above so that the lower end is free: *to* ~ *a lamp from the ceiling; curtains* ~*ing over the window.* **2.** (p.t. & p.p. *hanged*). put (sb.) to death by ~ing him with a rope round the neck. **3.** ~ *a door,* attach it with hinges to a frame; ~ *the head,* let it fall forward (when ashamed); ~ *fire,* (of a gun) be slow in going off; (of events) be slow in developing. **4.** (with adv. and prep.): ~ *about,* be or remain near, waiting or idling. ~ *back,* hesitate; show unwillingness to act. ~ *on to,* hold tightly; refuse to give up. ~ *together,* (of persons) support one another; (of a story, its parts) fit together well. *be hung up,* be delayed. *n.* **1.** the way in which sth. (esp. a garment) ~s. **2.** *get the* ~ *of sth.,* understand how to do or use sth. *not to care a* ~, not to care at all. '~**dog** *adj.* (of sb.'s look) sly and ashamed. ~**er** *n.* (esp.) wooden bar on which to ~ dresses, coats, etc. '~**er-'on** *n.* person forcing his company on others in the hope of profit or advantage. ~**ings** *n. pl.* curtains. ~**man** *n.* executioner by ~ing(2).

han·gar ['hæŋgə*] *n.* shed for aircraft.

hank [hæŋk] *n.* coil or twist of wool, silk, etc., thread.

hank·er ['hæŋkə*] *v.i.* ~ *after* (*for*), be continually wishing for.

han·som (cab) ['hænsəm ('kæb)] *n.* (no longer used) two-wheeled horse-cab for two passengers, with the driver's seat high at the back.

hap·haz·ard ['hæp'hæzəd] *adj., adv. & n.* (by) mere chance; (by) accident.

ha·p'orth = halfpennyworth. See *half.*

hap·pen ['hæpən] *v.i.* **1.** take place; come about. **2.** ~ *on,* find or meet by chance. ~**ing** *n.* event.

hap·py ['hæpi] *adj.* (*-ier, -iest*). 1. feeling or expressing pleasure; pleased; lucky. 2. (of words, ideas, suggestions) well suited to the situation. '~-**go**-'**luck·y** *adj.* taking what fortune brings; carefree. **hap·pi·ly** *adv.* **hap·pi·ness** *n.*

ha·rangue [hə'ræŋ] *v.t. & i. & n.* (make a) long, loud (often scolding) speech (to).

har·ass ['hærəs] *v.t.* trouble; worry; make repeated attacks on.

har·bin·ger ['hɑːbindʒə*] *n.* sb. or sth. that foretells the coming of sb. or sth.

har·bour ['hɑːbə*] *n.* place of shelter for ships; (fig.) place of safety. *v.t.* 1. keep safe; hide: *to ~ a criminal.* 2. hold (ill feeling, etc.) in the mind.

¹hard [hɑːd] *adj.* (*-er, -est*). 1. firm; solid; not easily cut or dented. *~ cash,* coins, notes, not a cheque or promise to pay. *~ water,* containing too much lime. *~ of hearing,* rather deaf. *~ labour,* imprisonment with ~ physical labour. *~ and fast* (rules, etc.), that cannot be altered to fit special cases. *~ luck, ~ lines,* worse fortune than is deserved. *~ times,* times of money shortage, unemployment, etc. *~en* *v.t. & i.* make or become ~. '~-'**head·ed** *adj.* unsentimental; shrewd; astute. '~-'**heart·ed** *adj.* pitiless, unfeeling. '~**i·hood** *n.* boldness. '~**ship** *n.* severe suffering; painful condition. '~**ware** *n.* metal goods such as pans, locks, nails.

²hard [hɑːd] *adv.* with great energy; with all one's force; severely; heavily; with difficulty. *~ up,* short of money. *be ~ put to it, ~ pressed,* be in difficult circumstances. *~ by,* near; *~ upon,* not far behind.

hard·ly ['hɑːdli] *adv.* 1. with difficulty; severely. 2. scarcely; only just. *~ any,* very few, very little.

har·dy ['hɑːdi] *adj.* (*-ier, -iest*). 1. strong; able to endure suffering or hardship. 2. (of plants)

not damaged by frost. **har·di·ly** *adv.* **har·di·ness** *n.*

hare [heə*] *n.* field animal with a divided upper lip, like, but larger than, a rabbit. '~-'**brained** *adj.* rash; wild.

ha·rem ['hɛərəm] *n.* women's part of a Muslim household.

har·i·cot ['hærikou] *n.* (also ~ *bean*) kidney bean; French bean.

hark [hɑːk] *v.i.* (chiefly imperative) Listen!

har·le·quin ['hɑːlikwin] *n.* comic character in pantomime.

har·lot ['hɑːlət] *n.* prostitute.

harm [hɑːm] *v.t. & n.* (cause) damage or injury (to). ~**ful** *adj.* causing ~. ~**less** *adj.* causing no ~.

har·mo·ni·um [hɑː'mounjəm] *n.* musical instrument like a small organ, but with reeds instead of pipes.

har·mo·ny ['hɑːməni] *n.* 1. agreement (of feeling, interests, opinions, etc.): *in ~ with.* 2. (music) pleasing combination of notes sounded together; pleasing association of colours seen together. **har·mo·ni·ous** [hɑː-'mounjəs] *adj.* in agreement; pleasingly combined or arranged; sweet-sounding; tuneful. **har·mo·nize** ['hɑːmənaiz] *v.t. & i.* bring into, be in, ~ (with); (music) add notes (to a melody) to make chords.

har·ness ['hɑːnis] *n.* all the leatherwork and metalwork by which a horse is controlled and fastened to whatever it pulls or carries. *in ~,* doing one's regular work. *v.t.* 1. put ~ on (a horse). 2. use (a river, waterfall) to produce (esp. electric) power.

harp [hɑːp] *n.* stringed musical instrument played with the fingers. *v.i.* play the ~. *~ on,* (fig.) talk repeatedly or tiringly about (e.g. one's misfortunes). ~**ist** *n.* player on the ~. See the picture on page 240.

har·poon [hɑː'puːn] *n.* spear attached to a rope, thrown by hand or fired from a gun, e.g. for catching whales.

harp·si·chord ['hɑːpsikɔːd] *n.*
piano-like instrument dating
from the 16th century.

har·py ['hɑːpi] *n.* (old Greek
stories) cruel creature with a
woman's face and bird's wings
and claws.

har·row ['hærou] *n.* heavy frame
with metal teeth or discs for
breaking up ground after
ploughing. *v.t.* pull a ~ over;
(fig.) distress (feelings).

har·ry ['hæri] *v.t.* lay waste and
plunder; attack frequently;
worry.

harsh [hɑːʃ] *adj.* (-*er*, -*est*). 1.
rough and disagreeable, esp. to
the senses. 2. stern, cruel, severe.
~·**ly** *adv.* ~·**ness** *n.*

har·um-scar·um ['hɛərəm-
'skɛərəm] *n.* reckless, impulsive
person.

har·vest ['hɑːvist] *n.* 1. (season
for) cutting and gathering in of
grain and other food crops;
quantity obtained. 2. con-
sequence(s) of action or behaviour. *v.t.* cut, gather, dig up,
a crop: *to ~ rice* (*potatoes*). ~·**er**
n. reaper; grain-~ing machine.

has, had, see *have*.

hash [hæʃ] *v.t.* cut up (meat) into
small pieces. *n.* dish of cooked
meat, ~ed and recooked. *make
a ~ of sth.*, (fig.) do it badly.

hash·ish, hash·eesh ['hæʃiːʃ] *n.*
dried hemp leaves made into a
drug for smoking or chewing.

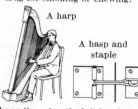

A harp

A hasp and
staple

hasp [hæsp] *n.* the left-hand part
of the metal fastening shown
in the picture above.

has·sock ['hæsək] *n.* cushion for
kneeling on (e.g. in church).

haste [heist] *n.* quickness of
movement; hurry. *make ~,*
hurry. *in* (*great*) ~, in a hurry;
hastily. **hast·en** ['heisn] *v.i. &*

t. 1. move or act with speed. 2.
cause (sb.) to hurry; cause (sth.)
to be done or to happen quickly
or earlier. **hast·y** *adj.* (-*ier,
-iest*). 1. said, made or done (too)
quickly. 2. quick-tempered.
hast·i·ly *adv.* **hast·i·ness** *n.*

hat [hæt] *n.* covering for the
head, usu. with a brim, worn
out of doors. (Cf. *cap, bonnet,*
without a brim.) *talk through
one's hat,* (colloq.) talk foolishly.

¹**hatch** [hætʃ] *n.* (movable covering over an) opening in a wall or
floor, esp. (~*way*) one in a ship's
deck. *under* ~*es,* below deck.

²**hatch** [hætʃ] *v.t. & i.* 1. (cause to)
break out (of an egg): *to ~
chickens* (*eggs*). 2. think out and
develop (a plot). ~·**er·y** *n.* place
for ~ing fish.

hatch·et ['hætʃit] *n.* axe with
a short handle. *bury the* ~, stop
quarrelling.

hate [heit] *v.t. & n.* (have a)
violent dislike (of). ~·**ful** *adj.*
showing, causing, ~. **hat·red**
['heitrid] *n.* = hate.

haugh·ty ['hɔːti] *adj.* (-*ier, -iest*).
arrogant. **haugh·ti·ly** *adv.*

haul [hɔːl] *v.t. & i.* pull (with
effort or force): *elephants* ~*ing
logs; to* ~ *at a rope.* ~ (*sb.*) *over
the coals,* find fault with; scold.
n. act of ~ing; amount gained
as the result of effort, esp. of
fish ~ed up in a net. ~·**age**
['hɔːlidʒ], *n.* transport of goods.

haunch [hɔːnʃ] *n.* (in man and
animals) part of the body round
the hips, or between the ribs
and thighs.

haunt [hɔːnt] *v.t.* visit, be with,
habitually or repeatedly: *idle
students who* ~ *dance-halls;
wrongdoers* ~*ed by fears of discovery. n.* place frequently
visited by person(s) named: *the
~ of criminals.* ~·**ed** *adj.* (of
a place) frequently visited by
ghosts.

have [hæv] *v.t.* (inf. [hæv, həf]);
pres. t. *have* [hæv, həv], *I've*
[aiv], *has* [hæz, həz], *haven't*
['hævnt], *hasn't* ['hæznt]; p.t. *had*
[hæd, həd], *hadn't* ['hædnt], *I'd*
[aid]; pres. p. *having* ['hæviŋ];
p.p. *had* [hæd, həd]). I. *aux.*

v. used to form the perfect tenses and the perfect infinitive. **II. 1.** (in sentences where *be* is possible): *Has June thirty-one days?* **2.** possess: *Has she blue eyes or brown?* **3.** experience in the mind: *I've no doubt about it. What reason ~ you for thinking so?* **4.** allow: *I won't ~ such behaviour in my house.* **5.** expressing obligation: *When ~ you to go to the dentist? We shall have to go soon.* **6.** suffer from: *Do you often ~ pain?* **7.** give birth to: *The cat has just had kittens.* **8.** receive; obtain: *What presents did you ~ at Christmas?* **9.** take; choose; accept: *What shall we ~ for dinner? Will you ~ me for a partner?* **10.** wish; expect: *What would you ~ me do in that case?* **11.** ~ *to do with*, be concerned with: *What has she to do with that?* (How is she concerned?). ~ *something (nothing) to do with*, be connected (be unconnected) with. ~ *something out with sb.*, discuss and settle (a matter under dispute).

ha·ven ['heivn] *n.* harbour; (fig.) place of safety or rest.

haver·sack ['hævəsæk] *n.* canvas bag, esp. as used by soldiers, for carrying food, etc.

hav·oc ['hævək] *n.* widespread damage; destruction.

haw [hɔ:] *n.* fruit (red berry) of the hawthorn bush.

¹**hawk** [hɔ:k] *n.* strong, swift, keen-sighted bird of prey.

²**hawk** [hɔ:k] *v.t.* go from street to street, house to house, with goods for sale. ~·**er** *n.*

haw·ser ['hɔ:zə*] *n.* thick, heavy rope; thin steel cable (used on ships).

haw·thorn ['hɔ:θɔ:n] *n.* thorny shrub with white or red blossom and red berries called haws.

hay [hei] *n.* grass cut and dried for use as animal food. *hay fever*, disease affecting the nose and throat, caused, e.g. by pollen (dust) from various plants.

¹**hay·rick**, ¹**hay·stack** *n.* mass of hay firmly piled in a field till needed.

haz·ard ['hæzəd] *n.* risk; danger: *exposed to the ~s of a life at sea. v.t.* **1.** take the risk of; expose to danger. **2.** venture to make (a guess, remark). ~·**ous** *adj.* risky.

haze [heiz] *n.* thin mist. **haz·y** *adj.* (-ier, -iest). misty; (fig.) vague; not clear.

ha·zel ['heizl] *n.* small nut-tree; (esp. of eyes) reddish-brown colour.

he [hi:] *pron.* male person or animal previously referred to.

head [hed] *n.* **1.** that part of the body which contains the brain, the mouth, etc. **2.** life: *to lose one's ~. It cost him his ~.* **3.** sth. like a ~ in form or position, e.g. the striking part of a hammer, the flat end of a nail, the top of a mast, foam on beer, a mass of leaves or flowers at the top of a stem, etc. **4.** brain; imagination; power to reason: *make sth. up out of one's ~. lose (keep) one's ~,* become overexcited (remain calm) in the face of difficulty, danger, etc. *off one's ~,* mad. *take it into one's ~ that,* come to believe that. (*talk) above their ~s,* beyond their power to understand. ~ *over heels,* upside-down; deeply and completely: *be ~ over heels in love.* **5.** picture or image of a ~ (esp. on coins): ~*s or tails; be unable to make ~ or tail of sth.,* be completely puzzled by it. **6.** one person: *5s. a ~, 5s.* for each person; *crowned ~s,* kings, queens. **7.** (pl. unchanged) unit of a flock or herd: *50 ~ of cattle.* **8.** chief position: *at the ~ of the list.* **9.** upper end: *the ~ of a valley (lake, bed).* **10.** ruler; chief; master: *the ~ of the school; the ~ waiter.* **11.** division in a speech or essay. **12.** *come to a ~,* a crisis or culmination. *v.t. & i.* **1.** be at the ~ of (e.g. a procession). **2.** move in the direction indicated: ~*ing south;* ~ *for home;* ~ *sb. off,* get in front in order to turn him back. **3.** strike with the ~: *to ~ the ball.* ¹~**-dress** *n.* (esp. ornamental) ~ covering. ~·**er** *n.* fall or dive

~ first. **~·ing** *n.* word(s) at the top of a section of printed matter. **'~·light** *n.* large lamp on a motor-car, etc. **'~·land** *n.* ²cape. **'~·line** *n.* newspaper ~ing, usu. in large type. **'~·long** *adj. & adv.* with the ~ first; thoughtless(ly) and hurried(ly). **'~·man** *n.* chief of a tribe or village. **'~·'mas·ter, '~·'mis·tress** *n.* teacher in charge of a school. **'~·'on** *adj. & adv.* (of vehicles) (colliding) directly, front to front. **'~·phones** *n. pl.* earphones. **'~·'quar·ters** *n. pl.* place from which (e.g. police, army) activities are controlled. **'~·strong** *adj.* self-willed; obstinate. **'~·way** *n.* progress. **'~·word** *n.* word used as a heading, esp. the first word, in heavy type, of a dictionary entry.

heal [hi:l] *v.t. & i.* make or become well: *to ~ a wound*; *wounds that ~ slowly*; (fig.) *to ~ a quarrel*.

health [helθ] *n.* **1.** condition of the body or the mind; *good (poor) ~*. **2.** (esp.) state of being free from illness. **3.** *drink sb's ~*, (as a social custom) raise one's glass and wish good ~ to. **~·y** *adj.* (*-ier, -iest*). having, showing, producing, good ~ : *~y exercise*.

heap [hi:p] *n.* **1.** number of things, mass of material, piled up like a small hill : *a ~ of books* (*sand*). **2.** (pl., colloq.) a large number; plenty : *to have ~s of books* (*time*). *~v.t.* **1.** put in a ~ ; make into a ~ : *to ~ (up) stones.* **2.** fill; load : *to ~ a plate with food* ; *to ~ favours upon a friend.*

hear [hiə*] *v.t. & i.* (p.t. & p.p. *heard* [hə:d]). **1.** become aware of (sound) through the ears. *~ from*, receive news, a message, from; *~ of*, have news, knowledge, about. **2.** (of a judge) try (a case) ; judge. **3.** *Hear! Hear!* cry expressing approval or agreement. **~·ing** *n.* **1.** ability to hear; distance within which one can hear: *within (out of) ~ing*, near enough (too far off) to be heard. **2.** trial. **'~·say** *n.* what one hears said, whether true or not.

hear·ken ['hɑ:kən] *v.i.* (old use) listen.

hearse [hə:s] *n.* carriage, car, for carrying a coffin.

heart [hɑ:t] *n.* **1.** that part of the body which pumps the blood through it. **2.** centre of the affection or emotions: *not have the ~ to (disappoint sb.)*, be too sympathetic to (do so); *lose ~*, feel discouraged ; *take ~*, be confident ; *take sth. to ~*, be much affected by it; *a change of ~*, change making one a better person; *after one's own ~*, of the sort most liked or approved. **3.** centre: *in the ~ of the forest*. **4.** playing-card marked with red ~(s). **'~·ache** *n.* deep sorrow. **'~-beat** *n.* one movement of the ~'s regular motion. **'~·breaking** *adj.* causing great sorrow. **'~·broken** *adj.* suffering from deep sorrow. **'~·burn** *n.* burning feeling below the ~, caused by indigestion. **'~·burning** *n.* envy; discontent. **~·en** *v.t.* give courage to: *~ening news.* **'~·felt** *adj.* (of feelings, esp. sympathy) sincere; deeply felt. **'~·less** *adj.* unkind; without pity. **'~·rending** *adj.* causing deep grief. **'~-strings** *n. pl.* deepest feelings. **'~·whole** *adj.* not yet in love. **~·y** *adj.* (*-ier, -iest*). **1.** sincere: *my ~y approval*; *a ~y welcome*. **2.** strong; healthy: *still hale and ~y at 95.* **3.** (of meals, appetites) big: *a ~y meal* (*eater, appetite*). **~·i·ly** *adv.*

hearth [hɑ:θ] *n.* floor of a fireplace; (fig.) home. (See the picture at **grate**.) **'~-rug** *n.* rug spread in front of a ~.

heat [hi:t] *n.* **1.** hotness. **2.** intense feeling: *in the ~ of the argument.* **3.** trial race, the winners of which take part in (the further races leading to) the finals. *v.t. & i.* make or become warm or hot. **~·er** *n.* apparatus for warming a room, motor-car, etc. **'cen·tral '~·ing** *n.* system that ~s a building from one source. **'~·wave** *n.* period of unusually hot weather. **~·ed·ly** *adv.* angrily.

heath [hi:θ] *n.* **1.** area of flat waste land. **2.** (sorts of) low-growing bush or shrub growing on ~s, hillsides, etc.

hea·then ['hi:ðən] *n. & adj.* (person) of a religion neither Christian, Muslim, Jewish, nor Buddhist; (fig.) savage.

heath·er ['heðə*] *n.* kind of heath (2) with small, light purple flowers.

heave [hi:v] *v.t. & i.* (p.t. & p.p. *heaved* or (nautical use) *hove* [houv]). **1.** raise, lift up (sth. heavy); pull (*at*, *on*, a rope). **2.** (colloq.) lift and throw: *to ~ one's luggage into a taxi.* **3.** rise and fall: *heaving waves; a heaving bosom.* **4.** (of a ship) ~ *in sight*, come into view; come to a stop: *The ship hove to.* *n.* act of heaving.

heav·en ['hevn] *n.* **1.** home of God and the Saints. **2.** place, condition, of great happiness. **3.** (often pl.) the sky. *Good H~s!* int. showing surprise. ~**·ly** *adj.* **1.** of, from, like, ~. **2.** very beautiful or pleasing.

heav·y ['hevi] *adj.* (*-ier*, *-iest*). **1.** having great weight; difficult to lift or move. **2.** of more than usual size, amount, force, etc.: ~ *crops* (*rain*, *work*, *blows*); ~ *roads* (e.g. because of mud); ~ *going* (of conditions that make progress difficult). **3.** (of persons, writing, etc.) dull; tedious. *adv.* (= heavily) *time hanging ~ on his hands*, passing slowly. '~**·weight** *n.* boxer weighing 175 lb. or more. **heav·i·ly** *adv.*

He·brew ['hi:bru:] *n.* (language, religion of a) Jew. *adj.* of the ~ language or people.

heck·le ['hekl] *v.t.* ask many troublesome questions at a public meeting. **heck·ler** *n.*

hec·tic ['hektik] *adj.* **1.** unnaturally red: ~ *cheeks* (*colouring*) (as of a person suffering from tuberculosis). **2.** full of excitement and without rest.

hec·to- ['hektou-] *prefix.* 100: ~*gramme*, ~*litre*.

hedge [hedʒ] *n.* row of bushes, tall plants, etc., usu. trimmed, forming a boundary (for a field, garden, etc.). *v.t. & i.* **1.** put a ~ or (fig.) barrier round: ~*d in with regulations*, unable to act freely. **2.** avoid giving a direct answer to a question. '~**·hog** *n.* small spine-covered animal which rolls itself into a ball when attacked. ~**·row** ['hedʒrou] *n.* = hedge.

heed [hi:d] *v.t. & n.* (pay) attention (to): *to ~ a warning; to take no ~ of what people say.* ~**·ful** *adj.* attentive. ~**·less** *adj.* inattentive.

¹**heel** [hi:l] *n.* back part of the human foot; part of sock, etc., covering this; part of shoe supporting this. *take to one's ~s, show a clean pair of ~s*, run away. *cool* (*kick*) *one's ~s*, be kept waiting. *come to ~*, (of a dog) walk at its master's ~s; (fig.) submit to control. *down at ~*, (of shoes) worn down at the ~s; (fig.) poorly dressed. *v.t.* put new ~s (on shoes, etc.).

²**heel** [hi:l] *v.i. & t.* (of a ship) (cause to) lean (*over*).

hef·ty ['hefti] *adj.* (*-ier*, *-iest*). (colloq.) big and strong.

heif·er ['hefə*] *n.* young cow that has not yet had a calf.

height [hait] *n.* **1.** distance from bottom to top; distance to the top of sth. from a level, esp. sea level: *the ~ of a mountain.* **2.** high place. **3.** utmost degree: *the ~ of his ambition; at its ~.* ~**·en** *v.t.* make high(er); make greater in degree.

hein·ous ['heinəs] *adj.* (of crime) very wicked; atrocious.

heir [εə*] *n.* person with the legal right to receive a title, property, etc., when the owner dies. ~**·ess** ['εəris] *n.* female ~. '~**·loom** *n.* sth. handed down in a family for several generations.

held, see hold.

hel·i·cop·ter ['helikəptə*] *n.* kind of aircraft, with horizontal rotor(s), that requires only a small landing-space. See the picture on page 244.

hel·i·port ['helipɔ:t] *n.* landing-place for helicopters.

hell [hel] *n.* **1.** (in some religions) place of punishment after death.

2. place, condition, of great suffering or misery. **3.** (as int.) expressing anger or disgust.

hel·lo *int.* = *hallo, hullo.*

helm [helm] *n.* handle (also *tiller*) or wheel for moving the rudder of a boat or ship.

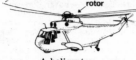

A helicopter

hel·met ['helmit] *n.* protective head-covering worn by soldiers, firemen, some workers, some policemen, etc.

help [help] *v.t. & i.* **1.** do sth. that eases another person's work or benefits him in some way; assist. **2.** escape; avoid: *I can't* ~ *doing it. It can't be* ~*ed.* **3.** serve with food or drink: ~*ing himself to the beer.* **n. 1.** act of ~ing; person or thing that ~s. **2.** escape; avoidance: *There's no* ~ *for it* (one cannot escape from it or avoid it). ~**'er** *n.* one who ~s. ~**'ful** *adj.* giving ~; useful. ~**'ing** *n.* portion of food served on a person's plate. ~**'less** *adj.* without ~; unable to look after oneself. '~**'mate** *n.* friend who ~s; (esp.) one's husband or wife.

hel·ter-skel·ter ['heltə'skeltə*] *adv.* in disorderly haste.

hem [hem] *n.* border or edge of cloth, esp. when turned and sewn down. *v.t.* (*-mm-*). **1.** make a hem on. **2.** *hem about* (*in*), confine; surround. '~**'stitch** *n.* ornamental stitching. *v.t.* decorate cloth with this.

hem·i- ['hemi-] *prefix.* half.

hem·i·sphere ['hemisfiə*] *n.* half a sphere; half the earth: *the Northern and Southern H*~*s.*

hemp [hemp] *n.* plant and its fibre, used in rope-making.

hen [hen] *n.* female of the domestic fowl. (Cf. ¹*cock.*) '**hen-pecked** *adj.* (of a man) ruled by his wife.

hence [hens] *adv.* **1.** from here; from now: *a week* ~, in a week's time. **2.** for this reason. ~**'forth** ['hens'fo:θ], ~**'forward** ['hens'fo:wəd] *adv.* from this time on.

hench·man ['hentʃmən] *n.* faithful, unquestioning supporter, esp. political supporter.

her [hə:*] *pron.* object form of *she: She's in the garden; I can see her.* **poss. adj.** *This is her book.* **hers** [hə:z] *poss. pron. This book is hers* (belongs to her).

her·ald ['herəld] *n.* **1.** (historical) person making public announcements for, carrying messages from, a ruler. **2.** person or thing foretelling the coming of sb. or sth.: *In England the cuckoo is a* ~ *of spring.* *v.t.* make known the coming of. **her·ald·ry** *n.* science dealing with coats of arms, descent and history of old families. **her·al·dic** [he'rældik] *adj.* of ~ry.

herb [hə:b] *n.* low, soft-stemmed plant that dies down after flowering, esp. one whose leaves are used in medicine or for flavouring food. ~**'al·ist** ['hə:bəlist] *n.* person who grows or sells ~s for medical use.

her·ba·ceous [hə:'beifəs] *adj.* ~ *border,* bed with plants which come up and flower year after year.

herb·age ['hə:bidʒ] *n.* grass and other field plants.

her·cu·le·an [,hə:kju'liən] *adj.* having, needing, great powers of body or mind.

herd [hə:d] *n.* number of cattle, etc., feeding or going about together. *the common* (*vulgar*) ~, (contemptuous) the mass of ordinary people. **herds·man** ['hə:dzmən] *n.* man who looks after ~s.

here [hiə*] *adv.* in, at, to, this point or place. ~ *and there,* in various places. *neither* ~ *nor there,* not important, not to the point. ~**'a·bouts** ['hiərə,bauts] *adv.* near or about ~. ~**'af·ter** [hiər'ɑ:ftə*] *adv. & n.* (in the) future; after this life on earth. ~**'up·on** ['hiərə'pɒn] *adv.* at this point. ~**'with** ['hiə'wið] *adv.* with this.

he·red·i·ta·ry [hi'redi/təri] *adj.* (having a position) passed on from parent to child, from one generation to following generations: ~ *rulers* (*beliefs*). **he'red·i·ty** [hi'rediti] *n.* tendency of living things to pass their characteristics on to offspring.

her·e·sy ['herisi] *n.* (holding of) belief or opinion contrary to what is generally accepted, esp. in religion. **her·e·tic** ['heritik] *n.* person supporting a ~. **he·ret·i·cal** [hi'retikl] *adj.* of ~ or heretics.

her·i·tage ['heritidʒ] *n.* that which has been or may be inherited.

her·met·ic [hə:'metik] *adj.* airtight. **her·met·i·cal·ly** *adv.* ~*ally sealed*, sealed so as to keep air in or out.

her·mit ['hə:mit] *n.* person (esp. man in early Christian times) living quite alone.

he·ro ['hiərou] *n.* (pl. *-oes*). **1.** boy or man respected for bravery or noble qualities. **2.** chief man in a poem, story, or play. ~**ine** ['herouin] *n.* woman ~. ~**ic** [hi'rouik] *adj.* of, like, fit for, a ~. **her·o·ism** ['herouizm] *n.* great courage; ~*ic* qualities and acts.

her·on ['herən] *n.* long-legged bird living in marshy places.

her·ring ['heriŋ] *n.* sea-fish much used for food.

her·self [hə:'self, hə-] *pron.* **1.** *She has hurt* ~. **2.** *She* ~ *did it* (nobody else). **3.** *She sat by* ~ (alone). *She did it by* ~ (without help).

hes·i·tate ['heziteit] *v.i.* show signs of uncertainty or unwillingness in speech or action. **hes·i·tant** ['hezitənt] *adj.* inclined to ~. **hes·i·tat·ing·ly**, **hes·i·tant·ly** *adv.* in a hesitating manner. **hes·i·ta·tion** [,hezi-'teiʃən] *n.*

hes·si·an ['hesiən] *n.* strong, coarse cloth of hemp or jute; sack-cloth.

het·er·o·dox ['hetərədɔks] *adj.* not orthodox. ~**y** *n.* opp. of orthodoxy.

het·er·o·ge·neous [,hetərou'dʒi:-njəs] *adj.* different; unlike; made up of different kinds.

hew [hju:] *v.t.* (p.t. *hewed* [hju:d], p.p. *hewn* [hju:n]). cut (by striking or chopping); shape by chopping: *to hew down a tree*; *hewn timber*.

hex·a·gon ['heksəgən] *n.* straight-sided figure with six (usu. equal) angles.

hex·am·e·ter [hek'sæmitə*] *n.* line of verse (esp. Greek or Latin) with six feet.

hey [hei] *int.* word used to attract attention or express surprise.

hey·day ['heidei] *n.* time of greatest prosperity or power.

hi·a·tus [hai'eitəs] *n.* space or gap in a series, making it incomplete.

hi·ber·nate ['haibəneit] *v.i.* (of some animals) pass the winter in a state like sleep.

hic·cup, hic·cough ['hikʌp] *v.i. & n.* (have a) sudden stopping of the breath with a cough-like sound.

hid, hidden, see ¹*hide*.

¹**hide** [haid] *v.t. & i.* (p.t. *hid*, p.p. *hidden*). put or keep out of sight; prevent from being seen, found, or known. **hid·ing** *n.* (of a person) *go into hiding*, ~ oneself; *be in hiding*, be hidden. ¹**hid·ing-place** *n.* place where sb. or sth. is or could be hidden.

²**hide** [haid] *n.* animal's skin, esp. as an article of commerce and manufacture; (humor.) human skin. ¹~**bound** *adj.* narrow-minded. **hid·ing** *n.* beating or whipping.

hid·e·ous ['hidiəs] *adj.* very ugly.

hi·er·ar·chy ['haiəra:ki] *n.* organization (esp. a Church) with grades of authority.

hi·er·o·glyph ['haiərouglif] *n.* picture of an object representing a word, syllable, or sound, as used in the ancient writing of the Egyptians and Mexicans. ~**ic** [,haiərou'glifik] *adj. & n.*

hig·gle·dy-pig·gle·dy ['higldi-'pigldi] *adj. & adv.* mixed up; without order.

high [hai] *adj.* (*-er, -est*). **1.** extending far upwards; measuring (the given distance) from bottom to top (cf. *tall* for men); chief; important; extreme; intense; noble; worthy. '~**lights**, parts of a picture, photograph, etc., reflecting most light. ~ **priest**, chief priest, esp. of Jews. '~**road**, important road. ~ **school**, one giving education more advanced than that of an elementary school. *the* ~ **seas**, the open ocean, away from the land. *a* ~ *sea*, one with big waves. ~ **tea**, early evening meal. *a man of* ~ (*worthy*) *principles*. **2.** (of time) at its peak: ~ *summer*. *It's* ~ *time you started*, is past the time for you to start. **3.** (of food) beginning to go bad. *adv.* in or to a ~ degree. *play* ~, play cards, etc., for large sums of money. *run* ~, (of the sea) be rough; (fig., of the feelings) be roused, excited. '~-**born** *adj.* born of a noble family. '~-**brow** *n. & adj.* (person) with tastes and interests considered superior to those of most people. '~-**flown** *adj.* (of speech, writing, etc.) sounding important but often not very sensible. '~-'**hand·ed** *adj.* overbearing. '~-**lands** *n. pl.* mountainous country, esp. the Highlands of NW. Scotland. '~-**land·er** *n.* native of these highlands. ~**ly** *adv.* in or to a ~ degree: *a* ~*ly paid man*; *to think* ~*ly of sb.* '~-'**mind·ed** *adj.* of morally ~ character. ~**ness** *n.* **1.** opp. of *lowness*. **2.** *His* (*Her, Your*) *H*~, title, form of respect, used of (to) princes(ses). '~-('**ly**)-'**strung** *adj.* sensitive; with nerves easily upset. '~-**way** *n.* public road, esp. main road. '~-**way·man** *n.* (in olden times) man, usu. on horseback, who robbed travellers by road after threatening violence.

hike [haik] *v.i. & n.* (go for a) long country walk. **hik·er** *n.*

hi·la·ri·ous [hi'lɛəriəs] *adj.* noisily merry. **hi·lar·i·ty** [hi'læriti] *n.*

hill [hil] *n.* small mountain; slope (on a road, etc.). **hil·ly** *adj.*
having many ~s. **hil·lock** *n.* small ~.

hilt [hilt] *n.* handle of a sword or dagger. *up to the* ~, completely.

him [him] *pron.* object form of *he*: *He loves my sister; and she loves him.* **him·self** [him'self] *pron.* *He cut himself. He said so, himself* (nobody else). *He did it by himself* (without help). *He sat by himself* (alone).

¹**hind** [haind] *n.* female deer.

²**hind** [haind] *adj.* (of things in pairs, front and back) at the back: *the* ~ *legs of a horse; the* ~ *wheels of a wagon.* ~**most** *adj.* farthest back.

hin·der ['hində•] *v.t.* obstruct; delay; prevent. **hin·drance** ['hindrəns] *n.* sth. that ~s.

Hin·du [hin'du:] *n.* person whose religion is Hinduism. **Hin·du·ism** ['hindu:izəm] *n.* a religion of India.

hinge [hindʒ] *n.* joint on which a lid, door, or gate, opens and shuts. *v.t. & i.* **1.** attach with a ~. **2.** ~ (*up*)*on*, (fig.) turn or depend upon.

Hinges

hint [hint] *n.* slight suggestion or indication. *v.t. & i.* give a ~: *I* ~*ed that he ought to work harder. I* ~*ed at his laziness.*

¹**hip** [hip] *n.* bony part of each side of the body just above the leg. See the picture at *back*.

²**hip** [hip] *n.* fruit of the wild rose.

³**hip** [hip] *int.* *Hip, hip, hurrah!* cry, cheer, of approval.

hip·po·drome ['hipədroum] *n.* place for horse or chariot races in ancient Greece and Rome; (modern use) open space or building for circuses or horse-riding displays, variety shows.

hip·po·pot·a·mus [,hipou'potəməs] *n.* large, thick-skinned African river animal. See the picture on page 247.

hire ['haiə*] *v.t.* obtain or allow the use or services of in return for fixed payment: to ~ a horse (a concert-hall); to ~ out boats. (Cf. *rent* for buildings occupied for a long period.) *n.* (money paid for) hiring: bicycles on ~; to pay for the ~ of a hall. '~'**ling** *n.* (usu. contemptuous) person whose services may be ~d. '~-'**pur·chase** *n.* system by which sth. ~d becomes the property of the ~r after a number of agreed payments have been made. **hir·er** *n.*

A hippopotamus

hir·sute ['hə:sju:t] *adj.* hairy.

his [hiz] *pron. and adj.* belonging to him.

hiss [his] *v.i. & t. & n.* (make the) sound of *s*, or that made by a snake; (make) such sounds to show disapproval: to ~ an actor off the stage; (make the) sound of water on a very hot surface.

his·to·ry ['histəri] *n.* (orderly description of) past events; branch of knowledge dealing with past events, political, social, economic, of a country or of the world. **his·tor·i·an** [his'tɔ:riən] *n.* writer of ~. **his·tor·ic** [his'tɔrik] *adj.* famous in ~; associated with past times. **his·tor·i·cal** [his'tɔrikl] *adj.* 1. of ~ (esp. as contrasted with legend and fiction): *historical events* (not imaginary). 2. based on ~: *historical novels and plays.*

his·tri·on·ic [,histri'ɔnik] *adj.* of drama, the theatre, acting: ~ *ability.* *n.* (pl.) theatrical display; speech and behaviour designed for effect, like that of an actor.

hit [hit] *v.t. & i.* (-tt-; p.t. & p.p. *hit*). 1. come against (sth.) with force; strike; give a stroke (1)

to. *hit it off with sb.*, agree with, get on well with. *be hard hit (by sth.)*, be much troubled; be severely affected. 2. hit (up)on (a plan, etc.), discover by chance. *n.* blow (1); stroke (1). *a lucky hit*, a successful attempt. *make a hit*, win general approval.

hitch [hitʃ] *v.t. & i.* 1. pull (up) with a quick movement: to ~ up one's trousers. 2. fasten, become fastened, on or to a hook, etc., or with a loop of rope, etc. *n.* 1. sudden pull. 2. kind of knot used by sailors. 3. sth. that stops progress: *Everything went off without a ~* (i.e. smoothly).

hitch-hike ['hitʃ'haik] *n.* travel by asking drivers of cars or lorries for free rides.

hith·er ['hiðə*] *adv.* (old use) here. ~'**to** [,hiðə'tu:] *adv.* up to now.

hive [haiv] *n.* 1. box (of wood, straw, etc.) made for bees to live in. 2. place full of busy people.

hoard [hɔ:d] *n.* carefully saved and guarded store of money, food, or other treasured objects; mass of facts. *v.i. & t.* save and store (up).

hoard·ing ['hɔ:diŋ] *n.* wooden fence round waste land, building work, etc., often covered with advertisements.

hoar-frost ['hɔ:frɔst] *n.* white frost; frozen moisture on the surface of leaves, roofs, etc.

hoarse [hɔ:s] *adj.* (-r, -st). (of the voice) rough and harsh; (of a person) having a ~ voice. ~**ly** *adv.*

hoar·y ['hɔ:ri, 'hɔəri] *adj.* grey or white with age; very old.

hoax [houks] *n.* mischievous trick played on sb. for a joke. *v.t.* deceive in this way.

hob [hɔb] *n.* flat metal shelf at the side of a fire-place where pans, etc., can be kept warm.

hob·ble ['hɔbl] *v.i. & t.* 1. walk as when lame, as when the feet or legs are hurting. 2. tie a horse's legs to keep it from going far away. *n.* limping way of walking.

hob·by ['hɔbi] *n.* interesting

occupation, not one's regular business, for one's leisure time. '~·**horse** *n.* wooden horse for children; (fig.) sb.'s favourite subject of conversation.

hob·gob·lin ['hɔb,gɔblin] *n.* imp.

hob·nail ['hɔbneil] *n.* short nail with a heavy head used for boot soles.

hob-nob ['hɔbnɔb] *v.i.* (-bb-). have a friendly talk, drink (*with* sb.).

hock [hɔk] *n.* middle joint of an animal's hind leg.

hock·ey ['hɔki] *n.* game played on a field or on ice by two teams of eleven or six players with curved sticks.

ho·cus-po·cus ['houkəs'poukəs] *n.* talk, behaviour, designed to draw away one's attention from sth.

hod [hɔd] *n.* light open box with a long handle used by workmen for carrying bricks, mortar, etc., on the shoulder.

hoe [hou] *n.* tool for loosening soil, cutting up weeds among growing crops. *v.t. & i.* work with a hoe.

hog [hɔg] *n.* castrated male pig; (fig.) dirty, greedy person. *go the whole hog,* do sth. thoroughly.

hoist [hɔist] *v.t. & n.* (lift up with) apparatus of ropes and pulleys, or kind of elevator (esp. on a warship): *ammunition ~s.*

¹**hold** [hould] *v.t. & i.* (p.t. & p.p. held). 1. have and keep fast in or with the hand(s) or some other part of the body, or with a tool, etc.; keep or support (oneself or a part of the body) in a certain position or manner. 2. (with adv. & prep.): ~ *back,* show unwillingness to do sth.; ~ *sth. back,* keep it secret; ~ *sb.* (oneself) *back,* restrain, deter; ~ *by* (*to*), keep to (a purpose, etc.); ~ *forth,* preach, talk at length; ~ *off,* keep at a distance; ~ *out,* (a) keep one's position or strength; (b) last; ~ *out sth.* (e.g. hopes), offer; ~ *sth. over,* postpone it; ~ *sb.* or *sth. up,* (a) delay; (b) stop by force for the purpose of robbery; ~ *with,* approve of. 3. (be able to) contain: *a trunk ~ing all my*

clothes. 4. have or keep in mind; consider: *to ~ strange opinions;* *to ~ (the view) that the soul is immortal.* 5. restrain; keep back: ~ *one's breath;* ~ *one's hand;* ~ *one's tongue* (*one's peace*), be silent. 6. be the owner or tenant of: *to ~ shares* (*land*); occupy (a place or office): *to ~ office,* to be in a position of authority. 7. have (a meeting, debate, conversation, examination). 8. remain the same; keep or stay in the same position, etc.: *How long will the fine weather ~?* ~ *good,* be still in force; be valid. *H~ hard!* (colloq.) Don't go on doing that! ~ *one's own* (*one's ground*), not give way; keep one's position. *n.* 1. act, manner, or power, of ~ing: *to catch* (*get, have, keep, lose*) ~ *of sth.* 2. part or place that may be used for ~ing. (Cf. *foot~.*) '~·**all** *n.* roomy, soft bag (q.v.), with handles, for carrying one's belongings. ~·**er** *n.* person who ~s sth.: 'office-~ers; thing that ~s sth.: 'pen-~er. ~·**ing** *n.* sth. held, esp. land ('small-~ings) or shares in a business. '~-**up** *n.* act of ~ing up (see *hold* (2) *up*): *a traffic ~up; a bank ~-up.*

²**hold** [hould] *n.* part of ship below decks where cargo is stored.

hole [houl] *n.* opening or hollow place in a solid body; animal's burrow; hollow place in the surface of the ground made by digging, etc. *pick ~s in,* find fault with. *in a ~,* (colloq.) in an awkward situation. ~ *and corner* (methods, etc.), secret; not open and straightforward. *v.t.* make ~s in; put into a ~.

hol·i·day ['hɔlədi, -idi] *n.* day(s) of rest from work. *bank ~,* weekday on which all the banks are closed by law, usu. a general ~.

ho·li·ness, see *holy.*

hol·low ['hɔlou] *adj.* 1. not solid; with a hole or empty space inside: *a ~ tree.* 2. (of sounds) as if coming from this ~. 3. (fig.) unreal; false; insincere: ~ *words* (*sympathy*). 4. sunken: ~ *cheeks;* ~-*eyed.* **adv.**

(colloq.) (*beat sb.*) ~, completely. *n.* ~ place; hole; valley. *v.t.* make a ~ in: *river banks* ~*ed out by water*.

hol·ly ['holi] *n.* evergreen bush with hard, dark-green, sharp-pointed leaves and red berries.

hol·ly·hock ['holihok] *n.* tall garden plant with brightly coloured flowers.

hol·o·caust ['holǝko:st] *n.* large-scale destruction, esp. of human lives by fire.

hol·ster ['houlstǝ*] *n.* leather case for a pistol or revolver.

ho·ly ['houli] *adj.* (-ier, -iest). 1. of God; associated with God or with religion: *the Holy Bible*; *the Holy Land*, where Jesus lived; *Holy Week*, before Easter. 2. devoted to religion: *a ~ man*; *living a ~ life*. **ho·li·ness** *n.* 1. being ~ or sacred. 2. *His* (*Your*) *Holiness*, title used of (to) the Pope.

ho·ly·stone ['houlistoun] *v.t. & n.* (clean with) soft sandstone (formerly) used for scrubbing the wooden decks of ships.

hom·age ['homidʒ] *n.* 1. expression of respect, tribute paid (*to* a person, his merits): *paying* ~ *to* (*the genius of*) *Shakespeare*. 2. (feudal) acknowledgement of loyalty to a lord or ruler.

home [houm] *n.* 1. place where one lives, esp. with one's family; the land of one's birth. *at* ~ (*to*), expecting and ready to receive (visitors, etc.). (*be, feel, make oneself*) *at* ~, as if in one's own ~; not feeling strange. 2. institution or place (for the care of children, old or sick people). 3. (attrib.) of the ~: ~ *life*; of or inside the country in question: ~ *industries*. *the Home Office*, department controlling local government, police, etc., in England and Wales. *adv.* to, at, in, one's ~ or country. *bring sth.* ~ *to sb.*, make him fully conscious of it. '~**·less** *adj.* '~**·like** *adj.* '~**·made** *adj.* '~**·sick** *adj.* sad because away from ~. '~**·spun** *n. & adj.* (cloth) made at ~. '~**·stead** *n.* farmhouse with land

and out buildings. '~**·ward** *adj. & adv.* (going) towards ~. '~**·work** *n.* work which a pupil is required to do at ~.

home·ly ['houmli] *adj.* 1. simple and plain, of the sort used every day. 2. causing one to think of home or to feel at home: *a ~ atmosphere* (*boarding-house*). 3. (U.S.A., of persons) plain faced.

hom·i·cide ['homisaid] *n.* killing, killer, of a human being. **hom·i·ci·dal** [,homi'saidl] *adj.*

hom·o·ge·neous [,homou'dʒi:-njǝs] *adj.* (formed of parts) of the same sort.

hom·o·nym ['homǝnim] *n.* word with the same form or sound as another but different in meaning, e.g. *pail, pale*.

hone [houn] *n.* stone used for sharpening tools. *v.t.* sharpen on a ~.

hon·est ['onist] *adj.* not telling lies; not cheating or stealing; straightforward. ~**·ly** *adv.* **hon·es·ty** *n.*

hon·ey ['hʌni] *n.* sweet, sticky, yellowish liquid made by bees from nectar. '~**·comb** *n.* structure of six-sided cells made by bees for ~ and eggs. *v.t.* fill with holes, tunnels, etc. **hon·eyed, hon·ied** ['hʌnid] *adj.* (of words, etc.) sweet. '~**·moon** *n.* holiday taken by a newly married couple. '~**·suck·le** *n.* sweet-scented climbing plant.

hon·o·ra·ri·um [,onǝ'rɛǝriǝm] *n.* fee offered (not claimed) for services.

hon·o·ra·ry ['onǝrǝri] *adj.* 1. (shortened to *hon.*) (of a position) unpaid: *the ~ secretary*. 2. (of a degree, rank, etc.) given as an honour, without the usual requirements: *an ~ vice-president*.

hon·our ['onǝ*] *n.* 1. high public regard; great respect: *win ~ in war*; *do ~ to the King*; *a guard of ~*; *a ceremony in ~ of sb.* 2. good personal character; reputation for good behaviour: *on my ~*, according to my reputation for telling the truth; *bound in ~* (but not by law) *to do sth.*; *word of ~*, solemn promise. 3. (as a polite formula): *May I have*

I

the ~ of your company at dinner?
4. (pl.) civilities to guests, visitors, etc.: *do the ~s (of),* act as host, guide, etc. **5.** *Your (His) H~,* form of address used to (of) some judges. **6.** person or thing bringing credit: *an ~ to the school.* **7.** (pl.) marks of respect, distinction, titles, etc.: *the ~s list* (of. titles, etc., conferred by the reigning Sovereign). *an ~s degree,* given for work with special distinction. *v.t.* **1.** feel ~ for; show ~ to; confer ~ on. **2.** accept and pay (a cheque, etc.) when due. *~ a promise,* keep it. **~·a·ble** ['ɒnər-əbl] *adj.* **1.** worthy of, bringing, consistent with, ~ (1), (2): *~able conduct (burial).* **2.** (shortened to *Hon.*) title of judges and other high officials, of members of the House of Commons (when referred to during a debate), and of children of some peers.

hood [hud] *n.* **1.** bag-like covering for the head and neck, often fastened to a cloak so that it can hang down at the back when not in use. **2.** folding roof of a carriage or motor-car. **3.** ~-shaped or ~-like thing. **~·ed** ['hudid] *adj.* having, wearing, a ~.

hood·wink ['hudwiŋk] *v.t.* deceive; trick; mislead.

hoof [hu:f] *n.* (pl. *hoofs* [hu:fs] or *hooves* [hu:vz]). horny part of the foot of a horse, etc.

hook [huk] *n.* **1.** curved or bent piece of metal, etc., for catching hold of sth. or for hanging sth. on. **2.** curved tool for cutting (grain, etc.) or chopping (branches, etc.). *by ~ or by crook,* by one means or another. *v.t. & i.* fasten, be fastened, catch, with a ~ or ~s: *a dress that ~s (is ~ed) at the back; to ~ a fish.* **hooked** [hukt] *adj.* made with, having, ~s; ~-shaped. **'~-worm** *n.* worm that ~s itself to the intestine and causes disease.

hool·i·gan ['hu:ligən] *n.* disorderly man (usu. one of a gang) making disturbances in the streets or other public places. **~ism** *n.*

hoop [hu:p] *n.* band of wood or metal (put round a barrel); similar band bowled along the ground as a plaything.

hoot [hu:t] *n.* **1.** cry of an owl. **2.** sound made by a motor-car horn, steam-whistle, etc. **3.** shout or cry expressing disapproval or scorn. *v.i. & t.* make a ~ or ~s (*at*); drive away by ~s: *to ~ an actor off the stage.* **~·er** *n.* siren (2) (e.g. in a factory).

hooves, see *hoof.*

¹hop [hop] *n.* tall climbing plant with flowers growing in clusters; (pl.) these flowers, dried and used in beer-making.

²hop [hop] *v.i. & t.* (*-pp-*). **1.** (of persons) jump with one foot; (of birds) jump forward on both feet. **2.** cross (*over*), go (*across*), by ~ping. *n.* action of ~ping; short jump; stage of journey by plane.

hope [houp] *n.* **1.** feeling of expectation and desire; feeling of trust or confidence. **2.** cause for ~; person, circumstance, etc., on which ~ is based. *v.t. & i.* expect and desire: *to ~ (for sth., that . . ., to have, etc.).* **~·ful** *adj.* having or giving ~. **~·ful·ly** *adv.* **~·less** *adj.* having no ~; giving or promising no ~; (of persons) incurable: *a ~less invalid.*

hop·per ['hopə*] *n.* **1.** structure like an inverted cone or pyramid through which grain passes to a mill, coal to a furnace, etc. **2.** young locust.

horde [hɔ:d] *n.* **1.** wandering tribe: *~s of Tartars.* **2.** (used scornfully) large crowd.

ho·ri·zon [hə'raizn] *n.* line at which earth or sea and sky seem to meet. **hor·i·zon·tal** [,hori-'zontl] *adj.* parallel to the ~; flat or level. **hor·i·zon·tal·ly** *adv.*

horn [hɔ:n] *n.* **1.** one of the hard, pointed, usu. curved, outgrowths on the heads of cattle, deer, and some other animals; the substance of these. **2.** ~-like part (e.g. on the head of a snail). *draw in one's ~s,* show less willingness to do sth.; draw back. **3.** (sorts of) wind-instrument: *a huntsman's ~;*

French ~ (made of brass); instrument for making warning sounds: *a fog-~*; *a motor-car ~*. **horned** *adj.* having ~s (1): *~ed cattle.* '~·**pipe** *n.* (music for) sailor's lively dance. ~·**y** *adj.* of, like, ~: *hands ~y from hard work.*

hor·net ['hɔ:nit] *n.* large insect of the wasp family with a powerful sting.

hor·o·scope ['hɔrəskoup] *n.* diagram of, observation of, the position of stars at a certain time (e.g. a person's birth).

hor·ror ['hɔrə*] *n.* (sth. causing) feeling of extreme fear or dislike. '~-**struck**, '~-,**strick·en** *adj.* overcome with ~. **hor·ri·ble** ['hɔrəbl] *adj.* **hor·rid** ['hɔrid] *adj.* causing ~; (colloq.) disagreeable; annoying. **hor·ri·fy** ['hɔrifai] *v.t.* fill with ~; shock.

hors de com·bat ['ɔ:də'kɔmba:] (French) *pred. adj.* wounded, disabled, and unable to continue (fighting).

hors-d'œuvre ['ɔ:'də:vrə] (Fr.) *n.* tasty dish served before the main meal.

horse [hɔ:s] *n.* **1.** see the picture, also *stallion, mare.* **2.** soldiers mounted on ~s: *~ and foot*, cavalry and infantry. **3.** wooden framework with legs (for jumping over in physical training). '~·**back** *n. on ~back*, (riding) on a ~. '~·**man**, '~·,**wom·an** *n.* one skilled in riding and managing ~s. '~·**man·ship** *n.* skill in riding ~s. '~·**play** *n.* rough, noisy fun. '~·**pow·er** *n.* (shortened to h.p.) unit of power (of engines, etc.). '~·,**rad·ish** *n.* plant with hot-tasting root used for meat sauces. '~·**sense** *n.* ordinary wisdom. '~·**shoe** *n.* ∩-shaped metal shoe for a ~. '~·**whip** *n. & v.t.* (-*pp*-). (thrash with a) whip for ~s. **hor·sy** *adj.* of ~s or ~-racing; (esp. of a person) showing by dress, speech, etc., a fondness for ~s.

hor·ti·cul·ture ['hɔ:tikʌltʃə*] *n.* (art of) growing flowers, fruit, and vegetables. **hor·ti·cul·tu·ral** [,hɔ:ti'kʌltʃərəl] *adj.*

¹**hose** [houz] *n.* rubber or canvas tube for directing water on to gardens, fires, etc. *v.t.* water (a garden, etc.) with a ~; wash (a motor-car, etc.) by using a ~.

²**hose** [houz] *n.* **1.** (trade name for) stockings. **2.** close-fitting outer garment from the waist to the knees or feet, worn by men in former times: *doublet and ~*. **ho·sier** ['houʒə*] *n.* shopkeeper who sells men's socks, collars, underwear, etc. **ho·siery** ['houʒəri] *n.* such goods.

hos·pice ['hɔspis] *n.* house of rest for travellers, esp. one kept by a religious order (e.g. in the Swiss mountains).

hos·pit·a·ble ['hɔspitəbl] *adj.* giving, liking to give, hospitality.

A horse   A horseshoe

hos·pi·tal ['hɔspitl] *n.* place where people are treated for, nursed through, their sickness or injuries.

hos·pi·tal·i·ty [,hɔspi'tæliti] *n.* friendly and generous reception and entertainment of guests, esp. in one's own home.

¹**host** [houst] *n.* **1.** person who entertains guests. **2.** innkeeper; hotel-keeper. '**hos·tess** *n.* '**air·**'**hos·tess** *n.* woman responsible for passengers' comfort during air-travel.

²**host** [houst] *n.* **1.** great number: *~s of friends*; *a ~ of difficulties*. **2.** (old use) army.

³**host** [houst] *n. the ~*, bread eaten at Holy Communion.

hos·tage ['hɔstidʒ] *n.* person (less often, thing) given or seized as a pledge that demands will be satisfied.

hos·tel ['hɔstəl] *n.* building in which board and lodging are provided (with the support of authorities concerned) for students and others under their care. *youth* ~, one for young people on walking-tours. ~·**ry** *n.* (old use) inn.

hos·tess, see ¹*host.*

hos·tile ['hostail] *adj.* of an enemy: *a ~ army*; feeling or showing enmity (*to*); ~ *looks*; ~ *to reform.* ~·**ly** *adv.* **hos·til·i·ty** [hos'tiliti] *n.* enmity; (pl.) (acts of) war.

hot [hot] *adj.* (*-tt-*). **1.** having great heat or high temperature (cf. *feverish*); producing a burning sensation on the tongue. *get into hot water*, get into trouble (for foolish acts). *hot air*, boastful or foolish talk. **2.** (of a scent in hunting) strong and fresh: *hot on the trail*, near to what is being pursued. **3.** (as *adv.*) eagerly; hotly: *blow hot and cold*, be favourable and unfavourable by turns. '**hot-bed** *n.* bed of earth heated by rotting manure to quicken growth; (fig.) place, conditions, favourable to growth (of crime, etc.). '**hot-'head(ed)** *n.* (*adj.*) impetuous (person). '**hot·house** *n.* heated building, usu. of glass, for growing delicate plants. '**hot-pot** *n.* dish of meat, potatoes, etc., cooked in a tight-lidded pot. **hot·ly** *adv.* (fig.) eagerly; passionately: *hotly pursued by the enemy.* **hot·ness** *n.*

hotch-potch ['hotʃpotʃ] *n.* jumble.

ho·tel [hou'tel] *n.* building where meals and rooms are provided for travellers.

hound [haund] *n.* **1.** (kinds of) dog used for hunting and racing: *fox~*; *blood~*; *grey~*. **2.** contemptible man. *v.t.* chase or hunt with, or as with, ~s: ~*ed by one's creditors.*

hour ['auə*] *n.* **1.** 60 minutes. *at the eleventh* ~, when almost too late. *the small* ~*s*, the three or four ~*s* after midnight. **2.** point of time by the clock: *a clock that strikes the* ~*s.* **3.** (pl.) fixed periods of time, esp. for work: *office* ~*s, 9.30 a.m. to 5.30 p.m.*; *to keep early (late, etc.) *~*s*, get up and go to bed

early (late, etc.). **4.** a particular, or the present, point in time: *in the* ~ *of danger*; *questions of the* ~ (i.e. now being discussed). ~·**ly** *adj. & adv.* (done, occurring) every ~.

house [haus] *n.* (pl. ['hauziz]). **1.** building, esp. one constructed as a home for a family (*dwelling-house*) (cf. *hotel, block of flats, offices, factory*); *keep* ~, manage the affairs of a ~hold. **2.** *Houses of Parliament*, buildings used by the British Parliament. **3.** (spectators, audience, in a) theatre: *a full* ~ (i.e. all seats filled); *bring down the* ~, (of an actor) win very loud applause. **4.** family line: *the H~ of Windsor* (the present British Royal Family). **5.** business firm. [hauz] *v.t.* **1.** provide ~s for: *the housing problem*; *a housing estate*, large group of dwelling-~s planned and built by one organization. **2.** store in a ~ or room: *Where to* ~ *all my books is a problem.* '~-·a·**gent** *n.* person who sells or lets ~s for others. '~·**boat** *n.* boat fitted up for living in on a river, etc. '~·**break·er** *n.* **1.** workman who pulls down old buildings. **2.** man who forces his way into a ~ by day (cf. *burglar* by night) to commit crime. '~·**hold** *n.* all persons (family and servants) living in a ~. '~·**hold·er** *n.* person leasing or owning and occupying a ~ (not one living in a hotel, in lodgings, etc.). '~·**keep·er** *n.* woman employed to manage the affairs of a ~hold. '~·**maid** *n.* woman servant in a ~, esp. one who cleans rooms. '~·**mas·ter** *n.* teacher in charge of a school boarding-~. '~·**wife** *n.* **1.** woman who does the cleaning, cooking, shopping, etc., for her family. (Cf. *housekeeper*.) **2.** ['hazif] small folding case of needles, thread, etc. '~·**work** *n.* work done in a ~ (cleaning, cooking, etc.).

hove, see *heave.*

hov·el ['hovl] *n.* small, dirty house.

hov·er ['hovə*] *v.i.* (of birds)

remain in the air over one place; (of persons) wait about. '**~craft** *n.* craft that can remain still or travel along while raised above the surface of land or water by air-pressure from its engines.

how [hau] *adv.* **1.** in what way or manner; by what means; in what degree; to what extent; in what state. **2.** introducing an indirect statement: *He told me how* (= that) *he had seen it in the newspaper.* **3.** introducing a question asking for an opinion, decision, etc.: *How about going for a walk* (shall we go or not)? *How's that for a beginner?* (expecting the answer, 'Very good'). **how·ev·er** [hau'evə*] *adv.* in whatever way or degree. *conj.* nevertheless; but yet.

how·dah ['haudə] *n.* (usu. covered) seat on an elephant's back.

howl [haul] *n.* long, loud cry (e.g., of a wolf); long cry of a person in pain or of sb. expressing scorn, amusement, etc. *v.i. & t.* utter such cries; make sounds suggesting these: *the wind ~ing through the trees*; *~ing with pain (laughter)*; *to ~ a speaker down.* **~·er** *n.* (colloq.) laughable mistake.

hub [hʌb] *n.* central part of a wheel; (fig.) centre of activity.

hub·bub ['hʌbʌb] *n.* confused noise (e.g. of many voices); uproar.

hud·dle ['hʌdl] *v.i. & t.* **1.** crowd or press together in disorder or distress: *sheep huddling together for warmth.* **2.** ~ (oneself) *up,* draw the knees up to the body for warmth.

¹**hue** [hju:] *n.* (shade of) colour.

²**hue** [hju:] *n. hue and cry,* general outcry of alarm (as when a criminal is being pursued, or when there is opposition to sth.).

huff [hʌf] *n. in a ~,* ill-tempered. **huf·fy** *adj.* (easily made) ill-tempered.

hug [hʌg] *v.t.* (-*gg*-). **1.** put the arms round tightly, esp. to show love. **2.** show fondness for (e.g. beliefs); (of a ship) keep close to (the coast). *n.* act of hugging.

huge [hju:dʒ] *adj.* very great.

hulk [hʌlk] *n.* **1.** old ship either not used or used (only in former times) as a prison. **2.** big clumsy person. **~·ing** *adj.* clumsy; big and awkward.

¹**hull** [hʌl] *v.t. & n.* (remove) outer covering (of beans, peas).

²**hull** [hʌl] *n.* body or frame of a ship.

hul·la·ba·loo [ˌhʌləbə'lu:] *n.* uproar; outcry; disturbance: *What a ~!*

hul·lo [hʌ'lou, hə-] *int.* cry expressing surprise, or to get attention; informal greeting.

hum [hʌm] *v.t. & i.* (-*mm*-). make a continuous sound like that made by bees; sing with closed lips: *to hum (a song) to oneself; a factory humming with activity; make things hum,* bring about a state of lively activity. *n.* humming sound: *the distant hum of traffic.* [hmm] *int.* used to express doubt. '**hum·ming-bird** *n.* bird whose rapidly moving wings make a humming sound.

hu·man ['hju:mən] *adj.* of man or mankind: *a ~ being,* a person. **~·ly** *adv.* (esp.) by ~ means: *all that was ~ly possible.*

hu·mane [hju'mein] *adj.* **1.** tender; kind-hearted. **2.** ~ *learning, studies,* other than science. **~·ly** *adv.* in a ~ (1) manner.

hu·man·ism ['hju:mənizəm] *n.* devotion to human interests; system concerned with ethical (not religious) standards and with the study of mankind.

hu·man·i·ta·ri·an [hju:ˌmæni'teəriən] *adj. & n.* (of, holding the views of, a) person working for the welfare of all human beings (by reducing suffering, reforming laws about punishment, etc.). **~·ism** *n.*

hu·man·i·ty [hju'mæniti] *n.* **1.** the human race; mankind. **2.** human nature. **3.** quality of being humane. **4.** *the humanities,* branches of learning concerned with Greek and Latin culture; literature, history, and philosophy.

hu·man·ize ['hju:mənaiz]

make or become human or humane (1).

hum·ble ['hʌmbl] *adj.* (-r, -st).
1. having or showing a modest opinion of oneself, one's powers, position, etc. **2.** poor; mean (1); low in rank, etc.: *men of ~ birth*; *~ occupations* (e.g. street-cleaning). *v.t.* make ~; make lower in rank or self-opinion. **hum·bly** *adv.*

hum·bug ['hʌmbʌg] *n.* dishonest and deceiving act, behaviour, talk, person, etc.; nonsense. *v.t.* (-*gg*-). deceive or trick (*sb. into, out of*).

hum·drum ['hʌmdrʌm] *adj.* dull; commonplace; monotonous.

hu·mid ['hju:mid] *adj.* (esp. of air, climate) damp. ~**i·ty** [hju:'miditi] *n.* dampness (of atmosphere).

hu·mil·i·ate [hju:'milieit] *v.t.* cause to feel ashamed or humble. **hu·mil·i·a·tion** [hju:ˌmili'eifən] *n.*

hu·mil·i·ty [hju:'militi] *n.* humble condition or state of mind.

hum·mock ['hʌmək] *n.* hillock.

hu·mour ['hju:mə*] *n.* **1.** (capacity to cause or feel) amusement: *a story full of ~*; *to have a good sense of ~*. **2.** person's state of mind (esp. at a particular time); temper: *in a good* (*bad*) *~*; *not in the ~ for work*, not feeling inclined to work. *v.t.* give way to, gratify (a person), his desires). **hu·mor·ist** *n.* humorous talker or writer. **hu·mor·ous** *adj.* having or showing a sense of ~; causing amusement: *humorous remarks.*

hump [hʌmp] *n.* fleshy lump, e.g. on a camel's back or (as a deformity) on a person's back. '~**back** *n.* person with a ~ on the back.

humph [hʌmf] *int.* used to show doubt or dissatisfaction.

hu·mus ['hju:məs] *n.* earth formed by decay of vegetable matter (dead leaves, plants, etc.).

hunch [hʌntʃ] *n.* **1.** hump. **2.** thick piece (of bread, etc.). **3.** (colloq.) *have a ~ that . . .*, have an idea or a feeling that

. . . . *v.t.* bend (*out, up*) to form a hump; *to ~ the shoulders.* '~**back** *n.* = humpback.

hun·dred ['hʌndrəd] *n. & adj.* 100. **hun·dredth** *adj. & n.* next in order after the 99th; ¹⁄₁₀₀. '~**weight** *n.* (written *cwt.*) ¹⁄₂₀ of a ton.

hung, see hang.

hun·ger ['hʌngə*] *n.* **1.** need, desire, for food: *to die of ~*; *to satisfy one's ~*. **2.** (fig.) any strong desire: *a ~ for adventure.* *v.i.* feel, suffer from, ~; have a strong desire (for). '~**strike** *n.* refusal to eat food in order to get release from prison, etc.

hun·gry ['hʌngri] *adj.* (-*ier, -iest*). feeling, showing signs of, ~. **hun·gri·ly** *adv.*

hunk [hʌnk] *n.* = hunch (2).

hunt [hʌnt] *v.t. & i.* **1.** go after (wild animals) for food or sport. **2.** look for; try to find: *to ~ for a lost book*; *to ~ sb. or sth. down,* look for, pursue, and find; *~ sth. up,* search for (e.g. records, bits of information). *n.* the action of ~ing. ~**er** *n.* '~**ress** *n.* '**hunts·man** *n.*

hur·dle ['hə:dl] *n.* **1.** movable oblong frame of wood, etc., used for making temporary fences (e.g. for sheep pens). **2.** light frame to be jumped over in a ~*race* (for running and jumping). **hurd·ler** *n.* runner in a ~ race.

hurl [hə:l] *v.t.* throw violently.

hur·ly-bur·ly ['hə:li,bə:li] *n.* noisy commotion; uproar.

hur·rah [hu'rɑ:], **hur·ray** [hu'rei] *int.* cry of welcome, joy, triumph.

hur·ri·cane ['hʌrikən, -kein] *n.* violent wind-storm.

hur·ry ['hʌri] *n.* haste; wish to get sth. done quickly; eager haste; (with neg. or in interr.) need for haste: *There's no ~. What's the hurry?* *in a ~*, acting, anxious to act, quickly. *v.t. & i.* (cause to) move or do sth. quickly or too quickly; *~ up,* be quick; *~ away*, go off quickly; *~ (over) one's work.* **hur·ried** *adj.* done in a ~. **hur·ried·ly** *adv.*

hurt [həːt] *v.t. & i.* (p.t. & p.p. *hurt*). cause injury or pain to ; come to harm. *n.* harm ; injury. ~**ful** *adj.* causing suffering to.

hurtle ['həːtl] *v.t. & i.* (cause to) rush violently.

hus·band ['hʌzbənd] *n.* man to whom a woman is married. *v.t.* use sparingly : *to ~ one's strength.* ~**'man** *n.* (old use) farmer. ~**'ry** *n.* farming.

hush [hʌʃ] *v.t. & i.* make or become silent ; (imperative) Be silent! ~ *sth. up*, prevent it from becoming public knowledge. *n.* silence ; quiet.

husk [hʌsk] *n.* dry outer covering of seeds, esp. grain. *v.t.* remove the ~s from. ~**'y** *adj.* **1.** (dry) like ~s. **2.** (of the voice) hoarse. ~**'i·ly** *adv.* ~**'i·ness** *n.*

hus·sar [hu'zaː] *n.* soldier of a light cavalry regiment.

hus·sy ['hʌzi] *n.* worthless woman ; ill-mannered girl.

hus·tle ['hʌsl] *v.t. & i.* push roughly ; (make sb.) act quickly and with energy. *n.* quick and energetic activity.

hut [hʌt] *n.* small, roughly made house or shelter.

hutch [hʌtʃ] *n.* box with a front of wire-netting, esp. one for rabbits.

hy·a·cinth ['haiəsinθ] *n.* kind of plant growing from a bulb ; its sweet-smelling flowers.

hy·ae·na = hyena.

hy·brid ['haibrid] *n. & adj.* (animal, plant, etc.) from parents of different sorts : *A mule is a ~ (animal).*

hy·dra ['haidrə] *n.* (in old Greek stories) great sea-serpent with many heads that grow again if cut off.

hy·drant ['haidrənt] *n.* pipe (esp. in a street) to which water hoses can be attached for street-cleaning, putting out fires, etc.

hy·drau·lic [hai'drɔːlik] *adj.* of water moving through pipes, etc. ; worked by water-power.

hy·dro- ['haidrou] *prefix.* **1.** of water. **2.** of hydrogen. '~**e·lec·tric** *adj.* of electricity produced by water-power. ~**'gen** ['haidrədʒən] *n.* gas without colour, taste, or smell, that combines with oxygen to form water. ~**'pho·bi·a** *n.* = rabies.

hy·e·na [hai'iːnə] *n.* flesh-eating wild animal, like a wolf, with a laugh-like cry.

hy·giene ['haidʒiːn] *n.* science of, rules for, healthy living. **hy·gien·ic** [hai'dʒiːnik] *adj.* of ~ ; likely to promote health ; free from disease germs. **hy·gien·i·cal·ly** *adv.*

hymn [him] *n.* song of praise to God, esp. one for use in a religious service. ~**al** ['himnəl] *n.* book of ~s.

hy·per- ['haipə*] *prefix.* too : ~*critical* ; ~*sensitive.*

hy·per·bo·le [hai'pəːbəli] *n.* exaggerated statement made for effect.

hy·phen ['haifən] *n.* the mark -, used for joining or dividing words : *Anglo-French.*

hyp·no·sis [hip'nousis] *n.* state like deep sleep in which a person's acts may be controlled by another person. **hyp·not·ic** [hip'nɔtik] *adj.* of ~. **hyp·no·tism** ['hipnətizm] *n.* production of ~. **hyp·no·tize** ['hipnətaiz] *v.t.* produce ~ in (sb.).

hy·poc·ri·sy [hi'pɔkrəsi] *n.* (making a) pretence of virtue or goodness. **hyp·o·crite** ['hipə-krit] *n.* person guilty of ~. **hyp·o·crit·i·cal** [,hipə'kritikl] *adj.* of ~ or a hypocrite. **hyp·o·crit·i·cal·ly** *adv.*

hy·po·der·mic [,haipou'dəːmik] *adj.* put in beneath the skin : ~ *needle (syringe),* used for giving ~ injections (of drugs).

hy·poth·e·sis [hai'pɔθisis] *n.* (pl. *-eses* [-isiːz]). idea, suggestion, put forward as a starting-point for reasoning or explanation. **hy·po·thet·i·cal** [,haipə'θetikl] *adj.* of, based on, a ~, not on certain knowledge.

hys·te·ri·a [his'tiəriə] *n.* **1.** disturbance of the nervous system, with outbursts of emotion, often uncontrollable. **2.** senseless, uncontrolled excitement. **hys·ter·i·cal** [his'terikl] *adj.* caused by, suffering from, ~. **hys·ter·ics** [his'teriks] *n. pl.* attack(s) of ~ : *go into hysterics.*

I

I [ai] ***pron.*** used by a speaker or writer in referring to himself.

An iceberg

ice [ais] ***n.*** frozen water. *break the ~*, get (people) on friendly terms; get well started on sth. ***v.t. & i.*** **1.** make (food, etc.) very cold: *~d water.* **2.** cover, become covered, with a coating of ~; cover (a cake) with sugary mixture. **'~·berg** ***n.*** mass of ~ (broken off a glacier) floating in the sea. **'~-cream** ***n.*** frozen cream or custard. **'~-bound** **('~-free)** ***adj.*** (of harbours, etc.) obstructed by (free from) ~. **'~-field, '~-pack** ***n.*** wide area of ~ covering the sea. **i·ci·cle** ['aisikl] ***n.*** hanging piece of ~ formed by the freezing of dripping water. **'ic·ing** ***n.*** **1.** sugary coating for (on) a cake. **2.** formation of ice on the wings of an aircraft. **i·cy** ['aisi] ***adj.*** (*-ier, -iest*). very cold; (fig.)unfriendly in manner; covered with ~. **i·ci·ly** ***adv.***

i·con ['aikɔn] ***n.*** (Eastern Church) painting of a sacred person.

i·dea [ai'diə] ***n.*** **1.** thought; picture in the mind. **2.** plan; scheme: *He's full of new ~s.*

i·deal [ai'diəl] ***adj.*** **1.** satisfying one's highest ideas; perfect: *~ weather.* **2.** (opposite of *real*) existing only as an idea; not likely to be achieved. ***n.*** idea, example, looked upon as perfect: *the high ~s of the Christian religion.* **~·ism** ***n.*** **1.** living according to, being guided by, one's ~s. **2.** (opposite of *realism*) (in art) imaginative treatment so that things are pictured in

perfect form. **~·ize** ***v.t.*** make, think of, as ~. **~·ly** ***adv.***

i·den·ti·cal [ai'dentikl] ***adj.*** the same. *~ with*, like in every way.

i·den·ti·fy [ai'dentifai] ***v.t.*** **1.** say, show, prove, who or what sb. or sth. is. **2.** *identify oneself with*, give support to, associate oneself with. **i·den·ti·fi·ca·tion** [ai,dentifi'keiʃən] ***n.***

i·den·ti·ty [ai'dentiti] ***n.*** **1.** state of being identical. **2.** who sb. is; what sth. is.

i·de·ol·o·gy [,aidi'ɔlədʒi] ***n.*** system of ideas, esp. for an economic or political system.

id·i·om ['idiəm] ***n.*** **1.** (special form of a) language peculiar to a class of people, a part of a country, etc. (e.g. *in order to*) **2.** word-group whose meaning must be learnt as a whole. **id·i·o·mat·ic** [,idiə'mætik] ***adj.***

id·i·o·syn·cra·sy [,idiə'siŋkrəsi] ***n.*** kind of behaviour, view, peculiar to sb.

id·i·ot ['idiət] ***n.*** stupid person; person of feeble mind. **id·i·o·cy** ['idiəsi] ***n.*** stupidity. **id·i·ot·ic** [,idi'ɔtik] ***adj.*** stupid. **id·i·ot·i·cal·ly** ***adv.***

i·dle ['aidl] ***adj.*** (*-r, -st*). **1.** not being worked; not being used: *~ machinery.* **2.** (of persons) not working: *~ because of trade disputes.* **3.** lazy; not working hard: *an ~, worthless boy.* **4.** useless; worthless: *~ gossip.* ***v.i. & t.*** be ~; do nothing: *~ away one's time*, pass one's time doing nothing. **i·dler** ***n.*** person who ~s. **i·dly** ***adv.*** **~·ness** ***n.***

i·dol ['aidl] ***n.*** **1.** image (in wood, stone, etc.) of a god. **2.** sb. or sth. greatly loved or admired. **~·a·ter** [ai'dɔlətə*] ***n.*** person who worships ~s. **~·a·trous** ***adj.*** of ~ worship. **~·a·try** ***n.*** worship of ~s. **~·ize** ['aidəlaiz] ***v.t.*** love or admire too much.

i·dyll ['aidil, 'idil] ***n.*** short description, usu. in verse, of a simple scene or event; scene, etc., suitable for this. **i·dyl·lic** [ai'dilik, i'dilik] ***adj.***

if [if] ***conj.*** **1.** on condition that; supposing that: *If you want to go there I will take you. If it* *rains, we shall not go.* **2.** when; whenever: *If I do not wear my spectacles I get a headache.* **3.** although: *I will do it, (even) if it takes me all day.* **4.** whether: *Do you know if Mr Smith is at home?* **5.** as *if,* see *as,* II, (9). **6.** *If only I had known that* (emphasizing one's regret that one did not know it).

ig·loo ['iglu:] *n.* Eskimo's winter hut made of blocks of hard snow.

ig·ne·ous ['igniəs] *adj.* (of rocks) formed by heat of volcanic action.

ig·nite [ig'nait] *v.t. & i.* set on fire; take fire. **ig·ni·tion** [ig-'nifən] *n.*

ig·no·ble [ig'noubl] *adj.* dishonourable; of low repute.

ig·no·min·i·ous [,ignə'miniəs] *adj.* bringing contempt, disgrace, shame; dishonourable. **ig·no·mi·ny** ['ignəmini] *n.* public dishonour or shame; dishonourable act or behaviour.

ig·no·rant ['ignərənt] *adj.* having, showing, little or no knowledge; not aware (*of* sth.). **ig·no·rance** *n.* the state of being ~. **ig·no·ra·mus** [,ignə'reiməs] *n.* (pl. *~es* [-iz]). ~ person.

ig·nore [ig'nɔ:ˈ] *v.t.* take no notice of; refuse to take notice of.

il- *prefix.* opposite of; not. **il·le·gal** [i'li:gəl], **il·leg·i·ble** [i'ledʒibl], **il·le·git·i·mate** [,ili'dʒitimit], **il·log·i·cal** [i'lɔdʒikl] *adj.*

ill [il] *adj.* **1.** (usu. predic.) in bad health: *fall ill; be taken ill.* **2.** (attrib.) bad: *ill health; ill breeding.* *n.* **1.** evil: *to do ill.* **2.** misfortune; trouble: *the many ills of life.* *adv.* badly; imperfectly; unfavourably. *ill at ease,* uncomfortable, embarrassed. *I can ill afford it,* can hardly afford the money for it. **ill-'bred** *adj.* badly brought up; rough in behaviour. **ill-'fat·ed** *adj.* destined to misfortune. **ill-'fa·voured** *adj.* (of a person) of unattractive appearance. **ill-'got·ten** *adj.* gained by wrong or unlawful methods. **ill-'na·tured** *adj.* bad-tempered. **ill·ness** *n.* being ill; disease.

ill-'treat, ill-'use *v.t.* treat badly or cruelly.

il·lic·it [i'lisit] *adj.* unlawful.

il·lit·er·ate [i'litərit] *n. & adj.* (person) with little or no education, unable to read or write. **il·lit·er·a·cy** *n.*

il·lu·mi·nate [i'lu:mineit] *v.t.* **1.** give light to; throw light on. **2.** decorate (streets, etc.) with bright lights (as a sign of rejoicing, etc.). **il·lu·mi·na·tion** [i,lu:mi'neifən] *n.* lighting; (esp. pl.) lights, etc., used to ~ (2) a town. **il·lu·mine** [i'lu:min] *v.t.* give light to or on.

il·lu·sion [i'lu:ʒən] *n.* (the seeing of) sth. that does not really exist or of sth. as different from the reality; false idea or belief. **il·lu·sive** [i'lu:siv], **il·lu·so·ry** [i'lu:səri] *adj.* unreal; caused by ~.

il·lus·trate ['iləstreit] *v.t.* explain by examples, pictures, etc.; provide (a book, etc.) with pictures, diagrams, etc. **il·lus·tra·tor** *n.* person making illustrations for a book, etc. **il·lus·tra·tion** [,ilə'streifən] *n.* illustrating sth. that ~s.

il·lus·tri·ous [i'lʌstriəs] *adj.* celebrated; greatly distinguished.

im- *prefix.* opposite of; not: **im·ma·'te·ri·al, im·ma·'ture, im·'meas·ur·a·ble, im·'mo·bile, im·'mod·er·ate, im·'mor·al, im·'mu·ta·ble, im·'pa·tient, im·'pen·i·tent, im·'per·fect, im·'pos·si·ble, im·'prob·a·ble, im·'pru·dent, im·'pure** *adj.*

im·age ['imidʒ] *n.* **1.** likeness or copy of the shape of sb. or sth., esp. one made in wood, stone, or metal. **2.** mental picture. **3.** simile. **4.** *be the (very) ~ of (sb.),* be exactly like. **im·a·ger·y** *n.* ~s(1); use of ~s (3) in writing.

i·mag·ine [i'mædʒin] *v.t.* **1.** form a picture of in the mind. **2.** think of (sth.) as probable; take (an idea, etc.) into one's head. **i·mag·in·a·ble** *adj.* that can be ~d. **i·mag·i·na·ry** *adj.* unreal; existing only in the mind. **i·mag·i·na·tion** [i,mædʒi'neifən] *n.* power of the mind to ~; sth. ~d. **im·ag·i·na·tive** [i'mædʒinətiv] *adj.* of, having, using, showing, imagination.

i·mam [i'mɑːm] *n.* title of various Muslim leaders.

im·be·cile ['imbisiːl] *adj.* weakminded; stupid. *n.* ~ person. **im·be·cil·i·ty** [ˌimbi'siliti] *n.* stupidity.

im·bed [im'bed] *v.t.* (*-dd-*). embed.

im·bibe [im'baib] *v.t.* drink; take in (ideas).

im·bue [im'bjuː] *v.t.* ~d *with*, filled with (patriotism, hatred).

im·i·tate ['imiteit] *v.t.* 1. copy the behaviour of; take as an example. 2. be like; make a likeness of. **im·i·ta·tion** [ˌimi'teiʃən] *n.* imitating; sth. that ~s; copy; (attrib.) not real. **im·i·ta·tive** ['imitətiv] *adj.* following the model or example of: *the imitative arts*, painting and sculpture. **im·i·ta·tor** *n.* one who ~s.

im·mac·u·late [i'mækjulit] *adj.* faultless; pure; correct in every detail.

im·ma·te·ri·al [ˌimə'tiəriəl] *adj.* 1. unimportant. 2. not having physical substance.

im·me·di·ate [i'miːdiət] *adj.* 1. without others coming between; nearest: *my ~ neighbours.* 2. occurring at once: *an ~ answer.* ~·ly *adv.* (esp.) at once; without delay.

im·me·mo·ri·al [ˌimi'mɔːriəl] *adj.* going back beyond the reach of memory.

im·mense [i'mens] *adj.* very large. ~·ly *adv.* **im·men·si·ty** *n.* great size.

im·merse [i'məːs] *v.t.* 1. put under the surface of (water or other liquid). 2. *be ~d in*, deep in (debt, difficulties, thought, a book). **im·mer·sion** [i'məːʃən] *n.* ~ *heater*, electrical apparatus ~d in (a tank of) water for heating it.

im·mi·grate ['imigreit] *v.i.* come (*into* a country) as a settler (i.e. to live there). **im·mi·grant** ['imigrənt] *n.* sb. who does this. **im·mi·gra·tion** [ˌimi'greiʃən] *n.*

im·mi·nent ['iminənt] *adj.* (esp. of danger) likely to come or happen soon. **im·mi·nence** *n.* nearness (of an event, etc.).

im·mor·tal [i'mɔːtl] *adj.* living for ever; never forgotten. *n.* ~ being. *the ~s*, the gods of ancient Greece and Rome. ~·ize *v.t.* give endless life or fame to. ~·ity [ˌimɔː'tæliti] *n.* endless life or fame.

im·mov·a·ble [i'muːvəbl] *adj.* 1. that cannot be moved: ~ *property* (e.g. buildings). 2. fixed (in purpose, etc.).

im·mune [i'mjuːn] *adj.* free, secure (*from* possibility of catching a disease, etc.). **im·mu·ni·ty** *n.* safety, security (*from* disease, etc.); exemption (*from* taxation, etc.). **im·mu·nize** ['imjunaiz] *v.t.* make ~ (*from*).

imp [imp] *n.* child of the devil; little devil; (playfully) mischievous child.

im·pact ['impækt] *n.* collision; striking (*on, against*, sth.) with force.

im·pair [im'peə*] *v.t.* weaken; damage.

im·pale [im'peil] *v.t.* pierce through, pin down, with a sharppointed stake, spear, etc.

im·part [im'pɑːt] *v.t.* give, pass on (a share of sth., a secret, news, etc. *to* sb.).

im·par·tial [im'pɑːʃəl] *adj.* fair (in giving judgements, etc.). ~·ly *adv.*

im·pass·a·ble [im'pɑːsəbl] *adj.* (of roads, etc.) that cannot be travelled on or through.

im·passe [im'pɑːs] *n.* place, position, from which there is no way out; deadlock.

im·pas·sioned [im'pæʃənd] *adj.* full of, showing, deep feeling.

im·pas·sive [im'pæsiv] *adj.* showing no sign of feeling; unmoved.

im·pa·tience [im'peiʃəns] *n.* lack of patience; hastiness.

im·peach [im'piːtʃ] *v.t.* 1. question, raise doubts about (sb.'s character, etc.). 2. accuse (sb. *of* or *with* wrongdoing); (esp.) accuse (sb.) of crime against the State.

im·pec·ca·ble [im'pekəbl] *adj.* faultless; incapable of doing wrong.

im·pe·cu·ni·ous [,impi'kju:niəs] *adj.* having little or no money.

im·pede [im'pi:d] *v.t.* get in the way of; hinder. **im·ped·i·ment** [im'pedimənt] *n.* (esp.) defect in speech (e.g. a stammer).

im·pel [im'pel] *v.t.* (*-ll-*). drive forward; force (sb. *to do* sth., *to* an action).

im·pend·ing [im'pendiŋ] *adj.* about to happen; imminent: *the ~ storm.*

im·pen·e·tra·ble [im'penitrəbl] *adj.* that cannot be penetrated.

im·per·a·tive [im'perətiv] *adj.* 1. urgent; needing immediate attention. 2. not to be disobeyed; done, given, with authority: *~ orders* (*looks, gestures*). 3. (grammar) form of verb expressing commands.

im·pe·ri·al [im'piəriəl] *adj.* 1. of an empire or its ruler: *~ trade.* 2. (of weights and measures) used by law in the U.K. 3. imperious. **~ism** *n.* belief in the value of colonies; policy of extending a country's empire and influence. **~ist** *n.* supporter of, believer in, *~ism.*

im·per·il [im'peril] *v.t.* (*-ll-*). put in, bring into, danger.

im·pe·ri·ous [im'piəriəs] *adj.* commanding; displaying authority.

im·per·son·al [im'pə:sənəl] *adj.* 1. not influenced by personal feeling. 2. not referring to a particular person: *~ remarks.* 3. (of verbs) used after *it*, as in *It is raining.*

im·per·so·nate [im'pə:səneit] *v.t.* 1. act the part of (in a play); pretend to be (another person). 2. personify.

im·per·ti·nent [im'pə:tinənt] *adj.* 1. not showing proper respect. 2. not bearing on the subject. **im·per·ti·nence** *n.*

im·per·tur·ba·ble [,impə'tə:-bəbl] *adj.* not easily moved or troubled; calm.

im·per·vious [im'pə:vjəs] *adj.* 1. (of materials) not allowing (water, etc.) to pass through. 2.

~ to, not moved or influenced by: *~ to argument.*

im·pet·u·ous [im'petjuəs] *adj.* moving quickly or violently; acting, inclined to act, energetically but with insufficient thought or care; done or said hastily.

im·pet·u·os·i·ty [im,petju'ositi] *n.*

im·pe·tus ['impitəs] *n.* (pl. *-es* [iz]). force with which a body moves; driving force.

im·pinge [im'pindʒ] *v.i.* fall or strike forcibly (*on, against*).

im·pious ['impjəs] *adj.* not pious; wicked.

im·plac·a·ble [im'plækəbl] *adj.* full of (hatred, enmity, etc.) that cannot be made less or ended.

im·plant [im'pla:nt] *v.t.* fix or put (ideas, feelings, etc., *in* the mind).

im·ple·ment ['implimənt] *n.* tool or instrument: *farm ~s.* ['impliment] *v.t.* carry (an undertaking, agreement, promise) into effect.

im·pli·cate ['implikeit] *v.t.* show that (sb.) has a share (*in* a crime, etc.). **im·pli·ca·tion** [,impli-'keiʃən] *n.* 1. implicating or being implicated. 2. implying; sth. implied.

im·plic·it [im'plisit] *adj.* 1. (cf. *explicit*) implied: *~ threats.* 2. unquestioning (belief, obedience, etc.).

im·plore [im'plɔ:*] *v.t.* request earnestly. **im·plor·ing·ly** *adv.*

im·ply [im'plai] *v.t.* give or make a suggestion; convey(2) the truth (beyond what is definitely stated): *Silence sometimes implies consent,* i.e. failure to say 'no' may be thought to mean 'yes'.

im·pon·der·a·ble [im'pondərəbl] *adj.* (fig.) of which the effect cannot be estimated.

im·port [im'pɔ:t] *v.t.* 1. bring (esp. foreign goods) into (a country). 2. mean; signify. ['impɔ:t] *n.* 1. (usu. pl.) goods *~ed*(1). 2. the act of *~ing*(1). 3. meaning. **~er** *n.* sb. who *~s*(1).

im·por·tant [im'pɔ:tənt] *adj.* 1. of great influence; to be treated seriously; having a great effect. **2.** (of a person) having a position of authority. ~**·ly** *adv.* im·**por·tance** *n.*

im·**por·tu·nate** [im'po:tʃunit] *adj.* **1.** (of persons) making repeated and inconvenient requests. **2.** (of affairs, etc.) urgent. im·**por·tu·ni·ty** [,impo:-'tʃu:niti] *n.*

im·**pose** [im'pouz] *v.t. & i.* **1.** lay or place (a duty, tax, etc., *upon* sb. or sth.). **2.** ~ *upon*, take advantage of (sb., his good nature); deceive. im·**pos·ing** *adj.* important-looking; causing admiration. im·**po·si·tion** [,impə'ziʃən] *n.* **1.** the act of imposing(1) (taxes, etc.). **2.** sth. ~d; tax, etc.; unreasonable demand. **3.** fraud; overcharge.

im·**pos·si·ble** [im'posəbl] *adj.* **1.** not possible. **2.** that cannot be endured: *It's an* ~ *situation!*

im·**pos·tor** [im'postə*] *n.* person pretending to be what he is not. im·**pos·ture** [im'postʃə*] *n.* act of deception by an ~.

im·**po·tent** ['impətənt] *adj.* lacking sufficient strength (to do sth.); unable to act. im·**po·tence** *n.*

im·**pound** [im'paund] *v.t.* take possession of by law or authority.

im·**pov·er·ish** [im'povəriʃ] *v.t.* cause to become poor; take away good qualities: ~*ed soil.*

im·**prac·ti·ca·ble** [im'præktikəbl] *adj.* **1.** that cannot be done or effected; impossible. **2.** (of routes) that cannot be used; impassable.

im·**pre·ca·tion** [,impri'keiʃən] *n.* curse.

im·**preg·na·ble** [im'pregnəbl] *adj.* that cannot be overcome or taken by force.

im·**preg·nate** [im'pregneit] *v.t.* fertilize; saturate; fill (*with* feelings, etc.).

im·**press** [im'pres] *v.t.* **1.** press (one thing *on* or *with* another); make a mark, etc., by doing this. **2.** have a strong influence on; fix deeply (on the mind, memory): *I was not much* ~*ed*, did not form a favourable opinion. im·**pres·sion** [im-'preʃən] *n.* **1.** mark made by pressing. **2.** print (of engraving, etc.). **3.** (printing of) number of copies forming one issue(4) of a book or newspaper. **4.** effect produced on the mind or feelings. **5.** (vague or uncertain) idea, belief: *under the* ~*ion that*, having the idea that. im·**pres·sion·a·ble** *adj.* easily influenced. im·**pres·sive** *adj.* ~ing(2) the mind or feelings.

im·**print** [im'print] *v.t.* print, stamp: *ideas* ~*ed on the mind.* ['imprint] *n.* sth. (e.g. a fingerprint) ~ed or impressed.

im·**prison** [im'prizn] *v.t.* put or keep in prison. ~**·ment** *n.*

im·**promp·tu** [im'promptju:] *adv. & adj.* without preparation.

im·**prop·er** [im'propə*] *adj.* not suited to the occasion; indecent; incorrect.

im·**prove** [im'pru:v] *v.t. & i.* (cause to) become better. ~ *upon*, do (sth.) better than (what is mentioned). ~**·ment** *n.*

im·**prov·i·dent** [im'provident] *adj.* wasteful; not looking to future needs. ~**·ly** *adj.*

im·**pro·vise** ['improvaiz] *v.t. & i.* **1.** compose music while playing, verse while reciting, etc. **2.** provide, make or do sth. quickly, in time of need, using whatever happens to be available.

im·**pu·dent** ['impjudənt] *adj.* shamelessly rude. im·**pu·dence** *n.*

im·**pugn** [im'pju:n] *v.t.* challenge, express doubt about a statement, act, etc.).

im·**pulse** ['impʌls] *n.* **1.** push or thrust; impetus: *an* ~ *to trade.* **2.** sudden inclination to act without thought: *seized with an* ~ *to do sth.* im·**pul·sive** [im-'pʌlsiv] *adj.* acting on, resulting from, ~(2).

im·**pu·ni·ty** [im'pju:niti] *n. with* ~, with freedom from punishment or injury.

im·**pute** [im'pju:t] *v.t.* ~ *sth. to*, consider as the act, quality, or outcome of: *innocent of the crime* ~*d to him*; ~ *a boy's failure to stupidity.* im·**pu·ta·tion**

[ˌimpjuˈteiʃən] *n.* accusation or suggestion of wrongdoing, etc.

¹**in** [in] *prep. & adv.* **I. prep. 1.** (of place; cf. *at*): *the highest mountain in the world*; *in Africa*; *children playing in the street*; *standing in the corner of the room* (cf. *the house at the corner*); *a holiday in the country* (cf. *at the seaside*); *lying in bed* (cf. *sitting on the bed*); *read about sth. in the newspapers.* **2.** (of direction): *in this* (*that*) *direction*; *in all directions.* **3.** (indicating direction of motion or activity) into: *He dipped his pen in the ink. Cut* (*break*) *it in two. They fell in love.* **4.** (of time when): *in the 20th century*; *in 1960*; *in my absence*; *in his youth*; *in old age*; *in these* (*those*) *days*; *in the morning* (*afternoon, evening*) (cf. *on Monday morning*). **5.** (of time) in the course of; within the space of: *I shall be back in a short time* (*in a few days, in a week's time, etc.*). **6.** (indicating inclusion): *seven days in a week.* **7.** (indicating ratio): *a slope* (*gradient*) *of one in five. Not one in ten of the boys could spell well.* **8.** (of dress, etc.): *dressed* (*clothed*) *in rags*; *the woman in white*, *wearing white clothes.* **9.** (indicating physical surroundings, circumstances, etc.): *go out in the rain*; *a temperature of 25° C. in the shade.* **10.** (indicating state or condition): *in a troubled state*; *in good order*; *in poor health.* **11.** (indicating form, shape, arrangement): *a novel in three parts.* **12.** (indicating method of expression, etc.): *speaking* (*writing*) *in English*; *written in ink* (*pencil*). **13.** (indicating degree or extent): *in large* (*small*) *quantities*; *in great numbers.* **in all**, as the total: *We were fifteen in all.* **14.** (indicating identity): *You will always have a good friend in me, I shall always be a friend to you.* **15.** (indicating relation, reference, respect): *in some* (*all*) *respects*; *in every way.* **16.** (indicating occupation, activity,

etc.): *He's in the army* (*in insurance*). *How much time do you spend in reading?* **17.** (used in numerous prepositional phrases, see the noun entries, e.g.): *in memory of*; *in touch with*; *in defence of*; *in justice to*; *in exchange for.* **18. in so far as, in as far as,** in such measure as; to the extent that: *He is a Russian in so far as he was born in Russia, but he became a French citizen in 1920.* **II. adv.** (contrasted with *out*). **1.** used with many verbs, as *come in* (= enter) and *give in* (= surrender); see the verb entries for these. **2.** (used with the verb *be*) (a) at home: *Is there anyone in?* (b) arrive: *Is the steamer in yet?* (*Has it arrived?*) (c) (of crops) harvested; brought in from the fields: *The wheat crop* (*The harvest*) *is safely in.* (d) in season; obtainable: *Strawberries are in now.* (e) in fashion: *Long skirts are in again.* (f) elected; in power; in office: *The Democrats are in. The Liberal candidate is in,* has been elected. (g) burning: *Is the fire still in?* (h) (cricket, baseball) batting: *Which side is in?* **3. in for,** (a) likely to experience: *I'm afraid we're in for a storm*, etc. (b) committed to, having agreed to take part in: *I'm in for the competition,* shall be a competitor. **in and out,** now in and then out: *He's always in and out of hospital,* is frequently ill and in hospital. **4.** (preceding a noun): *an in-patient,* one who lives in a hospital while receiving treatment (contrasted with *out-patient*).

²**in** [in] *n.* (only) *the ins and the outs,* the different parts; the details: *know all the ins and outs of a problem.*

³**in-** *prefix.* not; the opposite of: **in·ac·cu·rate, in·sin·cere(·ly).**

in·ad·ver·tent [ˌinədˈvəːtənt] *adj.* not paying or showing proper attention; (of actions) done thoughtlessly or not on purpose. ~·**ly** *adv.* **in·ad·ver·tence** *n.*

in·a·lien·a·ble [in'eiljənəbl] *adj.* (of rights, etc.) that cannot be given away or taken away.

in·ane [i'nein] *adj.* foolish. ~·ly *adv.* **in·an·i·ty** [i'næniti] *n.* foolish or purposeless behaviour, act, etc.

in·an·i·mate [in'ænimit] *adj.* lifeless; spiritless; ~ (i.e. dull) *conversation.*

in·a·ni·tion [,inə'niʃən] *n.* emptiness; extreme weakness from want of food.

in·apt [in'æpt] *adj.* unskilful; not bearing on the subject: ~ *remarks.*

in·as·much [,inəz'mʌtʃ] *adv.* ~ *as,* since; because.

in·au·gu·rate [in'ɔ:gjureit] *v.t.* **1.** introduce (a new official, professor, etc.) at a special ceremony. **2.** enter, with public formalities, upon (an undertaking, etc.); open (an exhibition, a public building) with formalities. **in·au·gu·ral** [i'nɔ:gjurəl] *adj.* of or for an inauguration. **in·au·gu·ra·tion** [i,nɔ:gju'reiʃən] *n.*

in·born ['in'bɔ:n] *adj.* (of a quality) possessed (by a person or animal) at birth: *an* ~ *love of mischief.*

in·bred ['inbred] *adj.* inborn.

in·breed·ing ['in'bri:diŋ] *n.* breeding from animals closely related.

in·can·des·cent [,inkæn'desnt] *adj.* giving out, able to give out, light when heated. **in·can·des·cence** *n.*

in·can·ta·tion [,inkæn'teiʃən] *n.* form of words used in magic.

in·ca·pac·i·tate [,inkə'pæsiteit] *v.t.* make incapable or unfit (*for*). **in·ca·pac·i·ty** [,inkə'pæsiti] *n.* inability; powerlessness (*for* sth.).

in·car·cer·ate [in'ka:səreit] *v.t.* imprison.

in·car·nate [in'ka:nit] *adj.* having (esp. a human) body: *a devil* ~. ['inka:neit] *v.t.* **1.** make ~. **2.** put (an idea, etc.) into a real or material form. **3.** (of a person) be a living form of (a quality): *a wife who* ~*s all the virtues.* **in·car·na·tion** [,inka:-

'neiʃən] *n.* **1.** (esp.) *the Incarnation,* the taking of bodily form by Jesus Christ. **2.** person looked upon as a type of a quality: *She's the incarnation of health.*

in·cen·di·a·ry [in'sendjəri] *n. & adj.* **1.** (person) setting fire to property unlawfully and with an evil purpose; (person) tending to stir up violence. **2.** (bomb) causing fire.

¹in·cense [in'sens] *v.t.* make angry.

²in·cense ['insens] *n.* (smoke of a) substance producing a sweet smell when burning.

in·cen·tive [in'sentiv] *n.* motive; that which encourages sb. to do sth.

in·cep·tion [in'sepʃən] *n.* start.

in·ces·sant [in'sesənt] *adj.* continual: *a week of* ~ *rain;* often repeated.

in·cest ['insest] *n.* sexual intercourse between near blood relations, e.g., brother and sister.

inch [intʃ] *n.* measure of length, one-twelfth of a foot: *by* ~*es,* bit by bit; *every* ~ (*a soldier*), completely, in every way.

in·ci·dence ['insidəns] *n. the* ~ *of a disease,* the range or extent of its effect; *the* ~ *of a tax,* the way it falls to certain people to pay it.

in·ci·dent ['insidənt] *n.* event, esp. one of less importance than others; happening that attracts general attention. **in·ci·den·tal** [,insi'dentl] *adj.* **1.** accompanying, but not forming a necessary part: ~*al music to a play.* **2.** ~*al expenses,* additional to the main expenses. **3.** ~*al to,* likely to occur in connexion with.

in·cin·er·ate [in'sinəreit] *v.t.* burn to ashes. **in·cin·er·a·tor** *n.* enclosed fire-place for burning rubbish, etc.

in·cip·i·ent [in'sipiənt] *adj.* beginning; in an early stage.

in·ci·sion [[in'siʒən] *n.* cutting; a cut (esp. one made in a surgical operation). **in·ci·sive** [in'saisiv] *adj.* sharp; (fig., of a person's mind, remarks) acute; clear-cut.

in·cite [in'sait] *v.t.* stir up, rouse (sb. *to* do sth., *to* anger, etc.). ~**ment** *n.*

in·clem·ent [in'klemənt] *adj.* (of weather) severe; cold and stormy. **in·clem·en·cy** *n.*

in·cli·na·tion [,inkli'neiʃən] *n.* 1. leaning (of the mind or heart, *to* sth.); liking or desire (*for* one thing rather than another, *to* do sth.). 2. slope or slant.

in·cline [in'klain] *v.i. & t.* 1. (cause to) slope or slant. 2. direct the mind in a certain direction; cause (sb.) to have a tendency or wish: *The news ~s me* (*I am ~d*) *to start at once.* ['inklain] *n.* upward or downward path.

in·clude [in'klu:d] *v.t.* bring in, reckon, as part of the whole: *Price 7s. 9d., postage ~d.* **in·clu·sion** [in'klu:ʒən] *n.* **in·clu·sive** [in'klu:siv] *adj.* including everything between named points: *inclusive terms*, e.g. at a hotel, the charge(3) for a bedroom and all meals, etc., during one's stay.

in·cog·ni·to [in'kɔgnitou] *adv.* with one's name kept secret: *to travel ~.*

in·come ['inkəm] *n.* money received during a given period (as salary, receipts from trade, interest from investments, etc.).

in·com·ing ['inkʌmiŋ] *adj.* coming in: *the ~ tide* (*tenant*).

in·com·mode [,inkə'moud] *v.t.* cause trouble or inconvenience to.

in·com·pa·ra·ble [in'kɔmpərəbl] *adj.* that cannot be compared (*to* or *with*); matchless; without equal.

in·con·gru·ous [in'kɔŋgruəs] *adj.* not in harmony or agreement (*with*); out of place. **in·con·gru·i·ty** [,inkɔŋ'gruiti] *n.*

in·con·se·quent [in'kɔnsikwənt] *adj.* not following naturally what has been said or done before; (of a person) saying ~ things. **in·con·se·quen·tial** [in,kɔnsi'kwenʃəl] *adj.* ~; unimportant.

in·con·ve·nience [,inkən'vi:njəns] *n.* (cause of) discomfort. *v.t.* cause ~ to (sb.).

in·cor·po·rate [in'kɔ:pəreit] *v.t. & i.* make, become, united in one body or group; (law) form into, become, a corporation(2). [in'kɔ:pərit] *adj.* formed into a corporation (2). **in·cor·po·ra·tion** [in,kɔ:pə'reiʃən] *n.*

in·cor·ri·gi·ble [in'kɔridʒəbl] *adj.* (of a person, his bad ways) that cannot be cured or corrected.

in·crease [in'kri:s] *v.t. & i.* make or become greater in size, number, degree, etc. ['inkri:s] *n.* increasing; growth; amount by which sth. ~s.

in·cre·ment ['inkrimənt] *n.* profit; increase; amount of increase.

in·crim·i·nate [in'krimineit] *v.t.* say, be a sign, that (sb.) is guilty of wrongdoing.

in·cu·bate ['inkjubeit] *v.t. & i.* hatch (eggs) by sitting on them or by artificial warmth; sit on eggs. **in·cu·ba·tor** *n.* apparatus for hatching eggs by artificial warmth or for rearing babies born too soon.

in·cul·cate ['inkʌlkeit] *v.t.* fix (ideas, etc.) well by repetition (*upon* sb., *in* his mind).

in·cum·bent [in'kʌmbənt] *adj.* ~ *upon* sb., resting upon him as a duty (*to* do sth.). *n.* rector or vicar.

in·cur [in'kə:*] *v.t.* (*-rr-*). bring (debt, danger, hatred, etc.) upon oneself.

in·cur·sion [in'kə:ʃən] *n.* sudden attack or invasion.

in·debt·ed [in'detid] *adj.* in debt, under an obligation (*to*).

in·deed [in'di:d] *adv.* really; truly. *int.* expressing surprise, interest, irony, etc.

in·de·fat·i·ga·ble [,indi'fætigəbl] *adj.* untiring; that cannot be tired out.

in·def·i·nite [in'definit] *adj.* vague. ~ *article*, (grammar) the word a(*n*).

in·del·i·ble [in'delibl] *adj.* that cannot be rubbed or wiped out.

in·del·i·cate [in'delikit] *adj.* (of a person, his behaviour, speech, etc.) not refined; immodest. **in·del·i·ca·cy** *n.*

in·dem·ni·fy [in'demnifai] *v.t.*

1. make (sb.) safe (*from, against* harm, loss, punishment, etc.). **2.** pay back (sb. *for* loss, expenses, etc.). **in·dem·ni·fi·ca·tion** [in‚demnifi'keiʃən] *n.* ~ing or being indemnified. **in·dem·ni·ty** [in'demniti] *n.* being indemnified; payment to compensate for loss.

in·dent [in'dent] *v.t.* **1.** break into the edge or surface of (as with teeth): *an* ~*ed* (i.e. very irregular) *coast-line*. **2.** start (a line of print or writing) further from the margin than the others. **3.** make an order (*upon* sb. *for* goods, etc.); order goods by means of an~. ['indent] *n.* trade order (placed esp. in the United Kingdom) for goods to be exported; official requisition for stores.

in·den·ture [in'dentʃə*] *n.* agreement (of which two copies are made), esp. one binding an apprentice to his master.

in·de·pen·dent [‚indi'pendənt] *adj.* **1.** not dependent on or controlled by (other persons or things); not relying on others; not needing to work for a living. **2.** self-governing. **3.** acting or thinking along one's own lines: *an* ~ *thinker*. *n.* (esp.) Member of Parliament not belonging to a political party. ~**ly** *adv.* **in·de·pen·dence** *n.* the state of being ~.

in·de·ter·mi·nate [‚indi'tə:minit] *adj.* not fixed; vague or indefinite.

in·dex ['indeks] *n.* (pl. ~*es, indices* ['indisi:z]). **1.** sth. that points to or indicates: *the* ~ *finger*, the forefinger, used for pointing. **2.** list of names, references, etc., in ABC order, at the end of a book, or on cards, etc. *v.t.* make an ~ for (a book, etc.); put in an ~.

In·dia ['indjə] *n.* ~ *paper*, very thin printing paper (e.g. for airmail editions of newspapers). **In·dian** *adj.* ~*n corn*, maize; *in* ~*n file*, in single file (see ²*file*). **'in·dia‚rub·ber** *n.* piece of rubber for rubbing out pencil marks.

in·di·cate ['indikeit] *v.t.* point to; point out; make known; be a sign of. **in·di·ca·tion** [‚indi'keiʃən] *n.* that which ~s. **in·dic·a·tive** [in'dikətiv] *adj.* **1.** *indicative mood*, form of a verb used in stating or asking for facts. **2.** *indicative of*, giving indications of. **in·di·ca·tor** ['indikeitə*] *n.* (esp.) pointer, recording apparatus, on a machine or vehicle (to show speed, pressure, direction).

in·di·ces, plural of *index*.

in·dict [in'dait] *v.t.* (legal) accuse (sb. *for* riot, *as* a rioter, *on* a charge of rioting, etc.). ~**a·ble** *adj.* who, for which sb., may be ~ed: ~*able offences*. ~**ment** *n.* written statement ~ing sb.

in·dif·fer·ent [in'difrənt] *adj.* **1.** ~ *to*, not interested in; neither for nor against. **2.** commonplace; not of good quality or ability: *an* ~ *book* (*footballer*). **in·dif·fer·ence** *n.* absence of interest or feeling; unimportance.

in·dig·e·nous [in'didʒənəs] *adj.* native (*to*); belonging naturally (*to* a country, etc.).

in·di·gent ['indidʒənt] *adj.* poor; without money. **in·di·gence** *n.*

in·di·ges·tion [‚indi'dʒestʃən] *n.* (pain from) difficulty in digesting food.

in·dig·nant [in'dignənt] *adj.* angry and scornful, esp. at injustice or because of undeserved blame, etc.: ~ *with sb. at a false accusation*; ~ *looks*. ~**ly** *adv.* **in·dig·na·tion** [‚indig'neiʃən] *n.*

in·dig·ni·ty [in'digniti] *n.* unworthy treatment causing shame or loss of respect: *subjected to numerous indignities by the rough soldiers*.

in·di·go ['indigou] *n.* deep blue (dye).

in·dis·cre·tion [‚indis'kreʃən] *n.* (esp.) indiscreet remark, act, behaviour.

in·dis·crim·i·nate [‚indis'kriminit] *adj.* acting, given, without enough care or taste: ~ *praise*; ~ *in making friends*.

in·dis·pen·sa·ble [‚indis'pensəbl]

adj. necessary; that one cannot do without.

in·dis·posed [‚indis¹pouzd] *adj.* **1.** unwell. **2.** not inclined (*for* sth., *to* do sth.). **in·dis·po·si·tion** [‚indispə¹ziʃən] *n.* (esp.) slight illness.

in·di·vid·ual [‚indi¹vidjuəl] *adj.* **1.** (opposite of *general*) specially for one person or thing. **2.** characteristic of a single person or thing: *an ~ style of speaking.* **3.** considered or taken by itself: *in this ~ case.* *n.* any one human being (contrasted with society). **~·ly** *adv.* separately; one by one. **in·di·vid·u·al·i·ty** [‚indi‚vidju¹æl1ti] *n.* the ~ character (esp. those features of it which are strongly marked).

in·doc·tri·nate [in¹doktrineit] *v.t.* fill the mind (*with* particular ideas or beliefs).

in·do·lent [¹indələnt] *adj.* lazy; inactive. **in·do·lence** *n.*

in·dom·i·ta·ble [in¹domitəbl] *adj.* unconquerable; unyielding.

in·door [¹indɔː*] *adj.* situated, carried on, inside a building. **in·doors** [¹in¹dɔːz] *adv.* in(to) a house, etc.

in·du·bi·ta·ble [in¹djuːbitəbl] *adj.* that cannot be doubted.

in·duce [in¹djuːs] *v.t.* **1.** persuade (sb. *to* do sth.). **2.** bring about: *illness ~d by overwork.* **~·ment** *n.* sth. that ~s(1).

in·duc·tion [in¹dakʃən] *n.* method of reasoning that obtains or discovers general laws from particular facts or examples; production (of facts) to prove a general statement. **in·duc·tive** *adj.* (of reasoning) based on ~.

in·dulge [in¹dald3] *v.t. & i.* gratify; give way to and satisfy (desires, etc.): *to ~ a sick child; to ~ in a holiday.* **in·dul·gence** [in¹dald3əns] *n.* **1.** sth. in which a person ~s (a cigar, a visit to the theatre). **2.** (R.C. Church) granting of freedom from punishment still due for sin. **in·dul·gent** *adj.* inclined to ~: *indulgent parents.*

in·dus·try [¹indəstri] *n.* **1.** quality of being hard working; constant employment in useful work. **2.** (branch of) trade or manufacture (often contrasted with distribution and commerce). **in·dus·tri·al** [in¹dastriəl] *adj.* of industries (2). **in·dus·tri·ous** [in¹dastriəs] *adj.* hard-working; showing ~ (1).

i·ne·bri·ate [i¹niːbrieit] *v.t.* intoxicate. [i¹niːbriit] *n. & adj.* (person who is habitually) intoxicated.

in·ef·fa·ble [in¹efəbl] *adj.* too great to be described in words: *~ beauty.*

in·ept [i¹nept] *adj.* absurd; said, done, at the wrong time. **in·ep·ti·tude** [i¹neptitjuːd] *n.* (esp.) *~ action,* etc.

in·ert [i¹nəːt] *adj.* **1.** without power to move or act: *~ matter.* **2.** (of a person) slow; dull. **3.** having no power to act chemically: *~ gases.* **in·er·tia** [i¹nəː·ʃə] *n.*

in·es·ti·ma·ble [in¹estiməbl] *adj.* too great to be estimated or given a value.

in·ev·i·ta·ble [in¹evitəbl] *adj.* that cannot be avoided; sure to happen.

in·ex·o·ra·ble [in¹eksərəbl] *adj.* relentless; unyielding.

in·ex·pe·ri·ence [‚iniks¹piəriəns] *n.* lack or want of experience.

in·ex·pres·si·ble [‚iniks¹presəbl] *adj.* that cannot be expressed in words.

in·ex·tric·a·ble [in¹ekstrikəbl] *adj.* that cannot be escaped from, solved, reduced to order or untied.

in·fa·mous [¹infəməs] *adj.* wicked; shameful. **in·fa·my** [¹in·fəmi] *n.* being ~; ~ act; ~ behaviour.

in·fant [¹infənt] *n.* baby; very young child. **in·fan·cy** [¹infənsi] *n.* **1.** state of being, period when one is, an ~. **2.** early stage of development: *Aviation is no longer in its infancy.* **in·fan·ti·cide** [in¹fæntisaid] *n.* crime of killing an ~. **in·fan·tile** [¹infəntail] *adj.* of, or as of, ~s: *~ile diseases.*

in·fan·try [¹infəntri] *n.* part of an army that fights on foot.

in·fat·u·ate [in'fætjueit] *v.t.* be ~d (*with*), be foolishly in love (with); be affected foolishly.
in·fat·u·a·tion [in,fætju'eiʃən] *n.*

in·fect [in'fekt] *v.t.* affect (a person, his body, mind) (*with* disease); give disease germs (fig. feelings, ideas) to: *a pupil whose high spirits ~ed the whole class.*
in·fec·tion [in'fekʃən] *n.* (esp.) disease that ~s. **in·fec·tious** [in'fekʃəs] *adj.* 1. ~ing with disease; (of disease) that can be spread by germs carried in air or water. (Cf. *contagious*.) 2. (fig.) quickly influencing others: *~ious laughter (yawns).*

in·fer [in'fə*] *v.t.* (-*rr*-). conclude (3); reach an opinion (from facts, reasoning). ~·ence ['infərəns] *n.* 1. process of ~ring: *by ~ence.* 2. sth. ~red; conclusion.

in·fe·ri·or [in'fiəriə*] *adj.* low(er) in rank, social position, importance, quality, etc.: *goods ~ to samples.* *n.* person who is ~ (in rank, etc.). ~·i·ty [in,fiəri'ɔriti] *n.* state of being ~: *~ity complex*, state of mind in which a feeling of being ~ to others causes a person to try to win importance for himself (e.g. by being aggressive).

in·fer·nal [in'fə:nl] *adj.* of hell; devilish; abominable: *~ cruelty.*
in·fer·no [in'fə:nou] *n.* hell.

in·fest [in'fest] *v.t.* (of rats, insects, brigands, etc.) be present in large numbers: *warehouses ~ed with rats.*

in·fi·del ['infidl] *n.* person with no belief in (what is considered to be) the true or accepted religion.

in·fi·del·i·ty [,infi'deliti] *n.* (act of) disloyalty or unfaithfulness (esp. to a wife or husband).

in·fil·trate ['infiltreit] *v.t. & i.* (cause to) pass through or into by filtering; (of troops) pass through defences without attracting notice; (of ideas) pass into people's minds. **in·fil·tra·tion** [,infil'treiʃən] *n.*

in·fi·nite ['infinit] *adj.* endless; without limits: *the ~, ~ space; the I~*, God. ~·ly *adv.* **in·fin·i·tes·i·mal** [,infini'tesiməl] *adj.* too small to be measured. **in·fin·i·tive** [in'finitiv] *adj. & n.* (of the) form of the verb not changed for person, number, or time, used with or without *to* (e.g. *let him go*; *allow him to go*). **in·fin·i·ty** [in'finiti] *n.* (maths.) infinite number, quantity, measure or distance.

in·firm [in'fə:m] *adj.* 1. physically weak, esp. from age. 2. mentally or morally weak: *~ of purpose.* **in·fir·ma·ry** [in'fə:məri] *n.* hospital. **in·fir·mi·ty** [in'fə:miti] *n.* weakness.

in·flame [in'fleim] *v.t. & i.* (cause to) become red, angry, overheated: *~d eyes; to ~ popular feeling.* **in·flam·ma·ble** [in'flæməbl] *adj.* easily set on fire or (fig.) excited. **in·flam·ma·tion** [,inflə'meiʃən] *n.* ~d condition (esp. of part of the body). **in·flam·ma·to·ry** [in'flæmətəri] *adj.* 1. of inflammation of the body. 2. (of speeches, etc.) likely to ~ (angry) feelings.

in·flate [in'fleit] *v.t. & i.* 1. fill (a tyre, balloon, etc.) with air or gas; cause to swell: (fig.) *~d with pride.* 2. take action to increase the amount of money in circulation so that prices rise. (Cf. *deflate*.) **in·fla·tion** [in'fleiʃən] *n.* **in·fla·tion·a·ry** *adj.*

in·flect [in'flekt] *v.t.* (grammar) change the ending or form of (a word) to show its relationship to other words in a sentence. **in·flec·tion, in·flex·ion** [in'flekʃən] *n.* 1. ~ing; an ending (e.g. *-ed*) used for ~ing. 2. rise or fall of the voice.

in·flict [in'flikt] *v.t.* ~ *sth. on sb.*, cause him to suffer by means of (a blow, wound, penalty, punishment, etc.): *~ oneself (one's company) (up)on sb.*, force one's company on. **in·flic·tion** [in'flikʃən] *n.*

in·flow ['inflou] *n.* flowing in.

in·flu·ence ['influəns] *n.* 1. action of natural forces (*on*): *the ~ of the moon* (on the tides), *of climate* (on vegetation). 2. power to affect sb.'s character, beliefs, or actions (through example, fear, admiration, etc.);

person or fact that exercises such power; the exercise of such power ((up)on sb., sth.). **3.** power due to wealth, position, etc.: *use one's ~ to get a job for a friend.* **v.t.** have, use, ~ upon. **in·flu·en·tial** [ˌinfluˈenʃəl] **adj.** having ~.

in·flu·en·za [ˌinfluˈenzə] **n.** infectious disease with fever and catarrh.

in·flux [ˈinflʌks] **n.** flowing in (e.g. of visitors).

in·form [inˈfɔːm] **v.t. & i.** 1. give knowledge to: *to ~ sb. that, to ~ sb. of sth.,* etc. **2.** ~ *against sb.,* bring an accusation against him to the police. **~·ant n.** person giving ~*ation.* **in·for·ma·tion** [ˌinfəˈmeiʃən] **n.** facts told; news or knowledge given: *a useful piece of ~ation.* **in·for·ma·tive adj.** instructive; giving ~ation. **~·er n.** (esp.) sb. who ~s the authorities of offences against the law.

in·for·mal [inˈfɔːməl] **adj.** not formal. **~·ly adv. ~·i·ty** [ˌinfɔːˈmæliti] **n.**

in·frac·tion [inˈfrækʃən] **n.** breaking (of a rule, law, etc.).

in·fringe [inˈfrindʒ] **v.t. & i.** 1. break (a rule, etc.). **2.** ~ *upon* (sb.'s rights), trespass upon. **~·ment n.**

in·fu·ri·ate [inˈfjuərieit] **v.t.** fill with fury; make very angry.

in·fuse [inˈfjuːz] **v.t. & i.** 1. put, pour (a quality, etc., into): *~ courage (new life) into soldiers.* **2.** pour (hot) liquid on leaves, herbs, etc., to flavour it; (of the liquid) be flavoured through this process. **in·fu·sion** [inˈfjuːʒən] **n.** sth. (e.g. tea) made by infusing.

in·ge·nious [inˈdʒiːnjəs] **adj.** 1. (of a person) clever and skilful (at making or inventing). **2.** (of things) skilfully made. **in·ge·nu·i·ty** [ˌindʒiˈnuiti] **n.**

in·gen·u·ous [inˈdʒenjuəs] **adj.** frank; innocent; natural.

in·glo·ri·ous [inˈɡlɔːriəs] **adj.** 1. shameful; dishonourable. **2.** obscure (2).

in·got [ˈiŋɡot] **n.** (usu. brick-shaped) lump of metal (esp. gold or silver).

in·grained [inˈɡreind] **adj.** (of habits, stains, etc.) deeply fixed; difficult to get rid of.

in·gra·ti·ate [inˈɡreiʃieit] **v.t.** bring (oneself) into favour (*with* sb.), esp. in order to win an advantage.

in·gre·di·ent [inˈɡriːdjənt] **n.** one of the parts of a mixture.

in·hab·it [inˈhæbit] **v.t.** live in. **~·a·ble adj.** that can be lived in. **~·ant n.** person living in a place.

in·hale [inˈheil] **v.t. & i.** take or draw (air, gas, smoke) into the lungs.

in·her·ent [inˈhiərənt] **adj.** existing (*in*) as a natural and permanent part or quality of.

in·her·it [inˈherit] **v.t.** 1. receive (property, a title, etc.) as heir. **2.** derive (qualities, etc.) from ancestors. **~·ance** [inˈheritəns] **n.** ~·ing; sth. ~ed.

in·hib·it [inˈhibit] **v.t.** hinder; restrain. **in·hi·bi·tion** [ˌinhiˈbiʃən] **n.** impulse or desire that is ~ed.

in·hu·man [inˈhjuːmən] **adj.** unfeeling; cruel. **~·i·ty** [ˌinhjuːˈmæniti] **n.**

in·im·i·cal [iˈnimikəl] **adj.** unfriendly or harmful (*to*).

in·im·it·a·ble [iˈnimitəbl] **adj.** too good, clever, etc., to be imitated.

in·iq·ui·tous [iˈnikwitəs] **adj.** very wicked or unjust. **in·iq·ui·ty** [iˈnikwiti] **n.**

in·i·tial [iˈniʃəl] **adj.** of or at the beginning. **n.** (pl.) first letters of a person's names (e.g. T.S. for Tom Smith). **v.t.** mark or sign (sth.) with one's ~s. **~·ly adv.** at the start.

in·it·i·ate [iˈniʃieit] **v.t.** 1. begin; set (a scheme, etc.) working. **2.** admit or introduce (sb. *into* a secret, a society, etc.); give (sb.) instruction (*in* mysteries, etc.). [iˈniʃiit] **n. & adj.** (person) who has been ~d (2). **in·i·ti·a·tion** [iˌniʃiˈeiʃən] **n. in·i·ti·a·tive** [iˈniʃiətiv] **n.** 1. first step: *take the initiative,* make the first move; *on one's own initiative,* without an order or suggestion from others. **2.** capacity or right to ~(1): *to have (the) initiative.*

in·ject [in'dʒekt] *v.t.* drive or force (a liquid, drug, etc., *into* sth.) with or as with a syringe; fill (sth. *with* a liquid, etc.) by ~ing. **in·jec·tion** *n.*

in·junc·tion [in'dʒʌŋkʃən] *n.* order, esp. written order from a law court demanding that sth. shall or shall not be done.

in·jure ['indʒə*] *v.t.* hurt; damage. **in·ju·ry** *n.* damage; wounding; wounded place; wrong. **in·ju·ri·ous** [in'dʒuə-riəs] *adj.* causing, likely to cause, injury.

in·jus·tice [in'dʒʌstis] *n.* 1. lack of justice. 2. unjust act: *do sb. an* ~, judge him unfairly.

ink [iŋk] *n.* coloured liquid used for writing and printing. *v.t.* mark, make dirty, with ink. **ink·y** *adj.* (*-ier, -iest*).

ink·ling ['iŋkliŋ] *n.* slight suggestion or idea (*of*).

in·land ['inlənd, -lænd] *adj.* 1. in the interior of a country. 2. carried on, obtained, within the limits of a country: ~ (= domestic) *trade*; ~ *revenue* (excluding customs). [in'lænd] *adv.* away from the coast.

in·lay [in'lei] *v.t.* (p.t. & p.p. *inlaid* [in'leid]). set pieces of (designs in) wood, metal, etc., in the surface of another kind of wood, metal, etc., so that the resulting surface is smooth and even: *ivory inlaid with gold.* ['inlei] *n.* inlaid work.

in·let ['inlet] *n.* strip of water extending into the land from a larger body of water, or between islands.

in·mate ['inmeit] *n.* one of a number of persons living together (esp. in a prison or other institution). (Cf. *in-patient.*)

in·most ['inmoust] *adj.* most inward; farthest from the surface.

inn [in] *n.* 1. public house where lodging, drink, and meals may be had. 2. *Inns of Court*, (buildings of) London law societies.

in·nate [i'neit, 'ineit] *adj.* (of a quality, etc.) in one's nature; possessed from birth.

in·ner ['inə*] *adj.* (of the) inside. ~**most** *adj.* = inmost.

in·nings ['iniŋz] *n.* time during which a player or team (cricket, etc.) is batting; (fig.) period of power or opportunity to show one's ability.

in·no·cent ['inəsənt] *adj.* 1. not guilty (*of* wrongdoing). 2. harmless: ~ *pastimes*. **in·no·cence** *n.*

in·noc·u·ous [i'nɔkjuəs] *adj.* causing no harm.

in·no·vate ['inouveit] *v.i.* make changes (*in* old customs, etc.); bring in sth. new. **in·no·va·tion** [,inou'veiʃən] *n.*

in·nu·en·do [,inju'endou] *n.* (pl. *-oes*). indirect reference (usu. sth. unfavourable to a person's reputation).

in·nu·mer·a·ble [i'nju:mərəbl] *adj.* too many to be counted.

in·oc·u·late [i'nɔkjuleit] *v.t.* introduce disease germs into (a person or animal) so that a mild form of the disease may keep him safe (*against* severe attacks). **in·oc·u·la·tion** [i,nɔkju'leiʃən] *n.*

in·op·er·a·ble [in'ɔpərəbl] *adj.* (of a tumour, etc.) that cannot be cured by operation (4).

in·pa·tient ['in'peiʃənt] *n.* person lodged at a hospital during treatment.

in·quest ['inkwest] *n.* official inquiry to learn facts, esp. concerning a death which may be the result of crime.

in·quire [in'kwaiə*] *v.t.* 1. ask to be told: ~ *sb's name* (*how to get somewhere*, etc.). 2. ~ *into*, try to learn the facts about; ~ *after*, ask about (sb.'s health or welfare); ~ *for* (sb.), ask to see (him). **in·quir·er** *n.* person who ~s. **in·quir·y** [in'kwaiəri] *n.* 1. asking; inquiring. 2. question; investigation: *hold an inquiry into sth.* **in·quis·i·tion** [,inkwi'ziʃən] *n.* thorough investigation, esp. one made officially. **in·quis·i·tive** [in-'kwizitiv] *adj.* fond of, showing a fondness for, inquiring into other people's affairs.

in·road ['inroud] *n.* sudden attack (*into* a country, etc.); (fig.)

make ~s *on*, use up (leisure, savings, etc.).

in·rush ['inrʌʃ] *n.* rushing in (of water, etc.).

in·sa·tia·ble [in'seiʃjəbl] *adj.* that cannot be satisfied; very greedy.

in·scribe [in'skraib] *v.t.* write (words, one's name, etc., *in* or *on*); mark (sth. *with* words, etc.). **in·scrip·tion** [in'skripʃən] *n.* sth. ~d (e.g. words on a coin).

in·scru·ta·ble [in'skru:təbl] *adj.* mysterious; that cannot be known.

in·sect ['insekt] *n.* sorts of small animal having six legs and no backbone (e.g. ant, fly, wasp); (incorrectly) any similar creeping or flying creature (e.g. a spider). **in·sec·ti·cide** [in'sektisaid] *n.* substance for killing ~s.

in·sen·sate [in'senseit] *adj.* unfeeling; stupid: ~ *rocks* (*cruelty*).

in·sen·si·ble [in'sensibl] *adj.* 1. unconscious (as the result of injury, illness, etc.). 2. unaware (*of* danger, etc.). 3. unfeeling; unsympathetic. 4. (of changes) too small or gradual to be observed. **in·sen·si·bly** *adv.* without being observed. **in·sen·si·bil·i·ty** [in,sensi'biliti] *n.*

in·sert [in'sə:t] *v.t.* put (sth. *in, into, between*): ~ *a key in a lock* (*an advertisement in a newspaper, etc.*). **in·ser·tion** [in'sə:ʃən] *n.* ~ing; sth. ~ed.

in·set ['inset] *n.* extra pages inserted in a book, etc.; small diagram, map, etc., within the border of a printed page or larger map.

in·side ['in'said] *n., adj., adv., prep.* I. *n.* 1. inner side or surface; part(s) within. ~ *out*, with the inner side outside. 2. part of a road, etc., on the inner side of a curve; part of a pavement or footpath farthest from the roadway. 3. (colloq.) stomach and bowels. II. *adj.* situated on or in, coming from, the inner part or inner edge. III. *adv.* on or in the ~. IV. *prep.* on the inner side of.

in·sid·i·ous [in'sidiəs] *adj.* doing harm secretly, unseen.

in·sight ['insait] *n.* power of seeing with the mind (*into* a problem, etc.); deep understanding.

in·sig·nia [in'signjə] *n. pl.* symbols of office (e.g. a king's crown).

in·sin·u·ate [in'sinjueit] *v.t.* 1. make a way for (oneself or sth.) gently and craftily (*into* sth.). 2. suggest unpleasantly and indirectly (*that*). **in·sin·u·a·tion** [in,sinju'eiʃən] *n.*

in·sip·id [in'sipid] *adj.* tasteless; uninteresting; dull.

in·sist [in'sist] *v.i. & t.* 1. urge with emphasis, against opposition or disbelief (*on* sth.); declare emphatically: *to* ~ *on one's innocence* (*that one is innocent*). 2. declare that a purpose cannot be changed: *He* ~s *on being present.* **in·sis·tent** *adj.* (esp.) demanding attention: ~*ent requests.* **in·sis·tence** *n.*

in·so·lent ['insələnt] *adj.* insulting; offensive; contemptuous. **in·so·lence** *n.*

in·som·ni·a [in'sɔmniə] *n.* inability to sleep.

in·so·much [,insou'mʌtʃ] *adv.* to such a degree or extent (*that*).

in·spect [in'spekt] *v.t.* examine carefully; visit officially to see that rules, etc., are obeyed. **in·spec·tion** [in'spekʃən] *n.* **in·spec·tor** *n.* (esp.) official who ~s (e.g. schools, factories, mines).

in·spire [in'spaiə*] *v.t.* 1. put uplifting thoughts, feelings, or aims into: *to* ~ *sb. with hope.* 2. fill with creative power: *an* ~*d poet.* **in·spi·ra·tion** [,inspi'reiʃən] *n.* 1. influence(s) causing the creation of works of art, music, etc. 2. person or thing that ~s. 3. good thought or idea that comes to the mind suddenly.

in·sta·bil·i·ty [,instə'biliti] *n.* lack of stability (usu. of character).

in·stall [in'stɔ:l] *v.t.* 1. place (sb.) in his new position of authority with the usual ceremony. 2. put (a heating system, telephone, etc.) into a building, ready for use. 3. settle (oneself) in a place. **in·stal·la·tion** [ˌin-stə'leiʃən] *n.* ceremony of ~ing (1); sth. ~ed (2).

in·stal·ment [in'stɔːlmənt] *n.* **1.** any one of the parts in which sth. is supplied over a period of time. **2.** any of the parts of a payment spread over a period of time: *paying for a radio by monthly ~s.*

in·stance ['instəns] *n.* **1.** example; fact, etc., supporting a general truth. *in the first ~,* firstly; *for ~,* as an example. **2.** *at the ~ of,* at the request of. *v.t.* give as an ~ (1).

in·stant ['instənt] *adj.* **1.** coming or happening at once. **2.** (trade correspondence) of this month; *your letter of the 9th inst.* **3.** (of coffee powder, etc.) quickly and easily made ready for use. **4.** urgent: *in ~ need of help.* *n.* **1.** point of time; moment. **2.** *this ~,* now; *the ~ (that),* as soon as. **~·ly** *adv.* at once. **in·stan·ta·ne·ous** [ˌin-stən'teinjəs] *adj.* happening, done, in an ~.

in·stead [in'sted] *adv.* in place (of).

in·step ['instep] *n.* upper surface of a foot or shoe between the toes and the ankle.

in·sti·gate ['instigeit] *v.t.* excite and urge (sb. to do sth.); cause (sth.) by doing this: *to ~ a strike.*

in·stil [in'stil] *v.t.* (-ll-). introduce (ideas, etc., *into* sb.'s mind) gradually.

in·stinct ['instiŋkt] *n.* natural tendency to behave in a certain way without reasoning. **in·stinc·tive** *adj.* based on ~: *an ~ive dread of fire.*

in·sti·tute ['institjuːt] *n.* society or organization for a special (usu. social or educational) purpose. *v.t.* establish, get started (an inquiry, rule, custom, etc.). **in·sti·tu·tion** [ˌinsti'tjuːʃən] *n.* **1.** instituting or being ~d. **2.** long-established law, custom, or practice. **3.** (building of an) organization with a charitable purpose or for social welfare (e.g. an orphanage).

in·struct [in'strʌkt] *v.t.* **1.**

teach. **2.** give orders to. **in·struc·tion** [in'strʌkʃən] *n.* **1.** teaching. **2.** (pl.) orders; directions. **in·struc·tive** *adj.* giving knowledge. **in·struc·tor** *n.*

in·stru·ment ['instrumənt] *n.* **1.** simple apparatus used in performing an action, esp. for delicate or scientific work: *optical ~s* (e.g. a microscope). (Cf. *tool, utensil.*) **2.** apparatus for producing musical sounds. **3.** person used by another for his own purposes. **in·stru·men·tal** [ˌinstru'mentəl] *adj.* **1.** (of music) played on ~s. **2.** serving as a means: *~al in (doing) sth.* **in·stru·men·tal·ist** *n.* player of an ~ (2).

in·sub·or·di·nate [ˌinsə'bɔːdinit] *adj.* disobedient; reckless. **in·sub·or·di·na·tion** [ˈinsəˌbɔːdi-'neiʃən] *n.*

in·suf·fer·a·ble [in'sʌfərəbl] *adj.* over-proud; unbearably conceited.

in·su·lar ['insjulə*] *adj.* of an island; of or like islanders; narrow-minded. **~·i·ty** [ˌinsju-'læriti] *n.*

in·su·late ['insjuleit] *v.t.* **1.** cover or separate (sth.) with non-conducting material to prevent loss of heat, electricity, etc. **2.** separate (sb. or sth.) *from* surroundings; . isolate. **in·su·la·tion** [ˌinsju'leiʃən] *n.* being ~d; act of insulating; insulating material. **in·su·la·tor** *n.* (esp.) substance, device, for insulating electric wire.

in·sult ['insʌlt] *n.* sth. said or done intended to hurt, or actually hurting, a person's feelings or dignity. [in'sʌlt] *v.t.* treat (sb.) with ~s.

in·su·per·a·ble [in'sjuːpərəbl] *adj.* (of difficulties, etc.) that cannot be overcome.

in·sup·port·a·ble [ˌinsə'pɔːtəbl] *adj.* that cannot be endured.

in·sur·ance [in'ʃuərəns] *n.* **1.** (undertaking, by a company, society, or the State, to provide) safeguard against loss, provision against sickness, death, etc., in return for regular payments. **2.** payment made to or by such a company, etc. ~ **pol·i·cy** *n.* agreement covering ~. **in·sure** [inˈʃuə*] *v.t.* make an agreement about ~: *to insure one's house against fire (one's life for £1,000).*

in·sur·gent [inˈsə:dʒənt] *adj.* rebellious. *n.* rebel soldier.

in·sur·mount·a·ble [ˌinsə-ˈmauntəbl] *adj.* that cannot be climbed or overcome.

in·sur·rec·tion [ˌinsəˈrekʃən] *n.* rising against the government.

in·tact [inˈtækt] *adj.* undamaged; untouched; complete.

in·take [ˈinteik] *n.* 1. place where water, gas, etc., is taken into a pipe, channel, etc. 2. quantity, number, entering (during a given period).

in·tan·gi·ble [inˈtændʒibl] *adj.* (esp.) that cannot be grasped by the mind.

in·te·ger [ˈintidʒə*] *n.* whole number (contrasted with a fraction); thing complete in itself.

in·te·gral [ˈintigrəl] *adj.* 1. necessary for completeness. 2. whole.

in·te·grate [ˈintigreit] *v.t.* make complete; combine (parts) into a whole. **in·te·gra·tion** [ˌintiˈgrei-ʃən] *n.* integrating or being ~d: *the integration of immigrants into the local community.*

in·teg·ri·ty [inˈtegriti] *n.* 1. quality of being honest and upright in character: *commercial* ~. 2. condition of being complete.

in·tel·lect [ˈintilekt] *n.* power of the mind to reason (contrasted with feeling and instinct). **in·tel·lec·tu·al** [ˌintiˈlektjuəl] *adj.* 1. of the ~. 2. having or showing good reasoning power: *an* ~*ual man (face). n. *~ual person.*

in·tel·li·gence [inˈtelidʒəns] *n.* 1. (power of) understanding and learning. 2. news; information. **in·tel·li·gent** *adj.* having, showing, ~. **in·tel·li·gent·si·a** [inˌteliˈdʒentsiə] *n.* that part of a nation which can be regarded as capable of serious independent thinking. **in·tel·li·gi·ble** [inˈtelidʒəbl] *adj.* clear to the mind; easily understood. **in·tel·li·gi·bil·i·ty** [inˌtelidʒiˈbiliti] *n.*

in·tend [inˈtend] *v.t.* have in mind as a purpose or plan.

in·tense [inˈtens] *adj.* 1. (of qualities) high in degree: ~ *heat.* 2. (of feelings, etc.) strong; violent. ~**ly** *adv.* **in·ten·si·fy** [inˈtensifai] *v.t. & i.* make, become, ~. **in·ten·si·fi·ca·tion** [inˌtensifiˈkeiʃən] *n.* **in·ten·si·ty** [inˈtensiti] *n.* being ~; strength (of feeling, etc.). **in·ten·sive** *adj.* deep and thorough: ~ *study.*

in·tent [inˈtent] *adj.* 1. (of looks) eager; earnest. 2. (of persons) ~ *on,* with the attention or desires directed towards. *n.* purpose: *shooting with ~ to kill; to all ~s and purposes,* in all essential points.

in·ten·tion [inˈtenʃən] *n.* purpose; intending. ~**al** *adj.* said or done on purpose. ~**al·ly** *adv.*

in·ter [inˈtə:*] *v.t.* (-rr-). bury.

in·ter- *prefix.* between; among; one with or on another.

in·ter·cede [ˌintəˈsi:d] *v.i.* plead (*with sb. for* or *on behalf of* sb. else). **in·ter·ces·sion** [ˌintə-ˈseʃən] *n.*

in·ter·cept [ˌintəˈsept] *v.t.* stop, catch, seize (sb. or sth.) between the starting-point and the destination.

in·ter·change [ˌintəˈtʃeindʒ] *v.t.* 1. make an exchange of (views, etc.). 2. put (each of two things) in the other's place. [ˈintə-tʃeindʒ] *n.*

in·ter·course [ˈintəkɔ:s] *n.* social dealings or communication: exchange (of trade, ideas, etc., between persons, societies, nations, etc.).

in·ter·est [ˈintrist] *n.* 1. condition of wanting to know or learn about sth.: *taking a great* ~ *in sport.* 2. quality that excites curiosity. 3. sth. with which one concerns oneself: *His chief ~s are horse-racing and football.* 4. importance: *a matter of considerable ~.* 5. (what is to sb.'s) advantage or profit: *to look after one's own ~s.* 6. legal right to a share in sth., esp. in its profits. 7. money charged or paid for the loan of capital: *a loan at 6 per cent ~*. ['intərest] *v.t.* cause (sb.) to give his attention to: *Can I ~ you in this question?* **in·ter·est·ed** ['intristid] *adj.* having an ~ (6) in; self-seeking: showing or taking ~ (1). ~**·ing** *adj.* holding the attention.

in·ter·fere [,intə'fiə*] *v.i.* 1. (of persons) ~ *in*, break in upon (other persons' affairs) without right or invitation. 2. ~ *with*, come into opposition with: *allowing pleasure to ~ with duty*; meddle with. **in·ter·fer·ence** *n.*

in·ter·im ['intərim] *n. in the ~*, meanwhile; between these two events; (attrib.) as an instalment; for the meantime.

in·te·ri·or [in'tiəriə*] *adj.* 1. situated inside; of the inside parts. 2. inland. 3. domestic (not foreign). *n.* 1. the inside parts of sth. 2. inland areas.

in·ter·ject [,intə'dʒekt] *v.t.* put in suddenly (a remark, etc.) between statements, etc., made by another. **in·ter·jec·tion** *n.* word(s) used as exclamation(s) (e.g. *Oh! Good! Indeed!*).

in·ter·lock [,intə'lɔk] *v.t. & i.* lock or join together; clasp firmly together.

in·ter·lop·er ['intəloupə*] *n.* person who (esp. for profit) pushes himself in where he has no right.

in·ter·lude ['intəlu:d] *n.* 1. interval between two events or two periods of time of different character, esp. the interval between two acts of a play. 2. music played during an interval.

in·ter·me·di·a·ry [,intə'mi:djəri] *n. & adj.* (sb. or sth.) acting between (persons, groups).

in·ter·me·di·ate [,intə'mi:djət] *adj.* situated or coming between (in time, space, degree, etc.).

in·ter·mi·na·ble [in'tə:minəbl] *adj.* endless; tedious because too long.

in·ter·mit·tent [,intə'mitənt] *adj.* with some intervals: ~ *fever*, fever that keeps coming and going.

in·tern [in'tə:n] *v.t.* compel (persons, esp. aliens during a

war) to live inside certain fixed limits or in a special camp. ~**·ment** *n.*

in·ter·nal [in'tə:nəl] *adj.* 1. of or in the inside. 2. of the home or domestic affairs of a country. 3. derived from within the thing itself: ~ *evidence* (e.g. of when a book was written). ~**·ly** *adv.*

in·ter·na·tion·al [,intə'næʃənəl] *adj.* existing, carried on, between nations.

in·ter·play ['intəplei] *n.* operation of two things on each other.

in·ter·po·late [in'tə:pəleit] *v.t.* make (usu. misleading) additions to a book, manuscript, etc. **in·ter·po·la·tion** [in,tə:-pə'leiʃən] *n.*

in·ter·pose [,intə'pouz] *v.t. & i.* 1. put forward (an objection, a veto, etc.) as an interference. 2. say (sth.) as an interruption. 3. come in (*between* others); mediate (*in* a dispute).

in·ter·pret [in'tə:prit] *v.t. & i.* 1. show, make clear, the meaning of (either in words or by artistic performance of music, etc.). 2. consider to be the meaning of. 3. act as ~er. ~**·er** *n.* person who gives an immediate translation of words spoken in another language. **in·ter·pre·ta·tion** [in,tə:pri'teiʃən] *n.*

in·ter·ro·gate [in'terəgeit] *v.t.* question. **in·ter·ro·ga·tion** [in,terə'geiʃən] *n.* questioning. **in·ter·rog·a·tive** [,intə'rɔgətiv] *adj.* of or for questions.

in·ter·rupt [,intə'rʌpt] *v.t. & i.* break the continuity of: *traffic ~ed by floods*; speak to sb. while he is saying sth. **in·ter·rup·tion** *n.* ~ing; sth. that ~s.

in·ter·sect [,intə'sekt] *v.t. & i.* 1. divide by cutting, passing, or lying across. 2. (of lines) cut or cross each other. **in·ter·sec·tion** *n.* (esp.) point where two lines, etc., cross.

in·ter·sperse [,intə'spə:s] *v.t.* place here and there (*between* or *among*).

in·ter·val ['intəvəl] *n.* 1. time (between two events or two parts of an action), esp. the time between two acts of a play, two parts of a concert, etc. **2.** space between (two objects or points): *at* ∼s, with ∼s between. **in·ter·vene** [,intə'vi:n] *v.i.* **1.** (of circumstances, events) come between (others) in time. **2.** (of persons) interfere so as to prevent sth. or change the result. **3.** (of time) come or be between. **in·ter·ven·tion** [,intə'venʃən] *n.* intervening (2).

in·ter·view ['intəvju:] *n.* meeting with sb. for discussion or conference; meeting of a newspaper reporter, broadcaster, with sb. whose views are requested. *v.t.* conduct an ∼ with.

in·tes·tate [in'testeit] *adj.* not having made a will before death occurs.

in·tes·tine [in'testin] *n.* (usu. pl.) lower part of the food canal below the stomach.

¹**in·ti·mate** ['intimit] *adj.* **1.** close and familiar: ∼ *friends*; *on* ∼ *terms*. **2.** innermost; private and personal: ∼ *details of one's life*. ∼**ly** *adv.* **in·ti·ma·cy** ['intiməsi] *n.* **1.** being ∼. **2.** ∼ action (e.g. a caress).

²**in·ti·mate** ['intimeit] *v.t.* make known; show clearly: ∼ *one's approval*. **in·ti·ma·tion** [,inti'meiʃən] *n.* (esp.) sth. ∼d; suggestion.

in·tim·i·date [in'timideit] *v.t.* frighten, esp. in order to force (sb.) *into* doing sth. **in·tim·i·da·tion** [in,timi'deiʃən] *n.*

in·to ['intu] *prep.* **1.** (indicating movement towards a point within): *Let us go* ∼ *the garden*. **2.** (indicating a change or a result from action): *He got himself* ∼ *serious trouble*.

in·tone [in'toun] *v.t.* recite (a prayer, etc.) in a singing voice; speak with a particular tone. **in·to·na·tion** [,intou'neiʃən] *n.* (esp.) the rise and fall of the voice in speaking.

in·tox·i·cate [in'toksikeit] *v.t.* **1.** make stupid with, cause to lose self-control as the result of taking, alcoholic drink. **2.** excite greatly, beyond self-

control: ∼*d with (by) success*. **in·tox·i·cant** *adj. & n.* (intoxicating) drink. **in·tox·i·ca·tion** [in,tɔksi'keiʃən] *n.*

in·trep·id [in'trepid] *adj.* fearless.

in·tri·cate ['intrikit] *adj.* complicated; puzzling. **in·tri·ca·cy** ['intrikəsi] *n.*

in·trigue [in'tri:g] *n.* secret plotting; plot; secret love-affair. *v.i.* engage in ∼: ∼ *with A against B*.

in·trin·sic [in'trinsik] *adj.* (of value, quality) belonging naturally; existing within, not coming from outside.

in·tro·duce [,intrə'dju:s] *v.t.* **1.** bring in or forward: *to* ∼ *a Bill before Parliament*. **2.** bring (sth.) into use or into operation for the first time; cause (sb.) to be acquainted with. **3.** make (persons) known by name *to* one another, esp. in the usual formal way. **4.** insert (*into*). **in·tro·duc·tion** [,intrə'dʌkʃən] *n.* introducing or being ∼d; sth. ∼d or that ∼s; (esp.) explanatory article at or before the beginning of a book. **in·tro·duc·to·ry** [,intrə'dʌktəri] *adj.* serving to ∼ sb. or sth.

in·tro·spec·tion [,introu'spekʃən] *n.* examination by oneself of one's thoughts and feelings. **in·tro·spec·tive** *adj.*

in·trude [in'tru:d] *v.t. & i.* force (oneself *into* a place, *upon* sb.); enter without invitation. **in·tru·der** *n.* **in·tru·sion** [in'tru:ʒən] *n.*

in·tu·i·tion [,intju'iʃən] *n.* (power of) immediate understanding of sth. without reasoning.

in·un·date ['inʌndeit] *v.t.* flood: ∼*d fields*; (fig.) overwhelmed: ∼*d with requests*. **in·un·da·tion** [,inʌn'deiʃən] *n.*

in·ure [i'njuə*] *v.t.* accustom.

in·vade [in'veid] *v.t.* **1.** enter (a country) with armed forces in order to attack. **2.** (fig., of feelings, diseases, etc.) attack. **3.** violate, interfere with: ∼ *sb.'s rights*. **in·vad·er** *n.* **in·va·sion** [in'veiʒən] *n.*

¹**in·val·id** ['invəli(:)d] *n. & adj.*

(person who is) weak or disabled through illness or injury; suitable for such a person: *an ~ chair (diet)*. (also [͵invə'li:d]) *v.t. & i.* (esp. of a member of the armed forces) remove from active service as an ~: *He was ~ed home.*

²in·val·id [in'vælid] *adj.* not valid.

in·val·u·a·ble [in'væljuəbl] *adj.* having a value too great to be measured.

in·va·sion, see *invade*.

in·vec·tive [in'vektiv] *n.* abusive language.

in·veigh [in'vei] *v.i.* ~ *against*, attack violently in words.

in·vei·gle [in'veigl] *v.t.* lure (sb. *into* a place, *into* doing sth., etc.) by using flattery, etc.

in·vent [in'vent] *v.t.* 1. create or design (sth. not existing before). 2. make up (a story, excuse, etc.). in·ven·tor *n.* in·ven·tive *adj.* able to ~: *an ~ive mind.* in·ven·tion [in'venʃən] *n.* ~ing; sth. ~ed; capacity to ~.

in·ven·to·ry ['invəntri] *n.* detailed list (of household goods, stocks, etc.).

in·verse ['in'və:s] *adj.* inverted: *in ~ proportion (ratio)*, that between two quantities one of which decreases in the same proportion that the other increases.

in·vert [in'və:t] *v.t.* put upside down or in the opposite order, position, or relation: *~ed commas, " " or ' '.* in·ver·sion [in'və:ʃən] *n.* ~ing or being ~ed.

in·vest [in'vest] *v.t. & i.* 1. put (money *in* a business, *in* stocks and shares, etc.). 2. ~ *in*, (colloq.) buy (sth. considered useful). 3. clothe, endow (*in* or *with* robes, insignia, authority). 4. surround (e.g. a town) with armed forces. in·ves·ti·ture [in'vestitʃə*] *n.* ceremony of ~ing(3) sb. with a rank, etc. ~·ment *n.* the ~ing of money; sum of money ~ed; business undertaking, etc., in which money is ~ed: *a good (bad) investment.* ~·or *n.* person who ~s money.

in·ves·ti·gate [in'vestigeit] *v.t.* examine, inquire into (e.g. the causes of an accident). in·ves·ti·ga·tion [in͵vesti'geiʃən] *n.*

in·vet·er·ate [in'vetərit] *adj.* (esp. of habits, prejudices) deep-rooted; long-established.

in·vid·i·ous [in'vidiəs] *adj.* likely to cause ill feeling (because of real or apparent injustice): *~ distinctions.*

in·vig·o·rate [in'vigəreit] *v.t.* make vigorous; make strong or confident.

in·vin·ci·ble [in'vinsibl] *adj.* too strong to be overcome or conquered.

in·vi·o·la·ble [in'vaiələbl] *adj.* not to be disturbed, disobeyed, or treated disrespectfully.

in·vi·o·late [in'vaiəlit, -eit] *adj.* unbroken; untouched; held in respect.

in·vite [in'vait] *v.t.* 1. ask (sb. to accept hospitality, do sth., come somewhere, etc.). 2. ask for (suggestions, etc.). 3. encourage; attract. in·vit·ing *adj.* attractive. in·vi·ta·tion [͵invi'teiʃən] *n.* (esp.) request to come or go somewhere, do sth.

in·vo·ca·tion, see *invoke*.

in·voice ['invɔis] *v.t. & n.* (make a) list of goods sold with the prices charged: *to ~ sb. for sth.*

in·voke [in'vouk] *v.t.* 1. call upon (God, the power of the law, etc.) for help or protection. 2. request earnestly. 3. summon (by magic). in·vo·ca·tion [͵invou'keiʃən] *n.* (prayer used for) invoking.

in·vol·un·ta·ry [in'vɔləntəri] *adj.* done without intention; done unconsciously.

in·volve [in'vɔlv] *v.t.* 1. cause (sb. or sth.) to be caught or mixed up (*in* trouble, etc.); get (sb. or sth.) into a complicated or difficult condition: *~d in debt (crime)*. 2. have as a necessary consequence: *plans that ~ further expenditure.* in·volved *adj.* complex.

in·ward ['inwəd] *adj.* 1. situated within; inner. 2. turned towards the inside. ~·ly *adv.*

(esp.) in mind or spirit. **in·ward(s)** *adv.* towards the inside; towards the mind.

i·o·dine ['aiədi:n] *n.* chemical substance used as an antiseptic and in dyeing and photography.

i·o·ta [ai'outə] *n.* the Greek letter i: *not an ~ of truth*, no truth at all.

I O U ['aiou'ju:] *n.* (= I owe you). signed paper acknowledging that one owes the sum of money stated.

ir- prefix. not, as in *irreverent, irresponsible*, etc.

i·ras·ci·ble [i'ræsibl] *adj.* easily made angry.

i·rate [ai'reit] *adj.* angry. **ire** ['aiə*] *n.* (liter.) anger.

i·ris ['aiəris] *n.* **1.** coloured part of the eyeball. **2.** flowering plant with sword-shaped leaves.

irk [ə:k] *v.t.* trouble; annoy: *It irks me to....* **irk·some** *adj.* tiresome.

i·ron ['aiən] *n.* **1.** commonest and most important metal, from which steel is made. *strike while the ~ is hot*, act while circumstances are favourable. *rule with an ~ hand (a rod of ~)*, rule with great severity. *a man of ~*, an unfeeling, merciless man. **2.** tool, etc., made of ~, esp. (*flat-~*) tool heated and used for smoothing clothes, etc. *too many ~s in the fire*, too many plans, etc., needing attention at the same time. **3.** (pl.) *~ chains* for a prisoner's hands or feet: *to put a man in ~s.* *v.t.* smooth (clothes, etc.) with a flat-~. '**~,mon·ger** *n.* dealer in goods made of metal. '**~·,mon·ger·y** *n.* business of an ~monger; his goods. '**~-mould** *n.* discoloration caused by ~-rust or ink.

i·ron·y ['aiərəni] *n.* **1.** the expression of one's meaning by saying sth. that is the direct opposite of one's thoughts, in order to make one's remarks forceful. **2.** event, situation, which is itself desirable, but which, because of the circumstances, is of no value: *the ~ of fate; one of life's ironies.* **i·ron·**

i·cal [aiə'rɔnikl] *adj.* of, using, showing, ~.

ir·re·proach·a·ble [,iri'prout∫əbl] *adj.* free from blame.

ir·re·sis·ti·ble [,iri'zistəbl] *adj.* that cannot be resisted; very attractive.

ir·re·spec·tive [,iri'spektiv] *adj.* ~ *of*, not paying consideration to.

ir·re·spon·si·ble [,iri'spɔnsəbl] *adj.* **1.** (esp. of behaviour) done without proper care. **2.** not responsible; not to be blamed.

ir·ri·gate ['irigeit] *v.t.* **1.** supply (land, crops) with water (by means of rivers, water-channels, etc.). **2.** construct reservoirs, canals, ditches, etc., for distribution of water (for crops). **ir·ri·ga·tion** [,iri'gei∫ən] *n.*

ir·ri·tate ['iriteit] *v.t.* **1.** make angry or annoyed. **2.** cause discomfort to (part of the body); make sore or inflamed. **ir·ri·ta·ble** ['iritəbl] *adj.* easily ~d. **ir·ri·tant** ['iritənt] *n. & adj.* (thing) causing irritation. **ir·ri·ta·tion** [,iri'tei∫ən] *n.*

Is·lam ['izla:m] *n.* faith, religion, taught by the prophet Muhammad; all Muslims; all the Muslim world.

is·land ['ailənd] *n.* piece of land surrounded by water; thing considered to be like an ~ because it is surrounded by sth. different. **~·er** *n.* person born on or living on an ~. **isle** [ail] *n.* (liter. except in proper names) ~.

i·so·bar ['aisouba:*] *n.* line on a map joining places with the same atmospheric pressure at a particular time.

i·so·late ['aisəleit] *v.t.* separate, put or keep away, from others. **i·so·la·tion** [,aisə'lei∫ən] *n.*

is·sue ['isju:, 'i∫ju:, 'ifu:] *v.i. & t.* **1.** come, go, flow, out: *smoke issuing from chimneys.* **2.** give or send out; publish (journals, etc.); distribute: *to ~ commands (bank-notes, orders).* *n.* **1.** outgoing: *the point of ~.* **2.** result, outcome, or consequence: *a problem with important ~s.* **3.** question that arises for discussion: *debating an ~; the point* *with sb.* (*on* sth.), argue with him (about it). **4.** publication, edition (of newspapers, etc.); sending out (*of* new coins, etc.); postage stamps, etc.). **5.** (legal) offspring: *to die without* ~ (i.e. childless).

isth·mus ['isməs] *n.* neck of land joining two larger bodies of land.

it [it] *pron.* (pl. *they, them*). **1.** used in referring to lifeless things, animals, infants: *Where's my book? Have you seen it?* **2.** used to refer to a phrase or clause which follows: *Is it difficult to learn Chinese?* **3.** used as a subject for the verb *be,* etc., balancing the complement: *It's raining. It's six o'clock. It's a cold day.* **4.** used to emphasize one part of a sentence: *It was John I gave the book to, not Harry.* **its** [its] *poss. adj.* of it: *The dog wagged its tail.* **it·self** [it'self] *pron. The dog got up and stretched itself.*

i·tal·ic [i'tælik] *adj.* (of letters) sloping: ~ *type.* **n. pl.** ~ letters. **i·tal·i·cize** [i'tælisaiz] *v.t.* print in ~s.

itch [itʃ] *v.i. & n.* **1.** (have a) feeling of irritation on the skin, causing one to want to scratch. **2.** (have a) restless longing (*for* sth., *to* do sth.). ~·y *adj.*

i·tem ['aitəm] *n.* **1.** single article or unit in a list, etc. **2.** detail or paragraph (of news). ~·ize ['aitəmaiz] *v.t.* give, write, every ~ of: *an ~ized account.*

i·tin·er·ant [i'tinərənt] *adj.* going from place to place: ~ *musicians.*

i·tin·er·a·ry [ai'tinərəri] *n.* (plan for, details or records of, a) journey; route.

i·vo·ry ['aivəri] *n.* white, bone-like substance forming the tusks of elephants, etc., used for ornaments, piano-keys, etc.

i·vy ['aivi] *n.* climbing, clinging, evergreen plant with dark, shiny (often five-pointed) leaves.

J

jab [dʒæb] *v.t.* (*-bb-*). force (a pointed weapon, the elbow, etc.) suddenly and roughly (*into* sb. or sth.); aim a blow (*at* sb. or sth.). *n.* blow of this sort.

jab·ber ['dʒæbə*] *v.i. & t.* talk excitedly; utter (words, sounds) fast and indistinctly. *n.* chatter; rapid, confused talk.

jack [dʒæk] *n.* **1.** device for raising heavy objects, e.g. cars, engines, off the ground, in order to remove wheels, etc. **2.** ship's flag to show nationality, esp. *the Union Jack* (of the United Kingdom). *v.t.* (~ *up*) raise with a ~. ~·**ass** ['dʒækæs] *n.* male ass; foolish person. **'~- of-'all-trades** *n.* person knowing something of many trades. **jack·al** ['dʒækɔ:l] *n.* wild dog-like animal.

jack·et ['dʒækit] *n.* **1.** short, sleeved coat. **2.** outer covering round a boiler; skin of a potato, etc.; loose paper wrapper to protect a book.

jade [dʒeid] *n.* hard, usu. green, stone, carved into ornaments. **jad·ed** ['dʒeidid] *adj.* tired out; wearied by excess: *a* ~ *appetite.*

jag [dʒæg] *n.* sharp, rough point of rock. **jag·ged** ['dʒægid] *adj.* with rough, uneven edges: *jagged rocks.*

jag·uar ['dʒægwɑ:*] *n.* large, fierce, cat-like animal, of Central and S. America.

jail [dʒeil] *n.* = gaol.

¹jam [dʒæm] *v.t. & i.* (*-mm-*). **1.** crush, be crushed, between two surfaces or things: *a ship jammed in the ice; logs that jam in a river* (i.e. become tightly packed). **2.** (of parts of a machine, etc.) (cause to) become fixed so that movement or action is prevented: *to jam on the brakes of a car. The brakes jammed.* **3.** push (things) together (into a mass or into sth.): *to jam clothes into a drawer; a corridor jammed by people.* **4.** *jam a broadcast,* interfere with the reception of a broadcast from another station. *n.* number of things or people crowded together so that movement is difficult: *a traffic jam.*

²**jam** [dʒæm] *n.* fruit boiled with sugar and preserved in jars, etc.

jamb [dʒæm] *n.* side post of a doorway or window.

jam·bor·ee [ˌdʒæmbəˈriː] *n.* merry meeting, rally, esp. of Scouts.

jan·gle [ˈdʒæŋgl] *v.i. & t. & n.* (give out, cause to give out a) harsh, metallic noise.

jan·i·tor [ˈdʒænitə*] *n.* door-keeper.

Jan·u·a·ry [ˈdʒænjuəri] *n.* the first month of the year.

¹**jar** [dʒɑ:*] *v.i. & t.* (*-rr-*). **1.** strike (*on* or *against* sth.) with a harsh, unpleasant sound. **2.** have an unpleasant effect (*on* sb., their ears or nerves): *sounds that jar on the ear.* **3.** *jar with,* be out of harmony with: *a jar-ring note.* *n.* **1.** jarring sound. **2.** bodily or mental shock. **3.** disagreement or quarrel.

²**jar** [dʒɑ:*] *n.* tall vessel, usu. round, with a wide mouth, of glass, stone, or earthenware.

A jam-jar   A javelin

jar·gon [ˈdʒɑ:gən] *n.* **1.** language difficult to understand, because it is either a bad form or spoken badly. **2.** language full of technical or special words: *the ~ of radio technicians.*

jas·min(e) [ˈdʒæsmin] *n.* (kinds of) shrub with sweet-smelling white or yellow flowers.

jaun·dice [ˈdʒɔ:ndis] *n.* disease, caused by stoppage of bile, marked by yellow skin; (fig.) mental outlook marked by spite and jealousy. **jaun·diced** *adj.* jealous and spiteful.

jaunt [dʒɔ:nt] *v.i. & n.* (take a) short journey for pleasure.

jaun·ty [ˈdʒɔ:nti] *adj.* (*-ier, -iest*). feeling or showing self-con-fidence and self-satisfaction. **jaun·ti·ly** *adv.* **jaun·ti·ness** *n.*

jave·lin [ˈdʒævlin] *n.* light spear. *throwing the ~* (a sport).

jaw [dʒɔ:] *n.* **1.** *lower* (*upper*) *jaw,* one or other of the bone structures containing the teeth. **2.** (pl.) the mouth, its bones and teeth; (fig.) mouth of a valley, etc.; (esp.) entrance to a danger-ous place. **3.** gripping part (e.g. of a ²*vice*). **4.** (colloq.) talk; tedious moral lecture. *v.t. & i.* (colloq.) talk; rebuke (sb.).

jay [dʒei] *n.* (sorts of) noisy, bright-coloured bird.

jazz [dʒæz] *n.* rhythmical music and dancing of American Negro origin. *adj.* (also *jazzy*) (e.g. of patterns) of strongly contrasted colours and shapes. *v.i.* play or dance ~; arrange as ~.

jeal·ous [ˈdʒeləs] *adj.* **1.** feeling or showing fear or ill will be-cause of possible or actual loss of rights or love: *a ~ husband*; *~ looks.* **2.** feeling or showing unhappiness because of the better fortune, etc., of others: *~ of sb. else's success.* **3.** taking watchful care (*of* one's reputa-tion, etc.). **~·ly** *adv.* **~·y** *n.* being ~.

jean [dʒi:n] *n.* strong cotton cloth; (pl.) workman's overalls; close-fitting trousers.

jeep [dʒi:p] *n.* strong, light motor vehicle, for use on rough ground.

jeer [dʒiə*] *v.i.* mock, laugh rudely (*at* sb.). *n.* ~ing remark.

jelly [ˈdʒeli] *n.* soft, semi-trans-parent food substance made from gelatin; similar substance made with fruit juice. *v.t. & i.* (cause to) become like ~. **'~-fish** *n.* ~-like sea animal.

A jelly-fish

jem·my ['dʒemi] *n.* short iron bar used (by burglars) for forcing windows, doors, drawers, etc., open.

jeop·ard·y ['dʒepədi] *n. in* ~, in danger. **jeop·ard·ize** ['dʒepədaiz] *v.t.* put in danger.

jerk [dʒəːk] *v.t. & i. & n.* **1.** (give a) sudden pull or twist: *The train stopped with a* ~ (~ed to *a stop*). *The old bus* ~ed *along.* **2.** (give a) sudden twitch of the muscles. **3.** *physical* ~s, (colloq.) physical exercises. ~·y *adj.* (-ier, -iest). with sudden stops and starts. ~·i·ly *adv.*

jer·kin ['dʒəːkin] *n.* short, close-fitting jacket, usu. of leather.

jer·ry-built ['dʒeribilt] *adj.* (of buildings) badly made of bad materials.

jer·sey ['dʒəːzi] *n.* close-fitting knitted woollen garment with sleeves.

jest [dʒest] *n.* sth. said or done to cause amusement; joke. *in* ~, not in earnest. *v.i.* make ~s; act or speak lightly. ~·er *n.* (esp.) man kept in former times by a king or noble to provide amusement by his ~s. ~·ing·ly *adv.*

¹**jet** [dʒet] *n.* **1.** strong stream of gas, liquid, steam, or flame, forced out of a small opening. *jet aircraft (engine)*, one driven forward by jets of gas directed backwards from it. **2.** the narrow opening from which a jet comes out.

²**jet** [dʒet] *n.* hard black mineral taking a brilliant polish and used for buttons, ornaments, etc. *adj.* black.

jet·sam ['dʒetsəm] *n.* goods thrown overboard from a ship at sea to lighten it (e.g. in a storm); such goods washed to the sea-shore. (Cf. *flotsam*.)

jet·ti·son ['dʒetisn] *v.t.* throw (goods) overboard in order to lighten a ship, e.g. during a storm.

jet·ty ['dʒeti] *n.* structure built as a breakwater or as a landing-place for boats or ships.

Jew [dʒuː] *n.* person of the Hebrew race. **Jew·ish** ['dʒuːiʃ] *adj.* of the Jews.

jew·el ['dʒuːəl] *n.* **1.** precious stone (e.g. a diamond or ruby); ornament with ~s set in it. **2.** sth. or sb. highly valued. *v.t.* (-*ll*-). adorn with ~s. ~·ler *n.* trader in ~s; person who sets ~s. ~·(le)ry *n.* ~s.

¹**jib** [dʒib] *n.* small triangular sail.

²**jib** [dʒib] *v.i.* (-*bb*-). **1.** (of a horse, etc.) stop suddenly; refuse to go forward; (fig.) refuse to proceed with sth. **2.** *jib at*, show unwillingness or dislike: *He jibbed at working overtime.*

jibe [dʒaib] *n. & v.i.* = gibe.

jif·fy ['dʒifi] *n.* (colloq.) *in a* ~, in a moment; very soon.

jig [dʒig] *n.* (music for a) quick, lively dance. *v.i. & t.* (-*gg*-). dance a jig; move up and down in a quick, jerky way. **jig·saw** *n.* = fret-saw. **jig·saw ,puz·zle** *n.* picture, map, etc., pasted on thin board and cut in irregularly shaped pieces which are to be fitted together again.

jilt [dʒilt] *v.t.* (usu. of a woman) give up, send away, a lover after giving him encouragement or a promise to marry. *n.* woman who does this.

jin·gle ['dʒiŋgl] *v.i. & t. & n.* (make a) light, ringing sound (as of coins or keys striking together, or small bells); succession of words having similar sounds.

jinks [dʒiŋks] *n. high* ~s, noisy merry-making; uncontrolled fun.

job [dʒɔb] *n.* **1.** complete(d) piece of work: *make a good job of it*, do it well; *odd jobs*, bits of work not connected with each other. **2.** *That's a good (bad) job*, that is (un)fortunate. **3.** regular employment: *out of a job*, unemployed; *looking for a job*. *v.t. & i.* (-*bb*-). **1.** do odd jobs (usu. present participle): *a jobbing gardener* (not working for one employer only). **2.** do business for others (as a broker on the Stock Exchange, in markets, etc.).

jock·ey ['dʒɔki] *n.* person (esp. a professional) who rides horses in races. *v.t. & i.* trick (sb.) (*out of* sth.; *into* doing sth.).

jo·cose [dʒə'kous] *adj.* humorous; playful. ~**ly** *adv.*

joc·u·lar ['dʒɔkjulə*] *adj.* humorous; given to joking. ~**i·ty** [ˌdʒɔkju'læriti] *n.* ~**ly** *adv.*

jo·cund ['dʒɔkənd] *adj.* merry; cheerful.

jog [dʒɔg] *v.t. & i.* (-gg-) *& n.* **1.** (give a) slight knock or push: *jog sb.'s elbow*; (fig.) *jog sb.'s memory*, cause him to remember sth. **2.** (run, move, at a) pace causing an unsteady, shaking motion: *The old bus jogged us up and down. We jogged along the bad roads.* **3.** *jog on, along*, (fig.) make slow, uneventful progress. '**jog·trot** *n.* slow, regular trot.

join [dʒɔin] *v.t. & i.* **1.** put or come together; unite or be united; connect (two points, things) with a line, rope, bridge, etc. **2.** become a member of (a society, the armed forces, etc.). **3.** come into the company of; associate with (sb. *in* sth.): *I'll soon ~ you. Will you ~ us in a game of cards? n.* = joint(1).

join·er ['dʒɔinə*] *n.* skilled workman who makes furniture and house fittings in wood. (Cf. *carpenter*.) ~**y** *n.* work of a ~.

joint [dʒɔint] *n.* **1.** place at which two things are joined. **2.** structure by which two things are joined (e.g. two pipes, two bones) are joined: *finger ~s.* **3.** limb or other division of a sheep, ox, etc., which a butcher serves to his customers. *adj.* held or done by, belonging to, two or more persons together: *~ ownership*; *~ stock*, capital(3) contributed by a number of persons. *v.t.* **1.** fit together by means of ~s (2): *a ~ed fishing-rod.* **2.** divide at a ~ (2).

Finger joints   A joint of meat

joist [dʒɔist] *n.* one of the parallel pieces of timber (from wall to wall) to which floor-boards are nailed.

joke [dʒouk] *n.* sth. said or done to cause amusement; circumstance that causes amusement. *practical ~*, trick played on sb. to make him seem ridiculous. *It's no ~*, it's a serious matter. *v.i.* make ~s. **jok·er** *n.* **jok·ing·ly** *adv.*

jol·ly ['dʒɔli] *adj.* (-ier, -iest). **1.** joyful; gay; merry. **2.** (colloq.) delightful. *adv.* (colloq.) very. **jol·li·fi·ca·tion** [ˌdʒɔlifi'keiʃən] *n.* merry-making; festivity. **jol·li·ty** *n.* ~ condition; fun.

jolt [dʒoult] *v.t. & i. & n.* **1.** (give sb. or sth. a) jerk or sudden shake. **2.** (of a cart, etc.) move with ~s: *The old bus ~ed along* (*~ed its passengers badly*).

jos·tle ['dʒɔsl] *v.t. & i.* push roughly (against); push (sb. *away*, or *from*).

¹**jot** [dʒɔt] *v.t.* (-tt-). *jot sth. down*, make a quick written note of it.

²**jot** [dʒɔt] *n.* very small amount. *not a jot*, not a bit, not at all.

jour·nal ['dʒə:nl] *n.* **1.** daily newspaper; other periodical. **2.** daily record of news, events, accounts(2), etc. ~**ese** [ˌdʒə:nə'li:z] *n.* style of English composition common in second-rate ~s. ~**ism** ['dʒə:nəlizm] *n.* work of writing for, editing, or publishing, newspapers. ~**ist** *n.* person engaged in ~ism.

jour·ney ['dʒə:ni] *n.* (distance travelled in) going to a place, esp. a distant place (usu. by land; cf. *voyage*): *a three days' ~; to go on* (make) *a ~* (*from . . . to . . .*). *v.i.* make a ~.

joust [dʒu:st, dʒaust] *v.i. & n.* (engage in a) fight on horseback with lances (as between knights in the Middle Ages).

jo·vial ['dʒouvjəl] *adj.* full of fun and good humour. ~**ly** *adv.* **jo·vi·al·i·ty** [ˌdʒouvi'æliti] *n.*

jowl [dʒaul] *n.* jaw; lower part of the face. *cheek by ~*, close together.

joy [dʒɔi] *n.* (sth. that gives) deep pleasure. **joy·ful** *adj.* filled with, showing, causing, joy. **joy·ful·ly** *adv.* **joy·less** *adj.* sad. **joy·less·ly** *adv.* **joy·ous** ['dʒɔiəs] *adj.* full of joy.

ju·bi·lant ['dʒu:bilənt] *adj.* triumphant; showing joy. **ju·bi·la·tion** [ˌdʒu:bi'leiʃən] *n.*

ju·bi·lee ['dʒu:bili:] *n.* (celebration of the) 50th anniversary of some event: *silver* ~, *25th*; *diamond* ~, *60th*.

Ju·da·ism ['dʒu:deiizəm] *n.* the religion of the Jews.

judge [dʒʌdʒ] *n.* **1.** public officer with authority to hear and decide cases(3) in a court of justice. **2.** person who decides a contest, competition, dispute, etc. **3.** person qualified and able to give opinions on merits or values: *a good* ~ *of horses.* *v.t. & i.* **1.** act as a ~(1) in a court of justice; state what punishment is to be given. **2.** give a decision (in a competition, etc.). **3.** estimate; consider; form an opinion about: *to* ~ *it better to postpone a meeting; to* ~ *a man by his actions.* **judg(e)·ment** ['dʒʌdʒmənt] *n.* **1.** judging or being ~d; decision of a ~(1) or court. **2.** power, ability, to ~(2),(3); good sense: *a man of* ~*ment.* **3.** misfortune considered as a punishment by God.

ju·di·ca·ture ['dʒu:dikitʃə*] *n.* administration of justice; body of judges.

ju·di·cial [dʒu:'diʃəl] *adj.* of or by a court of justice or a judge.

ju·di·cious [dʒu:'diʃəs] *adj.* showing or having good sense; prudent. ~**ly** *adv.* ~**ness** *n.*

ju·do ['dʒu:dou] *n.* Japanese style of wrestling and self-defence.

jug [dʒʌg] *n.* deep vessel for liquids, with a handle and lip.

jug·ger·naut ['dʒʌgənɔ:t] *n.* (fig.) cause or belief to which persons are sacrificed or to which they sacrifice themselves: *the* ~ *of war.*

jug·gle ['dʒʌgl] *v.i. & t.* **1.** perform (*with* objects, e.g. by throwing many balls up into the air and catching them). **2.** play tricks (*with* objects, facts, figures, etc.) in order to deceive. **jug·gler** *n.*

jug·u·lar ['dʒʌgjulə*] *adj.* ~ *veins,* those in the neck returning blood from the head to the heart.

juice [dʒu:s] *n.* liquid part of fruits, vegetables, meat; fluid in animal organs: *digestive* ~s. **juic·y** *adj.* (*-ier, -iest*). full of ~.

Ju·ly [dʒu:'lai] *n.* the seventh month of the year.

jum·ble ['dʒʌmbl] *v.t. & i.* mix, be mixed, in a confused way. *n.* confused mixture. '~**-sale** *n.* sale of a mixed collection of second-hand articles, usu. for charity.

jump [dʒʌmp] *v.i. & t.* **1.** move quickly, rise suddenly (*up*), by sudden use of the muscles. **2.** make a sudden movement (e.g. from fear). **3.** ~ *at* (an offer, etc.), accept eagerly; ~ (*up*)*on* (sb.), scold; punish. **4.** (cause to) pass over by ~ing: *to* ~ (*a horse over*) *a fence.* *n.* **1.** act of ~ing: *the long (high)* ~ (in athletic contests). **2.** sudden movement caused by fear. **3.** sudden rise (e.g. in prices). **jump·y** *adj.* (*-ier, -iest*). nervous.

jump·er ['dʒʌmpə*] *n.* outer garment pulled on over the head and coming down to the hips.

junc·tion ['dʒʌŋkʃən] *n.* (place of) joining, esp. railway station where lines join. **junc·ture** ['dʒʌŋktʃə*] *n.* joining. *at this* ~, now, with affairs as they are.

June [dʒu:n] *n.* the sixth month of the year.

jun·gle ['dʒʌŋgl] *n.* (land covered with) thickly growing trees and undergrowth (esp. in the tropics).

ju·nior ['dʒu:njə*] *n. & adj.* (person) younger, lower in rank, than another.

ju·ni·per ['dʒu:nipə*] *n.* kinds of evergreen tree with berries from which an oil is obtained.

¹**junk** [dʒʌŋk] *n.* old things of little or no value.

²**junk** [dʒʌŋk] *n.* flat-bottomed Chinese sailing-vessel.

A ²junk

jun·ket ['dʒʌŋkit] *n.* dish of milk curdled by the addition of acid, often sweetened and flavoured; feast. ~**·ing** *n.* feasting; merry-making.

ju·ris·dic·tion [ˌdʒuəris'dikʃən] *n.* administration of justice; legal authority; extent of this.

ju·ris·pru·dence [ˌdʒuəris'pruː-dəns] *n.* science of human law.

ju·rist ['dʒuərist] *n.* expert in law.

ju·ry ['dʒuəri] *n.* body of (usu. 12) persons who swear to give a true decision (a *verdict*) on a case (3) in a court of justice. **ju·ror**, ~**·man** *n.* member of a ~.

ju·ry-mast ['dʒuərimaːst] *n.* mast put up in place of one that has broken.

¹**just** [dʒʌst] *adv.* **1.** used with a verb to indicate the immediate past: *They have ~ gone* (i.e. they went a very short time ago). **2.** exactly: *It's ~ two o'clock. This is ~ as good as that.* **3.** at this (that) very time: *We're (We were) ~ going.* **4.** only ~, almost not: *We only ~ caught the train.* **5.** ~ now, at this moment: *I'm busy ~ now*; a short time ago: *Tom was here ~ now.* **6.** only; merely: *He's ~ an ordinary man.* **7.** (colloq.) absolutely: *Did you enjoy the party? Yes, it was ~ lovely.*

²**just** [dʒʌst] *adj.* **1.** fair; in accordance with what is right. **2.** well-deserved. ~**·ly** *adv.*

jus·tice ['dʒʌstis] *n.* **1.** ~ conduct; the quality of being right and fair: *to treat all men with justice. do justice to*, treat fairly;

show that one has a ~ opinion of or knows the value of. **2.** the law and its administration: *to bring a man to justice*; *a court of justice.* **3.** judge of the Supreme Court. **4.** *Justice of the Peace*, magistrate.

jus·ti·fy ['dʒʌstifai] *v.t.* **1.** show that (a person, statement, act, etc.) is right, reasonable, or proper. **2.** be a good reason for (doing sth.). **jus·ti·fi·a·ble** ['dʒʌstifaiəbl] *adj.* that can be justified. **jus·ti·fi·ca·tion** [ˌdʒʌstifi'keiʃən] *n.* (esp.) sth. that justifies.

jut [dʒʌt] *v.i.* (-*tt*-). *jut out*, stand out (*from* a line or edge on either side, or *over* sth. underneath).

jute [dʒuːt] *n.* fibre from the outer skin of certain plants, used for making canvas, rope.

ju·ve·nile ['dʒuːvənail] *n.* young person. *adj.* of, characteristic of, suitable for, ~s: ~ *books.*

jux·ta·pose ['dʒʌkstəpouz] *v.t.* place side by side. **jux·ta·po·si·tion** [ˌdʒʌkstəpə'ziʃən] *n.*

K

ka·lei·do·scope [kə'laidəskoup] *n.* (fig.) constantly changing pattern of bright scenes.

kan·ga·roo [ˌkæŋgə'ruː] *n.* Australian animal that jumps along.

Kangaroos

ka·pok ['keipɔk] *n.* soft cotton-like material (from seeds of a tropical tree) used for filling cushions, etc.

keel [kiːl] *n.* timber or steel structure on which the framework of a ship is built up. *on an even*

~, (fig.) steady. *v.i. & t.* ~ *over*, turn over on one side; overturn.

keen [ki:n] *adj.* (*-er*, *-est*). **1.** (of points and edges) sharp; (fig.) cutting: *a ~ wind.* **2.** (of interest, the feelings) strong; deep. **3.** (of the mind, the senses) active; sensitive; sharp: ~ *sight*; *a ~ intelligence.* **4.** (of persons, their character, etc.) eager; anxious to do things: *a ~ sportsman*; ~ *to help.* ~ *on*, interested in; fond of. ~**ly** *adv.* ~**ness** *n.*

keep [ki:p] *v.t. & i.* (p.t. & p.p. *kept* [kept]). **1.** continue to have; have and not give away; not lose: *May I ~ this? He always ~s old letters. K~ hold of it*, don't let go. ~ *sth. in mind*, remember it. ~ *one's temper*, remain calm. ~ *one's seat on a horse*, not fall off. **2.** pay proper regard to; celebrate (a ceremony, Christmas, the Sabbath); observe (the law); be faithful to (a promise, treaty, etc.). **3.** provide what is needed for; support: *earning enough to ~ oneself (one's family)*; *to ~ one's family in clothes (in comfort).* **4.** own and look after, esp. for profit: ~ *a shop (an inn)*; ~ *pigs.* **5.** ~ *house*, be responsible for cleaning, cooking, shopping, etc. (Cf. *housekeeper*.) **6.** make entries in or records of (business, etc.): ~ *a diary*; ~ *accounts (books)*. (Cf. *book-keeping*.) **7.** not let people know: ~ *secrets*; ~ *(back) nothing from a friend.* **8.** (cause to) continue in a certain place, direction, relation, condition, etc.: ~ *quiet*; ~ *the children quiet*; ~ *straight on*; *kept indoors by bad weather. Traffic in England ~s to the left*, i.e., runs on the left side of the road. **9.** (of food) not go bad: *Meat does not ~ in hot weather.* (fig.) *news that will ~* (i.e. may be told later). **10.** (cause to) do (sth.) frequently or repeatedly: *Why does she ~ giggling? My shoe-lace ~s coming undone.* **11.** ~ *sb. or sth. from (doing sth.)*, prevent or hold back: *What kept you from joining me?* **12.** (with adv. & prep.): ~ *at*, (cause to) work persistently at. ~ *away*, avoid going, prevent (sb.) from going, to or near. ~ *down*, hold under, make (expenses, etc.) low. ~ *from*, abstain from, prevent, or restrain (sb. or sth.) from (doing sth.). ~ *in*, restrain (one's feelings, etc.); see that (a fire) continues burning; confine (a boy) after school hours. ~ *in with (sb.)*, remain on good terms with. ~ *one's hand (eye) in*, practise in order to retain one's skill. ~ *off*, (cause to) stay at a distance; say nothing about (a question, etc.). ~ *on*, continue (to have, do, use, wear, etc.): *to ~ on although one is tired*; *to ~ one's hat on*; *to ~ an old servant on*; *to ~ on doing sth.*, do sth. repeatedly (used of actions, not states): *Don't ~ on asking silly questions.* ~ *under*, control; hold down. ~ *up*, prevent (one's courage, spirits) from sinking; observe (e.g. old customs); prevent or hinder (sb.) from going to bed; carry on (a correspondence *with* sb.); ~ *it up*, go on without slackening; ~ *up appearances*, behave as usual, in spite of a change in circumstances; ~ *up with*, go on at the same rate as. **13.** ~ *(oneself) to oneself*, avoid the society of others. ~ *sth. to oneself*, refuse to share it. ~ *early (good)* or *late (bad) hours*, finish work, go to bed, early (or late). ~ *pace with*, go at the same rate as. ~ *track of*, keep in touch with the progress of. ~ *watch*, be on watch (for sth.). ~ *one's feet (balance)*, not fall. *n.* **1.** (food needed for) support: *to earn one's ~.* **2.** *for ~s*, (colloq.) permanently. **3.** (history) strong tower. ~**er** *n.* (chiefly in compounds: see *shopkeeper*, *goalkeeper*, etc.), but (esp.) *gamekeeper* (see ¹*game*(5)). ~**ing** *n.* **1.** care; *in safe ~ing.* **2.** *in (out of) ~ing with*, in (not in) harmony or agreement with. ¹~**sake** *n.* sth. kept in memory of the giver.

keg [keg] *n.* small cask or barrel.

ken [ken] *n.* range of knowledge: *beyond (outside) my ken.*

ken·nel [ˈkenl] *n.* hut for a dog.

kept, see *keep*.

kerb [kə:b] *n.* stone edging of a raised path. '**~-stone** *n.* one of the stones in such an edging.

ker·chief ['kə:tʃif] *n.* piece of cloth or lace used as a head-covering.

ker·nel ['kə:nl] *n.* inner part (seed) of a nut or fruit-stone; (fig.) important part of a subject, problem, etc. (See *nut*.)

ker·o·sene ['kerəsi:n] *n.* = paraffin.

kes·trel ['kestrəl] *n.* small hawk.

ketch·up ['ketʃəp] *n.* sauce made from the juice of tomatoes, mushrooms, etc.

ket·tle ['ketl] *n.* metal vessel with a lid, spout, and handle, for boiling water. *a pretty ~ of fish,* an awkward state of affairs. '**~-drum** *n.* metal drum, shaped like a hemisphere, with skin stretched across.

key [ki:] *n.* **1.** metal instrument for moving the bolt of a lock; instrument for winding a watch or clock by tightening the spring. **2.** (fig.) sth. that provides an answer to a problem or mystery. **3.** set of answers to exercises or problems; a translation from or into a foreign language. **4.** (also attrib.) place that, from its position, gives control of a route or area: *the key to the Mediterranean; a key position.* **5.** (attrib.) *key industries,* those (e.g. coal-mining) essential to the carrying on of others. **6.** operating part of a piano, organ, typewriter, etc., pressed down by a finger. *keyboard,* row of keys (6). **7.** (music) scale of notes definitely related to each other and based on a particular note called the *keynote;* (fig., of thought, feelings, talk) general tone or style: *all in the same key* (i.e. monotonously). *v.t. key up,* tune (the strings of a musical instrument by tightening or loosening); (fig.) stimulate or raise the standard of (a person, his activity, etc.). '**key·stone** *n.* middle stone of an arch; (fig.) controlling or central principle.

kha·ki ['kɑ:ki] *n. & adj.* (cloth, military uniform, of a) dull yellowish-brown.

kick [kik] *v.t. & i.* strike with the foot; make movements as if doing this: *The baby was ~ing and screaming. to ~ a football. to ~ one's slippers off. ~ one's heels,* be kept waiting, wasting time. *~ against,* protest, show annoyance. *~ off,* (football) start. *~ up a row,* (colloq.) cause a disturbance (by protesting). *n.* **1.** act of ~ing; blow resulting from ~ing. **2.** (colloq.) thrill: *get a ~ out of sth.,* get pleasure and excitement. **3.** recoil of a gun when fired; (fig.) power to react: *with no ~ left in him,* i.e. no power to resist further.

kid [kid] *n.* **1.** young goat. **2.** leather made from its skin: *kid gloves. ~ 3.* (colloq.) child. **kid·dy** *n.* = kid (3). *v.t.* (-*dd*-). (colloq.) tease: *You're kidding* (me).

kid·nap ['kidnæp] *v.t.* (-*pp*-). steal (a child); carry away (sb.) by force and unlawfully. ~**per** *n.*

kid·ney ['kidni] *n.* one of a pair of organs in the abdomen separating waste liquid from the blood; ~ of sheep, etc. as food.

The kidneys   A kilt

kill [kil] *v.t. & i.* put to death; cause the death of; destroy; put an end to; spoil the effect of. ~ *time,* do sth. to interest oneself while waiting. *n.* act of ~ing (esp. by a sportsman); animal(s) ~ed in hunting.

kiln [kiln] *n.* large furnace or oven for burning (*lime-~*), baking (*brick-~*) or drying (*hop-~*).

ki·lo- ['ki(:)lou] *prefix.* 1,000, esp. in ~*gram,* ~*metre,* ~*watt.*

kilt [kilt] *n.* short, pleated skirt, esp. as worn by men in the Scottish Highlands.

ki·mo·no [ki'mounou] *n.* loose garment worn as a dressing-gown.

kin [kin] *n.* (collectively) family; relations. *next of kin*, nearest relation(s).

¹kind [kaind] *n.* **1.** race, natural group, of plants, animals: *mankind; the four-legged ~*. **2.** sort, class, or variety: *something of the ~*, something like the thing mentioned; *nothing of the ~*, not at all like it; *of a ~*, (a) of the same ~, (b) scarcely deserving the name: *coffee of a ~*. **3.** *pay in ~*, pay in goods instead of in money; *repay sb. in ~*, treat him as he has treated you.

²kind [kaind] *adj.* (*-er, -est*). having, showing, or thoughtfulness, sympathy, or love for others: *Will you be ~ enough to*, will you, please? *It was ~ of you to*, you were ~ to. *Give my ~ regards to Y*, tell Y that I have ~ thoughts of him. **~·ly** *adv. Will you ~ly tell me*, will you, please, tell me? **~·ly** *adj.* (*-lier, -iest*). behaving with, showing, ~·ness. **~·ness** *n.* ~ behaviour; ~ act.

kin·der·gar·ten [,kində'ga:tn] *n.* school for very small children.

kin·dle ['kindl] *v.t. & i.* **1.** (cause to) catch fire or burst into flame. **2.** (fig.) rouse, be roused, to a state of strong feeling, interest, etc. **'kind·ling** *n.* material (e.g. dry sticks) for starting a fire.

kind·ly, see **²kind**.

kin·dred ['kindrid] *n.* **1.** relationship by birth between persons: *to claim ~ with sb.* **2.** all one's relations. *adj.* **1.** related; having a common source. **2.** similar.

kine [kain] *n.* (old plural form) cows.

ki·net·ic [ki'netik] *adj.* of, due to, motion.

king [kiŋ] *n.* **1.** male (usu. hereditary) supreme ruler of an independent state. **2.** person of great influence, e.g. in industry: *an oil ~.* **~·dom** ['kiŋdəm] *n.* **1.** country ruled by a ~ or queen. **2.** any one of the three divisions of the natural world: *the animal, vegetable, and mineral ~doms.*

'~·,fish·er *n.* small, brightly coloured bird feeding on fish in rivers, etc. **~·ly** *adj.* royal; like or suitable for a ~.

kink [kiŋk] *n.* **1.** irregular or back twist in wire, pipe, cord, etc. **2.** abnormal way of thinking. *v.t. & i.* make a ~ in; form a ~.

kins·folk ['kinzfouk] *n. pl.* relations. **kin·ship** *n.* relationship. **kins·man** ['kinzmən], **kins·wom·an** ['kinzwumən] *n.* male, female, relation.

ki·osk ['ki:ɔsk] *n.* small enclosed stall, etc., for a public telephone or the sale of newspapers, etc.

kip·per ['kipə•] *n.* salted herring, dried or smoked.

kirk [kə:k] *n.* (Scot.) church.

kiss [kis] *v.t. & i.* touch with the lips to show affection or as a greeting. *n.* a touch given with the lips.

kit [kit] *n.* **1.** all the equipment (esp. clothing) of a soldier, sailor, or other person who travels. **2.** equipment needed by a workman for his trade: *a plumber's kit.* **3.** equipment needed for a special activity: *skiing kit.* **'kit-bag** *n.* bag for kit(1).

kit·chen ['kitʃin] *n.* room used for cooking. **'~ 'gar·den** *n.* garden where vegetables, etc., are grown. **'~-maid** *n.* servant who helps the cook.

kite [kait] *n.* **1.** bird of prey of the hawk family. **2.** framework of wood, etc., covered with paper or cloth, made to fly at the end of a long string or wire.

kith [kiθ] *n.* (only in) ~ *and kin*, friends and relations.

kit·ten ['kitn] *n.* young cat.

knack [næk] *n.* cleverness (acquired through practice) enabling one to do sth. skilfully: *There's a ~ in it.*

knap·sack ['næpsæk] *n.* canvas or leather bag carried on the back by soldiers, travellers, etc.

knave [neiv] *n.* dishonest man; man without honour. **knav·er·y** ['neivəri] *n.* dishonesty; dishonest act. **knav·ish** ['neiviʃ] *adj.* deceitful.

knead [ni:d] *v.t.* **1.** make (flour and water, wet clay, etc.) into a firm paste by working with the hands; make (bread, pots) in this way. **2.** massage (muscles).

knee [ni:] *n.* see the picture. *on the ~s of the gods,* yet uncertain. '**~-cap** *n.* flat bone forming the front part of the ~.

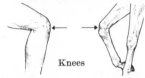

Knees

kneel [ni:l] *v.i.* (p.t. & p.p. *knelt* [nelt]). go down on one's knee(s); rest on one's knee(s).

knell [nel] *n.* slow sounding of a bell, esp. for a death or at a funeral; (fig.) sign of death or the coming end of sth.

knew, see *know.*

knick·er·bock·ers ['nikǝbɔkǝz] *n. pl.* loose, wide breeches gathered in below the knees.

knick·ers ['nikǝz] *n.pl.* woman's or girl's undergarment similar to *briefs* (q.v.).

knick-knack ['niknæk] *n.* small unimportant ornament, piece of jewellery, article of dress, piece of furniture, etc.

knife [naif] *n.* (pl. *knives* [naivz]). sharp steel blade with a handle, used to cut or stab. *get one's ~ into sb.,* have the wish to harm him. *v.t.* wound with a ~.

knight [nait] *n.* **1.** (in the Middle Ages) man, usu. of noble birth, raised to honourable military rank. **2.** (modern use) man on whom the title of honour *Sir* (before Christian name and surname) has been conferred, as a reward for services to his country. *v.t.* make (sb.) a ~ (2). ~·**hood** *n.* rank of a ~. ~·**ly** *adj.* brave and generous; like a ~ (1).

knit [nit] *v.t. & i.* (-*tt*-). **1.** make (an article of clothing, etc.) by looping wool, silk, yarn on long needles. **2.** unite firmly or closely: *to ~ broken bones;* a

closely·~ argument (of which the parts hold together firmly). **3.** ~ *the brows,* frown. ~·**ting** *n.* material being ~ted.

Knitting

knives, see *knife.*

knob [nɔb] *n.* **1.** rounded end of a door- or drawer-handle, of a walking-stick, etc. **2.** rounded swelling on, or rounded part standing out from, a surface (e.g. a tree trunk). **3.** small lump (e.g. of coal). ~·**bly** *adj.* having ~s (2).

knock [nɔk] *v.t. & i.* **1.** hit, strike; get (*down, in,* etc.) by hitting: ~ *the bottom of a box out;* ~ *a man down;* ~ *at a door* (*on a window*) (to call attention). ~ *sb. or sth. about,* treat roughly. ~ *about the world,* make many long journeys. ~ *sb. out,* (in boxing) send him to the floor with a blow so that he cannot continue; (fig.) overwhelm (with surprise, etc.). **2.** ~ *off work,* stop working. ~ *off* (a shilling from a bill), deduct. ~ *sb. up,* wake him by ~ing (at his door). ~ *sth. up,* make, put together, roughly and quickly. *be ~ed up,* be tired out. **3.** (of a petrol engine) make a ~ing sound. *n.* (short, sharp sound of a) blow. '**~-about** *adj.* (of a comic performance in a theatre) rough and noisy. ~·**er** *n.* (esp.) metal device for striking against a metal plate on a door to call attention. '**~-out** *n.* blow that ~s sb. out (see (1) above).

knoll [noul] *n.* small hill.

knot [nɔt] *n.* **1.** parts of one or more pieces of string, rope, etc., twisted together to make a fastening; (fig.) sth. that ties together. **2.** piece of ribbon, etc., twisted and tied as an ornament. **3.** difficulty; hard problem: *tie oneself* (*up*) *in*(*to*) ~s, get badly confused about sth. **4.** hard lump in timber where a branch grew out from a bough or trunk: ~-holes (in a board, as in the picture). **5.** group (of persons): *people standing about in* ~s. **6.** measure of speed for ships: *a vessel of 20* ~s, i.e. able to sail 20 nautical miles an hour (a nautical mile = 6,080 feet). *v.t. & i.* (-*tt*-). make a ~ or ~s in; tie (sth.) with ~s; form ~s. ~·**ty** *adj.* (-*ier*, -*iest*). (esp.) puzzling: *a* ~*ty problem*.

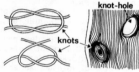

Knots

knout [naut] *n.* leather whip.
know [nou] *v.t. & i.* (p.t. *knew* [nju:], p.p. *known* [noun]). have news or information about; have in one's mind by learning or by experience; be acquainted with (sb.); be able to recognize or distinguish. *You ought to* ~ *better than to do that*, you ought to ~ that it is wrong, foolish, etc.; ~ *one's own mind*, be certain of one's purpose, ideas, etc.; ~ *what's what*, ~ *one's own business*, have common sense, good judgement, practical experience. *n.* (only) *in the* ~, having information not shared by all. ~·**ing** *adj.* having, showing that one has, intelligence, sharp wits, etc.: *a* ~*ing child*; ~*ing looks.* ~·**ing·ly** *adv.* **1.** consciously. **2.** in a ~ing manner. ~·**ledge** ['nolidʒ] *n.* **1.** ~ing; understanding. **2.** all that is ~n; what a person ~s: *to (the best of) my* ~*ledge*, as far as I ~. ~·**ledge·able** ['nolidʒ-əbl] *adj.* well-informed; having much ~ledge.
knuck·le ['nʌkl] *n.* bone at a finger-joint; (in animals) knee-joint or part joining leg to foot (esp. as food). *v.i.* ~ *under*, submit; yield.

kosh·er ['koufə*] *n. & adj.* (food, food-shop) fulfilling requirements of Jewish rites.
ko(w)·tow ['kau'tau] *v.i.* ~ *to*, show great humility to; pay too much respect to.
kraal [krɑ:l, krɔ:l] *n.* (in S. Africa) fenced-in village of huts; fence for enclosing domestic animals.
ku·dos ['kju:dos] (colloq.) honour and glory; credit.

L

la·bel ['leibl] *v.t. & n.* (-*ll*-). (stick, tie, or pin on sth. a) piece of paper, metal, etc., for describing sth., where it is to go, etc.
la·bial ['leibjəl] *adj.* of the lip(s).
la·bor·a·to·ry ['læbərətri, lə'bor-ətri] *n.* place for scientific experiments, esp. in chemistry.
la·bour ['leibə*] *n.* **1.** work. **2.** piece of work: *a* ~ *of love*, work undertaken for the pleasure of doing it or for the good of sb. one loves. **3.** workers as a class (contrasted with capitalists): *the L*~ *Party*, political party representing the interests of this class. **4.** pains of childbirth: *a woman in* ~. *v.i. & t.* **1.** work hard, esp. with the hands. **2.** try hard (*for* sth., *to* do sth.). **3.** move, breathe, slowly and with difficulty. **4.** ~ *under*, be the victim of (a disadvantage, delusion, etc.). **5.** work out in detail: ~ *the point*, treat it at too great length. **la·boured** *adj.* ~*ed breathing*, slow and troublesome; *a* ~*ed style*, not easy and natural. ~·**er** *n.* man who does heavy work with his hands. **la·bo·ri·ous** [lə'bo:riəs] *adj.* **1.** hard-working; needing great effort. **2.** showing signs of great effort.
lab·y·rinth ['læbərinθ] *n.* network of winding paths, roads, etc., through which it is difficult to find one's way without help.
lac, lakh [læk] *n.* (in India and Pakistan) 100,000 (esp. ~ *of rupees*, written Rs. 1,00,000).

lace [leis] *n.* **1.** delicate ornamental open-work fabric of threads: *gold* (*silver*) ~, braid for trimming uniforms. **2.** string or cord put through small holes in shoes, etc., to draw the sides together. *v.i. & t.* fasten, tighten, with ~s(2): *to ~ one's shoes* (*up*).

Lace (1)

lac·er·ate ['læsəreit] *v.t.* tear (the flesh, (fig.) the feelings). **lac·er·a·tion** [,læsə'reiʃən] *n.*

lach·ry·mose ['lækrimous] *adj.* tearful; in the habit of weeping.

lack [læk] *v.t.* **1.** be without; have less than enough of. **2.** be ~*ing*, be wanting: *Money for this plan was ~ing.* *n.* need; shortage: *no ~ of*, plenty of; *for ~ of*, because of the absence of.

lack·a·dai·si·cal [,lækə'deizikl] *adj.* appearing tired, uninterested, unenthusiastic.

lack·ey, lac·quey ['læki] *n.* manservant; slavish person.

la·con·ic [lə'kɔnik] *adj.* using, expressed in, few words. **la·con·i·cal·ly** *adv.*

lac·quér ['lækə*] *n.* (sorts of) varnish used to give a hard, bright coating for metal, etc. *v.t.* put ~ on.

lac·tic ['læktik] *adj.* of milk.

lac·y ['leisi] *adj.* (-*ier*, -*iest*) of or like lace (1).

lad(die) ['læd(i)] *n.* boy.

lad·der ['lædə*] *n.* **1.** two lengths of wood, metal, or rope, with cross-pieces (called *rungs*), used in climbing up and down walls, a ship's side, etc. **2.** fault in a stocking caused by broken thread. *v.i. & t.* (of stockings) develop a ~ in; make a ~ in.

la·den ['leidn] *ppl. adj.* ~ *with*, weighted or burdened with.

lad·ing ['leidiŋ] *n. bill of ~*, list of a ship's cargo.

la·dle ['leidl] *n.* large deep cup-shaped spoon for dipping out liquids. *v.t.* (often ~ *out*) serve with or as from a ~.

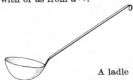

A ladle

la·dy ['leidi] *n.* **1.** woman of good manners; polite term for any woman. **2.** (*L~*) title (in Gt. Brit.) used of and to the wives and daughters of some nobles and the wife of a knight. ~*in-waiting*, ~ in attendance on a queen or princess. **3.** *Our L~*, Mary, Mother of Jesus. '~·like *adj.* behaving as a ~. '~·ship *n.* used (*Your*, *Her*, *L~ship*) in speaking to or of a titled lady.

lag [læg] *v.i.* (-*gg*-). (often *lag behind*) move too slowly. *n. time lag*, period of time by which sth. is slower or later. **lag·gard** ['lægəd] *n.* one who lags.

la·ger ['lɑːgə*] *n.* sort of light beer.

la·goon [lə'guːn] *n.* salt-water lake separated from the sea by sand-bank(s) or coral reef(s).

laid, see [1]*lay.*

lain, see [2]*lie.*

lair [lɛə*] *n.* wild animal's resting-place or den.

laird [lɛəd] *n.* landowner in Scotland.

lais·sez-faire ['leisei'fɛə*] (Fr.) *n.* policy of allowing individual activities (esp. in commerce) to be conducted without government control.

la·i·ty ['leiiti] *n. the ~*, laymen.

lake [leik] *n.* large area of water surrounded by land.

lamb [læm] *n.* young sheep; its flesh as food.

lame [leim] *adj.* **1.** not able to walk normally because of an injury or defect. **2.** (of an argument, etc.) unconvincing. *v.t.* make ~. ~·ly *adv.* ~·ness *n.*

la·ment [lə'ment] *v.t. & i.* show,

feel, express, great sorrow or regret. *n.* expression of grief; song or poem expressing grief.

lam·en·ta·ble ['læməntəbl] *adj.* regrettable; to be ~ed. **lam·en·ta·tion** [,læmen'teiʃən] *n.*

lamp [læmp] *n.* container for oil and wick, used to give light; other device for giving light: *gas and electric* ~s. **~·post** *n.* post for a street ~.

lam·poon [læm'pu:n] *n.* piece of writing attacking and ridiculing sb. *v.t.* write a ~ against.

¹lance [lɑ:ns] *n.* long spear used by soldiers on horseback. **lanc·er** *n.* soldier armed with a ~. **~-'cor·por·al** *n.* lowest grade of non-commissioned officer in the army.

²lance [lɑ:ns] *v.t.* cut into, cut open, with a lancet.

lan·cet ['lɑ:nsit] *n.* pointed, two-edged knife used by surgeons.

land [lænd] *n.* **1.** solid part of the earth's surface (cf. *sea, water*). **2.** ground, earth, used for farming, etc.: *working on the* ~; ~-*workers.* **3.** country: *one's native* ~. *v.t. & i.* **1.** go, come, put, on ~ (from a ship, aircraft, etc.); bring (a fish, aircraft) to ~. **2.** bring to, reach, a position or situation: *to* ~ *oneself in difficulties; to* ~ *on one's feet like a cat.* **'~ed** *adj.* owning ~. **'~·holder** *n.* owner or tenant of ~. **'~·ing** *n.* **1.** platform at the top of a flight of stairs on to which doors open; platform between two flights of stairs. **2.** act of ~ing: *to make a safe* ~*ing.* **3.** (usu. ~*ing-place,* ~*ing-stage*) platform on to which passengers ~ from a ship. **'~·,la·dy** *n.* woman keeping an inn or boarding-house, or letting rooms to tenants. **'~-locked** *adj.* (of a harbour, etc.) almost enclosed by ~. **'~·lord** *n.* person from whom another rents land or building(s); person keeping an inn, a hotel, a boarding-house. **'~·,lub·ber** *n.* (sailor's name for) person not accustomed to the sea. **'~·mark** *n.* **1.** sth. marking the boundary of a piece of land. **2.** object, etc.,

easily seen from a distance and helpful to travellers, etc. **3.** (fig.) event, etc., marking a stage or turning-point (e.g. in a nation's history). **'~·scape** ['lændskeip] *n.* (picture of) inland scenery; branch of art dealing with this. **'~·slide** *n.* sliding down of a mass of earth, rock, etc., from the side of a cliff, etc. **'~·slip** *n.* =~slide.

lane [lein] *n.* narrow country road; side-street; way made or left to allow people or traffic to move freely.

lan·guage ['læŋgwidʒ] *n.* **1.** words and their use. **2.** form of ~ used by a nation or race. **3.** manner of using words; words, phrases, etc., used by a profession: *legal* ~; *the* ~ *of diplomacy.* **4.** *bad (strong)* ~, ~ full of oaths (violent words). **5.** signs used as ~: *finger* ~ (to the deaf or by the dumb).

lan·guid ['læŋgwid] *adj.* lacking in energy; slow-moving. **lan·guish** ['læŋgwiʃ] *v.i.* become ~; lose health and strength; be unhappy because of a desire (*for* sth.); *languishing looks* (showing desire for sympathy or love). **lan·guor** ['læŋgə*] *n.* weakness; lack of energy; stillness.

lank [læŋk] *adj.* (of hair) long and lying limp or flat. **~·y** *adj.* (-*ier,* -*iest*). (of a person) tall and lean; (of arms or legs) long and thin.

lan·tern ['læntən] *n.* case (usu. metal and glass) protecting a light from wind, etc., outdoors. ~ *jaws,* long thin jaws.

lan·yard ['lænjəd] *n.* cord worn (by sailors and soldiers) for a whistle or knife; short rope used on a ship for fastening or moving sth.

¹lap [læp] *n.* resting-place formed by the legs when a person is seated: *sitting with her baby on (her hands in) her lap.* **'lap-dog** *n.* small pet dog.

²lap [læp] *v.t. & i.* (-*pp-*). **1.** fold (cloth, etc.) *round* or *in*: (fig.) *lapped in luxury.* **2.** arrange (cloth, etc.) so that the edge or border is folded back or over.

n. **1.** amount by which one thing laps over. **2.** one circuit round a race-track: *on the last lap.*

³**lap** [læp] *v.t. & i.* (*-pp-*). **1.** drink by taking *up* (water, etc.) with the tongue, as a cat does. **2.** (of waves, etc.) move (*against* sth.) with a lapping sound. *n.* act or sound of lapping.

la·pel [læ'pel] *n.* part of the breast of a coat folded back (forming a continuation of the collar).

The lapels

lapse [læps] *n.* **1.** slight error in speech or behaviour; slip of memory. **2.** falling away from what is right: *a ~ from virtue.* **3.** (of time) passing away; interval. **4.** (law) ending of a right, etc., e.g. from failure to use it. *v.i.* **1.** fail to keep one's position; fall *from* good ways *into* bad ways: *to ~ from virtue into vice.* **2.** (legal, of rights, etc.) be lost because not claimed or used.

lar·ce·ny ['lɑːsəni] *n.* the crime of theft.

larch [lɑːtʃ] *n.* tree with small cones and light-green leaves.

lard [lɑːd] *n.* pork fat prepared for use in cooking. *v.t.* put ~ on.

lard·er ['lɑːdə*] *n.* room or cupboard where meat and other kinds of food are stored.

large [lɑːdʒ] *adj.* (*-r, -st*). **1.** of considerable size; taking up much space; able to contain much. **2.** liberal; generous: *a ~- hearted man.* **3.** with a wide range; unrestricted: *a man with ~ ideas. at ~,* free; not in prison. *people (the world) at ~,* people in general. *by and ~,* taking everything into consideration. ~·**ly** *adv.* to a great extent.

¹**lark** [lɑːk] *n.* (sorts of) small song-bird, esp. the *skylark.*

²**lark** [lɑːk] *n.* bit of fun; sth. amusing. *v.i.* play (*about*).

lar·va ['lɑːvə] *n.* (pl. *larvae* ['lɑːviː]). insect in the first stage of its life-history, after coming out of the egg.

lar·ynx ['læriŋks] *n.* upper part of the wind-pipe where the vocal cords are. **lar·yn·gi·tis** [ˌlærin-'dʒaitis] *n.* inflammation of the ~.

The larynx   A latch (1)

las·civ·i·ous [lə'siviəs] *adj.* lustful.

lash [læʃ] *v.t. & i.* **1.** beat or strike violently (as) with a whip: *rain~ing (against) the windows.* **2.** make violent movements, move up and down: *The horse ~ed out at me,* tried to kick me. *The wounded animal ~ed its tail.* **3.** scold angrily; rouse or excite to anger: *to ~ oneself (one's audience) into a fury.* **4.** fasten tightly with rope, etc. *n.* **1.** part of whip with which strokes are given; stroke given with a whip. **2.** = eyelash. ~·**ing** *n.* **1.** whipping. **2.** cord or thin rope.

lass [læs], **las·sie** ['læsi] *n.* girl.

las·si·tude ['læsitjuːd] *n.* tiredness; state of being uninterested.

las·so [læ'suː] *n.* long rope looped with a slip-knot, for catching horses etc., as in America. *v.t.* (*p.t. & p.p. lassoed*). catch with a ~.

¹**last** [lɑːst] *adj., adv. & n.* **I.** *adj.* **1.** coming after all others in time or order. **2.** coming immediately before the present. **3.** the only remaining (one): *I've spent my ~ shilling.* **4.** least suitable, etc.: *He's the ~ person to trust with money.* **5.** final: *I've said my ~ word on this subject.* **II.** *adv.* **1.** after all others. **2.** on the ~ (2) occasion before the

present. **III.** *n.* that which comes at the end. *at* ~, in the end, after long delay. *to the* ~, till the end, till death. ~**·ly** *adv.*

²**last** [lɑːst] *v.i.* go on; be enough (for): *enough food to* (*us*) *three days.* ~**·ing** *adj.* continuing (for a long time): *a* ~*ing peace.*

³**last** [lɑːst] *n.* wooden model of the foot for making shoes on. *stick to one's* ~, not try to do things one cannot do well.

latch [lætʃ] *n.* **1.** simple fastening for a door, gate, or window: *on the* ~, fastened with a ~ but not locked. **2.** small spring lock for a house door opened from outside with a ~*key.* *v.t.* & *i.* fasten with a ~. (See the picture on page 289.)

late [leit] *adj.* **1.** (*later, latest*). after the right or usual time; far on in the day or some other period. **2.** no longer living: *her* ~ *husband.* **3.** who or which was until recently: *the* ~ *prime minister*; *the* ~ *political troubles.* **4.** *of* ~, recently; *of* ~ *years*, in the last few years. *adv.* **1.** after the usual, expected, or proper time. **2.** recently: *I saw him as* ~ *as yesterday* (i.e. very recently). **3.** *later on,* at a later time; afterwards. *sooner or later,* at some future time. ~**·ly** *adv.* a short time ago; recently. **lat·est** *adj.* the most recent; the newest (fashions, etc.). *at* (*the*) *latest,* before or not later than. **lat·ish** *adj.* rather ~.

la·tent [ˈleitənt] *adj.* (of qualities, etc.) present but not active and not seen: ~ *energy.*

lat·er·al [ˈlætərəl] *adj.* of, at, from, to, the side(s): ~ *buds.*

lath [lɑːθ] *n.* long, thin strip of wood, esp. as used for plaster walls and ceilings.

lathe [leið] *n.* machine for holding and turning pieces of wood or metal while they are being shaped, etc.

lath·er [ˈlæðə*] *n.* **1.** soft mass of white froth from soap and water (as made on a man's face before shaving). **2.** frothy sweat on a horse. *v.t.* & *i.* **1.** make ~ on. **2.** form ~.

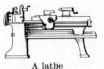

A lathe

Lat·in [ˈlætin] *n.* language of ancient Rome. *adj.* of the ~ language; of peoples speaking languages based on ~.

lat·i·tude [ˈlætitjuːd] *n.* **1.** distance north or south of the equator measured in degrees; (pl.) *high* (*low*) ~*s*, places a long way from (near to) the equator. **2.** (measure of) freedom in action or opinion; *to allow people great* ~ *in political belief.*

la·trine [ləˈtriːn] *n.* (in places where there are no sewers, e.g. army camps) pit or trench to receive waste matter from the human body.

lat·ter [ˈlætə*] *adj.* **1.** recent; belonging to the end (of a period). **2.** *the* ~, the second of two already named. (Cf. *former.*) ~**·ly** *adv.* nowadays; recently.

lat·tice [ˈlætis] *n.* framework of crossed laths or metal strips as a screen, etc.: ~ *window*, one with small square or diamond-shaped pieces of glass in a framework of lead.

A lattice window   Laughing

laud [lɔːd] *v.t.* praise. ~**·a·ble** *adj.* deserving praise. ~**·a·bly** *adv.*

laugh [lɑːf] *v.i.* & *t.* see the picture. ~ *in one's sleeve*, be secretly amused. *n.* sound or act of ~ing. *have* (*get*) *the* ~ *of sb.*, reverse a situation so that you may laugh at him; outwit him; *raise a* ~, cause amusement. '~**·ing-stock** *n.* person or thing causing general ridicule.

~**a·ble** *adj.* causing ~ter.
~**ter** *n.* ~ing.

¹**launch** [lɔ:ntʃ] *v.t. & i.* **1.** set
a ship (esp. one newly built)
afloat; send (a space rocket, etc.)
into space. **2.** send (a blow, a
spear, etc., *at* or *against*). **3.** get
started: *to ~ an attack (an
enterprise)*. **4.** ~ *out (into)*, make
a start on sth. new. *n.* ~ing a
ship. '~**·ing-pad** *n.* platform
from which space rockets and
missiles are ~ed.

²**launch** [lɔ:ntʃ] *n.* passenger-
carrying boat (on rivers, in
harbours) driven by steam,
petrol, or electricity.

laun·der ['lɔ:ndə*] *v.t. & i.* wash
and press (clothes). **laun·dress**
['lɔ:ndris] *n.* woman who ~s.
laun·dry ['lɔ:ndri] *n.* clothes-
washing place or business;
clothes (to be) ~ed. **laun·der·
ette** [,lɔ:ndə'ret] *n.* laundry at
which customers pay to ~ their
clothes in washing-machines.

lau·re·ate ['lɔ:riət] *n. Poet L~*,
poet appointed by the King or
Queen of Great Britain to write
poems on national occasions.

lau·rel ['lɒrəl] *n.* evergreen shrub;
(pl.) victory, honour (in war, art,
writing, etc.): *to gain one's ~s*.

la·va ['lɑ:və] *n.* molten matter
flowing from a volcano; this
substance when it has cooled
and hardened.

lav·a·to·ry ['lævətəri] *n.* room for
washing hands and face in;
water-closet.

lav·en·der ['lævində*] *n.* plant
with pale purple sweet-scented
flowers.

lav·ish ['læviʃ] *v.t.* give abundantly and generously: *~ing
care on an only child. adj.* giving,
producing, generously; given
generously or abundantly. ~**ly**
adv.

law [lɔ:] *n.* **1.** rule made by
authority for the proper regulation of a community or society
or for correct conduct in life.
2. *the law*, body of laws. **3.** such
a body of rules as a subject
of study and as a profession:
a law student. go to law, appeal
to the law courts. **4.** correct

statement of what always happens (in nature, in science) in
certain circumstances; regularity
in nature, e.g. the order of
the seasons: *the laws of nature;
Newton's law.* '**law-a·ˌbid·ing**
adj. obeying the law. **law
court** *n.* court of justice. **law·
ful** *adj.* allowed by, according
to, the law. **law·less** *adj.* not
obeying the law; contrary to
the law. '**law·suit** *n.* claim
made in a law court. **law·yer**
['lɔ:jə*] *n.* person who has
studied law and advises others
in matters of law.

¹**lawn** [lɔ:n] *n.* area of grass kept
closely cut and smooth. '~**-
ˌmow·er** *n.* machine for cutting
grass on ~s.

A lawn-mower   Leap-frog

²**lawn** [lɔ:n] *n.* kind of fine linen.
lax [læks] *adj.* **1.** negligent; inattentive. **2.** not strict or
severe: *~ morals.* **3.** relaxed.
~**i·ty** ['læksiti] *n.*

lax·a·tive ['læksətiv] *n. & adj.*
(substance, drug) causing the
bowels to empty easily.

¹**lay** [lei] *v.t. & i.* (p.t. & p.p. *laid*
[leid]). **1.** put on to a surface;
put down in a certain position
or place: *to lay linoleum on the
floor; to lay a submarine cable.*
2. (of birds and insects) produce
(eggs). **3.** (with various objects)
put down; cause to be down: *to
lay the dust; crops laid* (i.e.
flattened) *by rain-storms.* make
ready a trap, etc.: *to lay a snare
(ambush).* set (a meal) on the
table: *to lay the table; to lay
supper.* prepare: *to lay a fire.*
4. (special phrases) *lay about one*,
strike out in all directions. *lay
sth. aside*, save for future needs;
put down (e.g. a book); give up
(e.g. old habits). *lay bare*, reveal.
lay sth. by, save for future use.

lay claim to, claim as one's own.
lay down one's life, sacrifice it.
lay down the law, speak, give
opinions, as if with authority.
lay it down (that), declare firmly.
can't lay one's hands on sth.,
can't find where sth. is. *lay hold
of (on)*, get hold of. *lay in*, provide a store of. *lay (sb.) low*,
overcome, overthrow. *lay on*,
impose (taxes); apply (blows,
etc.) with violence; supply (gas,
water) through pipes into a
building. *lay out*, spread out on
view or in readiness; prepare
(a corpse) for burial; make a plan
for (a garden, a printed page,
the spending of money, etc.).
lay oneself out to, take pains to.
lay up, save, store. *be laid up
(aside)*, be forced to stay in bed
by illness, etc. **'lay-by** *n.* space
beside a main road where
vehicles may stop for a short
time without hindering traffic.

²lay, see *²lie*.

³lay [lei] *n.* song; poem intended
for singing.

⁴lay [lei] *adj.* (attrib. only). **1.** of,
for, done by, persons who are
not priests: *a lay brother*, a
member, but not a priest, of a
religious order. **2.** of, for, done
by, persons outside a class of
persons with expert knowledge;
non-professional (esp. in law and
medicine). **lay·man** *n.* lay
person.

lay·er ['leiə*] *n.* **1.** thickness of
material (esp. one of several)
laid or lying on or spread over a
surface or forming one horizontal
division: *a ~ of clay*. **2.** shoot
of a plant fastened down to
take root while still growing
from the parent plant.

lay·ette [lei'et] *n.* clothing, etc.,
needed for a newly born child.

lay·out ['leiaut] *n.* arrangement;
general design.

la·zy ['leizi] *adj.* (-*ier*, -*iest*).
unwilling to work; doing
little work. **laze** *v.i.* be ~; do
nothing. **'~-bones** *n.* (colloq.)
~ person. **laz·i·ly** *adv.* **laz·i·
ness** *n.*

lea [li:] *n.* (liter.) stretch (2) of
grassland.

¹lead [led] *n.* **1.** heavy soft grey
metal. **2.** lump of this, tied to
a line, for measuring the depth
of the sea. **3.** (also *black·~*)
stick of graphite as used in a
~ pencil. **~·en** *adj.* of ~;
heavy as ~; ~-coloured; suggesting ~: *~en clouds*.

²lead [li:d] *v.t. & i.* (p.t. & p.p.
led [led]). **1.** go in front, take,
guide, towards some place. **2.**
control; manage; direct by
example or persuasion: *to ~ an
army (expedition)*; *to ~ the singing (the choir)*. **3.** (cause sb. to)
pass, go through: *to ~ a good
life*; *to ~ sb. a dog's life* (i.e.
make his life wretched). **4.** ~
to, (of a road, etc.) go to; (of acts,
etc.) have as a result: *extrav-
agance that led to his bankruptcy*.
5. ~ *sb. to think (believe)*, cause
him to do so. *n.* **1.** action of
~ing or guiding: *to take the ~*;
to follow sb.'s ~ (example). **2.**
~ing position; distance by which
one ~s: *to have a ~ of five yards*.
3. strap, etc., for ~ing a dog.
4. (actor taking) chief part
in a play. **5.** (in card games)
right to start play. **~·er** *n.* person who ~s; ~ing article (see
below). **~·er·ship** *n.* **~·ing**
adj. chief; most important:
~ing lady, chief actress in a play;
~ing article, in a newspaper, one
giving editorial opinions on
events, policies, etc. *~ing
question*, one that suggests the
answer that is hoped for.

leaf [li:f] *n.* (pl. *leaves* [li:vz]). **1.**
one of the parts (usu. green and
flat) growing from the stem, etc.,
of a plant: *trees in ~ (coming
into ~)*. **2.** single sheet of paper
forming two pages of a book.
turn over a new ~, (fig.) make a
new and better start. **3.** hinged
or loose part of an extending
table. **4.** *gold ~*, gold hammered into very thin sheets.
~·less *adj.* without leaves.
~·let *n.* **1.** young ~. **2.** printed
sheet (unbound but sometimes
folded) with announcements,
etc. **~·y** *adj.* (-*ier*, -*iest*). of or
like, shaded by, leaves.

league [li:g] *n.* **1.** agreement

between persons, groups, or nations for their common welfare. **2.** group of sports clubs playing matches among themselves: ~ *football*. *v.t. & i.* form into, become, a ~.

²**league** [li:g] *n.* (old) measure of distance (about three miles).

leak [li:k] *n.* hole, crack, etc., through which liquid, gas, etc., may wrongly get in or out. *v.i. & t.* **1.** (let liquid, etc.) pass through a ~. **2.** (fig., of news, a secret) ~ *out*, become known; ~ *secret information to the press*, supply it purposely. ~**·age** ['li:kidʒ] *n.* ~ing; sth. that ~s out or in. ~**·y** *adj.* having a ~.

¹**lean** [li:n] *adj.* (-*er*, -*est*). **1.** (of persons, animals, meat) having less fat than usual. **2.** not productive: ~ *harvests* (*years*). *n.* meat without fat. ~**·ness** *n.*

²**lean** [li:n] *v.i. & t.* (p.t. & p.p. *leaned* or *leant* [lent]). **1.** be or put in a sloping position: *to ~ backwards*; *to ~ out of a window.* **2.** support: *to ~ a ladder against a wall* (*one's elbows on a table*). **3.** have a tendency (*towards*). **4.** ~ *upon*, (fig.) depend upon (*for* sth.). ~**ing** *n.* tendency (of mind, *towards* sth.). '~-'**to** *n.* building (e.g. a shed) whose roof is supported against the wall of another building.

leap [li:p] *v.i. & n.* (p.t. & p.p. *leapt* [lept] or *leaped*). jump. *by ~s and bounds*, rapidly. '~-**frog** *n.* game (see the picture on page 291). '~-**year** *n.* year in which February has 29 days.

learn [lə:n] *v.t. & i.* (p.t. & p.p. *learnt* [lə:nt]). **1.** gain knowledge of or skill in, by study, practice, or being taught. **2.** be told or informed (*that*, *how*, *whether*). ~**ed** ['lə:nid] *adj.* having or showing much knowledge: *the ~ed professions*, those needing much knowledge. ~**·ed·ly** *adv.* ~**ing** *n.* advanced knowledge gained by careful study.

lease [li:s] *n.* legal agreement by which the owner of land or a building agrees to let another have the use of it for a certain time for a regular payment (called *rent*). *a new ~ of life*, better chance of living longer or of being happier, more active. *v.t.* give, take possession of (land, etc.) by ~. '~-**hold** *n. & adj.* (land) held for a term of years (cf. *freehold*).

leash [li:ʃ] *n.* dog's ²**lead** (3). *hold in ~*, control. *v.t.* put a ~ on.

least [li:st] *adj.* (superl. of *little*) *& n.* smallest (quantity, degree, etc.). *at ~*, at any rate; not less, even if more is impossible. *adv.* in the ~ degree.

leath·er ['leðə*] *n.* material made by curing animal skins.

¹**leave** [li:v] *v.t. & i.* (p.t. & p.p. *left*). **1.** go away from. **2.** neglect or forget to take, bring, or do sth.: ~ *one's umbrella in the train*; ~ *half one's work until the next day*; ~ *the door open*; ~ (*sb.* or *sth.*) *alone*, not touch, trouble, interfere with. **3.** ~ *go* (*of*), stop holding. ~ *off*, stop, give up. ~ *out*, omit, neglect to think about. **4.** give (money, etc.) by will to sb., at one's death; ~ *behind* at one's death. **5.** pass (a place, etc.) so that it is in a certain relation, etc.: *L~ the church on your left and go straight on.* **6.** be left, remain: *There's nothing left for you.* **leav·ings** *n. pl.* what is left, esp. sth. unwanted or worthless.

²**leave** [li:v] *n.* permission, consent, authority (to do sth., esp. to be absent from duty in the armed forces or government service): *to ask for* (*go home on*) ~; *by your ~*, with your permission. **2.** period of such absence: *six months' ~*; *two ~s in six years.* **3.** *take one's ~*, *take ~ of sb.*, go away, say farewell. *take ~ of one's senses*, behave as if mad.

leav·en ['levn] *n.* substance (e.g. yeast) used to make bread rise before baking; (fig.) quality or influence spreading in and changing sth. *v.t.* add ~ to; act like ~ upon.

leaves, see *leaf*.

lec·tern ['lektə(:)n] *n.* sloping reading-desk for a Bible in church.

lec·ture ['lektʃə*] *v.i. & t. & n.*
1. (give a) talk (to an audience
or class) for the purpose of
teaching. **2.** (give sb. a) scolding
or reproof. **lec·tur·er** *n.* ~·
ship *n.* post as lecturer at a
university, etc.

led, see ²*lead.*

ledge [ledʒ] *n.* narrow shelf coming out from a wall, cliff, or
other upright surface: *a window* ~.

ledg·er ['ledʒə*] *n.* book in which
a business firm's accounts are
kept.

lee [li:] *n.* (place giving) protection against wind; (attrib.) of or
on the side sheltered from the
wind: *the lee side of a ship; a lee
shore* (towards which the wind
is blowing). **'lee·way** *n.* sideways drift (of a ship) in the
direction towards which the
wind is blowing; (fig.) *make up
leeway,* make up for lost time,
get back into position.

leech [li:tʃ] *n.* small blood-sucking worm living in wet places.
stick like a ~, be difficult to get
rid of.

leek [li:k] *n.* onion-like vegetable.

leer [liə*] *n.* unpleasant look that
suggests evil desire or ill will.
v.i. ~ *at,* look at in this way.

lees [li:z] *n. pl.* dregs(1).

¹left, see *¹leave.*

²left [left] *adj.* opposite of ²*right*(1);
(of, in, on, the) side of the body
which is towards the west when
one faces the north: *Few people
write with the* ~ *hand.* **'~-
'hand·ed** *adj.* using the ~ hand
more often or more easily than
the right. *the L*~, the more
radical political group(s), e.g.
Socialists, Communists.

leg [leg] *n.* **1.** one of the limbs
of a person's or animal's body
used in walking, running, and
jumping. *give sb. a leg up,* help
in time of need. *pull sb.'s leg,*
try, for a joke, to make him
believe sth. that is untrue. *not
have a leg to stand on,* have
nothing to support one's opinion,
defence, etc. *on its last legs,*
almost useless or at an end.
2. (of a journey) part that lies

between two turning points;
stage(4). **leg·gings** *n. pl.*
leather coverings for the lower
part of the legs. **leg·less** ['leglis]
adj. having no legs.

leg·a·cy ['legəsi] *n.* money, etc.,
(to be) received by a person
under the will of and at the
death of another person.

le·gal ['li:gl] *adj.* connected with,
in accordance with, authorized
or required by, the law: ~
tender, form of money which
must be accepted if offered in
payment. ~**·ly** *adv.* ~**·i·ty**
[li(:)'gæliti] *n.* being ~. ~**·ize**
['li:gəlaiz] *v.t.* make ~. ~**·i·za·**
tion [ˌli:gəlai'zeiʃən] *n.*

leg·ate ['legit] *n.* the Pope's
ambassador to a country.

le·ga·tion [li'geiʃən] *n.* (house,
offices, etc., of a) diplomatic
minister below the rank of
ambassador, with those under
him, representing his government in a foreign country.

leg·end ['ledʒənd] *n.* old story
handed down from the past, esp.
one of doubtful truth; literature
of such stories: *famous in* ~.
leg·en·da·ry *adj.* famous,
known only, in ~s.

leg·i·ble ['ledʒəbl] *adj.* (of handwriting, print) that can be read
easily. **leg·i·bly** *adv.* **leg·i·**
bil·i·ty [ˌledʒi'biliti] *n.*

le·gion ['li:dʒən] *n.* **1.** division
of several thousand men in an
old Roman army. **2.** very great
number.

leg·is·late ['ledʒisleit] *v.i.* make
laws. **leg·is·la·tion** [ˌledʒis-
'leiʃən] *n.* making laws; the laws
made. **leg·is·la·tive** ['ledʒis-
lətiv] *adj.* law-making: *legislative assemblies (councils).* **leg·is·**
la·tor ['ledʒisleitə*] *n.* member
of a law-making body. **leg·is·**
la·ture ['ledʒislətʃə*] *n.* law-
making body (e.g. Parliament
in U.K.).

le·git·i·mate [li'dʒitimit] *adj.* **1.**
lawful, regular: *the* ~ *king;*
~ *purposes.* **2.** reasonable; that
can be justified: ~ *absence from
school.* **3.** born of persons married to one another. **le·git·i·**
ma·cy *n.*

lei·sure ['leʒə*] *n.* spare time; time free from work. *at ~*, not occupied; when there is ~. *at one's ~*, when one has free time. **leis·ured** *adj.* having plenty of ~. **~·ly** *adj. & adv.* unhurried(ly).

lem·on ['lemən] *n.* (tree with) pale yellow fruit with acid juice used for drinks and flavouring. **~·ade** [ˌlemə'neid] *n.* drink made from ~s.

Lemons   A leopard

lend [lend] *v.t.* (p.t. & p.p. *lent*). **1.** give (sb.) the use of (sth.) for a period of time, after which it is to be returned. **2.** ~ *a hand*, help. ~ *oneself to*, give one's support to. ~ *itself to*, be useful or helpful for a purpose. **3.** contribute: *facts that ~ probability to a theory.* **~·er** *n.*

length [leŋθ] *n.* **1.** measurement from end to end (space or time). *at ~*, at last, for (after) a long time. *at full ~*, with the body stretched out and flat. *keep sb. at arm's ~*, avoid being friendly. *go to all ~s (any ~)*, do anything necessary to get what one wants. **2.** piece of cloth, etc., long enough for a purpose: *a dress ~.* **~·en** *v.t. & i.* make or become longer. **'~·wise**, **'~·ways** *adv.* in the direction of the ~. **~·y** *adj.* (*-ier*, *-iest*). (of speech, writing) very long; too long.

le·nient ['liːnjənt] *adj.* not severe: ~ *punishment*; ~ *towards wrongdoers.* **~·ly** *adv.* **le·nien·cy** ['liːnjənsi] *n.*

lens [lenz] *n.* piece of glass or glass-like substance with one or both sides curved, for use in eye-glasses, cameras, telescopes.

lent, see **lend**.

Lent [lent] *n.* (in the Christian Church) period of forty days before Easter.

len·til ['lentl] *n.* kind of bean plant; seed of this: ~ *soup*.

leop·ard ['lepəd] *n.* large flesh-eating animal with yellowish coat and dark spots.

lep·er ['lepə*] *n.* person with leprosy. **lep·ro·sy** ['leprəsi] *n.* skin disease that slowly eats into the body. **lep·rous** ['leprəs] *adj.* of, having, leprosy.

less [les] *comp. adj.* (cf. *little, least, few*). **1.** not so much (in amount); a smaller quantity or degree of. **2.** followed by *than*: *I have ~ money than* (not so much money as) *you.* *n.* smaller amount, time, quantity, etc.: *I want ~ of this and more of that.* *adv.* **1.** to a smaller extent; not so much: *He was ~ hurt than frightened.* **2.** not so: *Tom is ~ clever than his brother.* *prep.* minus; with (that stated) taken away: *£10 less £3 for taxes.* **les·sen** *v.t. & i.* make or become ~. **les·ser** *adj.* not so great as the other.

les·see [le'siː] *n.* person who holds land, a building, etc., on a lease.

les·son ['lesn] *n.* **1.** sth. to be learnt or taught; period of time given to teaching or learning. **2.** sth. experienced, esp. sth. serving as an example or warning: *Let this be a ~ to you!* **3.** reading from the Bible during a church service.

les·sor [le'sɔː*] *n.* person who grants a lease.

lest [lest] *conj.* for fear that; in order that . . . not; (after *fear, be afraid*) that.

let [let] *v.t. & i.* (*-tt-*, p.t. & p.p. *let*). **1.** allow: *to let sb. do sth.*; *to let the fire out* (on purpose or not). **2.** (with adv. & prep.): *let sth. down*, cause it to be down; make (a dress, etc.) longer by unstitching the hem. *let sb. down*, fail to help him in time of need. *let oneself (sb.) in for*, cause oneself (sb.) to be responsible for (esp. sth. troublesome). *let sb. into a secret, let a secret out*, share it. *let off*, fire or discharge (a gun, firework, etc.); allow (sb.) to go unpunished or with slight punishment. **let out**, make (a garment) wider or looser by undoing stitches; hire out (see 4). **3.** (other special phrases): **let** (*sth.* or *sb.*) **alone**, leave undisturbed, not touch or trouble. **let alone**, (as prep.) not to mention; far less (more) than. **let fly** (*at*), throw (sth.) violently (at), say angry words (to). **let go** (*of*), stop holding. **let oneself go**, stop controlling one's feelings. **4.** allow the use of a building in return for rent: *to let a house*; *houses to let*; (often *let out*) hire out: *to let out horses by the day.* **5.** (with first and third persons only, used to make suggestions or give orders): *Let's start at once! Let every man do his duty!* **6.** (with third person only, used to indicate a challenge): *Let him do his worst. Let them try to trespass on my land again!* *n.* letting (4); lease.

leth·al ['li:θəl] *adj.* causing, designed to cause, death: ~ *weapons*, guns, etc.

leth·ar·gy ['leθədʒi] *n.* (state of) being tired, uninterested; want of energy. **le·thar·gic** [le-'θɑ:dʒik] *adj.*

let·ter ['letə*] *n.* **1.** character or sign representing a sound; *capital* ~, A, etc.; *small letter*, a, etc. *keep the* ~ *of the law* (*an agreement*), carry out its stated conditions without regard to its spirit or true purpose. **2.** written message, etc., sent by one person to another. **3.** (pl.) literature; books: *a man of* ~*s*.

let·tuce ['letis] *n.* garden plant with green leaves used in salads.

lev·el ['levl] *n.* **1.** surface parallel with the horizon; such a surface with reference to its height: *at* (*above*) *sea·*~; *on a* ~ *with*, at the same height as. **2.** instrument for testing whether a surface is ~: *a spirit·*~. *adj.* **1.** having a horizontal surface: ~ *ground*; *a* ~ *crossing*, place where a railway crosses a road on the same ~. **2.** *have a* ~ *head*, *be* ~*-headed*, be steady and well balanced, able to judge well; *do one's* ~ *best*, do all that one can

do. **3.** on an equality (*with*): *a* ~ *race*, *to draw* ~ *with the other runners.* *v.t.* (*-ll-*). **1.** make ~; make equal by removing distinctions: *Death* ~*s all men.* **2.** ~ *up* (*down*), raise (lower) to a certain ~. **3.** pull or knock down: *to* ~ *a building to the ground.* **4.** aim (a gun, an accusation *at* or *against*).

le·ver ['li:və*] *n.* bar or other tool turned on a pivot to lift, force open, etc., as shown in the illustration. *v.t.* move (sth. *up*, *along*, *into position*, etc.) with a ~. ~·**age** ['li:vəridʒ] *n.* action of, power gained by using, a ~.

A lever

le·vi·a·than [li'vaiəθən] *n.* **1.** sea monster. **2.** anything of very great size and power.

lev·i·ty ['leviti] *n.* tendency to treat serious matters without respect; lack of seriousness.

lev·y ['levi] *v.t.* **1.** impose, collect by authority or force (taxes, a ransom); raise (an army) by using compulsion. **2.** ~ *war* (*upon*, *against*), declare and make war (on). *n.* act of ~*ing*; amount of money, number of men, so obtained: *capital* ~, seizure of part of the private wealth of persons in a community or union.

lewd [lu:d] *adj.* indecent; lustful.

lex·i·con ['leksikən] *n.* dictionary (esp. of Greek or Hebrew). **lex·i·cog·ra·phy** [ˌleksi'kɔgrəfi] *n.* dictionary-compiling. **lex·i·cog·ra·pher** *n.* compiler of a dictionary.

li·a·ble ['laiəbl] *adj.* **1.** ~ *for*, responsible according to law: *He is* ~ *for his wife's debts.* **2.** *be* ~ *to*, have a tendency to (make mistakes, etc.), be likely to (suffer, experience sth. undesirable), be subject to (tax, punishment, etc.). **li·a·bil·i·ty**

[,laiə'biliti] *n.* **1.** being ~:
liability for military service. **2.**
(pl.) debts or other personal
responsibilities.

li·ai·son [li'eizon] *n.* (army) connexion, link: ~ *officer,* one keeping two military units (esp. of
different nationalities) in touch
with each other.

li·ar ['laiə*] *n.* person who tells
untruths or who has told an
untruth.

li·ba·tion [lai'beifən] *n.* (pouring
out of an) offering of wine to a god.

li·bel ['laibl] *n.* **1.** (publishing of)
written or printed statement
about sb. that damages his
reputation. **2.** (colloq.) anything
that does not do justice or brings
discredit (*on*). *v.t.* (*-ll-*). publish
a ~ against; fail to do full justice
to. ~**lous** ['laibələs] *adj.*

lib·er·al ['libərəl] *adj.* **1.** giving
or given freely; generous. **2.**
open-minded; having, showing,
(of education) directed towards,
a broad mind free from prejudice. **3.** of the L~ (a British
political) Party. *n.* member of
the L~ party; person favouring
equality of opportunity for
all and opposing too much
government control. ~**·i·ty**
[,libə'ræliti] *n.* generosity;
broadmindedness.

lib·er·ate ['libəreit] *v.t.* set free.
lib·er·a·tor *n.* **lib·er·a·tion**
[,libə'reifən] *n.*

lib·er·tine ['libəti(:)n] *n.* man
who gives himself up to immoral pleasures.

lib·er·ty ['libəti] *n.* **1.** state of
being free: ~ *of conscience,* freedom to have one's own (esp.
religious) beliefs without interference. **2.** right or power to
decide for oneself what to do,
how to live, etc.: *You are at* ~
to leave whenever you wish. **3.**
take liberties with, behave without proper respect for.

li·bra·ry ['laibrəri] *n.* (building,
room, for a) collection of books.
li·bra·ri·an [lai'breəriən] *n.*
person in charge of a ~.

li·bret·to [li'bretou] *n.* book of
words of an opera or musical
play.

lice, see *louse.*

li·cence ['laisəns] *n.* **1.** (written
or printed statement giving)
permission from someone in
authority for sb. to do sth.: *a* ~
to drive a car; to marry by ~.
2. wrong use of freedom; disregard of laws, customs, etc.

li·cense *v.t.* give a ~ to: *shops
licensed to sell tobacco; licensed
premises,* hotels, restaurants,
where the sale of alcoholic drinks
is allowed.

li·cen·tious [lai'senfəs] *adj.* immoral (esp. in sexual relationships).

lich·en ['laikən, 'litfin] *n.* (sorts
of) small, dry-looking plant
without flowers growing like a
crust on stones, tree trunks, etc.

lick [lik] *v.t. & i.* **1.** pass the
tongue over: ~ *one's lips;* ~
sth. up (off), get it by ~ing; ~
a plate clean. **2.** (of flames,
waves) move gently over. **3.**
(colloq.) beat; whip. (fig.) ~
recruits into shape, train them.
n. act of ~ing with the tongue;
(also *salt-*~) place to which
animals go for salt. ~**ing** *n.*
(colloq.) beating; whipping;
defeat.

lid [lid] *n.* movable cover of a
container: *the lid of a box (kettle);*
eyelid.

¹lie [lai] *v.i. & n.* (p.t. & p.p.
lied [laid]). (make a) statement
that one knows to be untrue:
*to tell lies; in the habit of lying;
give a person the lie,* accuse him
of lying.

²lie [lai] *v.i.* (p.t. *lay* [lei], p.p. *lain*
[lein]). **1.** be, put oneself, flat
on a horizontal surface: *to lie in
bed.* **2.** be resting flat on sth.:
a book lying open on the table. **3.**
be kept, remain, in a certain
position or state: *ships lying at
anchor; money lying idle in the
bank; men who lay (= were) in
prison for years; a town lying in
ruins.* **4.** be spread out to view:
The valley lay before us. **5.** be
present; exist: *The blame lies at
your door,* you are responsible.
The trouble lies in the engine. **6.**
(with adv., etc.): *lie down under
(an insult, etc.),* fail to protest,

resist, etc. **lie in**, stay in bed after one's usual time; remain in bed to give birth to a child. **lie low**, (colloq.) keep out of the way to avoid being seen. **lie up**, stay in bed or in one's room (through illness, etc.). **n.** the way sth. lies: *the lie of the land*, its natural features; (fig.) the state of affairs.

lien [liən] **n.** (law) legal claim *upon* property till the owner has repaid a loan or debt connected with it.

lieu [lju:] **n.** *in ~ of*, instead of.

lieu·ten·ant [lef'tenənt] **n.** 1. army commissioned officer below a captain; junior officer in the navy. 2. (in compounds) officer with the highest rank under: *~-colonel*, *~-general* (army); *~-commander* (navy).

A lifebelt

A life-jacket

life [laif] **n.** (pl. **lives** [laivz]). 1. condition that distinguishes animals and plants from earth, rock, etc.: *How did ~ begin?* 2. living things in general; all living things: *Is there any ~ on the planet Mars?* 3. state of existence as a human being: *take sb.'s ~*, kill him; *to save sb.'s ~*. 4. period between birth and death, between one's birth and now. 5. way of living: *country ~ and town ~*. 6. written account of sb.'s ~. 7. activity, liveliness, interest: *children who are full of ~* (i.e. active and cheerful); *put more ~ into one's work*. 8. period during which sth. is active and useful: *the ~ of a steamship*. '~**belt n.** circular buoy thrown into the water to save sb. from sinking. '~**boat n.** one for saving lives of those in danger at sea or along the coast. '~**guard n.** expert swimmer on duty at places where people swim. **L~ Guards**

n. pl. cavalry regiment in the British Army. '~**-jack·et n.** belt of cork, etc., worn to keep a person afloat in the water. ~**·less adj.** 1. dead. 2. not lively. '~**long adj.** lasting throughout ~.

lift [lift] **v.t. & i.** 1. raise to a higher level or position: ~ (*up*) *a table*; ~ *sth. out*; ~ *up one's voice*, cry out. 2. (of clouds, mist) pass away; rise. 3. dig up (root crops). **n.** 1. act of ~ing: *give sb. a ~*, take him (into a car, etc.) to help him on a journey. 2. apparatus for taking persons or goods up or down to another floor.

lig·a·ment ['ligəmənt] **n.** band of strong tissue holding bones together in the body.

lig·a·ture ['ligətʃə*] **n.** bandage, piece of thread, etc., for binding or tying.

¹**light** [lait] **n.** 1. (opposite of *darkness*) that which enables things to be seen: *the ~ of the sun*; *reading by the ~ of a lamp*; *come to ~*, be brought to ~, become known as the result of inquiry, etc. 2. source of ~; sth. (e.g. candle, lamp) that gives ~. *strike a ~*, strike a match. 3. new knowledge helping to understand or explain sth.: *discoveries that throw new ~ on the problem*. **adj.** (opposite of *dark*) that is well provided with ~; pale-coloured. (See also ²*light*.) **v.t. & i.** (p.t. & p.p. **lit** or **lighted**). 1. cause to burn or shine. 2. (often ~ *up*) make (become) bright. 3. give ~ to: ~ *sb. on his way*. ~**·en** ['laitn] **v.t. & i.** 1. make or become ~(er). 2. send out lightning: *It thundered and lightened*. (See also under ²*light*.) ~**·er n.** device for producing flame: *a cigarette-~er*; *a fire-~er*. '~**·house n.** tower, building (on cliff, rocks, etc.) with a strong ~ to guide and warn ships. ~**·ning** ['laitniŋ] **n.** flash of bright ~ produced by natural electricity in the sky, with thunder. '**light·ning-rod, -con·duc·tor n.** metal rod fixed on top of high buildings

and connected with the earth, to prevent damage by ~ning. '~**ship** *n.* moored ship with the same purpose as a ~house.

²**light** [lait] *adj.* (*-er, -est*). **1.** of little weight, esp. for its size. **2.** not made to support anything heavy: *a ~ bridge (railway).* **3.** gentle, delicate: *a ~ wind; with ~ footsteps; to give sb. a ~ touch on the shoulder.* **4.** (of books, plays, etc.) for entertainment: *~ comedy*; (of food) easily digested; (of sleepers) easily waked; (of beer, wines) not very strong; (of punishment) not severe. (See also under ¹*light*.) *adv.* travel ~, with little luggage. ~**en** ['laitn] *v.t. & i.* make (become) ~(er): *~en a ship.* (See also under ¹*light*.) '~·'**fin·gered** *adj.* skilful in using the hands, esp. for stealing things from people's pockets. '~·'**head·ed** *adj.* dizzy. '~·'**heart·ed** *adj.* gay; free from care. '~·**weight** *adj.*, ~**weight** *n.* boxer weighing between 130 and 135 lb. ~·**ly** *adv.* ~**ness** *n.*

³**light** [lait] *v.i.* (p.t. & p.p. *lit*). ~ (*up*)*on*, find, come upon, by chance.

light·er ['laitə*] *n.* **1.** boat for carrying goods to and from ships in harbour. **2.** (See ¹*light*.)

¹**like** [laik] *adj.* **1.** similar; having the same qualities; such as; resembling; characteristic of; (after *feel*) in the mood for, ready for, likely to. *nothing ~ as (good, etc.)*, not nearly so (good, etc.). *prep.* in the manner of; to the same degree as. *adv.* as (which is considered to be more correct). *n.* ~ person or thing; that which is equal or similar: *We have never seen the ~ (e.g. such bad weather). He doesn't play chess and the ~ (indoor games).* ~·**ly** *adj.* (*-ier, -iest; more, most*). **1.** probable. **2.** that seems suitable, reasonable: *a ~ly excuse (reason for his absence).* **3.** (as adv.) probably: *I shall very ~ly be away tomorrow.* ~·**li·hood** ['laiklihud] *n.* degree to which sth. is ~ly: *not much ~lihood of finding him*

at home. **lik·en** ['laikn] *v.t.* point out the ~ness of one thing (to another): *to liken the heart to a pump.* ~**ness** *n.* quality of being ~: *The painting is a good ~ness of you.* '~**wise** *adv.* in the same way. *conj.* also.

²**like** [laik] *v.t.* **1.** be fond of; find satisfactory or agreeable; have a taste (4) for. **2.** (in negative sentences with *will*) be unwilling: *I didn't ~ to trouble him.* **3.** (with *would, should*) expressing a wish: *They would ~ to come. n.* (pl. only) things one ~s. **lik·a·ble** *adj.* pleasing; of a kind that is ~d. **lik·ing** *n.* *have a liking for*, be fond of, have a taste for; *to one's liking*, as one ~s it, satisfactory.

li·lac ['lailək] *n.* shrub with white or purple flowers growing in clusters; pale purple or pinkish purple.

lilt [lilt] *n.* (lively song or tune with) well-marked rhythm; *v.t. & i.* sing with a ~.

li·ly ['lili] *n.* (sorts of) plant growing from a bulb whose flowers are of many shapes, sizes, and colours.

limb [lim] *n.* leg, arm, or wing; bough of a tree.

lim·bo ['limbou] *n.* condition of being forgotten and unwanted; place for forgotten and unwanted things.

¹**lime** [laim] *n.* white substance obtained by burning limestone, used in making cement and mortar: *quick ~, dry ~; slaked ~,* after being acted upon by water. *v.t.* put ~ on (fields, etc.). '~·**light** *n.* intense white light formerly used for lighting the stage in theatres: *in the ~light,* receiving great publicity. '~·**stone** *n.* stone containing much ~.

²**lime** [laim] *n.* round juicy fruit like, but more acid than, a lemon.

³**lime** [laim] *n.* tree with smooth heart-shaped leaves and sweet-smelling yellow blossoms.

lim·er·ick ['limərik] *n.* humorous or nonsense poem of five lines.

lim·it ['limit] *n.* **1.** line or point

that may not or cannot be passed: *to set a ~ to one's expenses.* **2.** greatest or smallest amount, degree, etc., of what is possible, to be allowed, etc.: *That's the ~!* (colloq.) that's the most that can be accepted, endured, etc. *v.t.* put a ~ or ~s to; be the ~ of: *to ~ one's expenses (to £10).* **~ed** *adj.* (of quantity) small; (of views, etc.) restricted; narrow. **~ed liability company,** business company whose members are liable for its debts only to the extent of the capital sum they have provided. **~·less** *adj.* without ~s. **lim·i·ta·tion** [,limi'teiʃən] *n.* ~ing; condition that ~s; disability: *He knows his ~ations,* what qualities, abilities, etc., he lacks.

¹**limp** [limp] *adj.* (-er, -est). not stiff or firm; tired. **~·ly** *adv.*

²**limp** [limp] *v.i.* walk lamely or unevenly as when one leg or foot is hurt or stiff. *n.* a lame walk: *with a bad ~.* **~·ing·ly** *adv.*

lim·pet ['limpit] *n.* small shellfish that fastens itself tightly to rocks.

lim·pid ['limpid] *adj.* (of liquids, the atmosphere, the eyes) clear. **~·ly** *adv.*

linch·pin ['lintʃpin] *n.* pin passed through the end of an axle.

¹**line** [lain] *n.* **1.** mark made by drawing the point of a pen, etc., along a surface. **2.** length of thread, string, rope, or wire for various purposes: *fishing ~s; telephone ~s.* **3.** use of ~s (1) in drawing, etc.: *a ~ drawing.* **4.** row: *a ~ of trees; boys standing in (a) ~; in ~ with,* (fig.) in agreement with. **5.** railway: *the main (a branch) ~; to cross the ~ by the bridge.* **6.** organized system of transport: *a steamship ~; an air~.* **7.** row of words on a page of writing or print: *read between the ~s,* find more meaning than the words express. **8.** short letter: *Send me a ~ to say you have arrived.* **9.** series of connected military defence posts, trenches, etc.:

the front ~; behind the ~s; successful all along the ~. **10.** family, esp. several generations: *a long ~ of great kings.* **11.** direction; course; way of behaving, dealing with a situation, etc.: *to be studying a subject on sound ~s (on the wrong ~s),* i.e. by good (bad) methods; *taking one's own ~,* being independent. **12.** the equator: *cross the ~.* **13.** kind of business or commercial activity: *He's in the drapery ~. That's not much in my ~,* is sth. I know little about. **14.** class of commercial goods: *several good ~s in cheap underwear.* **15.** *Hard ~s!* Bad luck! *v.t. & i.* mark (sth.) with ~s; form a ~ or ~s: *roads ~d with trees; to ~ up soldiers; soldiers who ~ up smartly.* **lin·e·age** ['liniidʒ] *n.* family ~; ~ of descent. **lin·e·al** ['liniəl] *adj.* in the direct ~ of descent (from father to son, etc.). **lin·e·ar** ['liniə*] *adj.* of or in ~s: *linear designs;* (maths.) *linear measure,* of length only. **lin·er** *n.* ship, aircraft, of a ~ (6) of ships or aircraft. '**lines·man** *n.* (in sport) man who helps the referee, e.g. by signalling when the ball has crossed one of the ~s. '**~-up** *n.* way in which persons, States, etc., are allied: *a new ~-up of European powers.*

²**line** [lain] *v.t.* add a layer of (usu. different) material to the inside of (bags, boxes, articles of clothing): *fur-~d gloves.* **lin·ing** *n.* layer of material added to the inside of a garment, etc.; kind of material so used.

lin·e·a·ment ['liniəmənt] *n.* (usu. pl.) lines, details, etc., that mark the character (esp. of a face).

lin·en ['linin] *n. & adj.* (cloth) made of flax; articles made of ~, esp. shirts and collars, bedsheets, table-cloths.

lin·ger ['liŋgə*] *v.i.* be late or slow in going away; stay long(er than others) at a place. **~·ing** *adj.* (of an illness) lasting a long time.

lin·ger·ie ['lænʒəri] *n.* (genteel name for) women's underclothing.

lin·go ['liŋgou] *n.* (pl. -oes). (humor. or contemptuous) language, esp. one that one does not know.

lin·gua fran·ca ['liŋgwə'fræŋkə] *n.* language adopted as a means of general communication over an area in which several languages are spoken, e.g. Swahili in E. Africa.

lin·guist ['liŋgwist] *n.* person skilled in foreign languages.

lin·'guis·tic *adj.* of (the study of) languages.

lin·i·ment ['linimənt] *n.* liquid for rubbing on stiff or aching parts of the body.

lin·ing, see ²*line*.

link [liŋk] *n.* 1. one ring or loop of a chain. 2. (cuff-~s, sleeve-~s) pair of ~ed buttons for fastening the cuffs of a shirt. 3. person or thing that unites or connects two others. *v.t. & i.* join, be joined, with, or as with, ~s (together, to or with sth.).

links [liŋks] *n. pl.* golf-course.

li·no·leum [li'nouljəm] *n.* strong floor-covering of canvas treated with powdered cork and oil.

lin·seed ['linsi:d] *n.* flax seed.

lint [lint] *n.* linen, with one side scraped fluffy, used for dressing wounds.

lin·tel ['lintl] *n.* piece of wood or stone forming the top of a doorway or window-frame.

li·on ['laiən] *n.* see the picture. *the ~'s share,* the larger part. *~·ess n. ~·ize* ['laiənaiz] *v.t.* treat (sb.) as a celebrated person.

A lion

lip [lip] *n.* 1. one of the two fleshy edges of the opening to the mouth. 2. edge of a cup, etc.; part like a lip. **'lip-₁serv·ice** *n.* approval, respect, etc., given in words but not sincere. **'lip·**

stick *n.* (stick of) colouring material for the lips.

li·queur [li'kjuə*] *n.* sorts of strong flavoured alcoholic drink, usu. sipped after a meal.

liq·uid ['likwid] *n.* substance like water or oil that flows freely and is neither a solid nor a gas. *adj.* 1. in the form of a ~ : ~ *food.* 2. bright and moist-looking: ~ *eyes.* 3. (of sounds) clear, soft: ~ *notes.* 4. not fixed; easily changed: ~ *opinions.* 5. ~ *assets,* cash, property which can easily be changed into cash.

liq·ue·fy ['likwifai] *v.t.* make or become a ~. **liq·ue·fac·tion** [₁likwi'fækʃən] *n.*

liq·ui·date ['likwideit] *v.t. & i.* 1. pay (a debt). 2. bring (esp. an unsuccessful business company) to an end by dividing up its property to pay debts. 3. (of a company) go through this process. 4. get rid of (an enemy) by violence. **liq·ui·da·tion** [₁likwi-'deiʃən] *n. go into liquidation,* become bankrupt.

liq·uor ['likə*] *n.* 1. alcoholic drink. 2. liquid produced by boiling or fermenting a food substance.

lisp [lisp] *v.i. & t.* fail to use the sounds s and z correctly (e.g. by saying *thikthteen* for *sixteen*). *n.* a ~ing way of speaking.

lis·som ['lisəm] *adj.* quick and graceful in movement; lithe.

¹list [list] *n.* number of names (of persons, items, things, etc.) written or printed : *a shopping ~. v.t.* make a ~ of ; put on a ~.

²list [list] *v.i.* (esp. of a ship) lean over to one side (e.g. because of cargo that has shifted). *n.* ~ing of a ship : *a ~ to starboard.*

³list [list] *v.i. & t.* (old use) listen (to).

lis·ten ['lisn] *v.i.* try to hear; pay attention (to). ~ *in,* ~ to a radio programme. **~·er** *n.*

list·less ['listlis] *adj.* too tired to show interest or do anything.

lists [lists] *n. pl.* (olden times) enclosure for fights between men on horseback. *enter the ~s,* (fig.) send out, accept, a challenge to a contest.

lit, see ¹*light* (v.).

lit·a·ny ['litəni] *n.* form of prayer for use in church services, recited by a priest with responses from the congregation.

lit·er·a·cy ['litərəsi] *n.* being literate.

lit·er·al ['litərəl] *adj.* 1. connected with, expressed in, letters of an alphabet. 2. corresponding exactly to the original : *a ~ copy* (*translation*). ~·**ly** *adv.* giving, taking, words in their ordinary meaning, not figuratively.

lit·er·a·ry ['litərəri] *adj.* of literature or authors : ~ *style* (contrasted with colloquial, etc., styles).

lit·er·ate ['litərit] *n. & adj.* (person) able to read and write.

lit·er·a·ture ['litəritʃə*] *n.* 1. (the writing or study of) books, etc., valued as works of art (drama, fiction, essays, poetry, contrasted with technical books and journalism). 2. all the writings of a country or period ; the books dealing with a special subject : *travel literature* ; *18th-century literature.*

lithe [laið] *adj.* (of a person, body) bending, twisting or turning, easily.

lith·og·ra·phy [li'θɔgrəfi] *n.* process of printing from parts of a flat stone or metal surface that have been prepared to receive ink.

lit·i·gate ['litigeit] *v.i. & t.* go to law ; contest (sth.) at a court of law. **lit·i·gant** *n.* person engaged in a lawsuit. **lit·i·ga·tion** [,liti'geiʃən] *n.* **li·tig·ious** [li-'tidʒəs] *adj.* fond of going to law.

li·tre ['li:tə*] *n.* unit of measure in the metric system. 1 litre = about 1¾ pints.

¹**lit·ter** ['litə*] *n.* couch or bed arranged for carrying a person about.

²**lit·ter** ['litə*] *n.* 1. various articles, scraps of paper, etc., left lying about untidily. 2. straw, etc., used as bedding for animals. 3. newly-born young ones of an animal : *a ~ of puppies* (*pigs*). *v.t. & i.* 1. put, leave,

~ (1) *about* : *a room ~ed with books and papers.* 2. put ~ (2) down (for animals). 3. (of animals) give birth to a ~ (3).

lit·tle ['litl] *adj.* 1. small ; young ; not tall ; unimportant. 2. of the smaller or smallest size : *the ~ finger* (*toe*). 3. (*less, least*). not much. *a ~*, a small quantity or amount. *n.* small amount. *after* (*for*) *a ~*, after (for) a short time. *adv.* not much ; hardly at all. *a ~*, rather : *He's a ~ better this morning.* ~ *by ~*, gradually.

lit·tor·al ['litərəl] *n. & adj.* (that part of a country which is) along the coast.

lit·ur·gy ['litədʒi] *n.* fixed form of public worship used in a church.

live [liv] *v.i. & t.* 1. be alive ; have existence as an animal or plant. ~ *on*, have as food or diet : *to ~ on fruit* ; get what one needs for support from : *to ~ on one's income* (*friends*) ; ~ *sth. down*, by good living make people forget (earlier wrongdoing, mistakes, etc.) ; ~ *up to* (one's principles, faith, etc.), reach the standard which has been set. [laiv] *adj.* (attrib. only ; cf. *alive*) having life ; full of energy, activity, interest : ~ *coals*, burning ; ~ *shells*, not yet exploded ; ~ *wires*, charged with electric current. ~·**li·hood** ['laivlihud] *n.* means of living : *to earn one's ~lihood by farming.* ~·**long** ['livlɔŋ] *adj.* (only) *the ~long day*, etc., the whole length of the day, etc. ~·**ly** ['laivli] *adj.* (*-ier, -iest*). full of life and gaiety ; cheerful ; quick-moving. ~·**li·ness** *n.* **liv·en** ['laivn] *v.t. & i.* (often *liven up*) make or become ~ly. ~·**stock** ['laivstɔk] *n.* animals kept for use or profit.

liv·ing ['liviŋ] *adj.* 1. alive : *living creatures.* 2. (of a picture, etc.) true to life. *n.* 1. = ~lihood : *to make a living as a shopkeeper.* 2. manner of life : *plain living* ; *high standards of living* ; *living-room*, room for general use by day ; *a living wage*, one that is enough to ~ on.

liv·er ['livə*] *n.* reddish-brown organ in the body purifying the blood; animal's ~ as food. ~**ish**,~**y** *adj.* ill because the ~ is out of order.

liv·er·y ['livəri] *n.* **1.** special dress worn by menservants in a great household. **2.** ~ *stable*, one where horses are kept for owners; one from which horses may be hired. *adj.* see *liver.*

liv·id ['livid] *adj.* of the colour of lead: ~ *marks on the body* (e.g. because of bruises); ~ *with cold (anger).*

liz·ard ['lizəd] *n.* small, creeping, long-tailed, four-legged reptile.

A lizard

lla·ma ['lɑːmə] *n.* S. American animal, with a thick woolly coat, used as a beast of burden.

load [loud] *n.* **1.** that which is (to be) carried or supported; (fig.) weight of care, responsibility, etc. **2.** amount which a cart, etc., can take: *a cart-~ of hay.* *v.t. & i.* **1.** put a ~ (1) on or in; put (goods) into or on: *to ~ a donkey; to ~ coal on to carts.* **2.** put (a cartridge, shell, etc.) into (a gun). **1~·line** *n.* line painted on a ship's side to mark the highest safe water-level.

load·stone, see *lodestone.*

¹loaf [louf] *n.* (pl. *loaves* [louvz]). mass of bread cooked as a separate quantity.

²loaf [louf] *v.i. & t.* waste time; wait about idly: ~*ing at street corners.* ~**er** *n.*

loam [loum] *n.* rich soil with much decayed vegetable matter. ~**y** *adj.*

loan [loun] *n.* **1.** sth. lent, esp. a sum of money: *government ~s, capital lent to the government.* **2.** lending or being lent: *books on ~; ask for the ~ of.* *v.t.* lend.

loath, loth [louθ] *predic. adj.* unwilling (*to do* sth.). *nothing ~, quite glad (to).*

loathe [louð] *v.t.* dislike greatly; feel disgust for. **loath·ing** *n.* disgust. **loath·some** *adj.* disgusting.

loaves, see *¹loaf.*

lob·by ['lobi] *n.* entrance-hall; corridor: *in the hotel ~.*

lobe [loub] *n.* lower rounded end of the outer ear.

lob·ster ['lobstə*] *n.* shellfish as shown here; its flesh as food.

A lobster   A lock of hair

lo·cal ['loukl] *adj.* **1.** of a place or district: ~ *news; the ~ doctor; ~ government.* **2.** of a part, not of the whole: *a ~ pain.* ~**ly** *adv.* ~**i·ty** [lou'kæliti] *n.* thing's position; place; district; place where an event occurs. ~**ize** ['loukəlaiz] *v.t.* make ~, not general.

lo·cate [lou'keit] *v.t.* **1.** discover, show, the position of: *to ~ a town on a map.* **2.** *be ~d,* be situated. **3.** establish in a place: *to ~ a school in a new suburb.* **lo·ca·tion** [lou'keiʃən] *n.* locating or being ~d; position or place of or for sth.; (S. Africa) suburb for non-Europeans.

loch [lok] *n.* (Scotland). **1.** long narrow arm of the sea. **2.** lake.

¹lock [lok] *n.* portion of hair that naturally clings together.

A canal lock (3)

²lock [lok] *n.* **1.** mechanism, worked by turning a key, for sliding a bolt to fasten a door, gate, lid, etc. **2.** mechanism by which a gun is fired. ~, *stock, and barrel,* the whole of a thing; completely. **3.** section of a canal or other waterway, closed at each end by gates, in which boats are raised or lowered to another water-level. 4. *air-lock*, stoppage of a pump, etc., because of an air-bubble. *v.t. & i.* 1. fasten (a door, box, etc.) by turning the key of a ~: ~ (*sb.*) *in* (*out*), keep in (out) by ~ing the door (gate, etc.); ~ *sth. up*, put in a ~ed place, ~ the doors, etc., of a building. 2. become (cause to be) fixed and unable to move: *jaws tightly ~ed*; *~ed wheels*. '~**er** *n.* small cupboard with a ~. '~**-jaw** *n.* disease in which the jaws become tightly fixed. '~**-out** *n.* refusal of employers to allow workers to enter their place of work until they accept certain conditions. '~**smith** *n.* maker and repairer of ~s for doors, etc. '~**-up** *n.* (colloq.) (room used as a) prison.

lock·et ['lɒkit] *n.* small (often gold or silver) case for a portrait, lock of hair, etc., worn hung from the neck.

lo·co·mo·tion [ˌloukə'mouʃən] *n.* (power of) going from one place to another. **lo·co·mo·tive** ['loukəˌmoutiv] *adj.* of, having, causing ~. *n.* railway engine.

lo·cum te·nens ['loukəm 'ti:nenz] (Latin) *n.* priest, doctor, performing the duties of another who is away (e.g. on holiday).

lo·cust ['loukəst] *n.* winged insect which flies in great swarms and destroys crops and vegetation.

A locust

lo·cu·tion [lɔ'kju:ʃən] *n.* style of using words; phrase or idiom.

lode [loud] *n.* vein of metal ore. '~**star** *n.* the pole-star. '~**stone** *n.* kind of iron ore that is magnetic.

lodge [lɒdʒ] *n.* small house, at the gateway to a large private estate. *v.t. & i.* 1. supply (sb.) with room(s) for living in. 2. live (*in, at, with*) as a lodger. 3. enter and become fixed (*in*); cause to do this: *The bullet ~d in his jaw.* 4. put (money, etc.) for safety (*with* sb., *in* a place); place (a statement, complaint, etc.) with the proper authorities. **lodg·er** *n.* person paying for rooms, etc., in sb.'s house: *make a living by taking in ~rs.* **lodg·ing** *n.* (usu. pl.) place where one ~s (2), room(s) occupied by a ~r. '**lodg·ing-house** *n.*

loft [lɒft] *n.* room, place used for storing things, in the highest part of a house under the roof. **loft·y** ['lɒfti] *adj.* (*-ier, -iest*). 1. (not of persons) very high. 2. (of thoughts, aims, feelings) distinguished; noble. 3. (of manner) proud. **loft·i·ly** *adv.*

¹**log** [lɒg] *n.* rough length of a tree trunk that has been cut down; short piece of this for fuel.

²**log** [lɒg] *n.* 1. apparatus for measuring a ship's speed. 2. (also *log-book*) daily record of a ship's rate of progress, events of a voyage, etc.; motor-car owner's registration book.

log·a·rithm ['lɒgəriθəm] *n.* one of a series of numbers set out in tables which make it possible to work out problems in multiplication and division easily by adding and subtracting.

log·ger·head ['lɒgəhed] *n. at ~s* (*with*), on bad terms, in disagreement.

log·ic ['lɒdʒik] *n.* science, method, of reasoning; ability to argue and convince. **log·i·cal** ['lɒdʒikl] *adj.* in accordance with the laws of ~; able to reason rightly. **log·i·cal·ly** *adv.*

loin [lɔin] *n.* 1. (pl.) the lower part of the back between the hip-bones and the ribs. 2. joint of meat from this part of an animal: ~ *of mutton.*

loi·ter ['lɔitə*] *v.i.* go slowly and stop frequently on the way somewhere; stand about; pass time (*away*) thus. ~**er** *n.*

loll [lol] *v.i. & t.* rest, sit, or stand (*about*) in a lazy way; (of the tongue) hang (*out*); let (the tongue) hang (*out*).

lone [loun] *adj.* (attrib. only, chiefly liter.; *alone* and *lonely* are more usual) without companions; unfrequented. ~**ly** ['lounli] *adj.* (*-ier, -iest*). **1.** without companions. **2.** (of places) without many people; not often visited; far from inhabited places or towns: *a* ~*ly village*. **3.** *feeling* ~*ly*, feeling sad because alone. ~**li·ness** *n.* ~**some** ['lounsəm] *adj.* ~**ly**.

¹**long** [loŋ] *adj.* (*-er, -est*) *& n.* **1.** (contrasted with *short*) measuring much from end to end in space or time. **2.** (various uses) *a* ~ *face*, a sad, dismal look. *in the* ~ *run*, in the end, as the final result. *all day* ~, throughout the day. *before* ~, before a ~ *time has passed*. *the* ~ *and the short of it*, the general effect or outcome of it all. *two inches* (*six weeks*) ~, having the length indicated. *adv. as* (*so*) ~ *as*, for as ~ a time as; on condition that; ~ *drawn out*, taking an unnecessarily ~ time. '~**bow** *n.* bow bent by hand. *draw the* ~*bow*, tell untrue or exaggerated stories. **lon·gev·i·ty** [lon'dʒeviti] *n.* ~ life. '~**hand** *n.* ordinary writing (not shorthand). '~**shore·man** *n.* man who loads ships. '~**-'suf·fer·ing** *adj. & n.* patient and uncomplaining (behaviour). '~**ways**, '~**wise** *adv.* = lengthways. ~**wind·ed** [loŋ'windid] *adj.* (of talk, writing) tediously long.

²**long** [loŋ] *v.i.* desire earnestly (*for, to do,* sth.). ~**ing** *n.* strong desire. *adj.* showing, having, strong desire. ~**ing·ly** *adv.*

lon·gi·tude ['londʒitju:d] *n.* distance east or west (measured in degrees) from a meridian, esp. that of Greenwich, in London.

look [luk] *v.i. & t.* (p.t. & p.p. *looked* [lukt]). **1.** try to see; turn one's eyes towards: *L~ at him!*; inspect, examine: *They were* ~*ing at some books*. **2.** (with adv., prep.): ~ *after* (sb. or sth.), take care of, watch over. ~ *down on*, regard with contempt, have a low opinion of. ~ *for*, try to find, be on the watch for. ~ *forward to*, expect, wait for (usu. with pleasure). ~ *in on* (sb.), visit while passing. ~ *on*, be a spectator, not taking part. ~ (*up*)*on* sb. or sth. as, consider as. ~ *out*, be on one's guard, watch (*for* sth.). ~ *sth. over*, inspect it. ~ *sth. through*, glance at, read it. ~ *to*, attend to, take care about. ~ *up*, improve. ~ *sth. up*, find (e.g. a word in a dictionary). ~ *up to*, respect. **3.** (with adj., conj.): ~ *like*, seem to be, seem likely: *It* ~*s like rain*, rain seems likely. ~ *alive* (*sharp*), be quick, hurry. *n.* **1.** act of ~ing. **2.** appearance; what sth. suggests when seen: *angry* ~*s; a* ~ *of pleasure*. **3.** (pl.) person's appearance: *good* ~*s*, beauty. '~**er-'on** *n.* (pl. ~*ers-on*). spectator. '~**-in** *n.* not have a ~*-in*, not have a chance to win. '~**ing-glass** *n.* mirror made of glass. '~**-'out** *n.* **1.** (place for) keeping watch; person who keeps watch. **2.** prospect, future: *It's a poor* ~*-out for this generation* (i.e. their future seems dismal). **3.** *That's his* (*your, etc.*) ~*-out*, that's a (risk, etc.) for him (you) only.

¹**loom** [lu:m] *n.* machine for weaving cloth.

²**loom** [lu:m] *v.i.* appear indistinctly and in a threatening way.

Loops

loop [lu:p] *n.* (shape produced by a) curve crossing itself; part of a length of string, wire, ribbon, etc., in such a shape, esp. as a knot or fastening. *v.t. & i.* **1.** form or bend into a ~ or ~s. **2.** ~ *sth. up* (*back*), keep or fasten sth. up (back) in the form of, or with, a ~. '~**-hole** *n.* narrow opening in a wall; (fig.) way of escape from control, esp. one provided by careless or inexact wording of a rule: *to find a ~-hole in the law.*

loose [lu:s] *adj.* (*-r -st*). **1.** free; not held together, fastened, packed, or contained in sth.: *small change ~ in one's pocket* (i.e. not in a purse). **2.** not tight or close-fitting: *a ~ collar.* **3.** moving more freely than is right: *a ~ tooth* (*bowels, window-frame*). **4.** (of talk, behaviour, etc.) not sufficiently controlled: *~* (i.e. immoral) *conduct; living a ~ life; ~* (i.e. inexact or careless) *thinking; a ~* (i.e. badly connected) *argument.* **5.** not compact; not tightly packed, etc.: *a ~ soil.* **6.** *at a ~ end,* with nothing to do. *v.t.* make *~.* *~·ly adv.*

loos·en ['lu:sn] *v.t.* set or become *~*; make less tight.

loot [lu:t] *v.t. & i.* take (goods, esp. private property) unlawfully and by force, esp. in time of war: *soldiers ~ing the town.* *n.* property so taken.

¹lop [lop] *v.t.* (*-pp-*). cut (branches, etc.) *off* (from a tree, etc.); cut *off* or *away* with one blow.

²lop [lop] *v.i.* (*-pp-*). hang down loosely. **'lop-eared** *adj.* with drooping ears. **'lop-'sided** *adj.* with one side lower than the other.

lope [loup] *v.i.* move with long, easy steps or strides (as a hare does).

lo·qua·cious [lou'kweiʃəs] *adj.* talkative. **lo·quac·i·ty** [lou-'kwæsiti] *n.*

lord [lo:d] *n.* **1.** supreme ruler: *our sovereign ~ the King.* **2.** (*L~*) God: *the L~'s Prayer; the L~'s Day,* Sunday. **3.** peer; nobleman: *the House of Lords,* the upper division of Parliament. **4.** (person with) position of authority, official position: *the Lords of the Admiralty; the L~ Mayor of London.* *v.t. ~ it over,* rule over like a *~.* *~·ly adj.* like, suitable for, a *~.* **Lord·ship** *n. His* (*Your*) *Lordship,* used when speaking of (to) a *~.*

lore [lo:*] *n.* learning or knowledge, esp. handed down from past times (e.g. *folk~, gipsy ~*) or of a special subject (e.g. *bird ~*).

lor·gnette [lo:n'jet] *n.* eye-glasses on a long handle.

lor·ry ['lori] *n.* motor wagon (usu. long and low) for transporting heavy goods. (U.S.A. *truck.*)

lose [lu:z] *v.t. & i.* (p.t. & p.p. **lost** [lost]). **1.** have no longer; have taken away from one (by accident, carelessness, death, etc.). **2.** *~ one's way, ~ oneself, be lost,* not know where one is, be unable to find the right road, etc.; *~ track of,* not know what has happened to (sb. or sth.). **3.** fail to be in time for, fail to see, hear, etc.: *~ one's train* (*the post*); *~ the end of a sentence.* **4.** fail to keep: *~ one's hair; ~ one's temper,* get angry; *~ one's reason,* become insane; *~ one's head,* become too excited; *~ face,* fail to keep one's dignity, be made to look small. **5.** *~ no time* (*in doing sth.*), do it at once. **6.** *be lost to* (all sense of shame, etc.), be no longer affected by; *be lost in* (wonder, etc.), be filled with, wholly given up to. **7.** (of a watch or clock) go too slowly: *losing five minutes a day.* **los·er** *n.* person who *~s.* **loss** [los] *n.* losing; sth. lost; waste; disadvantage caused by losing sth. *at a loss,* perplexed; uncertain what to do or say: *at a loss for words.*

lost, see **lose.**

¹lot [lot] *n.* (colloq.) *the lot, the whole lot,* all; everything. *a lot* (*of*), *lots* (*of*), a great number or amount (of). *adv. a lot* (*better,* etc.), much.

²lot [lot] *n.* **1.** (one of a set of objects used in) the making of a selection or decision by methods depending on chance: *to draw* (*cast*) *lots; to decide sth. by lot.* **2.** that which comes to a person by luck or destiny: *His lot has been a hard one.* **3.** number of various objects offered for sale together, esp. by auction. **4.** *a bad lot,* (colloq.) bad person. **5.** (U.S.) plot (1).

loth, see **loath.**

lo·tion ['loufən] *n.* medicinal liquid for use on the skin.

lot·ter·y ['lɔtəri] *n.* arrangement to give money prizes to holders of numbered tickets previously bought by them and drawn by ²lot (1).

lo·tus ['loutəs] *n.* kinds of water-lily.

loud [laud] *adj.* (-er, -est). 1. easily heard; noisy; not quiet or soft. 2. (of a colour, behaviour, etc.) of the kind that forces itself on the attention. '~·'speak·er *n.* part of a radio receiver that changes electric waves into sound waves loud enough to be heard without earphones. ~·ly *adv.*

lounge [laundʒ] *v.i.* sit, stand about (leaning against sth.), in a lazy way. *n.* room (e.g. in a hotel) with comfortable chairs for lounging: *the hotel* ~. ~ suit *n.* man's suit of jacket and trousers (and waistcoat) for informal day wear.

louse [laus] *n.* (pl. *lice* [lais]). sorts of small insect living on the bodies of human beings and animals existing under dirty conditions; similar insect living on plants. **lous·y** ['lauzi] *adj.* (-ier, -iest). having lice.

lout [laut] *n.* clumsy, ill-mannered man. ~·ish *adj.* ~ish *behaviour*.

love [lʌv] *n.* warm and tender feeling as between parents and children, husband and wife, and close friends; fondness; affection. *in* ~ (*with*), having love and desire (for); *make* ~ *to*, show that one is in ~ with. *v.t.* 1. have strong affection and tender feeling for. 2. find pleasure in: *to* ~ *comfort* (*mountain-climbing*). **lov·a·ble** *adj.* deserving ~; having qualities that cause ~. ~·less *adj.* not feeling, showing, having, ~: *a* ~*less marriage.* **lov·er** *n.* 1. person who ~s sth.: *a lover of good food.* 2. man who is in ~. 3. (pl.) man and woman in ~. **lov·ing** *adj.* feeling or showing ~. **lov·ing·ly** *adv.* '~·sick *adj.* unhappy through feelings of unsatisfied ~.

love·ly ['lʌvli] *adj.* (-ier, -iest). 1. beautiful; pleasant; attractive. 2. delightful; amusing. **love·li·ness** ['lʌvlinis] *n.*

low [lou] *adj.* (-er, -est). 1. (contrasted with *high, tall*) not reaching far upwards; below the usual level; not loud or shrill. 2. not highly developed: *low forms of life.* 3. feeble: *in a low state of health; feeling low,* in low spirits, sad. 4. vulgar; common: *low manners; low tastes.* 5. *lower animals,* all except man; *lower deck,* (Navy) ratings, those who are not officers. *adv.* in or to a low position; in a low manner. *be laid low,* be forced to stay in bed through injury, illness, etc. *be running low,* (of supplies, etc.) be getting near the end. '**low-brow** *n. & adj.* (person) having or showing little taste for intellectual things, esp. art, music, and literature. '**low-down** *adj.* (colloq.) (of behaviour, etc.) dishonourable.

low·er ['louə*] *v.t.* 1. let down (a flag, sail, etc.). 2. make or become less high: *to* ~ *one's voice* (*prices*).

low·ly ['louli] *adj.* (-ier, -iest). humble; simple; modest.

loy·al ['lɔiəl] *adj.* true, faithful (to one's country, friends, etc.). ~·ly *adv.* ~·ist *n.* ~ subject, esp. during a revolt. ~·ty *n.*

loz·enge ['lɔzindʒ] *n.* 1. four-sided diamond-shaped figure. 2. small sweet, esp. one containing medicine: *cough* ~s.

£.₁s. d. ['eles'di:] (abbr.) pounds, shillings, and pence; money.

lu·bri·cate ['lu:brikeit] *v.t.* put oil or grease into (machine parts) to make (them) work smoothly. **lu·bri·cant** ['lu:brikənt] *n.* substance used for this purpose.

lu·cerne [lu:'sə:n] *n.* clover-like plant used for feeding animals.

lu·cid ['lu:sid] *adj.* 1. clear; easy to understand: *a* ~ *explanation.* 2. ~ *intervals,* periods of sanity between periods of insanity. ~·i·ty [lu:'siditi] *n.*

luck [lʌk] *n.* 1. good or bad fortune; chance; sth. that comes by chance: *in* (*out of*) ~, having (not having) good ~; *for* ~, to bring good ~. **2.** good fortune; the help of chance: *as ~ would have it . . .*; *try one's* ~. ~**·less adj.** unfortunate. ~**·y adj.** (*-ier, -iest*). having, bringing, resulting from, good ~. ~**·i·ly adv.**

lu·cra·tive ['lu:krətiv] **adj.** profitable.

lu·di·crous ['lu:dikrəs] **adj.** ridiculous.

lug [lʌg] **v.t.** (*-gg-*). pull or drag roughly and with much effort.

lug·gage ['lʌgidʒ] **n.** bags, trunks, etc., and their contents taken on a journey.

lug·ger ['lʌgə*] **n.** small ship with one or more four-cornered sails.

lu·gu·bri·ous [lu:'gju:briəs] **adj.** dismal; mournful; gloomy.

luke·warm ['lu:kwɔ:m] **adj.** neither hot nor cold; (fig.) not eager in either supporting or opposing.

lull [lʌl] **v.t. & i.** make or become quiet or less active: *to ~ a baby to sleep*; *to ~ sb.'s suspicions. The wind ~ed.* **n.** interval of quiet; period of lessened activity, etc.: *a ~ in the conversation.* **lul·la·by** ['lʌləbai] **n.** song for ~ing a baby to sleep.

lum·ba·go [lʌm'beigou] **n.** muscular pain in the lower part of the back.

lum·ber ['lʌmbə*] **n.** **1.** roughly prepared timber (e.g. planks, boards). **2.** useless or unwanted articles stored away or taking up space. **v.t. & i.** **1.** ~ *along* (*by, past*), move in a heavy, slow, and noisy way. **2.** ~ *up*, fill space inconveniently: *a room ~ed up with useless things.*

lu·mi·na·ry ['lu:minəri] **n.** star; the sun or moon; (fig.) moral or intellectual leader.

lu·mi·nous ['lu:minəs] **adj.** giving out light; bright. **lu·mi·nos·i·ty** [,lu:mi'nɔsiti] **n.**

lump [lʌmp] **n.** **1.** mass without regular shape: ~*s of clay*; *broken into* ~*s*. **2.** *a ~ sum*, one payment for a number of separate purchases. **3.** swelling or bump. **v.i. & t.** **1.** form into ~s. **2.**

put or group (*together*) in a mass; treat (things) as if they were the same. **3.** *If you don't like it, you can ~ it*, this must be endured, whether you like it or not. ~**·ish adj.** (of a person) clumsy; stupid. ~**·y adj.** full of, covered with, ~s.

lu·nar ['lu:nə*] **adj.** of the moon: *a ~ month*, 28 days.

lu·na·tic ['lu:nətik] **n.** madman.

lu·na·cy ['lu:nəsi] **n.** madness.

lunch [lʌntʃ] **n.** meal taken in the middle of the day. **v.i.** eat ~. ~**·eon** ['lʌntʃən] **n.** = lunch.

lung [lʌŋ] **n.** either of the two breathing organs in the chest of man and other animals.

lunge [lʌndʒ] **n.** sudden forward push (e.g. with a sword) or forward movement of the body (when striking a blow). **v.i.** make a ~.

¹lurch [lə:tʃ] **n.** (only) *leave sb. in the ~*, leave him when he is in difficulties and needing help.

²lurch [lə:tʃ] **n.** sudden change of weight to one side; sudden roll. **v.i.** move along with a ~ or ~es.

lure [luə*] **n.** sth. that attracts; the attraction or interest that sth. has: *the ~ of the sea for adventurous boys.* **v.t.** attract, tempt (to do sth., go somewhere): ~*d away from one's work.*

lu·rid ['luərid] **adj.** **1.** highly coloured, esp. suggesting flame and smoke: *a ~ sunset.* **2.** sensational; violent and shocking: *a ~ description*; ~ *details of a train smash.* ~**·ly adv.**

lurk [lə:k] **v.i.** be, keep, out of view, lying in wait or ready to attack.

lus·cious ['lʌʃəs] **adj.** rich and sweet in taste or smell; (of writing, music, art) too rich in ornament.

lush [lʌʃ] **adj.** (of grass, etc.) luxuriant.

lust [lʌst] **n.** intense desire: *a ~ for power* (*gold*); *the ~s of the flesh*, bodily desires. **v.i.** ~ *after* (*for*), have ~ for. ~**·ful adj.** full of ~.

lus·tre ['lʌstə*] *n.* quality of being bright, esp. of a polished or smooth surface: *the ~ of pearls*; (fig.) glory. **lus·trous** ['lʌstrəs] *adj.*

lust·y ['lʌsti] *adj.* (-ier, -iest). healthy and strong.

lute [l(j)u:t] *n.* stringed musical instrument dating from the 14th century.

lux·u·ri·ant [lʌg'zjuəriənt] *adj.* strong in growth; abundant: *~ vegetation.* **lux·u·ri·ance** *n.* ~ growth. **lux·u·ri·ate** [lʌg'zjuərieit] *v.i.* take great delight (*in* sth).

lux·u·ry ['lʌkʃəri] *n.* **1.** state of life in which one has and uses things that please the senses (good food, clothes, comfort, beautiful surroundings): *to live in ~.* **2.** sth. pleasing to have but not essential. **lux·u·ri·ous** [lʌk'sjuəriəs] *adj.* loving ~; having ~: *luxurious hotels (food).*

lying, see *lie.*

lynch [lintʃ] *v.t.* put to death without a lawful trial (sb. believed guilty of crime).

lynx [liŋks] *n.* short-tailed wild animal of the cat family, noted for its keen sight: *~-eyed.*

lyre ['laiə*] *n.* kind of harp with strings vertically fixed in a U-shaped frame, used by the ancient Greeks.

lyr·ic ['lirik] *adj.* of, composed for, singing. *n.* ~ poem; (pl.) ~ verses. **lyr·i·cal** *adj.* **1.** = lyric. **2.** full of emotion; enthusiastic.

M

ma [mɑ:] *n.* short for *mamma.*

ma'am [mɑ:m, məm] *n.* short for *madam.*

ma·ca·bre [mə'kɑ:br] *adj.* gruesome; grim; suggesting death.

ma·cad·am [mə'kædəm] *n.* ~ *road,* one with a surface of crushed rock or stone.

mac·a·ro·ni [,mækə'rouni] *n.* flour paste formed into tubes, cooked for food.

mace [meis] *n.* rod or staff carried as a sign of office or authority.

A mace

mach·i·na·tion [,mæki'neiʃən] *n.* evil plot(ting) or scheme.

ma·chine [mə'ʃi:n] *n.* **1.** apparatus or appliance with parts working together to apply power, often steam or electric power (*printing-~*), but sometimes human power (*bicycle, sewing-~*). **2.** persons organized to control a political group. ~-**gun** *n.* one firing continuously while the trigger is pressed. **ma·chin·er·y** [mə'ʃi:nəri] *n.* **1.** (parts or works of) ~s. **2.** methods, organization (e.g. of government). **ma·chin·ist** *n.* ~ (e.g. a sewing-~) worker.

mack·er·el ['mækrəl] *n.* small striped sea-fish much used as food.

mack·in·tosh ['mækintɔʃ] *n.* (colloq. abbr. *mac, mack*). rainproof coat made of cloth treated with rubber.

mad [mæd] *adj.* (-dd-). **1.** having, resulting from, a diseased mind. **2.** much distracted: *mad with pain*; *mad (angry) at missing the train.* **mad·den** *v.t.* make mad, esp. make angry. **'mad·cap** *n.* person acting recklessly or on impulse. **mad·ly** *adv.* **mad·ness** *n.*

mad·am ['mædəm] *n.* respectful form of address to a woman. (Cf. *sir.*) **Ma·dame** [mæ'dɑ:m] *n.* Mrs (used before names of married women not British).

made, see *make.*

Ma·dem·oi·selle [,mædəm(w)ə'zel] (French) *n.* title (cf. *Miss*) used before the name of an unmarried woman.

Ma·don·na [mə'dɔnə] *n.* (picture or statue of) Mary, Mother of Jesus Christ.

mad·ri·gal ['mædrigəl] *n.* short love song or poem; (esp.) song, usu. of five or six parts, for voice only.

mael·strom ['meilstroum] *n.* violent whirlpool or, (fig.) violent or destructive force, whirl of events : *the ~ of war.*

mag·a·zine [,mægə'zi:n] *n.* 1. store for arms, ammunition, explosives, etc. 2. chamber, e.g. for holding cartridges fed into the breech of a rifle or gun. 3. paper-covered (usu. weekly or monthly) periodical, with stories, articles, etc., by various writers.

ma·gen·ta [mə'dʒentə] *adj. & n.* bright crimson (substance used as a dye).

mag·got ['mægət] *n.* larva; grub, esp. as found in bad meat.

mag·ic ['mædʒik] *n.* 1. art of controlling events by the pretended use of supernatural forces. 2. the identification of a symbol with the thing it stands for (as when the wearing of a lion's skin is thought to give the wearer a lion's courage). 3. art of obtaining mysterious results by stage tricks. 4. mysterious quality. *adj.* (also ~al) done by, or as by, ~; possessing ~; used in ~. ~ *lantern,* (old name for) slide projector.

ma·gi·cian [mə'dʒiʃən] *n.* person skilled in ~ (1), (3).

mag·is·te·ri·al [,mædʒis'tiəriəl] *adj.* of a magistrate; having, showing, authority : *a ~ manner.*

mag·is·trate ['mædʒistr(e)it] *n.* civil officer acting as judge in the lowest courts; Justice of the Peace.

mag·nan·i·mous [mæg'næniməs] *adj.* having, showing, generosity. **mag·na·nim·i·ty** [,mægnə'nimiti] *n.*

mag·nate ['mægneit] *n.* wealthy, leading, man of business or industry.

mag·ne·sium [mæg'ni:zjəm] *n.* silver-white metal which burns brightly. **mag·ne·sia** [mæg'ni:ʃə] *n.* white tasteless powder, carbonate of ~, used in medicine.

mag·net ['mægnit] *n.* piece of iron able to attract iron. ~**ic** [mæg'netik] *adj.* of, like, produced by, a ~ : *a ~ic needle;* exercising attraction : *a ~ic smile.*

~**·ism** ['mægnitizəm] *n.* (science of) magnetic properties and phenomena. ~**ize** ['mægnitaiz] *v.t.* give properties of a ~ to; attract like a ~; mesmerize.

mag·ne·to [mæg'ni:tou] *n.* electrical apparatus for producing sparks in a petrol engine.

mag·ni·fi·cent [mæg'nifisənt] *adj.* splendid; remarkable; important-looking. **mag·ni·fi·cence** *n.*

mag·ni·fy ['mægnifai] *v.t.* 1. make (sth.) appear larger or more important. 2. give praise to (God).

mag·nil·o·quent [mæg'niloukwənt] *adj.* (of words, speech, etc.) pompous; (of a person) using pompous words.

mag·ni·tude ['mægnitju:d] *n.* size; (degree of) importance.

mag·pie ['mægpai] *n.* noisy black-and-white bird noted for thieving.

ma·hog·a·ny [mə'hɔgəni] *n.* (tropical tree with) red-brown wood much used for furniture.

ma·hout [mɑ:'haut] *n.* elephant-driver.

maid [meid] *n.* 1. (liter.) girl. 2. (old use) unmarried woman : *old ~,* elderly woman now unlikely to marry; ~ *of honour,* unmarried woman attending a queen or princess. 3. woman servant.

maid·en ['meidn] *n.* (liter.) girl; young unmarried woman. *adj.* (attrib. only) ~ *name,* woman's family name before marriage. ~ *speech,* sb.'s first speech made in public or in Parliament. ~ *voyage,* ship's first voyage.

¹**mail** [meil] *n.* body armour of metal rings or plates. **mailed** *adj. the ~ed fist,* armed force.

²**mail** [meil] *n.* 1. letters, parcels, etc., sent or delivered by post; the letters, etc., sent, collected, or delivered at one time. 2. government system of carrying and delivering letters, etc.: *by air~;* ~ *orders,* orders for goods to be delivered by post; ~*-coach,* horse-drawn coach in olden times carrying ~. *v.t.* send (a letter, etc.) by post.

maim [meim] *v.t.* wound so that some part of the body is useless.

main [mein] *adj.* chief; most important: *have an eye to the ~ chance*, look after one's own interests. *n.* **1.** *the ~s*, the principal pipes bringing water or gas, the principal wires transmitting electric current, from the source of supply (contrasted with pipes from a cistern in a building, etc.): *a ~s set*, a radio set to be connected to the ~s, not a battery set. **2.** *with might and ~*, with all one's physical strength. **3.** *in the ~*, for the most part. **4.** (poet.) the sea. **'~·land** *n.* country or continent without its islands. **~·ly** *adv.* chiefly; for the most part. **'~·spring** *n.* **1.** chief spring in a watch or clock. **2.** driving force or motive. **'~·stay** *n.* (fig.) chief support.

main·tain [mein'tein] *v.t.* **1.** keep in working order; keep up (e.g. friendship). **2.** support. **3.** *~ an opinion, ~ that . . .*, claim as true. **main·te·nance** ['meintənəns] *n.* (esp.) what is needed to support life.

maize [meiz] *n.* sort of grain plant, also called *Indian corn*.

A maize-cob

maj·es·ty ['mædʒisti] *n.* kingly or queenly appearance, conduct, speech, causing respect; stateliness; royal power. *His (Her, Your) M~*, form used when speaking of (to) a king or queen. **ma·jes·tic** [mə'dʒestik] *adj.* having, showing, ~.

ma·jor ['meidʒə*] *adj.* **1.** greater or more important of two (parts, etc.); elder of two brothers: *Smith M~*. **2.** *~ scale*, (music) that having two full tones between the keynote and the third note. *n.* army officer between a captain and a colonel. **'~·'do·mo** *n.* chief steward in a

great household. **'~·'gen·er·al** *n.* army officer next above a brigadier and under a lieutenant-general. **~·'i·ty** [mə'dʒɔriti] *n.* **1.** the greater number or part (of); the number by which votes for one side exceed those for the other side: *elected by a ~ity of 503*. **2.** legal age of reaching manhood or womanhood: *to reach one's ~ity*.

make [meik] *v.t. & i.* (p.t. & p.p. *made* [meid]). **1.** create, bring into existence, construct; produce; prepare: *~ cloth (machines, clothes)*; *~ a hole in sth.*; *~ a noise*; *made of wood*; *~ money (a profit, one's fortune)*; *~ (i.e. prepare) tea (the beds)*; *~ fun (game, sport) of (sb.)*, ridicule, laugh at; *~ light of (sth.)*, treat as not serious or not difficult; *~ the most of sth.*, use to the greatest advantage. **2.** compel, force: *to ~ sb. do sth.*, *to be made to do sth.*; persuade: *to ~ sb. believe sth.* **3.** cause to be, become, do, sth.; cause to take place: *~ sb. happy*; *~ sth. stronger*; *~ a man President*; *~ the fire burn up.* **4.** bring about the prosperity of: *The cotton trade made Manchester.* **5.** reach; accomplish: (of a ship) *to ~ port*; *making only nine knots*; *to make a journey in three hours.* **6.** reckon, consider to be: *What do you ~ the time (the total)?* **7.** (with adv. and prep. and in phrases): *~ for*, go towards; rush violently at. *~ off*, go or run away (esp. after doing sth. wrong). *~ off (away) with sth.*, steal it, take it without permission. *~ out*, write out (e.g. a cheque, a bill); succeed in seeing, reading, understanding; give the idea (that). *~ sth. over (to sb.)*, transfer the possession of sth. (esp. by a formal agreement). *~ up*, invent (a story); supply (what is needed for completion); prepare (medicine, etc.); put together (things into parcels, bundles, etc.); settle (a dispute); become friendly again (after a quarrel); prepare (an actor for the stage), put cosmetics on (the face). ~ *up one's mind* (*to*), determine (to). ~ *believe*, pretend. *n.* way a thing is made; structure: *cars of all* ~s; *of our own* ~, made by us. '~-be‚lieve *n.* pretending; a pretence. '~·shift *n.* sth. used until sth. better can be obtained. '~-up *n.* 1. arrangement, composition. 2. face-powder, rouge, etc. '~·weight *n.* small quantity added to ~ the weight right. 'mak·ing *n.* *be the making of*, cause the well-being of; *have the makings of*, have the necessary qualities for becoming.

mal- [mæl-] *prefix.* 1. bad(ly): *maltreat*, *malformation*, *maladjustment*. 2. not: *malcontent*.

mal·a·dy ['mælədi] *n.* disease; illness.

ma·lar·i·a [mə'lɛəriə] *n.* fever spread by a certain kind of mosquito. ma·lar·i·al *adj.* *malarial regions*.

mal·con·tent ['mælkəntent] *n.* person discontented and inclined to rebel.

male [meil] *adj.* of the sex that does not give birth to offspring. (Cf. *female*.) *n.* ~ person, animal.

mal·e·dic·tion [‚mæli'dikʃən] *n.* curse.

mal·e·fac·tor ['mælifæktə*] *n.* wrongdoer; criminal.

mal·ev·o·lent [mə'levələnt] *adj.* wishing evil to others; spiteful. ma·lev·o·lence *n.*

mal·for·ma·tion ['mælfɔ:'meiʃən] *n.* the state of being badly formed or shaped; badly formed part. mal·'formed *adj.* badly formed.

mal·ice ['mælis] *n.* active ill will; desire to harm others: *to bear sb. no* ~. ma·li·cious [mə'liʃəs] *adj.* feeling, showing, ~.

ma·lign [mə'lain] *v.t.* speak ill of (sb.); tell lies about. *adj.* (of things) injurious: *a* ~ *influence*. ma·lig·nant [mə'lignənt] *adj.* 1. (of persons, their actions) filled with, showing, desire to hurt. 2. (of diseases) harmful to life: ~*ant cancer*. ma·lig·nan·cy [mə'lignənsi] *n.* ma·lig·ni·ty [mə'ligniti] *n.*

ma·lin·ger [mə'liŋgə*] *v.i.* pretend to be ill (esp. in order to escape one's duty).

mal·le·a·ble ['mæliəbl] *adj.* 1. (of metals) that can be hammered or pressed into new shapes. 2. (fig., e.g. of character) easily trained or adapted.

mal·let ['mælit] *n.* wooden-headed hammer.

mal·nu·tri·tion ['mælnju:'triʃən] *n.* condition caused by not getting enough food or the right sort of food.

mal·o·do·rous [mæ'loudərəs] *adj.* ill-smelling.

mal·prac·tice [mæl'præktis] *n.* (legal) wrongdoing; neglect of duty.

malt [mɔ:lt] *n.* grain (usu. barley) prepared for use in beer-making. *v.t.* make (grain) into ~; prepare with ~.

mal·treat [mæl'tri:t] *v.t.* treat roughly or cruelly. ~·ment *n.*

mam·ma [mə'ma:] *n.* (child's word for) mother.

mam·mal ['mæml] *n.* any of the class of animals that feed their young with milk from the breast.

mam·mon ['mæmən] *n.* wealth (when looked upon as an evil influence).

mam·moth ['mæməθ] *n.* large kind of elephant now extinct; (attrib.) immense: *a* ~ *project*.

man [mæn] *n.* (pl. *men*). 1. adult male human being (i.e. not a woman, boy, or girl); human being, without regard to sex or age: *All men must die. the man in the street*, person looked upon as representing the interests and opinions of ordinary people. *man of the world*, one with wide experience of business and society. *man of letters*, writer. 2. the human race; all mankind. 3. male person under the authority of another: *masters and men* (= employees); *officers and men. v.t.* supply (ships, a fort, defences, etc.) with the men needed. 'man·ful *adj.* fearless; determined. 'man·ful·ly *adv.* 'man·‚han·dle *v.t.* move by physical strength;

(colloq.) handle roughly. **'man·hole** *n.* opening through which a man may enter (a boiler, tank, underground sewer, etc.). **'man·hood** *n.* **1.** the state of being a man: *to reach manhood.* **2.** manly qualities. **man·'kind** *n.* the human race; all men. **'man·like** *adj.* having the qualities (good or bad) of a man. **'man·ly** *adj.* (*-ier*, *-iest*). having the qualities expected of a man. **'man·nish** *adj.* (of a woman) manlike; more suitable for a man than for a woman. **man-o'-'war** *n.* (old use) warship. **man·slaugh·ter** ['mæn-slɔːtə*] *n.* act of killing a person unlawfully but not wilfully.

man·a·cle ['mænəkl] *n.* (usu. pl.) fetter or chain for the hands or feet. *v.t.* put ∼s on.

man·age ['mænidʒ] *v.t. & i.* **1.** control: *to ∼ a business.* **2.** succeed; be able (to do sth.): *I can't ∼ without help. He ∼d to keep* (succeeded in keeping) *his temper.* **'∼·a·ble** *adj.* that can be ∼d or controlled. **'∼·ment** *n.* **1.** managing or being ∼d: *failure caused by bad ∼ment.* **2.** *the ∼ment*, persons who ∼ a business. **man·a·ger** *n.* person who controls a business, hotel, etc. **man·a·ger·ess** ['mæni-dʒəres] *n.* **man·a·ge·ri·al** [,mænə'dʒiəriəl] *adj.* of managers.

man·da·rin ['mændərin] *n.* (old use) name for a high Chinese government official; form of Chinese used by educated classes and for official purposes.

man·date ['mændeit] *n.* **1.** order from a superior; command given with authority. **2.** control over certain territories authorized by the League of Nations after the First World War. **3.** authority given to representative(s) by voters, members of a trade union, etc. **man·dat·ed** [mæn'deitid] *adj.* under a ∼ (2).

man·do·lin ['mændəlin] *n.* musical instrument with 6 or 8 metal strings stretched in pairs on a rounded body.

mane [mein] *n.* long hair on the neck of some animals (esp. horse, lion).

man·ga·nese ['mæŋgəniːz] *n.* hard, brittle, light-grey metal.

mange [meindʒ] *n.* skin disease, esp. of dogs and cats. **man·gy** *adj.* (*-ier*, *-iest*). suffering from ∼; dirty, neglected.

man·ger ['meindʒə*] *n.* long open box or trough for horses or cattle to feed from.

¹**man·gle** ['mæŋgl] *v.t. & n.* (put through a) machine (= wringer) with rollers for pressing out water from and smoothing laundry, etc.

²**man·gle** ['mæŋgl] *v.t.* cut up, tear, damage badly.

man·go ['mæŋgou] *n.* (pl. *-oes*). tropical tree having pear-shaped fruit with yellow flesh.

man·grove ['mæŋgrouv] *n.* tropical tree growing in salt-water swamps and sending down new roots from its branches.

ma·nia ['meinjə] *n.* **1.** violent madness. **2.** great enthusiasm (*for* sth.). **ma·ni·ac** ['meiniæk] *n.* raving madman. **ma·ni·a·cal** [mə'naiəkl] *adj.*

man·i·cure ['mænikjuə*] *n.* care of the hands and nails. *v.t.* give ∼ treatment to.

man·i·fest ['mænifest] *adj.* clear and obvious. *v.t.* **1.** show clearly; give signs of. **2.** (of a thing) reveal (*itself*); appear. *n.* list of a ship's cargo. **man·i·fes·ta·tion** [,mænifes'teifən] *n.* **man·i·fes·to** [,mæni'festou] *n.* (pl. *-os*). public declaration of principles, purposes, etc., by a ruler, group of persons, etc.

man·i·fold ['mænifould] *adj.* having or providing for many uses, copies, etc.; many and various.

ma·nil·a [mə'nilə] *n.* plant fibre used for making rope, mats, etc.

ma·nip·u·late [mə'nipjuleit] *v.t.* operate, handle, use with skill (instruments, etc.); manage or control (sb. or sth.) cleverly, esp. by using one's influence. **ma·nip·u·la·tion** [mə,nipju'lei-fən] *n.*

man·kind, man·ly, see *man.*

man·na ['mænə] *n.* (in the Bible)

L

food provided by God for the Israelites.

man·ne·quin ['mænikin] *n.* person (now usu. called a *model*) employed to display new clothes for sale by wearing them.

man·ner ['mænə*] *n.* **1.** way a thing is done or happens. **2.** person's way of behaving towards others. **3.** (pl.) habits and customs. **4.** (pl.) social behaviour: *He has no ~s* (i.e. does not behave well). **5.** sort: *all ~ of*, every kind of; *by no ~ of means*, in no circumstances. **ill- (well-) man·nered** *adj.* having bad (good) ~s. '**~·ism** *n.* peculiarity of behaviour, esp. one that is habitual. '**~·ly** *adj.* well-bred; having good ~s.

ma·nœu·vre [mə'nu:və*] *n.* planned movement (of military forces); movement or plan, made to deceive or to escape from sb., to win or do sth. *v.i. & v.t.* (cause to) perform ~s; force (sb. or sth.) (*into* doing sth., *into* or *out of* a position) by clever handling.

man·or ['mænə*] *n.* unit of land under the feudal system; (modern use) piece of land over which the lord (or lady) of the ~ has or had certain rights. **ma·no·ri·al** [mə'nɔ:riəl] *adj.* of a ~.

manse [mæns] *n.* Presbyterian church minister's house.

man·sion ['mænʃən] *n.* **1.** grand house. **2.** (pl., in proper names) blocks of flats.

man·tel·piece ['mæntlpi:s] *n.* shelf above a fireplace.

man·tis ['mæntis] *n.* long-legged insect as shown here.

A mantis

man·tle ['mæntl] *n.* **1.** loose, sleeveless cloak; (fig.) overall cover: *a ~ of snow*. **2.** lace-like

cover fixed over the flame of a paraffin or gas lamp to make the light brilliant.

man·u·al ['mænjuəl] *adj.* of, done with, the hands: ~ *work*; ~ *labourers*. *n.* **1.** textbook, handbook. **2.** keyboard of an organ. ~**·ly** *adv.*

man·u·fac·ture [,mænju'fæk-tʃə*] *v.t.* make, produce (goods, etc.), esp. on a large scale by machinery. *n.* the making of goods; (pl.) ~d goods. **man·u·fac·tur·er** *n.*

ma·nure [mə'njuə*] *n.* animal waste or other material, natural or artificial, used for making soil fertile; fertilizer. *v.t.* put ~ on (land).

man·u·script ['mænjuskript] *n.* book, etc., as first written out by hand: *poems still in* ~.

man·y ['meni] *adj. & n.* (contrasted with *few*; see *more*, *most*). **1.** a large number, a lot of: *Were there ~ people at the meeting? There were a great ~* (a very large number). **2.** ~ *a* (with sing. n.): *M~ a man* (= ~ men) *would prefer to die than betray his country*. *be one too ~ for*, be cleverer than; outwit. '**~-,sid·ed** *adj.* (fig.) having ~ abilities, capabilities, aspects, etc.

map [mæp] *n.* see the picture. *v.t.* **1.** make a map of. **2.** *map out*, plan, arrange.

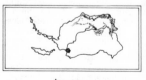

A map

ma·ple ['meipl] *n.* (wood of) sorts of tree. '**~-,sug·ar** *n.* from one kind of ~.

mar [ma:*] *v.t.* (*-rr-*). injure; spoil.

mar·a·thon (race) ['mærəθən 'reis] *n.* long-distance race on foot.

ma·raud·er [mə'rɔ:də*] *n.* person who makes raids in search of plunder.

mar·ble ['mɑ:bl] *n.* **1.** sorts of hard limestone used, when cut and polished, for building and sculpture. **2.** (pl.) works of art in ~. **3.** small ball of stone or glass used in children's games: *playing* ~s.

March [mɑ:tʃ] *n.* the third month of the year.

march [mɑ:tʃ] *v.t. & i.* walk as soldiers do, with regular and measured steps; cause to do this: *The soldiers* ~*ed (the prisoners) away. n.* **1.** act of ~ing: *a* ~ *of 10 miles;* music for ~ing to: *a dead* ~, one in slow time for a funeral. **2.** (fig.) progress; onward movement: *the* ~ *of events (time).*

mar·chion·ess ['mɑ:ʃənis] *n.* wife or widow of a marquis.

mare [meə*] *n.* female horse. ~*'s nest,* discovery that turns out to be false or worthless.

mar·gar·ine [ˌmɑ:dʒə'ri:n, ˌmɑ:-gə-] *n.* butter substitute made from animal or vegetable fat.

mar·gin ['mɑ:dʒin] *n.* **1.** blank space round the printed or written matter on a page. **2.** edge or border (e.g. of a lake). **3.** amount (of time, money, etc.) above what is estimated as necessary. **mar·gi·nal** *adj.* of or in a ~(1): ~*al notes.*

mar·guer·ite [ˌmɑ:gə'ri:t] *n.* kinds of large daisy.

ma·rine [mə'ri:n] *adj.* **1.** of, by, found in, produced by, the sea: ~ *products.* **2.** of ships; ~ *insurance. n.* **1.** *merchant* ~, all the merchant ships of a country. **2.** soldier serving on a warship and trained for fighting at sea or on land. **mar·i·ner** ['mærinə*] *n.* (liter. or official) sailor.

mar·i·o·nette [ˌmæriə'net] *n.* doll or puppet moved by strings on a small stage.

mar·i·tal ['mæritl] *adj.* of a husband; of or between husband and wife.

mar·i·time ['mæritaim] *adj.* of the sea: ~ *law;* near the sea: ~ *provinces.*

mark [mɑ:k] *n.* **1.** line, scratch, cut, stain, etc., that spoils the appearance of sth. **2.** noticeable spot on the body: *a white* ~ *on a horse's head; a birth-*~. **3.** natural sign or indication (of quality, character, intelligence). **4.** figure, design, line, etc., made as a sign or indication: *hall*~; *trade*~s. **5.** unit for measuring quality or result (e.g. of school work): *full* ~*s for science;* 95 ~*s out of 100 for English.* **6.** sth. aimed at: *beside (wide of) the* ~, not to the point, incorrect. **7.** normal level: *up to (below) the* ~, as good as (not so good as) the normal. **8.** *make one's* ~, become famous. *v.t.* **1.** put or be a ~(4) on or against: *to* ~ *prices on goods; to* ~ *a pupil absent.* **2.** *give* ~s(5): *to* ~ *examination papers.* **3.** pay attention to: ~ *how it is done.* **4.** ~ *time,* raise the feet as when marching but without moving forward; (fig.) wait and do nothing. **5.** ~ *sth. off,* separate by a limit. ~ *sth. out,* make lines to show the limits of (e.g. a tennis-court). ~ *sb. out for* (e.g. promotion), decide in advance (that he will be promoted later). **marked** [mɑ:kt] *adj.* clear; readily seen: *a* ~*ed difference; a* ~*ed man,* one who is watched with suspicion and who is to be attacked or punished. ~*ed·ly* ['mɑ:kidli] *adv.* ~*er n.* person or tool that ~s. ~*ing n.* (esp.) different colours of feathers, fur, etc. **marks·man** ['mɑ:ksmən] *n.* person skilled in shooting. **marks·man·ship** *n.*

mar·ket ['mɑ:kit] *n.* **1.** public place (open space or building) where people meet to buy and sell goods: *going to (the)* ~ *to sell eggs;* ~*-day,* one fixed by law for holding a ~; ~*-town,* (esp.) one where there is a cattle-~. **2.** trade in a certain class of goods: *the coffee* ~; state of trade as shown by prices, etc.: *a lively* ~. *The* ~ *rose,* i.e. prices advanced. **3.** buying and selling: *come into, be on, the* ~, be offered for sale. **4.** area, country, in which goods may be sold:

finding new ~s *for manufactures. v.i. & t.* take or send to ~ ; buy or sell in a ~ : *to ~ing* ; *to ~ one's goods.* ~**·a·ble** *adj.* that can be sold. **!~·₁gar·den** *n.* one where vegetables, etc., are grown for a ~.

mar·ma·lade ['mɑ:mǝleid] *n.* orange jam.

¹ma·roon [mǝ'ru:n] *adj. & n.* brownish-crimson (colour).

²ma·roon [mǝ'ru:n] *n.* firework, esp. the kind used as a warning signal.

³ma·roon [mǝ'ru:n] *v.t.* put (sb.) on a desert island, uninhabited coast, etc., and leave him there.

mar·quee [mɑ:'ki:] *n.* large tent.

mar·quis, mar·quess ['mɑ:-kwis] *n.* nobleman next in rank below a duke. (See *marchioness.*)

mar·riage, see *marry.*

mar·row ['mærou] *n.* 1. soft fatty substance that fills the hollow parts of bones. 2. (often *vegetable ~*) vegetable of the gourd family, used as food.

mar·ry ['mæri] *v.t. & i.* take a woman (or a man) to be one's wife (or husband); join as husband and wife; give (e.g. one's daughter) in marriage. **mar·riage** ['mæridʒ] *n.* union of a man and woman as husband and wife; state of being married; wedding ceremony. **mar·riage·a·ble** *adj.* (of an age) fit for marriage.

marsh [mɑ:ʃ] *n.* area of low-lying wet land. ~**·y** *adj.*

mar·shal ['mɑ:ʃl] *n.* 1. officer of highest rank: *Field-M~* (Army); *Air-M~* (Air Force). 2. official responsible for important public events. *v.t.* (*-ll-*). 1. arrange (military forces, railway waggons, facts, etc.) in the right order. 2. guide or lead (sb.) with ceremony.

mar·su·pi·al [mɑ:'sju:piǝl] *n. & adj.* (one) of the class of animals (e.g. the kangaroo) having a pouch in which to carry their young which are born before developing completely.

mar·tial ['mɑ:ʃl] *adj.* of, associated with, warfare: ~ *music.*

~ *law,* military government replacing the operation of ordinary law for a time.

mar·tin ['mɑ:tin] *n.* kind of swallow.

mar·ti·net [ˌmɑ:ti'net] *n.* person who expects and enforces very strict discipline.

mar·tyr ['mɑ:tǝ*] *n.* 1. person put to death or caused to suffer for his religious beliefs or for the sake of a great cause. 2. *be a ~ to* (e.g. rheumatism), suffer great pain because of. *v.t.* put to death, cause to suffer, as a ~. ~**·dom** *n.* ~'s suffering or death.

mar·vel ['mɑ:vl] *n.* 1. sth. causing great surprise, pleased astonishment: *the ~s of modern science.* 2. sb. or sth. showing a good quality in a surprising way. *She's a ~ of patience. v.i.* (*-ll-*). be much surprised : *to ~ at sth.*; *to ~ that (how, etc.).* ~**·lous** ['mɑ:vǝlǝs] *adj.* wonderful ; causing pleased surprise.

mas·cot ['mæskǝt] *n.* person, animal, or object considered likely to bring good fortune.

mas·cu·line ['mæskjulin] *adj.* of, like, the male sex ; of male gender.

mash [mæʃ] *n.* 1. grain, bran, etc., cooked in water for horses. 2. any substance softened and crushed. *v.t.* beat or crush into a ~ : ~*ed potatoes.*

mask [mɑ:sk] *n.* 1. covering for the face or part of the face. 2. (also *'gas-~*) covering for the head worn as a protection against gas (e.g. in mines). 3. false face worn by an actor. *v.t.* wear, cover with, a ~ ; keep (sth.) from view.

ma·son ['meisn] *n.* 1. stone-cutter; worker who builds with stone. 2. = freemason (see *free*). ~**·ic** [mǝ'sɔnik] *adj.* of free-masons. ~**·ry** *n.* stonework.

masque [mɑ:sk] *n.* drama in verse, usu. with music, dancing and fine dresses, common in the 16th and 17th centuries.

mas·quer·ade [ˌmæskǝ'reid] *n.* ²ball at which masks and other disguises are worn. *v.i.* appear, be, in disguise: *a prince who ~d as a shepherd.*

¹**mass** [mæs] *n.* **1.** lump, quantity of matter, without regular shape; large number, quantity or heap (of): *~es of dark clouds; the ~es*, the great body of ordinary working people; *a ~ meeting*, a large meeting (esp. of people wanting to express their views); *~ production*, manufacture of large numbers of identical articles. **2.** (science) quantity of matter in a body. *v.t. & i.* form or collect into a ~: *troops ~ing on the frontiers.*

²**Mass** [mæs] *n.* celebration (esp. Roman Catholic) of Holy Communion.

mas·sa·cre ['mæsəkə*] *n.* cruel killing of large numbers of (esp. defenceless) people. *v.t.* make a ~ of.

mas·sage ['mæsɑːʒ] *n.* rubbing and pressing of the body to lessen pain, stiffness, etc. *v.t.* apply ~ to. **mas·seur** [mæ-'sə:*], **mas·seuse** [mæ'sə:z] *n.* man, woman, trained in ~.

mas·sive ['mæsiv] *adj.* **1.** heavy and solid; heavy-looking. **2.** (fig.) substantial.

mast [mɑːst] *n.* upright support (wood or metal) for a ship's sails; tall staff (2) (for a flag); tall steel structure for aerials of a radio or television transmitter.

mas·ter ['mɑːstə*] *n.* **1.** man who has others working for or under him; male owner of a dog, horse, etc.; captain of a merchant ship; male head of a household; male teacher. **2.** M~ of Arts (Science, etc.), holder of this university degree. **3.** skilled workman self-employed: *a ~ builder.* **4.** *the old ~s*, great painters, esp. those of 1200–1700, and the pictures they painted. **5.** person who has control (of): *be ~ of one's fate; make oneself ~ of a subject*, learn it thoroughly. **6.** (with a boy's name) young Mr: *Master Tom; Master T. Smith.* *v.t.* become the ~ of; overcome: *~ one's temper*, control it. **~·ful**

adj. fond of controlling others. '**~-key** *n.* one that will open many different locks. **~·ly** *adj.* skilful; expert. '**~·piece** *n.* sth. made or done with great skill. **~·y** *n.* complete control or knowledge (of).

mas·ti·cate ['mæstikeit] *v.t.* soften, grind up, (food) with the teeth.

¹**mat** [mæt] *n.* piece of material used for a floor covering or (*doormat*) to wipe dirty shoes on; piece of material placed on a table, etc., to prevent damage (e.g. from hot dishes). **mat·ted** ['mætid] *adj.* (of hair, etc.) tangled; knotted.

²**mat(t)** [mæt] *adj.* (of a surface) dull (1) not glossy or polished.

mat·a·dor ['mætədɔː*] *n.* man whose task is to kill the bull in the sport of bull-fighting.

¹**match** [mætʃ] *n.* see the picture. '**~·wood** *n.* small broken bits of wood.

A box of matches

²**match** [mætʃ] *n.* **1.** contest, game: *a football ~.* **2.** person able to meet another as his equal in strength, skill, etc.: *find (meet) one's ~.* **3.** marriage: *They decided to make a ~ of it*, to marry; '**~·mak·er** *n.* person fond of bringing about marriages. **4.** person or thing exactly like, corresponding to, or combining well with, another: *colours (materials) that are a good ~.* *v.t. & i.* **1.** put in competition (*with* or *against*). **2.** be equal to or corresponding (with) (in quality, colour, etc.): *curtains that ~ the carpet; a brown dress with a hat to ~.* **3.** be, obtain, a ~ (2) for: *a well-~ed pair* (e.g. boxers about equal in skill, or a husband and wife fitted to live together happily). **~·less** *adj.* unequalled.

mate [meit] *n.* **1.** fellow workman. **2.** ship's officer below the

captain: *first* (*second, etc.*) ~.
3. one of a pair of birds or animals living together: *the lioness and her* ~. *v.t. & i.* unite, cause to unite (to produce young): *the mating season. The Zoo camels have not* ~*d this season.*

ma·te·ri·al [mə'tiəriəl] *n.* that of which sth. is or can be made or with which sth. is done: *raw* ~*s*, not yet used in manufacture; *dress* ~, cloth; *writing* ~*s*, pen, paper, etc. *adj.* **1.** made of, connected with, matter or substance (contrasted with *spiritual*): *the* ~ *world.* **2.** of the body; of physical needs: ~ *comforts and pleasures; a* ~ *point of view.* **3.** important; essential. ~**ism** *n.* **1.** theory, belief, that only physical things exist. **2.** interest in, attention to, ~ things (money, bodily comfort, and pleasures) only. ~**ist** *n.* believer in ~ism; person who ignores religion, art, music, etc. ~**ize** *v.t. & i.* (cause to) take a ~ form; (cause to) become fact.

ma·ter·nal [mə'tə:nl] *adj.* of or like a mother: ~ *aunt*, aunt on the mother's side of the family. ~**ly** *adv.* **ma·ter·ni·ty** [mə'tə:niti] *n.* motherhood.

math·e·mat·ics [,mæθə'mætiks] *n.* (sing. vb.) science of space and number. **math·e·mat·i·cal** *adj.* of ~. **math·e·ma·ti·cian** [,mæθəmə'tiʃən] *n.* expert in ~.

mat·i·née ['mætinei] *n.* afternoon performance at a theatre.

mat·ins ['mætinz] *n. pl.* morning prayer (Church of England); prayers at daybreak (Church of Rome).

mat·ri·arch ['meitriɑ:k] *n.* woman head of a family or tribe.

mat·ri·cide ['meitrisaid] *n.* killing by sb. of his own mother; person guilty of this.

ma·tric·u·late [mə'trikjuleit] *v.t. & i.* (allow to) enter a university as a student, usu. after passing an examination. **ma·tric·u·la·tion** [mə,trikju-'leiʃən] *n.* matriculating; special examination for this.

mat·ri·mo·ny ['mætriməni] *n.* state of being married. **mat·ri·mo·nial** [,mætri'mounjəl] *adj.*

ma·trix ['meitriks] *n.* (pl. *matrices* ['meitrisi:z] or ~*es*) mould into which hot metal, etc., is poured to be shaped; rock-mass in which gems, metals, etc., are found embedded.

ma·tron ['meitrən] *n.* **1.** woman housekeeper in a school or other institution. **2.** woman controlling nursing staff in a hospital. **3.** married woman or widow. ~**ly** *adj.* of or like a ~; dignified.

matt, see ²*mat.*

mat·ter ['mætə*] *n.* **1.** physical substance (in contrast with *mind* and *spirit*). **2.** *printed* ~, anything printed. **3.** subject; sth. to which thought or attention is given: *money* ~*s; a* ~ *I know little about; as a* ~ *of fact,* in reality, although you might not think so; *a* ~ *of course,* sth. naturally to be expected; *for that* ~, *for the* ~ *of that,* so far as that is concerned. **4.** what is said in (contrasted with *manner* of) a book, speech, etc. **5.** pus. **6.** *be the* ~ (*with*), be wrong (with); *no* ~ *what,* whatever; *no* ~ *when* (*where, who, how*), it is unimportant when, etc. *v.i.* be important (*to* sb.): *It doesn't* ~ *to me how you do it.* '~**-of·**'**fact** *adj.* keeping to facts; unimaginative; ordinary.

mat·ting ['mætiŋ] *n.* woven material for floor coverings, packing goods, etc.

mat·tock ['mætək] *n.* tool as shown here.

A mattock

mat·tress ['mætris] *n.* long, thick, flat, oblong pad of wool, hair, feathers, straw, etc., sometimes containing springs, on which to sleep. *spring* ~, framework of springs and wires as part of a bed or divan. See the picture on page 319.

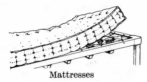

Mattresses

ma·ture [məˈtjuə*] *v.t. & i.* come or bring to full development or to a state ready for use. *adj.* ripe; fully grown or developed; carefully thought out; perfected; (of bills) due for payment. **ma·tur·i·ty** [məˈtjuəriti] *n.*

maud·lin [ˈmɔːdlin] *adj.* sentimental in a silly or tearful way.

maul [mɔːl] *v.t.* injure by rough or brutal handling.

mau·so·le·um [ˌmɔːsəˈliəm] *n.* magnificent tomb.

mauve [mouv] *adj. & n.* pale purple.

maw [mɔː] *n.* animal's stomach.

maw·kish [ˈmɔːkiʃ] *adj.* foolishly sentimental; sweet and sickly.

max·im [ˈmæksim] *n.* widely accepted general truth or rule of conduct expressed in few words.

max·i·mum [ˈmæksiməm] *n.* greatest possible or recorded degree, quantity, etc.; opposite of *minimum*.

May [mei] *n.* the fifth month of the year; (also *may-blossom*) hawthorn. **'May-day** *n.* 1st of May as a country festival or Labour Day. **'may·pole** *n.* flower-decorated pole danced round on May-day.

may [mei] *v.* (p.t. *might* [mait]; neg. *may not*, shortened to *mayn't* [meint], p.t. *might not*, *mightn't* [ˈmaitnt]). **1.** used to indicate possibility or probability: *That may or may not be true. That might be true one day* (i.e. in the future). *That might have been true then* (i.e. at some time in the past), *but it is not true now.* **2.** used to indicate (a request for) permission: *May I come in? Yes, you may.* **3.** used to express a wish: *May*

you live to be a hundred! **4.** used in clauses after *wish, fear,* etc., or to express purpose: *I fear you may blame me for this. Write to him today, so that he may know when to expect you.* **'may·be** *adv.* perhaps; possibly: *as soon as maybe,* as soon as possible.

may·on·naise [ˌmeiəˈneiz] *n.* thick dressing of eggs, oil, and vinegar, used on cold food, esp. salads.

mayor [mɛə*] *n.* head of a town corporation. **~·al·ty** [ˈmɛərəlti] *n.* ~'s (period of) office. **~·ess** [ˈmɛəris] *n.* ~'s wife or female relative helping in social duties.

maze [meiz] *n.* network of paths, lines, etc.; number of confusing facts, etc.: *in a ~,* bewildered; puzzled.

me [miː] *pron.* object form of the pronoun *I*.

mead [miːd] *n.* (poet.) meadow.

mead·ow [ˈmedou] *n.* piece of grassland, esp. one used for hay.

mea·gre [ˈmiːgə*] *adj.* thin; not enough.

¹meal [miːl] *n.* occasion of eating (e.g. breakfast); food for a ~.

²meal [miːl] *n.* grain (e.g. wheat) coarsely ground: *oat~.* **~·y** *adj.* (*-ier, -iest*). powdery, like ~.

¹mean [miːn] *v.t. & i.* (p.t. & p.p. *meant* [ment]). **1.** convey to the mind (through the eyes, the ears, etc.) sth. that can be understood; intend to convey (a sense) or indicate (an object): *By running round after you he ~s to show sympathy. No, I don't ~ you, I am pointing to him.* **2.** design, have in mind: *I ~ to go to America one of these days. This medicine is not ~t for children.* **3.** have as a purpose or plan: *He ~s mischief,* has an evil plan in his mind; *~ business,* be ready to act, not merely to talk; *~ sb. no harm,* have no intention to harm him. **4.** be a sign of: *Does this incident ~ war?* **5.** ~ *much* (*a great deal, little,* etc.) *to,* be of much, little, importance to. **~·ing** *n.* **1.** that which is meant. **2.** purpose. *adj.* *a ~ing look,* one that shows a purpose; one full of

~ing. ~ing·less adj. ~ing·ly adv.

¹mean [mi:n] adj. (-er, -est). 1. poor in appearance: a ~ house in a ~ street. 2. selfish; ungenerous. 3. (of behaviour) unworthy; discreditable. 4. (of intelligence, etc.) low in quality. ~ly adv. ~ness n.

²mean [mi:n] n. & adj. 1. (condition, quality, number) equally distant from two opposites or extremes: the ~ annual temperature. '~·time adv. & n. (in) the time between. '~·while adv. & n. = ~time.

⁴mean [mi:n] n. 1. (usu. pl., often with indef. art.). method, process, way, by which a result may be obtained: by ~s of, through; with the help of; by all ~s, certainly, at all costs; by no ~s, not at all; by some ~s (or other), somehow (or other). 2. (pl.) money, property, resources: a man of ~s, a rich man; live within one's ~s, not spend more than one's income.

me·an·der [mi'ændə*] v.i. wander here and there; (of a stream) wind about.

meant, see ¹mean.

mea·sles ['mi:zlz] n. (sing.). infectious disease causing fever and red spots on the body.

mea·sly ['mi:zli] adj. (colloq.) of poor quality; of small value or amount.

mea·sure ['meʒə*] n. 1. size, quantity, degree, etc.: give full (short) ~, give the full (less than the full) amount; (clothes) made to ~, specially made for sb. after taking his ~ments. 2. unit, standard, or system used in stating size, quantity, or degree: An inch is a ~ of length. liquid (dry) ~. 3. sth. with which to test size, quantity, etc.: a tape-~; a pint ~. 4. extent: in some ~, to some extent or degree; in a great ~, largely; beyond ~, very great(ly). 5. (proposed) law. 6. proceeding; step: take ~s against wrongdoers, do sth. to stop or punish them. 7. verse-rhythm; time in music. v.t. & i. 1. find the size,

amount, etc., of (sth. or sb.). 2. ~ out, give a ~d quantity of, mark out. 3. be (a certain length, etc.). meas·ured adj. 1. (esp. of language) carefully considered. 2. in slow and regular rhythm. ~ment ['meʒə-mənt] n. (esp. pl.) detailed figures about length, breadth, height, etc.

meat [mi:t] n. flesh of animals used as food; (old use) food of any kind.

me·chan·ic [mi'kænik] n. skilled workman, esp. one who makes or works machines. me·chan·ics n. science of motion and force; science of machinery. me·chan·i·cal adj. of, connected with, produced by, machines: ~al transport. me·chan·i·cal·ly adv. mech·a·nism ['mekənizm] n. working parts of a machine; way in which sth. works. mech·a·nize ['mekənaiz] v.t. use machines in or for: mechanized forces (e.g. in the army, using motor transport). mech·a·ni·za·tion [,mek-ənai'zeiʃən] n.

med·al ['medl] n. flat piece of metal, usu. shaped like a coin, with words and a design stamped on it, given as an award or made to commemorate an event. me·dal·lion [mi'dæljən] n. large ~; large flat circular ornamental design (e.g. on a carpet). ~·list n. person rewarded with a ~ after a competition.

med·dle ['medl] v.i. busy oneself without being invited, interfere (with others' things, in sb. else's affairs). '~·some adj. in the habit of meddling.

me·dia, see medium.

me·di·ate ['mi:dieit] v.i. act as go-between or peacemaker: ~ between employers and workers. me·di·a·tion [,mi:di'eiʃən] n. me·di·a·tor n.

med·i·cal ['medikl] adj. of the art of medicine: ~ students; the ~ ward of a hospital (cf. surgical). ~·ly adv. me·dic·a·ment [me-'dikəmənt] n. substance used in ~ treatment, internally or externally. med·i·cat·ed ['medikeitid] *adj.* (of a liquid, cloth, etc.) containing a substance used ~ly: *medicated gauze.* **me·di·ci·nal** [me'disinl] *adj.* having ~ properties: *medicinal preparations.* **med·i·cine** ['medsin] *n.* **1.** the art and science of the prevention and cure of disease. **2.** substance (esp. one taken through the mouth) used in medicine. **'med·i·cine-man** *n.* witch-doctor.

med·i·e·val, -i·ae·val [ˌmedi-'i:vl] *adj.* of the Middle Ages (about A.D. 1100–1500).

me·di·o·cre ['mi:dioukə*] *adj.* not very good; second-rate. **me·di·oc·ri·ty** [ˌmi:di'ɔkriti] *n.* (esp.) ~ person.

med·i·tate ['mediteit] *v.t. & i.* **1.** think about; consider: ~ *revenge.* **2.** give oneself up to serious thought: ~ *upon one's past life.* **med·i·ta·tion** [ˌmedi-'teiʃən] *n.*

me·di·um ['mi:djəm] *n.* **1.** that by which or through which sth. is done: *Newspapers are a ~ for advertising.* **2.** middle quality or degree: *the happy ~,* not extreme. **3.** (pl. often *media*). substance within which sth. exists or through which sth. (e.g. sound) moves. **4.** person acting as a go-between (esp. in spiritualism, as between living people and the spirits of the dead). *adj.* coming half-way between; not extreme: *of ~ height;* ~ *wave* (in radio).

med·ley ['medli] *n.* mixture of different articles, colours, sounds, etc.

meed [mi:d] *n.* (poet.) deserved portion (of praise or blame).

meek [mi:k] *adj.* (*-er, -est*). mild and patient; unprotesting. ~**ly** *adv.* ~**ness** *n.*

meet [mi:t] *v.t. & i.* (p.t. & p.p. *met*). **1.** come face to face with (sb. or sth. coming from the opposite or a different direction); come together from anywhere. **2.** ~ *with,* experience: *to ~ with misfortune.* **3.** go to a place and wait for the arrival of sb. or sth.: *to ~ a train; to ~ a friend at the airport.* **4.** be

introduced to; make the acquaintance of: *I'd like you to* ~ *my brother.* **5.** satisfy; come into agreement with (sb., his wishes): *Will this ~ the case* (be satisfactory)? *n.* gathering of persons for a fox-hunt. ~**ing** *n.* coming together of persons for some purpose, esp. discussion.

meg·a·phone ['megəfoun] *n.* horn for speaking through, to carry one's voice to a distance.

A megaphone

mel·an·cho·ly ['melənkəli] *n. & adj.* (being) sad, in low spirits.

mê·lée ['melei] (French) *n.* confused struggle; confused crowd of people.

mel·lif·lu·ous [me'lifluəs] *adj.* (of words, voices, music) smooth-flowing and sweet-sounding.

mel·low ['melou] *adj.* (*-er, -est*). **1.** soft and sweet in taste; soft, pure, and rich in colour or sound. **2.** made sympathetic and wise by experience. *v.t. & i.* make or become ~.

mel·o·dra·ma ['melədrɑːmə] *n.* exciting and emotional drama, usu. with a happy ending. **mel·o·dra·mat·ic** [ˌmelədrə'mætik] *adj.* (esp. of a person, his behaviour) theatrical; in the manner of an actor of ~.

mel·o·dy ['melədi] *n.* **1.** sweet music; tunefulness. **2.** song or tune; principal line or part in harmonized music. **me·lo·di·ous** [mi'loudjəs] *adj.* sweet-sounding.

mel·on ['melən] *n.* large juicy round fruit growing on a plant that trails along the ground.

melt [melt] *v.t. & i.* **1.** (cause to) become liquid through heating: ~*ing snow.* **2.** soften, be softened: *a heart ~ing with pity.* **3.** fade, go slowly (away): *The mists ~ed away. In the rainbow one colour ~s into* *another.* **mol·ten** ['moultən] (old p.p. now used only of minerals). ~ed: *molten steel* (*lava*).

mem·ber ['membə*] *n.* **1.** person belonging to a group, society, etc. **2.** (old use) part of the body (e.g. an arm, the tongue). ~**ship** *n.* the state of being a ~ (of a society, etc.); the number of ~s (in a society).

mem·brane ['membrein] *n.* soft, thin, skin-like substance covering or connecting inside parts of an animal or plant.

me·men·to [mi'mentou] *n.* (pl. -*oes*, -*os*) sth. that serves to remind one of a person or event.

mem·o. ['memou] *n.* short for *memorandum.* (See *memory.*)

mem·oir ['memwɑ:*] *n.* **1.** short life-history, esp. one by someone with first-hand knowledge. **2.** (pl.) person's own written account of his life or experiences.

mem·o·ry ['meməri] *n.* **1.** power of remembering: *to have a good* (*bad*) ~ ; *speaking from* ~ ; *to the best of my* ~, as far as I can remember. **2.** period over which the ~ can go back: *within living* ~, of all people now living. **3.** *in* ~ *of,* to keep (sb. or sth.) in the ~. **4.** sth. that is remembered; sth. from the past stored in the ~ : *memories of childhood.* **mem·o·ra·ble** ['memərəbl] *adj.* deserving to be remembered.

mem·o·ran·dum [,memə'rændəm] *n.* **1.** note or record for future use. **2.** informal business communication, usu. without a personal signature. **mem·o·rize** ['meməraiz] *v.t.* learn by heart; commit to ~. **me·mo·ri·al** [mi'mo:riəl] *n. & adj.* **1.** (sth.) made or done to remind people of an event or person: *a war memorial*; *a memorial service.* **2.** written statement, sent to authorities, for or against sth. **me·mo·ri·al·ize** [mi'mo:riəlaiz] *v.t.* present a memorial of (2) to.

men (pl. of *man*). **men·folk** ['menfouk] *n. pl.* (colloq.) men, esp. the male members of a family. **men·ace** ['menis] *n.* threat; danger. *v.t.* threaten. **men·ac·**

ing·ly *adv.* in a threatening manner.

me·nag·er·ie [mi'nædʒəri] *n.* collection of wild animals in cages, etc., esp. for a travelling show. (Cf. *zoo.*)

mend [mend] *v.t. & i.* **1.** remake, repair, or set right sth. broken or worn out or torn; restore to good condition or working order. **2.** = amend(1): *to* ~ *one's ways.* **3.** regain health. *n.* hole, damaged part, etc., that has been ~ed. *on the* ~, improving (in health, etc.).

men·da·cious [men'deiʃəs] *adj.* untruthful. **men·dac·i·ty** [men'dæsiti] *n.*

men·di·cant ['mendikənt] *n. & adj.* (person) getting a living by begging: ~ *friars.*

me·nial ['mi:njəl] *adj. & n.* (suitable for, to be done by, a) servant.

men·su·ra·tion [,mensjuə'reiʃən] *n.* mathematical rules for finding length, area, volume.

men·tal ['mentl] *adj.* of or in the mind: ~ *arithmetic,* done in the head, not on paper; ~ *patient,* person suffering from a diseased mind; ~ *home,* place where ~ patients are cared for. ~**ly** *adv.* ~**i·ty** [men'tæliti] *n.* general character of a person's mind.

men·tion ['menʃən] *v.t.* speak or write sth. about; say the name of. *n.* ~ing.

men·tor ['mento:*] *n.* adviser and helper (of an inexperienced person).

men·u ['menju:] *n.* list of food dishes to be served at a meal.

mer·can·tile ['mə:kəntail] *adj.* of trade and merchants: ~ *marine,* country's merchant ships and seamen.

mer·ce·na·ry ['mə:sinəri] *n. & adj.* (soldier fighting or sb.) working only for money or reward: ~ *politicians*; based on love of money : ~ *motives.*

mer·chan·dise ['mə:tʃəndaiz] *n.* goods bought and sold; trade goods.

mer·chant ['mə:tʃənt] *n.* (usu. wholesale) trader, esp. one doing

business with foreign countries:
~ *service*, ships and seamen
engaged in carrying goods and
passengers. '~**man** *n*. ~ ship.

mer·cu·ry ['mə:kjuri] *n*. heavy,
silver-coloured metal (usu. liquid, as in thermometers). **mer-
cu·ri·al** [mə:'kjuəriəl] *adj*. (also
fig.): *a mercurial* (lively) *tempera-
ment; a mercurial* (inconstant)
person.

mer·cy ['mə:si] *n*. **1.** (capacity
for) holding oneself back from
punishing, causing suffering to,
sb. whom one has the right to
punish or power to hurt: *to
show* ~ *to a defeated enemy; have
~ on* (*sb*.), treat him kindly; (*be*)
at the ~ *of*, in the power of; *be
left to the tender mercies of*, be
exposed to the probable unkind
or cruel treatment of. **2.** sth.
to be thankful for; piece of good
fortune. **mer·ci·ful** *adj*. having,
showing, ~. **mer·ci·less** *adj*.
without ~; cruel.

mere [miə*] *adj*. not more than;
only: *a* ~ (*the* ~*st*) *trifle*. ~**ly**
adv. only.

mer·e·tri·cious [ˌmeri'triʃəs]
adj. attractive on the surface
but of little value.

merge [mə:dʒ] *v.t. & i*. **1.** (cause
to) become part of or absorbed
into sth. greater; (esp. of two
companies) become, cause to
become, one. **2.** ~ *into*, become
absorbed in, swallowed up in.
merg·er *n*. (esp.) act of merging
business companies into one
company.

me·rid·i·an [mə'ridiən] *n*. **1.**
half-circle round the globe, passing through a given place and
the north and south poles: *the
~ of Greenwich*. **2.** highest point
reached by the sun or other star
as viewed from a point on the
earth's surface. **3.** (fig.) point
of greatest success, power, fame.

me·ringue [mə'ræŋ] *n*. cake
made of white of egg and sugar.

me·ri·no [mə'ri:nou] *n*. kind of
sheep; yarn or cloth made from
its long, fine wool or from wool
and cotton.

mer·it ['merit] *n*. **1.** praiseworthy quality. **2.** (pl.) what

is deserved (reward; less often,
punishment). *v.t.* deserve; be
worthy of. **mer·i·to·ri·ous**
[ˌmeri'tɔːriəs] *adj*. praiseworthy.

mer·maid ['mə:meid], **mer·man**
['mə:mæn] *n*. (in stories) woman,
man, with a fish's tail in place of
legs.

mer·ry ['meri] *adj*. (**-ier, -iest**).
happy, cheerful, bright: *make
~*, hold a ~ *party*. **mer·ri·ly**
adv. **mer·ri·ment** *n*. '~-
ˌmaking *n*. '~-go-ˌround *n*.
revolving machine with wooden
horses, etc., at a fun fair.

A merry-go-round

mesh [meʃ] *n*. one of the spaces
in netting; (pl.) net; (fig.) snares.
v.t. & i. **1.** catch in a net. **2.**
(of toothed wheels) interlock.

mes·mer·ism ['mezmərizm] *n*.
(method, power, of gaining)
control over sb.'s personality
and actions by the exercise of
will-power; the sleep-like condition thus produced in the person. **mes·mer·ize** ['mezməraiz]
v.t. exercise ~ on.

¹**mess** [mes] *n*. state of confusion,
disorder, or dirt: *make a ~ of
sth.; get into a ~*. *v.t. & i*.
make a ~ of: ~ *sth. up*, spoil it;
~ *about*, be busy with odd jobs
but without getting much done.
mes·sy *adj*. (**-ier, iest-**). dirty;
untidy.

²**mess** [mes] *n*. group of persons
taking meals together (esp. in the
armed forces); these meals; the
room in which they are eaten.
v.i. eat meals in a ~-*room*: ~*ing
allowance*, money for that purpose.

mes·sage ['mesidʒ] *n*. spoken
or written request or piece of
news sent to sb. **mes·sen·ger**
['mesindʒə*] *n*. person carrying
a ~.

Mes·si·ah [mi'saiə] *n*. person
expected by the Jews to come

and set them free; the Saviour, Jesus Christ.

Messrs ['mesəz] title used before names of business firms (*Messrs Smith, Brown & Co.*) and as plural of Mr: *Messrs John and Charles Smith.*

met, see *meet.*

met·al ['metl] *n.* **1.** any one of a class of mineral substances such as tin, iron, gold, and copper. **2.** *road-~,* broken stone used for road-making. **3.** (pl.) railway-lines. **me·tal·lic** [mi-'tælik] *adj.* of or like ~. **me·tal·lur·gy** [mi'tælədʒi] *n.* art of separating ~ from ore and working ~.

met·a·mor·pho·sis [ˌmetə'mɔ:-fəsis] *n.* change of form or character.

met·a·phor ['metəfə*] *n.* (an example of) the use of words to indicate sth. different from the literal meaning, as in: 'I'll make him *eat* his words'; 'He has a *heart of stone*'. *~·i·cal* [ˌmetə-'forikl] *adj.*

met·a·phys·ics [ˌmetə'fiziks] *n.* branch of philosophy dealing with the nature of existence, truth, and knowledge; (popular use) mere theory. **met·a·phys·i·cal** *adj.*

mete [mi:t] *v.t.* (liter., old use) ~ *out,* give (rewards, punishments).

me·te·or ['mi:tjə*] *n.* small body rushing from outer space into the earth's atmosphere and becoming bright. **me·te·or·ic** [ˌmi:ti'orik] *adj.* bright and swift like a ~. *~·ite* ['mi:tjərait] *n.* ~ that has fallen to earth. **me·te·or·ol·o·gy** [ˌmi:tjə'rolədʒi] *n.* science of the weather. **me·te·or·o·log·i·cal** [ˌmi:tjərə'lodʒ-ikl] *adj.* of the weather or the atmosphere.

me·ter ['mi:tə*] *n.* apparatus which measures, or indicates, esp. one that records the amount of whatever passes through it (e.g. gas, water).

meth·od ['meθəd] *n.* **1.** way of doing sth. **2.** system; orderliness. **meth·od·i·cal** [mi'θodikl] *adj.* following, done with, a ~; orderly. **me·thod·i·cal·ly** *adv.*

Meth·o·dism ['meθədizm] *n.* teaching and organization of Christian Churches started by John Wesley. **Meth·o·dist** *adj. & n.*

meth·yl·at·ed spir·it ['meθ-ileitid 'spirit] *n.* form of alcohol used for lighting and heating.

me·tic·u·lous [mi'tikjuləs] *adj.* giving, showing, great attention to details.

me·tre ['mi:tə*] *n.* **1.** unit of length (39·37 inches) in the metric system. **2.** (particular form of) verse-rhythm. **met·ric** ['metrik] *adj. metric system,* decimal measuring system based on the ~ as the unit of length. **met·ri·cal** ['metrikl] *adj.* **1.** of or in verse-rhythm. **2.** of measurement.

me·trop·o·lis [mi'tropəlis] *n.* chief city of a country. **me·tro·pol·i·tan** [ˌmetrə'politən] *adj.* of a ~.

met·tle ['metl] *n.* quality (of a person, horse) of endurance and courage: *be on one's ~, put sb. on his ~,* in a position that tests this quality and moves a person to do his best. *~·some adj.* high-spirited.

mews [mju:z] *n.* street or square of stables, buildings for coaches.

mi·ca ['maikə] *n.* transparent mineral substance easily divided into thin layers.

mice, see *mouse.*

mi·crobe ['maikroub] *n.* tiny living creature, esp. kind of bacteria causing diseases and fermentation.

mi·crom·e·ter [mai'kromitə*] *n.* instrument for measuring very small distances, etc.

mi·cro·phone ['maikrəfoun] *n.* instrument for changing sound waves into electrical waves, as used in telephones, radio, etc.

A microphone   A microscope

mi·cro·scope ['maikrəskoup] *n.* instrument with lenses for magnifying objects too small to be seen without it. See the picture on page 324. **mi·cro·scop·ic** [,maikrə'skɔpik] *adj.* too small to be seen except with a ~.

¹mid– [mid] *adj.* in the middle of; middle: *in mid-Atlantic*; *in mid-June*; *in mid-air*, high above the ground. **'mid·'day** *n.* noon. **the Mid·lands** ['midləndz] *n.pl.* the central counties of England. **'mid·most** *adj.* in the exact middle. **'mid·night** *n.* **1.** 12 o'clock at night. **2.** (often attrib.) the middle of the night. **'mid·sum·mer** *n. Midsummer Day*, 24 June. **'mid·'way** *adv.* half-way. **'mid·'win·ter** *n.*

²mid [mid] *prep.* (old use) amid, among.

mid·den ['midn] *n.* heap of dung or rubbish.

mid·dle ['midl] *n. & adj.* (point, position, or part, that is) at an equal distance from two or more points, etc., or between beginning and end. ~ *age*, period of life midway between youth and old age; ~*-aged*, of ~ *age*; *the M~ Ages*, time in (European history) from about A.D. 1100 to 1500; *the ~ class(es)*, those between the highest and lowest classes of society; *the ~ watch*, (on ships) period from midnight to 4 a.m. **'~·man** *n.* any trader through whose hands goods pass between producer and consumer. **'mid·dling** *adj.* of ~ or medium size, quality, etc.; moderately good. *adv.* moderately; fairly well.

midge [midʒ] *n.* small winged insect like a gnat.

mid·get ['midʒit] *n.* extremely small person or thing.

mid·ship·man ['midʃipmən] *n.* (colloq. *middy* ['midʒi]). boy training to become a junior naval officer.

midst [midst] *n. in the ~ of*, in the middle of; while occupied with; *in our ~*, among us. *prep.* (liter.) among; in the middle of.

mid·wife ['midwaif] *n.* (pl. -*wives*). woman trained to help

women in childbirth. **mid·wif·er·y** ['midwifri] *n.* the work of a ~.

mien [mi:n] *n.* (liter.) person's bearing, appearance (showing a mood, etc.).

¹might, see *may*.

²might [mait] *n.* great power or strength. ~·**y** *adj.* (-*ier*, -*iest*). of great power or size. *adv.* (colloq.) very.

mi·grate [mai'greit] *v.i.* **1.** move from one place to another (to live there). **2.** (of birds) come and go regularly, with the seasons. **mi·grant** ['maigrənt] *n. & adj.* (esp.) (bird) that ~s. **mi·gra·tion** [mai'greiʃən] *n.* **mi·gra·to·ry** ['maigrətəri] *adj.* migrating: *migratory birds.*

mike [maik] *n.* (colloq.) microphone.

milch [miltʃ] *adj.* giving milk: ~ *cow.*

mild [maild] *adj.* (-*er*, -*est*). **1.** soft; gentle; not severe: ~ *weather* (*punishment*). **2.** (of food, drink, tobacco) not sharp or strong in taste: ~ *ale.* ~·**ly** *adv.* ~·**ness** *n.*

mil·dew ['mildju:] *n.* (usu. destructive) growth of tiny fungi forming on plants, leather, food, etc., in warm wet weather.

mile [mail] *n.* measure of distance, 1760 yards. **mil(e)·age** ['mailidʒ] *n.* distance travelled, measured in ~s. **'~·stone** *n.* roadside stone marking distance in ~s.

mil·i·tant ['militənt] *adj.* actively engaged in (esp. spiritual) warfare.

mil·i·tary ['militəri] *adj.* of or for soldiers, an army, war on land: *in ~ uniform*; ~ *training. the ~*, soldiers; the army. **mil·i·ta·rism** ['militərizm] *n.* belief in, reliance upon, ~ strength and virtues.

mil·i·tate ['militeit] *v.i.* ~ *against*, act, operate, be an influence, against.

mi·li·tia [mi'liʃə] *n.* force of civilians trained as soldiers but not part of the regular army.

milk [milk] *n.* white liquid produced by female mammals as food for their young, esp. that of cows which is drunk by human beings and made into butter and cheese. *v.t.* draw the ~ from (a cow, etc.). '~`maid *n.* woman who ~s cows and makes butter, etc. '~`man *n.* man who delivers ~ to the houses of his customers. '~-tooth *n.* one of the first set of teeth. ~`y *adj.* of or like ~. *the Milky Way*, galaxy.

mill [mil] *n.* 1. (building with) machinery (driven e.g. by water-power) for grinding grain into flour. 2. building, factory, work-shop for industry: *paper-* (*cotton-, steel-, saw-*) ~s. 3. small machine for grinding: *a coffee-*~. *v.t. & i.* 1. put through a machine for grinding; produce by doing this: *to ~ grain (flour).* 2. ~ed edge, edge (esp. of a coin) crossed with regular cuts. 3. (of cattle, crowds of people) move round and round in a confused way. '~`stone *n.* either of the two round stones between which grain is ground; (fig.) a serious hindrance. mil`ler *n.* man who owns or works a flour-~.

mil·len·ni·um [mi'leniəm] *n.* 1. 1,000 years. 2. future time of complete happiness for all.

mil·let ['milit] *n.* grain plant with very small seeds.

mil·li· *prefix.* one thousandth part of: ~*gram*; ~*metre*.

mil·li·ner ['milinə*] *n.* person who makes or sells women's hats. ~`y *n.* (the business of making or selling) women's hats; things needed for these.

mil·lion ['miljən] *n.* 1,000,000. ~`aire [,miljə'neə*] *n.* extremely rich man.

mime [maim] *v. & n.* (act in a) simple kind of entertainment using gestures and facial movements but no words.

mim·ic ['mimik] *adj.* imitated or pretended; done in play: ~ *warfare.* *n.* person imitating others. *v.t.* (p.t. & p.p. *mimicked* ['mimikt]). 1. imitate, esp. to cause amusement. 2. be very like. ~`ry *n.* mimicking.

mi·mo·sa [mi'mouzə] *n.* shrub with clusters of sweet-smelling, ball-like, yellow flowers.

min·a·ret ['minəret] *n.* tall, slender spire (connected with a mosque) from which people are called to prayer. (See *mosque* and the picture on page 334.)

mince [mins] *v.t. & i.* 1. cut up (meat, etc.) into small pieces. 2. *not ~ matters*, speak bluntly, say frankly what one thinks. 3. speak, walk, with unnatural and exaggerated care. *n.* ~d meat. '~`meat *n.* mixture of ~d dried fruit, sugar, suet, etc. '~ 'pie *n.* small round pie filled with ~meat.

¹mind [maind] *n.* 1. memory: *keep (bear) sth. in ~*, remember it; *call to ~*, recall to the memory; *put sb. in ~ of*, remind him of. 2. what a person thinks; way of thinking, feeling, wishing; opinion; purpose: *make up one's ~*, come to a decision; *change one's ~*, change one's purpose or intention; *be in two ~s (about sth.)*, feel doubtful, hesitate; *speak one's ~*, say plainly what one thinks; (of two or more persons) *be of one ~*, be in agreement; *have a good ~ to*, be almost decided or ready to; *take one's ~ off*, turn one's attention from. 3. centre of one's thinking, reasoning, understanding, etc.: *out of one's ~*, *not in one's right ~*, mad; *presence of ~*, ability to decide or act quickly when there is danger, etc. 4. (person with) mental ability: *one of the greatest ~s of the age.* ~`ful *adj.* ~*ful of*, giving thought or care to. ~`less *adj.* ~*less of*, paying no attention to.

²mind [maind] *v.t. & i.* 1. take care of; attend to: ~*ing the baby.* ~ *the step*, take care not to stumble over it. ~ *your own business*, not interfere in the affairs of others. *Mind (out)!* Be careful! 2. be troubled by; feel objection to: *Do you ~ my smoking? Would you ~ shutting the door* (= please shut the door).

¹**mine** [main] **pron.** of or belonging to me.

²**mine** [main] **n. 1.** hole made in or under the earth to get coal, mineral ores; (fig.) source (of knowledge). **2.** (tunnel for) charge of high explosive; metal case filled with high explosive for use in or on the sea, or (land-~) dropped from the air or laid in or on the ground: *ships sunk by ~s*. **v.t. & i. 1.** dig (coal, metals, etc.) from the ground. **2.** put ~s(2) in (the sea) or under (e.g. a fort); destroy, sink, or damage with a ~(2). **3.** (also *under*~) make holes or tunnels under. '~-**field** *n.* (esp.) area of land or sea where ~s (2) have been laid. '~**·lay·er** (**·**·**sweep·er**) *n.* ship laying (sweeping up or destroying) ~s(2). **min·er** *n.* (esp.) man working in a ~(1).

min·er·al ['minərəl] *n.* substance (e.g. coal) not vegetable or animal, got from the earth by mining, etc. ~ **wat·er** *n.* water containing gas (and often a flavouring), as *soda-water*.

min·gle ['mingl] *v.t. & i.* mix (with): *truth ~d with falsehood*; *mingling with* (going about among) *the crowds*.

min·i- ['mini] *prefix.* very small, short, etc.: ~*bus*, ~*skirt*.

min·i·a·ture ['minitʃə*] *n.* very small picture of a person; small-scale copy or model of sth.; (used attrib.): ~ *railway*.·

min·i·mize ['minimaiz] *v.t.* reduce to, estimate at, the smallest possible amount or degree.

min·i·mum ['minimam] *n. & adj.* least possible or recorded amount, degree, etc. (of): *the ~ temperature*; ~ *wages*.

min·ion ['minjən] *n.* slave; lowest servant.

min·is·ter ['ministə*] *n.* **1.** person at the head of a Department of State: *M~ for Defence*; *Prime M~*. **2.** person representing his Government in a foreign country. **3.** Christian priest or clergyman. *v.i.* give help or service (*to*): ~*ing to the sick*.

min·is·te·ri·al [,minis'tiəriəl]

adj. of a M~ of State; of his Ministry; of a ~ of religion. **min·is·tra·tion** [,minis'treiʃən] *n.* giving of help or (esp. religious) service. **min·is·try** ['ministri] *n.* **1.** Department of State under a ~(1): *the Air Ministry*. **2.** all the ~s(1) forming a Government; the Cabinet. **3.** *enter the ministry*, become a ~(3). **4.** position of, time of being, duties of, a ~(3).

mink [mink] *n.* (valuable brown fur skin of a) small stoat-like animal.

min·now ['minou] *n.* sorts of very small freshwater fish.

mi·nor ['mainə*] *adj.* **1.** smaller; less important: *a broken leg and ~ injuries*. **2.** younger of two brothers: *Jones M~*. **3.** ~ ¹*scale* (7), having one-and-a-half tones between the keynote and third note. *n.* person not yet legally of age (2). ~**·i·ty** [mai'noriti] *n.* **1.** the state of being not legally of age. **2.** the smaller number or part, esp. of a total of votes.

min·ster ['minstə*] *n.* large or important church, esp. one that once belonged to a monastery. **min·strel** ['minstrəl] *n.* (formerly) travelling composer, player and singer of songs and ballads.

¹**mint** [mint] *n.* sort of plant whose leaves are used for flavouring.

²**mint** [mint] *n.* place where coins are made, usu. under State authority. *v.t.* make (coins) by stamping metal.

min·u·et [,minju'et] *n.* (music for) slow, graceful dance for two persons.

mi·nus ['mainəs] *prep.* less; with the deduction of: *7 minus 3 is 4* $(7-3 = 4)$. *adj. the ~ sign*, the sign −; *a ~ quantity*, a quantity less than 0, e.g. -21, $-2x^2$.

¹**min·ute** ['minit] *n.* **1.** one-sixtieth part of one hour. **2.** one-sixtieth part of a degree in the measurement of an angle. **3.** official record giving authority, advice, or making comments. **4.** (pl.) summary, records, of what is

said and decided at a meeting, esp. of a society or committee. **'~·book** *n.* for keeping ~s (4).

²mi·nute [mai'nju:t] *adj.* very small; giving small details: *a ~ description*.

minx [miŋks] *n.* sly, impertinent girl.

mir·a·cle ['mirəkl] *n.* **1.** act or event that does not follow the known laws of nature; remarkable and surprising event. **2.** remarkable specimen or example (of a quality): *a ~ of ingenuity*. **mi·rac·u·lous** [mi'rækjuləs] *adj.*

mi·rage ['mira:ʒ] *n.* **1.** effect, produced by air conditions, causing sth. distant to appear as if it were near, esp. in the desert. **2.** (fig.) any illusion.

mire ['maiə*] *n.* wet ground; soft deep mud.

mir·ror ['mirə*] *n.* polished (formerly metal, now less glass) surface reflecting images; looking-glass. *v.t.* reflect as a ~ does.

mirth [mə:θ] *n.* laughter; being merry.

mis- [mis] *prefix.* bad(ly); wrong(ly), as in *misbehave, miscount, mis-spell*, etc.

mis·ad·ven·ture [ˌmisəd'ventʃə*] *n.* (event caused by) bad luck.

mis·an·thrope ['misənθroup] *n.* person who hates mankind, avoids society. **mis·an·throp·ic** [ˌmisən'θrɔpik] *adj.*

mis·car·riage [mis'kæridʒ] *n.* **1.** ~ *of justice*, mistake in judging or punishing. **2.** failure to deliver to, or arrive at, a destination: ~ *of goods*. **3.** delivery of a baby before it is able to live.

mis·car·ry [mis'kæri] *v.i.* **1.** (of plans, etc.) fail; have a result different from what was hoped for. **2.** (of letters, etc.) fail to arrive at the right destination. **3.** give birth to a baby before it can live.

mis·cel·la·neous [ˌmisə'leinjəs] *adj.* of mixed sorts; having various qualities and characteristics. **mis·cel·la·ny** [mi'seləni, 'misələni] *n.* ~ collection (e.g. of writings on various subjects by various authors).

mis·chance [mis'tʃɑːns] *n.* bad luck.

mis·chief ['mistʃif] *n.* **1.** injury or damage done on purpose. *make ~ between*, cause ill feeling between (others) by gossip, etc. **2.** foolish or thoughtless behaviour likely to cause trouble: *boys who are always getting into (up to) ~.* **3.** light-hearted desire to tease: *eyes full of ~.* **mis·chie·vous** ['mistʃivəs] *adj.* causing, engaged in, fond of, showing a spirit of, ~: *as mischievous as a monkey*.

mis·con·ceive [ˌmiskən'si:v] *v.t.* have a wrong idea of. **mis·con·cep·tion** [ˌmiskən'sepʃən] *n.* *under a misconception*.

mis·con·duct [mis'kɔndʌkt] *n.* wrong behaviour or conduct (e.g. adultery). [ˌmiskən'dʌkt] *v.t.* manage (a business, etc.) badly; behave (*oneself*) badly.

mis·con·strue [ˌmiskən'stru:] *v.t.* form a wrong idea of (sb.'s words, acts).

mis·cre·ant ['miskriənt] *n.* scoundrel.

mis·deal [mis'di:l] *v.i. & t.* deal (playing cards) wrongly. *n.* such a mistake.

mis·deed ['mis'di:d] *n.* wicked act; crime.

mis·de·mean·our [ˌmisdi'mi:nə*] *n.* unlawful act of a not very serious sort.

mi·ser ['maizə*] *n.* person who loves wealth for its own sake and spends as little as possible. ~**ly** *adj.*

mis·er·a·ble ['mizərəbl] *adj.* **1.** wretched; very unhappy; causing wretchedness and unhappiness. **2.** poor in quality. **mis·er·a·bly** *adv.* **mis·er·y** ['mizəri] *n.* state of being ~; pain; suffering; poverty: *living in misery*.

mis·fire ['mis'faiə*] *v.i.* (of a gun) fail to go off; (of a motor-engine) fail to start. *n.* such a failure.

mis·fit ['mis'fit] *n.* article of clothing that does not fit well; (fig.) person not well suited to his position.

mis·for·tune [mis'fɔ:tʃən] *n.*

mis·giv·ing [mis'giviŋ] *n.* doubt, distrust.

mis·guid·ed [mis'gaidid] *adj.* foolish and wrong (because of bad guidance or influence).

mis·hap [mis'hæp] *n.* unfortunate accident (usu. not serious).

mis·lay [mis'lei] *v.t.* (p.t. & p.p. *mislaid* [mis'leid]). put (sth.) by chance where it cannot easily be found.

mis·lead [mis'li:d] *v.t.* (p.t. & p.p. *misled* [mis'led]). lead wrongly; cause to be or do wrong; give a wrong idea to.

mis·no·mer [mis'noumə*] *n.* wrong use of a name or word.

mis·place ['mis'pleis] *v.t.* 1. put in a wrong place. 2. (in the passive) give (love, affections) wrongly or unwisely.

mis·print ['mis'print] *v.t. & n.* (make an) error in printing.

mis·quote ['mis'kwout] *v.t.* quote wrongly. **mis·quo·ta·tion** ['miskwou'teiʃən] *n.*

mis·rule ['mis'ru:l] *n.* bad government.

miss [mis] *v.t. & i.* (p.t. & p.p. *missed* [mist]). 1. fail to hit (hold, catch, reach, see, be at) what it is desired to hit, etc.: *fire at a lion and ~ it*; *try to catch a ball and ~ it*; *~ the point of a joke*. 2. realize or learn or feel regret at the absence of: *She'd ~ her gardener if he left.* 3. ~ *sth. out*, omit; fail to put in or say. *n.* failure to hit, etc.: *a lucky ~*, *a fortunate escape.* **~·ing** *adj.* not to be found; not in the place where it ought to be: *a book with two pages ~ing*; *dead, wounded, and ~ing* (soldiers).

Miss [mis] *n.* prefix to the surname of an unmarried woman or girl.

mis·shap·en ['mis'ʃeipən] *adj.* (of the body) wrongly shaped; deformed.

mis·sile ['misail] *n.* object thrown (e.g. a stone, a spear) or sent through the air (e.g. an arrow, a bomb) in order to hurt or damage; rocket propelled into the air (as a weapon, e.g. to destroy enemy aircraft).

mis·sion ['miʃən] *n.* 1. (the sending out of a) number of persons entrusted with special work, usu. abroad: *a trade ~*; *religious ~s.* 2. work done by such persons; their building(s), organization, etc. 3. special work which a person feels called upon to do: *his ~ in life.* **~·a·ry** ['miʃənəri] *n.* person sent to preach his religion, esp. to people ignorant of it.

mis·spell ['mis'spel] *v.t.* (p.t. & p.p. *mis-spelled* or *mis-spelt*). spell wrongly. **mis·spel·ling** *n.*

mis·spent [mis'spent] *adj.* wasted; foolishly spent.

mis·sive ['misiv] *n.* (humor.) letter.

mist [mist] *n.* water vapour in the air, less dense than fog: *hills hidden in ~.* **~·y** *adj.* (*-ier, -iest*). 1. with ~: *~y weather.* 2. not clear: *a ~y idea.*

mis·take [mis'teik] *n.* wrong opinion, idea, or act; error: *by ~*, in error, as the result of carelessness, forgetfulness, etc. *v.t. & i.* (p.t. *mistook* [mis'tuk], p.p. *mistaken* [mis'teikn]). 1. be wrong, have a wrong idea, about. 2. ~ (*sb. or sth.*) *for*, wrongly suppose that (sb. or sth.) is another (person or thing).

mis·ter, see *Mr.*

mis·tle·toe ['mizltou] *n.* plant with small white berries, used for decoration at Christmas.

mis·took, see *mistake.*

mis·tress ['mistris] *n.* 1. housewife in charge of a household. 2. woman with knowledge or control (of sth.): *a ~ of needlework.* 3. woman school-teacher. 4. concubine.

mis·trust [mis'trʌst] *v.t. & n.* (feel) doubt or suspicion (about). **~·ful** *adj.* suspicious.

mis·un·der·stand ['misʌndə-'stænd] *v.t.* take a wrong meaning from (instructions, messages, etc.); form a wrong opinion of (sb. or sth.). **~·ing** *n.* failure to understand rightly, esp. when this has led or may lead to ill feeling.

mis·use [mis'ju:z] *v.t.* use wrongly or for a wrong purpose; treat unkindly. [mis'ju:s] *n.* using wrongly; instance of this.

mite [mait] *n.* **1.** (old use) small coin. **2.** very small child. **3.** tiny insect-like creature: *cheese ~s.*

mit·i·gate ['mitigeit] *v.t.* make less severe, violent, or painful. **mi·ti·ga·tion** [,miti'geiʃən] *n.*

mi·tre ['maitə*] *n.* **1.** tall cap worn by bishops. **2.** joint between two pieces of wood as shown here.

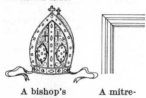

A bishop's   A mitre-
mitre   joint

mit·ten ['mitn] *n.* **1.** kind of glove covering four fingers together and thumb separately. **2.** covering for the back and palm of the hand only.

mix [miks] *v.t. & i.* (of different substances, people, etc.) put, bring, or come together so that the substances, etc., are no longer separate; make or prepare (sth.) by doing this: *mix flour and sugar; oil and water do not mix; mix a batter; be mixed up in (with)* (e.g. politics), be involved in; *feel mixed up (about sth.),* feel confused. **mixed** *adj.* of different sorts: *mixed feelings (pickles).* **mix·ture** ['mikstʃə*] *n.* **1.** mixing; being mixed. **2.** sth. that is mixed: *a smoking mixture* (made by mixing different kinds of tobacco).

moan [moun] *v.i. & n.* (utter, give, a) low sound of pain or regret or one suggesting distress.

moat [mout] *n.* deep wide ditch, with water, round a castle, etc., as a protection against attack.

mob [mɔb] *n.* **1.** disorderly crowd. **2.** the common people;

the masses. *v.t.* (-*bb*-). crowd round (either to attack or to show admiration, etc.).

mo·bile ['moubail] *adj.* moving, able to be moved, easily: ~ *troops;* easily and often changing: ~ *features.* **mo·bil·i·ty** [mou'biliti] *n.*

mo·bil·ize ['moubilaiz] *v.t. & i.* collect together (forces, resources, etc.) and prepare for service or use, esp. in war. **mo·bil·i·za·tion** [,moubilai'zeiʃən] *n.*

moc·ca·sin ['mɔkəsin] *n.* (shoe made from) soft deerskin leather.

mock [mɔk] *v.t. & i.* make fun of; ridicule (esp. by mimicking); ~ *at,* laugh at, make fun of. *adj.* (attrib. only) not real or genuine: *a ~ battle.* '~-**up** *n.* full scale model of sth. (e.g. a new book) intended to show what it will look like when manufactured. ~'**ing·ly** *adv.* ~'**er·y** *n.* **1.** ~ing; ridicule. **2.** sb. or sth. that is ~ed. **3.** bad or contemptible example (*of* sth.): *His trial was a ~ery of justice.*

mode [moud] *n.* way in which sth. is done; style or fashion (of dress).

mod·el ['mɔdl] *n.* **1.** small-scale copy of sth.; design to be copied; one of a series of different designs of the same thing (e.g. a motor-car). **2.** person or thing to be copied. **3.** mannequin. **4.** person employed by an artist as a ~ (2). **5.** (attrib.) deserving to be imitated: *a ~ wife.* *v.t.* (-*ll*-). **1.** shape (in some soft substance): *~ling in clay.* **2.** make from a ~; take as a copy or example: ~ *one's behaviour upon* (sb. else's). **3.** act as a ~ (3), (4).

mod·er·ate ['mɔdərit] *adj.* not extreme, midway (in opinions, habits); fairly large; fairly good: ~ *prices; a ~ appetite;* ~ *in his opinions.* *n.* person with ~ opinions (esp. in politics). ['mɔdəreit] *v.t. & i.* make, become, less violent or extreme: *to ~ one's demands (enthusiasm).* ~'**ly** *adv.* to a ~ extent. **mod·er·a·tion** [,mɔdə'reiʃən] *n.* quality of being ~: *moderation* in food and drink; in moderation, in a ~ way or amount.

mod·ern ['mɔdən] adj. **1.** of the present or recent times: ~ history (languages). **2.** new and up to date: ~ ideas (methods). ~·ize v.t. bring up to date; make suitable for present-day needs.

mod·est ['mɔdist] adj. **1.** having, showing, a not too high opinion of one's merits, abilities, etc. **2.** not very large, fine, etc.: a ~ demand; living in a ~ way. **3.** taking, showing, care not to do or say anything impure or improper: ~ in dress, speech, and behaviour. ~·ly adv. mod·es·ty n.

mod·i·cum ['mɔdikəm] n. moderate amount.

mod·i·fy ['mɔdifai] v.t. make changes in; make less severe, violent, etc. mod·i·fi·ca·tion [,mɔdifi'keiʃən] n.

mod·u·late ['mɔdjuleit] v.t. make a change in the tone, pitch, or key of. mod·u·la·tion [,mɔdju'leiʃən] n.

moist [mɔist] adj. slightly wet. ~·en ['mɔisn] v.t. make, become, ~. mois·ture ['mɔistʃə*] n. slight wetness; liquid in the form of vapour or in small drops on the surface of sth.

mo·lar ['moulə*] n. & adj. (one) of the teeth used for grinding food.

mo·las·ses [mə'læsiz] n. (with sing. v.) thick dark syrup drained from raw sugar.

¹mole [moul] n. small, dark-grey, fur-covered animal living in tunnels which it makes in the ground. ~·hill n. heap of earth thrown up by a ~.

²mole [moul] n. permanent dark-coloured spot on the skin.

³mole [moul] n. stone wall built in the sea as a breakwater or causeway.

mol·e·cule ['mɔlikju:l] n. smallest unit into which a substance could be divided without a change in its chemical nature. mo·lec·u·lar [mə'lekjulə*] adj.

mo·lest [mə'lest] v.t. trouble or annoy intentionally. mo·les·ta·tion [,moules'teiʃən] n.

mol·li·fy ['mɔlifai] v.t. make (a person, his feelings) calm.

mol·lusc ['mɔləsk] n. one of a class of animals with soft bodies, some with shells (e.g. oysters, snails) and some without (e.g. slugs).

mol·ly·cod·dle ['mɔlikɔdl] n. person who takes too much care of his health, etc. v.t. take too much care of (oneself, a person).

mol·ten, see melt.

mom [mɔm] n. (U.S.A.) mother.

mo·ment ['moumənt] n. **1.** point of time: in a ~, very soon; the ~ (that), as soon as. **2.** importance: affairs of great ~. mo·men·ta·ry adj. lasting for, done in, a ~. mo·men·tous [mou'mentəs] adj. very important or serious.

mo·men·tum [mou'mentəm] n. quantity of motion of a moving body; (fig.) gain in force and speed caused by motion.

mon·arch ['mɔnək] n. supreme ruler, esp. a king or an emperor. ~·ism n. ~·ist n. supporter of ~y. ~·y n. (country with) government by a ~.

mon·as·ter·y ['mɔnəstəri] n. building in which monks live.

mo·nas·tic [mə'næstik] adj. of monasteries and monks.

Mon·day ['mʌndi] n. the second day of the week.

mon·ey ['mʌni] n. metal coin; (paper ~) official notes (4) printed with values and accepted as payment in place of coins. '~ ,or·der n. official order (7) bought from a post office for money to be paid by another post office to a named person. mon·e·ta·ry ['mʌnitəri] adj. of ~.

mon·goose ['mɔngu:s] n. (pl. -s). small Indian animal clever at catching snakes.

mon·grel ['mʌngrəl] n. dog of mixed breed; any plant or animal of mixed origin; (attrib.) of mixed origin.

mon·i·tor ['mɔnitə*] n. **1.** schoolboy given authority over his fellows. **2.** person employed to listen to and report on foreign broadcasts. v.t. & i. act as a ~ (2).

monk [mʌŋk] *n.* one of a group of men living together under religious vows in a monastery.

mon·key ['mʌŋki] *n.* see the picture. *v.i.* play mischievously (*about with* sth.). **'~-nut** *n.* = groundnut, peanut.

A monogram   A monkey

mon·o- *prefix.* one, as ~*chrome* ['mɒnəkroum]. *n. & adj.* (painting) in one colour only.

mon·o·cle ['mɒnəkl] *n.* eyeglass for one eye only.

mo·nog·a·my [mə'nɒgəmi] *n.* practice of being married to only one person at a time.

mon·o·gram ['mɒnəgræm] *n.* two or more letters (esp. sb.'s initials) combined in one design.

mon·o·graph ['mɒnəgræf, -grɑːf] *n.* written study of a subject, esp. a report on research.

mon·o·lith ['mɒnəliθ] *n.* single upright block of stone (as a pillar or monument).

mon·o·logue ['mɒnəlɒg] *n.* scene in a play, etc., in which only one person speaks, by himself.

mon·o·plane ['mɒnəplein] *n.* aircraft with one wing on each side of the fuselage.

mo·nop·o·ly [mə'nɒpəli] *n.* 1. (possession of the) sole right to supply; the supply or service thus controlled. 2. complete possession of trade, talk, etc.: *In some countries tobacco is a government ~.* **mo·nop·o·list** *n.* person who has a ~. **mo·nop·o·lize** *v.t.* get, keep, a ~ of.

mon·o·syl·la·ble ['mɒnə,siləbl] *n.* word of one syllable. **mon·o·syl·lab·ic** [,mɒnəsi'læbik] *adj.*

mon·o·the·ism ['mɒnəˈθiːizm] *n.* belief that there is only one God.

mon·o·tone ['mɒnətoun] *n.* (keeping a) level tone in talking or singing. **mo·not·o·nous** [mə-

'nɒtənəs] *adj.* (uninteresting because) unchanging. **mo·not·o·ny** [mə'nɒtəni] *n.* sameness; wearisome lack of variety.

Mon·sieur [mə'sjə:*] *n.* (French for) Mr, sir, gentleman.

mon·soon [mɒn'su:n] *n.* wind blowing in the Indian Ocean from SW. in summer and from NE. in winter.

mon·ster ['mɒnstə*] *n.* 1. wrongly-shaped animal or plant; person or thing of extraordinary shape, size, or qualities. 2. (in stories) imaginary creature (e.g. half animal, half bird). 3. very cruel person. **mon·stros·i·ty** [mɒn'strɒsiti] *n.* ~ (1). **mon·strous** ['mɒnstrəs] *adj.* 1. of or like a ~; of great size. 2. absurd; impossible: *monstrous demands.*

month [mʌnθ] *n.* any period of 28 days; one of the twelve parts into which a year is divided; period as from, e.g., 3 March to 3 April. **~ly** *adj. & adv.* done, valid for, one ~. *n.* periodical issued once a ~.

mon·u·ment ['mɒnjumənt] *n.* 1. building, column, statue, etc., serving to keep alive the memory of a person or event. 2. work of scholarship of permanent value. **mon·u·men·tal** [,mɒnju'mentl] *adj.* 1. (of books, studies, etc.) of lasting value. 2. (of qualities, tasks, buildings) very great.

mood [mu:d] *n.* state of mind or spirits. **~y** *adj.* (*-ier, -iest*). having ~s that often change; gloomy. **~i·ly** *adv.*

moon [mu:n] *n.* see the picture.

Phases of the moon

¹**moor** [muə*, mɔ:*] *n.* area of open uncultivated land, esp. heather-covered land.

²**moor** [muə*, mɔ:*] *v.t.* make (a boat, ship) secure (to the land or buoys) by means of cables, etc. **~ings** *n. pl.* cables, etc., by which a ship is ~ed; place at which a ship is ~ed.

moose [mu:s] *n.* N. American sort of deer.

moot [mu:t] *adj.* ~ *point (question),* one about which there is uncertainty. *v.t.* raise, bring forward, for discussion.

mop [mɔp] *n.* **1.** bundle of coarse strings, cloth, etc., fastened to a stick for cleaning floors, etc. **2.** mass of thick untidy hair. *v.t.* (-*pp*-). clean with a mop; wipe up with, or as with, a mop: *mop up,* clean up; make an end of.

mope [moup] *v.i.* pity oneself, give way to sadness.

mo·ped [mouped] *n.* pedal bicycle fitted with a small petrol engine.

mor·al ['mɔrəl] *adj.* **1.** concerning principles (2). **2.** good and virtuous: *a ~ life; ~ books.* **3.** ~ *victory,* outcome of a struggle in which the weaker side is comforted because it has established the righteousness of its cause; ~ *certainty,* sth. so probable that there is little room for doubt. *n.* **1.** that which a story, event, experience, etc., teaches. **2.** (pl.) standards of behaviour; principles of right and wrong. ~**ist** *n.* person who points out ~s (1). **mo·ral·i·ty** [mə'ræliti] *n.* (standards, principles, of) good behaviour. ~**ize** ['mɔrəlaiz] *v.i.* deal with ~ questions; show the ~ meaning of; point out ~s (2). ~**ly** *adv.*

mo·rale [mə'rɑːl] *n.* confidence; fighting spirit (esp. of soldiers under discipline).

mo·rass [mə'ræs] *n.* stretch of low, soft, wet land; marsh.

mor·a·to·ri·um [ˌmɔrə'tɔːriəm] *n.* legal authorization to delay payment of debts.

mor·bid ['mɔːbid] *adj.* **1.** diseased: *a ~ growth* (e.g. a cancer). **2.** (of sb's mind or ideas) unhealthy: *a ~ imagination.* **3.** (of a person) having unhealthy or unnatural ideas and feelings. ~**ly** *adv.*

mor·dant ['mɔːdənt] *adj.* biting, sarcastic.

more [mɔː*] *adj., n. & adv.* (contrasted with *less* and *few;* cf. *much, many, most*). **I. adj.** greater in number, quantity, quality, size, etc.; additional. **II.** *n.* a greater amount, number, etc.; an additional amount. **III. adv. 1.** forming the comparative degree of many adjectives and adverbs: ~ *useful;* ~ *easily.* **2.** to a greater extent; in a greater degree: *You should sleep ~ than you do at present.* **3.** again: *Do it once ~. Do you want to go there any ~?* **4.** ~ *and ~,* increasingly. ~ *or less,* about: *It's an hour's journey,* ~ *or less. be no ~,* be dead. ~**·o·ver** [mɔː'rouvə*] *adv.* further; besides; in addition (to this).

mor·i·bund ['mɔribʌnd] *adj.* about to die or come to an end.

morn·ing ['mɔːniŋ] *n.* early part of the day between dawn and noon (or the midday meal). ~ *coat,* man's tail-coat with the front sloped away; ~ *watch,* (at sea) 4 a.m. to 8 a.m. **morn** *n.* (liter.) ~.

mo·roc·co [mə'rɔkou] *n.* soft leather made from goatskins.

mo·rose [mə'rous] *adj.* sullen; ill-tempered.

mor·phia ['mɔːfjə], **mor·phine** ['mɔːfiːn] *n.* drug for relieving pain.

mor·row ['mɔrou] *n. the ~,* (liter.) the next day (after the day or event indicated).

Morse [mɔːs] *n.* ~ *code,* system of dots and dashes representing letters of the alphabet to be signalled by lamp, wireless, etc.

mor·sel ['mɔːsl] *n.* tiny piece (esp. of food); bite.

mor·tal ['mɔːtl] *adj.* **1.** which must die; which cannot live for ever. **2.** causing death: ~ *injuries.* **3.** lasting until death: ~ *hatred;* ~ *combat* (only ended by death). **4.** extreme: *in ~ fear of death. n.* human being. ~**ly** *adv.* ~**i·ty** [mɔː'tæliti] *n.* **1.** being ~. **2.** the number of deaths caused by sth. (e.g. a disaster or disease).

mor·tar ['mɔːtə*] *n.* **1.** mixture of lime, sand, and water used in building. **2.** bowl of hard material in which substances are crushed to powder with a pestle.

3. short gun for firing shells at high angles. **'~-board** *n.* **1.** flat board with a short handle for holding ~ (1). **2.** square cap worn by members of a college.

mort·gage ['mɔːgidʒ] *v.t.* give a creditor a claim on (property) as a security for payment of debt. *n.* act of mortgaging; agreement about this.

mor·ti·fy ['mɔːtifai] *v.t. & i.* **1.** cause (sb.) to be ashamed, humiliated, or hurt in his feelings: *mortified by sb.'s rudeness*; *a ~ing defeat.* **2.** ~ *the flesh,* discipline bodily passions. **3.** (of flesh, e.g. round a wound) decay, be affected with gangrene. **mor·ti·fi·ca·tion** [,mɔːtifi'keiʃən] *n.*

mor·tise, -tice ['mɔːtis] *n.* hole cut in a piece of wood, etc., to receive the end of another piece. *v.t.* join thus.

A mortise and tenon

mor·tu·a·ry ['mɔːtjuəri] *n.* room or building to which dead bodies are taken to await burial.

mo·sa·ic [mou'zeiik] *n. & adj.* (form or work of art) in which designs, pictures, etc., are made by fitting together bits of differently coloured stone, etc.

mosque [mɔsk] *n.* building in which Muslims worship Allah.

minaret

A mosque

mos·qui·to [mɔs'kiːtou] *n.* small flying blood-sucking insect, esp. the sort spreading malaria.

moss [mɔs] *n.* sorts of small green or yellow plant growing in thick masses on wet surfaces. **mos·sy** *adj.* (-ier, -iest).

most [moust] *adj., n. & adv.* (contrasted with *least* and *fewest*; cf. *much, many, more*). **I.** *adj. & n.* **1.** (the) greatest in number, quantity, etc.: *Which is ~, 3, 13, or 30? Those who have the ~ money are not always the happiest.* **2.** the majority of: *M~ people like children.* **3.** *at (the) ~,* not more than. *make the ~ of,* use to the best advantage. *for the ~ part,* almost all; in the main. **II.** *adv.* forming the superl. degree of many adjectives and adverbs: *the ~ beautiful; ~ carefully. What pleased me ~ was his helpful nature. This is a ~* (= very) *interesting book.* **~·ly** *adv.* chiefly; almost all; generally.

mote [mout] *n.* particle (esp. of dust).

mo·tel [mou'tel] *n.* hotel designed for the convenience of travellers by motor-car.

moth [mɔθ] *n.* (sorts of) winged insect flying chiefly at night, attracted by lights.

moth·er ['mʌðə*] *n.* female parent. ~ *tongue,* one's native language. ~ *of pearl,* smooth, shining lining of some shells, esp. the pearl oyster. *v.t.* watch over as a ~ does her children. **~·hood** *n.* **~·less** *adj.* **~·ly** *adj.* having the tender qualities of a ~. **'~-in-law** *n.* ~ of one's wife or husband.

mo·tif [mou'tiːf] *n.* main idea or design in a work of art.

mo·tion ['mouʃən] *n.* **1.** (manner of) moving: *in ~,* moving. **2.** gesture; particular movement. **3.** proposal to be discussed and voted on at a meeting. *v.t.* direct (sb.) by a ~ (2): *to ~ sb. in (away, to a seat).* **~·less** *adj.* not moving.

mo·tive ['moutiv] *adj.* causing motion: ~ *power.* *n.* that which causes sb. to act: *actuated by low and selfish ~s.* **mo·ti·vate** ['moutiveit] *v.t.* give a ~ to; be a ~ of.

mot·ley ['mɔtli] *adj.* of various colours: *a ~ coat;* of various sorts: *a ~ crowd.*

mo·tor ['moutə*] *n.* **1.** machine

(esp. one worked by petrol or electricity) supplying motive power for a vehicle, lawn-mower or vessel. (Cf. *steam-engine, diesel engine, jet engine.*) **2.** muscle or nerve producing motion. **3.** (attrib.) worked or driven by a ~: ~*bicycle* (*-scooter, -car, -bus, -boat*). *v.i. & t.* travel, take (sb.), by ~*-car*.

mot·tled ['mɒtld] *adj.* irregularly marked with different colours.

mot·to ['mɒtou] *n.* (pl. *-oes*). short sentence or phrase used as a guide or rule of behaviour.

¹**mould** [mould] *n.* container into which liquid metal or a soft substance is put to take a desired shape; food (e.g. jelly) shaped in such a container. *v.t.* give a shape or form to: *to ~ a head in (out of) clay*; (fig.) *to ~ sb.'s character.*

²**mould** [mould] *n.* woolly or furry growth of fungi appearing on moist surfaces (e.g. leather, cheese). ~·**y** *adj.* covered with, suggesting, ~: ~*y bread*; *a ~y smell*; (fig.) out of date; old-fashioned.

³**mould** [mould] *n.* soft, fine, loose, earth. ~·**er** *v.i.* break up into ~; decay: ~*ering ruins of a house.*

moult [moult] *v.t. & i.* (of birds) lose (feathers) before a new growth.

mound [maund] *n.* mass of piled-up earth; small hill.

mount [maunt] *n.* **1.** (liter. except in proper names) mountain: *Mount (Mt.) Everest.* **2.** card, etc., which provides a margin for a picture or photograph fixed on it. **3.** horse, etc., on which a person rides or is to ride. *v.t. & i.* **1.** go up (a ladder, a hill); get on to (a horse, etc.); supply (sb.) with a horse: *the ~ed police. He ~ed (his horse) and rode off.* **2.** fix on to a card, stand, etc., for display or use: *to ~ pictures*; *to ~ a gun* (on a gun-carriage); *to ~ jewels* (e.g. in gold). **3.** ~ *up*, become greater in amount: *Our living expenses are ~ing up.* **4.** ~ *guard* (*over*), watch and protect; be on duty as a guard.

moun·tain ['mauntin] *n.* mass of very high land going up to a peak. ~·**eer** [ˌmaunti'niə*] *n.* person who lives among ~s or is clever at climbing ~s. ~·**ous** ['mauntinəs] *adj.* having many ~s; immense: ~*ous waves.*

moun·te·bank ['mauntibæŋk] *n.* sb. who persuades people by clever and humorous talk to buy worthless medicine, etc.

mourn [mɔːn] *v.t. & i.* feel or show sorrow for a death or loss: ~*ing the death of a friend*; ~*ing for (over) her dead child.* ~·**er** *n.* one who ~s, esp. at a funeral. ~·**ful** *adj.* sad. ~·**ful·ly** *adv.* ~·**ing** *n.* **1.** grief. **2.** (the wearing of) black clothes as a sign of grief: *go into ~ing (for sb.).*

mouse [maus] *n.* (pl. *mice* [mais]). see the picture.

Mice

mous·tache [məs'tɑːʃ] *n.* hair on the upper lip.

mouth [mauθ] *n.* (pl. *-s* [mauðz]). **1.** opening through which people and animals take in food; space behind this containing the tongue, etc. *down in the ~*, sad. **2.** opening or outlet (*of a* bag, bottle, cave, tunnel, river, etc.). [mauð] *v.t. & i.* speak (words) with too much movement of the ~. ~·**ful** *n.* as much as can be put into the ~ comfortably at one time. ~·**ˌor·gan** *n.* small musical wind-instrument played by passing it along the lips. ¹~·**piece** *n.* **1.** part of a tobacco pipe or musical instrument placed against or between the lips. **2.** person, newspaper, etc. expressing the opinions of others.

move [muːv] *v.t. & i.* **1.** (cause to) change position. ~ *house*, take one's furniture, etc., to another house; ~ *in (out)*, take one's furniture, etc., into (out of) a house, etc. **2.** work on the feelings of: ~d to tears; ~ sb. to do sth., cause him to do sth. **3.** put forward for discussion and decision (at a meeting): *Mr Chairman, I ~ that the money shall be used for library books.* **n. 1.** change of place or position: *~s in a game of chess.* **2.** sth. (to be) done to achieve a purpose: *What's the next ~?* **3.** *on the ~,* moving about: *large enemy forces on the ~.* **mov·a·ble** ['mu:vəbl] *adj.* that can be moved. **~·ment** ['mu:vmənt] *n.* **1.** moving or being ~d; activity. **2.** moving part of a machine or a particular group of such parts: *the ~ment of a clock.* **3.** united action and efforts of a group of people for a special purpose: *the ~ment to abolish slavery.* **4.** chief division of a musical work. **mov·ies** ['mu:viz] *n.* (colloq.) the cinema.

mow [mou] *v.t. & i.* (p.t. *mowed*, p.p. *mowed* or *mown* [moun]). cut (grass, etc.) with a scythe or machine (*lawn-mower*): *mowing the lawn; new-mown hay;* (fig.) *mown down by machine-gun fire.*

Mr ['mistə*], **Mrs** ['misiz] *n.* prefix to the surname of a man, woman, who has no other title.

much [mʌtʃ] *adj.* (*more, most,* cf. *little*), *n. & adv.* **I. adj. & n.** (cf. *many,* used with pl. nouns). a lot (of), plenty (of), a good deal (of), a large quantity (of): *There isn't ~ food in the house, so we must go out and buy some. You have given me too ~, I can't eat it all. as ~* (as), quantity equal to, same quantity as: *Give me as ~ as you did before. I've had as ~ trouble as I can bear.* **II. adv. 1.** modifying comp. and superl.: *He's ~ better today than yesterday. This is ~ the best essay* (far better than all others). **2.** modifying past participles, etc.: *I'm very ~ afraid your child is seriously ill. I'm ~ annoyed at his behaviour.* **3.** greatly: *~ to my surprise.* **4.** to a great extent or degree: *It doesn't matter ~* (*~ matter). I don't like mangoes ~. She likes them very ~.*

muck [mʌk] *n.* **1.** farmyard manure (animal droppings). **2.** dirt; anything looked upon as dirty or disgusting. *v.t. & i.* **1.** make dirty. **2.** *~ sth. up,* (colloq.) make a mess of it. **3.** *~ about,* (colloq.) spend time aimlessly. **~·y** *adj.* (*-ier, -iest*). dirty.

mu·cous ['mju:kəs] *adj.* *~ membrane,* moist skin lining the nose, mouth, food canal. **mu·cus** ['mju:kəs] *n.* sticky or slimy liquid produced by the ~ membrane.

mud [mʌd] *n.* soft wet earth. **mud·dy** *adj.* (*-ier, -iest*). **'mud·guard** *n.* curved strip covering the rim of a road-wheel.

mud·dle ['mʌdl] *v.t. & i.* bring into confusion and disorder; do (sth. badly). *n.* ~d state: *in a ~.*

mu·ez·zin [mu:'ezin] *n.* man who calls the faithful to prayer from the minaret of a mosque.

muff [mʌf] *n.* covering, usu. a padded bag of fur, open at both ends, used by women to keep their hands warm.

muf·fin ['mʌfin] *n.* light, flat, round tea-cake, usu. eaten hot with butter.

muf·fle ['mʌfl] *v.t.* **1.** cover up for warmth: *to ~* (*oneself*) *up well* (e.g. by putting a scarf round the neck). **2.** make the sound of sth. (e.g. a bell or drum) dull by wrapping it up in cloth, etc. **muf·fler** *n.* cloth, scarf, worn round the neck for warmth.

muf·ti ['mʌfti] *n. in ~,* (of sb. who normally wears uniform) wearing ordinary clothes.

mug [mʌg] *n.* **1.** straight-sided drinking-vessel of china or metal with a handle, for use without a saucer: *a beer-mug.* **2.** (colloq.) easily deceived person.

Mu·ham·mad [mə'hæməd] *n.* the founder of Islam.

mul·ber·ry ['mʌlbəri] *n.* (fruit of) tree whose leaves are used for feeding silkworms.

mulch [mʌltʃ] *n.* mixture of wet straw, leaves, peat, etc., used to protect roots of plants, trees, etc. *v.t.* cover with ~.

mulct [mʌlkt] *v.t.* punish by means of a fine: ~ *sb.* £10; deprive (sb. *of*): ~*ed of his money.*

mule [mju:l] *n.* offspring of an ass and a mare. **mul·ish** ['mju:liʃ] *adj.* stubborn.

mul·let ['mʌlit] *n.* sort of sea-fish, used as food.

mul·lion ['mʌljən] *n.* upright stone column between parts of a window.

mul·ti- ['mʌlti-] *prefix.* having many (of). ~**fa·ri·ous** [,mʌlti-'feəriəs] *adj.* many and various.

mul·ti·ple ['mʌltipl] *adj.* having many parts. *n.* number which contains another number an exact number of times: *28 is a ~ of 7.*

mul·ti·ply ['mʌltiplai] *v.t. & i.* 1. *6 multiplied by 5 is 30 (6×5 = 30).* 2. produce a great number of: *to ~ instances.* 3. make or become great in number: *Rabbits soon ~.* **mul·ti·pli·ca·tion** [,mʌltipli'keiʃən] *n.* ~ing or being multiplied. **mul·ti·pli·ci·ty** [,mʌlti'plisiti] *n.* great number or variety: *the multiplicity of his duties.*

mul·ti·tude ['mʌltitju:d] *n.* 1. great number (esp. of people gathered together). 2. *the ~,* the masses, the common people. **mul·ti·tu·di·nous** [,mʌlti'tju:-dinəs] *adj.* great in number.

mum [mʌm] *int. & adj.* keep mum about (sth.), say nothing about, keep secret. *Mum's the word !* Say nothing about it.

mum·ble ['mʌmbl] *v.t. & i.* say sth., speak (one's words), indistinctly. *n.* ~d words: *His only answer was a ~.*

mum·mer ['mʌmə*] *n.* actor in an old form of drama without words. ~**·y** *n.* (performance of) useless ceremonial.

An Egyptian ¹mummy

¹**mum·my** ['mʌmi] *n.* dead person preserved from decay by being embalmed, esp. as by the ancient Egyptians.

²**mum(my)** ['mʌm(i)] *n.* child's name for its mother.

mumps [mʌmps] *n.* contagious disease causing painful swellings in the neck.

munch [mʌntʃ] *v.t. & i.* eat with much movement of the jaw: ~*ing an apple.*

mun·dane ['mʌndein] *adj.* worldly (contrasted with spiritual): ~ *affairs.*

mu·ni·ci·pal [mju:'nisipl] *adj.* of a ~ity. ~**·i·ty** [mju:,nisi'pæliti] *n.* town or city governed by its own elected council; governing body of such a town.

mu·nif·i·cent [mju:'nifisənt] *adj.* very generous. **mu·nif·i·cence** *n.*

mu·ni·tions [mju:'niʃənz] *n. pl.* military supplies, esp. guns, shells, etc.

mu·ral ['mjuərəl] *adj.* of or on a wall: ~ *paintings. n.* ~ painting.

mur·der ['mə:də*] *n.* unlawful killing of a human being on purpose. *v.t.* kill (sb.) unlawfully and on purpose. ~**er** *n.* ~**ess** *n.* ~**ous** ['mə:dərəs] *adj.* planning, suggesting, designed for, ~ : ~*ous weapons.*

murk·y ['mə:ki] *adj.* (-ier, -iest). dark; gloomy.

mur·mur ['mə:mə*] *v.t. & i. & n.* 1. (make a) low, continuous, indistinct sound: *the ~ of bees; a ~ of pain; a stream ~ing over the stones.* 2. say (sth.), talk, in a low voice: ~*ing a prayer;* ~*ing against heavy taxes.*

mus·cle ['mʌsl] *n.* (band, bundle, of) elastic substance in an animal body that can be tightened or loosened to produce movement. **mus·cu·lar** ['mʌs-kjulə*] *adj.* of the ~s; having much ~.

Muscles of the arm

muse [mju:z] *v.i.* think deeply or dreamily (*on, upon, over,* sth.), ignoring what is happening around one.

mu·se·um [mju:'ziəm] *n.* building in which objects illustrating art, history, science, etc., are displayed.

mush·room ['mʌʃrum] *n.* **1.** kind of fast-growing fungus that can be eaten. **2.** (attrib.) ~ *growth*, rapid development.

mu·sic ['mju:zik] *n.* (art of producing) pleasing combinations of sounds in rhythm and harmony; written or printed signs for these: *face the* ~, meet one's critics, face difficulties, etc. **mu·si·cal** *adj.* of, fond of, skilled in, ~. *n.* stage play or film (3) with songs and dances. **mu·si·cal·ly** *adv.* **mu·si·cian** [mju:'ziʃən] *n.* person skilled in ~; composer of ~. '~-hall *n.* (building for) variety entertainment (singing, dancing, etc.).

musk [mʌsk] *n.* substance obtained from male deer (~-*deer*), used in making perfumes. '~-rat *n.* rat-like water-animal of N. America.

mus·ket ['mʌskit] *n.* old style of gun, now replaced by the rifle. ~·ry *n.* (science of, instruction in) shooting with rifles.

Mus·lim ['muslim] *n.* **1.** believer in Islam. **2.** member of the nation of Islam.

mus·lin ['mʌzlin] *n.* thin, fine, soft cotton cloth used for dresses, curtains, etc.

must [mʌst, məst] *aux. v.* (no infinitive, no participles; neg. ~ *not* may be contracted to *mustn't* ['mʌsnt]). **1.** expressing a past, present, or future obligation: *I said I* ~ *go. I* ~ *go now. I* ~ *go next week. Why* ~ *you keep worrying about your money?* **2.** expressing certainty or strong probability: *You* ~ *be hungry after your long walk. I think you* ~ *have made a mistake.*

mus·tang ['mʌstæŋ] *n.* small wild or half-wild horse of the American plains.

mus·tard ['mʌstəd] *n.* plant; seeds of this crushed to a yellow powder; hot-tasting sauce made from this powder.

mus·ter ['mʌstə*] *n.* assembly or gathering of persons, esp. for review: *pass* ~, be considered satisfactory. *v.t. & i.* collect, call, come, together: ~ *up one's courage*, overcome one's fears.

mus·ty ['mʌsti] *adj.* (*-ier*, *-iest*) stale; smelling, tasting, mouldy.

mu·ta·ble ['mju:təbl] *adj.* likely to change; liable to change. **mu·ta·bil·i·ty** [,mju:tə'biliti] *n.* **mu·ta·tion** [mju:'teiʃən] *n.* change.

mute [mju:t] *adj.* **1.** silent; making no sound. **2.** (of a person) unable to speak; dumb. **3.** (of a letter in a word) not sounded (as the *b* in *dumb*). *n.* person who cannot speak.

mu·ti·late ['mju:tileit] *v.t.* damage by tearing, breaking, or cutting off a part. **mu·ti·la·tion** [,mju:ti'leiʃən] *n.*

mu·ti·ny ['mju:tini] *n.* (esp. of soldiers and sailors) open rising against authority. *v.i.* rise against authority; be guilty of ~. **mu·ti·neer** [,mju:ti'niə*] *n.* person guilty of ~. **mu·ti·nous** ['mju:tinəs] *adj.* rebellious.

mut·ter ['mʌtə*] *v.t. & i.* speak, say (sth.), in a low voice not meant to be heard: ~*ing threats.*

mut·ton ['mʌtn] *n.* flesh of the sheep.

mu·tu·al ['mju:tjuəl] *adj.* **1.** (of love, respect, etc.) shared, exchanged. **2.** (of feelings, opinions, etc.) held in common with others. **3.** common to two or more: *our* ~ *friend.* ~·ly *adv.*

muz·zle ['mʌzl] *n.* **1.** animal's nose and mouth; device of straps or wires placed over an animal's ~ to prevent it from biting, etc. **2.** open end or mouth of a gun. *v.t.* put a ~ on (an animal); prevent (a person, newspaper, etc.) from expressing views freely.

muz·zy ['mʌzi] *adj.* confused in mind.

my [mai] *poss. adj.* **1.** belonging to me. **2.** in a form of address: *My Lord. My dear (John).* **3.** in exclamations: *Oh, my!* **my·self** [mai'self, mi-] *pron.* **my·op·ic** [mai'ɔpik] *adj.* short-sighted.

myr·i·ad ['miriəd] *n.* number beyond count.

myrrh [mə:*] *n.* sweet-smelling kind of gum or resin from trees, used for incense and perfumes.

myr·tle ['mə:tl] *n.* evergreen shrub with sweet-smelling white flowers and black berries.

mys·ter·y ['mistəri] *n.* 1. sth. of which the cause or origin is hidden or impossible to understand; condition of being secret or obscure: *wrapped in ~*. 2. (pl.) secret religious rites and ceremonies. 3. *~ play*, old play telling a Bible story. **mys·te·ri·ous** [mis'tiəriəs] *adj.* full of, suggesting, ~; wrapped in ~.

mys·tic ['mistik] *adj.* of hidden meaning or spiritual power; mysterious; causing feelings of awe and wonder. *n.* person who seeks union with God and, through that, the realization of truths beyond men's understanding. **mys·ti·cal** *adj.* = ~. **mys·ti·cism** ['mistisizm] *n.* beliefs, experiences, of a ~.

mys·ti·fy ['mistifai] *v.t.* puzzle, bewilder. **mys·ti·fi·ca·tion** [,mistifi'keiʃən] *n.* ~ing; sth. that mystifies.

myth [miθ] *n.* 1. story, handed down from olden times, containing the early beliefs of a race (esp. explanations of natural events). 2. false belief; nonexistent person, thing, etc. **~·i·cal** ['miθikl] *adj.* of ~s; unreal; non-existent. **my·thol·o·gy** [mi'θɔlədʒi] *n.* study of ~s; body or collection of ~s. **myth·o·log·i·cal** [,miθə'lɔdʒikl] *adj.* **my·thol·o·gist** [mi'θɔlədʒist] *n.* student of ~ology.

N

na·dir ['neidiə*] *n.* (fig.) lowest, weakest, point (of one's fortunes, hopes).

¹nag [næg] *n.* (colloq.) small horse.

²nag [næg] *v.t. & i.* (-gg-). scold (sb., *at* sb.) continuously; annoy thus.

nai·ad ['naiæd] *n.* (Greek stories) water-nymph.

nail [neil] *n.* 1. layer of hard substance over the outer tip of a finger or toe. 2. piece of metal, pointed at one end and with a head at the other, (to be) hammered into articles to hold them together, or into a wall, etc., to hang sth. on. *on the ~*, at once; *hit the ~ on the head*, say or do the right thing. *v.t.* make fast with a ~ or ~s.

A finger-nail   A nail (2)

na·ïve [nɑ:'i:v] *adj.* natural and innocent in speech and behaviour (e.g. because young or inexperienced). **~·ly** *adv.* **~·té** [nɑ:'i:vtei] *n.* being ~; ~ remark, etc.

na·ked ['neikid] *adj.* without clothes on; bare; without the usual covering: *trees ~ of leaves*; *with the ~ eye*, without the help of a telescope, microscope, etc. **~·ly** *adv.* **~·ness** *n.*

name [neim] *n.* 1. word(s) by which a person, animal, place or other thing is known and spoken to or of. *in the ~ of*, with the authority of (e.g. the law); for the sake of (e.g. common sense); *call sb. ~s*, call him insulting ~s (e.g. liar, coward); *not have a penny to one's ~*, be without money. 2. reputation: *win a good ~ for oneself. v.t.* 1. give a ~ to; say the ~ of: *~ sb. after*, give him the same ~ as. 2. mention, state: *~ your price*, say what price you want. **~·less** *adj.* 1. not having a ~, having an unknown ~. 2. too bad to be ~d. **~·ly** *adv.* that is to say: *Only one child, ~ly Mary, was absent.* '**~·sake** *n.* person with the same ~ as another.

nan·ny ['næni] *n.* (children's word for a) child's nurse.

¹nap [næp] *n.* short sleep (esp. during the day, not in bed). *be caught napping*, be taken by surprise, found not ready.

²**nap** [næp] *n.* surface of cloth, etc., consisting of soft short hairs or fibres, smoothed and brushed up.

na·palm ['neipɑ:m] *n.* ~ *bomb*, one containing petrol jelly.

nape [neip] *n.* back (of the neck).

naph·tha ['næfθə] *n.* liquid made from coal-tar, used for burning, for cleaning clothes, etc. ~**·lene** ['næfθəli:n] *n.* strong-smelling substance made from coal-tar, used for keeping insects out of clothes, etc.

nap·kin ['næpkin] *n.* 1. (table-~) piece of cloth used at meals for protecting clothing, for wiping lips, etc. 2. (colloq. *nappy*) towel folded between a baby's legs.

nar·cis·sus [nɑ:'sisəs] *n.* (pl. -*si* [-ai]). sorts of bulb plant with white or yellow flowers in spring.

nar·cot·ic [nɑ:'kɔtik] *n. & adj.* (substance) producing sleep or other insensible condition; harmful drug.

nar·rate [nə'reit] *v.t.* tell (a story); give an account of. **nar·ra·tor** *n.* **nar·ra·tive** ['nærətiv] *adj. & n.* (of, in the form of) story-telling; story.

nar·row ['nærou] *adj.* (-*er*, -*est*). 1. measuring little across in comparison with length. 2. small, limited: *a ~ circle of friends*. 3. with a small margin: *a ~ escape from death; by a ~ majority*. 4. strict, exact: *a ~ search*. ~**·ly** *adv.* 1. only just; with little to spare. 2. closely; carefully. '~**·mind·ed** *adj.* having no or little sympathy for other persons' opinions, beliefs, etc. ~**·ness** *n.*

na·sal ['neizl] *adj.* of the nose.

nas·ty ['nɑ:sti] *adj.* (-*ier*, -*iest*). 1. dirty; unpleasant. 2. threatening; dangerous; awkward(1).

na·tal ['neitl] *adj.* of birth.

na·tion ['neiʃən] *n.* body of people with a common language, history, and government. ~**·al** ['næʃənl] *adj.* of, common to a, ~. *n.* person of a certain ~: *British ~als in China*. ~**·al·ism** *n.* 1. political movement for ~al self-government. 2. strong devotion to one's ~. ~**·al·ist** *n.*

supporter of ~alism (1). ~**·al·i·ty** [,næʃə'næliti] *n.* being a member of a ~: *men of French ~ality*. ~**·al·ize** ['næʃənəlaiz] *v.t.* 1. transfer (e.g. land) from private to State ownership. 2. make into a ~. ~**·al·i·za·tion** [,næʃənəlai'zeiʃən] *n.*

na·tive ['neitiv] *adj.* 1. of the place, circumstances, etc., of one's birth: *This is my own, my ~ land!* 2. (of qualities) belonging to a person by nature, not by education: *Rather than instruct a lawyer to defend him he relied on his ~ wit.* 3. (of plants and animals) belonging by origin (to): *plants ~ to America.* *n.* 1. person belonging by birth to a place or country: *a ~ of Wales.* 2. animal or plant natural to and having its origin in a certain region: *The kangaroo is a ~ of Australia.*

na·tiv·i·ty [nə'tiviti] *n.* birth. *the N~*, the birth of Jesus Christ: *a Nativity play* (about the N~).

nat·u·ral ['nætʃərəl] *adj.* 1. of, concerned with, produced by, nature(1), (2): ~ *forces* (e.g. storms); ~ *history* (e.g. botany); *animals living in their* ~ (i.e. wild) *state.* 2. of, in agreement with, the nature(5) of a living thing: *a ~ orator; her ~ abilities.* 3. ordinary; normal; to be expected: *to die a ~ death*, not by violence, etc. *It is ~ for a bird to fly.* 4. simple, not cultivated or self-conscious: *speaking in a ~ voice; ~ behaviour.* ~**·ly** *adv.* 1. in a ~(3), (4) way. 2. by nature(5). 3. of course; as might be expected. ~**·ist** *n.* student of ~ history.

nat·u·ral·ize ['nætʃrəlaiz] *v.t.* 1. give (sb. from another country) rights of citizenship: *to become a ~d British subject.* 2. take (a word) from one language into another. **nat·u·ral·i·za·tion** [,nætʃrəlai'zeiʃən] *n.*

na·ture ['neitʃə*] *n.* 1. the whole universe and every created thing: ~ *study*, the study of plants, insects, animals, etc.; ~ *worship* (e.g. of trees, oceans, wind). 2. the forces that control life, weather, etc., in the world : *mankind's struggle against ~*. **3.** simple life without civilization, cultivation, etc.: *in a state of ~*, naked. **4.** essential qualities: *studying the ~ of gases*. **5.** general characteristics of a living thing: *a girl with a kind ~*; *proud by ~*; *human ~*; *good ~*, kindness, unselfishness. *It is the ~ of dogs to bark*. class: *things of this ~*; *in the ~ of*, almost the same as. **'good·'na·tured, 'ill-'na·tured** *adj.* having a good (ill) ~ (5).

naught [nɔːt] *n.* nothing.

naugh·ty ['nɔːti] *adj.* (*-ier, -iest*). (of children, their behaviour, etc.) disobedient; causing trouble; bad; wrong. **naugh·ti·ly** *adv.* **naugh·ti·ness** *n.*

nau·sea ['nɔːsjə] *n.* feeling of sickness (e.g. caused by bad food) or disgust. **nau·se·ous** ['nɔːsiəs] *adj.* disgusting. **nau·seate** ['nɔːsjeit] *v.t.* cause ~ to.

nau·ti·cal ['nɔːtikl] *adj.* of ships, sailors, or navigation.

na·val ['neivl] *adj.* of a navy: ~ *officers* (*warfare*).

nave [neiv] *n.* central part of a church where the congregation sits.

na·vel ['neivl] *n.* small depression in the surface of the belly.

nav·i·gate ['nævigeit] *v.t.* direct the course of (a ship or aircraft); sail or steam along (a river) or across (a sea). **nav·i·ga·ble** ['nævigəbl] *adj.* that can be ~d; (of ships) in good condition for sailing, etc. **nav·i·ga·tion** [,nævi'geiʃən] *n.* science of navigating. **nav·i·ga·tor** *n.*

nav·vy ['nævi] *n.* unskilled workman employed in making roads, canals, railways, etc.

na·vy ['neivi] *n.* a country's warships; their officers and men. ~ *blue*, dark blue.

nay [nei] *particle & adv.* (old) No; not only that, but also.

neap(-tide) ['niːp('taid)] *n.* tide when high-water level is at its lowest.

near [niə*] *adv., prep., & adj.* **I.** *adv.* (*-er, -est*). (contrasted with *far*) within a short distance

in space or time: *The station is quite ~*; *it is only two minutes' walk*. *The summer holidays are drawing ~*; *they start next week*. *He lives ~ by* (~ *at hand*). **II.** *prep.* Don't go ~ *the edge of the cliff, you may fall over it*. *It's getting ~ dinner-time*. **III.** *adj.* (*-er, -est*). **1.** close in relationship: *She's a ~ relative of mine. They are our ~ and dear friends*. **2.** (contrasted with *off*) on the side (of a vehicle or animal that runs) closer to the edge of the roadway (in Great Britain, the left side). **3.** ungenerous. *a ~ thing*, a narrow escape. *v.t. & i.* come ~ (to): *a ship ~ing land*. ~**·ly** *adv.* **1.** almost: *~ly six o'clock*. **2.** *not ~ly* (*enough*), far from (enough). ~**·ness** *n.*

neat [niːt] *adj.* (*-er, -est*). **1.** (liking to have everything) tidy, in good order with nothing out of place; done carefully: *a ~ worker* (*desk*); ~ *writing*. **2.** simple and pleasant; in good taste: *a ~ dress*. **3.** cleverly said or done: *a ~ answer* (*trick*). **4.** (of wines and spirits) unmixed with water. ~**·ly** *adv.* ~**·ness** *n.*

neb·u·la ['nebjulə] *n.* (pl. *-lae* [-liː]). group of very distant stars, mass of gas, seen in the night sky as an indistinct patch of light. **neb·u·lous** ['nebjuləs] *adj.* cloud-like; indistinct; vague.

nec·es·sa·ry ['nesisəri] *adj.* which has to be done; which must be; which cannot be done without or escaped from: *Sleep is ~ to health*. *n.* (usu. pl.) things ~ for living. **nec·es·sa·ri·ly** *adv.* as *a ~ result*. **nec·es·si·tate** [ni-'sesiteit] *v.t.* make ~. **nec·es·si·tous** [ni'sesitəs] *adj.* poor; needy. **nec·es·si·ty** [ni'sesiti] *n.* **1.** urgent need: *driven to steal by necessity; for use in case of necessity*. **2.** sth. that is ~: *Food and warmth are necessities*. **3.** condition of being poor: *in necessity*.

neck [nek] *n.* **1.** part of the body that connects the shoulders and the head. ~ and ~, (of competitors in a race) running level, side by side; ~ or nothing, with the alternative of complete victory or defeat; ~ and crop, roughly and thoroughly. **2.** anything like a ~ in shape: *the ~ of a bottle*. ~**·band** *n.* part of a shirt, etc., that goes round the ~. ~**·lace** *n.* string of beads, pearls, etc., worn round the ~ as an ornament. ~**·tie** *n.* narrow band of material worn with a collar and knotted in front.

A necklace   A necktie

nec·tar ['nektə*] *n.* sweet liquid in flowers, gathered by bees.

née [nei] (French) *adj.* (of a married woman) whose family name, before her marriage, was . . . : *Mrs Williams, née Jones.*

need [ni:d] *v.* **1.** want; require; be in need of; be necessary: *They ~ more food. His coat ~s mending.* **2.** be obliged to: *N~ you go home yet? No, I ~ not (~n't).* *n.* **1.** the condition of being without sth. that is necessary: *in ~ of money.* **2.** circumstances making sth. necessary: *no ~ to hurry.* **3.** sth. that is wanted or necessary: *earning enough for one's ~s.* ~**·ful** *adj.* necessary. ~**·less** *adj.* unnecessary. **needs** *adv.* (only in) *must ~s* or *~s must,* be compelled to, have to (do sth.). ~**·y** *adj.* (*-ier, -iest*). poor; not having what is necessary for living.

need·le ['ni:dl] *n.* **1.** small, thin pointed steel instrument with a hole (called *eye*) at one end for thread, used in sewing and darning. **2.** longer, thin needle-like instrument without an eye, of wood, bone, steel, etc., for

knitting. **3.** pointer in a compass or on the dial of a meter or gauge. **4.** ~-like part of a syringe. **5.** ~-like leaf (of pine and fir trees). '~·**woman** *n.* one who does ~work. '~·**work** *n.* sewing.

ne'er [neə*] *adv.* (poet.) never. ~**-do-well** ['neədu:wel] *n.* useless or good-for-nothing person.

ne·ga·tion [ni'geiʃən] *n.* act of denying: *Shaking the head is a sign of ~.*

neg·a·tive ['negətiv] *adj.* **1.** (of words and answers) indicating *no* or *not* (opp. *positive*). **2.** expressing the absence of clearly marked qualities: ~ *virtue.* **3.** (maths.) (of a quantity) that has to be subtracted from another or from zero (0): ~ *quantities.* **4.** ~ *electricity,* the kind produced at the cathode of a cell (4). **5.** (photography) with light and dark reversed. *n.* **1.** ~ word or statement. **2.** (maths.) ~ quantity. **3.** (photography) developed film or plate from which (positive) prints are made. *v.t.* **1.** prove (a theory, etc.) to be untrue. **2.** make useless; act against.

neg·lect [ni'glekt] *v.t.* **1.** fail to pay attention to; disregard. **2.** leave undone (what one ought to do); omit (to do sth.). *n.* ~ing or being ~ed: ~ *of duty; in a state of ~.* ~**·ful** *adj.* in the habit of ~ing.

neg·li·gent ['neglidʒənt] *adj.* taking too little care. ~**·ly** *adv.* **neg·li·gence** *n.* **neg·li·gi·ble** ['neglidʒəbl] *adj.* that need not be considered; of little or no importance or size.

ne·go·ti·ate [ni'gouʃieit] *v.i. & t.* **1.** discuss (sth. *with* sb.) in order to come to an agreement. **2.** arrange (*for* a sale, loan, etc.) by discussion; get or give money for (cheques, bonds, etc.). **3.** get past or over (an obstacle, etc.). **ne·go·ti·a·ble** *adj.* that can be ~d (3); (of cheques, etc.) that can be exchanged for cash. **ne·go·ti·a·tion** [ni,gouʃi'eiʃən] *n.*

Ne·gro ['ni:grou] *n.* (pl. *-oes*).

member (or, outside Africa, descendant) of one of the African races south of the Sahara. **Ne'gress** ['niːgris] *n.* woman ~.

neigh [nei] *v.i. & n.* (make the) cry of a horse.

neigh·bour ['neibə*] *n.* person living in a house, street, etc., near oneself; person, thing, or country that is near(est) another. ~·**hood** *n.* 1. (people living in a) district; area near the place, etc., referred to: *in the ~hood of Leeds* (*the post office*). 2. condition of being near. ~·**ing** *adj.* that border(s) upon: *~ing countries.* ~·**ly** *adj.* friendly. ~·**li·ness** *n.*

nei·ther ['naidə*, 'niːdə*] *adj. & pron.* (cf. *either*) not one nor the other (of two): *N~ statement is true. I like ~ of them. adv. & conj.* 1. ~ . . . *nor: He ~ knows nor cares what happened. N~ you nor I could have done this.* 2. nor; and not; no more than : *If you don't go, ~ shall I. I don't like it, ~ does she.*

nem. con. ['nem'kɔn] (abbreviated from Latin) *adv.* unanimously; without any objection : *The vote was carried ~.*

ne·me·sis ['nemisis] *n.* just punishment for wrongdoing; deserved fate.

neo- [niːou] *prefix.* new, later. ~·**lith·ic** [ˌniːou'liθik] *adj.* of the new or later stone age.

ne·on ['niːɔn] *n.* gas forming a very small proportion of the atmosphere, used in lamps for some electric signs.

neph·ew ['nevjuː] *n.* son of one's brother or sister.

nep·o·tism ['nepətizm] *n.* the giving of special favour (esp. employment) by a person in high position to his relatives.

nerve [nəːv] *n.* 1. fibre or bundle of fibres carrying feelings and impulses between the brain and parts of the body. 2. (pl.) condition of being easily excited, worried, irritated : *noises that get on my ~s* (i.e. worry me); *suffering from ~s.* 3. quality of being bold, self-reliant, etc.: *have enough ~ to drive a racing car;*

lose one's ~, become nervous(2). 4. (old use) sinew : *strain every ~,* make the utmost effort (to do sth.). *v.t.* give strength to : *~ oneself for a task* (*to face trouble*). ~·**less** *adj.* without energy or strength. **nerv·ous** ['nəːvəs] *adj.* 1. of the ~s : *the nervous system.* 2. having or showing ~s(2). **nerv·y** *adj.* (colloq.) = nervous(2).

nest [nest] *n.* 1. place made or chosen by a bird for its eggs; kind of place in which certain living things have and keep their young: *a wasps' ~.* 2. comfortable place : *a ~ of soft cushions.* 3. number of like things (esp. boxes, tables) fitting one inside another. *v.i.* make and use a ~. '~-**egg** *n.* sum of money saved for future use.

nes·tle ['nesl] *v.i. & t.* settle comfortably and warmly : *~ down among the cushions*; press oneself lovingly: *nestling closely to its mother.* **nest·ling** ['nesliŋ] *n.* bird too young to leave the nest. (Cf. *fledgeling.*)

¹**net** [net] *n.* open-work material of knotted string, hair, wire, etc.; such material made up for a special purpose : *fishing net; tennis net; mosquito net. v.t.* (*-tt-*). catch (fish, animals, etc.) with or in a net; cover (e.g. fruit trees) with a net. **net·ting** *n.* net material: *windows screened with wire netting.* '**net·work** *n.* complex system of lines that cross : *a network of railways* (*canals*); connected system : *a network of radio stations.*

²**net** [net] *adj.* remaining when nothing more is to be taken away : *net profit* (when working expenses have been deducted); *net price* (the lowest to be charged); *net weight* (of the contents only). *v.t.* (*-tt-*). gain as a net profit.

neth·er ['neðə*] *adj.* (old use) lower.

net·tle ['netl] *n.* common wild plant with leaves that sting when touched. *v.t.* (fig.) make rather angry; annoy.

neu·ral·gia [njuə'rældʒə] *n.*

sharp jumping pain in the nerves, esp. of the face and head.

neu·rot·ic [njuə'rɒtik] *n. & adj.* (person) suffering from nervous disorder; too nervous.

neu·ter ['nju:tə*] *adj.* (of plants) without male or female parts; (of words) neither feminine nor masculine.

neu·tral ['nju:trəl] *adj.* **1.** helping neither side in a war or quarrel; belonging to a ~ country: ~ *territory.* **2.** having no definite characteristics, not clearly one (colour, etc.) nor another. **3.** neither acid nor alkali. *n.* ~ (1) person, country. ~**i·ty** [nju:'træliti] *n.* state of being ~, esp. in war. ~**ize** ['nju:trəlaiz] *v.t.* **1.** make ~: *to ~ize a border territory.* **2.** take away the effect or special quality of sth. by means of sth. with an opposite effect or quality.

nev·er ['nevə*] *adv.* **1.** at no time; on no occasion. **2.** an emphatic substitute for *not*: *That will ~ happen if I can prevent it.* **3.** *N~ mind!* Don't worry about that. *Well, I ~!* How surprising! ~**more** *adv.* ~ again. ~**the·less** [,nevəðə'les] *conj.* in spite of that; yet.

new [nju:] *adj.* (**-er, -est**). **1.** not existing before; seen or heard of for the first time; recently introduced, etc. **2.** existing before, but only now discovered, etc. **3.** unfamiliar; freshly arrived. **4.** beginning again: *a new moon*; *a Happy New Year. adv.* newly; recently; just: *newcomers*, those recently arrived; *new-laid eggs*; *new-fangled*, new, strange and unwelcome. **new·ly** *adv.* recently; in a new way. **new·ness** *n.*

news [nju:z] *n.* report or account of what has recently happened, of new facts, etc.: *a piece of interesting ~.* '~**a·gent** *n.* shopkeeper selling ~papers, periodicals, etc. '~**boy** *n.* boy selling ~papers on the street. ~**paper** ['nju:s,peipə*] *n.* set of printed and folded sheets containing news, literary articles, etc., usu. one published daily.

'~**-reel** *n.* cinema film of recent events.

newt [nju:t] *n.* small lizard-like animal living in water.

next [nekst] **I.** *adj. & n.* **1.** coming nearest or immediately after, in space or in order. *I'm first, who's ~? Take the ~ turning to the right. Who lives ~ door?* **2.** immediately following in time: *We are going ~ Friday.* **II.** *adv.* **1.** after this (or that); then: *When you have finished this, what are you going to do ~?* **2.** in the nearest place (to): *Come and sit ~ to me.* **III.** *prep.* (= next to): *My seat is ~ to the door. ~ door, as next to the ~ house. ~ door to,* (fig.) almost.

nib [nib] *n.* pointed metal tip of a pen.

nib·ble ['nibl] *v.t. & i.* take tiny bites (*at*): *fish nibbling (at) the bait. n.* the act of nibbling (*at*).

nice [nais] *adj.* (**-r, -st**). **1.** pleasant; agreeable; good. **2.** needing care, exactness (in judging, deciding sth.). **3.** particular; fussy: *too ~ about one's food.* ~**ly** *adv.* **ni·ce·ty** ['naisiti] *n.* **1.** exactness; quality of doing things with delicate care: *~ty of judgement.* **2.** delicate distinction: *the ~ties of criticism; to a ~ty,* without error or misjudgement.

niche [nitʃ] *n.* recess (often with a shelf) in a wall, usu. for a statue or ornament; (fig.) suitable or fitting position: *to find the right ~ for oneself* (i.e. a position offering work that one can do well).

A niche

nick [nik] *v.t. & n.* (make a) small V-shaped cut (in sth.), esp. as a record. *in the ~ of time,* only just in time.

nick·el ['nikl] *n.* silver-white metal used in alloys; (U.S.A.) coin worth 5 cents.

nick·name ['nikneim] *n.* name given in addition to or altered from or used instead of the real name. *v.t.* give a ~ to.

nic·o·tine ['nikəti:n] *n.* poisonous liquid in tobacco leaves.

niece [ni:s] *n.* daughter of one's brother or sister.

nig·gard·ly ['nigədli] *adj.* ungenerous.

nigh [nai] *adv. & prep.* (old use) near (to).

night [nait] *n.* the dark hours between one day and the next. *all* ~ (*long*), throughout the whole ~. *Good* ~*!*, parting wish on going to bed or going home late. *Have you had a good* ~ (slept well)? *at* ~, during the ~. ~ *and day*, continuously. *make a* ~ *of it*, pass the ~ in pleasure-making, esp. at a party. '~**-dress**, '~**-gown** *n.* long, loose garment worn by a woman or a child in bed. '~**-fall** *n.* end of daylight. ~**·ly** *adj. & adv.* done, happening, at ~ or every ~. '~**·mare** *n.* terrible dream; horrible experience. '~**·shirt** *n.* long shirt formerly worn by a man or a boy in bed. '~**·watch·man** *n.* man employed to be on guard (e.g. in a factory) during the ~.

night·in·gale ['naitiŋgeil] *n.* small bird which sings sweetly at night as well as during the day.

nil [nil] *n.* nothing: *The result of the game was three–nil.*

nim·ble ['nimbl] *adj.* (-*r*, -*st*). quick-moving: *as* ~ *as a goat*; (of the mind) quick to understand; sharp. **nim·bly** *adv.*

nin·com·poop ['ninkəmpu:p] *n.* fool.

nine [nain] *n. & adj.* 9. *a* ~ *days' wonder*, sth. that excites attention for a few days only. ~**teen** ['nain'ti:n] *n. & adj.* 19. **ninth** [nainθ] *n. & adj.* next in order after *eighth*; ⅑. **nine·ti·eth** ['naintiiθ] *n. & adj.* 90th; 1/90. ~**·ty** *n. & adj.* 90.

nine·pins ['nainpinz] *n. pl.* game in which a ball is rolled along the ground at nine bottle-shaped pieces of wood.

¹nip [nip] *n.* **1.** small, quick bite or pinch. **2.** *a nip in the air*, a feeling of frost. *v.t. & i.* (-*pp*-). **1.** give a nip to. **2.** (of frost, etc.) stop the growth of; (esp. fig.) *nip in the bud*, stop the development of. **3.** (colloq.) hurry: *nip along* (*off, in*). **nip·per** *n.* **1.** (pl., colloq.) pincers, forceps, etc. **2.** (colloq.) small child.

²nip [nip] *n.* small drink (esp. of brandy or other spirits).

nip·ple ['nipl] *n.* part of the breast through which milk comes; thing shaped like a ~.

ni·tre ['naitə*] *n.* salt obtained from potash, used in making gunpowder. **ni·trate** ['naitreit] *n.* salt of nitric acid, esp. the kind used as fertilizer. **ni·tric** ['naitrik] *adj.* *nitric acid*, powerful acid that destroys most metals. **ni·tro·gen** ['naitrədʒən] *n.* gas without colour, taste, or smell, forming about four-fifths of air. **ni·tro·glyc·er·ine** [,naitrou'glisəri:n] *n.* powerful explosive.

no. ['nʌmbə*] *n.* number: *No. 7.*

no [nou] *adj., adv. & particle.* **I.** *adj.* **1.** not one, not any: *They have no food and will starve. We must go this way, because there is no other.* **2.** indicating the opposite of the following word: *He's no fool* (i.e. he's a clever man). *We got there in no time* (i.e. quickly). **3.** *No smoking!* (Smoking is not allowed here.) **II.** *adv.* not any: *We can go no farther* (we must stop here). **III.** *particle.* opp. *yes. Is it Monday today? No, it's Tuesday.*

no·ble ['noubl] *adj.* (-*r*, -*st*). **1.** having, showing, high character and qualities. **2.** (of families) of high rank or birth: *men of* ~ *rank.* **3.** splendid; that excites admiration: ~ *buildings.* *n.* person of ~ (2) birth; peer. **no·bil·i·ty** [nou'biliti] *n.* **1.** the ~s as a class. **2.** quality of being ~. **no·bly** *adv.* ~**·man** *n.* = noble.

no·bod·y ['noubədi] *n.* not any-body; no person. *a mere* ~, a person of no importance.

noc·tur·nal [nɔk'tə:nl] *adj.* of, in, or done, active, or happening in, the night.

nod [nɔd] *v.t. & i.* (-dd-). **1.** bow (the head) slightly and quickly as a sign of agreement or as a familiar greeting. *have a nodding acquaintance with*, have a slight acquaintance with or knowledge of. **2.** let the head fall forward when sleepy or when falling asleep. *n.* nodding movement (of the head). *the land of nod*, sleep.

No·el [nou'el] *n.* Christmas.

noise [nɔiz] *n.* sound, esp. loud, unpleasant sound. ~**·less** *adj.* silent. **nois·y** *adj.* (-ier, -iest). making much ~; full of ~. **nois·i·ly** *adv.*

noi·some ['nɔisəm] *adj.* offensive; (esp. of smell) disgusting.

no·mad ['noumæd] *n.* member of a tribe that wanders with no fixed home. **no·mad·ic** [nou-'mædik] *adj.* of ~s.

no·men·cla·ture [nou'menklə-tʃə*] *n.* system of naming: *botanical* ~.

nom·i·nal ['nɔminl] *adj.* **1.** existing, etc., in name or word only, not in fact: *the* ~ *ruler*; *the* ~ *value of shares.* **2.** *a* ~ *sum* (*rent*), one much below actual value given or received. ~**·ly** *adv.*

nom·i·nate ['nɔmineit] *v.t.* put forward sb.'s name for election to a position: ~ *sb. for the Presidency*, **nom·i·na·tion** [,nɔmi'neiʃən] *n.* (right of) nominating. **nom·i·na·tive** ['nɔminətiv] *adj. & n.* (of the) form of a n. or adj. when it is the subject of a sentence. **nom·i·nee** [,nɔmi'ni:] *n.* person ~d.

non- [nɔn] *prefix.* who (which) is not, who (which) does not, etc.: *non-smokers*; *non-combatant*, not taking part in fighting; *non-commissioned officers*, not having commissions (4); *non-committal*, not showing or giving a definite decision, etc.; *nonconformist*, Protestant not conforming to

the ritual, etc., of an established (4) church.

nonce [nɔns] *n. for the* ~, for the present only.

non·cha·lant ['nɔnʃələnt] *adj.* not having, or not showing, in-terest or enthusiasm.

non·de·script ['nɔndiskript] *n. & adj.* (person or thing) not easily classed, not having a definite character.

none [nʌn] *pron.* not any; not one: *Is there any beer in the house? No, (there's)* ~ *(at all). We invited several friends, but* ~ *came. N*~ *of them have (has) come yet. adv.* (only with com-paratives and *too*) not at all: ~ *too plentiful*; ~ *the worse for his experiences.*

non·en·ti·ty [nɔ'nentiti] *n.* un-important person.

non·plus ['nɔn'plʌs] *v.t.* (-ss-). surprise or puzzle (sb.) so much that he does not know what to do or say.

non·sense ['nɔnsəns] *n.* mean-ingless words; foolish talk, ideas, behaviour. **non·sen·si·cal** [nɔn'sensikl] *adj.*

¹noo·dle ['nu:dl] *n.* (pl.) mixture of flour and eggs prepared in long strips, used in soups, etc.

²noo·dle ['nu:dl] *n.* foolish person.

nook [nuk] *n.* quiet, out-of-the-way place; inside corner.

noon [nu:n] *n.* 12 o'clock in the middle of the day. '~**·day,** '~**·tide** *n.* (time about) ~.

noose [nu:s] *n.* loop of rope (with a running knot) that becomes tighter when the rope is pulled: *the hangman's* ~.

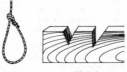

A noose   Notches

nor [nɔ:*] *conj.* **1.** (after *neither* or *not*) and not: *I should like to have a holiday, but can find neither the time nor the money. I have not the time nor the money* *to go on holiday.* **2.** and ... not : *He can't do it, nor can I.*

nor·mal ['nɔ:ml] *adj.* in agreement with what is representative, usual or regular. ~ *school,* one for training school-teachers. *n.* above (below) ~, above (below) what is ~. **~·ly** *adv.*

north [nɔ:θ] *n., adj., & adv.* **1.** one of the four cardinal points of the compass ; direction towards which the magnetic needle turns. **2.** situated in, coming from, etc., the N~. **~·er·ly** ['nɔ:ðəli] *adj. & adv.* (of winds) from the ~ ; towards the ~ ; in or to the ~. **~·ern** ['nɔ:ðən] *adj.* in or of the ~. **~·ward(s)** ['nɔ:θwəd(z)] *adv.* towards the ~.

nose [nouz] *n.* **1.** part of the face above the mouth, serving as the organ of smell. *pay through the* ~, pay a very high price. *poke one's* ~ *into sth.,* be inquisitive about it. **2.** sense of smell. *v.t. & i.* **1.** smell (*about, for*) ; discover by smelling : *The dog* ~*d out a rat.* **2.** go forward carefully : *a ship nosing (its way) through the ice.* **'~·dive** *v.i. & n.* (of an aircraft)(make a) quick descent with the ~ of the plane pointing to the earth. **'~·gay** *n.* bunch of cut flowers. **nos·y, nos·ey** *adj.* inquisitive.

nos·tal·gia [nɔs'tældʒə] *n.* homesickness ; longing for sth. one has known.

nos·tril ['nɔstril] *n.* either of the two openings into the nose.

not [nɔt] *adv.* used to make a finite verb negative (often contracted to *n't* as in *hasn't*): *Have they gone yet? Haven't they gone yet? They have not gone yet.*

no·ta·ble ['noutəbl] *adj.* deserving to be noticed ; worthy of attention. **no·ta·bly** *adv.* **no·ta·bil·i·ty** [,noutə'biliti] *n.* (esp.) important person.

no·ta·ry ['noutəri] *n.* (often ~ *public*) official with authority to do certain kinds of legal business, esp. to record that he has witnessed the signing of legal documents.

no·ta·tion [nou'teifən] *n.* system of signs or symbols representing numbers, amounts, musical notes, etc., e.g. Roman numerals, I, II, III, etc.

notch [nɔtʃ] *v.t. & n.* (make a) V-shaped cut (*in* or *on* sth.). See the picture on page 346.

note [nout] *n.* **1.** short record (of facts, etc.) made to help the memory. **2.** short letter : *a ~ of thanks* ; ~*paper* (for writing letters on) ; letter from one government to another. **3.** short comment on or explanation of a word or passage in a book. **4.** written or printed promise to pay money : *bank-~s* ; *a £5* ~ ; *a promissory* ~. **5.** single sound of a certain pitch and duration ; sign (e.g. ♩, ♪) used to represent such a sound in printed music ; any one of the keys of a piano or organ. **6.** quality (esp. of voice) showing the nature of sth., a feeling : *a ~ of self-satisfaction in his speech.* **7.** sign or mark used in writing and printing : ~ *of exclamation* (!). **8.** distinction ; importance : *a family of* ~. **9.** notice ; attention : *worthy of* ~. *Take* ~ *of what I say. v.t.* **1.** notice ; pay attention to. **2.** ~ *sth. down,* write down ; make a ~(1) of. **not·ed** ['noutid] *adj.* well-known ; famous. **~·worthy** ['nout,wə:ði] *adj.* deserving attention.

noth·ing ['nʌθiŋ] *n.* not anything. *come to* ~, fail, have no result or success. *make* ~ *of,* be unable to understand, fail to use (e.g. opportunities), treat as unimportant. *There is* ~ *for it but to ...,* the only possible way is to ... ; *we can only. ... adv.* not at all ; in no way : *The house is* ~ *near as large as I expected.*

no·tice ['noutis] *n.* **1.** (written or printed) news of sth. about to happen or sth. that has happened : *to put up a* ~ ; *a* ~*-board.* **2.** warning, esp. warning given to or by sb. about the ending of an agreement (e.g. to a servant by an employer, to a tenant by the house-owner) : *to give a* *servant a month's* ～ ; *at short* ～, with little warning. **3.** short particulars of a new book, play, etc., in a periodical. **4.** attention : *Take no* ～ *of* (pay no attention to) *what they say. Bring it to the* ～ *of the manager.* **v.t. & i.** take ～ of ; see. ～·a·ble **adj.** easily seen or ～d.

no·ti·fy ['noutifai] **v.t.** give notice of ; report (*to*) : *to* ～ *a loss to the police* (～ *the police of a loss*). no·ti·fi·a·ble **adj.** that must be notified (esp. of certain diseases which must be reported to the health authorities). no·ti·fi·ca·tion [ˌnoutifi'keiʃən] **n.**

no·tion ['nouʃən] **n.** idea ; opinion.

no·to·ri·ous [nou'tɔ:riəs] **adj.** widely known (esp. for sth. bad). no·to·ri·e·ty [ˌnoutə'raiəti] **n.**

not·with·stand·ing [ˌnotwið'stændiŋ] **prep.** in spite of. **conj.** although.

nought [nɔ:t] **n.** nothing ; 0.

noun [naun] **n.** (grammar) word by which a person, thing, quality, etc., is named.

nour·ish ['nʌriʃ] **v.t. 1.** make or keep strong with food. **2.** have or encourage (hope, hatred, etc.). ～·ment **n.** food ; power of ～ing.

¹nov·el ['nɔvl] **adj.** strange ; of a new kind not previously known. ～·ty **n. 1.** newness ; strangeness. **2.** previously unknown thing, idea, etc. ; (pl.) new kinds of fancy goods, toys, etc.

²nov·el ['nɔvl] **n.** made-up story in prose, long enough to fill one or more books, about either imaginary or historical people. ～·ist **n.** writer of ～s.

No·vem·ber [nou'vembə*] **n.** the eleventh month of the year.

nov·ice ['nɔvis] **n.** person who is still learning and who is without experience, esp. person who is to become a monk or a nun. no·vit·i·ate [nou'viʃiit] **n.** period of being a ～.

now [nau] **adv.** at the present time ; in the present circumstances. *now and again, now and then*, from time to time, sometimes. *Now then! Now, now!* used as a friendly warning or protest. **conj.** through or because of the fact (that) : *Now (that) you mention it, I do remember seeing you at the theatre.*

now·a·days ['nauədeiz] **adv.** in these days ; at the present time.

no·where ['nouhwɛə*] **adv.** not anywhere.

nox·ious ['nɔkʃəs] **adj.** harmful.

noz·zle ['nɔzl] **n.** metal end of a hose or bellows.

A nozzle

nu·cle·us ['nju:kliəs] **n.** (pl. *nuclei* ['nju:kliai]). central part, round which other parts are grouped or round which other things collect. nu·cle·ar **adj.** of a ～ : *nuclear physics*, science dealing with the nuclei of atoms and atomic energy.

nude [nju:d] **adj.** unclothed. **n.** ～ human figure (in art). nud·ist ['nju:dist] **n.** person who believes that exposing the naked body to sun and air is beneficial.

nudge [nʌdʒ] **v.t.** push slightly with the elbow to attract attention. **n.** push given in this way.

nug·get ['nʌgit] **n.** lump of metal, esp. gold, as found in the earth.

nui·sance ['nju:səns] **n.** thing, person, act, etc., that causes trouble or offence.

null [nʌl] **adj.** of no effect or force : ～ *and void*, (legal) without legal effect. nul·li·fy **v.t.** make ～.

numb [nʌm] **v.t. & adj.** (make) without power to feel or move : *fingers* ～(*ed*) *with cold* ; ～ *with grief*.

num·ber ['nʌmbə*] **n. 1.** 1, 13, and 103 are ～s. **2.** quantity or amount : *a large* ～ *of people* ; *fifteen in* ～ ; *times without* ～, very often. **3.** one issue of a periodical, esp. for one day, week, etc. : *the current* ～ ; *a back* ～, (also fig.) out-of-date person or thing. **4.** dance, song, etc., for the stage. *v.t.* **1.** give a ~ to; put a ~ on. **2.** add up to. **3.** ~ (*sb.*) *among*, include him, regard him as being, among. **~·less** *adj.* more than can be counted.

nu·mer·al ['nju:mərəl] *n.* word or sign standing for a number. **nu·mer·a·tor** ['nju:məreitə*] *n.* number above the line in a fraction, e.g. 3 in ¾. **nu·mer·i·cal** [nju:'merikl] *adj.* of, in, connected with, numbers. **nu·mer·ous** ['nju:mərəs] *adj.* very many; great in number.

num·skull ['nʌmskʌl] *n.* stupid person.

nun [nʌn] *n.* woman who, after taking religious vows, lives, with other women, a secluded life in the service of God. **nun·ner·y** *n.* house of nuns; convent.

nun·ci·o ['nʌnʃiou] *n.* ambassador or representative of the Pope in a foreign country.

nup·tial ['nʌpʃəl] *adj.* of marriage: ~ *bliss.* **nup·tials** *n. pl.* wedding.

nurse [nə:s] *n.* **1.** woman who looks after babies and small children for a living. **2.** person (usu. trained) who cares for people who are ill or injured: *hospital ~s.* *v.t.* **1.** act as a ~ (2). **2.** feed (a baby) at the breast. **3.** hold (a baby) in the arms or on the lap. **4.** look after carefully, try to cause the growth of (e.g. a new business). **nurs·er·y** ['nə:səri] *n.* **1.** room for the special use of young children. *~ry rhymes*, poems or songs for young children. **2.** place where young plants and trees are raised. **nurs·er·y·man** *n.* man who owns a plant ~ry.

nur·ture ['nə:tʃə*] *n.* training; care; education (of children). *v.t.* give ~ to.

nut [nʌt] *n.* **1.** eatable seed with a hard shell: *walnut*; *groundnut*. **2.** small piece of metal for screwing on to the end of a bolt. **'nut·,crack·ers** *n. pl.* device for cracking nuts. **'nut·shell** *n. in a nutshell*, in the smallest

possible space, in the fewest possible words.

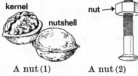

A nut (1)   A nut (2) and bolt

nut·meg ['nʌtmeg] *n.* hard nut of an East Indian tree, grated for use in flavouring food.

nu·tri·ment ['nju:trimənt] *n.* nourishing food. **nu·tri·tion** [nju:'triʃən] *n.* the process of supplying and receiving nourishment; the science of food values. **nu·tri·tious** [nju:'triʃəs] *adj.* having high value as food; nourishing.

nuz·zle ['nʌzl] *v.i. & t.* press or rub the nose (*against, into*); press the nose against: *The horse ~d (against) my shoulder.*

ny·lon ['nailən] *n.* man-made fibre used for making stockings, blouses, ropes, etc.

nymph [nimf] *n.* (Greek and Roman stories) one of the lesser goddesses, living in rivers, trees, hills, etc.

O

O, oh [ou] *int.* cry of surprise, fear, etc.

oak [ouk] *n.* (hard wood of) sorts of large tree common in many parts of the world.

oa·kum ['oukəm] *n.* loose fibre obtained by picking old ropes, used for filling spaces between boards of a ship.

oar [ɔ:*, ɔə*] *n.* pole with a flat blade used in rowing. **'oars·man** ['ɔ:zmən] *n.* person using an ~. See the picture on page 350.

o·a·sis [ou'eisis] *n.* (pl. *oases* [-si:z]). fertile place, with water and trees, in a desert.

An oarsman, rowing

oath [ouθ] *n.* (pl. *oaths* [ouðz]).
1. solemn undertaking with God's help to do sth.; solemn declaration that sth. is true: *take (make, swear) an ~; on (one's) ~, having taken an ~.* **2.** wrongful use of God's name or of sacred words to express strong feeling; swear-word.

oats [outs] *n. pl.* (seed grains of) plant grown in cool climates, providing food for men and horses. *sow one's wild ~,* lead an immoral life as a young man. *oatmeal,* ground ~.

ob·du·rate ['ɔbdjurit] *adj.* stubborn. **ob·du·ra·cy** ['ɔbdjurəsi] *n.*

o·be·dient [ou'bi:djənt] *adj.* doing, willing to do, what one is told to do. **~·ly** *adv.* **o·be·dience** *n.* being ~ : *in obedience to.*

o·bei·sance [ou'beisəns] *n.* deep ²bow (of respect or homage).

ob·e·lisk ['ɔbilisk] *n.* tall, pointed four-sided stone pillar, as a monument or landmark.

o·bese [ou'bi:s] *adj.* (of persons) very fat. **o·bes·i·ty** [ou'bi:siti] *n.*

o·bey [ou'bei] *v.t. & i.* do what one is told to do: *~ orders.*

o·bit·u·a·ry [ou'bitjuəri] *n.* printed notice of sb.'s death, often with a short account of his life.

¹ob·ject ['ɔbdʒikt] *n.* **1.** sth. that can be seen or touched; material thing: *an ~-lesson,* one (to be) taught or learnt from an example before the learner. **2.** person or thing to which action or feeling or thought is directed; purpose: *with no ~ in life; to succeed in one's ~; time (distance, money) no ~,* time (etc.) need not be considered.

²ob·ject [əb'dʒekt] *v.i.* say that one is not in favour of sth.; be opposed *(to)*: *He ~ed to working on Sundays.* **ob·jec·tion** [əb-'dʒekʃən] *n.* statement or feeling against sth.; cause of *~ing.* **ob·jec·tion·a·ble** *adj.* likely to be *~ed* to; unpleasant: *an ~ionable smell.* **ob·jec·tor** *n.* person who *~s* (to sth.): *conscientious ~or,* (usu.) man who objects to military service because of his religious beliefs, etc.

ob·jec·tive [əb'dʒektiv] *adj.* uninfluenced by thoughts and feelings; impersonal. *n.* object aimed at; purpose, esp. (military use) point to which armed forces are moving in order to capture it.

ob·la·tion [ou'bleiʃən] *n.* offering made to God or a god.

ob·li·ga·tion [,ɔbli'geiʃən] *n.* promise, duty, or condition that indicates what action ought to be taken (e.g. the power of the law, duty, a sense of what is right): *the ~s of good citizenship; under an ~ to sb. for his help* (i.e. feeling the need to repay him in some way). **ob·li·ga·to·ry** [əb'ligətəri] *adj.* that is necessary, required, by law, rule, or custom: *Is attendance at school obligatory?*

o·blige [ə'blaidʒ, ou-] *v.t.* **1.** bind by a promise; require (sb. to do sth.). **2.** do sth. for sb. as a favour or in answer to a request. *I'm much ~d to you,* I'm grateful to you for what you've done. **o·blig·ing** *adj.* willing to help.

ob·lique [ə'bli:k] *adj.* sloping; slanting. *~ angle,* any angle that is not a right angle (i.e. not 90°). (Cf. *acute, obtuse.*)

ob·lit·er·ate [ə'blitəreit] *v.t.* rub or blot out; remove all signs of; destroy. **ob·lit·er·a·tion** [əb,litə'reiʃən] *n.*

ob·liv·i·on [ə'blivian] *n.* state of being quite forgotten: *sink (fall) into ~.* **ob·liv·i·ous** [ə'blivias] *adj.* unaware *(of),* having no memory *(of).*

ob·long ['ɔblɔŋ] *n. & adj.* (figure) having four straight sides and angles of 90°, longer than it is wide.

ob·lo·quy ['ɔbləkwi] *n.* public shame or reproach.

ob·nox·ious [əb'nɔkʃəs] *adj.*
offensive; nasty.

ob·scene [ɔb'si:n] *adj.* (of words,
pictures, behaviour) likely to
arouse indecent thoughts, esp.
on sex. **ob·sce·ni·ty** *n.* ~ language, etc.

ob·scure [əb'skjuə*, ɔb-] *adj.* **1.**
dark; hidden; not clearly seen
or understood. **2.** not well
known: *an* ~ *young poet.* *v.t.*
make ~. **ob·scu·ri·ty** [əb'skjuə-
riti] *n.*

ob·se·quies ['ɔbsikwiz] *n. pl.*
funeral ceremonies.

ob·se·qui·ous [əb'si:kwiəs] *adj.*
too eager to obey, serve, show
respect.

ob·serve [əb'zə:v] *v.t. & i.* **1.**
see and notice; watch carefully.
2. pay attention to (laws, rules);
celebrate (festivals, birthdays,
anniversaries). **3.** say (*that*).
ob·serv·a·ble *adj.* that can be
or that deserves to be ~d (1).
ob·serv·ance *n.* observing (2)
(of a law, festival, etc.); act performed as part of a ceremony, as
a sign of respect or worship.
ob·serv·ant *adj.* quick at
noticing things; careful to ~ (1)
(laws, rules, etc.). **ob·serva-
tion** [,ɔbzə'veiʃən] *n.* **1.** observing or being ~d: *keep sb.
under observation,* watch him
carefully; *criminals trying to
avoid observation* (i.e. being
seen). **2.** remark, statement (on
what is ~d). **ob·serv·a·to·ry**
[əb'zə:vətəri] *n.* building from
which the sun and stars or other
natural phenomena may be ~d.
ob·serv·er *n.*

ob·sess [əb'ses] *v.t.* (of a fear,
fixed or false idea) continually
distress; occupy the mind of:
~*ed by fear of unemployment.*
ob·ses·sion [əb'seʃən] *n.* (influence of) idea, feeling, etc.,
that ~es sb.

ob·so·lete ['ɔbsəli:t] *adj.* no
longer in use; out of date: ~
words (*methods*). **ob·so·les·cent**
[,ɔbsə'lesənt] *adj.* becoming ~.

ob·sta·cle ['ɔbstəkl] *n.* sth. in
the way that stops progress or
makes it difficult.

ob·sti·nate ['ɔbstinit] *adj.* **1.**

resisting argument or persuasion: ~ *children.* **2.** not easily
overcome: *an* ~ *resistance* (*disease*). ~·**ly** *adv.* **ob·sti·na·cy** *n.*

ob·struct [əb'strʌkt] *v.t.* be, get,
put sth., in the way of; block
up (a road, passage, etc.); hinder
(free movement); make (the
development or progress of
sth.) difficult. **ob·struc·tion**
[əb'strʌkʃən] *n.* (esp.) sth. that
~s. **ob·struc·tive** *adj.* causing,
likely to cause, ~ion.

ob·tain [əb'tein] *v.t.* **1.**
buy; have lent or granted to
oneself. **2.** get, secure for oneself: *to* ~ *a position* (*experience,
etc.*). **3.** (of rules, customs, etc.)
be established or in use. ~·**a·ble**
adj. that can be ~ed.

ob·trude [əb'tru:d] *v.t. & i.*
push (oneself, one's opinions,
etc.) forward (*upon sb.*), esp.
when unwanted. **ob·tru·sive**
[əb'tru:siv] *adj.*

ob·tuse [əb'tju:s] *adj.* **1.** blunt.
2. (of an angle) between 90° and
180°. (Cf. *acute.*) **3.** slow in
understanding; stupid.

ob·vi·ate ['ɔbvieit] *v.t.* get rid of,
clear away (dangers, difficulties,
etc.).

ob·vi·ous ['ɔbviəs] *adj.* easily
seen or understood; plain; clear.
~·**ly** *adv.*

oc·ca·sion [ə'keiʒən] *n.* **1.** time
at which a particular event takes
place; right time (for sth.): *not
an* ~ (a suitable time) *for
laughter; rise to the* ~, show that
one is equal to what needs to be
done. **2.** reason, cause, need:
There's no ~ *for you to lose your
temper.* *v.t.* be the ~ (2) of;
cause: *Your late arrival* ~*ed
anxiety.* ~·**al** *adj.* infrequent:
to pay sb. ~*al visits.* ~·**al·ly**
adv. now and then; at intervals.

Oc·ci·dent ['ɔksidənt] *n. the O*~,
(liter.) the West (Europe and
America.)

oc·cult [ɔ'kʌlt] *adj.* **1.** hidden;
secret. **2.** mysterious; magical:
~ *sciences* (e.g. astrology).

oc·cu·py ['ɔkjupai] *v.t.* **1.** live
in, be in possession of (a house,
farm, etc.); take and keep possession of (towns, countries,

etc., in war). **2.** take up, fill (space, time, attention, the mind): *speeches ~ing two hours; anxieties that occupied my mind; ~ing himself with his homework.*

oc·cu·pi·er *n.*, **oc·cu·pant** [ˈɔkjupənt] *n.* person who occupies a house, etc. **oc·cu·pa·tion** [ˌɔkjuˈpeiʃən] *n.* **1.** act of ~ing (1) (a house, etc.). **2.** employment, business, trade, etc.

oc·cur [əˈkəː*] *v.i.* (-rr-). **1.** take place; happen. **2.** exist; to be found: *Which letter of the alphabet ~s most commonly?* **3.** ~ to, come into (sb.'s mind): *When did the idea ~ to you? It ~red to me that. . . .* ~**'rence** [əˈkʌrəns] *n.* happening: *an everyday ~rence; of frequent ~rence.*

o·cean [ˈouʃən] *n.* the vast body of water that surrounds the land masses; one of the great seas that divide the continents.

o·chre [ˈoukə] *n.* pale yellowish-brown colour.

o·clock [əˈklɔk] *particle* indicating the hour in telling the time: *What's the time? It's 5 ~.*

oc·ta·gon [ˈɔktəgən] *n.* plane figure with eight angles and sides. **oc·tag·o·nal** [ɔkˈtægənl] *adj.* eight-sided.

An octagon   An octopus

oc·tave [ˈɔktiv] *n.* (music) the note that is six whole tones above or below a given note; the interval of five whole tones and two semi-tones covered by a musical scale; a note and its ~ sounding together.

Oc·to·ber [ɔkˈtoubə*] *n.* the tenth month of the year.

oc·to·ge·na·ri·an [ˌɔktoudʒiˈnɛəriən] *n.* (person) aged between 79 and 89.

oc·to·pus [ˈɔktəpəs] *n.* sea-animal with a soft body and eight arms (tentacles) provided with suckers.

oc·u·lar [ˈɔkjulə*] *adj.* of, for or by the eyes; of seeing: ~ *proof* (i.e. by being shown). **oc·u·list** [ˈɔkjulist] *n.* eye-doctor.

odd [ɔd] *adj.* **1.** (of numbers) not even. 1, 3, 5, 7 are odd numbers. **2.** of one of a pair when the other is missing; of one or more of a set or series when not with the rest: *an odd sock; two odd volumes of an encyclopaedia.* **3.** with a little extra: *twelve pounds odd* (more than £12 but less than £13). **4.** (odder, oddest). strange; peculiar: *He's an odd (odd-looking) old man.* **5.** odd jobs, various, unconnected bits of work. *at odd times (moments),* at various and irregular times. **odd·i·ty** [ˈɔditi] *n.* **1.** quality of being odd (4); strangeness. **2.** peculiar person, thing, way of behaving, etc. **odd·ly** *adv.* strangely. *oddly enough,* strange to say. **odd·ments** *n. pl.* remnants; odds and ends (see below, (3)). **odds** *n. pl.* **1.** the chances in favour of or against sth. happening: *The odds are against us (in our favour). The odds are that . . . ,* it is likely that. . . . **2.** *be at odds (with),* be quarrelling (with). **3.** *odds and ends,* small articles, bits and pieces, of various sorts.

ode [oud] *n.* poem, usu. in irregular metre and expressing noble feelings.

o·di·ous [ˈoudiəs] *adj.* hateful; repulsive. **o·di·um** [ˈoudiəm] *n.* widespread hatred.

o·dour [ˈoudə*] *n.* **1.** smell. **2.** *in good (bad) ~ (with),* having (not having) the favour and approval (of). ~**'less** *adj.*

o·er [ˈouə*, əə*] *adv. & prep.* (in poetry) over.

of [ɔv, əv] *prep.* **1.** (indicating separation in space or time): *five miles south of Leeds.* **2.** (indicating authorship, origin): *the works of Shakespeare; a man of humble birth.* **3.** (cause): *die of grief.* **4.** (deliverance, loss): *be cured of a disease, be robbed of one's money.* **5.** (material): *a* table of dark oak. **6.** (description): *a man of tall appearance.* **7.** (indicating an object): *a maker of pots; love of money.* **8.** (indicating a subject): *the love of a mother for her children.* **9.** (portion or measure): *a sheet of paper; a yard of cloth.* **10.** (relationship): *a friend of mine; a portrait of the queen; an offer of help.* **11.** (time): *in days of old; of a Sunday* (= on Sundays). **12.** by: *a man beloved of all his friends.* **13.** about: *I often think of you.*

off [ɔːf, ɒf] ***prep., adv. & adj.*** **I. prep. 1.** (away) from: *He fell off the ladder. off the record,* not to be recorded, confidential. **2.** (reducing, etc.): *Will you take 2½% off the price if I pay cash?* **3.** *off duty,* free from duty (1). **4.** near to but not on; leading from: *a house just off the main road; a road off the High Street; an island off the coast.* **5.** *off colour,* (colloq.) unwell; *off one's food,* without appetite; *off one's head,* (slang) mad. **II. adv. 1.** I see *go off, show off,* etc. **2.** at or to a distance: *The town is five miles off.* **3.** (indicating departure): *We're just off to America.* **4.** (separation): *Take off your coat. Off with it!* (Take it off.) *Switch off the light.* **5.** (completion): *Finish off that job before starting another.* **6.** disconnected; no longer available: *The electricity is off.* (in a restaurant) *That dish is off, sir* (none left to eat). **7.** (decay): *This fish is off.* **8.** *off and on,* at times; at intervals. (*badly*) *well off,* (not) rich. **III. adj. 1.** the *off side,* the further or far side; (of horses, carriages) of the side further from the side of the road (in Gt. Brit. the *right* side): *the off rear wheel.* (Cf. *near.*) **2.** *on the off chance,* on the improbable chance. *off season,* period of little activity. *in one's off time,* when one has no duties, in one's spare time. **off·hand** [ˈɒfˈhænd] ***adj.*** (of behaviour) casual, careless; without enough respect: *in an offhand way.* ***adv.*** without

previous thought or preparation: *I can't say offhand.*

of·fal [ˈɒfl] ***n.*** **1.** those parts of an animal (e.g. heart, liver, kidneys) which are considered less valuable than the flesh as food. **2.** waste parts of an animal which has been cut up for food.

of·fence [əˈfens] ***n.*** **1.** wrongdoing; crime; sin; breaking of a rule: *an ~ against God and man* (*against the law, good manners*). **2.** the hurting of sb.'s feelings; condition of being hurt in one's feelings: *give ~ to sb.; take ~ easily.* **3.** that which annoys the senses or which makes sb. angry. **4.** attacking: *weapons of ~.* **of·fend** [əˈfend] ***v.t. & i.*** **1.** do wrong; commit an ~ (1) (against the law, custom, etc.). **2.** give ~ (2) to; hurt the feelings of. **3.** be displeasing to: *ugly sounds that offend the ear.* **of·fen·der** ***n.*** person who offends, esp. by breaking the law. **of·fen·sive** [əˈfensiv] ***adj.*** **1.** causing ~ (3): *an offensive smell; offensive language* (e.g. insults). **2.** used for attacking; connected with attack: *an offensive weapon* (*war*). ***n.*** attack: *take the offensive,* go into attack. **of·fen·sive·ly** ***adv.***

of·fer [ˈɒfə*] ***v.t. & i.*** **1.** hold out, put forward (a thing, suggestion, etc.), to be taken or refused; say what one is willing to pay, give or exchange for sth. **2.** present to God: *~* (*up*) *a prayer.* **3.** attempt: *~ing no resistance.* **4.** occur: *the first opportunity* (*chance, occasion*) *that ~s,* that there is. ***n.*** statement *~ing* to do or give sth.; that which is *~ed: make* (*accept*) *an ~; an ~ of marriage.* **~·ing** ***n.*** sth. *~ed* or presented, esp. the money collected at a church service. **~·to·ry** [ˈɒfətəri] ***n.*** money *~ing* in church.

of·fice [ˈɒfis] ***n.*** **1.** (often pl.) room(s) used as a place of business, for clerical work: *a lawyer's ~; working in an ~* (e.g. as a clerk). **2.** (buildings of a) government department, including the staff, their work and duties: *the Foreign O~*; *the Home O~*; *a post ~*. **3.** the work which it is sb.'s duty to do: *accept (enter upon, leave, resign) ~* (esp. of a position in the government service); *~-holders.* **4.** duty: *the ~ of chairman (host).* **5.** (pl.) attention, services, help: *through the good ~s (kind help) of a friend.* '**~-boy** *n.* boy employed to do the less important duties in an ~ (1).

of·fi·cer ['ɔfisə*] *n.* **1.** person appointed to command others in the armed forces, in merchant ships, aircraft, the police force, etc. **2.** person with a position of authority or trust, esp. in the government or civil service: *~s of state* (ministers in the government); *customs ~s*; *the ~s of a society* (e.g. the secretary).

of·fi·cial [ə'fiʃl] *adj.* **1.** of a position of trust or authority; said, done, etc., with authority: *~ statements (records, uniform).* **2.** characteristic of, suitable for, persons holding office (3): *in an ~ style.* *n.* person holding a government position or engaged in public work: *government ~s.* **~·ly** *adv.* in an ~ manner; with ~ authority.

of·fi·ci·ate [ə'fiʃieit] *v.i.* perform the duties of an office or position: *~ as chairman*; (of a priest or minister) *~ at a wedding.* **of·fi·cious** [ə'fiʃəs] *adj.* too eager or ready to help, offer advice, use authority, etc.

off·set ['ɔfset] *v.t.* (-*tt*-, p.t. & p.p. *offset*). balance, compensate for.

off·shoot ['ɔfʃu:t] *n.* stem or branch growing from a main stem, etc.

off·spring ['ɔfspriŋ] *n.* (pl. unchanged) child(ren); young of animals.

of·ten ['ɔfn] *adv.* (-*er*, -*est*; *more*, *most*). **1.** many times; in a large proportion of cases. **2.** *How ~?* At what intervals? How many times? *as ~ as*, each time that.

o·gle ['ougl] *v.i. & t.* look (*at* sb.) in a way suggesting love or longing; make eyes (*at*).

o·gre ['ougə*] *n.* (in fairy-tales) cruel man-eating giant.

Oh! [ou] *int.*

oil [ɔil] *n.* (sorts of) (usu. easily burning) liquid that does not mix with water, obtained from animals (*whale oil*), plants (*coco-nut oil*), or from wells (*petroleum*). *painted in oils*, painted in oil-colours (see below). *v.t.* put oil on or into (parts of a machine, etc.). '**oil·cake** *n.* cattle food made from seeds after oil has been pressed out. '**oil-,col·ours** *n. pl.* paint made from colouring matter and oil. '**oil·skin** *n.* (coat, etc., of) cloth treated with oil to make it keep out water. **oil·y** *adj.* of, like, oil; covered with oil.

oint·ment ['ɔintmənt] *n.* medicinal paste made from oil or fat and used on the skin.

o·kay [ou'kei] (abbr. O.K.) *adj. & adv.* (colloq.) all right; correct; approved. *v.t.* agree to; approve of. *n.* agreement; sanction.

old [ould] *adj.* (-*er*, -*est*; see also *elder*, *eldest*). **1.** of age: *She's twenty-two years old.* **2.** (contrasted with *young*) having lived a long time; past middle age. **3.** (contrasted with *new*, *modern*, *up-to-date*) belonging to past times; having been in existence or use for a long time. **4.** long known or familiar: *an old friend*; *my dear old boy* (a term of affection). **5.** having passed through a school: *an Old Boys' Dance*; having had much experience: *an old hand at carpentry.* *n. in days of old*, in past times. **old·en** *adj.* (liter.) *in olden days (times)*, in past times. '**old-'fash·ioned** *adj.* out of date; not according with modern ideas, tastes, etc.; keeping to old ways.

ol·i·gar·chy ['ɔligɑ:ki] *n.* (country having) government by a small group of all-powerful persons; such a group.

ol·ive ['ɔliv] *n.* (tree with) small fruit with a stone-like seed. *hold out the ~ branch*, show that one is ready to discuss peace-making.

adj. yellowish - green or yellowish-brown.

ome·lette ['ɔmlit] *n.* eggs beaten together, flavoured and fried.

o·men ['oumen] *n.* (thing, happening, regarded as a) sign of sth. good or of evil fortune: *an ~ of success.* **om·i·nous** ['ɔminəs] *adj.* of bad ~; threatening.

o·mit [ou'mit] *v.t.* (-*tt*-). 1. fail (to do sth.): *~ to do one's homework.* 2. leave out: *~ the next chapter*, not read it. **o·mis·sion** [ɔ'miʃən] *n.* ~ting; sth. ~ted.

om·ni·bus ['ɔmnibəs] *n.* 1. (former name for) bus. 2. (attrib.) for many purposes: *an ~ bill* (3); containing many: *an ~ volume* (several books bound in one cover).

om·nip·o·tent [ɔm'nipətənt] *adj.* having power over all. *the O~*, God. **om·nip·o·tence** *n.*

om·nis·ci·ent [ɔm'nisiənt] *adj.* knowing all things. *the O~*, God. **om·nis·ci·ence** *n.*

om·niv·o·rous [ɔm'nivərəs] *adj.* eating all kinds of food.

on [ɔn] *prep. & adv.* I. *prep.* 1. supported by; fastened to; covering (a surface); lying against; in contact with. 2. (indicating time): *on Sundays; on 1st May; on that occasion; on my arrival; on time* (i.e. punctually). 3. about: *a lecture on Shakespeare.* 4. (indicating membership): *be on the committee.* 5. (indicating direction): *drifting on the rocks.* 6. (expressing reason, basis, etc.): *retire on a pension.* 7. (indicating nearness): *a town on the coast.* 8. (indicating how occupied): *be on holiday.* 9. (indicating manner or state): *be on sale, on loan, on fire.* II. *adv.* 1. (expressing progress): *They hurried on* (= forward). *The time is getting on* (late). 2. (corresponding in meaning to the prep. (1) but omitting the noun): *Put your shoes on* (i.e. on your feet). 3. (contrasted with *off* (II. (6)): *Switch the light on.* 4. happening: *What's on at the cinema this week?*

once [wʌns] *adv.* 1. on one

occasion: *I only went ~.* 2. at some time in the past: *Once (upon a time) there was a princess.* 3. ever; at all: *He didn't ~ offer to help me.* 4. *~ in a way (while)*, occasionally. *~ and for all*, now and for the last time. *at ~*, now, immediately. *all at ~*, all together; suddenly. *conj.* from the moment that: *Once you begin to feel afraid.* . . . *n.* one time or occasion: *For ~ you're right.*

one [wʌn] *adj. & pron.* I. *adj. & pron.* 1. a single: *one book, two books, three books*; the figure, 1. 2. a particular single thing: *One day* (i.e. on a certain day that I have in mind) *we went to the Zoo. You can have one or the other, but not both. I want that one, not this one.* II. *impersonal pron.* 1. (used to indicate any person): *One should not do such an unkind thing as that* (i.e. nobody should do it). III. *personal pron. the Holy One* (God); *the absent one* (member of the family not present); *the little ones*, children. *one another*, each other: *They don't like one another. one by one*, one at a time, one after the other. *It's all one to me*, I have no preference. **one·self** [wʌn'self] *pron.* used by the speaker to refer to his own self or to persons in general: *One should not be too proud of oneself.* **'one-'sid·ed** *adj.* (esp.) concerned with, seeing, only one side: *a one-sided argument.*

on·er·ous ['ɔnərəs] *adj.* needing effort; burdensome: *~ duties.*

on·ion ['ʌnjən] *n.* vegetable plant with a round root, having a sharp taste and smell.

Onions

on·look·er ['ɔnlukə*] *n.* person who looks on at sth. happening.

on·ly ['ounli] *adj.* (with a singular noun) that is the one single example; single; (with a plural noun) that are all examples; the best: *He's the ~ man (They are the ~ men) fit to take the responsibility*. *adv.* solely; no one more; nothing more: *Only men allowed to swim here. Only five men were hurt in the explosion. if ~*, see *if* (6). *conj.* but one should add that: *The book would be helpful to you, ~ it's expensive*.

on·set ['ɔnset] *n.* 1. attack. 2. vigorous start: *the ~ of a disease*.

on·slaught ['ɔnslɔ:t] *n.* furious attack.

o·nus ['ounəs] *n.* (sing. only) responsibility for, burden of, doing sth.: *The ~ of proof rests on you*.

on·ward ['ɔnwəd] *adj. & adv.* forward. **~s** *adv.*

ooze [u:z] *n.* soft liquid mud, esp. on a river-bed, at the bottom of a pond, etc. *v.i.* (of thick liquids) pass slowly through small openings: *blood oozing from a wound*. (fig.) *Their courage ~d away*.

o·pal ['oupl] *n.* precious stone in which changes of colour are seen.

o·paque [ou'peik] *adj.* not allowing light to pass through; that cannot be seen through; dull.

o·pen ['oupn] *adj.* 1. not closed or enclosed, so that people and things can go in, out, or through; not covered in or over; spread out or unfolded; public, not restricted to a few people. 2. (special uses with nouns): *in the ~ air*, out of doors; *with ~ arms*, with affection or joy; *an ~ boat*, one with no deck; *~ competitions (scholarships, etc.)*, not limited to any special persons but for anyone to enter; *the ~ country*, land where distant views can be seen, land not covered with forests, not built over, etc.; *keep ~ house*, be always ready to welcome visitors; *have an ~ mind*, be ready to consider new ideas, etc.; *in ~ order*, (of troops) widely spread out in a line; *an ~ question (verdict)*, one not settled or decided; *the ~ sea*, sea far from the land; *~ water*,

free from ice. 3. *~ to*, (a) willing to listen to (reasons, arguments) or to consider (an offer, etc.); (b) offering room or reason for (doubt). *n. the ~*, the ~ air, the ~ country. *v.t. & i.* 1. make ~ or cause to be ~; unfasten; cut or make an ~ing in or a passage through. 2. *~ out*, unfold, spread out; *~ up*, make ~, make possible the development of (a country, etc.). 3. *~ fire (at, on)*, start shooting. 4. start (a banking account, a debate); announce that (an exhibition, a meeting) may start. **~·ing** *n.* 1. ~ space; way in or out. 2. beginning. 3. position (in a business firm, etc.) which is ~ or vacant: *no ~ings for stupid boys*. **~·ly** *adv.* without secrecy; frankly. **'~-'hand·ed** *adj.* generous. **'~-'heart·ed** *adj.* frank, sincere. **'~-work** *n.* material (e.g. lace) with ~ings in it as in a net.

op·e·ra ['ɔpərə] *n.* dramatic composition with music in which the words are sung. **'~-ˌglas·ses** *n. pl.* binoculars for use in a theatre. ˌope·'rat·ic *adj.*

op·er·ate ['ɔpəreit] *v.t. & i.* 1. (cause to) work, be in action, have an effect: *to ~ a machine; machinery that ~s night and day*. 2. *~ on sb.* (for sth.), perform a surgical operation (4) on. **op·er·a·tion** [ˌɔpə'reiʃən] *n.* 1. working; way in which sth. works: *in operation; come into operation*, become effective. 2. piece of work; sth. (to be) done: *begin operations*. 3. (pl.) movements of troops, ships, aircraft, etc., in warfare. 4. cutting of the body by a surgeon (to remove diseased parts, etc.). **op·er·a·tive** ['ɔprətiv] *adj.* operating; effective. *n.* worker, esp. in a factory. **op·er·a·tor** ['ɔpəreitə*] *n.* person who ~s sth.: *telegraph operators*.

o·pi·ate ['oupiət] *n.* drug containing opium, used to relieve pain or help sb. to sleep.

o·pin·ion [ə'pinjən] *n.* 1. belief or judgement not founded on complete knowledge; idea that sth. is probably true: *in my ~*, it seems likely to me that; *public ~*, what the majority of people think. 2. professional estimate or advice: *get a lawyer's ~*. o'pin'ion'at'ed [ə'pinjən-eitid] *adj.* obstinate in one's *~s*.

o'pium ['oupjəm] *n.* substance prepared from poppy juice, used to relieve pain, cause sleep, and as a drug to soothe the senses.

op'po'nent [ə'pounənt] *n.* person against whom one fights, struggles, plays (games), or argues.

op'por'tune ['opətju:n] *adj.* 1. (of time) favourable; good for a purpose. 2. done, coming, at a favourable time. op'por'tun'ist *n.* person who is more anxious to gain an advantage than to consider whether he is gaining it fairly. op'por'tu'ni'ty [,opə'tju:niti] *n.* favourable time or chance (*for* sth., *of* doing sth., *to* do sth.).

op'pose [ə'pouz] *v.t.* 1. set oneself, fight, against (sb. or sth.). 2. put forward as a contrast or opposite (*to*). op'po'site ['opə-zit] *adj.* 1. facing: *the house opposite* (*to*) *mine*. 2. entirely different; contrary: *in the opposite direction*. *n.* word or thing that is opposite. op'po'si'tion [,opə'ziʃən] *n.* 1. the state of being opposite; resistance. 2. *the Opposition*, M.P.s of the political party or parties opposing the Government.

op'press [ə'pres] *v.t.* 1. rule unjustly or cruelly; keep down by unjust or cruel government. 2. (fig.) weigh heavily on; cause to feel troubled or uncomfortable: *~ed by the heat*. op'pres'sion *n.* op'pres'sive *adj.* unjust: *~ive laws*; hard to bear: *~ive weather* (*taxation*). op'pres'sive'ly *adv.* op'pres'sor *n.*

op'pro'bri'ous [ə'proubriəs] *adj.* (of words, etc.) showing scorn or reproach. op'pro'bri'um *n.* scorn; disgrace; public shame.

op'ti'cal ['optikl] *adj.* of the sense of sight; for looking through;

to help eyesight: *~ instruments* (e.g. a microscope). op'ti'cian [op'tiʃən] *n.* person who makes or supplies *~* instruments, esp. eye-glasses.

op'ti'mism ['optimizm] *n.* belief that in the end good will triumph over evil; tendency to look upon the bright side of things; confidence in success. op'ti'mis'tic [,opti'mistik] *adj.* expecting the best; confident. op'ti'mist *n.* optimistic person.

op'tion ['opʃən] *n.* right or power of choosing; thing that is or may be chosen. *~'al adj.* which may be chosen or not as one wishes: *~al subjects at school*. *~'al'ly adv.*

op'u'lent ['opjulənt] *adj.* abundant; rich. op'u'lence *n.*

o'pus ['oupəs] *n.* complete musical composition.

or [ɔ:*, ə*] *conj.* 1. (introducing an alternative): *Is it green or blue? either . . . or*, see *either*. *or else*, otherwise; if not: *Hurry up, or else you will be late*. 2. (introducing a word that explains, or means the same as, another): *He carries a revolver, or pistol, in his belt*.

or'a'cle ['orəkl] *n.* 1. (in ancient Greece) (answer given at a) place where questions about the future were asked of the gods; priest(ess) giving the answers. 2. person considered able to give reliable guidance. o'rac'u'lar [ə'rækjulə*] *adj.* of or like an *~*; with a hidden meaning.

o'ral ['ɔ:rəl] *adj.* 1. using the spoken, not the written, word: *an ~ examination*. 2. (in anatomy) of the mouth. *~'ly adv.*

or'ange ['orindʒ] *n. & adj.* (evergreen tree with) round, yellow, thick-skinned juicy fruit; (of the) colour of an *~* (between yellow and red). See the picture on page 358.

o'rang-ou'tang [ɔ'ræŋu'tæŋ] *n.* large, long-armed ape of Borneo. See the picture on page 358.

o'ra'tion [ə'reiʃən] *n.* formal speech made in public: *a funeral ~*. or'a'tor ['orətə*] *n.* person who makes speeches (esp. a good speaker). **or·a·tor·i·cal** [ˌɔrəˈtorikl] *adj.* of speech-making. **or·a·to·ry** [ˈɔrətəri] *n.* **1.** art of public speech-making. **2.** small chapel for private worship or prayer.

Oranges   An orang-outang

or·a·to·ri·o [ˌɔrəˈtoːriou] *n.* musical composition for solo voices, chorus, and orchestra, usu. with a biblical subject.

orb [ɔːb] *n.* globe, esp. the sun, moon, or one of the stars.

or·bit [ˈɔːbit] *n.* path followed by one heavenly body round another: *the earth's ~ round the sun; satellites in ~ round the earth.*

or·chard [ˈɔːtʃəd] *n.* piece of ground (usu. enclosed) with fruit-trees.

or·ches·tra [ˈɔːkistrə] *n.* **1.** band of persons playing musical instruments (including stringed instruments) together. **2.** place in a theatre for an ~. **or·ches·tral** [ɔːˈkestrəl] *adj.*

or·chid [ˈɔːkid] *n.* sorts of plant, many of which have flowers of bright colours and unusual shapes.

or·dain [ɔːˈdein] *v.t.* **1.** (of God, law, authority) decide; give orders (*that*). **2.** make (sb.) a priest or minister.

or·deal [ɔːˈdiːl] *n.* **1.** (in former times) method of deciding sb.'s guilt or innocence by requiring him to pass a physical test, such as walking through fire unharmed: *~ by fire; trial by ~.* **2.** any severe test of character or endurance.

or·der [ˈɔːdə*] *n.* **1.** way in which things are placed in relation to one another: *names in alphabetical ~; in ~ of size.* **2.** condition in which everything is carefully arranged; working condition: *machinery in good working ~; out of ~.* **3.** (condition brought about by) good and firm government, obedience to the laws. **4.** rules usual at a public meeting: *called to ~ by the Chairman* (required to obey the rules); *protest on a point of ~.* **5.** command given with authority: *by ~ of the King.* **6.** request to supply goods; the goods supplied: *an ~ for two tons of flour; made to ~,* made according to special or personal requirements; *on ~,* asked for but not yet supplied. **7.** written direction (esp. to a bank or post office) to pay money. **8.** *in ~ that,* so that, with the intention that. *in ~ to (do sth.),* with the purpose of (doing sth.). **9.** rank or class in society: *the ~ of knights;* group of people belonging to or appointed to a special class (as an honour): *the O~ of Merit;* badge, sign, worn by members: *wearing his O~s.* **10.** (pl.) authority given by a bishop to perform church duties: *take holy ~s,* become a priest; persons on whom such ~s have been conferred: *the O~ of Deacons.* **11.** society of persons living under religious rules, esp. a brotherhood of monks. *v.t.* **1.** give an ~ (5), (6), (7) to (sb.) or for (sth.). **2.** put (sth.) in ~ (2); arrange. **~·ly** *adj.* **1.** well arranged; in good ~ (2). **2.** peaceful; well-behaved: *an ~ly crowd.* *n.* (army) officer's messenger; hospital attendant.

or·di·nal [ˈɔːdinl] *n. & adj.* (number) showing order or position in a series, as *first, second, third,* etc.

or·di·nance [ˈɔːdinəns] *n.* order made by an authority: *~s of the City Council.*

or·di·na·ry [ˈɔːdinəri] *adj.* normal; usual; average; *out of the ~,* exceptional, unusual. **or·di·nar·i·ly** *adv.*

or·di·na·tion [ˌɔːdiˈneiʃən] *n.* ceremony of ordaining (2) (a priest or minister).

ord·nance [ˈɔːdnəns] *n.* artillery.

Army O~ Department, responsible for military supplies; *O~ Survey maps*, detailed maps made for the Government.

ore [ɔ:*] *n.* rock, earth, etc., from which metal can be extracted.

or·gan [ˈɔ:gən] *n.* **1.** any part of an animal body or plant serving an essential purpose: *the ~s of speech* (i.e. the tongue, teeth, lips, etc.). **2.** means of getting work done; organization. **3.** means for making known what people think: *~s of public opinion* (e.g. newspapers). **4.** musical instrument from which sounds are produced by air forced through pipes, played by keys pressed with the fingers and pedals pressed with the feet. **~·ic** [ɔ:ˈgænik] *adj.* **1.** of the *~s* of the body. **2.** having bodily *~s*. **3.** *an ~ic whole*, an organized whole; *an ~ic part*, a structural part. **~·ism** [ˈɔ:gənizm] *n.* living being with parts which work together; (fig.) *the social ~ism.* **~·ist** *n.* person who plays the *~* (4).

or·gan·ize [ˈɔ:gənaiz] *v.t.* put into working order; arrange in a system; make preparations for: *~ an army (an expedition, one's work).* **or·gan·ized** *adj.* *highly ~d forms of life*, having highly developed organs (1). **or·gan·i·za·tion** [ˌɔ:gənaiˈzeiʃən] *n.* organizing or being *~d*; *~d body of persons*; *~d system.* **or·gan·i·zer** *n.* person who *~s*.

or·gy [ˈɔ:dʒi] *n.* occasion of wild merry-making: *a drunken ~.*

o·ri·ent [ˈɔ:riənt] *n.* *the O~*, (poetical name for) countries east of the Mediterranean. **o·ri·en·tal** [ˌɔ:riˈentl] *adj.* of the O~: *~al civilization (rugs).* *n.* *~al* person.

or·i·fice [ˈɔrifis] *n.* outer opening; mouth of a cave, etc.

or·i·gin [ˈɔridʒin] *n.* starting-point; (person's) parentage: *of humble ~.* **o·rig·i·nate** [əˈridʒi-ineit] *v.i. & t.* **1.** come into being. **2.** be the inventor of.

o·rig·i·nal [əˈridʒinl] *adj.* **1.** first or earliest: *the ~ inhabitants.*

2. newly formed or created; not copied or imitated: *~ ideas.* **3.** able to produce new ideas, etc.: *an ~ mind.* *n.* **1.** that from which sth. is copied. **2.** the language in which sth. was first written: *reading Homer in the ~* (i.e. in Greek). **~·ly** *adv.* **~·i·ty** [əˌridʒiˈnæliti] *n.* quality of being *~*; ability to create: *work that lacks ~ity.*

or·na·ment [ˈɔ:nəmənt] *n.* **1.** sth. designed or used to add beauty to sth. else. **2.** person, act, quality, etc., adding beauty, charm, etc. (*to*). *v.t.* be an *~* to; make beautiful. **or·na·men·tal** [ˌɔ:nəˈmentl] *adj.* of or for *~*.

or·nate [ɔ:ˈneit] *adj.* richly ornamented.

or·ni·thol·o·gy [ˌɔ:niˈθɔlədʒi] *n.* scientific study of birds.

or·phan [ˈɔ:fən] *n.* child who has lost one or both of its parents by death. *v.t.* cause to be an *~*: *~ed by war.* **~·age** [ˈɔ:fənidʒ] *n.* institution for *~s*.

or·tho·dox [ˈɔ:θədɔks] *adj.* (having opinions, beliefs, etc., that are) generally accepted or approved: *an ~ member of the Church*; *~ beliefs*; *~ behaviour.* **~·y** *n.* being *~*.

or·thog·ra·phy [ɔ:ˈθɔgrəfi] *n.* system of spelling.

os·cil·late [ˈɔsileit] *v.i. & t.* (cause to) swing or move to and fro between two points, as a pendulum does.

o·sier [ˈouʒə*] *n.* kind of willow tree, twigs of which are made into baskets.

os·ten·si·ble [ɔsˈtensibl] *adj.* (of reasons, etc.) put forward in an attempt to hide the real reason, etc. **os·ten·si·bly** *adv.*

os·ten·ta·tion [ˌɔstenˈteiʃən] *n.* display (of wealth, learning, etc.) to obtain admiration or envy. **os·ten·ta·tious** *adj.* fond of, showing, *~*.

os·tler [ˈɔslə*] *n.* man who looks after horses at an inn.

os·tra·cize [ˈɔstrəsaiz] *v.t.* banish from society; refuse to meet, talk to, etc. **os·tra·cism** *n.*

os·trich [ˈɔstritʃ] *n.* large, fast-running bird, unable to fly, bred for its valuable tail feathers.

other ['ʌðə*] *pron. & adj.* (person or thing) not the same as that already referred to. *on the ~ hand*, introducing sth. in contrast to an earlier statement. *the ~, the ~s: Give this to Jack and that to the ~ boy. You two boys can go home, but (all) the ~s must stay here. adv.* (= *otherwise*) in a different way: *I could not treat him ~ than fairly. the ~ day*, a few days ago. *some day (time) or ~*, one day, some time; *~ than*, different from. **~'wise** ['ʌðəwaiz] *adv.* differently; in different conditions; in ~ respects. *conj.* if not; or else.

ot·ter ['ɔtə*] *n.* fur-covered, fish-eating water-animal with four webbed feet; its fur.

ot·to·man ['ɔtəmən] *n.* long cushioned seat without a back or arms, often used as a box.

ought [ɔ:t] *v.* (neg. *ought not* contracted to *oughtn't*). **1.** (indicating obligation): *You ~ (~n't) to go.* **2.** (indicating what is advisable or right): *Your brother ~ to see (~ to have seen) a doctor at once.* **3.** (indicating probability): *If he started an hour ago he ~ to be here soon.*

ounce [auns] (abbr. *oz.*) *n.* unit of weight, one-sixteenth of a pound avoirdupois or one-twelfth of a pound troy.

our ['auə*] *adj.* of or belonging to us; that we are concerned with, etc. **ours** ['auəz] *pron. & adj.* (the one or ones) belonging to us. **our·selves** [auə'selvz] *pron.*

oust [aust] *v.t.* drive or push (sb.) out (*from* his employment, position, etc.).

out [aut] *adv.* away from (not in or at) a place; not in the usual condition; at an end, exhausted, etc. *out of*, without, beyond, not in: *out of date*, old-fashioned, not now being used, etc.; *out of breath*, breathless, breathing fast; *out of doors*, in the open air; *out of one's mind (senses)*, mad; *out of temper*, angry; *out-of-the-*

way, remote, uncommon, unusual. *have sth. out with sb.*, discuss a matter under dispute till an understanding is reached. *v.i.* become known: *The truth will out.* **out·er** ['autə*] *adj.* of or for the outside; further from the middle or inside: *the outer suburbs.* **out·er·most** *adj.*

out·bid [aut'bid] *v.t.* bid(1) higher than (sb. else) at a sale.

out·bound ['autbaund] *adj.* (of ships) outward (2) bound.

out·break ['autbreik] *n.* breaking out (see *break* v. (2)) (of war, disease, etc.).

out·build·ing ['autbildiŋ] *n.* small building (e.g. shed, stable) separate from the main building.

out·burst ['autbə:st] *n.* a bursting out (see *burst*, v. (2)) (of steam, anger, etc.).

out·cast ['autka:st] *n. & adj.* (person or animal) driven out from home or society; homeless and friendless.

out·class [aut'kla:s] *v.t.* be much better than; surpass.

out·come ['autkʌm] *n.* effect or result of an event, of circumstances.

out·crop ['autkrɔp] *n.* that part of a layer or vein (of rock, etc.) which can be seen above the ground's surface.

out·cry ['autkrai] *n.* loud shout (of fear, etc.); public protest (*against*).

out·dis·tance [aut'distəns] *v.t.* travel faster than, and so leave (e.g. other runners in a race) far behind.

out·do [aut'du:] *v.t.* do more or better than: *not to be outdone*, not willing to let sb. else do better.

out·door ['autdɔ:*] *adj.* for, done in, the open air: *~ games; live an ~ life.* **out·doors** [aut'dɔ:z] *adv.* outside, in the open air.

out·face [aut'feis] *v.t.* face boldly; stare at (sb.) until he turns his eyes away.

out·fit ['autfit] *n.* all the clothing or articles needed for a purpose: *a camping ~; his school ~.* **~'ter** *n.* shopkeeper selling clothes.

out·flank [aut'flæŋk] *v.t.* go or pass round the flank of (the enemy).

out·grow [aut'grou] *v.t.* grow too tall or too large for (e.g. one's clothes); grow faster or taller than (e.g. one's brother); leave behind, as one grows older (bad habits, childish interests, opinions, etc.).

out·growth ['autgrouθ] *n.* **1.** natural development or product. **2.** that which grows out of sth.; offshoot.

out·house ['authaus] *n.* stable, barn, etc., adjoining a main building.

out·ing ['autiŋ] *n.* *have (go for) an ~*, go away from home for a short pleasure trip.

out·land·ish [aut'lændiʃ] *adj.* looking or sounding strange or foreign.

out·last [aut'lɑːst] *v.t.* last or live longer than.

out·law ['autlɔː] *n.* (olden times) person punished by being placed outside the protection of the law; criminal. *v.t.* condemn (sb.) as an ~.

out·lay ['autlei] *n.* spending; money spent (on materials, work, etc.).

out·let ['autlet] *n.* **1.** way out for water, steam, etc.: *the ~ of a lake.* **2.** means of or occasion for releasing (one's feelings, energies, etc.).

out·line ['autlain] *n.* **1.** line(s) showing the shape or boundary: *a map in ~.* **2.** statement of the chief facts, points, etc.; *an ~ for an essay; an ~ of world history.* *v.t.* draw in ~ (1); give an ~ (2) of.

out·live [aut'liv] *v.t.* live longer than; live until (sth.) is forgotten.

out·look ['autluk] *n.* **1.** view on which one looks out. **2.** what seems likely to happen. **3.** person's way of looking at a problem, etc.

out·ly·ing ['autlaiiŋ] *adj.* far from a centre: *~ villages.*

out·num·ber [aut'nʌmbə*] *v.t.* be greater in number than.

out-pa·tient ['aut,peiʃənt] *n.* person visiting a hospital for treatment but not lodged there.

out·post ['autpoust] *n.* (soldiers in an) observation post far from the main body of troops.

out·put ['autput] *n.* quantity of goods, etc., produced.

out·rage ['autreidʒ] *n.* **1.** (act of) extreme violence or cruelty: *~s committed by the mob.* **2.** act that shocks public opinion: *an ~ upon decency.* *v.t.* be guilty of an ~ upon; do sth. that shocks (public opinion, etc.).

out·ra·geous [aut'reidʒəs] *adj.* shocking; very cruel, shameless, immoral.

out·right ['autrait] *adv.* **1.** openly, with nothing held back: *tell sb. ~ what one thinks.* **2.** completely; at one time: *to buy a house ~* (i.e. not by instalments); *kill sb. ~.* *adj.* positive, thorough: *an ~ denial.*

out·set ['autset] *n.* start.

out·side ['aut'said] *n., adj., adv. & prep.* (contrasted with *inside*). I. *n.* **1.** the outer side or surface; the outer part. **2.** *at the ~*, at the most. II. ['aut said] *adj.* **1.** of, on, nearer, the ~. **2.** the greatest possible or probable. **3.** not connected with or included in a group: *We shall need ~ help* (extra workers). III. *adv.* on or to the ~. IV. *prep.* **1.** at or on the outer side of. **2.** beyond the limits of. **out·'sid·er** *n.* person who is not, or is not considered fit to be, a member of a group, society, etc.

out·skirts ['autskəːts] *n. pl.* borders or outlying parts (esp. of a town).

out·spok·en [aut'spoukən] *adj.* saying freely what one thinks; frank.

out·stand·ing [aut'stændiŋ] *adj.* **1.** in a position to be easily noticed; attracting notice: *~ features of the landscape.* **2.** (of problems, work, payments, etc.) still to be attended to.

out·stay [aut'stei] *v.t.* stay longer than: *~ one's welcome,* stay too long.

out·strip [aut'strip] *v.t.* (*-pp-*).

do better than, pass (sb.) in a race, etc.

out·ward ['autwəd] *adj.* **1.** of or on the outside. **2.** going out: *the ~ voyage.* **~(s)** ['autwəd(z)] *adv.* towards the outside; away from home or the centre. **~·ly** *adv.* on the surface; to all appearances.

out·weigh [aut'wei] *v.t.* be greater in weight, value, or importance than.

out·wit [aut'wit] *v.t.* (*-tt-*). get the better of by being cléverer or more cunning.

out·work ['autwə:k] *n.* part of a military defence system away from the centre: *the ~s of the castle.*

o·val ['ouvl] *n. & adj.* ¹plane figure, outline, as shown here.

An oval   An overall

o·va·tion [ou'veiʃən] *n.* enthusiastic expression of welcome or approval.

ov·en ['ʌvn] *n.* enclosed box-like space which is heated for baking food, etc.

¹o·ver ['ouvə*] *adv. & prep.* I. *adv.* **1.** (indicating movement from an upright position, loss of balance, change from one side to the other, a twist): *fall ~, cross ~, change ~, roll ~ (and ~).* **2.** (indicating motion upwards and outwards): *boil ~.* **3.** from beginning to end: *Think it (Read it) ~.* **4.** (indicating repeated action): *Count it ~ (again).* **5.** remaining: *Is there any bread (left) over?* **6.** ended: *The meeting was ~ by ten o'clock.* **7.** more than is usual or necessary (see ²*over*)? **8.** on the whole surface: *I ache all ~ my body.* II. *prep.* resting on, and partly or completely covering, a surface; at or to a level higher than, but not touching; in or across every

part of; from one side to the other of; in command of: *ruling ~ a vast country*; throughout but not beyond: *stay ~ Sunday* (i.e. depart on Monday); more than: *speaking for ~ an hour.* ~ *and above*, in addition (to). *n.* (cricket) (end of) each bowler's turn (4) at bowling, usu. six times.

²o·ver- [-'ouvə*] *prefix.* too (much): *~-polite*; *~-tired*; *~-heated.*

o·ver·act [,ouvər'ækt] *v.t. & i.* act in an exaggerated way: *~ing (in) his part.*

o·ver·all(s) ['ouvərɔ:l(z)] *n.* loose-fitting garment worn over or-dinary clothes to keep them clean.

o·ver·awe [,ouvə'rɔ:] *v.t.* over-come or restrain with awe.

o·ver·bal·ance [,ouvə'bæləns] *v.i. & t.* (cause to) lose balance; fall over.

o·ver·bear [,ouvə'bɛə*] *v.t.* (p.t. *-bore*, p.p. *-borne*). overcome (by forcible argument, strong force, or authority): *objections over-borne in the argument.* **~·ing** *adj.* masterful; forcing others to one's will: *an ~ing manner.*

o·ver·board ['ouvəbɔ:d] *adv.* over the side of a ship into the water: *fall ~.*

o·ver·cast ['ouvəkɑ:st] *adj.* (of the sky, and fig.) darkened (as) by clouds.

o·ver·coat ['ouvəkout] *n.* long coat worn out of doors over ordinary clothes in cold weather.

o·ver·come [,ouvə'kʌm] *v.t.* (p.t. *-came*, p.p. *-come*). **1.** get the better of; be too strong for: *~ the enemy (bad habits).* **2.** make weak: *be ~ by emotion.*

o·ver·do [,ouvə'du:] *v.t.* (p.t. *-did*, p.p. *-done*). do too much; exaggerate; cook (meat) too much.

o·ver·draw [,ouvə'drɔ:] *v.t. & i.* (p.t. *-drew*, p.p. *-drawn*). draw a cheque for a sum in excess of (one's account at a bank). **o·ver·draft** ['ouvədrɑ:ft] *n.* amount of money by which a bank account is ~n.

o·ver·dress [,ouvə'dres] *v.t. & i.* dress too showily.

o·ver·due [ˌouvəˈdjuː] *adj.* beyond the time fixed (for arrival, payment, etc.).

o·ver·grown [ˌouvəˈgroun] *adj.* 1. having grown too fast: *an ~ boy.* 2. covered (with sth. that has grown over): *flower-beds ~ with weeds.*

o·ver·hang [ˌouvəˈhæŋ] *v.t. & i.* (p.t. & p.p. -*hung*). stick out over; be over like a shelf: *~ing branches; cliffs ~ing a river.*

o·ver·haul [ˌouvəˈhɔːl] *v.t.* 1. examine thoroughly in order to learn about the condition of; put into good condition: *~ an engine.* 2. overtake. [ˈouvəhɔːl] *n.* thorough examination for repairs, etc.

o·ver·head [ˌouvəˈhed] *adj.* 1. raised above the ground: *~ cables; an ~ railway* (built on supports above street level). 2. (business) *~ expenses (charges),* those needed for carrying on a business (e.g. for rent, advertising, salaries, light, and heating), not manufacturing costs. *adv.* above one's head; in the sky: *the stars ~.*

o·ver·hear [ˌouvəˈhiə*] *v.t.* (p.t. & p.p. -*heard*). hear without the knowledge of the speaker(s); hear what one is not intended to hear; hear by chance.

o·ver·joyed [ˌouvəˈdʒɔid] *adj.* greatly delighted (*at* sth.).

o·ver·lap [ˌouvəˈlæp] *v.t. & i.* (-*pp*-). partly cover and extend beyond one edge: *~ping tiles (boards).*

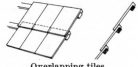

Overlapping tiles

o·ver·lay [ˈouvəˈlei] *v.t.* (p.t. & p.p. -*laid*). put a coating or layer over the surface of.

o·ver·look [ˌouvəˈluk] *v.t.* 1. have a view of from above: *~ing the harbour.* 2. fail to see or notice; pay no attention to: *~ an error.* 3. let pass without

punishing: *~ sb.'s wrong-doing.*

o·ver·night [ˌouvəˈnait] *adv.* 1. on the night before: *get everything ready ~.* 2. for the night: *Can you stay ~?* [ˈouvənait] *adj.* during or for the night: *an ~ journey; an ~ stop.*

o·ver·power [ˌouvəˈpauə*] *v.t.* overcome; be too strong for. *~ing adj.* too strong; very powerful: *an ~ing stink.*

o·ver·rate [ˌouvəˈreit] *v.t.* put too high a value on (e.g. sb.'s abilities).

o·ver·reach [ˌouvəˈriːtʃ] *v.t.* get the better of (by trickery). *~ oneself,* fail in one's object, damage one's own interests, by being too ambitious. *~ the mark,* go past it.

o·ver·ride [ˌouvəˈraid] *v.t.* (p.t. -*rode*, p.p. -*ridden*). prevail over (sb.'s opinions, decisions, wishes, claims, etc.).

o·ver·rule [ˌouvəˈruːl] *v.t.* decide against (esp. by using one's higher authority): *objections ~d by the judge; ~d by the majority.*

o·ver·run [ˌouvəˈrʌn] *v.t.* (p.t. -*ran*, p.p. -*run*). 1. spread over and occupy or injure: *a country ~ by enemy troops; a garden ~ with weeds.* 2. go beyond (a limit): *speakers who ~ the time allowed.*

o·ver·sea(s) [ˈouvəˈsiː(z)] *adj.* (at, to, from, for places) across the sea: *~ education (trade,* etc.). *adv.* go (live, come from) *~s.*

o·ver·see [ˌouvəˈsiː] *v.t.* (p.t. -*saw*, p.p. -*seen*). look after; control (work, workmen). **o·ver·seer** [ˈouvəsiə*] *n.* foreman.

o·ver·sight [ˈouvəsait] *n.* failure to notice sth.: *Your letter was unanswered through an ~.*

o·ver·state [ˌouvəˈsteit] *v.t.* state too much or more than is true about; exaggerate. *~ment n.*

o·ver·step [ˌouvəˈstep] *v.t.* (-*pp*-). go beyond: *~ one's authority.*

o·ver·strung [ˌouvəˈstrʌŋ] *adj.* (of a person, his nerves) intensely strained; quickly and easily excited.

o·vert [ˈouvəːt] *adj.* done openly, publicly, not secretly. *~ly adv.*

o·ver·take [ˌouvəˈteik] *v.t.* (p.t. -*took*, p.p. -*taken*). **1.** come or catch up with; outstrip: ~ *other cars on the road* (*arrears of work*). **2.** (of storms, troubles, etc.) come upon (sb.) suddenly, by surprise.

o·ver·throw [ˌouvəˈθrou] *v.t.* (p.t. -*threw*, p.p. -*thrown*). defeat; put an end to; cause to fail or fall: ~ *the government.* *n.* [ˈouvəθrou] defeat; fall.

o·ver·time [ˈouvətaim] *n. & adv.* (time spent at work) after the usual hours: *working* ~; *earning extra for* ~.

o·ver·ture [ˈouvətjuə*] *n.* **1.** (often pl., esp. *make* ~*s to*) approach made *to* sb. with the aim of starting discussions: *peace* ~*s.* **2.** musical composition played as an introduction to an opera or at a concert.

o·ver·whelm [ˌouvəˈhwelm] *v.t.* weigh down; submerge; overcome completely: ~*ed by grief* (*sb.'s kindness*); ~*ed by the enemy's forces; an* ~*ing victory.*

o·ver·wrought [ˌouvəˈrɔːt] *adj.* tired out by too much work or excitement; in a state of nervous illness.

owe [ou] *v.t. & i.* **1.** be in debt to (sb.) (*for* sth.): *owing £20 to one's tailor for an overcoat*; *owe one's success to hard work.* **2.** be under obligation to give: *owe loyalty to the king.* **ow·ing** *adj.* still to be paid. **ow·ing to** *prep.* because of.

owl [aul] *n.* night-flying bird with large eyes that lives on mice and small birds.

An owl   An oyster

own [oun] *adj.* (used with possessives to give emphasis to the ownership or special character of sth.): *This is my pen; it's my own* (*pen*), *my very own and no one else's. This is all my own work* (i.e. nobody helped me). *hold*

one's own, keep one's position against attack; not be defeated or overcome; not lose strength; *on one's own*, independent(ly); without a companion. *v.t. & i.* **1.** possess: *own a house.* **2.** agree; confess; recognize: *own that a claim is justified; own to having told a lie; own up* (*to a fault, etc.*), confess (to it). **own·er** *n.* person who owns (1) sth. **own·er·less** *adj.* having no (known) owner; *ownerless dogs.* **own·er·ship** *n.* of uncertain ownership.

ox [ɔks] *n.* (pl. *oxen* [ˈɔksn]). **1.** general name for domestic cattle. (Cf. *cow, bull, bullock.*) **2.** (esp.) fully grown castrated bullock, used as a draught animal.

ox·ide [ˈɔksaid] *n.* compound of oxygen with another element: *iron* ~. **ox·i·dize** [ˈɔksidaiz] *v.t. & i.* (cause to) combine with oxygen; make or become rusty.

ox·y·gen [ˈɔksidʒən] *n.* gas without smell, colour, or taste, necessary for life.

oy·ster [ˈɔistə*] *n.* kind of shellfish, usu. eaten uncooked, whose shell sometimes contains a pearl.

oz. written abbr. of *ounce*(*s*).

o·zone [ouˈzoun] *n.* form of oxygen with a sharp, refreshing smell; (popular use) pure, refreshing air as at the seaside.

P

pa [pɑː] *n.* (colloq.) short for *papa*.

pace [peis] *n.* **1.** (distance covered by the foot in a) single step in walking or running. **2.** rate of walking, running; (fig.) progress: *keep* ~ *with* (*sb.*), keep up with, progress at the same speed as. **3.** (esp. of horses) way of walking, running, etc.: *put sb. through his* ~*s*, test his abilities, etc. *v.i. & t.* **1.** walk with slow or regular steps: ~ (*up and down*) *a room.* **2.** measure by taking ~*s*: ~ *out* (*off*) *a distance.*

pa·cif·ic [pəˈsifik] *adj.* peaceful;

making or loving peace. **pac·i·fi·ca·tion** [ˌpæsifiˈkeiʃən] *n.* making or becoming peaceful; bringing about a state of peace. **pa·ci·fism** [ˈpæsifizm] *n.* principle that war should and could be abolished. **pac·i·fist** [ˈpæsifist] *n.* believer in pacifism. **pac·i·fy** [ˈpæsifai] *v.t.* calm and quieten.

pack [pæk] *n.* **1.** bundle of things tied or wrapped up together for carrying. ~-*horse*, ~-*animal*, one used for carrying ~s. **2.** number of dogs kept for hunting (*a* ~ *of hounds*) or of wild animals (e.g. wolves) that go about together (usu. contemptuous) number of persons or things: *a* ~ *of thieves* (*liars, lies*). **3.** complete set of (usu. 52) playing-cards. *v.t. & i.* **1.** put (things) into a box, bundle, bag, etc.; fill (a box, bag, etc.) with things: ~*ing his clothes for a journey*; ~*ing his trunks; start* ~*ing for the holidays.* **2.** crush or crowd (into a place): ~*ing people into a railway carriage; crowds* ~*ing into the cinemas.* **3.** put soft material into or round to keep sth. safe or to prevent loss or leakage: *glass* ~*ed in straw*; ~ *a leaking joint in a pipe.* **4.** ~ *sb. off, send sb.* ~*ing*, send him away quickly. ~·**age** [ˈpækidʒ] *n.* parcel, bundle, bale. ~·**et** [ˈpækit] *n.* small bundle, esp. of letters or papers. ~·**ing** *n.* material used in ~ing goods.

pact [pækt] *n.* agreement.

pad [pæd] *n.* **1.** cushion-like container filled with soft material, used to prevent damage, give comfort, improve the shape of sth., etc. **2.** guard for the leg, in cricket and other games. **3.** number of sheets of writing-paper fastened together along one edge. **4.** soft, fleshy under-part of the foot (of dogs, foxes, etc.). *v.t.* **1.** put pad(s)(1) on or in. **2.** (often *pad out*) make (a sentence, essay, book, etc.) longer by using unnecessary words or material. **pad·ding** *n.* material used for making pads (1).

pad·dle [ˈpædl] *n.* short oar with a broad blade at one or each end. *v.t. & i.* **1.** send (a canoe) through the water by using a ~ or ~s. **2.** walk with bare feet in water; move the hands about in water. '~-ˌsteam·er *n.* one with ~-wheels. '~-wheel *n.* wheel fitted with boards which strike the water in turn and so send the ship forward.

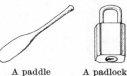

A paddle   A padlock

pad·dock [ˈpædək] *n.* small grass field (usu. for horses).

pad·dy [ˈpædi] *n.* growing rice; rice in the husk. '~-field *n.* rice-field.

pad·lock [ˈpædlɔk] *v.t. & n.* (fasten with a) lock of the kind shown above.

pad·re [ˈpɑːdrei, -dri] *n.* (army and navy slang) chaplain; (colloq.) clergyman.

pa·gan [ˈpeigən] *n. & adj.* (person who is) not a believer in one of the chief religions of the world. ~·**ism** *n.* beliefs, practices, of ~s.

¹**page** [peidʒ] *n.* one side of a leaf of paper in a book, periodical.

²**page** [peidʒ] *n.* boy servant (in a club, hotel, etc.).

pag·eant [ˈpædʒənt] *n.* **1.** public entertainment, often outdoors, in which historical events are acted in the costume of the period. **2.** public celebration, esp. one in which there is a procession of persons in fine costumes (e.g. a coronation). ~·**ry** *n.* rich, splendid display.

pa·go·da [pəˈgoudə] *n.* sacred tower of several storeys (India, Burma, China, Japan, etc.). See the picture on page 366.

paid, see *pay.*

pail [peil] *n.* bucket (as shown on page 366).

pain [pein] *n.* **1.** suffering of body or mind. **2.** (pl.) trouble.

take ∼s, do one's best; work
carefully. **3.** penalty: *on* ∼
(*death*), with the risk of suffering (death). *v.t.* cause ∼ to.
∼**·ful** *adj.* causing ∼. ∼**·ful·ly**
adv. ∼**·less** *adj.* without ∼;
causing no ∼. ∼**·less·ly** *adv.*
'pains·tak·ing *adj.* taking
trouble in doing sth.

A pagoda   A pail

paint [peint] *n.* colouring matter
(to be) mixed with oil or other
liquid. *v.t. & i.* **1.** cover a surface with ∼. **2.** make a picture
(of) with ∼: ∼ *flowers.* ∼**·er** *n.*
person who ∼s (buildings, etc.);
artist who ∼s (pictures). ∼**·ing**
n. ∼ed picture; the art of ∼ing
pictures.
paint·er ['peintə*] *n.* rope by
which a boat may be tied to a
ship, pier, etc.
pair [peə*] *n.* **1.** two things of
the same kind used together: *a*
∼ *of shoes*; single article with
two parts always joined: *a* ∼ *of
trousers* (*scissors*). **2.** two persons closely associated, e.g. a
man and woman who are (about
to be) married: *in* ∼s, in twos.
v.t. & i. form a ∼ or ∼s; join
in ∼s. ∼ *off*, form into ∼s;
arrange in ∼s.
pal [pæl] *n.* (colloq.) comrade;
friend.
pal·ace ['pælis] *n.* house of a ruler
(e.g. a king) or a bishop; any
large and splendid house. **pa·
la·tial** [pə'leiʃəl] *adj.* of or like
a ∼.
pal·an·quin [ˌpælən'ki:n] *n.* =
¹litter.
pal·ate ['pælit] *n.* **1.** roof of the
mouth. **2.** sense of taste. **pal·a·
ta·ble** ['pælətəbl] *adj.* agreeable
to the taste or the mind.
pal·av·er [pə'lɑ:və*] *n.* conference, esp. between explorers

and the people of the country.
v.i. talk idly for a long time.
¹**pale** [peil] *adj.* (*-r, -st*). **1.** (of
a person's face) having little
colour; bloodless. **2.** (of colours)
faint; not bright. *v.i.* become
∼.
²**pale** [peil] *n.* **1.** long, pointed
piece of wood used for fences.
2. limits of what is considered
good social behaviour: *beyond*
(*outside, within*) *the* ∼. **pal·
ing(s)** *n.* fence of ∼s.

Palings

pal·ette ['pælit] *n.* board (with a
hole for the thumb) on which an
artist mixes his colours.
pal·i·sade [ˌpæli'seid] *n.* fence of
strong, pointed wooden stakes.
¹**pall** [po:l] *v.i.* become uninteresting: *His long lecture* ∼ed *on me.*
²**pall** [po:l] *n.* heavy cloth spread
over a coffin; (fig.) any dark,
heavy covering: *a* ∼ *of smoke.*
pal·let ['pælit], **pal·li·asse**
['pæliæs] *n.* straw-filled mattress
for sleeping on.
pal·li·ate ['pælieit] *v.t.* lessen the
severity of (pain, disease); excuse the seriousness of (a crime,
etc.). **pal·li·a·tion** [ˌpæli'eiʃən]
n. **pal·li·a·tive** ['pæliətiv] *n. &
adj.* (sth.) serving to ∼.
pal·lid ['pælid] *adj.* pale(1); ill
looking.
pal·lor ['pælə*] *n.* paleness (of
face).
¹**palm** [pɑ:m] *n.* inner part of the
hand between wrist and fingers.
v.t. ∼ *sth. off on sb.*, persuade
sb., by trickery, to take sth. of
little value. ∼**·ist** *n.* one who
claims to tell a person's future
by examining lines on his ∼.
∼**·is·try** *n.* art of doing this.
²**palm** [pɑ:m] *n.* **1.** sorts of tree
growing in warm climates, with
no branches and a mass of large
wide leaves at the top: *date*-∼;
coconut-∼. **2.** ∼-leaf as a symbol
of victory: *carry off the* ∼, be
successful. *P*∼ *Sunday*, Sunday
before Easter. ∼**·y** *adj.* (*-ier,*

-iest). prosperous: *in my ~y days.*

pal·pa·ble ['pælpəbl] *adj.* that can be felt or touched; clear to the mind: *a ~ error.* **pal·pa·bly** *adv.*

pal·pi·tate ['pælpiteit] *v.i.* (of the heart) beat rapidly; (of a person, his body) tremble (with terror, etc.). **pal·pi·ta·tion** [,pælpi'teiʃən] *n.* palpitating of the heart (from disease, great efforts).

pal·ter ['pɔ:ltə*] *v.i. ~ with*, trifle with; be insincere when dealing with.

pal·try ['pɔ:ltri] *adj.* worthless; of no importance; contemptible.

pam·pas ['pæmpəs] *n. pl.* wide treeless plains of S. America.

pam·per ['pæmpə*] *v.t.* indulge too much; be unduly kind to.

pamph·let ['pæmflit] *n.* small paper-covered book, esp. on a topical question. **~·eer** [,pæmfli'tiə*] *n.* writer of ~s.

pan [pæn] *n.* flat dish, often shallow and without a cover, used for cooking and other household purposes. **'pan·cake** *n.* batter fried in a pan (and usu. eaten hot).

pan- [pæn] *prefix.* of or for all: *~-Asian.*

pan·a·ce·a [,pænə'siə] *n.* remedy for all diseases, troubles, etc.

pan·da ['pændə] *n.* bear-like animal of Tibet.

pan·de·mo·nium [,pændi'mounjəm] *n.* (scene of) wild and noisy disorder.

pan·der ['pændə*] *v.i. ~ to*, indulge (sb.), incite (his) unworthy desires or tastes.

pane [pein] *n.* single sheet of glass in (a division of) a window.

pan·e·gyr·ic [,pæni'dʒirik] *n.* speech, piece of writing, praising a person or event.

pan·el ['pænl] *n.* 1. separate part of the surface of a door, wall, ceiling, etc., usu. raised above or sunk below the surrounding area. 2. (list of names of) persons appointed to serve on a jury, take part in a discussion on the radio, etc. *v.t.* (-*ll-*). put ~s on or in. **~·ling** *n.* ~led work.

pang [pæŋ] *n.* sharp, sudden feeling of pain or remorse.

pan·ic ['pænik] *n.* unreasoning, uncontrolled, quickly-spreading fear. *adj.* (of fear) unreasoning. **pan·ick·y** *adj.*

pan·nier ['pæniə*] *n.* one of a pair of baskets placed across the back of a horse or ass for carrying things in.

pan·o·ply ['pænəpli] *n.* full suit of armour; (fig.) complete equipment.

pan·o·ra·ma [,pænə'rɑ:mə] *n.* wide, uninterrupted view; constantly changing scene: *the ~ of London life.*

pan·sy ['pænzi] *n.* flowering plant.

pant [pænt] *v.t. & i.* 1. take short, quick breaths. 2. have a strong wish (*for* sth., *to* do sth.). 3. say while ~ing: *~ing out his message. n.* short, quick breath; gasp.

pan·the·ism ['pænθiizm] *n.* belief that God is in everything.

pan·ther ['pænθə*] *n.* leopard.

pan·to·mime ['pæntəmaim] *n.* 1. drama, based on a fairy-tale, with music, dancing, and clowning. 2. acting without words.

pan·try ['pæntri] *n.* 1. room in which silver, glass, table-linen, etc., are kept. 2. room in which food is kept.

pants [pænts] *n. pl.* 1. drawers; two-legged undergarment hanging from the waist. 2. (colloq.) trousers. **pan·ties** *n. pl.* (colloq.) short knickers, as worn by a child or a woman.

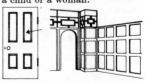

A panel   Panelling

pap [pæp] *n.* soft food for babies.

pa·pa [pə'pɑ:] *n.* (child's word for) father.

pa·pa·cy ['peipəsi] *n.* position of, authority of, the Pope; system of government by popes. **pa·pal**

['peipl] *adj.* of the Pope, the ~.

pa·pa·ya [pə'paijə], **pa(w)·paw** ['pɔːpɔː] *n.* tropical tree; its fruit, green outside and yellow inside.

pa·per ['peipə*] *n.* **1.** substance manufactured from wood-pulp, rags, etc., and used in sheets for writing, printing, wrapping, etc. **2.** newspaper. **3.** (pl.) documents showing who sb. is, what authority he has, etc. **4.** sth. written about a problem, etc., to be read aloud to a learned society, etc. **5.** set of examination questions on a given subject: *The biology ~ was difficult.* *v.t.* paste ~ on (walls, etc.). '~·**,hang·er** *n.* man whose trade is to put wall~ on walls of rooms. '~·**knife** *n.* blunt one for slitting folded paper, etc. '~·**weight** *n.* weight placed on loose ~s to prevent their being blown away.

pa·pier-mâ·ché ['pæpjei'mɑːʃei] *n.* paper pulped and used as a plastic.

pa·pist ['peipist] *n.* (unfriendly word for a) member of the Roman Catholic Church.

pa·py·rus [pə'paiərəs] *n.* (kind of paper made in ancient Egypt from a) tall water-plant or reed.

par [pɑː*] *n.* **1.** average or normal amount, degree, etc.: *above* (*at, below*) *par,* (of shares) above (at, below) the original price. **2.** *on a par with,* equal to.

par·a·ble ['pærəbl] *n.* story designed to teach a moral lesson.

par·a·chute ['pærəʃuːt] *n.* apparatus used for a jump from an aircraft or for dropping supplies. **par·a·chut·ist** *n.*

A   Parallel   A parallel-
parachute   lines   ogram

pa·rade [pə'reid] *v.t. & i.* **1.** (of troops) gather together for drilling, etc.; march in procession. **2.** make a display of; try to attract attention to: *to ~ one's abilities.* *n.* **1.** a parading of troops: *on ~.* ~-*ground,* area used for this. **2.** wide, often ornamental pathway, esp. on a sea-front. **3.** display (of one's wealth, virtues, etc.) made to impress.

par·a·dise ['pærədais] *n.* **1.** the Garden of Eden. **2.** Heaven. **3.** any place of perfect happiness.

par·a·dox ['pærədɔks] *n.* statement which seems to say sth. opposite to the truth but which may contain a truth (e.g. 'More haste, less speed' (proverb)). ~·**i·cal** [,pærə'dɔksikl] *adj.*

par·af·fin ['pærəfin] *n.* ~ *oil,* oil obtained from coal, petroleum.

par·a·gon ['pærəgən] *n.* model of excellence; apparently perfect person or thing.

par·a·graph ['pærəgrɑːf] *n.* division of a composition (usu. a group of several sentences dealing with one main idea) started on a new line.

par·a·keet ['pærəkiːt] *n.* sorts of small long-tailed parrot.

par·al·lel ['pærəlel] *adj.* **1.** (of lines) continuing at the same distance from one another; (of one line) having this relation (*to* another). **2.** exactly corresponding (*to*). *n.* **1.** ~ *of latitude,* line on a map ~ to the equator and passing through all places the same distance north or south of it. **2.** person, event, etc., precisely similar (*to*). **3.** comparison: *draw a ~ between....* *v.t.* **1.** be ~ to. **2.** produce sth. as a ~ (2) of. ~·**o·gram** [,pærə·'leləgræm] *n.* four-sided plane figure with opposite sides ~.

pa·ral·y·sis [pə'rælisis] *n.* loss of feeling or power to move, in any or every part of the body. **par·a·lyse** ['pærəlaiz] *v.t.* affect with ~; make helpless. **par·a·lyt·ic** [,pærə'litik] *n. & adj.* (person) suffering from ~; of ~.

par·a·mount ['pærəmaunt] *adj.* of supreme importance; having supreme authority.

par·a·pet ['pærəpit] *n.* (usu. low) protective wall at the edge of a flat roof, side of a bridge, etc.

par·a·pher·na·lia [ˌpærəfə'neiljə] *n. pl.* numerous small possessions, tools, esp. concerning sb.'s hobby or technical work.

par·a·phrase ['pærəfreiz] *v.t. & n.* (give a) restatement of the meaning of (a piece of writing) in other words.

par·a·site ['pærəsait] *n.* **1.** animal or plant living on or in another and getting its food from it. **2.** person supported by another and giving him nothing in return.

par·a·sol [ˌpærə'sɔl] *n.* sun-umbrella.

par·a·troop·er ['pærətru:pə*] *n.* (pl. *paratroops*). airborne soldier trained to land by parachute.

par·cel ['pɑ:sl] *n.* **1.** thing(s) wrapped and tied up for carrying, sending by post, etc. **2.** *part and ~ of,* an essential part of. *v.t.* (*-ll-*). ~ *out,* divide; distribute.

parch [pɑ:tʃ] *v.t.* **1.** (of heat, the sun, etc.) make (the throat, the land) dry. **2.** dry up by heating: ~ed peas.

parch·ment ['pɑ:tʃmənt] *n.* writing material made from the skin of a sheep or goat; ~-like paper.

par·don ['pɑ:dn] *v.t.* forgive; excuse. *n.* forgiveness. ~·a·ble *adj.* that can be ~ed. ~·a·bly *adv.*

pare [pɛə*] *v.t.* cut away the outer part, edge, or skin of: ~ *sth. down,* reduce (e.g. one's expenditure). **par·ing** ['pɛəriŋ] *n.* sth. ~d off: *nail parings.*

par·ent ['pɛərənt] *n.* father or mother; (fig.) origin. ~·age ['pɛərəntidʒ] *n. of unknown ~age* (having unknown ~s). **pa·ren·tal** [pə'rentl] *adj.* of a ~.

pa·ren·the·sis [pə'renθisis] *n.* (pl. *-es* [-i:z]). sentence within another sentence, marked off by commas, dashes or brackets; (pl.) the brackets ( ), used to mark off a ~: *in parentheses.* **par·en·thet·i·cal** [ˌpærenˈθetikl] *adj.*

par·i·ah ['pɛəriə] *n.* outcast. '~-

dog *n.* ownerless dog of mixed breed.

par·ish ['pæriʃ] *n.* division of a county with its own church and clergyman; division of a county for local government: ~ *church (council).* ~·ion·er [pəˈriʃənə*] *n.* person living in a (particular) ~, esp. a member of the ~ church.

par·i·ty ['pæriti] *n.* equality; being equal; being at par.

park [pɑ:k] *n.* **1.** public garden or recreation ground in a town. **2.** area of grassland with trees round a large country house. **3.** *car ~,* place where motor-cars, etc., may be left for a time. **4.** *national ~,* area of natural beauty (e.g. mountains, forest) set apart by the State for public enjoyment. *v.t.* put or leave (a motor-car, etc.) in a public place or in a car ~ (3). **'park·ing lot** *n.* (U.S.A.) outdoor car ~ (3). **'park·ing-ˌme·ter** *n.* coin-operated meter that registers the period for which a car is parked in a street.

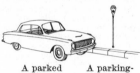

A parked   A parking
car   meter

par·lance ['pɑ:ləns] *n. in common ~,* in the usual way of speaking.

par·ley ['pɑ:li] *n.* conference, esp. between leaders of opposed forces. *v.i.* discuss terms (*with* sb.).

par·lia·ment ['pɑ:ləmənt] *n.* (esp. in Great Britain and other countries with representative government) supreme law-making council or assembly, formed (in G.B.) of the House of Commons and the House of Lords. **par·lia·men·ta·ri·an** [ˌpɑ:ləmenˈtɛəriən] *n.* person skilled in ~ary debate, rules, etc. **par·lia·men·ta·ry** [ˌpɑ:ləˈmentəri] *adj.* of ~.

par·lour ['pɑ:lə*] *n.* sitting-

room in a private house; private sitting-room at an inn. '~·
maid *n.* woman employee (in a private house) who waits at table. (Cf. *waitress*.)

pa·ro·chi·al [pə'roukiəl] *adj.* of a parish; (fig.) limited; narrow: *a ~ outlook (mind).*

par·o·dy ['pærədi] *n.* (piece of) writing intended to amuse by imitating the style of writing used by sb. else; weak imitation. *v.t.* make a ~ of: ~ *an author (a poem).* **par·o·dist** *n.*

pa·role [pə'roul] *n.* prisoner's promise, if given freedom for a time without a guard, that he will return and not try to escape: *a prisoner of war who is on ~.*

par·ox·ysm ['pærəksizm] *n.* sudden attack or outburst (of pain, etc.).

par·quet ['pɑːki] *n.* flooring of wooden blocks fitted together like bricks to form a design.

par·ri·cide ['pærisaid] *n.* **1.** person who murders his father, near relation, or sovereign ruler. **2.** any of those crimes.

par·rot ['pærət] *n.* sorts of bird with a hooked bill, some of which can be taught to say words; person who repeats what others say.

par·ry ['pæri] *v.t.* turn aside (a blow, (fig.) a question).

parse [pɑːz] *v.t.* describe (a word, a sentence) grammatically and point out how words are related.

par·si·mo·ny ['pɑːsiməni] *n.* (too much) care in the use of money, goods, etc. **par·si·mo·nious** [ˌpɑːsi'mounjəs] *adj.* too economical.

pars·ley ['pɑːsli] *n.* garden plant whose leaves are used in sauces and for decorating food.

pars·nip ['pɑːsnip] *n.* sort of root vegetable.

par·son ['pɑːsn] *n.* (colloq.) parish priest; any clergyman. ~·**age** ['pɑːsənidʒ] *n.* ~'s house; vicarage.

part [pɑːt] *n.* **1.** some but not all of a thing or number of things. *for the most ~,* in most cases, mostly. *in ~,* in some

degree. **2.** (pl.) *these (those)* ~s, this (that) ~ of the country, this (that) district. **3.** any one of a number of equal divisions: *A minute is the sixtieth ~ of an hour.* **4.** person's share in some activity; his duty or responsibility: *a man with a ~ in a play (in the recent conferences). on my (his, etc.) ~, on the ~ of Mr A.,* proceeding from, done by (me, him, Mr A.). *take ~ in* (an event, etc.), have a share in, help. *for my ~,* as far as I am concerned. **5.** what an actor in a play, cinema film, etc., says and does: *actors who are learning their ~s.* **6.** *take sb.'s ~,* support him, approve of what he does, says, etc. **7.** *take sth. in good ~,* not be offended at it. **8.** (grammar) ~ *of speech,* one of the classes of words (e.g. noun, verb, adjective). *v.t. & i.* **1.** (cause to) separate; divide: *The crowd ~ed. Let's ~ friends* (i.e. separate without ill will). ~ *company (with),* end a relationship (with), disagree (with). **2.** ~ *one's hair,* make a dividing line by combing the hair in opposite ways. **3.** ~ *with,* give up, give away: *a man who won't ~ with his money.* ~·**ing** *n.* (esp.) line where the hair is combed in opposite ways. ~·**ly** *adv.* in ~; to some extent. '~·**song** *n.* song with different ~s for three or more voices to form a harmony. '~·**time** *adj. & adv.* for only ~ of the working week: *~-time teaching; working ~-time only.*

par·take [pɑː'teik] *v.i. & t.* (p.t. *-took,* p.p. *-taken*). **1.** have or take a share (*in* sth.). **2.** have some (*of* the food, drink, etc., provided): ~ *of a meal.* **3.** have some of the characteristics (*of* sth.).

par·tial ['pɑːʃl] *adj.* **1.** forming only a part; not complete: *a ~ success.* **2.** ~ *to,* having a liking or taste for. **3.** showing too much favour to one person or one side. ~·**ly** *adv.* **par·ti·al·i·ty** [ˌpɑːʃi'æliti] *n.* **1.** being ~ (3) in treatment, judgement, etc. **2.** special taste or liking (*for*).

par·ti·ci·pate [pɑːˈtisipeit] *v.i.* have a share, take part (*in* a common act, feeling, etc.): ~ *in sb.'s suffering.* **par·ti·ci·pant** *n.* person who ~s. **par·ti·ci·pa·tion** [pɑːˌtisiˈpeiʃən] *n.*

par·ti·ci·ple [ˈpɑːtisipl] *n.* form of a verb: *'Writing' and 'written' are the present and past ~s of the verb 'write'.* **par·ti·cip·i·al** [ˌpɑːtiˈsipiəl] *adj.* of a ~: *participial adjective* (e.g. *loving* in 'a loving mother').

par·ti·cle [ˈpɑːtikl] *n.* 1. very small bit: ~s of dust. 2. (grammar) article (*a, an, the*), preposition or adverb (*up, in,* etc.), conjunction, or affix (e.g. *un-, in-, -ness, -ly*).

par·ti·col·oured [ˈpɑːtikʌləd] *adj.* differently coloured in different parts.

par·tic·u·lar [pəˈtikjulə*] *adj.* 1. relating to one as distinct from others: *in this ~ case.* 2. especial: *do sth. with ~ care.* 3. hard to satisfy: *very ~ about what he eats.* 4. giving or showing great attention to detail: *~ about what she wears.* in ~, especially. *n.* detail: *go into ~s, give details.* ~**ize** *v.t.* give ~s of; name one by one. ~**ly** *adv.* especially; distinctly.

par·ti·san [ˌpɑːtiˈzæn] *n.* person devoted to a party, group, or cause.

par·ti·tion [pɑːˈtiʃən] *n.* 1. division into parts. 2. that which divides, esp. a thin wall between rooms, etc. 3. part formed by dividing; section. *v.t.* divide: ~*ed off,* separated by means of a ~.

part·ner [ˈpɑːtnə*] *n.* 1. person who takes part with another or others in some activity, esp. one of the owners of a business. 2. one of two persons dancing together, playing tennis, cards, etc., together; husband or wife. *v.t.* be a ~ to. ~**ship** *n.*

par·took, see *partake*.

part·ridge [ˈpɑːtridʒ] *n.* sorts of bird of the same family as the pheasant; its flesh as food.

par·ty [ˈpɑːti] *n.* 1. body of persons united in opinion, in support of a cause, etc., esp. in politics. *the ~ line,* the declared policy of a political ~. See also (4). 2. system of government based on political parties: *the ~ system; putting public interest before ~.* 3. one of the persons or sides in a legal action, agreement, etc. 4. group of persons travelling or working together. *a ~ line,* telephone line shared by two or more subscribers. 5. meeting, by invitation, of a group of persons, e.g. at a private house, for pleasure: *a dinner (birthday,* etc.*) ~.* 6. person taking part in or approving of an action: *a ~ to an action.* 7. (humor.) person.

pass [pɑːs] *v.i. & t.* 1. go past (2), move towards and beyond (a person, place, or object): ~ *ing through the village; after ~ing the post office.* 2. give by handing: *a letter that was ~ed on to all the members of the family. P~ the salt, please.* 3. ~ *a remark,* speak (*about*). ~ *the time of day with,* give a greeting to. 4. change (*from* one state of things to another); change (*into* another state of things). 5. come to an end; die: *customs that are ~ing. He ~ed away* (died) *peacefully. The pain will soon ~ off.* 6. examine and accept; be examined and accepted (*in*): *Parliament ~ed the Bill. The Bill ~ed. The examiners ~ed the candidates. The boys ~ed* (the *examination*) *in French.* 7. take place, be done or said (*between* persons). 8. (of time) spend; be spent: *How shall we ~ the evening? Time ~ed quickly.* 9. (cause to) circulate: *imprisoned for ~ing forged bank-notes.* 10. (= surpass) be beyond the range of: *a story that ~es belief.* 11. give (an opinion, judgement, sentence *upon* sb. or sth.). 12. (with adv. & prep.): ~ *sb. or sth. by,* (a) go past, (b) pay no attention to. ~ *for,* be accepted as. ~ *off,* (of events) take place without trouble: *The meeting of the strikers ~ed off quietly.* ~ *sth.* (*sb., oneself*) *off as,* represent falsely, get people to believe that (it, he, etc.) is sth. different. ~ *out*, (colloq.) faint. ~ *sth. or sb. over*, pay no attention to, overlook. *n.* 1. success in satisfying examiners (without distinction or honours(7)): *a* ~ *in mathematics*; *a* ~ *degree*. 2. (paper, ticket, etc., giving) permission or authority to travel, leave or enter a building, occupy a seat in a theatre, etc. 3. (sing. only) serious condition: *Things have come to a sad* (*pretty*) ~. *come to* ~, happen; *bring to* ~, cause to happen. 5. act of ~ing the ball from one player to another (in football, etc.). 6. movement of the hand over or in front of sth. (as in conjuring, etc.). 7. forward movement, blow (in fencing, etc.). 8. narrow way over or between mountains.

pas·sa·ble ['pɑːsəbl] *adj.* 1. (of roads, etc.) that can be ~ed over. 2. that can be accepted as fairly good but not excellent. **pas·sa·bly** *adv.* '~·book *n.* book with a customer's bank account record. **pas·ser-by** ['pɑː- sə'bai] *n.* (pl. *passers-by*). one who goes past, esp. by chance. '~·key *n.* key opening a number of different locks. '~·word *n.* secret word which enables sb. to be known as a friend (e.g. by sentries).

pas·sage ['pæsidʒ] *n.* 1. act of going past, through, or across; journey by sea: *the* ~ *of time*; *to book one's* ~ *to New York*. 2. way through; corridor. 3. passing(6) of a Bill so that it becomes law. 4. short extract from a piece of writing.

pas·sen·ger ['pæsindʒə*] *n.* person being conveyed by bus, aircraft, train, ship, etc.

pas·sion ['pæʃən] *n.* 1. strong feeling or enthusiasm: *filled with* ~ *for sb.* 2. outburst of anger: *fly into a* ~. 3. *the P*~, the suffering and death of Jesus. ~·ate ['pæʃənit] *adj.* easily moved by ~; filled with, showing, ~.

pas·sive ['pæsiv] *adj.* 1. acted upon but not acting; not offering active resistance: *remain*

~; ~ *obedience*; ~ *resistance*. 2. (of verb forms) form used when the subject of the verb is affected, as in 'The letter *was written* yesterday'. ~·ly *adv.*

pas·si·vi·ty [pə'siviti] *n.*

Pas·so·ver ['pɑːsouvə*] *n.* Jewish feast.

pass·port ['pɑːspɔːt] *n.* 1. government document to be carried by a traveller abroad, giving personal particulars. 2. (fig.) means of attaining (*to* favour, success, etc.).

past [pɑːst] *adj.* of the time before the present. *n.* 1. ~ time; ~ events: *memories of the* ~. 2. person's ~ life or experiences. *prep.* 1. after: ~ *eleven o'clock*. 2. up to and farther than: *walk* ~ *the church*. 3. beyond: *pain that was* ~ *bearing*, too severe to be endured. *adv.* beyond in space; up to and farther than: *Walk* (*hurry*, etc.) ~ *and look the other way*.

paste [peist] *n.* 1. soft mixture of flour, fat, etc., for making pastry. 2. ~-like mixture made from meat, fish, etc. 3. mixture of flour and water used for sticking things together, esp. paper on walls or boards. 4. substance used in making artificial diamonds, etc. *v.t.* stick (things *down*, *together*, *on*, etc.) with ~ (3). '~·board *n.* cardboard.

pas·tel ['pæstəl] *n.* (picture drawn with) coloured chalk made into crayons: ~ *shades*, soft, light, delicate colours.

pas·teur·ize ['pæstəraiz] *v.t.* rid (milk, etc.) from disease germs by using the heating method of Pasteur.

pas·tille ['pæstil] *n.* small sweet, usu. containing medicine for the throat.

pas·time ['pɑːstaim] *n.* anything done to pass time pleasantly; a game.

pas·tor ['pɑːstə*] *n.* minister (esp. in a nonconformist church).

pas·tor·al ['pɑːstərəl] *adj.* 1. of a bishop: ~ *letter*, to the members of his diocese; ~ *staff*, bishop's emblem, like a shepherd's staff or crook. 2. of shepherds and country life: ~ *poetry*. **n.** ~ poem or drama.

pas·try ['peistri] **n.** paste of flour, fat, etc., baked in an oven, with fruit, meat, etc.; pies, tarts, etc.

pas·ture ['pɑːstʃə*] **n.** grassland for cattle; grass on such land. **v.t.** put cattle, sheep, etc., on ~; (of animals) eat the grass on (a ~). **pas·tur·age** ['pɑːstʃəridʒ] **n.** = ~.

pas·ty ['peisti] **adj.** like paste (1). *a ~ complexion*, white and unhealthy. (also ['pæsti]) **n.** meat covered in paste (1) and baked.

¹pat [pæt] **v.t.** (-*tt*-). hit gently again and again with the open hand or with something flat: *pat a dog; pat sb. on the back.* **n. 1.** touch of this kind. **2.** small mass of sth., esp. butter, shaped by patting it.

²pat [pæt] **adv.** at the right moment; at once and without hesitation: *The answer came pat.*

patch [pætʃ] **n. 1.** small piece of material put on over a hole or damaged place. **2.** differently coloured part of a surface: *a dog with a white ~ on its neck.* **3.** small area of ground, esp. for gardening: *the cabbage ~.* **4.** *not a ~ on*, not nearly so good as. **v.t. 1.** put a ~ or ~es on. **2.** ~ *up*, make roughly ready for use: *an old ~ed-up motor-bicycle*; (fig.) ~ *up a quarrel*, settle it for a time. '~**work n.** piece of material made of bits of cloth of various sizes, shapes, and colours sewn together. ~**·y adj.** (fig., of work) of uneven quality.

pate [peit] **n.** (colloq., humor.) head.

pat·ent ['peitənt] **adj. 1.** evident, easily seen: *It was ~ that he disliked the idea.* **2.** *letters ~* (usu. ['pætənt]), government authority to manufacture sth. invented and protect it from imitation. **3.** protected by letters ~: *a ~ medicine*, one made and sold by one manufacturer only. **n. 1.** (privilege granted by) letters ~. **2.** that which is given legal protection by letters ~ against imitation. **v.t.** obtain a ~ for (an invention, etc.).

~·**ee** [,peitən'tiː] **n.** person to whom a ~ has been granted.

pa·ter ['peitə*] **n.** (old-fashioned schoolboy slang) father.

pa·ter·nal [pə'təːnl] **adj.** of or like a father. ~·**ly adv. pa·ter·ni·ty** [pə'təːniti] **n.** being a father; origin on the father's side: *paternity unknown*; (fig.) source.

path [pɑːθ] **n.** (pl. ~*s* [pɑːðz]). **1.** (also ~*way*) way made (across fields, through woods, etc.) by people walking. **2.** (also *foot*~) prepared track for walkers along the side of a road. (Cf. *pavement*.) **3.** line along which sth. or sb. moves: *the moon's ~ round the earth.* '~·**way n.** = foot~.

pa·thet·ic [pə'θetik] **adj.** sad; pitiful. **pa·thet·i·cal·ly adv.**

pa·thol·o·gy [pə'θɔlədʒi] **n.** science of diseases. **path·o·log·i·cal** [,pæθə'lɔdʒikl] **adj.** of ~; of the nature of disease. **pa·thol·o·gist** [pə'θɔlədʒist] **n.** student of, expert in, ~.

pa·thos ['peiθɔs] **n.** quality that arouses feelings of pity.

pa·tience ['peiʃəns] **n. 1.** (power of) enduring trouble, suffering, inconvenience, without complaining; ability to wait for results, to solve problems calmly and without haste, etc.: *out of ~ with*, no longer able to endure. **2.** kind of card game (usu. for one person). **pa·tient** ['peiʃənt] **adj.** having or showing ~. **n.** person receiving medical treatment.

pa·tri·arch ['peitriɑːk] **n.** old man who is highly respected.

pa·tri·cian [pə'triʃən] **n. & adj.** (person) of noble birth (esp. of ancient Rome).

pat·ri·mo·ny ['pætriməni] **n.** property inherited from one's father or ancestors.

pat·ri·ot ['pætriət] **n.** person who loves and is ready to defend his country. ~·**ic** [,pætri'ɔtik] **adj.** ~·**ism** ['pætriətizm] **n.** feelings and qualities of a ~.

pa·trol [pə'troul] **v.t. & i.** (-*ll*-). go round (a camp, town, the streets, etc.) to see that all is well, to look out (for wrong-doers, the enemy, etc.). *n.* **1.** the act of ~ling: *soldiers on* ~ ; *constant sea and air* ~. **2.** person(s), ship(s), or aircraft on ~ duties.

pa·tron ['peitrən] *n.* **1.** person who supports financially, etc., the artistic or social work of a person or society. **2.** regular customer (of a shop). **3.** ~ *saint*, saint regarded as protecting (a church, town, travellers, etc.). **pat·ron·age** ['pætrənidʒ, 'peit-] *n.* **1.** support, etc., given by a ~ (1), (2). **2.** right of a ~ (1) (to appoint sb. to a position, to grant privileges, etc.). **3.** ~izing (2) manner. **pat·ron·ize** ['pæt·rənaiz] *v.t.* **1.** be a ~ (1), (2) to. **2.** treat (sb. whom one is helping, talking to, etc.) as if he were an inferior person.

¹pat·ter ['pætə*] *n.* sound of quick, light taps or footsteps: *the* ~ *of rain on a roof.* *v.i.* make this sound.

²pat·ter ['pætə*] *n.* **1.** kind of talk, words, used by a class of people : *thieves'* ~. **2.** rapid talk of a conjurer or comedian.

pat·tern ['pætən] *n.* **1.** excellent example : *a* ~ *of all the virtues.* **2.** sth : serving as a model, esp. the shape of a garment, cut out in paper, used as a guide in dressmaking. **3.** sample, esp. a small piece of cloth. **4.** ornamental design (on a carpet, wallpaper, etc.).

pat·ty ['pæti] *n.* small pie with meat, oysters, etc., in it.

pau·ci·ty ['pɔ:siti] *n.* smallness of number or quantity.

paunch [pɔ:ntʃ] *n.* fat belly.

pau·per ['pɔ:pə*] *n.* person with no income, esp. when he is supported by charity. ~·**ize** *v.t.* make a ~ of.

pause [pɔ:z] *n.* **1.** short interval or stop in the middle of (doing or saying sth.). **2.** *give* ~ *to,* cause (sb.) to stop and think. *v.i.* make a ~.

pave [peiv] *v.t.* put flat stones, bricks, etc., on (a road, etc.); (fig.) ~ *the way for,* make conditions easy for. **¹~·ment** *n.* ~d

way at the side of a street for people on foot.

pa·vil·ion [pə'viljən] *n.* **1.** ornamental building for concerts, dancing, etc. **2.** building on a sports ground for the use of players, spectators, etc. **3.** big tent.

paw [pɔ:] *n.* animal's foot that has claws or nails; (humor.) hand. *v.t.* (of animals) feel, scratch, with the paw(s); (of a horse) strike (the ground) with a hoof.

¹pawn [pɔ:n] *n.* least valuable piece in the game of chess; person made use of by others for their own advantage.

²pawn [pɔ:n] *v.t.* leave (clothing, jewellery, etc.) as pledge for money borrowed. *n.* (only) *in* ~, ~ed: *His watch is in* ~. '~·**brok·er** *n.* person licensed to lend money at interest on the security of goods, etc., left with him. '~·**shop** *n.*

paw·paw, pa·paw, see *papaya.*

pay [pei] *v.t. & i.* (p.t. & p.p. *paid* [peid]). **1.** give (sb.) money for goods, etc.: *pay sb. off,* pay him his wages and discharge (4) him. **2.** suffer pain or punishment (*for* what one has done). **3.** give (attention *to* sth.); make (a call, a visit, *on* sb.); offer (a compliment *to* sb.). **4.** *pay out* (rope), let (it) pass out through the hands. *n.* money paid for regular work or services, e.g. in the armed forces. **pay·a·ble** *adj.* which must or may be paid. **pay·ee** [pei'i:] *n.* person to whom money is (to be) paid. **pay·mas·ter** *n.* officer in the army, etc., responsible for pay. **pay·ment** *n.* paying or being paid; sum of money paid; reward or punishment.

pea [pi:] *n.* plant with seeds in pods, used as food; one of these seeds. (See the picture on page 375.) '**pea·nut** *n.* = ground-nut.

peace [pi:s] *n.* **1.** state of freedom from war and disorder: *at* ~ *with neighbouring countries.* **2.** rest; quiet; calm: ~ *of mind; hold one's* ~, say nothing, stop

talking. ~·a·ble *adj.* not quarrelsome; ~ful. ~·a·bly *adv.*
~·ful *adj.* 1. loving ~. 2. calm;
quiet. ~·ful·ly *adv.* '~·,mak·er
n. person who helps to bring
about ~, to end quarrels. '~·
,of·fer·ing *n.* sth. offered to show
that one is willing to make ~.

Peas in a pod

peach [pi:tʃ] *n.* (tree with) juicy
round fruit with delicate yellowish-red skin and a rough stone-
like seed; yellowish-red colour.
pea·cock ['pi:kɔk] *n.* large male
bird as shown here, noted for
its fine tail feathers. '**pea·hen**
n. female of ~.

A peacock   A pear

peak [pi:k] *n.* 1. pointed top,
esp. of a mountain. 2. pointed
front part of a cap, to shade the
eyes. 3. highest point or period
of use: *the ~ hours* (e.g. of traffic).
peal [pi:l] *n.* 1. loud ringing of a
bell, or of bells with different
notes. 2. set of bells tuned to be
played together. 3. loud echoing
noise: *~s of thunder (laughter)*.
v.t. & i. (cause to) ring or sound
loudly.
pear [pɛə*] *n.* (tree with) sweet
juicy fruit as shown above.
pearl [pə:l] *n.* 1. silvery-white
gem which forms in some oyster
shells, valued for its beauty. 2.
sth. that looks like a ~ (e.g. a
dewdrop); sb. or sth. very
precious.
peas·ant ['pezənt] *n.* countryman (not now in Great Britain,
U.S.A., etc.) working on the
land, either for wages or on a

very small farm which he rents
or owns: ~ *labour.* ~·ry *n.* the
~s of a country; ~s as a class.
peat [pi:t] *n.* plant material
partly decomposed by the action
of water; piece of this cut out
(to be) dried and burnt as fuel.
~·y *adj.*
peb·ble ['pebl] *n.* small stone
made smooth and round by rolling against other stones in the
sea or a river.
pec·ca·dil·lo [,pekə'dilou] *n.*
small unimportant weakness in
a person's character; small fault.
¹**peck** [pek] *n.* measure for dry
goods (e.g. beans) equal to two
gallons; (fig.) a lot: *a ~ of
troubles.*
²**peck** [pek] *v.t. & i.* 1. strike (*at*)
with the beak; get by doing
this: *hens ~ing corn*; make (a
hole) by doing this. 2. (colloq.)
~ *at one's food*, eat only small
bits of food, having no appetite.
n. stroke made by a bird with
its beak; (colloq.) quick, carelessly given kiss. ~·ish *adj.*
(colloq.) hungry.
pe·cu·liar [pi'kju:ljə*] *adj.* 1.
strange; unusual. 2. special. 3.
~ *to*, used, adopted, practised,
only by: *a style of dress ~ to this
tribe.* ~·ly *adv.* **pe·cu·li·ar·i·ty**
[pi,kju:li'æriti] *n.* sth. strange or
characteristic.
pe·cu·nia·ry [pi'kju:njəri] *adj.*
of money.
ped·a·gogue ['pedəgog] *n.*
schoolmaster; pedantic teacher.
ped·a·go·gy ['pedəgodʒi, -gogi]
n. science of teaching.
ped·al ['pedl] *n.* part of a machine or instrument (e.g. bicycle,
sewing-machine, piano) worked
by the foot or feet. *v.t. & i.*
(*-ll-*). use a ~ or ~s (for playing
an organ, riding a ~ bicycle).
ped·ant ['pedənt] *n.* person who
values book-learning, rules,
etc., too highly. **pe·dan·tic**
[pi'dæntik] *adj.* of a ~. ~·ry
['pedəntri] *n.* tiresome and unnecessary display of learning.
ped·dle ['pedl] *v.i. & t.* go from
house to house, selling small
articles. **ped·lar** *n.* one who
does this.

ped·es·tal ['pedistl] *n.* base of a column; base for a statue or other work of art.

pe·des·tri·an [pi'destriən] *n.* person walking in a street, etc. *adj.* 1. going on foot; connected with walking. 2. (of a person, what he says or writes) dull; uninspired.

ped·i·cab ['pedikæb] *n.* three-wheeled cab for two passengers and driver (in some Asian countries).

ped·i·gree ['pedigri:] *n.* line of ancestors; ancient descent. ~ *animals*, whose ~ is recorded.

ped·lar, see *peddle*.

peek [pi:k] *v.i.* peep (*at* sth.).

peel [pi:l] *v.t. & i.* 1. take the skin off (fruit, etc.). 2. (of the skin of the body, wallpaper, the bark of a tree, etc.) come off in bits or strips. *n.* skin of fruit, potatoes, young shoots. ~·**ings** *n. pl.* pieces ~ed off (e.g. *potato* ~*ings*).

peep [pi:p] *n.* 1. a short quick look, often one taken secretly or inquisitively. 2. a look through a narrow opening; an incomplete view. 3. the first light (of day). ~ *v.i.* 1. take a ~ at: ~*ing from behind the curtains.* 2. come into view slowly or partly: *The sun* ~*ed out from the clouds.*

¹peer [piə*] *v.i.* look (*at, into,* sth.) closely, as if or when unable to see well.

²peer [piə*] *n.* 1. person's equal in rank, merit, etc. 2. (in Gt. Brit.) nobleman; person with the right to sit in the House of Lords. ~·**age** ['piəridʒ] *n.* the ~s (2); the rank of ~ (2): *raised to the* ~*age;* book with a list of ~s. ~·**ess** ['piəris] *n.* woman ~; wife of a ~ (2). ~·**less** *adj.* without equal.

peev·ish ['pi:viʃ] *adj.* irritable. ~·**ly** *adv.*

peg [peg] *n.* 1. wooden or metal pin or bolt used to fasten parts of woodwork, etc., together, to hang things on (e.g. *hat-pegs*), to hold a rope (e.g. *tent-pegs*), to fasten laundered clothes to a line (*clothes-pegs*), to stop up a

hole in a barrel, etc. *a square peg in a round hole,* a person unfitted for his position. 2. (colloq.) alcoholic drink, esp. whisky. *v.t. & i.* (-*gg*-). 1. fasten with pegs: *peg a tent down.* 2. fix (prices, etc.) by regulation. 3. *peg away* (*at*), keep on working (at). *peg out,* (colloq.) die.

pe·kin·ese [ˌpi:ki'ni:z] *n.* small Chinese dog with long silky hair.

pel·i·can ['pelikən] *n.* large water-bird with a long bill under which hangs a pouch.

pel·let ['pelit] *n.* 1. small ball of sth. soft (e.g. wet paper, bread), made, for example, by rolling between the fingers; pill. 2. small ball of lead for a gun.

pell-mell ['pel'mel] *adv.* in a hurrying disorderly manner.

¹pelt [pelt] *n.* animal's skin with the hair or fur on it.

²pelt [pelt] *v.t. & i.* 1. attack (with stones, mud, etc.). 2. (of rain, etc.) beat down; fall heavily: *hail* ~*ing against the roof. It is* ~*ing with rain. n. at full* ~, at full speed.

pel·vis ['pelvis] *n.* cavity composed of the hip-bones and the lower part of the backbone, holding the bowel, bladder, etc.

pem·mi·can ['pemikən] *n.* dried lean meat beaten and mixed into cakes (as) by N. American Indians.

¹pen [pen] *n.* instrument for writing in ink, consisting of a metal nib in a holder, or (*fountain-pen*) a nib fixed in a hollow container ('barrel') of ink, or (*ball-pen*) a tiny metal ball revolving at the end of a narrow tube filled with special ink. *v.t.* (-*nn*-). write (a letter, etc.). **¹pen·man·ship** *n.* art or style of handwriting. **¹pen·knife** *n.* small folding pocket-knife.

²pen [pen] *n.* small closed-in space for cattle, sheep, pigs, etc. *v.t.* (-*nn*-). *pen sb. up* (*in*), shut up in or as in a ~.

pe·nal ['pi:nl] *adj.* connected with punishment: ~ *laws; a* ~ *offence,* one for which there is legal punishment; ~ *servitude,* imprisonment for three years or more with hard labour. **pe·nal·ize** ['pi:nəlaiz] *v.t.* make (an act) ~; give a ~ty to (a player, competitor, etc.). **pe·nal·i·za·tion** [ˌpi:nəlai'zeiʃən] *n.* **pen·al·ty** ['penəlti] *n.* 1. punishment for wrongdoing, for failure to obey rules or keep an agreement, etc.; suffering which wrongdoing brings. 2. (in sport, competitions, etc.) loss of points, disadvantage, etc., imposed for breaking a rule.

pen·ance ['penəns] *n.* punishment which sb. imposes upon himself to show repentance, as on the advice of a priest: *do ~ for one's sins.*

pence, see *penny.*

pen·cil ['pensl] *n.* instrument for drawing or writing with, especially a thin rod of wood enclosing a stick of graphite or coloured chalk sharpened to a point. *v.t.* (-ll-). write or draw with a ~.

pend·ant ['pendənt] *n.* hanging ornament, esp. one fastened to a necklace, etc.

pend·ing ['pendiŋ] *adj.* waiting to be settled or decided. *prep.* 1. while waiting for (e.g. sb.'s arrival). 2. during the continuance of (e.g. discussions).

pen·du·lum ['pendjuləm] *n.* weighted rod hung from a fixed point so that it swings freely, esp. one regulating the movement of a clock. *the swing of the ~*, (fig.) the movement(3) of public opinion from one extreme to the other.

A pendulum

A penguin

pen·e·trate ['penitreit] *v.t. & i.* 1. make a way into or through; pierce; (fig.) see into or through. 2. spread through: *bad smells that ~d (through) the building.* **pen·e·trat·ing** *adj.* (of a person, his mind) keen; able to see and understand quickly and clearly;

(of cries, voices) piercing; loud and clear. **pen·e·tra·tion** [ˌpeni'treiʃən] *n.*

pen·guin ['peŋgwin] *n.* sea-bird of the Antarctic with wings used for swimming, not for flying.

pe·nin·su·la [pə'ninsjulə] *n.* area of land (e.g. Italy) almost surrounded by water. **pe·nin·su·lar** *adj.* of or like a ~.

pen·i·tence ['penitəns] *n.* sorrow and regret for wrongdoing. **pen·i·tent** *n. & adj.* (person) feeling regret; showing ~: *penitent looks.* **pen·i·ten·tial** [ˌpeni'tenʃl] *adj.* of ~ or of penance. **pen·i·ten·tia·ry** [ˌpeni'tenʃəri] *n.* prison, esp. one in which reform of the prisoners is the chief aim.

pen·nant ['penənt], **pen·non** ['penən] *n.* long, narrow (usu. triangular) flag.

pen·ny ['peni] *n.* (pl. *pennies*, a number of coins; *pence* [pens], for value or cost). British coin, see the Appendix, p. 628. '~·worth, 'pen·n'orth ['penəθ] *n.* as much as a ~ will buy. 'pen·ni·less *adj.* without money or property.

pen·sion ['penʃən] *n.* regular payment made by the State or by a former employer to sb. on completion of a term of service, or on retirement, disablement, etc. *v.t.* give a ~ to. ~·er *n.* person receiving a ~.

pen·sive ['pensiv] *adj.* deep in thought.

pent [pent] *adj.* shut (*up*) in; penned up: *~-up feelings.*

pen·ta·gon ['pentəgən] *n.* plane figure with five sides and five internal angles.

pent·house ['penthaus] *n.* sloping roof supported against a wall, esp. one for a shelter or shed; flat(4) built on the roof of a tall building.

pen·ul·ti·mate [pi'nʌltimit] *n. & adj.* (word, syllable, etc., which is) last but one.

pen·u·ry ['penjuəri] *n.* poverty. **pe·nu·ri·ous** [pi'njuəriəs] *adj.* poor; not generous.

pe·o·ny ['piəni] *n.* garden plant

with large round white, pink, or red flowers.

peo·ple ['pi:pl] *n.* **1.** men and women in general. **2.** all those persons forming a nation or race : *government of the ~ by the ~ for the ~.* **3.** *the ~,* those who are not nobles, not high in rank, position, etc. **4.** (with indef. art. and in pl.) race, nation : *the ~s of Asia; a brave and intelligent ~.* *v.t.* fill with people : *in : a thickly-~d district.*

pep [pep] *n.* (slang) energy.

pep·per ['pepə*] *n.* **1.** hot-tasting powder made from the dried berries of certain plants, used on food. **2.** red, yellow, or green seed-pods of certain plants, used as a vegetable. *v.t.* **1.** put ~ on (food). **2.** ~ *sb. with* (stones, questions, etc.), pelt with. '~·mint** *n.* (plant producing) hot-tasting oil used in medicine and for flavouring sweets. **~·y** *adj.* tasting of ~ ; hot-tempered.

per [pə*] *prep.* for each, in each : *per annum* (year), *per pound*, *per man*, *per cent* (hundred). **per·cen·tage** [pə'sentidʒ] *n.* rate or number per cent.

per·ad·ven·ture [pərəd'ventʃə*] *adv.* (old use) perhaps ; by chance.

per·am·bu·la·tor [pə'ræmbjuleitə*], **pram** [præm] *n.* four-wheeled hand-pushed carriage for a baby.

per·ceive [pə'si:v] *v.t.* become aware of, esp. through the eyes or the mind. **per·cep·ti·ble** [pə'septibl] *adj.* that can be ~d. **per·cep·ti·bly** *adv.* **per·cep·tion** [pə'sepʃən] *n.* act or power of perceiving. **per·cep·tive** [pə'septiv] *adj.* having or connected with perception.

perch [pə:tʃ] *n.* **1.** bird's resting-place (e.g. a branch); rod or bar provided for this purpose. **2.** any high position occupied by a person or building. **3.** measure of distance, 5½ yards. *v.t. & i.* **1.** come to rest (on); take up position (*on a high place*): *~ed on a high stool (on sb.'s shoulders)*. **2.** (of a building) be situated : *~ed on the top of the hill.*

per·chance [pə'tʃɑ:ns] *adv.* (old use) perhaps ; possibly ; by chance.

per·co·late ['pə:kəleit] *v.i. & t.* **1.** (of liquid) pass slowly (*through*); filter (*through*). **2.** cause (liquid, etc.) to ~. **per·co·la·tor** *n.* (esp.) apparatus in which boiling water ~s through coffee.

per·cus·sion [pə'kʌʃən] *n.* the striking together of two (usu. hard) objects; ²tapping : ~ *instruments,* musical instruments played by ~, e.g. drums.

per·di·tion [pə'diʃən] *n.* complete ruin; everlasting damnation.

per·e·gri·na·tion [,perigri'neiʃən] *n.* journey; travelling about.

per·emp·to·ry [pə'remptəri] *adj.* (of commands) not to be disobeyed or questioned; (of a person, his manner) (too) commanding; insisting on obedience. **per·emp·to·ri·ly** *adv.*

per·en·ni·al [pə'reniəl] *adj.* **1.** continuing throughout the whole year. **2.** lasting for a very long time. **3.** (of plants) living for more than two years. *n.* ~ plant.

per·fect ['pə:fikt] *adj.* **1.** complete, with everything needed. **2.** without fault; excellent. [pə:'fekt] *v.t.* make ~. **~·ly** *adv.* completely. **per·fec·tion** [pə'fekʃən] *n.* ~ing or being ~ed ; ~ quality, person, etc.: *the ~ion of beauty.*

per·fi·dy ['pə:fidi] *n.* treachery; breaking of faith with sb.; treacherous act. **per·fid·i·ous** [pə:'fidiəs] *adj.* treacherous.

per·fo·rate ['pə:fəreit] *v.t. & i.* make a hole or holes through, esp. a line of small holes in paper so that part may be torn off easily. **per·fo·ra·tion** [,pə:fə'reiʃən] *n.* (esp.) line of holes made through paper (as between stamps).

per·force [pə'fɔ:s] *adv.* of necessity.

per·form [pə'fɔ:m] *v.t. & i.* **1.** do (a piece of work, sth. one is ordered to do, sth. one has promised to do, etc.). **2.** act (a play); play (music), sing, do tricks, etc., before an audience. ~**ance** *n.* **1.** ~ing; (esp.) sth. done or acted: *a fine* ~*ance*. **2.** the ~ing of a play; a concert: *two* ~*s daily*. ~**er** *n.* one who ~s, esp. in a play or at a concert. ~**ing** *adj.* (of animals) trained to ~ stage tricks: ~*ing elephants*.

per·fume ['pə:fju:m] *n.* (prepared liquid with a) sweet smell, esp. that of flowers. [pə'fju:m] *v.t.* give a ~ to; put ~ on.

per·func·to·ry [pə'fʌŋktəri] *adj.* done as a duty but without care or interest; (of a person) doing things thus; casual. **per·func·to·ri·ly** *adv.*

per·go·la ['pə:gələ] *n.* structure of posts for climbing-plants shading a garden walk.

per·haps [pə'hæps, præps] *adv.* possibly; it may be.

per·il ['peril] *n.* serious danger. ~**ous** *adj.* dangerous; risky.

per·im·e·ter [pə'rimitə*] *n.* (length of the) outer boundary of a closed figure.

pe·ri·od ['piəriəd] *n.* **1.** length or portion of time marked off by events that recur (e.g. a month). **2.** indefinite portion of time in the life of a person, nation, etc.: *the* ~ *of the French Revolution*. **3.** (grammar) complete sentence or statement, usu. complex. **4.** the pause at the end of a sentence; the mark (also called *full stop*) indicating this in writing. ~**ic** [ˌpiəri'ɔdik] *adj.* occurring or appearing at regular intervals. ~**i·cal** *adj.* = ~ic. *n.* ~ic publication (e.g. a magazine, a newspaper). ~**i·cal·ly** *adv.*

per·i·pa·tet·ic [ˌperipə'tetik] *adj.* going about from place to place; wandering.

per·i·scope ['periskoup] *n.* instrument with mirrors and lenses arranged to reflect a view down a tube, etc., so that the viewer may get a view as from a level above that of his eyes; used in submarines, trenches.

per·ish ['periʃ] *v.i. & t.* **1.** (cause to) be destroyed, come to an end, die; decay. **2.** ~*ed with cold*, feeling very cold. ~**a·ble** *adj.* (esp. of food) quickly or easily going bad.

per·i·wig ['periwig] *n.* = wig.

per·jure ['pə:dʒə*] *v.t.* ~ *oneself*, knowingly make a false statement after taking an oath to tell the truth. **per·jured** *adj.* having ~d oneself. **per·ju·ry** *n.* act of perjuring oneself.

perk [pə:k] *v.i. & t.* **1.** (of a person) ~ *up*, become lively and active. **2.** (of a horse, etc.) ~ *up (its head, tail)*, lift up as a sign of interest, liveliness, etc. ~**y** *adj.* (-*ier*, *iest*). lively; showing interest or confidence, ~**i·ly** *adv.* ~**i·ness** *n.*

per·ma·nent ['pə:mənənt] *adj.* going on for a long time; intended to last: *the* ~ *way*, railway track; ~ *wave*, style of hairdressing in which waves or curls are set in the hair so that they last several months. ~**ly** *adv.* **per·ma·nence** *n.*

per·me·ate ['pə:mieit] *v.t. & i.* ~ *through*, spread, pass, into every part of. **per·me·a·ble** ['pə:miəbl] *adj.* that can be ~d by fluids; porous.

per·mit [pə'mit] *v.t. & i.* (-*tt*-). **1.** allow: *Smoking not* ~*ted. P*~ *me to say that. . . . ***2.** ~ *of*, admit (3): *a situation that* ~*s of no delay*. ['pə:mit] *n.* written authority to do sth., go somewhere, etc. **per·mis·si·ble** [pə'misibl] *adj.* which is ~ted. **per·mis·sion** [pə'miʃən] *n.* consent; statement, etc., that ~s.

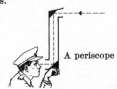

A periscope

per·mu·ta·tion [ˌpə:mju'teiʃən] *n.* change of the order in which a number of things are arranged.

per·ni·cious [pə'niʃəs] *adj.* harmful; injurious: ~ *influences* (*habits*).

per·nick·e·ty [pə'nikəti] *adj.* fussy; worrying about unimportant details.

per·o·ra·tion [ˌperə'reiʃən] *n.* last part of a speech; summing up.

per·ox·ide [pə'rɔksaid] *n.* (esp.) chemical substance used as a disinfectant and for bleaching (e.g. hair).

per·pen·dic·u·lar [ˌpə:pən'dik-julə*] *adj.* 1. at an angle of 90° to (another line or surface). 2. upright; crossing the horizontal at an angle of 90°. *n.* ~ line.

per·pe·trate ['pə:pitreit] *v.t.* commit (a crime, an error); do (sth. wrong). **per·pe·tra·tor** *n.* **per·pe·tra·tion** [ˌpə:pi'treiʃən] *n.*

per·pet·u·al [pə'petjuəl] *adj.* 1. never-ending; going on for a long time or without stopping. 2. often repeated. ~**ly** *adv.* **per·pet·u·ate** [pə'petjueit] *v.t.* preserve from being forgotten or from going out of use. **per·pe·tu·i·ty** [ˌpə:pi'tjuiti] *n.* being ~: *in perpetuity*, for ever.

per·plex [pə'pleks] *v.t.* 1. puzzle, bewilder. 2. make (a question, etc.) more complex or confusing. **per·plexed** *adj.* ~**ed·ly** [pə'pleksidli] *adv.* ~**i·ty** [pə'pleksiti] *n.* 1. ~ed condition. 2. ~ing thing.

per·qui·site ['pə:kwizit] *n.* profit, allowance, etc., taken in addition to regular wages or salary.

per·se·cute ['pə:sikju:t] *v.t.* 1. punish, treat cruelly, esp. because of religious beliefs. 2. allow no peace to; worry (*with* questions, etc.). **per·se·cu·tor** *n.* **per·se·cu·tion** [ˌpə:si'kju:-ʃən] *n.* persecuting or being ~d.

per·se·vere [ˌpə:si'viə*] *v.i.* keep on, continue (*at, in, with*). **per·se·ver·ance** [ˌpə:si'viərəns] *n.*

per·sist [pə'sist] *v.i.* 1. ~ *in*, refuse, in spite of opposition, failure, etc., to make any change in (what one is doing, one's beliefs, etc.). 2. continue to exist.

~**ence** *n.* ~**ent** *adj.* ~**ing;** continuing. ~**ent·ly** *adv.*

per·son ['pə:sn] *n.* 1. man, woman, or child. 2. living body of a ~: *attacks against the* ~, bodily attacks; *be present in* ~, be present oneself (not represented by sb. else). ~**a·ble** *adj.* good-looking. ~**age** *n.* (important) ~. ~**al** *adj.* 1. private; individual; of a ~, not of a group: ~*al needs* (*opinions*). 2. done, etc., by a ~ himself: *a* ~*al call* (*interview*). 3. of a ~'s looks, abilities, qualities, etc.: ~*al beauty.* 4. of, about, against, a ~: ~*al remarks.* ~**al·ly** *adv.* 1. in ~; oneself; not through others. 2. as a ~. 3. speaking for oneself: *P*~*ally I see no objection.* ~**al·i·ty** [ˌpə:sə'næliti] *n.* 1. existence as a ~. 2. qualities that make up a ~'s character: *a strong* ~*ality; a man with little* ~*ality.* 3. person well known in certain circles: *a TV* ~*ality.* 4. (pl.) impolite remarks about sb.'s looks, habits, etc. ~**i·fy** [pə'sɔnifai] *v.t.* 1. regard or represent (sth.) as a ~. 2. be an example of (a quality). ~**i·fi·ca·tion** [pəˌsɔnifi'keiʃən] *n.* ~**nel** [ˌpə:sə'nel] *n.* staff; ~s employed in any work, esp. public undertakings and the armed forces.

per·spec·tive [pə'spektiv] *n.* 1. art of drawing solid objects on a flat surface so as to give the right impression of their relative size, distance, etc. 2. apparent relation between different aspects of a problem, etc.: *see sth. in the right* ~.

per·spi·ca·cious [ˌpə:spi'keiʃəs] *adj.* quick to judge and understand. **per·spi·ca·ci·ty** [ˌpə:-spi'kæsiti] *n.*

per·spic·u·ous [pə'spikjuəs] *adj.* expressed clearly; expressing things clearly.

per·spire [pə'spaiə*] *v.i.* sweat. **per·spi·ra·tion** [ˌpə:spi'reiʃən] *n.*

per·suade [pə'sweid] *v.t.* cause (sb.) by reasoning (*to do sth.,* etc.); convince (sb. *of* the truth of sth., *that* sth. is true, etc.).

per·sua·sion [pə'sweiʒən] *n.*
persuading; being ~d; con-
viction or belief. **per·sua·sive**
[pə'sweisiv] *adj.* able to ~;
convincing.

pert [pəːt] *adj.* saucy; not showing proper respect: *a ~ child
(answer).*

per·tain [pə'tein] *v.i.* ~ *to*, belong to (as a part); have reference to.

per·ti·na·cious [,pəːti'neiʃəs]
adj. not easily giving up (what
has been started); determined.
per·ti·na·ci·ty [,pəːti'næsiti] *n.*

per·ti·nent ['pəːtinənt] *adj.* referring directly (*to* the question,
etc.).

per·turb [pə'təːb] *v.t.* trouble,
make anxious: ~*ing rumours.*

pe·ruke [pə'ruːk] *n.* long wig.

pe·ruse [pə'ruːz] *v.t.* read carefully. **pe·ru·sal** *n.*

per·vade [pə'veid] *v.t.* spread
through, get into every part of.
per·va·sive [pə'veisiv] *adj.*
tending to ~: *pervasive
ideas.*

per·verse [pə'vəːs] *adj.* 1. (of
persons) wilfully continuing in
wrongdoing. 2. (of behaviour)
contrary to reason; (of circumstances) contrary (to one's
wishes).

per·vert [pə'vəːt] *v.t.* 1. turn
(sth.) to a wrong use. 2. cause
(a person, his mind) to turn
away from right behaviour,
beliefs, etc. ['pəːvəːt] *n.* ~ed
person. **per·ver·sion** [pə'vəː-
ʃən] *n.* ~ing or being ~ed.

pes·si·mism ['pesimizm] *n.* tendency to believe that the worst
thing is most likely to happen.
pes·si·mist *n.* person subject
to ~. **pes·si·mis·tic (-ti·cal·ly)**
[,pesi'mistik(əli)] *adj. & adv.*

pest [pest] *n.* troublesome or destructive thing, animal, etc.;
garden ~s (e.g. insects); (old use)
= pestilence. ~**·i·lence** ['pes-
tiləns] *n.* fatal, infectious, quickly spreading disease. ~**·i·len·-
tial** [,pesti'lenʃəl] *adj.* causing
harm; (colloq.) annoying.

pes·ter ['pestə*] *v.t.* trouble;
annoy: ~ed *with flies (requests
for money).*

pes·tle ['pesl] *n.* instrument used
for crushing substances in a
mortar.

A pestle
and mortar

¹pet [pet] *n.* 1. animal, etc., kept
as a companion: *a pet dog.* 2.
person treated as a favourite;
sb. especially loved. *one's pet
name*, name other than the real
name, used affectionately. *v.t.*
(-*tt*-). treat with affection; touch
lovingly.

²pet [pet] *n.* fit of ill temper, esp.
about sth. unimportant. **pet·
tish** *adj.*

pet·al ['petl] *n.* one of the leaf-
like divisions of a flower: *rose
~s.*

pe·ter ['piːtə*] *v.i.* ~ *out*, come
gradually to an end.

pe·ti·tion [pi'tiʃən] *n.* prayer;
earnest request, esp. one made
to an authority and signed by
a number of people. *v.t.* make
a ~ to (sb. *for* sth.).

pet·rel ['petrəl] *n.* long-winged
black and white sea-bird.

pet·ri·fy ['petrifai] *v.t. & i.*
(cause to) change into stone;
(fig.) take away power to think,
feel, act, etc. (through terror,
surprise, etc.). **pet·ri·fac·tion**
[,petri'fækʃən] *n.* ~ing or being
petrified.

pet·rol ['petrəl] *n.* refined petroleum used to drive engines (in
motor-cars, etc.). **pe·tro·le·um**
[pi'trouljəm] *n.* mineral oil from
which ~, paraffin, etc., are
obtained.

pet·ti·coat ['petikout] *n.* woman's underskirt.

pet·ti·fog·ging ['petifɔgiŋ] *adj.*
(of persons) worrying about
small and unimportant details;
(of methods) concerned with
small matters.

pet·ty ['peti] *adj.* 1. unimportant: ~ *troubles.* 2. having or
showing a narrow mind; mean:
~ *spite.* 3. ~ *cash* (business)
money for or from small pay-

ments. **4.** ~ *officer,* naval officer below commissioned rank.

pet·u·lant ['petjulənt] *adj.* unreasonably impatient or irritable. ~**ly** *adv.* **pet·u·lance** *n.*

pew [pju:] *n.* long bench with a back, usu. fixed to the floor, in a church.

pew·ter ['pju:tə*] *n.* grey alloy of tin and lead; vessels made of ~.

pha·lanx ['fælæŋks] *n.* (ancient Greece) body of soldiers in close ranks for fighting.

phan·tasm ['fæntæzm] *n.* phantom. **phan·tas·mal** [fæn'tæzməl] *adj.* of or like a ~. **phan·ta·sy** ['fæntəzi] *n.* = fantasy.

phan·tom ['fæntəm] *n.* ghost; sth. without reality, as seen in a dream or vision.

Pha·raoh ['fɛərou] *n.* title of the kings of ancient Egypt.

phar·ma·cy ['fɑ:məsi] *n.* the preparation of medicines, etc.; chemist's shop. **phar·ma·ceu·ti·cal** [,fɑ:mə'sju:tikl] *adj.*

phase [feiz] *n.* **1.** stage of development: *a ~ of history.* **2.** (of the moon) amount of bright surface visible from the earth (new moon, full moon, etc.). (See *quarter* (7) and the picture at *moon.*)

pheas·ant ['feznt] *n.* long-tailed game bird; its flesh as food.

phe·nom·e·non [fi'nɔminən] *n.* (pl. *phenomena*). **1.** thing that appears to or is perceived by the senses. **2.** remarkable or unusual person or thing. **phe·nom·e·nal** [fi'nɔminl] *adj.* (esp.) extraordinary; unusual.

phi·al ['faiəl] *n.* small bottle, esp. one for medicine.

phi·lan·der [fi'lændə*] *v.i.* make love, be in the habit of making love, without serious intentions. ~**er** *n.*

phil·an·thro·py [fi'lænθrəpi] *n.* love of mankind; practice of helping other people, esp. those who are needy. **phil·an·thro·pist** *n.* person who helps others, esp. those who are poor and in trouble. **phil·an·throp·ic** [,filən'θrɔpik] *adj.* of ~; kind and

helpful: *philanthropic institutions* (e.g. a home for blind people).

phi·lat·e·ly [fi'lætəli] *n.* postage-stamp collecting. **phi·lat·e·list** *n.* stamp-collector.

phi·lol·o·gy [fi'lɔlədʒi] *n.* science of the nature and development of (a) language. **phi·lol·o·gist** *n.* expert in ~. **phi·lo·log·i·cal** [,filə'lɔdʒikl] *adj.* of ~.

phi·los·o·phy [fi'lɔsəfi] *n.* **1.** the search for knowledge, esp. concerning nature and the meaning of existence. **2.** system of thought resulting from such a search. **3.** calm acceptance of events; self-control in the face of suffering or danger. **phi·los·o·pher** *n.* **1.** person studying ~ or having a system of ~. **2.** person whose mind is untroubled by his passions and hardships; person who lets reason govern his life. **phi·lo·soph·i·cal** [,filə'sɔfikl] *adj.* of, devoted to, ~; guided by ~; resigned.

phil·tre ['filtə*] *n.* love-potion.

phlegm [flem] *n.* **1.** thick semifluid substance forming on the skin of the throat and in the nose and brought up by coughing. **2.** quality of being slow to act or feel emotion, interest, etc. **phleg·mat·ic** [fleg'mætik] *adj.* having the quality of ~ (2).

pho·bi·a ['foubiə] *n. & suffix.* fear and dislike of. (See *hydro~.*)

phoe·nix ['fi:niks] *n.* mythical bird.

phone [foun] *n. & v.t. & i.* (colloq.) telephone.

pho·net·ic [fou'netik] *adj.* corresponding to the sounds of speech: ~ *spelling* (e.g. *flem* for *phlegm*); *a ~ language,* one in which the same letters are always used for the same sounds. **pho·net·ics** *n.* (sing. v.) study and science of speech sounds and the symbols used to represent them. **pho·net·i·cal·ly** *adv.* **pho·ne·ti·cian** [,founi'tiʃən] *n.*

pho·ney ['founi] *adj.* (slang) sham.

pho·no·graph ['founəgrɑ:f, -græf] *n.* (U.S.A.) gramophone.

phos·phate ['fɔsfeit] *n.* any salt

of phosphorus, esp. fertilizer containing such salts.

phos·phor·us ['fosfərəs] *n.* yellowish non-metallic element which catches fire easily and gives out a faint light in the dark. **phos·phor·es·cent** [ˌfosfə'resənt] *adj.* giving out a faint light without burning. **phos·phor·es·cence** *n.*

pho·to·graph ['foutəgrɑːf, -græf] *n.* picture made by means of the chemical action of light on a specially prepared glass plate or film. *v.t.* take a ~ of. **pho·tog·ra·pher** [fə'togrəfə*] *n.* **pho·tog·ra·phy** [fə'togrəfi] *n.* art or process of taking ~s. ~**ic** [ˌfoutə'græfik] *adj.* ~**i·cal·ly** *adv.*

phrase [freiz] *n.* small group of words forming part of a sentence (e.g. *in the garden, in order to*). *v.t.* express in words. **phra·se·ol·o·gy** [ˌfreizi'olədʒi] *n.* wording; choice of words.

phys·ic ['fizik] *n.* (colloq.) medicine.

phys·i·cal ['fizikl] *adj.* 1. of material (contrasted with moral and spiritual) things: *the ~ world.* 2. ~ *geography,* of the earth's structure. 3. of the body: ~ *strength (beauty).* 4. of the laws of nature: *It's a ~ impossibility to be in two places at once.* ~**ly** *adv.*

phy·si·cian [fi'ziʃən] *n.* doctor of medicine and surgery.

phys·ics ['fiziks] *n.* (sing. v.) group of sciences dealing with matter and energy (e.g. heat, light, sound), but usu. excluding chemistry and biology. **phys·i·cist** ['fizisist] *n.* expert in ~.

phys·i·og·no·my [ˌfizi'onəmi] *n.* (art of judging character from) the face; general features of a country.

phys·i·ol·o·gy [ˌfizi'olədʒi] *n.* science of the normal functions of living things. **phys·i·o·log·i·cal** [ˌfizio'lodʒikl] *adj.*

phy·sique [fi'ziːk] *n.* structure and development of the body: *a man of strong ~.*

pia·no ['pjænou, pi'ɑːnou] *n.* see the picture at *pierrot.* *n.*

pi·a·nist ['piənist] *n.* person who plays the ~.

pic·co·lo ['pikəlou] *n.* small flute.

¹**pick** [pik] *n.* 1. (also ~*axe*) heavy tool with an iron head having two sharp ends, used for breaking up hard surfaces (e.g. brickwork, roads). 2. small, sharp-pointed instrument: *a tooth~.*

²**pick** [pik] *v.t. & i.* 1. take or gather (flowers, fruit) from plants, bushes, trees; get the meat off (a bone); tear or separate with the fingers: ~*ing rags*; ~*ing sth. to pieces.* 2. choose; select: ~ *only the best;* ~ *one's words;* ~ *one's way (steps) along a muddy road;* ~ *sth. out,* distinguish it, choose it from, among others. 3. ~ *up,* take hold of and lift up (e.g. sth. on the floor); acquire (e.g. bits of information); (of a train, bus, etc.) take (passengers) on to or into; recover or regain one's health (spirits, etc.); meet, talk to, make the acquaintance of (sb.); ~ *oneself up,* get to one's feet after a fall. 4. ~ *sb.'s pocket,* steal sth. from his pocket; ~ *sb.'s brains,* use his ideas as if they were one's own; ~ *a lock,* open it by using a pointed instrument, a piece of wire, etc.; ~ *a quarrel (with sb.),* start one on purpose; ~ *holes in sth.,* point out the faults, etc., in it. *n.* act of ~ing; that which is ~ed or chosen: *the ~ of the bunch,* the best or finest. '~-**a·back** *adv.* (of the way a child is carried) on sb.'s back or shoulders. ~**ings** *n. pl.* small bits left over; odds and ends from which a profit may be made; these profits. '~-**me-up** *n.* sth. (e.g. a drink) that gives new strength or cheerfulness. '~·ˌpock·et *n.* person who steals from a person's pocket. '~-**up** *n.* 1. that part of a record-player which holds the stylus (needle). 2. small, general-purpose van used by builders, farmers, etc.

pick·et ['pikit] *n.* 1. pointed stake, etc., set upright in the ground. 2. small group of men on police duty or sent out to watch the enemy, etc.; one or more workers on guard during a strike, to try to stop others from going to work. **v.t. 1.** put ~s (1) round; fasten (a horse) to a ~ (1). **2.** place a ~ (2) in or round. **3.** act as a ~ (2).

pic·kle ['pikl] *n.* **1.** salt water, vinegar, etc., for keeping meat, vegetables, etc., in good condition. **2.** (usu. pl.) vegetables kept in ~. **3.** *in a (sad, etc.)* ~, in an embarrassing position, in a dirty state. **v.t.** preserve in, treat with, ~ (1).

pic·nic ['piknik] *n.* pleasure trip on which food is carried for eating outdoors. **v.i.** (pres.p. *-king*, p.t. & p.p. *-ked*). go on a ~.

pic·to·ri·al [pik'tɔ:riəl] *adj.* of, having, represented in, pictures.

pic·ture ['piktʃə*] *n.* **1.** painting, drawing, sketch, of sth., esp. as a work of art. **2.** beautiful person, thing, view. **3.** *be the* ~ *of* (health, etc.), appear to have (it) in a high degree. **4.** *the* ~s, (colloq.) the cinema. **v.t.** make a ~ of; describe in words; have or form a ~ of in one's mind; imagine. **pic·tur·esque** [,piktʃə'resk] *adj.* **1.** (of scenes, places, etc.) striking or charming in appearance. **2.** (of a person, his language or behaviour) striking; original; full of colour.

pid·gin ['pidʒin] *n.* ~ *English*, mixture of English and native words and idioms used in some parts of Asia, West Africa, etc.

pie [pai] *n.* meat or fruit covered with pastry and baked in a dish.

pie·bald ['paibɔ:ld] *adj.* (of a horse) having white and dark patches of irregular shape.

piece [pi:s] *n.* **1.** part or bit of a solid substance: *in* ~s, broken; *come (take, break) to* ~s. **2.** separate instance or example: *a* ~ *of news (advice, luck, etc.)*. **3.** unit or definite quantity in which goods are prepared for distribution: *a* ~ *of cloth*; *sold only by the* ~; ~*-goods* (esp. cotton and silk, in standard lengths). **4.** single composition (in art, music, etc.): *a fine* ~ *of*

work (*music, poetry, etc.*). **5.** single thing out of a set: *a tea service of thirty* ~s; one of the wooden, metal, etc., objects moved on a board in such games as chess. **6.** coin: *a shilling* ~. **v.t.** put (parts, etc., *together*), make by joining or adding ~s together. '~·meal *adv.* (done) bit by bit, a ~ at a time. '~·work *n.* work paid for according to the amount done, not by the time taken.

pier [piə*] *n.* **1.** structure of wood, iron, etc., built out into the sea as a landing-stage or for walking on for pleasure. **2.** pillar supporting a span of a bridge, etc.; brickwork between windows or other openings.

pierce [piəs] **v.t. 1.** (of sharp-pointed instruments) go into or through; make (a hole) by doing this. **2.** (fig., of cold, pain, sounds, etc.) force a way into or through; affect deeply.

pier·rot ['piərou] *n.* member of a party of concert artistes who appear in loose white clothes and tall caps.

A pierrot troupe with a piano

pi·e·ty ['paiəti] *n.* being pious.

pif·fle ['pifl] *n.* (slang) nonsense.

pig [pig] *n.* **1.** see the picture. **2.** oblong mass of iron (*pig-iron*) extracted from ore and shaped in a mould. '**pig·head·ed** *adj.* obstinate. '**pig·sty** *n.* building for pigs. '**pig·tail** *n.* plait of hair hanging down over the back of the neck.

A pig   A pigeon

pi·geon ['pidʒin] *n.* bird, wild or tame, of the dove family, some kinds being trained to carry letters. '~-**hole** *n.* one of a number of small open boxes above a desk for keeping papers, etc., in. *v.t.* put (papers, etc.) in a ~-hole and forget them : (fig.) *The scheme was ~-holed* (i.e. consideration of it was postponed).

pig·ment ['pigmənt] *n.* colouring matter for making dyes, paint, etc.; the natural colouring matter in the skin, hair, etc., of living beings.

pig·my ['pigmi] *n.* = pygmy.

¹**pike** [paik] *n.* spear formerly used by soldiers fighting on foot: *as plain as a ~staff*, easy to see or understand.

²**pike** [paik] *n.* large river-fish.

pil·chard ['piltʃəd] *n.* small sea-fish.

¹**pile** [pail] *n.* heavy piece of timber driven into the ground, esp. under water, as a foundation for a building, etc. '~-ₗ**driv·er** *n.* machine for driving in ~s.

²**pile** [pail] *n.* **1.** number of things lying one upon another. **2.** large high building. **3.** (colloq.) *make a ~*, make a fortune. *v.t.* put in a ~; make a ~ of : *~ logs*; *~ things up*.

³**pile** [pail] *n.* soft, thick, hair-like surface of velvet, some carpets, etc.

pil·fer ['pilfə*] *v.t. & i.* steal things of small value in small numbers or quantities.

pil·grim ['pilgrim] *n.* person who travels to a sacred place: *~s to Mecca*. ~**age** *n.* journey of a ~.

pill [pil] *n.* ball of medicine for swallowing whole.

pil·lage ['pilidʒ] *n., v.t. & i.* plunder.

pil·lar ['pilə*] *n.* column, either as a support or as an ornament; (fig.) strong supporter (*of a* cause, organization, etc.). '~-**box** *n.* box set up in the street in which letters are posted.

pil·lion ['piljən] *n.* seat for a second person behind the rider of a horse; seat for a passenger behind the driver of a motor-bicycle.

pil·lo·ry ['piləri] *n.* wooden framework in which the heads and hands of wrongdoers were secured as a punishment. *v.t.* (fig.) call public attention to faults, mistakes, etc.

pil·low ['pilou] *n.* soft cushion for the head, esp. in bed. '~-**case,** '~-**slip** *n.* cotton or linen cover for a ~.

pi·lot ['pailət] *n.* **1.** person trained to take ships into or out of a harbour, up a river, etc. *~ scheme*, experiment for testing how sth. new would work, before it is used on a large scale. **2.** person trained to control aircraft in flight. **3.** guide. *v.t.* act as a ~ to.

pim·ple ['pimpl] *n.* small, hard, inflamed spot on the skin.

pin [pin] *n.* short piece of stiff wire with a sharp point and a rounded head, used for fastening together pieces of cloth, paper, etc. *safety-pin*, see the picture. *don't care a pin*, don't care at all. *pins and needles*, pricking sensation in the body caused by fallen flowing again when circulation has been checked for a time. *v.t.* (-*nn*-). **1.** fasten (things *together, up, to* sth., etc.) with a pin or pins. **2.** prevent from moving: *pinned down by fallen timber*; *pin sb. down* (to a promise, etc.), make him do what he ought to do. '**pin·prick** *n.* (fig.) small act, remark, etc., causing annoyance.

Pins   Pincers

pin·a·fore ['pinəfɔ:*] *n.* loose article of clothing worn over a child's dress to keep it clean.

pin·cers ['pinsəz] *n. pl.* instrument for gripping things, pulling out nails, etc.

pinch [pintʃ] *v.t. & i.* **1.** take or have in a tight grip between the thumb and finger, or between two hard things which are pressed together: *He ~ed his finger in the doorway. He ~ed the top of the plant off.* **2.** be too tight, hurt by being too tight: *shoes that ~ (the feet).* **3.** *be ~ed for money,* have not enough. *~ed with cold,* suffering from the cold. **4.** (colloq.) steal; take without permission. *n.* **1.** painful squeeze; act of *~ing* (1). (fig.) *feel the ~* (of poverty). **2.** amount which can be taken up with the thumb and finger: *a ~ of salt.* **3.** *at a ~,* if there is need and no other way is possible. *if it comes to the ~,* if it becomes absolutely necessary.

¹**pine** [pain] *n.* kinds of evergreen tree with needle-shaped leaves, and cones; wood of this tree.

²**pine** [pain] *v.i.* **1.** waste away through sorrow or illness. **2.** have a strong desire (*for* sth., *to* do sth.).

pine·ap·ple [ˈpainæpl] *n.* (tropical plant with) sweet juicy fruit.

A pineapple

¹**pin·ion** [ˈpinjən] *n.* bird's wing, esp. the outer joint. *v.t.* hold or bind fast (sb.'s arms) to his sides.

²**pin·ion** [ˈpinjən] *n.* small cogwheel with teeth fitting into those of a larger cog-wheel.

pink [piŋk] *n. & adj.* **1.** pale red (colour). **2.** garden plant with sweet-scented flowers. **3.** *in the ~,* (colloq.) very well.

pin·nace [ˈpinis] *n.* ship's boat with (usu.) eight oarsmen; ship's boat driven by steam or petrol.

pin·na·cle [ˈpinəkl] *n.* **1.** tall, pointed ornament built on to a roof. **2.** (fig.) highest point: *at the ~ of his fame.*

pint [paint] *n.* unit of measure for liquids and certain dry goods, one-eighth of a gallon: *a ~ of milk (of lentils).*

pi·o·neer [ˌpaiəˈniə*] *n.* **1.** person who goes first into a country to develop it; first student of a new branch of study, etc.; explorer. **2.** one of an advance party of soldiers (e.g. clearing or making roads). *v.i. & t.* act as a ~.

pi·ous [ˈpaiəs] *adj.* **1.** having or showing deep love for religion. **2.** (old use) dutiful to parents. *~·ly adv.*

pip [pip] *n.* **1.** seed, esp. of a lemon, orange, apple, or pear. **2.** note of a time-signal on the telephone or radio.

pipe [paip] *n.* **1.** tube through which liquids or gases can flow. *pipeline,* line of *~s,* e.g. for carrying petroleum from the well to a port for shipment. **2.** musical wind-instrument (tube with holes stopped with the fingers). **3.** *the ~s,* bagpipes. **4.** (sound of) whistle used by a boatswain. **5.** tube with a bowl, used for smoking tobacco. *v.t. & i.* **1.** convey (water, etc.) through *~s* (1). **2.** play (a tune) on a ~ (2), (3). **3.** summon (sailors) by blowing a ~ (4): *~ all hands on deck.* **pip·er** *n.* player on a ~, esp. bag-~s. **pip·ing** *n.* length of *~s* (1), esp. for water and drains: *ten feet of lead piping. adj.* like the sound of a ~ (2): *a piping voice. adv. piping hot,* very hot.

pi·quant [ˈpiːkənt] *adj.* pleasantly sharp to the taste; pleasantly exciting to the mind. **pi·quan·cy** *n.*

pique [piːk] *v.t.* **1.** hurt the pride or self-respect of. **2.** stir the curiosity or interest (of). **3.** *~ oneself on* (sth.), feel proud about. *n.* feeling one has when one's feelings are hurt or one's curiosity is not satisfied; ill temper.

pi·rate [ˈpaiərit] *n.* **1.** sea-robber; sea-robbers' ship. **2.** person who infringes sb. else's copyright. *v.t.* infringe copyright of (a book, etc.). **pi·ra·cy** [ˈpaiərəsi] *n.*

pir·ou·ette [ˌpiruˈet] *n.* dancer's rapid turn on the point of the toe. *v.i.* make a ~ or series of ~s.

pis·tol ['pistl] *n.* small fire-arm held in one hand.

pis·ton ['pistən] *n.* (in a pump or engine) short cylinder or round plate fitting closely inside another cylinder, forced backwards and forwards by gas or steam pressure. '~-**rod** *n.* rod to which a ~ is fixed (see the picture at *cylinder*).

pit [pit] *n.* **1.** deep hole in the earth, with steep sides, esp. one from which material is dug out: *a chalk-pit; a coal-pit.* **2.** (people in) seats in the back part of the ground floor of a theatre. **3.** small dent in the skin, as left by smallpox, etc. *v.t.* (-*tt*-). **1.** mark with pits (3): *a face pitted with smallpox.* **2.** match (a person or animal *against*) another in a fight, etc.: *pit one's strength against a rival.* '**pit·fall** *n.* pit (1) with a covered opening, to trap wild animals; (fig.) unsuspected danger.

¹**pitch** [pitʃ] *v.t. & i.* **1.** put up (a tent, etc.). **2.** throw (a ball, etc.), esp. throw (sb. or sth. *out, aside*) with impatience or energetic dislike: *P~ the drunkard out!* **3.** (cause to) fall forwards or outwards: *He (was) ~ed from the carriage. He ~ed on his head.* **4.** (of a ship) move up and down as the bows rise and fall (cf. *roll*). **5.** (music) set in a certain key: ~ *a tune too high (in a lower key).* ~ *in,* set to work with energy. ~ *into,* attack violently. ~ *upon* (sb.), select by chance. **7.** give a slope to (a roof). **8.** ~ed *battle,* one for which two sides have made full preparations. *n.* **1.** place where sb. (esp. a street trader) usually does business. **2.** (cricket) part of the ground between the wickets. **3.** act of ~ing (2). **4.** amount of slope (esp. of a roof). **5.** (music and speech) degree of highness or lowness: *the ~ of his voice.* **6.** degree (of a quality): *expectation raised to the highest* ~. **7.** (of a ship) process of ~ing (4). '~-**fork** *n.* long-handled· two-

pointed fork for lifting hay, etc. *v.t.* lift or move with a ~fork.

²**pitch** [pitʃ] *n.* black sticky substance made from coal-tar or turpentine, used to fill cracks, cover roofs, etc. *v.t.* put ~ on. '~-'**black,** '~-'**dark** *adj.* quite black or dark.

pitch·er ['pitʃə*] *n.* large jug.

pit·e·ous ['pitiəs] *adj.* arousing pity.

pith [piθ] *n.* **1.** soft substance filling the stems of some plants. **2.** (fig.) most necessary or important part (of a speech, etc.). ~·**y** *adj.* (esp.) full of forceful meaning; concise. ~·**i·ly** *adv.*

pit·tance ['pitəns] *n.* low, insufficient payment or allowance (for work, etc.).

pi·ty ['piti] *n.* **1.** feeling of sorrow for the troubles, sufferings, etc., of another: *have (take)* ~ *on* (sb.), help (sb. in trouble). **2.** (event that gives) cause for regret or sorrow: *What a* ~ *that* .... *v.t.* feel ~ for. **pit·i·a·ble** ['pitiəbl] *adj.* exciting ~; miserable; deserving only contempt. **pit·i·ful** *adj.* feeling ~; causing ~; arousing contempt. **pit·i·ful·ly** *adv.* **pit·i·less** *adj.* feeling no ~; merciless. **pit·i·less·ly** *adv.*

piv·ot ['pivət] *n.* central pin or point on which sth. turns; (fig.) sth. on which an argument or discussion depends. *v.t. & i.* place on, supply with, a ~; turn (*on* sth.) as on a ~.

pix·ie, pix·y ['piksi] *n.* small fairy.

plac·ard ['plækɑːd] *n.* sheet of paper with an announcement, displayed publicly. *v.t.* put ~s on (walls, etc.); make known by means of ~s.

pla·cate [plə'keit] *v.t.* soothe; take away (sb.'s) angry feelings.

place [pleis] *n.* **1.** particular part of space occupied by sth. or sb.; city, town, village, etc.; building or area of land used for a purpose that is stated: ~ *of worship,* church, etc.; ~s *of amusement,* cinemas, theatres, etc. **2.** *in* (*out of*) ~, in (not in) the right ~. *take* ~, (of an event) be held; happen. **give ~ to**, have one's ~ (or job) taken by. **in ~ of**, instead of. **3.** passage or part of a book, etc., reached in reading, esp. *find (lose) one's ~*. **4.** work : *lose one's ~*, become unemployed. **5.** (in a competition) position among those whose success is recorded (e.g. the first three in a horse-race). **6.** position in social order, etc. : *keep sb. in his ~*, not allow him to be too familiar. **v.t. 1.** put (sth.) in a certain ~; find a ~ for. **2.** give (an order to a tradesman); put (confidence in sb., etc.). **3.** give a ~ (5) to : *The horse I backed wasn't ~d.*

plac·id ['plæsid] *adj.* calm; untroubled; (of a person) not easily irritated. **~·ly** *adv.* **pla·cid·i·ty** [plæ'siditi] *n.*

pla·gia·rize ['pleidʒjəraiz] *v.t.* take and use (e.g. in an essay) sb. else's ideas, words, etc., as if they were one's own. **pla·gia·rism** *n.* **pla·gia·rist** *n.*

plague [pleig] *n.* **1.** = pestilence. **2.** cause of trouble, annoyance or disaster : *a ~ of locusts.* **v.t.** annoy, esp. with repeated requests or questions.

plaice [pleis] *n.* kind of flat seafish.

plaid [plæd] *n.* long piece of woollen cloth worn over the shoulders by Scottish Highlanders.

¹**plain** [plein] *adj.* (-*er*, -*est*). **1.** easy to see, hear, or understand : *~ sailing*, (fig.) course of action that is simple and free from difficulties. **2.** simple; ordinary; without luxury or ornament : *~ food* (*cooking*); *a ~ dress*; *a ~ blue dress* (i.e. of blue material without a design on it); *in ~ clothes*, (esp.) in ordinary clothes, not in uniform. **3.** (of thoughts, actions, etc.) straightforward; frank : *in ~ words*; *to be ~ with you* (i.e. to speak openly); *~ dealing.* **4.** (of sb.'s appearance) not pretty or handsome. **adv.** clearly. **~·ly** *adv.* **~·ness** *n.*

²**plain** [plein] *n.* area of level country.

plain·tiff ['pleintif] *n.* person

who brings an action in a law court.

plain·tive ['pleintiv] *adj.* sounding sad.

plait [plæt] *v.t.* weave or twist (three or more lengths of hair, straw, etc.) under and over one another into one rope-like length. *n.* sth. made in this way : *wearing her hair in a ~* (as shown here).

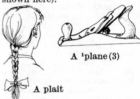

A ¹plane (3)

A plait

plan [plæn] *n.* **1.** outline drawing (of or for a building) showing the relative size, positions, etc., of the parts, esp. as if seen from above (cf. *elevation*). **2.** diagram (of the parts of a machine). **3.** diagram showing how a garden, park, or other area of land has been, or is to be, laid out. **4.** arrangement for doing or using sth., considered in advance : *~s for the summer holidays*; *working according to ~*. **v.t.** (-*nn*-). make a ~ of or for; make ~s (*to do sth.*); *~ (sth.) out*, consider and arrange in advance.

¹**plane** [plein] *n.* **1.** flat or level surface. **2.** stage or level of development : *not in the same ~ as*, not at the same level (of thought, skill, etc.) as. **3.** tool with a blade for smoothing wood, etc. **4.** wing of an aircraft. **v.t. & i.** make smooth with a ~ (3): *~ down* (irregular surfaces). **adj.** perfectly flat; forming or lying along a ~ (1): *a ~ figure.*

²**plane** [plein] *n.* sorts of tree with spreading branches and broad leaves.

plan·et ['plænit] *n.* one of the heavenly bodies (e.g. Mars) moving round the sun; one that moves round another ~ (as the moon moves round the earth). **~·a·ry** ['plænitəri] *adj.* of ~s.

plank ['plæŋk] *n.* **1.** long, flat piece of wood; board. **2.** one of the items in a political platform (3). *v.t.* **1.** cover with ~s. **2.** (colloq.) ~ *sth. down*, put sth. down (e.g. money for a purchase) on a table, counter, etc.

plant [plɑ:nt] *n.* **1.** living, growing thing other than an animal, esp. (*garden* ~) one with leaves, flowers, and roots, and smaller than a tree or shrub. **2.** the machinery, etc., used in an industrial process, etc.: *The farm has its own lighting* ~ (e.g. a generator for producing electric light). *v.t.* **1.** put ~s in (a garden, etc.). **2.** put (bulbs, plants, trees, etc.) in the ground to grow. **3.** place firmly in position: ~ *oneself in the doorway*, stand there; ~ *one's feet wide apart*, stand thus. **4.** establish (a colony, colonists). **plan·ta·tion** [plæn'teɪʃən] *n.* **1.** area of land ~ed with trees. **2.** large estate producing tea, tobacco, cotton, etc. ~**·er** *n.* person growing crops on a ~ation (2): *rubber* ~*ers.*

plan·tain ['plæntin] *n.* kind of large banana; tree producing this fruit.

plaque [plɑ:k] *n.* flat metal or porcelain plate on a wall as an ornament or as a memorial.

plas·ter ['plɑ:stə*] *n.* **1.** paste of lime, sand, water, etc., used for coating walls and ceilings. **2.** medical preparation spread on a piece of cloth, etc., for use on the body (to relieve pain, cover a wound, etc.). *v.t.* **1.** put ~ (1) on (walls, etc.); put **a** ~ (2) on (the body). **2.** cover thickly (*with*): *hair* ~*ed with oil.* ~**·er** *n.* workman who ~s walls, etc.

plas·tic ['plæstik] *adj.* **1.** (of materials) easily shaped: *Clay is a* ~ *substance.* (of goods) made of such materials. **2.** of the art of modelling: *the* ~ *arts*; ~ *surgery.* **3.** (fig.) easily bent or changed: *the* ~ *mind of a child.* *n.* substance derived from ~ material. **plas·tics** *n.* science of ~ substances. **plas·ti·ci·ty** [plæs'tisiti] *n.*

plate [pleit] *n.* **1.** circular, almost flat, dish, usu. made of china, from which food is eaten; ~*ful: a* ~ *of beef.* **2.** flat, thin sheet of metal, glass, etc., e.g. steel ~s for building ships, ~ glass (thick glass in large sheets for windows, etc.), photographic ~s (for use in cameras). **3.** oblong piece of metal (usu. brass) with a person's, firm's, name, etc., fixed to the door or gate. **4.** (usu. photographic) book illustration printed separately from the text; metal, etc., ~ (2) of a page for use in reprinting. **5.** gold or silver articles (e.g. spoons, dishes) for use at meals: ~*-powder* (for cleaning such articles). **6.** *dental* ~, frame with artificial teeth, fitting the upper or lower jaw. *v.t.* **1.** cover (a ship, etc.) with metal ~s (2). **2.** coat (one metal) with another: *silver-*~*d spoons.* ~**·ful** *n.* the amount that a ~ holds. '~'**,lay·er** *n.* workman who lays rails, keeps the railway track in order.

pla·teau ['plætou, plæ'tou] *n.* (pl. ~*x* [-z]). expanse of level land high above sea-level.

plat·form ['plætfɔ:m] *n.* **1.** flat surface built at a higher level than the railway lines at a station, for use by passengers. **2.** flat structure raised above floor-level for speakers in a hall, teachers in a classroom, etc. **3.** programme of a political party, esp. as stated before an election.

plat·i·num ['plætinəm] *n.* white, easily worked heavy metal of great value.

plat·i·tude ['plætitju:d] *n.* statement that is obviously true, esp. one often heard before but made as if it were new.

plat·ter ['plætə*] *n.* large (usu. wooden) plate, e.g. for a loaf of bread at table.

plau·dit ['plɔ:dit] *n.* (usu. pl.) clapping, cry, etc., of approval or praise.

plau·si·ble ['plɔ:zibl] *adj.* **1.** (of excuses, arguments, etc.) seeming to be right or reasonable. **2.**

(of persons) clever at producing ~ arguments, etc.: *a ~ rogue*.

plau·si·bil·i·ty [ˌplɔːziˈbiliti] *n*.

play [plei] *v.i. & t*. **1.** (contrasted with *work*) amuse oneself; have fun: *~ games*. **2.** perform (on a musical instrument); act, take a part, in a stage drama: *~ing (the part of) Hamlet*; *~ the fool*, act foolishly; *~ the man*, be brave and honourable. **3.** (special uses with nouns): *~ a trick (a practical joke) on sb.*, perform, carry out, a trick against sb. *~ tricks with sth.*, misuse it. **4.** (special uses with adv. & prep.): *~ at sth.*, do it in a not very serious spirit. *~ with*, treat lightly, trifle with, allow the mind to think about. *~ up*, (usu. imperative) put all one's energies into a game. *~ up to (sb.)*, flatter him to win approval for oneself. *~ upon (sb.'s fears, etc.)*, make use of them for one's own advantage. *~ into sb.'s hands*, behave so that one gives him an advantage over oneself. *be ~ed out*, be tired out, have no strength or value left. **5.** (of light, water) move about in a lively way: *sunlight ~ing on the water*; *fountains ~ing in the park*. **6.** send, be sent; direct (light, water, on or over sth.): *search-lights ~ing on the clouds*; *firemen ~ing their hoses on a burning building*. *n.* **1.** (contrasted with *work*) what is done for amusement; recreation: *in ~*, not seriously. **2.** drama: *the ~s of Shakespeare*. **3.** gambling: *~ing cards for money: lose £50 in an hour's ~*; *high ~* (for large sums of money). **4.** *a ~ on words*, see *pun*. **5.** the *~ing* (5) of sunlight, etc. **6.** (space for) free and easy movement: *give one's fancy full ~*, allow one's imagination to be quite free. *a joint with too much ~*, one that is not tight enough. **7.** *come into ~*, begin to͜operate. *be in full ~*, be in full operation. *bring into ~*, bring into use. *~'er n*. one who *~s* games; one who *~s* a musical instrument. **'~·bill** *n*. theatre poster. **'~·ˌfel·low**, **'~·mate** *n*. child who *~s* with another. **'~·ful** *adj*. full of fun; ready for *~*; not serious. *~·ful·ly adv*. **'~·ˌgo·er** *n*. person who often goes to the theatre. **'~·thing** *n*. toy. **'~·wright** *n*. person who writes *~s* for the theatre.

plea [pliː] *n*. **1.** (law) statement made by or for a person charged in a law court. **2.** request: *~s for help*. **3.** excuse offered for wrongdoing.

plead [pliːd] *v.i. & t*. **1.** make a plea (1); speak for either side in a law court: *get a lawyer to ~ one's case*; *~ guilty* (admit that one is guilty). **2.** ask earnestly: *~ for mercy*; *~ with sb. to show mercy*. **3.** offer as an excuse: *The thief ~ed poverty*.

pleas·ant [ˈpleznt] *adj*. (-er, -est). giving pleasure; agreeable; friendly. *~·ly adv*. *~·ness n*. *~·ry n*. joking remark; humour.

please [pliːz] *v.i. & t*. give satisfaction to; be agreeable to: *(if you) ~*, polite word(s) used in making a request. **pleas·ing** *adj*. agreeable; giving pleasure.

pleas·ure [ˈpleʒə*] *n*. **1.** feeling of being happy or satisfied: *take ~ in*, enjoy; *with ~*, willingly. **2.** thing that gives happiness. **pleas·u·ra·ble** [ˈpleʒərəbl] *adj*. giving *~*.

pleat [pliːt] *n*. fold made by doubling cloth on itself. *v.t.* make *~s* in: *a ~ed skirt*.

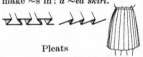

Pleats

A pleated skirt

ple·be·ian [pliˈbiːən] *n. & adj*. (person who is) of the lower classes.

pleb·i·scite [ˈplebisit] *n*. (decision made upon a political question by the) votes of all qualified citizens.

pledge [pledʒ] *n*. **1.** sth. left with sb. to be kept by him until the giver has done sth. that he is under obligation to do;

article left with a pawnbroker.
2. sth. given as a sign of love,
favour, approval, etc.; promise
or agreement: *a ~ of my friendship*; *under ~ of secrecy.* *v.t.*
1. give (sth.) as a ~; give (sb.)
a promise, make an undertaking
(to do sth.). **2.** drink the health
of.

ple·na·ry ['pli:nəri] *n.* (of powers)
unlimited; (of a meeting) attended by all who have the
right to attend.

plen·i·po·ten·tia·ry [ˌplenipə-
'tenʃəri] *n. & adj.* (person,
e.g. representative, ambassador)
having full power to act, make
decisions, etc. (on behalf of his
government, etc.).

plen·ty ['plenti] *n.* more than
enough (of). **plen·ti·ful** *adj.*
in large quantities or numbers.
plen·teous ['plentjəs] *adj.*
(liter.) plentiful.

pleu·ri·sy ['pluərisi] *n.* serious
illness in which the skin of the
lungs and the chest wall is
inflamed.

pli·a·ble ['plaiəbl] *adj.* easily
bent or twisted; (of the mind)
easily influenced; open to suggestion. **pli·a·bil·i·ty** [ˌplaiə-
'biliti] *n.*

pli·ant ['plaiənt] *adj.* = pliable.

pli·ers ['plaiəz] *n. pl.* tool, hinged
like scissors, for holding, bending, turning, or twisting things.

¹plight [plait] *n.* sad or serious
condition: *His affairs were in a
sad ~.*

²plight [plait] *v.t.* ~ *one's word,*
give one's word, promise; ~
one's troth, ~ *oneself,* engage
oneself to be married or to
marry.

plinth [plinθ] *n.* square block or
base supporting a column.

plod [plod] *v.i.* (*-dd-*). continue
walking, working, etc., slowly
but without resting: *~ding
away at one's work*; *~ding along
the road.* **plod·der** *n.* (esp.) slow
but earnest worker.

plot [plot] *n.* **1.** small piece of
land. **2.** plan or outline of the
events in a story (esp. a novel or
a drama). **3.** secret plan: *a ~
to overthrow the government.* *v.t.*

(*-tt-*). **1.** make secret plans (4) (*to
do sth., for* or *against* sth.):
~ *sb.'s ruin*; *~ting against the
State.* **2.** represent, mark the
position of, sth. on a chart or
graph: ~ *a temperature curve.*
~ter *n.*

plough [plau] *n.* instrument for
cutting and turning up the soil.
v.t. **1.** break up (land) with a ~;
use a ~. **2.** force (a way)
through: *a ship ~ing through the
heavy waves.* **3.** reject a candidate in an examination. **'~·
boy,** '**~·man** *n.* one who guides
a ~. '**~·share** *n.* blade of a ~.

A plough

plow [plau] *n.* (U.S.A. spelling)
plough.

pluck [plʌk] *v.t. & i.* **1.** pull the
feathers off (a hen, goose, etc.).
2. pick (flowers, etc., fruit); pull
(weeds, etc., *up* or *out*). **3.** snatch
(*at* sth.); take hold of and pull
(*at*). **4.** ~ *up courage,* summon
one's courage; overcome one's
fears. *n.* courage; spirit: *a boy
with plenty of ~.* **~·y** *adj.* (*-ier,
-iest*). brave. **~·i·ly** *adv.*

plug [plʌg] *n.* **1.** piece of wood,
metal, etc., used to stop up a
hole (e.g. in a barrel or wash-
basin). **2.** device for making a
connexion with a supply of electric current. **3.** sparking-plug.
v.t. & i. (*-gg-*). **1.** stop up (a
hole) with a ~ (1). **2.** (colloq.) ~
away at, work hard at. **3.** ~ *in,*
make a connexion with a ~ (2).

A plug   An electric   A sparking-
(1)   plug (2)   plug (3)

plum [plʌm] *n.* **1.** (tree having)
soft, round, smooth-skinned
fruit with a stone-like seed. **2.**

sth. considered good and desirable, esp. well-paid employment. '~-'**cake,** '~-'**pudding** *n.* one made with currants and raisins.

plum·age ['plu:midʒ] *n.* bird's feathers.

plumb [plʌm] *n.* piece of lead tied to the end of a cord or rope (~-*line*) for finding the depth of water or testing whether a wall is perpendicular. *adv.* exactly. *v.t.* (fig.) get to the root of (a question, mystery).

plumb·er ['plʌmə*] *n.* man who fits pipes (for water, etc.) into buildings and repairs them.

plumb·ing ['plʌmiŋ] *n.* 1. the work of a ~. 2. the pipes, water-tanks, etc., in a building.

plume [plu:m] *n.* feather, esp. one used for decorating; ornament of feathers; sth. suggesting a feather by its shape: *a ~ of steam. v.t.* 1. (of a bird) ~ *itself (its feathers),* smooth the feathers. 2. ~ *oneself (on),* congratulate oneself.

¹**plump** [plʌmp] *adj.* (-*er,* -*est*). (of an animal, a person) rounded; fat in a pleasant-looking way: ~ *cheeks. v.t. & i.* (often ~ *up* or *out*) make or become ~.

²**plump** [plʌmp] *v.i. & t.* 1. (cause to, allow to) fall, drop, suddenly and heavily: ~ (*oneself*) *down in a chair.* 2. ~ *for,* choose, vote for, with confidence. *adv.* suddenly; abruptly.

plun·der ['plʌndə*] *v.t. & i.* take goods from (places) by force, rob (people), esp. during war or civil disorder. *n.* ~ing; goods taken.

plunge [plʌndʒ] *v.t. & i.* 1. put (sth.) or go, suddenly and with force (*into*): ~ *one's hand into water (a hole);* ~ *into a lake;* (fig.) ~ *a room into darkness* (e.g. by putting out the lights). 2. (of a horse, a ship) move forward or downward violently. *n.* act of plunging (*into* water from a diving-platform into water); (fig.) *take the* ~, decide to do sth. risky or difficult.

plu·ral ['pluərəl] *n. & adj.* (form

of word) used with reference to more than one: *The ~ of ox is oxen.*

plus [plʌs] *prep.* with the addition of: *Two ~ five is seven* (2 + 5 = 7). *adj.* ~-*fours,* wide, loose-fitting knickerbockers.

plush [plʌʃ] *n.* kind of silk or cotton cloth with a soft ²nap.

plu·toc·ra·cy [plu:'tɔkrəsi] *n.* (government by a) rich and powerful class. **plu·to·crat** ['plu:təkræt] *n.* person who is powerful because of his wealth. **plu·to·crat·ic** [,plu:tə'krætik] *adj.*

¹**ply** [plai] *n.* layer of wood or thickness of cloth; one strand in wool, yarn, rope, etc.: *three-ply wood; three-ply wool for knitting.*

²**ply** [plai] *v.t. & i.* 1. work with (an instrument): *plying her needle.* 2. (of ships, buses, etc.) go regularly (*between, from . . . to*): *ships that ply between Glasgow and New York.* 3. *ply a trade,* work at it. 4. *ply sb. with,* keep him constantly supplied with (food and drink, questions, news, etc.).

pneu·mat·ic [nju:'mætik] *adj.* worked or driven by, filled with, compressed air: ~ *drills (tyres).*

pneu·mo·nia [nju:'mounjə] *n.* serious illness with inflammation of the lung(s).

¹**poach** [poutʃ] *v.t.* cook (an egg) by dropping the contents into boiling water.

²**poach** ['poutʃ] *v.t. & i.* (go on sb. else's land and) take (pheasants, hares, salmon, etc.) illegally. ~·**er** *n.*

pock [pɔk] *n.* spot on the skin caused by smallpox: ~-*marked,* with pits left after smallpox.

pock·et ['pɔkit] *n.* 1. small bag in an article of clothing for carrying things in. *in (out of)* ~, having gained (lost) money as the result of doing sth. 2. string bag on a billiard table. 3. hole in rock, etc., containing gold or ore. *v.t.* 1. put in one's ~. 2. keep (money, etc.) for oneself, esp. when this is wrong. 3. hide, conceal: ~ *one's pride (feelings).*

'~-book *n.* small notebook; leather case for paper money.

'~-₁money *n.* money for small needs, esp. money given to children.

pod [pod] *n.* long seed-vessel of various plants, esp. peas and beans. *v.t. & i.* (-*dd*-). take (peas, etc.) out of pods; form pods.

pod·gy ['pɔdʒi] *adj.* (-*ier*, -*iest*). short and fat.

po·em ['pouim] *n.* piece of writing in verse form, esp. one expressing deep feeling or noble thought in beautiful language.

po·et ['pouit] *n.* writer of ~s.

po·et·ess ['pouitis] *n.* woman poet.

po·et·i·c(al) [pou'etik(l)] *adj.* of poets or poetry; in the form of verse: *poetic drama.*

po·et·ry ['pouitri] *n.* the art of a poet; poems; quality producing feeling like that produced by poetry: *the poetry of motion.*

poign·ant ['poinənt] *adj.* 1. sharp in taste or smell: ~ *sauces.* 2. distressing to the feelings; deeply moving; keen: ~ *sorrow* (*regret, memories*).

poin·set·ti·a [poin'setiə] *n.* plant with large, bright-red leaves like flower petals.

point [point] *n.* 1. sharp end (of a pin, pencil, ²cape, etc.). 2. dot made by or as by the ~ of a pencil, etc., on paper: *a decimal* ~. 3. mark, position (real or imagined), in space or time: ~ *of view*, position from which sth. is looked at; (fig.) way of looking at a question, etc.: *a* ~ *of departure*; *a turning-*~ *in his career*; *at this* ~ (at this place or moment); *be on the* ~ *of doing sth.*, be about to do it; *when it comes to the* ~, when it is time for action or decision. 4. mark on a scale; degree: *the boiling-*~ *of water. The cost of living has gone up five* ~s. 5. one of thirty-two marks on the compass: ~s *of the compass* (e.g. NNE). 6. chief idea, purpose, etc., of sth. said, done, planned, etc.: *miss* (*see*) *the* ~ *of a joke*; *come to the* ~, reach the most important part of an explanation, etc.; *carry* (*gain*) *one's* ~, persuade

others to agree to one's purpose, etc.; *off* (*away from*) *the* ~; *to the* ~, concerned with what is being discussed, etc. 7. detail, step, division, esp. one marking stages in the development of an argument, theory, etc.: *the first* ~ *of my argument*; *explain a theory,* ~ *by* ~. 8. marked quality; characteristic: *What are her best* ~s *as a secretary?* 9. unit for measuring scores in some games and sports: *score twenty* ~s. *The boxer won on* ~s (not by a knock-out). 10. (pl.) tapering movable rails by which a train can move from one track to another. *v.t. & i.* 1. ~ *to*, show the position or direction of, indicate; suggest, be a sign of: *Everything* ~*ed to his guilt.* 2. ~ *at*, direct attention to: ~ *a finger accusingly at sb.*; aim, direct, at: *The rocket was* ~*ed at* (*towards*) *the moon.* 3. ~ *out*, call attention to, show, (a fact, *that . . .*). 4. make a ~ (1) on (e.g. a pencil); give sharpness to (advice, a moral). '~-'blank *adj.* aimed, fired, at very close range; (fig., of sth. said, e.g. a refusal) in a way that leaves no room for doubt. *adv.* in a ~-blank manner. '~-₁du·ty *n.* work of a policeman stationed at a particular ~, e.g. to direct traffic. ~·ed *adj.* 1. (fig.) directed definitely against a person or his behaviour: *a* ~*ed reproof*; *showing* ~*ed attentions to the pretty film star.* 2. (of wit) sharp. ~·er *n.* stick used to ~ to things on a map, blackboard, etc.; indicator on a dial. ~·less *adj.* (fig.) with little or no sense, aim, or purpose.

poise [poiz] *v.t. & i.* be or keep balanced; support in a particular place or manner. *n.* balance; way in which one holds oneself or one's head; (fig.) quiet self-confidence.

pois·on ['poizn] *n.* substance causing death or harm if absorbed by a living thing (animal or plant); (fig.) principle, idea, etc., that is harmful to society, etc. *v.t.* give ~ to; put ~ on;

kill with ~ ; (fig.) injure morally.
~·'er n. ~·'ous adj.

poke [pouk] v.t. & i. 1. push
(with a stick, one's finger, etc.):
~ the fire, ~ sth. in (down, etc.).
2. make (a hole) by pushing sth.
in or through; get (a stick, etc.)
into or through sth. by pushing.
3. ~ fun at, make fun of. n. act
of poking.

¹pok·er ['poukə*] n. metal bar for
stirring or breaking up the coal
in a fire.

²pok·er ['poukə*] n. card-game
for two or more players.

pok·y ['pouki] adj. (-ier, -iest). (of
a room, etc.) small; narrow.

¹pole [poul] n. 1. North P~, South
P~, two ends of the earth's axis;
two points in the sky about
which the stars appear to turn:
~-star, star near the North P~
of the sky. 2. either of the two
ends of a magnet or the terminal
points of an electric battery:
the negative (positive) ~. po·lar
adj. of or near the North or
South P~: polar bear, the kind
living near the North P~.

²pole [poul] n. 1. long thick rod
of wood or metal as used for
supporting telegraph wires,
tents, etc., or for flying a flag.
2. unit for measuring distance:
5½ yards.

po·lem·ic [pə'lemik] adj. & n.
(of) dispute or argument.

po·lice [pə'li:s] n. department
of government, body of men,
concerned with the keeping of
public order; the ~, members of
this body. v.t. keep order in (a
place) with ~, or as with ~.
'~-court n. law court for small
offences. ~·man n. member of
the ~ force. ~·,sta·tion n.
office of the ~ in a district.

¹pol·i·cy ['polisi] n. 1. plan of
action, esp. one made by a
government, business company,
etc. 2. wise, sensible conduct.

²pol·i·cy ['polisi] n. written statement of the terms of a contract
of insurance.

pol·ish ['polij] v.t. & i. 1. make
or become smooth and shiny by
rubbing. 2. (esp. in p.p.) improve in behaviour, intellectual

interests, etc. 3. ~ (sth.) off,
finish quickly. n. 1. (surface,
etc., obtained by) ~ing. 2. substance used for ~ing: shoe-~.

po·lite [pə'lait] adj. (-r, -st).
1. having, showing the possession of, good manners and consideration for other people. 2.
refined: ~ society. ~·ly adv.
~·ness n.

pol·i·tic ['politik] adj. 1. (of
persons) acting or judging
wisely. 2. (of actions) well
judged; prudent.

po·lit·i·cal [pə'litikl] adj. of the
State; of government; of public affairs: ~ prisoners (imprisoned for opposing the
government); ~ geography (of
boundaries, communications,
etc.); ~ economy (= economics).
~·ly adv.

pol·i·tics ['politiks] n. pl. the
science or art of government;
political views, affairs, questions, etc.: party ~; local ~.
pol·i·ti·cian [,poli'tiʃən] n. person taking part in ~ or much
interested in ~.

poll [poul] n. 1. voting at an
election; list of voters; counting
of votes; place where voting
takes place: go to the ~; at the
head of the ~ (i.e. having won).
2. (old use) the head. v.t. & i.
1. vote at an election; receive
(a certain number of) votes. 2.
cut off the top of (the horns of
animals); (= pollard) cut off the
top of (a tree). '~-tax n. tax
to be paid equally by every
person. 'pol·ling-booth n. place
where voters go to record votes.

pol·lard ['poləd] v.t. cut off the
top of (a tree) so that a thick
head of new branches grows out.
n. ~ed tree.

pol·len ['polən] n. fine powder
(usu. yellow) formed on flowers,
that fertilizes other flowers when
carried to them by the wind,
insects, etc. pol·li·nate ['poli-
neit] v.t. make fertile with ~.

pol·lute [pə'lju:t, pə'lu:t] v.t.
make dirty. pol·lu·tion n.

po·lo ['poulou] n. ball game
played on horseback with mallets.

pol·y- *prefix.* many. **~·ga·my** [pə'ligəmi] *n.* (custom of) having more than one wife at the same time. **~·glot** ['poliglot] *adj.* knowing, using, written in, many languages. *n.* ~glot person or book. **~·gon** *n.* ['poligon] *n.* figure with five or more straight sides. **~·syl·la·ble** ['poli,siləbl] *n.* word of several (usu. more than three) syllables. **~·tech·nic** [,poli'teknik] *n.* school where many subjects, esp. trades, are taught.

po·made [pə'mɑːd] *n.* ointment for use on the hair.

pome·gran·ate ['pomgrænit] *n.* (tree with) thick-skinned fruit which, when ripe, has a reddish centre full of seeds.

pom·mel ['pʌml] *n.* part of a saddle which sticks up at the front. (also **pum·mel**) *v.t.* (-ll-). strike repeatedly with the fists.

pomp [pomp] *n.* splendid display, esp. at a public event.

pom·pous ['pompəs] *adj.* full of, showing, self-importance; over-dignified. **~·ly** *adv.* **pom·pos·i·ty** [pom'positi] *n.*

pond [pond] *n.* small area of still water, esp. one made or used as a drinking-place for cattle.

pon·der ['pondə*] *v.t. & i.* consider; be deep in thought.

pon·der·a·ble ['pondərəbl] *adj.* that can be weighed or measured.

pon·der·ous ['pondərəs] *adj.* 1. not moved or moving easily because of weight. 2. (fig.) dull; tedious.

pon·iard ['ponjəd] *n.* dagger.

pon·tiff ['pontif] *n.* 1. the Pope. 2. (old use) chief priest; bishop.

pon·toon [pon'tuːn] *n.* 1. flat-bottomed boat. 2. one of a number of such boats, or a floating hollow metal structure, supporting a roadway over a river, etc.: *a ~ bridge.*

po·ny ['pouni] *n.* horse of small breed.

poo·dle ['puːdl] *n.* kind of dog with thick hair, kept as a pet.

pooh [puː] *int.* expression of contempt. **pooh-'pooh** *v.t.* treat (an idea, etc.) with contempt.

¹pool [puːl] *n.* 1. small area of still water, esp. one naturally formed. 2. water or liquid lying on the floor, on a road, etc. 3. part of a river where the water is quiet and deep.

²pool [puːl] *n.* 1. (gambling) total of money staked by a group of gamblers: *football ~s.* 2. arrangement by business firms to share business and divide profits; common fund or service provided by or shared among many. 3. game for several players played on a billiard-table. *v.t.* put (money, etc.) together for the use of all who contribute: *They ~ed their savings and bought a car.*

poop [puːp] *n.* (raised deck at the) stern of a ship.

poor [puə*] *adj.* (-er, -est). 1. having little money; not having and not able to buy enough food, clothing, etc. 2. deserving or needing help or sympathy. 3. small in quantity: *a ~ supply of teachers.* 4. low in quality: *~ soil (food); in ~ health.* **'~-house** *n.* = workhouse. **'~-'spir·it·ed** *adj.* lacking in courage. **~·ly** *adv.* 1. badly; with little success. 2. *~ly off*, having little money. *pred. adj.* (colloq.) ill; in ~ health. **~·ness** *n.* quality of being ~; lack of some good quality.

¹pop [pop] *v.t. & i.* (-pp-). 1. (cause to) make a sharp, quick sound (as when a cork comes out of a bottle). 2. (cause to) go or come (in, out, etc.) quickly: *always popping in and out; popping his head in at the door.* *n.* 1. sharp sound like that heard when a cork is pulled out of a bottle. 2. (colloq.) bottled drink with gas in it.

²pop [pop] *adj.* (colloq. abbr. of) popular: *pop music (singers, records)* (e.g. those popular on radio and TV).

Pope [poup] *n.* (Bishop of Rome as) head of the Roman Catholic Church.

pop·lar ['poplə*] *n.* (wood of) tall, straight, quickly-growing tree.

pop·lin ['pɔplin] *n.* cloth of silk and wool with raised lines on it; kind of strong, shiny cotton cloth used for shirts, etc.

pop·py ['pɔpi] *n.* sorts of plant, wild and cultivated, with large flowers, esp. red; from the juice of one sort opium is made.

pop·u·lace ['pɔpjuləs] *n.* the ~, the common people; the general public.

pop·u·lar ['pɔpjulə*] *adj.* **1.** of or for the people: ~ *govern-ment*; ~ (= low) *prices*. **2.** suited to the tastes, educational level, etc., of the general public: ~ *science*. **3.** liked and admired by the public: ~ *film actors*. ~·**i·ty** [ˌpɔpjuˈlæriti] *n.* condition of being ~ (3). ~·**ize** *v.t.* make ~ (2), (3).

pop·u·late ['pɔpjuleit] *v.t.* people. **pop·u·la·tion** [ˌpɔpjuˈleiʃən] *n.* (number of) people living in a place, country, etc., or a special section of them. **pop·u·lous** ['pɔpjuləs] *adj.* thickly ~d.

porce·lain ['pɔːslin] *n.* (articles, e.g. cups, plates, made of a) fine china with a coating of trans-parent material called *glaze*.

porch [pɔːtʃ] *n.* built-out roofed doorway or entrance to a build-ing.

por·cu·pine ['pɔːkjupain] *n.* small rat-like animal covered with quills.

¹pore [pɔː*] *n.* tiny opening in the skin through which sweat passes.

²pore [pɔː*] *v.i.* ~ *over*, study (a book, etc.) with close attention; ~ *upon*, give one's close atten-tion to (problems).

pork [pɔːk] *n.* meat of a pig, esp. unsalted. (See *ham*, *bacon*.)

po·rous ['pɔːrəs] *adj.* allowing liquid to pass through (as sandy soil does).

por·poise ['pɔːpəs] *n.* sea-animal about five feet long.

por·ridge ['pɔridʒ] *n.* soft food made by boiling oatmeal in water or milk.

¹port [pɔːt] *n.* (town with a) har-bour.

²port [pɔːt] *n.* **1.** doorway in a ship's side for loading or unload-ing. **2.** small glass window in a ship's side that closes a ~-hole. **port·hole** ['pɔːthoul] *n.* opening for admission of light and air to a cabin in a ship.

³port [pɔːt] *n.* left side of a ship or aircraft as one looks forward. *v.t.* turn (a ship's helm) to ~. (Cf. *starboard*.)

⁴port [pɔːt] *n.* sweet (usu. red) wine.

por·ta·ble ['pɔːtəbl] *adj.* that can be carried about; not heavy or fixed: ~ *radios* (*typewriters*).

por·tage ['pɔːtidʒ] *n.* (cost of) carrying goods, esp. when goods have to be carried overland between two rivers or parts of a river.

por·tal ['pɔːtl] *n.* doorway, esp. an imposing one of a large building.

port·cul·lis [pɔːtˈkʌlis] *n.* iron grating lowered in front of the gateway of castles, etc., in former times, to keep out attackers.

por·tend [pɔːˈtend] *v.t.* be a sign or warning of (a future event, etc.). **por·tent** ['pɔːtent] *n.* thing, esp. sth. marvellous or mysterious, which ~s sth. **por·ten·tous** [pɔːˈtentəs] *adj.* extraordinary; marvellous; (humor.) solemn.

por·ter ['pɔːtə*] *n.* **1.** person whose work is to carry luggage, etc., at railway stations, hotels, etc. **2.** door-keeper or gate-keeper.

port·fo·lio [pɔːtˈfouliou] *n.* **1.** holder (usu. leather) for loose papers, documents, etc. **2.** position as a Minister of State: *He resigned his ~.*

por·ti·co ['pɔːtikou] *n.* roof sup-ported by columns, esp. at the entrance of a building.

por·tion ['pɔːʃən] *n.* **1.** part, esp. a share, (to be) given when sth. is distributed. **2.** amount; some (of). *v.t.* divide into ~s.

port·ly ['pɔːtli] *adj.* (usu. of elderly persons) stout.

port·man·teau [pɔːtˈmæntou] *n.* oblong square-shouldered leath-er case for clothes, opening on a hinge into two equal parts.

por·trait ['pɔːtrit] *n.* painted picture, drawing, photograph, of a person or animal; vivid description in words. **por·trai·ture** ['pɔːtritʃə*] *n.* art of portraying; ~. **por·tray** [pɔː'trei] *v.t.* make a picture of; describe vividly in words; act the part of. **por·tray·al** [pɔː'treiəl] *n.* portraying; description.

pose [pouz] *v.t. & i.* **1.** put (sb.) in a position before making a painting, photograph, etc., of him; take up such a position. **2.** behave in an affected way hoping to impress people; set oneself up (as): ~ *as an expert on art.* **3.** put forward (a difficult question or problem). *n.* **1.** position taken when posing (1) for a picture, etc. **2.** behaviour, attitude, intended to impress people. **pos·er** *n.* awkward or difficult question. **po·seur** [pou-'zɔː*] *n.* person posing(2) for effect.

posh [pɔʃ] *adj.* (colloq.) smart.

po·si·tion [pə'ziʃən] *n.* **1.** place where sth. or sb. is or stands, esp. in relation to others. **2.** right place for sth. or sb.: *in (out of)* ~. **3.** way in which the body is placed: *in a comfortable* ~. **4.** person's place or rank in relation to others, in employment, in society. **5.** condition; circumstances: *not in a* ~ *to help,* unable to help. **6.** standpoint; views; opinions: *What's your* ~ *on this problem?*

pos·i·tive ['pozitiv] *adj.* **1.** definite; sure; leaving no room for doubt: ~ *orders.* **2.** (of persons) quite certain, esp. about opinions: *Are you* ~ *it was after midnight?* **3.** practical and constructive; that definitely helps: *a* ~ *suggestion;* ~ *help.* **4.** (maths.) greater than 0. *the* ~ *sign,* +. **5.** (of electricity) that which is produced at the anode of a cell (4). **6.** (grammar, of adjectives and adverbs) of the simple form, not the comparative or superlative degree. *n.* ~ (6) degree; photograph printed from a (negative) plate or film. **~·ly** *adv.* definitely.

pos·sess [pə'zes] *v.t.* **1.** own; have. **2.** keep control over: ~ *one's soul in patience,* be patient. **3.** ~ *oneself of,* become the owner of: *be* ~*ed of,* have. **4.** *be* ~*ed,* be mad, be controlled by an evil spirit: *He fought like one* ~*ed.* **pos·ses·sion** [pə-'zeʃən] *n.* **1.** ~*ing: in* ~*ion (of),* owning, having; *in the* ~*ion of,* owned by. **2.** (often pl.) property; sth. ~*ed: lose all one's* ~*ions.* **pos·ses·sive** [pə'zesiv] *adj.* **1.** of ~*ion;* eager to ~ or retain. **2.** (grammar) showing ~*ion: the* ~*ive case* (e.g. *Tom's, boy's, my*). **pos·ses·sor** *n.* owner.

pos·si·ble ['posibl] *adj.* **1.** that can be done; that can exist or happen. **2.** that is reasonable or satisfactory for a purpose: *a* ~ *answer to a problem.* **pos·si·bly** *adv.* **1.** by any possibility. **2.** perhaps. **pos·si·bil·i·ty** [‚posi-'biliti] *n.* **1.** state of being ~; (degree of) likelihood. **2.** sth. that is ~: *a scheme with great possibilities.*

¹post [poust] *n.* **1.** place where a soldier is on watch; place of duty; place occupied by soldiers, esp. a frontier fort. **2.** *last* ~, military bugle call sounded towards bedtime, and at funerals. **3.** trading station. **4.** position or appointment; job. *v.t.* put at a ~(1): ~ *sentries at the gates;* send to a ~(1).

²post [poust] *n.* government transport and delivery of letters and parcels; one collection or distribution of letters, etc.; letters, etc., delivered at one time; ~-office or pillar-box: *take letters to the* ~; *send sth. by* ~. *v.t. & i.* **1.** send (letters, etc.) by ~; put (letters, etc.) in a pillar-box or take to the ~-office for forwarding by ~. **2.** (old use) travel by stages; make a quick journey: ~*ing from London to York.* **3.** ~ (*up*), (business) write items in a ledger: ~ (*up*) *export sales.* **4.** *keep sb.* ~*ed,* keep him supplied with news. **~·age** ['poustidʒ] *n.* payment for the carrying of letters, etc. ~·**al** ['poustl] *adj.* of the ~ or ~-office : ~*al order*, official paper receipt for a small sum paid in by the sender to be cashed by the receiver at another ~-office in order to avoid sending money by ~. '~·**card** *n.* card for a short message to be sent by ~. '~-'**free** *adj.* without charge for ~age; (of a price) including a charge for ~age. '~-'**haste** *adv.* in great haste. '~·**man** *n.* man employed to collect and deliver letters. '~·**mark** *n.* official mark stamped on letters, etc., and cancelling the ~age stamp(s). '~·,**mas·ter**, '~·,**mis·tress** *n.* man, woman, in charge of a ~-office. '~·,**of·fice** *n.* government department in charge of the ~al service; office, building, in which ~al work is carried on. '~-'**paid** *adj. & adv.* with ~age already paid.

³**post** [poust] *n.* upright piece of wood, metal, etc., supporting or marking sth.: *gate-~s; the winning-~; bed-~s; lamp-~s.* *v.t.* 1. ~ *sth. up*, display publicly on a ~, on a notice-board, etc. 2. make known by means of a ~ed notice: ~ *a ship as missing.* ~·**er** *n.* public advertisement (to be) ~ed up (on a wall, etc.).

⁴**post-** [poust-] *prefix.* after, later than. '~-'**date** *v.t.* put (on a letter, cheque, etc.) a date later than the date of writing. '~-'**grad·u·ate** *adj.* (of studies, etc.) done after having taken a degree. ~·**hu·mous** ['postjuməs] *adj.* (of a child) born after the death of its father; coming or happening after death: ~*humous fame.* '~-**script** *n.* (*PS.*) sentence(s) added to a letter after the signature. ~-**war** ['poust'wɔ:*] *adj.* after, later than, the (last) war.

poste res·tante ['poust'resta:nt] *n.* post-office department to whose care letters may be addressed, to be kept until called for.

pos·te·ri·or [pɔs'tiəriə*] *adj.* 1. later in time or order. 2. placed behind; at the back. *n.* buttocks.

pos·ter·i·ty [pɔs'teriti] *n.* 1. person's descendants (his children, their children, etc.). 2. those coming after; later generations.

pos·til·ion [pɔs'tiljən, pəs-] *n.* man riding on one of the two or more horses pulling a carriage or coach.

post·pone [pous'poun, pəs-] *v.t.* put off until another time. ~·**ment** *n.*

pos·tu·late ['postjuleit] *v.t.* demand, put forward, take for granted, as a necessary fact, as a basis for reasoning, etc. ['postjulit] *n.* sth. ~d.

pos·ture ['postʃə*] *n.* 1. attitude of the body: *in a reclining ~.* 2. muscular control of the body; attitude of body or mind: *Good ~ helps you to keep well.* *v.i.* take up a ~: *a vain girl posturing before a mirror.*

po·sy ['pouzi] *n.* small bunch of cut flowers.

pot [pɔt] *n.* round vessel of earthenware, glass, metal, etc., for holding things in, for cooking, etc.: *a flower-pot; a coffee-pot. keep the pot boiling*, earn enough money to buy one's food, etc. *pots of money*, (slang) very much money. *v.t.* (*-tt-*). 1. put (meat, fish paste, etc.) in a pot to preserve it. 2. plant in a flower-pot. '**pot-hole** *n.* 1. hole in a road made by rain and traffic. 2. deep hole worn (e.g. in limestone caves) in rock by water. '**pot-hol·er** *n.* explorer of pot-holes (2). **pot luck** *n.* whatever is being prepared for a meal: *Come home with me and take pot luck.* **pot·ter** *n.* maker of pottery. **pot·ter·y** *n.* pots; earthenware; work of a potter.

Pots   Potatoes

pot·ash ['pɒtæʃ] *n.* substance used in making soap and glass, and as a fertilizer.

po·ta·to [pə'teitou] *n.* (pl. *-oes*). plant with rounded tubers eaten as a vegetable; one of the tubers. See the picture on page 398.

po·tent ['poutənt] *adj.* strong; powerful; effective: ~ *forces* (*reasons*, *charms*). **po·ten·cy** ['poutənsi] *n.* **po·ten·tate** ['poutənteit] *n.* powerful person; ruler.

po·ten·tial [pə'tenʃl] *adj.* that can or may come into existence or action: *the ~ sales of a new book.*

po·tion ['pouʃən] *n.* drink of medicine or poison.

¹pot·ter, pot·ter·y, see *pot*.

²pot·ter ['pɒtə*] *v.i.* work (*at* sth.) with little energy; move (*about*) from one little job to another.

pot·ty ['pɒti] *adj.* (colloq.) (of jobs) unimportant; (of persons) mad; strange in behaviour.

pouch [pautʃ] *n.* **1.** small bag (e.g. for pipe tobacco). **2.** baglike formation (e.g. that in which a kangaroo carries its young); puffy area of skin (e.g. under the eyes of sick people).

poul·tice ['poultis] *n.* soft mass of linseed, mustard, etc., heated and put on the skin to lessen pain, etc. *v.t.* put a ~ on.

poul·try ['poultri] *pl. n.* hens, ducks, geese, etc. **poul·ter·er** ['poultərə*] *n.* dealer in ~.

pounce [pauns] *v.i. & n.* (make a) sudden attack or downward swoop (*on*).

¹pound [paund] *n.* **1.** unit of weight, 16 ounces avoirdupois, 12 ounces troy. **2.** (£1) unit of money, 100 pence (formerly 20s.).

²pound [paund] *v.t. & i.* **1.** strike heavily and repeatedly (at, on): ~*ing at the door with a stick*; ~*ing (on) the piano.* **2.** crush to powder; break to pieces; *a ship ~ing (being ~ed) on the rocks.*

³pound [paund] *n.* closed area in a village, etc., where (lost) animals can be kept (until claimed).

pour [pɔ:*] *v.t. & i.* **1.** (of liquids, or substances that flow like liquids) flow, cause to flow, in a continuous stream: ~*ing tea out of a pot*; *sweat ~ing off his face*; (fig.) ~*ing out a story of misfortunes.* **2.** (of people) come (*in*, *out*, etc.) in large numbers: *people ~ing into the railway station.* **3.** (of rain) come down heavily: *a ~ing wet day.*

pout [paut] *v.t. & i.* push out (the lips), esp. when discontented, bad-tempered, etc. *n.* act of ~ing.

pov·er·ty ['pɒvəti] *n.* state of being poor. '~-ˌstrick·en *adj.* very poor; looking very poor; shabby-looking.

pow·der ['paudə*] *n.* **1.** substance that has been crushed, rubbed or worn to dust; special kind of ~, e.g. for use on the skin (*face-* ~) or as a medicine. **2.** gun~. *v.t. & i.* put ~ on; use ~ on the face; make into ~. '~-ˌmag·aˌzine *n.* place for storing gun~ and other explosives. ~·y *adj.* of, like, covered with, ~.

pow·er ['pauə*] *n.* **1.** ability to do or act: *He gave me all the help in his ~.* **2.** strength; force: *the ~ of a blow.* **3.** energy or force that can be used to do work: *water-~*; *electric ~*; *an engine of sixty horse-~.* **4.** right; control; authority: *the ~ of the law*; *have sb. in one's ~*, be able to do what one wishes with him. **5.** person or organization having great authority or influence; State having great authority and influence in international affairs. **6.** (maths.) *the fourth ~ of 3,* (3 × 3 × 3 × 3 = 81). **7.** capacity to magnify: *the ~ of a lens*; *a telescope of high ~.* '~-ˌhouse, '~-ˌsta·tion *n.* place where ~ (3) (esp. electrical) is produced or distributed. ~·ful *adj.* having or producing great ~. ~·less *adj.* without ~; unable (*to do* sth.).

prac·tice ['præktis] *n.* **1.** performance; the doing of sth. (contrasted with *theory*): *put a plan into ~.* **2.** way of doing sth. that is common or habitual; sth. done regularly: *the ~ of* *closing shops on Sundays.* **3.** frequent or regular repetition of sth., in order to become skilful: *in (out of)* ~, having (not having) lately practised. **4.** work of a doctor or lawyer; all those who consult a certain doctor or lawyer: *retire from* ~ ; *a doctor with a large* ~ (i.e. many patients). **5.** *sharp* ~, not strictly honest or legal way of doing business. **prac·ti·ca·ble** ['præktikəbl] *adj.* that can be put into ~ ; that can be done or used. **prac·ti·cal** ['præktikl] *adj.* **1.** concerned with ~ (1): *practical difficulties.* **2.** (of persons) clever at doing and making things; fond of action. **3.** useful; doing well what it is intended to do. **prac·ti·cal·ly** *adv.* **1.** in a practical manner. **2.** really. **3.** almost.

prac·tise ['præktis] *v.t. & i.* **1.** do sth. repeatedly in order to become skilful: ~ *the piano.* **2.** make a custom of: ~ *early rising*; ~ *what one preaches* (2). **3.** ~ *the law (medicine),* work as a lawyer (a doctor). **prac·tised** *adj.* skilled; having had much practice. **prac·ti·tion·er** [præk-'tiʃənə*] *n.* person practising medicine or the law.

prai·rie ['preəri] *n.* wide area of level land with grass but no trees, esp. in N. America.

praise [preiz] *v.t.* **1.** speak with approval of; say that one admires. **2.** give honour and glory to (God). *n.* act of praising; expressions of admiration. '~·worthy *adj.* deserving ~.

pram [præm] *n.* short for *perambulator.*

prance ['prɑːns] *v.i.* (of a horse) rise up on the hind legs and jump about; (of a person) jump or move about gaily; walk arrogantly.

prank [præŋk] *n.* playful or mischievous trick: *play a* ~ *on sb.*

prate [preit] *v.i. & t.* talk foolishly or boastfully; talk too much.

prat·tle ['prætl] *v.i. & t.* talk, say sth., in a simple way; go on talking as a child does, about

unimportant things. *n.* such talk.

prawn [prɔːn] *n.* shellfish like a large shrimp.

pray [prei] *v.i. & t.* **1.** commune with God; offer thanks, make requests known (*to God, for* sth. or *for* the good of sb.). **2.** ask (sb.) (*for, to do* sth.) as a favour. **3.** (formal) if you please: *P*~ *don't speak so loud.* **prayer** [prɛə*] *n.* ~ing to God; thing ~ed for; form of worship (*Morning Prayer*) or of words for use in ~ing: *the Lord's Prayer.*

pre- [priː-] *prefix.* before, as in *prefix, prepaid, pre-war.*

preach [priːtʃ] *v.t. & i.* **1.** deliver (a sermon); give a talk, esp. in church, about religion or morals; give moral advice (*to*). **2.** recommend, urge, as right or desirable. ~·**er** *n.*

pre·am·ble [priː'æmbl] *n.* introduction to a talk, statement, piece of writing.

pre·ca·ri·ous [pri'kɛəriəs] *adj.* uncertain; depending upon chance.

pre·cau·tion [pri'kɔːʃən] *n.* care taken in advance to avoid a risk: *take* ~s *against fire.*

pre·cede [priː'siːd] *v.t. & i.* come or go before (in time, place, or order). **pre·ced·ence** [pri'siːd-əns] *n.* (right to a) higher or earlier position: *a question which takes* ~nce *of (over) all others,* which must be considered first. **prec·e·dent** ['presidənt] *n.* earlier happening, decision, etc., taken as an example of or as a rule for what comes later.

pre·cept ['priːsept] *n.* rule or guide, esp. for behaviour.

pre·cinct ['priːsiŋkt] *n.* **1.** space enclosed by outer walls or boundaries, esp. of a sacred or official building. **2.** (pl.) neighbourhood of, places near (a town).

pre·cious ['preʃəs] *adj.* **1.** of great value: *the* ~ *metals* (gold, silver). **2.** highly valued; dear (*to*).

prec·i·pice ['presipis] *n.* perpendicular or very steep face of a rock, cliff, or mountain.

pre·cip·i·tate [pri'sipiteit] *v.t.* **1.** throw or send (stones, oneself) violently down from a height. **2.** cause (an event) to happen suddenly, quickly, or in haste. **3.** condense (vapour) into drops which fall as rain, dew, etc. **4.** separate (solid matter) from a solution. [pri'sipitit] *n.* that which is ~d (4). *adj.* violently hurried; hasty; (done, doing things) without enough thought. **pre·cip·i·ta·tion** [pri,sipi'teiʃən] *n.* ~ action; fall of rain, snow, etc.

pre·cip·i·tous [pri'sipitəs] *adj.* like a precipice; steep.

pré·cis ['preisi] *n.* chief ideas, points, etc., of a speech or piece of writing restated in a shortened form.

pre·cise [pri'sais] *adj.* **1.** exact; correctly stated; free from error. **2.** taking care to be exact, not to make errors. ~**ly** *adv.* (esp. in agreeing with sb.) quite so. **pre·ci·sion** [pri'siʒən] *n.* accuracy; freedom from error.

pre·clude [pri'klu:d] *v.t.* prevent (sb. *from* doing sth.); make impossible.

pre·co·cious [pri'kouʃəs] *adj.* (of a person) having some faculties developed earlier than is normal; (of actions, knowledge, etc.) marked by such development.

pre·con·ceive ['pri:kən'si:v] *v.t.* form (ideas, opinions) in advance (before getting knowledge or experience). **pre·con·cep·tion** [,pri:kən'sepʃən] *n.* ~d idea.

pre·cur·sor [pri:'kə:sə*] *n.* person or thing coming before, a sign of what is to follow.

pred·a·to·ry ['predətəri] *adj.* of plundering and robbery: ~ *tribesmen* (*habits*).

pre·de·ces·sor ['pri:disesə*] *n.* person who held a position before (the person mentioned).

pre·des·tine [pri:'destin], **pre·des·ti·nate** [pri:'destineit] *v.t.* settle or decide in advance.

pre·dic·a·ment [pri'dikəmənt] *n.* awkward or unpleasant situation from which escape seems difficult.

pred·i·cate ['predikeit] *v.t.* declare to be true or real. ['predikit] *n.* (grammar) part of a statement that says sth. about the subject. **pre·dic·a·tive** [pri'dikətiv] *adj.* ~ *adjective*, one used only in a ~ (e.g. *asleep*, *alive*).

pre·dict [pri'dikt] *v.t.* say, tell in advance (sth. that will come, *that* sth. will happen): ~ *that it will rain* (*a good harvest*). **pre·dic·ta·ble** *adj.* that can be ~ed. **pre·dic·tion** [pri'dikʃən] *n.* ~ing; sth. ~ed.

pre·di·lec·tion [,pri:di'lekʃən] *n.* special liking; preference (*for*).

pre·dis·pose [,pri:dis'pouz] *v.t.* cause (sb.) to be inclined or liable before the event (*to* sth., *to do* sth.). **pre·dis·po·si·tion** ['pri:,dispə'ziʃən] *n.*

pre·dom·i·nant [pri'dɔminənt] *adj.* having most power or influence; prevailing or supreme (*over*); most noticeable. **pre·dom·i·nance** *n.* **pre·dom·i·nate** *v.t.* be ~.

pre-em·i·nent [pri:'eminənt] *adj.* superior; best of all. **pre-em·i·nence** *n.*

preen [pri:n] *v.t.* **1.** (of a bird) smooth (itself, its feathers) with its beak. **2.** (fig., of a person) show self-satisfaction.

pre·fab·ri·cate ['pri:'fæbrikeit] *v.t.* manufacture complete sections (of a house, ship, etc.) in advance of building, ready to be put together on the site.

pref·ace ['prefis] *n.* author's explanatory remarks at the beginning of a book. *v.t.* begin (a talk, etc., *with* sth.).

pre·fect ['pri:fekt] *n.* **1.** title of a governor in ancient Rome; title of a government official in France. **2.** school pupil given responsibility for keeping order.

pre·fer [pri'fə:*] *v.t.* (*-rr-*). **1.** choose rather; like better. **2.** put forward, submit (a complaint, request, etc.). **3.** appoint (sb.) to a higher position. ~**a·ble** ['prefərəbl] *adj.* superior (*to*); to be ~red. ~**a·bly** *adv.* by choice or ~ence. ~**ence** ['prefərəns] *n.* **1.** ~ring; sth. ~red. **2.** the favouring of one person, country, etc., more than another. **3.** *P~ence Stock*, on which dividend payments must be made before profits are distributed to holders of Ordinary Stock. ~·**en·tial** [ˌprefəˈrenʃəl] *adj.* (esp. of taxes, tariffs) of or giving ~ence (2). ~·**ment** *n.* giving or receiving a higher position (esp. in the Church).

pre·fix [ˈpriːfiks] *n.* **1.** word or syllable (e.g. *hydro-, co-*) forming the first part of a compound word to add to or change the meaning. **2.** word placed before another. [priːˈfiks] *v.t.* add a ~ to or in front of; add (a note, etc., *to* sth.) at the beginning.

preg·nant [ˈpregnənt] *adj.* **1.** (of a woman or female animal) carrying offspring in the process of development before birth. **2.** (of words, actions) full of meaning; important for the future. **preg·nan·cy** [ˈpregnənsi] *n.*

pre·his·tor·ic [ˌpriːhisˈtɔrik] *adj.* of the time before recorded history.

prej·u·dice [ˈpredʒudis] *n.* **1.** opinion, like or dislike, formed before one has adequate knowledge or experience: *a ~ against (in favour of) modern poetry*. **2.** *to the ~ of*, with (possible) injury to (sb.'s interests, etc.). *v.t.* **1.** cause (sb.) to have a ~ (1). **2.** injure (sb.'s interests, etc.). **prej·u·di·cial** [ˌpredʒuˈdiʃəl] *adj.* causing ~ or injury (*to*).

prel·ate [ˈprelit] *n.* bishop or other churchman of equal or higher rank.

pre·lim·i·na·ry [priˈliminəri] *adj.* coming first and preparing for what follows. *n.* ~ step, action, etc.

prel·ude [ˈpreljuːd] *n.* introductory action or event; piece of poetry or music that introduces a main work. (Cf. *preface, prologue*.)

pre·ma·ture [ˈpremətjuə*] *adj.* done, happening, doing sth., before the right or usual time. ~·**ly** *adv.*

pre·med·i·tate [priˈmediteit] *v.t.* consider, plan (sth.) in advance: *a ~d crime.*

pre·mier [ˈpremjə*, ˈpriː-] *adj.* first in position, importance, etc. *n.* prime minister; head of government.

prem·ise [ˈpremis] *n.* **1.** (also *premiss*) statement on which reasoning is based. **2.** (pl.) house or building with its land.

pre·mium [ˈpriːmjəm] *n.* **1.** amount or instalment paid for an insurance policy or a lease. **2.** reward; bonus: *put a ~ on* (behaviour, an act); make it profitable for sb. (to do sth., behave in a certain way). **3.** *at a ~,* (of stocks and shares) at more than the par value.

pre·mo·ni·tion [ˌpriːməˈniʃən] *n.* feeling of uneasiness considered as a warning (of approaching danger, etc.).

pre·oc·cu·py [priːˈɔkjupai] *v.t.* take all the attention of (sb., his mind) so that attention is not given to other matters: *pre-occupied by (with) family troubles.* **pre·oc·cu·pa·tion** [priːˌɔkjuˈpeiʃən] *n.* (esp.) sth. that takes up all a person's thoughts.

pre·or·dain [ˌpriːɔːˈdein] *v.t.* (of God) determine (2) in advance.

prep [prep] *n.* (schoolboy slang for) *preparation* (1) (of lessons) and for *preparatory* (see below).

pre·pare [priˈpɛə*] *v.t. & i.* **1.** get or make ready: ~ *one's lessons*; ~ *to do sth.*; ~ *for work.* **2.** *be ~d to,* be able and willing to. **prep·a·ra·tion** [ˌprepəˈreiʃən] *n.* **1.** preparing or being ~d; (time given to) preparing school lessons. **2.** kind of food, medicine, etc., specially ~d. **pre·par·a·to·ry** [priˈpærətəri] *adj.* introductory; needed for preparing: *preparatory measures*; *preparatory schools* (preparing young children for entry to a higher school). **pre·pared·ness** [priˈpɛədnis] *n.* being ~d.

pre·pay [ˈpriːˈpei] *v.t.* pay in advance.

pre·pon·der·ate [priˈpɔndəreit] *v.i.* be greater in number, strength, influence, etc. **pre·pon·der·ant** *adj.* **pre·pon·der·ance** *n.*

prep·o·si·tion [ˌprepəˈziʃən] *n.*

word used with a noun or pronoun to mark its relation with another word, as in: go *from* home; walk *to* school; swim *in* the river; a pound *of* tea. ~·al **adj.** ~al phrase (e.g. in front of).

pre·pos·ses·sing [ˌpriːpəˈzesiŋ] **adj.** making a favourable impression; attractive. pre·pos·ses·sion [ˌpriːpəˈzeʃən] **n.** favourable feeling formed in advance; prejudice.

pre·pos·ter·ous [priˈpɒstərəs] **adj.** completely contrary to reason or sense.

pre·req·ui·site [ˈpriːˈrekwizit] **n. & adj.** (thing) required as a condition for sth. else: *Matriculation is a ~ of entrance to the University.*

pre·rog·a·tive [priˈrɒgətiv] **n.** special right(s) or privilege(s) (of a ruler).

pres·age [ˈpresidʒ] **n.** feeling that sth. (usu. evil) will happen; sign looked upon as a warning. [priˈseidʒ] **v.t.** be a sign of.

pre·sci·ent [ˈpreʃiənt] **adj.** knowing about, able to see into, the future.

pre·scribe [prisˈkraib] **v.t. & i.** 1. order the use of: ~d text-books; (esp.) order as a possible cure for illness: *The doctor ~d castor oil (complete rest).* 2. say, with authority, what course of action, etc., is to be followed: *penalties ~d by the law.* pre·scrip·tion [prisˈkripʃən] **n.** sth. ~d, esp. (written directions for preparing) medicine.

¹pres·ent [ˈpreznt] **adj.** 1. at the place referred to: ~ *company,* those who are here. 2. existing now: *the ~ government.* 3. not past or future: *at the ~ time.* **n.** the ~ time; (grammar) the ~ tense. *at ~,* now. *for the ~,* for now; until later. pres·ence [ˈpreznz] **n.** 1. being ~ in a place: *in the presence of his friends,* with his friends there. 2. *presence of mind,* ability to act quickly and sensibly in time of danger, etc. ~·ly **adv.** soon.

²pre·sent [priˈzent] **v.t.** 1. give; offer; put forward; submit: ~ *a cheque at the bank* (for payment);

~ *a petition to the mayor.* 2. introduce (sb., esp. to a person of high rank): *be ~ed at Court.* 3. ~ *oneself,* appear, attend (for examination, trial, etc.). 4. hold (a rifle, etc.) in a certain way as a salute, etc.: *P~ arms!* pres·ent [ˈpreznt] **n.** sth. given: *birthday ~s.* ~·a·ble [priˈzentəbl] **adj.** fit to appear, be shown, etc., in public. pres·en·ta·tion [ˌprezənˈteiʃən] **n.** ~ing or being ~ed; sth. ~ed, esp. at a public ceremony.

pre·sen·ti·ment [priˈzentimənt] **n.** feeling that sth. (esp. sth. bad) is about to happen.

pre·serve [priˈzəːv] **v.t.** 1. keep safe; keep from danger, loss, risk of going bad, etc.: ~ *eggs* (one's eyesight). 2. care for or protect land and rivers, with the animals, birds, and fish, esp. to prevent these from being taken by poachers. **n.** 1. woods, streams, etc., where animals, birds and fish are ~d: *a game (5) ~*; (pl., fig.) activities, interests, etc., looked upon as belonging specially to sb.: *poaching on sb. else's ~s.* 2. (usu. pl.) jam. pres·er·va·tion [ˌprezəˈveiʃən] **n.** 1. condition of sth. ~d: *in a good state of preservation* (i.e. well ~d). 2. act of preserving. pre·serv·a·tive [priˈzəːvətiv] **n. & adj.** (substance) used for preserving (e.g. food).

pre·side [priˈzaid] **v.i.** have, take, the position of authority (*over* a business, etc., *at* a meeting).

pres·i·dent [ˈprezidənt] **n.** 1. elected head of a republic. 2. head of certain government departments, of some business companies, colleges, societies, etc. pres·i·den·cy [ˈprezidənsi] **n.** (term of) office of a ~. pres·i·den·tial [ˌpreziˈdenʃl] **adj.** of a ~ or his duties.

¹press [pres] **v.t. & i.** 1. push against: ~ *the trigger of a gun* (the button of an electric bell); *crowds ~ing against the gates.* 2. use force or weight to make sth. flat, to get sth. into a smaller space, to get juice out of fruit, etc.: ~ *grapes* (to make wine);

~ *juice out of oranges*; ~ *clothes* (with an iron (2), to make them smooth). **3.** keep close to and attack: ~ *the enemy*; ~ *an attack* (continue to attack vigorously). **4.** ~ *for*, make repeated requests for. **5.** *be* ~*ed for* (time, money, etc.), have hardly enough; be in great need of. **6.** demand action or attention: *The matter is* ~*ing*. **7.** *Time* ~*es*, there is no time to lose. **8.** ~ *sb.'s hand*, grasp it to show affection, sympathy, etc. **9.** ~ *sth. on sb.*, urge him again and again to take (e.g. food, money). *n.* **1.** act of ~*ing*. **2.** machine, apparatus, etc., for ~*ing*: *a wine-*~. **3.** machine for printing: *in the* ~, being printed. **4.** business for printing (and sometimes publishing) books or newspapers. **5.** *the* ~, printed periodicals; the newspapers generally. ~ *cutting, paragraph, article, etc.*, cut out from a newspaper. **6.** = pressure (work, business, etc.). **7.** crowd: *The boy was lost in the* ~. **8.** cupboard for clothes, books, etc. **pres·sing** *adj.* (of business) needing attention at once; (of persons, their requests) insistent. '~·**man** *n.* newspaper reporter.

²**press** [pres] *v.t.* **1.** ~ *into service*, make use of because of urgent need. **2.** compel (sb.) to become a soldier or sailor. '**press-gang** *n.* body of men formerly employed to ~ men into the Navy. **pres·sure** ['preʃə*] *n.* **1.** pressing; (the amount of) force exerted continuously on or against sth. by sth. that touches it: ~ *gauge*, apparatus for measuring the ~ of a liquid or gas at a given point; *atmospheric* ~, weight of the atmosphere as measured by a barometer at a given point and time. '~·**cooker**, airtight container for cooking food quickly under high ~. **2.** *bring* ~ *to bear on sb.*, *put* ~ *on sb.*, do sth. that forces him (to do what is required). ~ *group*, organized group of members · of an association, union, etc., that exerts its influence for the benefit of its members. **3.** *work at high* ~, work with great energy and speed. **pres·sur·ized** ['preʃəraizd] *adj.* (of aircraft cabins) constructed so that air-pressure, temperature, etc., in them can be adjusted for flying at great heights without discomfort.

pres·tige [pres'tiːʒ] *n.* respect resulting from the good reputation (of a person, nation, etc.); power or influence caused by this.

pre·sume [pri'zjuːm] *v.t. & i.* **1.** take for granted (*that*); suppose to be true. **2.** venture; dare: *May I* ~ *to advise you?* **3.** ~ *upon*, make a wrong use of, take an unfair advantage of (sb.'s kind nature, etc.). **pre·sump·tion** [pri'zʌmpʃən] *n.* **1.** sth. ~d (1); sth. which seems likely although there is no proof. **2.** behaviour which is too bold, which takes unfair advantage, etc. **pre·sump·tive** [pri'zʌmptiv] *adj.* based on presumption (1): *the heir* ~, person who is the heir (to the throne, etc.) until sb. with a stronger claim is born. **pre·sump·tu·ous** [pri'zʌmptjuəs] *adj.* (of behaviour, etc.) too bold or self-confident.

pre·sup·pose [ˌpriːsə'pouz] *v.t.* **1.** assume beforehand (*that*). **2.** require as a condition; imply: *Good health* ~*s enough sleep.* **pre·sup·po·si·tion** [ˌpriːsʌpə'ziʃən] *n.* sth. ~d.

pre·tend [pri'tend] *v.t. & i.* **1.** make oneself appear (to be sth., to be doing sth.) either in play or to deceive others: ~ *to be asleep*; *children* ~*ing that they are soldiers.* **2.** do this as an excuse or reason or to avoid danger, difficulty, etc.: *to* ~ *sickness.* **3.** claim; say falsely: ~ *to like sb.* **4.** ~ *to*, put forward a false claim to. ~·**er** *n.* person who ~s (4) to a position (e.g. the throne). **pre·tence** [pri'tens] *n.* ~*ing*; make-believe; false claim or untrue reason. **pre·ten·sion** [pri'tenʃən] *n.* **1.** (statement of) a) claim. **2.** being pretentious. **pre·ten·tious** [pri'tenʃəs] *adj.* suggesting a claim to great merit or importance.

pret·er·ite ['pretərit] *adj.* ~ *tense*, the simple past tense (e.g. *he went*).

pre·text ['pri:tekst] *n.* false reason for an action: *under the ~ of (that)*.

pret·ty ['priti] *adj.* (*prettier*, *-iest*). pleasing and attractive without being beautiful or magnificent. *adv.* (colloq.) quite; rather: ~ *late (good)*. **pret·ti·ly** *adv.* **pret·ti·ness** *n.*

pre·vail [pri'veil] *v.i.* 1. gain victory (*over*); get control (*over*); fight successfully (*against*). 2. be widespread; be generally seen, done, etc. 3. ~ *upon* (sb. to do sth.), persuade. **prev·a·lent** ['prevələnt] *adj.* common, seen or done everywhere (at the time referred to): *the prevalent fashions*. **prev·a·lence** *n.* *the prevalence of influenza in winter*.

pre·var·i·cate [pri'værikeit] *v.i.* make untrue or partly untrue statements. **pre·var·i·ca·tion** [pri,væri'keifən] *n.*

pre·vent [pri'vent] *v.t.* 1. stop (sth.) from happening: ~ *an accident*. 2. keep (sb. *from* doing sth.): ~ *sb. from falling.* ~·**a·ble** *adj.* that can be ~ed. **pre·ven·tion** [pri'venfən] *n.* **pre·ven·tive** *adj.* serving to ~: ~*ive medicine.*

pre·vi·ous ['pri:vjəs] *adj.* coming earlier in time or order: *a ~ engagement.* ~ *to*, before. ~·**ly** *adv.*

prey [prei] *n.* 1. animal, bird, etc., hunted for food by another: *bird of ~* (e.g. an eagle), kind that kills and eats other birds and animals. 2. *be a ~ to fears (disease*, etc.), be greatly troubled by. *v.i.* ~ *upon*, take, hunt, (other animals, etc.) as ~ (1); (of fears, disease, losses, etc.) trouble greatly.

price [prais] *n.* money for which sth. is (to be) sold or bought; that which must be done, given, or experienced to obtain or keep sth.: *the ~ of liberty (independence)*. *v.t.* fix the ~ of sth.; mark (goods) with a ~. ~·**less** *adj.* too valuable to be ~d.

prick [prik] *v.t. & i.* 1. make a hole or mark in (sth.) with a sharp point: ~ *a toy balloon*; make (a hole or mark in sth.) in this way. 2. hurt with a sharp point: ~ *one's finger with a needle.* 3. cause sharp pain to: *Thorns ~*. 4. feel sharp pain: *My finger ~s*. 5. ~ *up the ears* (esp. of dogs, horses) raise the ears; (fig., of persons) pay sharp attention. *n.* small mark or hole, pain, caused by the act of ~ing. ~·**le** ['prikl] *n.* pointed growth on the stem, etc., of a plant or on the skin of some animals (e.g. a hedgehog). *v.t. & i.* give or have a ~ing feeling. ~·**ly** *adj.* having ~les; ~ling: ~*ly heat*, rash with irritation of the skin caused by hot weather.

pride [praid] *n.* 1. feeling of satisfaction arising from what one has done, or from persons, things, etc., one is concerned with: *take ~ in one's work (the success of one's school*, etc.). 2. object of such feeling: *a girl who is her mother's ~*. 3. (also *proper ~*) self-respect; knowledge of one's own worth and character: ~ *that prevented him from doing anything dishonourable.* 4. too high an opinion of oneself, one's position, possessions, etc. *v.t.* ~ *oneself (up)on*, take ~ in; be pleased and satisfied about.

priest [pri:st] *n.* 1. clergyman of a Christian Church, esp. one who is between a deacon and a bishop in the Church of England or the Roman Catholic Church. 2. (of non-Christian religions) person trained to perform special acts of religion. ~·**ess** *n.* woman ~ (2). ~·**hood** *n.* the whole body of ~s of one religion. ~·**ly** *adj.*

prig [prig] *n.* self-satisfied, self-righteous person. ~·**gish** *adj.*

prim [prim] *adj.* (*primmer*, *primmest*). neat; formal; disliking, showing a dislike of, anything improper: *a ~ old lady.*

pri·ma·cy ['praiməsi] *n.* 1. being of highest rank, quality, etc. 2. position of an archbishop.

pri·ma don·na ['pri:mə'dɔnə] *n.* leading woman singer in an opera.

pri·ma·ry ['praiməri] *adj.* 1. leading in time, order, or development: *of* ~ (i.e. chief) *importance*; *a* ~ *school*. 2. ~ *colours*, red, blue, and yellow, from which all others can be obtained by mixing two or more.

pri·mate ['praimit] *n.* archbishop.

prime [praim] *adj.* 1. chief; most important: ~ *minister* (= premier). 2. of best quality: ~ *beef*. 3. ~ *number*, one that cannot be divided exactly except by itself and the number 1 (e.g. 7, 17). *n.* the first or finest part: *the* ~ *of the year*; *in the* ~ *of life*, the time when one's powers are fully developed. *v.t. & i.* get ready for use or action: ~ *a pump* (by putting water into it); *well* ~*d with facts*, well supplied.

prim·er ['praimə*] *n.* first textbook of any school subject.

pri·me·val [prai'mi:vl] *adj.* 1. of the earliest time in the world's history. 2. very ancient: ~ *forests*.

prim·i·tive ['primitiv] *adj.* of the earliest times; at an early stage of social development; simple: ~ *man*; ~ *weapons*.

prim·rose ['primrouz] *n.* pale yellow (flower).

prince [prins] *n.* 1. ruler, esp. of a small State. 2. son of a ruler, esp. of a king or emperor. **prin·cess** [prin'ses, 'prinses] *n.* wife of a ~; daughter, granddaughter, of a sovereign. ~**ly** *adj.* of or for a ~; magnificent; very generous: *a* ~*ly gift*.

prin·ci·pal ['prinsipl] *adj.* highest in order of importance: *the* ~ *towns of France*. *n.* 1. head of certain organizations, esp. colleges. 2. person for whom another acts as agent in business. 3. money lent, put into a business, etc., on which interest is payable. ~**ly** *adv.* chiefly.

prin·ci·pal·i·ty [,prinsi'pæliti] *n.* country ruled by a prince.

prin·ci·ple ['prinsipl] *n.* 1. basic truth; general law of cause and effect. 2. guiding rule for behaviour: *Gambling is against my* ~*s*. *on* ~, because of, obey-

ing, a ~ (2), not because of self-interest, etc. *a man of* ~, an honest, upright man. **prin·ci·pled** *adj.* (in compounds) following, having the kind of ~ (2) indicated, as *high-*~*d*, *loose-*~*d*.

print [print] *v.t.* 1. make marks on (paper, etc.) by pressing it with inked type, etc.; make (books, pictures, etc.) in this way. 2. make (a photograph) on paper, etc., from a negative film or plate. 3. shape (one's letters, etc.) like those used in ~. *n.* 1. mark(s), letters, etc., made by ~ing (1) on paper, etc.; ~ (of a book) ~ed and on sale; *out of* ~, (of a book) no more ~ed copies available from the publisher. 2. (in compounds) mark made on a surface by sth. pressed on it: *finger-*~*s*. 3. (any special kind of) ~ed lettering: *in large, clear* ~. 4. picture, design, etc., made by ~ing; photograph ~ed from a negative. 5. cotton cloth with coloured designs, etc., ~ed with it. ~**·a·ble** *adj.* (esp.) fit to be ~ed. ~**er** *n.* workman who ~s books, etc.; owner of a ~ing business. '~**·ing-press** *n.* machine for ~ing books, etc.

¹**pri·or** ['praiə*] *adj.* earlier in time or order. *adv.* ~ *to*, before. ~**·i·ty** [prai'oriti] *n.* being ~; right to have or do sth. before others.

²**pri·or** ['praiə*] *n.* head of a religious order or house. ~**ess** *n.* woman ~. ~**·y** *n.* house governed by a ~ or ~ess.

prise, see ²*prize*.

prism ['prizm] *n.* solid figure of the kind here illustrated; body with this form, esp. glass ~ that breaks up white light into the colours of the rainbow. **pris·mat·ic** [priz'mætik] *adj.* 1. of the shape of a ~. 2. (of colours) brilliant; varied.

A prism

pris·on ['prizn] *n.* building in which wrongdoers serve their sentences (2); place where a person is shut up against his will. **~·er** *n.* person held in ~ for crime, etc., or until tried in a law court; person captured in war: *to take a soldier* ~*er.*

pri·vate ['praivit] *adj.* **1.** (opp. of *public*) of, for the use of, concerning, one person or a group of persons, not people in general. *living on* ~ *means*, on an income not earned as salary, etc.; *a* ~ *letter*, about personal, not business, matters; ~ *theatricals*, for family and friends. **2.** secret; kept secret: ~ *information.* **3.** having no official position: *a* ~ *person; retiring to* ~ *life.* **4.** ~ *soldier*, ordinary soldier of the lowest rank. *n.* **1.** ~ soldier. **2.** *in* ~, confidentially; not in the presence of others. **~·ly** *adv.* in ~; alone. **pri·va·cy** ['pri-visi, 'praivisi] *n.*

pri·va·teer [ˌpraivə'tiə*] *n.* (formerly) armed vessel under private ownership, allowed to attack enemy shipping during a war.

pri·va·tion [prai'veiʃən] *n.* **1.** lack of the necessaries of life: *suffering many* ~*s.* **2.** state of being deprived of sth.: *He found it a great* ~ *not being allowed to smoke in prison.*

priv·i·lege ['privilidʒ] *n.* right or advantage available only to a person, class, holder, of a certain position, etc. **priv·i·leged** *adj.* having, granted, a ~ or ~s.

priv·y ['privi] *adj.* **1.** (old use, except in law) secret; private: ~ *to*, having private knowledge of. *P~ Council*, committee of persons appointed by the king (queen), advising on some government business; ~ *purse*, money provided by Parliament for a sovereign's personal use.

¹**prize** [praiz] *n.* **1.** sth. (to be) awarded to one who succeeds in a competition, lottery, etc. **2.** sth. worth working for. **3.** sth. (esp. a ship, its cargo) captured from the enemy in war. **4.** (attrib.) given as a ~; awarded a ~: *a* ~ *scholarship*; ~ *cattle.* *v.t.* value highly: *his most* ~*d*

possessions. '**~-fight** *n.* boxing-match for which a money ~ is given. '**~-ring** *n.* the enclosed area in which a boxing-match for a ~ is fought; the sport of ~-fighting.

²**prize, prise** [praiz] *v.t.* use force to get (a box, lid) (*open, up, off*).

pro [prou] *n.* (colloq., short for) *professional* (player, etc.).

pro- [prou] *prefix.* supporting; favouring: *pro-British.* **pros and cons** *n. pl.* the arguments for and against.

prob·a·ble ['prɔbəbl] *adj.* likely to happen or to prove true or correct. **prob·a·bly** *adv.* **prob·a·bil·i·ty** [ˌprɔbə'biliti] *n.* being ~; chance; sth. that is ~: *in all probability*, very probably, most likely.

pro·bate ['proubit] *n.* the official process of proving that a will is drawn up in correct legal form; copy of a will with a certificate that it is correct.

pro·ba·tion [prou'beiʃən] *n.* **1.** testing of a person's conduct, abilities, qualities, etc., before he is finally accepted for a position, admitted into a society, etc.: *two years'* ~; *on* ~ (i.e. undergoing ~). **2.** (law) *the* ~ *system*, that by which the (esp. young) offenders are allowed to go unpunished for their first offence while they continue to live an honest life. ~ *officer*, one who watches over the behaviour of such offenders. **~·er** *n.* person on ~, esp. a hospital nurse receiving training.

probe [proub] *n.* slender instrument with a blunt end, used by doctors for learning about the depth or direction of a wound, etc. *v.t.* examine with a ~; press a sharp instrument into; (fig.) inquire deeply into (sb.'s thought, the causes of sth.).

pro·bi·ty ['proubiti] *n.* uprightness of character; straightforwardness.

prob·lem ['prɔbləm] *n.* question to be solved or decided, esp. sth. difficult. **~·at·ic, ~·at·i·cal** [ˌprɔblə'mætik(l)] *adj.* (esp. of a result) doubtful.

pro·ce·dure [prə'si:djuə*, -dʒə*] *n.* (regular) order of doing things, esp. in legal and political affairs.

pro·ceed [prou'si:d] *v.i.* **1.** go forward (*to* a place); continue, go on (*to do* sth., *with* one's work, etc.). **2.** come, arise (*from* a cause). **3.** take legal action (*against* sb.). ~·ing *n.* **1.** action; sth. done or being done. **2.** (pl.) take, start, ~ings (*against* sb.), take legal action. **3.** (pl.) records (of the activities of a society, etc.). **pro·ceeds** ['prou-si:dz] *n. pl.* financial results, profits, of an undertaking.

pro·cess ['prouses] *n.* **1.** connected series of actions, changes, etc.: *the* ~ *of digestion.* **2.** method, esp. one used in industry. **3.** forward movement; progress: *in* ~ *of time*, as time goes on; *in* ~ *of completion*, being completed. *v.t.* put (materials) through a ~ (2); treat in order to preserve: *to* ~ *leather* (*cheese*).

pro·ces·sion [prə'seʃən] *n.* number of persons, vehicles, etc., moving forward and following each other in an orderly way: *a funeral* ~; *march in* ~ *through the town.*

pro·claim [prə'kleim] *v.t.* make known publicly or officially: ~ *a public holiday*; ~ *sb.* king. **proc·la·ma·tion** [ˌprɔklə'mei-ʃən] *n.* act of ~ing; sth. ~ed.

pro·cliv·i·ty [prə'kliviti] *n.* tendency or inclination (*towards*, *to* sth., *to do* sth., *for* doing sth.).

pro·cras·ti·nate [prou'kræsti-neit] *v.i.* delay action. **pro·cras·ti·na·tion** [prouˌkræsti-'neiʃən] *n.*

proc·tor ['prɔktə*] *n.* university official with the duty of keeping students in order.

pro·cure [prə'kjuə*] *v.t.* **1.** obtain, esp. with care or effort. **2.** (old use) bring about, cause. **pro·cur·a·ble** *adj.*

prod [prɔd] *v.t. & i.* (-*dd*-). push or poke (*at*) with sth. pointed: ~*ding the animal with her umbrella. n.* poke or thrust.

prod·i·gal ['prɔdigl] *adj.* wasteful (*of* sth.); spending or using too much (*of*). *n.* ~ person.

pro·dig·ious [prə'didʒəs] *adj.* enormous; surprisingly great; wonderful.

prod·i·gy ['prɔdidʒi] *n.* sth. surprising because it seems contrary to the laws of nature; person who has unusual or remarkable abilities or who is a wonderful example of some quality: *a* ~ *of learning.*

pro·duce [prə'dju:s] *v.t.* **1.** put or bring forward to be looked at or examined: ~ *proofs of a statement*; ~ *one's railway ticket when asked to do so.* **2.** manufacture, make; create (works of art, etc.). **3.** bring forth, yield (crops, etc.); give birth to (young); lay (eggs). **4.** cause; bring about: *success* ~*d by long study.* **5.** (maths.) make (a line) longer. **6.** ~ *a play*, organize its performance. **prod·uce** ['prɔdju:s] *n.* sth. ~d, esp. by farming: *garden* ~ (vegetables, etc.). **pro·duc·er** [prə'dju:sə*] *n.* **1.** person who ~s goods (contrasted with *consumer*). **2.** person who prepares actors for a stage performance, who advises persons who are to broadcast, etc. **prod·uct** ['prɔd-əkt] *n.* **1.** sth. ~d (by nature or by man): *farm products.* **2.** quantity obtained by multiplying numbers. **pro·duc·tion** [prə'dʌkʃən] *n.* process of producing; sth. ~d; quantity ~d. **pro·duc·tive** [prə'dʌktiv] *adj.* **1.** able to ~; fertile: *productive land.* **2.** tending to ~: *discussions that are productive only of quarrels.* **prod·uc·tiv·i·ty** [ˌprɔdʌk'tiviti] *n.* being productive; capacity to ~; rate at which goods are ~d per man per hour.

pro·fane [prə'fein] *adj.* **1.** (contrasted with *holy, sacred*) worldly. **2.** having or showing contempt for God or sacred things: ~ *language* (*practices*); *a* ~ *man.* *v.t.* treat (sacred or holy places, things) with contempt, without proper reverence. ~·ly *adv.* **pro·fan·i·ty** [prə'fæniti] *n.* conduct or speech; use of swearwords.

pro·fess [prə'fes] *v.t.* **1.** declare

that one has (beliefs, likes, ignorance, interests, etc.). 2. have as one's profession: to ~ *law* (*medicine*). 3. claim; represent oneself (*to be, to do* sth.): *Don't ~ to be an expert* (*to have an expert's knowledge*). *a ~ed friend*, one who claims to be a friend, but is not. **pro·fes·sed·ly** [prə-'fesidli] *adv*. according to one's own account or claims.

pro·fes·sion [prə'feʃən] *n*. 1. occupation, esp. one requiring advanced education and special training (the law, architecture, medicine, the Church). 2. statement or declaration of belief, feeling, etc.: *a ~ of faith* (*friendship, loyalty*). ~**al** *adj*. 1. of a profession (1): *~al skill*; *~al men* (e.g. lawyers, doctors). 2. connected with, engaged in, the doing of sth. for payment or to make a living (opp. of *amateur*): *~al football*(*ers*). *n*. person who teaches or engages in some kind of sport for money; person who does sth. for payment that others do for pleasure: *~al musicians*.

pro·fes·sor [prə'fesə*] *n*. university teacher of the highest grade.

prof·fer ['prɒfə*] *v.t. & n.* offer.

pro·fi·cient [prə'fiʃnt] *adj*. skilled; expert (*in, at,* sth.). **pro·fi·cien·cy** *n*.

pro·file ['proufail] *n*. 1. side view, e.g. of the face. 2. edge or outline of sth. seen against a background. 3. short biography, as given in a newspaper article, radio talk, etc.

prof·it ['prɒfit] *n*. 1. advantage or good obtained from sth.: *gain ~ from one's studies*. 2. money gained in business: *making a ~ of a shilling on every article sold*. *v.t. & i.* 1. get ~ (*from*); bring ~ to. 2. ~ *by*, be helped by, use to one's advantage: *~ by sb. else's experience*. ~·**a·ble** *adj*. bringing ~. **prof·i·teer** [ˌprɒfi'tiə*] *v.i.* make large ~s, esp. by taking advantage of times of difficulty or scarcity, e.g. in war. *n*. person who does this.

prof·li·gate ['prɒfligit] *adj*. 1.

(of a person, his behaviour) shamelessly immoral. 2. (of the spending of money) reckless; very extravagant. *n*. ~ (1) person. **prof·li·ga·cy** *n*.

pro·found [prə'faund] *adj*. 1. deep: *a ~ sleep* (*sigh, interest*). 2. needing, showing, having, great knowledge: *~ books* (*writers, thinkers*). 3. needing much thought or study to understand: *~ mysteries*. ~·**ly** *adv*. deeply; sincerely. **pro·fun·di·ty** [prə-'fʌnditi] *n*.

pro·fuse [prə'fju:s] *adj*. 1. very plentiful or abundant: *my ~ thanks*. 2. ~ *in* (*of*), giving, using, producing very (or too) generously: *He was ~ in his apologies*. ~·**ly** *adv*. **pro·fu·sion** [prə'fju:ʒən] *n*. great quantity: *roses growing in profusion*.

prog·e·ny ['prɒdʒəni] *n*. offspring; descendants; children.

prog·nos·ti·cate [prɒg'nɒstikeit] *v.t.* foretell; predict. **prog·nos·ti·ca·tion** [prɒgˌnɒsti'keiʃən] *n*. prediction.

pro·gramme ['prougræm] *n*. 1. list of items, events, etc. (e.g. for a concert, play at the theatre). 2. plan of what is to be done: *political ~s. What's the ~ for tomorrow? What are we going to do?* *v.t.* prepare a ~ for (e.g. a computer).

pro·gress ['prougres] *n*. 1. forward movement; advance: *making fast ~*. 2. development: *~ in civilization*; *now in ~*, now being done or carried on. 3. improvement: *The patient is making good ~*, is getting better. [prou'gres] *v.i.* make ~. **pro·gres·sion** [prə'greʃən] *n*. ~·ing: *modes of ~ion* (e.g. crawling). **pro·gres·sive** [prə'gresiv] *adj*. 1. making continuous forward movement. 2. increasing by regular degrees: *~ive taxation of incomes*. 3. undergoing improvement; getting better (e.g. in civilization); supporting or favouring ~: *a ~ive nation* (*policy, political party*). *n*. person supporting a ~ive policy.

pro·hib·it [prə'hibit] *v.t.* forbid, prevent (by law, etc.) (sb.

from doing sth.); order that sth. must not be done: *smoking ~ed.*

pro·hib·i·tive [prəˈhibitiv] *adj.* (esp. of prices) high enough to prevent purchase or use: *~ive rents.*

pro·hi·bi·tion [ˌprouiˈbiʃən] *n.* ~ing; order ~ing sth., esp. law ~ing the sale of alcoholic drink.

proj·ect [ˈprɔdʒekt] *n.* (plan for a) scheme or undertaking. **pro·ject** [prəˈdʒekt] *v.t. & i.* **1.** make plans for: *to ~ a new dam.* **2.** cause (a shadow, an outline, a picture from a film or slide) to fall on a surface (e.g. a wall or screen). **3.** stand out beyond the surface nearby: *~ing eyebrows.* **pro·jec·tile** [prəˈdʒektail] *n.* sth. (to be) shot forward, esp. from a gun. **pro·jec·tion** [prəˈdʒekʃən] *n.* 1. ~ing (2), (3). **2.** sth. ~ed, esp. sth. that stands out; prominent part. **pro·jec·tor** *n.* apparatus for ~ing pictures by rays of light on to a screen: *a film ~or.*

pro·le·ta·ri·at [ˌprouleˈtɛəriæt] *n.* the whole body of unskilled workers or wage-earners. **pro·le·ta·ri·an** *n. & adj.* (member) of the ~.

pro·lif·ic [prəˈlifik] *adj.* producing much or many: *a ~ author,* writing many books; *~ of new ideas.*

pro·lix [ˈprouliks] *adj.* (of a speaker, writer, speech, etc.) tedious, tiring because too long. *~·i·ty* [prouˈliksiti] *n.*

pro·logue [ˈproulog] *n.* **1.** introductory part of a poem; poem recited at the beginning of a play. **2.** (fig.) first of a series of events.

pro·long [prəˈlɔŋ] *v.t.* make longer. **pro·longed** *adj.* continuing for a long time. **pro·lon·ga·tion** [ˌproulɔŋˈgeiʃən] *n.* (esp.) part added to sth. to ~ it.

prom·e·nade [ˌprɔmiˈnɑːd] *n.* (place suitable for, specially made for, a) walk or ride taken for pleasure in public. *v.i. & t.* go up and down a ~; take (sb.) up and down a ~: *~ (one's children) along the sea-front.*

prom·i·nent [ˈprɔminənt] *adj.* **1.** (of a part) standing out;

projecting (3). **2.** easily seen. **3.** important; distinguished. **prom·i·nence** *n.* **1.** being ~. **2.** ~ part or place.

pro·mis·cu·ous [prəˈmiskjuəs] *adj.* **1.** made up of a mixture; unsorted. **2.** without careful choice: *~ friendships.* **prom·is·cu·i·ty** [ˌprɔmisˈkjuːiti] *n.* (state of) being ~.

prom·ise [ˈprɔmis] *n.* **1.** written or spoken undertaking to do or not to do sth., to give sth., etc.: *a ~ of help*; *make (keep, break) a ~.* **2.** (sth. that gives) hope of success or good results: *boys who show ~,* who are likely to be successful, etc. *v.t. & i.* **1.** make a ~ (1) to: *~ help*; *~ to do sth.*; *~ that.* . . . **2.** give cause or hope for expecting: *clouds that ~ rain*; *a situation that ~s well,* seems likely to develop well. **prom·is·ing** *adj.* seeming likely to do well, to have good results, etc. **prom·is·so·ry** [ˈprɔmisəri] *adj. promissory note,* signed ~ to pay a stated sum of money.

prom·on·to·ry [ˈprɔməntəri] *n.* headland; high point of land standing out from the coast.

pro·mote [prəˈmout] *v.t.* **1.** give (sb.) higher position or rank: *~d to the position of manager.* **2.** help forward; encourage; support: *~ peace (a plan for a new park).* **3.** help to organize and start (new business companies, etc.). **pro·mot·er** *n.* (esp.) person who ~s business companies. **pro·mo·tion** [prəˈmouʃən] *n.*

¹prompt [prɔmpt] *adj.* acting, done, sent, given, without delay: *a ~ answer*; *~ to volunteer.* *~·ly adv.* *~·ness n.* **promp·ti·tude** [ˈprɔmptitjuːd] *n.*

²prompt [prɔmpt] *v.t.* **1.** be the reason causing sb. (to do sth.): *~ed by patriotism.* **2.** follow the text of a play and remind actors, where necessary, of their lines. *~·er n.* person who ~s actors.

prom·ul·gate [ˈprɔməlgeit] *v.t.* **1.** make public, announce officially (a decree, a new law, etc.). **2.** spread widely (beliefs, knowledge). **prom·ul·ga·tion** [ˌprɔməlˈgeiʃən] *n.*

prone [proun] *adj.* **1.** (stretched out, lying) face downwards. **2.** ~ **to**, inclined to: ~ *to error*.

prong [prɔŋ] *n.* each one of the pointed parts of a fork.

pro·noun ['prounaun] *n.* word used in place of a noun, e.g. *I*, *you*, *he*, *mine*. **pro·nom·i·nal** [prou'nɔminl] *adj.*

pro·nounce [prə'nauns] *v.t. & i.* **1.** say, make, the sound of (a word, etc.). **2.** declare, announce (esp. sth. official): ~ *judgement* (*sentence*). **3.** give one's opinion (*on*, *for* or *against*, *in favour of*, sth.). ~·**a·ble** *adj.* (of sounds, words) that can be ~d. **pro·nounced** *adj.* definite; strongly marked. ~·**ment** *n.* decision; formal statement of opinion. **pro·nun·ci·a·tion** [prə₍nʌnsi'eiʃən] *n.* way of pronouncing a word; way in which sb. usually ~s his words.

proof [pru:f] *n.* **1.** fact(s), method(s), reasoning, etc., showing that sth. is true, that sth. is a fact: *supply* ~(*s*) *of a statement*; ~ *of the prisoner's guilt*. **2.** act of testing whether sth. is true, a fact, etc.: *capable of* ~; *put sth. to the* ~ (i.e. test it). **3.** trial copy of a book, picture, etc., for approval before other copies are printed. *adj.* giving safety or protection (*against* sth.): ~ *against temptation*; *a bomb-~ shelter*; *a rain-~ coat*.

prop [prɔp] *n.* **1.** support used to keep sth. up: *pit-~s* (holding up the roof in a mine). **2.** person who supports sth. or sb.: *the* ~ *of his parents during their old age.* *v.t.* (*-pp-*). (often ~ *up*) support; keep in position.

prop·a·gan·da [₍prɔpə'gændə] *n.* (means of, measures for, the) spreading of information, opinions, ideas, etc.: *health* ~.

prop·a·gate ['prɔpəgeit] *v.t.* **1.** increase the number of (plants, animals) by natural reproduction: ~ *by seed* (*cuttings*). **2.** spread (news, knowledge, etc.) more widely. **prop·a·ga·tion** [₍prɔpə'geiʃən] *n.* propagating or being ~d: *the propagation of disease by insects.*

pro·pel [prə'pel] *v.t.* (*-ll-*). drive forward. ~·**ler** *n.* shaft with blades for ~ling a ship or aircraft.

pro·pen·si·ty [prə'pensiti] *n.* natural tendency (*to sth.*, *to do* sth., *for doing sth.*).

prop·er ['prɔpə*] *adj.* **1.** right, correct, fitting (*for doing sth.*, *to do sth.*, *to an occasion*, etc.). **2.** in conformity with the conventions of society: ~ *behaviour*. **3.** rightly or strictly so named: *architecture* ~ (i.e. excluding, for example, the water-supply, etc.). **4.** ~ *noun* (*name*), name used for one special person, place, etc. (e.g. Mary). **5.** (colloq.) great, thorough: *a* ~ *mess*. ~·**ly** *adv.* in a ~ manner: *behave* ~*ly* ; ~*ly* (i.e. strictly) *speaking*.

prop·er·ty ['prɔpəti] *n.* **1.** that which a person owns; possession(s): (esp.) land, or land and building(s). **2.** special quality belonging to sth.: *the* ~ *of dissolving grease*. **3.** (usu. pl.) things (not scenery) used on the stage in the performance of a play.

proph·e·cy ['prɔfisi] *n.* power of telling, statement of, what will happen in the future. **proph·e·sy** ['prɔfisai] *v.t.* say what will happen in the future: *prophesy war* (*that there will be war*).

proph·et ['prɔfit] *n.* **1.** person who teaches religion and claims that his teaching comes to him directly from God: *the prophet Isaiah* ; *Muhammad, the Prophet of Islam.* **2.** teacher of a new theory, cause, etc. **3.** person who tells what will happen in the future. **proph·et·ess** *n.* woman prophet. **pro·phet·ic** [prə'fetik] *adj.* of a prophet or of prophesying.

proph·y·lac·tic [₍prɔfi'læktik] *n. & adj.* (substance, treatment) serving to protect from disease.

pro·pin·qui·ty [prə'piŋkwiti] *n.* nearness (in time, place, relationship).

pro·pi·ti·ate [prə'piʃieit] *v.t.* pacify; do sth. to take away the anger of; win the favour or support of. **pro·pi·ti·a·tion** [prə₍piʃi'eiʃən] *n.*

pro·pi·tious [prə'pɪʃəs] *adj.* favourable; likely to bring success.

pro·por·tion [prə'pɔːʃən] *n.* **1.** relationship of one thing to another in quantity, size, etc.; relation of a part to the whole: *wide in ~ to the height.* **2.** (often pl.) the correct relation of parts or of the sizes of the several parts: *a room of admirable ~s.* **3.** (pl.) size; measurements: *a coat of ample ~s.* **4.** part; share: *A large ~ of N. Africa is desert.* **5.** (maths.) equality of relationship between two sets of numbers (e.g. 4 and 8, 6 and 12). *v.t.* put into ~ or right relationship: *~ what one spends to what one earns;* arrange the ~s of; divide into right shares. **~·al** *adj.* in proper ~; corresponding in size, amount, etc. (*to*): *payment ~al to the work done.* **~·ate** *adj.* = *~al.*

pro·pose [prə'pəʊz] *v.t. & i.* **1.** offer or put forward for consideration, as a suggestion, plan, or purpose: *~ an early start (to start early, that we start early).* **2.** offer marriage (*to* sb.). **3.** put forward (sb.'s name) for an office: *I ~ Mr X for President.* **pro·po·sal** *n.* **1.** sth. ~d; plan or scheme. **2.** offer (esp. of marriage). **prop·o·si·tion** [ˌprɒpə'zɪʃən] *n.* **1.** statement. **2.** question or problem (with or without the answer or solution). **3.** proposal.

pro·pound [prə'paʊnd] *v.t.* put forward for consideration or solution: *~ a theory (riddle).*

pro·pri·e·ta·ry [prə'praɪətərɪ] *adj.* owned or controlled by sb.; held as property: *~ medicines* (patented).

pro·pri·e·tor [prə'praɪətə*] *n.* person owning property; owner, esp. of a hotel, store, or land. **pro·pri·e·tress** *n.* woman ~.

pro·pri·e·ty [prə'praɪətɪ] *n.* **1.** state of being proper(2) in behaviour: *observe the proprieties,* the details of polite behaviour. **2.** correctness, suitability.

pro·pul·sion [prə'pʌlʃən] *n.* propelling force: *jet ~.*

pro ra·ta [prəʊ'rɑːtə] *adv.* in proportion; according to the share, etc., of each.

pro·rogue [prə'rəʊg] *v.t.* bring (a session of Parliament, etc.) to an end for a time.

pro·sa·ic [prəʊ'zeɪɪk] *adj.* dull; uninteresting; commonplace.

pro·scribe [prəʊs'kraɪb] *v.t.* declare to be dangerous; outlaw.

prose [prəʊz] *n.* language not in verse form. (Cf. *poetry*.)

pros·e·cute ['prɒsɪkjuːt] *v.t.* **1.** continue with (a trade, one's studies, an inquiry). **2.** start legal proceedings against: *Trespassers will be ~d.* **pros·e·cu·tion** [ˌprɒsɪ'kjuːʃən] *n.* **1.** act of prosecuting(1): *in the prosecution of my inquiries.* **2.** prosecuting(2) or being ~d(2). **3.** (law) person, and his advisers, who ~(2): *the case for the prosecution.* **pros·e·cu·tor** ['prɒsɪkjuːtə*] *n.* person who ~s(2): *Public Prosecutor,* person who ~s(2) on behalf of the State.

pros·e·lyte ['prɒsɪlaɪt] *n.* person converted to different religious, political, or other opinions or beliefs.

pros·o·dy ['prɒsədɪ] *n.* science of verse metres or rhythms.

pros·pect ['prɒspekt] *n.* **1.** wide view over land or sea or (fig.) before the mind, in the imagination. **2.** sth. expected, hoped for, or looked forward to; expectation: *not much ~ of recovering his health.* [prəs'pekt] *v.t. & i.* search (*for*): *~ing for gold.* **pros·pec·tive** [prəs'pektɪv] *adj.* hoped for; looked forward to: *~ive wealth; his ~ive bride.* **pros·pec·tor** [prəs'pektə*] *n.* person who ~s (for gold, etc.).

pro·spec·tus [prə'spektəs] *n.* printed account giving details of and advertising sth. (e.g. a school, a new business enterprise).

pros·per ['prɒspə*] *v.i. & t.* **1.** succeed; do well. **2.** (of God) cause to ~. **~·i·ty** [prɒs'perɪtɪ] *n.* good fortune; state of being successful. **~·ous** ['prɒspərəs] *adj.* ~ing; successful; favourable.

pros·ti·tute ['prɔstitjuːt] *n.* woman who hires herself out for sexual indulgence. *v.t.* put to wrong or immoral uses: ~ *oneself* (*one's energies*). **pros·ti·tu·tion** [ˌprɔsti'tjuːʃən] *n.*

pros·trate ['prɔstreit] *adj.* lying stretched out on the ground, usu. face downward (e.g. because tired out, or to show submission, deep respect); overcome (with grief, etc.). [prɔs'treit] *v.t.* 1. make ~: *trees ~d by the wind.* 2. ~ *oneself,* make oneself ~. 3. *be ~d,* be overcome (with grief, etc.); be made helpless. **pros·tra·tion** [prɔs'treiʃən] *n.* (esp.) complete exhaustion.

pros·y ['prouzi] *adj.* (*-ier, -iest*). dull; tedious. **pros·i·ly** *adv.* **pros·i·ness** *n.*

pro·tag·o·nist [prou'tægənist] *n.* chief person in a contest, play, novel, etc.

pro·tect [prə'tekt] *v.t.* 1. keep safe (*from, against,* danger, etc.); guard. 2. help (home industry) by taxing imports. **pro·tec·tion** [prə'tekʃən] *n.* ~ing or being ~ed; sth. that ~s. **pro·tec·tive** *adj.* giving ~ion: *the ~ive colouring of the tiger.* **pro·tec·tor** *n.* person who ~s; sth. made or designed to give ~ion. **pro·tec·tor·ate** [prə'tektərit] *n.* country under the ~ion of one of the great powers.

pro·té·gé ['prouteʒei] *n.* person cared for by another; person to whom another gives protective help.

pro·tein ['proutiːn] *n.* body-building substance essential to good health, in such foods as milk, eggs, meat.

pro tem(po·re) ['prou'tem(pəri)] *adv.* for the present time only.

pro·test [prə'test] *v.t. & i.* 1. declare against opposition (*that*). 2. raise an objection, say sth. (*against*). 3. express disapproval, say that one is displeased, (*about*). ['proutest] *n.* statement ~ing: *do sth. under* ~, unwillingly, with the feeling that what one is doing is not right.

pro·tes·ta·tion [ˌproutes'teiʃən] *n.* ~ing; solemn declaration: ~*ations of innocence* (*friendship*).

Prot·es·tant ['prɔtistənt] *n. & adj.* (member) of any of the Christian bodies except the Roman Catholic and Greek Orthodox Churches.

pro·to·col ['proutəkɔl] *n.* first written form of an agreement (esp. between States), signed by those making it, in preparation for a treaty.

pro·ton ['prouton] *n.* unit of positive electricity forming part of an atom. (Cf. *electron.*)

pro·to·type ['proutətaip] *n.* first or original example from which others have been or are to be copied or developed.

pro·tract [prə'trækt] *v.t.* lengthen the time taken by: *a ~ed visit* (*argument*). **pro·trac·tor** *n.* instrument for measuring angles.

A protractor

pro·trude [prə'truːd] *v.t. & i.* (cause to) stick out or project: ~ *the tongue; a shelf protruding from a wall.*

pro·tu·ber·ant [prə'tjuːbərənt] *adj.* curving or swelling outwards. **pro·tu·ber·ance** *n.* sth. that is ~; bulge or swelling.

proud [praud] *adj.* (*-er, -est*). 1. having or showing pride (1), (3), (4): ~ *of one's success; too* ~ *to ask for help.* 2. of or on which one may be justly ~: *a* ~ *day; a* ~ *sight.*

prove [pruːv] *v.t. & i.* 1. supply proof of: ~ *sb.'s guilt* (*that he is guilty*). 2. make certain of, by experiment or test: ~ *sb.'s worth.* 3. be seen or found in the end (to be): *The new typist~d* (*to be*) *useless.* 4. (legal) establish that (a will) is genuine and in order.

prov·en·der ['prɔvində*] *n.* food for horses, cattle; fodder.

prov·erb ['prɒvə:b] *n.* popular short saying, with words of advice or warning. **pro·ver·bi·al** [prə'və:bjəl] *adj.* widely known and talked about. **pro·ver·bi·al·ly** *adv.*

pro·vide [prə'vaid] *v.t. & i.* 1. give, supply (what is needed, esp. what a person needs in order to live): ~ *for one's family*; ~ *one's children with clothes*; ~d *with all one wants*. 2. make ready, do what is necessary (*for* an event, *for* the future); take steps to guard (*against* danger, shortages, etc.). **pro·vid·ed** *conj.* on condition (*that*). **pro·vid·ing** *conj.* on the condition or understanding (*that*).

prov·i·dence ['prɒvidəns] *n.* 1. (old use) care about future needs; thrift. 2. (P~) God; God's care for human beings and all He has created. **prov·i·den·tial** [ˌprɒvi'denʃl] *adj.* through, coming as from, P~: *a providential escape.*

prov·i·dent ['prɒvidənt] *adj.* (careful in) providing for future needs, esp. in old age: *a ~ fund for the staff.*

prov·ince ['prɒvins] *n.* 1. large administrative division of a country. *the ~s*, all the country outside the capital. 2. branch of learning; department: *the ~ of science*; *outside my ~*, not sth. with which I can or need deal. **pro·vin·cial** [prə'vinʃl] *adj.* 1. of a ~. 2. narrow in outlook; having or typical of the speech, manners, views, etc., of a person living in the ~s. *n.* person from the ~s.

pro·vi·sion [prə'viʒən] *n.* 1. providing; preparation (esp. for future needs). ~ *merchants, grocers.* 2. (pl.) food. 3. legal condition (e.g. a clause in a will). 4. *make ~ for*, provide for. **~·al** [prə'viʒən] *adj.* for the present time only, and to be changed or replaced later: *the ~al government.* **~·al·ly** *adv.*

pro·vi·so [prə'vaizou] *n.* (clause containing a) limitation (esp. in a legal document): *with the ~ that....*

pro·voke [prə'vouk] *v.t.* 1. make angry; vex. 2. cause, arouse (discussion, argument, etc.). 3. drive (sb. *to do* sth., *into doing* sth., *to* a state of anger, etc.). **pro·vok·ing** *adj.* annoying. **prov·o·ca·tion** [ˌprɒvə'keiʃən] *n.* provoking or being ~d; sth. that ~s: *under provocation*, when ~d. **pro·voc·a·tive** [prə'vɒkətiv] *adj.* causing, likely to cause, anger, argument, interest, etc.

prov·ost ['prɒvəst] *n.* head of certain colleges; (Scotland) mayor.

prow [prau] *n.* pointed front of a ship or boat.

prow·ess ['prauis] *n.* bravery; brave act(s); skill in fighting.

prowl [praul] *v.i.* go about cautiously looking for a chance to get food (as wild animals do), to steal, etc. *n. on the ~*, ~ing.

prox·im·i·ty [prɒk'simiti] *n.* nearness.

prox·y ['prɒksi] *n.* (document giving sb.) authority to represent or act for another (esp. in voting at an election); person given a ~.

prude [pru:d] *n.* person who is too modest and delicate in behaviour. **prud·er·y** *n.* **prud·ish** *adj.*

pru·dent ['pru:dənt] *adj.* careful; acting only after careful thought or planning. **~·ly** *adv.* **pru·dence** *n.*

¹prune [pru:n] *n.* dried plum.

²prune [pru:n] *v.t.* cut away parts of (trees, bushes, etc.), in order to control growth or shape; (fig.) take out unnecessary parts from.

pru·ri·ent ['pruəriənt] *adj.* having, showing, too much interest in impure things (esp. in regard to sex).

prus·sic ['prʌsik] *adj.* ~ *acid*, a violent and deadly poison.

¹pry [prai] *v.i. pry into*, inquire too curiously into (other people's affairs or conduct).

²pry [prai] *v.t.* lift *up*, get *open* by force, esp. with a lever; (fig.) *pry a secret out of sb.*

psalm [sɑ:m] *n.* sacred song or

hymn, esp. one of those (*the Psalms*) in the Bible.

pseu·do- ['sju:dou-] *prefix.* false; seeming to be, but not really being: ∼*archaic.*

pseu·do·nym ['sju:dənim] *n.* name taken, esp. by a writer, instead of his real name. **pseu·don·y·mous** [sju'dɔniməs] *adj.*

pshaw [ʃɔ:] *int.* exclamation to indicate contempt, impatience, etc.

psy·chic ['saikik] *adj.* of the soul or the mind. **psy·chi·a·try** [sai'kaiətri] *n.* treatment of mental illness. **psy·chi·a·trist** *n.* expert in psychiatry. **psy·cho·a·nal·y·sis** [ˌsaikouə'nælisis] *n.* science of the mind and its processes, based on the division of the mind into the conscious and the unconscious. **psy·chol·o·gy** [sai'kɔlədʒi] *n.* science, study, of the mind and its processes. **psy·chol·o·gist** *n.* expert in psychology. **psy·cho·log·i·cal** [ˌsaikə'lɔdʒikl] *adj.*

pto·maine [tou'mein] *n.* poison which is found in decaying food.

pub [pʌb] *n.* (colloq.) short for *public house.*

pu·ber·ty ['pju:bəti] *n.* age at which a person becomes physically able to be a parent.

pub·lic ['pʌblik] *adj.* (opp. of *private*) of, for, connected with, owned by, done for or done by, known to, people in general: *a* ∼ *library* (*park*); *a matter of* ∼ *knowledge* (i.e. known to all). ∼ *house*, house (not a hotel or club) whose chief business is to sell alcoholic drinks, to be drunk in the building. ∼ *school*, (in England) type of boarding-school for older pupils, supported by endowments and managed by a board of governors; ∼ *elementary and secondary schools*, government-controlled schools providing free education. ∼ *spirit*, readiness to work for the welfare of the community. *n.* *the* ∼, people in general, or of a particular class (e.g. *the theatregoing* ∼). *in* ∼, openly, not in private or in secret. ∼*ly adv.* in ∼; openly. **pub·li·can** *n.*

keeper of a ∼ house. **pub·li·cist** ['pʌblisist] *n.* newspaper man who writes on questions of ∼ interest; expert in international law. **pub·li·ci·ty** [pʌb'lisiti] *n.* 1. the state of being known to, seen by, everyone: *avoid* ∼*ity.* 2. advertisement; (measures (6) used for) the obtaining of ∼ notice. **pub·li·cize** ['pʌblisaiz] *v.t.* give ∼ity (2) to. **pub·li·ca·tion** [ˌpʌbli'keiʃən] *n.* 1. act of publishing. 2. sth. published, e.g. a book or periodical.

pub·lish ['pʌbliʃ] *v.t.* 1. make known to the public: ∼ *the news.* 2. have (a book, periodical, etc.) printed and announce that it is for sale. ∼*er* *n.* person whose business is the ∼ing of books, etc.

puck·er ['pʌkə*] *v.t. & i.* draw together into small folds or wrinkles. *n.* small fold or wrinkle.

pud·ding ['pudiŋ] *n.* dish of food, usu. a soft sweet mixture, served as part of a meal, generally eaten after the meat course.

pud·dle ['pʌdl] *n.* small dirty pool of rain-water, esp. on a road.

pu·er·ile ['pjuərail] *adj.* childish; suitable only for a child.

puff [pʌf] *n.* 1. (sound of a) short, quick sending out of breath or wind; amount of steam, smoke, etc., sent out at one time. 2. (*powder-*∼) piece or ball of soft material for putting powder on the skin. *v.t. & t.* 1. send out ∼s (1); move along with ∼s (1); breathe quickly (as after running); (of smoke, steam, etc.) come out in ∼s (1). *The train* ∼*ed out of the station. He* ∼*ed at his cigar. He* ∼*ed* (= blew) *out the candle.* 2. cause to swell out with air: ∼*ing out his chest with pride.* ∼*ed up*, filled with pride, conceited. **puf·fy** *adj.* (*-ier, -iest*). easily made short of breath (by running, etc.); swollen.

puf·fin ['pʌfin] *n.* N. Atlantic sea-bird with a large bill.

pu·gi·list ['pju:dʒilist] *n.* boxer. **pu·gi·lism** *n.* boxing.

pug·na·cious [pʌgˈneiʃəs] *adj.* fond of, in the habit of, fighting.

pug·nac·i·ty [pʌgˈnæsiti] *n.*

pull [pul] *v.t. & i.* **1.** (opp. of *push*) take hold of and use force upon (sth. or sb.) so as to bring it (him) closer to oneself, or to take it along as one moves, or to remove it from where it is fixed (~ *up a weed*, ~ *a tooth out*, ~ *a cart*). **2.** (with adv.): ~ *sb. or sth. about*, ~ in different directions; treat roughly. ~ (*sth.*) *down*, destroy it, break it down. ~ (*sb.*) *down*, (of illness) make him weak. ~ *sth. off*, (fig.) be successful in winning it. ~ *round*, recover from illness, etc. ~ *sb. round*, help him to recover from illness, etc. ~ *through*, come safely through illness, misfortune, etc. ~ *oneself together*, get control of oneself, one's feelings, etc. ~ *up, stop.* ~ *sth. or sb. up*, cause to stop. **3.** (with nouns): ~ *a face*, show dislike, disgust, disappointment, etc. ~ *one's weight*, do one's fair share of work with others. ~ *sb.'s leg*, try to deceive him in order to have a joke. *n.* **1.** act of ~*ing*; force used in ~*ing*. **2.** *a ~ at the bottle*, a drink. **3.** (colloq.) power to get help or attention through influence (e.g. with people in high positions). 'ˈ~ˌover *n.* knitted garment ~ed on over the head.

pul·let [ˈpulit] *n.* young hen.

pul·ley [ˈpuli] *n.* wheel with rope or chain, used for lifting things. 'ˈ~-block *n.* wooden block in which a ~ is fixed.

A pulley (-block and tackle)

pulp [pʌlp] *n.* **1.** soft fleshy part of fruit. **2.** soft mass of other material, esp. of wood fibre as used for making paper. *v.t. & i.* make into ~ or like ~; become (like) ~; take out the ~ from.

pul·pit [ˈpulpit] *n.* small raised and enclosed structure in a church, used by the preacher.

pulse [pʌls] *n.* **1.** the regular beat of the arteries (e.g. as felt at the wrist) as the blood is pumped through them by the heart. **2.** any regular rhythm. *v.i.* throb. **pul·sate** [pʌlˈseit] *v.i.* expand and contract by turns; throb.

pul·ver·ize [ˈpʌlvəraiz] *v.t. & i.* **1.** grind to powder; smash completely. **2.** become powder or dust.

pu·ma [ˈpjuːmə] *n.* large American animal of the cat family.

pum·ice [ˈpʌmis] *n.* (also ~-*stone*) light porous stone (lava) used for cleaning and polishing.

pum·mel [ˈpʌml] *v.t.* (-*ll*-). beat repeatedly with the fist(s).

¹**pump** [pʌmp] *n.* machine for forcing liquid, gas, or air into or out of sth. (e.g. water from a well, air into a tyre). *v.t. & i.* use a ~; force (water, etc.) (*out, up, into* sth.); make (a tyre, etc.) full (of air, etc.), by using a ~.

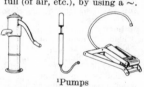

¹Pumps

²**pump** [pʌmp] *n.* sort of light shoe of soft, shiny leather, worn for dancing.

pump·kin [ˈpʌmpkin] *n.* (plant with a) large round yellow fruit with many seeds in it, used as a vegetable.

pun [pʌn] *n.* humorous use of words which sound alike or of words with two meanings. *v.i.* (-*nn*-). make puns; make a pun (*on, upon*, another word).

¹**punch** [pʌntʃ] *v.t.* strike hard with the fist. *n.* blow given with the fist.

²**punch** [pʌntʃ] *n.* tool, machine, for making holes (e.g. in leather, in bus tickets). *v.t.* use a ~ to make (a hole in): ~ *tickets*; ~ *holes in cards*.

³**punch** [pʌntʃ] *n.* drink made of wine, hot water, lemon juice.

punc·til·i·ous [pʌŋk'tiliəs] *adj.* very careful to carry out correctly details of conduct and ceremony ; careful in performing duties. ~**ly** *adj.*

punc·tu·al ['pʌŋktjuəl] *adj.* neither early nor late ; coming, doing sth., at the right time ; (of a person) in the habit of being ~. ~**ly** *adv.* ~**i·ty** [ˌpʌŋktju·'æliti] *n.*

punc·tu·ate ['pʌŋktjueit] *v.t.* 1. put marks (e.g. . , : ;) into a piece of writing. 2. interrupt from time to time : *a speech ~d with cheers.* **punc·tu·a·tion** [ˌpʌŋktju'eiʃən] *n.*

punc·ture ['pʌŋktʃə]* *n.* small hole (esp. in a bicycle or car tyre) made by sth. pointed. *v.t. & i.* make a ~ in ; get a ~ in.

pun·dit ['pʌndit] *n.* learned man ; scholar ; authority on a subject.

pun·gent ['pʌndʒənt] *adj.* (of smells, tastes) sharp ; biting ; stinging.

pun·ish ['pʌniʃ] *v.t.* 1. cause (sb.) suffering or inflict a penalty for wrongdoing. 2. treat roughly ; knock about. ~**ment** *n.* (method of) ~ing or being ~ed.

pu·ni·tive ['pju:nitiv] *adj.* (intended for) ~ing.

pun·ka(h) ['pʌŋkə] *n.* (formerly, in India) large piece of cloth kept in movement to make a current of air.

punt [pʌnt] *n.* flat-bottomed boat with square ends, moved by pushing a long pole against the river-bed. *v.t. & i.* go in a ~ ; move a ~.

pu·ny ['pju:ni] *adj.* (-ier, -iest). small and weak.

pup [pʌp] *n.* short for *puppy*.

pu·pa ['pju:pə] *n.* (pl. -ae ['pju:-pi:]). chrysalis.

¹**pu·pil** ['pju:pl] *n.* one who is being taught at school or by a private teacher. (Cf. *student*.)

²**pu·pil** ['pju:pl] *n.* circular opening in the centre of the eye, regulating the passage of light.

pup·pet ['pʌpit] *n.* doll, or small figure of an animal, etc., with jointed limbs moved by wires,

etc. : *a ~ show* ; (fig.) person, etc., controlled completely by another : *a ~ government.*

pup·py ['pʌpi] *n.* 1. young dog. 2. conceited young man.

pur·chase ['pə:tʃis] *v.t.* buy. *n.* 1. buying. 2. sth. bought. 3. firm hold or grip (for pulling or raising sth. or to prevent sth. from slipping).

pur·dah ['pə:də] *n.* (esp. in Muslim communities) curtain or veil for, convention of, keeping women out of sight of men : *in ~.*

pure [pjuə*] *adj.* (-r, -st). 1. unmixed with any other substance, etc. : *~ water.* 2. clean ; without evil or sin : *~ in body and mind.* 3. (of sounds) clear and distinct. 4. complete : *~ nonsense,* nothing but nonsense ; *a ~ accident,* one caused completely by chance, no one being to blame. 5. *~ mathematics (science),* dealing with theory only, not applied. ~**ly** *adv.* (esp.) entirely ; completely ; merely. ~**ness** *n.* **pu·ri·ty** ['pjuəriti] *n.* **pu·ri·fy** ['pjuərifai] *v.t.* make ~. **pu·ri·fi·ca·tion** [ˌpjuərifi'keiʃən] *n.* **pur·ist** *n.* person paying great attention to correct use of words, grammar, style, etc.

purge [pə:dʒ] *v.t.* 1. make clean or free (*of, from,* physical or moral impurity). 2. empty (the bowels) of waste matter by means of medicine. *n.* purging ; medicine for purging. **pur·ga·tive** ['pə:gətiv] *n. & adj.* (substance) having the power to ~ (2). **pur·ga·to·ry** ['pə:gətəri] *n.* condition of temporary suffering.

pu·ri·tan ['pjuəritən] *n.* 1. (P~) (16th and 17th centuries) member of a division of the Protestant Church which wanted simpler forms of church ceremony. 2. person who is strict in morals and religion. *adj.* of or like a P~ or ~. ~**i·cal** [ˌpjuəri-'tænikl] *adj.* strict and severe.

pur·lieus ['pə:lju:z] *n.* ground, districts, bordering on (a place) ; outskirts (of a town, etc.).

pur·loin [pə:'lɔin] *v.t.* steal.

pur·ple ['pə:pl] *n. & adj.* colour of red and blue mixed together. *the ~*, the ~ robes of a Roman emperor or a cardinal.

pur·port ['pə:pət] *n.* the general meaning or intention of sth. said or written; the likely explanation of a person's actions, etc. [pə:'pɔ:t] *v.t.* **1.** seem to mean. **2.** claim (to be); be intended or designed (to be).

pur·pose ['pə:pəs] *n.* **1.** what one means to do, get, be, etc.; plan; intention. **2.** that for which a thing is designed. **3.** determination; power of forming plans and keeping to them: *weak of ~*. **4.** *on ~*, by intention, not by chance. *to little (no) ~*, with little (no) result or effect; *to the ~*, useful for one's ~; *to the point. serve one's ~*, be satisfactory. *v.t.* have as a ~ (1). *~·ful adj.* having a conscious ~ (1). *~·ly adv.* on ~.

purr [pə:*] *v.i.* (of a cat) make a low murmuring sound as a sign of contentment or pleasure. *n.* this sound.

purse [pə:s] *n.* **1.** small bag, usu. of leather, for money. **2.** sum of money collected or offered as a prize, gift, etc. *v.t.* draw (the lips) together in tiny folds or wrinkles.

purs·er ['pə:sə*] *n.* officer responsible for ship's accounts, stores, etc.

pur·su·ance [pə'sjuəns] *n. in ~ of*, in the carrying out of or performance of (one's duties, a plan, etc.).

pur·sue [pə'sju:] *v.t.* **1.** go after in order to catch up with, capture, or kill: *~ a robber (a bear)*. **2.** go on with; work at: *~ one's studies after leaving school*. **3.** have as an aim or a purpose: *~ pleasure*. **pur·suit** [pə'sju:t] *n.* **1.** pursuing: *in pursuit of rabbits*. **2.** sth. at which one works or to which one gives one's time: *engaged in literary pursuits*.

pu·ru·lent ['pjuərulənt] *adj.* containing pus.

pur·vey [pə:'vei] *v.t. & i.* supply (food) *(to)* customers; supply provisions *(for)*: *a firm ~ing (meat) for the Navy*. *~·or n.*

pur·view ['pə:vju:] *n.* range of operation or activity; extent.

pus [pʌs] *n.* thick yellowish-white liquid formed in and coming out from a poisoned place in the body.

push [puʃ] *v.t. & i.* **1.** (opp. of *pull*) use force on (sb. or sth.) so as to cause him (it) to move away; move (sth. or sb. *up, over*, etc.) in this way; exert pressure *(against)*. **2.** *~ on (along, forward)*, go on with one's journey, one's work, etc.; *be ~ed for* (time, etc.), have hardly enough for one's needs. **3.** (fig.) urge, force, or drive (sb., oneself, *to do* sth.); force (one's goods, etc.) on the attention of other persons. *n.* **1.** act of ~ing; vigorous effort. **2.** determination to make one's way, attract attention, etc. **3.** *at a ~*, if compelled by need or circumstances.

puss [pus], **pus·sy** ['pusi] *n.* (words used for, or to call, a) cat or kitten.

put [put] *v.t.* (p.t. & p.p. *put*). **1.** cause to be in a certain place or position or in a certain relation or condition. **2.** (with *adv.*): *be much put about*, be troubled or worried. *put (an idea, etc.) across*, (colloq.) persuade people to accept it or approve of it. *put sth. away*, put into the proper place, the place where it is usually kept. *put back*, move (the hands of a clock) backwards to an earlier time; slow down or delay the development of sth. *put by*, save for future use. *put down*, write down; suppress; suppress (e.g. a rebellion) by force or (e.g. gambling) by authority. *put sb. down as*, consider him to be. *put forth*, exert (e.g. all one's strength). *put forward*, put (a theory, etc.) before people for their consideration. *put in*, advance (a claim); pass or spend (time); submit (a document); make a stop (at a port). *put in for*, apply for (a position). *put in an appear-*

ance, go to, be present (*at* a meeting, etc.). *put off*, postpone; make the time (of an event, for doing sth.) later. *put sb. off*, make excuses and try to evade doing sth. one has promised to do or that one ought to do for sb. *put sb. off his game*, cause him to play badly by taking his attention from it. *put sb. off his food*, cause him not to want it. *put on*, give oneself, pretend to have (a certain appearance, etc.); move (the hands of a clock) forwards; arrange for, make available (e.g. extra trains); increase (e.g. speed); bet (money) on. *put out*, cause (sth.) to stop burning; cause (sb.) to be troubled, inconvenienced or annoyed; (of ships) move out (from harbour, etc.). *put sth. through*, complete it successfully, get it done; connect (e.g. by telephone). *put up*, raise; offer (a prayer); offer (goods) for sale; pack (goods) (*in* boxes, barrels, etc.); provide, obtain, food and lodging; give (sb.'s name) as a candidate, esp. for election by voting. *put up a fight*, not give way without a struggle. *put sb. up to sth.*, suggest it to him, tell him about it. *put up with*, endure, bear patiently, without protest. **3.** (in phrases): *put an end to*, cause to end. *be hard put to it*, be in difficult or embarrassed circumstances. *put to death*, kill. *put sb. in mind of*, cause him to recall. *put sb. in the wrong*, cause him to feel or seem at fault. *put sth. in hand*, make a start in doing sth. **4.** state; express in words: *I put the matter clearly to them.*

pu·tre·fy ['pju:trifai] *v.t. & i.* (cause to) become rotten or putrid. **pu·tre·fac·tion** [ˌpju:tri-'fækʃən] *n.* **pu·tres·cent** [pju:-'tresnt] *adj.* becoming putrid. **pu·trid** ['pju:trid] *adj.* having gone rotten; decomposed and ill-smelling: *putrid fish.*

put·tee ['pʌti] *n.* long band of cloth wound round the leg from ankle **to** knee.

put·ty ['pʌti] *n.* soft paste of powder and oil used for fixing glass in window frames, etc. *v.t.* fix with ~.

puz·zle ['pʌzl] *n.* **1.** question, problem, difficult to understand or answer. **2.** problem (e.g. *crossword* ~) or toy designed to test a person's knowledge or skill. *v.t. & i.* **1.** cause (sb.) to be perplexed; make hard thought necessary. **2.** ~ *over a problem*, think deeply about it; ~ *sth. out* (try to) find the answer or solution by hard thought.

pyg·my ['pigmi] *n.* member of a race of very short persons in Africa; (attrib.) small; insignificant.

py·ja·mas [pi'dʒɑːməz] *n. pl.* loose-fitting jacket and trousers for sleeping in.

py·lon ['pailən] *n.* tall steel framework for supporting power cables.

pyr·a·mid ['pirəmid] *n.* solid figure with a triangular or square base and sloping sides meeting at a point; structure with this shape, esp. one of those built in ancient Egypt; pile of objects in the form of a ~.

A pyramid   Egyptian pyramids

pyre ['paiə*] *n.* large pile of wood for burning a dead body.

py·thon ['paiθən] *n.* large snake that kills its prey by twisting itself round it and crushing it.

Q

¹quack [kwæk] *v.i. & n.* (make the) cry of a duck.

²quack [kwæk] *n.* person dishonestly claiming to have knowledge and skill (esp. in medicine); (attrib.) of, used by, sold by, such persons: ~ *remedies.*

quad·ran·gle ['kwɔdræŋgl] *n.* plane figure with four sides, esp. a square or rectangle; space in the form of a ~ wholly or nearly surrounded by buildings, esp. in a college. **quad·ran·gu·lar** [kwɔd'ræŋgjulə*] *adj.* in the form of a ~.

quad·rant ['kwɔdrənt] *n.* 1. a fourth part of a circle or its circumference. 2. instrument used for measuring angles (of altitude) in astronomy and navigation.

quad·ri·lat·er·al [ˌkwɔdri'lætərəl] *adj. & n.* four-sided (plane figure).

quad·ru·ped ['kwɔdruped] *n.* four-footed animal.

quad·ru·ple ['kwɔdrupl] *adj.* made up of four parts; agreed to by four persons, parties, etc. *n.* number or amount four times as great as another. *v.t. & i.* make or become four times as great (as). **quad·ru·plet** *n.* one of four babies born at one birth.

quaff [kwɔf] *v.t.* (liter.) drink deeply.

quag·mire ['kwægmaiə*] *n.* area of soft wet land; bog; marsh.

quail [kweil] *v.i.* feel or show fear (*at, before*, danger, etc.).

quaint [kweint] *adj.* (-er, -est). attractive or pleasing because unusual or old-fashioned. ~·ly *adv.* ~·ness *n.*

quake [kweik] *v.i.* (of the earth) shake; tremble; (of a person) tremble (*with* fear, cold, etc.). *n.* earthquake.

Quak·er ['kweikə*] *n.* member of the Society of Friends, a Christian group holding informal meetings without priests.

qual·i·fy ['kwɔlifai] *v.t. & i.* make or become trained or entitled (*to do* sth., *for doing* sth., for a post, *as* a doctor, etc.): *Are you qualified to teach English?* 2. limit; make less inclusive, less general. 3. (grammar) *Adjectives* ~ (describe, give the qualities of) *nouns.* 4. describe (*as*) : ~ *sb. as selfish.* **qual·i·fi·ca·tion** [ˌkwɔlifi'keiʃən] *n.* 1. training, test, etc., that qualifies (1) a person : *a doctor's quali-*

fications. 2. statement, fact, circumstance, etc., that qualifies (2) or limits.

qual·i·ty ['kwɔliti] *n.* 1. (degree, esp. high degree, of) goodness or worth : *material of the best* ~; *a poor* ~ *of cloth.* 2. sth. that is special in sth. or sb.; that which distinguishes a person or thing : *One* ~ *of pine timber is that it can be sawn easily.* 3. (old use) high social position. **qual·i·ta·tive** ['kwɔlitətiv] *adj.* of ~ : *qualitative analysis.*

qualm [kwɑːm] *n.* 1. feeling of doubt (esp. about whether one is doing or has done right); misgiving. 2. temporary feeling of sickness in the stomach.

quan·da·ry ['kwɔndəri] *n.* state of doubt or perplexity.

quan·ti·ty ['kwɔntiti] *n.* 1. the property of things which can be measured (e.g. size, weight, amount, number) : *prefer quality to* ~. 2. certain amount or number; (often pl.) a large amount or number : *buy things in* ~ (*in large quantities*). 3. *an unknown* ~, a person or thing whose action cannot be foreseen. **quan·ti·ta·tive** ['kwɔntitətiv] *adj.* of ~.

quar·an·tine ['kwɔrənti:n] *n.* (period of) separation from others until it is known that there is no danger of spreading disease : *in* ~ *for a week.* *v.t.* put or keep in ~ : ~*d because of yellow fever.*

quar·rel ['kwɔrəl] *n.* 1. angry argument; violent disagreement : *have a* ~ *with sb. over* (*about*) *sth.* 2. cause for being angry; reason for protest or complaint. *v.i.* (-*ll*-). have, take part in, a ~ ; find fault (*with*). ~·some *adj.* in the habit of ~ling; fond of ~ling.

¹**quar·ry** ['kwɔri] *n.* place where stone, slate, etc., is got out of the ground (for building, etc.). *v.t.* get (stone, etc.) from a ~.

²**quar·ry** ['kwɔri] *n.* animal, bird, etc., which is hunted.

quart [kwɔːt] *n.* measure of capacity equal to two pints.

quar·ter ['kwɔːtə*] *n.* 1. ¼ : *the*

first ~ of this century (1901–25).
2. period of three months ending on a ~-day (see below). **3.** joint of meat including a leg: *a ~ of mutton.* **4.** direction; part: *men running from all ~s; travel in every ~ of the globe* (i.e. in all parts). **5.** (U.S.A.) (coin worth) 25 cents. **6.** district, part (esp. part of a town): *the business ~; the Chinese ~ of San Francisco.* **7.** one-fourth of a lunar month; the moon's phase at the end of the first or third week. **8.** unit of grain measure, 8 bushels. **9.** unit of weight, 28 lb. **10.** mercy to a defeated enemy: *give (receive, ask for) ~.* **11.** (pl.) lodgings; place to stay in: *take up ~s with a friend;* (esp.) place where soldiers are lodged: *All troops to return to ~s at once.* **12.** *at close ~s,* close together. *v.t.* **1.** divide into ~s (1). **2.** find ~s (11) for; place (soldiers) in lodgings. **'~-day** *n.* one of four days in the year on which three-monthly accounts are due. **'~-deck** *n.* part of the upper deck reserved for a warship's officers. **~·ly** *adj. & adv.* (happening) once in each three months. *n.* periodical published once a ~ (2). **'~·,mas·ter** *n.* army officer in charge of stores, etc.; sailor in charge of steering the ship.

quar·tet(te) [kwɔ:'tet] *n.* (piece of music for) four players or singers.

quartz [kwɔ:ts] *n.* sorts of hard mineral, including agate and other semi-precious stones.

qua·si- ['kweisai-] *prefix.* seeming(ly); half: *a ~-official position.*

quat·rain ['kwɔtrein] *n.* verse of four lines.

qua·ver ['kweivə*] *v.t. & i.* **1.** (of the voice or a sound). shake; tremble. **2.** say or sing in a shaking voice. *n.* **1.** ~ing sound. **2.** musical note (♪) half as long as a crotchet.

quay [ki:] *n.* (usu. stone) landing-place built for ships in a harbour or on a river bank.

quea·sy ['kwi:zi] *adj.* **1.** (of food) causing a feeling of sickness in

the stomach. **2.** (of the stomach) easily upset. **3.** (of a person) easily made sick; (fig.) easily shocked (because over-delicate).

queen [kwi:n] *n.* **1.** wife of a king. **2.** woman ruler. **3.** (~ bee, ~ wasp, etc.) egg-producing (bee, etc.). **~·ly** *adj.* of, like, suitable for, a ~.

queer [kwiə*] *adj.* (-er, -est). **1.** strange; unusual. **2.** causing doubt or suspicion. **3.** (colloq.) unwell; feeling as if about to faint. *v.t.* (colloq.) put out of order; cause to go wrong. **~·ly** *adv.* **~·ness** *n.*

quell [kwel] *v.t.* subdue (a rebellion).

quench [kwentʃ] *v.t.* put out (flames, fire); satisfy (thirst); put an end to (hope, etc.).

quer·u·lous ['kweruləs] *adj.* full of complaints; fretful.

que·ry ['kwiəri] *n.* **1.** question, esp. one raising a doubt about the truth of sth. **2.** the mark ? put against sth. as a sign of doubt. *v.t. & i.* ask (*if, whether*); express doubt about.

quest [kwest] *n.* search (*for* sth.): *in ~ of,* seeking for, trying to find.

ques·tion ['kwestʃən] *n.* **1.** kind of sentence that asks for information, permission, etc., and expects an answer. **2.** sth. about which there is discussion; sth. that needs to be decided: *out of the ~,* impossible. *It is only a ~ of time,* it will certainly come (happen, etc.), sooner or later; *(the man,* etc.) *in ~,* being talked about. **3.** (the putting forward of) doubt, objection: *beyond ~,* without doubt; *call sth. in ~,* raise objections to, express doubt about. *v.t. & i.* ask ~(s) of. **2.** express doubt about; feel doubt. **~·a·ble** *adj.* which may be ~ed (2). **'~-mark** *n.* the sign ?. **~·naire** [,kwestʃə'nɛə*] *n.* list of ~s to be answered by a number of people, esp. to get facts, information about their views.

queue [kju:] *n.* line of people waiting for their turn (e.g. to enter a bus, buy sth., etc.), *v.i.*(often ~ *up*) get into, be in , a ~.

quib·ble ['kwibl] *n.* secondary or doubtful use of word(s) in order to escape giving an honest answer or argument. *v.i.* use ~s; argue about small points or differences.

quick [kwik] *adj.* (-*er*, -*est*). **1.** moving fast; done in a short time; able to move fast and do things in a short time. **2.** lively; bright; active; prompt: ~ *to understand*; *a* ~ *ear for music*; ~-*witted*, ~ at seeing and making jokes, etc.; ~ at understanding things; ~ *to take offence*, ~-*tempered*, easily made angry. **3.** (old use) living: *the* ~ *and the dead*. *n.* sensitive part of flesh (esp. under the nails): *cut to the* ~, (fig.) hurt in one's feelings. *adv.* (-*er*, -*est*). colloq. = ~*ly*. ~**·ly** *adv.* ~**·ness** *n.* ~**·en** *v.t. & i.* **1.** make or become ~er. **2.** (cause to) become (more) lively or active. '~**·lime** *n.* unslaked lime (see ¹*lime*). '~**·sand** *n.* (area of) loose, wet, deep sand which sucks down men, animals, etc., that try to walk on it. '~**·set** *adj.* (of a hedge or fence) made of living bushes, etc. (not stakes). '~**·sil·ver** *n.* mercury.

¹**quid** [kwid] *n.* piece of tobacco to be chewed.

²**quid** [kwid] *n.* (colloq.) £1.

qui·es·cent [kwai'esnt] *adj.* at rest; motionless; passive.

qui·et ['kwaiət] *adj.* (-*er*, -*est*). **1.** with little or no movement or sound: *a* ~ *sea* (*evening*). **2.** free from excitement, trouble, anxiety: *a* ~ *life* (*mind*). **3.** gentle; not rough: ~ *children*. **4.** (of colours) not bright. *n.* being ~ (1), (2): *living in peace and* ~; *an hour's* ~. *v.t. & i.* make or become ~(1), (2). ~**·ly** *adv.* ~**·ness** *n.* **qui·et·en** *v.t.* make ~(er). **qui·e·tude** ['kwaiitju:d] *n.* stillness; calmness.

quill [kwil] *n.* **1.** large wing or tail feather; (hollow stem of) such a feather as formerly used for writing with. **2.** long sharp stiff spine of a porcupine.

quilt [kwilt] *n.* bed-covering placed over blankets.

quince [kwins] *n.* (tree with) hard, acid, pear-shaped fruit.

qui·nine [kwi'ni:n] *n.* bitter liquid made from the bark of a tree and used as a medicine for fevers.

quin·tes·sence [kwin'tesns] *n.* perfect example: *the* ~ *of politeness*.

quin·tet(te) [kwin'tet] *n.* (piece of music for a) group of five players or singers.

quip [kwip] *n.* clever, witty or sarcastic remark or saying.

quire ['kwaiə*] *n.* twenty-four sheets of writing-paper.

quit [kwit] *v.t. & i.* (-*tt*-; p.t. & p.p. ~*ted*). **1.** go away from; leave. **2.** stop (doing sth.). **3.** (old use) acquit: *They* ~*ed themselves well. adj.* be ~ *of*, be free of, no longer burdened with.

quits *adj.* be ~*s*, be on even terms (*with* sb.) by paying a debt (of money, punishment).

quite [kwait] *adv.* **1.** completely. **2.** rather; somewhat: ~ *cool this evening. He's* ~ *a scholar*. **3.** (in answers) ~ (*so*), expressing understanding or agreement.

¹**quiv·er** ['kwivə*] *v.t. & i.* (cause to) tremble slightly: *leaves* ~*ing in the wind; in a* ~*ing voice*.

²**quiv·er** ['kwivə*] *n.* archer's bag for carrying arrows.

qui vive ['ki:'vi:v] (Fr.) *n. on the* ~, on the alert; watchful.

quix·ot·ic [kwik'sotik] *adj.* generous, unselfish, imaginative, and acting in disregard of one's own welfare.

quiz [kwiz] *v.t.* (-*zz*-). **1.** ask questions of, as a test of knowledge. **2.** (old use) make fun of. *n.* such a test. ~**·zi·cal** ['kwizikl] *adj.* **1.** comical; causing amusement. **2.** teasing: *a* ~*zical smile*.

quod [kwɔd] *n.* (colloq.) prison.

quoit [kɔit] *n.* ring (metal, rubber, rope) to be thrown in the game called ~s, and in deck tennis.

quor·um ['kwɔ:rəm] *n.* number of persons who must, by the rules, be present at a meeting (of a committee, etc.) before its proceedings can have authority.

quo·ta ['kwoutə] *n.* limited share, amount, or number, esp. quantity of goods or number of immigrants allowed to enter a country.

quote [kwout] *v.t.* 1. repeat, write (words used by another); repeat or write words (*from a book*, etc.). 2. give (a reference, etc.) to support a statement: ~ *a recent instance.* 3. name, mention (a price). **quo·ta·tion** [kwou'teiʃən] *n.* sth. ~d (1), (2). *quotation marks*, the marks ' ' or " " placed before and after the words ~d.

quoth [kwouθ] *v.t.* (old use) said.

quo·tient ['kwouʃənt] *n.* number obtained by dividing one number by another.

R

rab·bi ['ræbai] *n.* teacher of the Jewish law; (title of) Jewish priest.

rab·bit ['ræbit] *n.* small animal living in a burrow.

rab·ble ['ræbl] *n.* disorderly crowd.

rab·id ['ræbid] *adj.* 1. furious; unreasoning; violent. 2. (of dogs) mad.

ra·bies ['reibi:z] *n.* disease causing madness in dogs.

¹**race** [reis] *n.* 1. contest or competition in speed (e.g. running, to see who can do best). 2. strong, fast current of water in the sea, a river, etc. *v.i. & t.* 1. run a ~ (1) (*with* sb., *against* time, etc.). 2. cause (a horse, etc.) to take part in a ~ (1). 3. (cause to) move at great speed. **rac·ing** *n.* (esp.) horse-racing. '~·course *n.* ground or track prepared for horse ~s. '~·horse *n.* sort of horse specially bred for racing.

²**race** [reis] *n.* 1. tribe or nation (group of tribes or nations) having, or thought to have, the same original ancestors: *the*

Anglo-Saxon ~. 2. main division of any living things: *the human* ~, mankind; *the feathered* ~, birds. **ra·cial** ['reiʃl] *adj.* of ~ : *racial pride*.

¹**rack** [ræk] *n.* 1. wooden or metal framework for holding food (esp. hay) for animals. 2. framework with bars, pegs, etc., for holding things, hanging things on, etc.: *a plate-* ~ ; *a hat-*~. 3. shelf in a railway carriage, bus, etc., for light luggage. 4. instrument formerly used for torturing a victim by stretching. 5. rod, bar, or rail with teeth or cogs into which the teeth on a wheel fit (used, for example, on special railways up steep hill-sides). *v.t.* 1. torture by stretching on the ~(4) ; cause severe pain to: ~ed *with grief.* 2. ~ *one's brains* (for an answer, etc.), make great mental efforts.

²**rack** [ræk] *n.* (only in) *go to* ~ *and ruin*, fall into a ruined state.

¹**rack·et** ['rækit] *n.* 1. uproar; loud noise. 2. time of social activity, hurry, and bustle. 3. (colloq.) dishonest way of getting money by deceiving or threatening people, selling worthless goods, etc. ~·**eer** [,ræki'tiə*] *n.* person engaged in a ~ (3).

²**rack·et, rac·quet** ['rækit] *n.* light bat used for hitting the ball in tennis and other games.

ra·cy ['reisi] *adj.* (of speech or writing) lively. **ra·ci·ly** *adv.*

ra·dar ['reidɑ:*] *n.* radio apparatus that indicates on a screen solid objects that come within its range, used by pilots, etc., esp. in fog or darkness.

ra·diant ['reidjənt] *adj.* 1. sending out rays of light; shining. 2. (of a person's looks, eyes) bright; showing joy or love. ~·**ly** *adv.* **ra·diance** *n.*

ra·di·ate ['reidieit] *v.t. & i.* 1. send out rays (of light or heat) ; come or go out in rays: *a stove radiating warmth* ; *heat radiating from a stove.* 2. give out, show (joy, etc.). 3. spread out like radii from a centre. **ra·di·a·tion** [,reidi'eiʃən] *n.* radiating; sth. ~d. **ra·di·a·tor** ['reidieitə*] *n.*

1. apparatus for radiating heat, esp. heat from steam or hot water supplied through pipes. 2. device for cooling a motor-car's engine by radiating the heat.

rad·i·cal ['rædikl] *adj.* 1. of or from the root or base: ~ (= thorough and complete) *reforms.* 2. (politics) favouring great changes. *n.* person with ~(2) opinions. ~**ly** *adv.*

ra·di·o ['reidiou] *n.* 1. wireless telegraph or telephone; broadcasting. 2. (also ~ *set*) apparatus for receiving broadcast programmes. 3. (attrib.) of, used in, sent out, by ~: *a ~ telescope.* *v.t. & i.* send by ~. '~**gram** *n.* combined ~ set and gramophone.

ra·di·o- ['reidiou-] *prefix.* of rays, esp. of X-rays. '~·**'ac·tive** *adj.* (of such metals as radium and uranium) having the property of giving off rays which pass through solids and produce electrical effects. '~·**'ac·tiv·i·ty** *n.* '~·**graph** *n.* X-ray photograph.

rad·ish ['rædiʃ] *n.* small salad plant with a solid root.

ra·di·um ['reidjəm] *n.* radioactive metal used in the treatment of some diseases (e.g. cancer).

ra·di·us ['reidjəs] *n.* (pl. *-ii* [-iai]). 1. straight line from the centre of a circle or sphere to any point on the circumference or surface. 2. circular area measured by its ~.

raf·fi·a ['ræfiə] *n.* fibre from the leaf-stalks of a kind of palm, used for making baskets, hats.

raf·fle ['ræfl] *n.* sale of an article by a lottery. *v.t.* sell (sth.) by this method.

raft [rɑːft] *n.* number of tree trunks or pieces of roughly-shaped timber fastened together in order to float down a river or to serve as a boat.

raf·ter ['rɑːftə*] *n.* one of the sloping beams forming the structure of a roof, supporting tiles, slates, etc.

¹**rag** [ræg] *n.* 1. odd bit of cloth.

2. (pl.) old or torn clothes: *dressed in rags.* 3. (humor.) newspaper which one considers contemptible. **rag·a·muf·fin** ['rægəmʌfin] *n.* dirty person, esp. a small boy dressed in rags.

rag·ged ['rægid] *adj.* 1. (with clothes) badly torn or in rags. 2. having rough or irregular edges or outlines or surfaces: *a dog with a ragged coat of hair.*

²**rag** [ræg] *v.t. & i.* (*-gg-*). (colloq.) tease; play practical jokes on. *n.* ragging.

rage [reidʒ] *n.* 1. (outburst of) furious anger; violence. 2. strong desire (*for* sth.); *all the ~,* (colloq.) the fashion. *v.i.* be violently angry; (of storms, etc.) be violent.

raid [reid] *v.t. & i. & n.* (make a) sudden attack (*on*), a surprise visit (to): *air ~s on London.* ~**er** *n.* person, ship, aircraft, etc., making a ~.

¹**rail** [reil] *n.* 1. wood or metal bar or rod, or a number of such bars or rods placed end to end, as a fence or barrier, to hang things on, etc. 2. steel bar forming part of a railway or tramcar track: *go off the ~s,* (of a train, etc.) leave the track; (fig.) become out of order, out of control. *v.t.* put ~s (1) round; shut (*in* or *off*), separate, by means of ~s (1). ~**ing** *n.* (often pl.) fence made with ~s (e.g. at the side of steps). '~**road** *n.* (U.S.A.) = ~way. '~**way** *n.* track on which trains run; system of such tracks, with the engines, coaches, etc., used on them.

²**rail** [reil] *v.i.* complain, speak angrily (*against, at,* sth. or sb.). ~**ler·y** ['reiləri] *n.* good-humoured teasing.

rai·ment ['reimənt] *n.* (liter.) clothing.

rain [rein] *n.* 1. water falling in drops from the sky. 2. thick, fast fall of sth. like ~: *a ~ of bullets.* 3. *the ~s,* the rainy season in some tropical countries. *v.t. & i.* 1. *It is ~ing* (~ *is falling*). 2. come, fall, send (*down upon*), like ~: *tears ~ing* *down his cheeks.* '**~·bow** *n.* many-coloured arch seen in the sky or in spray when the sun shines through falling drops of water. '**~fall** *n.* (esp.) amount of ~ falling on a plane in a certain period (e.g. as measured in inches or cm.). '**~·gauge** *n.* instrument for measuring ~fall. '**~·proof** *adj.* able to keep ~ out. **~·y** *adj.* (*-ier, -iest*). having much ~. *save for a ~y day*, put money aside for a possible time of need.

raise [reiz] *v.t.* 1. lift up (e.g. a weight, one's hat, one's voice, etc.); make (e.g. prices, the temperature, sb.'s hopes, etc.) higher; erect or build (e.g. a monument). 2. cause to rise or appear: *motor-buses raising the dust.* 3. bring up for attention or discussion: ~ *a new point*; ~ *a question (a protest)*. 4. grow or produce (crops); breed (sheep, cattle, etc.); bring up (a family). 5. get or bring together; manage to get: ~ *an army (a loan, money for the holidays)*. 6. ~ *a siege (blockade)*, end it.

rai·sin ['reizn] *n.* dried grape (as used in cakes, etc.).

ra·ja(h) ['rɑːdʒə] *n.* Indian prince; Malayan chief.

¹**rake** [reik] *n.* long-handled tool with teeth (*n*), used for smoothing soil, gathering dead leaves, straw, hay, etc., together. *v.t. & i.* 1. use a ~ on (soil, etc.) for smoothing. 2. get (sth. *together, up, out,* etc.) with a ~. 3. search (*through* or *over* old records, papers, etc.) for facts, etc. ~ *sth. up*, bring to people's knowledge (sth. forgotten, e.g. a charge of wrongdoing). 4. fire with guns at (a ship, etc.) from end to end.

²**rake** [reik] *n.* dissolute man.

rak·ish ['reikiʃ] *adj.* 1. (of a ship) looking as if built for speed. 2. *at a ~ angle*, at a sharp angle. 3. of or like a ²rake.

¹**ral·ly** ['ræli] *v.t. & i.* 1. (cause to) come together, esp. after defeat or confusion, to make a stand and new efforts. 2. give new strength to; (cause to)

recover (health, strength): *The patient is ~ing.* *n.* 1. ~ing. 2. public meeting, esp. to support a cause. 3. gathering of drivers of cars or motor-cycles for a competitive drive, or to test reliability.

²**ral·ly** ['ræli] *v.t.* tease in a good-humoured way; make fun of.

ram [ræm] *n.* 1. male sheep. 2. instrument for ramming or battering. *v.t.* (*-mm-*). strike and push heavily. '**ram·rod** *n.* iron rod for ramming gunpowder, etc., into old-fashioned guns.

ram·ble ['ræmbl] *v.i.* walk for pleasure, with no special destination; (fig.) wander in one's talk. *n.* rambling walk. **ram·bler** *n.* person who ~s; climbing rose. **ram·bling** *adj.* (esp. of buildings, streets, towns) extending in various directions irregularly, as if built without planning; (fig.) of conversation.

ram·i·fy ['ræmifai] *v.i. & t.* form or produce branches; make or become like a network. **ram·i·fi·ca·tion** [,ræmifi'keiʃən] *n.*

¹**ramp** [ræmp] *n.* rising bank of earth; sloping way from one level to another.

²**ramp** [ræmp] *n.* (colloq.) attempt to obtain much too high a price; swindle.

ram·page [ræm'peidʒ] *v.i.* rush about in excitement or rage. *n. on the ~*, rampaging.

ram·pant ['ræmpənt] *adj.* 1. (esp. of diseases, social evils) unchecked; beyond control. 2. (of animals) on the hind legs.

ram·part ['ræmpɑːt] *n.* wide bank of earth, often with a wall, built to defend a fort, etc.

ram·shack·le ['ræmʃækl] *adj.* almost collapsing: *a ~ old house.*

ran, see ¹**run**.

ranch [rɑːntʃ] *n.* (esp. U.S.A.) large farm, esp. for raising cattle but also for fruit, chickens, etc. ~**er** *n.*

ran·cid ['rænsid] *adj.* (esp. of fat, butter) stale, bad, ill-smelling.

ran·cour ['ræŋkə*] *n.* deep and long-lasting feeling of bitterness. **ran·cor·ous** *adj.*

ran·dom ['rændəm] *n.* (only in) at ~, without aim or system. *adj.* done or made at ~: ~ *remarks*.

rang, see ²*ring*.

range [reindʒ] *n.* 1. row, line, or series of things, esp. mountains. 2. area of ground with targets for firing at: *a rifle-*~. 3. distance to which a gun will shoot or to which a shell, etc., can be fired: *in* (*beyond, out of*) ~; distance between a gun, etc., and what is fired at: *at short* (*long*) ~. 4. extent; distance between limits: *a wide* ~ *of prices* (*colours*); *the annual* ~ *of temperature* (e.g. from 35° to 106° F.); *the* ~ *of her voice* (i.e. between her top and bottom notes). 5. area over which plants are found growing or in which animals are found living. 6. area included in or concerned with sth.: *a subject that is outside my* ~ (that I know nothing about). 7. cooking-stove, with a flat metal top and an oven. *v.t. & i.* 1. put in a row or rows; arrange in order. 2. go, move, wander (*over, through*, etc.), the woods, hills, etc.). 3. extend, run in a line: *a boundary ranging N. and S.* 4. vary between limits: *prices ranging from 3s. to 10s.* (*between 3s. and 10s.*). 5. ~ *oneself*, place oneself: *men who* ~*d themselves with* (*against, on the side of*) *the rebels.* '~-,**find·er** *n.* instrument for measuring the distance of sth. to be fired at.

rank [ræŋk] *n.* 1. line of persons or things: *a taxi-*~. 2. (army) line of soldiers placed side by side: *the* ~*s, the* ~ *and file, other* ~*s,* private(4) soldiers and corporals. 3. position in a scale, esp. grade in the armed forces: *promoted to the* ~ *of captain*; *people of all* ~*s.* *v.t. & i.* 1. put or arrange in a ~ or ~s. 2. have, give (sb.), a certain ~ (3) compared with others: ~ (sb.) *with the world's greatest actors.*

²**rank** [ræŋk] *adj.* 1. (of plants and land) overgrown. 2. having

a bad, strong taste or smell: ~ *tobacco.* 3. unmistakably bad: *a* ~ *traitor.*

ran·kle ['ræŋkl] *v.i.* continue to be painful or bitter in the mind: *insults that* ~*d.*

ran·sack ['rænsæk] *v.t.* 1. search (a place, etc.) thoroughly (*for* sth.). 2. rob; plunder (*of* things).

ran·som ['rænsəm] *n.* freeing of a captive upon payment; the money paid: *hold sb. to* ~, hold him captive and demand ~. *v.t.* obtain the freedom of (sb.), set (sb.) free, in exchange for ~.

rant [rænt] *v.i. & t.* speak wildly, violently, or boastingly: *a bad actor* ~*ing his words.* ~·**er** *n.*

¹**rap** [ræp] *v.t. & i.* (-*pp-*). 1. knock (1) repeatedly: *sb. rapping at the window.* 2. rap sth. out, say suddenly or sharply. *n.* (sound of a) knock.

²**rap** [ræp] *n. not care a rap,* not care at all.

ra·pa·cious [rə'peiʃəs] *adj.* greedy (esp. for money). **ra·pac·i·ty** [rə'pæsiti] *n.* greed; avarice.

¹**rape** [reip] *v.t.* 1. seize and carry off by force. 2. force (sb.) to have sexual intercourse unwillingly. *n.* act of raping.

²**rape** [reip] *n.* plant grown as food for sheep and pigs; plant grown for the oil obtained from its seeds.

rap·id ['ræpid] *adj.* 1. quick. 2. (of a slope) steep. *n.* (usu. pl.) part of a river where a steep slope makes the water flow fast. ~·**ly** *adv.* **ra·pid·i·ty** [rə'piditi] *n.*

ra·pier ['reipjə*] *n.* light, slim sword used in ²*fencing.*

rapt [ræpt] *adj.* so deep in thought, so carried away by feelings, that one is unaware of other things: ~ *in a book*; *listening with* ~ *attention.* **rap·ture** ['ræptʃə*] *n.* (state, expression of) great joy. **rap·tur·ous** *adj.*

rare [rɛə*] *adj.* (-*r, -st*). 1. unusual; uncommon; not often happening, seen, etc. 2. unusually good. 3. (of a substance, esp. the atmosphere) thin, not dense. ~·**ly** *adv.* seldom. **rar·e·fied** ['rɛərifaid] *adj.* = ~ (2):

the ~fied air of the mountain tops.

rar·i·ty ['reəriti] *n.* being ~ (1), (3) ; ~ (1) thing.

ras·cal ['rɑːskl] *n.* **1.** dishonest person. **2.** (playfully) mischievous person (esp. a child), fond of playing tricks.

¹rash [ræʃ] *n.* (breaking out of) many tiny red spots on the skin.

²rash [ræʃ] *adj.* (-er, -est). too hasty ; overbold ; done, doing things, without enough thought of the consequences. ~·ly *adv.* ~·ness *n.*

rash·er ['ræʃə*] *n.* slice of bacon or ham (to be) fried.

rasp [rɑːsp] *n.* metal tool like a file with surfaces covered with sharp points, used for scraping. *v.t. & i.* **1.** scrape with a ~. **2.** make a grating sound ; (fig.) have an irritating effect on (nerves).

rasp·ber·ry ['rɑːzbəri] *n.* (bush with) small, sweet, red or yellow berries.

rat [ræt] *n.* animal like but larger than a mouse. *smell a rat*, (fig.) suspect that sth. wrong is being done.

A rat   A ratchet

ratch·et ['rætʃit] *n.* gear-wheel whose cogs, engaging (5) with a spring catch, allow it to turn in one direction only.

¹rate [reit] *n.* **1.** standard of reckoning, by bringing two numbers or amounts into relationship : *walking at the ~ of 5 miles in 65 minutes ; buy things at the ~ of 5s. a hundred ; an annual death ~ of 25 per 1,000.* **2.** *at this ~*, if this is true, if this state of affairs continues ; *at any ~*, in any case, whatever happens. **3.** *the ~s*, charges levied on householders, businesses, etc. by local authorities for water-supply, education, and other local services : *the water-~.* **4.** *first ~*, excellent ; *second ~*, fairly good ; *third ~*, rather poor.

v.t. & i. judge or estimate the work or value of ; consider.

²rate [reit] *v.t. & i.* scold.

rath·er ['rɑːðə*] *adv.* **1.** more willingly ; by preference : *Don't come today, I would ~ you came* (would prefer you to come) *to-morrow.* **2.** more precisely : *He arrived late last night, or ~, in the early hours this morning.* **3.** somewhat : *Do you see that ~ tall boy standing over there ?* **4.** (colloq. answer) indeed so : A. *Are you comfortable?* B. *Yes, ~!*

rat·i·fy ['rætifai] *v.t.* confirm (an agreement) by signature or other formality. **rat·i·fi·ca·tion** [,ræti-fi'keiʃən] *n.*

rat·ing ['reitiŋ] *n.* **1.** class or grade, esp. of ships (according to tonnage). **2.** (in a ship) person's rank. **3.** (Navy) sailor who is not an officer.

ra·tio ['reiʃiou, -fou] *n.* relation between two amounts expressed by dividing one by the other : *The ~s 1 to 5 and 20 to 100 are the same.*

ra·tion ['ræʃən] *n.* fixed quantity, esp. of food, allowed to one person. *v.t.* limit (people, goods) to ~s.

ra·tion·al ['ræʃənl] *adj.* of reason or reasoning ; able to reason ; sensible ; that can be tested by reason : ~ *conduct (explanations).* ~·ly *adv.*

rat·tan [ræ'tæn] *n.* (E. Indian palm with) cane-like stem, used for building, basketwork, etc.

rat·tle ['rætl] *v.t. & i.* **1.** (cause to) make short, sharp sounds quickly, one after the other : *windows that ~ in the wind.* **2.** talk, say, or repeat sth., quickly and in a thoughtless or lively way : ~ *off a poem one has learnt by heart.* **3.** move, fall, travel fast and with a rattling noise : *A cart full of milk-bottles ~d past.* *n.* (baby's toy producing a) rattling noise. ~·snake *n.* poisonous American snake that makes a rattling noise with its tail.

rau·cous ['rɔːkəs] *adj.* (of sounds) harsh ; rough ; hoarse.

rav·age ['rævidʒ] *v.t. & i.* **1.**

destroy; damage badly: *forests ~d by fire.* **2.** rob with violence. *n.* destruction; destructive effects (of): *the ~s of time.*

rave [reiv] *v.i.* **1.** talk wildly, violently, angrily. **2.** talk with foolish enthusiasm (*of* or *about*).

rav·ings *n. pl.* foolish or wild talk (e.g. of a madman).

rav·el ['rævl] *v.t. & i.* (*-ll-*). **1.** (of knitted or woven things) separate into threads; become untwisted; fray: *Bind the edge so that it will not ~.* **2.** cause (threads) to twist together; (fig.) make confused.

rav·en ['reivn] *n.* large black bird like a crow. *adj.* (esp. of hair) black.

rav·en·ous ['rævinəs] *adj.* very hungry.

ra·vine [rə'viːn] *n.* deep narrow valley.

rav·ish ['rævif] *v.t.* **1.** fill with delight: *a ~ing view.* **2.** (old use) seize and carry off.

raw [rɔː] *adj.* **1.** uncooked. **2.** in the natural state, not manufactured or prepared for use: *raw hides* (not yet tanned); *raw materials.* **3.** (of persons) untrained; unskilled; inexperienced: *raw recruits.* **4.** (of the weather) damp and cold. **5.** (of a place on the flesh) with the skin rubbed off; sore and painful. **6.** harsh; unjust: *get a raw deal.*

ray [rei] *n.* **1.** line, beam, of radiant light, heat, energy: *the rays of the sun; X-rays.* **2.** any one of a number of lines coming out from a centre.

ray·on ['reion] *n.* silk-like material made from cellulose.

raze [reiz] *v.t.* destroy completely (towns, buildings), esp. by knocking them down to the ground.

ra·zor ['reizə*] *n.* instrument with a sharp blade, used for shaving.

re [riː] *prep.* (law) concerning.

re- [riː-] *prefix.* **1.** again: *re-appear, re-count.* **2.** again and in a different way: *rearrange.*

reach [riːtʃ] *v.t. & i.* **1.** stretch (the hand): *to ~ out one's hand*

for sth.; to ~ for a book. **2.** stretch out the hand for and take sth., give sth. to: *Please ~ me that book.* **3.** get to, go as far as: *~ London* (the end of a chapter); *as far as the eye can ~.* *n.* **1.** (extent or distance of) *~ing: within easy ~ of London; out of ~; beyond the ~ of all help.* **2.** straight stretch, esp. of a river, between two bends.

re·act [ri'ækt] *v.t.* **1.** have an effect (*on* the person or thing acting): *Applause ~s upon a speaker* (e.g. has the effect of giving him confidence). **2.** *~ to*, behave differently, be changed, as the result of being acted upon: *Children ~ to kind treatment by becoming more self-confident.* **3.** *~ against,* respond to sth. with a feeling of dislike: *~ing against flattery.* **re·ac·tion** [ri'ækfən] *n.* action or state resulting from (in response to) sth., esp. a return of an earlier condition after a period of the opposite condition: *After these days of excitement, there was a ~ion* (e.g. a period when life seemed dull). **re·ac·tion·a·ry** [ri'ækfənəri] *n. & adj.* (person) supporting political reaction; opponent of progress. **re·ac·tor** [ri'æktə*] *n.* nuclear reactor, apparatus for the controlled production of nuclear energy.

read [riːd] *v.t. & i.* (p.t. & p.p. *read* [red]). **1.** look at and (be able to) understand (sth. written or printed); say (aloud or silently) what is written or printed. **2.** study (a subject, esp. at a university): *~ing physics at Cambridge.* **3.** give a certain impression, seem (good, bad, etc.) when read: *The play ~s well.* **4.** *~ between the lines,* see line (7). *n.* period of time given to *~ing: having a quiet ~.* *~'a·ble adj.* capable of being *~;* that is easy or pleasant to *~. ~·er n.* **1.** person who *~s* (esp. one who *~s* a great deal). **2.** school *~ing-book.* **3.** university teacher junior to a professor. *~·ing n.* **1.** knowledge, esp. of books: *a man of wide ~ing.* **2.** way in which sth. is interpreted or understood: *my solicitor's ~ing of this clause in the agreement* (i.e. what he says it means). **3.** figure of measurement, etc., as shown on a dial, scale, etc., at a particular time: *the ~ings on my thermometer last month*. **4.** alternative wording of a passage in an author's original text that has occurred in copying or reprinting.

read·y ['redi] *adj.* **1.** in the condition needed for use; in the condition for doing sth.; willing (to do sth.): *~ for school; ~ to start; get things ~.* **2.** (*-ier, -iest*). quick; prompt: *be too ~ with excuses. He always has a ~ answer.* **3.** *~ money*, money in the form of coins and notes, which can be used for payment at the time goods are bought; cash payment: *He wants ~ money. ~ reckoner*, book of answers to various common calculations needed in business, etc. *~-made*, (esp. of clothes) made in standard sizes, not made specially to the wearer's measurements. **read·i·ly** *adv.* willingly; without difficulty or trouble. **read·i·ness** *n. in readiness for, ~ (1) for.*

real [riəl] *adj.* **1.** existing in fact; not imagined or supposed; not made up or artificial: *~ silk (gold); the ~ (= true) reason; a ~ (= complete, thorough) cure.* **2.** (law) *~ estate*, land and buildings. *~·ism* ['riəlizm] *n.* **1.** (in art and literature) showing of *~* life, facts, etc., in a true way. **2.** behaviour based on the facing of facts and disregard of sentiment and convention. *~·is·tic* [riə'listik] *adj.* marked by *~ism* (1); concerned with what is *~* and practical; not sentimental. **re·al·i·ty** [ri'æliti] *n.* **1.** quality of being *~: in ~ity,* in actual fact. **2.** sth. *~;* sth. actually seen, experienced, etc.: *the grim ~ities of war. ~·ly adv.* truly. **real·ize** ['riəlaiz] *v.t.* **1.** be fully conscious of; understand: *~ one's mistake; ~ that one is wrong.* **2.** convert (a hope, plan,

etc.) into a fact: *~ one's ambitions.* **3.** exchange (property, business shares, etc.) for money; (of property, etc.) obtain as a price for or profit (*on*). **real·i·za·tion** [,riəlai'zeiʃən] *n.*

realm [relm] *n.* **1.** kingdom. **2.** region (fig. of knowledge, imagination).

ream [ri:m] *n.* 480 sheets (of paper).

reap [ri:p] *v.t. & i.* cut (grain, etc.); gather in a crop of grain from (a field, etc.). *~·er n.* person or machine that *~s.*

¹rear [riə*] *n.* **1.** back part: *in the ~ of the house.* **2.** last part of an army, fleet, etc.: *attack the enemy in the ~,* from behind; *bring up the ~,* come (be) last. **3.** (attrib.) at the back: *leave the bus by the ~ entrance.* '~**·'ad·mir·al** *n.* naval officer below a vice-admiral. '~·**guard** *n.* soldiers guarding the *~* (2).

²rear [riə*] *v.t. & i.* **1.** cause or help to grow, bring up: *~ poultry;* take care of, foster: *~ing a family.* **2.** (esp. of a horse) rise on the hind legs. **3.** raise, put up (the head). **4.** (liter.) set up, build (e.g. an altar).

rea·son ['ri:zn] *n.* **1.** (fact put forward or serving as) cause of or justification for sth.: *my ~ for saying so; the ~ why I said so. by ~ of,* because of. **2.** power of the mind to understand, form opinions, etc.; common sense: *It stands to ~ (that),* it is clear to the mind (that); *sensible people agree (that); do anything in ~,* do anything that is moderate or sensible. *v.i. & t.* **1.** make use of one's *~* (2) (*about* sth.). **2.** argue, use *~s* (1) (*with* sb.) in order to convince him. **3.** put forward as a *~* (1) or argument: *He ~ed that. . . . * **4.** *~ sb. into (out of) doing sth.,* persuade him, by giving *~s* (1), to do (not to do) sth. **5.** *~ sth. out,* think about a question in order to be clear about it. *~·a·ble* ['ri:zənəbl] *adj.* **1.** having ordinary common sense; able to *~.* **2.** acting, done, in accordance with

~ (2); willing to listen to ~. **3.** moderate; neither more nor less than seems right or acceptable: *a ~able excuse (price).* **~·a·bly** *adv.*

re·as·sure [ˌriəˈʃuə*] *v.t.* remove the fears or doubts of (sb.). **re·as·sur·ance** *n.*

re·bate [ˈriːbeit] *n.* sum of money by which a payment is (to be) reduced; discount.

re·bel [riˈbel] *v.i.* (-ll-). **1.** take up arms to fight (*against* the government). **2.** show resistance: *children who ~ against too much homework.* **reb·el** [ˈrebl] *n.* person who ~s; (attrib.) *the ~ army.* **re·bel·lion** [riˈbeljən] *n.* ~ling, esp. an armed rising against a government. **re·bel·lious** [riˈbeljəs] *adj.* acting like a ~; taking part in a ~lion; not easily controlled: *a child with a ~lious temper.*

re·bound [riˈbaund] *v.i.* spring or bounce back after hitting sth. *n.* (often [ˈriːbaund]) act of ~ing.

re·buff [riˈbʌf] *n.* refusal of an offer of, or request for, friendship, help, etc.; ¹snub. *v.t.* give a ~ to.

re·buke [riˈbjuːk] *v.t.* speak severely to (sb. for doing wrong, etc.); reprove. *n.* words used in rebuking sb.

re·but [riˈbʌt] *v.t.* (-tt-). prove (a charge, piece of evidence, etc.) to be false. **~·tal** *n.*

re·cal·ci·trant [riˈkælsitrənt] *adj.* disobedient; resisting authority.

re·call [riˈkɔːl] *v.t.* **1.** summon back (e.g. an ambassador). **2.** bring back (an event, etc.) to the mind. **3.** take back; cancel (an order, a decision). *n.* order to return and give up a position. *beyond (past) ~,* that cannot be brought back.

re·cant [riˈkænt] *v.t. & i.* give up (an opinion, a belief); take back (a statement) as being false. **re·can·ta·tion** [ˌriːkænˈteiʃən] *n.*

re·ca·pit·u·late [ˌriːkəˈpitjuleit] *v.t. & i.* repeat, go through again, the chief points of (an

argument, etc.). **re·ca·pit·u·la·tion** [ˈriːkəˌpitjuˈleiʃən] *n.*

re·cast [ˈriːˈkɑːst] *v.t.* give a new shape or arrangement to: *~ a sentence.*

re·cede [riˈsiːd] *v.i.* **1.** (appear to) go back or away from the observer or from an earlier position. **2.** become less in value. **3.** slope away from the front or from the observer: *a receding chin.*

re·ceipt [riˈsiːt] *n.* **1.** receiving or being received: *on ~ of the news.* **2.** (pl.) money received (in a business, etc.). **3.** written statement that sth. (esp. money) has been received. **4.** recipe. *v.t.* write out and sign a ~(3).

re·ceive [riˈsiːv] *v.t. & i.* **1.** accept; take (sth. offered, sent, etc.): *~ insults (punishment, a warm welcome).* **2.** allow to enter, be ready to see, welcome, entertain. **re·ceived** *adj.* widely accepted as correct: *the ~d opinion (text).* **re·ceiv·er** *n.* **1.** person who ~s (esp. stolen goods). **2.** part of a telephone apparatus that is held to the ear. **re·ceiv·ing-set** *n.* apparatus for receiving and reproducing radio signals.

re·cent [ˈriːsənt] *adj.* (having existed, been made, happened) not long before; begun not long ago. **~·ly** *adv.*

re·cep·ta·cle [riˈseptəkl] *n.* container or holder in which things may be put away or out of sight.

re·cep·tion [riˈsepʃən] *n.* **1.** way or manner of receiving sth. or sb. *Is radio ~ good in your district?* **2.** formal party: *a wedding ~.* **3.** (attrib.) of receiving (visitors, etc.): *~ desk* (in a hotel). **re·cep·tive** [riˈseptiv] *adj.* quick or ready to receive new ideas, suggestions, etc.

re·cess [riˈses] *n.* **1.** period of time when work is stopped (e.g. when Parliament, the law courts, are not in session). **2.** part of a room where the wall is set back from the main part; alcove. **3.** dark or secret inner place or part: *the ~es of a cave; a mountain ~.* **re·ces·sion** [riˈseʃən] *n.* slump in trade.

rec·i·pe ['resipi] *n.* directions for preparing (a cake, any dish of food, etc.) or for getting any result.

re·cip·i·ent [ri'sipiənt] *n.* person who receives sth.

re·cip·ro·cal [ri'siprəkl] *adj.* given and received in return; mutual: ~ *help* (*gifts, affection*).

re·cip·ro·cate [ri'siprəkeit] *v.t. & i.* 1. (of two persons) give and receive, to and from each other. 2. give in return. 3. (of parts of a machine) (cause to) move backwards and forwards in a straight line (like the piston of an engine).

re·cite [ri'sait] *v.t. & i.* 1. say (esp. poems) aloud from memory. 2. give a list of, tell one by one (names, facts, etc.). **re·cit·al** [ri'saitl] *n.* 1. telling of facts; account: *the recital of his complaints* (*adventures*). 2. musical performance by one person or a small group or of the works of one composer. **rec·i·ta·tion** [ˌresi'teiʃən] *n.* 1. reciting. 2. sth. (to be) ~d, e.g. a poem.

reck·less ['reklis] *adj.* rash; not thinking: ~ *of the consequences.*

reck·on ['rekn] *v.t. & i.* 1. find out (the quantity, number, cost, etc.) by working with numbers. ~ *up,* add up; ~ *in,* include, take into account, when ~ing. 2. ~ *with,* take into account; settle accounts with. 3. look upon (*as*); be of the opinion, suppose (*that*). 4. ~ *on, ~ upon,* depend on; base one's hopes or plans on. **~·ing** *n.* (esp.) bill (for charges at a hotel, restaurant, etc.). *day of* ~*ing,* time when one's acts (esp. wrongdoing) must be accounted for; *out in one's* ~*ing,* mistaken in one's calculations.

re·claim [ri'kleim] *v.t.* 1. bring back (waste land, etc.) to a useful condition. 2. request that sth. be returned. 3. reform. **rec·la·ma·tion** [ˌreklə'meiʃən] *n.*

re·cline [ri'klain] *v.t. & i.* be, place oneself, in a position of rest; put (one's arms, etc.) in a resting position; lie down.

re·cluse [ri'klu:s] *n.* person who lives alone and avoids others.

rec·og·nize ['rekəgnaiz] *v.t.* 1. know, (be able to) identify again, (sb. or sth.) that one has seen, heard, etc., before: *I ~ that tune.* 2. be willing to accept (sb. or sth.) as what he or it claims to be: *refuse to ~ a new government.* 3. be aware (*that*): ~ *that one is not qualified for a post.* 4. be ready to admit: ~ *the danger of an undertaking.* 5. acknowledge: *His long years of service have been* ~*d.* **rec·og·ni·tion** [ˌrekəg'niʃən] *n.* recognizing or being ~d.

re·coil [ri'kɔil] *v.i.* 1. jump back (*from,* e.g. in fear). 2. (of a gun) kick back (on being fired). *n.* act of ~ing.

rec·ol·lect [ˌrekə'lekt] *v.t. & i.* call back to the mind; succeed in remembering. **rec·ol·lec·tion** [ˌrekə'lekʃən] *n.* 1. time over which the memory goes back. 2. sth. ~ed; a memory. 3. act or power of ~ing.

rec·om·mend [ˌrekə'mend] *v.t.* 1. speak favourably of; say that one thinks sth. is good (*for* sth.) or that sb. is fitted (*for* a post, etc., *as* a teacher, etc.). 2. suggest as wise or suitable; advise: *I ~ you to do what your doctor says.* 3. (of a quality, etc.) cause to be or appear pleasing, satisfactory: *His bad conduct does not ~ him.* **rec·om·men·da·tion** [ˌrekəmen'deiʃən] *n.* (esp.) statement that ~s sb. or sth.

rec·om·pense ['rekəmpens] *v.t.* 1. reward or punish; make payment to: ~ *sb. for his trouble.* 2. pay (sb.) (*for* loss or injury). *n.* reward; payment.

rec·on·cile ['rekənsail] *v.t.* 1. cause (persons) to become friends after they have quarrelled. 2. settle (quarrels); bring (differing opinions) into harmony, cause to agree: ~ *what sb. says with the facts.* 3. ~ *oneself to sth.,* overcome one's objection to it. **rec·on·cil·i·a·tion** [ˌrekənsili'eiʃən] *n.*

rec·on·dite ['rekəndait] *adj.* (of knowledge) known to few people;

obscure; (of an author) having ~ knowledge.

re·con·di·tion [ˌriːkənˈdiʃən] *v.t.* put into good condition again.

re·con·nais·sance [riˈkɔnisəns] *n.* act of reconnoitring.

re·con·noi·tre [ˌrekəˈnɔitə*] *v.t. & i.* go to or near (a place or area occupied by enemy forces) to learn about their position, strength, etc.

re·cord [riˈkɔːd] *v.t.* **1.** set down in writing for reference. **2.** preserve for later use, by writing or in other ways (e.g. by means of photographs, tape-~ers, gramophone discs, etc.): *The radio programme was ~ed. The volume ~s the history of the regiment.* **3.** (of an instrument) mark or indicate on a scale: *What temperature does the thermometer ~?* **re·cord·ing** *n. They bought the latest ~ing of Beethoven's Third Symphony.* **rec·ord** [ˈrekɔːd] *n.* **1.** written account of facts, events, etc.: *on ~, ~ed(1); bear ~ to,* give evidence supporting the truth of. **2.** ~ed (1) facts about sb. or sth., esp. past history: *an airline with a bad ~* (e.g. many accidents to its aircraft). **3.** disc on which music, etc., has been ~ed (2). **4.** limit, score, point, attainment, mark, etc. (high or low), not reached before; (esp. in sport) the best yet done: *break (beat) the ~,* do better (worse) than ever before. **5.** (attrib.) that is a ~ (4): *a ~ rice crop; a ~ score.* **rec·ord-play·er** [ˈrekɔːdˌpleiə*] *n.* gramophone.

¹re·count [riˈkaunt] *v.t.* give an account of; tell.

²re-count [ˈriːˈkaunt] *v. t. & n.* count(ing) again.

re·coup [riˈkuːp] *v.t.* compensate (sb., oneself, *for* loss, etc.).

re·course [riˈkɔːs] *n. have ~ to,* turn to for help; seek help from.

re·cov·er [riˈkʌvə*] *v.t. & i.* **1.** get back (sth. lost, etc.); get back the use of (one's sight, hearing, etc.). **2.** become well, happy, etc., again. **3.** ~ *oneself,* regain control of oneself; become calm or normal. **~·y** *n.*

rec·re·ant [ˈrekriənt] *adj. & n.* (liter.) coward(ly); unfaithful (person).

rec·re·a·tion [ˌrekriˈeiʃən] *n.* (form of) play or amusement; sth. that pleasantly occupies one's time after work is done.

re·crim·i·na·tion [riˌkrimiˈneiʃən] *n.* accusation in return for one already made.

re·cru·des·cence [ˌriːkruːˈdesns] *n.* (of disease, violence, etc.) breaking out again; new outburst.

re·cruit [riˈkruːt] *n.* new member of a society, group, etc., esp. a soldier in his early days of training. *v.t. & i.* **1.** get ~s for; get (sb.) as a ~. **2.** get a sufficient quantity or store of; bring back to what is usual: ~ *supplies* (one's strength).

rec·tan·gle [ˈrektæŋgl] *n.* oblong. **rec·tan·gu·lar** [rekˈtæŋgjulə*] *adj.*

rec·ti·fy [ˈrektifai] *v.t.* put right; take out mistakes from. **rec·ti·fi·ca·tion** [ˌrektifiˈkeiʃən] *n.*

rec·ti·tude [ˈrektitjuːd] *n.* honesty; upright or straightforward behaviour.

rec·tor [ˈrektə*] *n.* **1.** (Church of England) clergyman in charge of a parish the tithes of which were not withdrawn (e.g. to a monastery or university) at or after the time when the English Church separated from the Church of Rome. (Cf. *vicar.*) **2.** head of certain universities, colleges, etc. **~·y** *n.* ~'s residence.

re·cum·bent [riˈkʌmbənt] *adj.* (esp. of a person) lying down.

re·cu·per·ate [riˈkjuːpəreit] *v.t. & i.* make or become strong again after illness. **re·cu·per·a·tion** [riˌkjuːpəˈreiʃən] *n.*

re·cur [riˈkəː*] *v.i.* (-rr-). **1.** come, happen, again; be repeated. **2.** go back (*to* sth.) in words or thought: ~*ring to what I said yesterday.* **~·rence** [riˈkʌrəns] *n.* ~ring; repetition: *Let there be no ~rence of this mistake.* **~·rent** [riˈkʌrənt] *adj.* ~ring frequently or regularly.

red [red] *adj. & n.* (of) the colour

of fresh blood. *the Red Cross,* (sign) of) international organization (*Red Crescent* in Muslim countries) for helping the sick and wounded in war, relieving suffering caused by natural disasters, etc. *red tape,* (fig.) too much attention to rules, esp. in public affairs and when causing delay. *see red,* lose control of oneself when angry. **red·den** ['redn] *v.t. & i.* make or become red. **'red-'hand·ed** *adj.* take (*catch*) *sb.* red-handed, in the act of doing sth. wrong. **'red-let·ter 'day** *n.* day on which some happy or important event happens. **'red·skin** *n.* (old name for) N. American Indian.

re·deem [ri'di:m] *v.t.* **1.** get (sth.) back by payment or by doing sth.: ~ *a pawned watch* (*one's honour*). **2.** perform (a promise, obligation). **3.** set free by payment; rescue: ~ *a slave* (*prisoner*); (by Jesus) make free from the power of sin. **4.** compensate: *his ~ing feature,* the feature or quality which balances his faults, etc. **the Re· deem·er** *n.* Jesus Christ. **re· demp·tion** [ri'dempʃən] *n.* ~ing; deliverance or rescue (esp. from evil ways): *past redemption,* too bad to be ~ed (3).

re·do ['ri:'du:] *v.t. & i.* do again.

red·o·lent ['redələnt] *adj.* having a smell or suggestion (*of* sth.).

re·double [ri'dʌbl] *v.t. & i.* make or become greater or stronger.

re·doubt·a·ble [ri'dautəbl] *adj.* formidable; to be feared.

re·dound [ri'daund] *v.i.* contribute greatly in the end (*to* one's credit, advantage, etc.); promote (2).

re·dress [ri'dres] *v.t.* **1.** set (a wrong) right again; make up for, do sth., that compensates for (a wrong). **2.** ~ *the balance,* make things equal again. *n.* ~ing; sth. (e.g. payment) ~ing.

re·duce [ri'dju:s] *v.t. & i.* **1.** make less; make smaller in size, appearance, price, etc.: ~ *speed* (*one's expenses,* etc.). **2.** ~ *to,* bring or get to a certain condition, way of behaving, etc.:

~ *a class of noisy children to order.* **3.** ~ *to,* change to: ~ *pounds to pence* (*wood logs to pulp*). **re·duc·tion** [ri'dʌkʃən] *n.* **1.** reducing or being ~d: *a reduction in price*; *sell sth. at a reduction.* **2.** copy, on a smaller scale, of a picture, map, etc.

re·dun·dant [ri'dʌndənt] *adj.* beyond what is needed: ~ *labour,* surplus workers. **re· dun·dan·cy** *n.*

reed [ri:d] *n.* **1.** (tall firm stem or stalk of) kinds of water plant: *a roof thatched with* ~(*s*). **2.** *a broken* ~, a person or thing that has failed to give the expected support. **3.** (in wind-instruments, organs) part that vibrates to produce sound. **~·y** *adj.* (of sounds, voices) shrill.

¹reef [ri:f] *n.* that part of a sail which can be rolled up or folded so as to reduce its area. *v.t.* reduce the area of (a sail) by rolling up or folding part of it. **¹~-knot** *n.* ordinary double knot.

²reef [ri:f] *n.* ridge of rock, stones, etc., just below or above the surface of the sea: *wrecked on a* ~.

reek [ri:k] *n.* strong bad smell (e.g. of stale tobacco smoke). *v.i.* smell strongly and unpleasantly (*of*).

¹reel [ri:l] *n.* cylinder, roller, or similar device on which cotton, wire, photographic film, etc., is wound. *v.t.* **1.** roll or wind on to, or with the help of a ~. ~ *off* (*a story,* etc.), tell quickly and easily. **2.** walk unsteadily, moving from side to side. **3.** be dizzy; (of things) seem to be going round: *The street* ~*ed before my eyes.* **4.** be shaken or shocked: *His mind* ~*ed when he heard the news.*

²reel [ri:l] *n.* (music for a) lively Scottish dance.

re·fec·to·ry [ri'fektəri] *n.* dining-hall (in a monastery, convent, college).

re·fer [ri'fə:*] *v.t. & i.* (*-rr-*). **1.** send, take, hand over (*to* sb. or sth.) to be dealt with, decided, etc.: ~ *a dispute to the United*

Nations; ~ *sb. to the Manager.* **2.** turn to, go to, for information, etc.: ~ *to one's notes.* **3.** ~ *to,* (of a speaker) speak about or of: *I was not ~ring to you.* **4.** ~ *to,* (of a statement) be connected with, apply to: *What I have said ~s to all of you.* **ref·er·ee** [‚refə'ri:] *n.* **1.** person to whom questions are ~red for decision. **2.** (in football, boxing, etc.) person who controls the players or contestants, according to the rules. *v.i.* act as ~ee. ~·**ence** ['refrəns] *n.* **1.** ~ring: *a ~ence book* (e.g. a dictionary); *a ~ence library* (where books may be ~red (2) to but not taken away). **2.** (person willing to make a) statement about a person's character or abilities: *excellent ~ences from former employers.* **3.** note, direction, etc., telling where certain information may be found: *a cross-~ence*, one to another passage in the same book. **4.** *in* (*with*) ~*ence to*, concerning; about; *without ~ence to*, irrespective of. **ref·er·en·dum** [‚refə'rendəm] *n.* the ~ring (1) of a political question to a direct vote of the citizens.

re·fine [ri'fain] *v.t. & i.* **1.** free (e.g. gold, sugar) from other substances; make or become pure. **2.** cause to be more cultured, polished in manners; get rid of what is coarse or vulgar: *~d speech* (*tastes, manners*). ~'**ment** *n.* **1.** refining or being ~d. **2.** purity of feeling, taste, language, etc.; delicacy of manners. **3.** delicate or ingenious development of sth.: *~ments of cruelty* (*meaning*). **re·fin·er·y** *n.* place, building, etc., where sth. is ~d (1): *a sugar refinery.*

re·fit ['ri:'fit] *v.i. & t.* (*-tt-*). make (a ship) ready for use again by renewing or repairing; (of a ship) be made fit for further voyages. *n.* ~ting.

re·flect [ri'flekt] *v.t. & i.* **1.** (of a surface) throw back (light, heat, sound); (of a mirror, etc.) send back an image of. **2.** express; show the nature of: *sad looks that ~ed the thoughts pass-*

ing through his mind. **3.** (of actions, results) bring (credit or discredit *upon*). **4.** ~ *upon*, hurt the good reputation of: *Such behaviour ~s upon his honesty* (suggests that he is dishonest). **5.** consider; think (*on, that, how,* etc.). **re·flec·tion, re·flex·ion** [ri'flekʃən] *n.* **1.** ~ing or being ~ed (1); sth. ~ed, esp. an image ~ed in a mirror or still water. **2.** thought: *lost in ~ion*; *on ~ion*, after careful thought. **3.** expression of a thought in speech or writing. **4.** expression of blame: *cast a ~ion upon sb.*; action that brings discredit. **re·flec·tive** *adj.* thoughtful; in the habit of ~ing (5). **re·flec·tor** *n.* sth. that ~s (1).

re·flex ['ri:fleks] *adj.* ~ *action*, one that is involuntary (e.g. a sneeze, shivering). *n.* ~ action. ~·**ion** *n.* see *reflection*.

re·flex·ive [ri'fleksiv] *adj. & n.* (word or form) showing action on or referring back to the subject: *a ~ verb* (e.g. *cut* oneself); *a ~ pronoun* (e.g. manifest *itself*).

¹**re·form** [ri'fɔ:m] *v.t. & i.* make or become better by removing or putting right what is bad or wrong: ~ *the world* (*a sinner, one's character*). *n.* ~ing; improvement; change made with this purpose in view. **ref·or·ma·tion** [‚refə'meiʃən] *n.* change for the better in morals, habits, methods, etc., or in society, the church. ~·**a·tory** [ri'fɔ:mətəri] *adj.* tending to, designed to, ~. *n.* (former type of) school or institution for ~ing young offenders against the law. ~·**er** *n.* person actively supporting ~s.

²**re·form** ['ri:'fɔ:m] *v.t. & i.* form again.

re·fract [ri'frækt] *v.t.* (of water, glass, etc.) bend aside (a ray of light where it enters): *Light is ~ed when it enters a prism.* **re·frac·tion** [ri'frækʃən] *n.*

re·frac·to·ry [ri'fræktəri] *adj.* resisting control, discipline, or (of metals, diseases) treatment.

¹**re·frain** [ri'frein] *v.i.* hold oneself back (*from* sth., *from* doing sth.).

²re·frain [ri'frein] n. lines of a song which are repeated, esp. at the end of each verse.

re·fresh [ri'freʃ] v.t. 1. give new strength to; make fresh: ~ oneself with a cup of tea (a warm bath). 2. ~ one's memory, freshen it by referring to notes, etc. ~·ing adj. strengthening; pleasant and welcome: a ~ing sleep (breeze). ~·ment n. that which ~es, esp. (often pl.) food or drink (between meals).

re·frig·er·ate [ri'fridʒəreit] v.t. make cool or cold; preserve (food) by keeping it very cold. re·frig·er·a·tor n. box or room in which food is kept cold.

ref·uge ['refju:dʒ] n. (place giving) shelter or protection from trouble, danger, or pursuit. ref·u·gee [,refju:'dʒi:] n. person taking ~ (e.g. from floods, war, persecution).

re·fund [ri'fʌnd] v.t. & i. pay back (money to sb.). ['ri:fʌnd] n. ~ing; money ~ed.

¹re·fuse [ri'fju:z] v.t. & i. say 'no' to; show unwillingness to accept sth. offered, or to do sth. that one is asked to do. re·fus·al [ri'fju:zl] n. 1. refusing. 2. right of deciding whether to accept or ~ sth. before it is offered to others.

²ref·use ['refju:s] n. waste material.

re·fute [ri'fju:t] v.t. prove (statements, opinions, etc.) to be wrong or mistaken; prove (sb.) wrong in his opinions, etc. ref·u·ta·tion [,refju'teiʃən] n.

re·gain [ri:'gein] v.t. 1. get possession of again. 2. get back to (a place or position).

re·gal ['ri:gl] adj. of, for, fit for, by, a king or queen. ~·ly adv.

re·gale [ri'geil] v.t. give pleasure or delight to (sb., oneself) (with food, drink, etc.). ~ oneself on, enjoy oneself by eating.

re·ga·lia [ri'geiljə] n. pl. emblems (crown, sceptre, etc.) of royalty; emblems and ornaments of a society.

re·gard [ri'gɑ:d] v.t. 1. look closely at. 2. consider: ~ sb. with awe; ~ed as the best dentist

in the town. 3. pay attention to; respect: ~ sb.'s advice (wishes); ~ sb. highly, have great respect for him. 4. as ~s, ~ing, concerning, in the matter of. n. 1. long or steady look: His ~ was fixed on the horizon. 2. attention; concern: with little ~ for the feelings of others. 3. respect; approval; kindly feeling: win sb.'s ~; held in high ~. 4. (pl.) (esp. at the end of a letter) kindly thoughts and wishes. 5. in (with) ~ to, concerning; about. ~·ful adj. ~ful of, paying attention to. ~·less adj. ~less of, paying no attention to.

re·gat·ta [ri'gætə] n. meeting for boat races (e.g. between yachts).

re·gen·er·ate [ri'dʒenəreit] v.t. & i. 1. reform spiritually; raise morally. 2. give new strength or life to. re·gen·er·a·tion [ri,dʒenə'reiʃən] n.

re·gent ['ri:dʒənt] n. & adj. (person) performing the duties of a ruler who is too young, old, ill, etc., or who is absent: the Prince R~. re·gen·cy ['ri:dʒənsi] n. (time of) office, authority, etc., of a ~.

ré·gime [rei'ʒi:m] n. method or system of government or of living.

reg·i·ment ['redʒimənt] n. 1. (army) permanent unit divided into battalions or batteries, commanded by a colonel. 2. large number (of). v.t. organize; discipline. reg·i·men·ta·tion [,redʒimen'teiʃən] n. strict political or other discipline.

re·gion ['ri:dʒən] n. area or division with or without definite boundaries or characteristics: the Arctic ~s; in the ~ of the heart. ~·al adj. of ~s: a ~al geography. ~·al·ly adv.

reg·is·ter ['redʒistə*] n. 1. (book containing a) record or list (e.g. of births, marriages, or deaths). 2. mechanical device for keeping records: a cash ~. 3. range of a voice or musical instrument. v.t. & i. 1. make a written record of, in a list. 2. put or get sb.'s name, one's own name, on a ~ (e.g. at a hotel). 3. (of instruments, e.g. a thermometer) indicate; record. **4.** (of sb.'s face) show (a feeling). **5.** send (a letter, parcel) by special post, paying a fee and getting a receipt, for insurance. **reg·is·trar** ['redʒistrɑ:*, ˌredʒis'trɑ:*] *n.* person who keeps ~s or records. **reg·is·tra·tion** [ˌredʒis'treiʃən] *n.* **reg·is·try** ['redʒistri] *n.* place where ~s are kept: *registry* (sometimes *register*) *office*, place for marriages before a registrar (without a religious ceremony); *servant's registry office*, employment agency for domestic servants.

re·gret [ri'gret] *n.* feeling of sadness at the loss of sth., or of annoyance or disappointment because sth. has or has not been done. *v.t.* (*-tt-*). have ~ for; be sorry (*that*). **~·ful** *adj.* sad; sorry. **~·ful·ly** *adv.* **~·ta·ble** *adj.* (esp. of behaviour) that should be ~ted.

reg·u·lar ['regjulə*] *adj.* **1.** evenly arranged; symmetrical: ~ *teeth* (*features*). **2.** coming, happening, again and again at even intervals: ~ *breathing*. **3.** normal; orderly: *a man of ~ habits*. **4.** not amateur; full-time or professional: *a ~ doctor* (not a quack); *the ~ army*. **5.** in keeping with standards of correctness, e.g. of etiquette. *n.* soldier of the ~ army. **~·i·ty** [ˌregju'læriti] *n.* **~·ize** ['regjuləraiz] *v.t.* make lawful or correct. **~·ly** *adv.* in a ~ manner; at ~ intervals or times.

reg·u·late ['regjuleit] *v.t.* **1.** control by means of a system or by rule(s). **2.** adjust (apparatus, a mechanism) to obtain a desired result: ~ *a clock*. **reg·u·la·tion** [ˌregju'leiʃən] *n.* **1.** regulating or being ~d; rule or order. **2.** (attrib.) correct, as required by rules: *regulation dress.* **reg·u·la·tor** *n.* (esp.) part of a clock, machine, etc., that ~s (2) (speed, etc.).

re·ha·bil·i·tate [ˌri:ə'biliteit] *v.t.* **1.** restore (e.g. old buildings) to a good condition. **2.** restore (sb.) to former rank, position, or reputation. **3.** bring back (a disabled, etc. person) to a normal life by special treatment.

re·hearse [ri'hə:s] *v.t. & i.* **1.** practise (a play, etc.) for public performance. **2.** say over again; give an account of: ~ *the day's happenings.* **re·hears·al** *n.*

reign [rein] *n.* (period of) rule: *the ~ of George VI.* *v.i.* **1.** rule (over). **2.** prevail: *Silence ~s*, there is not a sound of any kind.

re·im·burse [ˌri:im'bə:s] *v.t.* repay (a person who has spent money, the amount spent). **~·'ment** *n.* repayment of expenses.

rein [rein] *n.* (often pl.) long narrow strap fastened to a bridle for controlling a horse. *v.t.* control with, or as with, ~s.

rein·deer ['reindiə*] *n.* kind of large deer used in Lapland for transport, etc.

re·in·force [ˌri:in'fɔ:s] *v.t.* make stronger by adding or supplying more material, men, etc. **~·ment** *n.* (esp. in pl.) men, ships, etc., sent to ~.

re·in·state [ˌri:in'steit] *v.t.* put back, establish, in a former position or condition. **~·ment** *n.*

re·it·er·ate [ˌri:'itəreit] *v.t.* say or do again several times. **re·it·er·a·tion** [ri:itə'reiʃən] *n.*

re·ject [ri'dʒekt] *v.t.* put aside, throw away, as not fit to be kept; refuse to accept: ~ *an offer.* ['ri:dʒekt] *n.* ~ed article. **re·jec·tion** [ri'dʒekʃən] *n.*

re·joice [ri'dʒɔis] *v.i. & t.* be or make glad; show signs of great happiness: ~ *at your success*; *success that ~d your parents.* **re·joic·ing** *n.* (often pl.) celebration(s) for a happy event.

¹**re·join** [ri'dʒɔin] *v.i. & t.* answer. **~·der** *n.* answer (esp. to an argument).

²**re·join** ['ri:'dʒɔin] *v.t. & i.* join (together) again.

re·ju·ve·nate [ri'dʒu:vəneit] *v.t. & i.* make or become young again in nature or appearance. **re·ju·ve·na·tion** [riˌdʒu:və'neiʃən] *n.*

re·lapse [ri'læps] *v.i.* fall back into bad ways; become ill again,

after improving: ~ *into error.*
n. falling back, esp. after recovering from illness.

re·late [ri'leit] **v.t. & i.** **1.** tell
(a story); give an account of
(facts, adventures, etc.). **2.**
connect in thought or meaning:
~ *results to* (*with*) *their causes.* **3.**
be ~d (*to*), have reference to;
concern. **re·lat·ed adj.** connected (esp. by family) (*to*).

re·la·tion [ri'leiʃən] **n.** **1.** relating (1); sth. related(1) (a tale,
an account). **2.** connexion; what
there is between one thing, person, idea, etc., and another or
others: *the* ~ *between mother and
child; the* ~*s expressed by prepositions* (e.g. time, place, direction); *effort and expense that bear
no* ~ (*that are out of all* ~) *to
the results* (i.e. are not propor-
tional to the results); *in* ~ *to,*
as regards, concerning. **3.** (often
pl.) dealings; what one person,
group, country, etc., has to do
with another: *have business*
~*s with a firm in London;
friendly* ~*s between countries.*
4. = relative(1). ~**·ship n.**
= relation (2).

rel·a·tive ['relətiv] **adj.** **1.** ~ *to,*
having a connexion with: *the
facts* ~ *to this problem.* **2.** comparative: *the* ~ *advantages of
two methods. They are living in*
~ *comfort* (i.e. compared with
other people, or with themselves
at an earlier time). **3.** considered
in relation (2) each to each: *the
~ duties of a ruler and his subjects.* **4.** (grammar) ~ *pronoun*
(e.g. *whom* in 'the man whom I
met'); ~ *adverb* (e.g. *where* in
'the place where I met him'). **n.**
1. person to whom one is related
(an uncle, aunt, cousin, nephew,
etc.). **2.** ~ pronoun or adverb.
~**·ly adv.** comparatively; in
proportion (*to*).

re·lax [ri'læks] **v.t. & i.** **1.** (cause
to) become less tight or stiff;
(allow to) become less severe
or strict; weaken: ~ *discipline.* **2.**
a ~*ing climate,* one that causes
an inclination to be lazy. ~**·a-
tion** [ˌri:læk'seiʃən] **n.** (esp.)
recreation.

re·lay n. [ri'lei] **1.** supply of fresh
men or horses to replace tired
ones: *working in* ~s. **2.** ~ *race*
['ri:lei'reis], one between two
teams, each member of the team
running one section of the total
distance. **3.** ['ri:'lei] ~ed radio
programme. ['ri:'lei] **v.t.** (p.t. &
p.p. ~ed). send on further (e.g.
a radio programme received
from another station).

re·lease [ri'li:s] **v.t.** **1.** allow to
go; set free; unfasten. **2.** allow
(news) to be published; allow
(a film) to be exhibited publicly.
n. releasing or being ~d.

rel·e·gate ['religeit] **v.t.** **1.** hand
over (a question, task, etc., *to*
sb. for decision, etc.). **2.** dismiss to a lower place or condition. **rel·e·ga·tion** [ˌreli'gei-
ʃən] **n.**

re·lent [ri'lent] **v.i.** become less
harsh; begin to show mercy.
~**·less adj.** without pity.

rel·e·vant ['relivənt] **adj.** connected with what is being discussed.

re·li·a·ble [ri'laiəbl] **adj.** that can
be relied upon. **re·li·a·bly adv.**
re·li·a·bil·i·ty [ri,laiə'biliti] **n.**

re·li·ance [ri'laiəns] **n.** trust.
re·li·ant adj. having trust;
trusting.

rel·ic ['relik] **n.** **1.** part of the
body or dress, etc., of a saint,
kept after his death. **2.** sth.
that has survived from the past
and that serves to keep memories alive.

re·lief [ri'li:f] **n.** **1.** the lessening
or ending or removal of pain,
anxiety, etc. **2.** that which
brings ~(1); food, clothes,
money, etc. (to be) given to
people in trouble: *a* ~ *fund.
R~ was sent to those made homeless by the floods.* **3.** sth. that
adds interest to what would,
without it, be dull or monotonous. **4.** freedom from duty (esp.
keeping watch); the person(s)
replacing other person(s) on
duty. **5.** method of carving or
moulding in which a design or
figure stands out from the surface; design or carving made in
this way. **6.** degree of clearness of

outline : *standing out in sharp* ~ (i.e. clearly); *a* ~ *map*, one showing (e.g. by colours) comparative height above, depth below, sea level. **re·lieve** [ri'li:v] *v.t.* 1. be, give, or bring, ~ to : *relieve one's feelings*, provide an outlet for them (e.g. by crying or swearing). 2. *relieve sb. of sth.*, take it from him.

re·li·gion [ri'lidʒən] *n.* 1. belief in God as creator and controller of the universe. 2. system of faith and worship based on such belief : *the Christian* ~. **re·li·gious** [ri'lidʒəs] *adj.* 1. of ~. 2. (of a person) devout; godfearing. 3. conscientious.

re·lin·quish [ri'liŋkwiʃ] *v.t.* give up (e.g. hope); let go (e.g. one's hold of sth.).

rel·ish ['reliʃ] *n.* 1. special taste or flavour; sth. that gives an attractive flavour or quality. 2. liking (*for*). *v.t.* enjoy; get pleasure from.

re·luc·tant [ri'lʌktənt] *adj.* (slow to do sth. because) unwilling. **re·luc·tance** *n.*

re·ly [ri'lai] *v.i.* ~ (*up*)*on*, depend upon, look to, (sb.) for help.

re·main [ri'mein] *v.i.* 1. be still present after a part has gone or has been taken away. 2. continue in some place or condition; continue to be. ~**·der** *n.* that which ~s; those who ~; the rest. **re·mains** *n. pl.* 1. what is left (e.g. of a meal). 2. ruins (e.g. of ancient Rome). 3. dead body.

re·mand [ri'mɑ:nd] *v.t.* send (an accused person) back to prison (from a court of law) until more evidence is obtained. *n.* ~ing.

re·mark [ri'mɑ:k] *v.t. & i.* 1. notice; see. 2. say (*that*); say sth. (*on* or *about*). *n.* 1. notice; looking at : *nothing worthy of* ~. 2. comment; sth. said. ~**·a·ble** *adj.* out of the ordinary; deserving notice. ~**·a·bly** *adv.*

rem·e·dy ['remidi] *n.* cure (for a disease, etc.); method of, sth. used for, putting right sth. that is wrong. *v.t.* provide a ~ for. **re·me·dial** [ri'mi:djəl] *adj.* providing a ~ : *remedial measures.*

re·mem·ber [ri'membə*] *v.t. & i.* 1. keep in the memory; call back to the mind. 2. ~ *sb. to* (sb. else), give or carry greetings (kind words) to. **re·mem·brance** [ri'membrəns] *n.* 1. ~ing or being ~ed; memory : *in remembrance of.* 2. sth. given or kept in memory of sb. or sth. 3. (pl.) regards (4) (sent in a letter or by a third person).

re·mind [ri'maind] *v.t.* cause (sb.) to remember (*to do* sth., *that*); cause (sb.) to think (*of* sth. or sb.). ~**·er** *n.* sth. (e.g. a letter) that helps one to remember sth.

rem·i·nis·cence [,remi'nisəns] *n.* 1. remembering; the recalling of past experiences. 2. (pl.) account of what sb. remembers : ~*s of the days when he was a sailor.* **rem·i·nis·cent** *adj.* 1. reminding one (*of*); suggestive (*of*). 2. remembering the past : *become reminiscent.*

re·miss [ri'mis] *adj.* careless; not doing one's duty properly : ~ *in one's duties.* ~**·ness** *n.*

re·mis·sion [ri'miʃən] *n.* 1. pardon or forgiveness (of sins, by God). 2. freeing (from debt, punishment). 3. lessening or weakening (of pain, efforts, etc.).

re·mit [ri'mit] *v.t. & i.* (*-tt-*). 1. (of God) forgive (sins). 2. excuse (sb.) payment (of a debt or punishment). 3. send (money, etc.) by post. 4. make or become less : ~ *one's efforts.* 5. take or send (a question to be decided) to some authority. ~**·tance** *n.* the sending of money, sum of money sent, to sb. at a distance.

rem·nant ['remnənt] *n.* 1. small part that remains. 2. (esp.) piece of cloth offered cheap after the greater part has been sold.

re·mon·strate [ri'monstreit] *v.i.* make a protest (*against* sth.); argue in protest (*with* sb., *that*). **re·mon·strance** [ri'monstrəns] *n.* remonstrating; protest (*against*).

re·morse [ri'mɔ:s] *n.* deep, bitter regret for wrongdoing. ~**ful**

adj. feeling ~. **~·less** *adj.* without ~.

re·mote [ri'mout] *adj.* (-r, -st).
1. far away in space or time. 2. widely separated (in feeling, interests, etc., *from*). 3. slight : *a ~ possibility* ; *not the ~st idea.*

re·move [ri'mu:v] *v.t. & i.* 1. take off, away, or to another place : *~ one's hat* (*one's hand from sb.'s shoulder*) ; *~ a boy from school.* 2. (usu. *move*) change one's dwelling-place ; go to live elsewhere. **re·mov·a·ble** *adj.* (e.g. of officials) that can be ~d (from office at any time). **re·mov·al** *n.* act of removing : *a removal van* (for removing furniture).

re·mu·ner·ate [ri'mju:nəreit] *v.t.* pay (sb.) for work or services ; reward. **re·mu·ner·a·tion** [ri-,mju:nə'reiʃən] *n.* payment or reward. **re·mu·ner·a·tive** [ri'mju:nərətiv] *adj.* profitable.

re·nais·sance [rə'neisəns] *n.* 1. (*the R~*) (period of) revival of art and literature in Europe in the 14th, 15th, and 16th centuries, based on ancient Greek learning. 2. any similar revival.

rend [rend] *v.t. & i.* (p.t. & p.p. *rent*) (liter.). 1. pull or divide forcibly : *a country rent* (*in two*) *by civil war.* 2. tear or pull (*off, away*) violently.

ren·der ['rendə*] *v.t.* 1. give in return or exchange or as sth. due : *~ thanks to God* ; *~ good for evil* ; *~ help to those in need.* 2. present ; offer ; send in (an account for payment). 3. perform or sing (a piece of music) ; give a performance of (e.g. a drama, a character in a drama) ; give a translation of (*in another language*). 4. cause to be (in some condition) : *~ed helpless by an accident.* 5. (of fat) make clear by melting.

ren·dez·vous ['rondivu:] *n.* (place decided upon for a) meeting at a time agreed upon.

re·new [ri'nju:] *v.t.* 1. make new ; make as good as new. 2. replace (sth.) with a new thing of the same sort : *snakes ~ing their skins.* 3. begin again : *~*

an attack. 4. get, make, say, or give again : *~ a lease.* **~·al** *n.* ~ing or being ~ed ; sth. ~ed.

re·nounce [ri'nauns] *v.t.* 1. say that one will no longer have anything to do with, that one no longer recognizes (sb. or sth. having a claim to one's care, affection, etc.). 2. give up ; surrender (a claim, right, privilege, etc.). **re·nun·ci·a·tion** [ri,nʌn-si'eiʃən] *n.*

re·no·vate ['renouveit] *v.t.* restore (e.g. old buildings) to good or strong condition. **re·no·va·tion** [,renou'veiʃən] *n.*

re·nown [ri'naun] *n.* fame. **re·nowned** *adj.* famous.

¹**rent,** see *rend.*

²**rent** [rent] *n.* torn place (in cloth, etc.) ; split.

³**rent** [rent] *n.* regular payment for the use of land, a building, a room, machinery, etc. *v.t. & i.* 1. pay ~ for. 2. allow (sb.) to occupy or use in return for ~. **~·al** *n.* amount of ~ paid or received.

re·nun·ci·a·tion, see *renounce.*

¹**re·pair** [ri'pɛə*] *v.i.* 1. mend ; put (sth. damaged or worn) into good condition : *~ the roads.* 2. put right ; make up for. *n.* 1. ~ing : *road under ~.* 2. work or process of ~ing. **~·a·ble** *adj.* that can be ~ed. **rep·a·ra·ble** ['repərəbl] *adj.* (esp. of losses) that can be made good. **rep·a·ra·tion** [,repə'reiʃən] *n.* act of, payment, compensating for loss or damage.

²**re·pair** [ri'pɛə*] *v.i.* go (*to*) (esp. go frequently *to*, go in large numbers *to*).

rep·ar·tee [,repɑ:'ti:] *n.* witty, clever answer(s).

re·past [ri'pɑ:st] *n.* (formal word for a) meal.

re·pat·ri·ate [ri:'pætrieit] *v.t.* send or bring (sb.) back to his own country. **re·pat·ri·a·tion** ['ri:pætri'eiʃən] *n.*

re·pay [ri:'pei] *v.t. & i.* (p.t. & p.p. *repaid*). pay back (money, etc.) ; give in return for : *~ sb.'s kindness.* **~·ment** *n.*

re·peal [ri'pi:l] *v.t.* revoke, put an end to (a law). *n.* ~ing.

re·peat [ri'pi:t] *v.t. & i.* **1.** say or do again : ~ *a word* (*a mistake*) ; ~ *oneself*, say or do what one has already said or done before. **2.** say (what sb. else has said or what one has learnt by heart). **~·ed·ly** *adv.* again and again. **rep·e·ti·tion** [ˌrepi-'tiʃən] *n.* ~ing or being ~ed ; sth. ~ed ; further occurrence.

re·pel [ri'pel] *v.t.* (-*ll*-). **1.** drive back or away : ~ *the enemy* (*a temptation*). **2.** cause a feeling of dislike : ~*led by his long beard.* **~·lent** *adj.* tending to ~ ; unattractive ; uninviting.

re·pent [ri'pent] *v.t. & i.* wish one had not done sth. ; be or feel sorry (esp. about wrongdoing) : ~ (*of*) *one's sins.* **re·pen·tance** [ri'pentəns] *n.* regret for wrongdoing. **~·ant** *adj.* feeling or showing ~ance.

re·per·cus·sion [ˌri:pə'kʌʃən] *n.* **1.** coming or springing back (after striking sth. with force) ; echoing sound. **2.** (usu. pl.) far-reaching and indirect effect of an event.

re·per·toire ['repətwɑ:*], **rep·er·to·ry** ['repətəri] *n.* plays, songs, pieces, etc., which a theatrical company, actor, musician, etc., is prepared to perform.

rep·e·ti·tion, see *repeat.*

re·pine [ri'pain] *v.i.* be discontented.

re·place [ri:'pleis] *v.t.* put back in its place ; take the place of : *Have buses* ~*d trams in your town?*

re·plen·ish [ri'pleniʃ] *v.t.* fill up (sth.) again with : ~ *one's wardrobe with new clothes.*

re·plete [ri'pli:t] *adj.* filled : ~ *with food* ; well provided (*with*). **re·ple·tion** [ri'pli:ʃən] *n.* being ~.

rep·li·ca ['replikə] *n.* exact copy (esp. one made by an artist of one of his own pictures).

re·ply [ri'plai] *v.i. & t. & n.* answer.

re·port [ri'pɔ:t] *v.t. & i.* **1.** give an account of (sth. seen, heard, done, etc.) ; give as news : ~ *speeches made in Parliament.* **2.**

go to sb., go somewhere, and say that one has come, that one is ready for work, etc. : ~ *to the manager.* **3.** make a complaint about (*to* sb. in authority) : *The soldier was* ~*ed for insolence.* *n.* **1.** account of, statement about, sth. heard, seen, done, etc. **2.** common or general talk ; rumour. **3.** noise of an explosion : *the* ~ *of a gun.* **~·er** *n.* person who ~s for a newspaper, the radio, TV., etc.

re·pose [ri'pouz] *v.t. & i.* **1.** rest ; give rest or support to : *A girl was reposing in the hammock.* **2.** be supported or based (*on*). **3.** place or put (belief, confidence, etc., *in* sb., *in* sb.'s honesty, promise, etc.). *n.* **1.** rest ; sleep. **2.** quietness ; restful or quiet behaviour or appearance.

re·pos·i·to·ry [ri'pɔzitəri] *n.* place where things are or may be stored.

rep·re·hen·si·ble [ˌrepri'hensibl] *adj.* deserving reproof.

rep·re·sent [ˌrepri'zent] *v.t.* **1.** be, give, make, a picture, sign, symbol, or example of : *a painting that* ~*s the Garden of Eden.* **2.** describe (*as*) : ~ *oneself as an expert.* **3.** make clear ; explain : ~ *one's grievances to the management.* **4.** act or speak for ; be an agent for ; be M.P. for. **rep·re·sen·ta·tion** [ˌreprizen'teiʃən] *n.* **rep·re·sen·ta·tive** [ˌrepri'zentətiv] *adj.* **1.** serving as an example of a class or group ; containing examples of a number of classes or groups : *models* ~*ative of primitive tools.* **2.** ~*ative government,* government by persons who are elected by the public to ~ (4) them. *n.* **1.** example, typical specimen (of a group or class). **2.** person who ~s (4) others.

re·press [ri'pres] *v.t.* keep or put down or under ; prevent from finding an outlet : ~ *an impulse.* **re·pres·sion** [ri'preʃən] *n.* **re·pres·sive** *adj.*

re·prieve [ri'pri:v] *v.t.* **1.** say that the execution (of sb. condemned to death) will not take place. **2.** give relief for a short time from (trouble, danger, etc.). **n. 1.** (order giving authority for) not carrying out punishment (esp. by death). **2.** temporary relief from trouble, danger, etc.

rep·ri·mand ['reprimɑ:nd] *v.t.* reprove severely. *n.* severe reproof.

re·pri·sal [ri'praizl] *n.* action taken in revenge; paying back injury with injury.

re·proach [ri'prəutʃ] *v.t.* blame regretfully or reluctantly; scold: *I have nothing to ~ myself with* (i.e. I don't feel that I am in the wrong). *n.* **1.** (words used for) ~ing. **2.** sth. that may bring ~; cause of shame or discredit. ~·**ful** *adj.* full of, expressing, ~.

rep·ro·bate ['reprəubeit] *v.t.* disapprove strongly of. *n. & adj.* (person who is) very immoral.

re·pro·duce [ˌri:prə'dju:s] *v.t. & i.* **1.** copy; cause to be seen, heard, etc., again: *~ music from a gramophone record.* **2.** produce offspring; bring about a natural increase: *plants that ~ by spores* (e.g. ferns). **re·pro·duc·tion** [ˌri:prə'dʌkʃən] *n.* process of reproducing; sth. ~d (1); copy of sth. **re·pro·duc·tive** *adj.*

re·proof [ri'pru:f] *n.* (words of) blame or disapproval. **re·prov·al** [ri'pru:vl] *n.* reproving; ~. **re·prove** [ri'pru:v] *v.t.* find fault with; say sharp words to.

rep·tile ['reptail] *n.* cold-blooded animal that creeps or crawls (e.g. a lizard, tortoise, or snake).

re·pub·lic [ri'pʌblik] *n.* (country with) system of government in which the elected representatives of the people are supreme and the head of the government (the President) is elected. **re·pub·li·can** *adj.* of a ~.

re·pu·di·ate [ri'pju:dieit] *v.t. & i.* refuse to accept (a statement, sb.'s authority), to pay (a debt), to acknowledge (a friend); say that one will have nothing more to do with (e.g. a wicked son). **re·pu·di·a·tion** [riˌpju:di'eifən] *n.*

re·pug·nant [ri'pʌgnənt] *adj.* distasteful; causing a feeling of dislike or opposition. **re·pug·nance** *n.* strong dislike (*to* sth.); unwillingness to do sth.

re·pulse [ri'pʌls] *v.t.* **1.** drive back (the enemy); resist (an attack) successfully. **2.** refuse to accept (help, friendly offers); treat (sb. offering help, etc.) coldly. *n.* repulsing or being ~d. **re·pul·sion** [ri'pʌlʃən] *n.* feeling of dislike or distaste. **re·pul·sive** [ri'pʌlsiv] *adj.* causing strong dislike.

rep·u·ta·tion [ˌrepju'teifən] *n.* the general opinion about the character of sb. or sth.: *a man of high ~; live up to one's ~,* act as people expect one to act. **rep·u·ta·ble** ['repjutəbl] *adj.* respected; honourable. **re·pute** [ri'pju:t] *n. =* (usu. good) reputation. **re·put·ed** *adj.* generally considered (*to* be).

re·quest [ri'kwest] *n.* **1.** act of asking. **2.** thing asked for. **3.** *in ~,* required, being ~ed, by people. *v.t.* make a ~ (*for* sth., *that*).

re·qui·em ['rekwiem] *n.* (music for) Mass for the dead.

re·quire [ri'kwaiə*] *v.t.* **1.** need. **2.** order (sb. to do sth.). **3.** demand (as a right or by authority). ~·**ment** *n.*

req·ui·site ['rekwizit] *n. & adj.* (thing) needed or required.

req·ui·si·tion [ˌrekwi'zifən] *v.t. & n.* (make a) demand for the supply of (food, etc.) or use of (houses, etc.); make demands upon (a town, etc., *for* supplies).

re·quite [ri'kwait] *v.t.* pay back; reward or avenge. **re·quit·al** *n.* repayment.

re·scind [ri'sind] *v.t.* cancel (a law, etc.).

res·cue ['reskju:] *v.t.* deliver from danger or harm; set free (from captivity, the power of enemies, etc.). *n.* rescuing or being ~d: *come* (*go*) *to the ~.*

re·search [ri'sə:tʃ] *n.* investigation undertaken in order to discover new facts. *v.i.* make ~es.

re·sem·ble [ri'zembl] *v.t.* be like; be similar to. **re·sem·blance**

[ri'zembləns] *n.* (point of) likeness.

re·sent [ri'zent] *v.t.* feel bitter, indignant, or angry at : ~ *being called stupid.* ~·ful *adj.* ~ing. ~·ment *n.*

re·serve [ri'zə:v] *v.t.* 1. store for later use. 2. set apart (*for* or *to* one's own or sb. else's use, or *for* a special purpose): *This room is* ~*d for children (television).* *n.* 1. sth. that is being or has been stored for later use: *the bank's* ~*s* (of money). 2. state of being stored: *have some money in* ~. 3. (pl.) military forces kept in ~, to be used if needed. 4. area of land kept and used for a special purpose: *a game* ~ (e.g. in Africa, for wild animals). 5. condition that limits or restricts: *accept a statement without* ~, believe every word of it ; ~ *price* (esp. at an auction) the lowest price that will be accepted. 6. self-control in speech and behaviour; keeping silent or saying little, not showing one's feelings : *break through sb.'s* ~, get him to talk and be more sociable. re·ser·va·tion [,rezə'veiʃən] *n.* reserving or being ~d. *without reservation*, without any limiting condition. re·served *adj.* (esp.) having or showing ~ (6). res·er·voir ['rezəvwɑ:*] *n.* place (often an artificial lake) where water is stored (e.g. for supplying a town); (fig.) supply (*of* facts, knowledge).

re·side [ri'zaid] *v.i.* have one's home (*in, at,* etc.). res·i·dence ['rezidəns] *n.* (formal, for the) building in which one ~s. res·i·dent ['rezidənt] *adj.* residing: *the* ~*nt population* (i.e. excluding visitors). *n.* 1. person who ~s in a place (contrasted with a visitor). 2. (*R*~*nt*) British political agent in some States. res·i·den·cy ['rezidənsi] *n.* residence of a British political representative. res·i·den·tial [,rezi-'denʃl] *adj.* of, with, private houses: *the residential part of the town* (contrasted with the business or industrial parts).

res·i·due ['rezidju:] *n.* that which remains after a part is taken or used.

re·sign [ri'zain] *v.t. & i.* 1. give up (a position, claim, etc.). 2. ~ *oneself to*, submit to ; be ready to accept or endure without protest. re·signed *adj.* having or showing patient acceptance of sth. re·sig·na·tion [,rezig'neiʃən] *n.* 1. ~ing a position; letter to one's employer, proposing this. 2. being ~ed to conditions.

re·sil·i·ence [ri'ziliəns] *n.* quality or property of quickly recovering the original shape or condition after being pulled, crushed, etc. re·sil·i·ent *adj.* having or showing ~.

res·in ['rezin] *n.* sticky substance that flows out from plants and trees, esp. fir- and pine-trees.

re·sist [ri'zist] *v.t. & i.* 1. oppose; use force against in order to prevent the advance of. 2. be undamaged or unaffected by : *a kind of glass dish that* ~*s heat* (i.e. that does not crack or break in a hot oven). 3. (usu. neg.) keep oneself back from. ~·ance [ri'zistəns] *n.* 1. (power of) ~ing : *make (offer) no* ~*ance to the enemy.* 2. opposing force. ~·less *adj.* that cannot be ~ed.

res·o·lute ['rezəlu:t] *adj.* fixed in determination or purpose; firm. res·o·lu·tion [,rezə'lu:ʃən] *n.* 1. quality of being resolute. 2. sth. that is resolved(1): *pass a* ~; (also) motion(3) put to a meeting to be resolved(1).

re·solve [ri'zɔlv] *v.t. & i.* 1. decide or determine (*that, to do* sth.): *He* ~*d to succeed.* 2. put an end to (doubts, difficulties, etc.) by providing the answer. 3. break up, separate (*into* parts). *n.* determination; sth. ~d (1).

res·o·nant ['rezənənt] *adj.* 1. (of sounds) resounding; continuing to resound. 2. tending to make sounds ~ : ~ *walls* (which echo and prolong sounds). res·o·nance *n.*

re·sort [ri'zɔ:t] *v.i.* ~ *to.* 1. make use of for help or to gain one's

purpose, etc.: *compelled to ~
to force.* **2.** go often (*to* a place).
n. **1.** ~ing(1): *in the last ~,*
as a last attempt, when all else
has failed. **2.** thing or person
~ed(1) to. **3.** place visited
frequently or by large numbers
of people: *a seaside (health) ~.*

re·sound [ri'zaund] *v.i. & t.*
1. (of a voice, instrument, sound)
echo and re-echo; fill a place
with sound. **2.** (of a place) be
filled with sound, echo back
sound. **3.** (fig., of fame, an
event, etc.) be much talked
about.

re·source [ri'sɔːs] *n.* **1.** (pl.)
wealth, supplies of goods, etc.,
which a person or country has
or can use: *natural ~s,* minerals,
water-power, etc. **2.** sth. which
helps in doing sth. or in escaping
trouble; pastime (e.g. reading,
music). **3.** skill in finding ~s(2):
a man of ~. ~**·ful** *adj.* good
or quick at finding ~s(2).

re·spect [ris'pekt] *n.* **1.** honour;
high opinion or regard: *pay
(show) ~ to one's teachers.* **2.**
attention; consideration; care:
have ~ for the needs of the public.
with ~ to, concerning. *in ~ to
(of),* as concerns; with regard to.
without ~ to, leaving out of the
question; paying no attention
to. **3.** (pl.) greetings: *Give my ~s
to your father.* **4.** detail, particular: *in this one ~; in some
(all, no, many) ~s.* *v.t.* **1.** have
~ (1), (2) for: ~ *one's elders.* **2.**
refrain from hurting, interfering
with, breaking, etc.: ~ *a person's feelings (wishes);* ~ *the law.*
re·spec·ta·ble [ris'pektəbl] *adj.*
1. deserving ~ (1), (2). **2.** (of
a person, his clothes, behaviour,
etc.) of a sort considered right
or good enough. **3.** fairly high
in degree or amount: *a ~able
income.* **re·spec·ta·bly** *adv.* **re·
spec·ta·bil·i·ty** [ris,pektə'biliti]
n. being ~able (2). ~**·ful** *adj.*
showing ~ (to). ~**·ing** *prep.*
with reference to. ~**·ive** [ris-
'pektiv] *adj.* for, belonging to,
of, each of those in question.
~**·ive·ly** *adv.* separately or in
turn, and in the order men-

tioned: *Tom, Dick, and Harry
are 12, 14 and 15 years old,
~ively.*

re·spire [ris'paiə*] *v.i.* breathe;
breathe in and out. **res·pi·ra·
tor** ['respireitə*] *n.* apparatus
for breathing through (in a
place where the air is impure).
res·pi·ra·tion *n.*

res·pite ['respait, -pit] *n.* **1.**
time of relief or rest (*from* toil,
suffering, anything unpleasant).
2. postponement (of punishment, esp. sentence of death).
v.t. give a ~ to; reprieve for a
time.

re·splen·dent [ris'plendənt] *adj.*
very bright; splendid. **re·splen·
dence** *n.*

re·spond [ris'pond] *v.i.* **1.** answer. **2.** act in answer *to.* **3.**
react (*to*): ~ *to kindness (a
medicine).* **re·sponse** [ris'pons]
n. ~ing; answer; reaction. **re·
spon·sive** *adj.* answering; ~ing
easily or quickly.

re·spon·si·ble [ris'ponsəbl] *adj.*
1. (of persons) ~ *for,* in a position
where one has sth. in one's care
and can be blamed for loss,
failure, etc.; *be ~ (to),* have to
give an account of what one
does (*to* sb.). **2.** deserving credit
or blame (*for*). **3.** trustworthy;
able to be ~ for important
business, etc.: *Give the task to
a ~ person.* **4.** (of work, a
position, etc.) needing a ~(3)
person. **re·spon·si·bil·i·ty** [ris-
,ponsi'biliti] *n.* **1.** being ~:
He did it on his own responsibility
(i.e. without being told or
authorized to do it). **2.** sth.
for which a person is ~; duty:
*the heavy responsibilities of the
prime minister.*

¹**rest** [rest] *n.* **1.** condition of
being free from activity, movement, disturbance; (period of)
quiet or sleep: *be at ~; be laid
to ~,* be buried. **2.** support, for
keeping sth. in position: *a head-
~.* **3.** (music) (sign marking an)
interval of silence. *v.i. & t.* **1.**
be still or quiet; be free from
activity, movement, disturbance, etc. **2.** give a ~ to: ~
one's horse (eyes). **3.** (cause to)

be supported (*on* or *against* sth.): ~ *one's elbows on the table.* ~**·ful** *adj.* quiet; peaceful; giving ~ or a feeling of ~. ~**·ive** *adj.* (of horses) refusing to stand still; (of persons) impatient of control or discipline. ~**·less** *adj.* never still or quiet; unable to ~.

²**rest** [rest] *n.* (always *the* ~) what is left; the others. *v.i.* **1.** remain, continue to be, in some condition or position: *You may* ~ *assured that. . . .* **2.** depend: *A great deal ~s on his answer.* **3.** *It ~s with you to decide,* you are the one who must decide.

res·tau·rant ['restərɔŋ, 'restə-rənt] *n.* place where meals can be bought and eaten.

res·ti·tu·tion [,resti'tjuːʃən] *n.* restoring (of sth. stolen, etc.) to its owner.

re·store [ri'stɔ:*] *v.t.* **1.** give back (sth. stolen, etc.). **2.** bring back into use (e.g. old customs); put (sb.) back into a former position. **3.** repair, rebuild as before: ~ *an old house.* **4.** make well or normal again: ~*d to health.* **res·to·ra·tion** [,restə-'reiʃən] *n.* restoring or being ~d.

re·strain [ris'trein] *v.t.* hold back; keep under control; prevent (sb. or sth. *from* doing sth., etc.). **re·straint** *n.* ~ing or being ~ed; sth. that ~s.

re·strict [ris'trikt] *v.t.* limit; keep within limits. **re·stric·tion** [ris'trikʃən] *n.* ~ing or being ~ed; sth. that ~s. **re·stric·tive** [ris'triktiv] *adj.* ~ing; tending to ~.

re·sult [ri'zʌlt] *n.* that which is produced by an activity or other cause. *v.i.* be a ~; have the kind of ~ indicated: ~ *in failure.*

re·sume [ri'zjuːm] *v.t.* **1.** go on after stopping for a time. **2.** take or occupy again: ~ *one's seat.* **re·sump·tion** [ri'zʌmp-ʃən] *n.*

res·ur·rect [,rezə'rekt] *v.t.* **1.** take up from the grave. **2.** bring back into use or to the memory. **res·ur·rec·tion** [,rezə-'rekʃən] *n. the R~,* the rising of

Jesus from the tomb; the rising of all the dead on the Last Day.

re·sus·ci·tate [ri'sʌsiteit] *v.t. & i.* bring back (sb. nearly drowned, etc.) to consciousness. **re·sus·ci·ta·tion** [ri,sʌsi'teiʃən] *n.*

re·tail ['riːteil] *n.* selling of goods to the general public, not for resale (cf. *wholesale*): *sell by* ~; ~ *prices.* [riː'teil] *v.t. & i.* **1.** sell (goods) by ~. **2.** (of goods) be sold by ~ (*at* or *for* a price). **3.** repeat (what one has heard, esp. gossip) bit by bit or to several persons in turn. ~**·er** *n.* tradesman who sells by ~.

re·tain [ri'tein] *v.t.* **1.** keep; continue to have or hold; keep in place: *a pot that does not* ~ *water.* **2.** get the services of (a barrister) by payment. ~**·er** *n.* **1.** (formerly) servant of sb. of high rank. **2.** fee paid to ~ sb.'s services if needed.

re·tal·i·ate [ri'tælieit] *v.i.* return the same sort of ill treatment as one has received. **re·tal·i·a·tion** [ri,tæli'eiʃən] *n.*

re·tard [ri'taːd] *v.t.* check; hinder (esp. progress, development).

retch [riːtʃ] *v.i.* make the sound and motion of vomiting but without the result.

re·ten·tive [ri'tentiv] *adj.* having the power of retaining (1) things. **re·ten·tion** *n.* retaining or being retained.

ret·i·cent ['retisənt] *adj.* (in the habit of) saying little; reserved. **ret·i·cence** *n.*

ret·i·nue ['retinjuː] *n.* number of persons (servants, officers, etc.) travelling with a person of high rank.

re·tire [ri'taiə*] *v.i. & t.* **1.** withdraw, go away (*from* a place, *from* company, *to* a place). **2.** give up one's work, business, or position: ~ *on a pension;* cause (sb.) to do this. **3.** go to bed. **re·tired** *adj.* **1.** having ~d(2); *a* ~*d civil servant.* **2.** quiet, secluded. ~**·ment** *n.* condition of being ~d: *living in* ~*ment.* **re·tir·ing** *adj.* avoiding society; reserved.

¹**re·tort** [ri'tɔ:t] *v.i. & t.* answer back quickly and sharply (esp. to an accusation or challenge); get equal with sb. by returning (insults, attacks, etc.). *n.* such an answer.

²**re·tort** [ri'tɔ:t] *n.* vessel with a long narrow neck sloping downwards, used to heat liquids (to distil them).

re·touch ['ri:'tʌtʃ] *v.t.* improve (a photograph, painting, etc.) by making small changes.

re·trace ['ri:'treis] *v.t.* 1. go back over or along: ~ *one's steps*. 2. go over (past actions, etc.) in one's mind.

re·tract [ri'trækt] *v.t. & i.* 1. take back or withdraw (a statement, an offer or opinion). 2. draw back or in (a part of the body, the undercarriage of an aircraft, etc.). ~·**a·ble** *adj.* that can be ~ed.

re·treat [ri'tri:t] *v.i.* go back; withdraw: *force the enemy to* ~. *n.* 1. act of ~ing: *in full* ~; *make good one's* ~, ~ *safely*. 2. signal (on a bugle or drum) for ~. 3. (place for) period of quiet and rest: *go into* ~.

re·trench [ri'trentʃ] *v.t. & i.* cut down, reduce (expenses, etc.); economize. ~·**ment** *n.*

ret·ri·bu·tion [,retri'bju:ʃən] *n.* deserved punishment.

re·trieve [ri'tri:v] *v.t. & i.* 1. get possession of again. 2. put right (an error). 3. restore (one's fortunes).

ret·ro- ['retrou-] *prefix.* backwards; back again. ,~·'**ac·tive** *adj.* = ~spective. '~·'**grade** *adj.* moving backwards; becoming worse; likely to cause worse conditions, etc. ,~·'**gres·sion** *n.* return to a less advanced state. ,~·'**gres·sive** *adj.* '~·'**spect** *n.* review of past events, etc.: *in* ~*spect*, when looking back (at sth. in the past). ,~·'**spec·tion** *n.* ,~·'**spec·tive** *adj.* 1. of ~spection. 2. (of laws, etc.) applying to the past: ~*spective legislation*.

re·turn [ri'tə:n] *v.i. & t.* 1. come or go back. 2. give, put, send, pay, back: ~ *a borrowed book*.

3. say in reply. 4. (of a constituency) send (sb.) as representative to Parliament. *n.* 1. ~ing or being ~ed: *on his* ~ *home*; *in* ~ (*for*), as repayment or in exchange; *a* ~ *ticket*, one for a journey to a place and back again. 2. (often *pl.*) profit (on an investment or undertaking). 3. official report or statement: *the election* ~*s*. ~·**a·ble** *adj.* that can be, or is to be, ~ed.

re·u·nion [ri:'ju:njən] *n.* (esp.) meeting of old friends, former colleagues, after long separation.

re·veal [ri'vi:l] *v.t.* allow or cause to be seen; make known (a secret, a spiritual truth). **rev·e·la·tion** [,revi'leiʃən] *n.* ~ing; sth. ~ed, esp. a piece of surprising knowledge.

re·veil·le [ri'væli] *n.* (in the army) signal to men to get up in the morning: *sound the* ~.

rev·el ['revl] *v.i.* (-*ll-*). 1. make merry; have a gay, lively time. 2. ~ *in*, take great pleasure in. *n.* joyful merry-making. ~·**ry** *n.* wild or noisy merry-making.

rev·e·la·tion, see *reveal*.

re·venge [ri'vendʒ] *v.t.* 1. do sth. to get satisfaction for (wrong): ~ *an insult*; ~ *one's friend* (i.e. do equal harm to sb. in return for a wrong done by him to one's friend). 2. *be* ~*d* (*on sb. for sth.*), ~ *oneself*. *n.* act of revenging; desire to ~. ~·**ful** *adj.* feeling or showing a desire for ~: ~*ful looks*.

rev·e·nue ['revənju:] *n.* income, esp. the total annual income of the State: *Inland R*~, income from government taxes, etc.; ~ *officer*, customs and excise officer.

re·ver·ber·ate [ri'və:bəreit] *v.t. & i.* (esp. of sound) send back; be sent back. **re·ver·ber·a·tion** [ri,və:bə'reiʃən] *n.*

re·vere [ri'viə*] *v.t.* have deep respect for (esp. sacred things). **rev·er·ence** ['revərəns] *n.* deep respect; feeling of wonder and awe: *hold sb. or sth. in* ~*nce*. *v.t.* treat with ~nce. **rev·er·end** ['revərənd] *adj.* 1. deserving to be treated with respect (because of age, character, etc.). **2.** *the Reverend* (usu. shortened in writing to *the Rev.*) as a title for clergymen : *The Rev. T. Wells.*

rev·er·ent ['revərənt] *adj.* feeling or showing ~nce. **rev·er·en·tial** [ˌrevə'renʃl] *adj.* caused or marked by ~nce.

rev·er·ie ['revəri] *n.* (state of enjoying) dreamy pleasant thoughts : *lost in* ~ ; *indulge in* ~s *of the future.*

re·verse [ri'vəːs] *adj.* **1.** contrary ; in the ~ direction. **2.** back or under : *the* ~ *side of a gramophone record.* *n.* **1.** the opposite or contrary : *do the* ~ *of what one is asked to do.* **2.** ~ side (of cloth, a coin, a medal, etc.). **3.** defeat ; change to bad fortune : *suffer a financial* ~. *v.t.* **1.** put in ~ position : ~ *arms,* carry rifles so that they point downwards. **2.** (cause to) go in the opposite direction. **3.** do the opposite of (sth. done earlier). **4.** cancel (a decision) ; revoke (an order). **re·ver·sal** *n.* reversing or being ~d. **re·ver·si·ble** *adj.* that can be ~d (esp. of cloth, either side of which can be used on the outside).

re·vert [ri'vəːt] *v.i.* return (*to* a former state, problem, an earlier question, etc.)

re·view [ri'vjuː] *v.t. & i.* **1.** consider or examine again ; go over again in the mind : ~ *last week's lesson.* **2.** inspect formally (troops, a fleet, etc.). **3.** write an account of (new books, etc.) for periodicals. *n.* **1.** act of ~ing. **2.** critical account of a new book, play, film, etc. **3.** periodical with articles on current events, ~s of new books.

re·vile [ri'vail] *v.t. & i.* swear at ; call bad names.

re·vise [ri'vaiz] *v.t.* reconsider ; read through carefully, esp. in order to correct and improve. **re·vi·sion** [ri'viʒən] *n.* revising or being ~d ; ~d version.

re·vive [ri'vaiv] *v.t. & i.* **1.** come or bring back to consciousness, strength, health, or an earlier state : *flowers that* ~ *in*

water. Our hopes ~d. **2.** come, bring, into use again : ~ *old customs.* **re·viv·al** [ri'vaivl] *n.* **1.** reviving or being ~d : *the Revival of Learning,* the Renaissance. **2.** (esp.) (meetings intended to produce an) increase of interest in religion. **re·viv·al·ist** *n.* person organizing a revival(2).

re·voke [ri'vouk] *v.t.* repeal ; cancel ; withdraw (a decree, etc.). **re·vo·ca·tion** [ˌrevə'keiʃən] *n.*

re·volt [ri'vəlt] *v.i. & t.* **1.** rise in rebellion. **2.** be filled with disgust or horror (*at* or *against* a crime, a stink, etc.). **3.** cause a feeling of disgust in : *sights that* ~ed *all who saw them.* *n.* rebellion.

rev·o·lu·tion [ˌrevə'luːʃən] *n.* **1.** journeying round : *the* ~ *of the earth round the sun.* **2.** one complete turn of a wheel : *sixty-five* ~s *a minute.* **3.** complete change (in conditions, ways of doing things, esp. in methods of government when caused by the overthrow of one system by force). ~'a·ry *adj.* of a ~(3) ; bringing, causing, favouring, great (and often violent) changes. *n.* supporter of (political) ~. ~·ize *v.t.* make a complete change in.

re·volve [ri'vəlv] *v.i. & t.* **1.** (cause to) go round in a circle (as the rim of a wheel does). **2.** turn over in the mind ; think about all sides of (a problem). (Cf. *rotate.*)

re·volv·er [ri'vəlvə*] *n.* pistol that can be fired a number of times without being reloaded.

re·vue [ri'vjuː] *n.* theatrical entertainment of songs, dances, satire on current events, etc.

re·vul·sion [ri'vʌlʃən] *n.* sudden and complete change of feeling.

re·ward [ri'wɔːd] *n.* sth. offered, given, or obtained in return for work or services or for the capture of a criminal, etc. *v.t.* give a ~ to (sb. *for* sth.) ; be a ~ to (sb.).

rhap·so·dy ['ræpsədi] *n.* enthusiastic expression of delight (in speech, poetry, music).

rhet·or·ic [ˈretərik] *n.* **1.** (art of) using words impressively in speech and writing. **2.** language with too much display and ornamentation. **rhet·or·i·cal** [riˈtorikl] *adj.* in, using, a style appealing to the emotions. *a ~al question,* one asked for the sake of effect (2), not because an answer is needed or expected. **rhet·o·ri·cian** [ˌretəˈriʃən] *n.* person skilled in ~ (1) or fond of ~al language.

rheu·ma·tism [ˈruːmətizm] *n.* disease causing pain and swollen joints. **rheu·ma·tic** [ruːˈmætik] *adj.* of ~; causing, caused by, ~; suffering from, liable to have, ~.

rhi·noc·er·os [raiˈnosərəs] *n.* thick-skinned animal of Africa and Asia.

A rhinoceros

rhu·barb [ˈruːbɑːb] *n.* (plant with) thick juicy stalks which are cooked and used like fruit.

rhyme [raim] *n.* **1.** sameness of sound in endings of words, esp. at ends of lines of verse (e.g. *sea, key; rhyme, time*). **2.** verse(s) with ~: *nursery ~s,* poems or songs for small children. **3.** word that ~s with another. *v.t. & i.* **1.** (of words or lines of verse) be in ~: '*father*' ~s with '*rather*'. **2.** use (a word) as a ~: '*Poets* ~ '*love*' *with* '*above*''. **3.** write verse(s) with ~. **rhymed** *adj.* having ~s.

rhythm [ˈriðm] *n.* regular succession of weak and strong stresses, accents, sounds, or movements (in speech, music, dancing, etc.). **rhyth·mic(mi·cal)** [ˈriðmik(l)] *adj.*

rib [rib] *n.* **1.** any one of the curved bones extending from the backbone round the chest to the front of the body. **2.** sth. like a rib, e.g. curved timber in the sides of a ship, a thick vein in

a leaf. **ribbed** [ribd] *adj.* (esp. of cloth) having rib-like markings or ridges.

rib·ald [ˈribəld] *adj.* (of a person) using indecent or irreverent language; (of talk, laughter, etc.) coarse, mocking. ~·ry *n.* ~ language or talk.

rib·bon [ˈribn] *n.* **1.** (length or piece of) silk or other material woven in a long narrow strip or band, used for ornamenting or for tying things. **2.** sth. like a ~: *a typewriter ~.*

rice [rais] *n.* (plant with) white grain used as food, esp. in the East.

rich [ritʃ] *adj.* (-*er,* -*est*). **1.** having much money or property. **2.** (of clothes, jewels, furniture, etc.) costly; splendid. **3.** (of land, etc.) producing much; abundant (*in*). **4.** (of food) containing much fat, many eggs, etc. **5.** (of colours, sounds, etc.) deep; strong; full. ~·es *n. pl.* wealth; abundance. ~·ly *adv.* **1.** in a ~ (2) manner. **2.** fully (esp. ~*ly deserve*). ~·ness *n.* the quality of being ~.

rick [rik] *n.* pile of hay, straw, etc., built and covered for storage. *v.t.* make into a ~.

rick·ets [ˈrikits] *n.* disease of childhood, marked by softening and malformation of the bones. **rick·et·y** [ˈrikiti] *adj.* weak, esp. in the joints; likely to break and collapse: *rickety furniture.*

rick·shaw [ˈrikʃɔː] *n.* (old style) two-wheeled carriage pulled by a man.

ric·o·chet [ˈrikəʃei] *n.* jumping or skipping movement (of a stone, bullet, etc.) after hitting the ground or the surface of water. *v.i.* (of sth. shot from a gun, etc.) skip or bound off.

rid [rid] *v.t.* (p.t. *rid* or *ridded,* p.p. *rid*). make free (of): *rid a house of mice; get rid of a cough.* **rid·dance** [ˈridns] *n.* clearing away; being free from.

rid·den [ˈridn] p.p. of *ride* (esp. in compounds). oppressed or dominated by: *disease-~ slums.*

¹rid·dle [ˈridl] *n.* puzzling question; puzzling thing, situation.

²rid·dle ['ridl] *n.* large kind of sieve (for stones, earth, etc.). *v.t.* 1. put (material) through a ~. 2. make many holes in (sth.) (e.g. by firing bullets into it).

ride [raid] *v.i. & t.* (p.t. *rode* [roud], p.p. *ridden* ['ridn]). 1. sit on (a horse, bicycle, etc.) and be carried along : *riding* (*on*) *a camel.* 2. be carried along (*in* a bus, train, etc.). 3. be supported by ; float on water : *a ship riding at anchor.* *n.* journey on horseback, on a bicycle, as a passenger in a car, etc. : *go for a* ~. **rid·er** *n.* 1. person who ~s a horse, etc. 2. additional observation following a statement, verdict, etc.

ridge [ridʒ] *n.* 1. upper edge of two surfaces that slope together : *the* ~ *of a roof (the nose).* 2. long narrow stretch of high land ; chain of hills, etc., forming a watershed. 3. raised narrow strip (e.g. on ploughed land, between the furrows). *v.t.* make into, cover with, ~s.

rid·i·cule ['ridikju:l] *v.t.* cause (sb. or sth.) to appear foolish ; make fun of. *n.* words, acts, used to show humorous contempt. **ri·dic·u·lous** [ri'dik-juləs] *adj.* deserving ~ ; foolish ; unreasonable.

rife [raif] *adj.* (predic. only). 1. widespread ; common. 2. ~ *with,* having many or much, full of : *a country* ~ *with superstition.*

riff-raff ['rifræf] *n.* ill-behaved people of the lowest class.

¹ri·fle ['raifl] *v.t.* search and rob : *The thieves* ~*d every drawer in the house.*

²ri·fle ['raifl] *v.t.* cut spiral grooves in (the barrel of a gun). *n.* gun with a long, ~d barrel.

rift [rift] *n.* split or crack : *a* ~ *in the clouds.*

rig [rig] *v.t.* (-*gg*-). 1. supply (a ship) with masts, rigging, sails, etc. 2. *rig sb. out* (*with*), provide with necessary clothes, equipment, etc. ; *rig sth. up,* make, put together, quickly with any materials available : *rig up a shelter.* *n.* 1. design of a ship's mast(s) and rigging. 2.

(colloq.) style of dress ; clothing ; person's general appearance resulting from his clothing. 3. *oil-rig,* structure (2) with apparatus for drilling in search of petroleum or natural gas under the sea. **rig·ging** *n.* ropes, etc., which support a ship's masts and sails.

¹right [rait] *adj., adv. & n.* (opp. *left*). *In Britain traffic keeps to the left, not to the* ~ (*side*) *of the road. He looked neither* ~ *nor left. Take the first turning to the* ~. *the R*~ (*wing*), (politics) the Conservative party. ~-*hand man,* valuable or chief helper.

²right [rait] *adj.* (opp. *wrong*). 1. (of conduct) just ; morally good ; according to law or duty. 2. *the* ~ *side* (of cloth, etc.), the side intended to be seen. 3. true ; correct ; satisfactory : *the* ~ *time* ; *on the* ~ *road* ; *the* ~ *man for the job.* 4. ~ *angle,* one of 90° : *These two roads cross at* ~ *angles.* *n.* 1. that which is ~ : *know the difference between* ~ *and wrong* ; *be in the* ~, have justice or truth on one's side. 2. sth. to which one has a just claim ; sth. one may do or have by law : *by* ~(*s*), justly, correctly ; *by* ~ *of,* because of, on account of. *v.t.* put, bring, or come back, into the ~, or an upright, condition ; make sth. ~ again. ~·**ful** *adj.* 1. according to law or justice : *the* ~*ful owner* (*king*). 2. (of actions) justifiable. ~·**ly** *adv.* justly ; correctly : *if I am* ~*ly informed.*

³right [rait] *adv.* 1. straight, directly : *Go* ~ *on until you get to the church.* 2. ~ *away,* immediately : *I'll go* (*come*) ~ *away.* 2. completely ; all the way : *turn* ~ *round* ; *a* ~-*about turn,* a turn continued until one is facing in the opposite direction. 3. exactly : ~ *in the middle.*

right·eous ['raitʃəs] *adj.* obeying the law ; just. ~·**ly** *adv.* ~·**ness** *n.*

rig·id ['ridʒid] *adj.* 1. stiff ; unbending ; that cannot be bent. 2. firm ; strict ; not changing ; not to be changed : *a* ~ *rule* ; ~ *discipline.* ~·**ly** *adv.* **ri·gid·i·ty** [ri'dʒiditi] *n.*

rig·ma·role ['rɪgməroul] *n.* long, wandering story or statement that does not mean much.

rig·our ['rɪgə*] *n.* **1.** sternness; strictness. **2.** (often pl.) severe conditions (esp. of climate). **rig·or·ous** *adj.* **1.** strict. **2.** harsh; severe.

rile [raɪl] *v.t.* (colloq.) make angry.

rill [rɪl] *n.* (liter.) small stream.

rim [rɪm] *n.* **1.** raised or thickened edge, esp. of sth. round: *the rim of a bowl.* **2.** outer ring of a wheel (to which a tyre is fitted). *v.t.* (-mm-). make or be a rim for; provide with a rim: *a pool rimmed with flowers.*

rime [raɪm] *n.* (liter.) hoar-frost.

rind [raɪnd] *n.* hard outside skin or covering (of some fruits, e.g. melons, or of bacon and cheese).

¹ring [rɪŋ] *n.* **1.** circle: *children dancing in a ~.* **2.** circular band: *a wedding-~; a key-~* (on which keys are carried). **3.** enclosed space for a circus, a cattle-show, etc. **4.** square platform for boxing matches; boxing as a sport. **5.** group of persons who combine for a selfish purpose, e.g. to control prices. *v.t.* (p.t. & p.p. ~ed). **1.** surround; put a ~ round or over. **2.** put a ~ in the nose of (e.g. a bull). **'ring·lead·er** *n.* person who leads others in a rising against authority. **'~·worm** *n.* skin disease causing round red patches.

²ring [rɪŋ] *v.i.* & *t.* (p.t. rang, p.p. rung). **1.** give out a clear musical sound as when metal is struck: *The telephone bell rang.* **2.** cause sth., esp. a bell, to ~; do this in order to get attention, give a warning, etc.: *~ the church bells (a bicycle bell); ~ for the waiter. ~ (sb.) up*, get into communication by telephone; *~ off*, end a telephone conversation. *~ the changes (on sth.)*, do or use sth. in all possible different ways. **3.** (of a place) resound *(with)*. *n.* ~ing(1) sound.

ring·let ['rɪŋlɪt] *n.* small curl of hair.

rink [rɪŋk] *n.* sheet of artificial ice for skating; specially made floor for roller-skating.

rinse [rɪns] *v.t.* (often ~ *out*) wash with clean water in order to remove unwanted substances: *~ the clothes; ~ out the soap; ~ out the teapot. n.* act of rinsing: *Give your hair a good ~.*

ri·ot ['raɪət] *n.* **1.** violent outbreak of lawlessness by people in a district. **2.** noisy uncontrolled behaviour (e.g. by students making merry). *run ~*, throw off discipline, be out of control. *v.i.* **1.** take part in a ~. **2.** indulge *(in)*; revel *(in)*. **~·er** *n.* person who ~s. **~·ous** ['raɪətəs] *adj.* taking part in a ~; disorderly.

rip [rɪp] *v.t.* & *i.* (-pp-). **1.** pull, tear, or cut (sth.) quickly and violently (to get it off, out, open, etc.): *rip a letter open; rip the cover off; rip a piece of cloth in two.* **2.** (of material) be ripped. *n.* torn place; long cut.

ripe [raɪp] *adj.* (-r, -st). **1.** (of fruit, grain) ready to be gathered and used. **2.** fully developed: *~ judgement.* **3.** *~ for*, ready for (e.g. mischief). **rip·en** *v.t.* & *i.* (cause to) become ~.

rip·ple ['rɪpl] *n.* (sound of) small wave(s) (esp. travelling along the surface); gentle rise and fall (of laughter, etc.). *v.i.* & *t.* (cause to) move in ~s; make ~s in.

rise [raɪz] *v.i.* (p.t. rose, p.p. risen). **1.** go or come up or higher. **2.** stand up; get out of bed. **3.** come to the surface of a liquid: *bubbles rising from the bottom of a pond.* **4.** have as a starting-point: *The river ~s in Turkey.* **5.** rebel *(against* the government, etc.). **6.** *~ to an occasion*, show that one has the ability to deal with it. **7.** (of Parliament, a committee, etc.) adjourn(2). *n.* **1.** small hill; upward slope. **2.** increase (in value, temperature, wages, etc.). **3.** *give ~ to*, be the cause of; *take (get) a ~ out of sb.*, cause him to show annoyance by teasing him. **ris·ing** *adj. the rising generation*, the young people of the time referred to; *rising twelve*, getting near the age of twelve. *n.* (esp.) rebellion.

risk [risk] *n.* possibility or chance of meeting danger, suffering loss or injury, etc.: *take (run) ~s; at the ~ of one's life. v.t.* put or be in danger: *~ one's neck (~ losing one's life)*; take the chance of: *~ failure.* *~·y adj. (-ier, -iest).*

ris·sole ['risoul] *n.* small ball of minced meat or fish, mixed with potato, etc., and fried.

rite [rait] *n.* act or ceremony (esp. in religious services): *~s of baptism.* **rit·u·al** ['ritjuəl] *n.* system of *~s. adj.* of or connected with *~s: the ritual dances of an African tribe.*

ri·val ['raivl] *n.* **1.** person who competes with another (because he wants the same thing, or to do better than the other): *business ~s.* **2.** (attrib.) competing: *~ shops. v.t. (-ll-).* be a *~* of; claim to be (almost) as good as. *~·ry n.* being *~s*; competition.

riv·er ['rivə*] *n.* natural stream of water flowing to the sea, etc.: *the ~ Nile.*

riv·et ['rivit] *n.* metal pin or bolt for fastening metal plates (in a ship's sides, etc.). *v.t.* **1.** fasten with *~s.* **2.** fix (the eyes, one's attention) *upon* (sth.); attract, keep (the attention).

Rivets

riv·u·let ['rivjulit] *n.* small stream.

road [roud] *n.* specially constructed way for travellers on foot or riding from place to place; such a way with pavements, houses, shops, etc., on either side (*= street*): *on the ~, travelling; in the ~*, on the surface of the *~; in my (your, etc.) ~*, in my (etc.) way. *~·_met·al n.* broken stone for making or repairing *~s.* **roads**, *~·stead n.* stretch of water near the shore where ships can

anchor. *~·way n.* (usu. *the ~way*) that part of a *~* used by traffic (contrasted with the footpath or pavement).

roam [roum] *v.i. & t.* wander.

roan [roun] *adj.* (of animals) with a coat in which the chief colour is thickly mixed with grey or white. *n.* *~* horse, etc.

roar [rɔː*] *n.* loud, deep, lengthy sound (e.g. as made by a lion): *~s of laughter, applause. v.t. & i.* **1.** make such sounds. **2.** shout (*out*) (commands, etc.).

roast [roust] *v.t. & i.* **1.** cook, be cooked, over or in front of a fire or (of meat) in an oven. **2.** heat, be heated: *~ coffee-beans. n.* *~ed* meat.

rob [rob] *v.t. (-bb-).* deprive (sb.) of his property; take property from (a place) unlawfully (and often by force); *rob sb. of his wallet*; *rob a bank.* **rob·ber** *n.* **rob·ber·y** *n.* act of robbing.

robe [roub] *n.* long, loose (usu. official) outer garment: *the king in his ~s of state. v.t. & i.* put a *~* or *~s* on.

rob·in ['robin] *n.* small bird with a red breast.

ro·bot ['roubot] *n.* mechanism made to act like a man; machine-like person.

ro·bust [rou'bʌst] *adj.* vigorous; healthy; (of the mind) sensible; straightforward.

¹**rock** [rok] *n.* **1.** the solid stony part of the earth's crust: *a house with a foundation built on ~.* **2.** mass of *~* standing out from soil or the sea-floor: *as firm as a ~; on the ~s*, (of a ship) wrecked on *~s*; (fig.) very short of money. **3.** separate lump of *~: ~s falling down the mountainside.* *~·'bot·tom adj.* (of prices) the lowest. *'~·_gar·den, ~·er·y n.* (part of) garden with soil packed between *~s* for growing mountain plants, etc. *~·y adj. (-ier, -iest).* full of *~s*; hard like *~.*

²**rock** [rok] *v.t. & i.* **1.** roll backwards and forwards or from side to side: *~ a baby to sleep.* **2.** shake: *The town was ~ed by an earthquake.*

rock·et ['rɔkit] *n.* tube-shaped case filled with fast-burning material, which launches itself into the air (as a firework or as a signal of distress), or is used to drive shells through the air, to launch a space-craft, etc. *v.i.* go up fast like a ~.

rod [rɔd] *n.* **1.** thin straight piece of wood or metal: *curtain-rods*; *a fishing-rod*; *piston-rod*. **2.** stick used for punishing. **3.** measure of length, 5½ yards.

rode, see *ride*.

ro·dent ['roudənt] *n.* animal (e.g. rat, rabbit, squirrel) that gnaws things.

ro·de·o [rou'deiou] *n.* **1.** driving of cattle together for marking them. **2.** exhibition by cowboys (of horse-riding, roping cattle).

¹roe [rou] *n.* mass of eggs in fish.

²roe [rou] *n.* small kind of deer.

rogue [roug] *n.* rascal. **ro·guer·y** ['rougəri] *n.* conduct of a ~.

ro·guish ['rougiʃ] *adj.* (esp.) playful or mischievous.

rois·ter·er ['rɔistərə*] *n.* rough, noisy merry-maker.

role [roul] *n.* actor's part in a play; person's task or duty in an undertaking.

roll [roul] *v.t. & i.* **1.** move along on wheels; move along by turning over and over; ~ *a barrel*; *a ~ing stone*. **2.** turn or fold over and over into the shape of a ball or cylinder: ~ *string round a ball*; ~ *up a map*; ~ *oneself up in a blanket*. **3.** make flat or smooth by pressing with a ~ing cylinder of wood, metal, etc.: ~ *out pastry*. **4.** rock or sway from side to side: *The ship was ~ing in the storm*. **5.** (of surfaces) have long slopes that rise and fall: *miles of ~ing country*. **6.** make, say (sth.) with, long deep sounds as of thunder: *The thunder ~ed in the distance*. **7.** ~ *in* (*along*, *up*), come in large numbers. *be ~ing in money*, be very rich. ~ *up*, (esp.) increase in number. **8.** ~*ed gold*, thin coating of gold on another metal. *n.* **1.** sth. made roughly into the shape of a cylinder by being ~ed (2) or folded; sth. in this shape, however formed: *a ~ of cloth*; *a man with ~s of fat on him*. **2.** a ~ing (4) movement: *the heavy ~ of a ship*. **3.** ~ing (6) sound: *a ~ of drums*. **4.** official list, esp. of names: *call the ~*. **roll·er** *n.* cylinder-shaped object of wood, metal, rubber, etc., usu. part of a machine, for pressing, smoothing, crushing, printing, road-making, etc. '~*er-skates*, skates with four small wheels for use on a smooth floor. **'roll·ing-pin** *n.* ~er about one foot long used for ~ing out dough, etc. **'roll·ing-stock** *n.* railway's coaches, wagons, etc.

rol·lick·ing ['rɔlikiŋ] *adj.* noisy and jolly; full of good humour.

Ro·man ['roumən] *adj.* of (esp. ancient) Rome. ~ *Catholic*, of the Church of Rome. ~ *numerals* (e.g. I, II, IV, X = 1, 2, 4, 10).

ro·mance [rou'mæns] *n.* **1.** story or novel of adventure; love story, esp. one in which the events are quite unlike real life. **2.** real experience, esp. a love-affair, considered to be remarkable or worth description: *Their meeting was quite a ~*. **ro·man·tic** [rou'mæntik] *adj.* **1.** (of persons) having ideas, feelings, etc., suited to ~; imaginative. **2.** of, like, suggesting, ~: *romantic scenes* (*tales*, *lives*). **3.** (in art and literature) marked by feeling rather than by intellect; neither classical nor realistic.

romp [rɔmp] *v.i.* (esp. of children) play about, esp. running, jumping, and being rather rough. *n.* rough noisy play. ~*ers* ['rɔmpəz] *n. pl.* loose-fitting garment worn by a child for ~ing.

roof [ru:f] *n.* top covering of a building, tent, bus, etc. *v.t.* put a ~ on; be a ~ for.

¹rook [ruk] *n.* large black bird like a crow. ~*er·y* *n.* place (a group of trees) where many rooks have their nests.

²rook [ruk] *n.* person who cheats when gambling, esp. at cards and dice. *v.t.* **1.** swindle (esp.

at cards and dice). **2.** charge (sb.) far too high a price.

room [rum, ru:m] *n.* **1.** one of the separate divisions of a building, enclosed by its floor, ceiling, and walls; (pl.) set of these occupied by one person or family. (Cf. *apartments*.) **2.** space that is or might be occupied or that is enough for a purpose: *Standing ~ only*. **3.** ~ *for*, scope or opportunity, for (improvement, etc.). **roomed** *adj. a three-~ed house*, a house with three ~s. **~ful** *n.* **~·y** *adj.* (*-ier*, *-iest*) having much ~(2) in it.

roost [ru:st] *n.* branch, pole, etc., on which a bird rests, esp. one in a henhouse. *v.i.* sleep on a ~. **~·er** *n.* (U.S.A.) cock; male domestic fowl.

root [ru:t] *n.* **1.** that part of a plant, tree, etc., which is normally in the soil and which takes food from it: *take* (*strike*) ~, *send down a* ~; begin to grow. **2.** (also ~*-crop*) plant with a ~ used as food (e.g. carrot, turnip). **3.** part of a hair, tooth, the tongue, which corresponds to a ~. **4.** (fig.) that from which sth. grows: *get to the* ~ *of the trouble*. **5.** (part of a) word on which other forms of that word are based. *v.t. & i.* **1.** (of plants, cuttings) (cause to) send out ~s and begin to grow. **2.** ~ *sth. up* (*out*), pull up together with the ~s; (fig.) get rid of completely.

rope [roup] *n.* **1.** (piece or length of) thick strong cord or wire made by twisting finer cords or wires together. *know the* ~*s*, know how to set about some activity or business. **2.** number of things twisted together or threaded on a line together: *a ~ of onions* (*pearls*). *v.t.* tie (*up*, *together*) with ~; enclose or mark off. *~ sb. in*, (fig.) get him to help in some activity.

ro·sa·ry ['rouzəri] *n.* string of beads used in keeping count while reciting a number of prayers.

¹rose, see *rise*.

²rose [rouz] *n.* **1.** sweet-smelling flower (white, red, yellow, pink),

growing on a bush with thorny stems. **2.** pinkish-red colour. *look at things through ~-coloured spectacles*, see them as bright and hopeful. **ro·se·ate** ['rouziət] *adj.* ~-coloured. **ro·sette** [rou-'zet] *n.* small ~-shaped ornament (e.g. of silk ribbon). **'~·wood** *n.* hard dark-red wood.

ros·y ['rouzi] *adj.* (*-ier*, *-iest*) **1.** (esp. of a person's cheeks) pink; reddish. **2.** (fig.) bright: *a rosy future*.

ros·ter ['rostə*, 'roustə*] *n.* list of names of persons showing duties to be performed by each in turn.

ros·trum ['rostrəm] *n.* platform or pulpit for public speaking.

rot [rot] *v.i. & t.* (*-tt-*). **1.** go bad, spoil, by natural process: *fruit rotting on the ground*. **2.** (fig.) waste away; decay. **3.** cause to rot. *n.* **1.** decay; condition of being bad: *a tree affected by rot*. **2.** (colloq.) nonsense: *Don't talk rot!* **rot·ten** ['rotn] *adj.* **1.** decayed; having rotted: *rotten eggs*. **2.** (colloq.) bad; disagreeable.

ro·ta ['routə] *n.* list of persons who are to do things, list of duties to be performed, in turn.

ro·ta·ry ['routəri] *adj.* **1.** (of motion) round a central point. **2.** (of an engine) working by ~ motion.

ro·tate [rou'teit] *v.i. & t.* **1.** (cause to) move round a central point. **2.** (cause to) take turns or come in succession. **ro·ta·tion** [rou'teiʃən] *n. in rotation*, in turn.

rote [rout] *n.* (only) *by ~*, by heart; from memory without thinking: *do* (*say*, *know*) *sth. by ~.*

rot·ten, see *rot*.

ro·tor ['routə*] *n.* rotating blade(s) of a helicopter.

ro·tund [rou'tʌnd] *adj.* **1.** (of a person, his face) round and fat. **2.** (of the voice) rich and deep. **ro·tun·di·ty** [rou'tʌnditi] *n.* **ro·tun·da** *n.* round building, esp. one with a dome.

rou·ble ['ru:bl] *n.* unit of Russian money.

rouge [ruːʒ] *n.* red substance for colouring the cheeks or lips. *v.i. & t.* put ~ on (the face).

rough [rʌf] *adj.* (*-er, -est*). **1.** not level, smooth or polished; of irregular surface; (of roads, etc.) not easy to walk or ride on. **2.** not calm or gentle; moving or acting violently : ~ *children (behaviour)*; stormy : *a ~ sea*. **3.** made or done without attention to detail, esp. as a first attempt : *a ~ sketch (translation)*. ~ *and ready*, good enough for practical purposes although not exact or refined. **4.** (of sounds) harsh : *in* ~ *a ~ voice*. **5.** without comfort or conveniences : *the ~ life of an explorer*. *n.* **1.** bad-mannered and violent person. **2.** ~ state : *take the ~ with the smooth*, accept the unpleasant things as well as the pleasant things ; *in the ~*, in an unfinished state. *v.t.* **1.** make ~. **2.** ~ *sth. out*, make a ~(3) plan or outline. **3.** ~ *it*, do without the usual comforts of life (e.g. while camping). **'~·cast** *n.* mixture of cement with pebbles or gravel, applied to outside walls. ~**en** *v.t. & i.* make or become ~. **'~·'hew** *v.t.* carve ~ly into shape. ~**ly** *adv.* (esp.) approximately ; about : *It will cost ~ly £25.* **'~·shod** *adj.* (of a horse) with shoes provided with special nails to prevent slipping. *ride ~shod over*, (fig.) treat harshly or without sympathy.

rou·lette [ruːˈlet] *n.* gambling game played with a revolving wheel or disc.

round [raund] *adj.* **1.** shaped like a circle or ball. *a ~ trip (journey)*, one that starts and ends at the same place. *in ~ numbers (figures)*, roughly ; given in 10s, 100s, 1,000s, etc. *a ~ game*, one in which there are no teams or partners and in which there may be any number of players. **2.** full ; complete : *a ~ dozen*; large : *a good ~ sum (of money)*. *n.* **1.** ~ slice. **2.** regular series or succession or distribution (of duties, pleasures, etc.) : *my daily ~* ; *the postman's*

~ ; *go the ~s*. **3.** (amount of ammunition needed for firing a) single shot : *have only five ~s left*. **4.** one stage in a competition : *a fight (boxing-match) of ten ~s*. **5.** action, etc., performed by a number of people : ~ *after ~ of cheers*. *adv.* **1.** in a circle or in a half-circle : *look ~* (i.e. behind) ; *all the year ~*, throughout the year. **2.** on all sides : *gather ~*. **3.** from one to another of a group in turn : *Hand these papers ~. not enough food to go ~* (i.e. not enough for everyone). **4.** by a longer route : *We came the long way ~* (i.e. not by the nearest or most direct route). **5.** *bring sb. ~*, cause him to become conscious again ; *come ~*, become conscious again. **6.** to or from a place where sb. is or will be : *Come ~ and see me some time*. *prep.* **1.** on all sides of ; in a circle ~ : *a town with a wall ~ it*. **2.** so as to be or go ~ : *fly ~ the world*. *v.t. & i.* **1.** make or become ~ : *stones ~ed by the action of water*. **2.** go ~ : *to ~ a corner*. **3.** ~ *sth. off*, make it complete, add a suitable finish. ~ *up* (esp. animals), get them together. ~ *(up)on sb.*, turn on him and attack him. ~**·a·bout** [ˈraundəbaut] *adj.* not going by or using the shortest or most direct way : *I heard the news in a ~about way*. *n.* **1.** circular platform with wooden horses, etc., which carry children for amusement. **2.** circular enclosure at a road-junction, causing traffic to go ~ instead of across.

A roundabout (2)

roun·ders *n.* ball game. ~**ly** *adv.* with vigour ; bluntly : *tell sb. ~ly that he is behaving badly*. **'rounds·man** *n.* tradesman or his employee going ~ (to customers' houses) to ask for and to deliver orders.

rouse [rauz] *v.t. & i.* **1.** wake

(*up*). **2.** cause (sb.) to be more active, interested, etc.: ~ *sb. to action*; ~*d to anger* (made angry) *by insults*; *rousing cheers*.

¹**rout** [raut] *v.t. & n.* (cause) complete defeat and disorderly flight.

²**rout** [raut] *v.i.* ~ *sb. up* (*out*), force him out (of bed, etc.).

route [ru:t] *n.* way taken or planned from one place to another. '~**-march** *n.* march made by soldiers in training.

rou·tine [ru:'ti:n] *n.* fixed and regular way of doing things: *a matter of* ~; *the* ~ (i.e. usual) *procedure*.

rove [rouv] *v.i.* roam; wander.

¹**row** [rou] *n.* line of persons or things: *a row of houses*; (esp.) line of seats: *sitting in the front row*.

²**row** [rou] *v.t. & i.* move (a boat) by using oars; carry or take (sb. or sth.) in a boat with oars: *row sb. across a river.* *n.* journey or outing in a rowing-boat: *go for a row.* **row·lock** ['rolək] *n.* pivot for an oar on the side of a boat.

³**row** [rau] *n.* **1.** noisy or violent argument or quarrel: *have a row with one's neighbours*; (colloq.) uproar. **2.** trouble: *get into a row for being late at the office.*

row·dy ['raudi] *adj.* (*-ier, -iest*) *& n.* rough and noisy (person). **row·di·ly** *adv.* **row·di·ness** *n.* **row·dy·ism** *n.* rowdy behaviour.

roy·al ['roiəl] *adj.* of, like, suitable for, belonging to the family of, a king or queen: *His R~ Highness*; *the R~ Navy.* ~**ly** *adv.* ~**ist** *n.* supporter of (government by) a king. ~**ty** *n.* **1.** ~ persons: *in the presence of* ~*ty*. **2.** position, dignity, power, etc., of a ~ person. **3.** payment of money by a mining company to the owner of land (e.g. *oil* ~*ties*); sum (to be) paid to the owner of a copyright or patent.

rub [rʌb] *v.t. & i.* (*-bb-*). **1.** move (one thing) backwards and forwards on the surface of (another): *rub one's hands with soap*;

rub one's hands together; *rub oil on the skin*; *rub sth. out* (*off*), remove (esp. marks) by rubbing. **2.** dry, clean, polish, bring a surface to a certain condition, by rubbing: *rub up the silver spoons. rub up your French*, (fig.) freshen your knowledge of it. *n.* **1.** act of rubbing. **2.** sth. that causes trouble.

¹**rub·ber** ['rʌbə*] *n.* **1.** elastic substance made from the juice of certain trees and used for making tyres, balls, etc. **2.** person or thing that rubs; sth. used for rubbing, esp. (also *india*~) for rubbing out pencil marks.

²**rub·ber** ['rʌbə*] *n.* (cards) three successive games between the same sides: *win the* ~, win two games in succession or two out of three.

rub·bish ['rʌbiʃ] *n.* **1.** waste material; things thrown away or destroyed as worthless. **2.** nonsense.

rub·ble ['rʌbl] *n.* bits of broken stone, rock, or brickwork.

ru·bi·cund ['ru:bikənd] *adj.* (of a person's face) ruddy.

ru·bric ['ru:brik] *n.* title or heading printed in red or special type, esp. a direction given in a prayer-book.

ru·by ['ru:bi] *n.* red jewel; deep red colour.

¹**ruck** [rʌk] *n. the* (*common*) ~, ordinary commonplace people or things.

²**ruck** [rʌk] *n.* irregular fold or crease (esp. in cloth). *v.i. & t.* (often ~ *up*) make into ~s; be pulled into ~s.

ruck·sack ['ruksæk] *n.* canvas bag strapped on one's back.

ruc·tion ['rʌkʃən] *n.* (usu. pl.) (colloq.) quarrel; angry words or protest.

rud·der ['rʌdə*] *n.* flat broad piece of wood or metal hinged on the stern of a boat or ship for steering.

rud·dy ['rʌdi] *adj.* (*-ier, -iest*). (of the face) red, as showing good health: ~ *cheeks.*

rude [ru:d] *adj.* (*-r, -st*). **1.** (of a person, his behaviour, speech, etc.) impolite; not showing respect or consideration. **2.** startling; violent; rough: *get a ~ shock.* **3.** primitive; without refinement: *our ~ forefathers.* **4.** roughly made; simple: *the ~ ornaments made by the Saxons.* **~·ly** *adv.* **~·ness** *n.*

ru·di·ment ['ru:dimənt] *n.* **1.** (pl.) first steps or stages (of an art or science). **2.** (in animals and plants) imperfectly developed part or organ. **ru·di·men·ta·ry** [,ru:di'mentəri] *adj.* **1.** elementary. **2.** undeveloped; having stopped at an early stage.

rue [ru:] *v.t.* repent of; think of with sadness or regret.

ruff [rʌf] *n.* **1.** ring of differently coloured or marked feathers round a bird's neck or of hair round an animal's neck. **2.** wide stiff frill worn as a collar (16th century).

ruf·fian ['rʌfjən] *n.* violent, cruel man.

ruf·fle ['rʌfl] *v.t. & i.* disturb the peace, calm, or smoothness of: *easily ~d,* easily made bad-tempered, annoyed. *n.* strip of material gathered into folds; frill used to ornament a dress.

rug [rʌg] *n.* **1.** floor mat of thick material. **2.** thick, usu. woollen, covering or wrap: *a travelling-~.*

Rug·by ['rʌgbi] *n.* *R~* football, form of football played by two teams of usu. fifteen players using an oval-shaped ball which may be handled.

rug·ged ['rʌgid] *adj.* **1.** rough; uneven; rocky: *a ~ coast.* **2.** irregular; wrinkled: *~ features* (i.e. face). **3.** rough but kindly and honest: *a ~ old peasant; ~ manners.*

rug·ger ['rʌgə*] *n.* (colloq.) Rugby football.

ru·in ['ru:in] *n.* **1.** destruction; overthrow; serious damage: *the ~ of my hopes; bring sb. or sth. to ~.* **2.** cause of this: *Gambling was his ~.* **3.** sth., esp. a building, that has fallen to pieces: *The old fort is now only a ~.* *in ~s,* having fallen to pieces. *v.t.* cause the ~ of: *crops ~ed by the storm; be ~ed,* have lost one's

property, position, etc. **~·a·tion** [,ru:i'neiʃən] *n.* being ~ed; bringing to ~. **~·ous** ['ru:inəs] *adj.* causing ~; in ~s.

rule [ru:l] *n.* **1.** law or custom that guides or controls behaviour or action; decision made by an organization, etc., about what must or must not be done: *obey the ~s of the game; the ~(s) of the road,* ~s for driving cars, etc., safely along the road. **2.** that which is usually done; habit: *Make it a ~ to read one English book a week. as a ~,* usually, more often than not. **3.** government; authority: *the ~ of the people; under French ~.* **4.** strip of wood, etc., used to measure: *a foot-~* (12 inches long). *v.t. & i.* **1.** govern; have authority (*over*): *~ the country; ~ over a large empire.* **2.** *~ sth. out,* declare that it cannot be considered, etc. **3.** give as a decision (*that*). **4.** *~ a line,* make a line on paper with a *~r; ~ paper,* make parallel lines on paper with a *~r; ~ sth. off,* separate it by ruling a line. **rul·er** *n.* **1.** person who ~s(1). **2.** straight strip of wood, metal, etc., used for drawing straight lines. **rul·ing** *n.* (esp.) decision made by sb. in authority, esp. a judge.

¹**rum** [rʌm] *n.* alcoholic drink made from sugar-cane juice.

²**rum** [rʌm] *adj.* (colloq.) queer; odd.

rum·ble ['rʌmbl] *v.i. & n.* (make a) deep heavy continuous sound: *thunder (gun-fire) rumbling in the distance.*

ru·mi·nate ['ru:mineit] *v.i.* turn over in the mind; meditate.

rum·mage ['rʌmidʒ] *v.i. & t.* turn things over, move things about, while looking for sth.: *~ in a drawer; ~ through old papers.* ¹**~-sale** *n.* sale of old articles for charity.

ru·mour ['ru:mə*] *n.* hearsay: *according to ~.* *v.t.* tell as ~: *It is ~ed that. . . .*

rump [rʌmp] *n.* animal's buttocks.

rum·ple ['rʌmpl] *v.t.* crease; crumple.

rum·pus ['rʌmpəs] *n.* (colloq.) disturbance; noise; uproar.

¹run [rʌn] *v.i. & t.* (-nn-; p.t. *ran*, p.p. *run*). **1.** (of men and animals) move with quick steps, faster than when walking. **2.** (of vehicles) go along; make a journey: *The buses run every ten minutes.* **3.** (of machines, etc.) keep going: *leave the engine running.* **4.** (of liquids) flow; cause to flow: *leave the water (the tap) running.* **5.** become; get: *run into debt; run short of money; supplies running low.* **6.** (cause to) pass or move quickly or lightly (over, through, etc.): *A shiver ran down his spine. Doubts kept running through his mind. He ran his fingers over the keys of the piano. She ran a comb through her hair. He ran his eyes over the page.* **7.** (of roads, lines, etc.) go; extend: *The road runs due north. Shelves ran round two walls.* **8.** (of colours in a material) spread when wet: *Will the dye run when the blouse is washed?* **9.** force; cause (sth.) to go (against, into, through): *run a splinter into one's finger; run one's head against a wall.* **10.** control, manage (a business, a theatre, the home). **11.** (of a play in the theatre) continue to be performed; (of an agreement) continue in force; (of the sale of books) reach: *The book ran into (through) six editions.* **12.** *run a risk*, take the chance. **13.** get past: *run a blockade.* **14.** get (goods) into a country illegally: *engaged in running contraband.* **15.** be a candidate (for). (Cf. *stand for.*) **16.** cause to run (a horse in a race). **17.** (of a series of words, musical notes) have, be in, a certain order: *How does the verse run?* **18.** (of woven or knitted materials) become unwoven; drop stitches. **19.** be on the average; tend to be: *prices running high.* **20.** (with adv. & prep.): *run across (sb. or sth.)*, meet or find by chance. *run after (sb.)*, try to catch. *run away*, try to escape. (of expenses) *run away with* (a lot of money, etc.), use it up. *run down*, (of a clock, etc.) stop because the spring is un-wound. *be run down*, (of a person) be tired, exhausted. *run (sb.) down*, say unkind things about him. *run sb. in*, (of the police) arrest him and put him in prison. *run into*, collide with, meet unexpectedly. *run on*, be joined together; continue; talk continuously. *run out (of)*, become exhausted; have no more. *run over*, (of a vessel or its contents) overflow. *run over sb. or sth.*, knock down and pass over: *The dog was run over by a bus. run up (a flag)*, raise. *run up (a bill, etc.)*, let the bill, etc., grow larger. **'run·a·way** *n.* (often attrib.) (horse, person, etc.) running away: *a runaway slave.* **run·ner** *n.* **1.** person, animal, etc. that runs. **2.** (in compounds) smuggler: *gun-runners.* **3.** messenger. **4.** part on which sth. slides: *the runners of a sledge.* **5.** stem coming from a plant and taking root: *strawberry runners.* **6.** long piece of cloth (for a side-board, etc.); long piece of carpet. **'run·ner-'up** *n.* person taking the second place in a competition. **run·ning** *adj.* **1.** done, made, carried on, while running: *a running jump.* **2.** continuous, uninterrupted: *a running commentary,* a description given while the event is taking place. **3.** (after a plural noun) one after the other with nothing in between: *five times (nights) running.* **4.** with liquid coming out: *a running tap (sore).* *n. in (out of) the running,* having (not having) a chance of success in a race, etc.: *make the running,* be the leading runner; set the pace.

²run [rʌn] *n.* **1.** act of running; drive(1): *go for a run; on the run,* running away; continuously busy. **2.** (usu. large enclosed) space for domestic animals: *a chicken run; a cattle run.* **3.** quick fall: *prices coming down with a run.* **4.** series of performances: *The play had a run of six* months. **5.** unit of score in cricket and baseball. **6.** period; succession: *a run of ill luck*; *in the long run*, finally. **7.** *have*, *give sb.*, *the run of (the house)*, the right to enter it, use it, etc. **8.** *a run on the bank*, a rush by many people to withdraw money. **9.** *the common run of mankind*, ordinary, average people. **10.** (music) series of notes sung or played quickly and in the order of the scale. **'run·way** *n.* (esp.) track on which aircraft move when taking off and landing.

¹rung, see *²ring.*

²rung [rʌŋ] *n.* crosspiece forming a step in a ladder or joining the legs of a chair to strengthen it.

ru·pee [ru:'pi:] *n.* monetary unit in India, Pakistan, etc.

rup·ture ['rʌptʃə*] *n.* act of breaking apart or bursting; ending of friendly relations. *v.t.* break (e.g. a blood-vessel); end (a connexion, etc.).

ru·ral ['ruərəl] *adj.* in, of, characteristic of, suitable for, the country: ~ *life (customs).* (Cf. *urban.*)

ruse [ru:z] *n.* trick; deceitful way of doing sth., getting sth.

¹rush [rʌʃ] *v.i.* & *t.* **1.** (cause to) go or come with violence or speed: ~*ing out of school*; ~*ing fresh troops to the front.* **2.** act quickly and without enough thought. **3.** capture by a sudden attack; get through or over by pressing eagerly forward: ~ *the gates of the sports ground.* *n.* act of ~*ing*: *swept away by the ~ of the flood*; *the ~-hours* (when, in a big town, everyone is travelling to or from work).

²rush [rʌʃ] *n.* (tall stem of) marsh plant.

rusk [rʌsk] *n.* piece of bread baked hard and crisp; kind of crisp biscuit.

rus·set ['rʌsit] *adj.* & *n.* reddish brown; apple with rough ~ skin.

rust [rʌst] *n.* reddish-brown coating formed on iron by the action of water and air. *v.t.* & *i.* (cause to) become covered with ~; (fig.) become poor in quality because not used. ~**·y** *adj.*

(*-ier*, *-iest*). covered with ~; (fig. of a person) out of practice (3).

rus·tic ['rʌstik] *adj.* **1.** rural; in rough, country style. **2.** of country people (contrasted with smart city people); simple: ~ *dress*; ~ *speech.* *n.* peasant; simple country person.

rus·tle ['rʌsl] *n.* gentle light sound (as of leaves moved by a breeze). *v.t.* & *i.* make this sound; move with such a sound.

rut [rʌt] *n.* line or track made by wheel(s) in soft ground. *get into a rut*, get into a fixed way of living so that it becomes difficult to change.

ruth·less ['ru:θlis] *adj.* cruel; without pity; showing no mercy.

rye [rai] *n.* (plant with) grain used for making flour and as animal fodder.

S

Sab·bath ['sæbəθ] *n.* weekly day of rest, Saturday for Jews, Sunday for Christians.

sa·ble ['seibl] *n.* (valuable fur of) small dark-coated animal. *adj.* (liter.) black.

sab·o·tage ['sæbətɑ:ʒ] *n.* & *v.t.* (take part in) the wilful damaging of machinery, materials, etc., during an industrial or political dispute or during war; commit ~ on; wreck (a plan, etc.). **sab·o·teur** [ˌsæbə'tə:*] *n.* person who commits ~.

sa·bre ['seibə*] *n.* sword with a curved blade used by soldiers on horseback.

sa·chet ['sæʃei] *n.* small scented bag: *a handkerchief ~.*

¹sack [sæk] *n.* large bag of strong material (for heavy goods, e.g. coal, flour, potatoes). *v.t.* put (things) into ~s. **'~·cloth** *n.* woven material of which ~s are made. (*clothed*) *in ~cloth and ashes*, (fig.) showing regret and grief. ~**·ing** *n.* ~cloth.

²sack [sæk] *v.t.* (colloq.) dismiss (sb.) from employment. *n.* *get* the ~, be dismissed; give sb. the ~, dismiss him.

²sack [sæk] **v.t.** rob, plunder violently (a town, etc., captured in war). **n.** act of plundering (a captured town, etc.).

sac·ra·ment ['sækrəmənt] **n.** solemn religious ceremony in the Christian Church (e.g. Baptism, Marriage); (esp.) Holy Communion. **sac·ra·men·tal** [ˌsækrə'mentl] **adj.** of a ~: the ~al wine.

sa·cred ['seikrid] **adj.** 1. of God; connected with religion: a ~ building (e.g. a church); ~ music. 2. solemn: a ~ promise. **~·ly** **adv.** **~·ness n.**

sac·ri·fice ['sækrifais] **n.** 1. the offering of sth. precious to a god; the thing offered: the ~ of an ox to Jupiter. 2. the giving up of sth. of value to oneself for a special purpose or to benefit sb. else: parents who make ~s (go without things) in order to educate their children. 3. sth. given up in this way. 4. sell sth. at a ~, sell it below its true value. **v.t. & i.** make a ~; give up as a ~ (2): He ~ed his life to save the child from drowning. **sac·ri·fi·cial** [ˌsækri'fiʃl] **adj.** of, like, a ~.

sac·ri·lege ['sækrilidʒ] **n.** disrespectful treatment of, injury to, what should be sacred. **sac·ri·le·gious** [ˌsækri'lidʒəs] **adj.**

sac·ro·sanct ['sækrousæŋkt] **adj.** (to be) protected from all harm, because sacred or holy.

sad [sæd] **adj.** (-dd-). unhappy; causing unhappy feelings. **sad·ly** **adv.** **sad·ness n.** **sad·den** ['sædn] **v.t. & i.** make or become sad.

sad·dle ['sædl] **n.** 1. leather seat for a rider on a horse or bicycle. 2. line or ridge of high land rising at each end to a high point. **v.t.** 1. put a ~ on (a horse). 2. put a heavy responsibility on (sb.): ~d with big debts. '**~·bag n.** one of a pair of bags laid over a horse's back; small bag (e.g. for tools) hung on a bicycle ~. **sad·dler n.** maker of ~s and leather goods for horses.

sa·dism ['seidizm] **n.** enjoyment

of cruelty; cruelty inflicted for pleasure. **sa·dist n.** person who gets pleasure from cruelty. **sa·dis·tic** [sə'distik] **adj.**

sa·fa·ri [sə'fɑːri] **n.** overland journey, esp. in East and Central Africa. (Cf. trek.)

safe [seif] **adj.** (-r, -st). 1. free from, protected from, danger. 2. unhurt or undamaged. 3. not causing or likely to cause harm or danger: travelling at a ~ speed. 4. cautious; not taking risks: a ~ driver; on the ~ side, with more precaution than may be necessary. **n.** 1. metal chest, with a strong lock, for keeping valuables in. 2. cool airy cupboard for food: a meat-~. '**~·conduct n.** (document giving) the right to visit or pass through a dangerous area, esp. in time of war. '**~·guard n.** something that gives protection, prevents harm. **v.t.** protect. '**~·keeping n.** care; keeping ~. **~·ly** **adv.** **~·ty n.** being ~; freedom from danger: play for ~ty, take no risks; in ~ty, ~ly; ~ty-pin, one with a guard for the point; ~ty-valve, one that releases pressure when it becomes too great; (fig.) way of releasing feelings of anger, etc., harmlessly.

sag [sæg] **v.i.** (-gg-). 1. sink or curve down in the middle under weight or pressure: a sagging roof. 2. hang down unevenly; hang sideways. **n.** (degree of) sagging.

sa·ga ['sɑːgə] **n.** old story of heroic deeds, esp. of Icelandic or Norwegian heroes.

sa·ga·cious [sə'geiʃəs] **adj.** showing wisdom, common sense, or (of animals) intelligence. **sa·gac·i·ty** [sə'gæsiti] **n.** sound judgement.

¹sage [seidʒ] **adj.** (-r, -st). wise. **n.** wise man; man who is believed to be wise. **~·ly** **adv.**

²sage [seidʒ] **n.** garden plant with grey-green leaves used to flavour food.

sa·go ['seigou] **n.** starchy food, in the form of hard, white grains, made from the pith of certain palm-trees.

sa·hib ['sɑːhib] *n.* (Indian title) sir; gentleman.

said, see *say.*

sail [seil] *n.* **1.** sheet of canvas spread to catch the wind and move a boat or ship forward: *under* ~, with ~s spread; *in full* ~, with all ~s spread; *set* ~, begin a voyage. **2.** short excursion on water for pleasure: *go for a* ~. **3.** ~ing-ship: *a fleet of fifty* ~. *v.i. & t.* **1.** move forward across the sea, a lake, etc., by means of a ~ or ~s. **2.** begin a voyage. **3.** voyage across or on: ~ *the Pacific.* **4.** control (a boat). **5.** move smoothly like a ship with ~s. ~·**or** *n.* **1.** seaman; member of a ship's crew. **2.** *a bad* (*good*)~*or*, a person (not) usually seasick in rough weather.

saint [seint] *n.* **1.** holy person. **2.** one declared by the Church to have won by his holy living on earth a place in Heaven. ~·**ed** ['seintid] *adj.* declared to be, regarded as, a ~. ~·**ly** *adj.* (*-ier, -iest*). very holy or good; like a ~. ~·**li·ness** *n.*

saith [seθ] *v.* (old use) says.

sake [seik] *n. for the* ~ *of, for my* (*your, the country's, etc.*) ~*, for the welfare or interest of; because of an interest in or desire for: *be patient for the* ~ *of peace.*

sa·laam [sə'lɑːm] *n.* oriental greeting meaning 'peace'; low bow.

sal·a·ble ['seiləbl] *adj.* suitable for selling; likely to sell.

sal·ad ['sæləd] *n.* **1.** uncooked (and usu. green) vegetables (lettuce, onion, celery, etc.) prepared as food: ~ *dressing*, mixture of oil, vinegar, cream, etc., used with ~s. **2.** mixture of different kinds of cold food prepared with ~ (1): *fish* ~; *chicken* ~. **3.** *fruit* ~, mixed sliced fruits.

sal·a·ry ['sæləri] *n.* (usu. monthly or quarterly) payment for regular employment on a yearly basis: *a* ~ *of £900 per annum.* (Cf. *a weekly wage.*) **sal·a·ried** *adj.* receiving a ~.

sale [seil] *n.* **1.** exchange of goods for money; act of selling sth.: *on* (*for*) ~, offered for pur-

chase. **2.** the offering of goods at low prices for a period (to get rid of old stock, etc.). **3.** occasion when goods or property are put up for ~ by auction. **'sales·man, 'sales·,wo·man** *n.* person selling goods in a shop or (on behalf of wholesalers) to shopkeepers. **'sales·man·ship** *n.* skill in selling goods.

sa·lient ['seiljənt] *adj.* outstanding; easily noticed: *the* ~ *points of a speech.* *n.* forward wedge driven into the enemy's battle front.

sa·line ['seilain] *adj.* containing salt.

sa·li·va [sə'laivə] *n.* the natural liquid present in the mouth; spittle.

sal·low ['sælou] *adj.* (of the skin) of an unhealthy yellow colour.

sal·ly ['sæli] *n.* **1.** sudden breaking-out by soldiers who are surrounded by the enemy: *make a successful* ~. **2.** witty remark. *v.i.* **1.** make a ~(1). **2.** ~ *forth* (*out*) go out (on a journey, for a walk).

salm·on ['sæmən] *n.* (pl. unchanged). large fish valued for food; the colour of ~ flesh, orange-pink.

sal·on ['sælon] *n.* **1.** large room for entertaining guests. **2.** (place for) exhibition of works of art.

sa·loon [sə'luːn] *n.* **1.** room for social use in a ship, public house, etc.: *the ship's dining*-~; *the* ~ *bar* (for drinks in a hotel, etc.). **2.** (U.S.A.) place where alcoholic drinks are bought and drunk. (Cf. *public house.*) **3.** motor-car with wholly enclosed seating space for 4–7 passengers.

salt [soːlt] *n.* **1.** white substance obtained from mines, present in sea-water, used to flavour and preserve food. *take* (*a statement*) *with a grain of* ~, feel doubt about whether it is altogether true. *not worth one's* ~, not deserving one's pay. *the* ~ *of the earth,* the finest citizens. **2.** (chemistry) chemical compound of a metal and an acid. **3.** *an old* ~, an experienced sailor. *v.t.* put ~ on or in food. *adj.* (also ~·**y**) containing ~; tasting of ~.

sa·lu·bri·ous [sə'lu:briəs] *adj.* (esp. of climate) health-giving.

sal·u·tar·y ['sælju:təri] *adj.* having a good effect (on body or mind): ~ *exercise* (*advice*).

sal·u·ta·tion [ˌsælju'teiʃən] *n.* (act or expression of) greeting: *raise one's hat in* ~.

sa·lute [sə'lu:t] *n.* sth. done to welcome sb. or to show respect or honour, esp. (military ~) the raising of the hand to the forehead, the firing of guns, the lowering and raising of a flag. *v.t. & i.* 1. make a ~ to (sb.). 2. greet (with a bow, by raising the hat, etc.).

sal·vage ['sælvidʒ] *n.* 1. the saving of property from loss (by fire or other disaster). 2. (payment due for saving) such property. 3. waste materials (e.g. paper, to be collected and re-used). *v.t.* save from loss in a fire, wreck, etc.

sal·va·tion [sæl'veiʃən] *n.* 1. the act of saving, the state of having been saved, from the power of sin. 2. that which saves sb. from loss, disaster, etc.

salve [sælv] *n.* 1. oily substance used on wounds, sores, or burns. 2. (fig.) sth. that comforts wounded feelings or soothes an uneasy conscience. *v.t.* 1. put ~(1)on. 2. be a ~(2) to.

sal·ver ['sælvə*] *n.* tray, usu. round and made of silver or other metal, on which letters, drinks, etc., are presented.

sal·vo ['sælvou] *n.* (pl. *-oes, -os*). the firing of a number of guns together (e.g. as a salute).

same [seim] *adj. & pron.* (with *the*). 1. unchanged; not different; identical: *We have lived in the* ~ *house for twenty years. He is the* ~ *age as his wife.* 2. come to the ~ *thing*, make no difference; *be all (just) the* ~ *to*, make no difference to; *all the* ~, in spite of the fact that, although that is the case; *at the* ~ *time*, however, nevertheless, yet. *adv. the* ~, in the same way: *If you leave me I shall never feel the* ~ *again*.

sam·pan ['sæmpæn] *n.* small flat-bottomed boat used in China.

sam·ple ['sɑ:mpl] *n.* specimen; one of a number, part of a whole, taken to show what the rest is like. *v.t.* take a ~ or ~s of; test a part of.

san·a·to·ri·um [ˌsænə'tɔ:riəm] *n.* hospital, esp. one for people with weak lungs or for convalescent people.

sanc·ti·fy ['sæŋktifai] *v.t.* make holy; set apart as sacred. **sanc·ti·fi·ca·tion** [ˌsæŋktifi'keiʃən] *n.*

sanc·ti·mo·nious [ˌsæŋkti'mounjəs] *adj.* making a show of sanctity.

sanc·tion ['sæŋkʃən] *n.* 1. right or permission given by authority to do sth. 2. approval, encouragement (of behaviour, etc.), by general custom or tradition. 3. penalty intended to restore respect for law or authority: ~*s against aggressors.* *v.t.* give ~ (1), (2) to.

sanc·ti·ty ['sæŋktiti] *n.* holiness; sacredness.

sanc·tu·a·ry ['sæŋktuəri] *n.* 1. holy or sacred place, esp. a church. 2. (historical) place (esp. church altar) where persons were protected by Church law. 3. *bird* ~, area where wild birds are left undisturbed.

sanc·tum ['sæŋktəm] *n.* 1. holy place. 2. (colloq.) person's private room.

sand [sænd] *n.* 1. tiny grains of worn rock as seen on the seashore, in deserts, etc. 2. *the* ~*s*, expanse of ~ exposed at low tide. '~**bag** *n.* bag filled with ~ used as a defence. '~·**pa·per** *n.* strong paper with ~ glued to it, used for rubbing rough surfaces smooth. '~·**stone** *n.* rock formed mostly of ~. ~·**y** *adj.* (*-ier, -iest*). 1. covered with ~. 2. (esp. of hair) yellowish red.

san·dal ['sændl] *n.* kind of shoe made of a sole with straps to hold it on the foot.

sand·wich ['sænwidʒ] *n.* two slices of bread with meat, etc., between. *v.t.* put (one thing, or person) between two others, esp. where there is little space.

sane [sein] *adj.* (*-r, -st*). 1. healthy

in mind, not mad. **2.** sensible: ~ *views* (*policies*). ~**·ly** *adv.*

sang, see *sing*.

sang-froid ['sɑːŋ'frwɑː] (Fr.) *n.* calmness in face of danger.

san·gui·na·ry ['sæŋgwinəri] *adj.* with much bloodshed: *a* ~ *battle*; fond of bloodshed; delighting in cruel acts: *a* ~ *ruler*.

san·guine ['sæŋgwin] *adj.* **1.** hopeful; optimistic. **2.** redfaced.

san·i·ta·ry ['sænitəri] *adj.* **1.** clean; free from dirt which might cause disease: ~ *conditions*. **2.** of, concerned with, the protection of health. **san·i·ta·tion** [ˌsæni'teiʃən] *n.* arrangements to give ~ conditions (e.g. for the removal of sewage).

san·i·ty ['sæniti] *n.* being sane; soundness of judgement.

sank, see *sink*.

¹**sap** [sæp] *n.* liquid in a plant, carrying necessary food to all parts. *v.t.* (-*pp*-). drain off sap; weaken; take away the life and strength of: *sapped by disease* (*an unhealthy climate*). **sap·ling** *n.* young tree. **sap·py** *adj.* full of sap; young and vigorous.

²**sap** [sæp] *n.* tunnel or covered trench made to get nearer to the enemy. *v.t. & i.* (-*pp*-). make a sap; weaken (a wall, etc.) by digging under it; (fig.) destroy (sb.'s faith, confidence, etc.). **sap·per** *n.* soldier engaged in engineering work (e.g. road and bridge building).

sap·phire ['sæfaiə*] *n.* clear, bright, blue jewel.

sar·casm ['sɑːkæzm] *n.* (use of) bitter remarks intended to wound the feelings. **sar·cas·tic** [sɑː'kæstik] *adj.* of, using, ~. **sar·cas·ti·cal·ly** *adv.*

sar·coph·a·gus [sɑː'kɒfəgəs] *n.* stone coffin (esp. as used in ancient times).

sar·dine [sɑː'diːn] *n.* small fish (usu.) tinned in oil.

sar·don·ic [sɑː'dɒnik] *adj.* scornful; mocking. **sar·don·i·cal·ly** *adv.*

sa·ri ['sɑːri] *n.* length of cotton or silk material draped round the body, worn by Hindu women.

sa·rong [sə'rɒŋ] *n.* broad strip of material wrapped round the middle of the body by Malays.

sar·to·ri·al [sɑː'tɔːriəl] *adj.* of tailors and their work; of men's clothing.

¹**sash** [sæʃ] *n.* narrow strip of cloth worn over clothing round the waist or one shoulder for ornament or as part of a uniform.

²**sash** [sæʃ] *n.* ~ *window,* one that slides up and down (cf. *casement*); ~*cord,* cord (with weight) running over a pulley to keep the window balanced in any desired position.

sat, see *sit*.

Sa·tan ['seitn] *n.* the Evil One; the Devil. ~**·ic** [sə'tænik] *adj.* of ~; wicked.

satch·el ['sætʃl] *n.* leather or canvas bag, as for schoolbooks.

sate [seit] *v.t.* = satiate.

sat·el·lite ['sætəlait] *n.* **1.** planet moving round another: *The moon is a* ~ *of the earth.* **2.** artificial object put in orbit round the earth. **3.** (fig.) person, State, depending upon and taking the lead from another.

sa·ti·ate ['seiʃieit] *v.t.* satisfy (too) fully. ~*d with food* (*pleasure*). **sa·ti·e·ty** [sə'taiəti] *n.* condition or feeling of being ~d.

sat·in ['sætin] *n.* silk material smooth and shiny on one side. *adj.* like ~.

sat·ire ['sætaiə*] *n.* form of writing holding up a person or society to ridicule or showing the foolishness of an idea, custom, etc.; piece of writing that does this. **sa·tir·i·cal** [sə'tirikl] *adj.* **sa·tir·i·cal·ly** *adv.* **sat·i·rist** ['sætərist] *n.* writer of ~(s). **sat·i·rize** ['sætəraiz] *v.t.* attack with ~(s).

sat·is·fy ['sætisfai] *v.t.* **1.** give (sb.) what he wants or needs; make contented. **2.** be enough for (one's needs); be equal to (what one hopes or desires). **3.** convince (sb., oneself, *of* sth., *that* . . .). **sat·is·fac·tion** [ˌsætis'fækʃən] *n.* ~*ing* or being satisfied; sth. that satisfies; feeling of pleasure. **sat·is·fac·to·ry** [ˌsætis'fæktəri] *adj.* giving pleasure or satisfaction; ~ing a need or desire; good enough for a purpose. **sat·is·fac·to·ri·ly** *adv.*

sat·u·rate ['sætʃəreit] *v.t.* **1.** make thoroughly wet; soak with moisture (or, fig., *with* learning, prejudice, etc.). **2.** (science) cause (one substance) to absorb the greatest possible amount of another: *a ~d solution of salt.* **sat·u·ra·tion** [ˌsætʃə'reiʃən] *n.*

Sat·ur·day ['sætədi] *n.* the seventh day of the week.

sat·ur·nine ['sætə:nain] *adj.* gloomy.

sat·yr ['sætə*] *n.* (Greek and Roman stories) immortal creature, half man and half animal.

sauce [so:s] *n.* **1.** liquid served with food to give it extra flavour. **2.** (colloq.) impudence. **sau·cy** *adj.* (*-ier, -iest*). impudent. **sau·ci·ly** *adv.*

sauce·pan ['so:spən] *n.* deep, round, metal cooking pot, usu. with a lid and a handle.

sau·cer ['so:sə*] *n.* small circular dish on which a cup stands.

saun·ter ['so:ntə*] *v.i.* walk in a leisurely way. *n.* leisurely walk.

saus·age ['sosidʒ] *n.* chopped-up meat, etc., flavoured and stuffed into a tube of skin; one section of such a tube.

sav·age ['sævidʒ] *adj.* **1.** in a primitive or uncivilized state: ~ *tribes* (*countries*). **2.** fierce; cruel. *n.* a person. ~·**ry** ['sæv-idʒri] *n.* ~(1) condition; ~(2) behaviour.

sa·van·na(h) [sə'vænə] *n.* treeless plain (esp. of Central America).

sav·ant ['sævənt] *n.* man (esp. scientist) of great learning.

save [seiv] *v.t. & i.* **1.** make or keep safe (from loss, injury, etc.): ~ *sb. from drowning;* ~ *sb.'s life;* ~ *a person from himself,* from the results of his own foolishness. **2.** keep or store for future use (esp. ~ of money): ~ *half your salary;* ~ *some of the meat for tomorrow.* **3.** avoid; make unnecessary: *If you walk, you'll* ~ *spending money on bus fares.* **4.** keep (sb.) from the

necessity to use (money, etc.): *That will* ~ *me a lot of trouble.* **5.** (in the Christian religion) set free from the power of (or eternal punishment for) sin. **prep. & conj.** except: *all* ~ *him.*

sav·ing *adj.* the saving grace of (*humour, etc.*), the one good quality that redeems sb. from other bad qualities. *n.* **1.** way of saving; amount that is ~d; *a saving of time and money.* **2.** (pl.) money ~d up: *Keep your savings in the bank.* **'sav·ings-bank** *n.* bank which holds, gives interest on, small savings(2).

sav·iour ['seivjə*] *n.* person who rescues, saves, sb. from danger. *The S~, Our S~,* Jesus Christ.

sa·vour ['seivə*] *n.* taste or flavour (*of* sth.); suggestion (*of* a quality). *v.i.* ~ *of,* suggest. ~·**y** *n. & adj.* (food dish) having a sharp or salt, not a sweet, taste.

¹saw, see *see.*

²saw [so:] *n.* wood- or metal-cutting tool with a tooth-edged steel blade. *v.t. & i.* (p.t. *sawed,* p.p. *sawn* [so:n]). use a saw: *saw sth. up,* cut it into pieces with a saw. **'saw·dust** *n.* tiny bits of wood falling off when wood is sawn. **'saw·mill** *n.* workshop, etc., where wood is sawn by machinery. **'saw·yer** *n.* man whose work is sawing wood.

sax·o·phone ['sæksəfoun] *n.* musical wind-instrument made of brass.

say [sei] *v.t. & i.* (pres. t., 3rd person sing. *says* [sez], p.t. & p.p. *said* [sed]). **1.** use one's voice to utter words, sentences: *Say ' Thank you' when you are given something. Now say it again.* **2.** *What do you say to* . . .? What do you think about (the suggestion, etc.)? *go without saying,* be obvious. *that is to say,* in other words. *n.* have (*say*) *one's say,* state one's opinions, views. *have a say in the matter,* have an opportunity to share in a discussion, decision. **say·ing** *n.* common remark: *It was a saying of his that.* . . .

scab [skæb] *n.* **1.** dry crust

formed over a wound or sore.
2. skin disease (esp. of sheep).
3. (colloq.) blackleg. ~**·by** *adj.*
covered with ~s.

scab·bard ['skæbəd] *n.* case for
the blade of a sword, dagger, or
bayonet.

sca·bies ['skeibi:z] *n.* kind of skin
disease.

scaf·fold ['skæfəld] *n.* **1.** structure put up for workmen and
materials around a building
which is being erected or repaired. **2.** platform on which
criminals are executed. ~**·ing**
n. (materials for a) ~ (e.g. poles,
planks, steel tubes).

scald [skɔ:ld] *v.t.* **1.** hurt with
hot liquid or steam : ~ *one's hand
with hot fat.* **2.** clean (dishes,
etc.) with boiling water or
steam. **3.** heat (milk) almost
to boiling-point. *n.* injury from
hot liquid or steam.

¹scale [skeil] *n.* **1.** series of marks
at regular intervals for the
purpose of measuring (as on a
ruler or a thermometer). **2.**
system of units for measuring:
the decimal ~. **3.** tool or instrument marked for measuring. **4.**
arrangement in steps or degrees: *a* ~ *of wages; a person
who is high in the social* ~. **5.**
proportion between the size of
sth. and the map, plan, diagram, etc., which represents it:
a map on the ~ *of one inch to a
mile.* **6.** relative size, extent,
etc.: *making preparations on a
large* ~. **7.** (music) series of
tones arranged in order of
pitch, esp. a series of eight starting on a keynote. *v.t.* **1.** climb
(a wall, cliff, etc.) (with a ladder,
etc.). **2.** make a copy or representation of, according to a
certain ~(5). **3.** ~ *up (down)*, increase (decrease) by a certain
proportion: *All prices (wages)
were* ~d *up ten per cent.*

²scale [skeil] *n.* **1.** one of the two
pans of a balance. **2.** (pl. often
pair of ~s). balance; instrument
for measuring weight. *turn the*
~(s), decide the result of sth.
which is in doubt; *hold the* ~s
even, judge fairly (between).

²Scales (2)

³scale [skeil] *n.* **1.** one of the
thin, flat plates of hard material
covering the skin of some fishes
and reptiles. **2.** chalky deposit
inside boilers, water-pipes, or
on teeth. *v.t. & i.* **1.** take ~s
from (e.g. fish). **2.** come (*off*)
in flakes: *paint scaling off a wall.*

scal·ly·wag ['skæliwæg] *n.*
scamp.

scalp [skælp] *n.* skin and hair of
the top of the head. *v.t.* cut the
~ off.

scalp·el ['skælpl] *n.* small knife
used by surgeons.

scamp [skæmp] *n.* worthless
person; (playfully) rascal. *v.t.*
do (work) carelessly or too
quickly.

scam·per ['skæmpə*] *v.i.* (esp.
of small animals, e.g. mice and
rabbits, when frightened, or of
children and dogs at play) run
quickly. *n.* short quick run:
take the dog for a ~.

scan [skæn] *v.t. & i.* (-*nn*-). **1.**
look at attentively; run the
eyes over every part of: ~ *the
horizon (sb.'s proposals).* **2.** test
the metre of (a line of verse) by
noting the division into feet
(see *foot*(4)). **3.** (of a line of
verse) be metrically correct.

scan·dal ['skændl] *n.* **1.** (actions,
behaviour, etc., that cause)
general feeling of indignation;
shameful or disgraceful action.
2. harmful gossip; unkind talk
that hurts sb.'s reputation.
~**·ize** ['skændəlaiz] *v.t.* shock;
fill with indignation. ~**·ous**
adj. **1.** very wrong; shocking.
2. (of reports, rumours) containing ~(2). **3.** (of persons) fond of
spreading ~: ~*ous neighbours.*

scant [skænt] *adj.* (having)
hardly enough : ~ *of breath; pay
~ attention to what sb. says.* ~**·y**
adj. (-*ier*, -*iest*). barely sufficient;
small in size or amount. ~**·i·ly**
adv.

scape·goat ['skeipgout] *n.* person blamed or punished for the mistake(s) or wrongdoing of others.

scar [ska:*] *n.* mark remaining on the surface (of skin, furniture) as the result of injury or damage. *v.t.* (-rr-). mark with a ~ or ~s: *an arm ~red by numerous vaccinations.*

scar·ab ['skærəb] *n.* kinds of beetle; carving in the shape of a ~.

scarce [skɛəs] *adj.* (scarcer, scarcest). **1.** rare; not available in sufficient quantity: *Eggs were ~ here last winter.* **2.** uncommon; not often seen or found. **~·ly** *adv.* not quite; almost not; barely: *Scarcely anyone knows what happened.* **scar·ci·ty** *n.*

scare [skɛə*] *v.t.* frighten. *n.* fright; state of widespread alarm: *The news from X caused a war ~.* **'~·crow** *n.* figure made of sticks and old clothes, put in a field to frighten birds from crops. **'~·,mon·ger** *n.* person who starts a ~.

scarf [ska:f] *n.* long strip of material (silk, wool, etc.) worn over the shoulders, round the neck, or over the hair.

scar·let ['ska:lit] *n. & adj.* bright red. ~ *fever,* infectious disease that causes ~ marks on the skin.

scath·ing ['skeiðiŋ] *adj.* (of words, criticism, etc.) harsh; cutting.

scat·ter ['skætə*] *v.t. & i.* **1.** send, go, in different directions. **2.** throw or put here and there: *~ seed; ~ sand on an icy road.* **scat·tered** *adj.* not situated together: *~ed villages.*

scav·en·ger ['skævindʒə*] *n.* **1.** animal or bird (e.g. a vulture) that lives on decaying flesh. **2.** (old use) street-cleaner.

sce·na·ri·o [si'na:riou] *n.* outline of events, details of scenes, etc., in a drama, esp. for a film production.

scene [si:n] *n.* **1.** place of an actual or imagined event: *the ~ of a famous battle.* **2.** view; sth. that is seen: *boats in the harbour making a pretty ~; go abroad for a change of ~.* **3.** one of the parts, shorter than an act, into which a play is divided: *Act I, S~ ii.* **4.** painted background, woodwork, canvas, etc., on the stage of a theatre, representing a place. *behind the ~s,* at the back of the stage, hidden from the audience, and so (fig., of a person) having information about matters not known by the general public. **5.** angry outburst; noisy argument; display of bad temper in the presence of other people: *Don't make a ~.* **scen·er·y** ['si:nəri] *n.* **1.** stage ~ (4). **2.** general natural features of a district: *mountain ~ry.* **scen·ic** ['si:nik] *adj.* of ~ry.

scent [sent] *n.* **1.** smell, esp. of sth. pleasant: *the ~ of roses.* **2.** (usu. liquid) preparation made from flowers; perfume: *a bottle of ~. She put some ~ on her hair.* **3.** smell left by an animal by which dogs can follow its track: *on (off) the ~,* following (not following) the right ~; *throw sb. off the ~,* mislead him, deceive him, by giving wrong suggestions, etc. **4.** sense of smell (in dogs, etc.): *hunt by ~.* *v.t.* **1.** learn the presence of by smell: *My dog ~ed a fox.* **2.** (fig.) suspect; become aware of: *~ a plot (a crime).* **3.** put ~ (2) on. **4.** give a ~ (1) to.

scep·tic ['skeptik] *n.* person who doubts whether sth. is true, esp. one who doubts the truth of religious teachings. **scep·ti·cal** *adj.* **scep·ti·cism** ['skeptisizm] *n.* doubting state of mind.

scep·tre ['septə*] *n.* rod or staff carried by a ruler as a sign of power or authority.

sched·ule ['ʃedju:l] *n.* list or statement of details, esp. of times for doing things: *according to ~,* as planned. *v.t.* make a ~ of; put in a ~.

scheme [ski:m] *n.* **1.** arrangement; ordered system: *a colour ~* (e.g. for a room, so that colours of curtains, rugs, etc., are in harmony). **2.** plan or design for work or activity: *a ~*

(= syllabus) *for the term's work.*
3. secret and dishonest plan.
v.t. & i. make a ~ or ~s (esp.
dishonest) (*for sth., to do sth.*).
schem·er *n.* **schem·ing** *adj.*
(esp.) (of a person) making dishonest ~s.

schism ['sizm] *n.* division (esp.
of a Church) into groups, esp.
because of difference of opinion;
the offence of causing such a
division. **schis·mat·ic** [siz-
'mætik] *adj.* causing, likely to
cause, ~.

schol·ar ['skolə*] *n.* **1.** (old-
fashioned use) boy or girl at
school. **2.** student who, after
a competitive examination, is
awarded money or other help so
that he may attend school or
college: *a Rhodes ~.* **3.** person
with much knowledge (usu. of
a particular subject): *Professor
X, the famous Greek ~.* **~·ly**
adj. having or showing much
learning; of or befitting a ~(3);
fond of learning. **~·ship** *n.* **1.**
learning or knowledge obtained
by study. **2.** money given to a
~(2) so that he may continue
his studies. **scho·las·tic** [skə-
'læstik] *adj.* of schools or education.

¹**school** [sku:l] *n.* **1.** building,
institution, where children or
adults are taught; all the pupils
in a ~. **2.** group of persons
having the same principles or
characteristics, e.g. of technique,
or influenced by the same
teacher, esp. a group of artists.
v.t. train; control; discipline:
~ed by adversity. **¹~·fel·low,**
¹~·mate *n.* one educated or
being educated at the same ~ as
another. **~·ing** *n.* education at
~. **¹~·mas·ter, ¹~·mis·tress**
n. man, woman, teaching in a ~.

²**school** [sku:l] *n.* large number
(*of* fish) swimming together.

schoon·er ['sku:nə*] *n.* kind of
sailing-ship with two or more
masts.

sci·ence ['saiəns] *n.* **1.** knowledge arranged in a system, esp.
knowledge obtained by observation and testing of facts. **2.**
branch of such knowledge (e.g.

physics, chemistry, biology). **3.**
skill; expertness (e.g. in sport).
sci·en·tif·ic [,saiən'tifik] *adj.* **1.**
of, for, connected with, used
in, ~; guided by the rules of ~:
scientific farming. **2.** having,
using, needing, skill or expert
knowledge: *a scientific boxer.*
sci·en·tif·i·cal·ly *adv.* **sci·en·
tist** ['saiəntist] *n.* person expert
in one of the natural or physical
~s.

scin·til·late ['sintileit] *v.i.*
sparkle.

sci·on ['saiən] *n.* young member
of (usu. an old or a noble
family).

scis·sors ['sizəz] *n. pl.* (often
pair of ~) cutting instrument
with two blades which cut as
they come together.

scoff [skof] *v.i.* speak contemptuously; mock (*at*). *n.* mocking
words. **scof·fer** *n.*

scold [skould] *v.t. & i.* blame
(sb.) with angry words; speak
angrily in protest. *n.* woman
who ~s.

scone [skon] *n.* soft flat cake
of barley meal or wheat flour
baked quickly.

scoop [sku:p] *n.* **1.** (sorts of) deep
shovel-like tool for taking up
and moving quantities of flour,
sand, earth, etc.; such a part of
a machine with that purpose. **2.**
(colloq.) piece of news obtained
and published by one newspaper
before others. *v.t.* **1.** lift (*up*
or *out*) with, or as with, a ~.
2. make (a hole or a hollow *in*
sth.) as with a ~.

scoot [sku:t] *v.i.* (colloq., humor.)
run off quickly.

scoot·er ['sku:tə*] *n.* (motor-)
cycle with small wheels and
a low saddle.

scope [skoup] *n.* **1.** outlook;
range of action or observation.
2. opportunity; outlet: *work
that gives ~ for one's abilities.*

scorch [skɔ:tʃ] *v.t. & i.* **1.** burn
or discolour the surface of (sth.)
with dry heat. **2.** (colloq., of
motorists, cyclists, etc.) travel
(*along*) at very high speed.

¹**score** [skɔ:*] *n.* **1.** cut or scratch
made on a surface; line drawn

on a board for the purpose of keeping a record. **2.** record kept by ~s (1), esp. of money owing. *run up a ~*, get into debt. *pay off (wipe off, settle) old ~s*, (fig.) get even with someone for past offences; have one's revenge. **3.** (record of) points, goals, runs, etc., made by a team or player in sport. **4.** *on the ~ of*, because of. *on that ~*, as far as that point is concerned. **5.** copy of orchestral, etc., music showing what each instrument is to play, each voice to sing. *v.t. & i.* **1.** make (cuts, scratches, lines) on: *a composition ~d with corrections in red ink.* **2.** make or keep a record (esp. for games). **3.** make as points in a game, etc.: *~ a goal; a batsman who failed to ~.* **4.** win an advantage; do well: *~ off sb.*, get the better of him (in an argument, etc.). **5.** write, in a ~(5), instrumental or vocal parts for a musical composition. **scor·er** *n.* (esp.) person who keeps the ~(3) (e.g. for a game of cricket).

²score [skɔ:*] *n.* (set of) twenty.

scorn [skɔ:n] *n.* **1.** contempt; feeling that sb. or sth. deserves no respect. **2.** person, action, etc., that is despised or looked down on. *v.t.* **1.** feel or show contempt for: *We ~ liars.* **2.** refuse, be unwilling (*to do* sth.), because it is wrong or unworthy. ~·**ful** *adj.* showing or feeling ~. ~·**ful·ly** *adv.*

scor·pion ['skɔ:pjən] *n.* small animal of the spider group with a poisonous sting in its long tail.

Scotch [skɔtʃ], **Scot·tish** ['skɔtiʃ] *adj.* of Scotland or its people. *n.* (*Scotch*) ~ whisky.

scot-free ['skɔt'fri:] *adv.* go (*get off, escape*) ~, unharmed, unpunished.

scoun·drel ['skaundrəl] *n.* wicked person. ~·**ly** *adj.* wicked.

¹scour ['skauə*] *v.t.* **1.** rub (a dirty surface) bright or clean. **2.** get (rust, marks, etc., *off, out, away*) by rubbing. *n.* act of ~·ing.

²scour ['skauə*] *v.t.* go rapidly into every part of (a place) looking (*for* sb. or sth.): *~ing the woods for a lost child.*

scourge [skə:dʒ] *n.* whip for punishment; (fig.) cause of suffering (e.g. an outbreak of disease). *v.t.* whip; punish; bring pain or suffering to.

¹scout [skaut] *n.* **1.** person (not a spy) or ship sent out to get information about the enemy's movements, strength, etc. **2.** (*S~*) member of the world-wide organization for boys founded by Baden-Powell. *v.i.* go out as a ~(1): *~ about, ~ round (for)*, go about looking (for things or people wanted).

Scouts (2)

²scout [skaut] *v.t.* consider (an idea or suggestion) worthless or ridiculous.

scowl [skaul] *v.i. & n.* (have a) bad-tempered look on the face.

scrag·gy ['skrægi] *adj.* (*-ier, -iest*). thin and bony.

scram·ble ['skræmbl] *v.i.* **1.** climb or crawl (*up, over, along, into*, etc.): *~ up a cliff.* **2.** struggle with others (*for* sth.). **3.** cook (eggs) by beating them in milk and then heating them in melted butter. *n.* **1.** climb or walk over or through obstacles, rough ground, etc. **2.** rough struggle (*for* sth.).

¹scrap [skræp] *n.* **1.** small (usu. unwanted) piece. **2.** waste or unwanted articles, esp. those of value only for the material they contain: *~ iron*, articles of iron and steel to be melted down. ¹~·**book** *n.* book of blank pages on to which pictures, etc., cut from periodicals are pasted. ¹~-**heap** *n.* pile of waste or unwanted material or articles. ~·**py** *adj.* (*-ier, -iest*). made up of bits; not complete or properly arranged. *v.t.* (*-pp-*). throw away as useless or worn out.

²scrap [skræp] *n. & v.i.* (*-pp-*). (colloq.) fight.

scrape [skreip] *v.t. & i.* **1.** make clean, smooth, or level by drawing or pushing the hard edge of a tool, or sth. rough, along the surface; remove (mud, grease, paint, etc.) in this way: *to ~ paint off the door.* **2.** injure or damage by scraping. **3.** go, get, *through* or *past* another object, touching or almost touching it. *~ through an examination,* (fig.) only just pass. **4.** collect with effort or difficulty: *~ up enough money to pay the rent.* **5.** rub with a harsh or rough sound. **6.** make by scraping (1): *~ (out) a hole in the sand. n.* **1.** act or sound of scraping. **2.** ~d place. **3.** awkward situation resulting from foolish behaviour: *a boy who is always getting into ~s.* **scrap·er** *n.* tool used for scraping.

scratch [skrætʃ] *v.t. & i.* **1.** make lines on or in a surface with sth. pointed or sharp; break or cut lightly (a surface) in this way: *~ the paint on a door; ~ out a word* (with a knife, or by drawing a line through it). **2.** make (a hole) by ~ing. **3.** rub (the skin) with the finger-nails, etc., to relieve itching: *~ one's head.* **4.** draw or write carelessly. **5.** rub with a harsh noise; make a harsh noise: *This pen ~es.* **6.** withdraw (a horse, a candidate, oneself) from a contest. *n.* **1.** mark, cut, injury, sound, made by ~ing: *escape without a ~* (i.e. quite unhurt). **2.** act of ~ing. **3.** starting line for a race: *start from ~,* start from the beginning or without any advantages; *come up to ~,* be ready to do what one is expected or required to do. *adj.* formed or done with whatever is available: *a ~ team* (collected hastily); *a ~ dinner.* ~·**y** *adj.* (*-ier, -iest*). (of drawings, writing) done carelessly; (of a pen) that makes a ~ing noise.

scrawl [skrɔ:l] *v.i. & t.* write or draw quickly and carelessly. *n.* ~ed writing; sth. ~ed.

scream [skri:m] *v.i. & t.* **1.** give a loud sharp cry of, or as of, fear or pain; cry (sth.) in a loud high voice. *~ with laughter,* laugh in a noisy, uncontrolled way. **2.** (of the wind, machines, etc.) make a loud, shrill noise. *n.* loud, shrill, piercing cry or noise.

screech [skri:tʃ] *v.i. & t.* **1.** make a harsh, piercing sound. **2.** scream in anger or pain; cry out in high tones: *monkeys ~ing in the trees. n.* ~ing cry or noise.

screed [skri:d] *n.* long (and usu. uninteresting) letter.

screen [skri:n] *n.* **1.** (often movable) upright framework, often made so as to fold, used to hide sb. or sth. from view or to protect from draughts or too much heat or light, etc. **2.** anything that gives shelter or protection as a ~(1) does: *a ~ of trees* (hiding a house from the road); *a smoke ~* (used in war to hide ships, etc., from the enemy). **3.** frame with fine wire netting (*~-window, ~-door*) to keep out flies, mosquitoes, etc. **4.** sieve (for coal, etc.). **5.** smooth surface on to which slides, films, TV pictures, etc., are projected; (attrib.) of the cinema: *~ play (actor, etc.). v.t.* **1.** shelter, protect, hide from view, with a ~(1), (2); (fig.) protect (sb.) from punishment, blame, discovery, etc. **2.** provide (windows, a house, etc.) with wire ~s (3). **3.** separate (coal, etc.) into different sizes by passing through a ~(4).

A screen   A scrubbing-brush

screw [skru:] *n.* **1.** metal peg with a spiral groove round its length driven into wood (metal, etc.) by twisting under pressure, for fastening and holding things together. **2.** sth. turned like a ~ and used for exerting pressure, tightening, etc. *put the ~ on sb.*, use one's power to force him to do sth. **3.** propeller of a ship or (*air~*) of an aircraft. *v.t. & i.* **1.** fasten or tighten with a ~ or ~s (1): *S~ down the lid.* **2.** twist round: ~ *the lid of a jar on* (*off*); ~ (*turn*) *one's head round.* **3.** ~ *up one's eyes* (*mouth, face*), cause the skin there to wrinkle. ~ *up one's courage*, overcome one's fears. **4.** exert pressure; force (*out of*). '~·₁driv·er *n.* tool for turning ~s (1).

scrib·ble ['skribl] *v.i. & t.* write hastily or carelessly; make meaningless marks on paper, etc. *n.* sth. ~d.

scribe [skraib] *n.* professional letter-writer; (Bible) teacher of Jewish law.

scrim·mage ['skrimidʒ] *n.* confused struggle. *v.i.* take part in a ~.

script [skript] *n.* **1.** handwriting; type that imitates handwriting. **2.** (short for) manuscript or typescript (esp. of an actor's part in a play, a talk to be broadcast, etc.).

scrip·ture ['skriptʃə*] *n.* **1.** *The Holy Scriptures*, the Bible. **2.** study of the Bible. **scrip·tur·al** *adj.* based on the Bible.

scroll [skroul] *n.* roll of paper or parchment for writing on; ancient book written on a ~.

¹**scrub** [skrʌb] *v.t. & i.* (*-bb-*). clean by rubbing hard, esp. with a stiff brush, soap, and water. *n.* ~·bing. '~·bing-brush *n.* brush as shown on page 467.

²**scrub** [skrʌb] *n.* (land covered with) trees and bushes of poor quality; brushwood. ~·by *adj.* (*-ier, -iest*). insignificant; stunted; unshaven: *a ~by chin.*

scruff [skrʌf] *n.* back of the neck (esp. of an animal). **scruf·fy** *adj.* (colloq.) untidy and rough looking.

scru·ple ['skru:pl] *n.* (hesitation caused by) uneasiness of conscience: *Have you no ~s about borrowing things without per-*

mission? v.i. ~ *to do sth.*, have ~s about doing it. **scru·pu·lous** ['skru:pjuləs] *adj.* **1.** careful to do nothing morally wrong. **2.** paying great attention to small points (esp. of conscience).

scru·ti·ny ['skru:tini] *n.* thorough and detailed examination. **scru·ti·nize** *v.t.* make a ~ of.

scuf·fle ['skʌfl] *n.* rough confused fight or struggle. *v.i.* take part in a ~.

scull [skʌl] *n.* one of a pair of oars used together; single oar used with a twisting stroke at the stern of a boat. *v.t. & i.* row (a boat) with ~s or propel (a boat) with one ~ at the stern.

scul·ler·y ['skʌləri] *n.* room in which pots, pans, dishes, etc., are washed.

sculp·ture ['skʌlptʃə*] *n.* **1.** art of making representations in stone, wood, metal, etc., by carving, modelling, etc. **2.** (a piece of) such work. *v.t. & i.* make a ~ of; ornament with ~: *a ~d column.* **sculp·tor** ['skʌlptə*] *n.* artist who makes ~s. **sculp·tur·al** *adj.*

scum [skʌm] *n.* **1.** froth, dirty substance that comes to the surface of a boiling liquid, a pond, etc. **2.** (fig.) worst or seemingly worthless part (*of* the population, etc.).

scup·per ['skʌpə*] *n.* opening in a ship's side for draining water from the deck.

scurf [skə:f] *n.* small bits of dead skin, esp. on the scalp, loosened as new skin grows. ~·y *adj.*

scur·ri·lous ['skʌriləs] *adj.* using, full of, violent words of abuse: *a ~ attack on the Council.*

scur·ry ['skʌri] *v.i.* run, esp. with short, quick steps. *n.* act or sound of ~ing.

scur·vy ['skə:vi] *adj.* contemptible: *a ~ trick.* ~. disease caused by lack of fresh fruit and vegetables to eat.

¹**scut·tle** ['skʌtl] *n.* (also *coal-~*) container for a supply of coal at the fireside.

²**scut·tle** ['skʌtl] *v.t.* make, open, a hole in (a ship) below the water-line, esp. to sink it and

so prevent its being captured by the enemy.

ˢscut·tle ['skʌtl] *v.i.* scurry (*off, away*).

scythe [saið] *n.* tool, as shown here, for cutting long grass, etc. *v.t.* cut with a ~.

A scythe

sea [si:] *n.* **1.** (any part of the) expanse of salt water that surrounds the continents (cf. *ocean*); name given to certain large areas of inland water, e.g. the Black Sea, the Caspian Sea, the Dead Sea (cf. Lake Victoria, Lake Erie). (*all*) *at sea*, (fig.) puzzled; *at a loss. go to sea*, become a sailor. *put* (*out*) *to sea*, leave the land, leave harbour. **2.** big wave coming over a ship, etc.: *swept overboard by a huge sea*. **3.** large area or stretch (*of* sth.); large quantity: *a sea of up-turned faces*. **'sea·board** *n.* coast region. **'sea·borne** *adj.* (of trade) carried in ships. **'sea-,far·ing** *adj.* of work or voyages on the sea. **'sea·front** *n.* part of a town facing the sea. **'sea-gull** *n.* common sea-bird with long wings. **'sea-legs** *n. pl. get one's sea-legs*, become used to the heaving motion of a ship. **'sea lev·el** *n.* level of the sea's surface used in reckoning height of land and depth of sea. **'sea-,li·on** *n.* large seal of the Pacific Ocean. **'sea·man** ['si:mən] *n.* sailor, esp. one who is not an officer. **'sea·man·ship** *n.* art of, skill in, managing a ship. **'sea·port** *n.* town with a harbour. **'sea·shore** *n.* land at the sea's edge. **'sea·sick** *adj.* sick from the motion of a ship. **'sea·side** *n.* (place, town) by the sea. **'sea·weed** *n.* plant(s) growing in the sea or on rocks washed by the sea. **'sea·,worth·y** *adj.* (of ships) fit for a sea voyage; well built.

ˢseal [si:l] *n.* **1.** piece of wax, lead, etc., often stamped with a design, attached to a document to show that it is genuine; or to a letter, box, door, etc., to guard against its being opened by un-authorized persons. **2.** piece of metal, etc., on which is the design to be stamped on a ~. **3.** act, event, regarded as giving effect to sth.; guarantee: *under the ~ of secrecy. v.t.* **1.** put a ~(1) on; stamp a ~(1). **2.** close tightly: ~ *a crack in a pipe*; ~ *a jar of fruit* (i.e. make it airtight). **3.** ~ *a bargain*, settle it. *His fate is* ~*ed*, is definitely decided. **'~·ing-wax** *n.* kind of wax, melted to ~ letters, etc.

A ˢseal(1)   A ²seal

ˢseal [si:l] *n.* fish-eating sea-animal valued for its fur.

seam [si:m] *n.* **1.** line where two edges, esp. of cloth or leather, are turned back and sewn to-gether. **2.** layer of coal, etc., between layers of other material (e.g. rock, clay). **3.** line or mark like a ~(1). *v.t.* (esp. in the p.p.; of the face) ~*ed with*, marked with (lines, scars, etc.). ~**stress** ['semstris] *n.* woman who makes a living by sewing. ~**y** *adj. the* ~*y side* (*of life*), the evils of poverty, crime, etc.

sear [siə*] *v.t.* burn the surface of, esp. with a heated iron; (fig.) make (sb.'s heart) hard and un-feeling.

search [sə:tʃ] *v.t. & i.* **1.** ex-amine, look carefully at, through or into (*for*, in order to find) sth. or sb.: ~ *a criminal to see what he has in his pockets.* **2.** go deeply into; go into every part of: *a* ~*ing wind. n.* act of ~*ing*: *go in* ~ *of a missing child.*

~·**ing** adj. (of a look) taking in all details; (of a test, etc.) thorough. '~·**light** n. powerful electric lamp for ~ing the sky, sea, etc. '~·**war·rant** n. official authority given to policemen when it is necessary to ~ a house (for stolen goods, etc.).

sea·son ['si:zn] n. 1. one of the divisions of the year according to the weather (e.g. spring, summer, etc.; the dry (rainy) ~). 2. period suitable or normal for sth.: the football ~; the nesting ~. in (out of) ~, (of fish, fruit, etc.) to be had (not to be had) in good condition and at ordinary prices. in ~ and out of ~, at all times. 3. period (in a town) when most of the social events take place. 4. (old use) for a ~, for a short time. v.t. & i. 1. make or become suitable for use (through the effects of time, the weather, or treatment): well-~ed wood, wood that has become dry and hard. 2. flavour (food) (with salt, pepper, etc.). ~·**a·ble** adj. 1. (of the weather) of the kind to be expected at the time of year. 2. (of help, advice, gifts, etc.) coming at the right time; opportune. ~·**al** adj. dependent on the ~s (1); changing with the ~s (1): ~al occupations (e.g. fruit picking). ~·**ing** n. sth. that adds flavour (e.g. salt). '~·'**tick·et** n. one giving the owner the right to travel between two places or to go to a place of amusement, etc., as often as he wishes during a certain period.

seat [si:t] n. 1. sth. made or used for sitting on (e.g. a chair, box, rug). 2. part of a chair, stool, etc., on which one sits. 3. part of the body (the buttocks) on which one sits; part of a garment (e.g. of trousers, a skirt) covering this. 4. place in which one has the right to sit: have a ~ in Parliament (i.e. be a Member). 5. country ~, large house with land, in the country. 6. place where sth. is or is carried on: the ~ of government (the capital); a ~ of learning (e.g.

a university). v.t. 1. ~ oneself, sit down; be ~ed, sit. 2. have ~s for: a hall that ~s 200.

se·cede [si'si:d] v.i. (of a group) withdraw from membership of a church, federation, etc.). **se·ces·sion** [si'seʃən] n.

se·clude [si'klu:d] v.t. keep (a person, oneself) apart from the company of others: lead a ~d life. **se·clud·ed** adj. (esp. of a place) hidden away; solitary. **se·clu·sion** [si'klu:ʒən] n. secluding or being ~d; ~d place; retirement: live in seclusion.

¹**sec·ond** ['sekənd] adj. 1. next after the first in position, time, order, etc. ~ childhood, old age when accompanied by mental weakness. ~ lieutenant, lowest commissioned rank in the army. ~ nature, habit. ~ sight, ability to see future events or events happening at a distance as if present. 2. additional; extra. 3. another; of the same kind as one that has gone before: a ~ Napoleon. n. 1. person or thing that comes next after the first. 2. person who supports or helps another in a duel or a boxing match. 3. (pl.) goods below the best quality. v.t. 1. support (esp. in a duel or boxing match). 2. (at a meeting) speak in support of a motion (after it has been proposed). 3. (official use, pronounced [si'kɒnd]) take (sb.) from his ordinary duty and give him a special duty. '~·**best** adj. next after the best. '~·**class** adj. of the class next after the first; inferior. '~·'**hand** adj. 1. already used by sb. else: ~-hand clothes (books). 2. (of news, knowledge) obtained from others, not based on personal observation, etc. '~·'**rate** adj. not of the best quality.

²**sec·ond** ['sekənd] n. 1. sixtieth part of a minute of time or angular measurement (indicated by the mark "): the ~ hand of a watch. 2. (colloq.) moment, short time.

sec·on·da·ry ['sekəndəri] adj. following what is first or primary: ~ school (education), between the primary school and the university; less important than chief or prime (1).

se·cret ['si:krit] *adj.* **1.** (to be) kept from the knowledge or view of others; of which others have no knowledge. **2.** (of a place) secluded. **3.** (of a person) = secretive. *n.* **1.** sth. ~ : *keep a ~*, not tell anyone else ; *in the ~*, among those allowed to know it. **2.** hidden cause ; explanation, way of doing sth., that is not widely known : *What is the ~ of his success?* **3.** *in ~*, = ~ly. **~·ly** *adv.* in a ~ manner. **se·cre·cy** ['si:krəsi] *n.* **1.** keeping things ~ ; ability to do this. **2.** state of being (kept) ~. **~·ive** ['si:krətiv] *adj.* having the habit of keeping things ~.

sec·re·ta·ry ['sekritri] *n.* **1.** person employed to send letters, keep papers and records, make business arrangements and appointments, etc., for another or for an organization. **2.** (*S~ of State*) minister in charge of a government department or a branch of a department. **sec·re·ta·ri·al** [ˌsekri'tɛəriəl] *adj.* of a ~ or a ~'s work. **sec·re·ta·ri·at** [ˌsekrə'tɛəriæt] *n.* staff of secretaries.

se·crete [si'kri:t] *v.t.* **1.** put or keep in a secret place. **2.** produce by secretion. **se·cre·tion** [si'kri:ʃən] *n.* **1.** process by which certain substances in a plant or animal body are separated (from sap or blood, etc.) for use or as waste. **2.** substance ~d (e.g. saliva, bile).

sect [sekt] *n.* group of people united by (esp. religious) beliefs or opinions that differ from those more generally accepted. **sec·ta·ri·an** [sek'tɛəriən] *n. & adj.* (member, supporter) of a ~ or ~s.

sec·tion ['sekʃən] *n.* **1.** part cut off; slice. **2.** one of a number of completed parts to be put together to make a structure : *fit together the ~s of a shed.* **3.** division of a piece of writing, of a town, country, or community : *the residential ~.* **4.** (also *cross-*

~) view or representation of sth. seen as if cut straight through. **~·al** *adj.* **1.** made or supplied in ~s(2) : *a ~al book-case.* **2.** of a ~(3) or ~s(2) : *~al jealousies* (e.g. between ~s of a community).

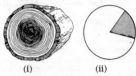

(i)   (ii)

(i) A cross-section of a tree trunk
(ii) A sector of a circle

sec·tor ['sektə] *n.* **1.** one of the areas into which a battle area is divided for the purpose of controlling operations. **2.** part of a circle as shown above.

sec·u·lar ['sekjulə] *adj.* worldly or material, not religious or spiritual : *~ art (music, education).*

se·cure [si'kjuə] *adj.* **1.** safe (*from* or *against* risk, etc.). **2.** firmly or tightly fixed; not likely to slip or break. *v.t.* **1.** make ~ : *a ~ village from (against) floods by building embankments.* **2.** make fast : *~ the doors and windows.* **3.** obtain : *~ tickets for a concert.* **~·ly** *adv.*

se·cu·ri·ty [si'kjuəriti] *n.* **1.** (sth. that provides) safety. **2.** sth. valuable (e.g. a life-insurance policy) given as a pledge for the repayment of a loan or the fulfilment of a promise or undertaking. **3.** document, certificate, etc., showing ownership of property (esp. bonds, stocks, and shares).

se·dan(-chair) [si'dæn(tʃɛə)] *n.* covered chair carried on poles by two men, used in the 17th and 18th centuries.

se·date [si'deit] *adj.* (of a person, his behaviour) calm; serious; grave. **~·ly** *adv.*

sed·a·tive ['sedətiv] *n. & adj.* (medicine) tending to calm the nerves.

sed·en·ta·ry ['sedəntəri] *adj.* (of

work) done sitting down (at a desk, etc.); (of persons) spending much of their time seated.

sed·i·ment ['sedimənt] *n.* matter (sand, gravel, mud, dirt) that settles to the bottom of a liquid (e.g. mud left on fields after a river has been in flood over them).

se·di·tion [si'diʃən] *n.* words, actions, intended to make people rebel against authority. **se·di·tious** [si'diʃəs] *adj.*

se·duce [si'djuːs] *v.t.* persuade (sb.) to do wrong (e.g. by offering money); (esp.) persuade (a woman) to give up her chastity. **se·duc·er** *n.* **se·duc·tion** [si-'dakʃən] *n.* seducing or being ~d; sth. very attractive and tempting. **se·duc·tive** *adj.* alluring; captivating.

sed·u·lous ['sedjuləs] *adj.* persevering; done with persistence.

¹**see** [siː] *v.i. & t.* (p.t. *saw* [sɔː], p.p. *seen* [siːn]) **1.** have (use) the power of sight; understand. **2.** (with adv. & prep.): *see about*, attend to; take steps to do (sth.) or to get (sth.). *see after*, look after; attend to. *see into*, inquire into. *see sb. off*, go to a railway station, ship, etc., to see sb. start a journey. *see sb. out*, go with him to the door when he is leaving. *see through* (*sb. or sth.*), not be deceived by. *see* (*sb. or sth.*) *through*, support for as long as is necessary. *see to*, attend to. *see to it that*, take care, make certain, that. **3.** (with n. & adj.): *see the back of* (*sb.*), get rid of him. *see the last of*, have done with. *see double*, see two things where there is only one. *see red*, become violently angry. *see life*, have wide experience of many kinds of activity, etc. **4.** (various uses) *I'll see*, I will consider the matter. *Let me see*, give me time to think or recall.

²**see** [siː] *n.* district under a bishop. *the Holy S~*, the Papacy.

seed [siːd] *n.* (pl. *seed* or *seeds*). **1.** flowering plant's element of life, from which another plant can grow. *run* (*go*) *to* ~, stop

flowering and produce ~; (fig.) become careless of one's appearance and clothes. **2.** cause, origin (*of a tendency, development*). **3.** ~ed player: *No. 3* ~, the third best. *v.t. & i.* **1.** (of plants) produce ~. **2.** take the ~ out of (e.g. dried fruit). **3.** ~*ed players*, (esp. tennis) tested and proved of high standard. ~·**ling** *n.* plant newly grown from a ~. '**seeds·man** *n.* dealer in ~s. ~·**y** *adj.* (*-ier, -iest*). **1.** shabby. **2.** (colloq.) unwell.

seek [siːk] *v.t. & i.* (p.t. & p.p. *sought* [sɔːt]). **1.** look for; try to find: ~ *shelter*; ~ *safety in flight*. **2.** ~ *for*, look for. **3.** ~ *to do sth.*, try to do sth. **4.** *sought after*, wanted; in demand.

seem [siːm] *v.i.* have or give the impression or appearance of being or doing; appear to be: *Things far off* ~ (*to be*) *small*. ~·**ing** *adj.* apparent but perhaps not real: *his* ~*ing friendship*. ~·**ing·ly** *adv.* in appearance; apparently.

seem·ly ['siːmli] *adj.* (*-ier, -iest*). (of behaviour) proper or correct (for the occasion or circumstances); decent; decorous.

seen, see *see.*

seep [siːp] *v.i.* (of liquids) ooze out or through; trickle. ~·**age** ['siːpidʒ] *n.*

seer [siə*] *n.* person claiming to see into the future; prophet.

see·saw ['siːsɔː] *n.* (board and pivot for a) game, as shown here; up-and-down or to-and-fro motion. *v.i.* move or play in this way.

A seesaw

seethe [siːð] *v.i.* **1.** (of liquids) boil; bubble; (of crowds, etc.) move about excitedly. **2.** (of a person) be excited: *seething with anger*; (of a place) be full of excited people or excited feelings.

seg·ment ['segmənt] *n.* **1.** part cut off or marked off by a line: *a ~ of a circle.* **2.** division or section: *a ~ of an orange.*

seg·re·gate ['segrigeit] *v.t.* separate, put apart, from others.

seg·re·ga·tion [ˌsegri'geiʃən] *n.*

seis·mic ['saizmik] *adj.* of earthquakes.

seis·mo·graph ['saizməgrɑːf] *n.* instrument which records the strength and the distance away of an earthquake.

seize [siːz] *v.t. & i.* **1.** take possession of (property, etc.) by law: *~ sb.'s goods for payment of debt.* **2.** take hold of, suddenly and violently: *~ a thief by the collar; ~ an opportunity,* use it promptly. **3.** *~ upon an idea,* see and use it. **sei·zure** ['siːʒə*] *n.* **1.** seizing. **2.** sudden attack of illness (esp. of heart trouble).

sel·dom ['seldəm] *adv.* rarely; not often: *She was ~ seen there.*

se·lect [si'lekt] *v.t.* choose (as being the most suitable, etc.). *adj.* **1.** carefully chosen. **2.** (of a school, society, etc.) of or for carefully chosen persons; not open to all. **se·lec·tion** [si'lekʃən] *n.* **1.** ~ing. **2.** collection or group of ~ed things or examples; number of things from which to ~. **se·lec·tive** *adj.* having the power to ~. **se·lec·tor** *n.* (esp.) member of a committee ~ing a team.

self [self] *n.* (pl. *selves* [selvz]). person's nature, special qualities; interests; etc., considered from one's own point of view: *one's better ~,* one's better nature and desires; *a woman with no thought of ~,* an unselfish woman.

self- *prefix.* short for *itself, myself, himself, oneself,* etc., as in *~-taught,* taught by oneself, *~-control,* control of oneself. **'~-as'ser·tive** *adj.* insisting on one's own claims; pushing oneself forward. **'~-as'ser·tion** *n.* **'~-'cen·tred** *adj.* interested chiefly in oneself, one's own affairs. **'~-'col·oured** *adj.* of the same colour all over. **'~-com·'mand** *n.* power of commanding one's feelings. **'~-'con·scious** *adj.* (esp.) shy, unnatural in behaviour because unable to forget oneself. **'~-con·'tained** *adj.* (esp. of a flat) complete in itself and with its own private entrance; (of a person) reserved. **'~-de'ni·al** *n.* voluntary sacrifice of pleasures to save money, etc. **'~-de·ˌter·mi·'na·tion** *n.* (esp.) right of a nation to decide the kind of government it shall have. **'~-'ev·i·dent** *adj.* clear without proof or more evidence. **'~-im·'por·tant** *adj.* pompous; having too high an opinion of oneself. **'~-in·'dul·gent** *adj.* giving way to desires for one's own comfort, pleasures, etc. **'~-'made** *adj.* (esp. of persons) having succeeded by their own efforts, esp. after beginning life without money, education, or influence. **'~-pos·'sessed** *adj.* calm, cool, confident. **'~-pos·'ses·sion** *n.* **'~-ˌpres·er·'va·tion** *n.* (instinct for) keeping oneself from harm or destruction. **'~-re·'li·ant** *adj.* having or showing confidence in one's own powers, etc. **'~-re·'li·ance** *n.* **'~-re·'spect** *n.* proper regard for one's own character and reputation. **'~-'right·eous** *adj.* convinced of one's own goodness; feeling that one is better than others. **'~-'sac·ri·fice** *n.* the giving up of one's own interests for the sake of other persons. (the) **'~-'same** *adj.* the very same. **'~-'seek·ing** *adj. & n.* selfish (behaviour). **'~-'ser·vice** *adj.* (of restaurants, shops) having goods, etc., on counters, from which customers serve themselves. **~-'sown** *adj.* (of plants) growing from seed dropped by a plant. **'~-'styled** *adj.* using a name, title, etc., to which one has no right. **'~-suf·'fi·cient** *adj.* needing no help from others; overconfident. **'~-'will** *n.* wilfulness. **'~-'willed** *adj.* obstinate; refusing advice or guidance.

Q

self·ish ['selfiʃ] *adj.* chiefly thinking of (interested in) one's own needs and welfare; without care for others. ~·ly *adv.* ~· ness *n.*

sell [sel] *v.t. & i.* (p.t. & p.p. *sold* [sould]). **1.** give in exchange for money. ~ *off*, ~ (stocks of goods) cheaply. ~ *out*, ~ part or all of one's share in a business; ~ all of one's stock (*of sth.*). ~ (*sb.*) *up*, ~ his goods for payment of debt. **2.** (of shopkeepers, etc.) keep stocks for sale; find buyers; (of goods) be sold. **sel·ler** *n.* person who ~s: *a book~er*; sth. that is sold, esp. *a best ~er*, a book that ~s(2) in large numbers.

sel·vage, sel·vedge ['selvidʒ] *n.* edge of cloth woven so that threads do not unravel.

selves, see *self.*

sem·a·phore ['seməfɔ:*] *n.* system for sending signals by using arms on a post or flags held in the hands. *v.t. & i.* send (messages) by ~.

sem·blance ['sembləns] *n.* likeness; appearance.

se·mes·ter [si'mestə*] *n.* half of a school or university year (esp. U.S.A.).

sem·i- ['semi-] *prefix.* **1.** half: *a ~-circle.* **2.** almost; partly: ~*-civilized*; ~*-conscious*; ~*-official.* **3.** occurring twice in (a year, etc.): ~*-annual.* '~· **'co·lon** *n.* the sign ; used in writing and printing. '~-**de**'**tached** *adj.* (of a house) joined to another on one side only. '~-**'fi·nal** *n.* the last match (contest) but one in a competition.

sem·i·nar ['seminɑ:*] *n.* class of students in a university, studying a problem and meeting for discussions with a teacher.

sem·i·na·ry ['seminəri] *n.* Roman Catholic training college for priests.

sen·ate ['senit] *n.* **1.** Upper House (usu. smaller) of the two parts of Parliament, esp. in France and U.S.A. **2.** governing council of some universities. **3.** highest council of state in An-

cient Rome. **sen·a·tor** ['senətə*] *n.* member of a ~.

send [send] *v.t. & i.* (p.t. & p.p. *sent*). **1.** cause (sb. or sth.) to go, come, or be carried; get (sb. or sth.) taken. ~ *away*, ~ to a distance; dismiss (a servant, etc.). ~ *for*, ask or order sb. to come; ask or order that sth. shall be sent. ~ *forth*, produce (leaves, etc.). ~ *in*, enter (one's name, work, etc., *for* a competition, exhibition, etc.). ~ *off* (letters, goods, etc.), dispatch. ~ *on*, forward; ~ in advance (e.g. one's luggage). ~ *out*, give forth (light, heat); distribute (circulars, etc.) by post, messengers, etc. ~ *word*, send news, a message, etc. **2.** cause to become: ~ *sb. mad.* '~-**off** *n.* meeting (e.g. at a railway station) of a traveller's friends to wish him a good journey, to show respect, etc.

se·nile ['si:nail] *adj.* showing signs of, caused by, old age. **se·nil·i·ty** [si'niliti] *n.* weakness (of body or mind) in old age.

se·nior ['si:njə*] *adj.* **1.** older in years; higher in rank, authority, etc. (often ~ *to*). **2.** (after a person's name) indicating the elder person with the same name: *Tom Brown Senior (Sen.).* *n.* ~ person. **se·ni·or·i·ty** [ˌsi:ni'ɔriti] *n.* condition of being ~ (in age, rank, etc.).

sen·sa·tion [sen'seiʃən] *n.* **1.** feeling: *a ~ of warmth (smoothness, dizziness).* **2.** (sth. that causes) deep interest or excitement. ~**al** *adj.* causing deep interest: *a ~al crime*; (of newspapers, etc.) presenting news in a manner designed to cause excitement.

sense [sens] *n.* **1.** any one of the special powers of the body by which a person is conscious of things: sight, hearing, smell, taste, and feeling. **2.** feeling; consciousness: *a ~ of pleasure.* **3.** power of judging; practical wisdom: *a man of ~*; *have ~ enough not to waste money on useless things.* **4.** appreciation or understanding of the value or worth (*of*): *a ~ of humour*; *the moral ~*; *my ~ of duty*. **5.** meaning: *a word with several ~s*; *make ~*, have a meaning that can be understood. **6.** (pl.) normal state of mind: *out of one's ~s*, mad; *bring sb. to his ~s*, get him to stop behaving foolishly; *come to one's ~s*, stop behaving foolishly. **~·less** *adj.* **1.** foolish. **2.** unconscious.

sen·si·bil·i·ty [ˌsensi'biliti] *n.* power of feeling, esp. delicate emotional impressions; susceptibility (*to*).

sen·si·ble ['sensibl] *adj.* **1.** having or showing good sense(3): *a ~ answer*. **2.** aware (*of*).

sen·si·tive ['sensitiv] *adj.* **1.** quick to receive impressions: *~ skin. The eyes are ~ to light*. **2.** easily hurt in the spirit or offended: *~ to criticism*. **3.** (of instruments) able to record small changes. **4.** (of photographic film, paper, etc.) affected by light. **sen·si·tiv·i·ty** [ˌsensi'tiviti] *n.* quality, degree, of being ~. **sen·si·tize** ['sensitaiz] *v.t.* make (film, paper, etc.) ~ (4) (for photographic purposes).

sen·so·ry ['sensəri] *adj.* of the senses(1) or sensation(1).

sen·su·al ['sensjuəl] *adj.* of, given up to, the pleasures of the senses only. **~·ist** *n.* ~ person. **sen·su·ous** ['sensjuəs] *adj.* affecting, noticed by, appealing to, the senses.

sent, see *send*.

sen·tence ['sentəns] *n.* **1.** words, esp. with subject and predicate, that form a statement, question, or request, making complete sense. (Cf. *clause, phrase*.) **2.** (statement by a judge, etc., of) punishment: *under ~ of death*. *v.t.* state that (sb.) is to have a certain punishment: *~ a thief to six months' imprisonment*.

sen·ten·tious [sen'tenʃəs] *adj.* having, putting on, an air of wisdom; pompous.

sen·tient ['senʃənt] *adj.* that feels or is able to feel.

sen·ti·ment ['sentimənt] *n.* **1.** mental feeling (e.g. of admiration, pity, loyalty). **2.** (tendency

to be moved by) (display of) tender feeling (instead of reason). **3.** expression of feeling; opinion or point of view. **sen·ti·men·tal** [ˌsenti'mentl] *adj.* easily moved by, full of, tender feelings; designed to have an effect on the feelings: *~al girls* (*novels*); *for ~al reasons*. **sen·ti·men·tal·ist** *n.* person moved by ~ rather than by reason. **sen·ti·men·tal·i·ty** [ˌsentimen'tæliti] *n.* false or exaggerated ~.

sen·ti·nel ['sentinl] *n.*, **sen·try** ['sentri] *n.* soldier keeping watch or guard. **'sen·try-box** *n.* hut or cabin for a sentry. **'sen·try-go** *n.* (duty of) pacing up and down as a sentry: *on sentry-go*.

sep·a·rate ['sepərit] *adj.* apart; not joined; distinct; individual: *keep this ~ (from the others)*. ['sepəreit] *v.t. & i.* **1.** make, keep, or become, ~ : *~ the sheep from the goats*. **2.** (of a number of people) go in different ways. **sep·a·ra·ble** ['sepərəbl] *adj.* that can be ~d. **sep·a·ra·tion** [ˌsepə'reiʃən] *n.* (period of) being ~d; act of separating.

se·pia ['si:pjə] *n.* dark brown (paint).

Sep·tem·ber [sep'tembə*] *n.* the 9th month of the year.

sep·tic ['septik] *adj.* infected; causing, caused by, infection (with disease germs): *~ poisoning. a ~ tank*, one to which sewage flows for sterilization.

sep·tu·a·ge·na·ri·an ['septjuə-dʒi'nɛəriən] *n.* person 69 to 79 years old.

se·pul·chre ['sepəlkə*] *n.* tomb. *the Holy S~*, that of Jesus Christ. **se·pul·chral** [si'pʌlkrəl] *adj.* **1.** of a ~; of burial. **2.** (of a voice, etc.) deep and mournful.

se·quel ['si:kwəl] *n.* **1.** that which follows or arises out of (an earlier happening): *in the ~*, later on. **2.** later story about the same people.

se·quence ['si:kwəns] *n.* a following on; connected line of events, ideas, etc.: *in ~*, one after another, in order.

se·ques·ter [si'kwestə*] *v.t.* keep

(sb.) away or apart from other people; withdraw oneself to a quiet place: *a ~ed life.*

se·rag·li·o [se'rɑːliou] *n.* harem.

ser·aph ['serəf] *n.* (pl. ~s or ~*im*). angel. ~·ic [si'ræfik] *adj.* angelic; happy and beautiful as a ~.

ser·e·nade [ˌseri'neid] *n.* music (intended to be) sung or played outdoors at night. *v.t. & i.* sing or play a ~ to (sb.).

se·rene [si'riːn] *adj.* clear and calm. ~·ly *adv.* se·ren·i·ty [si'reniti] *n.*

serf [səːf] *n.* (in olden times) person not allowed to leave the land on which he worked. ~·dom ['səːfdəm] *n.* social system in which land was cultivated by ~s; ~'s condition of life.

serge [səːdʒ] *n.* hard-wearing woollen cloth.

ser·geant ['sɑːdʒənt] *n.* 1. non-commissioned army officer above a corporal and below a ~-major. 2. police officer with rank below that of an inspector. ~-'ma·jor *n.* warrant-officer, between a non-commissioned and a commissioned army officer.

se·ri·al ['siəriəl] *adj.* 1. of, in, or forming, a series: *the ~ number of a bank-note.* 2. (of a story, etc.) appearing in parts (in a periodical, etc.). *n.* ~ story. ~·ly *adv.*

se·ries ['siəriːz] *n.* (pl. unchanged). 1. number of things, events, etc., each of which is related in some way to the others, esp. to the one before it. 2. succession: *a ~ of wet days.*

se·ri·ous ['siəriəs] *adj.* 1. solemn; thoughtful; not frivolous. 2. important because of possible danger: *a ~ illness (situation).* 3. in earnest; sincere; not playful. ~·ly *adv.* ~·ness *n.*

ser·mon ['səːmən] *n.* spoken or written address on a religious or moral subject, esp. one given in church.

ser·pent ['səːpənt] *n.* snake. ser·pen·tine *adj.* curving and twisting like a ~.

ser·ried ['serid] *adj.* (of per-

sons in lines or ranks) close together.

se·rum ['siərəm] *n.* watery part of the blood; such a fluid taken from an animal and used for inoculation.

ser·vant ['səːvənt] *n.* wage-earning person, esp. one engaged to do housework, etc.; member of a (company's, etc.) staff. *public* ~*s,* State officials. *civil* ~, member of the Civil Service.

serve [səːv] *v.t. & i.* 1. work for; be a servant to (sb.): *serving as cook (gardener, etc.).* 2. perform duties (for): ~ *one's country in Parliament;* ~ *a year in the Army;* ~ *on* (be a member of) *a committee.* 3. attend to (customers in a shop, etc.); supply (*with* goods or services); place (food, etc.) on the table for a meal; give (food, etc.) to people at a meal: *Dinner is ~d. S~ the coffee in the next room.* 4. be satisfactory for a need or purpose: *a box that ~d as a seat; an excuse that will not ~,* that is not good enough. 5. act towards, treat (sb. in a certain way): ~ *sb. shamefully* (behave badly towards him). *It ~s him right,* this is a suitable punishment for or consequence of his behaviour. 6. ~ *one's time (apprenticeship),* pass the usual or normal number of years (learning a trade, etc.); go through one's term of office, etc. 7. ~ *time,* ~ *a sentence,* undergo a period of imprisonment. 8. (legal) deliver (a summons, etc.) to the person named in it: ~ *a summons on sb.;* ~ *sb. with a writ.*

serv·ice ['səːvis] *n.* 1. being a servant; position as a servant: *go into* ~, become a domestic servant. 2. department or branch of public work, government employment, etc.: *the Civil (Diplomatic) S~; the fighting* ~*s,* the Navy, Army, Air Force; *on active* ~, engaged on military duties in time of war; ~ *dress (rifle, etc.),* military dress, etc. 3. sth. done to help or benefit another: *get the* ~*s of a* doctor (lawyer); his ~s to the State. **4. at** your ~, ready and willing to do what you want; ready for you to use. **5.** system or arrangement that supplies public needs, esp. for communications: a bus (train, etc.) ~; the telephone ~. **6.** form of worship and prayer to God: three ~s every Sunday; religious ceremony for a special purpose: the marriage (burial) ~. **7.** complete set of plates, dishes, etc., for use at table: a tea (dinner) ~ of 50 pieces. **8.** act or work of serving food and drink (in hotels, etc.); work done by domestic servants, hotel servants, etc.: add 10% to the bill for ~; a ~ flat, one whose rent includes the cost of cleaning, etc. **v.t.** put into, keep, in good order: Cars ~d here. ~'

a·ble ['sə:visəbl] **adj. 1.** able to help. **2.** strong and lasting.

ser·vi·ette [ˌsə:vi'et] **n.** table napkin.

ser·vile ['sə:vail] **adj. 1.** of or like slaves. **2.** suggesting the attitude of a slave to his master: ~ flattery. **ser·vil·i·ty** [sə:-'viliti] **n.**

ser·vi·tude ['sə:vitjuːd] **n.** condition of being forced to work for others and of having no freedom.

ses·sion ['seʃən] **n.** (meeting of a) law court, law-making body, etc.; time occupied by discussions at such a meeting; series of such meetings. **in** ~, assembled for business, etc.

¹set [set] **v.t. & i.** (p.t. & p.p. set, pres. p. setting). **1.** (of the sun, etc.) go down below the horizon. **2.** put or place (sth. in a certain position, condition, or relation): set a box on its end; set a stake in the ground. **3.** (with prep. & adv.): set about one's work, set about doing sth., make a start. set apart, set aside, put separately; reserve. set sb. or sth. back, stop or slow down the progress of; move back (e.g. the hands of a clock). set forth, start a journey; state clearly (e.g. one's views). set in, (of a

type of weather, a disease, etc.) start and seem likely to continue; (of tides, winds) begin to flow (in towards the shore). set off, start a journey; explode (a mine, a firework, etc.); cause (sb.) to begin laughing (talking, etc.); make more striking by contrast: a large hat setting off a pretty little face. set on sb., attack him. set (sb. or sth.) on, cause or urge to attack. set out, start a journey, etc. set sth. out, make known (e.g. reasons); put on view. set to, begin vigorously (to do sth.); begin fighting. set up, begin business (as a carpenter, etc.). set (sb. or sth.) up, get (sb.) started (in business); get a business started; make (sb.) strong after an illness, etc.; arrange (type) in order ready for printing; put forward (e.g. a defence). well set up (with), well provided. set upon, attack. **4.** (with certain objects): set a (broken) bone, bring the parts together so that they may unite; set a clock (watch), move the hands to show a certain time; set eggs, place them under a hen; set (sb.) an example, show, by one's own behaviour, how others should behave; never set eyes on, never see; set one's face against (sth.), be firmly opposed to; set a fashion, start one to be copied; set fire (a light) to sth., cause it to begin burning; set one's heart on (sth.), direct and fix one's hopes on; set a hen, place it on eggs (for hatching); set one's name (hand, seal, etc.) (to a document), sign or seal; set the pace, go at a pace which others must keep up with; set sail, begin a voyage; set a saw, (sharpen and) adjust its teeth; set much (little, etc.) store by sth., value it greatly (little, etc.); set one's teeth, close the jaws tightly, showing firm determination; set a trap (for), arrange or adjust it. **5.** cause (sb. or sth.) to be in a certain state, relation, etc.: set sth. straight; set a prisoner free; set sb.'s doubts at rest (sb.'s mind at ease); set sb. (the law) at *defiance*; *set things to rights*, restore them to order. **6.** cause (sb.) to do sth.; give as a task, etc.: *set* (*sb.*) *a difficult problem*; *set the men to chop wood.* **7.** (of liquids, soft substances, etc.) become hard or solid: *The mortar* (*jam, jelly*) *hasn't set yet.* **8.** (of plants, esp. fruit-trees, their blossom) form or develop fruit. **9.** put (a jewel, etc.) firmly in gold or in a framework (e.g. of other jewels). **10.** *set sth. to music*, compose a tune for (words, a verse, etc.). **11.** (special uses of the passive past participle): *set fair*, (of the weather) good and unlikely to change; *set fast*, tightly fixed, unable to move; *a set time* (*date*), arranged in advance; *a set smile* (*look*), fixed, unchanging; *set opinions*, fixed; *a set book*, one on which an examination will be held.

²**set** [set] *n.* **1.** direction (of current, wind, tide); tendency (of opinion). **2.** number of things or persons of a similar kind, that go together: *a set of golf-clubs*; *a tea set* (*dinner set*). **3.** apparatus: *a television set.* **4.** position or angle; posture: *the set of sb.'s head* (*shoulders*). **5.** young plant, cutting or bulb ready to be planted. **6.** group of games in tennis. **7.** place prepared for a scene in a film play: *Everyone to be on the set at 8.30 a.m.* **8.** *make a dead set at*, attack vigorously; try to win the friendship of. '**set-back** *n.* (cause of) check to progress or development. '**set-square** *n.* three-sided piece of wood, etc., for drawing lines at certain angles (e.g. 30°, 60°, and 90°). **set·ting** *n.* **1.** framework in which sth. (e.g. a jewel) is fixed. (See ¹*set* v. (9)). **2.** music composed for a poem, etc. **3.** place, scene, etc., considered as the background or framework of a story, event, etc. '**set-'to** *n.* fight; argument.

set·tee [se'ti:] *n.* long soft seat like a sofa (q.v.), with sides and a back, for two or more persons. ¹**set·tle** ['setl] *n.* long wooden (usu.

fixed) seat with arms and a high back.

²**set·tle** ['setl] *v.t. & i.* **1.** (often ~ *down*) (cause to) come to rest: ~ (*oneself*) *down in an armchair*; (cause to) become used to a new way of life or occupation: ~ *down to a new job*; ~ *one's son in business*; *married and* ~*d down.* **2.** make or become calm, untroubled: *I can't* ~ (*down*) *to anything* (i.e. I am restless). *let the excitement* ~ *down*; *a period of* ~*d weather.* **3.** make one's home (*in, at*): ~ *in the country.* **4.** go to and live *in* (as colonists); establish colonists in: *The Dutch* ~*d in S. Africa.* **5.** reach an agreement about; decide: *That* ~*s the matter. Nothing is* ~*d yet.* ~ *one's affairs* (e.g. by making one's will). ~ (*up*)*on*, decide or resolve (to do sth., have sth., etc.). **6.** pay (a debt, etc.): ~ *a hotel bill*; ~ *up with your creditors*, come to an arrangement with them about debts; *have an account to* ~ *with sb.*, (fig.) have some unpleasant business to discuss. **7.** (of dust, etc., in the air, solid substances in a liquid, etc.) sink, cause to sink, to the floor, the ground, the bottom of a container, etc.: *The dust* ~*d on the floor. The rain* ~*d the dust.* **8.** (of a liquid) (cause to) become clear (as sediment, etc., ~*s*(7)). **9.** (of the ground, the foundation of a building, etc.) sink gradually to a lower level. **10.** (law) give (sb. property, etc.) for use during his lifetime: ~ *part of one's estate on one's son.* ~'**ment** *n.* **1.** the act of settling (an argument, a debt, etc.). **2.** property, etc., ~*d*(10) on sb.: *a marriage* ~*ment.* **3.** group of colonists; new colony; process of settling(4) colonists. **4.** group of persons engaged in social welfare work in a slum area: ~*ments in the East End of London.* **set·tler** *n.* person who ~*s*(4) in a new country: *the Dutch* ~*rs in S. Africa.*

sev·en ['sevn] *n. & adj.* 7. **sev·enth** *n. & adj.* 7th, ⅐. in

the ~*th heaven*, extremely happy.
~'teen ['sevn'ti:n] *n. & adj.* 17.
~'teenth *n. & adj.* 17th, $\frac{1}{17}$.
~'ty ['sevnti] *n. & adj.* 70.
~'ti·eth ['seventiiθ] *n. & adj.* 70th, $\frac{1}{70}$.

sev·er ['sevə*] *v.t & i.* 1. cut
(e.g. a rope) in two; break off
(relations, a friendship). 2. (of
a rope, etc.) break.

sev·er·al ['sevrəl] *adj.* 1. three or
rather more; some. 2. separate;
individual: *They went their* ~
ways, each went his own way.
pron. a moderate number, not
many; some. ~'ly *adv.* separately.

se·vere [si'viə*] *adj.* (*-r, -st*). 1.
stern; unkind; strict. 2. (of the
weather, a disease) violent,
harsh. 3. (of a test) hard. 4. (of
style, etc.) simple; without
ornament. ~'ly *adv.* se·ver·i·
ty [si'veriti] *n.*

sew [sou] *v.t. & i.* (p.t. *sewed*,
p.p. *sewed* or *sewn* [soun]). work
with a needle and thread; fasten
with stitches; make (a garment)
by stitching. sew·ing *n.* work
(clothes, etc.) being sewn. 'sew·
ing-ma·,chine *n.*

sew·er ['sjuə*] *n.* large, usu.
underground, drain that collects
and carries away water and
organic waste matter from
buildings and roadways. sew·
age ['sjuidʒ] *n.* waste matter
carried away in ~s. ~'age
['sjuəridʒ] *n.* waste removal by
~s; system of ~s.

sewn, *see* sew.

sex [seks] *n.* the state of being
male or female; males or females
collectively. sex·u·al ['sekʃuəl]
adj. of sex or the sexes.

sex·tant ['sekstənt] *n.* instrument used for measuring the
altitude of the sun, etc. (in order
to determine a ship's position).

sex·ton ['sekstən] *n.* man who
takes care of a church building,
digs graves, rings the church
bell, etc.

shab·by ['ʃæbi] *adj.* (*-ier, -iest*).
1. in bad condition because
much used, worn, etc.; wearing
~ clothes. 2. (of behaviour)
mean; unfair. shab·bi·ly *adv.*

shack [ʃæk] *n.* small, roughly
built hut or shelter.

shack·le ['ʃækl] *n.* one of a pair
of iron rings joined by a chain
for fastening a prisoner's wrists
or ankles; (fig., pl.) sth. that
prevents freedom of action. *v.t.*
put ~s on; prevent from acting
freely.

shade [ʃeid] *n.* 1. partly dark
area sheltered from direct rays
of light: *sitting in the* ~. 2.
darker part(s) of a picture, etc.:
not enough light and ~ *in your
drawing*. 3. degree or depth of
colour: *various* ~*s of colour.* 4.
degree of difference: *a word with
many* ~*s of meaning.* 5. sth.
(e.g. for a lamp) that shuts out
light or lessens its brightness.
6. ghost; (pl.) the Greek under-
world or home of spirits. *v.t. &
i.* 1. keep direct rays of light
from: *He* ~*d his eyes with his
hand.* 2. cover (a light, lamp,
etc.). 3. darken (parts of a
drawing, etc.) to give an appearance of solidity, etc. 4. change
by degrees (*into, from . . . to*):
pink shading into red. shad·y
adj. (*-ier, -iest*). 1. giving ~ from
sunlight; in the ~: *the shady side
of a street.* 2. (colloq., of behaviour) of doubtful honesty.

shad·ow ['ʃædou] *n.* 1. area of
shade, dark shape thrown on
the ground, on a wall, floor, etc.,
by sth. which cuts off the direct
rays of light. 2. least sign or
appearance: *without a* ~ *of
doubt.* *v.t.* 1. darken. 2. keep
a secret watch on; follow all the
movements of (e.g. a suspected
criminal). ~'y *adj.* of or like
a ~.

shaft [ʃɑːft] *n.* 1. the long slender
stem of an arrow or spear.
2. long handle of an axe, etc.
3. one of the two wooden poles
between which a horse is har-
nessed to pull a cart, etc. 4. long
narrow space, usu. vertical, e.g.
for a lift in a building, for ven-
tilation, for going down into a
coal-mine, etc. 5. main part of
a column(1). 6. bar or rod joining parts of a machine or causing parts to turn.

shag·gy [ˈʃægi] *adj.* (-*ier*, -*iest*). **1.** rough and coarse; ~ *eyebrows*. **2.** covered with ~ hair: *a* ~ *dog*.

shake [ʃeik] *v.t. & i.* (p.t. *shook* [ʃuk], p.p. *shaken* [ˈʃeikn]). **1.** move, be moved, from side to side, up and down, forwards and backwards: ~ *one's head*, move it from side to side to indicate 'No' or doubt, disapproval, etc.; ~ *hands* (*with sb.*), take sb.'s hand at meeting or parting, or to show sympathy, etc.; ~ *off* (e.g. a cold, a bad habit), get free from. **2.** shock; trouble; weaken: ~ *sb.'s faith* (*courage*); *be* ~*n by bad news*. **3.** (of sb.'s voice) tremble; become weak or faltering (from old age, strong feeling). *n.* a shaking. **shak·y** *adj.* (-*ier*, -*iest*). **1.** (of a person, his movements) unsteady. **2.** (of things) unsafe; unreliable. **shak·i·ly** *adv.*

shale [ʃeil] *n.* soft rock that splits easily into thin layers.

shall [ʃæl, ʃəl] *v.* (see **shalt**; *shall not* is often shortened to *shan't* [ʃɑ:nt]; p.t. form *should* [ʃud, ʃəd, ʃd]; *should not* is often shortened to *shouldn't* [ˈʃudnt]). **1.** used in expressing the future tense (cf. *will*): *We* ~ *arrive tomorrow. Shall we come tomorrow? I told him that I should see him the following day.* **2.** used in expressing (a) the speaker's determination: *You say you won't go, but I say you* ~ *go*; (b) a promise: *If you work well today you* ~ *go home early.* **3.** used in statements or questions concerning wishes, commands, duties, etc.: *Shall I* (= Do you want me to) *open the window? You shouldn't* (= ought not to) *behave like that.* **4.** used in expressing purpose (cf. *may*, *might*): *I lent him an umbrella so that he should not get wet.* **5.** in reported speech: (*He said,* '*You will fail*'.) *He told me that I should fail.*

shal·low [ˈʃælou] *adj.* (-*er*, -*est*). of little depth; (fig.) not earnest or serious. *n.* (often pl.) ~ place in a river, lake, etc.

shalt [ʃælt] *v.* form of *shall* used with 'thou': *Thou* ~ *not steal.*

sham [ʃæm] *v.t. & i.* (-*mm*-). pretend: ~*ming illness* (*sleep*). *n.* person who ~s; sth. intended to deceive: *His kindness is only a* ~ (i.e. he is not really kind). *adj.* false; pretended: *a* ~ *fight* (as in training).

sham·ble [ˈʃæmbl] *v.i.* walk unsteadily without lifting the feet enough.

sham·bles [ˈʃæmbəlz] *n. pl.* (often as if sing., *a* ~). scene of bloodshed; place or scene of complete disorder.

shame [ʃeim] *n.* **1.** distressed feeling; loss of self-respect, caused by wrong or dishonourable or foolish behaviour (of oneself, one's family, etc.); capacity for experiencing this feeling: *be quite without* ~. **2.** dishonour: *bring* ~ *on one's family*; *put sb. to* ~, cause him to be disgraced. **3.** sth. unworthy; sth. that causes ~: *What a* ~ *to deceive the old man!* *v.t.* **1.** cause ~ (2) to; cause (sb.) to feel ~(1). **2.** frighten or force (sb. *into* or *out of* doing sth.) by causing him to feel ~. ~**'faced** *adj.* showing ~; looking distressed through ~. ~**'fa·ced·ly** [ˈʃeimˈfeisidli] *adv.* ~**'ful** *adj.* causing or bringing ~. ~**'ful·ly** *adv.* ~**'less** *adj.* feeling no ~; done without ~. ~**'less·ly** *adv.*

sham·poo [ʃæmˈpu:] *n.* (special soap, powder, etc., for a) washing of the hair. *v.t.* wash (the hair of the head).

sham·rock [ˈʃæmrɔk] *n.* clover-like plant with (usu.) three leaves on each stem.

shank [ʃæŋk] *n.* **1.** leg, esp. from knee to ankle. **2.** straight, slender part of an anchor, key, spoon, etc.

shan't [ʃɑ:nt] *v.* shall not.

¹shan·ty [ˈʃænti] *n.* poorly made house or shed.

²shan·ty [ˈʃænti] *n.* sailor's song.

shape [ʃeip] *n.* outward form; appearance; outline: *The Earth has the same* ~ *as an orange. in any* ~ *or form*, of any kind, in any way. *take* ~, (of ideas, etc.)

become orderly, well arranged; (of plans, buildings) approach completion. *v.t. & i.* **1.** give a certain ~ to. **2.** take ~; develop: *plans that are shaping well.* **~·less** *adj.* without a clear or graceful ~; without order. **~·ly** *adj.* well ~d; having a pleasing ~.

¹**share** [ʃeə*] *n.* **1.** part or division which sb. has in, receives from, or gives to, a stock (7) held by several or many persons, or which he contributes to a fund, expenses, etc.: *go ~s in,* divide (*with* others); become part owner (*with* others). **2.** part taken by sb. in an action, undertaking, etc. **3.** one of the equal parts into which the capital of a business company is divided, giving (to the owner of *preference* ~s) a right to a fixed rate of dividend or (to the owner of *ordinary* ~s) a right to part of the profits. *v.t. & i.* **1.** give a ~ of to others; divide and distribute. **2.** have or use (*with*): *~ a hotel bedroom with a stranger.* **3.** have a ~ (*in*): *Let me ~ in the cost of the outing.* '~·,hold·er *n.* owner of ~s in a business company. '~-out *n.* distribution (among members of a group).

²**share** [ʃeə*] *n.* blade of a plough.

shark [ʃɑ:k] *n.* large sea-fish that eats other fish and is dangerous to bathers, etc.

sharp [ʃɑ:p] *adj.* (*-er, -est*). **1.** with a good cutting edge; not blunt: *a ~ knife*; with a fine point: *a ~ needle.* **2.** well-defined; clear-cut; distinct: *a ~ outline.* **3.** (of curves, slopes, bends) abrupt; changing direction quickly: *a ~ curve in the road.* **4.** (of sounds) shrill; piercing: *a ~ cry of distress.* **5.** quickly aware of things: ~ *eyes*; *a ~ sense of smell* (*hearing*). **6.** (of feelings, taste) keen; suggesting cutting or pricking: *a ~ pain*; *a sauce with a ~ flavour.* **7.** harsh; severe: ~ *rebukes.* **8.** quick in mind: *a ~ child*; *a ~ witted boy.* **9.** quick; brisk: *a ~ walk*; *a ~* (violent) *struggle.*

10. quick to take advantage; unscrupulous: *a ~ lawyer*; ~ *practice.* **11.** (music) above the normal pitch; (of a note) raised half a tone in pitch: *C ~.* *n.* (music) (the symbol ♯ used to indicate a) note that is raised half a tone: ~*s and flats.* *adv.* **1.** punctually: *at 5 o'clock ~.* **2.** suddenly; abruptly: *turn ~ to the left.* **3.** (music) above the true pitch: *sing ~.* ~·**en** *v.t. & i.* make or become ~ (1), (8). ~·**er** *n.* swindler, esp. one who makes a living by cheating at cards. ~·**ly** *adv.* ~·**ness** *n.*

shatter [ˈʃætə*] *v.t. & i.* **1.** break suddenly into small pieces. **2.** (fig.) end (sb.'s hopes); shock (sb.'s nerves).

shave [ʃeiv] *v.t. & i.* **1.** cut (hair) off the chin, etc., with a razor. **2.** cut off (a thin layer, slice, etc.). **3.** pass very close to, almost touching. *n.* **1.** shaving (of the face). **2.** *a close* (*narrow*) ~, a fortunate escape from disaster, injury, loss, etc. **shav·en** [ˈʃeivn] *adj.* (old p.p. of ~, now only in compounds). *clean-~n, well-~n,* having been ~d clean (well). **shav·er** *n.* (joking style) boy. '**shav·ing-brush** *n.* one for spreading lather over the face before shaving. **shav·ings** *n. pl.* thin slices ~d off wood, esp. with a ¹plane (3). (Cf. *sawdust.*)

shawl [ʃɔ:l] *n.* large (usu. square) piece of material worn about the shoulders or head by women or wrapped round a baby.

she [ʃi:] *pron.* **1.** female person, etc., already referred to. (Cf. *her.*) **2.** *prefix.* female: *a she-goat.*

sheaf [ʃi:f] *n.* (pl. *sheaves* [ʃi:vz]). bundle of corn, barley, etc., stalks tied together after reaping; bundle of papers, etc.

shear [ʃiə*] *v.t. & i.* (p.p. *shorn* [ʃɔ:n]). cut the wool off (a sheep) with shears: *a sheep shorn of its wool.* **shears** *n. pl.* large scissors of various kinds for ~ing sheep, cutting cloth, grass, etc.

sheath [ʃi:θ] *n.* **1.** case for the blade of a sword, dagger, etc.

2. long, folded covering, esp. as part of a plant. **sheathe** [ʃi:ð] *v.t.* 1. put (a sword, etc.) into a ~. 2. encase in protective material: *sheathe a ship's bottom with copper.*

shed [ʃed] *n.* building, roughly made structure, used for storing things, sheltering animals, etc.

²**shed** [ʃed] *v.t.* (-dd-; p.t. & p.p. shed). 1. let (tears, leaves, feathers, etc.) fall or come off: *trees ~ding their leaves.* 2. cause (blood) to flow to: ~ *sb.'s blood,* kill or wound him. 3. give forth: *a fire that ~s warmth*; ~ *light on,* (fig.) help to explain (sth. obscure).

sheen [ʃi:n] *n.* shiny quality (of a surface).

sheep [ʃi:p] *n.* (pl. unchanged). grass-eating animal kept for its flesh as food (mutton) and its wool. '~·**dog** *n.* dog trained to help a shepherd to look after ~. ~·**ish** *adj.* awkwardly self-conscious; timid like a ~.

¹**sheer** [ʃiə*] *adj.* 1. complete; thorough; absolute: ~ *nonsense*; *a ~ waste of time.* 2. (of textiles, etc.) finely woven and almost transparent: *stockings of ~ silk.* 3. straight up or down: *a ~ drop of fifty feet.* *adv.* straight up or down.

²**sheer** [ʃiə*] *v.i.* (esp. of a ship) change direction.

sheet [ʃi:t] *n.* 1. large piece of linen or cotton cloth, esp. for a bed. 2. broad thin flat piece (*of* glass, iron, paper, etc.); wide expanse (*of* water, ice, etc.). 3. cord fastened to the lower corner of a sail, used to hold and regulate it. ~·**ing** *n.* material (e.g. cotton, linen) used for ~s.

sheik(h) [ʃeik] *n.* Arab chieftain.

shelf [ʃelf] *n.* (pl. *shelves* [ʃelvz]). 1. level board fastened at right angles to a wall, or in a bookcase, cupboard, etc., to stand things on. 2. ~-like piece of rock on a cliff, mountain side, etc. **shelve** [ʃelv] *v.t.* 1. put on a ~; (fig., of problems, etc.) postpone dealing with. 2. (of

land, the seashore) slope gradually.

shell [ʃel] *n.* 1. hard outer covering of bird's eggs, nuts, some seeds and fruits, and of some water animals (called ~*fish,* e.g. oysters, lobsters). 2. outer structure, walls, of an unfinished or ruined building. 3. metal case, filled with explosive, to be fired from a gun.' *v.t.* 1. take out of a ~ (1): ~*ing peas.* 2. fire ~s (3) at (from artillery). 3. ~ *out,* (colloq.) pay for, give money for, sth. '~·**fish** *n.* see *shell* (1). '~·**shock** *n.* nervous or mental disorder caused by the noise and blast of bursting ~s.

shel·ter [ˈʃeltə*] *n.* 1. condition of being protected or safe (e.g. from rain, the heat of the sun, danger). 2. sth. that gives safety or protection, esp from the weather: *an air raid ~.* *v.t. & i.* 1. give ~ to; protect. 2. take ~ (*in, under,* etc., sth.; *from* the rain, etc.).

shelve, shelves, see *shelf.*

shep·herd [ˈʃepəd] *n.* man who takes care of sheep. *the Good S~,* Jesus Christ. *v.t.* take care of; guide or direct (people).

sher·iff [ˈʃerif] *n.* 1. chief officer of the Crown in counties and certain cities, with legal and ceremonial duties. 2. (U.S.A.) officer with power to enforce law and order.

sher·ry [ˈʃeri] *n.* kinds of yellow or brown wine from Spain.

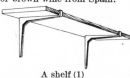

A shelf (1)

shield [ʃi:ld] *n.* 1. piece of armour (leather, steel, etc.) carried on the arm to protect the body in a fight. 2. sth. designed to keep out dust, wind, etc., to protect from danger (e.g. in a machine) or damage. 3. design in the shape of a ~ (1) in a coat of arms. *v.t.* protect; keep safe; save (sb.) from punishment or suffering.

shift [ʃift] *v.t. & i.* **1.** move, be moved, from one place to another: ~ *the blame* (*on*) *to sb. else*; ~ *the scenes* (on the stage of a theatre). **2.** ~ *for oneself*, manage to get a living, look after oneself, without help from others. *n.* **1.** change; group of workmen who start work as another group finishes; period for which such a group works: *on the day* (*night*) ~; *doing an eight-hour* ~. **2.** changed way of dealing with a situation: *make* ~ (*to do sth.*), do as well as one can without proper materials, tools, etc. ~**·less** *adj.* without ability to find ways of succeeding. ~**·y** *adj.* (*-ier, -iest*). untrustworthy; apt to use tricks.

shil·ling [ˈʃiliŋ] *n.* **1.** (formerly) British coin, value 1*s.* (= 5p). **2.** basic monetary unit of Kenya, Tanzania and Uganda. ~**'s worth** [ˈʃiliŋzwəːθ] *n.* as much as a ~ will buy.

shim·mer [ˈʃimə*] *v.i. & n.* (shine with a) wavering soft light: *moonlight* ~*ing on the lake*; *the* ~ *of pearls*.

shin [ʃin] *n.* front of the leg between the knee and the ankle.

shine [ʃain] *v.i. & t.* (p.t. & p.p. *shone* [ʃɔn]). **1.** give out or reflect light; be bright; make bright; polish. **2.** (fig.) be good (*at* or *in* sth.): *He doesn't* ~ *at tennis.* *n.* polish; brightness. **shin·y** *adj.* (*-ier, -iest*).

¹**shin·gle** [ˈʃiŋgl] *n.* small smooth pebbles on (or from) the seashore.

A shield (1)

A shield (3)

²**shin·gle** [ˈʃiŋgl] *n.* small, flat, square or oblong piece of thin wood used (like tiles) for covering a roof or wall. *v.t.* cover (a roof, etc.) with ~s.

ship [ʃip] *n.* seagoing vessel of considerable size: *a sailing-*~;

Ships

a steam-~. *v.t. & i.* (*-pp-*). **1.** put, take, send (goods, etc.), in a ~. **2.** ~ *water*, (at sea) be flooded by water breaking over the side; ~ *oars*, take them out of the water into the boat. **3.** agree to serve in a ~ for a voyage: *He* ~*ped as a steward.* '~**·mate** *n.* fellow sailor in a ~. '~**·ment** *n.* putting of goods on a ~; amount of goods ~ped at one time. '~**·per** *n.* person who arranges for goods to be ~ped. ~**·ping** *n.* ~s of a country, port, etc. '~**·shape** *adj.* in good order. '~**·wreck** *n.* loss or destruction of a ~ at sea by storm, etc. *v.t.* (cause to) suffer ~wreck. '~**·wright** *n.* ~builder. '~**·yard** *n.* place where ~s are built.

shire [ˈʃaiə*] *n.* county (chiefly in compounds, as *Yorkshire* [ˈjɔːkʃə*]).

shirk [ʃəːk] *v.t. & i.* avoid, try to escape (doing sth., responsibility, duty, sth. unpleasant, etc.). ~**·er** *n.*

shirt [ʃəːt] *n.* loose-fitting undergarment of cotton, etc., as worn by men under a suit. *in one's* ~*sleeves*, with no jacket on.

¹**shiv·er** [ˈʃivə*] *v.i.* tremble, esp. from cold or fear. *n.* ~ing.

²**shiv·er** [ˈʃivə*] *n.* one of many small broken pieces (of glass, etc.). *v.t. & i.* break into ~s.

¹**shoal** [ʃoul] *n.* great number of fish swimming together.

²**shoal** [ʃoul] *n.* shallow place in the sea, esp. where there are sandbanks.

¹**shock** [ʃɔk] *n.* number of sheaves of grain placed together and supporting each other in a field to dry after harvest.

²**shock** [ʃɔk] *n.* rough untidy mass of hair (on sb.'s head). '~-'**head·ed** *adj.* with such hair.

³**shock** [ʃɔk] *n.* **1.** violent blow or shaking caused by a collision or explosion. ~ *troops*, soldiers specially trained for fierce attacks. **2.** *electric* ~, disturbing effect of the passage of electric current through the body. **3.** sudden and violent disturbance of the feelings or the nervous system (caused by strong emotion, bad news, severe injury, etc.); condition caused by this: *suffering from* ~. *v.t.* (of news, etc.) cause ~ (3) to; fill with surprised disgust, horror, etc. ~'**ing** *adj.* very bad or wrong: ~*ing behaviour*: causing ~ (3).

shod, see *shoe*, v.

shod·dy ['ʃɔdi] *adj.* (-*ier*, -*iest*). of worse quality than it seems to be; below standard: *a* ~ *piece of work*.

shoe [ʃuː] *n.* outer covering for the foot, esp. one that does not reach above the ankle (cf. *boot*, *slipper*, *sandal*). *v.t.* **1.** put ~s on (a horse). **2.** (esp. p.p. *shod*): *well* (*poorly*) *shod for wet weather*, having, wearing, strong (poor) ~s. '~'**horn** *n.* device for getting the heel easily into a tight-fitting ~.

Shoes

shone, see *shine*.

shoo [ʃuː] *int.* cry used for driving away birds, etc. *v.t.* drive (birds, etc., *off*, *away*) by crying 'Shoo!'.

shook, see *shake*.

shoot [ʃuːt] *v.t. & i.* (p.t. & p.p. *shot* [ʃɔt]). **1.** move, come, go, send, suddenly or quickly (*out*, *in*, *up*, *forth*, etc.): *flames* ~*ing up from a burning house. The snake shot out its tongue.* **2.** (of plants, bushes) sprout; send out new leaves, etc., from a stem. **3.** (of pain) go repeatedly along (a part of the body) suddenly and swiftly: ~*ing pains. The*

pain shot up his arm. **4.** (of boats) move, be moved, rapidly over or through: ~ *the rapids*. **5.** (with a rifle, etc.) fire (4) a bullet from it; loose (an arrow): hit with a shell, bullet, arrow etc.; wound or kill (sb.) by doing this: ~ *a lion*; *be shot in the leg*; ~ *away all one's ammunition*. **6.** take a cinema picture of (a scene). *n.* **1.** new young growth on a plant or bush. **2.** = chute ~'**ing** *n.* act of ~ing a gun, etc.; right of ~ing (birds, etc.) over sb.'s land. ~'**ing star** *n.* meteor.

shop [ʃɔp] *n.* **1.** building or room where goods are shown and sold to the public. ~ *assistant*, sb. employed to serve customers in a ~. **2.** (also *workshop*) place where goods (esp. machines) are manufactured or repaired: *closed* (*open*) ~, works where only (not only) trade-union members are accepted. *v.i.* (-*pp-*). go to ~s(1) to buy things (often *go* ~*ping*; *have some* ~*ping to do*). '~'**keep·er** *n.* owner of a retail ~. '~'**lift·er** *n.* person who steals things from ~s while pretending to be a customer '~-**soiled,** '~-**worn** *adj.* damaged or dirty as the result of being put on view or handled in a ~. '~-**stew·ard** *n.* trade-union official in a workshop. '~'**walk·er** *n.* person who directs customers to the right counters, departments, etc., in a large ~.

shore [ʃɔː*] *n.* land bordering the sea, a lake, etc. *on* ~, on land.

²**shore** [ʃɔː*] *n.* wooden support placed against a shaky wall or the side of a ship on ¹shore. *v.t.* ~ *up*, support with a ~ or ~s.

shorn, see *shear*.

short [ʃɔːt] *adj.* (-*er*, -*est*). **1.** measuring little from end to end in space or time (opp. of *long*, *tall*). **2.** less than the usual, stated, or required (amount, distance, weight, etc.): *The shop keeper was fined for giving* ~ *weight* (*measure*). *a factory working* ~ *time*, fewer hours per day, fewer days per week, than usual. *a* ~ *cut*, a way of getting somewhere, doing sth., quicker than usual. ~ *of*, not having enough of : ~ *of money*; ~ *of breath*, (quickly becoming) breathless. **3.** (of a person) saying as little as possible; (of what he says) expressed in few words : *He* (*His answer*) *was* ~ *and to the point. for* ~, as a ~er form (of a name): *Benjamin, called ' Ben' for* ~. *in* ~, in a few words (used after a longer description or explanation). **4.** (of cake, pastry) easily breaking or crumbling. *adv.* **1.** suddenly; abruptly: *stop* ~; *pull up* ~. **2.** *come* (*fall*) ~ *of*, fail to reach (what is required, expected, etc.). ~ *of*, without going so far as; apart from. ~**·age** [ˈʃɔːtidʒ] *n.* condition of not having enough : *food* ~*ages*; *a* ~ *age of rice.* '~**·ˌcom·ing** *n.* fault; failure to be as good as is required or expected. ~**·en** *v.t. & i.* make or become ~er. ~**·en·ing** *n.* fat (lard, butter, etc.) used in making cakes, pastry, etc. '~**·hand** *n.* system of rapid writing using special signs. '~-**'hand·ed** *adj.* having not enough workers. '~-**'lived** *adj.* brief. ~**·ly** *adv.* **1.** after a ~ time. **2.** ~*ly before* (*after*), ~ time before (after). **3.** briefly; in a few words. **4.** sharply; curtly. ~**'ness** *n.* **shorts** *n. pl.* garment as shown below. '~-**'sight·ed** *adj.* **1.** unable to see things at a distance clearly. **2.** (fig.) not thinking sufficiently of future needs, etc. '~-**'tem·pered** *adj.* easily made angry. '~-**'wind·ed** *adj.* (easily made) breathless.

(A pair of)   A shovel
shorts

¹**shot** [ʃɔt] *n.* **1.** (sound of) firing of a gun, etc. (*do sth.*) *like a* ~, at once, without hesitation; *off*

like a ~, off at great speed. **2.** attempt to hit sth., hitting of sth. (e.g. with a stone); attempt to do sth., answer a question, etc.: *Let me have a* ~ (= try). **3.** that which is fired from a gun, esp. (pl. unchanged) a quantity of tiny balls of lead contained in the cartridge of a sporting gun (instead of a single bullet). **4.** person who shoots, with reference to his skill: *a good* (*poor*) ~. '~-**'gun** *n.* sporting gun firing ~ (3).

²**shot** [ʃɔt] *adj.* (of cloth) woven to show different colours when looked at from different angles.

should, see *shall.*

shoul·der [ˈʃouldə*] *n.* **1.** that part of the body of a human being or animal where an arm or foreleg is joined to the trunk; or where the wing of a bird joins its neck: *They were standing* ~ *to* ~ (side by side, close together). *straight from the* ~, (fig. of a rebuke, etc.) frankly put. **2.** (pl.) the top part of the back (q.v.). **3.** animal's foreleg as meat. **4.** ~-like part (of a bottle, mountain, etc.). *v.t.* **1.** take on one's ~(s). **2.** push with the ~: ~ *one's way through a crowd.* '~-**blade** *n.* one of the two flat bones of the ~s, behind and below the neck.

shout [ʃaut] *n.* loud call or cry. *v.i. & t.* give a ~; speak, say (sth.), in a loud voice.

shove [ʃʌv] *v.t. & i. & n.* (colloq.) push.

shov·el [ˈʃʌvl] *n.* spade-like tool, used for moving coal, sand, snow, etc. *v.t.* (*-ll-*). **1.** take (*up*), move, with a ~. **2.** make, clear (a path, etc.), with a ~. ~**·ful** *n.*

show [ʃou] *v.t. & i.* (p.t. ~*ed*, p.p. *shown*, rarely *shewn* [ʃoun]). **1.** allow to be seen; bring before the sight. **2.** (with adv.): ~ *sb. in* (*out*), lead him to a room (out to the doorway of a building). ~ *off*, make a display of one's accomplishments, powers, possessions, etc. ~ *sth. off*, display it to advantage, help to make its beauty, etc., noticeable. ~ *up*, (colloq.) be present (at a meeting, etc.). ~ (sb. or sth.) up, make the truth about (sb. or sth. dishonest, etc.) known to others. **3.** (with nouns): ~ *fight*, give signs of being ready to fight; ~ *one's hand*, make known one's plans; ~ *the way*, (fig.) set an example. **n. 1.** ~ing: *a ~ of hands*, (voting by) raising of hands for or against (a proposal). **2.** collection of things publicly displayed, esp. for competition: *a flower ~; a travelling ~ of wild animals*; *on ~*, exhibited. **3.** display (of one's possessions, abilities, etc.) for effect, to impress others: *a room furnished for ~, not for comfort*. **4.** public entertainment, theatrical performance, etc. *put up a good ~*, perform, do, well. **5.** (colloq.) sth. going on; undertaking: *give the (whole) ~ away*, let people know what is being done or planned. '~·**down** *n.* (slang) full and frank declaration of one's strength, intentions, etc. ~·**ing** *n.* *on one's own ~ing*, as made clear by oneself; *make a poor ~ing*, give a poor impression. '~·**man** *n.* organizer of public entertainments, esp. a circus. '~·**man·ship** *n.* art of attracting public attention (e.g. to what one is trying to sell). '~·**room** *n.*, '~·**case** *n.*, '~·**win·dow** *n.* one in which goods are displayed. ~·**y** *adj.* (-*ier*, -*iest*). likely to attract attention; (too much) decorated; (too) brightly coloured. ~·**i·ly** *adv.*

show·er ['ʃauə*] *n.* **1.** short fall of rain, etc.; large number of things, arriving together: *a ~ of sparks (arrows, leaves, etc.)*. **2.** (also '~-*bath*) (taking of a bath by standing under a) ~ or spray of water coming from a pipe fixed overhead. *v.i. & t.* fall, send, give, in a ~. ~·**y** *adj.* (of the weather) with frequent ~s.

shrank, see *shrink*.

shrap·nel ['ʃræpnl] *n.* shell that scatters bullets or pieces of metal when it explodes.

shred [ʃred] *n.* strip or piece cut or torn or broken off sth.;

fragment: *torn to ~s*; *not a ~ of evidence against the accused man*. *v.t. & i.* (-*dd*-). make into ~s; become ~s.

shrew [ʃru:] *n.* bad-tempered, scolding woman; small mouse-like animal. ~·**ish** *adj.* sharp-tongued.

shrewd [ʃru:d] *adj.* (-*er*, -*est*). **1.** having, showing, sound judgement and common sense. **2.** (of a guess) near the truth. ~·**ly** *adv.* ~·**ness** *n.*

shriek [ʃri:k] *v.i. & t. & n.* scream.

shrift [ʃrift] *n.* *give sb. (get) short ~*, little time (to prepare for punishment, get sth. done, etc.).

shrill [ʃril] *adj.* (of sounds, etc.) sharp; piercing; high-pitched.

shrimp [ʃrimp] *n.* small shellfish, cooked as food; very small person. *v.i.* *go ~ing*, catch ~s in nets.

shrine [ʃrain] *n.* **1.** tomb or casket containing holy relics. **2.** building or place associated with sth. or sb. especially respected.

shrink [ʃriŋk] *v.i. & t.* (p.t. *shrank* [ʃræŋk], p.p. *shrunk* [ʃrʌŋk]). **1.** make or become less, smaller (esp. of cloth through wetting). **2.** move back, show unwillingness to do sth. (*from* fear, shame, because it is unpleasant). ~·**age** ['ʃriŋkidʒ] *n.* process of ~ing; degree of ~ing.

shrive [ʃraiv] *v.t.* (p.t. ~*d* or *shrove*, p.p. ~*n* ['ʃrivn]). (old use, of a priest) hear the confession of a penitent sinner and absolve him from the spiritual consequences of his sin(s).

shriv·el ['ʃrivl] *v.t. & i.* (-*ll*-). (cause to) become dried or curled up (through heat, frost, dryness, old age).

shroud [ʃraud] *n.* **1.** cloth or sheet wrapped round a corpse. **2.** sth. that covers and hides: *a ~ of mist*. **3.** (pl.) ropes supporting a ship's mast. *v.t.* wrap or cover in a ~.

shrub [ʃrʌb] *n.* plant with woody stem, lower than a tree and (usu.) with several separate stems from the root. ~·ber·y ['ʃrʌbəri] n. place planted with ~s.

shrug [ʃrʌg] v.t. & i. (-gg-). lift (the shoulders) slightly (to show indifference, doubt, etc.). n. such a movement.

shrunk, see *shrink*.

shud·der ['ʃʌdə*] v.i. shake; tremble with fear or disgust: ~ *at the sight of*. . . . n. uncontrollable trembling.

shuf·fle ['ʃʌfl] v.i. & t. 1. walk (*along*) without raising the feet properly. 2. mix (playing-cards) before dealing; put (papers, etc.) into disorder. 3. do sth. in a careless way: ~ *into one's clothes*; ~ *one's clothes on* (*off*); ~ *through one's work*.

shun [ʃʌn] v.t. (-nn-). keep away from; avoid: ~ *temptation* (*publicity*).

shunt [ʃʌnt] v.t. & i. send (a railway wagon, etc.) from one track to another; (of a train, etc.) be ~ed to a siding.

shut [ʃʌt] v.t. & i. (-tt-; p.t. & p.p. *shut*). 1. move (e.g. a door, the lips) so as to close an opening; (of a window, door, etc.) become closed; keep (sb. or sth. *out*), e.g. by closing a door, etc. 2. (with adv.): ~ *down*, (of a factory, etc.) stop work. be ~ *in*, (of a building, etc.) be cut off (from a view, from easy access, etc., e.g. by trees, other high buildings, etc.). ~ *off*, stop the supply of (gas, water, etc.). be ~ *off from*, be kept away from, be separated, from (society, etc.). ~ *up*, fasten doors, windows, etc., in a building (for safety); (colloq.) stop talking; make (sb.) stop talking.

shut·ter ['ʃʌtə*] n. 1. movable cover (wooden board or screen) for a window (to keep out light or thieves): *put up the ~s*, close a shop; stop doing business. 2. (in a camera) device that opens to allow light to pass through the lens.

shut·tle ['ʃʌtl] n. part of a loom or sewing-machine that carries the thread from side to side. v.t. & i. move backwards and forwards like a ~.

¹shy [ʃai] adj. (-er, -est). 1. (of persons) self-conscious and uncomfortable in the presence of others. 2. (of behaviour) showing such self-consciousness: *a shy look* (*smile*). 3. (of animals) easily frightened; unwilling to be seen. 4. *fight shy of*, be inclined to avoid. v.i. (of a horse) turn aside in fear or alarm: *The horse shied at a white object in the hedge*. shy·ly adv. shy·ness n.

²shy [ʃai] v.t. & i. & n. (colloq.) throw.

sick [sik] adj. 1. (predic. only) be ~, throw up food from the stomach: *sea~ on the first day of the voyage*; *feel ~*, feel that one is about to throw up food from the stomach. 2. unwell; ill. *go ~*, report to (army) doctor for medical treatment. 3. (colloq.) ~ *at* (*about*), feeling regret or annoyance at. ~ *for*, filled with a longing for. ~·en ['sikn] v.i. & t. 1. be ~ening for, be in the first stages of (an illness). 2. make or become tired (*of*), disgusted. ~·en·ing adj. disgusting; unpleasant: *a ~ening smell*. ~·ly adj. (-ier, -iest). 1. causing a ~ feeling. 2. frequently in bad health; weak: *a ~ly child*. 3. suggesting unhappiness or illness: *a ~ly smile*. ~·ness n. ill health; illness.

sick·le ['sikl] n. short-handled tool with a curved blade for cutting grass, wheat, etc.

A shuttle

side [said] n. 1. one of the flat or fairly flat surfaces of an object; one of these which is not the top or bottom: *A box has a top, a bottom, and four sides*; either of the two surfaces of a piece of paper, cloth or other very thin, flat object; the two surfaces of a house or the human body that are not the front or the back of it; one of the lines enclosing a square or a triangle. *on all ~s, on every ~,* everywhere around. *by the ~ of,* (fig.) compared with. *~ by ~,* touching or close together. *put sth. on one ~,* put it away, save it for future use. **2.** team of players: *take ~s (with),* support one party in a dispute. **3.** (colloq.) pretence of being superior or important: *He puts on too much ~.* *v.i.* (only) *~ with,* support (in a dispute). '~**board** *n.* table, usu. with drawers and cupboards, placed against the wall of a dining-room. '~-**car** *n.* small two-wheeled car fastened to the ~ of a motor-cycle. '~-**is·sue** *n.* question of less importance (in relation to the main one). '~-**light** *n.* one of two small lamps at the front of a motor-car; (fig.) sth. that throws extra, incidental, light on a problem. '~-**line** *n.* occupation that is not one's main work; class of goods sold in addition to the chief classes of goods; (pl.) (ground bordering the) lines at the sides of a football-pitch, tennis-court, etc. '~-**long** *adj. & adv.* (directed) to or from one ~: *a ~long glance.* '~-,**sad·dle** *n.* woman's saddle, made so that both feet may be on the same ~ of the horse. *adv.* on a ~-saddle. '~-**show** *n.* small show at a fair or exhibition; activity of small importance in relation to the main activity. '~-**step** *v. & n.* (avoid by taking a) sudden step to one ~. '~-**track** *n.* branch road or way. *v.t.* postpone or avoid discussion of (a proposal, etc.); turn (sb.) away from his main purpose to sth. less important. '~-**walk** *n.* (U.S.A.) paved footpath. ~-**ways** *adv.* to, towards, from, the ~; with the ~ or edge first. **sid·ing(s)** *n.* short railway track(s) at the ~ of the main line. **si·dle** ['saidl] *v.i.* walk (*up to, away from,* sb.) in a shy or nervous way.

siege [si:dʒ] *n.* (period of) operations of armed forces to capture

a fortified place. *lay ~ to,* besiege.

si·es·ta [si'estə] *n.* afternoon rest, esp. as taken in hot countries.

sieve [siv] *n.* utensil with wire network to separate finer grains from coarse grains, or solids from liquids.

sift [sift] *v.t. & i.* **1.** separate by putting through a sieve: *~ ashes from cinders;* (fig.) *~ evidence,* examine it carefully. **2.** shake through a sieve: *~ sugar on to a cake.*

sigh [sai] *v.i.* **1.** take a deep breath that can be heard (showing sadness, tiredness, relief, etc.); (of the wind) make a ~-like sound. **2.** *~ for,* feel a longing for. *n.* act or sound of ~ing.

sight [sait] *n.* **1.** (power of) seeing: *lose one's ~,* become blind; *have long (short or near) ~,* be able to see things well only at long (short) range; *know sb. (only) by ~,* by appearance, not as an acquaintance; *lose ~ of,* see no longer, (fig.) be out of touch with, fail to keep in mind; *catch ~ of,* begin to see, succeed in seeing; *at (on) ~,* as soon as (sth. or sb.) is seen; *in (out of) ~,* that can (cannot) be seen. **2.** opinion: *Do what is right in your own ~.* **3.** sth. seen or to be seen, esp. sth. remarkable; (pl.) noteworthy buildings, places, etc., in a town or district: *Come and see the ~s of London.* **4.** *a ~,* (colloq.) a person or thing that excites ridicule or unfavourable comment: *What a ~ she looks in that old dress!* **5.** device helping to aim or observe when using a rifle, telescope, etc.; observation taken with such a device. '~-**seer** *n.* person visiting the ~s (3) of a town, etc. *v.t.* **1.** catch ~ of; see (by coming near to): *~ land.* **2.** observe (a star, etc.) by using ~s (5); adjust the ~s (5) of a gun, etc. ~-**less** ['saitlis] *adj.* ¹blind.

sign [sain] *n.* **1.** mark, object, used to represent sth.: *mathematical ~s* (e.g. $+$, $-$, $\times$, $\div$). **2.** word(s), design, etc., on a board or plate to warn sb. of or direct sb. towards sth.: *traffic ~s* (e.g. to give warning of a speed limit). **3.** sth. that gives evidence, points to the existence or likelihood, of sth.: *~s of suffering on a person's face.* **4.** movement of the hand, head, etc., used with or instead of words. **5.** = ~board. *v.t. & i.* **1.** write one's name on (a letter, document, etc.) to show that one is the writer or that one agrees with the contents. *~ away*, give up (rights, property, etc.) by ~ing one's name. *~ on (up)*, ~ an agreement about employment. **2.** make known (to sb.) an order or request by using ~s (4): *The policeman ~ed to (for) us to stop.* '~**board** *n.* board with a notice or advertisement on it, e.g. one giving the name of an inn. '~**post** *n.* post showing names and directions of towns, villages, etc.

¹**sig·nal** ['signəl] *n.* **1.** (making of) sign(s), movement(s), showing of light(s), to give warning, instructions, news, etc., esp. to sb. at a distance. **2.** *railway ~*, post, etc., for ~s to drivers of trains. **3.** event which is a starting-point for a series of events. *v.i. & t.* (*-ll-*). **1.** make a ~ or ~s (*to, sb., to do* sth., *that*). **2.** use ~s. **3.** send (news) by ~(s). '~**box** *n.* building on a railway from which railway ~s are worked. ~**ler** *n.* person who sends and receives ~s in the Army. '~**man** *n.* person who sends and receives ~s (on railways, in the Navy, etc.).

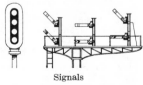

Signals

²**sig·nal** ['signəl] *adj.* remarkable; outstanding: *win a ~ victory.* ~**ly** *adv.* ~**ize** *v.t.* make (an event) ~.

sig·na·to·ry ['signətəri] *n. &*

adj. (person, country) that has signed an agreement.

sig·na·ture ['signətʃə*] *n.* person's name signed by himself.

sig·ni·fy ['signifai] *v.t. & i.* **1.** show by a sign; make known: *~ one's approval.* **2.** mean; be a sign of. **3.** *~ much (little)*, be of much (little) importance. **sig·nif·i·cance** [sig'nifikəns] *n.* meaning; importance. **sig·nif·i·cant** *adj.* important; having a special or suggestive meaning. **sig·ni·fi·ca·tion** [signifi'keiʃən] *n.* (exact) meaning (of a word).

si·lage ['sailidʒ] *n.* green cattle food stored in a silo.

si·lence ['sailəns] *n.* condition of being quiet or silent: *listen to sb. in ~.* *v.t.* make (sb. or sth.) silent; cause to be quiet. **si·lenc·er** *n.* device that reduces the noise made by a petrol engine, etc. **si·lent** ['sailənt] *adj.* **1.** making no or little sound; still; without sound. **2.** saying little or nothing; giving no answer, no news. **si·lent·ly** *adv.*

sil·hou·ette [silu'et] *n.* picture in solid black showing only the shape; shape of sth. or sb. seen against a light background. *v.t.* show or make a ~ of: *a mountain ~d against the sky at daybreak.*

silk [silk] *n.* thin soft thread from the cocoons of certain insects; material made from this; made of ~: *~ stockings.* *take ~*, become K.C. or Q.C. '~**en** *adj.* (liter.) soft and smooth: *~en hair; a ~en voice.* '~**worm** *n.* caterpillar that produces ~. ~**y** *adj.* (*-ier, -iest*). soft, shiny, smooth, like ~.

sill [sil] *n.* shelf, block of wood or stone at the base of a window.

sil·ly ['sili] *adj.* (*-ier, -iest*). foolish; weak-minded. **sil·li·ness** *n.*

si·lo ['sailou] *n.* (pl. *-os*). airtight structure in which green food (silage) for farm animals is stored.

silt [silt] *n.* sand, mud, etc., deposited by moving water (at the mouth of a river, in a harbour, etc.). *v.t. & i.* (of a harbour, etc.) (cause to) become stopped (*up*) with ~.

sil·van ['silvən] *adj.* of trees or a wood (2); rural.

sil·ver ['silvə*] *n.* **1.** shining white metal used for making coins, ornaments, spoons, etc. **2.** things made of ~, esp. ~ coins and table ~ (spoons, forks, dishes, etc.). **3.** (attrib.) ~-coloured; (of sounds) soft and clear. *v.t.* coat with ~ or material like ~; make (sth.) bright like ~. ~·**y** *adj.* like ~; clear-toned.

sim·i·lar ['similə*] *adj.* like; of the same sort. ~ *to*, almost the same as. ~·**ly** *adv.* ~·**i·ty** [,simi'læriti] *n.* likeness.

sim·i·le ['simili] *n.* (use of) comparison of one thing to another (e.g. He is as brave as a lion).

sim·mer ['simə*] *v.i. & t.* **1.** keep (a pot, food, etc.) almost at boiling-point. **2.** be filled with (*anger*, etc.) which is just kept under control: ~*ing with rage.*

sim·per ['simpə*] *v.i. & n.* (give a) silly self-conscious smile.

sim·ple ['simpl] *adj.* (*simpler*, *simplest*). **1.** unmixed; not divided into parts; having only a small number of parts; *a ~ substance;* ; *a ~ machine.* **2.** plain; not much decorated or ornamented: *~ food (buildings).* **3.** not highly developed: *~ forms of plant life.* **4.** easily done or understood; not causing trouble: *a ~ task; written in ~ language.* **5.** innocent, straightforward: *behave in a pleasant and ~ way.* **6.** foolish; inexperienced. **7.** with nothing added; absolute: *a ~ fact; the truth, pure and ~.* ~·**ton** *n.* foolish, easily-deceived person.

sim·plic·i·ty [sim'plisiti] *n.* the state of being ~. **sim·pli·fy** ['simplifai] *v.t.* make ~(r); make easier to understand or deal with. **sim·pli·fi·ca·tion** [,simplifi'keiʃən] *n.* simplifying; sth. that is simplified. **sim·ply** *adv.* **1.** in a ~ manner. **2.** quite. **3.** only.

sim·u·late ['simjuleit] *v.t.* pre-

tend to be; pretend to have or feel.

sim·ul·ta·ne·ous [,siməl'teinjəs] *adj.* happening or done at the same time.

sin [sin] *n.* **1.** breaking of, act which breaks, God's laws. **2.** sth. looked upon as contrary to good manners, common sense, etc.: *It's a sin to make the children do too much homework.* *v.i.* (-*nn*-). commit sin ; do wrong. **sin·ful** *adj.* wicked. **sin·less** *adj.* free from sin. **sin·ner** *n.* person who sins.

since [sins] *adv.* **1.** (with the perfect tenses) after a date in the past; before the present time; between some time in the past and the present time: *Last Tuesday he went out for a walk and has not been seen ~. ever ~ : I met him ten years ago and have admired him ever ~.* **2.** ago: *She left here many years ~.* **prep.** during a period of time after: *We haven't met ~ her marriage.* **conj.** **1.** from the past time when: *Where have you been ~ I last saw you? It is just a week ~ we arrived here.* **2.** as: *S~ we have no money we can't buy anything.*

sin·cere [sin'siə*] *adj.* **1.** (of feelings, behaviour) genuine; not pretended. **2.** (of a person) straightforward; not in the habit of expressing feelings that are not genuine. ~·**ly** *adv.* **sin·cer·i·ty** [sin'seriti] *n.*

si·ne·cure ['sainikjuə*] *n.* position for which one receives credit or payment without having to work or take responsibility.

sin·ew ['sinju:] *n.* **1.** tendon (strong cord) joining a muscle to a bone. **2.** (pl.) muscles; energy; physical strength. ~*s of war,* money.

sing [siŋ] *v.i. & t.* (p.t. *sang* [sæŋ], p.p. *sung* [sʌŋ]). **1.** make continuous musical sounds (tunes) with the voice; utter words or sentences set to a tune. ~ *out,* call loudly (*for*). ~ *up,* ~ with more force. **2.** make a whistling or humming sound : *The kettle is ~ing on the fire*. **3.** (often ~ *of*) celebrate in poetry. **~·song** ['siŋsɒŋ] *n.* **1.** *in a ~song*, in a rising and falling tone of monotonous regularity. **2.** meeting of friends to ~ songs together.

singe [sindʒ] *v.t. & i.* **1.** burn off the tips or ends (esp. of hair). **2.** blacken the surface of (cloth, etc.) by burning.

sin·gle ['siŋgl] *adj.* **1.** one only. ~ *ticket*, for a journey to a place, not there and back. **2.** for the use of, used for, done by, one person, etc. : *a ~ bed*. **3.** unmarried. *v.t.* ~ *out*, select from others (for special attention, etc.). **'~-'hand·ed** *adj. & adv.* without help from others. **'~-'mind·ed** *adj.* intent on, devoted to one cause or purpose. **sin·gly** *adv.* one by one ; by oneself.

sin·glet ['siŋglit] *n.* undershirt ; vest.

sin·gu·lar ['siŋgjulə*] *adj.* **1.** uncommon ; strange. **2.** outstanding (courage, etc.). **3.** (grammar) of the form used in speaking of one person or thing. *n.* ~ (3) form (of a word). **~·ly** *adv.* **~·ity** [ˌsiŋgju'læriti] *n.* sth. that is ~ (1) ; the quality of being ~ (1).

sin·is·ter ['sinistə*] *adj.* **1.** suggesting evil or coming misfortune : *a ~ beginning*. **2.** showing ill will : *a ~ face*.

sink [siŋk] *v.i. & t.* (p.t. *sank* [sæŋk], p.p. *sunk* [sʌŋk]). **1.** go down, esp. below the horizon or the surface of a liquid ; cause or allow (a ship) to ~. **2.** slope downwards ; become lower or weaker : *The foundations have sunk*. (fig.) *His heart sank at the news.* **3.** make by digging, etc. : *a ~ well*. **4.** (of liquids, and fig.) go deep (*into*) : *The rain sank into the dry ground. The warning sank into his mind*. **5.** put (money) into an undertaking, esp. one from which it cannot easily be taken out again. *n.* fixed basin (of stone, porcelain, etc.) with a drain for taking off water, used for washing dishes, etc. **~·a·ble**

adj. that can be sunk. **~·er** *n.* (esp.) lead weight for ~ing a fishing-line or net. **~·ing** *adj.* ~*ing feeling*, feeling in the stomach caused by hunger or fear ; ~*ing fund*, money from revenue put aside by a government, business company, etc., for gradual repayment of a debt.

sin·u·ous ['sinjuəs] *adj.* winding ; full of curves and twists.

sip [sip] *v.t. & i.* (-*pp*-). drink, taking (the liquid in) a very small quantity at a time. *n.* (quantity taken in) one act of sipping.

si·phon ['saifən] *n.* **1.** bent or curved tube so arranged that liquid will flow up and then down through it. **2.** bottle from which soda-water, etc., can be forced out by pressure of gas in it. *v.t. & i.* (cause to) draw (out, off) through a ~.

A siphon   A soda-siphon

sir [sə:*] *n.* **1.** respectful form of address to a man, used in speaking and writing : *Good morning, sir. Here is your coffee, sir. Dear Sir, . . .* (Cf. *madam*.) **2.** prefix to the name of a knight or baronet : *Sir* [sə*] *Walter Scott.*

sire ['saiə*] *n.* (old use). **1.** father or male ancestor. **2.** title of respect used when addressing a king or emperor.

si·ren ['saiərən] *n.* **1.** (in old Greek stories) one of a number of winged women whose songs charmed sailors and caused their destruction. **2.** woman who attracts and is dangerous to men. **3.** ship's whistle for sending warnings and signals ; device for producing a loud shrill noise (as a warning, etc.).

sir·loin ['sə:lɔin] *n.* best part of loin of beef.

sis·al ['saisl] *n.* plant with strong fibre used for making rope.

sis·ter ['sistə*] *n.* **1.** daughter of the same parents as oneself or another person referred to. **2.** senior hospital nurse. **3.** member of a ~hood; nun: *Sisters of Mercy.* **4.** (attrib.) of the same design, type, etc.: ~ *ships.* ~**hood** *n.* society of women who devote themselves to charitable work or who live together in a religious order (11). '~**-in-law** *n.* ~ of one's wife or husband; wife of one's brother. ~**ly** *adj.* of or like a ~.

sit [sit] *v.i. & t.* (*-tt-* ; p.t. & p.p. *sat* [sæt]). **1.** rest the body on the buttocks. **2.** (with adv. & prep.): *sit down under* (insults, etc.), suffer without complaint; *sit for*, represent (a town, etc.) in Parliament; *sit for an examination*, take an examination; *sit for one's portrait*, have one's portrait painted while sitting before an artist; *sit on a committee, etc.*, be a member of one; *sit (up)on a question, etc.*, (of a jury, etc.) inquire into it; *sit (up)on sb.*, (colloq.) snub him; *sit out (a play)*, remain to the end; *sit up*, take an upright position after lying flat; not go to bed (until later than the usual time); *make sb. sit up*, shock or surprise him. **3.** (of Parliament, a court of law, a committee, etc.) hold meetings, etc. **4.** keep one's seat on (a horse). **5.** (of clothing) fit: *a coat that sits well* (*loosely*, etc.) *on sb.* **6.** (of birds) perch; (of hens) be on a nest, covering eggs in order to hatch them. **sit·ting** *n.* (esp.) time during which a court of law, Parliament, etc., sits (3), or during which a person is engaged on one task: *finish reading a book at one sitting.*

si·tar ['sitɑ:*] *n.* Indian stringed musical instrument played with the fingers.

site [sait] *n.* place where sth. was, is, or is to be: *the ~ of a battle; a ~ for a new school.*

sit·u·at·ed ['sitjueitid] *adj.* (of a town, building, etc.) placed; (of a person) in (certain) circum-stances. **sit·u·a·tion** [ˌsitju-'eifən] *n.* **1.** position (of a town, building, etc.). **2.** condition, state of affairs (esp. at a certain time). **3.** work, employment (esp. as a domestic servant).

six [siks] *n. & adj.* 6. *at sixes and sevens*, in confusion. **six·pence** ['sikspəns] *n.* British coin, see Appendix, p. 628. **six·teen** ['siks'ti:n] *n. & adj.* 16. **sixth** [siksθ] *n. & adj.* 6th; ⅙. **six·ty** ['siksti] *n. & adj.* 60. **six·ti·eth** ['sikstiiθ] *adj. & n.* 60th.

¹size [saiz] *n.* **1.** degree of large-ness or smallness: *about the ~ of*, about as large as; *of some ~*, fairly large. **2.** one of the stan-dard and (usu.) numbered ~s in which articles of clothing, etc., are made: ~ *six shoes. v.t.* **1.** arrange in ~s. **2.** ~ *up*, form an opinion or a judgement of. **siz·a·ble** *adj.* of a fairly large ~.

²size [saiz] *n.* sticky substance used to glaze textiles, paper, etc.

siz·zle ['sizl] *v.i. & n.* (make the) hissing sound as of sth. cooking in fat.

¹skate [skeit] *n.* one of a pair of sharp-edged steel blades to be fastened to a boot for moving smoothly over ice. *v.i.* go on ~s. (Cf. *roller-~s*, see *roll.*)

A ¹skate   Skiing

²skate [skeit] *n.* large flat sea-fish, valued as food.

skein [skein] *n.* length of silk or wool yarn coiled into a bundle.

skel·e·ton ['skelitn] *n.* **1.** bones of an animal body in the same relative positions as in life. **2.** hard framework of an animal or plant. **3.** framework of a build-ing or of an organization, plan, theory, etc. **4.** (attrib.) ~ *key*, one that will open a number of different locks; ~ *staff* (*crew*, *etc.*), one reduced to the smallest possible number needed for maintenance.

sketch [sketʃ] *n.* **1.** rough, quickly-made drawing. **2.** short account or description. **3.** short, humorous play or piece of writing. *v.t. & i.* make a ~ of. ~ *sth out*, give a rough plan of. ~·y *adj.* (-*ier*, -*iest*). done roughly and without detail or care; incomplete. ~·i·ly *adv.*

skew·er [ˈskjuə*] *n.* pointed stick of wood or metal for holding meat together while cooking. *v.t.* fasten with, or as with, a ~.

ski [skiː] *n.* (pl. *ski* or *skis*). one of a pair of long, narrow strips of wood, strapped to the boots, for moving over snow. *v.i.* move over snow on skis. (See the picture on page 492.)

skid [skid] *n.* **1.** piece of wood or metal fixed under the wheel of a cart, etc., to prevent it from turning, and in this way check the speed when going downhill. **2.** slipping movement of the wheels of a car, etc., on a slippery road. *v.i.* (-*dd*-). (of a car, etc.) move or slip (sideways).

skies, see *sky.*

skiff [skif] *n.* small light boat, esp. one rowed or sculled by one person.

skill [skil] *n.* ability to do sth. well and expertly. **skilled** *adj.* trained; experienced: ~*ed workmen*; needing ~: ~*ed work*. **skil·ful** *adj.* having or showing ~. **skil·ful·ly** *adv.*

skim [skim] *v.t. & i.* (-*mm*-). **1.** remove the cream, scum, etc., from the surface of (a liquid): ~ *the cream off*; ~ *the milk*. **2.** move lightly over (a surface), not touching or only occasionally touching it: *a bird* ~*ming (over) a lake*. **3.** read through sth. quickly, noting only the chief points. 'ˈ~ **milk** *n.* milk from which the cream has been ~med.

skimp [skimp] *v.t. & i.* supply, use, less than enough of what is needed.

skin [skin] *n.* **1.** elastic substance forming the outer covering of the body of a person or animal. **2.** animal ~ with or without the hair or fur; material made from this; ²hide. **3.** outer covering of a fruit: *banana* ~s. **4.** container made of ~ for holding liquids, etc. *v.t. & i.* take the ~ off. 'ˈ~-ˈdeep *adj.* not going deep; of or on the surface only. 'ˈ~·flint *n.* miser. ~·ny *adj.* (-*ier*, -*iest*). having little flesh.

skip [skip] *v.i. & t.* (-*pp*-). **1.** jump lightly and quickly: ~ *out of the way of the bus.* **2.** jump over a rope which is turned over the head and under the feet as one jumps. **3.** go from one point to another; (esp.) go from one part of a book, etc., to another without reading what is between: ~ *the next chapter.* *n.* ~ping movement.

Skipping   A sledge or toboggan

skip·per [ˈskipə*] *n.* captain, esp. of a small merchant ship.

skir·mish [ˈskəːmiʃ] *n.* (usu. unplanned) fight between small parts of armies or fleets.

skirt [skəːt] *n.* **1.** woman's loose garment that hangs from the waist. **2.** part of a dress, etc., below the waist. **3.** (pl.) = outskirts. *v.t.* be on, pass along, the ~s (3) of. 'ˈ~·ing-board *n.* board fixed along the bottom of the walls of a room.

skit [skit] *n.* short piece of humorous writing, short play, copying and making fun of sth. or sb.

skit·tish [ˈskitiʃ] *adj.* (of horses and persons) lively; full of play and fun.

skit·tle [ˈskitl] *n.* one of the bottle-shaped pieces of wood to be knocked down by a ball rolled towards them in the game of ~s.

skulk [skʌlk] *v.i.* hide, move secretly, through cowardice, or to avoid work or duty, or with an evil purpose.

skull [skʌl] *n.* bony framework of the head. '~-**cap** *n.* brimless, close-fitting cap.

skunk [skʌŋk] *n.* small N. American animal which sends out a bad-smelling liquid when attacked; its fur.

sky [skai] *n.* (pl. *skies*). the space in which we see the sun, moon, stars, and clouds. '**sky·'high** *adj. & adv.* up in(to) the sky. '**sky·lark** *n.* small bird that sings as it flies high into the sky. '**sky·light** *n.* window in a roof. '**sky·line** *n.* outline of things (mountains, buildings, etc.) seen against the sky. '**sky·ˌscrap·er** *n.* very tall building.

slab [slæb] *n.* thick flat piece (of stone or other solid substance).

slack [slæk] *adj.* (*-er, -est*). 1. giving little care or attention to one's work; having or showing little energy. 2. dull; inactive; with not much business or work needing to be done. 3. loose; not tight: *a ~ rope. n.* 1. *the ~*, that part of a rope, etc., which hangs loosely. 2. coal-dust. 3. (pl.) loose-fitting trousers. *v.i.* be lazy or careless in one's work: *~ off (up)*, reduce speed, do less work. ~·**en** *v.t. & i.* make or become slower, looser, or less active. ~·**er** *n.* (colloq.) sb. who tries to avoid his proper share of work. ~·**ly** *adv.* ~·**ness** *n.*

slag [slæg] *n.* waste matter remaining when metal has been extracted from ore.

slain, see *slay*.

slake [sleik] *v.t.* 1. satisfy or make less strong (thirst, desire for revenge, etc.). 2. change the chemical nature of (lime) by adding water.

slam [slæm] *v.t. & i.* (*-mm-*). 1. shut violently: *~ the door. The door ~med.* 2. put (*down*), throw or knock with force: *~ sth. down. n.* noise of a door, window, etc., being ~med.

slan·der ['slɑːndə*] *v.t. & i. & n.* (make a) false statement that damages a person's reputation. ~·**ous** *adj.* making such statements; containing ~s.

slang [slæŋ] *n.* (always singular). 1. words, meanings, phrases, commonly used in talk but not suitable for good writing or serious occasions. 2. kind of ~ used by a trade or social group: *schoolboy ~.* 3. (attrib.) ~ *words. v.t.* use scolding language to. ~·**y** *adj.* (*-ier, -iest*). fond of using ~; full of ~; of the nature of ~: *~y expressions.*

slant [slɑːnt] *v.i. & n.* slope: *on the ~*, ~ing, sloping.

slap [slæp] *n.* quick blow with the open hand or with sth. flat. *v.t.* (*-pp-*). 1. hit with a ~. 2. put (sth. *down*) with a ~ping noise. '~-**dash** *adj. & adv.* careless(ly); reckless(ly).

slash [slæʃ] *v.t. & i.* make long cuts in (or *at*) sth. with a sweeping stroke; strike with a whip. *n.* act of ~ing; long cut.

slat [slæt] *n.* long, thin, narrow piece of wood or metal.

slate [sleit] *n.* 1. kind of blue-grey stone that splits easily into thin, smooth, flat layers; square or oblong piece of this used for roofs. 2. sheet of ~ in a wooden frame for writing on: *a clean ~*, (fig.) a good record (2). 3. colour of ~, blue-grey. *v.t.* 1. cover (a roof) with ~s. 2. (colloq.) scold. **slat·y** *adj.* like, containing, ~.

slat·tern ['slætən] *n.* dirty, untidily dressed woman. ~·**ly** *adj.*

slaugh·ter ['slɔːtə*] *v.t.* kill (an animal) for food; kill (people) in great numbers. *n.* killing of animals for food or of many people (in war). '~-**house** *n.* place where animals are killed for food.

slave [sleiv] *n.* 1. person who is the property of another and bound to serve him; person compelled to work very hard for someone else. 2. *a ~ to (of)*, sb. completely in the power of, under the control of, an impulse, habit, etc. *v.i.* work hard (*at* sth., *for* a living, etc.). '~-ˌdriv·er *n.* man in charge of ~s; employer, etc., forcing those under him to work very hard. **slav·er** *n.* ship or person trading in ~s. **slav·er·y** ['sleivəri] *n.* condition of being a ~; custom of having ~s; hard, esp. badly paid, employment. **slav·ish** *adj.* 1. in the manner of ~s; (esp.) weak and submissive. 2. without originality: *a slavish imitation.* **slav·ish·ly** *adv.*

slay [slei] *v.t.* (p.t. **slew** [slu:], p.p. **slain** [slein]). kill; murder.

sled [sled], **sledge** [sledʒ] *n.* vehicle with runners (long narrow strips of wood or metal) instead of wheels, used on snow. *v.i. & t.* travel, carry, by ~. (See the picture on page 493.)

sledge (**-ham·mer**) ['sledʒ (-ˌhæmə*)]*n.* heavy hammer used by blacksmiths.

sleek [sli:k] *adj.* 1. (of hair, an animal's fur, etc.) soft and smooth. 2. (of a person or animal) having ~ hair or fur. 3. (of a person, his behaviour) over-anxious to please. *v.t.* make ~(1); smooth with the hand.

sleep [sli:p] *n.* completely restful and inactive condition of the body such as that which normally comes each night for several hours in bed; period of this: *to have a good ~. v.i. & t.* (p.t. & p.p. **slept**). 1. rest in the condition of ~; be or fall asleep. 2. ~ *sth. off,* recover from (e.g. a headache) by ~ing. 3. (of a hotel, etc.) have enough beds for: *a hotel that can ~ sixty guests.* ~**er** *n.* 1. person who ~s, esp. *a heavy* (*light*) ~*er.* 2. wooden beam, etc., as a support for railway lines. 3. (bed in a) ~ing-car(riage). '~**ing-car,** (**-ˌcar·riage**) *n.* railway carriage with beds(berths). '~**ing-pill** *n.* medicine to cause a person to ~. ~**ing part·ner** *n.* person who puts money into a business but plays no active part in it. ~**less** *adj.* without ~; unable to get ~: *a ~less night.* ~**less·ly** *adv.* ~**less·ness** *n.* '~-ˌwalk·er *n.* person who walks while asleep. ~**·y** *adj.* (-ier, -iest). 1. needing, ready for, ~. 2. inactive: *a ~y village.* ~**·i·ly** *adv.* ~**·i·ness** *n.*

sleet [sli:t] *n.* falling snow or hail mixed with rain. *v.i. It was ~-ing,* ~ *was falling.*

sleeve [sli:v] *n.* that part of a garment which covers the arm. *laugh up one's ~,* be secretly amused; *have sth. up one's ~,* have an idea, plan, etc., which one keeps secret for future use.

sleigh [slei] *n.* sledge, esp. one drawn by a horse.

sleight [slait] *n.* (only in) ~ *of hand,* expertness in using the hand(s) in performing tricks, in juggling, etc.

slen·der ['slendə*] *adj.* (-er, -est). 1. small in width or circumference compared with height or length: *a ~ stem.* 2. not fat; graceful: *a ~ girl; a ~ waist.* 3. slight; small; inadequate: *a ~ chance of success.*

slept, see *sleep.*

sleuth(-hound) ['slu:θ(-haund)] *n.* bloodhound; dog that follows a scent; (colloq., *sleuth*) detective.

¹**slew,** see *slay.*

²**slew** [slu:] *v.i. & t.* force or turn *round* into a new direction.

slice [slais] *n.* 1. thin, wide, flat piece cut off sth., esp. bread or meat. 2. utensil with a wide flat surface for cutting, serving, or lifting (e.g. cooked fish). *v.t.* cut into ~s; cut (a piece *off*).

slick [slik] *adj.* (colloq.) 1. smooth. 2. (of a person, his manners) too smooth; tricky.

slide [slaid] *v.t. & i.* (p.t. & p.p. **slid**). 1. (cause to) move smoothly, slip along, over a polished surface, ice, etc.: *children sliding on the ice.* 2. (of things) move easily and smoothly: *drawers that ~ in and out. The book slid from my knee to the floor.* 3. *let things ~,* not trouble about things. 4. pass gradually, without being aware (*into* a condition, e.g. dishonesty). *n.* 1. act of sliding(1). 2. smooth stretch of ice, hard snow, etc., on which to ~(1). 3. smooth slope down which things or persons can ~(1). 4. picture, etc., on a glass plate to be slid into a projector and shown on a screen. 5. glass plate on which is placed sth. to be examined under a microscope. 6. part of a machine, etc., that ~s. 7. ~ rule, rule with a sliding part, used for mathematical calculations. **slid·ing scale** n. scale by which one thing (e.g. salary) goes up or down in relation to changes in sth. else (e.g. cost of living).

¹**slight** [slait] adj. (-er, -est). 1. slim; slender. 2. small; not serious or important: a ~ head-ache. ~·ly adv. (esp.) a little: ~ly better.

²**slight** [slait] v.t. treat (sb.) without proper respect or courtesy. n. (behaviour, words, showing a) lack of proper respect.

slim [slim] adj. (-mm-). 1. slender. 2. small; insufficient: a ~ attendance (excuse). v.i. (-mm-). eat less, take physical exercise, etc., to reduce one's weight and become ~(1).

slime [slaim] n. 1. soft, thick mud. 2. sticky substance from snails, etc. **slim·y** adj. (-ier, -iest). of, like, covered with, ~.

sling [sliŋ] n. band of material, rope, chain, etc., looped round an object (e.g. a broken arm, a barrel) to support, throw, or lift it. v.t. & i. (p.t. & p.p. slung [slʌŋ]). 1. throw with force: ~ stones at a window. 2. support (sth.) so that it can swing, be lifted, etc.: ~ a hammock.

slink [sliŋk] v.i. (p.t. & p.p. slunk [slʌŋk]). go (about, away, by, off) in a secret, guilty, or ashamed manner.

slip [slip] v.i. & t. (-pp-). 1. lose one's balance; fall or almost fall as the result of this: He ~ped and broke his leg. 2. go or move quietly or quickly, esp. without attracting attention: He ~ped past me. The years ~ped by. 3. move, get away, escape, fall, by being hard to hold or by not being held firmly: The fish ~ped out of my fingers. The blanket ~ped off the bed. 4. put; pull on or push off with a quick easy movement: ~ into (out of) a dress; ~ a coat on (off); ~ a

coin into sb.'s hand. 5. make a small mistake, esp. by being careless: ~ in one's grammar. 6. escape, get free, from: The dog ~ped its collar. It ~ped my memory. n. 1. act of ~ping. give sb. the ~, get away from him. 2. small mistake, esp. ~ of the pen (tongue), error in writing (speaking), etc. 3. loose cover for a pillow, etc. 4. kind of petti-coat. 5. narrow strip of paper. '~-**knot** n. knot which ~s along its own cord to form a noose which becomes tight. ~·**per** n. loose-fitting light shoe worn indoors. ~·**per·y** adj. (-ier, -iest). smooth, wet, polished, so that it is difficult to hold, to stand on or to move on: a ~pery road. '~-**shod** adj. slovenly; careless.

slit [slit] n. long, narrow cut, tear, or opening. v.t. & i. (-tt-; p.t. & p.p. slit). make a ~ in; cut or tear into narrow pieces; open (an envelope, etc.) by ~ting.

slith·er ['sliðə*] v.i. slide.

slob·ber ['slɔbə*] v.t. & i. 1. let spit run from the mouth. 2. ~ over (sb. or sth.), show foolish or excessive love or admiration for.

slo·gan ['slougən] n. striking and easily remembered phrase used to advertise sth. or to make clear the aim of a group, organization, campaign, etc.

sloop [slu:p] n. 1. small one-masted sailing-ship. 2. small warship used for anti-submarine escort duty.

slop [slɔp] v.i. & t. (-pp-). 1. (of liquids) spill over the edge. 2. cause (liquid) to do this: ~ coffee on the table. **slops** n. pl. 1. dirty, waste water from the kitchen, etc. 2. liquid food (e.g. milk, soup), esp. for sick people. ~·**py** adj. (-ier, -iest). 1. wet and dirty with rain or ~s(1): ~py roads. 2. (of food) consisting of ~s(2). 3. (of a person) foolishly sentimental; (of sentiment) fool-ish and weak. 4. (colloq.) care-less; untidy.

slope [sloup] n. 1. slanting line,

position or direction, at an angle of less than 90° to the earth's surface or to some other line or flat surface: *the ~ of the roof.* **2.** area of rising or falling ground. *v.i. & t.* have a ~; cause to ~; give a ~ to. ~ **arms,** place and hold rifle(s) in a sloping position on the left shoulder(s).

slot [slɔt] *n.* narrow opening through which sth. (e.g. a coin) is to be put. *v.t.* (*-tt-*). make a ~ or ~s in. '~-**ma,chine,** from which, e.g. matches, a ticket, can be obtained by putting a coin through a ~.

sloth [slouθ] *n.* laziness; idleness.

slouch [slautʃ] *v.i.* stand, sit, move, in a lazy, tired way.

¹slough [slau] *n.* swamp; marsh.

²slough [slʌf] *n.* cast-off skin of a snake. *v.t. & i.* put, come, or throw (*off*).

slov·en·ly ['slʌvnli] *adj.* dirty, untidy, or careless (in dress, habits, work, etc.). **slov·en** *n.* ~ person. **slov·en·li·ness** *n.*

slow [slou] *adj.* (*-er, -est*). **1.** taking a long time; not quick; at less than the usual speed; dull, not quick at learning; not lively enough: *What a ~ entertainment!* **2.** (of a clock) showing a time that is earlier than the correct time. *v.t. & i.* (cause to) go at a ~er speed than before: *The train ~ed down.* '~**coach** *n.* person who acts or thinks ~ly. *adv.* (*-er, -est*). at a low speed: *Go ~ till you feel better. Go ~er or you will fall.* ~**ly** *adv.* *Try to walk more ~ly.* ~**ness** *n.*

sludge [slʌdʒ] *n.* thick mud; thick dirty oil or grease.

slug [slʌg] *n.* slow-moving creature like a snail but without a shell.

slug·gard ['slʌgəd] *n.* lazy, slow-moving person. **slug·gish** ['slʌgiʃ] *adj.* inactive; slow-moving.

sluice [slu:s] *n.* **1.** apparatus (~-*gate,* ~-*valve*) for regulating the level of water by controlling the flow into or out of (a canal, lake, etc.). **2.** channel

carrying off surplus water; current of water through a ~. **3.** thorough washing with a stream of water. *v.t. & i.* **1.** send a stream of water over; wash with a stream of water. **2.** (of water) come (*out*) in a stream.

slum [slʌm] *n.* **1.** street of poor, dirty, crowded houses. **2.** (pl.) part of a town where there are ~s (1).

slum·ber ['slʌmbə*] *v.i. & n.* (liter.) sleep.

slump [slʌmp] *v.i.* **1.** ~ *down* (*into*), drop or fall heavily. **2.** (of prices, trade, activity) fall steeply or suddenly. *n.* period of time during which prices, trade activity, etc., have ~ed.

slung, see *sling.*

slunk, see *slink.*

slur [slə:*] *v.t. & i.* (*-rr-*). **1.** join words, syllables, musical notes, etc., so that they cannot be separately distinguished. **2.** ~ *over,* deal quickly with in the hope of concealing: ~ *over sb.'s faults.* *n.* **1.** reproach; sth. that damages one's reputation. **2.** act of ~ring sounds.

slush [slʌʃ] *n.* soft melting snow; slimy mud.

slut [slʌt] *n.* slovenly woman.

sly [slai] *adj.* (*-er, -est*). **1.** deceitful; keeping or doing things secretly; seeming to have, suggesting, secret knowledge: *a sly look; on the sly,* secretly. **2.** playfully mischievous.

¹smack [smæk] *n.* (sound of) blow given with the open hand. *v.t.* **1.** strike with the open hand. **2.** ~ *one's lips,* make a ~ing sound with the lips to show pleasure (at food, etc.). *adv.* in a sudden and violent way: *run ~ into a brick wall.*

²smack [smæk] *n.* sort of small sailing-boat for fishing.

³smack [smæk] *v.i. & n.* (have a) slight flavour or suggestion (*of*).

small [smɔ:l] *adj.* (*-er, -est*). opp. of *large*: *Lions are large, dogs are ~, and rats are ~er still. look (feel) ~,* look (feel) foolish or humbled. ~ *change,* coins of small value. *the ~ hours,* the early hours (1 a.m. to 4 a.m.). ~ talk, talk about unimportant things. on the ~ side, a little too ~. '~-arms n. pl. weapons light enough to be carried in the hand. '~-pox n. serious contagious disease which leaves permanent marks on the skin.

¹smart [smɑːt] v.i. & n. (feel or cause) sharp pain (in body or mind).

²smart [smɑːt] adj. (-er, -est). 1. bright; new-looking; clean; well dressed. 2. clever; skilful; having a good quick brain. 3. fashionable. 4. (of a walk) quick; brisk. 5. severe: a ~ blow (punishment). ~en v.t. & i. ~en up, make or become ~ (1). ~ly adv. ~ness n.

smash [smæʃ] v.t. & i. 1. break, be broken, into pieces. ~ up, break violently. 2. rush, force a way, violently (into, through, etc.). 3. defeat utterly. n. (sound of) ~ing; violent fall, blow, collision; accident.

smat·ter·ing ['smætəriŋ] n. a ~ of, a slight knowledge of (a subject).

smear [smiə*] v.t. & i. 1. cover or mark with sth. oily or sticky. 2. make dirty greasy marks on. 3. (of wet ink, etc.) spread and make dirty marks, etc. n. mark made by ~ing.

smell [smel] n. that one of the five senses which is special to the nose; that which is noticed by means of the nose; bad or unpleasant quality that affects the nose: What a ~! v.t. & i. (p.t. & p.p. smelt). 1. be aware of by means of the sense of ~; use the nose for its special purpose of detecting a ~; sniff in order to enjoy, etc., the ~ of sth. ~ of, have the ~ of; suggest. ~ out, discover by means of the sense of ~; (fig.) discover (a secret, etc.) by careful inquiry. 2. give out a ~: His breath ~s of beer. 'smel·ling-salts n. pl. sharp-smelling substance used to relieve headache or faintness.

smelt [smelt] v.t. melt (ore); separate (metal) from ore by doing this. (See also smell.)

smile [smail] v.i. & t. & n. (have a) pleased, happy expression on the face. ~ (up)on, look with favour or approval on. smil·ing·ly adv. with a ~.

smirch [sməːtʃ] v.t. make dirty; (fig.) dishonour. n. (fig.) stain (on one's reputation).

smirk [sməːk] n. habitual or silly self-satisfied smile. v.i. smile thus.

smite [smait] v.t. & i. (p.t. smote [smout], p.p. smitten ['smitn]) (liter. or humor. only). 1. strike; hit hard. 2. defeat utterly. smitten by (with), deeply attracted by; attacked by (an illness).

smith [smiθ] n. worker in iron or other metals, esp. a black~. ~·y ['smiði] n. black~'s workshop.

smock [smɔk] n. loose garment like an overall.

smoke [smouk] n. 1. black, grey, etc., vapour that can be seen coming from a burning substance with particles of carbon. (Cf. steam.) end in ~, have no satisfying result. 2. act of smoking tobacco; (colloq.) cigar; cigarette. v.i. & t. 1. give out ~. 2. (of a fire or fire-place) send out ~ into the room. 3. breathe in and out the ~ of burning tobacco from a cigarette, cigar, or pipe between one's lips. 4. dry,and preserve (meat, fish) with ~. 5. stain, darken, or dry, with ~: ~d glasses. 6. drive out with ~; send ~ on to (insects, plants). smok·er n. person who ~s tobacco; railway carriage in which passengers may smoke (2). smok·y adj. (-ier, -iest). 1. giving out ~; full of ~: smoky chimneys. 2. like ~ in taste, appearance, etc. ~·less adj. burning without ~: ~less coal; free from ~: a ~less atmosphere. '~-screen n. cloud of ~ intended to hide military or naval operations. '~-stack n. tall factory chimney; outlet for ~ and steam from a steamship or railway engine.

smooth [smuːð] adj. (-er, -est). 1. having a surface like that of glass; (of the sea) without waves; (of movement) free from shaking, bumping, etc. **2.** (of a liquid mixture) free from lumps; well beaten or mixed. **3.** (of sounds, speech) flowing easily. **4.** (of a person, his manner or words) flattering; pleasant but perhaps insincere. *v.t. & i.* **1.** make ~ (often ~ *down, out*). **2.** free from difficulties, troubles, etc.: ~ *away sb.'s objections*. ~'ly *adv.* ~'ness *n.* '~-faced *adj.* (fig.) pleasant in behaviour and appearance but insincere. '~-,spok·en, '~-tongued *adj.* using ~ (4) words.

smote, see *smite*.

smoth·er ['smʌðə*] *v.t. & i.* **1.** cause the death of, by stopping the breath of or by keeping air from. **2.** cover thickly or completely: ~*ed in dust*; ~ *a child with kisses*. **3.** keep back, suppress (a yawn, one's anger, etc.). **4.** put out (a fire), cause (a fire) to burn slowly, by covering it with ashes, sand, etc.

smoul·der ['smouldə*] *v.i.* burn slowly without flame. *n.* ~ing fire.

smudge [smʌdʒ] *n.* dirty mark, esp. one where wet ink has been rubbed. *v.t. & i.* make a ~ on; mark with ~s.

smug [smʌg] *adj.* (*-gg-*) self-satisfied; too fond of comfort and respectability. ~'ly *adv.*

smug·gle ['smʌgl] *v.t. & i.* **1.** get (goods) secretly and illegally (*into, out of*, a country, *through* the customs, etc.). **2.** take (sth. or sb.) secretly (*into*, etc.): ~ *a letter to sb. in prison*. **smug·gler** *n.*

smut [smʌt] *n.* (mark or stain made by a) bit of soot, dirt from burning coal, etc. ~'ty *adj.* (*-ier, -iest*). dirty with ~s; improper: ~*ty stories*.

snack [snæk] *n.* light, usu. hurriedly eaten, meal.

snag [snæg] *n.* rough or sharp object, root of tree, hidden rock, which may be a source of danger; (colloq.) unexpected hindrance or difficulty.

snail [sneil] *n.* kinds of small soft animal, most of them with a spiral shell, as shown here.

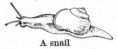

A snail

snake [sneik] *n.* long, legless, crawling reptile. **snak·y** *adj.* of or like a ~; infested with ~s.

snap [snæp] *v.t. & i.* (*-pp-*). **1.** make a sudden, often noisy, bite (*at*); (try to) snatch (*at* sth.). **2.** ~ *sb.'s head off*, speak suddenly and impatiently to him. **3.** break with a sharp noise; open or close with a sudden cracking noise; make a sharp noise: ~ *one's fingers*. **4.** take a ~shot of. *n.* **1.** act or sound of ~ping. **2.** *a cold* ~, a sudden, short period of cold weather. **3.** = ~shot. **4.** (attrib.) done quickly and without much warning: *a* ~ *election (vote)*. *adv.* with a ~ (1). ~'py *adj.* (*-ier, -iest*). lively. '~·shot *n.* casual, informal photograph taken with a hand camera.

snare [snɛə*] *n.* trap, esp. one with a slip-knot, for catching small animals and birds; (fig.) trick; temptation. *v.t.* catch in a ~.

snarl [snɑːl] *v.i. & t.* (of dogs) show the teeth and growl. *n.* act or sound of ~ing.

snatch [snætʃ] *v.t. & i.* **1.** put out the hand suddenly and take: ~ *sth. up* (*down, away, off*, etc.). **2.** ~ *at*, try to get by ~ing. **3.** get quickly or when the chance occurs: ~ *an hour's sleep*. *n.* **1.** sudden stretching out of the hand to get sth. **2.** short outburst or period (*of* sth.): ~*es of song*.

sneak [sniːk] *v.i. & t.* **1.** go quietly and secretly (*away, in, off*, etc.). **2.** (colloq.) take away (sb. else's property) without permission. *n.* cowardly, treacherous person.

sneer [sniə*] *v.i. & n.* (show contempt by a) scornful smile or words: ~ *at sb. or sth.* ~'ing·ly *adv.*

sneeze [sniːz] *n.* sudden uncontrollable outburst of air through the nose and mouth. *v.i.* make a ~.

sniff [snif] *v.i. & t.* **1.** draw air in through the nose so that there is a sound; do this (~ *at*) to show disapproval or contempt. **2.** draw (sth.) in through the nose as one breathes: ~ *up powdered medicine*; smell by doing this: *dogs ~ing (at) a lamp-post*. *n.* act or sound of ~ing; a breath (*of* air, etc.). **snif·fle** *v.i.* = snuffle.

snig·ger ['snigə*] *n.* half-suppressed laugh (esp. at sth. improper). *v.i.* ~ *at (over)* sth., laugh in this way.

snip [snip] *v.t. & i.* (-*pp*-). cut with scissors: ~ *the ends off*. *n.* cut made by ~ping; sth. ~ped off.

¹**snipe** [snaip] *n.* game (5) bird with a long bill, living in marshes.

²**snipe** [snaip] *v.i. & t.* shoot (*at* sb.) from a hiding-place or in darkness; kill or wound by firing shots in this way. **snip·er** *n.* soldier who ~s.

snip·pet ['snipit] *n.* small piece cut off; (pl.) small bit (*of* information, news, etc.).

sniv·el ['snivl] *v.i.* (-*ll*-). cry with pretended grief, sorrow, or fear; whine. *n.* tearful state or talk.

snob [snob] *n.* person who pays too much respect to social position or wealth. ~·**bish** *adj.* ~·**bish·ly** *adv.* ~·**bish·ness** *n.*

snoop [snu:p] *v.i.* pry into other persons' affairs. ~·**er** *n.* person who does this.

snooze [snu:z] *v.i. & n.* (colloq.) (take a) short sleep.

snore [sno:*] *v.i.* breathe roughly and noisily while sleeping. *n.* sound of snoring. **snor·er** ['sno:rə*] *n.*

snort [sno:t] *v.i. & t.* force air violently out through the nose; do this (*at* sb.) *with* impatience, contempt, etc. *n.* act or sound of ~ing.

snout [snaut] *n.* nose (and mouth) of an animal (esp. a pig); pointed front of sth. like an animal's ~.

snow [snou] *n.* frozen vapour

falling from the sky in flakes; mass of such flakes on the ground, etc. *v.i. & t.* **1.** (of ~) come down from the sky. **2.** come or send (down, etc.) like ~, in large quantities. **3.** *be ~ed up (in)*, be prevented by ~ from going out. '~·**ball** *n.* lump of ~ pressed together for throwing in play; (fig.) sth. that increases quickly in size as it moves forward. '~·**bound** *adj.* unable to travel because of heavy falls of ~. '~·**drift** *n.* bank of ~ heaped up by wind. '~·**drop** *n.* bulb plant with small white flowers in early spring. '~·**flake** *n.* feather-like piece of falling ~. '~·**plough** *n.* device for pushing ~ from roads and railways. '~·**shoe** *n.* frame with leather straps for walking on soft ~. '~·**y** *adj.* (-*ier*, -*iest*). of or like ~; covered with ~.

¹**snub** [snʌb] *v.t.* (-*bb*-). treat (esp. a younger or less senior person) with cold behaviour or contempt; reject (an offer) thus. *n.* blunt words or behaviour.

²**snub** [snʌb] *adj.* *a* ~ *nose*, ('~-*nosed*, with a) short, thick, slightly turned-up nose.

¹**snuff** [snʌf] *v.i. & t.* = snuffle. *n.* powdered tobacco to be taken up into the nose. ~·**col·oured** *adj.* brownish-yellow.

²**snuff** [snʌf] *v.t. & i.* cut or pinch off the end of the wick of a candle; put out (a candle light) by doing this.

snuf·fle ['snʌfl] *v.i.* make sniffing sounds; breathe noisily, talk through the nose, esp. when it is partly stopped up. *n.* act or sound of snuffling.

snug [snʌg] *adj.* (-*gg*-). **1.** warm and comfortable; sheltered. **2.** neat and tidy; rightly or conveniently placed or arranged. ~·**gle** ['snʌgl] *v.i.* lie or get (close to sb.) so as to be warm or comfortable: *~gle up*.

so [sou] *adv.* **1.** to such an extent: *Why are you so unkind? He is not so stupid as that. He was so ill that we had to call a doctor. Now we have come so far* (as far as this), *we may as* *well go all the way.* **so long as,** on condition that: *You may borrow the book, so long as you keep it clean.* **so far from,** instead of: *So far from helping, he hindered us.* **2.** in this (that) way: *As you treat me, so will I treat you. Stand so* (like this). *It happened (just) so* (as we had expected). **so that,** (a) in order that: *Speak clearly, so that we can hear you;* (b) with the result that: *He remained still, so that people thought he had died.* **so as to,** in order to: *I will hurry, so as not to delay you.* **3.** used instead of a word, phrase, etc.: *I told you so!* (That is what I told you.) **4.** also: *You are learning English and so are they.* **5.** about: *She is forty or so* (about forty). **conj. 1.** therefore; that is why: *She asked me to go, so I went.* **2.** (as an exclamation): *So you've come back at last!* **'so-and-'so pron.** used for sb. or sth. not named. **'so-'called adj.** described thus (esp. without good reason).

soak [souk] *v.t. & i.* **1.** become wet through, by being in liquid or by absorbing liquid: *Let the clothes ~ in soapy water.* **2.** cause (sth.) to absorb as much liquid as possible: *~ bread in milk (dirty clothes in water).* **3.** (of rain, etc.) make very wet; enter, pass *(through, into, etc.).* **4.** *~ up,* (of substances) take up, absorb (liquid). *n.* act of *~ing;* heavy fall of rain.

soap [soup] *n.* fatty substance used with water to remove dirt by washing and scrubbing. **soft ~,** (fig.) flattery. **'~-,bub·ble n.** filmy ball, of *~y* water with changing colours, filled with air. **'~-suds n. pl.** mass of foam or lather made from *~* and water. **~·y adj.** of or like *~;* (fig.) over-anxious to please. *v.t.* rub *~* on; wash with *~.*

soar [sɔ:] *v.i.* go, float high, in the air; rise beyond what is ordinary: *a ~ing eagle. Prices ~ed.*

sob [sɔb] *v.i. & t.* (-*bb*-). draw in the breath sharply and irregu-

larly from sorrow or pain, esp. while crying; say (sth.) while doing this. *n.* act or sound of sobbing.

so·ber ['soubə*] *adj.* **1.** self-controlled; temperate; serious in thought, etc.; calm. **2.** avoiding drunkenness; not drunk. **3.** (of colours) not bright. *v.t. & i.* make or become *~.* **so·bri·e·ty** [sou'braiəti] *n.* quality or condition of being *~.*

soc·cer ['sɔkə*] *n.* (colloq.) association football.

so·cia·ble ['souʃəbl] *adj.* fond of the company of others; friendly; showing friendliness. **so·cia·bly adv. so·cia·bil·i·ty** [,souʃə'biliti] *n.*

so·cial ['souʃəl] *adj.* **1.** living in groups, not separately. **2.** of people living in communities; of relations (3) between persons or communities: *~ customs; ~ reform; ~ welfare.* **3.** of or in society: *one's ~ equals* (i.e. persons of the same class in a society (1)). *n.* friendly meeting, usu. for talk and entertainment, esp. one organized by a club, etc. **~·ism n.** theory that land, transport, chief industries, etc., should be owned and managed by the State or public bodies in the interests of the community as a whole. **~·ist n.** supporter of *~ism.* **~·is·tic** [,souʃə'listik] *adj.* of, tending towards, *~ism.* **~·ize** ['souʃəlaiz] *v.t.* make *~istic;* transfer to public ownership.

so·ci·e·ty [sə'saiəti] *n.* **1.** social community; persons living together as a group or as a nation; the organization, customs, etc., of such a group. **2.** the persons of fashion or distinction in a place, district, country, etc.; the upper classes. **3.** company; companionship: *spend an evening in the ~ of one's friends.* **4.** organization of persons formed with a purpose; club; association: *the school debating ~.*

so·ci·ol·o·gy [,sousi'ɔlədʒi] *n.* science of the nature and growth of society. **so·ci·ol·o·gist n.** expert in *~.*

sock [sɔk] *n.* **1.** short stocking not reaching the knee. **2.** loose sole put inside a shoe.

sock·et ['sɔkit] *n.* hollow into which sth. fits or in which sth. turns.

sod [sɔd] *n.* (cut lump of) surface of grassland with the roots and earth.

so·da ['soudə] *n.* common chemical substance used in making soap, glass, etc. *washing* ~, for softening water, cleaning, etc.; *baking* ~, used in cooking; ~-*water*, water charged with gas to make it bubble. '~-,**foun·tain** *n.* (U.S.A.) counter from which ~-water, ices, etc., are served.

sod·den ['sɔdn] *adj.* **1.** wet through: *clothes* ~ *with rain.* **2.** stupid through too much drinking. **3.** (of bread, etc.) heavy and dough-like.

so·dium ['soudjəm] *n.* silverwhite metal occurring naturally only in compounds.

so·fa ['soufə] *n.* long, cushioned seat, with a back and arms for two or three persons.

soft [sɔft] *adj.* (*-er*, *-est*). **1.** opp. of *hard*: *As soon as we left the road our car stuck in the* ~, *wet soil.* **2.** (of cloth) smooth; delicate. **3.** (of light, colours) not bright; restful to the eyes. **4.** (of sounds) subdued; not loud. **5.** (of words, answers, etc.) mild; intended to please. **6.** ~ *drinks*, cold nonalcoholic drinks, esp. fruit juices; ~ *water*, water (e.g. rainwater) easy to wash with. ~**en** ['sɔfn] *v.t. & i.* make or become ~. ~**ly** *adv.*

sog·gy ['sɔgi] *adj.* (*-ier*, *-iest*). (esp. of ground) heavy with water.

¹**soil** [sɔil] *n.* ground; earth, esp. the earth in which plants grow.

²**soil** [sɔil] *v.t. & i.* make or become dirty.

so·journ ['sɔdʒəːn] *v.i. & n.* (make a) stay (*with* sb., *at* or *in*) for a time.

sol·ace ['sɔləs] *n.* (that which gives) comfort or relief (when one is in trouble, pain). *v.t.* give ~ to.

so·lar ['soulə*] *adj.* of the sun.

sold, see *sell.*

sol·der ['sɔldə*] *n.* easily melted metal used to join surfaces of harder metals, wires, etc. *v.t.* join with ~. '~-**ing-,i·ron** *n.* tool used for ~ing.

sol·dier ['souldʒə*] *n.* member of an army. ~**ly**, ~**like** *adj.* like a ~; smart, brave, etc.

¹**sole** [soul] *n.* the under part of the foot or of a sock, shoe, etc. *v.t.* fasten a ~ on (a shoe, etc.).

²**sole** [soul] *n.* flat sea-fish with a delicate flavour.

³**sole** [soul] *adj.* **1.** one and only; single. **2.** restricted to one person, etc.: *have the* ~ *right of selling this article.* ~**ly** *adv.* **1.** alone. **2.** only.

sol·e·cism ['sɔlisizm] *n.* error in the use of language; offence against good manners.

sol·emn ['sɔləm] *adj.* **1.** performed with religious or other ceremony; causing deep thought or respect. **2.** serious-looking; grave; important. ~**ly** *adv.* **so·lem·ni·ty** [sə'lemniti] *n.* (esp.) ~ ceremony. **sol·em·nize** ['sɔlemnaiz] *v.t.* perform (a religious ceremony, esp. a wedding) with the usual rites.

sol-fa ['sɔl'faː] *n.* system of syllables each representing a musical note.

so·lic·it [sə'lisit] *v.t. & i.* ask (*for*) earnestly or repeatedly: ~ *sb. for help;* ~ *sb.'s help* (*trade*).

so·lic·i·tor [sə'lisitə*] *n.* lawyer who prepares legal documents (e.g. wills) and advises his clients on legal matters. (Cf. *barrister*.)

so·lic·i·tous [sə'lisitəs] *adj.* troubled, anxious (*about*); eager (*to* do sth.); considerate (*for*).

so·lic·i·tude [sə'lisitjuːd] *n.*

sol·id ['sɔlid] *adj.* **1.** not in the form of a liquid or gas; not (easily) changing its shape when pressed. **2.** without holes or spaces; not hollow. **3.** of strong or firm material or construction: ~ *buildings.* **4.** having length, breadth, and thickness: *a figure* (e.g. a cube). **5.** that can be depended on: ~ *arguments;* *a* ~ *business firm.* **6.** firmly united in support of sth.: ~ *in defence of the country.* **7.** of

the same substance throughout:
~ *gold.* **8.** continuous; without
a break: *waiting for a ~ hour.*
n. body or substance that is
~, not a liquid or a gas. **~·ly**
adv. **sol·i·dar·i·ty** [ˌsoliˈdæriti]
n. unity resulting from common
interests or feelings: *national*
~arity in the face of danger.
so·lid·i·fy [səˈlidifai] *v.t. & i.*
make or become ~. **so·lid·i·ty**
[səˈliditi] *n.* quality of being ~.
so·lil·o·quy [səˈliləkwi] *n.* act of
speaking one's thoughts aloud.
so·lil·o·quize [səˈliləkwaiz] *v.i.*
talk to oneself.
sol·i·tary [ˈsolitəri] *adj.* **1.**
(living) alone; without companions; lonely. **2.** only one.
3. (of places) seldom visited.
sol·i·tude [ˈsolitju:d] *n.* being
~ ; ~ place or condition.
so·lo [ˈsoulou] *n.* piece of music
(to be) performed by one person.
adv. alone. **~·ist** [ˈsoulouist]
n. person who performs a ~.
sol·stice [ˈsolstis] *n.* either time
at which the sun is farthest N.
or S. of the equator.
sol·u·ble [ˈsoljubl] *adj.* that can
be dissolved (*in* a liquid). **sol·
u·bil·i·ty** [ˌsoljuˈbiliti] *n.*
so·lu·tion [səˈlu:ʃən] *n.* **1.** answer (*to* a question, etc.); way of
dealing with a difficulty, etc.
2. process of dissolving a solid
or gas in a liquid; the liquid
that results: *a ~ of salt in water.*
solve [solv] *v.t.* find the answer
to (a problem, etc.); find a way
out of (a difficulty, etc.).
sol·vent [ˈsolvənt] *adj.* **1.** (of a
substance, usu. a liquid) able
to dissolve other substances. **2.**
having money enough to pay
one's debts. *n.* ~ (1) substance:
Petrol is a ~ of grease. **sol·
ven·cy** *n.* being ~ (2).
som·bre [ˈsombə*] *adj.* dark-
coloured; gloomy; dismal.
some [sʌm, səm] *adj. & pron.*
I. *adj.* **1.** (cf. *any*) used with a
material noun to indicate an
amount or quantity of it that
is not fixed: *Won't you have some*
(any) sugar with your cereal? **2.**
(cf. *any*) used as a plural of *a,*
an, one: Have they any children?

Yes, they have some, but I don't
know how many. No, they
haven't any. **3.** used with *more*:
Do you want ~ (any) more
writing-paper? **4.** used to indicate an unknown person,
place, etc.: *He's staying at ~*
hotel (or other) in London. **5.**
a considerable quantity of: *I*
shall be away ~ (a fairly long)
time. **II.** *pron. some of* and *any*
of are equivalent to *a few of, a*
little of, part of: S~ of these
books are dirty. S~ of this paper
is torn. **~·bod·y** [ˈsʌmbədi],
~·one [ˈsʌmwʌn] *pron.* **1.** ~
(indefinite) person. **2.** a person
of importance: *He's ~body in*
his own town, if not elsewhere.
~·thing [ˈsʌmθiŋ] *pron.* (indefinite) an object, event, etc.:
There is ~thing moving behind
the trees. If ~thing should delay
your departure then telephone to
let us know. (Cf. *anything.*) **~·**
times [ˈsʌmtaimz] *adv.* from
time to time ; now and then: *We*
~times go to the cinema. S~·
times I travel by train, at other
times I take the car. **~·what**
[ˈsʌmhwot] *adv.* in ~ degree ;
rather. **~·where** [ˈsʌmhwɛə*]
adv. in, at, some place : *You will*
find the book you want ~where in
his office. (Cf. *anywhere.*)
som·er·sault [ˈsʌmə,so:lt] *n. & v.*
jump and turn heels over head
before landing on one's feet.
som·no·lent [ˈsomnələnt] *adj.*
sleepy; almost asleep; causing
sleep. **som·no·lence** *n.*
son [sʌn] *n.* male child of a
parent. **'son-in-law** *n.* daughter's husband.
so·na·ta [səˈnɑ:tə] *n.* kind of
musical composition in three or
four movements, for one or two
instruments.
song [soŋ] *n.* music for, or produced by, the voice. *for a ~,*
very cheaply.
son·ic [ˈsonik] *adj.* relating to
sound, sound-waves, or the
speed of sound. ~ *bang (boom),*
noise made when an aircraft
exceeds the speed of sound.
son·net [ˈsonit] *n.* kind of poem
containing 14 lines each of 10

syllables and with a formal pattern of rhymes.

so·no·rous [sə'nɔːrəs] *adj.* **1.** having a full, deep sound. **2.** (of language, style, etc.) making a deep impression.

soon [suːn] *adv.* (*-er, -est*). **1.** not long after the present time or the time spoken of; in a short time. **2.** early. **3.** *as ~ as*, at the moment that; when; no later than. **4.** *would as ~ (would ~er)*, would with equal (with more) pleasure or willingness.

soot [sut] *n.* black powder in smoke, or left by smoke on surfaces. ~·y *adj.* (*-ier, -iest*).

soothe [suːð] *v.t.* **1.** make (a person, his nerves) quiet or calm. **2.** make (pains, aches) less sharp or severe. **sooth·ing·ly** *adv.*

sooth·say·er ['suːθseiə*] *n.* fortune-teller.

sop [sɔp] *n.* **1.** piece of bread, etc., soaked in milk, soup, etc. **2.** sth. offered to sb. to prevent trouble or to give temporary satisfaction. *v.t.* (*-pp-*). soak (bread, etc.) in milk, gravy, etc.; take (*up*) liquid, etc. **sop·ping** *adj. & adv.* wet through.

soph·ism ['sɔfizm] *n.* false reasoning intended to deceive. **soph·ist** ['sɔfist] *n.* person who uses clever but misleading arguments. **so·phis·ti·cat·ed** [sə'fistikeitid] *adj.* having lost natural simplicity; (of apparatus, etc.) with the latest technical developments. **so·phis·ti·ca·tion** [sə,fisti'keifən] *n.*

soph·o·more ['sɔfəmɔː*] *n.* (U.S.A.) person in his second year at college, etc.

so·po·rif·ic [,sɔpə'rifik] *n. & adj.* (substance, drink, etc.) producing sleep.

sop·py ['sɔpi] *adj.* (*-ier, -iest*). **1.** very wet. **2.** (colloq.) too sentimental (cf. *sloppy*).

so·pra·no [sə'prɑːnou] *n. & adj.* (person having) highest singing voice of women or boys.

sor·cer·er ['sɔːsərə*] *n.* man who practises magic with the help of evil spirits. **sor·cer·ess** *n.* woman~. **sor·cer·y** ['sɔːsəri] *n.* witchcraft.

sor·did ['sɔːdid] *adj.* **1.** (of conditions) wretched; shabby; comfortless. **2.** (of behaviour, etc.) contemptible; prompted by self-interest or meanness.

sore [sɔː*] *adj.* (*-r, -st*). **1.** (of a part of the body) tender and painful; hurting when touched or used: *a ~ knee (throat)*. **2.** filled with sorrow: *a ~ heart*. **3.** causing sorrow or annoyance: *a ~ point (subject)*, one that hurts the feelings when talked about. **4.** (old use, also as an adv.) grievous(ly): *in ~ need*; *~ oppressed*. *n.* ~ place on the body. ~·ly *adv.* greatly: *~ly tempted*.

sor·row ['sɔrou] *n.* (a cause of) grief or sadness; regret. *v.i.* feel ~ (*at, over, for*, sth.). ~·ful *adj.* ~·ful·ly *adv.*

sor·ry ['sɔri] *adj.* (*-ier, -iest*). **1.** (predic. only) feeling regret or sadness: *be ~ for (about) sth.*; *~ to hear that*. **2.** pitiful: *in a ~ state*; worthless: *a ~ excuse*.

sort [sɔːt] *n.* **1.** group or class of persons or things which are alike in some ways: *What ~ of people does he think we are?* **2.** *a good ~*, (esp.) a person who is likable, who has good qualities. **3.** *out of ~s*, (colloq.) feeling unwell; rather ill. *v.t. & i.* (often ~ *out*) arrange in groups (according to size, destination, etc.): *~ing letters*; separate things of one ~ from others: *~ out the good apples from those that are going bad*; *~ out a quarrel (a muddle)*, set it right. ~·er *n.* (esp.) post-office worker who ~s letters.

sor·tie ['sɔːti] *n.* short sudden attack by besieged soldiers, military aircraft, etc.

SOS ['esou'es] *n.* message for help (sent by radio, etc.) from a ship, aircraft, etc., when in danger; any urgent call for help.

sot [sɔt] *n.* habitual drunkard.

sough [sau, sʌf] *v.i. & n.* (make a) moaning or sighing sound (as of the wind in trees, etc.).

sought, see *seek.*

soul [soul] *n.* **1.** non-material part of a human being that is believed to exist for ever. **2.**

person's real self, the centre of his feelings, thoughts, etc. **3.** human being : *not a ~ to be seen.* **4.** person regarded as the pattern or personification of some virtue or quality : *He is the ~ of honour.* **~·ful** *adj.* having, affecting, showing, deep feeling : *~ful looks.* **~·less** *adj.* without higher or deep feelings.

¹sound [saund] *n.* that which can be heard : *the ~ of voices ; within ~ of the guns,* near enough to hear them ; *vowel (consonant) ~s.* *v.i. & t.* **1.** make or produce *~ ;* make (sth.) produce *~ ; ~ a trumpet ; ~ an alarm.* **2.** make a certain impression on the ear or the mind : *His explanation ~s reasonable.* **3.** test or examine (e.g. with an instrument, tool, etc., and by listening) : *~ the wheels of a railway coach. The doctor ~ed my chest.* **¹~-proof** *adj.* that *~s* cannot pass into or through : *a ~-proof room (ceiling).*

²sound [saund] *n.* narrow strip of water joining two larger areas of water ; inlet of the sea. *v.t. & i.* **1.** test and measure the depth of the sea, etc., with a lead weight on a rope (*a ~ing-line*) or with *~ing-apparatus.* **2.** (fig.) try to learn sb.'s views (*on a subject*).

³sound [saund] *adj.* (-*er*, -*est*). **1.** healthy ; in good condition : *~ fruit (teeth).* **2.** dependable ; based on reason ; prudent : *a ~ argument (policy).* **3.** thorough ; complete : *a ~ sleep (thrashing).* *adv.* (only in) *~ asleep,* in a deep sleep. **~·ly** *adv.* **1.** with good judgement. **2.** thoroughly. **~·ness** *n.*

soup [su:p] *n.* liquid food made by boiling meat, vegetables, etc., in water. *in the ~,* (colloq.) in trouble.

sour ['sauə*] *adj.* (-*er*, -*est*). **1.** having a sharp, acid taste (like that of unripe fruit). **2.** (of milk, etc.) having spoiled. **3.** bad-tempered ; sharp-tongued. *v.t. & i.* make or become *~* (2), (3). **~·ly** *adv.* **~·ness** *n.*

source [so:s] *n.* starting-point,

esp. of a river ; origin ; place (e.g. book) where sth. (e.g. information) can be or was obtained.

souse [saus] *v.t.* **1.** throw into water ; throw water over. **2.** put (fish) into salted water, vinegar, etc., to preserve it.

south [sauθ] *n., adj., & adv.* (abbr. S.) one of the four cardinal points of the compass, opp. *North* and on the right of a person facing the sunrise. **~·er·ly** ['sʌðəli] *adj. & adv.* (of winds) from the *~* ; to or towards the *~.* **~·ern** ['sʌðən] *adj.* in or of the *~.* **~·ward(s)** ['sauθwəd(z)] *adv.* towards the *~.* **sou'wester** [ˌsau'westə*] *n.* **1.** strong SW. wind. **2.** oilskin hat with a wide flap at the back to protect the neck.

sou·ve·nir ['su:vəniə*] *n.* sth. taken, bought, or received as a gift, and kept as a reminder of a person, place, or event.

sov·er·eign ['sɒvrin] *adj.* **1.** (of power) highest ; without limit. **2.** (of a state, a ruler) having *~* power. **3.** excellent ; of proved or undoubted value : *no ~ remedy for leprosy.* *n.* **1.** ruler, e.g. a king or emperor. **2.** British gold coin (not now in general circulation). **~·ty** *n.* *~* power.

so·vi·et ['souviet] *n.* one of the councils of workers, etc., in any part of the U.S.S.R. (Union of Soviet Socialist Republics) ; any of the higher groups to which these councils give authority, forming part of the system of government of the U.S.S.R. : *S~ Russia ; the S~ Union.*

¹sow [sou] *v.t. & i.* (p.t. *sowed* [soud], p.p. *sown* [soun] or *sowed*). put (seed) in the ground ; plant (land) *with* seed.

²sow [sau] *n.* female pig.

so·ya (bean) ['sɔiə (bi:n)] *n.* plant grown as food and for the oil obtained from its seeds.

spa [spɑ:] *n.* (place where there is a) ¹*spring* (2) of mineral water having medicinal properties.

space [speis] *n.* **1.** that in which all objects exist or move : *The universe exists in ~.* **2.** the interval or distance between two or more objects: *the ~s between printed words*; *separated by a ~ of ten feet*. **2.** area or volume: *an open ~*, land, esp. in or near a town, not built on. **3.** limited or unoccupied place or area: *not enough ~ in this classroom for thirty desks*. **5.** period of time: *in the ~ of ten years*. *v.t.* place (esp. words, letters) with regular ~s(2) between. '**~-craft** *n.*, '**~-ship** *n.* rocket or other device able to travel in outer space (e.g. in orbit round the earth, or to the moon). **spa·cious** ['speiʃəs] *adj.* having much ~; with plenty of room. (Cf. *spatial*.)

spade [speid] *n.* **1.** tool for digging. **2.** playing-card with black design(s) as shown here. *v.t.* (often ~ *up*) dig with a ~. '**~·work** *n.* hard work needed at the start of an undertaking. **~·ful** *n.*

A spade (1)　　The four of spades (2)

spa·ghet·ti [spə'geti] *n.* thin kind of macaroni.

span [spæn] *n.* **1.** distance (about 9 inches) between the tips of a man's thumb and little finger when stretched out. **2.** distance or part between supports of an arch: *a bridge that crosses the river in a single ~*. **3.** length in time, from beginning to end of sth.: *our ~ of life*. *v.t.* (-*nn*-). **1.** extend across (from side to side): *a river ~ned by many bridges*. **2.** measure by hand-~s.

span·gle ['spæŋgl] *n.* tiny disc of shining metal, esp. one of many used for ornament on a dress, etc. *v.t.* cover with, or as with, ~s: *the sky ~d with stars*.

span·iel ['spænjəl] *n.* (sorts of) dog with long silky hair and large drooping ears.

spank [spæŋk] *v.t.* **1.** punish (a child) by slapping (on the buttocks) with the open hand. **2.** (esp. of a horse or ship) go (*along*) at a good pace. *n.* slap. **~·ing** *n.* giving several ~s. *adj.* (colloq.) excellent; (of a breeze) fresh, strong.

span·ner ['spænə*] *n.* tool for gripping and turning nuts (2).

Spanners

¹spar [spɑ:*] *n.* strong pole used for a ship's mast, yard, etc.

²spar [spɑ:*] *v.i.* (-*rr*-). make the motions of attack and defence with the fists (as in boxing); (fig.) dispute or argue. *~·ring partner*, man with whom a boxer ~s as part of his training.

spare [speə*] *v.t. & i.* **1.** refrain from hurting, damaging, or destroying; show mercy to: *~ sb.'s life*, not kill him. **2.** *~ no pains (expense)*, do everything that hard work (money) can do; *not ~ oneself*, use all one's energy. **3.** find (time, money, etc., *for*) by being careful: *We can't ~ the time for a holiday at present. Can you ~ me a gallon of petrol?* **4.** use in small quantities; be careful of: *Be sparing with the butter, we haven't much left.* **5.** have enough *and to ~*, have more than is needed. *adj.* **1.** additional to what is needed: *I have no ~ time (cash)*, no time (money) that I need not use. **2.** kept in reserve for use when needed: *a ~ tyre*; *~ parts* (for a machine, etc., to replace broken or worn-out parts); *a ~ room* (esp. one kept for guests). **3.** (of persons) thin; lean. **4.** small in quantity: *a ~ meal (diet)*. *n.* ~(2) part for a machine, etc. **spar·ing** *adj.* economical. **spar·ing·ly** *adv.*

spark [spɑ:k] *n.* tiny glowing bit thrown off from a burning substance or still present in ashes, etc., or produced by striking hard metal and stone together; flash produced by the breaking of an electric current; (fig.) sign of life, energy, etc.; flash of wit. *v.i.* give out ~s. '~**ing-plug** *n.* device for firing the gas in a petrol engine, etc. (See the picture at *plug*.)

spark·le ['spɑːkl] *v.i. & n.* (send out) flashes of light; gleam.

spar·row ['spærou] *n.* small brownish-grey bird common near houses.

sparse [spɑːs] *adj.* thinly scattered: *a ~ population*; not dense or thick: *a ~ beard*. ~·**ly** *adv.* **spar·si·ty** *n.*

spar·tan ['spɑːtn] *n. & adj.* (person) caring little for comfort, unafraid of pain or hardship; (of living conditions) hard because without comforts.

spasm ['spæzəm] *n.* 1. sudden and involuntary tightening of the muscles. 2. sudden fit of pain, outburst of grief, etc. **spas·mod·ic** [spæz'mɔdik] *adj.* 1. taking place, done, at irregular intervals. 2. caused by, affected by, ~s (1).

spat, see *spit*.

spate [speit] *n.* sudden rush (of water, business): *rivers in ~*.

spa·tial ['speiʃəl] *adj.* of, in relation to, existing in, space.

spat·ter ['spætə*] *v.t. & i.* splash, scatter, in all directions. *n.* a ~ing.

spawn [spɔːn] *n.* 1. eggs of fish and certain water-animals (e.g. frogs). 2. thread-like matter from which fungi grow. *v.i.* produce ~.

speak [spiːk] *v.i. & t.* (p.t. *spoke* [spouk], p.p. *spoken* ['spoukn]). say sth. aloud in one's ordinary (not a singing) voice; have a conversation: *speak to sb. about sth.*; know and be able to use (a language); address an audience; make a speech. ~ *out (up)*, ~ *clearly*, give one's views openly. ~ *one's mind*, say exactly what one thinks, even if it is unwelcome to the hearer(s). *nothing to ~ of*, nothing worth

mentioning, not much. *not on ~ing terms with*, no longer friendly with. ~ *well for*, be evidence in favour of. *a ~ing likeness*, (of a portrait, etc.) one that is life-like. ~·**er** *n.* (esp.) person ~ing in public; (*the S~er*) presiding officer of the House of Commons.

spear [spiə*] *n.* weapon with a metal point on a long shaft. *v.t.* pierce, wound, make a (hole) in, with a ~.

spe·cial ['speʃəl] *adj.* 1. of a particular or certain sort; not common, usual, or general; of or for a certain person, thing, purpose, etc. 2. (= *especial*) exceptional in degree: *give sb. ~ treatment*. 3. ~ *constable*, man enrolled to help the ordinary police in time of need; ~ *train*, extra train for a ~ purpose. ~·**ist** *n.* person who is an expert in a ~ branch of work, esp. in medicine: *a ~ist in diseases of the ear*. **spe·ci·al·i·ty** [speʃi'æliti] *n.* 1. ~ quality or characteristic of sb. or sth. 2. work, article, product, etc., for which a person, place, etc., is well known. ~·**ize** ['speʃəlaiz] *v.i. & t.* be or become a ~ist (*in sth.*); give ~ or particular attention to; develop in a particular way; adapt for a particular purpose. ~·**i·za·tion** [speʃəlai-'zeiʃən] *n.* ~·**ty** ['speʃəlti] *n.* ~ity (2).

spe·cie ['spiːʃi] *n.* money in the form of coins (not bank-notes).

spe·cies ['spiːʃiːz] *n.* 1. group having some common characteristics; division of a *genus*. 2. (colloq.) sort.

spe·cif·ic [spi'sifik] *adj.* 1. detailed and precise: *~ orders*. 2. relating to one particular thing, etc.; not general: *to be used for a ~ purpose*; *a ~ remedy* (for one particular disease). ~ *gravity*, the weight of any substance relative to that of an equal volume of water. *n.* ~ remedy. **spec·i·fy** ['spesifai] *v.t.* mention definitely; give the name or details of. **spec·i·fi·ca·tion** [spesifi'keiʃən] *n.* (esp. in pl.)

details, instructions, for the design, materials, etc., for doing or making sth.

spec·i·men ['spesimin, -mən] *n.* 1. sample; one of a class as an example: ~*s of rocks and ores.* 2. part taken to represent the whole: ~ *pages of a new book.*

spe·cious ['spi:ʃəs] *adj.* seeming true or right but not really so.

speck [spek] *n.* 1. small spot of dirt or colour. 2. tiny bit (of dust, etc.). **specked** *adj.* marked with ~s (1). ~'**le** ['spekl] *n.* small mark, esp. one of many, distinct in colour, on the skin, feathers, etc. ~'**led** ['spekəld] *adj.* marked with ~les: *a ~led hen.*

spec·ta·cle ['spektəkl] *n.* 1. public display, procession, etc., esp. one with ceremony. 2. sth. seen, sth. taking place before the eyes, esp. sth. fine, remarkable, or noteworthy. 3. *make a ~ of oneself,* behave, dress, etc., ridiculously. 4. (pl. often *a pair of ~s*) pair of glasses to help the eyesight or protect the eyes. **specs** *n. pl.* colloq. short form of ~s (4). **spec·tac·u·lar** [spek-'tækjulə*] *adj.* making a fine ~ (1), (2), attracting public attention. **spec·ta·tor** [spek'teitə*] *n.* onlooker.

spec·tre ['spektə*] *n.* ghost; haunting fear of future trouble, etc. **spec·tral** ['spektrəl] *adj.* of or like a ~.

spec·trum ['spektrəm] *n.* (pl. *spectra*). image of a band of colours (as seen in a rainbow) formed by rays of light which have passed through a prism.

spec·u·late ['spekjuleit] *v.i.* 1. consider, form opinions (without having considerable knowledge) (*about* sth.); guess (*how* to do sth., etc.). 2. buy and sell goods, stocks and shares, etc., with risk of loss and hope of profit through changes in their market value. **spec·u·la·tor** *n.* person who ~s (2). **spec·u·la·tion** [ˌspekju'leiʃən] *n.* speculating.

sped, see *speed.*

speech [spi:tʃ] *n.* 1. power, act,

manner, of speaking. 2. talk given in public: *make a ~.* '~·**day** *n.* annual school celebration with ~es and distribution of prizes. ~'**less** *adj.* unable to speak, esp. because of deep feeling.

speed [spi:d] *n.* 1. rate of moving: *travelling at full ~; at a ~ of thirty miles an hour. exceed the ~ limit,* go faster than the law allows. 2. swiftness: *more haste, less ~.* *v.t. & i.* (p.t. & p.p. *sped*). 1. (cause to) go quickly: ~ *up the train service; cars ~ing past the school.* 2. (old use) *God ~ you!* May God prosper you. ~'**om·e·ter** [spi'dɔmitə*] *n.* instrument recording the ~ of a motor-car, etc. ~'**way** ['spi:d-wei] *n.* racing track for motorcycles, etc. ~'**y** *adj.* (-*ier,* -*iest*) quick; coming, done, without delay. ~'**i·ly** *adv.*

¹**spell** [spel] *v.t. & i.* (p.t. & p.p. *spelt* or *spelled*). 1. name or write the letters of (a word) in their proper order. 2. have as a consequence: *Does laziness always ~ failure in life?* **spel·ling** *n.* way a word is spelt.

²**spell** [spel] *n.* words used as a charm, supposed to have magic power; overpowering attraction: *under a ~,* mastered or controlled by, or as by, a ~. '~·**bound** *adj.* with the attention held by, or as by, a ~: *The speaker held his audience ~bound.*

³**spell** [spel] *n.* period of time: *a ~ of cold weather*; period of activity or duty, esp. one at which two or more persons take turns.

spend [spend] *v.t. & i.* (p.t. & p.p. *spent*). 1. pay out (money) for goods, services, etc. 2. use up (energy, time, material, etc.). '~·**thrift** *n.* person who wastes money. **spent** *adj.* exhausted.

sperm [spə:m] *n.* fertilizing fluid of a male animal. '~·**whale** *n.* whale valuable for a white fatty substance, used for candles, etc.

spew [spju:] *v.t. & i.* vomit.

sphere [sfiə*] *n.* 1. form of a ball or globe; star; planet. 2.

person's interests, activities, surroundings, etc.: *distinguished in many ~s.* **3.** *~ of influence,* foreign area where a country claims, or is allowed, special rights. **spher·i·cal** ['sferikl] *adj.* shaped like a ~. **sphe·roid** ['sfiǝroid] *n.* body almost spherical.

sphinx [sfinks] *n.* stone statue in Egypt with a lion's body and a woman's head; person who keeps his thoughts and intentions secret.

spice [spais] *n.* **1.** sorts of substances (e.g. pepper, ginger, nutmeg) used to flavour food. **2.** (fig.) interesting flavour, suggestion or trace (*of*): *a ~ of humour* (*danger*). *v.t.* add flavour to (sth.) with ~, or as with ~.

spick [spik] *adj.* (only in) *~ and span,* bright, clean, tidy.

spi·der ['spaidǝ*] *n.* (sorts of) creature with eight legs. Most sorts spin webs (see the picture at *web*), in which insects are caught.

spied, see *spy.*

spike [spaik] *n.* **1.** sharp point; pointed piece of metal (e.g. on iron railings or in running-shoes). **2.** ear of grain (e.g. corn); long, pointed cluster of flowers on a single stem. *v.t.* **1.** put ~s on (shoes, etc.). **2.** pierce or injure with a ~.

¹**spill** [spil] *v.i. & t.* (p.t. & p.p. *spilt* or *spilled*). **1.** (of liquid or powder) (allow to) run over the side of the container: *Don't ~ the milk.* **2.** (of a horse, carriage, etc.) upset; cause (the rider, a passenger, etc.) to fall. *n.* fall from a horse, carriage, etc.

²**spill** [spil] *n.* thin strip of wood, rolled or twisted piece of paper, used to light candles, etc.

spin [spin] *v.t. & i.* (-*nn-*; p.t. *spun* [spʌn] or *span* [spæn], p.p. *spun*). **1.** form (thread) by twisting cotton, etc. **2.** form by means of threads: *spiders ~ning their webs.* **3.** (often *~ round*) (cause to) go round and round as a wheel does. **4.** *~ sth. out,* make it last for a long time; *~ a yarn,*

tell a story. *n.* **1.** ~ning motion, esp. as given to a ball in some games. **2.** short drive in a motor-car, ride on a cycle, etc.: *go for a ~.* **~·dle** ['spindl] *n.* **1.** thin rod used for twisting and winding thread. **2.** bar or pin on which sth. turns. **~·dle** *adj.* long and thin. **'~·ning-wheel** *n.* simple machine for ~ning(1) on a ~dle turned by a large wheel.

spin·ach ['spinidʒ] *n.* plant with green leaves used as a vegetable.

spine [spain] *n.* **1.** backbone. **2.** one of the sharp needle-like parts on some plants (e.g. a cactus) and animals (e.g. a porcupine). **spi·nal** ['spainl] *adj.* of the ~ (1): *the spinal column,* the backbone; *the spinal cord,* nerve-fibres in the ~. **~·less** *adj.* having no ~ (1); (fig.) without power to make decisions. **spin·y** *adj.* having ~s (2).

spin·et [spi'net] *n.* old type of keyboard instrument like a piano.

spin·ster ['spinstǝ*] *n.* (esp. legal or official use) unmarried woman.

spi·ral ['spaiǝrǝl] *adj. & n.* (in the form of an) advancing or ascending continuous curve winding round a central point. *v.i.* (-*ll-*). move in a ~.

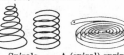

Spirals   A (spiral) spring

spire ['spaiǝ*] *n.* tall pointed structure on a church or tower. (See the picture at *steeple.*)

spir·it ['spirit] *n.* **1.** the soul. **2.** this part of a human being thought of as separate from the body; supernatural being: *the abode of ~s* (i.e. where the ~s of dead persons are). **3.** fairy, elf, goblin. **4.** quality of courage, vigour, liveliness: *a man of ~; put more ~ into one's work.* **5.** mood: *done in a ~ of mischief.* **6.** person considered from the intellectual, moral, or emotional point of view: *He is one of the leading ~s of the reform movement.* **7.** real meaning or purpose underlying a law, etc.: *Obey the ~, not the letter, of the law.* **8.** (pl.) state of mind (as being happy, hopeful, etc., or the opposite): *in high ~s,* cheerful; *in poor (low) ~s, out of ~s,* sad, depressed, hopeless. **9.** (pl.) distilled alcoholic drinks (e.g. whisky, brandy). **10.** industrial alcohol. ~*-lamp,* one in which this is burned. ~*-level,* instrument for testing whether a surface is level. *v.t.* take (sb. or sth. *away, off*) secretly or mysteriously. ~**·ed** *adj.* full of ~(4); lively; courageous. ~**·less** *adj.* without energy or courage; depressed. ~**·u·al** ['spiritʃuəl] *adj.* **1.** of the ~(1) or soul; of religion, not of material things. **2.** caring much for ~ual things. *n.* (*Negro* ~ual) emotional hymn of N. American Negroes. ~**·u·al·ism** *n.* belief in the possibility of receiving messages from the ~s of the dead; practice of attempting to do this. ~**·u·al·ist** *n.* believer in ~ualism. ~**·u·ous** ['spiritʃuəs] *adj.* (of liquids) containing distilled alcohol.

spit [spit] *v.t. & i.* (*-tt-*; p.t. & p.p. *spat* [spæt]). send liquid, (*out*) from the mouth; (of a cat, etc.) make an angry ~ting noise; utter (words) sharply. *n.* **1.** act of ~ting. **2.** ~tle. **'**~**'fire** *n.* hot-tempered person. ~**'tle** *n.* liquid of the mouth. ~**'toon** [spi'tu:n] *n.* pan to ~ into.

spite [spait] *n.* ill will; desire to cause pain or damage: *have a ~ against sb.; done from (out of) ~. in ~ of,* notwithstanding; not being, not to be, prevented by: *They went out in ~ of the rain. v.t.* injure or annoy because of ~. ~**'ful** *adj.* having, showing, ~. ~**'ful·ly** *adv.*

splash [splæʃ] *v.t. & i.* **1.** cause (a liquid) to fly about in drops; (of a liquid) fly about and fall in drops. **2.** make (sb. or sth.) wet by ~ing. **3.** move, fall, etc. (*into* sth.) so that there is ~ing: ~*ing (their way) across the stream;*

~*ing into the swimming-pool. n.* (sound, spot, or mark made by) ~ing. *make a ~,* (fig.) attract attention by making a show (esp. of one's wealth).

splay [splei] *v.t. & i.* (of an opening) slope outwards; become, make wider. *adj.* (of feet) broad, flat, and turned outwards.

spleen [spli:n] *n.* **1.** organ in the abdomen that causes changes in the blood. **2.** bad temper: *vent one's ~ on sb.; in a fit of ~.*

splen·did ['splendid] *adj.* **1.** magnificent: *a ~ sunset (house, victory).* **2.** (colloq.) satisfactory: *a ~ idea.* **splen·dour** ['splendə*] *n.* magnificence; brightness.

splice [splais] *v.t.* join (two ends of rope, etc.) by weaving the strands of one into the strands of the other; join (two pieces of wood) by fastening them so that they overlap. *n.* join made by splicing.

A spliced rope   A spliced board

splint [splint] *n.* strip of wood, etc., bound to an arm, leg, etc., to keep a broken bone in the right position.

splin·ter ['splintə*] *n.* sharp-pointed or sharp-edged bit of hard material (wood, stone, glass, etc.) split, torn or broken off a larger piece. *~ group,* division within a group, political party, etc., caused by difference of opinion. *v.t. & i.* break into ~s; come (*off*) as a ~.

split [split] *v.t. & i.* (*-tt-*; p.t. & p.p. *split*). **1.** break, cause to break, be broken, into two or more parts, esp. from end to end along the line of natural division: ~*ting logs; wood that ~s easily.* **2.** divide: *The enemy were unwise to ~ their forces.*

3. break (*open*) by bursting. **4.**
~ *one's sides*, laugh violently.
a ~*ting headache*, a very severe
one. ~ *hairs*, make very fine
distinctions (in an argument,
etc.). ~ *on sb.*, (colloq.) give
away his secret; give information about him. *n.* a ~*ting*;
crack made by ~*ting*.

splut·ter ['splʌtə*] *v.i.* & *t.* **1.**
speak quickly and confusedly
(from excitement, etc.). **2.**
sound as of spitting; spit (*out*
words).

spoil [spɔil] *v.t.* & *i.* (p.t. & p.p.
~*t* or ~*ed*). **1.** make useless or
unsatisfactory: *fruit* ~*t by
insects*; *holidays* ~*t by bad
weather*. **2.** harm the character
or temper of, by wrong upbring-
ing or lack of discipline: *parents
who* ~ *their children*. **3.** pay
great attention to the comfort
and wishes of: *His wife* ~*s him*.
4. (of food, etc.) become bad,
unfit for use. **5.** *be* ~*ing for* (*a
fight*), be eager for. *n.* (usu. pl.)
1. stolen goods; plunder. **2.**
profits gained from political
power, etc.

¹spoke, see *speak*.

²spoke [spouk] *n.* any one of the
bars or wires connecting the hub
(centre) of a wheel with the rim
(outer edge).

spo·ken, see *speak*.

spokes·man ['spouksmən] *n.*
person speaking, chosen to
speak, on behalf of a group.

sponge [spʌndʒ] *n.* **1.** kinds of
simple sea-animal. **2.** its light
structure of soft elastic material
full of holes and able to absorb
water easily; one of these, or
sth. of similar fabric, used for
washing, cleaning, etc. *throw up
the* ~, admit defeat or failure.
v.t. & *i.* **1.** wash, clean, wipe,
with a ~; take (*up* liquid) with
a ~. **2.** ~ *on sb.*, (colloq.) live
on sb., get money from sb.,
without giving anything in
return. '~-*cake n.* soft, light,
yellow cake. **spong·er** *n.* person
who ~s (2) on others. **spong·y**
adj. soft, porous, and elastic
like a ~: *spongy, moss-covered
land*.

spon·sor ['sponsə*] *n.* **1.** person
(e.g. a godfather or godmother),
making himself responsible for
another. **2.** person who first
puts forward or guarantees a
proposal; person, firm, etc.,
responsible for a commercial
radio or TV programme. *v.t.*
act as a ~ for.

spon·ta·neous [spon'teinjəs]
adj. done, happening, from
natural impulse, not caused or
suggested from outside. ~ *com-
bustion*, burning caused by
chemical changes, etc., inside
the material, not by the application of fire from outside.

spoof [spu:f] *v.t.* & *n.* (colloq.)
hoax.

spook [spu:k] *n.* ghost.

spool [spu:l] *n.* reel (for thread,
wire, photographic film, etc.).

spoon [spu:n] *n.* utensil, as shown
here, used for stirring, serving,
and taking up food, etc. *v.t.*
take (*up*, *out*) with a ~. '~-**fed**
adj. given very much help and
encouragement; looked after
too carefully. ~**ful** *n.*

A sponge　　　　A spoon

spoor [spuə*] *n.* track or scent
of an animal, enabling it to be
followed.

spo·rad·ic [spo'rædik, spə-] *adj.*
occurring, seen, only here and
there or occasionally.

spore [spɔ:*] *n.* germ, single cell,
by which a flowerless plant
(e.g. a fern) reproduces itself.

sport [spɔ:t] *n.* **1.** activity engaged in for amusement or fun,
esp. outdoor exercise. **2.** particular form of (usu.) outdoor
activity (e.g. swimming, wrestling, fishing, or games such as
football). **3.** (pl.) meeting for
athletic contests (e.g. running,
jumping): *the school* ~*s*. **4.** fun;
jest. *make* ~ *of sb.*, make him seem
ridiculous; *say sth. in* ~, in fun,

not seriously. **5.** (colloq.) = ~s-man (2). ***v.i. & t.* 1.** play about; amuse oneself: *a kitten ~ing with its tail.* **2.** (colloq.) have or wear for proud display: *~ a moustache (a diamond ring).* ~**'ing** *adj.* **1.** of ~. **2.** fond of, interested in, ~. **3.** willing to take a risk of losing; involving risk of losing: *a ~ing offer.* **spor'tive** *adj.* playful. **sports'man** *n.* **1.** person who takes part in, is fond of, ~. **2.** person who plays fairly, who is willing to take risks, and is cheerful if he loses. **sports'man·like** *adj.* fair and honourable; ready to obey the rules. **sports'man·ship** *n.*

spot [spot] *n.* **1.** small (esp. round) mark different in colour from what it is on: *white dress material with red ~s.* **2.** dirty mark or stain. **3.** small red place, blemish, on the skin. **4.** particular place or area: *the ~ where he was murdered. do sth. on the ~,* do it there and then; *the man on the ~,* the man present at the place in question. **5.** ~ *cash,* payment on delivery of goods; ~ *prices,* prices quoted for such payment. ***v.t. & i.*** (*-tt-*). **1.** mark, become marked, with ~s: *desks ~ted with ink.* **2.** pick out, recognize, see (one thing or person out of many): *~ a friend in a crowd; ~ the winner in a race,* pick out the winner before the start. ~**'less** *adj.* (esp.) quite clean. '~**'light** *n.* (lamp giving a) strong light directed on to a particular place or person (esp. on the stage of a theatre). ~**'ty** *adj.* (*-ier, -iest*). marked with ~s: *a ~ty face.*

spouse [spauz] *n.* (poet. or old use) husband or wife.

spout [spaut] *n.* **1.** pipe or lip through or from which liquid pours (e.g. for carrying rain-water from a roof, or tea from a teapot). **2.** stream of liquid coming out with great force. ***v.i. & t.*** **1.** (of liquid) come or send out with force: *water ~ing from a broken pipe.* **2.** (colloq.) speak, recite (verses), pompously.

sprain [sprein] ***v.t.*** injure (a joint, e.g. in the wrist or leg) by twisting violently so that there is pain and swelling. *n.* injury so caused.

sprang, see *spring.*

sprat [spræt] *n.* small sea-fish.

sprawl [spro:l] ***v.i.*** **1.** sit or lie with the arms and legs loosely spread out; fall so that one lies in this way: *be sent ~ing in the mud.* **2.** (of plants, handwriting) spread out loosely and irregularly. *n.* ~ing position.

spray [sprei] *n.* **1.** liquid sent through the air in a shower (by the wind or through an apparatus called a spray or ~er). **2.** twig or shoot with its leaves or flowers, esp. one used for decoration. ***v.t.*** scatter liquid, etc., on (sth.) in the form of ~: *~ mosquitoes (a fruit bush);* change (a liquid) into ~.

Spray(er)s

spread [spred] ***v.t. & i.*** (p.t. & p.p. *spread*). **1.** extend the surface or width of sth. by unfolding or unrolling; cover by doing this: *~ a cloth on a table (a table with a cloth); ~ out a map (one's arms).* **2.** put (a substance) on a surface and cover by flattening, etc.: *~ butter on bread (bread with butter).* **3.** extend in time: *payments ~ over six months.* **4.** (cause to) become more widely extended or distributed: *water ~ing over the floor; disease ~ by flies; a rumour ~ing through the district.* *n.* **1.** extent; breadth: *the ~ of a bird's wings.* **2.** ~ing (4); extension: *the ~ of education (disease).* **3.** (colloq.) feast; table ~ (3) with food.

spree [spri:] *n. have a ~,* have a lively, merry time: *be on the ~,* be having a ~.

sprig [sprig] *n.* small twig (of a plant or tree) with leaves, etc.

spright·ly ['spraitli] *adj.* (*-ier,
-iest*). lively; brisk.

¹spring [spriŋ] *v.i. & t.* (p.t.
sprang, p.p. *sprung* [sprʌŋ]). **1.**
jump suddenly from the ground;
move suddenly (*up, down, out,*
etc.) from rest or concealment:
~ *to one's feet*; ~ *out of bed*. **2.**
(often ~ *up*) appear; grow up
quickly from the ground or from
a stem, etc.: *weeds* ~*ing up
everywhere*. **3.** arise or come
(*from*). **4.** bring forward suddenly: ~ *a surprise on sb.* **5.**
~ *a trap* (*a mine*), cause it to go
off (burst). **6.** (of wood) split or
crack. ~ *a leak*, (of a ship) crack
or burst so that water enters. *n.*
1. act of ~*ing*(1); ~*ing*(1)
movement. **2.** (place where
there is) water coming up from
the ground. **3.** device of twisted,
bent, or coiled metal or wire
that tends to return to its
shape or position when pulled
or pushed: *the* ~*s of a motor-car.*
(See the picture at *spiral.*) **4.**
elastic quality: *rubber bands
that have lost their* ~. **5.** cause or
origin. **6.** (attrib.) containing,
resting on, a ~(3) or ~s(3):
a ~ *mattress; a* ~ *balance; a*
~*-board* (e.g. for diving from).
7. ~*-tide* (opp. of *neap-tide*), very
high tide after full and new moon.
~·**y** *adj.* (*-ier, -iest*). elastic.

²spring [spriŋ] *n.* season of
the year in which vegetation
sprouts; season between winter
and summer. ¹~·**tide** (liter.) cf.
¹*spring*(7). ¹~·**time** *n.* the
season of ~.

sprin·kle ['spriŋkl] *v.t. & i.*
direct, throw, a shower of (sand,
water, flour, etc.) on to (a surface): ~ *water on a dusty road*
(~ *a dusty road with water*). *n.*
small shower. **sprink·ler** *n.*
(esp.) apparatus for sprinkling
water. **sprink·ling** *n.* small
quantity or number (e.g. of
people at a meeting).

sprint [sprint] *v.i. & n.* run at
full speed; burst of speed at the
end of a race.

sprite [sprait] *n.* elf or fairy.

sprout [spraut] *v.i. & t.* **1.** start
to grow; put out leaves, etc.:

weeds ~*ing everywhere.* **2.** cause
to grow: *The rain* ~*ed the corn.*
3. have, develop, produce (hair,
horns, etc.). *n.* shoot, newly
~ed part, of a plant, etc.
Brussels ~s, tight heads of green
leaves ~*ing* from the stalk of a
cabbage-like plant.

¹spruce [spru:s] *adj.* neat and
smart in dress or appearance.
v.t. & i. ~ (*oneself*) *up*, make
oneself ~.

²spruce [spru:s] *n.* sort of fir-tree.

sprung, see *spring.*

spry [sprai] *adj.* lively; quick-
witted.

spud [spʌd] *n.* (colloq.) potato.

spue [spju:] *v.t. & i.* vomit.

spume [spju:m] *n.* foam.

spun, see *spin.*

spur [spə:*] *n.* **1.** sharp-toothed
wheel fitted to the heel of a
rider's boot to make a horse go
faster. **2.** (fig.) sth. that urges a
person on to activity. *act on the
~ of the moment*, on a sudden
impulse. **3.** sharp point at the
back of a cock's leg. **4.** ridge
extending from a mountain or
hill. *v.t.* (*-rr-*). urge on with, or
as with, ~s (1), (2).

Spurs

spu·ri·ous ['spjuəriəs] *adj.* false;
not genuine.

spurn [spə:n] *v.t.* kick or push
away contemptuously; treat with
contempt.

spurt [spə:t] *v.i. & t.* **1.** (of
liquid, flame, etc.) (cause to)
come (*out*) in a sudden burst. **2.**
make a sudden short effort, esp.
in a race or other contest. *n.*
sudden bursting forth: ~s *of
water* (*flame, energy*).

spy [spai] *n.* person who tries
to get secret information, esp.
about the military affairs of
foreign countries; person who
secretly watches the movements and activities of others.
v.i. & t. **1.** *spy* (*up*)*on,* watch
secretly; act as a spy on. **2.**

see; observe; discover. **'spy-glass** *n.* small telescope.

squab·ble ['skwɔbl] *v.i. & n.* quarrel noisily (about sth. unimportant).

squad [skwɔd] *n.* small group of soldiers, police, etc., working or being trained together. (Cf. *gang*.)

squad·ron ['skwɔdrən] *n.* 1. division of a cavalry regiment (120–200 men). 2. number of warships or military aircraft forming a unit.

squal·id ['skwɔlid] *adj.* dirty; wretched; uncared-for. **squal·or** ['skwɔlə*] *n.* ~ condition.

squall [skwɔ:l] *n.* 1. loud cry of pain or fear (esp. from a baby or child). 2. sudden, violent wind-storm, often with rain or snow. *v.i.* give ~s (1).

squan·der ['skwɔndə*] *v.t.* waste (time, money, etc.).

square [skwɛə*] *n.* 1. plane figure with four equal sides and four right angles. 2. object with the shape of a ~. 3. ~ space in a town, with buildings round it. 4. result obtained when a number is multiplied by itself: *The ~ of 7 is 49.* *adj.* 1. having the shape of a ~ (1). 2. having or forming a right angle: ~ *corners* (*shoulders*). 3. level or parallel (*with*). 4. (of dealings, business, etc.) fair; honest: *a ~ deal*, arrangement, etc., in which everyone is treated fairly, has equal opportunities, etc. 5. (of accounts, etc.) balanced: *get ~ with sb.*, settle accounts with, pay debts to, (fig.) have one's revenge on him. 6. ~ *inch* (*foot, etc.*), area equal to that of a ~ with sides of one inch (foot, · etc.); ~ *root (of 16)*, number which when multiplied by itself gives (16). 7. *a ~ meal*, one that is satisfying because there is enough good food. *adv.* = ~ly. *v.t. & i.* 1. make ~. 2. cause one line, surface, etc., to be at right angles to another: ~ *a length of timber*. 3. make straight or level: ~ *one's shoulders*. 4. get the ~ (4) of (a number). 5. mark (*off*) in ~s. 6. (often ~ *up*)

settle, balance (accounts). 7. ~ *with*, make or be consistent with: ~ *your practice with your principles*. 8. (colloq.) bribe. ~·ly *adv.* ~·ness *n.*

¹squash [skwɔʃ] *v.t. & i.* 1. crush; press flat or *into* a small space. 2. snub. *n.* 1. number of persons ~ed together. 2. *lemon* (*orange, etc.*) ~, drink made from fruit juice.

²squash [skwɔʃ] *n.* kinds of gourd, like a pumpkin, used as food.

squat [skwɔt] *v.i.* (-*tt*-). sit on one's heels; (colloq.) sit (*down*). *adj.* (of a person, building, etc.) short in height, length, in comparison with breadth. ~·ter *n.* person who occupies public land, an unoccupied building, etc., without legal right; (in Australia) sheep-farmer.

squaw [skwɔ:] *n.* N. American Indian woman or wife.

squawk [skwɔ:k] *v.i. & n.* (utter a) loud, harsh cry (esp. of hens, ducks).

squeak [skwi:k] *n.* 1. short, shrill cry (e.g. of a mouse) or sound (e.g. from an unoiled hinge). 2. *a narrow* ~, a narrow escape from danger or failure. *v.i. & t.* make a ~; say in a ~ing voice.

squeal [skwi:l] *n.* shrill cry or sound, longer and louder than a squeak, and indicating terror or pain. *v.i. & t.* give a ~; say in a ~ing voice.

squeam·ish ['skwi:miʃ] *adj.* 1. having a delicate stomach and easily made sick; feeling sick. 2. too particular or strict about what is right; easily disgusted or offended.

squeeze [skwi:z] *v.t. & i.* press on from opposite or from all sides; change the shape, size, etc., of sth. by doing this; get juice, water, etc. (*out of* sth.) by doing this; force (*into*, etc.) by pressing: ~ *a lemon*; ~ *the juice out*; ~ (*one's way*) *through a crowd* (*into a crowded bus*); ~ *sb.'s hand*, press it to show sympathy, etc. *n.* act of squeezing; condition of being ~d; close fit.

squelch [skwelt∫] *v.i. & t.* make a sucking sound as when feet are lifted from stiff, sticky mud.

squib [skwib] *n.* small firework of the kind thrown by hand.

squint [skwint] *v.i.* 1. have one eye turned in a different direction from the other; be cross-eyed. 2. look sideways or with half-shut eyes or through a narrow opening (*at, through*). *n.* 1. ~ing position of the eyeballs: *a man with a* ~. 2. (colloq.) look or glance (*at*).

squire ['skwaiə*] *n.* 1. (in England) chief landowner in a country parish. 2. (in olden times) knight's attendant.

squirm [skwə:m] *v.i.* twist the body, wriggle (from discomfort or shame).

squir·rel ['skwirəl] *n.* small bushy-tailed animal with red or grey fur, living in trees.

squirt [skwə:t] *v.t. & i.* (of liquid or powder) force out, be forced out, in a thin stream or jet. *n.* instrument for ~ing liquid, etc.; jet of liquid, etc.

stab [stæb] *v.t. & i.* (-*bb*-). 1. pierce or wound with a sharp-pointed weapon or instrument; push (a knife, etc.) into. 2. produce a sensation as of being ~bed: ~*bing pains in the back*. *n.* ~bing blow.

¹**sta·ble** ['steibl] *n.* building in which horses are kept. *v.t.* put or keep (horses) in a ~.

²**sta·ble** ['steibl] *adj.* firm; fixed; not likely to move or change. **sta·bil·i·ty** [stə'biliti] *n.* quality of being ~. **sta·bi·lize** ['steibilaiz] *v.t.* make ~. **sta·bi·li·za·tion** [ˌsteibilai'zei∫ən] *n.*

stac·ca·to [stə'ka:tou] *adj. & adv.* (of music) (to be played) with successive notes distinct, not slurred.

stack [stæk] *n.* 1. large pile of hay, straw, etc., usu. covered, for storage. 2. neatly arranged pile (*of* books, wood, etc.). 3. (also *chimney·*~) tall factory chimney; number of chimneys side by side on a roof. 4. (col-

loq.) ~*s of* (*food*, etc.), great quantities of. *v.t.* make into a ~ or ~s; pile up.

sta·dium ['steidjəm] *n.* enclosed area of land for games, athletic competitions, etc., usu. with stands for spectators.

staff [sta:f] *n.* 1. strong stick used as a support when walking, etc. 2. pole serving as a support: *a flag*~. 3. group of assistants under a manager or head: *the headmaster and his* ~ (i.e. the teachers). 4. group of senior army officers engaged in organization but not in actual fighting; (attrib.) ~ *officers*. 5. (music, pl. *staves* [steivz]). the five parallel lines and the spaces between them on which notes are written. *v.t.* provide with, act as, a ~ (3).

stag [stæg] *n.* male deer.

stage [steidʒ] *n.* 1. raised platform or structure, esp. the part of a theatre on which actors appear; (fig.) scene of an action. 2. theatrical work; the profession of acting: *go on the* ~, become an actor; ~ *fright*, nervousness felt when facing an audience. 3. point, period, or step in development: *at an early* ~ *in our history*. 4. journey, distance, between two stopping-places along a road or route: *by easy* ~*s*. *v.t. & i.* put (a play) on the ~ (1); arrange for (an event) so as to make it successful and effective. ¹~-**coach** *n.* public horse-drawn vehicle which carried passengers and goods by ~s(4) on a regular route. **stag·er** *n.* (only *old* ~*r*) person of long experience. **stag·ing** *n.* scaffolding.

stag·ger ['stægə*] *v.t. & i.* 1. walk or move unsteadily (from weakness, a heavy burden, drunkenness, etc.); (of a blow) cause (sb.) to do this. 2. (of news, etc.) shock deeply; cause worry or confusion to: ~*ed by the high cost of living* (*the difficulty of the examination questions*). 3. arrange (times of events, etc.) so that they occur one after another: ~ *annual* *holidays to avoid closing the works.* **n.** ~ing movement.

stag·nant ['stægnənt] **adj. 1.** (of water) without current or tide; still and stale. **2.** (fig.) unchanging; inactive. **stag·nate** [stæg'neit] **v.i.** be ~; (fig.) be(come) dull through disuse, etc.

staid [steid] **adj.** (of persons, their behaviour, etc.) quiet and serious.

stain [stein] **v.t. & i. 1.** (of liquids, other substances) change the colour of; make coloured patches or dirty marks on: *blood-~ed fingers; a tablecloth ~ed with gravy.* **2.** colour (wood, fabrics, etc.) with a substance that penetrates (the wood, etc.) to some extent. **3.** colour (glass) during manufacture: *~ed-glass windows.* **4.** (of material) become discoloured or soiled: *a dress that ~s easily.* **n. 1.** liquid used for ~ing (2) wood, etc. **2.** ~ed place; dirty mark or patch: *ink ~s*; (fig.) *a ~ on one's reputation.* ~**·less adj. 1.** without a ~: *a ~less* (i.e. pure) *reputation.* **2.** (esp. of a certain kind of steel) that resists rust and ~s.

stair [stɛə*] **n.** (often pl.) (any one of a) series (or flight) of fixed steps leading from one floor of a building to another: *sitting on the bottom ~.* '~·**case n.** ¹flight (5) of ~s inside or outside the walls of a building.

stake [steik] **n. 1.** strong pointed stick (to be) driven into the ground as a post, a support for sth., etc. **2.** such a post, as used in olden times, to which a person was tied before being burnt to death as a punishment (for heresy): *condemned to the ~.* **3.** sum of money risked on the unknown result of a future event, e.g. a horse-race. *at ~,* to be won or lost, depending upon the outcome of sth. **v.t. 1.** support with a ~ (1). **2.** mark *out* or *off* with ~s (1): *~ out a claim* (to land). **3.** risk, place (money, one's hopes, etc., *on*). '~·₁**hold·er n.** person holding ~s

(3) for other persons until the result is known.

stal·ac·tite ['stæləktait] **n.** pencil-shaped deposit of lime growing downwards from the roof of a cave as water runs through it. **stal·ag·mite** ['stæləgmait] **n.** similar deposit mounting upwards from the floor of a cave as water containing lime drips on to it from above.

Stalactites (above) and stalagmites

stale [steil] **adj.** (*staler, stalest*). **1.** (of food) dry and unappetizing because not fresh. **2.** uninteresting because heard before: *~ news* (*jokes*). **stale·mate** ['steilmeit] **n.** position of the pieces in chess in which no further move is possible; (fig.) any stage of a dispute at which further action by either side appears impossible.

¹**stalk** [stɔːk] **n.** non-woody part of a plant that supports a flower or flowers, a leaf or leaves, or (a) fruit.

²**stalk** [stɔːk] **v.t. & i. 1.** move quietly and cautiously towards a wild animal, etc. **2.** walk with slow, stiff strides, esp. in a proud, self-important, or grim way.

stall [stɔːl] **n. 1.** compartment for one animal in a stable or cattle-shed. **2.** small, open-fronted shop; table, etc., used by a trader in a market, on a street, in a railway station, etc.: *a flower-~; a book~.* **3.** seat in the part of a theatre nearest to the stage. **v.t. & i. 1.** place or keep (an animal) in a ~ (1). **2.** (of a motor-car engine) (cause to) fail to keep going through insufficient power or speed. **3.** (of aircraft) cause to be, become, out of control through loss of speed.

stal·lion [ˈstæljən] *n.* male horse, esp. one used for breeding.

stal·wart [ˈstɔːlwət] *adj.* tall and strong; solidly built; firm and resolved; ~ supporters.

sta·men [ˈsteimen] *n.* male part of a flower, bearing pollen.

stam·i·na [ˈstæminə] *n.* reserve of energy enabling a person or animal to work hard for a long time.

stam·mer [ˈstæmə*] *v.i. & t.* speak haltingly with a tendency to repeat certain sounds (e.g. g-g-give me that b-b-book); say sth. in this confused or hesitating way: ~ *out a request.* *n.* (tendency to) ~*ing talk.* ~'**er** *n.*

stamp [stæmp] *v.t. & i.* 1. put (one's foot) down with force (on sth.): ~*ing about the room;* ~ *sth. down (flat);* ~ *out a fire;* ~ *on a spider.* (fig.) ~ *out (put an end to) a disease (a rebellion).* 2. print (design, lettering, etc.) by using a ~(2) on paper, cloth, etc.: ~ *one's address on an envelope (an envelope with one's address);* ~ *a pattern on cloth.* 3. crush (ores, etc.). 4. put a postage ~(4) on (a letter, etc.). 5. (of behaviour, etc.) ~ *sb. as,* label as having (a certain quality, etc.): *His opinions* ~ *him as a man of high principles.* *n.* 1. act of ~*ing*(1) with the foot. 2. article (as illustrated) used for ~*ing*(2) designs, etc.: *a rubber* ~ *of your name and address.* 3. design, word(s), etc., made by ~*ing* (2) on a surface; (fig.) sign or label of sth.: *a face that bears the* ~ *of suffering.* 4. piece of printed paper stuck on (envelopes, etc.) to show the postage paid, or the duty paid on legal documents. 5. *men of that* ~, of that kind.

A postage stamp

An office stamp

stam·pede [stæmˈpiːd] *n.* sudden rush of frightened people or animals. *v.i. & t.* take part in a ~; cause to ~.

stanch *v.t. & adj.* = staunch.

stan·chion [ˈstɑːnʃən] *n.* upright post supporting sth.

stand [stænd] *v.i. & t.* (p.t. & p.p. *stood* [stud]). 1. have, take, keep, an upright position. ~ *up,* rise to the feet. 2. be of a certain height when ~*ing:* *He* ~*s five foot ten.* 3. remain without change: *Let the words* ~. 4. place (sth.) upright: *S*~ *them in a row.* *S*~ *the ladder against the wall.* 5. endure; undergo: *can't* ~ *the hot weather;* ~ *his trial for theft.* 6. be in a certain condition or situation: *We* ~ *in need of help.* *as affairs now* ~. ~ *well with* (be well thought of by) *one's employer.* 7. (colloq.) provide and pay for: ~ *drinks all round,* pay for drinks for all the company; ~ *sb. a good dinner.* 8. ~ *a (good, poor, etc.) chance (of),* have a prospect (of doing sth., etc.). ~ *one's ground,* not give way to force, argument, etc. *It* ~*s to reason (that),* all reasonable persons must agree. ~ *on ceremony,* pay too much attention to formalities of behaviour. ~ *to win (lose),* be in a position where one is likely to win (lose). 9. (with adv. & prep.): ~ *away (back),* move away (from an advanced position). ~ *by,* be an inactive onlooker; be ready (for action); show oneself to be faithful to (e.g. a friend). ~ *for,* (a) represent: £ ~*s for 'pound'; the Christian religion and all it* ~*s for;* (b) be a candidate for (Parliament, an office, etc.); support, contend for (a principle, etc.). ~ *off,* remain at a distance. ~ *out,* (a) be easily seen above or among others; (b) continue to resist; continue firm (*against* or *for* sth., esp. after others have stopped struggling). ~ *up for,* fight in the cause of (e.g. free speech). ~ *up to,* face boldly, show readiness to fight. *n.* 1. *come to a* ~, stop. *bring (sth. or sb.) to a* ~, cause to stop. *make a* ~, fight in defence (*for* or *against* sth.). *take one's ~*, base one's argument, point of view (*on* or *upon* sth.). **2.** small piece of furniture, support, etc., on or in which things may be placed: *an umbrella-~*; *a music-~*; *an ink-~*; *a news-~* (from which newspapers, etc., are sold). **3.** *cab~*, place in a street, etc., where cabs ~ in line waiting to be hired. **4.** structure (usu. sloping) where people may ~ or sit to watch races, sports-meetings, etc. '~·by **n.** reliable support in time of need. ~·ing **n. 1.** of long ~*ing*, that has existed for a long time. **2.** established position or reputation: *men of high ~ing*. **adj.** established and permanent; ready for use: *a ~ing army*; *a ~ing order* (for sth. to be done or delivered regularly). ~·off·ish ['stænd'ofiʃ] **adj.** cold and distant in behaviour. '~·point **n.** point of view. '~·still **n.** stop: *come to* (*bring to, be at*) *a ~still*.

stand·ard ['stændəd] **n. 1.** flag, esp. one to which loyalty is given or asked. **2.** (often attrib.) sth. used as a test or measure for weights, lengths, qualities, etc., or for the required degree of excellence: *the ~ of height required for army recruits*; *~ weights and measures*; *~ authors* (of long-established reputation); *a high ~ of living*; *work that is not up to ~* (not so good as is required); *~ time* (as officially adopted for a country or part of it). **3.** (often attrib.) upright support: *a ~ lamp* (one on a tall support with its base on the floor). **4.** class in a primary school. ~·ize **v.t.** make of one size, shape, quality, etc., according to fixed ~s(2): *Motor-car parts are usually ~ized.* ~·i·za·tion [ˌstændədai'zeiʃən] **n.**

stank, see *stink.*

stan·za ['stænzə] **n.** group of lines forming a division of a poem.

¹**sta·ple** ['steipl] **n.** U-shaped metal bar with pointed ends, hammered into a wall, etc., to hold sth. (see the picture at *hasp*); piece of wire for stitching sheets of paper together.

²**sta·ple** ['steipl] **n. 1.** chief sort of article or goods produced or traded in: *Cotton is one of the ~s of Egypt.* **2.** chief material or element of sth.; (attrib.) forming the ~: *the ~ product of Brazil* (i.e. coffee).

star [stɑ:*] **n. 1.** any one of the bodies in space seen as a distant point of light in the sky at night, esp. one that is not a planet. **2.** figure or design with points, asterisk, as shown: ★ *. the S~s and Stripes*, flag of the U.S.A. **3.** person famous as an author, singer, actor, actress, etc.: *film ~s.* **4.** planet or other heavenly body regarded as influencing a person's fortune, etc.: *born under a lucky ~.* **v.t. & i.** (*-rr-*). **1.** mark or decorate with a ~ or ~s. **2.** be a ~(3) actor, etc. (*in* a play or film). ~·ry **adj.** lighted by, shining like, ~s. '~·fish **n.** ~-shaped sea-animal.

star·board ['stɑ:bəd] **n.** right side of a ship from the point of view of a person looking forward (cf. *port*).

starch [stɑ:tʃ] **n. 1.** white tasteless food substance, plentiful in potatoes, grain, etc. **2.** this substance prepared in powder form and used for stiffening cotton clothes. **v.t.** make (e.g. shirt collars) stiff with ~. ~·y **adj.** like, containing, ~; (fig.) stiff; formal.

stare [stɛə*] **v.i. & t.** look (*at*) fixedly; (of eyes) be wide open. *~ him in the face, ~ at his face*; (of an object) be right in front of him. **star·ing adj.** (of colours, etc.) too conspicuous.

stark [stɑ:k] **adj. 1.** stiff, esp. in death. **2.** complete. **adv.** completely: *~ naked.*

star·ling ['stɑ:liŋ] **n.** small bird.

start [stɑ:t] **v.i. & t. 1.** begin a journey, begin an activity, etc.: *At last the train ~ed. S~ work at nine o'clock. It ~ed to rain* (*~ed raining*). **2.** (cause to) come into existence; set going:

Who ~ed *the fire? How did the fire* ~? **3.** jump (as) from fear, surprise, etc.: *He* ~ed *from his seat.* ~ *back* (*forward, aside, etc.*). *n.* **1.** act of ~ing (1): *make an early* ~; *the* ~ *of a race.* **2.** sudden jump because of fear, surprise, etc. **3.** amount of time or distance by which one person ~s(1) in front of (other) competitors: *We gave the small boy a* ~ *of ten yards.* **4.** *by fits and* ~s, irregularly.

star·tle ['stɑːtl] *v.t.* give a shock or surprise to; cause to move or jump.

starve [stɑːv] *v.i. & t.* (cause to) suffer or die from hunger: ~ *the enemy into submission*, force them to submit from lack of food; *be starving* (*for food*), be very hungry. **star·va·tion** [stɑː- 'veiʃən] *n.*

¹state [steit] *n.* **1.** way in which sth. or sb. is (in circumstances, appearance, mind, health, etc.): *in a poor* ~ *of health. The house was in a dirty* ~. *What a* ~ *he's in!* (i.e. How anxious, dirty, untidy, etc., he is!). **2.** rank in society; position in life. **3.** (often attrib.) dignity; ceremonial formality: *The King drove through the streets in* ~ *to open Parliament. the* ~ *coach* (used e.g. by a ruler for ceremonial rides). *lie in* ~, (of a dead person) be placed where the public may pay respect before his burial. **4.** self-governing country or self-governing division of a country: *Railways in Great Britain belong to the S*~. **5.** one of the political units forming a federal republic: *the S*~ *of New York; the United States of America,* (colloq.) *the States.* ~·**ly** *adj.* (-*ier*, -*iest*). dignified. '~·**room** *n.* private sleeping-compartment in a ship. **states·man** ['steitsmən] *n.* person who takes an important part in public affairs. '**states·man·like** *adj.* gifted with, showing, wisdom and a broad-minded outlook in politics, etc.

²state [steit] *v.t.* express in words, esp. carefully, fully, and clearly: ~ *one's views* (*reasons*); ~ *that*

(*why, how*). **stat·ed** ['steitid] *adj.* made known; announced: *at* ~*d times.* ~·**ment** *n.* stating of facts, views, a problem, etc.: *make* (*issue*) *a* ~*ment.*

stat·ic ['stætik] *adj.* at rest; in a state of balance.

sta·tion ['steiʃən] *n.* **1.** position (to be) taken up by sb. for some purpose. **2.** post of observation or service, esp. local branch or establishment of an organization, e.g. army, navy, police, fire service, missionary society: *a fire* ~ (for fire-engines, etc.). **3.** stopping-place for railway trains; the buildings, offices, etc., connected with it: *a railway* ~; *a bus* ~; *a goods* ~. **4.** social position: *people in all* ~s *of life.* *v.t.* put (sb., oneself) at a certain ~ (1). '~·**,mas·ter** *n.* man in charge of a railway ~. '~·**wagon** *n.* (U.S.A.) estate car.

sta·tion·a·ry ['steiʃənəri] *adj.* **1.** not intended to be moved about. **2.** not moving or changing.

sta·tion·er ['steiʃənə*] *n.* dealer in ~y. ~·**y** *n.* writing-materials.

sta·tis·tics [stə'tistiks] *n. pl.* **1.** facts shown in numbers collected and arranged for comparison, etc. **2.** (sing. v.) the science of ~. **sta·tis·ti·cal** [stə'tistikl] *adj.* of ~. **stat·is·ti·cian** [ˌstætis'tiʃən] *n.* person expert in ~.

stat·ue ['stætjuː] *n.* figure of a person, animal, etc., in wood, stone, bronze, etc. **stat·u·esque** [ˌstætju'esk] *adj.* like a ~, esp. in having clear-cut outlines, in being motionless. **stat·u·ette** [ˌstætju'et] *n.* small ~.

stat·ure ['stætʃə*] *n.* (person's) height.

sta·tus ['steitəs] *n.* **1.** person's legal, social, or professional position, relation to others. **2.** position of a community in relation to others. **3.** (Latin) ~ *quo* (*ante*), as it was before a recent change or as it is now.

stat·ute ['stætjuːt] *n.* law passed by Parliament or other law-making body. **stat·u·to·ry** ['stætjutəri] *adj.* fixed, done, required, by ~.

¹staunch [stɔ:ntʃ] **v.t.** stop the flow of blood from (a wound).

²staunch [stɔ:ntʃ] **adj.** (of a friend, supporter, etc.) trustworthy; firm.

stave [steiv] **n. 1.** one of the curved pieces of wood used for the side of a barrel. **2.** see *staff* (5). **v.t.** (p.t. & p.p. *staved* or *stove*). **1.** ~ *in*, break, smash, make a hole in (by smashing planks in a door, the side of a ship, etc.). **2.** ~ *off*, keep off, delay (danger, disaster, etc.).

stay [stei] **v.i. & t. 1.** be, keep, remain (at a place, in a position or condition): ~ *where you are*; ~ *in the house*; ~ *up late*, not go to bed until late. **2.** live for a time (e.g. as a guest): ~ *at a hotel*; ~ *with friends.* **3.** stop, delay, postpone, check: ~ *the progress of a disease.* **4.** endure; be able to continue (work, etc.): ~*ing-power*, endurance. **n. 1.** (period of) ~ing (2): *a short* ~ *at a friend's house.* **2.** support, esp. a rope or wire supporting a mast. **3.** (pl.) corset.

stead [sted] **n. 1.** *in a person's* ~, in his place; instead of him. **2.** *stand sb. in good* ~, be useful or helpful to him in time of need.

stead·fast ['stedfəst] **adj.** firm and unchanging; keeping firm (*to*).

stead·y ['stedi] **adj.** (-*ier*, -*iest*). **1.** standing firm; well balanced; not likely to fall over. **2.** regular in movement, direction, etc.: *a* ~ *wind*; *a* ~ *rate of progress.* **3.** regular in behaviour, habits, etc.: *a* ~ *young man.* **4.** constant; unchanging: *a* ~ *faith* (*purpose*). **v.t. & i.** make or become ~; keep ~. **stead·i·ly adv. stead·i·ness n.**

steak [steik] **n.** thick slice of meat or fish cut off before cooking.

steal [sti:l] **v.t. & i.** (p.t. *stole* [stoul], p.p. *stolen*). **1.** take (sb. else's property) secretly, without right, unlawfully. **2.** move, come or go (*in, out, away,* etc.), secretly and quietly. **3.** obtain by surprise or a trick: ~ *a march on sb.*, do sth. before him and so win an advantage over him.

stealth [stelθ] **n.** do sth. by ~, do

sth. secretly. ~**y** **adj.** (-*ier*, -*iest*). doing sth., done, quietly and secretly. ~**i·ly adv.**

steam [sti:m] **n.** gas or vapour into which boiling water changes: ~-*heated buildings. get up* ~, increase pressure of ~ in an engine sufficiently to drive it. **v.i. & t. 1.** give out ~. **2.** move, work, etc., (as if) under the power of ~: *a ship* ~*ing up the Red Sea.* **3.** cook, soften, clean, by means of ~. '~-,**en·gine**, '~·**ship n.** engine, ship, etc., worked or driven by pressure of ~. ~**er n. 1.** ~ship. **2.** vessel in which food is cooked by being ~ed. ~**y adj.** (-*ier*, -*iest*). of, like, full of, ~.

steed [sti:d] **n.** (liter.) horse.

steel [sti:l] **n.** hard alloy of iron and carbon or other elements, used for knives, tools, machines, etc. **v.t.** make (*oneself, one's will*) strongly determined (*to do sth., against sth.*). ~**y adj.** like ~ in hardness, brightness. '~'**yard n.** apparatus for weighing, with an arm along which a weight slides.

¹steep [sti:p] **adj.** (-*er*, -*est*). **1.** (of a slope) rising or falling sharply. **2.** (of a roof, etc.) with a ~ slope. **3.** (colloq.) (of a demand) unreasonable.

²steep [sti:p] **v.t. & i.** soak.

stee·ple ['sti:pl] **n.** high church tower, with a spire. '~·**chase n.** cross-country horse-race or race on foot with obstacles such as hedges and ditches. '~-**jack n.** workman who climbs and repairs ~s and other high structures.

A steeple
(a) The spire
(b) The tower

(A pair of)
steps

¹steer [stiə*] **n.** young bullock.

²steer [stiə*] **v.t. & i.** direct the course of (a boat, motor-car, etc.). **'steers·man** *n.* (formerly) man who ~s a ship.

steer·age ['stɪərɪdʒ] *n.* part of a ship for passengers travelling at the lowest fares.

stel·lar ['stelə*] *adj.* of the stars.

¹stem [stem] *n.* **1.** part of a plant coming up from the roots. **2.** part of a leaf, flower, fruit, that joins it to the stalk, branch, etc. **3.** anything that joins like a ~, e.g. the part of a wineglass between the bowl and the base. **4.** main part of a word (e.g. *man* in *unmanly*) from which other words are made by addition. **5.** main upright timber at the ³bow of a ship : *from ~ to stern*. *v.i.* (*-mm-*). ~ *from*, branch out from ; (fig.) arise from.

²stem [stem] *v.t.* (*-mm-*). **1.** check, stop (a current of water, etc.). **2.** make progress against the resistance of (the tide, etc.).

stench [stentʃ] *n.* bad smell.

sten·cil ['stensl] *n.* thin sheet of metal, cardboard, waxed paper, etc., with letters, designs, etc., cut through it ; lettering, designs, etc., printed by inking paper, etc., through a ~. *v.t.* (*-ll-*). print (words, etc.) by means of a ~.

ste·nog·ra·phy [ste'nɔɡrəfi] *n.* shorthand. **ste·nog·ra·pher** *n.* typist who can use shorthand.

sten·to·ri·an [sten'tɔːriən] *adj.* (of a voice) loud and strong.

step [step] *v.i. & t.* (*-pp-*). **1.** move the foot, or one foot after the other, forward, or in the direction indicated : ~ *on to* (*off*) *the platform* ; ~ *into a boat* ; ~ *across a stream*. ~ *aside*, (fig.) let sb. else take one's place. ~ *out*, walk quickly. **2.** walk by ~ping: *S*~ (= come) *this way, please*. **3.** ~ *up* (production), raise, increase. *n.* **1.** act of ~ping once ; distance covered by doing this : *walking with slow* ~*s* ; ~ *by* ~, gradually. **2.** (also *foot*~) sound made by sb. walking. **3.** person's way of walking (seen or heard) : *I recognize his* ~. **4.** *in* (*out of*) ~, putting (not putting) the same foot to the ground at the same time as others (in walking, marching, dancing). **5.** place for the foot when going from one level to another : *Mind the* ~*s down into the cellar*. **6.** ~*s, a pair of* ~*s*, ~*-ladder*, folding ladder with flat ~*s* (not rungs). (See the picture on page 520.) **7.** one action in a series of actions designed to effect a purpose : *take* ~*s to prevent illness*. **8.** grade ; rank ; a rise to a higher position.

step- [step-] *prefix.* **'~·child, '~·son, '~·daugh·ter** *n.* child of an earlier marriage of one's wife or husband. **'~·fath·er, '~·moth·er** *n.* later husband, wife, of one of one's parents. **'~·broth·er, '~·sis·ter** *n.* child of an earlier marriage of one's ~father or ~mother.

steppe [step] *n.* level treeless plain, esp. in Russia.

ster·e·o·(phon·ic) [ˌsterɪə'fɔnik)] *adj.* (of apparatus) reproducing sound as if coming from more than one direction. (Cf. *mono*.)

ster·e·o·scope ['sterɪəskoup] *n.* apparatus by which two photographs of sth., taken from slightly different angles, are seen as if united and with the effect of depth and solidity. **ster·e·o·scop·ic** [ˌsterɪə'skɔpik] *adj.*

ster·e·o·typed ['sterɪətaipt] *adj.* (of phrases, ideas, etc.) fixed in form ; used and repeated without change ; unoriginal.

ster·ile ['sterail] *adj.* **1.** not producing, not able to produce, seeds or offspring. **2.** (of land) barren. **3.** (fig.) having no result. **4.** free from living germs. **ster·il·i·ty** [stə'riliti] *n.* **ster·i·lize** ['sterilaiz] *v.t.* make ~. **ster·i·li·za·tion** [ˌsterilai'zeiʃən] *n.*

ster·ling ['stəːliŋ] *adj.* **1.** (of gold and silver) of a standard quality fixed by the government. **2.** genuine ; of excellent quality. *n.* British money : *payable in* ~.

¹stern [stəːn] *adj.* **1.** demanding or enforcing obedience. **2.** unkind ;. hard. ~·ly *adv.* ~·ness *n.*

²**stern** [stə:n] *n.* hindmost part of a ship or boat.

steth·o·scope ['steθəskoup] *n.* instrument used by doctors for listening to the beating of the heart, sounds of breathing, etc.

ste·ve·dore ['sti:vido:*] *n.* man who works in a ship in harbour, loading or unloading.

stew [stju:] *v.t. & i.* cook, be cooked, in water or juice, slowly in a closed dish, etc. *n.* **1.** dish of ~ed meat, etc. **2.** (colloq.) *in a ~*, in a nervous, anxious condition.

stew·ard [stjuəd] *n.* **1.** man who arranges for the supply of food, etc., in a club, college, etc. **2.** attendant for passengers in a ship or aircraft: *the baggage (cabin, deck, etc.) ~.* **3.** man responsible for organizing details of a dance, public meeting, etc. **4.** man who manages another's property (esp. a large house or estate). ~**ess** *n.* woman ~ (esp. in a ship or airliner). ~**ship** *n.* rank, duties, period of office of, a ~ (4).

¹**stick** [stik] *n.* **1.** thin branch of a tree or bush, cut for some purpose (e.g. *a walking-~, a drum~*): *gather ~s to make a fire.* **2.** rod-shaped piece (*of* chalk, sealing-wax, etc.). *v.t.* (p.t. & p.p. *sticked*). support with ~s: *to ~ peas.*

²**stick** [stik] *v.t. & i.* (p.t. & p.p. *stuck* [stʌk]). **1.** push sth. pointed (*into, through*, etc.): ~ *a fork into a potato.* **2.** (of a pointed thing) be, remain, in a position by the point: *a needle stuck in one's finger; find a nail ~ing in a tyre.* **3.** (cause to) be or become joined or fastened with, or as with, paste, glue, etc.: ~ *a stamp on a letter; stamps stuck together.* **4.** (colloq.) put (in some position), esp. quickly or carelessly: ~ *papers in a drawer. He stuck his hands in his pockets.* **5.** be or become fixed; fail to work properly: *with the key stuck in the lock.* **6.** (with adv. & prep.): ~ *at,* stop short of, hesitate at: ~ *at trifles.* ~ *at nothing,* be ready to do any-

thing, however difficult, wrong, etc., it may be. ~ *out,* (cause to) project, stand out: *with his chest stuck out. Don't ~ your tongue out at me.* ~ *out for,* refuse to give way until one is given (e.g. a higher salary). ~ *it out* (colloq.) endure (hardships, etc.) to the end. ~ *to,* be faithful to (one's word, a friend). ~ *up for,* defend, support. '~**ing-**,**plas·ter** *n.* plaster for ~ing on and protecting a cut, injury, etc. ~**y** *adj.* (-*ier, -iest*). that ~s (3) or tends to ~(3) to anything that touches it. ~**i·ly** *adv.* ~**i·ness** *n.*

stick·ler ['stiklə*] *n. a ~ for,* a person who insists upon the importance of (accuracy, discipline, formality, etc.).

stiff [stif] *adj.* (-*er, -est*). **1.** not easily bent or changed in shape: *a ~* (= starched) *collar; feel ~ in the joints.* **2.** hard to stir, work, move, do, etc.: *mix flour and milk to a ~ paste; a ~ climb.* **3.** (of unfriendly behaviour) formal; cold. **4.** (of a breeze, of alcoholic drinks) strong. **stif·fen** *v.t. & i.* (cause to) become ~(er). ~**ly** *adv.* ~**ness** *n.*

sti·fle ['staifl] *v.t. & i.* **1.** smother; make breathing difficult or impossible. **2.** suppress (e.g. a rebellion, a yawn). **3.** cause a feeling of oppression: *The heat in Calcutta was stifling.*

stig·ma ['stigmə] *n.* (fig.) mark of shame or disgrace. ~**tize** ['stigmətaiz] *v.t.* ~*tize sb. as,* describe him scornfully as (e.g. a liar, a coward).

stile [stail] *n.* step(s) for climbing over a fence.

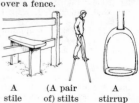

| A | (A pair | A |
| stile | of) stilts | stirrup |

sti·let·to [sti'letou] *n.* small dagger.

¹still [stil] *adj. & adv.* without movement or sound; quiet: *stand ~. ~ life*, picture of fruit, flowers, etc. *n. the ~ of night*, etc., time when everything is ~. *v.t.* make calm; cause to be at rest. **'~·born** *adj.* dead when born.

²still [stil] *adv.* **1.** even up to the present or some other moment: *He has (had) been working all day but ~ has (had) not finished.* **2.** (with a comp.) even; yet; in a greater degree: *This is good but that is better ~ (~ better).*

³still [stil] *n.* apparatus for making alcohol by distilling.

stilt [stilt] *n.* one of a pair of poles, each with a ledge for the foot, used for raising a walker above the ground. (See picture on p. 522.) **~ed** ['stiltid] *adj.* (of talk, writing, behaviour) stiff and unnatural; too formal.

stim·u·lant ['stimjulənt] *n.* drink (e.g. coffee, brandy), drug, etc., that increases bodily or mental activity.

stim·u·late ['stimjuleit] *v.t.* excite; rouse; quicken thought or feeling: *~ sb. to activity (to work harder).* **stim·u·lus** ['stimjuləs] (pl. *-li* [lai]). *n.* sth. that *~*s.

sting [stiŋ] *n.* **1.** sharp, often poisonous, pointed organ (1) of some insects and plants (e.g. scorpions, nettles). **2.** sharp pain caused by the ~ (1) of an insect or by touching, e.g. nettles; (fig.) any sharp pain of the body or mind: *the ~ of the wind (of criticism).* *v.t. & i.* (p.t. & p.p. *stung* [stʌŋ]). **1.** prick or wound with a ~; have the power to ~. **2.** cause sharp pain to; (of the body) feel sharp pain.

stin·gy ['stindʒi] *adj.* (*-ier, -iest*). **1.** spending, using, unwillingly; niggardly: *~ with the sugar.* **2.** scanty: *a ~ allowance from his father.*

stink [stiŋk] *v.i.* (p.t. *stank* [stæŋk] or *stunk* [stʌŋk], p.p. *stunk*) & *n.* (have a) nasty or offensive smell.

stint [stint] *v.t. & i.* keep (sb.) to a small allowance: *She ~ed herself of food in order to give the children enough.* *n.* without ~, freely; without limit.

sti·pend ['staipend] *n.* (esp. clergyman's) salary.

stip·ple ['stipl] *v.t.* draw or paint with dots instead of lines, etc.

stip·u·late ['stipjuleit] *v.t. & i.* **1.** state, put forward, as a necessary condition (*that*). **2.** *~ for*, require (as part of an agreement): *~ for the best materials to be used.* **stip·u·la·tion** [,stipju'leiʃən] *n.* sth. *~*d; condition.

stir [stə:*] *v.t. & i.* (*-rr-*). **1.** be moving; cause to move: *The wind ~red the leaves. Nobody in the house was ~ring.* **2.** move a spoon, etc., round and round in a liquid, etc., in order to mix it thoroughly: *~ milk into a cake mixture.* **3.** (often *~ up*) excite: *~ the blood; a story that ~red (up) one's feelings.* *n.* **1.** act or process of *~*ring. **2.** feeling or display of general interest: *Her new novel made quite a ~.* **~·ring** *adj.* exciting.

stir·rup ['stirəp] *n.* foot-rest, hanging down from a saddle, for the rider of a horse. (See the picture on p. 522.)

stitch [stitʃ] *n.* **1.** (sewing) the passing of a needle and thread in and out of cloth, etc.; (knitting, etc.) one complete turn of the wool, etc., over the needle. **2.** the thread, etc., seen between two holes made by a needle: *take the ~es out of a wound.* **3.** (sing. only) sharp pain in the side caused by running, etc. *v.t. & i.* sew; put ~es in.

stoat [stout] *n.* small furry animal larger than a rat; weasel; ermine.

stock [stɔk] *n.* **1.** lower part of a tree trunk. **2.** base, support, or handle of an instrument, tool, etc.: *the ~ of a rifle (plough).* **3.** line of ancestry: *a woman of Irish ~. He comes of farming ~.* **4.** store of goods available for sale or use, esp. goods kept by a trader or shopkeeper: *The book is in (out of) ~. take ~*, examine and list goods in ~; *take ~ of*, (fig.) review (a situation); estimate (sb.'s abilities, etc.). **5.** (also *live*~ ['laivstɔk]) farm animals: ~-*farmer*; ~-*breeding*. **6.** liquid in which bones, etc., have been stewed, used for making soup, gravy, etc. **7.** money lent to a government in return for interest; shares(4) in the capital of a business company. *the S*~ *Exchange*, place where ~s and shares are bought and sold. **8.** (attrib. use) usually kept in ~ (4): ~ *sizes in hats*; commonly or regularly used: ~ *arguments* (*jokes*). **9.** *the* ~s, framework with holes for the feet in which wrongdoers used to be locked in a sitting position. **10.** (pl.) framework supporting a ship while it is being built or repaired. **11.** sorts of sweet-smelling garden flower. *v.t.* **1.** (of a shop, etc.) have a ~ (4) of, keep in ~. **2.** supply or equip (*with*): ~ *a farm with animals and machinery*. '~:,brok·er *n.* man whose business is the buying and selling of ~(s)(7). '~-in-'trade *n.* things needed for sb.'s business, trade, activity, etc. '~-,pil·ing *n.* process of building up ~s(4) of raw materials, etc. (esp. for war purposes). '~-'still *adv.* motionless. '~-yard *n.* place where farm animals are kept before being killed or marketed.

stock·ade [stɔ'keid] *n.* line or wall of upright stakes, built as a defence. *v.t.* put a ~ round.

stock·ing ['stɔkiŋ] *n.* tight-fitting covering of silk, cotton, wool, etc., for the foot and leg, reaching to or above the knee.

stock·y ['stɔki] *adj.* (-*ier*, -*iest*). (of persons, animals, plants) short, strong, and stout.

stod·ġy ['stɔdʒi] *adj.* **1.** (of food) heavy and solid. **2.** (of books, etc.) uninterestingly written.

stoep [stu:p] *n.* (S. Africa) veranda.

sto·ic ['stouik] *n.* person who has great self-control, who bears pain and discomfort without complaint. **sto·i·cal** ['stouikl] *adj.* of or like a ~. **sto·i·cal·ly** *adv.* **sto·i·cism** ['stouisizm] *n.*

stoke [stouk] *v.t. & i.* put (coal, etc.) on (a fire); put coal, etc., on the fire of (an engine, furnace, etc.). '~-hole, '~-hold *n.* place where a ship's furnaces are ~d. **stok·er** *n.* workman who ~s a furnace, etc.

¹**stole, stol·en**, see *steal*.

²**stole** [stoul] *n.* strip of silk, etc., worn (round the neck with the ends hanging down in front) by Christian priests during services; woman's shoulder wrap.

stol·id ['stɔlid] *adj.* not easily excited; slow to show the feelings.

stom·ach ['stʌmək] *n.* **1.** bag-like part of the body into which food passes to be digested. **2.** *have no* ~ *for*, have no wish or inclination for (fighting, etc.). **3.** (genteel word for) belly. *v.t.* (usu. neg. or interr.) endure; put up with.

stone [stoun] *n.* **1.** solid mineral matter other than metal; rock; piece of this of any shape, usu. broken off: *a house built of* ~; *a* ~ *house*; *a heap of* ~s; *cut one's foot on a sharp* ~. **2.** jewel: *precious* ~s. **3.** unit of weight, 14 lb. **4.** hard shell and seed in such fruits as the peach, plum, cherry. *v.t.* **1.** throw ~s at (sb. in order to kill or injure). **2.** take ~s(4) from (fruit). '~-'blind (-'dead, -'deaf) *adj.* completely blind, etc. '~-,ma·son *n.* man who cuts ~, builds with ~. '~-'s 'throw *n.* short distance. '~-ware *n.* pottery made from flinty clay. **ston·y** *adj.* (-*ier*, -*iest*). **1.** having many ~s. **2.** hard, cold, and unsympathetic: *a stony heart*.

stood, see *stand*.

stool [stu:l] *n.* **1.** seat without a back, usu. for one person. **2.** (usu. *foot*~) low support on which to rest the feet.

stoop [stu:p] *v.i. & t.* **1.** bend the body forwards and downwards; bend the neck so that the head is forward and down: ~*ing with old age*; ~ *to pick sth. up.* **2.** (fig.) lower oneself morally: ~ *to cheating.* *n.* ~ing position of the body, esp. with the shoulders curved and the head bent forward: *walk with a ~*.

stop [stɔp] *v.t. & i.* (*-pp-*). **1.** put an end to (the movement or progress of sb. or sth.); prevent; hinder; discontinue; come to rest; halt. **2.** fill or close (a hole, opening, etc.): *~ a decayed tooth; ~ a leak in a pipe; ~ up a mouse-hole; ~ one's ears* (e.g. by covering them with the hands). **3.** discontinue payment: *~ sb.'s wages. ~ a cheque*, order the bank not to let it be cashed. **4.** stay, remain (*at home, in bed*, etc.). *n.* **1.** ~ping or being ~ped: *The train came to a sudden ~. put a ~ to*, end. **2.** place where buses, etc., ~ regularly: *the nearest bus-~*. **3.** (in a flute, etc.) hole or key for altering the ¹pitch(5); (in an organ (4)) set of pipes producing tones of one quality (e.g. of a bassoon); knob that brings this into action. **4.** (in writing, printing) punctuation mark, esp. *full ~*. **5.** *~-press*, latest news added to a newspaper already on the printing machines. '~·**cock** *n.* valve for controlling the flow of liquid or gas through a pipe. '~·**gap** *n.* thing or person filling the place of another for a time. ~·**page** ['stɔpidʒ] *n.* condition of being ~ped up; obstruction or interruption. ~·**per** *n.* cork or plug for closing an opening, esp. the mouth of a bottle. '~-**watch** *n.* watch with a hand that can be started and ~ped when desired, used to time events such as races to a fraction of a second.

store [stɔ:*] *n.* **1.** quantity or supply of sth. kept for use as needed. *in ~*, kept ready for future use; *in ~ for sb.*, ready for him, coming to him: *trouble in ~ for that careless assistant.* **3.** (pl.) goods, etc., of a particular kind or for a special purpose: *naval and military ~s.* **4.** place where goods are kept; warehouse. **5.** (pl.) shop selling many varieties of goods; (U.S.A., sing.) any kind of shop: *a clothing ~.* **6.** *set great ~ on* (*sth.*), value

highly. *v.t.* **1.** (often ~ *up*) collect, keep, for future use. **2.** put (e.g. furniture) in a warehouse for safe keeping. **3.** fill, supply (*with*): *~ the shed with wood* (*one's mind with facts*).

stor·age ['stɔ:ridʒ] *n.* (space used for, money charged for) the storing of goods, etc.: *fish kept in cold storage.* '~·**house** *n.*

sto·rey ['stɔ:ri] *n.* (pl. *storeys*) or · **sto·ry** (pl. *stories*) floor or level in a building: *a house of two ~s* (i.e. with rooms on the ground floor and one floor upstairs). '**two-**'~**ed,** '**four-**'**sto·ried** *adj.* having (two, four) ~s (stories).

stork [stɔ:k] *n.* large, long-legged, usu. white bird.

storm [stɔ:m] *n.* **1.** violent weather conditions: *a thunder-* (*snow-, sand-*, etc.) *~*. **2.** violent outburst of feeling: *a ~ of protest, etc.* **3.** *take (a place) by ~*, capture by a sudden and violent attack. *v.t. & i.* **1.** shout angrily (*at*). **2.** force (a way) *into* (a building, etc.); capture (a place) by sudden and violent attack. *~·y adj.* (*-ier, -iest*). *~·i·ly adv.*

sto·ry ['stɔ:ri] *n.* **1.** account of real events: *the ~ of Columbus.* **2.** account of imaginary events: *a ghost ~.* **3.** (in children's language) lie; untrue statement.

stout [staut] *adj.* (*-er, -est*). **1.** strong, thick, not easily broken or worn out: *~ shoes.* **2.** determined and brave: *~ companions; ~-hearted.* **3.** (of a person) rather fat. *n.* kind of strong dark beer. *~·ly adv.* in a *~* (2) manner.

¹**stove** [stouv] *n.* enclosed apparatus for producing heat for cooking, warming rooms, etc.

²**stove**, see **stave** (v.).

stow [stou] *v.t.* pack, esp. carefully and closely: *~ cargo in a ship's holds; ~ a trunk with clothes.* '~·**a·way** *n.* person who hides himself in a ship or aircraft (until after it leaves) in order to make a journey without paying.

strad·dle ['strædl] *v.t. & i.* **1.** stand with the legs wide apart. **2.** sit or stand across (sth.) with the legs widely separated: ~ *a ditch* (a horse).

strag·gle ['strægl] *v.i.* **1.** be, wander, here and there in an untidy way: *a straggling village*; *vines that* ~*d over the fences*. **2.** drop behind while on the march. **strag·gler** *n.* person who ~s (2).

straight [streit] *adj.* (*-er, -est*). **1.** without a curve or bend; continuing in one direction: *a* ~ *line* (road); ~ *hair* (without curls). **2.** parallel to (sth. else, esp. the horizon): *Put your hat on* ~. **3.** in good order; tidy: *Put your desk* ~ *before you leave*. **4.** (of a person, his behaviour, etc.) honest, frank, upright: *Give me a* ~ *answer*. **5.** *a* ~ *fight*, one between only two persons, sides, etc. (cf. *three-cornered contest*); *keep a* ~ *face*, refrain from smiling or laughing. *adv.* **1.** in a ~ line; by or in the shortest way; without delay: *Come* ~ *home*. **2.** ~ *away* (off), at once, without delay; ~ *on* (across, in, out, etc.), directly on, etc.; *say sth.* ~ *out*, openly, without hesitation. *n. out of the* ~, crooked. ~·**en** *v.t. & i.* make or become ~. ~·**for·ward** *adj.* **1.** honest; upright. **2.** simple; easy to do or understand.

strain [strein] *v.t. & i.* **1.** stretch tightly by pulling (*at*): ~ (*at*) *a rope*. **2.** cause (sb., oneself) to do as much as possible; make the greatest possible use of (powers, muscles, etc.); injure or weaken by doing this: ~ *every nerve to do sth.*; ~ *one's eyes* (heart, ankle, etc.); ~*ing at the oars*. **3.** (fig.) stretch the meaning of; twist from the true purpose or meaning. ~ *the truth*, say sth. that is almost a lie. **4.** hold (sb.) tightly (*to* oneself, *in* one's arms). **5.** pass (liquids) through a·cloth, a net-work of wire, etc., to separate solid matter: ~ *the soup. n.* **1.** condition of being stretched; force exerted: *The rope broke under the* ~. **2.** sth. that tests and ~s one's powers; severe demand on one's strength, etc.: *the* ~ *of sleepless nights*. **3.**

injury caused by ~ing; *suffering from over-~*. **4.** (pl.) music, song, or verse (of the kind indicated): *the* ~*s of an organ*. **5.** manner of speaking or writing: *in a cheerful* ~. **6.** tendency (esp. inherited) in sb.'s character: *a* ~ *of insanity in the family*. **strained** *adj.* (esp. of feelings and behaviour) forced, un-natural. ~*ed relations*, relations (3) at risk through loss of patience. ~·**er** *n.* vessel with small holes or a network of wire, etc., for ~ing (5) liquids.

strait [streit] *n.* **1.** (sometimes pl.) channel of water connecting two seas: *the S~ of Gibraltar*. **2.** (pl.) trouble; difficulty: *in great* ~*s*; *in financial* ~*s. adj.* (old use) narrow: ~*-laced*, severely moral (2). ~·**en** *v.t.* in ~*ened circumstances*, in financial ~*s* (2); hard up.

¹**strand** [strænd] *n.* (liter.) sandy shore of a lake, sea, or river. *v.i. & t.* **1.** (of a ship) run aground. **2.** be ~*ed*, (fig.) be left helpless, without money, friends, etc.: ~*ed in a foreign country*.

²**strand** [strænd] *n.* any one of the threads, wires, etc., twisted together into a rope or cable.

strange [streindʒ] *adj.* (*-r, -st*). **1.** not seen, heard, known, or experienced, before; foreign; surprising. **2.** (predic.) unaccustomed (*to*). ~·**ly** *adv.* ~·**ness** *n.* **stran·ger** *n.* person in a place or in company that he does not know.

stran·gle ['stræŋgl] *v.t.* kill by squeezing the throat of; hinder the breathing of. '~·**hold** *n.* (usu. fig.) deadly grip. **stran·gu·la·tion** [ˌstræŋgjuˈleiʃən] *n.*

strap [stræp] *n.* band (e.g. leather) to fasten things together or to keep sth. (e.g. a wrist-watch) in place. *v.t.* (*-pp-*). **1.** fasten or hold in place with a ~ or ~s. **2.** beat with a ~. ~·**ping** *adj.* (esp. of a person) tall and strong.

stra·ta, see *stratum*.

strat·a·gem ['strætidʒəm] *n.* (use of) trick or device to deceive sb. (esp. the enemy in war).

strat·e·gy ['strætidʒi] *n.* art of

planning operations in war, esp. the movements of armies and navies into favourable positions for fighting. **stra·te·gic** [strə-'tiːdʒik] *adj.* of, by, serving the purpose of, ~. **strat·e·gist** ['strætidʒist] *n.* expert in ~.

strat·o·sphere ['strætousfiə*] *n.* very high layer of atmosphere, beginning about seven miles above the earth.

stra·tum ['streitəm] *n.* (pl. *strata* ['straːtə]). layer of rock, etc., in the earth's crust; (fig.) social class or division.

straw [strɔː] *n.* cut stalks of dried grain plants (e.g. wheat, rice); one such stalk: *a roof thatched with ~. the last ~*, addition to a task, burden, etc., that makes it intolerable. *catch at a ~*, try to seize any chance, however small, in the hope of escaping from danger, etc.

straw·ber·ry ['strɔːbəri] *n.* (plant having) small juicy red fruit covered with tiny yellow seeds.

stray [strei] *v.i.* wander (*from* the right path, *from* one's companions, etc.). *adj.* **1.** having ~ed: ~ *cats.* **2.** occasional; seen or happening now and then. *n.* ~ed animal or person (esp. a child): *waifs and ~s*, homeless children.

streak [striːk] *n.* **1.** long, thin, usu. irregular line or band: ~s *of lean and fat* (in meat); *like a ~ of lightning* (i.e. very fast). **2.** trace (*of some quality*): *a ~ of vanity* (*cruelty*). *v.t.* mark with ~(s). ~·**y** *adj.* marked with, having, ~s.

stream [striːm] *n.* **1.** river. **2.** steady flow or current (of liquid, gas, persons, things, etc.). *go with the ~*, (fig.) act, think, etc., as the majority does. *v.i.* move as a ~; flow freely: *crowds ~ing out of the cinemas; flags ~ing (out) in the wind.* ~·**er** *n.* long narrow flag; long narrow ribbon of paper, etc. '~·**lined** *adj.* (of a car, aircraft, etc.) designed to offer little resistance to the flow of air, etc.; simplified for efficiency.

street [striːt] *n.* town or village

road, with houses, shops, etc., on either or both sides. *not in the same ~* (*as*), not nearly so good (as).

strength [streŋθ] *n.* **1.** quality of being strong; that which makes sb. or sth. strong. *on the ~ of*, relying on. **2.** number of persons present or that can be used: *The enemy were in (great) ~.* ~·**en** *v.t. & i.* make or become strong(er).

stren·u·ous ['strenjuəs] *adj.* using or needing great effort: ~ *work(ers).*

stress [stres] *n.* **1.** pressure; conditions causing hardship, etc.: *under the ~ of poverty (fear); driven by ~ of weather; times of ~*, times of trouble and danger. **2.** weight or force (*on*): *a school that lays ~ on domestic science.* **3.** (result of) extra force, used in speaking, on a particular word or syllable. **4.** tension. *v.t.* put ~ on; emphasize.

stretch [stretʃ] *v.t. & i.* **1.** make wider, longer, or tighter, by pulling; be or become wider, etc., when pulled: *S~ the rope tight. Rubber ~es easily. ~ one's arms*, extend them (e.g. after sleeping). *~ one's legs*, go for a short walk. *~ out* (= reach out) *one's arm for a book.* **2.** ~ *oneself out (on)*, lie at full length (on). **3.** make (a word, law, etc.) include or cover more than is strictly right. *~ a point (in sb.'s favour)*, treat (him) more favourably than is right or usual. **4.** extend (*for a certain distance or in a certain direction*): *forests ~ing for hundreds of miles. n.* **1.** act of ~ing or being ~ed. **2.** unbroken or continuous period of time or extent of country, etc. ~·**er** *n.* framework (of poles, canvas, etc.) for carrying a sick or injured person.

strew [struː] *v.t.* (p.t. ~ed, p.p. ~ed or *strewn* [struːn]). scatter (sand, flowers, etc., *on* a surface); spread (a surface *with* sand, etc.).

strick·en ['strikn] *adj.* affected or overcome: *terror-~. ~ in years*, very old.

strict [strikt] **adj.** (-er, -est). **1.** stern; demanding obedience. **2.** clearly and exactly defined or limited: *in the ~ sense of the word*; *the ~ truth*. **3.** requiring exact observance: *in ~ confidence*; *a ~ rule against smoking.* **~·ly adv. ~·ness n.**

stric·ture ['striktʃə*] **n.** severe criticism or blame.

stride [straid] **v.i. & t.** (p.t. **strode** [stroud]). **1.** walk with long steps. **2.** pass (*over* or *across* sth.) with one step. **n.** (distance covered in) one step. *take sth. in one's ~,* do it without special effort. *make great ~s,* make rapid progress.

stri·dent ['straidənt] **adj.** (of sounds) shrill; loud and harsh.

strife [straif] **n.** quarrelling.

strike [straik] **v.i. & t.** (p.t. & p.p. **struck** [strʌk]). **1.** hit; aim a blow (*at*): *~ sb. on the chin*; *~ a blow for freedom*; *~ at the root of the trouble.* **2.** (with adv.): *~ off* (*out*), cross out (a word, etc.) by drawing a line through. *~ out,* (esp.) begin swimming: *~ out for the shore. ~ out for oneself,* begin a new activity, esp. start business on one's own account. *~ up,* begin (playing music, a friendship with sb., etc.). **3.** (cause to) sound by striking: *The clock struck four.* **4.** lower, take down (a flag, sail, tent). **5.** make (a coin, medal, etc.) by stamping out of metal. **6.** *~ a match,* light it by scraping. **7.** find; discover; arrive at: *~ an average,* reach one (*between* amounts); *~ a bargain,* make one; *~ a balance,* balance accounts; *~ oil* (*gold*); *~ the right path through the forest.* **8.** take (a certain direction): *We struck* (*out*) *across the fields.* **9.** *~ terror* (*fear, etc.*) *into* (*the enemy*), fill (the enemy) with terror, etc. *be struck dumb* (*blind, etc.*), be suddenly made dumb, etc. **10.** have (usu. a strong) effect upon the mind; attract the attention of: *How does the plan ~ you?* **11.** (of·an idea) occur to (sb. suddenly): *It has struck me that* .... **12.** (of workers) stop working, in order to get better conditions (e.g. higher pay or shorter hours), or in protest against sth. **13.** (of plants) (cause to) grow roots: *The cutting soon struck* (root). **n. 1.** act of striking(12): *The workers are on ~.* **2.** act of striking(7) (oil, etc.) in the earth. **'~-,break·er n.** worker who takes the place of one on ~. **strik·er n. 1.** (esp.) worker on ~. **2.** (football) front-line player. **strik·ing adj.** attracting attention; unusual.

string [striŋ] **n. 1.** (piece or length of) fine cord or ribbon used for tying things. **2.** series of things threaded on a ~: *a ~ of beads*; number of things in, or as in, a line: *a ~ of buses* (*lies*). **3.** tightly-stretched length of cord, gut, or wire (e.g. in a violin or piano) for producing musical sounds: *the ~s,* musical instruments of the violin family played with a ¹bow(2). **4.** *pull the ~s,* control the actions of others (as if they were puppets on ~s). **v.t. & i.** (p.t. & p.p. **strung** [strʌŋ]). **1.** put a ~ or ~s on (a violin, a tennis racket, etc.). **2.** put (beads, etc.) on a ~. **3.** tie or hang on ~ or on rope: *~ lamps among the trees for a garden-party*; put (facts, etc.) together. **4.** *strung up, high(ly) strung,* (of a person) with the nerves in a tense state. **~'y adj.** (-ier, -iest). like ~: *~y meat* (full of tough ~-like fibres).

strin·gent ['strindʒənt] **adj.** (of rules) strict; that must be obeyed.

strip [strip] **v.t. & i.** (-pp-). **1.** take off (clothes, covering, etc.): *~ the bark off a tree*; *~ (off one's clothes) and jump into a lake.* **2.** take away the belongings, rights, contents, etc., of: *~ped of all his wealth. n.* long, narrow piece of (material, land, etc.).

stripe [straip] **n. 1.** long, narrow band of different colour or material: *the tiger's ~s*; *the Stars and S~s* (the American flag). **2.** (usu. V-shaped) badge showing rank (of a soldier, etc.). **3.** (old use) blow with a whip.

strip·ling ['striplɪŋ] *n.* young man not yet fully grown.

strive [straiv] *v.i.* (p.t. *strove* [strouv], p.p. *striven* ['strivn]). **1.** struggle (*with* sb., *against* sth.). **2.** make great efforts (*to do* sth., *for* sth.).

strode, see *stride.*

¹**stroke** [strouk] *n.* **1.** blow: *the ~ of a hammer.* **2.** one of a series of regularly repeated movements, esp. as a way of swimming or rowing: *swimming with a slow ~; a strong ~* (in rowing). **3.** single movement of the hand(s) or arm(s), esp. in games (e.g. cricket); mark made with a pen or brush: *with one ~ of the pen.* **4.** single effort: *a good ~ of business; not do a ~ of work all day; a ~ of luck,* a piece of good fortune. **5.** sound made by a bell striking the hours: *on the ~ of three,* at three o'clock. **6.** sudden attack of illness caused by the bursting of a blood-vessel in the brain, with loss of feeling, power to move, etc.: *suffering from a ~.* **7.** oarsman who regulates the stroke (2) for the others in a boat. *v.t.* act as ~ (7).

²**stroke** [strouk] *v.t.* pass the hand along a surface, usu. again and again: *~ a cat.* *n.* act of stroking.

stroll [stroul] *v.i. & n.* (go for a) quiet, unhurried walk.

strong [strɔŋ] *adj.* (*-er, -est*). **1.** (opp. of *weak*) having power to resist; not easily hurt, damaged, broken, etc.; having great power of body, mind, or spirit. **2.** having much of some substance in relation to the water, etc.: *~ coffee; a ~ solution.* **3.** *~ drink,* containing alcohol (esp. spirits). **4.** having a considerable effect on the mind or senses: *~ language,* full of forcible expressions; *a ~ smell of gas.* **5.** *~ verb,* one that forms the past tense by a vowel change (e.g. *sing, sang*), not by adding *-(e)d* or *-t.* *~·ly adv.* '*~-box,* '*~-room n.* one that is ~ly built

for keeping valuables. '*~·hold n.* fort or fortified building; (fig.) place where a cause is ~ly supported.

strove, see *strive.*

struck, see *strike.*

struc·ture ['strʌktʃə*] *n.* **1.** way in which sth. is built, put together, organized, etc. **2.** building; any complex whole; framework or essential parts of a building, etc. **struc·tur·al** ['strʌktʃərəl] *adj.* of a ~, esp. the framework: *structural alterations.*

strug·gle ['strʌgl] *v.i.* fight, make violent efforts (*to get free, to do* sth., *for* sth., etc.). *n.* struggling; great effort.

strum [strʌm] *v.i. & t.* (-*mm*-). play music carelessly or without skill.

strung, see *string* (v.).

¹**strut** [strʌt] *v.i.* (-*tt*-). walk (*about, around,* etc.) in a stiff, self-satisfied way. *n.* such a way of walking.

²**strut** [strʌt] *n.* piece of wood or metal used as a support, esp. in a framework.

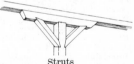

Struts

stub [stʌb] *n.* short remaining end of a pencil, cigarette, etc. *v.t.* (-*bb*-). *~ one's toe,* strike it against sth.

stub·ble ['stʌbl] *n.* **1.** ends of grain plants left in the ground after harvest. **2.** short stiff growth of beard.

stub·born ['stʌbən] *adj.* obstinate.

stub·by ['stʌbi] *adj.* (*-ier, -iest*). short and thick: *~ fingers.*

stuc·co ['stʌkou] *n.* sorts of plaster, hardening when dry, used for covering and decorating outside walls.

stuck, see ²*stick.*

¹**stud** [stʌd] *n.* **1.** small button-like device put through two buttonholes to fasten a collar,

shirt-front, etc. **2.** large-headed nail or knob, usu. one of many, on the surface of sth. (e.g. a door) as ornament or (e.g. the sole of a boot) for protection. *v.t.* (*-dd-*). ~*ded with* (*jewels*, etc.), having (jewels, etc.) set or scattered in or on the surface.

²**stud** [stʌd] *n.* number of horses kept by one owner for a special purpose (esp. racing, breeding).

stu·di·o ['stju:diou] *n.* **1.** well-lit workroom of a painter, sculptor, photographer, etc. **2.** hall, etc., where cinema films are acted and photographed. **3.** room from which radio or television programmes are broadcast.

stud·y ['stʌdi] *v.t. & i.* **1.** give time and attention to learning or discovering sth.: ~ *medicine*; ~*ing to be an engineer*; ~ *a map*. **2.** give care and consideration to: ~ *the wishes of one's friends*. **3.** (in p.p.) intentional: *a studied insult.* *n.* **1.** ~*ing* (1): *make a ~ of history*; *begin one's studies*. **2.** room used by sb. for ~*ing* and writing. **3.** sketch, etc., made for practice or experiment. **stu·dent** ['stju:dənt] *n.* person who is ~*ing*, esp. at a university or an art school. **stu·dious** ['stju:djəs] *adj.* **1.** having or showing the habit of ~*ing*. **2.** painstaking.

stuff [stʌf] *n.* **1.** material or substance. **2.** material of which the name is uncertain, unknown, unimportant; material of poor quality. **3.** (old use) woollen cloth. *v.t.* **1.** press (sth.) tightly (*into*); fill (sth.) tightly (*with*): ~ *feathers into a bag* (*a bag with feathers*). **2.** fill (a bird or animal) with material (e.g. plaster) so that it can be displayed (e.g. in a museum) or with seasoning (before cooking). **stuf·fing** *n.* material with which to ~ (e.g. cushions). **stuf·fy** *adj.* (*-ier, -iest*). (of a room) badly ventilated.

stul·ti·fy ['stʌltifai] *v.t.* cause to seem foolish or to be useless.

stum·ble ['stʌmbl] *v.i.* **1.** strike the foot against sth. and almost fall. **2.** ~ (*up*)*on*, find by chance. **3.** speak in a hesitating way,

esp. because of difficulty in finding the word(s) needed. *n.* act of stumbling. '**stum·bling-block** *n.* sth. causing difficulty or hesitation.

stump [stʌmp] *n.* **1.** part of a tree remaining when the trunk has fallen or has been cut down just above the ground. **2.** anything remaining after the main part has been cut or broken or has worn off. **3.** (cricket) one of the three upright sticks (*the wicket*) at which the ball is bowled. *v.t. & i.* **1.** walk (*along, about*, etc.) with stiff, heavy movements. **2.** (colloq.) be too hard for; leave at a loss: *The question ~ed me.* **3.** (cricket) end the innings of (a batsman) by touching the ~s (3) with the ball while the batsman is out of position. ~·**y** *adj.* (*-ier, -iest*). short and thick.

stun [stʌn] *v.t.* (*-nn-*). **1.** make unconscious by a blow, esp. one on the head. **2.** shock: ~*ned by the bad news.*

stung, see *sting.*

stunk, see *stink.*

¹**stunt** [stʌnt] *v.t.* stop or check the growth of.

²**stunt** [stʌnt] *n.* (colloq.) sth. sensational done to attract attention.

stu·pe·fy ['stju:pifai] *v.t.* make (sb.'s mind or senses) dull; make clear thought impossible: *stupefied with drink* (*amazement*). **stu·pe·fac·tion** [,stju:pi'fækʃən] *n.*

stu·pen·dous [stju'pendəs] *adj.* tremendous; amazing (in size, degree).

stu·pid ['stju:pid] *adj.* slow-thinking; foolish. ~·**i·ty** [stju-'piditi] *n.*

stu·por ['stju:pə*] *n.* almost unconscious condition caused by shock, drugs, drink, etc.

stur·dy ['stə:di] *adj.* (*-ier, -iest*). strong and solid; vigorous. **stur·di·ly** *adv.*

stut·ter ['stʌtə*] *v.i. & t.* stammer.

¹**sty** [stai] *n.* (pl. *sties*). pigsty.

²**sty** [stai] (pl. *sties*), **stye** (pl. *styes*). *n.* inflamed swelling on the edge of an eyelid.

style [stail] *n.* **1.** manner of writing or speaking (contrasted with the subject-matter); manner of doing anything, esp. when it is characteristic of an artist or a period of art, etc. **2.** quality that marks out anything done or made as superior, fashionable, or distinctive: *do things in ~*, not in a commonplace way; *the latest ~s* (fashions) *in dress*. **3.** general appearance, form, or design; kind or sort: *made in three ~s*. **4.** right title (to be) used when addressing sb. *v.t.* describe by a certain name or ~ (4): *He should be ~d 'Right Honourable'*. **styl·ish** ['stailiʃ] *adj.* having ~ (2); fashionable. **styl·ist** ['stailist] *n.* person, esp. a writer, who pays much attention to ~ (1). **styl·is·tic** [stai'listik] *adj.* of ~ in writing.

sty·lus ['stailəs] *n.* (esp.) tiny pointed sapphire or diamond used in playing gramophone records.

suave [swɑ:v] *adj.* smooth in manner; agreeably polite.

sub- [sʌb-] *prefix.* **1.** (with names of officials or official organizations) deputy or junior: *sublieutenant*; *subcommittee*. **2.** not quite; not altogether: *subhuman*; *subtropical*. **3.** forming a division between two others: *a subspecies*.

sub·al·tern ['sʌbəltən] *n.* commissioned army officer of lower rank than a captain.

sub·con·scious [ˌsʌb'kɒnʃəs] *adj. & n.* (of) those mental activities of which we are not (wholly) aware.

sub·con·ti·nent [ˌsʌb'kɒntinənt] *n.* mass of land, part of a continent, large enough to be regarded separately (esp. *the S~* of India and Pakistan).

sub·di·vide [ˌsʌbdi'vaid] *v.t. & i.* divide into further divisions.

sub·due [səb'dju:] *v.t.* **1.** overcome; bring under control. **2.** make quieter, softer, less strong: *~d light*.

sub·head·ing ['sʌbhediŋ] *n.* words showing contents of part of an article, etc. (in a newspaper, etc.).

sub·ject ['sʌbdʒikt] *n.* **1.** any member of a State except the supreme ruler: *British ~s*. **2.** sth. (to be) talked or written about or studied: *the ~ of an essay*; *change the ~*, talk about sth. different. *adj.* **1.** under foreign government or protection: *~ races* (nations). **2.** *~ to*, having a tendency to, liable to: *traffic ~ to delays in bad weather*. **3.** (also as adv.): *~ to*, conditional on: *~ to your approval*. [səb'dʒekt] *v.t.* **1.** bring, get (a country, nation, person) under control. **2.** cause to undergo or experience; expose: *~ oneself* (one's friends) *to criticism*. **sub·jec·tion** [səb'dʒekʃən] *n.* **1.** *~ing* (1): *the ~ion of the rebels*. **2.** being *~ed* (1).

sub·ju·gate ['sʌbdʒugeit] *v.t.* subdue (1); conquer. **sub·ju·ga·tion** [ˌsʌbdʒu'geiʃən] *n.*

sub·let ['sʌb'let] *v.t. & i.* rent to sb. else (a room, house, etc., of which one is a tenant).

sub·lieu·ten·ant ['sʌblef'ten-ənt] *n.* naval officer with rank next below that of a lieutenant.

sub·lime [sə'blaim] *adj.* of the greatest and highest sort; causing wonder or reverence: *~ scenery*.

sub·ma·rine ['sʌbməri:n] *n. & adj.* (ship able to travel) under the surface of the sea.

sub·merge [səb'mə:dʒ] *v.t. & i.* **1.** put under water; cover with water. **2.** sink out of sight; (of submarines) go down under water.

sub·mit [səb'mit] *v.t. & i.* (-tt-). **1.** put (oneself) under the control of another; surrender (to). **2.** put forward for opinion, discussion, decision, etc.: *~ plans* (reports, etc.) *to sb.* **3.** suggest (that). **sub·mis·sion** [səb'miʃən] *n.* *~ting*; theory, etc. *~ted* (2). **sub·mis·sive** [səb'misiv] *adj.* obedient.

sub·nor·mal ['sʌb'nɔ:ml] *adj.* below normal.

sub·or·di·nate [sə'bɔ:dinit] *adj.* junior in rank or position (to). *n.* sb. in a ~ position; sb. working

under another. [sə'bɔ:dineit]
v.t. treat as ~; make ~ (to).

sub·scribe [səb'skraib] **v.t. & i.**
1. (agree to) pay (a sum of
money), in common with other
persons (to a cause, for sth.) : ~
£5 to a flood relief fund. **2.** ~ to
(a newspaper, new book, etc.),
place an order for it. **3.** ~ to
(views, opinions, etc.), show that
one agrees with (them). **sub·
scrib·er** **n.** **sub·scrip·tion**
[səb'skripʃən] **n.** (esp.) money
~d (for charity, for receiving
a newspaper, etc.).

sub·se·quent ['sʌbsikwənt] **adj.**
later; following. ~·ly **adv.** later
on.

sub·ser·vient [səb'sə:vjənt] **adj.**
giving too much respect.

sub·side [səb'said] **v.i.** **1.** (of
flood water) sink to a lower
or to the normal level. **2.** (of
land) sink. **3.** (of buildings)
settle lower down in the ground.
4. (of winds, passions, etc.) become quiet after being violent.
sub·si·dence [səb'saidəns] **n.**

sub·sid·ia·ry [səb'sidjəri] **adj.** **1.**
serving as a help or a support
(to) but not of first importance.
2. ~ company, one controlled
by a larger one.

sub·si·dy ['sʌbsidi] **n.** money
granted, esp. by a government or
society, to an industry or other
cause needing help, or to an ally
in war, or (e.g. food subsidies)
to keep prices at a desired
level. **sub·si·dize** ['sʌbsidaiz]
v.t. give a ~ to.

sub·sist [səb'sist] **v.i.** exist; be
kept in existence (on food).
~·ence [səb'sistəns] **n.** existence; means of existing : my
means of ~ence, how I get
money to live on.

sub·stance ['sʌbstəns] **n.** **1.**
material; particular kind of
matter : Iron is a hard ~. **2.**
most important part, chief or
real meaning, of sth., e.g. of a
speech or argument. **3.** firmness; solidity. **4.** money; property : a man of ~. **sub·stan·
tial** [səb'stænʃəl] **adj.** **1.** strongly
or solidly built or made. **2.** real;
having physical existence. **3.**

large; considerable : a substantial meal (improvement). **4.**
wealthy. **5.** in substantial agreement, agreeing on all important
points. **sub·stan·ti·ate** [səb-
'stænʃieit] **v.t.** give facts to
support (a claim, statement).

sub·sti·tute ['sʌbstitju:t] **n.** person or thing taking the place of
or acting for another. **v.t.** put
or use as a ~ (for). **sub·sti·tu·
tion** [ˌsʌbsti'tju:ʃən] **n.**

sub·ter·fuge ['sʌbtəfju:dʒ] **n.**
trick, excuse, esp. one used to
escape trouble or sth. unpleasant.

sub·ter·ra·nean [ˌsʌbtə'reinjən]
adj. underground.

sub·tle ['sʌtl] **adj.** (-r, -st). **1.**
difficult to perceive or describe
because fine or delicate; mysterious : a ~ charm (flavour);
~ humour (smiles). **2.** quick and
clever at seeing or making
delicate differences; sensitive : a
~ observer (critic). **3.** ingenious;
elaborate; complex : a ~ argument (design). ~·ty ['sʌtəlti] **n.**

sub·tract [səb'trækt] **v.t.** take
(a number, quantity) away (from
another number, etc.). **sub·
trac·tion** [səb'trækʃən] **n.**

sub·urb ['sʌbə:b] **n.** outlying
district of a town or city. ~·an
[sə'bə:bən] **adj.** of or in a ~ :
~an shops.

sub·vert [səb'və:t] **v.t.** destroy,
overthrow (religion, a government, etc.), by weakening
the people's trust or belief.
sub·ver·sive [səb'və:siv] **adj.**
tending to ~.

sub·way ['sʌbwei] **n.** **1.** underground passage or tunnel, esp.
one to enable people to get from
one side of a busy street to the
other. **2.** (U.S.A.) underground
electric railway in a town.

suc·ceed [sək'si:d] **v.i. & t.** **1.**
do what one is trying to do;
gain one's purpose : ~ in (passing) an examination. **2.** do well;
go well; have a good result : The
plan ~ed. **3.** come next after
and take the place of : Who
~ed him as Prime Minister? **4.**
~ to, inherit; have (a title,
position, property) on the death

of the owner: ~ *to the throne.*
suc·cess [sək'ses] *n.* **1.** ~ing
(1), (2); doing well; good fortune. **2.** person or thing that
~s (1), (2); activity, etc., that
~s (1), (2). **suc·cess·ful** *adj.*
having success (*in*). **suc·ces·**
sion [sək'seʃən] *n.* **1.** the coming of one thing after another in
time or order: *the succession of
the seasons*; *in succession,* one
after the other. **2.** number of
things in succession: *a succession
of wet days.* **3.** (right of) ~ing
(3) to a title, to property, etc.;
persons having this right: *first
in succession to the throne.* **suc·**
ces·sive [sək'sesiv] *adj.* coming
one after the other: *win five
successive games.* **suc·ces·sor**
[sək'sesə*] *n.* person or thing
that ~s (3) another.
suc·cinct [sək'siŋkt] *adj.* expressed briefly and clearly.
suc·cour ['sʌkə*] *n.* help given
in time of need. *v.t.* give ~ to.
suc·cu·lent ['sʌkjulənt] *adj.* (of
fruit) juicy. **suc·cu·lence** *n.*
suc·cumb [sə'kʌm] *v.i.* yield (*to*
a temptation, etc.); die.
such [sʌtʃ] *adj. & pron.* **I.** *adj.*
1. of the same kind or degree
(*as*): *I have never seen ~ heavy
rain as this.* **2.** *You can borrow
my bicycle, ~ as it is* (suggesting
that it is not a good one). *His
illness is not ~ as to cause*
(not of a kind that might cause)
anxiety. **3.** *His rudeness was ~
that* (was so marked that) *his
parents were ashamed.* **4.** *Don't
be in ~* (so great) *a hurry.* **II.**
pron. ~ *persons or things: I
haven't many books on that
subject, but ~ as I have* (= those
that I have) *I will lend you.
He's a good businessman and is
recognized as ~* (i.e. as a good
businessman).
suck [sʌk] *v.t.* **1.** draw (liquid)
into the mouth by the use of lip
muscles: ~ *the juice from an
orange*; ~ *an orange dry.* **2.** hold
(sth.) in the mouth and lick,
roll about, squeeze, etc., with
the tongue: ~ *one's thumb* (*a
toffee*). **3.** take (liquid *in* or *up*);
absorb: *plants ~ing up moisture*

from the soil. **4.** draw into the
mind. ~ *sb.'s brains,* get ideas,
information, etc., from him for
one's own use. *n.* act or process of ~ing. **~·le** ['sʌkl] *v.t.*
feed with milk from the breast
or udder. **~·ling** *n.* baby or
young animal still being ~led
by its mother.
suck·er ['sʌkə*] *n.* **1.** shoot (1)
coming up from an underground
root or stem, not from the main
plant. **2.** organ in some animals
enabling them to rest on a surface by suction.
suc·tion ['sʌkʃən] *n.* **1.** the
action of sucking; removal of
air, liquid, etc., from a vessel or
cavity so as to produce a partial vacuum and enable air-
pressure from outside to force
in liquid, dust, etc.: *Some pumps
and all vacuum cleaners work by
~.* **2.** similar process enabling
sth. (e.g. a concave rubber disc)
to be held in contact with a
surface by means of a vacuum.
sud·den ['sʌdn] *adj.* happening
quickly or unexpectedly. *n.
all of a ~,* ~ly. **~·ly** *adv.*
suds [sʌdz] *n. pl.* froth, mass of
tiny bubbles, on soapy water.
sue [sjuː] *v.t. & i.* (present participle *suing* ['sjuːiŋ]; p.t. & p.p.
sued). **1.** go to law against: *sue
one's employer for unpaid wages.*
2. beg, ask: *sue* (*the enemy*) *for
peace; suing for mercy.*
suede [sweid] *n.* kind of soft
leather used for making gloves,
shoes, etc.
suet [sjuit] *n.* solid fat covering
the kidneys of sheep and oxen,
used in cooking.
suf·fer ['sʌfə*] *v.t & i.* **1.** feel
or have (pain, loss, etc.): ~
from (often have) *headaches. His
business ~ed during the war.* **2.**
allow; tolerate: *can't ~ such
insolence.* **~·ance** *n.* permission
implied by absence of objection: *He's here on ~ance,* allowed to be here but not wanted.
~·ing *n.* pain; (pl.) feelings of
pain; painful experiences.
suf·fice [sə'fais] *v.i. & t.* be
enough: *Will that ~ for your
needs* (~ *you*)? **suf·fi·cient**

[sə'fiʃənt] *adj.* enough. **suf·fi·cien·cy** *n.* sufficient quantity (*of*).

suf·fix ['sʌfiks] *n.* letter or syllable(s) added at the end of a word to make another word (as in rust*y*), or as an inflexion (as in ox*en*).

suf·fo·cate ['sʌfəkeit] *v.t. & i.* choke; kill by stopping the breathing or; cause or have difficulty in breathing. **suf·fo·ca·tion** [ˌsʌfə'keiʃən] *n.*

suf·frage ['sʌfridʒ] *n.* (right to) vote in elections.

suf·fuse [sə'fju:z] *v.t.* (esp. of colours, tears) spread slowly over the surface of : *the evening sky ~d with crimson.*

sug·ar ['ʃugə*] *n.* sweet substance obtained from various plants, esp. the '~-**cane** and the '~-**beet**. *v.t.* sweeten or mix with ~. ~**y** *adj.* tasting of ~; (fig. of music, etc.) too sweet (3).

sug·gest [sə'dʒest] *v.t.* propose; put forward for consideration, as a possibility : *~ a visit to the theatre* (*that we should go to the theatre*). **2.** bring (an idea, etc.) into the mind : *The look on his face ~ed fear* (caused others to think he was frightened). **sug·ges·tion** *n.* **1.** idea, plan, etc., that is ~ed. **2.** slight indication : *speaking with a ~ion of a foreign accent.* **sug·ges·tive** *adj.* tending to bring ideas, etc., to the mind : *a ~ive lecture.*

su·i·cide ['sjuisaid] *n.* self-murder(er). **su·i·ci·dal** [sjui'saidl] *adj.* very harmful to one's own interests.

suit [su:t, sju:t] *n.* **1.** set of articles of outer clothing of the same material : *a ~ of armour*; *a man's ~*, jacket (,waistcoat,) and trousers; *a woman's ~* (coat and skirt). **2.** request made to a superior, esp. to a ruler. **3.** (also *law~*) case in a law court. **4.** any of the four sets of cards (spades, hearts, diamonds, clubs) used in many card games. *follow ~*, (fig.) do what someone else does. *v.t.* **1.** satisfy; meet the needs of; be convenient to or right for : *Does*

the climate ~ you? **2.** (esp. of clothes) look well when worn : *That hat doesn't ~ you.* **3.** ~ *sth. to*, make fit or appropriate : *~ the punishment to the crime.* **4.** (p.p.) *be ~ed for* (*to*), be fitted : *Is he ~ed for teaching* (*to be a teacher*) (i.e. is he the right sort of man)? ~**·a·ble** ['sju:təbl] *adj.* right for the purpose or occasion. ~**'a·bly** *adv.* ~**·a·bil·i·ty** [ˌsju:tə'biliti] *n.* '~**·case** *n.* stiff, flat-sided case for carrying one's clothes, etc., when one is travelling. ~**·or** *n.* **1.** person bringing a law~. **2.** man courting(1) a woman.

suite [swi:t] *n.* **1.** personal attendants of an important person (esp. a ruler). **2.** complete set of rooms or articles of furniture : *a bedroom ~.*

sulk [sʌlk] *v.i.* be in a bad temper and show this by refusing to talk, etc. **the sulks** *n. pl.* condition of ~ing. ~**y** *adj.* (*-ier, -iest*). ~ing; having a tendency to ~. ~**·i·ly** *adv.*

sul·len ['sʌlən] *adj.* **1.** silently bad-tempered; unforgiving. **2.** (of the sky, etc.) dark and gloomy.

sul·ly ['sʌli] *v.t.* stain or discredit (sb.'s reputation, etc.).

sul·phur ['sʌlfə*] *n.* light-yellow substance that burns with a blue flame and a strong smell.

sul·tan ['sʌltən] *n.* Muslim ruler.

sul·try ['sʌltri] *adj.* (of the weather) hot and airless.

sum [sʌm] *n.* **1.** total obtained by adding together numbers or amounts. **2.** amount of money. **3.** problem in arithmetic. *in ~*, in a few words. *v.t. & i.* (*-mm-*). ~ *up.* **1.** give the total of. **2.** express briefly (the chief points of what has been said, etc.). **sum·ma·ry** ['sʌməri] *n.* brief account of the chief points. *adj.* done or given without delay or attention to small matters : *~mary justice.* **sum·ma·rize** ['sʌməraiz] *v.t.* be or make a ~mary of.

sum·mer ['sʌmə*] *n.* (in temperate climates) the warmest season of the year. (*~ time,* see *daylight-saving*.) ~-**house**, garden shelter with seats. *v.i.* spend the ~ (*at*, *in*, etc.).

sum·mit ['sʌmit] *n.* highest point; top: (fig.) *the ~ of his ambition*; *a ~ meeting*, one between heads of governments.

sum·mon ['sʌmən] *v.t.* 1. command (sb.) to come (esp. to appear in a law court); call (people) together for a meeting, etc.: ~ *Parliament*. 2. ~ *up*, gather together (one's energy, courage) (*to do* sth., *for* a task, etc.). **sum·mons** *n.* (pl. ~ses). 1. order to appear before a judge. 2. command to do sth. or appear somewhere. *v.t.* serve a ~s(1) on.

sump [sʌmp] *n.* 1. inner casing of a petrol engine, containing oil. 2. hole into which waste liquid drains.

sump·tu·ous ['sʌmptjuəs] *adj.* costly-looking; magnificent: *a ~ feast*.

sun [sʌn] *n.* 1. the heavenly body from which the Earth gets warmth and light. 2. the light or warmth of the sun: *have the sun in one's eyes*; *sitting in the sun*. *v.t.* (-*nn*-) put in the rays of the sun: *The cat was sunning itself on the path.* '**sun·blind** *n.* shade or awning fixed outside a window. '**sun·burn** *n.* darkening or blistering of the skin caused by the sun. '**sun·di·al** *n.* device that shows the time by the shadow of a rod or plate on a dial(1). '**sun·down** *n.* sunset. '**sun·flow·er** *n.* tall plant with large yellow flowers.

A sunblind

A sundial

'**sun·lit** *adj.* lighted by the sun. **sun·ny** *adj.* (-*ier*, -*iest*). (fig.) cheerful: *her sunny smiles*. '**sun·rise** *n.* (time of) sun's appearance above the horizon. '**sun·set** *n.* (time of) sun's disappear-

ance below the horizon; colours seen in the sky at this time. '**sun·shade** *n.* sort of umbrella used for keeping off sunlight. '**sun·shine** *n.* bright sunny weather: *six hours' sunshine.* '**sun·spot** *n.* dark patch on the sun at times. '**sun·stroke** *n.* illness caused by excessive exposure to the sun.

sun·dae ['sʌndi] *n.* portion of ice-cream served with fruit, nuts, etc., over it.

Sun·day ['sʌndi] *n.* the first day of the week. ~ *school*, one held on ~ for religious teaching.

sun·dry ['sʌndri] *adj.* various; a number of different kinds of. *all and ~*, each and all. **sun·dries** *n. pl.* various small items not separately named.

sung, see *sing*.

sunk [sʌŋk] p.t. & p.p. of *sink*. ~·**en** *adj.* (esp. of sb.'s face or eyes) fallen in; hollow-looking.

su·per- ['sju:pə*-] *prefix.* 1. more or greater than: ~*human*, ~*normal*, etc. 2. to an unusually high degree: ~-*charged*, ~-*heated*, ~-*abundant*, etc. 3. above; on the top: ~*impose*.

su·per·an·nu·ate [ˌsju:pər'ænjueit] *v.t.* give a pension to (an employee) when he is old or unable to work; dismiss (sb.) because of age or weakness. **su·per·an·nu·a·tion** [ˌsju:pə,rænju'eiʃən] *n.*

su·perb [sju:'pə:b] *adj.* magnificent.

su·per·cil·i·ous [ˌsju:pə'siliəs] *adj.* showing contemptuous indifference.

su·per·er·o·ga·tion [ˌsju:pə,rerə'geiʃən] *n.* the doing of more work than duty requires.

su·per·fi·cial [ˌsju:pə'fiʃl] *adj.* 1. of or on the surface only; not going deep: *a ~ wound.* 2. with no depth of knowledge or feeling. ~·**ly** *adv.*

su·per·fine ['sju:pəfain] *adj.* unusually fine in quality.

su·per·flu·ous [sju:'pə:fluəs] *adj.* more than is needed or wanted. **su·per·flu·i·ty** [ˌsju:pə'flu:iti] *n.* ~ quantity.

su·per·in·tend [ˌsju:pərin'tend] *v.t. & i.* manage; watch and

direct (work, etc.). ~·**ence** *n.*
~·**ent** *n.* manager.

su·pe·ri·or [sju:'piəriə*] *adj.* **1.**
better than the average : ~ *cloth* ;
~ *grades of coffee.* **2.** greater in
number : *The enemy attacked
with ~ forces (were in ~ numbers).*
3. ~ *to,* better than ; higher in
rank or position than ; not influenced by, not giving way to (e.g.
flattery, temptation). *n.* **1.** person
of higher rank, authority, etc.,
than another or who is better,
etc., than another (*in* sth.). **2.**
(*S*~) head of a monastery or
convent : *Father S~.* ~·**i·ty**
[sju:ˌpiəri'ɔriti] *n.*

su·per·la·tive [sju:'pə:lətiv] *adj.*
1. of the highest degree or
quality : *a man of ~ wisdom.* **2.**
(grammar) *the ~ degree,* the form
of an adj. and adv. expressing
the highest degree (e.g. *best,
most foolishly*).

su·per·mar·ket ['sju:pəˌmɑ:kit]
n. large self-service store for
food, household articles, etc.

su·per·nat·u·ral [ˌsju:pə'nætʃə-
rəl] *adj.* spiritual ; of that which
is not controlled or explained
by physical laws.

su·per·sede [ˌsju:pə'si:d] *v.t.*
take the place of ; put or use sb.
or sth. in the place of : *Electric
light has ~d gaslight in most
towns.*

su·per·son·ic [ˌsju:pə'sɔnik]
adj. (of speeds) greater than
that of sound ; (of aircraft) able
to fly at ~ speed.

su·per·sti·tion [ˌsju:pə'stiʃən]
n. **1.** unreasoning belief in, fear
of, what is unknown or mysterious, esp. belief in magic. **2.** idea,
practice, etc., founded on such
belief. **su·per·sti·tious** *adj.*
of, showing, resulting from,
~.

su·per·struc·ture ['sju:pəˌstrʌk-
tʃə*] *n.* structure built on sth.
else ; parts of a ship above the
main deck.

su·per·vene [ˌsju:pə'vi:n] *v.i.*
come or happen so as to interrupt or to change.

su·per·vise ['sju:pəvaiz] *v.t.*
watch and direct (work, workers, an organization). **su·**

per·vi·sor *n.* **su·per·vi·sion**
[ˌsju:pə'viʒən] *n.*

su·pine ['sju:pain] *adj.* **1.** lying
flat on the back. **2.** inactive ;
slow to act.

sup·per ['sʌpə*] *n.* evening meal
when dinner is eaten in the
middle of the day.

sup·plant [sə'plɑ:nt] *v.t.* **1.**
supersede : *Trams are being ~ed
by buses.* **2.** take the place of
(sb.), esp. after getting him out
of office, etc., by unfair means :
~ *a rival.*

sup·ple ['sʌpl] *adj.* easily bent ;
not stiff : *the ~ limbs of a child* ;
a ~ mind, (fig.) quick to respond
to ideas.

sup·ple·ment ['sʌplimənt] *n.* **1.**
sth. added later to improve or
complete (e.g. a dictionary). **2.**
extra and separate addition to
a periodical. [ˌsʌpli'ment] *v.t.*
make additions to. **sup·ple·
men·ta·ry** [ˌsʌpli'mentəri] *adj.*
additional ; extra : ~*ary esti-
mates.*

sup·pli·cate ['sʌplikeit] *v.t. & i.*
ask humbly and earnestly (*for*
sth.). **sup·pli·ant** ['sʌpliənt] *n.
& adj.* (person) supplicating
for sth.

sup·ply [sə'plai] *v.t.* **1.** give or
provide (sth. needed or asked
for) : ~ *customers with food
(food for the children).* **2.** meet
(a need) : ~ *the need for more
houses. n.* **1.** ~*ing* ; that which
is supplied ; stock or amount of
sth. which is obtainable. **2.** (pl.)
(esp.) stores necessary for some
public, esp., military need.

sup·port [sə'pɔ:t] *v.t.* **1.** bear
the weight of ; hold up or keep
in place. **2.** strengthen ; help
(sb. or sth.) to go on : ~ *a claim
(a hospital, a political party).*
3. provide (a person, one's
family) with food, clothes, etc.
4. endure. *n.* ~*ing* or being
~*ed* ; sb. or sth. that ~*s. in ~
of,* in order t· ·elp or to promote.

sup·pose [sə'pouz] *v.t.* **1.** let it
be thought that ; take it as a
fact that : *S~ the world were flat.*
2. guess ; think : *What do you ~
he wanted?* **3.** make necessary ;

imply: *The Creation ~s a Creator.*
4. (forming an imperative, or
used to make suggestions): *S~
we go* (= let's go) *for a swim.
S~ you have another try.* **5.** *be
~d to,* be expected to: *You're
~d to know the rules.* **sup·pos·
ing** *conj.* if. **sup·posed** *adj.*
accepted as being so: *his ~d
generosity.* **sup·pos·ed·ly** [sə-
'pouzidli] *adv.* as is (or was) ~d.
sup·po·si·tion [ˌsʌpə'ziʃən] *n.*
1. supposing: *based on supposition.* **2.** sth. ~d; guess.

sup·press [sə'pres] *v.t.* **1.** put an
end to the activity or existence
of: ~ *a rising (the slave-trade,
etc.).* **2.** prevent from being
seen or known: ~ *a yawn (the
news).* **sup·pres·sion** *n.*

sup·pu·rate ['sʌpjuəreit] *v.i.*
form pus.

su·preme [sju:'pri:m] *adj.* highest in rank or authority; of the
greatest importance or value.
the S~ Being, God. ~**ly** *adv.*
su·prem·a·cy [sju'preməsi] *n.*

sur·charge ['sə:tʃɑ:dʒ] *n.* payment demanded in addition to
the usual charge (e.g. as a penalty for an understamped letter).

sure [ʃuə*, ʃɔ:*] *adj.* (-r, -st). **1.**
~ *of,* ~ *that,* free from doubt;
certain: *feel ~ of oneself,* feel
self-confident. **2.** *be ~ to* (come,
etc.), do not fail to . . . . *make
~,* satisfy oneself; do what is
needed in order to feel certain,
to get sth., etc. **3.** proved or
tested; trustworthy: *a ~ remedy; a ~ messenger.* **adv.** ~
enough, certainly; as expected.
~**ly** *adv.* **1.** probability. **2.** if
experience or probability can be
trusted. ~**ty** ['ʃuərti] *n.* (sth.
given as a) guarantee; person
who makes himself responsible
for the conduct or debt(s) of
another: *stand ~ty for sb.*

surf [sə:f] *n.* waves breaking in
white foam on the sea-shore or
on reefs.

sur·face ['sə:fis] *n.* **1.** the outside
of any object, etc.; any of the
sides of an object; the top of a
liquid. **2.** outward appearance.
v.i. (e.g. of a submarine) rise to
the ~ of the sea.

sur·feit ['sə:fit] *n.* too much of
anything, esp. food and drink;
feeling of heaviness, sickness,
caused by a ~. *v.t.* overeat
(*oneself on* sth.).

surge [sə:dʒ] *v.i.* move forward,
roll on, in or like waves: *The
floods ~d over the valley. The
crowds ~d out of the railway
station.* *n.* forward rush of
waves: *the ~ of the ocean;*
(fig.) *a ~ of anger.*

sur·geon ['sə:dʒən] *n.* doctor
who performs operations(4).

sur·ger·y ['sə:dʒəri] *n.* **1.** treatment of injuries and diseases by
a ~. **2.** doctor's room where
patients come to consult him.

sur·gi·cal ['sə:dʒikl] *adj.* of or
by surgery.

sur·ly ['sə:li] *adj.* (-ier, -iest).
bad-tempered and unfriendly.
sur·li·ness *n.*

sur·mise [sə:'maiz] *v.t. & i. &
n.* guess(ing); conjecture.

sur·mount [sə:'maunt] *v.t.* **1.**
overcome (difficulties, etc.; get
over (obstacles). **2.** *be ~ed by
(with),* have on or over the top.

sur·name ['sə:neim] *n.* that part
of a person's name common to
all members of the family.

sur·pass [sə:'pɑ:s] *v.t.* do or be
better than; exceed.

sur·plice ['sə:plis] *n.* loose-fitting
(usu.) white gown with wide
sleeves worn by some priests
and choirs in church.

sur·plus ['sə:pləs] *n.* amount
(esp. money) that remains after
needs have been supplied. (Cf.
deficit.)

sur·prise [sə'praiz] *n.* (feeling
caused by) sth. sudden or unexpected. *v.t.* **1.** give a feeling of
~ to. **2.** catch (sb., the enemy)
unexpectedly, when they are
unprepared. **sur·pris·ing** *adj.*
causing ~.

sur·ren·der [sə'rendə*] *v.t. & i.*
1. give up (oneself, a ship, town,
etc.) (*to* the enemy, the police,
etc.). **2.** give up possession of
(freedom, liberty, etc., *to* sb.). **3.**
~ *oneself to,* yield or give way to
(a habit, an emotion such as
despair, etc.). *n.* act of ~ing.

sur·rep·ti·tious [ˌsʌrəp'tiʃəs]

S

adj. (of actions) done secretly or stealthily.

sur·round [sə'raund] *v.t.* be, go, all round; shut in on all sides. **~·ings** *n. pl.* everything around and about a place; conditions that may affect a person, etc.: *living in pleasant ~ings.*

sur·tax ['sə:tæks] *n.* additional tax on high personal incomes.

sur·vey [sə'vei] *v.t.* **1.** take a general view of. **2.** examine the general condition of sth.: *~ the international situation.* **3.** measure and map out the position, size, boundaries, etc., of (land, a country, coast, etc.). ['sə:vei] *n.* **1.** general view. **2.** piece of land-~ing; map or record of this. **~·or** *n.* man whose business is the ~ing of land or buildings.

sur·vive [sə'vaiv] *v.t. & i.* continue to live or exist; live or exist longer than; remain alive after: *those who ~d the earthquake.* **sur·viv·al** *n.* **1.** surviving. **2.** person, custom, belief, etc., that has ~d but is looked upon as belonging to past times. **sur·viv·or** *n.* person who has ~d: *the survivors of a shipwreck.*

sus·cep·ti·ble [sə'septəbl] *adj.* **1.** easily influenced by feelings: *a girl with a ~ nature.* **2.** ~ *to,* affected by, sensitive to: *~ to flattery (pain, etc.).* **3.** ~ *of,* that can receive or be given: *~ of proof.* **sus·cep·ti·bil·i·ty** [sə,septə'biliti] *n.* sensitiveness; (pl.) personal beliefs, ideas, etc., about which one is sensitive.

sus·pect [səs'pekt] *v.t.* **1.** have an idea or feeling (concerning the possible existence of): *He ~ed that the enemy were hiding among the trees. He ~ed an ambush.* **2.** feel doubt about: *~ the truth of an account.* **3.** have a feeling that sb. may be guilty (*of*): *~ed of telling lies.* ['sʌspekt] *n.* person ~ed of wrongdoing. *predic. adj.* of doubtful character; ~ed.

sus·pend [səs'pend] *v.t.* **1.** hang up: *a lamp ~ed from the ceiling.* **2.** be ~ed (in the air, in a liquid), remain in place as if hanging: *dust (smoke) ~ed in the still air.* **3.** stop for a time: *~ payment,* stop payment (e.g. when bankrupt, etc.). **4.** say that (sb.) cannot be allowed to perform his duties, enjoy privileges, etc., for a time. **5.** delay, esp. *~ judgement.* **~·er** *n.* elastic band, etc., to hold up socks or stockings. **sus·pen·sion** [səs'penʃən] *n.* ~ing or being ~ed. *suspension bridge,* bridge ~ed on or by means of steel cables.

A suspension bridge

sus·pense [səs'pens] *n.* uncertainty (about news, events, decisions, etc.): *keep sb. in ~,* keep him waiting for news about sth.

sus·pi·cion [səs'piʃən] *n.* **1.** feeling of a person who suspects; feeling that sth. is wrong: *above ~,* so good, honest, etc., that ~ is out of the question. **2.** slight taste or suggestion (*of*). **sus·pi·cious** [səs'piʃəs] *adj.* having, showing, or causing ~.

sus·tain [səs'tein] *v.t.* **1.** keep from falling or sinking. **2.** (enable to) keep up or last: *~ing food* (i.e. giving strength); *~ an argument (an attempt).* **3.** suffer: *~ a loss (a defeat).* **4.** (law) decide in favour of; admit; uphold. **sus·tained** *adj.* continued, going on, for a long time. **sus·te·nance** ['sʌstinəns] *n.* food and drink.

su·ze·rain ['su:zərein] *n.* State or ruler in relation to another country over which it or he has some control or authority.

swab [swɔb] *n.* mop or pad for cleaning; sponge, ball of cotton wool, etc., for medical use. *v.t.* (-*bb*-). clean with a ~; take (*up* liquid) with a ~.

swag [swæg] *n.* (slang) stolen goods.

swag·ger ['swægə*] *v.i.* walk or behave in a self-important or self-satisfied manner.

¹**swal·low** ['swɔlou] *v.t. & i.* **1.** cause or allow to go down one's throat. ~ *one's lunch*, eat it quickly. **2.** take in; use (*up*); absorb: *earnings that were ~ed up by doctor's bills*. **3.** ~ *a story*, believe it too easily; ~ *an insult*, accept it meekly; ~ *one's anger*, not show it; ~ *one's words*, take them back, express regret for them. *n.* act of ~ing.

²**swal·low** ['swɔlou] *n.* kinds of small, fast-flying, fork-tailed bird associated in Europe with summer.

swam, see *swim.*

swamp [swɔmp] *n.* (area of) soft wet land; marsh. *v.t.* **1.** flood, soak (e.g. a boat, the people or things in it) with water. **2.** (fig.) overwhelm (*with*): *~ed with work* (*orders for goods, etc.*). ~**·y** *adj.*

swan [swɔn] *n.* large, graceful, long-necked (usu. white) water-bird. '~**'s-down** *n.* ~'s soft under-feathers.

swank [swæŋk] *v.i.* (colloq.) swagger; behave or talk boast-fully (*about*).

swap [swɔp] *v.t. & i.* (-*pp-*). = swop.

sward [swɔːd] *n.* (liter.) (area of) turf.

¹**swarm** [swɔːm] *n.* **1.** colony, large number, of insects, birds, etc., moving about together: *a ~ of ants* (*bees*). **2.** (esp. pl.) large numbers (*of* children, etc.). *v.i.* **1.** (esp. of bees forming a new colony) move or go in large numbers. **2.** ~ *with*, be crowded, filled, or covered with: *a dog ~ing with fleas. The Zoo ~ed with visitors.*

²**swarm** [swɔːm] *v.i. & t.* climb (*up* a tree, rope, etc.) by gripping with the knees and hands.

swarth·y ['swɔːði] *adj.* (-*ier, -iest*). of a dark colour.

swas·ti·ka ['swɔstikə] *n.* kind of cross shown here. 卐.

swat [swɔt] *v.t.* (-*tt-*). (colloq.). ~ *a fly*, hit it with a sharp blow.

swathe [sweið] *v.t.* wrap or bind tightly: *His leg was ~d in bandages.*

sway [swei] *v.i. & t.* **1.** move, be moved, unsteadily, first to one side and then to the other: *The branches ~ed in the wind.* **2.** control or influence; govern the direction of: *~ed by his feelings*; *a speech that ~ed the voters. n.* **1.** ~ing movement. **2.** rule or control: *under the ~ of a dictator.*

swear [swɛə*] *v.t. & i.* (p.t. *swore* [swɔː*], p.p. *sworn* [swɔːn]). **1.** say solemnly or with em-phasis: ~ *to do sth.*; ~ *that one will do sth.* **2.** take (an oath); cause (sb.) to take an oath: ~ *sb. to secrecy.* **3.** ~ *by sth.*, (col-loq.) use and have great con-fidence in (e.g. a medicine). **4.** use curses and bad words, pro-fane language. '~**-word** *n.* word used in ~ing (4).

sweat [swet] *n.* **1.** moisture that is given off by the body through the skin. **2.** condition of a per-son when covered with ~: *in a ~.* **3.** ~-like moisture on a sur-face. **4.** (colloq.) hard work. *v.i. & t.* **1.** give out ~. **2.** work hard. **3.** make (sb.) work very hard at the lowest possible wages: *~ed labour.* ~**'er** *n.* knitted jacket or jersey, usu. of thick wool. ~**·y** *adj.* (-*ier, -iest*). (e.g. clothing) wet with, smelling of, ~.

swede [swiːd] *n.* kind of turnip.

sweep [swiːp] *v.t. & i.* (p.t. & p.p. *swept*). **1.** clear away (dust, dirt, etc.) with a brush or broom; clean by doing this: ~ *up the dust*; ~ *a floor* (*a chimney*). **2.** move or pass quickly over or along, esp. so as to overcome or remove anything in the way: *Houses were swept away by the floods. The waves swept me off my feet.* **3.** stretch in an un-broken line or curve or expanse: *The coast ~s northwards.* **4.** move in a stately manner: *She swept out of the room. n.* **1.** act of ~ing with, or as with, a brush, etc.; ~ing movement. *make a clean ~* (of sth.), (fig.) get rid of (e.g. old ways of doing things). **2.** long curving stretch of coun-try or of a road or river. **3.** range (4) of sth. moving or moved in a wide curve: *Don't go within the ~ of the scythe.* **4.**

(also *chimney-~*) man whose work is ~ing soot from chimneys. **~·er** *n.* person or thing that ~s: *street-~ers; carpet-~er.* **~·ing** *adj.* far-reaching; taking in very much: *~ing changes; a ~ing statement* (i.e. ignoring many exceptions to sth.). '**~· stake(s)** *n.* form of gambling, esp. on a horse-race.

sweet [swiːt] *adj.* (*-er, -est*). **1.** tasting like sugar or honey. **2.** fresh and pure: *~ milk.* **3.** pleasant or attractive: *a ~ scent* (*voice*); *a ~ temper; a ~ little boy. n.* **1.** dish of ~ food (tart, pudding, etc.) as part of a meal. **2.** piece of boiled and flavoured sugar, chocolate, etc. **~·en** *v.t. & i.* make or become ~. **~· en·ing** *n.* substance that ~ens. '**~·heart** *n.* either of a pair of lovers. '**~·meat** *n.* plum, etc., preserved in sugar.

swell [swel] *v.i. & t.* (p.t. ~ed, p.p. ~ed or *swollen* ['swoulən]). **1.** (cause to) become greater in volume, thickness or force: *Wood often ~s when wet.* (fig.) *He* (*His heart*) *was ~ing with pride. suffering from ~ed head,* from conceit. **2.** ~ *up* (*out*), (cause to) have a curved surface: *sails ~ing out in the wind. n.* **1.** gradual increase of sound: *the ~ of an organ.* **2.** slow rise and fall of the sea's surface after a storm. **3.** (colloq.) smartly dressed or important person. *adj.* (colloq.) well dressed; smart; distinguished. **~·ing** *n.* swollen place on the body (e.g. the result of a blow or of a diseased tooth).

swel·ter ['sweltə*] *v.i.* be uncomfortably warm; suffer from the heat.

swept, see *sweep.*

swerve [swəːv] *v.i. & t.* (cause to) change direction suddenly: *The car ~d to avoid knocking the boy down. n.* swerving movement.

¹swift [swift] *adj.* (*-er, -est*). quick. **~·ly** *adv.*

²swift [swift] *n.* small insect-eating bird with long wings.

swill [swil] *v.t. & i.* (often ~ *out*) rinse. *n.* pig's food, mostly liquid.

swim [swim] *v.i. & t.* (*-mm-*; p.t. *swam*, p.p. *swum* [swʌm]). **1.** move the body through water by using arms, legs, fins, tail, etc.; cross by ~ming: *Fish ~.* ~ (*across*) *the river. go ~ming.* **2.** be covered (*with*), overflowing (*with*), or as if floating (*in*): *eyes ~ming with tears; meat ~ming in gravy.* **3.** seem to be moving round and round; have a dizzy feeling: *The room swam before his eyes. His head swam. n.* **1.** act of ~ming (1): *go for a ~.* **2.** be *in* (*out of*) *the ~,* be (not be) taking part in, aware of, what is going on. **~·ming·ly** *adv.* easily and without trouble: *getting along ~mingly.*

swin·dle ['swindl] *v.t. & i.* cheat (sb. *out of money,* etc.); get (money, etc. *out of* sb.) by cheating. *n.* piece of swindling; sth. sold, etc., that is less valuable than it is described to be. **swin· dler** *n.* person who ~s.

swine [swain] *n.* (old use or liter., pl. unchanged) pig.

swing [swiŋ] *v.i. & t.* (p.t. & p.p. *swung* [swʌŋ]). **1.** (of sth. fixed at one end or side) (cause to) move forwards and backwards or in a curve: *swing one's arms. The door swung open.* **2.** walk or run with a free, easy movement: *soldiers advancing at a ~ing trot.* **3.** (cause to) turn in a curve: *The car swung round the corner. n.* **1.** ~ing movement or walk. **2.** strong rhythm: *go with a ~,* go easily, without trouble; *in full ~,* active, in full operation. **3.** seat held by ropes or chains for ~ing on, as shown here.

A swing (3)

swipe [swaip] *v.t. & n.* (hit hard with a) swinging blow; (slang) steal.

swirl [swə:l] *v.i. & t.* (of liquid, air, dust, etc.) (cause to) move or flow at different rates of speed, with twists and turns: *dust ~ing about the streets.* *n.* ~ing movement; eddy.

swish [swiʃ] *v.t. & i.* **1.** swing (a stick or whip) through the air so that it can be heard. **2.** make this kind of sound or a rustling sound (e.g. of skirts) or the sound made by rain falling heavily. *n.* sound of, sound suggesting, a cane or whip being ~ed.

switch [switʃ] *n.* **1.** device for making or breaking a connexion between railway points (to cause trains to go from one track to another) or between wires in an electric circuit. **2.** thin twig or stick (e.g. one for whipping a horse). *v.t. & i.* **1.** turn (electric current *off* or *on*); move (a train, tram) on to another track; (fig.) turn (one's thoughts, a conversation) from one subject to another. **2.** whip with a ~(2). **3.** move or swing with a jerk: *The horse ~ed its tail.* '~·**back** *n.* railway that twists and turns up and down steep slopes, esp. one in an amusement park. '~·**board** *n.* apparatus with numerous ~es(1), esp. for making connexions by telephone.

A switch

A swivel

swivel ['swivl] *n.* kind of joint (2) between two parts of a chair, coat-hook, etc., which allows one part to revolve without the other: *a ~ chair (chain).* *v.t.* (*-ll-*). (cause to) turn on, or as on, a ~.

swol·len, p.p. of *swell* (esp. when used as an adj.).

swoon [swu:n] *v.i. & n.* faint.

swoop [swu:p] *v.i.* come with a rush: *The eagle ~ed (down) on its prey.* *n.* ~ing movement.

swop [swɔp] *v.t. & i.* (*-pp-*). (colloq.) exchange (one thing *for* another).

sword [sɔ:d] *n.* long steel blade fixed in a hilt, used as a weapon. *put to the ~,* kill. *cross ~s with,* (fig.) dispute with. '~·**fish** *n.* large sea-fish with a long ~-like upper jaw. '**swords·man** *n.* man skilled in using a ~.

swore, sworn, see *swear.*

swot [swɔt] *v.i.* (*-tt-*). (slang) study hard. *n.* person who ~s, esp. one who is much more interested in books than in sport.

swum, see *swim.*

swung, see *swing.*

syc·a·more ['sikəmɔ:*] *n.* large tree valued for its hard wood.

syc·o·phant ['sikəfənt] *n.* person who tries to win favour by flattering rich or powerful people.

syl·la·ble ['siləbl] *n.* unit of pronunciation containing one vowel sound; word or division of a word with one vowel sound in it: *Arithmetic is a word of four ~s.* **syl·lab·ic** [si'læbik] *adj.* of or in ~s.

syl·la·bus ['siləbəs] *n.* outline or summary of a course of studies; programme of school lessons.

syl·lo·gism ['silədʒizm] *n.* form of reasoning in which a conclusion is reached from two statements, e.g.: *All men must die: I am a man; therefore I must die.*

sylph [silf] *n.* slender, graceful girl or woman.

syl·van ['silvən] *adj.* = silvan.

sym·bol ['simbl] *n.* sign, mark, object, etc., looked upon as representing or recalling sth.: *The Cross is the ~ of Christianity.* ×, ÷, +, *and* − *are common mathematical ~s.* ~·**ic** [sim·'bɔlik] *adj.* of, using, used as, a ~. ~·**i·cal·ly** *adv.* ~·**ize** ['simbəlaiz] *v.t.* be a ~ of ; make use of a ~ or ~s for.

sym·me·try ['simitri] *n.* (beauty resulting from) right relation of parts; quality of harmony or agreement (in size, design, etc.) between parts. **sym·met·ri·cal** [si'metrikl] *adj.* having ~ ; (of a design, etc.) having (usu. two) exactly similar parts on either side of a dividing line.

sym·pa·thy ['simpəθi] *n.* (capacity for) sharing the feelings of others, feeling pity or tenderness: *in ~ with*, agreeing with, approving of (e.g. a proposal); *feel ~ for* (the victims of an accident). **sym·pa·thet·ic** [ˌsimpə'θetik] *adj.* having or showing ~; caused by ~. **sym·pa·thize** ['simpəθaiz] *v.i.* feel or express ~ (*with*).

sym·pho·ny ['simfəni] *n.* elaborate musical composition in three or four parts for (usu. a large) orchestra.

sym·po·sium [sim'pouzjəm] *n.* collection of opinions of several persons on a problem or subject.

symp·tom ['simptəm] *n.* 1. change in the body's condition that indicates illness. 2. sign of the existence of sth. **symp·to·mat·ic** [ˌsimptə'mætik] *adj.* serving as a ~ (*of*).

syn·a·gogue ['sinəgog] *n.* (building used for an) assembly of Jews for religious teaching and worship.

syn·chro·nize ['siŋkrənaiz] *v.t. & i.* (cause to) happen at the same time; agree in time (*with*): ~ *watches*, make them show exactly the same time.

syn·di·cate ['sindikit] *n.* business association, esp. one that supplies articles, cartoons, etc., to several newspapers. ['sindikeit] *v.t.* publish in numerous newspapers through a ~.

syn·od ['sinəd] *n.* meeting of church officers to discuss and decide questions of policy, government, teaching, etc.

syn·o·nym ['sinənim] *n.* word with the same meaning as another in the same language. **syn·on·y·mous** [si'noniməs] *adj.*

syn·op·sis [si'nopsis] *n.* (pl. *-ses* [-si:z]). summary or outline (of a book, play, etc.).

syn·tax ['sintæks] *n.* (rules for) sentence building.

syn·the·sis ['sinθisis] *n.* (pl. *-ses* [-si:z]). combination of separate parts, substances, etc., into a whole or into a system; that which results from this process.

syn·thet·ic [sin'θetik] *adj.* produced by ~; (of substances) artificially made: *synthetic rubber*.

sy·phon, = siphon.

sy·ringe ['sirindʒ] *n.* device for drawing in liquid by suction and forcing it out again in a fine stream, used for washing out wounds, injecting liquids into the body, in spraying plants.

syr·up ['sirəp] *n.* thick, sweet liquid made from sugar-cane juice or by boiling sugar with water.

sys·tem ['sistim] *n.* 1. group of things or parts working together in a regular relation: *the nervous ~*. 2. ordered group of principles, ideas, etc.: *a ~ of government*. 3. the human body: *Too much alcohol is bad for the ~*. **~·at·ic** [ˌsisti'mætik] *adj.* methodical; done or arranged in harmony with a ~. **~·at·i·cal·ly** *adv.*

T

tab [tæb] *n.* small piece or strip of cloth, etc., fixed to a garment, etc., as a badge, distinguishing mark, or holder.

ta·ble ['teibl] *n.* 1. piece of furniture with a flat top and (usu. four) legs: *a dining- ~*. 2. people seated at a ~: *His talk amused the whole ~*. 3. *keep a good ~*, provide good meals. 4. list, orderly arrangement, of facts, information, etc.: *a railway time-~*; *multiplication ~s*. *v.t.* ~ *a motion (a bill)*, postpone discussion of. **'~-cloth** *n.* one (to be) spread over a ~. **'~·land** *n.* plateau. **'~·spoon** *n.* large spoon for serving food on to plates at ~.

ta·ble d'hôte ['tɑ:bl'dout] (Fr.). *n.* ~ *dinner*, restaurant or hotel meal at a fixed price.

tab·let ['tæblit] *n.* 1. (old use) flat sheet of wood, stone, etc., for cutting words on (e.g. as used

by the ancient Romans). **2.**
flat surface with words cut or
written on it, e.g. one fixed to a
wall in memory of sb. or sth. **3.**
number of sheets of writing-
paper fastened together along
one edge. **4.** lump of hard soap;
small flat hard piece of prepared
medicine (e.g. aspirin); flat hard
sweet.

A mural tablet(2)

ta·boo, ta·bu [tə'bu:] *n.* act or
thing which (esp. primitive)
religion or custom regards as
forbidden, not to be touched,
spoken of, etc. *adj.* forbidden;
consecrated. *v.t.* put under a
~; forbid or prohibit: *a subject
that was ~ed.*

tab·u·lar ['tæbjulə*] *adj.* arranged or displayed in tables
(4). **tab·u·late** ['tæbjuleit] *v.t.*
arrange (facts, figures, etc.) in
~ form.

tac·it ['tæsit] *adj.* unspoken;
understood without being put
into words: ~ *agreement* (*consent*).

tac·i·turn ['tæsitə:n] *adj.* (in the
habit of) saying very little. **tac·
i·tur·ni·ty** [ˌtæsi'tə:niti] *n.*

tack [tæk] *n.* **1.** short, flat-
headed nail. **2.** long, loose stitch
used in fastening pieces of cloth
together loosely or temporarily.
3. sailing-ship's direction as
fixed by the direction of the
wind and the position of the
sails, esp. *on the port* (*starboard*)
~, with the wind on the port
(starboard) side; (fig.) *on the
right* (*wrong*) ~, following a wise
(unwise) course of action. **4.**
(among sailors) *hard* ~, hard
ship-biscuit. *v.t. & i.* **1.** fasten
(*down*) with ~s(1). **2.** fasten
with ~s(2). **3.** sail a zig-zag
course.

tack·le ['tækl] *n.* **1.** set of ropes
and pulleys for working a ship's

sails, or for lifting weights, etc.
2. equipment, apparatus, for
doing sth.: *fishing-~.* **3.** act of
tackling(2). *v.t. & i.* **1.** deal
with, attack (a problem, a piece
of work). **2.** seize, lay hold of
(e.g. a thief or, in rugger, a player
who has the ball).

tact [tækt] *n.* (use of) skill and
understanding shown by sb. who
handles people and situations
successfully and without causing
offence. ~**ful(ly)** *adj.* (*adv.*)
~**less(ly)** *adj.* (*adv.*)

tac·tics ['tæktiks] *n. pl.* (often
with sing. vb.) art of placing or
moving fighting forces for use
during battle (cf. *strategy*); (fig.)
plan(s) or method(s) for carrying
out a policy. **tac·ti·cal** ['tæk-
tikl] *adj.* of ~. **tac·ti·cian**
[tæk'tiʃən] *n.* expert in ~.

tad·pole ['tædpoul] *n.* young of
the frog or toad before full
development.

A tadpole   A tail

taf·fe·ta ['tæfitə] *n.* thin, shiny,
rather stiff silk material.

taff·rail ['tæfreil] *n.* rail round a
ship's stern.

tag [tæg] *n.* **1.** loose or ragged
end. **2.** metal point at the end
of a string, shoe-lace, etc. **3.**
label (e.g. for showing prices,
addresses). **4.** phrase or sentence
often quoted: *Latin tags. v.t. & i.*
(*-gg-*). **1.** join (sth., esp. a piece
of writing, *to* or *on* to sth. else).
2. follow closely: *children tagging
after their mother.* **3.** fasten a
tag(3) to.

tail [teil] *n.* **1.** movable part at
the lower end of the back of an
animal, bird, fish, or reptile
which it can wave, wag, or
switch. **2.** sth. like a ~ in
position: *the ~ of a kite* (*comet,
aircraft*). **3.** (often pl.) side of a
coin not having the monarch's
head on it: (in spinning a coin to
decide sth.) *heads or ~s? v.t.
& i. ~* (*sb., after sb.*), follow close
behind; ~ *off*, become smaller in
number, size, etc.

tail·or [ˈteilə*] *n.* maker of suits and overcoats, esp. for men. *v.t.* cut out and sew. *a well-~ed man*, with well-made clothes.

taint [teint] *n.* trace of some bad quality, decay, or infection. *v.t. & i.* make or become infected: *~ed meat*.

take [teik] *v.t. & i.* (p.t. *took* [tuk], p.p. *taken* [ˈteikn]). **1.** get hold of with the hand(s), etc., or with an instrument, etc. (cf. *leave, let go of*): *~ sb.'s hand*; *~ sth. (up) with one's fingers*; *~ hold of sth.*, hold it, seize it. **2.** capture; catch (sb. or sth.) by surprise or pursuit; win; become ill with (a disease); attract: *~ a fortress*; *~ 500 prisoners*; *a rabbit ~n in a trap*; *~ first prize in a competition*; *~ cold* (become ill with a cold); *be ~n ill*; *~ fire*, begin to burn; *~* (attract) *the fancy*; *not much ~n with* (attracted by) *the idea*. **3.** carry, accompany (sb. or sth.): *~ a letter to the post*; *~ a friend home in one's car*; *~ a box upstairs*. **4.** have; eat or drink; give, allow or get for oneself: *~ a bath* (*a holiday, dinner, some medicine, a deep breath*); *~ pride* (*an interest*) *in one's work*; *~* (i.e. hire) *a taxi*; *~* (i.e. rent) *a seaside cottage for the holidays*. **5.** accept; receive; subscribe to: *I will ~ £5 for it. Which newspaper do you ~?* **6.** make a record (1): *~ notes of a lecture*; *~ a photograph*. **7.** need: *The work took four hours. It ~s two to make a quarrel.* **8.** suppose; conclude: *I took him to be an honest man. ~ sth. for granted*, accept it as true, certain to happen. **9.** (with adv. & prep.): *~ after* (sb.), resemble (a parent or relation) in looks, etc. *~ sth. back*, (esp.) withdraw sth. one has said. *~ (sth.) down*, lower; write down (notes, etc.). *~ sb. down*, lower his pride. *~ (sb.) in*, receive (him) as a guest, etc.; get the better of by a trick. *~ (sth.) in*, understand, receive into the mind; see at a glance; receive (a newspaper, etc.) regularly; reduce the area, width,

etc., of (e.g. a garment); include or comprise. *~ (sb. or sth.) for*, consider to be, esp. wrongly suppose to be: *He was ~n for an Englishman. ~ off*, (esp.) ridicule by imitation; (of aircraft) start a flight. *~ on*, undertake (work); engage (workers); assume (a quality or appearance). *~ out*, obtain (an insurance policy, a licence, a summons, etc.); remove (a stain). *~ (sth.) over*, succeed to the management or ownership of; accept the transfer of (duties, etc.): *When does the new manager ~ over? ~ to*, adopt as a habit or practice: *~ to gardening on retirement*; use, go to, as a means of escape: *~ to flight*; *~ to one's heels*; *~ to the woods*; *~ to the boats* (abandon ship); conceive a liking for: *I took to the man at once. ~ up*, absorb; dissolve; occupy (time, space); begin to give one's attention to; proceed to deal with. **10.** (esp. of vaccine) have effect; act. *n.* amount (of fish, etc.) *~n* (2).

tak·ing *adj.* attractive. *n. pl.* money *~n* by a shop, etc., during a stated period; gains.

tale [teil] *n.* **1.** story: *fairy ~s*. **2.** report or account. *tell ~s*, tell about sb.'s wrongdoing.

tal·ent [ˈtælənt] *n.* **1.** natural power to do sth.; ability: *a man of great ~*; *a ~ for painting*. **2.** people with ~: *local ~*. *~·ed adj.* having ~.

tal·is·man [ˈtælizmən] *n.* sth. considered as bringing luck; charm (2).

talk [tɔ:k] *v.i. & t.* say things; speak to give information (*to*); discuss matters (*with*); have the power of speech: *Some parrots can ~. ~ over*, discuss it; *~ sb. out of doing sth.*, persuade him not to do it; *~ sb. round*, get his support or agreement by *~ing. n.* **1.** *~ing*; informal lecture. **2.** *small ~*, conversation on unimportant subjects. *the ~ of the town*, sth. or sb. everyone is *~ing about. ~·a·tive* [ˈtɔ:kətiv] *adj.* liking to *~* a lot.

tall [tɔ:l] *adj.* (*-er*, *-est*). **1.** (esp. of persons) of more than ordinary height: *a ~ man*; *six foot ~*. **2.** *a ~ story*, one that is difficult to believe; *a ~ order*, a task difficult to perform; an unreasonable request.

tal·low ['tælou] *n.* hard (esp. animal) fat used for making candles, etc.

tal·ly ['tæli] *v.i. & t.* (of stories, amounts, etc.) correspond, agree. *n.* reckoning.

tal·ly-ho [ˌtæli'hou] *int.* huntsman's cry on catching sight of the fox.

tal·on ['tælən] *n.* claw of a bird of prey (e.g. an eagle).

tame [teim] *adj.* (*-r*, *-st*). **1.** (of animals) used to living with human beings; not wild or fierce. **2.** dull; uninteresting. *v.t.* make ~. **tam·er** *n.* person who ~s wild animals.

tam·per ['tæmpə•] *v.i.* meddle or interfere (*with*).

tan [tæn] *n. & adj.* yellowish-brown; brown colour of sun-burnt skin. *v.t. & i.* (*-nn-*). **1.** make (an animal's skin) into leather. **2.** make or become brown with sunburn. **tan·ner** *n.* workman who tans skins. **tan·ner·y** *n.* place where skins are tanned.

tan·dem ['tændəm] *n.* ~ *bicycle*, one for two persons to ride, one behind the other.

tang [tæŋ] *n.* sharp taste or smell.

tan·gent ['tændʒənt] *n.* straight line touching but not cutting a curve. *go* (*fly*) *off at a ~*, change suddenly from one line of thought, action, etc., to another.

tan·ger·ine [ˌtændʒə'ri:n] *n.* small, sweet, loose-skinned orange.

tan·gi·ble ['tændʒibl] *adj.* **1.** that can be touched. **2.** clear and definite: *~ proof*.

tan·gle ['tæŋgl] *n.* confused mass (of string, hair, etc.). *v.t. & i.* make or become disordered.

tan·go ['tæŋgou] *n.* slow S. American dance for two persons.

tank [tæŋk] *n.* **1.** (usu. large) container for liquid or gas: *the petrol ~ of a motor-car*. **2.** (India and Pakistan) artificial (usu. rectangular) pond for storing water. **3.** armoured fighting vehicle. ~**er** *n.* ship with ~s, lorry with a large cylindrical ~, for carrying oil, milk, etc.

A tank (3)

tank·ard ['tæŋkəd] *n.* metal mug, esp. one for beer.

tan·ta·lize ['tæntəlaiz] *v.t.* raise hopes that are to be disappointed; keep just out of his reach sth. that sb. desires.

tan·ta·mount ['tæntəmaunt] *adj.* (only) ~ *to*, equal in effect to.

tan·trum ['tæntrəm] *n.* fit of bad temper or anger: *in one of his ~s*.

¹**tap** [tæp] *n.* device for controlling the flow of a liquid or gas from a pipe, barrel, etc. *on tap*, (of beer, etc.) in a barrel with a tap; ready for use. *v.t.* (*-pp-*). **1.** let liquid out from (through a tap in a barrel); cut (the bark of a tree) and get (sap, etc.): *tapping rubber trees*. **2.** (fig.) try to obtain (money, information, etc.) from: *tap a friend for a loan*. *tap the telephone wires*, make a connexion in order to listen secretly to conversation.

²**tap** [tæp] *n.* quick light blow. *v.t. & i.* (*-pp-*). give a tap or taps: *tap one's foot on the floor*; *tap at* (*on*) *the door*; *tap sb. on the shoulder*.

tape [teip] *n.* **1.** long narrow strip of cloth, paper, etc., used for tying up parcels, in dress-making, for recording sound, etc. **2.** narrow strip of paper on which telegraph instruments automatically print news, etc. '~·ˌmeas·ure *n.* ~ marked in inches for measuring. ~ re·cord·er ['teip riˌkɔ:də•] *n.*

apparatus that records sound on magnetic ~.

¹**ta·per** ['teipə*] n. length of thread with a thin coating of wax, burnt to give a light.

²**ta·per** ['teipə*] v.t. & i. make or become gradually narrower towards one end: ~ing fingers; one end ~ing off to a point.

tap·es·try ['tæpistri] n. cloth with designs or pictures made by weaving coloured threads into it, used esp. for hanging on walls.

tap·i·o·ca [,tæpi'oukə] n. starchy food (in the form of hard white grains) from the root of a plant.

tar [ta:*] n. black substance, thick and sticky when melted, obtained from coal. (-rr-). coat with tar. **tar·ry** adj. ¹**tar·mac** n. mixture of tar and crushed stone used for road surfaces, runways on airfields.

tar·dy ['ta:di] adj. (-ier, -iest). late; slow. **tar·di·ly** adv. **tar·di·ness** n.

tar·get ['ta:git] n. 1. sth. to be aimed at. 2. thing, plan, etc., against which criticism, etc., is directed.

tar·iff ['tærif] n. 1. list of fixed charges, esp. for meals, rooms, etc., at a hotel. 2. list of taxes on goods imported or (less often) exported; tax on a particular class of imported goods.

tar·mac, see tar.

tar·nish ['ta:nif] v.i. & t. (esp. of metal surfaces) lose, cause loss of, brightness.

tar·pau·lin [ta:'pɔ:lin] n. (sheet or cover of) canvas made waterproof, esp. with tar.

tar·ry ['tæri] v.i. (liter.) wait (for); be slow or late in coming, going, or appearing; stay (at, in, etc.). See tar.

¹**tart** [ta:t] adj. acid; sharp in taste; (fig.) sharp: a ~ answer. ~·ly adv.

²**tart** [ta:t] n. 1. fruit pie. 2. circle of pastry with fruit or jam on it.

tar·tan ['ta:tən] n. Scottish woollen fabric woven with coloured crossing stripes.

task [ta:sk] n. piece of (esp. hard)

work (to be) done. take sb. to ~, scold him (for, about, sth.). ~-force, military, naval, or air unit with a special mission. v.t. (of a ~) put a strain on (sb.'s powers). '~·,mas·ter n. person who imposes hard ~s on others.

tas·sel ['tæsl] n. bunch of threads, etc., tied together at one end and hanging (from a flag, hat, etc.) as an ornament. **tas·selled** adj. having ~s.

taste [teist] n. 1. sense by which flavour is known: sweet to the ~. 2. quality of substances made known by this sense, e.g. by putting on the tongue: Sugar has a sweet ~. 3. small quantity (of sth. to eat or drink). 4. liking or preference (for): He has a ~ for modern art. not to my ~, not to my liking. 5. ability to enjoy beauty, esp. in art and literature; ability to choose and use the best kind of behaviour, etc.: a man of ~. in good (bad) ~, pleasing (displeasing) to people with ~(5). v.t. & i. 1. be aware of the ~(2) of sth. 2. (of food, etc.) have a particular ~(2): It ~s sour. It ~s of onions. 3. test the ~(2) of: The cook ~d the soup. 4. experience: ~ the joys of freedom. ~·ful adj. showing good ~(5); in good ~. ~·ful·ly adv. ~·less adj. 1. (of food) having little or no flavour. 2. without ~(5); in bad ~. ~·less·ly adv. tast·y adj. (-ier, -iest). pleasing to the ~(1).

tat·ter ['tætə*] n. (usu. pl.) rag; piece of cloth, paper, etc., torn off or hanging loosely from sth.: in ~s, in rags or torn strips. **tat·tered** adj. ragged.

tat·tle ['tætl] v.i. chatter; prattle; gossip. n. trivial talk or gossip.

¹**tat·too** [tə'tu:] n. & v.t. (mark sb. with) permanent designs or patterns by pricking the skin and inserting colouring matter.

²**tat·too** [tə'tu:] n. 1. beating of drum(s) to call soldiers back to quarters. 2. public entertainment, with music, marching, etc., by soldiers.

taught, see teach.

taunt [tɔ:nt] n. remark intended

to hurt sb.'s feelings. **v.t.** attack
(sb.) with ~s: ~ *a man with
having failed.* ~**ing·ly** *adv.*

taut [tɔːt] *adj.* (of ropes, nerves,
etc.) tightly stretched; tense.
~**·ly** *adv.*

tau·tol·o·gy [tɔːˈtɔlədʒi] *n.* the
saying of the same thing again
in different words.

tav·ern [ˈtævən] *n.* (old use) inn.

taw·dry [ˈtɔːdri] *adj.* (-ier, -iest).
showy, brightly coloured or
decorated, but in bad taste.

taw·ny [ˈtɔːni] *adj.* brownish-
yellow.

tax [tæks] *n.* **1.** sum of money
(to be) paid by citizens (according to income, value of purchases, etc.) to the government
for public purposes. **2.** *a tax on*
(one's strength, patience, etc.),
sth. that is a strain or a burden
on. **v.t. 1.** put a tax (1) on; get
a tax: *to tax sugar (the rich).* **2.**
be a tax (2) on (one's patience,
memory, etc.). **3.** *tax sb. with
sth.*, accuse him of: *They taxed
me with having neglected the work.*

tax·a·ble *adj.* that can be
taxed (1). **tax·a·tion** [tækˈsei-
ʃən] *n.* system of raising money
by taxes; taxes (to be) paid.
'**tax-'free** *adj.* (of goods) not
taxed; (of dividends, etc.) after
payment of tax by the company.

tax·i [ˈtæksi] *n.* (pl. *taxis* [ˈtæksiz])
(rarely ~-*cab*). motor-car, usu.
with a ~meter, which may be
hired. **v.i. 1.** go in a ~. **2.** (of
aircraft) move on wheels on the
ground: *The plane ~ed across
the tarmac.* ~**·me·ter** *n.* (usu.
meter) device which automatically records the fare for a journey
in a ~.

tax·i·der·my [ˈtæksiˌdəːmi] *n.*
art of preparing and stuffing the
skins of animals, birds, and fish
so that they look as they did
when living.

tea [tiː] *n.* **1.** (dried leaves of)
evergreen shrub of eastern Asia;
drink made by pouring boiling
water on these leaves. **2.** occasion (in the late afternoon) on
which tea is drunk. *high tea,*
meal (with tea to drink) taken in

the early evening in place of a
later supper or dinner. '**tea·
cloth** *n.* **1.** small cloth for a
tea-table. **2.** cloth for drying
dishes, etc. '**tea·set**, '**tea-
ˌserv·ice** *n.* number of cups,
saucers, plates, with teapot,
milk jug, etc., usu. of the same
pattern, for use at tea (2). '**tea-
things** *n. pl.* (colloq.) cups,
plates, etc., needed for tea.

teach [tiːtʃ] *v.t. & i.* (p.t. & p.p.
taught [tɔːt]). give instruction to
(sb.); cause (sb.) to know or be
able to do (sth.); give lessons at
school; do this for a living. ~**·er**
n. ~**·ing** *n.* (esp.) that which is
taught: *the ~ing(s) of Christ.*

teak [tiːk] *n.* (large tree of India,
Burma, Malaysia, etc., with)
hard wood used in shipbuilding.

team [tiːm] *n.* **1.** two or more
oxen, horses, etc., pulling a cart,
plough, etc., together. **2.** number of persons playing together
and forming one side in certain
games (e.g. football or cricket).

¹**tear** [tɛə*] *v.t. & i.* (p.t. *tore* [tɔː*],
*toə**], p.p. *torn* [tɔːn]). **1.** pull
sharply apart or to pieces; make
(a hole *in* sth.) by pulling sharply: ~ *a piece of paper in two* (or
to pieces, to bits); ~ *into
small pieces*; ~ *a dress on a nail*;
a torn coat. **2.** cause (sth.) to be
down, off, etc., by pulling sharply: ~ *a page out of a book*; ~
down a notice. **3.** (usu. passive)
destroy the peace of: *a country
torn by civil war.* **4.** become torn:
Paper ~s easily. **5.** go in excitement or at a great speed: *children ~ing out of school.* *n.* torn
place (e.g. in a coat).

²**tear** [tiə*] *n.* drop of salty water
coming from the eye. *in ~s,*
crying. ~**ful** *adj.* crying; wet
with ~s: *a ~ful face.* ~**·ful·ly**
adv.

tease [tiːz] *v.t.* make fun of (sb.)
playfully or unkindly; worry
with jokes, questions, etc.;
annoy: *It's unkind to ~ a child
because he stutters.* *n.* person
fond of teasing others. **teas·er**
n. (colloq.) difficult question or
task. **teas·ing·ly** *adv.*

teat [tiːt] *n.* nipple.

tech·ni·cal ['teknikl] *adj.* of, connected with, special to, one of the mechanical or industrial arts (e.g. printing, weaving) or with the methods used by experts: ~ *terms*; *the* ~ *skill of a pianist.* ~**i·ty** [,tekni'kæliti] *n.* ~ word, phrase, point, etc. **tech·ni·cian** [tek'niʃən] *n.* person expert in the technique of a particular art, etc. **tech·nique** [tek'ni:k] *n.* method of doing sth. expertly, esp. mechanical skill (often contrasted with feeling or expression, e.g. in music and art). **tech·nol·o·gy** [tek'nolədʒi] *n.* science of industrial arts.

te·dious ['ti:djəs] *adj.* slow and uninteresting: *a* ~ *lecture.* **te·dium** ['ti:djəm] *n.* ~ state; boredom; monotony.

teem [ti:m] *v.i.* 1. be present in great numbers. 2. ~ *with,* have in great numbers: *rivers* ~*ing with fish.*

teens [ti:nz] *n. pl.* the numbers 13 to 19: *girls in their* ~, 13 to 19 years of age. **teen·ag·er** ['ti:neidʒə*] *n.* person in his (her) ~.

teeth, see **tooth.**

teethe [ti:ð] *v.i.* (of a baby) be getting its first teeth.

tel·e- ['teli-] *prefix.* long distance. ~**gram** ['teligræm] *n.* message sent by ~graph. ~**graph** ['teligrɑ:f] *n.* means of, apparatus for, sending messages by the use of electric current along wires or by wireless. *v.t. & i.* send (news, etc.) by ~graph. ~**graph·ic** [,teli'græfik] *adj.* **te·leg·ra·phist** [ti'legrəfist] *n.* person trained to send and receive messages by ~graph. **te·leg·ra·phy** [ti'legrəfi] *n.* use, science, of the ~graph. ~**phone** ['telifoun] *n.* means, apparatus, for talking to sb. at a distance by using electric current or radio. *v.t. & i.* send (news, etc.) by ~phone; use the ~phone. ~**vi·sion** ['teliviʒən] *n.* process of transmitting a view of events, plays, etc. (while these are taking place, or from films or tapes) by radio to a distant ~vision receiving set. ~**vise** ['telivaiz] *v.t.* send views of (an event, a play, etc.) by ~vision.

te·lep·a·thy [ti'lepəθi] *n.* direct communication of thoughts or feelings from one mind to another at a distance without the use of signs, sounds, or words.

tel·e·scope ['teliskoup] *n.* tube-like instrument with lenses for making distant objects appear nearer and larger. *v.t. & i.* make or become shorter by means of or in the manner of sections that slide one within the other. **tel·e·scop·ic** [,teli'skopik] *adj.* 1. of, containing, able to be seen with, a ~. 2. having sections which slide one within the other: *a telescopic aerial.*

tell [tel] *v.t. & i.* (p.t. & p.p. *told* [tould]). 1. make known (in spoken or written words); inform about (one's name, etc.); relate (a story, etc.); utter (a lie, etc.); order: *T~ her to go away.* 2. (esp. with *can, be able to*) know apart, distinguish: *Can you* ~ *the difference between them? Can you* ~ *Mary from her twin sister?* 3. *there is no* ~*ing* (what will happen, etc.), it is impossible to say. 4. have a marked effect (*upon*); influence the result of: *All this hard work is* ~*ing on him,* is affecting his health. 5. (old use) count: ~ *one's beads,* say one's prayers with a rosary. *all told,* altogether. ~ *off,* count one by one and give orders (*for* a task, *to do* sth.); (colloq.) scold. **tel·ler** *n.* 1. person who receives and pays out money over a bank counter. 2. man who counts votes (e.g. in the House of Commons). **tell·ing** *adj.* effective: *a* ~*ing speech.* '~**tale** *n. & adj.* (person) making known a secret, sb.'s feelings, etc.

te·mer·i·ty [ti'meriti] *n.* rashness.

tem·per ['tempə*] *n.* 1. degree of hardness, toughness, elasticity, of a substance, esp. of steel. 2. state or condition of the mind: *in a good (bad)* ~, calm and pleasant (angry); *keep* (*lose*) one's ~, keep (fail to keep) one's anger under control; *out of* ~ (*with*), angry. *v.t. & i.* **1.** give the required ~ (1) to (steel, etc.) by heating and cooling, etc. **2.** soften or modify (sth. *with*): ~ *justice with mercy*, be merciful when giving a just punishment. **tem·pered** *adj.* (in compounds) having or showing a given kind of ~ (2): *a sweet-~ed child*.

tem·per·a·ment ['tempərəmənt] *n.* person's disposition or nature, esp. as this affects his way of thinking, feeling, and behaving: *a girl with a nervous* (*an artistic*) ~. **tem·per·a·men·tal** [ˌtempərə'mentl] *adj.* **1.** caused by ~: *a boy with a ~al dislike of study.* **2.** easily excited; having quickly-changing moods.

tem·per·ance ['tempərəns] *n.* moderation, self-control, in speech, behaviour, and (esp.) in the use of alcoholic drinks. **tem·per·ate** *adj.* **1.** showing, behaving with, ~. **2.** (of climate, parts of the world) free from extremes of heat and cold.

tem·per·a·ture ['tempritʃə*] degree of heat or cold. *take sb.'s* ~, measure it with a thermometer; *have a* ~, have a fever.

tem·pest ['tempist] *n.* violent storm. **tem·pes·tu·ous** [tem-'pestjuəs] *adj.* (of the weather, also fig.) violent.

¹**tem·ple** ['templ] *n.* building (esp. in ancient times) dedicated to a god; place of worship.

²**tem·ple** ['templ] *n.* flat part of either side of the head between the forehead and the ear.

tem·po ['tempou] *n.* speed at which music is (to be) played.

tem·po·ral ['tempərəl] *adj.* **1.** of, existing in, time. **2.** of this physical life only, not spiritual.

tem·po·ra·ry ['tempərəri] *adj.* lasting for, designed to be used for, a short time only: ~ *employment.* **tem·po·ra·ri·ly** *adv.*

tem·po·rize ['tempəraiz] *v.i.* delay making a decision, giving an answer, stating one's purpose, etc.; act so as to gain time.

tempt [tempt] *v.t.* **1.** (try to)

persuade (sb.) to do sth. wrong or foolish. **2.** attract (sb.) to have or do sth.: *The weather ~ed him to go for a swim.* **temp·ta·tion** [temp'teiʃən] *n.* ~ing or being ~ed; sth. that ~s. ~**·er** *n.* (esp.) *the Tempter*, Satan. ~**·ing·ly** *adv.*

ten [ten] *n. & adj.* **10. tenth** *n. & adj.* 10th; ⅒.

ten·a·ble ['tenəbl] *adj.* **1.** that can be defended successfully: *a fortress* (*position, argument*) *that is* ~. **2.** (of an office or ¹post (4)) that can be held (*by sb. for a certain period*).

te·na·cious [ti'neiʃəs] *adj.* holding tightly; refusing to let go *of*: *a* ~ *memory*; ~ *of our liberties.* **te·nac·i·ty** [ti'næsiti] *n.*

ten·ant ['tenənt] *n.* person who pays rent for the use of land, a building, room, etc. *v.t. (esp.) tenanted*, used by a ~. **ten·an·cy** ['tenənsi] *n.* use of land, etc., as a ~; length of time during which a ~ uses land, etc.

¹**tend** [tend] *v.t.* watch over, take care of (e.g. people who are ill).

²**tend** [tend] *v.i.* **1.** have a ~ency: *Prices are ~ing upwards.* **2.** move or be directed: *Their steps ~ed towards the bridge.* ~**·en·cy** ['tendənsi] *n.* turning or inclination (*to, towards, to* do sth.): *Your work shows a ~ency to improve.*

¹**ten·der** ['tendə*] *n.* **1.** wagon for coal and water behind a steam locomotive. **2.** small ship attending a larger one to carry stores, put on or take off passengers, etc. **3.** person who looks after sth.: *a bar—*.

²**ten·der** ['tendə*] *v.t. & i.* **1.** offer: ~ *payment* (of a debt); ~ *one's services* (*resignation*). **2.** make an offer (to carry out work, supply goods, etc.): ~ *for the construction of a bridge*, submit an offer to do it for a stated price. *n.* **1.** statement of the price at which one offers to supply goods or services, to do sth. **2.** sth. offered, esp. *legal* ~, form of money which must by law be accepted in payment of a debt.

³**ten·der** ['tendə*] *adj.* (*-er, -est*).

1. delicate; easily hurt or damaged; quickly feeling pain. **2.** (of meat) easily chewed; not tough. **3.** kind; loving: ~ *looks.* ~·**ly** *adv.* ~·**ness** *n.*

ten·don ['tendən] *n.* tough, thick cord that joins muscle to bone.

ten·dril ['tendril] *n.* thread-like part of a climbing plant (e.g. a vine) that twists round any support near by.

ten·e·ment ['tenəmənt] *n.* dwelling-house, esp. a large one for the use of many families at low rents.

ten·et ['ti:net, 'tenet, 'tenit] *n.* principle; belief; doctrine.

ten·nis ['tenis] *n.* game for two (four) players who hit a ball backwards and forwards over a net.

ten·on ['tenən] *n.* end of a piece of wood shaped to go into a mortise to make a joint. (See *mortise.*)

¹ten·or ['tenə*] *n.* general routine or direction (*of* one's life); general meaning or thread (*of* a speech, etc.).

²ten·or ['tenə*] *n.* (person with) highest normal adult male voice. (See *alto.*)

¹tense [tens] *n.* verb form that shows time.

²tense [tens] *adj.* (-r, -st). **1.** tightly stretched. **2.** showing or feeling excitement, etc.: *faces ~ with anxiety.* ~·**ly** *adv.* ~·**ness**, **ten·si·ty** ['tensiti] *n.*

ten·sile ['tensail, -sil] *adj.* **1.** of tension. **2.** capable of being stretched.

ten·sion ['tenʃən] *n.* **1.** state of, degree of, being tense: *the ~ of a violin string.* **2.** condition when feelings are tense, when relations between two persons, groups, states, etc., are strained: *political ~.*

tent [tent] *n.* shelter made of canvas supported by poles and ropes.

ten·ta·cle ['tentəkl] *n.* slender, flexible, snake-like, boneless part of certain animals (e.g. the octopus), used for feeling, holding, moving, etc.

ten·ta·tive ['tentətiv] *adj.* made or done as a trial, to see the

effect: *only a ~ suggestion.* ~·**ly** *adv.*

ten·ter·hooks ['tentə,huks] *n. pl.* (only) *on* ~, in a state of anxious suspense.

tenth, see **ten.**

ten·u·ous ['tenjuəs] *adj.* thin; flimsy.

ten·ure ['tenjuə*] *n.* (period of, time of, conditions of) holding (e.g. a political office) or using (land): ~ *of office; security of* ~.

tep·id ['tepid] *adj.* lukewarm.

ter·cen·te·na·ry [,tə:sen'ti:nəri] *n.* 300th anniversary.

term [tə:m] *n.* **1.** fixed or limited period of time: *a ~ of imprisonment;* period during which law courts, schools, etc., are open. **2.** (pl.) conditions offered or agreed to: ~*s of surrender; come to (make)* ~*s (with sb.),* reach an agreement; *inquire about* ~*s* (i.e. prices) *for a stay at a hotel.* **3.** (pl.) *on good* ~*s with sb.,* friendly with him. **4.** word(s) expressing a definite idea, etc., esp. in a branch of study: *scientific* ~*s.* **5.** (pl.) words: *in* ~*s of high praise; in abusive* ~*s.* *v.t.* name; give a certain ~ (4) to.

ter·mi·na·ble ['tə:minəbl] *adj.* that can be ended.

ter·mi·nal ['tə:minl] *adj.* **1.** of, taking place, each term (1): ~ *examinations.* **2.** of, forming, the point or place at either end (e.g. of a railway). *n.* ~ part or point (e.g. either of the free ends of an electric circuit).

ter·mi·nate ['tə:mineit] *v.t. & i.* come to an end; put an end to. ~ *in,* have at the end. **ter·mi·na·tion** [,tə:mi'neiʃən] *n.* ending (e.g. of a word).

ter·mi·nol·o·gy [,tə:mi'nolədʒi] *n.* system of names or terms (4) used in a science or art: *grammatical* ~.

ter·mi·nus ['tə:minəs] *n.* (pl. -*i,* -*uses* [ai, əsiz]). station at the end of a railway; end of a tram, bus, or air route.

ter·mite ['tə:mait] *n.* ant-like insect (often called *white ant*) which causes great damage to wood, etc.

ter·race ['terəs] *n.* **1.** level(led) piece of ground on a slope. **2.** continuous row of houses, esp. along the top of a slope. **ter·raced** *ppl. adj.* cut into ~s; having ~s: *a ~d lawn.*

ter·ra - cot·ta ['terə'kɔtə] *n.* (Latin) hard, reddish-brown pottery.

ter·ra fir·ma ['terə'fə:mə] (Latin) *n.* dry land; solid ground.

ter·rain [tə'rein] *n.* stretch of country, esp. as regards its physical features.

ter·res·tri·al [ti'restriəl] *adj.* of, on, living on, the earth or land.

ter·ri·ble ['teribl] *adj.* causing great fear, sorrow, or discomfort. **ter·ri·bly** *adv.* (colloq.) very (much).

ter·ri·er ['teriə*] *n.* kinds of small active dog.

ter·rif·ic [tə'rifik] *adj.* **1.** causing fear; terrible. **2.** (colloq.) very great; extreme.

ter·ri·fy ['terifai] *v.t.* fill with fear.

ter·ri·to·ri·al [,teri'tɔ:riəl] *adj.* **1.** of land, esp. land forming a division of a country. ~ *waters,* the sea near a country's coast. **2.** *the T~ Army,* force of soldiers (1908–67) organized for the defence of Great Britain, civilian members being trained in their spare time.

ter·ri·to·ry ['teritəri] *n.* **1.** land, esp. land under one ruler or government: *Portuguese ~ in Africa.* **2.** land or district, esp. its extent: *a business salesman who has a large ~ to travel.*

ter·ror ['terə*] *n.* (person, thing, etc., causing) great fear. ~·**ism** *n.* use of ~, esp. for political purposes. ~·**ist** *n.* person who uses violence to cause ~ for political ends.

terse [tə:s] *adj.* (-r, -st). (of speech, style, speakers) brief and to the point (6). ~·**ly** *adv.*

test [test] *n.* examination, trial (of sth.), to find its quality, value, composition, etc.; trial or examination (e.g. of sb.'s powers or knowledge): *put sth. to the ~. a ~ pilot,* one who takes newly-built aircraft on ~ flights.

v.t. **1.** put to the ~; examine: ~ *ore for gold.* **2.** be a ~ of: *The long climb ~ed our powers of endurance.* '~-**tube** *n.* slender glass tube, closed at one end, used in chemical ~s.

tes·ta·ment ['testəmənt] *n.* **1.** (often *last will and* ~) see ³*will.* **2.** *Old T~, New T~,* two main divisions of the Bible.

tes·ti·fy ['testifai] *v.t. & i.* **1.** give evidence (in a court of law *against, on behalf of, that*). **2.** state publicly, declare (*that*). **3.** ~ *to,* be a sign or evidence of: *Your work testifies to your ability.*

tes·ti·mo·nial [,testi'mounjəl] *n.* **1.** written statement testifying to a person's merits, abilities, qualifications, etc. **2.** sth. given to sb. to show appreciation of services, usu. sth. subscribed for by several or many persons. **tes·ti·mo·ny** ['testiməni] *n.* statement, esp. in a court of law, testifying that sth. is true; proof or evidence; open declaration of one's religious beliefs.

tes·ty ['testi] *adj.* easily annoyed.

tête-à-tête ['teitɑ:'teit] (Fr.) *n.* private meeting between two persons; their talk.

teth·er ['teðə*] *n.* rope or chain by which an animal is fastened while grazing. *at the end of one's* ~, (fig.) at the end of one's powers, resources, etc. *v.t.* fasten with a ~.

text [tekst] *n.* **1.** main body of a book (contrasted with notes, an index, etc.). **2.** sentence, esp. of Scripture, as the subject of a sermon or discussion. '~·**book** *n.* book giving instruction in a branch of learning.

tex·tile ['tekstail] *adj.* of the making of cloth. *n.* woven material; material suitable for spinning and weaving.

tex·ture ['tekstʃə*] *n.* **1.** the arrangement of the threads in a textile fabric: *cloth with a loose* ~. **2.** structure of a substance, esp. when felt or looked at.

than [ðæn, ðən] *conj.* **1.** (introducing the second part of a comparison): *John is taller than*

Jack. **2.** *no(ne) other* ~, not any other person but: *I met no(ne) other* ~ *my old friend, Philip, today. nothing else than,* only, entirely: *It was nothing else than bad luck that they lost the game.*

thank [θæŋk] *v.t.* express gratitude (to sb. *for* sth.) **thanks** *n. pl.* **1.** words of gratitude. **2.** (colloq.) Thank you (= 'Please accept my ~s'). *~s to,* as the result of; because of. *Give* ~s, (esp.) ~ God for food, etc.; say grace. ~**·ful** *adj.* ~**·ful·ly** *adv.* ~**·less** *adj.* (esp. of actions) for which no ~s are offered: *a* ~*less task.* ~**·less·ly** *adv.* **'thanks·giv·ing** *n.* (form of prayer used in) expression of ~s to God (e.g. for victory in war, the harvest).

that [ðæt] *adj. & pron.* (pl. *those* [ðouz]) (contrasted with *this, these*). **1.** *Look at* ~ *man* (*those men*) *over there. This photograph is much clearer than* ~ (*one*). **2.** *My new car is of a different make from* ~ *which I had before. Those who want to go swimming must put their names down on the list. adv.* (colloq.) *I couldn't walk* ~ *far* (= as far as ~). [ðæt, ðət] *rel. pron.* (pl. unchanged). *The letter* ~ *came this morning is from my father. Give help to anyone* ~ *needs it.* (Cf. *which, who.*) *conj.* **1.** *I will see* ~ *a meal is ready for you when you get home tonight.* **2.** *Bring it to the light, so* ~ *I can see it better.* **3.** *His manners are so bad* ~ *nobody invites him to a party.* **4.** *You may go on condition* ~ *you will not come home alone.* **5.** (in exclamations): *Oh,* ~ *I could see you again!* (How I wish it were possible for us to meet again!)

thatch [θætʃ] *n.* (roof covering of) dried straw, reeds, etc. *v.t.* cover (a roof, etc.) with ~.

thaw [θɔː] *v.i. & t.* **1.** *It is* ~*ing,* the temperature has risen above freezing-point, snow and ice are beginning to melt. **2.** (cause anything frozen to) become liquid or soft again. **3.** (of persons, their behaviour) (cause to) become less formal, more friendly.

n. (state of the weather causing) ~ing.

the [ðə, (before vowel sounds) ðiː] *definite article.* weak form of *this, that, these, those. adv.* by so much; by that amount: *The more he has, the more he wants.*

the·a·tre [ˈθiətə*] *n.* **1.** building for the acting of plays. **2.** hall or room with seats in rows rising one behind another for lectures, scientific demonstrations, etc. **3.** *operating* ~, room in a hospital where surgical operations are performed. **4.** *the* ~, drama; the writing and acting of plays. **the·at·ri·cal** [θiˈætrikl] *adj.* **1.** of or for the ~(1): *theatrical scenery.* **2.** (of behaviour, etc.) unnatural; exaggerated; designed for effect.

thee [ðiː] *pron.* object form of *thou.*

theft [θeft] *n.* (the act of) stealing.

their [ðɛə*] *adj.* of them: *They have lost* ~ *dog.* **theirs** [ðɛəz] *pron. That dog is not* ~s, *it's ours.*

the·ism [ˈθiːizəm] *n.* belief in the existence of a God who has made Himself known to mankind.

them, see *they.*

theme [θiːm] *n.* **1.** idea which is the subject of a talk or piece of writing. **2.** (music) short tune which is repeated, expanded, etc. (e.g. in a sonata or symphony). **3.** ~ *song,* one that is often repeated in a musical play, etc.

then [ðen] *adv. & conj.* **1.** at that time (past or future): *We were living in Scotland* ~. *Will you still be here* ~? *from* ~, from that time onwards. *since* ~, between that time and now. **2.** next; after that; afterwards: *We'll go to Paris first,* ~ *to Rome.* **3.** in that case: *You say you feel ill;* ~ *why don't you call the doctor?* **4.** and also: *T~ there's James, oughtn't he to come, too?* **5.** (in warning, protesting, to call attention): *Now then. . . .*

thence [ðens] *adv.* from there. ~**·'forth,** ~**·'for·ward** *adv.* from that time onwards.

the·ol·o·gy [θiˈɔlədʒi] *n.* science of the nature of God and of the foundations of religious belief. **the·ol·o·gian** [ˌθiːəˈloudʒjən] *n.* advanced student of ~. **the·o·log·i·cal** [ˌθiːəˈlɔdʒikl] *adj.*

the·o·rem [ˈθiərəm] *n.* **1.** statement which reasoning shows to be true. **2.** (maths.) statement for which a reasoned proof is required.

the·o·ry [ˈθiəri] *n.* **1.** (explanation of) general principles of an art or science (contrasted with *practice*). **2.** reasoned supposition put forward to explain facts or events: *Darwin's ~ of evolution*. **the·o·ret·ic, -i·cal** [θiəˈretik(l)] *adj.* based on ~, not on practice or experience. **the·o·rize** [ˈθiəraiz] *v.i.* make theories (*about*). **the·o·rist** *n.* person who forms theories.

there [ðɛə*] *adv.* (contrasted with *here*). **1.** in, at, or to, that place: *Put my box down ~.* **2.** *T~ goes the fox. T~ it goes.* **3.** calling attention: *There's a hole in your shoe. Look out, ~!* **4.** with *seem, appear*, etc.: *T~ seems to be no escape. T~ appears to be nobody here.* *int.* (in comforting): *T~, ~, dry your tears!* (in triumph): *T~, now, I was right!* (in dismay): *T~, I've upset the ink!* **'~·a·bouts** *adv.* near that place, number, quantity, etc. **'~·'af·ter** *adv.* afterwards. **'~·'by** *adv.* by that means; in that way. **'~·'fore** *adv.* for that reason. **'~·'up·'on** *adv.* then; as the result of that.

therm [θəːm] *n.* unit of heat. **~·al** *adj.* of heat: *~al springs*, springs of warm or hot water. **ther·mom·e·ter** [θəˈmɔmitə*] *n.* instrument for measuring temperature.

these, see *this*.

the·sis [ˈθiːsis] *n.* (pl. *theses* [ˈθiːsiːz]). statement or theory (to be) put forward and supported by arguments, esp. a written essay submitted for a university degree.

thews [θjuːz] *n. pl.* muscles; sinews.

they [ðei] *pron.* subject form pl. of *he, she, it.* **them** [ðem, ðəm, əm] *pron.* object form of *they.*

thick [θik] *adj.* (-er, -est). **1.** (opp. of *thin*) of comparatively great (or of a given) measurement, from one side to the other or from the upper surface to the lower surface: *a ~ line, ~ ice, three inches ~.* **2.** having a large number of units close together: *~ hair; a ~ forest.* **3.** (of liquids, the atmosphere) semi-solid; not clear: *~ soup; a ~ fog.* **4.** *~ with,* full of, holding a mass of: *air ~ with dust* (*snow*). **5.** (of the voice) indistinct (e.g. because one has a cold). *n.* ~est part; part where activity is greatest: *in the ~ of the fight. through ~ and thin,* whatever the conditions may be. *adv.* ~ly. *come ~ and fast,* come quickly and in large numbers. **~·en** *v.t. & i.* make or become ~. **'~·'head·ed** *adj.* stupid. **~·ly** *adv.* **~·ness** *n.* (esp.) layer. **'~·'set** *adj.* **1.** (of a person) short and stout. **2.** closely massed or planted. **'~·'skinned** *adj.* (fig.) not easily hurt by insults, reproaches, etc.; without delicate feelings.

thick·et [ˈθikit] *n.* mass of trees, shrubs, undergrowth, growing thickly together.

thief [θiːf] *n.* (pl. *thieves* [θiːvz]). person who steals, esp. secretly and without violence. (Cf. *robber, burglar.*) **thieve** [θiːv] *v.t. & i.* steal.

thigh [θai] *n.* part of the leg above the knee.

thim·ble [ˈθimbl] *n.* cap (of metal, etc.) used to protect the end of the finger when pushing a needle through cloth, etc. **~·ful** *n.* (colloq.) sip (of liquid).

thin [θin] *adj.* **1.** (-nn-; opp. of *thick*). having opposite surfaces close together; of small diameter: *a ~ sheet of paper; a ~ piece of string.* **2.** having not much flesh: *~ in the face.* **3.** (of liquids, e.g. soup) watery; without much substance. **4.** (colloq.) *a ~ excuse,* one that is easily seen through. *have a ~ time,* have a dull, or uncomfortable, time. *v.t. & i.* (-nn-).

make or become ~ : ~ *the plants
out*, take out some so that the
rest grow better. *adv.* ~·ly. *n.
through thick and* ~, through bad
times as well as good. '~·ly *adv.*
~·ness *n.* '~·'skinned *adj.*
sensitive (to criticism, etc.);
easily offended.

thine [ðain] *poss. adj. & pron.*
(old use) your(s) (sing.).

thing [θiŋ] *n.* **1.** any material
object : *A rose is a lovely* ~. **2.**
(pl.) general conditions or circumstances : *T~s are getting
better every day.* **3.** (pl. & colloq.) your (*his etc.*) ~s, belongings, esp. clothes : *Have you
packed your* ~*s yet?* **4.** *the* (*very*)
~, just what is needed, or what
is considered right or usual : *not
at all the* ~ *to do. This is the very
~ I wanted.*

think [θiŋk] *v.t. & i.* (p.t. & p.p.
thought [θɔ:t]). **1.** use the mind
in order to form an opinion, etc.
2. consider; be of the opinion :
~ *highly* (*well, little, nothing*) *of*
(*sb. or sth.*), have a high (good,
etc.) opinion of; ~ *nothing of*
(*doing sth.*) (e.g. walking thirty
miles), consider it not unusual
or remarkable; ~ *better of* (*doing
sth.*), reconsider (and give up);
~ *sth. out*, consider carefully and
make a plan; ~ *sth. over*, consider further before deciding it.

third [θə:d] *adj. & n.* next in
order after the second; ⅓.
~·ly *adv.* '~·'rate *adj.* of poor
quality.

thirst [θə:st] *n.* **1.** feeling caused
by a desire or need to drink;
suffering caused by this : *die of*
~. **2.** (fig.) strong desire (*for*
knowledge, etc.). *v.i.* have ~;
(fig.) be eager (*for* revenge, etc.).
~·y *adj.* (*-ier, -iest*). having or
causing ~ : ~*y work.* '~·i·ly *adv.*

thir·teen ['θə:'ti:n] *adj. & n.* 13.
thir·teenth ['θə:'ti:nθ] *adj. & n.*
next in order after the twelfth; ⅓.
thir·ty ['θə:ti] *adj. & n.* 30.
thir·ti·eth ['θə:tiiθ] *adj. & n.*

this [ðis] *adj. & pron.* (pl. *these*
[ði:z]). (contrasted with *that,
those*): *Look at* ~ *picture here,
and then at that picture over there.
T*~ is by far the better picture.*

this·tle ['θisl] *n.* (sorts of) wild
plant with prickly leaves and
yellow, white or purple flowers.
'~·'down *n.* ~ seed(s).

thith·er ['ðiðə*] *adv.* (old use) to
that place; in that direction.

thong [θɔŋ] *n.* narrow strip of
leather (e.g. as reins, a whip).

thor·ax ['θɔ:ræks] *n.* middle of
the three main sections of an
insect.

thorn [θɔ:n] *n.* **1.** sharp-pointed
growth on the stem of a plant.
2. shrub or bush with ~s (e.g.
haw~). ~·y *adj.* (*-ier, -iest*). **1.**
having ~s. **2.** (fig. of questions,
etc.) full of trouble and difficulty; causing argument.

thor·ough ['θʌrə*] *adj.* complete
in every way; not forgetting or
overlooking anything; detailed :
give the room a ~ *cleaning; a
~ worker; receive* ~ *instruction
in English.* ~·ly *adv.* ~·ness
n. '~·'bred *n. & adj.* (animal,
esp. a horse) of pure breed. '~·
fare *n.* street or road, esp. one
much used by traffic. *No* ~*fare*,
warning that a road is private
or that one end is closed.
'~·₁go·ing *adj.* complete.

thou [ðau] *pron.* (old or liter.
form of) you (sing.).

though [ðou] *conj.* (= *although*). **1.** in spite of the fact
that : (*Al*)*though poor, he was
always neatly dressed.* **2.** even
if : *T~ you hate me, I will serve
you faithfully.* **3.** *as though*, =
as if. **4.** and yet; all the same :
I'll try, ~ *I don't think I shall
succeed.* **5.** but yet; however.

thought [θɔ:t] *n.* **1.** (power, process, way, of) thinking : *lost in* ~;
modern ~; *take* ~ *for*, be concerned about. **2.** idea, opinion,
intention, formed by thinking :
He had no ~ *of* (no intention of)
causing you anxiety. ~·ful *adj.*
1. full of ~; showing ~ : ~*ful
looks.* **2.** considerate; thinking
of, showing ~ for, the needs of
others. ~·ful·ly *adv.* ~·ful·
ness *n.* ~·less *adj.* **1.** selfish;
inconsiderate (*of* others). **2.** unthinking; careless. ~·less·ly
adv. ~·less·ness *n.*

thou·sand(th) [ˈθauzənd(θ)] *n. & adj.* 1,000(th).

thrall [θrɔːl] *n.* (often fig.) (condition of being a) slave: *a ~ to drink.* **thral·dom** *n.* slavery.

thrash [θræʃ] *v.t. & i.* 1. beat with a stick, a whip, etc. 2. defeat. 3. ~ *out* (a problem), discuss thoroughly. 4. thresh. ~·**ing** *n.* beating; defeat: *give sb. (get) a good ~ing.*

thread [θred] *n.* 1. length of spun cotton, silk, flax, wool, etc., esp. for use in sewing and weaving. 2. chain or line (*of* thought, an argument, etc.). 3. spiral ridge round a screw. *v.t.* 1. put ~ through (a needle); put (beads, etc.) on a ~. 2. make (*one's way*) through (a crowd of people, etc.), by going in and out among them. '~·**bare** *adj.* 1. (of cloth) worn thin; shabby. 2. (fig. of arguments, etc.) old; much used and therefore uninteresting.

threat [θret] *n.* 1. statement of an intention to punish or hurt sb., esp. if he does not do as one wishes. 2. sign or warning of coming trouble, danger, etc. ~·**en** *v.t. & i.* 1. use ~(s) to: ~*en sb. with sth.*; ~*en to shoot sb.* 2. give warning of (danger, trouble, etc.): *clouds that ~en rain.* 3. (of sth. unpleasant) seem likely to come. ~·**en·ing·ly** *adv.*

three [θriː] *n. & adj.* 3. '~-'**ply**, see *ply.* ~·**pence** [ˈθrepəns] *n.* 3*d.* ~·**pen·ny** [ˈθrepəni] *adj.* costing or worth ~pence.

thresh [θreʃ] *v.t. & i.* beat the grain out of (wheat, etc.); beat wheat, etc., for this purpose.

thresh·old [ˈθreʃhould] *n.* stone or plank under a doorway; (fig.) start, beginning: *on the ~ of your career as a teacher.*

threw, see *throw.*

thrice [θrais] *adv.* three times.

thrift [θrift] *n.* care, economy, in the use of money or goods. ~·**y** *adj.* (-*ier. -iest*). using ~; economical.

thrill [θril] *n.* (experience causing) excited feeling passing like a wave along the nerves. *v.t. & i.* 1. feel a ~ or ~s: ~ *with pleas-*

ure. 2. cause a ~ or ~s in: *a play that ~ed the audience.*

thril·ler *n.* exciting story, play, or film.

thrive [θraiv] *v.i.* (p.t. *throve* [θrouv], p.p. *thriven* [ˈθrivn]). succeed; grow strong or healthy: *Children ~ on good food.*

throat [θrout] *n.* 1. front part of the neck. 2. passage in the neck through which food passes to the stomach and air to the lungs. ~·**y** *adj.* (-*ier, -iest*). (of the voice) thick (as when one has a cold); guttural.

throb [θrɔb] *v.i.* (-*bb-*). (of the heart, pulse, etc.) beat, esp. more rapidly than usual: ~*bing with excitement; a wound ~bing with pain.* *n.* a ~bing or vibration.

throe [θrou] *n.* (usu. pl.) sharp pain (e.g. of childbirth). *in the ~s of,* struggling with.

throne [θroun] *n.* 1. ceremonial chair or seat of a king, queen, bishop, etc.; (fig.) royal authority. 2. *the T~,* the sovereign.

throng [θrɔŋ] *n. & v.i. & t.* crowd.

throt·tle [ˈθrɔtl] *v.t* 1. seize (sb.) by the throat and stop his breathing. 2. control the flow of petrol, etc., to an engine. *n.* valve controlling the flow of petrol, etc., to an engine.

through [θruː] *prep.* 1 (of places) from end to end or side to side of; entering at one side, on one surface, etc. and coming out at the other: *The River Thames flows ~ London. The road goes (right) ~ the forest.* 2. (fig.) *We must go ~ (examine) the accounts.* 3. (of time) from beginning to end of: *He will not live ~ the night* (i.e. he will die before morning). 4. (indicating the cause, etc.): *The accident happened ~ no fault of yours. adv.* 1. from end to end, side to side, beginning to end: *I've read the letter ~ twice and cannot understand it.* 2. to the end; till complete: *see a job ~.* 3. all the way: *Does this train go ~ to Bombay?* (Also, modifying the noun: *a ~ train to Bombay.*)

4. connected by telephone: *Can you put me ~ to the manager?* **~·'out** [θruːˈaut] *adv. & prep.* in every part (of); from end to end (of).

throve, see *thrive.*

throw [θrou] *v.t. & i.* (p.t. *threw* [θruː], p.p. *thrown* [θroun]). **1.** cause (sth.) to go through the air, usu. with force, by a movement of the arm or by mechanical means. **2.** put (articles of clothing) *on, off, over,* etc., quickly or carelessly. **3.** move (one's arms, legs, etc.) *out, up, down, about,* violently: *~ one's chest out* (*one's arms about*). **4.** (of a horse) cause the rider to fall to the ground; (of a wrestler) force an opponent to the floor. **5.** (in phrases): *~ away,* lose by foolishness or neglect: *~ away one's advantages.* (*sth.*) *in,* (esp.) give sth. extra, without addition to the price. *~ oneself into* (an activity), take part in with vigour and enthusiasm. *~ off,* get rid of; become free from. *~ open,* make (e.g. a competition) open to all persons. *~ out,* make (a suggestion); give (a hint) in a casual way; reject (a Bill). *~ over,* abandon (a plan, a friend). *~ up,* vomit (food); resign from (a position). *n.* ~ing or being ~n; distance to which sth. is or can be ~n. *within a stone's ~,* quite near.

thrum [θrʌm] *v.t. & i.* (*-mm-*). play (a stringed instrument) by pulling the strings, esp. carelessly or idly.

thrush [θrʌʃ] *n.* (sorts of) songbird.

thrust [θrʌst] *v.t. & i.* push suddenly or violently; make a forward stroke with a sword, etc. *n.* act of ~ing; (in war) strong attempt to push forward into the enemy's lines (9), etc.

thud [θʌd] *v.i. & n.* (*-dd-*). (strike, fall with, a) dull sound as of a blow on sth. soft.

thug [θʌg] *n.* violent criminal.

thumb [θʌm] *n.* short, thick finger set apart from the other four. *under sb.'s ~,* under his influence and control. *rule of*

~, one based on experience or practice. *v.t.* turn over (pages, etc.); make dirty by doing this: *a well-~ed book.*

thump [θʌmp] *v.t. & i.* strike heavily, esp. with the fist(s); (of the heart) beat fast. *n.* (sound of a) heavy blow.

thun·der [ˈθʌndə*] *n.* **1.** loud noise coming after lightning. **2.** loud noise like or suggesting ~: *the ~ of the guns.* *v.i. & t.* **1.** *It ~ed,* there was ~. **2.** make a loud noise like ~: *sb. ~ing at the door.* **3.** speak in a loud voice, make an attack (*against*). **'~·bolt** *n.* lightning and crash of ~; (fig.) unexpected and destructive event. **'~·storm** *n.* storm of ~ and lightning, usu. with heavy rain. **'~·struck** *adj.* amazed. **~·y** *adj.* (of weather) giving signs of ~.

Thurs·day [ˈθəːzdi] *n.* the fifth day of the week.

thus [ðʌs] *adv.* in this way; so: *~ far,* to this point.

¹thwart [θwɔːt] *v.t.* obstruct a person or his plans.

²thwart [θwɔːt] *n.* seat across a rowing-boat for an oarsman.

thy [ðai] *adj.* (old use) your (singular).

thyme [taim] *n.* plant with sweet-smelling leaves used to flavour food.

ti·a·ra [tiˈɑːrə] *n.* coronet for a woman; crown worn by the Pope.

¹tick [tik] *n.* **1.** light regular sound, esp. of a clock or watch. **2.** small mark (often √) put against names, figures, etc., in a list or to show that sth. is correct. **3.** *on ~,* (slang) on credit. *v.i. & t.* **1.** (of a clock, etc.) make ~s (1). **2.** put a ~ (2) *against:* ~ (*off*) *the items in a list.* **3.** *~ sb. off,* (slang) rebuke him. **'~·er** *n.* (colloq.) watch; the heart. **'~·er-tape** *n.* telegraphic tape.

²tick [tik] *n.* small insect that fastens itself on the skin and sucks blood.

tick·et [ˈtikit] *n.* card, piece of paper, giving the holder the right to travel in a train, bus, etc., or to a seat in a theatre, etc., or showing the cost of sth. *v.t.* put a ~ on (esp. sth. to be sold).

tick·le ['tikl] *v.t. & i.* **1.** excite the nerves of the skin by touching or rubbing lightly, esp. at sensitive parts, often so as to cause laughter: ~ *sb. in the ribs. The rough blanket* ~*s (me).* **2.** have an itching feeling (as of being ~d): *My nose* ~*s.* **3.** please (one's sense of humour or of taste). *n.* act of tickling sb.; sensation of being tickled. **tick·lish** *adj.* **1.** (of a person) easily made to laugh or wriggle when ~d. **2.** (of a problem, piece of work) needing delicate care or caution.

tide [taid] *n.* **1.** regular rise and fall in the level of the sea, caused by the attraction of the moon: *at high* (low) ~; *washed up by the* ~. **2.** flow or tendency of opinion, public feeling, etc.). *v.t.* ~ *over*, get over, enable (sb.) to get over (a period of difficulty, etc.): *Will £3* ~ *you over until you get your wages?* **tid·al** ['taidl] *adj.* of the ~(s): *a tidal wave*, a great one such as may accompany an earthquake.

ti·dings ['taidiŋz] *n. pl.* news.

ti·dy ['taidi] *adj.* (-*ier*, -*iest*). neat, orderly: *a* ~ *room* (person); ~ *habits. v.t. & i.* (often ~ *up*) make ~. **ti·di·ly** *adv.* **ti·di·ness** *n.*

tie [tai] *v.t. & i.* (present participle *tying*, p.p. *tied*). **1.** fasten with string, etc.: *tie a man's feet together; tie up a parcel.* **2.** make (a knot). **3.** (fig., of conditions in an agreement, etc.) restrict; limit the freedom of. **4.** (of players, teams; often, *tie with*) make the same score (as). *n.* **1.** (fig.) sth. that holds people together: *ties of friendship; family ties.* **2.** sth. that takes up one's attention and limits one's freedom of action: *Small children are often a tie.* **3.** equal score in a game, etc.: *The match ended in a tie.* **4.** = necktie.

tier [tiə*] *n.* row (esp. of seats), shelf, etc., esp. one of a number rising in parallel lines.

tiff [tif] *n.* slight quarrel.

tif·fin ['tifin] *n.* (in the East) lunch.

ti·ger ['taigə*] *n.* large fierce animal of Asia, yellow-skinned with black stripes. **ti·gress** ['taigris] *n.* female ~.

tight [tait] *adj.* (-*er*, -*est*). **1.** fixed or fitting closely: *a* ~ *cork.* **2.** (of knots, etc.) not easily unfastened. **3.** fully stretched: ~ *ropes.* **4.** closely or firmly put together or packed so that all the space is occupied: *Stuff the cushions until they are* ~. **5.** produced by or needing pressure: *a* ~ *squeeze; in a* ~ *corner* (place), (fig.) in a dangerous or difficult situation from which escape is difficult; *a* ~ *fit*, (fig.) condition in which there is no room for any more things, etc. **6.** (in compounds, as *air*~, *water*~, etc.) made so that air, water, etc., can neither enter nor escape. *adv.* = ~ly. ~'en *v.t. & i.* (often ~*en up*) make or become ~ (not loose): ~*en one's belt.* '~-'fist·ed *adj.* mean; ungenerous. **tights** *n. pl.* skin-tight garment as worn by women, dancers, etc. ~'ly *adv.* ~'ness *n.*

tile [tail] *n.* square or oblong plate of baked clay for covering roofs, etc.

¹**till** [til] *prep. & conj.* until.

²**till** [til] *n.* money-drawer in a shop; drawer of a cash register.

³**till** [til] *v.t.* cultivate (land). **til·ler** *n.*

til·ler ['tilə*] *n.* handle fixed to the rudder of a small boat.

tilt [tilt] *v.i. & t.* **1.** (cause to) come into a sloping position: *T*~ *the barrel up* (to empty it, etc.). *The table* ~*ed.* **2.** (in former times, of men on horseback) ride *at* one another with lances; (fig.) attack in speech or writing: ~*ing at gamblers. n.* **1.** ~*ing*(1); sloping position. **2.** act of ~*ing*(2) with lances. (*at*) *full* ~, at full speed and with great force.

tim·ber ['timbə*] *n.* **1.** wood prepared for use in building, etc. **2.** beam forming a support (e.g. in a roof or a ship). **3.** trees large enough for use as ~ (1). **tim·bered** *adj.* (of buildings) made of ~ or with a framework of ~.

tim·bre ['tæmbə*] *n.* characteristic quality of sound produced by a particular voice or instrument.

time [taim] *n.* **1.** all the days of the past, present, and future; the passing of all the days and years, taken as a whole: *The world exists in space and ~.* **2.** portion or measure of ~ ; a point of ~ stated in hours and minutes: *The ~ is five o'clock.* **3.** *in ~*, (a) early enough: *We are in ~ for the meeting.* (b) after a period of ~, soon enough: *You will speak English in ~.* (c) *in good ~*, early; in due course. (d) *in no ~*, (colloq.) very soon; very quickly. *at one ~*, during a certain period of ~ in the past. *at the same ~*, yet, even if that is true. *from ~ to ~*, occasionally. *~ and (~) again*, repeatedly; often. *~ out of mind*, period of ~ further back than memory can go. *(work) against ~*, (work) fast because ~ is limited. **4.** (pl.) multiplied by: *Three ~s five is fifteen.* **5.** (often pl.) period of ~ associated with sth. or sb.: *in ancient ~s*; *the ~(s) of the Stuarts* (i.e. when the Stuart kings ruled). **6.** system of measuring ~: *Greenwich ~*; *summer ~* (see *daylight-saving*). **7.** length of a musical note; speed at which a piece of music is played; style of musical movement according to the number of beats in a bar. *in (out of) ~*, in (not in) accordance with the ~ of the music. *beat ~*, show the ~ of music by movements of the hand, etc. *v.t.* **1.** choose, arrange, or decide the ~ for (sth. to happen). **2.** measure the ~ taken by (e.g. a runner) or for (e.g. a race). **'~-,hon·oured** *adj.* respected because old. **~'less** *adj.* unending. **~'ly** *adj.* coming, occurring, at the right ~, when needed, etc. **~'·** **ta·ble** *n.* (book with) list of ~s at which things are to be done, esp. of arrivals and departures of trains, ships, etc. **'~-work** *n.* work for which payment is by the hour or day. (Cf. *piece-work*.)

tim·id ['timid] *adj.* easily frightened. **~'ly** *adv.* **ti·mid·i·ty** [ti'miditi] *n.*

tim·o·rous(ly) ['timərəs(li)] *adj. (adv.)* = timid(ly).

tin [tin] *n.* **1.** soft white metal used for coating iron sheets. **2.** tin-plated container for food, etc., esp. one sealed so as to be air-tight (= U.S.A. *can*). *v.t.* (*-nn-*). **1.** coat (sheet iron, etc.) with tin. **2.** pack (food, tobacco, etc.) in tins (3). **'tin-plate** *n.* sheet iron coated with tin.

tinc·ture ['tiŋktʃə*] *n.* **1.** medical substance dissolved in alcohol. **2.** small amount, trace, suggestion (*of*).

tin·der ['tində*] *n.* material that easily catches fire from a spark.

tinge [tindʒ] *v.t.* **1.** colour slightly (*with* red, etc.). **2.** affect slightly: *admiration ~d with envy.* *n.* slight colouring or mixture (*of*).

tin·gle ['tiŋgl] *v.i. & n.* (have a) pricking or stinging feeling in the skin: (fig.) *tingling with excitement.*

tin·ker ['tiŋkə*] *n.* tin-plate worker who travels from place to place and repairs kettles, pans, etc. *v.i.* (try to) do repairs, usu. without expert knowledge: *~ with (~ away at) sth.*

tin·kle ['tiŋkl] *v.i. & t.* (cause to) make a succession of slight ringing sounds (e.g. of a small bell). *n.* such sounds: *the ~ of a bell.*

tin·sel ['tinsl] *n.* glittering metallic substance made in sheets, strips, and threads, used for ornament; (fig.) cheap, showy brilliance.

tint [tint] *n.* (esp. pale) shade or variety of colour: *~s of green in the sky.* *v.t.* give a ~ to; put a ~ on.

ti·ny ['taini] *adj.* (*-ier, -iest*). very small.

¹tip [tip] *n.* **1.** pointed or thin end of sth.: *the tips of one's fingers.* **2.** small piece put on the end of sth. **'tip·toe** *v.i. & adv.* (walk quietly, be) on the toes: *stand-*

ing on tiptoe; tiptoe out of the room.

²tip [tip] *v.t. & i.* (*-pp-*). **1.** (often tip *up, over*) (cause to) lean or slant, rise on one side at or at one end; (cause to) overbalance or overturn: *He was tipped out of the cart into the ditch.* **2.** empty (contents of sth.) *out of* or *into* by tipping: *Tip the water out of the pail.* *n.* place where rubbish, etc., may be tipped (2).

³tip [tip] *v.t.* (*-pp-*). **1.** touch or strike lightly: *His bat just tipped the ball.* **2.** give or hand (sth. to sb.) in an informal way; give a tip (2) to: *He tipped the porter handsomely.* *n.* **1.** light blow; tap. **2.** gift of extra money to a porter, waiter, etc., for personal services. **3.** piece of advice on how to do sth., esp. of secret information about the probable winner of a horse-race, on the future state of business shares, etc. **tip·ster** ['tipstə*] *n.* person who gives tips (3) about races.

tip·ple ['tipl] *v.i. & t.* be in the habit of taking much alcoholic liquor; drink (wine, etc.). *n.* (colloq.) alcoholic drink. **tip·pler** *n.* person who ~s.

tip·sy ['tipsi] *adj.* intoxicated.

tip·toe, see ¹*tip.*

ti·rade [tai-, ti'reid] *n.* long, angry or scolding speech.

¹tire, see *tyre.*

²tire [taiə*] *v.t. & i.* make or become weary, in need of rest, or uninterested. ~ *of,* lose interest in. **tired** *adj.* weary in body or mind. ~*d out,* exhausted. ~·**less** *adj.* not easily ~d; ceaseless: *a ~less worker;* ~*less energy.* ~·**some** *adj.* troublesome.

ti·ro, ty·ro ['taiərou] *n.* beginner; person with little experience.

tis·sue ['tisju:, 'tiʃju:] *n.* **1.** any fine woven fabric. **2.** any of the substances forming part of an animal or plant: *skin (nervous, muscular)* ~. **3.** (fig.) web or network (*of* lies, etc.). **4.** = '~·ıpa·per *n.* thin soft paper used for wrapping, paper handkerchiefs, etc. *toilet (face)* ~*s.*

¹tit [tit] *n.* small bird, of various

kinds, e.g. blue-tit, coal-tit, titmouse.

²tit [tit] *n.* (only) *tit for tat,* blow in return for blow.

ti·tan·ic [tai'tænik] *adj.* immense.

tit·bit ['titbit] *n.* choice and attractive bit (*of* food, news).

tithe [taið] *n.* tenth part of farm produce formerly given by ancient custom for the support of (Church of England) parish priests.

ti·tle ['taitl] *n.* **1.** name of a book, poem, picture, etc. **2.** word used to show a person's rank or occupation (e.g. Lord, Prince, Professor). **3.** right (*to* sth., *to do* sth.), esp. (law) right to the possession of property. **ti·tled** ['taitəld] *adj.* having a ~ (2) of nobility. '~·**deed** *n.* document proving a ~ (3) to property. '~·**page** *n.* page of a book that gives the ~ (1), author's name, etc. **tit·u·lar** ['titjulə*] *adj.* existing in name but not having authority or duties: *the titular ruler.*

tit·ter ['titə*] *v.i. & n.* (give a) silly, half-suppressed little laugh.

tit·tle-tat·tle ['titl'tætl] *n. & v.i.* gossip.

to [tu:, tu, tə] *prep.* **1.** in the direction of; towards: *walk to the station; fall to the ground.* **2.** towards (a condition, quality, etc.): *go to sleep; slow to anger.* **3.** (introducing the indirect object): *Give it to her.* **4.** towards (a time, the end of a period, etc.): *a quarter to two; stay to the end of the play.* **5.** (indicating a comparison): *prefer walking to climbing; win by six goals to three.* **particle** marking the infinitive: *He wants me to go.* *adv.* **1.** to or in the usual or required position, esp. a closed position: *Please push the door to.* **2.** *to and fro,* backwards and forwards, from side to side.

toad [toud] *n.* frog-like animal that lives chiefly on land. '~·**stool** *n.* (usu. poisonous) kind of umbrella-shaped fungus.

toad·y ['toudi] *v.t. & i. & n.* flatter(er), esp. in the hope of gain.

¹toast [toust] *n.* sliced bread heated before a fire, etc., till crisp and scorched on both sides. *v.t. & i.* **1.** heat (sliced bread, etc.) in this way. **2.** (of oneself) make or become warm before a fire.

²toast [toust] *v.t.* wish happiness, success, etc., to (sb. or sth.) while raising a glass of wine : ~ *the bride and bridegroom. n.* act of ~ing ; person, etc., ~ed.

to·bac·co [tə'bækou] *n.* (plant having) leaves (to be) dried and used for smoking (in pipes, cigarettes, etc.). ~**nist** [tə'bækənist] *n.* shopkeeper who sells ~.

to·bog·gan [tə'bɔgən] *n.* long narrow sledge for sporting purposes. *v.i.* go down a snow- or ice-covered slope on a ~.

toc·sin ['tɔksin] *n.* (bell rung to give a) signal of alarm.

to·day [tə'dei] *adv. & n.* (on) this day ; (at) this present period or age (3).

tod·dle ['tɔdl] *v.i.* walk with short uncertain steps as a baby does. **tod·dler** *n.* baby who can ~.

tod·dy ['tɔdi] *n.* sweetened drink of alcoholic spirits and hot water.

to-do [tə'du:] *n.* (colloq.) fuss ; commotion : *What a ~ ! What a lot of excitement and talk!*

toe [tou] *n.* **1.** one of the five divisions of the front part of the foot ; similar part in an animal's foot. **2.** part of a sock, shoe, etc., covering the toes. *v.t.* touch, reach, with the toes. *toe the line,* stand with the toes on the starting-line ready for a race ; (fig.) obey orders given to one as a member of a group.

tof·fee, tof·fy ['tɔfi] *n.* (piece of) hard, sticky sweet made by boiling sugar, fat, etc.

to·geth·er [tə'geðə*] *adv.* (opp. of *separately*) one with another ; in company : *They went to the jeweller's ~ and bought a wedding ring. ~ with,* as well as ; in addition to ; also : *They bought a hairbrush, ~ with a case to keep it in.*

toil [tɔil] *v.i.* **1.** work hard (at a task). **2.** move with difficulty (*up* a mountain, *through*, etc.). *n.* hard work. ~·**er** *n.* person who ~s(1).

toil·et ['tɔilit] *n.* **1.** process of dressing, arranging the hair, etc. : *She spends only five minutes on her ~.* **2.** (style of) dress or costume. **3.** (as adj.) of or for the ~ : ~ *articles ; a ~ set,* brush, comb, hand-mirror, etc. ; ~ *table,* dressing-table. **4.** W.C. **5.** ~*paper,* paper for use in the W.C.

toils [tɔilz] *n. pl.* nets ; snares : *caught in the ~ of the law.*

to·ken ['toukn] *n.* **1.** sign, evidence, guarantee, or mark (of sth.) : *in ~ of,* as evidence of. **2.** ~ *payment,* payment of a small part of what is owed, made to show that the debt is recognized.

told, see *tell.*

tol·er·ate ['tɔləreit] *v.t.* allow or endure without protest. **tol·er·a·ble** ['tɔlərəbl] *adj.* **1.** that can be ~d. **2.** fairly good. **tol·er·ance** *n.* quality of tolerating opinions, customs, behaviour, etc., different from one's own. **tol·er·ant** *adj.* having or showing tolerance. **tol·er·a·tion** [ˌtɔlə'reifən] *n.* tolerance, esp. the practice of allowing religious freedom.

¹toll [toul] *n.* **1.** payment required or made for the use of a road, bridge, harbour, etc. **2.** *take ~ of,* take or destroy a part of : *The war took a heavy ~ of the nation's manhood.* '~**-bar,** '~**gate** *n.* one at which a ~(1) must be paid.

²toll [toul] *v.i. & t.* **1.** (of a bell) ring with slow regular strokes : ~*ing for sb.'s death.* **2.** cause (a bell) to ring in this way. *n.* sound made by the ~ing of a bell.

tom·a·hawk ['tɔməhɔ:k] *n.* light axe used as a tool and weapon by N. American Indians.

to·ma·to [tə'ma:tou] *n.* (pl. *-oes*). (plant with) soft juicy red or yellow fruit usually eaten with meat and in salads.

tomb [tu:m] *n.* place for a dead

body, dug in the ground, cut out of rock, etc., esp. one with a monument over it. '~**stone** *n.* stone set up over a ~.

tom·boy ['tɔmbɔi] *n.* girl who likes rough noisy games.

tome [toum] *n.* large, heavy book.

tom·fool ['tɔm'fu:l] *n.* fool. ~·er·y *n.* senseless behaviour; stupid joke.

to·mor·row [tə'mɔrou] *adv. & n.* (on) the day after today.

tom·tom ['tɔmtɔm] *n.* Indian drum.

ton [tʌn] *n.* 1. measure of weight (2,240 lb. in Gt. Brit.; 2,000 lb. in U.S.A.). 2. (colloq.) *tons* of (*money*, *etc.*), a great quantity of.

tone [toun] *n.* 1. sound, esp. with reference to its quality: *the sweet ~*(*s*) *of a violin*; *speak in an angry* (*entreating*, *etc.*) ~. 2. (contrasted with *stress*) rise or fall of the voice in speaking. 3. (music) any of the five larger intervals between one note and the next which, with two semi-~s, make up an octave. 4. general spirit, character, morale of a community: *the ~ of the school*. 5. shade (of colour); degree (of light). *v.t. & i.* 1. give a particular ~ of sound or colour to: ~ *down*, make or become less intense; ~ *up*, make or become higher, brighter, in ~. 2. (esp. of colours) be in harmony (*with*). **toned** *adj.* having a particular kind of ~ (1): *silver-~d trumpets*. ~**less** *adj.* dull; lifeless: *in a ~less voice*.

tongs [tɔŋz] *n. pl.* (often *a pair of* ~) tool for taking up and holding (a piece of coal, a lump of sugar, a block of ice, etc.).

tongue [tʌŋ] *n.* 1. movable organ in the mouth, used in talking, tasting, and licking. *have one's ~ in one's cheek*, say sth. that one does not mean to be taken seriously; *hold one's ~*, be silent. 2. language: *our mother ~*. 3. sth. like a ~: *the ~ of a bell*; *~s of flame*. '~**-tied** *adj.* unable to speak (esp. through fear or shyness).

ton·ic ['tɔnik] *n. & adj.* 1. (sth., esp. medicine) giving strength or energy: *the ~ quality of sea air*; *a bottle of* ~. 2. (music) keynote. ~ **sol-fa** [sɔl'fɑ:] (in teaching singing) method of showing musical notes by means of syllables, e.g. *sol*, *fa*, *doh*.

to·night [tə'nait] *adv. & n.* (on) the night of today.

ton·nage ['tʌnidʒ] *n.* 1. cubic capacity of a ship (100 cubic feet = 1 ton); cargo-carrying capacity of a ship (1 ton per 40 cubic feet). 2. total ~ (1) of a country's merchant shipping. 3. charge per ton on cargo, etc., for transport.

ton·sil ['tɔnsil] *n.* either of two small oval masses of tissue in the throat. **ton·sil·li·tis** [ˌtɔnsi'laitis] *n.* inflammation of the ~s.

ton·sure ['tɔnʃə*] *n.* shaving of the top of the head of a person about to become a priest or monk; the part so shaved.

too [tu:] *adv.* also; in addition; moreover; in a higher degree than is wanted, bearable, etc.

took, see *take*.

tool [tu:l] *n.* 1. implement held in the hand(s) and used by workmen, e.g. gardeners, carpenters, builders. (Cf. *instrument*.) *machine* ~, metal-cutting ~ operated by power, used in making machinery. 2. person who is used by another for dishonest purposes.

toot [tu:t] *n.* short, sharp warning sound from a horn, trumpet, etc. *v.i. & t.* (cause to) give out a ~ or ~s.

tooth [tu:θ] *n.* (pl. *teeth* [ti:θ]). (See the picture on page 562.) 1. each of the small, white, bony structures rooted in the jaws, used for biting and chewing. *fight ~ and nail*, fight bitterly, with all one's force. *in the teeth of*, against the full force of. 2. ~-like part, esp. of a comb, saw, or rake. '~**ache** *n.* continuous pain in a ~ or teeth. ~**less** *adj.* without teeth. '~**some** *adj.* (of food) pleasant to the taste.

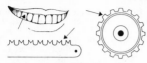

Teeth

top [tɒp] *n.* **1.** highest part or point. **2.** utmost degree; fullest capacity: *at the top of his voice*, as loudly as possible. **3.** (attrib.) of or at the top; highest in position or degree: *the top shelf*; *at top speed*. **top hat**, man's silk hat. *v.t.* (-pp-). **1.** provide a top for; be a top to. **2.** reach the top of (e.g. a slope); be at the top of. **3.** cut the top(s) off (e.g. plants). **'top·coat** *n.* overcoat. **'top-'heav·y** *adj.* too heavy at the top; ill-balanced. **'top·mast** *n.* upper part of a mast. **'top·most** *adj.* highest. **'top·ping** *adj.* (colloq.) excellent.

²**top** [tɒp] *n.* toy that spins and balances on a point. (*sleep*) *like a top*, soundly.

to·paz ['toupæz] *n.* semi-precious stone, usu. yellow.

to·pee, to·pi ['toupi] *n.* sun-helmet.

top·ic ['tɒpik] *n.* subject for discussion. **top·i·cal** *adj.* of present interest: *~al news.*

to·pog·ra·phy [tə'pɒgrəfi] *n.* (description of the) features (e.g. rivers, roads, etc.) of a place or district. **top·o·graph·i·cal** [,tɒpə'græfikl] *adj.*

top·ple ['tɒpl] *v.i. & t.* (cause to) be unsteady and overturn.

top·sy-tur·vy ['tɒpsi'tə:vi] *adj.* upside down; in confusion.

torch [tɔ:tʃ] *n.* **1.** piece of wood treated with oil, etc., used as a flaming light; (fig.) sth. that gives enlightenment: *the ~ of learning.* **2.** electric hand-light and battery.

tore, see ¹*tear.*

tor·ment ['tɔ:ment] *n.* (cause of) severe bodily or mental suffering. [tɔ:'ment] *v.t.* cause severe suffering to; annoy. **tor·men·tor** [tɔ:'mentə*] *n.*

torn, see ¹*tear.*

tor·na·do [tɔ:'neidou] *n.* (pl. -*os*, -*oes*). violent local (thunder-) storm, esp. in W. Africa and U.S.A.; whirlwind.

tor·pe·do [tɔ:'pi:dou] *n.* (pl. -*oes*). cigar-shaped self-propelling shell filled with explosive, aimed at ships and launched to travel below the surface of the water. *v.t.* strike, damage, sink, with a ~. ~**-boat** *n.* small fast warship from which ~es are fired.

tor·pid ['tɔ:pid] *adj.* **1.** dull and slow; inactive. **2.** (of animals that hibernate) not moving or feeling. ~**·i·ty** [tɔ:'piditi], **tor·por** ['tɔ:pə*] *n.* ~ condition.

tor·rent ['tɒrənt] *n.* violent rushing stream of liquid, esp. water: *rain falling in ~s*; (fig.) violent outburst (*of* angry words, etc.). **tor·ren·tial** [tə'renʃl] *adj.* of, like, caused by, a ~: ~*ial rain.*

tor·rid ['tɒrid] *adj.* (of the weather, a country) very hot; tropical.

tor·so ['tɔ:sou] *n.* human trunk; (esp.) statue of the human body without head, arms, and legs.

tor·toise ['tɔ:təs] *n.* slow-moving four-legged animal with a hard shell. '~**-shell** *n.* (attrib.) of the clouded dark brown and yellow colour of ~-shell.

A tortoise

tor·tu·ous ['tɔ:tjuəs] *adj.* full of twists and bends; (fig.) not straightforward.

tor·ture ['tɔ:tʃə*] *v.t. & n.* (cause) severe suffering (*of*): ~ *a man to make him confess*; *suffer ~ from toothache.* **tor·tur·er** *n.*

To·ry ['tɔ:ri] *n.* = Conservative.

tosh [tɒʃ] *n.* (slang) nonsense.

toss [tɒs] *v.t. & i.* **1.** (cause to) move restlessly from side to side or up and down. *Ships ~ing about on the stormy sea.* **2.** throw up into or through the air: ~ *one's hat on a shelf. The horse*

~ed its rider. **3.** ~ (up) a coin, spin a coin up into the air and guess which side (head or tail) will be on top when it falls; ~ for it, decide sth. by doing this. **4.** ~ one's head, jerk it up and back (to suggest contempt or indifference). **5.** ~ sth. off, drink it straight down. **n. 1.** ~ing movement: a ~ of the head. **2.** win (lose) the ~, guess rightly (wrongly) when a coin is ~ed up. a ~-up, sth. of which the outcome depends upon chance.

¹tot [tɒt] **n. 1.** very small child. **2.** small portion of spirits (e.g. rum).

²tot [tɒt] **v.t. & i.** (-tt-). (colloq.) add up: expenses totting up to £5.

to·tal ['toutl] **adj. & n.** (complete or entire) sum or amount: his ~ debts; a ~ of £20. **v.t.** (-ll-). find the ~ of; reach the ~ of; amount to. **~·ly adv.** completely.

to·tal·i·ta·ri·an [ˌtoutæli'tɛəriən] **adj.** ~ State, one in which only one political party is allowed and no rival loyalties are recognized (2).

to·tal·i·za·tor ['toutəlaiˌzeitə*] **n.** machine for registering numbers of bets on races (esp. between horses or greyhounds) and money due to backers.

tote [tout] **n.** (colloq.) = totalizator.

to·tem ['toutəm] **n.** (carved pole representing) natural object, esp. an animal, considered, esp. by N. American Indians, to have a close connexion with a family group. '~-pole **n.** one on which a ~ is carved or painted.

tot·ter ['tɒtə*] **v.i. 1.** walk with weak, unsteady steps. **2.** be almost falling. **~·y adj.** unsteady.

touch [tʌtʃ] **v.i. & t. 1.** (of two or more objects) not be entirely separate, one from the other(s); (cause to) be in contact with; put (a finger, hand, etc.) on or against (3), (5). **2.** affect a person or his feelings; concern: The sad story ~ed us (our hearts). **3.** (usu. in neg.) compare with, be equal

to: No one can ~ him as an actor of tragic roles. **4.** (with adv. & prep.): ~ at, (of a ship) visit (a port) for a short stay. ~ down, (of an aircraft) come down to land. ~ (up)on, say sth. about, refer to (a subject, etc.). ~ up, make small changes in (a picture, piece of writing, etc.) to improve it. **n. 1.** act or fact of ~ing. **2.** (sense giving) feeling by ~ing: soft (rough, etc.) to the ~. **3.** stroke made with a pen, brush, etc.: add a few finishing ~es to a painting. **4.** slight quantity, trace (of sth.): a ~ of frost in the air. **5.** connexion, esp. in (out of) ~ (with), in (not in) regular communication, having (not having) information about: in ~ with old friends; lose ~ (with), become out of ~ (with). **6.** style or manner of ~ing the keys, strings, etc., of a musical instrument, of workmanship (in art): the ~ of a master (i.e. expert style). **~-and-go adj.** of uncertain outcome: It was ~-and-go whether he would arrive in time. **touched predic. adj.** (colloq.) mentally disordered. **~ing adj.** arousing pity or sympathy. **prep.** concerning. '~·stone **n.** sth. used as a test or standard (of purity, etc.). **~·y adj.** (-ier, -iest). easily or quickly offended. **~·i·ness n.**

tough [tʌf] **adj.** (-er, -est). **1.** (of meat) hard to cut or to get one's teeth into. **2.** not easily cut, broken, or worn out: ~ leather. **3.** strong; able to endure hardships: ~ soldiers. **4.** (of work, problems) difficult: a ~ job. **5.** (of persons) rough and violent: a ~ criminal. **n.** ~(5) man. **~·en v.t. & i.** make or become ~.

tour [tuə*] **n.** journey out and home again during which several or many places are visited. **v.t. & i.** make a ~ (of): ~ Europe. **~·ist n.** person making a ~ for pleasure.

tour·na·ment ['tɔː-, 'tuənəmənt] **n. 1.** series of contests of skill between a number of players: a tennis (chess) ~. **2.** (historical) contest between armed knights on horseback. **tour·ney** ['tuəni] *n.* ~ (2).

tour·ni·quet ['tuəniket, -kei] *n.* device for stopping bleeding by twisting sth. tightly against an artery.

tou·sle ['tauzl] *v.t.* put (esp. the hair) into disorder by pulling it about, rubbing it, etc.

tout [taut] *n.* person who worries others to buy sth., use his services, etc., esp. one who sells information about race-horses. *v.i.* act as a ~ : ~*ing for custom.*

¹**tow** [tou] *v.t.* pull (a ship, motor-car, etc.) along by a rope or chain. *n.* towing or being towed : *have (take) (a boat, etc.) in tow,* have charge of, be in attendance on (fig. of persons). **'tow(ing)-path** *n.* path along the side of a river or canal for use in towing.

²**tow** [tou] *n.* broken fibres of flax, hemp, etc. (for rope, etc.).

to·ward(s) [tə'wo:d(z), tə:d(z)] *prep.* **1.** in the direction of ; approaching. **2.** near. **3.** for the purpose of helping. **4.** as regards ; in relation to.

tow·el ['tauəl] *n.* cloth for drying oneself after washing, for drying dishes, etc.

tow·er ['tauə*] *n.* tall strong building ; tall part of a building, usu. square or round, esp. as part of a castle or church. (See the picture at *steeple.*) *v.i.* rise to a great height, be very tall, esp. in relation to the height of the surroundings. ~ *above,* (fig.) greatly exceed in ability, moral qualities, etc. *in a ~ing rage,* violently angry.

town [taun] *n.* **1.** place (bigger than a village) with streets, shops, houses, etc., where people live in large numbers. (Cf. *country* (4).) **2.** the people of a ~ : *The whole ~ was talking about it.* **3.** business, shopping, etc., part of a ~ (contrasted with the suburbs, etc.): *go to ~ to do some shopping.* **4.** nearest big centre of population, esp. (in England) London. **5.** ~ *hall,* building, offices, for local government and public events (e.g. meetings, concerts).

tox·ic ['toksik] *adj.* of, caused by, poison ; poisonous.

toy [toi] *n.* child's plaything. *v.i.* *toy with (sth.),* handle absent-mindedly ; touch with the fingers ; think not very seriously about it.

trace [treis] *v.t.* **1.** outline ; mark (out) : ~ *out the plan of a house.* **2.** copy, e.g. by drawing on transparent paper the lines, etc., of (a map, design, etc.) placed underneath. **3.** follow or discover (sb. or sth.) by observing marks, tracks, bits of evidence, etc. : ~ *a rumour back to the person who started it.* *n.* **1.** mark, sign, etc., showing that sb. or sth. has been present, that sth. has existed or happened : ~*s of an ancient civilization.* **2.** small, least possible, amount (*of* sth.) : *not a ~ of fear in his character.* **trac·ing** *n.* copy (of a map, etc.) made by tracing (2).

trac·er·y ['treisəri] *n.* ornamental arrangement of designs (e.g. in frost on glass ; stone-work in a church window).

Tracery   A tractor

track [træk] *n.* **1.** line or series of marks left by a cart, person, animal, etc., in passing along : ~*s in the snow ; on the ~ of,* in pursuit of ; *make ~s for,* (colloq.) go towards. **2.** path made by frequent use. *off the ~,* (lit. & fig.) on a wrong path or course of action. **3.** course ; line taken by sth. : *the ~ of a comet (storm).* **4.** set of rails for trains, etc. : *single (double) ~,* one pair (two pairs) of rails. **5.** endless belt used instead of wheels on some tractors, tanks, etc. (hence ~*ed vehicles*). **6.** prepared path for racing: *a running-~*; ~ *events*, running races contrasted with other events. *v.t.* follow (an animal, etc.), along its ~s (1): ~ *down a bear*, find by ~ing. ~' **less** *adj.* having no ~s (2).

¹**tract** [trækt] *n.* stretch or area (*of* forest, farm land, water).

²**tract** [trækt] *n.* short printed essay on sth., esp. a moral or religious subject.

trac·ta·ble ['træktəbl] *adj.* easily controlled or guided.

trac·tion ['trækʃən] *n.* (power used in) pulling or drawing sth. over a surface: *steam* ~.

trac·tor ['træktə*] *n.* powerful motor vehicle used for pulling ploughs, guns, etc. (See the picture on page 564.)

trade [treid] *n.* **1.** buying and selling of goods; exchange of goods for money or other goods; particular branch of this: *the cotton* (*book*) ~. ~ *wind*, strong wind blowing always towards the equator from the SE. and NE. **2.** occupation; way of making a living, esp. a handicraft: *He's a carpenter* (*shoemaker, tailor*) *by* ~. **3.** the people, organizations, etc., engaged in a ~: ~ *union*, ~s *union*, organized association of workers in a ~ or group of ~s, formed to protect their interests, improve their conditions, etc. ~ *mark*, design, special name, etc., used to distinguish a manufacturer's goods from others. *v.i. & t.* **1.** engage in ~ (1): *trading in furs*; ~ (= barter) *furs for tools.* **2.** ~ (*up*)*on*, take a wrong advantage of, use (sb.'s sympathy, one's good reputation), in order to get sth. **trad·er** *n.* merchant.

'**trades·man** *n.* shopkeeper.

tra·di·tion [trə'diʃən] *n.* (handing down from generation to generation of) opinions, beliefs, customs, etc.; opinion, belief, etc., handed down from the past. ~**'al** *adj.*

tra·duce [trə'djuːs] *v.t.* slander.

traf·fic ['træfik] *n.* **1.** (movement of) people and vehicles along

roads and streets: ~ *lights*, coloured signals for controlling ~. **2.** transport business done by a railway, shipping line, etc. **3.** trading: *illegal drug* ~. *v.i.* (-ck-). ~ *in*, trade in.

trag·e·dy ['trædʒidi] *n.* **1.** play for the theatre, branch of drama, of a serious and solemn kind, usu. with a sad ending. **2.** sad event or experience in real life. **tra·ge·dian** [trə'dʒiːdjən] *n.* writer of, actor in, ~ (1). **trag·ic** ['trædʒik] *adj.* of ~(1); very sad. **trag·i·cal·ly** *adv.*

trail [treil] *n.* **1.** line, mark(s), traces, left by sb. or sth. that has passed by: *a* ~ *of smoke* (from a steam-engine); *a* ~ *of destruction* (left by a violent storm, etc.). **2.** track or scent followed in hunting: (*The hounds were*) *hot on the* ~, close behind. **3.** path through rough country. *v.t. & i.* **1.** pull or be pulled along behind: *a child* ~*ing a toy cart*; *a long dress* ~*ing on the ground.* **2.** (of plants) grow along or over the ground, down a wall, etc. **3.** walk wearily (*along*, etc.). ~**er** *n.* **1.** vehicle towed by another (e.g. a small cart, a caravan). **2.** ~ing plant.

train [trein] *v.t. & i.* **1.** give teaching and practice to (e.g. a child, a soldier, an animal) in order to bring to a desired standard of behaviour, efficiency, or physical condition: ~ *children to be good citizens*; ~ *a horse for a race.* **2.** cause (a plant) to grow in a required direction. **3.** ~ *a gun* (*up*)*on*, aim it at. *n.* **1.** (engine and) railway coaches, wagons, etc., joined together. **2.** number of persons, animals, carriages, etc., moving in a line: *a* ~ *of camels.* **3.** series or chain (*of* thoughts, ideas, events). **4.** group of attendants travelling with a king, etc. **5.** part of a long dress or robe on the ground or floor. **6.** line of gunpowder leading to a mine, etc., (hence) *in* ~, in readiness. ~**ee** [trei'niː] *n.* person receiving (usu. industrial) ~ing. ~**er** *n.* person who ~s (1) (athletes, animals for the circus, race-horses, etc.). ~·**ing** *n*. ~*ing* college, (esp.) one for ~*ing* teachers ; *in* (*out of*) ~*ing*, in (not in) good physical condition (for some athletic activity).

trait [trei] *n*. distinguishing quality or characteristic.

trai·tor ['treitə*] *n*. person who betrays a friend, is disloyal to his country, a cause, etc. ~·**ous** *adj*. **trai·tress** ['treitris] *n*. woman ~.

tra·jec·to·ry ['trædʒəktəri] *n*. curved path of a projectile (e.g. a bullet).

tram [træm] *n*. (also ~*car*) electric car of a railway running (usu.) along public roads or streets. '~·**line**, '~·**way** *n*. line of rails for ~s.

A tram(car)

tram·mel ['træml] *v.t.* (-*ll*-). hamper ; make progress difficult. *n*. (pl.) sth. that ~s : *the* ~*s of routine*.

tramp [træmp] *v.i. & t.* **1.** walk with heavy steps. **2.** walk (esp. for a long distance); walk through or over : ~ *through Wales* ; ~ *the hills*. *n*. **1.** sound of heavy footsteps (e.g. of soldiers marching). **2.** long walk. **3.** person (usu. homeless) who goes from place to place and does no regular work. **4.** cargo boat that goes to any port(s) where cargo can be picked up.

tram·ple ['træmpl] *v.t. & i.* tread heavily (*on*) ; crush under the feet : ~ *on the flowers* ; ~ *the grass down*.

trance [trɑ:ns] *n*. **1.** sleep-like condition. **2.** abnormal, dreamy state.

tran·quil ['træŋkwil] *adj*. calm ; quiet. ~·**ly** *adv*. ~·**li·ty** [træŋ-'kwiliti] *n*.

trans- [træns-, trænz-, trɑ:ns-, trɑ:nz-] *prefix*. across ; on or to the other side of : ~*atlantic*, ~*continental*. (See footnote.)

*****trans·act** [træn'zækt] *v.t.* do, conduct (business *with* sb.). **trans·ac·tion** *n*. **1.** (~*ing of a*) piece of business. **2.** (pl.)(records of) proceedings of a society (4), esp. lectures to a learned society.

†**tran·scend** [træn'send] *v.t.* be or go beyond or outside the range of (experience, imagination). **tran·scen·dent** *adj*. surpassing : *of* ~*ent genius*.

†**tran·scribe** [træns'kraib] *v.t.* copy in writing, esp. write (sth.) in full from shorthand notes. **tran·script** ['trænskript] *n*. sth. ~d. **tran·scrip·tion** [træns-'kripʃən] *n*. transcribing ; sth. ~d, esp. into a special form of writing : *phonetic transcription*.

†**tran·sept** ['trænsept] *n*. (either end of the) shorter part of a cross-shaped church.

†**trans·fer** [træns'fə:*] *v.t. & i.* (-*rr*-). **1.** change position, move *from* one place to another. **2.** hand over (property, etc.) to sb. ['trænsfə:*] *n*. ~*ring* ; document ~*ring* sb. or sth. ~·**a·ble** *adj*. that càn be ~red. ~·**ence** *n*. [træns'fə:rəns] ~*ring*, esp. from one job to another.

†**trans·fig·ure** [træns'figə*] *v.t.* change the shape or appearance of, esp. so as to make glorious or exalted. **trans·fig·u·ra·tion** [ˌtrænsfigju'reiʃən] *n*. change of this sort, esp. (*the T*~) that of Jesus, as described in the Bible (Matthew xvii).

†**trans·fix** [træns'fiks] *v.t.* **1.** pierce (with a pointed weapon, etc.). **2.** cause (sb.) to be unable to move, think, etc. : ~*ed with fear* (*surprise*).

†**trans·form** [træns'fɔ:m] *v.t.* change the shape, appearance, quality, or nature of. **trans·**

The first syllable of words marked * may be pronounced [træns-], [trɑ:ns-], [trænz-], or [trɑ:nz-]. The first syllable of words marked † may be pronounced either [træns-] or [trɑ:ns-].

for·ma·tion [ˌtrænsfəˈmeiʃən] *n.*
~·**er** *n.* (esp.) apparatus that ~s
electric current from one voltage
to another.

†**trans·fuse** [trænsˈfjuːz] *v.t.*
transfer (sth., esp. blood) from
one living person to another.

trans·fu·sion *n.* transfusing,
esp. of blood: *The patient had
several blood transfusions.*

*trans·gress** [trænsˈgres] *v.t. &
i.* **1.** overstep bounds; break (a
law, treaty, agreement). **2.** do
wrong; sin. **trans·gres·sion** *n.*
trans·gres·sor *n.* wrongdoer;
sinner.

†**tran·si·ent** [ˈtrænziənt] *adj.* lasting for a short time only;
brief.

†**tran·sis·tor** [trænˈsistə*] *n.* elec-
tronic device, much smaller than
a valve(3), used in radio sets,
etc.: *a ~ radio*; radio set with
this device.

*tran·sit** [ˈtrænsit] *n. lost (delayed) in ~,* while being taken
or carried from one place to
another.

*tran·si·tion** [trænˈsiʒən] *n.*
change from one condition or set
of circumstances to another.

†**tran·si·tive** [ˈtrænsitiv] *adj.* (of
a verb) taking a direct object.

*tran·si·to·ry** [ˈtrænsitəri] *adj.*
transient.

*trans·late** [trænsˈleit] *v.t.* give
the meaning of (sth. said or
written) in another language.
trans·la·tion *n.* process of
translating; sth. ~d.

*trans·lu·cent** [trænzˈluːsnt] *adj.*
allowing light to pass through,
but not transparent.

*trans·mit** [trænzˈmit] *v.t.* (-tt-).
1. pass or hand on; send on: ~
a message by radio; ~ *a disease.*
2. let through or along: *Iron ~s
heat.* **trans·mis·sion** [trænz-
ˈmiʃən] *n.* **1.** ~ting or being
~ted. **2.** part of a motor-engine
that ~s power to turn the axle(s).
~·**ter** *n.* (esp.) part of a telegraph,
radio apparatus, for sending out
signals, radio programmes, etc.

†**trans·par·ent** [trænsˈpɛərənt,
-ˈpær-] *adj.* **1.** that can be seen
through, like clear glass. **2.**
unmistakable or undoubted: *a
~ lie.* **3.** clear; easily understood: *a ~ style.* **trans·par·
ence, trans·par·en·cy** *n.*

†**trans·pire** [trænsˈpaiə*] *v.i.* (of
an event, a secret) become
known; come to light.

†**trans·plant** [trænsˈplɑːnt] *v.t.*
take up (plants, etc. with their
roots) and plant in another
place. [ˈtrænsplɑːnt] *n.* replace-
ment (by surgical operation) of a
diseased organ with a healthy
one from another body.

†**trans·port** [trænsˈpoːt] *v.t.* **1.**
carry (persons, goods) from one
place to another. **2.** (in former
times) send (a criminal) to a
distant colony as punishment.
3. *be ~ed with,* be overcome with
(joy, etc.). [ˈtrænspoːt] *n.* **1.** ~-
ing(1). **2.** (attrib.) of or for
~ing(1): *London's ~ system.* **3.**
ship, aircraft, for carrying soldiers. **4.** (often pl.) *in a ~ (in ~s)
of delight (rage, etc.),* carried away
by strong feelings of pleasure,
rage, etc. **trans·por·ta·tion**
[ˌtrænspoːˈteiʃən] *n.* (esp.) ~ing
(2) or being ~ed(2).

†**trans·pose** [trænsˈpouz] *v.t.*
cause (two or more things) to
change places. **trans·po·si·tion**
[ˌtrænspəˈziʃən] *n.*

†**trans·verse** [trænzˈvəːs] *adj.*
lying or placed across. ~·**ly** *adv.*

trap [træp] *n.* **1.** device for
catching animals, etc. **2.** plan
or trick for making a person do
or say sth. he does not wish to
do or say: *set a ~ to catch a
thief; fall into a ~,* be caught by
a trick. **3.** light, two-wheeled
carriage pulled by a horse or
pony. *v.t.* (-pp-). take in a ~
(1), (2); capture by a trick.
'~·**door, n.** door in a floor or
roof. ~·**per** *n.* man who ~s
animals for their skins.

tra·peze [trəˈpiːz] *n.* horizontal
bar or rod supported by two

The first syllable of words marked * may be pronounced [træns-],
[trɑːns-], [trænz-], or [trɑːnz-]. The first syllable of words marked †
may be pronounced either [træns-] or [trɑːns-].

ropes, used by acrobats and persons doing physical training.

trap·pings ['træpiŋz] *n. pl.* ornaments or decorations, esp. as a sign of public office: *the ~ of royalty*.

trash [træʃ] *n.* worthless material or writing. *~·y adj.* worthless.

trav·ail ['træveil] *n.* pains of childbirth; hard work.

trav·el ['trævl] *v.i. & t.* (*-ll-*). **1.** make (esp. long) journeys. **2.** go; move: *Light ~s faster than sound. n.* **1.** ~ling: *fond of ~.* **2.** (pl.) journeys, esp. to other countries: *Is he back from his ~s yet?* *~·ler n. commercial ~ler,* ~ling salesman.

trav·erse ['trævə:s] *v.t.* travel, pass, or lie, across.

trav·es·ty ['trævisti] *n.* imitation or description of sth. that is, often on purpose, unlike and inferior to the real thing: *His trial was a ~ of justice. v.t.* make or be a ~ of.

trawl [trɔ:l] *v.i. & t. & n.* (go fishing with, drag along the sea-bottom, a) large wide-mouthed net. *~·er n.* boat used in ~ing.

tray [trei] *n.* flat piece of wood, metal, etc., with raised edges, for holding small light things: *a tea-~ ; a pen-~.*

treach·er·ous ['tretʃərəs] *adj.* **1.** false or disloyal (to a friend, a cause, etc.). **2.** deceptive; not to be relied on: *The ice (My memory) is ~.* **treach·er·y** ['tretʃəri] *n.* being ~ ; ~ act(s).

trea·cle ['tri:kl] *n.* thick, sticky, dark liquid produced while sugar is being refined.

tread [tred] *v.i. & t.* (p.t. *trod,* p.p. *trodden* ['trɔdn]). **1.** walk, put the foot or feet down (*on*): *~ on sb.'s toes.* **2.** stamp or crush in, down, etc., with the feet: *~ out a fire in the grass.* **3.** make by walking: *The cattle had trodden a path to the river. n.* **1.** way or sound of walking: *with a heavy (loud) ~.* **2.** part of a step or stair on which the foot is placed. **3.** part of a tyre that touches the ground.

tread·le ['tredl] *n.* part that

drives a machine (e.g. a sewing-machine) and is worked by pressure of the foot or feet. *v.i.* work a ~.

trea·son ['tri:zn] *n.* treachery to one's ruler or government; disloyalty. *~·a·ble adj.* having the nature of ~.

treas·ure ['treʒə*] *n.* (store of) gold and silver, jewels, etc.; wealth; highly valued object or person: *art ~s. v.t.* **1.** store up for future use; keep; remember: *~ (up) old letters.* **2.** value highly. **treas·ur·er** *n.* person in charge of money, etc., belonging to a society, etc.

treas·ur·y ['treʒəri] *n.* **1.** department of government that controls a country's public money. **2.** place where ~s are kept; funds of a society, organization, etc.

treat [tri:t] *v.t. & i.* **1.** act or behave towards: *~ sb. kindly; ~ sb. as (if he were) a child.* **2.** consider: *~ sth. lightly (as a joke).* **3.** discuss; deal with: *He ~ed the subject thoroughly.* **4.** (of a lecture, book, etc.) *~ of,* be about: *The essay ~s of insect pests.* **5.** give medical or surgical care to (a person, disease). **6.** put (a substance) through a process (in manufacture, etc.): *~ a substance with acid.* **7.** *~ sb. to sth.,* supply him with food or drink, entertainment, etc.) at one's own expense: *~ a friend to a good dinner.* **8.** discuss or arrange terms (*with*). *n.* pleasure, esp. sth. not often enjoyed: *What a ~ to get out of the noisy town!* *~·ise* ['tri:tiz] *n.* book, etc., that deals carefully with a subject. *~·ment n.* way of ~ing sb. or sth.; particular kind of medical ~ment.

treat·y ['tri:ti] *n.* agreement made and signed between States: *a ~ of peace; a trade ~.*

¹**tre·ble** ['trebl] *v.t. & i. & adj.* (make or become) three times as much, etc.

²**tre·ble** ['trebl] *n.* (boy's voice, instrument, that takes the) highest part in music. *adj.* of or for the ~.

tree [tri:] *n.* see the picture. *family* ~, diagram or list showing or giving family descent.

A tree   A trestle table

trek [trek] *v.i. & n.* (-kk-). (S. Africa) (go on a) long journey, esp. by ox-wagon.

trel·lis ['trelis] *n.* upright framework of strips of wood, etc., crossing one another, e.g. for supporting climbing plants.

trem·ble ['trembl] *v.i.* shake (with fear, anger, cold, etc.); be agitated or worried. *n.* a trembling.

tre·men·dous [tri'mendəs] *adj.* very great; enormous. ~**ly** *adv.*

trem·or ['tremə*] *n.* **1.** shaking or trembling. **2.** thrill (of fear, excitement, etc.).

trem·u·lous ['tremjuləs] *adj.* trembling; timid; nervous.

trench [trenʃ] *n.* ditch dug in the ground (e.g. for draining off water, or as a protection for soldiers against the enemy's fire). *v.t. & i.* make a ~ or ~es in.

trench·ant ['trenʃənt] *adj.* (of language) vigorous; decisive.

trend [trend] *n.* general direction; tendency. *v.i.* have a certain ~: *The coast ~s (towards the) south.*

trep·i·da·tion [,trepi'deiʃən] *n.* alarm; excited state of mind.

tres·pass ['trespəs] *v.i.* **1.** ~ (*on, upon*), go on to privately-owned land without right or permission; (fig.) encroach (*upon sb.'s time, etc.*). **2.** (old use) do wrong (*against*). *n.* act of ~ing. **tres·pas·ser** *n.*

tress [tres] *n.* portion or lock of hair on the head; (pl.) long hair.

tres·tle ['tresl] *n.* wooden structure, as shown above, used as a support for a table top, a work-man's bench, etc. '~ 'bridge, one supported on a timber or metal framework.

tri- [trai-] *prefix.* three.

tri·al ['traiəl] *n.* **1.** testing; test: *a ~ of strength*; *give sth. a ~*, use it to learn whether it is good, useful, etc.; *a ~ flight* (e.g. of a new aircraft, to test it); *on ~*, for the purpose of testing. **2.** sth. or sb. troublesome or annoying: *a boy who is a ~ to his teachers.* **3.** examination before a judge (and jury): *on ~ for theft.*

tri·an·gle ['traiæŋgl] *n.* **1.** plane figure with three straight sides; any three points not in a straight line. **2.** musical instrument made of a steel rod in the shape of a ~, struck with a steel rod. **tri·an·gu·lar** [trai'æŋgjulə*] *adj.* **1.** in the shape of a ~. **2.** in which three persons, etc., take part.

tribe [traib] *n.* racial group, esp. one united by language and customs, living as a community under one or more chiefs. **tribes·man** *n.* member of a ~. **trib·al** *adj.*

trib·u·la·tion [,tribju'leiʃən] *n.* great trouble; (cause of) grief.

tri·bu·nal [trai-, tri'bju:nl] *n.* place of judgement; judges appointed for special duty, e.g. to hear appeals against high rents, military service, etc.

trib·ute ['tribju:t] *n.* **1.** (usu. regular) payment which one government or ruler exacts from another. **2.** sth. done, said, or given to show respect or admiration: *pay ~ to the founders of a school.* **trib·u·ta·ry** ['tribjutəri] *n. & adj.* **1.** (country, ruler, etc.) paying ~(1) to another. **2.** (river) flowing into another.

¹trice [trais] *v.t.* ~ *up*, pull up and tie (a sail) in place.

²trice [trais] *n.* (only) *in a ~*, in an instant; at once.

trick [trik] *n.* **1.** sth. done in order to deceive, to outwit, outdo, sb.; sth. done to make a person appear ridiculous: *play a ~ on sb.* **2.** action, usu. needing

T

skill or practice, done to deceive and amuse people: *card* (*conjuring*) ~*s*. **3.** way of behaving that is peculiar to a person: *He has a ~ of pulling his left ear when he's thinking.* **4.** the right way of doing sth., usu. a way that must be learnt by practice: *There's a~ in it. You'll soon get the ~ of it.* **5.** (cards played in) one round (of bridge, etc.): *take* (*win*) *a* ~, win one round. *v.t.* deceive by a ~(1): ~ *sb. out of sth.* (*into doing sth.*). ~·'**er·y** *n.* deception; cheating. **tricks·ter** *n.* person who has the habit of ~ing(1) people. ~·**y** *adj.* (*-ier*, *-iest*). **1.** (of persons, their actions) deceptive. **2.** (of work, etc.) requiring skill; full of hidden difficulties.

trick·le ['trikl] *v.i.* & *t.* (of liquid) (cause to) flow in drops or in a thin stream. *n.* weak or thin flow: *The stream had shrunk to a* ~.

tri·col·our ['trikələ*] *n.* flag (e.g. the French flag) with three bands of colour.

tri·cy·cle ['traisikl] *n.* three-wheeled cycle.

tri·dent ['traidənt] *n.* spear with three points.

tri·en·nial [trai'enjəl] *adj.* lasting for, happening or done, every three years. *n.* ~ event.

tri·fle ['traifl] *n.* **1.** thing, event, etc., of little value or importance. **2.** small amount (esp. of money). **3.** sweet dish of cake, jam, cream, etc. **4.** *a* ~, (as adv.) a little. *v.i.* & *t.* **1.** talk or act lightly, without serious purpose: *He's not a man to be* ~d *with.* **2.** ~ *away*, waste: ~ *away a whole hour.* **tri·fling** *adj.* unimportant.

trig·ger ['trigə*] *n.* lever for releasing a spring, esp. of a firearm.

trig·o·nom·e·try [,trigə'nɔmitri] *n.* branch of mathematics that deals with the relations between sides and angles of triangles.

tri·lat·er·al [trai'lætərəl] *adj.* three-sided.

trill [tril] *n.* shaking or quavering sound made by the voice, etc.

v.i. & *t.* say, sing, or play with a ~.

tril·lion ['triljən] *n.* & *adj.* (Gt. Brit.) one million × million × million; (U.S.A.) one million × million.

tri·lo·gy ['trilədʒi] *n.* group of three plays, operas, novels, etc., each complete in itself but with a common subject.

trim [trim] *adj.* (*-mer*, *-mest*). in good order; neat and tidy. *v.t.* & *i.* (*-mm-*). **1.** make ~, esp. by taking or cutting away uneven, irregular, or unwanted parts: ~ *a hedge* (*one's beard, the wick of a lamp*). **2.** decorate or ornament (a hat, dress, etc., with lace, etc.). **3.** adjust the balance of (a boat, an aircraft) by arranging the position of cargo, passengers, etc.; arrange (sails) to suit the wind. *n.* state or degree of preparedness (*for* sth.): *get into* ~ *for the sports meeting.* ~·'**ming** *n.* (esp.) material (lace, ribbon, etc.) for ~ming(2) dresses or hats.

trin·i·ty ['triniti] *n.* group of three. *the T~*, (in Christian teaching) union of Father, Son, and Holy Ghost, one God.

trin·ket ['triŋkit] *n.* small jewel or ornament, of little value.

tri·o ['tri:ou] *n.* group of three; (musical composition for) group of three singers or players.

trip [trip] *v.i.* & *t.* (*-pp-*). **1.** run with quick light steps. **2.** (cause to) stumble; (almost) fall after striking the foot on sth.: ~ *over the root of a tree.* **3.** (often ~ *up*), make a mistake, (cause sb. to) fail. *n.* **1.** journey, esp. for pleasure. **2.** a fall or stumble. ~·'**per** *n.* person making a (usu. short) ~(1) for pleasure: *week-end* ~*pers*.

tri·par·tite ['trai'pɑ:tait] *adj.* **1.** (of an agreement) in which three parties have a share. **2.** having three parts.

tripe [traip] *n.* **1.** part of a cow's stomach used as food. **2.** (slang) worthless talk, writing, ideas.

tri·ple ['tripl] *adj.* made up of three (parts or parties(3)). *v.t.* & *i.* make, become, be, three times as much or as many : ~ *your income.*

trip·let ['triplit] *n.* **1.** one of three children born at one birth. **2.** (pl.) three such children. **3.** set of three.

trip·li·cate ['triplikit] *adj.* of which there are three alike made. *n.* one of three like things, esp. documents : *in* ~, one original and two copies. ['triplikeit] *v.t.* make in ~.

tri·pod ['traipɔd] *n.* three-legged support (e.g. for a camera).

tri·sect [trai'sekt] *v.t.* divide (a line, angle, etc.) into three (esp. equal) parts.

trite [trait] *adj.* (of remarks, ideas, feelings) commonplace ; not new.

tri·umph ['traiəmf] *n.* (joy or satisfaction at) success or victory : *return home in* ~ ; *shouts of* ~. *v.i.* win a victory (*over*); exult (*over*); show joy because of success. **tri·um·phal** [trai'ʌmfl] *adj.* of, for, a ~ ; expressing ~. **tri·um·phant** [trai'ʌmfənt] *adj.* (rejoicing at) having ~ed.

triv·i·al ['triviəl] *adj.* **1.** of small value or importance. **2.** (of persons) trifling. **~·i·ty** [ˌtrivi'æliti] *n.* ~ thing, idea, etc.

trod(den), see *tread.*

trog·lo·dyte ['trɔglədait] *n.* cave-dweller in ancient times.

trol·ley ['trɔli] *n.* (pl. ~s). **1.** two- or four-wheeled handcart ; (also *tea·*~) small table, running on castors, for serving refreshments. **2.** small, low truck running on rails. **3.** small contact-wheel between a tramcar or bus (~·*bus*) and an overhead cable.

trom·bone [trɔm'boun] *n.* large, loud, brass wind-instrument with a sliding tube.

troop [tru:p] *n.* **1.** group of persons or animals, esp. when moving : ~*s of children* ; *a* ~ *of antelope.* **2.** unit of cavalry. **3.** (pl.) soldiers. *v.i.* come or go together in a group : *children* ~*ing out of school.* **~·er** *n.* soldier in a cavalry regiment. **~·ship** *n.* ship to carry soldiers.

tro·phy ['troufi] *n.* sth. kept in

memory of a victory or success (e.g. in hunting, games, etc.).

trop·ic ['trɔpik] *n.* **1.** line of latitude 23° 27' north (*T~ of Cancer*) or south (*T~ of Capricorn*) of the equator. **2.** *the* ~*s,* the part of the world between these lines. **trop·i·cal** *adj.* of, or as of, the ~*s* : ~*al fruit* ; ~*al temperatures.*

trot [trɔt] *v.i. & t.* (*-tt-*). **1.** (of horses, etc.) go at a pace faster than a walk but not so fast as a gallop. **2.** (of a person) run with short steps. **3.** cause to ~. *n.* ~*ting pace* ; *period of* ~*ting* : *at a steady* ~ ; *go for a* ~.

troth [trouθ] *n.* (old use, only in) *plight one's* ~, promise to marry.

trou·ba·dour ['tru:bədɔːˀ] *n.* travelling poet and singer in France and Italy, in the 11th to 13th centuries.

trou·ble ['trʌbl] *v.t. & i.* **1.** cause worry, discomfort, anxiety or inconvenience to : ~*d by bad health* (*with a cough*). **2.** *May I trouble you* (*for sth., to do sth.*)? Will you please (give me . . ., do sth.)? **3.** give oneself worry or inconvenience : *Don't* ~ *to do that. Don't* ~ *about that.* *n.* **1.** (person or happening causing) worry, anxiety, discomfort, unhappiness, possible punishment. *be in* ~, *get into* ~, do, have done, sth. likely to bring ~. **2.** extra work ; effort ; difficulty : *It will be no* ~. *have* ~ *with one's lessons,* find them difficult. *take* ~ (*to do sth., with* or *over* sth.), take pains, use great care. **~·some** *adj.* causing ~ ; needing much care.

trough [trɔf] *n.* **1.** long, open box for animals to feed or drink from. **2.** hollow in the sea's surface between two waves.

trounce [trauns] *v.t.* beat ; thrash ; defeat.

troupe [tru:p] *n.* company, esp. of actors or members of a circus.

trou·sers ['trauzəz] *n. pl.* (often *a pair of* ~) outer garment for the legs, reaching from waist to ankles.

trous·seau ['tru:sou] *n.* outfit of clothing, etc., for a woman on marrying.

trout [traut] *n.* freshwater fish valued as food.

trow·el ['trauəl] *n.* **1.** flat-bladed tool for spreading mortar on bricks, plaster on walls, etc. **2.** hand-tool with a scoop for lifting plants, etc.

Trowels

troy [trɔi] *n.* British system of weights, used for gold and silver, in which 1 pound = 12 ounces.

tru·ant ['tru:ənt] *n.* child who stays away from school without good reason: *play* ~, *be a* ~.

truce [tru:s] *n.* (agreement for) the stopping of fighting for a time (e.g. to take away the wounded).

¹truck [trʌk] *n.* **1.** open railway wagon for heavy goods (e.g. coal). **2.** railway porter's barrow. **3.** lorry.

²truck [trʌk] *n.* barter; exchange. *have no* ~ *with*, have no dealings with; have nothing to do with.

truck·le ['trʌkl] *v.i.* ~ *to*, submit to in a servile or cowardly way.

truc·u·lent ['trʌkjulənt] *adj.* looking for, desiring, a fight; ready to make trouble. ~·**ly** *adv.* **truc·u·lence** *n.*

trudge [trʌdʒ] *v.i.* walk wearily or heavily: *trudging through deep snow.* *n.* long tiring walk.

true [tru:] *adj.* (-*r*, -*st*). **1.** in accordance or agreement with fact: *come* ~, (of a hope or dream) become fact, happen. **2.** loyal, faithful (*to* a friend, etc.). **3.** genuine; rightly so named. **4.** correct: *a* ~ *copy*. **tru·ism** ['tru:izəm] *n.* statement that is obviously ~ and need not have been made. **tru·ly** *adv.* **1.** sincerely. **2.** truthfully. **3.** certainly; genuinely: *a truly brave action.*

trump [trʌmp] *v.t.* ~ *up*, invent (an excuse, a false story, etc.) ʾo deceive sb.

trump·er·y ['trʌmpəri] *adj.* showy, but of little value: ~ *ornaments*.

trum·pet ['trʌmpit] *n.* **1.** musical wind-instrument of brass: *blow one's own* ~, praise oneself. **2.** sth. shaped like a ~. *v.i. & t.* play a ~ or (e.g. of an elephant) make a ~-sound. ~·**er** *n.*

trun·cate [trʌŋ'keit] *v.t.* shorten by cutting the top, tip, or end from.

trun·cheon ['trʌnʃən] *n.* short thick club (e.g. used by the police).

trun·dle ['trʌndl] *v.t. & i.* (of sth. heavy or awkward in shape) roll along: *tanks*(3) *trundling along.*

trunk [trʌŋk] *n.* **1.** main stem of a tree. **2.** body without head, arms, or legs. **3.** large box for holding clothes, etc., while travelling. **4.** long nose of an elephant. **5.** (attrib.) ~-*call*, telephone call to a distant place. ʾ~-*line*, main line of a railway; telephone cable for ~-calls.

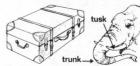

A cabin   An elephant's trunk
trunk   and tusks

truss [trʌs] *n.* **1.** bundle (of hay or straw). **2.** framework supporting a roof, bridge, etc. *v.t.* bind or fasten: ~ (*up*) *a chicken*, pin the wings to the body before roasting it.

trust [trʌst] *n.* **1.** confidence, strong belief, in the goodness, strength, reliability, of sth. or sb.: *on* ~, without proof; on credit. **2.** person or thing confided in. **3.** responsibility: *a position of great* ~. **4.** (law) property held and managed by one or more persons (~*ees*) for another's benefit; the legal relation (*in* ~) between the ~ee(s) and the property; such property. **5.** association of business firms to achieve some special object. *v.t. & i.* **1.** have

~ (1) in : ~ *in God*. **2.** give into the care of : *T~ your business affairs to me*. *T~ me with your affairs*. **3.** allow credit to a customer, etc. **4.** hope : *I ~ you will be able to help us*. **5.** allow (sb.) to have sth., to do sth., without a feeling of doubt or anxiety. **trus·tee** [trʌs'tiː] *n.* person who has charge of property in ~ (4) or of the business affairs of an institution. **trus·tee·ship** *n.* position of ~ee ; (esp.) responsibility for a territory, granted by the United Nations. **~·ful** *adj.* ready to ~ others ; not suspicious. **~·ing** *adj.* having or showing ~ (1). '~·', **wor·thy** *adj.* deserving ~ (1) ; dependable. **~·y** *adj.* (old use ; liter.) ~-worthy.

truth [truːθ, pl. truːðz] *n.* **1.** quality or state of being true. **2.** that which is true. **3.** fact ; belief, etc., accepted as true : *the ~s of religion*. **~·ful** *adj.* **1.** (of persons) in the habit of telling the ~. **2.** (of statements) true.

try [trai] *v.i. & t.* (p.t. & p.p. *tried* [traid]). **1.** make an attempt. **2.** *try for*, make an attempt to get (esp. a position). **3.** use sth., do sth., as an experiment or test, to see whether it is satisfactory : *Have you tried quinine? try sth. on*, put on (a garment, a shoe, etc.) to see whether it fits, looks well, etc. *try one's hand at sth.*, make a first attempt at it. *try sth. out*, use or experiment in order to test. **4.** inquire into (a case) in a law court : *He was tried and found guilty of theft*. **5.** cause annoyance or suffering (to) ; afflict ; strain : *try sb.'s patience (courage)*. *Small print tries the eyes*. *n.* attempt : *Let me have a try*. **try·ing** *adj.* causing trouble or annoyance ; difficult to endure.

tryst [trist] *n.* (old use) (time and place for, agreement to have, a) meeting, esp. between lovers.

tset·se ['tsetsi] *n.* (in tropical Africa) fly whose bite causes (often fatal) disease in cattle, horses, etc.

tub [tʌb] *n.* **1.** large open vessel, usu. round and made of wood. **2.** (colloq.) bath : *have a cold tub*. **tub·by** *adj.* (-ier, -iest). short, fat, and round.

tube [tjuːb] *n.* **1.** pipe, e.g. of glass or rubber. **2.** soft metal container with a screw-cap, used for tooth-paste, etc. **3.** underground railway (e.g. in London). **4.** (U.S.A.) valve for use in radio, etc. **tub·ing** *n.* length of ~ : *two yards of rubber tubing*. **tu·bu·lar** ['tjuːbjulə*] *adj.* ~-shaped ; having ~s : *a tubular boiler*.

tu·ber ['tjuːbə*] *n.* thick, swollen part, formed on a stem underground, from which new plants will grow. See *potato*.

tu·ber·cu·lo·sis [tjuːˌbəːkjuˈlousis] *n.* wasting disease affecting various parts of the body's tissues, esp. the lungs. **tu·ber·cu·lar** [tjuˈbəːkjulə*], **tu·ber·cu·lous** *adj.* of, affected by, ~.

tuck [tʌk] *n.* **1.** flat, stitched fold of material in a garment, for shortening or for ornament. **2.** (slang) food, esp. cakes and sweets. *v.t. & i.* **1.** roll, fold, or push (e.g. part of one's clothing) into a more convenient or secure position. **2.** ~ *sb.* (oneself) *up* (*in*), cover warmly by pulling bed-clothes over, round, etc. **3.** (colloq.) ~ *in*, eat heartily. '**~-shop** *n.* shop (for school-children) selling sweets, pastries.

Tues·day ['tjuːzdi] *n.* the third day of the week.

tuft [tʌft] *n.* bunch of hairs, bristles, grass, feathers, etc., growing closely or held firmly together at one end.

tug [tʌg] *v.i. & t.* (-gg-). pull hard or violently ; pull (*at* sth.). *n.* **1.** sudden or violent pull. **2.** small powerful boat for towing ships, etc. **tug of war** *n.* competition in which two teams pull against each other on a rope.

tu·i·tion [tjuˈiʃən] *n.* (fee for) teaching.

tu·lip ['tjuːlip] *n.* bulb plant having, in spring, a large up-turned bell-shaped flower.

tum·ble ['tʌmbl] *v.i. & t.* **1.** fall, esp. quickly or violently :

~ *down the stairs*; ~ *off a bicycle*. **2.** cause to fall: *The earthquake ~d us out of bed.* **n.** fall. **'~down** *adj.* (of buildings) unsafe; likely to collapse.

tum·bler ['tʌmblə*] *n.* drinking-glass with no stem; acrobat.

tum·brel, tum·bril ['tʌmbril] *n.* cart, esp. of the kind that carried prisoners to the guillotine during the French Revolution.

tum·my ['tʌmi] *n.* colloq. name for stomach.

tu·mour ['tjuːmə*] *n.* diseased growth in some part of the body.

tu·mult ['tjuːmʌlt] *n.* **1.** uproar; disturbance. **2.** mental excitement: *He(His mind)was in a ~.* **tu·mul·tu·ous** [tjuːˈmʌltjuəs] *adj.* disorderly; noisy and violent.

tun·dra ['tʌndrə] *n.* treeless plain, often marshy land, in the arctic regions; partially frozen desert.

tune [tjuːn] *n.* **1.** succession of notes forming a melody (of a song, hymn, etc.). **2.** correct pitch; agreement or harmony: *sing (play) in ~,* so that the notes are correctly pitched. **3.** (fig.) harmony: *out of ~ with one's companions (surroundings),* not happy with them. *v.t. & i.* **1.** adjust strings, etc., of a musical instrument to the right pitch. **2.** ~ *up,* (of an orchestra) put the instruments in ~. **3.** ~ *in,* adjust a radio receiver so as to get the programme from the station required. **~ful** *adj.* having a pleasing ~.

tu·nic ['tjuːnik] *n.* close-fitting, military-style jacket.

tun·nel ['tʌnl] *v.i.* (-*ll*-) *& n.* (make an) underground passage, esp. through a hill, etc., for a road, railway, canal, etc.

tup·pence ['tʌpəns] *n.* twopence.

tur·ban ['təːbən] *n.* man's head-dress made by winding a length of cloth round the head.

tur·bid ['təːbid] *adj.* (of liquids) thick; muddy; not clear.

tur·bine ['təːbain] *n.* engine or motor whose driving-wheel is turned by a strong current of water, steam, or air.

tur·bot ['təːbət] *n.* large, flat sea fish valued as food.

tur·bu·lent ['təːbjulənt] *adj.* violent; disorderly; uncontrolled: ~ *waves (passions, mobs).* **tur·bu·lence** *n.*

tu·reen [tjuˈriːn] *n.* deep dish with a lid, from which soup, vegetables, etc., are served at table.

turf [təːf] *n.* **1.** soil-surface with grass roots growing in it; piece of this cut out (pl. *turves*). **2.** *the* ~, horse-racing. *v.t.* cover with ~.

tur·gid ['təːdʒid] *adj.* **1.** swollen (e.g. by disease). **2.** (of language) pompous; full of high-sounding words.

tur·key ['təːki] *n.* large bird used as food.

tur·moil ['təːmoil] *n.* noise; confusion.

turn [təːn] *v.t. & i.* **1.** (cause to) move round a point; (cause to) move so as to face in a different direction. **2.** (with *adv. & prep.*): ~ *about,* ~ so as to face in the opposite direction. ~ *down,* reduce (the flame of a lamp, etc.) by ~ing a tap, etc.; reject (an offer, the person making it). ~ *in,* (colloq.) go to bed. ~ *off (on),* stop (start) the flow of (water, electric current, etc.) by ~ing a tap, switch, etc. ~ *out,* stop the flow of (gas) by ~ing a tap; expel; put out by force; produce (goods); empty (drawers, one's pockets, a room, etc., e.g. when searching for sth. or when cleaning); (cause to) go or come out for some purpose; prove to be, be in the end: *The day ~ed out wet.* ~ *over,* give the control of (a business, etc. *to* sb.) ~ *to,* go to (*sb.* or *sth.,* esp. for help, comfort); begin work. ~ *up,* (of persons) arrive; (of objects) be found, esp. by chance; (of a chance, etc.) appear. **3.** (cause to) change in nature, quality, etc.: *Frost ~s water into ice. The milk has ~ed* (become sour). *His hair is ~ing grey.* **4.** shape (sth.) while it is ~ing on a lathe. **5.** remake a garment (e.g. a coat) so that the

inner surface is the outer surface.
6. reach and pass : *He has not ~ed
forty yet. It has just ~ed two
o'clock.* **7.** (with nouns): ~ *sb.'s
brain*, make him mad ; ~ *the
corner*, (fig.) pass a crisis successfully ; ~ *sb.'s head*, make him
too vain ; ~ *one's hand to*, be
able to do ; ~ *one's stomach*,
make one (want to) vomit. ***n.***
1. ~ing movement. **2.** change
of direction : ~*s in the road.*
3. change in condition : *Affairs
took a ~ for the better*, became
better. **4.** occasion or opportunity for doing sth., esp.
in one's proper order among
others : *wait*(*until it is*) *one's ~* ;
in ~ ; ~ *and ~ about*, (of two
persons) first one and then the
other ; *out of ~*, before or after
the right or regular time ; *take* ~*s
at* (*sth.*), do it in ~. **5.** short
period of activity : *take a ~ at
the oars* ; *go for a ~* (a walk) *in
the park.* **6.** performance (e.g.
a song or dance) by one person
or a group of persons, forming
part of an entertainment. **7.** (*do
sb.*) *a good* (*bad*) ~, a kind (unkind) act. **8.** natural tendency :
a boy with a mechanical ~, interested in, clever at, mechanical things. **9.** *serve one's* ~, be
satisfactory for one's purpose.
done to a ~, cooked enough but
not too much. '~·**coat** *n.* person who changes his opinions
or the party he supports. ~·**er**
n. person who works a lathe.
~·**ing** *n.* place where a road ~s,
esp. where one road branches off
from another ; such a branch
road. '~·**ing·point** *n.* place or
point at which sb. or sth. ~s (1) ;
(fig.) a crisis. '~·**out** *n.* attendance of people at a meeting,
etc. ; general appearance of a
person's equipment ; act of
emptying sth. (e.g. a room) out ;
that which is moved out in this
way. '~·,**o·ver** *n.* amount of
business done (usu. within a
named period of time). '~·**stile**
n. revolving gate that admits
only one person at a time.
tur·nip ['tə:nip] *n.* (plant with)
large round root used as a

vegetable and as food for
cattle.
tur·pen·tine ['tə:pəntain] *n.* oil
obtained from certain trees, used
for mixing paint and var-
nish.
tur·pi·tude ['tə:pitju:d] *n.* wickedness.
tur·quoise ['tə:kwoiz] *n.* (colour
of) greenish-blue precious stone.
tur·ret ['tʌrit] *n.* **1.** small tower,
usu. at the corner of a building.
2. steel structure protecting
gunners, often made so as to
revolve with the gun(s).
tur·tle ['tə:tl] *n.* sea-animal with
a soft body protected by a hard
shell like that of a tortoise. *turn
~*, (of a ship) turn upside down ;
capsize.
turves, see *turf.*
tusk [tʌsk] *n.* long pointed tooth.
esp. one coming out from the
mouth as in the elephant or
walrus. (See the pictures at
trunk and *walrus.*)
tus·sle ['tʌsl] *v.i. & n.* (have a)
hard fight or struggle (*with*).
tu·tor ['tju:tə*] *n.* **1.** private
teacher. **2.** university teacher
who guides the studies of a
number of students. *v.t. & i.*
act as ~ to (sb.). **tu·to·ri·al** [tju-
'to:riəl] *adj.* of a ~ or his duties :
~*ial classes.*
twad·dle ['twodl] *n.* foolish
talk.
twain [twein] *n.* (old use)
two.
twang [twæŋ] *n.* sound of a tight
string or wire being plucked.
v.t. & i. (cause sth. to) make this
sound.
tweak [twi:k] *v.t. & n.* pinch
and twist.
tweed [twi:d] *n.* thick soft woollen cloth, usu. woven of mixed
colours.
twee·zers [' twi:zəz] *n. pl.* small
pair of pincers for picking up or
pulling out very small things.
twelve [twelv] *n. & adj.* 12.
twelfth [twelfθ] *n. & adj.* next
in order after eleventh ; $\frac{1}{12}$.
twen·ty ['twenti] *n. & adj.* 20.
twen·ti·eth ['twentiiθ] *n. & adj.*
next in order after nineteenth ;
$\frac{1}{20}$.

twice [twais] *adv.* two times.

twid·dle ['twidl] *v.t. & i.* twist or turn idly or aimlessly: ~ *one's thumbs.*

twig [twig] *n.* small woody shoot on a branch (of a tree or bush).

twi·light ['twailait] *n.* faint half-light before sunrise or after sunset.

twin [twin] *n.* **1.** either of two children born together of the same mother; (attrib.) ~ *brothers.* **2.** (usu. attrib.) (thing) completely like and associated with another: *a steamer with ~ screws* (two identical propellers).

twine [twain] *n.* thin string. *v.t. & i.* twist; wind: ~ *flowers into a wreath.*

twinge [twindʒ] *n.* sudden, sharp pain: *a ~ of toothache (conscience).*

twin·kle ['twiŋkl] *v.i.* shine with a light that gleams unsteadily: *stars twinkling in the sky; eyes twinkling with fun.* *n.* twinkling light. **twink·ling** *n. in a twinkling,* in an instant.

twirl [twə:l] *v.t. & i.* (cause to) rotate quickly.

twist [twist] *v.t. & i.* **1.** wind or turn (a number of strands, etc.) one around another. **2.** turn the two ends of sth. in opposite directions; turn one end of sth.: ~ *the cap off a fountain-pen.* **3.** force (sb.'s words, etc.) out of their true meaning. **4.** (e.g. of a road) turn and curve in different directions. *n.* ~ing or being ~ed; ~ed place; sth. made by ~ing. ~**·er** *n.* dishonest person.

twit [twit] *v.t.* (-tt-). tease (sb. *with* having made a mistake, etc.).

twitch [twitʃ] *n.* **1.** sudden, quick, usu. uncontrollable movement of a muscle. **2.** sudden, quick pull. *v.t. & i.* **1.** make a ~ (1): *His nose ~ed as he passed the kitchen door.* **2.** jerk: *The wind ~ed the paper out of her hand.*

twit·ter ['twitə*] *v.i.* (of birds) chirp; make a succession of soft,

short sounds. *n.* such sounds. *in a ~,* in a nervous or excited state.

two [tu:] *n. & adj.* **2. two·pence** ['tʌpəns] *n.* the sum or value of two pennies (2p, formerly 2d.) **two·pen·ny** ['tʌpni] *adj.* costing 2p.

type [taip] *n.* **1.** person, thing, event, etc., considered as an example of its class or group. **2.** class or group considered to have common characteristics: *men of this ~.* **3.** letters, etc., cast in a block of metal, for use in printing; any form of these: *in large ~; italic ~.* *v.i. & t.* write with a ~writer: ~ *a letter. She ~s well.* '~**·₁set·ter** *n.* worker or machine that sets ~ for printing. '~**·write** *v.t. & i.* (usu. *type*) use a ~writer: *a ~written letter.* '~**·₁writ·er** *n.* machine with which one prints letters on paper, using the fingers on a keyboard. **typ·i·cal** ['tipikl] *adj.* serving as a ~; representative or characteristic. **typ·i·cal·ly** *adv.* **typ·i·fy** ['tipifai] *v.t.* be a symbol of; be representative of. **ty·pist** ['taipist] *n.* person who types, esp. in order to earn a living. **ty·pog·ra·phy** [tai'pogrəfi] *n.* art or style of printing. **ty·phoid** ['taifoid] *n.* (often ~ *fever*) serious disease which attacks the intestines. **ty·phus** ['taifəs] *n.* disease causing red spots on the body and great weakness.

ty·phoon [tai'fu:n] *n.* violent windstorm, esp. in the China seas.

ty·rant ['taiərənt] *n.* cruel or unjust ruler, esp. one who has obtained complete power by force. **ty·ran·ni·cal** [ti'rænikl], **ty·ran·nous** ['tirənəs] *adj.* acting like a ~; of a ~. **ty·ran·nize** ['tirənaiz] *v.i.* (often *tyrannize over*) make a cruel and wrong use of authority. **ty·ran·ny** ['tirəni] *n.* cruel and unjust use of power; government by a ~.

tyre ['taiə*] *n.* (also *tire*) band of metal or rubber round the rim of a wheel.

ty·ro ['taiərou] *n.* = tiro.

U

u·biq·ui·tous [ju'bikwitəs] *adj.* present everywhere or in several places at the same time. **u·biq·uity** *n.* quality of being ~.

U-boat ['ju:bout] *n.* German submarine.

ud·der ['ʌdə*] *n.* part of a cow, goat, etc., from which milk comes.

ug·ly ['ʌgli] *adj.* (-ier, -iest). **1.** unpleasant to look at; hideous. **2.** threatening: *The sky looks* ~ (i.e. suggests bad weather). *an* ~ *customer*, a dangerous person.

u·ku·le·le [ju:kə'leili] *n.* kind of four-stringed musical instrument.

ul·cer ['ʌlsə*] *n.* open sore in which there is pus.

ul·te·ri·or [ʌl'tiəriə*] *adj.* situated beyond; beyond what is at first seen or said: ~ *motives*, motives other than those expressed.

ul·ti·mate ['ʌltimit] *adj.* last; furthest; basic: ~ *principles* (*truths, etc.*). ~*ly adv.* finally.

ul·ti·ma·tum [ˌʌlti'meitəm] *n.* final statement of conditions to be accepted without discussion, esp. one that threatens war if the conditions are not accepted.

ul·tra- ['ʌltrə-] *prefix.* beyond what is reasonable, natural, or usual; excessively: ~*-critical*, ~*-modern*.

ul·tra·ma·rine [ˌʌltrəmə'ri:n] *adj. & n.* brilliant pure blue (colour).

um·brage ['ʌmbridʒ] *n.* feeling that one has been treated unfairly or without proper respect: *take* ~ (*at*).

um·brel·la [ʌm'brelə] *n.* folding frame (with stick and handle), covered with silk, cotton, etc., cloth, used to shelter the person holding it from rain or sun.

um·pire ['ʌmpaiə*] *n.* person chosen or asked to act as judge in a dispute, or to see that the rules of a game (e.g. cricket) are followed by the players. (Cf. *referee* for football.) *v.t. & i.* act as ~ (in).

un- [ʌn-] *prefix.* **1.** (before adj., adv.) not: *uncertain(ly)*. **2.** (before v.) do the opposite of, reverse the action of, what is indicated by the verb: *undress*; *unscrew*; *untie*. **3.** (before nouns) indicating absence of: *uncertainty*, *unwillingness*.

un·a·bat·ed [ˌʌnə'beitid] *adj.* (of a storm, etc.) (continuing) as strong, violent, etc., as before.

un·ac·count·a·ble [ˌʌnə'kauntəbl] *adj.* strange; for which no explanation can be found.

u·nan·i·mous [ju'næniməs] *adj.* **1.** in complete agreement: *a* ~ *vote*. **2.** all holding the same opinion: *We are* ~ *in our support of the policy*. ~*ly adv.* **u·na·nim·i·ty** [ˌju:nə'nimiti] *n.* complete agreement or unity.

un·as·sum·ing [ˌʌnə'sju:miŋ] *adj.* not pushing oneself forward; not drawing attention to oneself; modest.

un·a·wares [ˌʌnə'wɛəz] *adv.* by surprise; unexpectedly; without being aware.

un·bal·anced [ʌn'bælənst] *adj.* (esp.) (of a person, his mind) not quite sane.

un·bend [ʌn'bend] *v.t. & i.* (esp.) relax; become less stiff or formal in behaviour.

un·bos·om [ʌn'buzəm] *v.t.* ~ *oneself*, confide one's troubles, etc. (*to* sb.).

un·bri·dled [ʌn'braidld] *adj.* (esp.) uncontrolled; violent (rage, etc.).

un·bur·den [ʌn'bə:dn] *v.t.* (esp.) ~ *oneself*, get relief by confessing sth., telling one's troubles (*to* sb.).

un·called-for [ʌn'kɔ:ldfɔ:*] *adj.* neither desirable nor necessary.

un·can·ny [ʌn'kæni] *adj.* unnatural; mysterious.

un·cle ['ʌŋkl] *n.* brother of one's father or mother; husband of one's aunt.

un·con·scion·a·ble [ʌn'kɔnʃənəbl] *adj.* unreasonable: *for an* ~ *time*.

un·couth [ʌn'ku:θ] *adj.* (of persons, their behaviour) rough, awkward, clumsy, uncultured.

unc·tion [ˈʌŋkʃən] *n.* **1.** act of anointing with oil, esp. as a religious rite. **2.** pretended (insincere) earnestness in speaking, in tone of voice. **unc·tu·ous** [ˈʌŋktjuəs] *adj.* insincere in speech or manner.

un·der [ˈʌndə*] *prep.* in or to a position lower than; in and covered by; less than: ~ *age*, not yet 21; under the legal age for sth. ~ *discussion* (*repair, etc.*), being discussed, etc. ~ *protest*, unwillingly, after protesting. ~ *fire*, (being) fired at. ~ *orders*, having received orders, been ordered (*to do* sth. etc.). *marching* ~ (weighed down by) *a heavy load of equipment. adv.* in or to a lower place: *The ship went* ~ (i.e. sank).

un·der- [ˈʌndə*] *prefix.* **1.** (before nouns) worn or placed under: ~*clothes;* ~*carriage* (aircraft's landing gear). **2.** (before verbs) not sufficiently; not so much as is necessary: ~*charge;* ~*stamp;* ~*value.*

un·der·cur·rent [ˈʌndəkʌrənt] *n.* current flowing below the surface; (fig.) tendency (of thought or feeling) lying below what is first seen: *an* ~ *of opposition* (*melancholy*).

un·der·cut [ˌʌndəˈkʌt] *v.t.* offer (goods, services) at a lower price than competitors.

un·der·dog [ˈʌndədɔg] *n.* poor and helpless person usually oppressed by others.

un·der·done [ˌʌndəˈdʌn] *adj.* (esp. of meat) not completely cooked throughout.

un·der·go [ˌʌndəˈgou] *v.t.* **1.** experience (hardship, trials, suffering). **2.** go through (a process).

un·der·grad·u·ate [ˌʌndəˈgrædjuit] *n.* university student working for a bachelor's degree.

un·der·ground [ˈʌndəgraund] *adj. & adv.* below the ground. *n. the U*~, railway built below the surface.

un·der·growth [ˈʌndəgrouθ] *n.* shrubs, bushes, low trees, growing under taller trees.

un·der·hand [ˈʌndəhænd] *adj. & adv.* **1.** (bowling in cricket)

with the hand kept below the shoulder. **2.** deceitful(ly); sly(ly).

un·der·lie [ˌʌndəˈlai] *v.t.* (esp.) be the foundation of (a theory, etc.).

un·der·line [ˌʌndəˈlain] *v.t.* draw a line under (a word, etc.); (fig.. emphasize.

un·der·ling [ˈʌndəliŋ] *n.* (usu contemptuous) person in an unimportant position under another.

un·der·mine [ˌʌndəˈmain] *v.t.* **1.** make a hollow or tunnel under; weaken at the base: *cliffs* ~*d by the sea.* **2.** weaken gradually: ~ *sb.'s authority; health* ~*d by overwork.*

un·der·neath [ˌʌndəˈniːθ] *adv. & prep.* under; below.

un·der·pin [ˌʌndəˈpin] *v.t.* (-*nn-*). put timber, stones, etc., under (a wall) to support (it).

un·der·sell [ˌʌndəˈsel] *v.t.* sell (goods) at a lower price than (competitors).

un·der·signed [ˈʌndəsaind] *adj. the* ~, the person(s) signing below.

un·der·stand [ˌʌndəˈstænd] *v.t. & i.* (p.t. & p.p. -*stood* [-ˈstud]). **1.** know the meaning, nature, explanation, of (sth.): *make oneself understood,* make one's meaning clear. **2.** learn (from information received): *I* ~ (*that*) *you are now married.* **3.** supply (a word or words) mentally. ~·**a·ble** *adj.* that can be understood. ~·**ing** *adj.* (good at) ~ing or realizing other persons' feelings, points of view, etc. *n.* **1.** power of clear thought. **2.** capacity for sympathizing, seeing from another person's point of view, etc. **3.** agreement; realization of another's views or feelings towards oneself: *reach* (*come to*) *an* ~*ing with sb.* **4.** condition: *on this* ~*ing; on the* ~*ing that.*

un·der·stud·y [ˈʌndəˌstʌdi] *n.* person learning to, able to, take the place of another (esp. an actor). *v.t.* act as ~ for; rehearse a part so as to ~ for (sb.).

un·der·take [ˌʌndəˈteik] *v.t.* (p.t. -*took*, p.p. -*taken*). **1.** make oneself responsible for: ~ *a task*; ~ *to do sth.* **2.** start (a piece of work). **3.** affirm; promise (*that, to do* sth.). **un·der·tak·ing** *n.* **1.** work that one has undertaken (1) to do. **2.** promise.

un·der·tak·er ['ʌndə,teikə*] *n.* person whose business is to prepare the dead for burial or cremation and manage funerals.

un·der·tone ['ʌndətoun] *n.* low, quiet note, esp. *talk in* ~s, with subdued voices.

un·der·tow ['ʌndətou] *n.* current caused by the backward flow of a wave after breaking on the beach.

un·der·wear ['ʌndəwɛə*] *n.* underclothing.

un·der·world ['ʌndəwə:ld] *n.* **1.** (in Greek, etc., stories) the place of departed spirits of the dead. **2.** part of society that lives by vice and crime.

un·der·write [,ʌndə'rait] *v.t.* (p.t. -*wrote*[-rout], p.p.-*written*[-ritn]). undertake (3) to bear all or part of possible loss (by signing an agreement about insurance, esp. of ships). **un·der·writ·er** ['ʌndə,raitə*] *n.*

un·dies ['ʌndiz] *n. pl.* (colloq.) underclothes.

un·do [ʌn'du:] *v.t.* (p.t. -*did*, p.p. -*done*[-'dʌn]). **1.** untie, unfasten (knots, buttons, etc.). **2.** destroy the result of; bring back the state of affairs that existed before: *He has undone all the good work of his predecessor.* **3.** *be undone*, be brought to ruin or disaster. ~**ing** *n.* (cause of) ruin: *Drink was his ~ing.*

un·due ['ʌn'dju:] *adj.* improper; more than is right: *with* ~ *haste.* **un·du·ly** *adv.*

un·du·late ['ʌndjuleit] *v.i.* (of surfaces) have a wavy motion or look: *a field of wheat undulating in the breeze.*

un·earth [ʌn'ə:θ] *v.t.* discover and bring to light; uncover (e.g. by digging): ~ *a buried treasure*; ~ *new facts about the life of Nelson.*

un·earth·ly [ʌn'ə:θli] *adj.* **1.** supernatural. **2.** mysterious; ghostly; frightening: ~ *screams.*

un·eas·y [ʌn'i:zi] *adj.* uncomfortable in body or mind; troubled or anxious. **un·eas·i·ly** *adv.*

un·er·ring [ʌn'ə:riŋ] *adj.* accurate: *with* ~ *aim.*

un·ex·am·pled [,ʌnig'za:mpld] *adj.* of which there is no other example that can be compared with it: *the* ~ *heroism of our soldiers.*

un·fail·ing [ʌn'feiliŋ] *adj.* **1.** never coming to an end. **2.** always to be depended upon; loyal: *an* ~ *friend.*

un·fold [ʌn'fould] *v.t.* (esp. fig.) reveal, make known (one's intentions, etc.).

un·found·ed [ʌn'faundid] *adj.* without foundation: ~ (i.e. false) *rumours.*

un·frock [ʌn'frɔk] *v.t.* dismiss from the priesthood (for bad conduct).

un·gain·ly [ʌn'geinli] *adj.* clumsy; awkward; ungraceful.

un·gov·ern·a·ble [ʌn'gʌvənəbl] *adj.* that cannot be kept under control: *an* ~ *temper.*

un·guard·ed [ʌn'ga:did] *adj.* (esp. of a statement) careless; allowing sth. secret to become known.

un·heard-of [ʌn'hə:dɔv] *adj.* extraordinary; without earlier example.

un·hinged [ʌn'hindʒd] *adj.* (of a person, his mind) unbalanced.

u·ni·corn ['ju:nikɔ:n] *n.* (in old stories) horse-like animal with one long horn in the middle of its forehead.

u·ni·form ['ju:nifɔ:m] *adj.* the same; never varying: *of* ~ *length*; *to be kept at a* ~ *temperature.* *n.* style of dress worn by all members of an organization, etc. (e.g. the armed forces, the police). ~**ly** *adv.* ~**i·ty** [,ju:ni'fɔ:miti] *n.* ~ *condition.*

u·ni·fy ['ju:nifai] *v.t.* **1.** form into one; unite. **2.** make uniform. **u·ni·fi·ca·tion** [,ju:nifi'keiʃən] *n.* ~**ing**: *The unification of Europe is vital to peace.*

un·im·peach·a·ble ['ʌnim'pi:tʃəbl] *adj.* that cannot be questioned or doubted: ~ *honesty.*

u·nion ['ju:njən] *n.* **1.** uniting

or being united; joining or being joined (e.g. of two or three towns into one, of two persons in marriage). **2.** agreement or harmony: *in perfect ~.* **3.** group, association, etc., formed by the uniting of persons, smaller groups, etc.: *a trade ~; the Soviet U~; the U~ Jack* (the British flag). **4.** (old use) workhouse. **~ist** *n.* member of a trade ~.

u·nique [ju:'ni:k] *adj.* having no like or equal; being the only one of its sort. **~·ly** *adv.* **~·ness** *n.*

u·ni·son ['ju:nizən] *n.* concord or agreement: *acting in ~; sing in ~,* all singing the same notes, not harmonizing.

u·nit ['ju:nit] *n.* **1.** single person or thing or group regarded as complete in itself: *The family is often taken as the ~ of society.* **2.** quantity or amount used as a standard of measurement: *The metre is a ~ of length.* **3.** (maths.) the number, 1.

u·nite [ju'nait] *v.t. & i.* **1.** make or become one; join together. **2.** act or work together: *Let us ~ in fighting disease and poverty!* **u·nit·ed** *adj. the United Kingdom,* Great Britain and Northern Ireland; *a ~d effort.* **u·ni·ty** ['ju:niti] *n.* **1.** the state of being ~d; (an) arrangement of parts to form a complete whole. **2.** harmony, agreement (of aims, feelings, etc.).

u·ni·verse ['ju:nivə:s] *n. the ~,* everything that exists everywhere; all the stars, planets, etc. **u·ni·ver·sal** [,ju:ni'və:sl] *adj.* of or for all; used by, done by, affecting, all: *a universal rule,* one with no exceptions; *the universal misery caused by world wars.* **u·ni·ver·sal·ly** *adv.*

u·ni·ver·si·ty [,ju:ni'və:siti] *n.* institution giving more advanced education than is given in schools, awarding degrees, and engaging in research.

un·kempt [ʌn'kempt] *adj.* untidy; (esp. of the hair) uncombed.

un·less [ʌn'les] *conj.* if not; except when.

un·let·tered [ʌn'letəd] *adj.* uneducated; unable to read.

un·looked-for [ʌn'luktfɔ:*] *adj.* unexpected.

un·man [ʌn'mæn] *v.t.* (*-nn-*) weaken the courage and self-control of.

un·matched [ʌn'mætʃt] *adj.* without an equal.

un·mean·ing [ʌn'mi:niŋ] *adj.* without meaning or purpose.

un·men·tion·a·ble [ʌn'menʃən-əbl] *adj.* so bad, etc., that it cannot even be spoken of.

un·mis·tak·a·ble [,ʌnmis'teik-əbl] *adj.* clear; about which no mistake is possible.

un·mit·i·gat·ed [ʌn'mitigeitid] *adj.* complete; absolute: *an ~ scoundrel.*

un·nerve [ʌn'nə:v] *v.t.* cause to lose self-control, power of decision, or courage.

un·par·lia·men·ta·ry [,ʌnpɑ:lə-'mentəri] *adj.* (of language, conduct) not suitable (e.g. because abusive, disorderly) for parliament.

un·pleas·ant·ness [ʌn'plezənt-nis] *n.* quarrel; bad feeling (between persons).

un·prec·e·dent·ed [ʌn'presiden-tid] *adj.* without precedent.

un·pre·tend·ing [,ʌnpri'tend-iŋ], **un·pre·ten·tious** [,ʌnpri-'tenʃəs] *adj.* modest; not trying to seem important.

un·prin·ci·pled [ʌn'prinsipəld] *adj.* without moral principles; dishonest.

un·pro·fes·sion·al [,ʌnprə'feʃənl] *adj.* (esp. of conduct) contrary to the rules or customs of a profession.

un·rav·el [ʌn'rævl] *v.t. & i.* (*-ll-*). **1.** separate the threads of; pull or become separate: *The cuff of my sleeve has ~led.* **2.** make clear, solve (a mystery, etc.).

un·re·mit·ting [,ʌnri'mitiŋ] *adj.* unceasing: *~ care.*

un·re·quit·ed [,ʌnri'kwaitid] *adj.* (of love, etc.) not returned or rewarded.

un·rest [ʌn'rest] *n.* (esp.) disturbed condition(s): *social ~* (e.g. caused by unemployment).

un·ru·ly [ʌnˈruːli] *adj.* not easily controlled; disorderly.

un·sa·vour·y [ʌnˈseivəri] *adj.* (esp. of scandal, a story) nasty; disgusting.

un·scathed [ʌnˈskeiðd] *adj.* unharmed; unhurt.

un·scru·pu·lous [ʌnˈskruːpjuləs] *adj.* not guided by conscience; not held back by scruples from doing wrong.

un·seat [ʌnˈsiːt] *v.t.* **1.** remove from office: *Mr X was ~ed at the General Election*, lost his seat in Parliament. **2.** *be ~ed*, be thrown from a horse.

un·seen [ʌnˈsiːn] *n.* passage to be translated, without preparation, from a foreign language into one's own.

un·set·tle [ʌnˈsetl] *v.t.* make troubled, anxious or uncertain. *~d weather*, uncertain, changeable weather.

un·sight·ly [ʌnˈsaitli] *adj.* displeasing to the eye: *~ advertisements in the countryside.*

un·sound [ʌnˈsaund] *adj.* (esp.) *of ~ mind*, unbalanced in mind.

un·speak·a·ble [ʌnˈspiːkəbl] *adj.* that cannot be described in words: *~ joy (wickedness).*

un·strung [ʌnˈstrʌn] *adj.* (esp.) with little or no control over the nerves, mind, or feelings.

un·stud·ied [ʌnˈstʌdid] *adj.* (of behaviour) natural; not aimed at impressing other persons.

un·think·a·ble [ʌnˈθiŋkəbl] *adj.* such as one cannot have any real idea of, belief in; not to be considered.

un·think·ing [ʌnˈθiŋkiŋ] *adj.* thoughtless; done without thought of the effect.

un·til [ʌnˈtil] *prep. & conj.* up to (the time when): *Wait ~ to-morrow. Wait ~ his return. Go straight on ~ you come to the post office and then turn left.*

un·time·ly [ʌnˈtaimli] *adj.* coming at a wrong or unsuitable time or too soon: *~ remarks.*

un·to [ˈʌntu] *prep.* (old use) to.

un·told [ˈʌnˈtould] *adj.* (esp.) too much or too many to be measured, counted, etc.: *a man of ~ wealth.*

un·to·ward [ʌnˈtouəd] *adj.* unfavourable; unfortunate.

un·ut·ter·a·ble [ʌnˈʌtərəbl] *adj.* that cannot be expressed in words: *~ joy.*

un·var·nished [ʌnˈvɑːniʃt] *adj.* (esp.) *the ~ truth*, plain and straightforward.

un·wield·y [ʌnˈwiːldi] *adj.* awkward to move or control because of size, shape, or weight.

un·wit·ting [ʌnˈwitiŋ] *adj.* unknowing; unaware; unintentional.

up [ʌp] *adv. & prep., adv. particle.* **1.** e.g. *stand up, blow up*, see under the verbs; to or in an erect or vertical position: *John's already up* (i.e. out of bed). **2.** to or in a high(er) or (more) important place, degree, etc.: *Pull your socks up. Are you going up to London* (i.e. from the country) *soon? go up and down*, backwards and forwards, higher and lower. **3.** *up to*, occupied or busy with: *What's he up to? He's up to no good*, doing sth. wrong, etc. **4.** *up to much*, not very good. *I don't feel up to doing much*, don't feel well enough to do much. **5.** *What's up?* (slang) What's the matter? *The game's up, it's all up, We're beaten*, we've lost. *n. ups and downs*, (fig.) changes of fortune.

up- [ʌp-] *prefix.* in an upward direction: *an 'upturned nose; the 'up-stroke; with 'upraised hands.*

up·braid [ʌpˈbreid] *v.t.* scold.

up·bring·ing [ˈʌpbriŋiŋ] *n.* training and education during childhood.

up·heav·al [ʌpˈhiːvl] *n.* great and sudden change (fig., in conditions).

up·hill [ˈʌphil] *adj.* difficult; needing effort: *an ~ task.* *adv.* (often [ʌpˈhil]) up a slope: *to walk ~.*

up·hold [ʌpˈhould] *v.t.* (p.t. & p.p. *upheld*). support (a decision).

up·hol·ster [ʌpˈhoulstə*] *v.t.* provide (seats, etc.) with padding, springs, covering material, etc.; provide (a room) with carpets, curtains, cushioned seats, etc. ~·**er** *n.* person whose trade is to ~. ~·**y** *n.* (materials used in, business of) ~ing.

up·keep [ˈʌpkiːp] *n.* (cost of) keeping sth. in good condition.

up·land [ˈʌplənd] *n.* (often pl.) high part(s) of a country ; (attrib.) *an* ~ *region*.

up·lift [ʌpˈlift] *v.t.* lift (esp. thoughts, feelings) to a higher level.

up·on [əˈpɒn] *prep.* on. *put* ~ *sb.*, make him do more than is right.

up·per [ˈʌpə*] *adj.* higher. *get (have) the* ~ *hand*, get (have) control (over sb.). *n.* part of a shoe or boot above the sole. ~·**most** *adj. & adv.* highest ; on, to, at, the top or surface.

up·right [ˈʌprait] *adj.* 1. erect ; placed vertically (at right angles to the ground) : *an* ~ *post.* 2. honourable ; straightforward in behaviour : *an* ~ *man.* *adv.* in an ~ manner or position. *n.* ~ support in a structure. ~·**ly** *adv.*

up·ris·ing [ʌpˈraiziŋ] *n.* revolt.

up·roar [ˈʌprɔː*] *n.* outburst of noise and excitement : *The meeting ended in (an)* ~. ~·**i·ous** [ʌpˈrɔːriəs] *adj.* very noisy : *an* ~*ious meeting*, (esp.) with much loud laughter.

up·root [ʌpˈruːt] *v.t.* pull up (sth.) with its root(s).

up·set [ʌpˈset] *v.t. & i.* ; (-*tt*- ; p.t. & p.p. *upset*). 1. overturn : *The boat.* *Don't* ~ *the boat. Who has* ~ *the milk?* 2. trouble ; cause (sth. or sb.) to be disturbed : ~ *the enemy's plans. Don't* ~ *your stomach by eating too much rich food.* [ˈʌpset] *n.* ~ting or being ~.

up·shot [ˈʌpʃɒt] *n.* result or outcome : *What was the* ~ *of it all?*

up·side-down [ˈʌpsaidˈdaun] *adv.* with the upper side underneath or at the bottom ; (fig.) in disorder.

up·stairs [ʌpˈstɛəz] *adv.* 1. to or on a higher floor. 2. (attrib. [ˈʌpstɛəz]) : *an* ~ *room.*

up·stream [ˈʌpˈstriːm] *adv.* against the current.

up·take [ˈʌpteik] *n. quick (slow) on the* ~, (colloq.) quick (slow) to see the point of sth. said, to understand what is meant.

up-to-date [ˈʌptəˈdeit] *adj.* of the present time ; of the newest sort.

up·ward [ˈʌpwəd] *adj.* moving or directed up : *the* ~ *trend of prices.* ~(**s**) *adv.* towards a higher place, etc. ~*s of*, more than.

u·ra·ni·um [juəˈreinjəm] *n.* heavy white metal with radioactive properties, a source of atomic energy.

ur·ban [ˈəːbən] *adj.* of or in a town : ~ *districts.* ~·**ize** *v.t.* change from a rural to an ~ character.

ur·bane [əːˈbein] *adj.* polite ; polished in manners. ~·**ly** *adv.* **ur·ban·i·ty** [əːˈbæniti] *n.*

ur·chin [ˈəːtʃin] *n.* troublesome small boy, esp. one who roams the streets.

urge [əːdʒ] *v.t.* 1. push or drive (sth. or sb.)(*on, onward, forward*) : ~ *one's horse on.* 2. request (sb.) earnestly, try to persuade (sb. *to do* sth.). 3. press (*upon* sb.) requests and arguments : *He* ~*d upon his pupils the importance of hard work. n.* strong desire : *He has an* ~ *to travel.* **ur·gen·cy** [ˈəːdʒənsi] *n.* need for, importance of, haste or prompt action.

ur·gent [ˈəːdʒənt] *adj.* needing prompt decision or action ; (of a person, his voice, etc.) showing that sth. is ~nt. **ur·gent·ly** *adv.*

u·rine [ˈjuərin] *n.* waste liquid which collects in the bladder and is discharged from the body.

urn [əːn] *n.* 1. vase, usu. with stem and base, esp. as used for holding the ashes of a person whose body has been cremated. 2. large metal container in which a drink such as tea or coffee is made or kept warm (in restaurants, canteens, etc.).

us, see *we*.

us·age [ˈjuːzidʒ] *n.* 1. way of using sth. : *Machines soon wear out under rough* ~. 2. sth. commonly said or done ; general custom or practice.

use [ju:z] *v.t.* (p.t. & p.p. *used* [ju:zd]). **1.** employ for a purpose: *use a knife to cut bread.* **2.** *use up*, consume the whole of: *We've used up all our oil, we have no oil left.* **3.** behave towards: *Use others as you would like them to use you.* [ju:s] *n.* **1.** purpose for which sth. or sb. may be employed; work which sth. or sb. is able to do: *a tool with many uses.* **2.** using or being used: *in use*, being used; *come into use*, begin to be used; *go (fall) out of use*, be no longer used. **3.** value; advantage: *Is this of any use to you?* **4.** power of using: *lose the use of one's legs.* **5.** right to use: *have the use of a good library.* **used** [ju:st] *ppl. adj.* accustomed (to): *get used to sth.* **used to** ['ju:sttu] *v.* indicating a constant or frequent practice in the past, or the existence of something in the past: *He used to play football when he was a boy. There used to be a theatre at this corner years ago.* **use·ful** *adj.* helpful. **use·ful·ly** *adv.* **use·ful·ness** *n.* **use·less** *adj.* worthless. **use·less·ly** *adv.* **use·less·ness** *n.* **us·er** ['ju:zə*] *n.* person who uses sth.: *How many telephone users are there in your town?*

ush·er ['ʌʃə*] *n.* **1.** person who shows people to their seats in theatres, etc. **2.** doorkeeper in a law court, etc. **3.** (old use) assistant schoolmaster. *v.t.* go with (sb.) as ~ (1); take (*into* a room, etc.): *I was ~ed in by the servant.* **~ette** [ˌʌʃə'ret] *n.* girl or woman ~ (1).

u·su·al ['ju:ʒuəl] *adj.* such as commonly happens; customary. **~·ly** *adv.*

u·surp [ju:'zə:p] *v.t.* take (sb.'s power, authority, position) wrongfully. **~·er** *n.* person who ~s (e.g. the throne).

u·su·ry ['ju:ʒəri] *n.* (practice of) lending money, esp. at a rate of interest generally considered to be too high; such high interest. **u·su·rer** *n.* person whose business is ~.

u·ten·sil [ju:'tensl] *n.* tool, instrument, etc., esp. for use in the house: *kitchen ~s* (pots, pans, brushes).

u·til·i·ty [ju:'tiliti] *n.* **1.** quality of being useful. **2.** *public utilities*, public services, etc., supplying water, gas, electricity; bus or railway services, etc. **u·til·i·ta·ri·an** [ˌju:tili'tɛəriən] *adj.* for use rather than for decoration, etc. **u·til·ize** ['ju:tilaiz] *v.t.* make use of; find a use for. **u·til·i·za·tion** [ˌju:tilai'zeiʃən] *n.*

ut·most ['ʌtmoust] *adj.* **1.** farthest: *the ~ ends of the earth.* **2.** greatest: *in the ~ danger.* *n.* the most that is possible: *do one's ~; enjoy oneself to the ~.*

U·to·pia [ju:'toupjə] *n.* imaginary perfect social and political system. **U·to·pian** *adj.* attractive and desirable but impracticable.

¹ut·ter ['ʌtə*] *adj.* complete; total: *~ darkness.* **~·ly** *adv.*

²ut·ter ['ʌtə*] *v.t.* send out (a sound) so as to be heard: *~ a sigh (a cry of pain)*; say: *the last words she ~ed.* **~·ance** ['ʌtərəns] *n.* **1.** way of speaking: *a clear ~ance.* **2.** *give ~ance to one's feelings*, express them in words. **3.** sth. said.

ut·ter·most ['ʌtəmoust] *adj.* utmost.

V

va·cant ['veikənt] *adj.* **1.** empty: *~ space*; not occupied by anyone: *a ~ room* (in a hotel). *The position is ~* (i.e. there is no one to do the work). **2.** (of the mind) unoccupied with thought; (of the eyes, looks, etc.) showing no signs of thought or interest. **~·ly** *adv.* **va·can·cy** *n.* **1.** empty space. **2.** being ~ (2). **3.** position in business, etc., for which sb. is needed: *good vacancies for clerks and typists.*

va·cate [və'keit] *v.t.* give up living in (a house, rooms, etc.); leave unoccupied: *~ one's seat.*

va·ca·tion [vəˈkeiʃən] *n.* **1.** vacating (e.g. of a position). **2.** weeks during which universities and law courts stop work. **3.** (esp. U.S.A.) period of holidays.

vac·ci·nate [ˈvæksineit] *v.t.* protect (sb.) against smallpox, etc., by injecting vaccine (e.g. into the arm). **vac·ci·na·tion** [ˌvæksiˈneiʃən] *n.* **vac·cine** [ˈvæksiːn] *n.* a preparation of disease germs (or viruses) used for the protection of persons against smallpox and some other diseases.

vac·il·late [ˈvæsileit] *v.i.* waver, hesitate, be uncertain (*in* opinion, etc., *between* different opinions, etc.). **vac·il·la·tion** [ˌvæsiˈleiʃən] *n.*

vac·u·ous [ˈvækjuəs] *adj.* vacant (2).

vac·u·um [ˈvækjuəm] *n.* space completely empty of substance or air; space in container from which air has been pumped out. ~ *cleaner*, apparatus which takes up dust, dirt, etc., by suction; ~ *flask*, flask with two walls having a ~ between them, for keeping contents at an unchanging temperature.

va·ga·bond [ˈvægəbɔnd] *adj.* having no fixed living-place; habitually wandering: *lead a* ~ *life*; ~ *gipsies.* *n.* ~ person; tramp.

va·ga·ry [vəˈgɛəri] *n.* strange, unusual act or idea, esp. one for which there seems to be no good reason: *the vagaries of fashion.*

va·grant [ˈveigrənt] *adj.* leading a wandering life: ~ *beggars.* *n.* ~ person; vagabond or tramp. **va·gran·cy** *n.* being a ~.

vague [veig] *adj.* (*-r, -st*). **1.** not clear; indistinct: ~ *outlines*; ~ *demands.* **2.** (of persons, their looks, etc.) uncertain (about needs, intentions, etc.). ~ **ly** *adv.* ~ **ness** *n.*

vain [vein] *adj.* (*-er, -est*). **1.** without use, value, meaning, or result: *a* ~ *attempt.* **2.** having too high an opinion of one's looks or abilities, etc.; conceited. **3.** *in* ~, without the desired result:

Our efforts were in ~. ~ **ly** *adv.* ~ **ˈglo·ry** *n.* extreme vanity or pride in oneself. ~ **ˈglo·ri·ous** *adj.*

vale [veil] *n.* (liter.) valley.

val·en·tine [ˈvæləntain] *n.* (letter, card, etc., sent anonymously on St. V~'s Day, 14 Feb., to a) sweetheart.

val·et [ˈvælei] *n.* manservant who looks after his employer's clothes.

val·iant [ˈvæljənt] *adj.* brave.

val·id [ˈvælid] *adj.* **1.** (law) effective because made or done with the correct formalities: *The claim (marriage) was not* ~. **2.** (of contracts, etc.) having force in law: ~ *for three months.* **3.** (of arguments, reasons, etc.) well based; sound. ~ **ly** *adv.* **val·i·date** *v.t.* make ~. **va·lid·i·ty** [vəˈliditi] *n.*

va·lise [vəˈliːz] *n.* bag for clothes, etc., during a journey; kit-bag.

val·ley [ˈvæli] *n.* stretch of land between hills or mountains, often with a river flowing through it.

val·our [ˈvælə*] *n.* bravery, esp. in war. **val·or·ous** *adj.*

val·ue [ˈvæljuː] *n.* **1.** quality of being useful or desirable. **2.** worth of sth. in terms of money or other goods for which it can be exchanged. **3.** what sth. is considered to be worth: *I've been offered £5 for the ring but its* ~ *is much higher.* *v.t.* **1.** estimate the money ~ of. **2.** have a high opinion of: *I* ~ *your advice.* **val·u·a·ble** [ˈvæljuəbl] *adj.* of much ~. *n.* (often pl.) thing(s) of much ~, e.g. jewels, gold objects. **val·u·a·tion** [ˌvæljuˈeiʃən] *n.* process of deciding ~(3); the ~ (3) decided upon.

valve [vælv] *n.* **1.** (sorts of) mechanical device for controlling the flow of air, liquid or gas into a tube, pipe, etc. **2.** structure in the heart or in a blood-vessel allowing the blood to flow in one direction only. **3.** vacuum tube (used in radio and television sets, etc.). See the picture on page 585.

¹van [væn] *n.* **1.** covered or roofed vehicle for delivering goods by road: *the baker's van*; *a furniture van*. **2.** roofed railway wagon.

²van [væn] *n.* **1.** front or leading part of an army or fleet in battle. **2.** those persons who lead a procession or (fig.) a movement: *in the van of scientific progress*.

van·guard *n.* advance party of an army, etc., as a guard against surprise attacks, etc.

van·dal [ˈvændl] *n.* person who wilfully destroys or damages works of art, spoils the beauties of nature, etc. ~**ism** *n.*

vane [vein] *n.* **1.** arrow, etc., on the top of a building, turned by the wind so as to show its direction. **2.** blade of a propeller, sail of a windmill, etc.

van·ish [ˈvæniʃ] *v.i.* **1.** disappear suddenly; fade away gradually. **2.** go out of existence.

van·i·ty [ˈvæniti] *n.* **1.** conceit; having too high an opinion of one's looks, abilities, etc. **2.** worthlessness; quality of being unsatisfying, without true value: *the ~ of earthly greatness*.

van·quish [ˈvæŋkwiʃ] *v.t.* defeat.

vap·id [ˈvæpid] *adj.* tasteless; uninteresting. **va·pid·i·ty** [vəˈpiditi] *n.*

va·pour [ˈveipə*] *n.* **1.** steam; mist. **2.** gaseous form of a substance which is normally liquid or solid. **va·por·ize** [ˈveipəraiz] *v.t. & i.* (cause to) change into ~ (2).

va·ri·e·ty, va·ri·e·gat·ed, see *vary.*

var·nish [ˈvɑːniʃ] *n.* (liquid used to give a) hard, shiny, transparent coating on the surface of wood, etc. *v.t.* put ~ on.

va·ry [ˈvɛəri] *v.i. & t.* be, become, or make, different: ~*ing prices.* **va·ri·a·ble** *adj.* ~*ing;* changeable; that can be changed.

va·ri·a·bil·i·ty [ˌvɛəriəˈbiliti] *n.* **va·ri·ance** *n.* ~*ing;* condition of being in disagreement: *at variance with.* **va·ri·ant** *adj.* different or alternative: '*Tire*' and '*tyre*' are variant spellings. *n.* variant form (esp. of a word, its spelling). **va·ri·a·tion** [ˌvɛəriˈeiʃən] *n.* (degree of) ~*ing: variations of temperature; with little variation of speed.* **va·ried** *ppl. adj.* **1.** of different sorts. **2.** continually or often changing: *a varied career.* **va·ri·e·gat·ed** [ˈvɛəriəgeitid] *adj.* marked irregularly with differently coloured patches. **va·ri·e·ty** [vəˈraiəti] *n.* **1.** quality of not being all the same or not the same at all times: *We want more variety in our food.* **2.** number or group of different things: *for a variety of reasons.* **3.** division of a species. **4.** *variety show,* stage entertainment of songs, dances, short plays, etc. **va·ri·ous** [ˈvɛəriəs] *adj.* different; several: *for various reasons.*

vase [vɑːz] *n.* vessel of glass, pottery, etc., used for ornament, for holding flowers, etc.

vas·sal [ˈvæsl] *n.* person who, in former times, held land in return for military help to the owner of the land. ~**age** [ˈvæsəlidʒ] *n.* condition of being a ~.

vast [vɑːst] *adj.* immense; extensive.

vat [væt] *n.* tank or great vessel for holding liquids, esp. in brewing, dyeing, and tanning.

vau·de·ville [ˈvoudəvil] *n.* = *variety* (4).

¹vault [vɔːlt] *n.* **1.** arched roof; series of arches forming a roof. **2.** underground room or cellar, esp. for storing wine or valuables. **3.** burial chamber. ~**ed** *ppl. adj.* having, built with, ~s.

Valves (1), (3)

A vaulted roof

²**vault** [vɔːlt] *v.i. & t.* jump in a single movement, with the hand(s) resting on sth. or with the help of a pole: ~ (*over*) *a fence*. *n.* jump made in this way.

vaunt [vɔːnt] *n., v.i. & t.* boast.

veal [viːl] *n.* flesh of a calf as food.

veer [viə*] *v.i.* (esp. of wind, fig. of opinion) change direction: *The wind ~ed round to the north.*

veg·e·ta·ble [ˈvedʒitəbl] *adj.* of, from, relating to, plants or plant life: ~ *oils*. *n.* plant, esp. of the sort used for food (e.g. potatoes, beans, carrots, cabbages). **veg·e·ta·ri·an** [ˌvedʒiˈteəriən] *n.* person who does not eat meat; (attrib.) of ~s: *a vegetarian diet.* **veg·e·ta·tion** [ˌvedʒiˈteiʃən] *n.* plants of all kinds; plants growing in a place or area: *tropical vegetation.*

ve·he·ment [ˈviːəmənt] *adj.* (of feelings) strong; eager; (of persons, their speech, etc.) filled with, showing, strong or eager feeling. **ve·he·mence** *n.*

ve·hi·cle [ˈviːikl] *n.* 1. any conveyance (usu. wheeled, but also a sledge) for goods or passengers on land. 2. means by which thought, feeling, etc., can be conveyed: *use the newspapers as a ~ for political views.* **ve·hic·u·lar** [viˈhikjulə*] *adj.* of transport ~s: *This road is closed to vehicular traffic.*

veil [veil] *n.* 1. covering of fine net or other material to protect or hide a woman's face, or as part of a head-dress. *take the ~,* become a nun. 2. sth. that hides: *a ~ of mist. v.t.* put a ~ over; (fig.) conceal: ~ *one's distrust.*

vein [vein] *n.* 1. blood-vessel along which blood flows back to the heart. 2. one of the ~-like lines in a leaf, in the wing of an insect; coloured line in some kinds of stone (e.g. marble). 3. crack or fissure in rock, filled with coal, ore, etc. 4. mood; state of mind: *He talked in a merry ~ for several minutes.*

veld [felt] *n.* (stretch of) rocky grassland of the S. African plateau.

vel·lum [ˈveləm] *n.* parchment.

ve·loc·i·ty [viˈlɔsiti] *n.* (of objects) rate of motion; speed.

vel·vet [ˈvelvit] *n.* 1. cloth wholly or partly made of silk, with thick, soft ²nap on one side. 2. (attrib.) made of ~; soft like ~.

ve·nal [ˈviːnl] *adj.* 1. (of persons) willing to do wrong for money. 2. (of conduct, etc.) influenced by, done for, (possible) payment.

vend [vend] *v.t.* (chiefly legal) sell. ~·**or** *n.* seller: *news ~or,* seller of newspapers, etc.

ven·det·ta [venˈdetə] *n.* quarrel between families in which each commits murders in revenge for previous murders.

ve·neer [vəˈniə*] *n.* 1. thin layer of fine quality wood glued to the surface of cheaper wood (in furniture, etc.). 2. (fig.) surface appearance (of politeness, civilization, etc.) covering the true nature. *v.t.* put a ~(1) on (wood, etc.).

ven·er·a·ble [ˈvenərəbl] *adj.* deserving respect because of age, character, associations, etc. **ven·er·ate** [ˈvenəreit] *v.t.* regard with deep respect. **ven·er·a·tion** [ˌvenəˈreiʃən] *n.* deep respect.

ven·geance [ˈvendʒəns] *n.* 1. revenge; the return of injury for injury: *take ~ upon sb.,* have one's revenge. 2. *with a ~,* (colloq.) thoroughly, very much: *It's raining with a ~.* **venge·ful** *adj.* desiring ~.

The veins of a leaf

ve·ni·al [ˈviːniəl] *adj.* (of a sin or error) excusable; not serious.

ven·i·son [ˈvenizn] *n.* deer meat.

ven·om [ˈvenəm] *n.* 1. poison of snakes, etc. 2. hate; spite; ill feeling. ~·**ous** *adj.* deadly; spiteful.

vent [vent] *n.* 1. hole serving as

inlet or outlet for air, gas, liquid, etc. 2. (fig.) outlet for one's feelings: *give ~ to one's feelings*, express them. *v.t.* provide an outlet for.

ven·ti·late ['ventileit] *v.t.* 1. cause air to move freely in and out of: ~ *a room*. 2. make (a question, a grievance) widely known and cause it to be discussed. **ven·ti·la·tion** [,venti'leiʃən] *n.* **ven·ti·la·tor** ['ventileitə*] *n.* device for ventilating (1).

ven·tril·o·quism [ven'trilə-kwizəm] *n.* art of producing voice-sounds so that they seem to come from a person or place at a distance from the speaker. **ven·tril·o·quist** *n.* person skilled in this art.

ven·ture ['ventʃə*] *n.* undertaking in which there is risk: *at a ~*, without definite aim; trusting to chance. *v.t. & i.* 1. take the risk of danger or loss; be brave enough (*to do* sth.): ~ *near the edge of a cliff*. 2. put forward (an opinion); go so far as; dare: *I ~ to say that ...*; *if I may ~ to disagree*. **~·some** *adj.* ready to take risks; daring; (of acts) risky.

ve·ra·cious [və'reiʃəs] *adj.* true; truthful. **ve·rac·i·ty** [və'ræsiti] *n.*

ve·ran·da(h) [və'rændə] *n.* roofed and floored open space along the side(s) of a house, etc.

verb [və:b] *n.* word or phrase indicating what sth. or sb. does, what state sb. or sth. is in, what is becoming of sth. or sb.

ver·bal ['və:bl] *adj.* 1. of or in words: *a ~ error*. 2. spoken, not written: *a ~ message*. 3. word for word: *a ~ translation*. 4. of verbs: ~ *noun*, verb form used as a noun, e.g. *Dancing is good exercise*. **~·ly** *adv.* in spoken words, not in writing.

ver·ba·tim [və:'beitim] *adv.* word for word, exactly as spoken or written: *a speech reported ~*.

ver·bose [və:'bous] *adj.* using, containing, more words than are needed. **ver·bos·i·ty** [və:-'bositi] *n.*

ver·dant ['və:dənt] *adj.* (esp. of grass, fields, etc.) fresh and green. **ver·dure** ['və:dʒə*] *n.* greenness of growing things; fresh, green growth.

ver·dict ['və:dikt] *n.* 1. decision reached by a jury on a question of fact in a law case. 2. decision or opinion given after a test, etc.: *the ~ of the electors*.

ver·di·gris ['və:digri(:)s] *n.* green substance formed on copper surfaces.

verge [və:dʒ] *n.* 1. border (e.g. strip of grassy ground at the side of a road); edge of a lawn. 2. *be on the ~ of doing* sth., be about to do it. *v.i.* 1. incline: *The sun was verging towards the horizon.* 2. ~ *upon*, be near to: *The country was verging upon bankruptcy.*

ver·ger ['və:dʒə*] *n.* person who shows people to their seats in an Anglican church.

ver·i·fy ['verifai] *v.t.* 1. test the truth or accuracy of (statements, etc.). 2. (of an event, etc.) show the truth of (sth. said, etc.). **ver·i·fi·a·ble** *adj.* that can be verified. **ver·i·fi·ca·tion** [,verifi-'keiʃən] *n.*

ver·i·ly ['verili] *adv.* (old use) truly.

ver·i·si·mil·i·tude [,verisi'mili-tju:d] *n.* appearance, semblance, of truth.

ver·i·ta·ble ['veritəbl] *adj.* real; rightly named.

ver·i·ty ['veriti] *n.* truth (of a statement, etc.); true statement; sth. that really exists.

ver·mil·ion [və'miljən] *n. & adj.* bright red (colour).

ver·min ['və:min] *n.* 1. wild animals (e.g. rats) harmful to plants, birds, etc. 2. insects (e.g. lice) sometimes found on the bodies of human beings or animals. **~·ous** *adj.* 1. infested with fleas, lice, etc. 2. caused by insect ~: ~*ous diseases*.

ver·nac·u·lar [və'nækjulə*] *adj.* (of a word, a language) of the country in question: *the ~ languages of Indonesia*. *n.* language or dialect of a country or district.

ver·nal ['və:nl] *adj.* (liter.) of, in, as in, the season of spring.

ver·sa·tile ['və:sətail] *adj.* interested in and clever at many different things. **ver·sa·til·i·ty** [,və:sə'tiliti] *n.*

verse [və:s] *n.* **1.** (form of) writing arranged in groups of lines, each conforming to a pattern of accented and unaccented syllables and often having a rhyming syllable at the end. **2.** one line of ~ (1). **3.** group of such lines forming a unit in a poem, hymn, etc.: *a poem of five ~s.* **4.** one of the short, numbered divisions ·of a chapter in the Bible.

versed [və:st] *adj.* ~ *in*, skilled or experienced in.

ver·sion ['və:ʃən] *n.* **1.** translation into another language: *a new ~ of the Bible.* **2.** account of an event, etc., from the point of view of one person, etc.: *contradictory ~s of what was said.*

ver·sus ['və:səs] (Latin) *prep.* (in law and sport, often shortened to *v.* in writing and print) against.

ver·te·brate ['və:tibrit] *n.* & *adj.* (animal, bird, etc.) having a backbone.

ver·ti·cal ['və:tikl] *adj.* at right angles to the earth's surface or to another line (cf. *horizontal*): *a ~ line (cliff).*

ver·ti·go ['və:tigou] *n.* dizziness.

verve [və:v] *n.* spirit and force in the work of an artist, writer, musician.

ver·y ['veri] *adv.* to a great extent; to a marked degree: ~ *good,* ~ *well,* excellent(ly). *adj.* actually this and no other: *in this ~ place; the ~ thing I wanted.*

ves·pers ['vespəz] *n. pl.* church service in the evening; evensong.

ves·sel ['vesl] *n.* **1.** container for liquids (e.g. a bucket, bottle, cup). **2.** ship or large boat.

vest [vest] *n.* **1.** garment worn on the upper part of the body next to the skin. **2.** (U.S.A.) waistcoat.

ves·ti·bule ['vestibju:l] *n.* lobby or entrance hall of a building (e.g. where hats and coats may be left).

ves·tige ['vestidʒ] *n.* trace or sign; small remaining bit that is evidence of what once existed: *Not a ~ of the castle remains.*

vest·ment ['vestmənt] *n.* garment, esp. one worn by a priest in church; ceremonial robe.

ves·try ['vestri] *n.* **1.** part of a church where ~s are kept. **2.** parish committee of ratepayers.

vet [vet] *n.* (colloq.) veterinary surgeon. *v.t.* (-*tt-*; colloq.). **1.** give (sb.) a medical examination. **2.** examine and correct (a piece of writing).

vet·er·an ['vetərən] *n.* & *adj.* (person) having had much or long experience, esp. as a soldier.

vet·er·i·na·ry ['vetərinəri] *adj.* of or concerned with the diseases of animals: *a ~ surgeon (college).* *n.* ~ surgeon.

ve·to ['vi:tou] *n.* (pl. -*oes*). right to prevent a bill from becoming law; right to reject or forbid sth.; statement rejecting or prohibiting sth.: *put a ~ on sth.,* forbid it. *v.t.* use a ~ against; prohibit: *The meeting was ~ed by the President.*

vex [veks] *v.t.* annoy; distress; trouble. *a vexed question,* difficult question causing much discussion. **vex·a·tion** [vek'seiʃən] *n.* being vexed; sth. that vexes. **vex·a·tious** [vek'seiʃəs] *adj.* annoying: *vexatious regulations.*

via [vaiə] (Latin) *prep.* by way of: *travel from London to Paris via Dover.*

vi·a·duct ['vaiədʌkt] *n.* bridge with arches carrying a road or railway across a valley or low ground.

vi·brate [vai'breit] *v.i.* & *t.* **1.** (cause to) move rapidly and continuously backwards and forwards like the string of a violin: *The building ~s whenever a lorry passes.* **2.** (of stretched strings, the voice) throb: *a voice vibrating with passion.* **vi·brant** ['vaibrənt] *adj.* vibrating: *the vibrant notes of a 'cello.* **vi·bra·tion**

[vai'breiʃən] *n.* vibrating movement.

vic·ar ['vikə*] *n.* (Church of England) clergyman in charge of a parish the tithes of which were wholly or wholly payable to another person or body (e.g. a college) for whom the ~ acts. ~·**age** ['vikəridʒ] *n.* ~'s residence.

vi·car·i·ous [vi'kɛəriəs] *adj.* done, undergone, by one person for another or others.

¹**vice** [vais] *n.* **1.** (any particular kind of) evil conduct or immorality. **2.** (in a horse) bad habit (e.g. kicking) which makes control difficult.

²**vice** [vais] *n.* apparatus with strong jaws in which things can be held tightly while being worked upon.

A ²vice

vice- [vais-] *prefix.* acting for (another); holding rank next below: ~·**admiral**, ~·**chairman**. ~·**roy** ['vaisroi] *n.* (formerly) person governing a colony, etc., as the Sovereign's representative. ~·**re·gal** [vais'ri:gl] *adj.* of a ~roy.

vi·ce ver·sa ['vaisi'və:sə] (Latin) *adv.* the other way round: *We gossip about them and* ~ (i.e. they gossip about us).

vi·cin·i·ty [vi'siniti] *n.* nearness; neighbourhood: *in close* ~ *to the school*; *no school in the* ~.

vi·cious ['viʃəs] *adj.* **1.** of ¹vice; given up to ¹vice: *a* ~ *man* (*life, habit*). **2.** spiteful: *a* ~ *look* (*kick, temper*). **3.** (of a horse) having bad habits such as biting and kicking. **4.** having faults: *a* ~ *argument.* ~·**ly** *adv.*

vi·cis·si·tude [vi'sisitju:d] *n.* change, esp. in sb.'s fortunes.

vic·tim ['viktim] *n.* **1.** living creature killed and offered as a religious sacrifice. **2.** person, animal, etc., suffering injury, pain, loss, etc., because of circumstances, an event, the ill will of sb. else, etc.: *He is the* ~ *of his own foolishness* (*of his brother's anger*). ~·**ize** *v.t.* make a ~ of (sb.).

vic·tor ['viktə*] *n.* person who conquers or wins. **vic·to·ry** *n.* success (in a battle, contest, game, etc.). **vic·to·ri·ous** [vik-'tɔ:riəs] *adj.* having gained ~y.

vict·ual ['vitl] *n.* (usu. pl.) food and drink; provisions. *v.t. & i.* (*-ll-*). **1.** supply with ~s: ~ *a ship.* **2.** obtain stores. ~·**ler** ['vitlə*] *n.* trader in ~s.

vie [vai] *v.i.* (3rd person sing. pres.t. **vies**, p.t. & p.p. **vied**, pres. participle **vying**). rival or compete (with): *vying with one another for first place.*

view [vju:] *n.* **1.** sight (of): *be in* ~, *come into* ~, in(to) a position where (it) can be seen; *on* ~, being shown or exhibited. **2.** sth. (to be) looked at, esp. a stretch of natural scenery: *a house with a* ~. **3.** opinion: *We take a serious* ~ *of his conduct,* it is, in our opinion, bad. *in* ~ *of,* considering, taking into account. **4.** purpose; plan; intention: *fall in with* (*meet*) *sb.'s* ~*s,* agree with his wishes. *with a* ~ *to,* with intention to. *v.t.* look at; examine; consider.

vig·il ['vidʒil] *n.* staying awake to keep watch or to pray. **vig·i·lance** *n.* keeping watch; watchfulness. **vig·i·lant** *adj.* watchful.

vig·our ['vigə*] *n.* mental or physical strength; energy. **vig·or·ous** ['vigərəs] *adj.* strong; energetic.

vile [vail] *adj.* **1.** shameful and disgusting: ~ *habits.* **2.** (colloq.) bad: ~ *weather.* **vil·i·fy** ['vilifai] *v.t.* slander; say evil things about (sb.).

vil·la ['vilə] *n.* house in its own grounds or garden, esp. one on the outskirts of a town.

vil·lage ['vilidʒ] *n.* place smaller than a town, where there are houses, shops, etc.

vil·lain ['vilən] *n.* (esp. in drama) wrongdoer; wicked man. ~·**ous**

adj. very bad. ~·y *n.* evil conduct or act.

vim [vim] *n.* (colloq.) energy.

vin·di·cate ['vindikeit] *v.t.* show or prove the truth, justice, etc. (of sth. that has been attacked or disputed). **vin·di·ca·tion** [,vindi'keiʃən] *n.*

vin·dic·tive [vin'diktiv] *adj.* unforgiving; having or showing a desire for revenge.

vine [vain] *n.* climbing plant, esp. the kind that bears grapes. ~·yard ['vinjəd] *n.* area of land planted with grape-~s.

vin·e·gar ['vinigə*] *n.* acid liquid (from malt or wine) used in cooking, for flavouring and preserving food.

vin·tage ['vintidʒ] *n.* **1.** (period of) grape harvesting. **2.** (wine from) grapes of a particular year.

¹**vi·o·la** [vi'oulə] *n.* tenor violin, of larger size than the ordinary violin.

²**vi·o·la** ['vaiələ] *n.* kind of pansy.

vi·o·late ['vaiəleit] *v.t.* **1.** break (an oath, a treaty, etc.); act contrary to (what one's conscience tells one to do, etc.). **2.** act towards (a sacred place, sb.'s seclusion, etc.) without proper respect. **vi·o·la·tion** [,vaiə'leiʃən] *n.*

vi·o·lent ['vaiələnt] *adj.* **1.** using, showing, accompanied by, great force: *a ~ wind (attack)*; ~ *passions*. **2.** caused by ~ attack: ~ *death*. **3.** severe: ~ *toothache*. ~·ly *adv.* **vi·o·lence** *n.* being ~; ~ conduct: *crimes of violence*; *an outbreak of violence* (rioting).

vi·o·let ['vaiəlit] *n.* (bluish-purple colour of) small wild or garden sweet-smelling flower. *adj.* blue-red.

vi·o·lin [vaiə'lin] *n.* four-stringed musical instrument played with a bow, as shown here. ~·ist *n.* player of a ~. **vi·o·lon·cel·lo** [,vaiələn'tʃelou] (or **'cel·lo**) *n.* large-sized ~, deeper in tone, played while held between the knees.

vi·per ['vaipə*] *n.* small, poisonous snake.

vir·gin ['və:dʒin] *n.* girl or woman who has not experienced sexual union. *adj.* **1.** pure and untouched: ~ *snow*. **2.** in the original condition; unused: ~ *soil (forests)*. ~·al *adj.* of, like, a ~; pure. ~·i·ty [və:'dʒiniti] *n.*

vir·ile ['virail] *adj.* having or showing strength, energy, manly qualities; having the powers of a full-grown man. **vi·ril·i·ty** [vi'riliti] *n.*

vir·tu·al ['və:tjuəl] *adj.* being in fact, acting as, what is described, but not accepted openly or in name as such: *the ~ head of the business*; *a ~ defeat*. ~·ly *adv.*

vir·tue ['və:tju:] *n.* **1.** (any particular kind of) goodness or excellence (e.g. patience, chastity). **2.** *by (in) ~ of*, because of. **vir·tu·ous** ['və:tjuəs] *adj.* having or showing ~; (of women) chaste. **vir·tu·ous·ly** *adv.*

vir·u·lent ['virulənt] *adj.* (of poison) strong, deadly; (of ill feeling, hatred) bitter; (of words, etc.) full of ill feeling; (of diseases, sores) poisonous. **vir·u·lence** *n.*

vi·rus ['vaiərəs] *n.* poisonous element causing spread of infectious disease: *the ~ of influenza*.

vi·sa ['vi:zə] *n.* stamp or signature put on a passport to show that it has been examined and approved by the officials of the foreign country which the owner intends to visit or leave. *v.t.* put a ~ on.

vis·age ['vizidʒ] *n.* (liter.) face.

vis-à-vis [,vi:za:'vi:] (Fr.) *prep. & adv.* facing (one another).

vis·count ['vaikaunt] *n.* nobleman higher in rank than a baron.

Playing the violin   A viper

vis·i·ble ['vizibl] *adj.* that can be seen; that is in sight. **vis·i·**

bil·i·ty [ˌvizi'biliti] *n.* (esp.) condition of the atmosphere for seeing things at a distance.

vi·sion ['viʒən] *n.* **1.** power of seeing or imagining. **2.** sth. seen, esp. during sleep or in imagination: *have a ~ of the future.* **~·a·ry** ['viʒənəri] *adj.* **1.** existing only in the imagination, not practical or possible: *~ary ideas (plans, scenes).* **2.** (of persons) having ~ary ideas; dreamy. *n.* ~ary (2) person.

vis·it ['vizit] *v.t. & i.* **1.** go to see (sb.); go to (a place) for a time. **2.** (biblical use) (*upon* a person) punish; give punishment for (a sin): *~ the sins of the fathers upon the children.* *n.* act of ~ing (1); time of ~ing: *pay sb. a ~; on a short ~ to an aunt.* **vis·i·tor** *n.* person who ~s. **vis·i·ta·tion** [ˌvizi'teiʃən] *n.* (esp.) trouble, disaster, looked upon as punishment from God.

vis·ta ['vistə*] *n.* long, narrow view; (fig.) series of events looked back on or forward to.

vis·u·al ['vizjuəl] *adj.* concerned with, used in, seeing: *~ aids in teaching* (e.g. pictures, cinema films). **~·ize** *v.t.* bring (sth.) as a picture before the mind.

vi·tal ['vaitl] *adj.* **1.** of, connected with, necessary for, living. *a ~ wound,* one causing death. **2.** supreme: *of ~ importance.* **~·ly** *adv.* **~·i·ty** [vai'tæliti] *n.* **1.** ~ power; capacity to endure. **2.** liveliness; driving force. **~·ize** *v.t.* fill with ~ity; put vigour into.

vit·a·min ['vitəmin, 'vai-] *n.* sorts of substance, present in certain foods, that are essential to good health.

vi·ti·ate ['viʃieit] *v.t.* lower the quality of; weaken or destroy the force of.

vit·ri·ol ['vitriəl] *n.* sulphuric acid. **~·ic** [ˌvitri'ɔlik] *adj.* (fig., of words, feelings) biting; full of invective.

vi·tu·per·ate [vai'tju:pəreit] *v.t.* abuse in words; curse. **vi·tu·per·a·tive** *adj.* **vi·tu·per·a·tion** [ˌvaitju:pə'reiʃən] *n.*

vi·va·cious [vi'veiʃəs] *adj.* lively; high-spirited. **vi·vac·i·ty** [vi'væsiti] *n.*

vi·va vo·ce ['vaivə'vousi] (Latin) *adj. & adv.* oral(ly). *n.* oral (part of an) examination.

viv·id ['vivid] *adj.* **1.** (of colours, etc.) intense; bright. **2.** (of descriptions) giving a clear and distinct picture. **3.** lively: *a ~ imagination.* **~·ly** *adv.*

viv·i·sect [ˌvivi'sekt] *v.t.* cut up or experiment on (living animals) for scientific research. **viv·i·sec·tion** *n.*

vix·en ['viksn] *n.* female fox.

viz. (Latin, usu. read as *namely*). *adv.* that is to say; namely.

vi·zier [vi'ziə*] *n.* official of high rank in some Muslim countries.

vo·cab·u·la·ry [və'kæbjuləri] *n.* **1.** book containing a list of words; list of words used in a book, etc., usu. with definitions or translations. **2.** (range of) words known to or used by a person, by sb. in a profession.

vo·cal ['voukl] *adj.* of, for, with or using, the voice: *the ~ organs,* the tongue, lips, etc.; *~ music,* to be sung. **vo·cal·ist** *n.* singer.

vo·ca·tion [vou'keiʃən] *n.* **1.** feeling that one is called to (and qualified for) a certain kind of work, esp. religious work. **2.** person's trade or profession. **~·al** *adj.* of or for a ~ (2): *~al guidance,* advice on the choice of a ~ (2).

vod·ka ['vodkə] *n.* strong alcoholic drink distilled from rye.

vogue [voug] *n.* fashion (1): *all the ~,* popular everywhere; *have a great ~,* be popular or fashionable.

voice [vois] *n.* **1.** sounds made when speaking or singing; power of making such sounds: *He has lost his ~,* cannot speak or sing (e.g. because of a bad cold). **2.** (right to give an) opinion: *I have no ~ in the matter.* *v.t.* put into words: *The spokesman ~d the feelings of the crowd.*

void [void] *adj.* **1.** empty. **2.** *~ of,* without. **3.** (law, often *null and ~*) without force; invalid.

vol·a·tile ['vɒlətail] *adj.* (of a liquid) that easily changes into gas or vapour; (of a person) lively; gay; changeable.

vol·ca·no [vɒl'keinou] *n.* (pl. -oes). mountain with opening(s) through which gases, lava, ashes, etc., come up from below the earth's crust. **vol·can·ic** [vɒl-'kænik] *adj.* of, from, like, a ~.

vo·li·tion [vou'liʃən] *n.* act, power, of using one's will, of choosing, making a decision.

vol·ley ['vɒli] *n.* 1. hurling or shooting of a number of missiles (stones, arrows, bullets, etc.) together. 2. number of oaths, curses, questions, directed together, or in quick succession, at sb. '~·ball *n.* game in which players on each side keep a ball in motion by hitting it with their hands back and forth over a net without letting it touch the ground.

volt [voult] *n.* unit of electrical force. ~·age ['voultidʒ] *n.* electrical force measured in ~s.

vol·u·ble ['vɒljubl] *adj.* talking, able to talk, very quickly and easily; (of speech) fluent. **vol·u·bly** *adv.* **vol·u·bil·i·ty** [ˌvɒlju-'biliti] *n.*

vol·ume ['vɒljuːm] *n.* 1. book, esp. one of a set of books. 2. amount of space occupied by a substance, a liquid, or a gas. 3. large mass or amount, esp. (pl.) rounded masses of steam or smoke. 4. (of sound) loudness; sonority: *a voice of great ~.* **vo·lu·mi·nous** [vəl'juːminəs] *adj.* 1. (of writing) great in quantity; (of a writer) producing much. 2. spacious, occupying much space: *a voluminous correspondence.*

vol·un·ta·ry ['vɒləntəri] *adj.* 1. done, doing or ready to do things, willingly, without being compelled: ~ *helpers; a* ~ *statement.* 2. carried on, supported, by ~ work and gifts. **vol·un·ta·ri·ly** *adv.*

vol·un·teer [ˌvɒlən'tiə*] *n.* 1. person who offers to do sth., esp. sth. unpleasant or dangerous.

2. soldier who is not conscripted. *v.t. & i.* come forward as a ~; offer (help, service, *to do* sth.).

vo·lup·tu·ous [və'lʌptjuəs] *adj.* of, for, arousing, given up to, sensual pleasure.

vom·it ['vɒmit] *v.t. & i.* 1. bring back from the stomach through the mouth. 2. send out in large quantities: *factory chimneys* ~*ing smoke.* *n.* food that has been ~ed.

vo·ra·cious [və'reiʃəs] *adj.* very hungry or greedy; desiring much: *a* ~ *reader.* **vo·ra·ci·ty** [vɒ'ræsiti] *n.*

vor·tex ['vɔːteks] *n.* water or wind circling violently; quickly circling mass.

vote [vout] *n.* 1. (right to) expression of opinion or will, given by persons for or against sb. or sth., esp. by ballot or by putting up of hands: *put sth. to the* ~, decide it by asking for ~s. 2. total number of ~s (to be) given to a political party, etc.: *The Labour* ~ *is expected to decrease.* *v.i. & t.* 1. give a ~ (*for* or *against* sth. or sb.); announce a proposal (*that . . .*). 2. approve by ~s: ~ *a sum of money for Education.* 3. (colloq.) declare by general agreement: *The new captain was* ~*d a fine fellow.* **vot·er** *n.* person with the right to ~ in elections.

vouch [vautʃ] *v.i.* ~ *for* (*sb. or sth.*), be responsible for (a person, his honesty, the truth of a statement, etc.). ~·er *n.* receipt or document showing payment of money or correctness of accounts, etc.

vouch·safe [vautʃ'seif] *v.t.* be kind enough to give (sth.) or to do (sth.): ~ *a reply;* ~ *to help.*

vow [vau] *n.* solemn promise or undertaking: *marriage vows; under a vow of silence,* having promised not to speak about sth.; *break a vow.* *v.i.* make a vow (*that . . ., to do* sth.).

vow·el ['vauəl] *n.* 1. vocal sound made without audible stopping of the breath. 2. letter or symbol used to represent such a sound (e.g. the letters *a, e, i, o, u*, the symbols ʌ and ə).

voy·age ['vɔiidʒ] *v.i. & n.* (make a) journey by ship: *a ~ up the Nile.*

vul·can·ite ['vʌlkənait] *n.* plastic made from rubber and sulphur.

vul·can·ize ['vʌlkənaiz] *v.t.* treat (rubber) with sulphur at great heat to harden it.

vul·gar ['vʌlgə*] *adj.* ill-mannered; in bad taste(5); rough and noisy: *~ language.* **~·i·ty** [vʌl'gæriti] *n.* ~ behaviour.

vul·ner·a·ble ['vʌlnərəbl] *adj.* that is liable to be damaged; not protected against attack.

vul·ture ['vʌltʃə*] *n.* large bird, usu. with head and neck almost bare of feathers, that lives on the flesh of dead animals.

vy·ing, see *vie.*

W

wad [wɔd] *n.* **1.** lump of soft material for keeping things apart or in place, or to stop up a hole. **2.** number of papers or bank-notes pressed or rolled together. *v.t.* (-*dd*-). put wad(s) or wadding into or round sth.

wad·ding *n.* soft material, esp. raw cotton, used for packing.

wad·dle ['wɔdl] *v.i.* walk with slow steps and a sideways roll, as a duck does. *n.* this kind of walk.

wade [weid] *v.i. & t.* walk (*through* water, *across* a stream, etc.); (fig.) make one's way with effort (*through* a book). **wad·ers** *n.* high rubber boots used by men when fishing in rivers.

wa·di ['wɑːdi] *n.* (in northern Africa and the Middle East) rocky watercourse, dry except after heavy rain.

wa·fer ['weifə*] *n.* thin flat biscuit (e.g. as eaten with ice-cream).

waft [wɑːft, wɔft] *v.t.* carry lightly and smoothly through the air.

wag [wæg] *v.t. & i.* (-*gg*-). (cause

to) move from side to side or up and down: *The dog wagged its tail.* set chins (tongues) wagging, cause people to talk (esp. scandal). *n.* **1.** wagging movement. **2.** merry person fond of making jokes.

¹wage [weidʒ] *n.* (often pl.) payment made or received (usu. weekly) for work or services (cf. *salary, fee*).

²wage [weidʒ] *v.t.* carry on, engage in (a war, a campaign).

wa·ger ['weidʒə*] *v.t. & i. & n.* bet.

wag·gle ['wægl] *v.t. & i.* wag.

wag(g)·on ['wægən] *n.* **1.** four-wheeled cart for carrying goods, pulled by horses or oxen. **2.** open railway truck (e.g. for coal).

waif [weif] *n.* homeless person, esp. a child; homeless cat or dog.

wail [weil] *v.i. & t.* cry or complain with a loud, usu. high, voice: *~ (over) one's misfortunes*; (of the wind) sound like a person ~ing. *n.* ~ing cry; complaint.

waist [weist] *n.* part of the body between the ribs and hips; part of a garment which goes round the ~. **~·coat** ['weskət, 'weiskət] *n.* close-fitting sleeveless upper garment reaching to the ~ and buttoned down the front.

wait [weit] *v.t. & t.* **1.** stay where one is, delay acting, until sb. or sth. comes or until sth. happens: *~ for sb.*; *~ until the rain stops*; *~ to see what happens. ~ up*, stay up, not go to bed. **2.** *~ upon* (*sb.*), act as a servant to, fetch and carry things for; *~ at table*, serve food, carry away dishes, etc. *n.* act or time of ~ing: *We had a long ~ for the bus. lie in ~* (*for*), be in hiding in order to attack, etc. **~·er, ~·ress** ['weitris] *n.* man, woman, who ~s at table in a restaurant, hotel, etc.

waive [weiv] *v.t.* give up (a right or claim); not insist upon.

¹wake [weik] *v.i. & t.* (p.t. *woke* [wouk] or ~*d*, p.p. ~*d, woke,* or *woken*). **1.** (often ~ *up*) (cause to) stop sleeping. **2.** stir up (sb.), rouse: *~ memories.* **~·ful** *adj.* unable to sleep; with little sleep: *pass a ~ful night.* **wak·en** ['weikn] *v.t. & i.* = ~.

²wake [weik] *n.* track left by a ship on water. *in the ~ of,* after; following.

walk [wo:k] *v.i. & t.* **1.** (of persons) move by putting forward each foot in turn, without having both feet off the ground at once (cf. *run*); (of animals) move forward at their slowest pace (cf. *trot, gallop*). **2.** ~ *away (off) with,* carry off; steal. **3.** cause to ~: ~ *a horse up a hill.* *n.* **1.** journey on foot, esp. for pleasure or exercise; manner or style of ~ing. **2.** path for ~ing: *numerous pleasant ~s in the district.* **3.** ~ *of life,* person's social position, trade, or profession. '~-·,o'ver *n.* (colloq.) easy victory (because there is no, or only weak, opposition).

wall [wo:l] *n.* continuous, vertical, and strong structure of stone, brick, concrete, wood, etc., forming one of the sides of a room or building, or enclosing a garden, court-yard. *with one's back to the ~,* fighting where escape or retreat is impossible. *go to the ~,* be pushed aside as weak or helpless. *v.t.* close (*up* an opening, e.g. a window) with a ~ of bricks, etc. '~-·,flow'er *n.* garden plant with sweet-smelling yellow or dark-red flowers.

Walls

wal·la·by ['woləbi] *n.* (sorts of) small kangaroo.

wal·let ['wolit] *n.* **1.** folding pocket-case, usu. of leather, for papers, bank-notes, etc. **2.** (old use) bag for food, etc., carried on a journey.

wal·low ['wolou] *v.i.* roll about (in mud, etc.) as a pig does.

wal·nut ['wo:lnət] *n.* (tree producing) edible nut in a hard

shell; wood of this tree, used for making furniture.

wal·rus ['wo:lrəs] *n.* large sea-animal with two tusks pointing down from the mouth.

A walrus

waltz [wo:ls] *n.* (music for) kind of dance in which partners go round and round. *v.i.* dance a ~.

wan [won] *adj.* (of a person, his looks, etc.) looking ill or tired; (of light, the sky) pale; not bright. **wan·ly** *adv.*

wand [wond] *n.* **1.** baton(2). **2.** thin stick or rod, esp. as used by a fairy or a magician (e.g. in a pantomime).

wan·der ['wondə*] *v.i.* **1.** go from place to place without any special plan; leave the right path or road. **2.** be absent-minded; allow the thoughts to go from subject to subject. ~·er *n.* ~·ings *n. pl.*

wane [wein] *v.i.* **1.** (of the moon; cf. *wax*) show a smaller bright area after full moon. **2.** become less or weaker: *His influence has ~d.* *n.* process of waning, esp. *on the ~.*

wan·gle ['wæŋgl] *v.t.* (slang) get, arrange (sth.) by cajolery or trickery.

want [wont] *v.t. & i.* **1.** require; be in need of. **2.** *be ~ing,* be missing or lacking: *A few pages of this book are ~ing. He is ~ing in courtesy,* is not polite. **3.** wish for; have a desire for: ~ *for nothing,* have all one needs. *n.* **1.** lack; scarcity; state of being absent: *The plants died for ~ of water.* **2.** need; absence of a necessary thing: *He's always in ~ of money.* ~·ing *prep.* without; in the absence of.

wan·ton ['wontən] *adj.* **1.** playful: ~ *breezes.* **2.** uncontrolled, disorderly: *a ~ growth of weeds.* **3.** wilful; serving no useful purpose; done without good reason: ~ *damage (insults).* **4.** immoral;

unchaste : ~ *thoughts*. *n.* (esp.)
~ (4) woman. ~**·ly** *adv.* in a ~
(3) manner.

war [wɔ:*] *n.* use of armed force,
(period of) fighting, between
nations or groups : *declare* (*make*)
war upon ; *be at war* (*with*) ; *go to
war against*. *have been in the
wars*, (colloq.) have been injured,
etc. *v.i.* (*-rr-*). fight ; make war :
*war against neighbouring coun-
tries*. **'war·fare** *n.* making war ;
condition of being at war ;
fighting. **'war·like** *adj.* ready
for war ; suggesting war ; fond
of war. **'war·path** *n.* (only)
on the warpath, ready for, engaged in, a fight or quarrel.
war·ring *ppl. adj.* (of tendencies, etc.) not in harmony. **'war·
ship** *n.* ship armed (1) for use
in war. **'war-worn** *adj.* exhausted by war.

war·ble ['wɔ:bl] *v.i. & t.* (esp. of
birds) sing, esp. with a gentle
trilling note. *n.* warbling ; bird's
song.

ward [wɔ:d] *n.* **1.** young person
under the guardianship of an
older person or of law authorities. **2.** *keep watch and* ~, guard
or protect. **3.** division of a town
for purposes of government. **4.**
division of, separate room in, a
building, esp. a prison or hospital : *the fever* ~. *v.t.* ~ *off*,
keep away, avoid (a blow, danger, etc.). ~**·en** *n.* person having control or authority (e.g. the
heads of some colleges and
schools in Gt. Brit., persons in
charge of hostels) : *a traffic* ~
(responsible for the parking of
cars). ~**·er**, ~**·ress** ['wɔ:dris] *n.*
man, woman, acting as guard in
a prison. '~**·room** *n.* room for
use by a warship's officers.

ward·robe ['wɔ:droub] *n.* cup-
board-like piece of furniture in
which to hang up clothes ; a
person's stock of clothes.

ware [wɛə*] *n.* **1.** (chiefly in compounds) manufactured goods :
silver~, *iron*~, *tin*~. **2.** (pl.)
articles offered for sale. '~**·
house** *n.* building for storing
goods, furniture, etc. *v.t.* store
in a ~house.

war·i·ly, see *wary*.

warm [wɔ:m] *adj.* (*-er*, *-est*).
having a sufficient degree of heat
to be comfortable to the body
(between *cool* and *hot*) ; (of clothing) serving to keep the body ~ ;
(of relationships, behaviour between persons) kindly, enthusiastic, affectionate : *a* ~ *welcome*.
make things ~ *for sb.*, make
things unpleasant for him ; make
trouble for him ; punish him.
v.t. & i. (often ~ *up*) make
or become ~ ; (fig.) become more
enthusiastic about what one is
doing or saying. *n.* act of ~-
ing : *Come by the fire and have a*
~. ~**·ly** *adv.* '~**·'blood·ed**
adj. (of animals) having ~ blood
(contrasted with snakes, etc.) ;
(fig.) having feelings which are
quickly excited. '~**·'heart·ed**
adj. kind and sympathetic.
warmth [wɔ:mθ] *n.* state of
being ~ ; (fig.) excitement,
passion.

warn [wɔ:n] *v.t.* make (sb.) aware
of possible danger or unpleasant-
ness. ~**·ing** *n.* that which ~s ;
words, happening, etc., which
~.

warp [wɔ:p] *v.t. & i.* (cause to)
become bent or twisted from the
usual or natural shape : *The hot
sun* ~*ed the boards*. (fig.) *His
mind is* ~*ed*. *n.* **1.** part (e.g. of
a board) in a ~ed state. **2.** long
threads over and under which
other threads (the *weft*) are
passed when cloth is woven on
a loom.

war·rant ['wɔrənt] *n.* **1.** justification ; sth. giving right or
authority (for action, etc.) : *He
has no* ~ *for saying so*. **2.** written
order giving official authority
for sth. : *a* ~ *to arrest a suspected
criminal* ; *sign his death*-~. **3.**
certificate appointing a man as
a ~-officer (see below). *v.t.*
1. be a ~ (1) for. **2.** guarantee
(the quality, etc., of goods).
'~**·'of·fi·cer** *n.* member of the
armed forces (e.g. sergeant-
major) of the highest rank below
commissioned officers.

war·ren ['wɔrən] *n.* area of land
with many rabbit holes.

war·ri·or ['wɒriə*] *n.* (liter.) soldier.

wart [wɔːt] *n.* small, tough growth on the skin.

wa·ry [ˈwɛəri] *adj.* cautious; in the habit of looking out for possible danger or trouble: ~ *of giving offence.* **war·i·ly** *adv.* **was,** see *be.*

wash [wɒʃ] *v.t. & i.* 1. make clean with or in water or other liquid. ~ *(sth.) out (off),* remove by ~ing; ~ *up,* (esp.) ~ dishes, cutlery, etc., after a meal. 2. (of materials) be capable of being ~ed without damage: *Does this stuff* ~ *well?* 3. (of the sea, a river, etc.) flow past or against; carry (sth.) *away, off,* etc.: ~ed *overboard by a big wave; wood* ~ed *up on the beach by the tide.* *n.* 1. act of ~ing; being ~ed. 2. clothing, bed-sheets, etc., to be ~ed or being ~ed; place where they are ~ed: *All my shirts are at the* ~. *She was hanging out the* ~. 3. wake (2); swirl of water (e.g. made by a ship's propellers). 4. (in compounds) liquid prepared for a special kind of ~ing: *white*~ (for walls); *mouth-*~ (disinfectant). ~·**er** *n.* 1. machine for ~ing clothes. 2. small, flat ring of rubber or leather for making a joint or screw tight. ~·**ing** *n.* = ~ (2). '~·**ing-ma·chine** *n.* machine for ~ing clothes. '~·**(-hand)-stand** *n.* table with basin, jug, etc., for ~ing oneself (in a bedroom). '~·**leath·er** *n.* soft leather for cleaning and polishing. '~·**out** *n.* carrying away of earth, rock, etc., by floods: *trains delayed by a* ~*out*; (colloq.) useless or unsuccessful person, thing, event, etc. ~·**y** *adj.* (of colour) pale; (of liquids, etc.) thin, watery.

wasp [wɒsp] *n.* flying insect with a narrow waist and a powerful sting in the tail. ~·**ish** *adj.* ill-tempered.

wast [wɒst] *v.* (old form) *thou wast,* you were.

waste [weist] *adj.* 1. (of land) that is not, cannot, be used; no longer of use; barren: *reclaim* ~ *land.* 2. useless; thrown away because not wanted: ~ *paper.* *v.t. & i.* 1. make no use of; use with no good purpose; use more of (sth.) than is necessary: ~ *one's time and money*; ~ *water.* 2. make (land) ~. 3. (cause to) lose strength by degrees: *He's wasting away.* *n.* 1. wasting or being ~d: *a* ~ *of energy (time)*; *run (go) to* ~, be ~d. 2. ~ material; bits and pieces remaining and unwanted. 3. area of ~ land: *the* ~*s of the Sahara.* **wast·age** [ˈweistidʒ] *n.* amount ~d; loss by ~. ~·**ful** *adj.* causing ~; using more than is needed. '~·**pipe** *n.* pipe for carrying away ~ water, e.g. from a kitchen sink. **wast·er, wast·rel** [ˈweistrəl] *n.* ~ful, good-for-nothing person.

watch [wɒtʃ] *v.t. & i.* 1. look at; keep the eyes on; look out (*for* sb. or sth. expected, danger, etc.); be on guard (*over* sth.). 2. (old use) remain awake: ~ *at the bedside of a sick child.* *n.* 1. act of ~ing, esp. to see that all is well: *keep* ~, look out for danger; *on the* ~ (*for*), ~ing for sb. or sth., esp. possible danger. 2. (in former times) body of men, called ~*men,* employed to go through the streets and protect people, their property, esp. at night. 3. (in ships) period of duty (4 or 2 hours) for part of the crew: *the middle* ~, midnight to 4 a.m.; the men working in such a ~. 4. small timepiece that can be carried in the pocket or worn on the wrist. ~·**ful** *adj.* on the ~. '~·**man** *n.* 1. see ~ (2). 2. (modern use) man employed to guard a building (e.g. a bank) against thieves, etc., esp. at night. '~·**word** *n.* 1. password. 2. slogan.

wat·er [ˈwɔːtə*] *n.* 1. liquid as in rivers, seas, etc.: *rain-*~. *under* ~, flooded. *get into (be in) hot* ~, get into (have) trouble because of foolish behaviour, etc. *throw cold* ~ *on (a plan, etc.),* discourage (it). *hold* ~, (of a theory) be sound when tested. 2. state of the tide: *at high (low)* ~; *in low* ~, (fig.) short of money. **3.** (often pl.) mass of ~: *The ~s of the lake pour out over the rocks.* **4.** solution, etc., of a substance in ~: *soda-~; rose-~.* *v.t. & i.* **1.** put ~ on. **2.** give ~ to (e.g. a horse). **3.** (of the eyes or mouth) fill with ~, have much liquid: *The smoke made my eyes* ~. *The smell made my mouth* ~, made me want (the food, etc.). **4.** add ~ to: ~ *the milk;* ~ *sth. down,* (fig.) weaken it. **'~-,clos·et** *n.* (or *W.C.*) small room where waste from the body is washed down a drain-pipe by ~ from a cistern. **'~-,col·our** *n.* **1.** (pl.) paints (to be) mixed with ~, not with oil. **2.** picture painted with ~-colours. **'~·course** *n.* (channel of) small river. **'~·cress** *n.* plant that grows in ~, with hot-tasting leaves. **wat·ered** *adj.* (of silk) having a pattern of wavy lines. **'~·fall** *n.* fall of ~ (esp. in a river over a cliff or over rocks). **'~·front** *n.* part of a town beside a river, lake, or harbour. **'~-ing-place** *n.* **1.** spa. **2.** pool, etc., where animals go for ~. **3.** seaside town visited by people for holidays. **'~-line** *n.* line along which the surface of the ~ touches the ship's side. **'~-logged** *adj.* **1.** (of wood, a boat, etc.) so full of ~ that it can hardly float. **2.** (of ground) swampy; very wet. **'~·mark** *n.* paper manufacturer's design, seen when the paper is held against the light. **'~-,mel·on** *n.* large smooth-skinned melon with juicy pink or red flesh inside. **'~·proof** *n. & adj.* (coat) which does not let ~ through. *v.t.* make (sth.) ~-proof. **'~·shed** *n.* line of high land separating river systems. **'~·spout** *n.* (esp.) column of ~ drawn up from the sea by a whirlwind to meet a funnel-shaped cloud. **'~·tight** *adj.* made, fastened, etc., so that ~ cannot get out or in; (fig., of an agreement, etc.) drawn up so that there is no escape from any of the provisions, etc. **'~-**

works *n. pl.* system of reservoirs, pipes, etc., for supplying ~ to a town or area. **~·y** *adj.* of or like ~; containing too much ~; (of colour) pale.

watt [wɒt] *n.* unit of electrical power.

wat·tle ['wɒtl] *n.* structure of sticks or twigs intertwined with thicker sticks at right angles, used for fences, walls, etc. ~ *and daub,* this structure covered with clay, for walls or roofs.

wave [weiv] *v.i. & t.* **1.** move or be moved to and fro, up or down, as a flag moves in the wind. **2.** cause (sth.) to move in this way: ~ *one's hand (to sb.);* ~ *one's umbrella.* make a signal to sb. by this means: ~ *sb. on (away, etc.).* **3.** (of a line or surface, of hair) be in a series of curves, like this: ⌇⌇⌇⌇; cause to be like this. *n.* **1.** long ridge of water, esp. on the sea, between two hollows (or troughs, furrows); such a ridge curling over and breaking on the shore. **2.** act of waving; waving movement: *a* ~ *of the hand.* **3.** curve like a ~ of the sea: *the ~s in her hair.* **4.** steady increase and spreading *(of sth.):* *a* ~ *of enthusiasm (indignation); a 'crime-~; a 'heat (cold)-~,* a period of weather much hotter (colder) than usual. **5.** ~-like motion by which heat, light, sound, or electricity is spread or carried. **'~·length** *n.* distance between the highest point (crest) of one ~ and that of the next, esp. with reference to wireless telegraphy. **wav·y** ['weivi] *adj.* having ~-like curves: *a wavy line* (see ~ (3)).

wav·er ['weivə*] *v.i.* **1.** move uncertainly or unsteadily: ~-*ing shadows.* **2.** hesitate (*between* two opinions, etc.). **3.** (of troops, etc.) show signs of giving way, become unsteady in attack or defence.

¹wax [wæks] *v.i.* **1.** (esp. of the moon, cf. *wane*) show a larger bright area. **2.** (old use) become (indignant, merry, etc.).

²wax [wæks] *n.* **1.** soft yellow

substance made by bees and used by them for honeycomb cells; this substance made white and pure, used for making candles, for modelling, etc. **2.** substance similar to bees-wax, e.g. paraffin wax, sealing-wax. **wax·en** *adj.* of or like wax. **'wax·work** *n.* human figure modelled in wax.

way [wei] *n.* **1.** road, street, path, etc., esp. in compound words (*highway, railway*). *pave the way for,* prepare (people) for. **2.** route, road (to be) used from one place to another: *the quickest way from A to B; lose (find) one's way; buy some on the way home.* **3.** direction: *look this way; go that way; the wrong way round,* facing the wrong direction. **4.** distance: *We're a long way from home.* **5.** method or plan: *the right way to do it; do it in this way; ways and means,* (esp.) methods of providing money for sth. needed. **6.** (often pl.) method of behaving; habit or custom: *British ways of living. It's not his way to be mean. She has winning ways* (i.e. behaves so as to win the confidence and affection of people). **7.** point or detail: *They're in no way similar. He's clever in some ways.* **8.** space or freedom for movement: *You're in my way. Get out of the way. All traffic must make way for the fire-engine.* **9.** (phrases): *by the way,* often used to introduce a remark not connected with the subject of conversation. *by way of,* for the purpose of: *by way of introduction;* in the course of: *by way of business. in a way,* to some extent or degree. *in a bad (etc.) way,* in a bad condition, very ill, etc. *in a small way,* on a small scale. *have (get) one's own way,* have (do, get) what one wants. *give way,* break, bend, yield (*under, to*). **10.** progress; forward movement: *make one's way home; gather (lose) way,* (of ships) gain (lose) speed; *be under way,* (of ships) be moving forward. **11.** structure of heavy

timber down which a newly-built ship slides into the water. **'way·far·er** *n.* (liter.) person travelling on foot. **'way·side** *adj. & n.* (of, at) the side of the road: *wayside flowers* (*inns*).

way·lay [wei'lei] *v.t.* (p.t. & p.p. *waylaid*). (wait somewhere to) attack, rob, or speak to (sb.) as he passes.

way·ward ['weiwəd] *adj.* self-willed; not easily controlled or guided.

we [wi:] *pron.* (object form *us* [ʌs]) used by a speaker or writer in referring to himself and another or others.

weak [wi:k] *adj.* (*-er, -est*). **1.** (opp. of *strong*) below the usual standard of strength; easily bent or broken; unable to resist attack, hard wear or use. **2.** (of a solution) having little of some substance in relation to the water, etc.: ~ *beer; a* ~ *solution.* **3.** (of the senses) below normal: ~ *sight.* **4.** ~ *verb,* one that forms the past tense and p.p. by the addition of *-ed, -d,* or *-t* (e.g. *walked, dealt*). ~**'en** *v.t. & i.* make or become ~(er). **'~-'kneed** *adj.* (fig.) ~ in character; lacking determination. ~**'ling** *n.* ~ person or animal. ~**'ly** *adj.* delicate in health; sickly. *adv.* in a ~ manner. **'~-'mind·ed** *adj.* (esp.) easily influenced by others. ~**'ness** *n.* **1.** state of being ~. **2.** fault or defect of character. **3.** *have a* ~*ness for,* a special or foolish liking for.

¹weal [wi:l] *n.* well-being: *for the general (public)* ~, the welfare of all.

²weal [wi:l] *n.* mark on the skin made by a blow from a stick, whip, etc.

wealth [welθ] *n.* **1.** (possession of a) great amount of money, property, etc.; riches. **2.** great amount or number (*of*): *a* ~ *of illustrations.* ~**'y** *adj.* (*-ier, -iest*). having ~ (1); rich.

wean [wi:n] *v.t.* **1.** accustom (a baby, a young animal) to food other than its mother's milk.

2. cause (sb.) to turn away (*from* bad habits, companions, etc.).

weap·on ['wepən] *n.* sth. designed for, or used for, fighting or struggling (e.g. guns, fists, a strike by workmen).

wear [weə*] *v.t. & i.* (p.t. *wore* [wo:*, woə*], p.p. *worn* [wo:n]). **1.** have on the body or (of looks) on the face : *He was ~ing a hat (spectacles, a troubled look, a beard, a ring on his finger, heavy shoes).* ~ *one's hair long,* allow it to be long. **2.** (cause to) become less useful, be in a certain condition, etc., by being used: *This material has worn thin. My socks have worn into holes. The steps (The inscription on the stone) had worn away.* **3.** (be of a sort to) endure continued use; remain in a certain condition: *Good leather will ~ for years. This cloth has worn well (badly).* **4.** (fig. uses with adv.): ~ *off,* pass away: *The feeling of strangeness soon wore off.* ~ *on,* (of time) pass slowly away. ~ *out,* make or become exhausted: *His patience wore out (was worn out) at last. worn out by hard work.* *n.* **1.** use as clothing: *a suit for everyday ~ ; showing signs of ~* (i.e. no longer new-looking); *the worse for ~,* having been worn or used a long time and no longer in a good and useful condition. **2.** damage or loss of quality from use. *The carpets are showing ~. (fair) ~ and tear,* damage, loss in value, resulting from (normal) use. **3.** (esp. in compounds) things to ~ (1): *foot~; under~; a shop selling children's ~.*

wea·ry ['wiəri] *adj.* (*-ier, -iest*). **1.** tired. **2.** causing tiredness: *a ~ journey. v.t. & i.* make or become ~. **wea·ri·ly** *adv.* **wea·ri·ness** *n.* **wea·ri·some** *adj.* tiring; long and dull.

wea·sel ['wi:zl] *n.* small, fierce animal with red-brown fur, living on rats and rabbits, birds' eggs, etc.

weath·er ['weðə*] *n.* conditions over a particular area and time with reference to sunshine, temperature, wind, rain, etc. *v.t. & i.* **1.** come safely through (a storm, a crisis). **2.** become affected by the ~: *rocks ~ed by wind and water; leave wood to ~* (= season (1)). '~·,beat·en *adj.* (of sb.'s face) showing the result of exposure to sun, wind, etc. '~-bound *adj.* unable to make or continue a journey because of bad ~. '~·cock, -vane *n.* device, often in the shape of a cock, turning with the wind and showing its direction.

weave [wi:v] *v.t. & i.* (p.t. *wove* [wouv], p.p. *woven* ['wouvn]). **1.** make (by hand or by machine) (threads) into cloth, etc.; make (cloth, etc.) from threads. **2.** make (garlands, baskets, etc.) by a similar process; (fig.) put together, compose (a story, romance, etc.) from incidents. *n.* style of weaving: *a loose (coarse, plain, etc.) ~.* **weav·er** *n.*

web [web] *n.* **1.** network (usu. fig.): *a web of lies.* **2.** sth. made of threads by some creatures: *a spider's web.* **3.** skin joining the toes of water-birds, bats, and some water-animals (e.g. frogs). **webbed** [webd] *adj.* having webs (3) between the toes. **web·bing** *n.* band of coarse woven material used in belts, seats of chairs, etc.

A spider's web   A wedge

wed [wed] *v.t. & i.* (p.t. & p.p. *wedded* ['wedid]). marry. *wedded to,* devoted to (e.g. a hobby, an opinion). **wed·ding** *n.* marriage ceremony. '**wed·lock** *n.* state of being married.

wedge [wedȝ] *n.* V-shaped piece, esp. of wood or metal, for splitting or securing. *the thin end of the ~,* a small change or demand likely to lead to big changes or demands. *v.t.* fix tightly (as) with a ~; fasten (sth.) tightly with a ~.

Wednes·day ['wenzdi] *n.* the fourth day of the week.

wee [wi:] *adj.* (Scot.) (very) small.

weed [wi:d] *n.* wild plant growing where it is not wanted (e.g. in a garden, a field of wheat). *v.t. & i.* **1.** take ~s out of (the ground). **2.** ~ *out*, remove, get rid of (what is of lower value than the rest). ~·y *adj.* (*-ier, -iest*). **1.** with many ~s growing. **2.** tall, thin, and weak: ~y *young men.*

weeds [wi:dz] *n. pl.* (usu. *widow's* ~) mourning (black clothes) as worn by widows in some countries.

week [wi:k] *n.* **1.** period of seven days, esp. Saturday midnight to Saturday midnight. **2.** the six working days (i.e. except Sunday). '~-day *n.* any day except Sunday. '~-'end *n.* Saturday and Sunday (as a period of rest or holiday): *a ~-end visit.* ~·ly *adj. & adv.* (happening) once a ~, every ~; of, for, or lasting a ~: *a ~ly wage of £30; ~ly visits.* *n.* periodical published once a ~.

weep [wi:p] *v.i. & t.* (p.t. & p.p. *wept*). cry; let tears fall from the eyes: ~*ing for joy;* ~*ing over her dead son.* ~·ing *adj.* (of trees, esp. birch and willow) with branches drooping gracefully.

wee·vil ['wi:vil] *n.* small beetle with a hard shell, feeding on nuts, grain, and other seeds.

weft [weft] *n.* cross-threads taken over and under the warp in weaving.

weigh [wei] *v.t. & i.* **1.** learn how heavy sth. is. **2.** show a certain measure when put on a scale, etc.: *The box ~s 10 pounds.* **3.** compare, balance, the value or importance of (one thing *with* or *against* another): ~ *the consequences;* ~ *one's words,* choose them carefully. **4.** ~ *with,* have an effect upon, appear important to. **5.** ~ (*sth. or sb.*) *down,* pull down by being heavy, (fig.) make troubled or anxious; ~ *upon,*

(fig.) be heavy on. **6.** ~ *anchor,* raise it, begin a voyage. **weight** *n.* **1.** force with which a body tends towards the centre of the earth. **2.** how heavy a body is; this expressed in some scale (e.g. in tons, kilogrammes) as measured on a weighing-machine, etc.: *Are bananas sold by ~t or at so much apiece?* **3.** piece of metal of a certain ~t used in ~ing things (*an ounce ~t*) or in a machine (e.g. *a clock worked by ~ts*). **4.** (degree of) importance or influence: *arguments of great ~t.* *v.t.* **1.** put a ~t (3) or ~ts (3) on; make heavy. **2.** ~t *down,* burden with: *He was ~ted down with packages.* ~·ty *adj.* (*-ier, -iest*). **1.** of great ~t; burdensome. **2.** influential; important: ~*ty arguments.*

weir [wiə*] *n.* wall or similar structure built across a river to control the flow of water.

weird [wiəd] *adj.* (*-er, -est*). **1.** unnatural; unearthly. **2.** (colloq.) strange; difficult to explain or understand. ~·ly *adv.*

wel·come ['welkəm] *adj.* **1.** received with, giving, pleasure: *a ~ visitor* (rest). *make sb. ~,* show him that his coming is ~. **2.** *you are ~ to . . . ,* it gives me pleasure to give (lend, etc.) you . . . . *n.* words, behaviour, etc., used when sb. arrives, when an offer is received, etc.: *We had a warm* (*cold, enthusiastic*) ~. *v.t.* show pleasure or satisfaction at the arrival of sb. or sth.; greet (in the way indicated): ~ *a suggestion* (*warmly, coldly*).

weld [weld] *v.t. & i.* **1.** join or unite (pieces of metal, usu. heated) by hammering, pressing together, etc.; make (material into sth.) by doing this. **2.** (of iron, etc.) be capable of being ~ed. *n.* ~ed joint. ~·er *n.*

wel·fare ['welfɛə*] *n.* condition of having good health, a comfortable home, etc. ~ *state,* state in which the ~ of all classes is aided by national insurance, medical services, old-age pensions, etc.

¹**well** [wel] *n.* **1.** hole, usu. lined

with brick or stone, made in the ground for a water-supply (see the picture at *windlass*). **2.** hole bored for mineral oil. **3.** (old use, or in place-names) spring or fountain of water. **4.** deep, enclosed space in a building, often from roof to basement, for a staircase or lift. *v.i.* flow (*up* or *out*) as water flows from a ~ (3).

²**well** [wel] *adj.* (*better*, *best*). **1.** in good health: *be* (*look*, *feel*) ~ ; in a satisfactory condition: *Is all ~ with you?* (Are you happy, etc.?) **2.** *it would be ~ to*, it would be wise or desirable to. *~ and good*, all right, I agree (accept). *adv.* **1.** in a good, right, or satisfactory manner: *children behaving ~* ; with approval: *We think ~ of him.* **2.** *as ~* (*as*), in addition (to); also. **3.** *be ~ out of* (sth.), be the happier because not concerned with. **4.** with good reason: *You may ~ be surprised.* **5.** *We may as ~* (begin now, etc.), there is no reason why we should not. *n.* *wish sb.* ~, wish him success; *let ~ alone*, not change what is already satisfactory. *int.* expressing surprise, expectation, acceptance, etc.

well- [wel-] *prefix.* '~-'**be·ing** *n.* welfare; health, happiness, and prosperity. '~-'**born** *adj.* of a family with good social position. '~-'**con·'nec·ted** *adj.* ~-born. '~-'**dis·'posed** *adj.* having kind feelings (*towards*); ready to help. '~-'**do·ing** *n.* good deeds. '~-'**in·'ten·tioned**, '~-'**mean·ing**, '~-'**meant** *adj.* having, resulting from, good intentions. '~-'**nigh** *adv.* almost. '~-'**timed** *adj.* done, said, etc., at a suitable time. '~-to-'**do** *adj.* wealthy. '~-'**tried** *adj.* (of methods, remedies) tested and proved useful. '~-'**worn** *adj.* much used.

wel·ling·tons ['weliŋtənz] *n. pl.* high boots reaching to the knees.

welt [welt] *n.* **1.** strip of thick leather to which the sole and the upper part of a shoe are stitched. **2.** = ²*weal*.

wel·ter ['weltə*] *v.i.* wallow. *n.* confused mixture or state (*of*).

wench [wentʃ] *n.* (old use) girl or young woman, esp. a household servant.

wend [wend] *v.t.* ~ *one's way* (home, etc.), go, make one's way.

went, see *go*.

wept, see *weep*.

wert [wɔːt] *v. thou wert*, you were.

west [west] *n.* that part of the horizon where the sun is seen to set; that part of the world, of a country, etc., in this direction; cardinal point of the compass that is on the left of a person facing north; coming from the ~: *a ~ wind.* *adj.* situated, dwelling, in or towards the ~: *the W~ Indies*; *the ~ African peoples.* *adv.* to the ~: *sail from Southampton to New York.* ~'**er·ly** *adj. & adv.* (of direction) towards the ~; (of winds) from the ~. ~'**ern** *adj.* of (in, from) the ~: *~ern civilization*, that of Europe and America. ~'**ern·ize** *v.t.* introduce ~ern civilization (in)to. ~'**ward** *adj.* towards the ~. ~'**ward(s)** *adv.*

wet [wet] *adj.* (*wetter*, *wettest*). **1.** covered or soaked with water. **2.** rainy: *a wet day.* *n.* moisture; rain: *Come in out of the wet.* *v.t.* (*-tt-*). make wet. **wet·ting** *n.* becoming or being made wet: *get a wetting.* '**wet-nurse** *n.* woman who suckles another woman's child.

weth·er ['weðə*] *n.* castrated male sheep.

whack [hwæk] *v.t.* strike (sb. or sth.) with a blow hard enough to be heard. *n.* (sound of a) sharp blow.

whale [hweil] *n.* largest sea-animal in existence, valued for its oil. '~-**bone** *n.* thin, horny, springy substance from the upper jaw of some kinds of ~. **whal·er** *n.* ship or man engaged in hunting ~s.

wharf [hwɔːf] *n.* (pl. ~s or *wharves* [hwɔːvz]). wooden or stone structure at which ships are moored for (un)loading cargo. ~'**age** ['hwɔːfidʒ] *n.* (payment for) use of a ~.

U

what [*h*wot] *adj.* (cf. *which*) asking for one or more out of several people or things to be identified : *W~ books have you read on this subject? W~ time is it? W~ authors do you like best?* **pron.** *W~* (= ~ thing) *would you like for breakfast? Do ~* (that thing which) *you think is right.* **~·ev·er** [*h*wot-'evə*] **pron. & adj.** any sort or degree of : *W~ever* (service) *you give, give it willingly. ~ever he says,* it does not matter ~ he says. *no doubt ~ever,* no doubt at all.

wheat [*h*wi:t] *n.* (plant producing) grain from which flour (as used for bread, etc.) is made. **~·en** *adj.* of (coarse) ~ flour : *~en bread.*

whee·dle ['*h*wi:dl] *v.t.* make oneself pleasant to sb., flatter or coax, to get sth. one wants : *The child ~d sixpence out of her father (~d her father into giving her sixpence).*

wheel [*h*wi:l] *n.* circular frame or disc which turns on an axle (in a machine, on a bicycle, cart, motor-car, etc.). *at the ~,* driving a car, etc. ; steering a ship. *v.t. & i.* 1. push or pull (sth. on ~s, e.g. a barrow), convey sth. (in a handcart, etc.). 2. (cause to) turn in a curve or a circle. '~·**bar·row** *n.* small one-~ed vehicle with two legs and two handles, for moving small loads. '~·**wright** *n.* man who makes and repairs ~s.

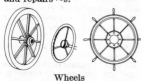

Wheels

wheeze [*h*wi:z] *v.i.* breathe noisily, esp. with a whistling sound in the chest or windpipe ; (of a pump, etc.) make a similar sound. **wheez·y** *adj.*

whelp [*h*welp] *n.* young dog (lion, tiger, etc.) ; ill-bred boy or young man.

when [*h*wen] *adv.* 1. at what time? on what occasion? : *W~ can you come to see us?* 2. (after day, time, etc.) at or on which : *Sunday is the day ~ I am least busy.* **conj.** 1. at or during the time that : *It was late ~ we arrived.* 2. although : *He stands ~ he might sit down.* 3. since ; considering that : *Why should I be polite to him ~ he is rude to me?* 4. at or during which time : *I will come and see you ~ I have an hour to spare.* **~·'ev·er** [*h*wen'evə*] *adv.* at every time ~.

whence [*h*wens] *adv.* 1. (in questions) from what place or cause? 2. (in statements) from which place. 3. to the place from which : *Return ~ you came.*

where [*h*weə*] *adv.* 1. in or to what place or position? ; in what direction? : *W~ does she live?* 2. what place? *W~ are you going to (does he come from)?* 3. in or at which : *That's the place ~ I was born.* '~·**a·'bouts** *adv.* in or near what place. *n.* place where sb. or sth. is. **~·'as** *conj.* taking into consideration that. '~·**fore** *adv.* (old use) why. *conj.* for which reason ; why. ‚~·**up·'on** *adv.* after which ; and then. **where·'ev·er** *adv.* in, to, or at, whatever place ; at those places ~. '~·**with·al** *n.* money with which to do sth. : *I haven't the ~withal to marry.*

whet [*h*wet] *v.t.* (-*tt*-). sharpen (a knife, etc.) ; excite (the appetite). '~·**stone** *n.* stone for ~ting edged tools.

wheth·er ['*h*weðə*] *conj.* 1. (cf. *if,* introducing an indirect question) : *I don't know ~ I can come or not.* 2. (introducing an infinitive phrase) : *I don't know ~ to accept or refuse.*

whey [*h*wei] *n.* liquid part of sour milk after separation of curds (for making cheese).

which [*h*witʃ] *adj.* (cf. *what*). *W~ way shall we go,* to the right or to the left of the wood? *Tell me ~ books on my shelf you would like to borrow.* **pron.** 1. ~ things ; ~ persons : *W~ is taller,*

Tom or Dick? **2.** relative pronoun referring to things, not persons: *This river, ~ flows through London, is called the Thames. The hotel at ~ we stayed was the cheapest in the town.* (Cf. *that*.) **~·'ev·er** *pron. & adj.* any one or ones (of a limited number, esp. two).

whiff [*h*wif] *n.* slight breath (of air, smoke, etc.); smell: *the ~ of a cigar.*

while [*h*wail] *conj.* **1.** during the time that; for as long as; at the same time as: *W~ there's life there's hope. W~ in London he studied music.* **2.** whereas. **3.** although: *W~ I admire your courage, I think you ought not to go on this dangerous journey.* *n.* (period of) time: *Where have you been all this ~? once in a ~,* occasionally; *worth one's ~,* repaying the time, effort, etc., needed. *v.t. ~ away the time,* pass the time pleasantly.

whim [*h*wim] *n.* sudden desire or idea, often sth. unusual or unreasoning.

whim·per ['*h*wimpə*] *v.i. & n.* (make a) weak cry of pain or fear (e.g. as of a baby when ill).

whim·sy ['*h*wimzi] *n.* whim; fanciful idea or wish. **whim·si·cal** ['*h*wimzikl] *adj.* full of whimsies; odd; quaint.

whine [*h*wain] *n.* low, long-drawn, complaining cry (e.g. made by a miserable dog or child). *v.t. & i.* make, say (sth.) with, such a cry; ask (for help, etc.) in a piteous way.

whin·ny ['*h*wini] *n.* gentle neigh made by a horse to show pleasure. *v.i.* make this sound.

whip [*h*wip] *n.* length of cord, strip of leather, etc., fastened to a handle. *have the ~ hand of* (*sb.*), have mastery over, be in a position to control. *v.t. & i.* **1.** strike with a ~. **2.** beat (eggs, cream, etc.) with a fork, etc., to mix thoroughly and make stiff. **3.** move or take suddenly: *~ out a knife; ~ off your coat.* **~·'ping** *n.* beating with a ~ as punishment.

whir(r) [*h*wə:*] *n.* sound (as of) bird's wings moving quickly or of wheels, etc., turning fast. *v.i.* make such sounds.

whirl [*h*wə:l] *v.t. & i.* **1.** (cause to) move quickly round and round: *fallen leaves ~ing in the wind.* **2.** (of the brain, the senses) be giddy; seem to ~. **3.** take, be taken, rapidly (*off, away,* etc.) in a car, etc. *n.* ~ing movement: *a ~ of dust.* '~' **pool** *n.* place where there are ~ing currents of water. '~' **wind** *n.* swift, circling current of air.

whisk [*h*wisk] *n.* **1.** small brush for removing dust, flies, etc. **2.** metal device (e.g. coiled wire) for whipping (2) eggs, etc. **3.** light, brushing movement (e.g. of a horse's tail). *v.t. & i.* **1.** brush (*off, away,* etc.) lightly and quickly. **2.** take (sb. or sth.), go (*off, away*) quickly and suddenly: *He was ~ed off to prison.* **3.** wave or move quickly: *The cow ~ed her tail.*

whisk·er ['*h*wiskə*] *n.* **1.** (usu. pl.) hair left to grow down the sides of a man's face (cf. *beard, moustache*). **2.** one of the long, stiff hairs growing near the mouth of a cat, etc.

whis·ky ['*h*wiski] *n.* strong alcoholic drink distilled from grain.

whis·per ['*h*wispə*] *v.i. & t.* speak, say (sth.) very softly, using the breath but not the vocal cords; (of leaves, the wind, etc.) make soft sounds. *n.* ~ing sound; sth. ~ed; (esp.) sth. ~ed secretly, a rumour.

whist [*h*wist] *n.* card-game for four players.

whis·tle ['*h*wisl] *n.* **1.** (usu. high) clear note made by forcing a stream of air or steam through a small opening, or by the wind; musical sound made by birds. **2.** instrument for producing such sounds: *a steam-~ ; the referee's ~.* *v.i. & t.* make a ~ (1) (e.g. by blowing through the rounded lips); make a musical series of notes in this way: *~ a tune;* make a signal (*to* sb., *to* a dog, etc.) with such sounds.

Whit, see *Whitsun*.

white [*h*wait] *adj*. (-*r*, -*st*). of the colour of fresh snow on the paper on which this book is printed. *the* ~ *flag*, the symbol of surrender. *a* ~ *lie*, a lie considered to be harmless, esp. one told for the sake of being polite. *n*. (esp.) the colourless liquid in an egg, ~ when boiled or fried (cf. *yolk*). **whit·en** ['*h*waitn] *v.t. & i*. make or become ~(r). **whit·ing** *n*. powdered ~ chalk used in ~wash. '~**·wash** *n*. mixture of powdered chalk or lime and water used for coating walls, ceilings, etc. *v.t.* put ~-wash on; (fig.) try to make (sb., his reputation) appear blameless.

whith·er ['*h*wiðə*] *adv*. (old use) where.

Whit·sun ['*h*witsən] *n*. (also *Whit Sunday*) 7th Sunday after Easter. ~**·tide** *n*. ~ and the weekend or the following week (often *Whit Monday*, etc.).

whit·tle ['*h*witl] *v.t. & i*. (often ~ *down or away*) cut thin slices or strips off (wood); cut (*at* sth.) in this way; (fig.) reduce by degrees: ~ *down their salaries*.

whiz(z) [*h*wiz] *v.i. & n*. (make the) sound of sth. rushing through the air: *An arrow* ~*ed past my ear*.

who [hu:] *pron*. (object form *whom* [hu:m]; possessive, *whose* [hu:z]). used as the subject, and only of persons. **1**. what person(s): *Who is that man? Who are those men? Do you know who she is? Do you know who(m) you are speaking to? To whom did you give it?* (formal style). *Who did you give it to?* (colloq.). **2**. *This is the man who asked to see you. My son, whom you met last week, wants to see you again.* ~**·'ev·er** *pron*. any person ~; the person ~.

whole [houl] *adj*. **1**. *the* ~ *truth*, all the truth; *his* ~ *energies*, all his energies. **2**. undamaged; unbroken: *escape with a* ~ *skin*; *not a* ~ (i.e. uncracked or unbroken) *plate in the house*. **3**. complete; entire: *cook a* ~ *sheep*; *rain for three* ~ *days*; *a* ~ *num-*

ber, one without a fraction. *n*. **1**. sth. complete: *A* ~ *is greater than any of its parts*. **2**. all there is of sth.: *He lost the* ~ *of his money*. **3**. (*up*)*on the* ~, taking everything into consideration. '~**·'heart·ed(ly)** *adj. & adv*. (in a manner) not weakened by doubt or hesitation. '~**·sale** *n*. (cf. *retail*) selling of goods (esp. in large quantities) to shop-keepers, etc., for resale to the public. '~**·some** *adj*. healthy; favourable to the health: ~*some food* (*surroundings*). **whol·ly** *adv*. completely.

whom, see *who*.

whoop [hu:p] *n*. loud cry: ~*s of joy*. '~**·ing-cough** *n*. children's disease with short violent coughs after long indrawing of breath.

whose, see *who*.

why [*h*wai] *adv*. for what reason?: *Why are you so late? The reason why he did it is not clear*. *int*. indicating surprise: *Why, even a child knows that!*; in protest: *Why, I could have told you the answer if you had asked me*.

wick [wik] *n*. (length of) thread which runs through a candle; strip of woven material by which oil in an oil-lamp or stove is drawn up to burn.

wick·ed ['wikid] *adj*. **1**. (of a person, his acts) bad, wrong, immoral. **2**. spiteful; intended to injure: ~ *rumours*. ~**·ly** *adv*. ~**·ness** *n*.

wick·er ['wikə*] *n*. twigs or canes woven together, usu. for baskets or furniture: *a* ~ *chair*. '~**·work** *n*. things made of ~.

wick·et ['wikit] *n*. **1**. (also ~-*door*, ~-*gate*) small door or gate, esp. one at the side of, or made in, a larger one. **2**. small opening (e.g. one with a sliding window) at which tickets, etc., are sold. **3**. (cricket) three stumps (with cross pieces called *bails*) at which the ball is bowled; the stretch of grass between the two ~s: *A soft* ~ *helps the bowlers*. *take a* ~, defeat a bats-man. '~**·₁keep·er** *n*. the player stationed behind the ~ (3).

wide [waid] *adj.* (-r, -st). **1.** measuring much from side to side or in comparison with length; broad: *a ~ road*; *sixty feet ~.* **2.** of great extent: *a man with ~ interests* (i.e. in many subjects). **3.** *~ of*, far from (what is aimed at or desired): *Your answer was ~ of the mark.* *adv.* **1.** in many directions: *searching far and ~.* **2.** fully: *~ open*; *~ awake.* **3.** *~ apart*, with *~ space(s) between.* **4.** far from what is aimed at: *The arrow fell ~ (of the mark).* **wid·en** *v.t. & i.* make or become *~(r).* **'~·spread** *adj.* (esp.) found, distributed, over a large area. **~·ly** *adv.* **1.** at *~* intervals. **2.** to a large extent. **3.** over a large area.

wid·ow ['widou] *n.* woman who has not married again after her husband's death. **~·er** *n.* man who has not married again after his wife's death. **wid·owed** *adj.* made a *~* or *~er*: *~ed by the war.*

width [widθ] *n.* **1.** quality of being wide. **2.** measurement from side to side: *ten feet in ~.* **3.** piece of material of a certain *~* (2); *join two ~s of cloth.*

wield [wi:ld] *v.t.* have and use: *~ an axe* (fig. *control, authority*).

wife [waif] *n.* (pl. *wives* [waivz]). woman who has a husband: *Smith and his ~.* (See **marry**.)

wig [wig] *n.* head-covering of false hair (e.g. as worn by judges in law courts, by actors, etc.).

wig·gle ['wigl] *v.t. & i.* (cause to) move with quick, short, side-to-side movements: *The baby ~d its toes.*

wild [waild] *adj.* (-er, -est). **1.** (of animals) living in natural conditions (e.g. lions and tigers); not tamed; (of plants) growing in natural conditions, not cultivated. **2.** uncultivated; unsettled: *~ and mountainous areas.* **3.** violent; uncontrolled; stormy: *~ seas* (weather); *~ with anger*; *driven ~ with anxiety.* **4.** reckless; done or said without proper thought or care: *~ schemes* (guesses). **5.** be *~*

about sth. or sb., *~* to do sth., (colloq.) have a strong desire for, love of, etc. *adv.* without care or control. *n.* the *~s*, uncultivated and (often) unpeopled areas: *the ~s of Africa.* **~·ly** *adv.* **~·ness** *n.* **'~·fire** *n.* (only in) *spread like ~fire*, (of news, etc.) spread very quickly.

wil·der·ness ['wildənis] *n.* wild, uncultivated waste land; desert.

wile [wail] *n.* trick; bit of cunning: *the ~s of the Devil.* *v.t.* entice, trick (sb. *away, into* doing sth.).

wil·ful ['wilful] *adj.* **1.** (of a person) obstinate; determined to have one's own way. **2.** (of bad acts) done on purpose: *~ murder.* **~·ly** *adv.*

¹will [wil] *aux. v.* (negative *~ not* or *won't* [wount]; p.t. *would* [wud, wəd, əd, d], negative *would not* or *wouldn't* ['wudnt]). **1.** used (cf. *shall*) in the future tense: *you, he, they, ~ go.* **2.** used (1st person) to express willingness, etc.: *All right, I ~ come.* **3.** in requests: *W~ you (Won't you) come in?* **4.** indicating strong purpose, etc.: *She ~ have her own way.* **5.** in refusing: *I won't let you go.* **6.** *would* is used (2nd and 3rd persons) in conditional statements and questions: *If a car had no brakes there would soon be an accident. would rather,* see *rather.*

²will [wil] *v.t.* (p.t. *would* [wud], no other forms used). **1.** (old use) wish: *Let him do what he ~.* **2.** (expressing wishes): *Would that it were true*, I wish it were true. **3.** make use of one's mental power in an attempt to do or get sth.: *We cannot achieve success merely by ~ing it.* **4.** (p.t. & p.p. *~ed*). leave (property, etc. to) by means of a testament (or *³will*(6)): *He ~ed most of his money to charities.*

³will [wil] *n.* **1.** mental power by which a person can direct his thoughts and actions, and influence those of others. **2.** (also *~·power*) control exercised over oneself, one's impulses: *have no ~ of one's own.* **3.** determination; desire or purpose: *work (do sth.) with a ~. He always has his ~* (or, colloq., *his own way*). *God's ~ be done. married against her ~,* i.e. to sb. she did not wish to marry. **4.** *at ~,* whenever and however one pleases. **5.** *good (ill) ~,* kind (unkind) feeling towards others. **6.** (often *last ~ and testament*) statement in writing saying how sb. wishes his property to be distributed after his death.

wil·ling ['wiliŋ] *adj.* **1.** ready to help, to do what is needed: *~ workers; ~ to work.* **2.** done, given, etc., readily, without hesitation: *~ obedience.* **~·ly** *adv.* **~·ness** *n.*

will-o'-the-wisp ['wiləðə,wisp] *n.* (fig.) sth. or sb. that one pursues unsuccessfully because (it or he) is difficult to grasp or reach.

wil·low ['wilou] *n.* (wood of) tree with thin, easily-bent branches. **~·y** *adj.* (of persons) slender and graceful in movement.

wil·ly-nil·ly ['wili'nili] *adv.* whether he wishes or not.

¹wilt [wilt] *v.* (old use) *thou wilt,* you will.

²wilt [wilt] *v.i. & t.* (of plants, etc.) (cause to) droop, lose freshness.

wil·y ['waili] *adj.* (*-ier, -iest*) full of wiles; cunning: *as ~ as a fox.*

win [win] *v.t. & i.* (*-nn-*; p.t. & p.p. *won* [wʌn]). **1.** get by means of hard work, perseverance, as the result of competition, etc.; do best in (*a fight,* etc.): *win a race (a battle, a scholarship, a prize, fame and fortune). Which team won?* **2.** persuade (sb.) by argument, etc. (*to do sth.*): *win (sb.) over,* overcome his objections to sth. **3.** reach by effort: *win the summit (shore).* *n.* success in a game, competition, etc. **win·ner** *n.* **win·ning** *adj.* (esp. of looks, behaviour) attractive; likely to win favour, etc.: *a winning smile; winning ways.*

win·nings *n. pl.* (esp.) money won in gambling.

wince [wins] *v.i. & n.* (make a)

sudden movement (in fear or pain): *He ~d at the insult.*

winch [wintʃ] *n.* windlass.

¹wind [wind] *n.* **1.** air blowing along as the result of natural forces: *A cold ~ blew from the north. The ~ carried my hat away. in the ~,* being secretly planned or going forward. (*see, find out*) *how the ~ blows,* what people are thinking, what is likely to happen. *take the ~ out of sb.'s sails,* prevent him from doing or saying sth. by doing or saying it first. **2.** breath needed for running, etc.: *The runner soon lost his ~.* **3.** scent carried by the ~ (1); *get ~ of,* (fig.) get news of; suspect. **4.** gas formed in the bowels and causing discomfort: *suffer from ~.* **5.** meaningless or valueless talk. **6.** (sound of) orchestral *~-instruments.* *v.t.* (p.t. & p.p. *~ed* ['windid]). **1.** cause to be out of breath: *The blow ~ed me.* **2.** rest (a horse which is out of breath). **'~·fall** *n.* fruit blown down by the *~;* (fig.) unexpected piece of good fortune, esp. money, coming to sb. **'~·,in·stru·ment** *n.* musical instrument (e.g. a trumpet or flute) from which sound is produced by forcing air through it. **'~·mill** *n.* mill worked by the *~* acting on large wooden sails, used for grinding grain or pumping up water. **'~·pipe** *n.* passage for air from the throat to the lungs. **'~·screen** *n.* window in front of the driver's seat in a motor-car, etc. **'~·ward** *adj. & adv.* (side) in the direction from which the *~* blows. **~·y** *adj.* (*-ier, -iest*). with much *~: a ~y day;* open to the *~: a ~y cliff.*

²wind [waind] *v.i. & t.* (p.t. & p.p. *wound* [waund]). **1.** go or move in a curving, circular, spiral, or twisting manner: *The river ~s (its way) to the sea. a ~ing staircase.* **2.** twist (string, wool, yarn, etc.) into a ball or round or on to sth. (e.g. a reel). **3.** turn (a handle, e.g. of a *~lass*); raise (sth.) by doing this: *~ up ore from a mine;* tighten the spring (of a clock, etc.) to put or keep its works in motion. **4.** ~ up, come or bring to an end: *It's time for him to ~ up his speech. ~ up a business company, one's affairs*, put everything in order before bringing to an end. **5.** *be wound up*, be tense with (excitement, etc.). *n.* bend or twist. '~**ing-sheet** *n.* sheet (to be) wound round a corpse.

³**wind** [waind] *v.t.* (p.t. & p.p. *winded* or *wound* [waund]). blow or sound (a horn, a bugle, a call *on* a horn, etc.).

wind·lass ['windləs] *n.* machine for lifting or pulling.

A windlass   Windows

win·dow ['windou] *n.* opening in a wall, etc., to let in light and air; framed pane(s) of glass for or in a ~ opening: *Please shut the ~.*

wine [wain] *n.* alcoholic drink made from the juice of grapes; ~-like drink made from other fruits or plants.

wing [wiŋ] *n.* **1.** one of the organs of a bird or insect with which it beats the air; one of the flat surfaces on each side of an aircraft that support it in the air. *on the ~*, in flight. *under sb.'s ~*, (of a person) cared for by, protected by, sb. **2.** part of a building, army, etc., stretching out at the side: *build a new ~ to a hospital.* **3.** (pl.) sides of the stage in a theatre (not visible to the audience).

A wing   The wings

wink [wiŋk] *v.i. & t.* **1.** shut and open (one's eyes or, usu., one

eye) quickly; do this (with one eye *at* sb.) as a private signal or hint (e.g. of amusement). **2.** ~ *at* (sth.), deliberately ignore (misconduct). *n.* **1.** act of ~ing, esp. as a hint or signal. **2.** *forty* ~*s*, a short sleep (esp. during the day); *not sleep a ~, not have a ~ of sleep*, have no sleep.

win·now ['winou] *v.t.* **1.** use a stream of air to separate dry outer coverings from grain. **2.** (fig.) separate what is true, good, useful, etc., from what is false, worthless, etc.

win·ter ['wintə*] *n.* season between autumn and spring, when (except in the tropics) the weather is usually cold. *v.i.* pass the ~: ~ *in the south.* **win·try** *adj.* of or like ~; cold; *a wintry sky.*

wipe [waip] *v.t.* **1.** clean or dry (sth.) by rubbing with a cloth, etc.: ~ *the dishes;* ~ *sth. dry;* ~ *your tears away.* **2.** ~ *off,* remove by wiping; ~ *out,* clean the inside of; remove (e.g. a mark or (fig.) disgrace); destroy completely; ~ *up,* soak up (liquid) by wiping. *n.* act of wiping. **wip·er** *n.* sth. that ~s clean: *windscreen-~r* (on a car).

wire ['waiə*] *n.* **1.** (piece or length of) strong metal thread: *telephone* ~*s.* **2.** (colloq.) telegram. *v.t. & i.* **1.** fasten (sth.) with ~. **2.** put ~(s) into: ~ *a house for electric current.* **3.** send a telegram to. **wir·ing** ['waiəriŋ] *n.* system of ~s for carrying electric current in a house, apparatus, etc. **wir·y** ['waiəri] *adj.* (esp. of persons) lean and with strong sinews.

wire·less ['waiəlis] *n.* radio; broadcasting: *listen to a concert on* (over) *the ~.*

¹**wise** [waiz] *adj.* (-r, -st). having or showing experience, knowledge, good judgement, prudence, etc.: ~ *men* (*acts*). ~·**ly** *adv.* **wis·dom** ['wizdəm] *n.* **1.** quality of being ~. **2.** thoughts, sayings, etc.: *the wisdom of our ancestors.* '~·₁**a·cre** *n.* person who tries to seem much ~r than he really is.

²**wise** [waiz] *n.* (only in) *in no ~,
in this ~*, in no (this) way.

wish [wiʃ] *v.t. & i.* **1.** have a
desire: *I ~ I knew* (I feel that I
should like, or ought, to know,
but I don't know). **2.** want:
When do you ~ to leave (*~ me to
leave*)? **3.** hope or desire (sth.)
for (sb.): *~ sb. a pleasant journey*. **4.** *~ for*, feel that one would
like to receive (sth.); pray for:
*can't ~ for anything better; have
everything you can ~ (for)*. *n.* **1.**
desire or longing: *in obedience
to your ~es*. **2.** *with all good ~es,
~ing* (3) you well. *~·**ful** adj.*
~ful thinking, thinking that sth.
is true merely because one ~es
it were true.

wisp [wisp] *n.* small bundle or
twist (*of* straw, hair, etc.);
spiral (*of* smoke).

wist·ful ['wistful] *adj.* having,
moved by, showing, an un-
satisfied and often vague desire:
~ eyes. *~·**ly** adv.*

wit [wit] *n.* **1.** intelligence;
quickness of mind. *have one's
wits about one*, be quick to see
what is happening, ready to act.
be at one's wits' end, not know
what to do or say. *live by one's
wits*, live by clever, not always
honest, methods. **2.** (person
noted for) clever and humorous
expression of ideas: *conversation
full of wit*. **wit·ti·cism** ['witi-
sizm] *n.* humorous remark. **wit·
ty** *adj.* (*-ier, -iest*). full of humour. **wit·ti·ly** *adv.*

witch [witʃ] *n.* woman said to
use magic, esp. for evil purposes.
'*~·**craft** n.* use of such magic.
'*~-**doc·tor** n.* male *~*. *~·**er·y**
n.* **1.** *~craft*. **2.** fascination;
charm.

with [wið] *prep.* **1.** having;
carrying: *a coat ~ four pockets;
a man ~ a bad arm* (*no legs*). **2.**
to indicate what is used: *writing
~ a pen; fill a barrow ~ sand*.
3. association: *live ~ one's
parents; mix one thing ~ another*.
4. opposition: *fight ~, argue ~
sb*. **5.** manner: *do sth. ~ pleasure*.
6. at the same time as; in the
same way as: *A tree's shadow
moves ~ the sun*. **7.** in regard to:

Be patient ~ children. **8.** separation: *I parted ~ her after many
years*. **9.** support; agreement:
*Are you ~ me or against me in
this matter?*

with·draw [wið'drɔː] *v.t. & i.*
(p.t. *-drew* [-druː], p.p. *-drawn*
[-drɔːn]). **1.** pull or draw back.
2. take out, away: *~ savings
from the bank; ~ a child from
school*. **3.** take back (a statement, an accusation, an offer).
4. move or go back or away: *~
troops from a place*. *~·**al** n.*

with·er ['wiðə*] *v.t. & i.* **1.**
(often *~ up, away*) (cause to)
become dry, faded, or dead: *The
flowers ~ed. The hot summer ~ed
(up) the grass*. **2.** (cause (sb.) to
be covered with shame or confusion: *She gave him a ~ing
look*.

with·hold [wið'hould] *v.t.* (p.t.
& p.p. *-held*). keep back; refuse
to give.

with·in [wið'in] *adv.* (old use)
inside. *prep.* inside; not beyond: *live ~ one's income; ~
hearing*, near enough to hear or
be heard; *~ a mile of the church*,
not more than a mile away.

with·out [wið'aut] *adv. & prep.*
1. (opposite of *with*) not having.
2. (old use) outside.

with·stand [wið'stænd] *v.t.* (p.t.
& p.p. *withstood*). resist; hold
out against (pressure, attack).

wit·ness ['witnis] *n.* **1.** person
who gives evidence under oath
in a law court. **2.** evidence;
what is said about sb. or an
event. *bear ~ to sb.'s character*,
speak about it from knowledge.
3. person who adds his own signature to a document to testify
that another person's signature
on it is genuine. **4.** sb. or sth.
that is a sign or proof of sth.:
My clothes are a ~ of my poverty.
v.t. & i. **1.** be a *~* (3) to (an
agreement, etc.). **2.** be a *~* (1)
of (an event). **3.** give *~* (2) (in
a law court, etc.). **4.** be a *~*
(4) of (sth.).

wit·ti·cism, wit·ty, see *wit*.

wit·ting·ly ['witiŋli] *adv.* consciously; knowingly; on purpose.

wives, see *wife*.

wiz·ard ['wizəd] *n.* **1.** magician. **2.** person with amazing abilities: *He's a ~ at mathematics.*

wiz·ened ['wiznd] *adj.* (esp. of the face) wrinkled; shrivelled.

wob·ble ['wɔbl] *v.i. & t.* (cause to) move unsteadily from side to side; (fig.) be uncertain (in opinions, in making decisions, etc.). **wob·bly** *adj.*

woe [wou] *n.* **1.** sorrow; grief; distress: *a tale of woe.* **2.** (pl.) causes of woe: *poverty, illness and other woes.* **woe·ful** *adj.* sorrowful; causing woe.

woke, see ¹*wake*.

wolf [wulf] *n.* (pl. *wolves* [wulvz]). wild, flesh-eating animal of the dog family, hunting in packs. *keep the ~ from the door,* be able to buy enough food, etc., for oneself and family. *v.t.* (colloq.) *~ one's food,* eat it quickly and greedily.

wom·an ['wumən] *n.* (pl. *women* ['wimin]). adult female human being; the female sex. **~·hood** *n.* women in general; the state of being a ~: *to reach ~hood.* **~·ish** *adj.* (of a man) like a ~ (in feeling, behaviour, etc.); (of things) more suitable for women than men. **~·ly** *adj.* proper to a ~: *~ly modesty.*

womb [wu:m] *n.* part of a female mammal in which offspring is held and nourished while developing before birth.

won, see *win*.

won·der ['wʌndə*] *n.* feeling caused by sth. unusual or surprising; thing or event causing such a feeling: *look at sth. in ~; be filled with ~; no ~ that . . ., it is not surprising that . . .; for a ~,* it is surprising (that); *work ~s,* produce amazing results. *v.i. & t.* **1.** feel ~ (*at*). **2.** ask oneself (*about* sth., *who, what, why, whether,* etc.). **~·ful** *adj.* causing ~; remarkable. **~·ment** *n.* surprise. **won·drous** ['wʌndrəs] *adj.* (old or liter.) ~ful.

wont [wount] *n.* what sb. is accustomed to doing: *He went to bed much later than was his ~.*

predic. adj. he was ~ to . . ., it was his custom to. . . . **~·ed** ['wountid] *adj.* customary; usual.

won't = *will not.*

woo [wu:] *v.t. & i.* **1.** woo a woman, try to win her love; pay court (5) to her. **2.** try to win (fame, fortune, sleep).

wood [wud] *n.* **1.** hard solid substance of a tree inside the bark. **2.** (often pl.) area of land covered with growing trees. *out of the ~,* free from troubles or difficulties. '**~·cut** *n.* print from a design or picture cut on a block of ~. **~·ed** *adj.* covered with ~s (2). **~·en** *adj.* made of ~: (fig.) stiff, clumsy, as if made of ~. '**~·land** *n.* tree-covered land. '**~·work** *n.* **1.** things made of ~, esp. the ~en parts of a building. **2.** carpentry. **~·y** *adj.* **1.** ~ed. **2.** of or like ~.

wool [wul] *n.* soft, curly hair of sheep, goats, camels, and some other animals; thread, yarn, cloth, clothing, made from this. **~·len** *adj.* made of ~. *n.* (usu. pl.) cloth, etc., made of ~. **~·ly** *adj.* made of, looking like, covered with, ~; (fig., of ideas, arguments) not clear. *n.* (pl. *woollies*). knitted ~len garment(s).

word [wə:d] *n.* **1.** unit of language as spoken, written, or printed: *put one's thoughts into ~s.* **2.** sth. said; talk; statement. *have a ~ with sb.,* speak to him. *have ~s (with sb.),* quarrel. *by ~ of mouth,* in spoken ~s, not in writing. *take sb. at his ~,* act on the belief that he means what he has said. **3.** news: *Leave ~ for me at the office. Send me ~ tomorrow.* **4.** promise; assurance: *break (keep, give sb.) one's ~, be as good as one's ~,* do all one has promised. *v.t.* express in ~s: *How shall we ~ the letter?* **~·ing** *n.* choice of ~s to express meaning. '**~·'per·fect** *adj.* knowing, able to repeat, sth. (e.g. a part in a play) perfectly. **~·y** *adj.* using, expressed in, a large number of ~s, esp. unnecessary ~s.

wore, see *wear*.

work [wə:k] *n.* **1.** use of bodily or mental powers with the purpose of doing or making sth. (esp. contrasted with play or amusement); use of energy supplied by steam, electricity, etc.: *Machines do much of the ~ formerly done by man.* set (get) to ~, begin doing sth. *make short ~ of sth.,* finish it quickly. **2.** what a person does to earn a living; employment. *in* (*out of*) ~, having (not having) employment. *at* ~, at one's place of employment; busy with one's ~. **3.** sth. (to be) done by ~ (1): *have a lot of ~ to do.* **4.** things needed or used for ~: *She took her ~* (e.g. sewing) *into the garden.* **5.** sth. produced by ~: *the ~ of silversmiths;* also in compounds, as *needle~, stone~, wood~.* **6.** product of the intellect or imagination: *a ~ of art; the ~s* (plays and poems) *of Shakespeare.* **7.** (pl.) moving parts of a machine (e.g. a clock): *sth. wrong with the ~s;* building(s) where industrial or manufacturing processes are carried on: *an iron~s. The ~s have closed.* **8.** *public ~s,* the building of roads, embankments, etc., by government authorities. *v.i. & t.* (p.t. & p.p. ~*ed,* see *wrought*). **1.** do ~. **2.** (of a machine, apparatus, bodily organ) be in operation, do what it is required or designed to do: *The lift* (*bell, etc.*) *is not ~ing.* **3.** (of a plan, method, etc.) have the desired outcome; be successful: *Will the method ~?* **4.** cause to ~; set in motion: *He ~s his wife too hard. The machines are ~ed by electricity.* **5.** produce as the result of effort; perform: ~ *miracles* (*a cure, harm, mischief*); ~ *out* (plan) *a scheme.* **6.** (cause to) move or go, usu. by degrees and often with difficulty (*in, out, through,* or *into* some condition): *The screw has ~ed loose. Can you ~ the stone into position? The men ~ed their way forward.* ~ *into,* introduce (e.g. a few jokes into a lecture). ~ *off,* get rid of; deal with: ~ *off one's superfluous energy.* ~ *up,* create by degrees: ~ *up a business;* excite: ~ *up sb.'s feelings* (*a rebellion*). **7.** make or shape by hammering, kneading, etc.: *wrought iron* (cf. *cast iron*): ~ *clay* (knead it with water). **8.** cause a change to come about in; have (esp. a disturbing) influence *upon: The sufferings of the refugees ~ed upon our feelings. The idea ~ed like madness in his brain.* **9.** make by stitching; embroider: ~ *a design on a cushion cover.* ~**'a·ble** *adj.* that can be ~ed; practicable: *a ~able scheme.* '~**a·day** *adj.* commonplace; dull: *a ~aday life.* '~**-bag,** '~**bas·ket,** '~**-box** *n.* one for holding (esp. needle~) materials. ~**er** *n.* person who ~s: ~man. '~**house** *n.* (old use) public institution for homeless people. ~**ing** *n.* (esp.) part of a mine or quarry. ~**man** *n.* man who earns a living by physical labour or in a factory, etc. ~**man·like** *adj.* characteristic of a good ~man. ~**man·ship** *n.* quality as seen in sth. made: *articles of poor ~manship.* '~**shop** *n.* room or building where things (esp. machines) are made or repaired.

world [wə:ld] *n.* **1.** the earth, its countries and people. **2.** persons, institutions, etc., connected with a special class of people or of interests: *the ~ of sport; the academic ~.* **3.** *the Old W~,* Europe, Asia, and Africa as known to the ancients; *the New W~,* America. **4.** *a ~ of,* a great amount of; *for all the ~ like,* like in every way. ~**'ly** *adj.* **1.** material: *my ~ly goods,* my property. **2.** (contrasted with *spiritual*) of this ~: *~ly pleasures.*

worm [wə:m] *n.* small, boneless, limbless creature of many sorts, esp. (*earth~*) the kind living in the ground. *v.t.* (often ~ *one's way*) go or get slowly (*through, into*); win by perseverance and patience, etc.: ~ *one's way into favour;* ~ *a secret out of sb.*

¹~·,eat·en *adj.* (of wood, etc.) full of holes made by ~s.

worn, see *wear.*

wor·ry ['wʌri] *v.t. & i.* (p.t. & p.p. worried). **1.** trouble; give (sb.) no peace of mind: ~ *sb. with foolish questions* ; ~ *sb. to do sth.* **2.** be troubled; be anxious or uneasy: *Don't ~ about trifles.* **3.** (usu. of dogs) seize and shake with the teeth: *The dog was ~ing a rat.* *n.* **1.** sth. that worries; cause of anxiety: *Is your life full of worries?* **2.** condition of being troubled: *show signs of ~.*

worse [wəːs] *comp. adj. & adv.* (= more bad(ly)): *Your work is bad but hers is ~; mine is worst of all. He behaved far ~ than she did.* *the ~ for wear,* in a bad condition as the result of being worn or used. *~ off,* poorer, less well treated. **wors·en** *v.t. & i.* make or become ~.

wor·ship ['wəːʃip] *n.* **1.** reverence and respect paid to God: *public ~, church service; place of ~,* church or chapel. **2.** admiration and respect shown to or felt for sb. or sth.: *hero-~.* **3.** *your (his) W~,* title of respect used to (of) a magistrate or mayor. *v.t. & i.* **1.** give ~(1), (2) to. **2.** attend church service. *~·per n.*

worst [wəːst] *adj. & adv.* (= most bad(ly), cf. *worse*): *get the ~ of it,* be defeated. *If the ~ comes to the ~,* if things are as bad as they possibly can be. *v.t.* defeat.

wor·sted ['wustid] *n.* twisted woollen yarn or thread; cloth made of this.

worth [wəːθ] *predic. adj.* **1.** having a certain value; of value equal to that of; possessing: *He died ~ £5,000.* **2.** giving a satisfactory return or reward for: *The book is well ~ reading. It was ~ it (~ our while),* ~ the money, time, etc., given to it. *n.* value; what sb. or sth. is ~: *a discovery of great ~; a pound's ~ [-wəθ] of stamps,* as many as £1 will buy. *~·less adj.* ¹~-¹while *adj.* that is ~ the time, money,

etc., needed: *a ~-while experiment.*

wor·thy ['wəːði] *adj.* (-ier, -iest). **1.** deserving (support, etc.): ~ *of respect; a ~ cause* (i.e. one deserving support). **2.** deserving respect: *a ~ gentleman.* *n.* (old use) person well known and respected. **wor·thi·ly** *adv.*

would, see ¹*will* and ²*will.*

¹**wound** [waund] *v.* see ²*wind* and ³*wind.*

²**wound** [wuːnd] *n.* **1.** hurt or injury to the body done by cutting, shooting, tearing, etc., esp. as the result of attack. **2.** pain given to a person's feelings: *a ~ to his pride.* *v.t.* give a ~ to: *ten killed and fifty ~ed in the battle* (cf. *injured* in an accident).

wove, wov·en, see *weave.*

wran·gle ['ræŋgl] *v.i. & n.* (take part in a) noisy or angry argument.

wrap [ræp] *v.t. & i.* (-pp-). **1.** (often ~ *up*) put (soft material, a blanket, etc.) round; cover or roll up (*in* paper or other soft material, etc.). **2.** *be ~ped up in,* be deeply interested in, devoted to. *n.* extra outer garment or covering (e.g. a scarf, cloak, rug). *~·per n.* paper cover for food, a newspaper, book, etc. (esp. for sending by post). *~·ping n.* (material for) covering or packing.

wrath [rɔːθ] *n.* (liter.) deep anger; strong indignation. *~·ful adj.* angry.

wreak [riːk] *v.t.* ~ *one's fury* (*indignation, etc.*) *upon sb.,* give effect to, give expression to.

wreath [riːθ] *n.* (pl. ~s [riːðz]). flowers or leaves twisted or woven together in a circle; ring or curving line (*of* smoke, etc.). **wreathe** [riːð] *v.t. & i.* encircle; cover: *hills ~ed in mist; a face ~ed in smiles,* a smiling face.

wreck [rek] *n.* ruin or destruction, esp. of a ship; ship that has suffered destruction or that has sunk; motor-car, building, etc., that has been badly damaged or that has fallen into ruin. *v.t.* cause the ~ of: *The*

ships (My hopes) were ~ed. ~·
age ['reikidʒ] *n.* ~ed material,
fragments: *The ~age of the aircraft was scattered over a wide
area.* **wrecked ppl. adj.** (of
sailors, etc.) having suffered
ship~.

wren [ren] *n.* small song-bird.

wrench [rentʃ] *n.* **1.** sudden and
violent twist or pull. **2.** (pain
caused by) sad parting or separation. **3.** tool for gripping and
turning nuts, bolts, etc.; span-
ner. *v.t.* **1.** twist or pull violently: *~ sth. off (away, open).*
2. injure (e.g. one's ankle) by
twisting.

wrest [rest] *v.t.* **1.** take (sth.)
violently away *(from): I ~ed
the sword from him (out of his
hand).* **2.** get by hard work:
~ a living from the soil.

wres·tle ['resl] *v.i. & t.* struggle
(with) in an effort to throw (sb.)
down without hitting (him); (fig.)
~ with a problem. **wres·tler**
n. person who ~s, esp. in sport.

wretch [retʃ] *n.* **1.** unfortunate
and miserable person. **2.** contemptible, mean person. ~**·ed**
['retʃid] *adj.* **1.** miserable; likely to cause misery: *living in ~ed
conditions.* **2.** of poor quality;
bad: *~ed food (weather).*

wrig·gle ['rigl] *v.i. & t.* **1.** twist
and turn (the body or a part of
it); move along by twisting:
*children who~ in their seats. The
fish ~d out of my fingers.* **2.** (fig.)
~ out of (doing sth., a difficulty),
escape from. *n.* wriggling movement.

wring [riŋ] *v.t.* (p.t. & p.p. *wrung*
[rʌŋ]). twist and squeeze tightly;
force (esp. water *out)* by doing
this: *~ (out) wet clothes; ~ water
out of a cloth; ~ a chicken's neck;*
(fig.) *~ money (a confession) out
of sb.,* get it by persuasion, etc.
~ing wet, (of clothes, etc.) so
wet that water can be wrung out
of them. ~**·er** *n.* (or *mangle)*
machine for ~ing clothes.

wrin·kle ['riŋkl] *n.* **1.** small fold
or line in the skin of the face
or on the surface of sth. (e.g. a
dress): *iron out the ~s.* **2.** (colloq.) useful hint or suggestion.

v.t. & i. make or get ~s in: *~
(up) one's forehead.*

A wringer

wrist [rist] *n.* joint between the
hand and arm. ~**·let** ['rislit] *n.*
band or ornament for the
~.

writ [rit] *n.* **1.** written order
issued in the name of a ruler or
sb. in authority to an official or
other person to do or not to do
sth. **2.** *Holy W~,* the Bible.

write [rait] *v.i. & t.* (p.t. *wrote*
[rout], p.p. *written* ['ritn]). make
letters or other symbols on a
surface, esp. with a pencil or
pen on paper; record (on paper)
by means of words, etc.: *write
(down) the address.* ~ *out,* copy
neatly; set down on paper a full
list, etc. *~ up,* (esp.) describe,
write about (an event, etc.), esp.
praising. **writ·er** *n.* one who
writes, esp. an author or jour-
nalist. **writ·ing** *n.* **1.** handwriting. **2.** (usu. pl.) literary work:
the writings of Swift.

writhe [raið] *v.i.* twist or roll
about in pain; (fig.) suffer mental agony: *~ under insults.*

wrong [roŋ] *adj.* (opp. of *right)* not
morally right; incorrect; unjust;
mistaken; unsuitable; out of
order; in a bad condition. *adv.*
in a *~ manner: You've spelt my
name ~* (cf. *~ly). go ~,* take to
evil ways; take a *~ road;* (of
plans) have a poor result; get
out of order. *n.* what is morally
~; evil; injustice; instance of
unjust treatment: *You've done
me a great ~ by blaming me for
this. in the ~,* having done or
said sth. ~; in error. *put sb. in
the ~,* cause him to seem in the
~. *v.t.* do ~ to; judge (sb.)
unfairly; make (sb.) appear
worse than he is. '~**·do·ing** *n.*
doing ~; crime; sin. ~**·ful adj.**
unjust; unlawful. ~**·ful·ly adv.**

~·**ly** *adv.* (esp. with a p.p.)
I was ~ly informed.

wrote, see *write.*

wroth [rouθ] *adj.* (liter.) angry.

wrought [rɔːt] old p.t. and p.p. of
work. **1.** ~ *iron,* forged or rolled
iron, not cast iron. **2.** *in a ~-up
state,* with the feelings excited or
disturbed.

wrung, see *wring.*

wry [rai] *adj.* pulled or twisted
out of shape: *make a wry face*
(usu. showing disgust, disappointment).

X

Xmas ['krisməs] *n.* common ab-
breviation (not used in speaking)
for *Christmas.*

X-rays ['eks'reiz] *n.* short-wave
rays that penetrate solids and
enable doctors to see into the
body. *n. sing.* **1.** apparatus for
using ~. **2.** (attrib.) *an X-ray
photograph.* **X-ray** *v.t.* examine
or treat with ~.

Y

yacht [jɔt] *n.* **1.** light sailing-
boat built specially for racing.
2. small (usu. privately-owned)
(power-driven or sailing-) ship
used for pleasure-cruising.

yak [jæk] *n.* long-haired ox of
Central Asia.

yam [jæm] *n.* climbing plant of
tropical countries; its tuber as
food.

yap [jæp] *v.i. & n.* (*-pp-*). (utter
a) short, sharp bark (as of an
excited puppy).

¹**yard** [jɑːd] *n.* **1.** unit of length,
3 feet or 36 inches. **2.** pole
fastened to a mast for supporting
a sail. ~**-arm** *n.* either half
of a ~ (2).

²**yard** [jɑːd] *n.* **1.** (usu. unroofed)
enclosed or partly enclosed
space near or round building(s),
often with a paved or stone
floor: *the school ~* (playground);
a farm~. **2.** enclosure for a
special purpose; *marshalling ~s*
(where goods trains are made
up). See also *dock~, ship~.*

yarn [jɑːn] *n.* **1.** thread prepared
for knitting, weaving, etc., esp.
woollen thread. **2.** (colloq.) story;
traveller's tale. *v.i.* tell ~s (2).

yawn [jɔːn] *v.i.* **1.** open the
mouth wide and breathe in
deeply, as when needing sleep or
when bored. **2.** be wide open:
a ~ing gulf. *n.* act of ~ing (1).

¹**ye** [jiː] *pron.* old form of *you:
How d'ye do?*

²**ye** [ji, (before a vowel) jiː] *adj.*
(old form of) *the: Ye olde Bull
and Bush* (as an inn-sign).

yea [jei] *adv. & int.* (old use) yes.

year [jiə•] *n.* **1.** time taken by
the earth in making one revolution round the sun, 365¼ days.
2. period from 1 January to 31
December; period of the same
length but starting on a different
day, e.g. *the academic ~.* *Leap
Y~,* see *leap.* ~**ling** *n.* animal
between one and two years old.
~**ly** *adj. & adv.* (taking place)
every ~, once every ~.

yearn [jɜːn] *v.i.* have a strong
desire (*for, to do* sth.). ~·**ing** *n.*
longing (*after, for*). ~·**ing·ly**
adv.

yeast [jiːst] *n.* substance used in
the brewing of beer and the
making of bread; added to
the dough it produces gas and so
makes the bread ²*light* (4).

yell [jel] *v.i. & t. & n.* (utter a)
loud cry of pain, excitement,
etc.; say (sth.) in a ~ing voice.

yel·low ['jelou] *n. & adj.* the
colour of gold or the yolk of a
hen's egg. ~ *fever,* tropical
disease causing the skin to turn
~. *v.i. & t.* (cause to) become ~.

yelp [jelp] *v.i. & n.* (esp. of dogs)
(utter a) short, sharp cry (of
pain, anger, or excitement).

yeo·man ['joumən] *n.* (pl. *-men*).
(old use) working farmer who
owned his land. *do ~('s) service,*
give valuable help in time of
need. ~**ry** *n.* cavalry force of
volunteers, not part of the
regular army.

yes [jes] *particle* indicating agreement, consent, etc., contrasting with *no*.

yes·ter·day ['jestədi] *n. & adv.* (on) the day before to-day.

yet [jet] *adv.* by this or that time; up to now; up to then; so far; still; at some future time. (Cf. *already.*) *conj.* but still; nevertheless.

yew [ju:] *n.* (wood of) evergreen tree with dark-green leaves.

yield [ji:ld] *v.t. & i.* **1.** give a natural product, a result or profit: *trees that ~ fruit; investments ~ing 10 per cent.* **2.** give way, esp. to force; surrender: *~ a town to the enemy.* **3.** *~ to none*, refuse to admit that anyone else is more fond of, zealous for, etc. *n.* amount produced: *the ~ per acre.* **~·ing** *adj.* easily giving way or bending; (*fig.*) not obstinate.

yoke [jouk] *n.* **1.** shaped piece of wood placed across the necks of oxen pulling a cart, plough, etc. **2.** *a ~ of oxen*, two oxen working together. **3.** *pass* (*come*) *under the ~*, acknowledge and accept defeat; *throw off the ~* (of servitude, etc.), rebel, refuse to obey. **4.** piece of wood shaped to fit a person's shoulders, used to support the weight of buckets, etc. **5.** part of a dress, etc., fitting the shoulders and the upper part of the chest. *v.t.* **1.** *~d to*, united to. **2.** put a ~ (1) on (oxen).

A yoke

yo·kel ['joukl] *n.* simple-minded countryman.

yolk [jouk] *n.* yellow part of an egg.

yon [jɔn], **yon·der** ['jɔndə*] *adj. & adv.* (that is, that can be seen) over there.

yore [jɔ:*, jɔə*] *n.* (liter.) *of ~*, of olden days; of the past.

you [ju:] *pron.* **1.** the person(s) addressed: *You are my friend(s).* **2.** (colloq.) any person: *You never know who may become your enemy* (one never knows who . . .). **your** [jɔ:*, jɔə*] *adj.* belonging to, relating to, you. **you're** [jɔ:*] = you are.

yours [jɔ:z, jɔəz] *pron. & predic. adj.* of you. **your·self** [jɔ:'self] *pron.* (pl. *~selves* [-selvz]). *Did you hurt ~self when you fell down? Did you do it by ~self* (without help)? *You ~self* (nobody else) *said so.*

young [jʌŋ] *adj.* (*-er, -est*). **1.** (contrasted with *old*) not far advanced in life, growth, etc.; of recent birth or origin: *a ~ woman* (*tree, animal, nation,* etc.). **2.** still near its beginning: *The night is still ~. n. ~ offspring. the ~, ~ people; ~ ones* (of animals and birds). **~·ish** *adj.* fairly ~. **~·ster** ['jʌŋstə*] *n.* child, esp. a boy.

youth [ju:θ] *n.* **1.** the state of being young. **2.** young persons: *the ~ of the nation; a Y~ Hostel.* **3.** (pl. *~s* [ju:ðz]). young man. **~·ful** *adj.* young; having the qualities, etc., of young people: *~ful appearance.*

yule [ju:l] *n.* (also *~-tide*). Christmas.

Z

zeal [zi:l] *n.* enthusiasm; warm interest (*for a cause, one's work,* etc.). **~·ot** ['zelət] *n.* person who shows much ~ for a cause. **~·ous** ['zeləs] *adj.* having, showing, acting with, ~. **~·ous·ly** *adv.*

ze·bra ['zi:brə] *n.* horse-like wild animal of Africa, with dark stripes on its body.

zen·ith ['zeniθ] *n.* part of the sky directly overhead; (*fig.*) highest point (of one's fame, fortune).

zeph·yr ['zefə*] *n.* west wind; (poet.) soft, gentle breeze.

ze·ro [ˈziərou] *n.* **1.** the figure 0 ; nought. **2.** the point between + and – on a scale, esp. a thermometer.

zest [zest] *n.* **1.** great interest or pleasure. **2.** pleasing or stimulating quality or flavour: *The possible danger gave* ~ *to the adventure.*

zig·zag [ˈzigzæg] *n.* line or path that turns right and left alternately at sharp (equal or unequal) angles: (attrib.) *a* ~ *path up the hillside.* **adv.** in a ~. *v.i.* (-gg-). go in a ~ course.

A zigzag A zipper

zinc [ziŋk] *n.* white metal used in alloys, and for coating sheet iron for roofing, etc.

zip [zip] *n.* sound as of a bullet going through the air. **zip·per,** ˈzip-ˌfast·en·er *n.* device for locking together two toothed metal edges by means of a sliding tab, used for fastening bags, dresses, etc.

zo·di·ac [ˈzoudiæk] *n.* belt of the sky in which the sun, moon, and planets move, divided into twelve parts having names (the signs of the ~).

zone [zoun] *n.* **1.** belt or band round sth. and distinguished from it by colour, appearance, etc. **2.** one of the five parts into which the earth is divided by imaginary lines parallel to the equator (the *torrid,* the *N. & S. temperate,* and the *arctic* or *frigid* ~s). **3.** area with particular features, purpose or use: *the war* ~; *the* ~ *of submarine activity.* **zon·al** *adj.* of, arranged in, ~s.

zoo [zu:] *n.* zoological gardens.

zo·ol·o·gy [zouˈɔlədʒi] *n.* science of the structure, forms, and distribution of animals. **zo·o·log·i·cal** [ˌzouəˈlɔdʒikl] *adj.* of ~ : *zoological gardens,* park (usu. public) in which many kinds of animals are kept for exhibition. **zo·ol·o·gist** [zouˈɔlədʒist] *n.* expert in ~.

about - acerca de
Above - acima de
Across - através de
after - depois
Against - contra
Among - entre (mais de)
between - entre (dois)
At, em, no, aos, a
before - antes de
behind - atrás de
below - por baixo de
Beneath - por baixo de
beside - ao lado de
besides - além de
by - junto de
For - para
From - de
In - dentro de
near - perto de
of - de
off - fora de
on - em cima de
over - acima de
past - para além de
since - desde
TO - para

COMMON PREFIXES AND SUFFIXES

The following lists are given for reference and study.

The meanings of prefixes are given under their entries in the dictionary; but suffixes, as such, do not appear in the body of the dictionary and are therefore explained here.

COMMON PREFIXES

aero-	dis-	milli-	self-
air-	ex-	mis-	semi-
Anglo-	fore-	multi-	step-
ante-	grand-	non-	sub-
anti-	great-	out-	super-
arch-	hecto-	over-	tele-
be-	hydro-	pan-	trans-
bi-	il-	poly-	tri-
by-	im-	post-	ultra-
co-	in-	pre-	un-
contra-	ir-	pro-	under-
de-	kilo-	pseudo-	vice-
deci-	mal-	radio-	well-
demi-	mid-	re-	

COMMON SUFFIXES

-able, -ible (Used to make adjs.) (*a*) that can be, is liable to be : *curable* (that can be cured); *eatable*; *conceivable*; *justifiable*; *compressible*; *taxable*; *digestible*. (*b*) having the qualities of: *comfortable*; *peaceable*. (*c*) likely to: *suitable*; *knowledgeable* (likely to know).

-ably, -ibly (Used to make advs. from adjs. in *-able*, *-ible*.) *peaceably*; *conceivably*; *suitably*.

-age (Used to make nouns.) (*a*) charge for ... ing, cost of ... ing: *cartage*. (*b*) system of: *coinage*. (*c*) condition of: *bondage*. (*d*) action of: *leverage*.

-al (Used to make adjs.) *monumental*, of, serving as, a monument; *baptismal*, of baptism; *national*, of a nation; *constitutional*, of, in accordance with, a constitution.

-(a)n (Used to make nouns and adjs.) *African*; *American*; *Asian*; *republican*; *Anglican*. (See also **-ian**.)

-ance, -ence (Used to make nouns.) (*a*) act or fact of ... ing: *avoidance*; *dependence*. (*b*) quality or state (indicated by the corresponding verb or adj.): *annoyance* (being annoyed); *absence* (being absent); *prudence* (being prudent); *ignorance* (being ignorant). (*c*) what is ... (e)d: *inheritance*; *contrivance*. (*d*) thing that ... s: *hindrance* (sth. that hinders); *conveyance* (sth. that conveys, e.g., passengers).

-ant, -ent (*a*) (Used to make adjs. from verbs.) *triumphant* (feeling or showing triumph); *indulgent* (in the habit of indulging, showing indulgence); *persistent*. (*b*) (Used to make nouns.) indicating an agent or instrument, a person who does (what the verb indicates): *applicant*; *irritant*; *assistant*; *inhabitant*; *president*; *superintendent*; *student*.

-ary, -ory (a) (Used to make adjs.) serving or tending to: *exemplary* (serving to provide an example); *advisory*; *explanatory*; *cautionary*. (b) (Used to make nouns.) person or thing that is or does: *commentary*; *boundary*. (c) (Used to make adjs.) being: *customary* (being the custom); *honorary*; *secondary*; *supplementary*; *contradictory* (that is a contradiction); *obligatory* (that is an obligation).

-dom (Used to make nouns.) (a) state of being: *freedom*; *martyrdom*. (b) rank, position, lands of: *kingdom, dukedom*.

-ed, -d (Used to make past tense and past participle.) *forced*; *bridged*.

-en (Used to make verbs.) (a) from adjs.: *shorten*; *deepen*; *soften*; *harden*. (b) from nouns: *lengthen*; *heighten*; *strengthen*; *hearten*.

-(e)n (Used to make adjs.) (a) denoting material: *wooden*; *woollen*. (b) showing resemblance to: *silken*; *golden*.

-(e)r (Used to form the comparative.) *stronger*; *smaller*; *wider*.

-er, -or (Used to make nouns.) (a) person or thing that does sth.: *admirer*; *learner*; *actor*; *survivor*; *elevator*; *tin-opener*; *oil-burner*. (b) person who lives in: *villager*; *Londoner*; *New Yorker*.

-(e)ry (Used to make nouns.) (a) place for . . . ing: (*oil, sugar*) *refinery*; (*fish*) *cannery*. (b) state or condition of being: *slavery*. (c) occupation: *archery, embroidery*. (d) class of goods: *confectionery, jewellery*.

-ese (Used with names of some countries, towns, to make adjs. or nouns.) of (the country or town); inhabitant, language (of the country or town): *Japanese*; *Milanese*.

-ess female: *poetess*; *hostess*; *heiress*; *lioness*; *tigress*.

-(e)st (Used to form the superlative.) *strongest*; *smallest*; *widest*.

-ful (a) (Used with abstract nouns to make adjs.) full of: *hopeful*; *graceful*. (b) (Used with concrete nouns to make nouns.) full: *handful*; *cupful*. (c) (Used with verbs to make adjs.) *forgetful*.

-hood (Used to make nouns.) (a) time or condition of being: *manhood*; *boyhood*. (b) group or society of: *priesthood*; *brotherhood*.

-ian (Used to make nouns and adjs.) of; having to do with: *Christian*; *electrician*; *musician*; *Austrian*. (See also **-an.**)

-ic(al) (Used to make adjs.) having the properties or nature of: *alcoholic*; *sulphuric*; *artistic*; *alphabetic(al)*; *geometric(al)*.

-ify (Used to make vbs.) make or become: *simplify*; *solidify*; *glorify*.

-ing Added to roots of verbs to make (a) the present participle; (b) the participial adj.: *interesting*; *amusing*; (c) the gerund: *swimming*; (d) thing produced: the *binding* of a book; floor *sweepings*; iron *filings*; (e) collective nouns: *shipping*; *bedding*; *washing*.

-ish (Used to make adjs.) (a) as of: like; suitable for: *foolish*; *childish*. (b) somewhat: *oldish*. (c) (esp., with names of colours) tending towards; rather: *greenish*; *yellowish*.

-ism (Used to make abstract nouns.) (a) from verbs. in *-ise, -ize*, as *baptism*; *criticism*. (b) system or doctrine: *communism*; *socialism*; *conservatism*. (c) quality, state, characteristic; *heroism*; *barbarism*; *paganism*; *realism*.

-ist (Used to make nouns.) person concerned with: *tobacconist*; *balloonist*; esp. player of a musical instrument: *pianist*; *violinist*.

-itis (Used to make nouns, esp. names of inflammatory diseases.) *appendicitis*; *bronchitis*.

-ize (Used to make verbs) make or become: *harmonize* (bring into harmony); *anglicize* (make English in form, etc.); *legalize*; *centralize*; *italicize*; *materialize*.

-less (Used to make adjs.) (*a*) without: *childless*; *homeless*; *treeless*; *countless* or *numberless* (too many to count); *hopeless*; *useless*; *harmless*; *thoughtless*. (*b*) that does not: *ceaseless*; *endless*; *tireless*.

-logist (Used to make nouns.) expert in, student of: *geologist*; *biologist*.

-logy (Used to make nouns, names of doctrines or sciences.) *geology*; *biology*; *theology*; *etymology*.

-ly (*a*) (Used to make adverbs from adjs.) *recently*; *quickly*; *slightly*. (*b*) (Used to make adjs. from nouns.) like; of; suited to: *manly*; *brotherly*; *ghostly*. (*c*) (Used to make adjs. and adverbs from nouns.) *gloomily*; *hourly*; *daily*; *weekly*; *monthly*; *yearly*.

-ment (Used to make nouns.) act, fact, or state of . . . ing or being . . . (e)d: *enjoyment*; *management*; *improvement*; *amazement*.

-most (Used with prepositions, etc., to make superlative adjs.) *inmost*; *topmost*.

-ness (Used to make nouns.) condition of being: *goodness*; *blackness*; *carefulness*; *preparedness*.

-(i)ous (Used to make adjs.) of, like, having: *ambitious*; *religious*; *dangerous*; *zealous*; *joyous*.

-ship (Used to make nouns.) (*a*) state or quality of being: *membership*; *friendship*; *ownership*. (*b*) skill: *horsemanship*. (*c*) position or rank: *headship* (being a headmaster); *governorship*.

-tion (Used to make nouns.) (*a*) act or state of . . . ing: *opposition*; *action*; *addition*. (*b*) condition of being . . . ed: *exhaustion*. (Compare *revision*; *admission*.)

-tude (Used to make nouns, usually from Latin adjectives.) *gratitude*; *altitude*.

-ty, -ety, -ity (Used to make abstract nouns.) *loyalty*; *penalty*; *piety*; *seniority*; *priority*; *profanity*.

-wise (Used to form adverbs of direction.) *coastwise*; *clockwise*; *lengthwise*.

-y (Used to make adjs. from nouns.) like, covered with, having the nature of: *icy*; *muddy*; *smoky*; *rocky*; *funny*; *wiry*; *woolly*.

COMMON ABBREVIATIONS

Abbreviations that consist of initial capital letters followed by full stops are sometimes printed without the full stops (e.g. HQ, TV, UK, UNESCO).

A.1., in the highest class or best condition.
A.B., able-bodied seaman.
A.B.C., alphabet(ical order).
a.c., alternating current.
A/C, Acc., account.
A.D., after the birth of Jesus Christ.
A.D.C., high officer's personal assistant.
advt., advertisement.
A.H., in the Muslim Era (since A.D. 622).
a.m., before noon.
Apr., April.
arr., arrives.
asst., assistant.
Aug., August.
avdp., avoirdupois.
Ave., avenue.

b., born.
B.A., Bachelor of Arts.
Bart., Baronet.
B.B.C., British Broadcasting Corporation.
B.C., before the birth of Jesus Christ.
B.D., Bachelor of Divinity.
B.E.A., British European Airways.
B.F.B.S., British and Foreign Bible Society.
B.Litt., Bachelor of Letters.
B.M.A., British Medical Association.
B.O.A.C., British Overseas Airways Corporation.
bot., bought.
Bp., Bishop.
B.R., British Rail(ways).
Brig., Brigadier.
Bros., Brothers.
B.Sc., Bachelor of Science.
B.V.M., The Blessed Virgin Mary.
B.W.I., British West Indies.

C., Centigrade.
c., cent(s); century; about; around; cubic; centimetre; centum (100).
Cantab., of Cambridge University.
Cantuar., (Archbishop) of Canterbury.
Capt., Captain.
Card., Cardinal.
Cent., Centigrade; century.
C.E., Church of England.
C.F., Chaplain to the Forces.
cf., compare.
ch., chap., chapter.
Chas., Charles.
C.I.D., Criminal Investigation Department.
c.i.f., cost, insurance and freight.
C.-in-C., Commander-in-Chief.
cm., centimetre.
C.O., commanding officer; conscientious objector to military service.
Co., company; county.
c/o, (used in addressing letters to sb. in the) care of. . . .
C.O.D., cash to be paid on delivery.
C. of E., Church of England.
Col., Colonel.
Coll., College.
Co-op., Co-operative Society.
Corp., Cpl., Corporal.
cp., compare.
Cr., creditor.
cub., cubic.
C.U.P., Cambridge University Press.
cwt., hundredweight.

d., daughter; died; penny, pence.
d.c., direct current.
D.C.L., Doctor of Civil Law.
D.D., Doctor of Divinity.
Dec., December.
deg., degree.
dep., departs.
dept., department.
D.Lit., Doctor of Literature.

D.M., Doctor of Medicine.
D.Mus., Doctor of Music.
do., ditto.
dol., dollar(s).
doz., dozen.
Dr, Doctor; debtor.
dram. pers., the characters in a play.
D.Sc., Doctor of Science.
D.V., if God so wills.

E., East.
E. and O.E., errors and omissions excepted.
Ebor., (Archbishop) of York.
E.C., East Central (London postal district).
ed., editor; edited by.
E.E.C., European Economic Community.
E.F.T.A., European Free Trade Association.
e.g., for example.
E.L.B.S., English Language Book Society.
E.R., Elizabeth Regina (Queen Elizabeth II).
Esq., Esquire.
etc., etcetera.
et seq., and what follows.
exc., except.

F., Fahrenheit.
f., feminine.
Feb., February.
fig., figure, diagram.
F.O., Foreign Office; Flying Officer.
f.o.b., free on board.
Fr., Father; French.
fr., franc.
Fri., Friday.
F.R.S., Fellow of the Royal Society.
ft., foot, feet.
fur., furlong.

gal., gallon(s).
G.B., Great Britain.
Gen., General.
G.H.Q., General Headquarters.
G.L.C., (from 1965) Greater London Council.
gm., gramme(s).
G.M.T., Greenwich Mean Time.
G.P.O., General Post Office.
gr., grain(s); grammar.
gym., gymnasium.

h. & c., hot water and cold water.
H.E., His Excellency.
H.H., Her (His) Highness; His Holiness (the Pope).
H.M., Her (His) Majesty.
H.M.S., Her (His) Majesty's Ship.
H.O., Home Office.
Hon., The Honourable; Honorary.
Hon. Sec., Honorary Secretary.
h.p., horse-power; hire purchase.
H.Q., Headquarters.
hr(s)., hour(s).

i/c, in charge.
i.e., that is.
I.L.E.A., Inner London Education Authority.
in., inch(es).
incog., incognito.
inst., of this month.
I.O.U., I owe you.
I.T.A., Independent Television Authority.

Jan., January.
J.P., Justice of the Peace (magistrate).
jr., jun., junior.
Jun., June.
Jul., July.

K.C., King's Counsel (barrister); Knight Commander.
kg., kilogram.
km., kilometre.
Kt., Knight.
kw., kilowatt.

L., Latin.
l., left; line; litre.
lat., latitude.
Lat., Latin.
lb., pound(s) in weight.
L.C.C., (until 1965) London County Council.
Lieut., Lieutenant.
Litt. D., Doctor of Letters.
ll., lines.
LL.B., Bachelor of Laws.
LL.D., Doctor of Laws.
long., longitude.
L.S.D., pounds, shillings, and pence.
Lt., Lieutenant.
Ltd., Limited.

M., Monsieur (French for Mr); thousand.

m., masculine; married; metre; mile; million; minute(s).

M.A., Master of Arts.

Maj., Major.

Mar., March.

matric., matriculation.

M.C., Master of Ceremonies.

M.Ch., Master of Surgery.

M.D., Doctor of Medicine.

memo., memorandum.

Messrs (see dictionary).

mg., milligram(s).

misc., miscellaneous.

Mlle, Mademoiselle.

MM., Messieurs (pl. of M.).

mm., millimetre(s).

Mme, Madame.

M.O., Medical Officer; money order.

M.P., Member of Parliament; Military Police.

m.p.g., m.p.h., miles per gallon, miles per hour.

Mr, Mrs (see dictionary).

M.Sc., Master of Science.

Mt., mountain, Mount.

M.V., motor vessel.

Mus.B., Bachelor of Music.

N., North; New. **N.E.,** northeast. **N.W.,** north-west.

n., neuter; nominative; noon; noun.

N.A.A.F.I., Naafi, Navy, Army, and Air Force Institutes.

N.A.T.O., North Atlantic Treaty Organization.

N.B., note carefully.

N.C.O., non-commissioned officer.

N.H.S., National Health Service.

No., Number. **Nos.,** Numbers.

Nov., November.

nr., near.

N.T., New Testament.

N.U.T., National Union of Teachers.

N.Y., New York.

N.Z., New Zealand.

O.A.U., Organization for African Unity.

ob., died.

O.C., officer commanding.

Oct., October.

o.d., (banking account) overdrawn.

O.H.M.S., On Her (His) Majesty's Service.

O.K., all correct, agreed.

opp., opposite.

O.T., Old Testament.

O.U.P., Oxford University Press.

Oxon., of Oxford University.

oz., ounce(s).

P, (car) park.

p., page; past; (new) penny.

P.A., personal assistant (*to*).

p.a., per annum.

P.A.Y.E., pay (income tax) as you earn (by deduction from one's wages).

P. & T., Posts and Telegraphs Department.

par., paragraph.

P.C., police constable; Privy Council(lor); Provincial Commissioner.

p.c., per cent; postcard.

pd., paid.

per pro., on behalf of.

P.G., paying guest.

Ph.D., Doctor of Philosophy.

pl., plural.

P.M., Prime Minister.

p.m., after noon.

P.M.G., Postmaster-General.

P.O., Petty Officer; Pilot Officer; postal order; Post Office.

pop., population.

p.p., past participle.

pp., pages.

pr., pair.

Pres., President.

P.R.O., Public Relations Officer.

Prof., Professor.

pro tem., for the time.

prox., of next (month).

PS., postscript.

P.T., physical training.

pt., part; pint; port.

P.T.O., please turn over.

P.W.D., Public Works Department.

Q., Queen.

Q.C., Queen's Counsel.

Q.E.D., which had to be shown.

qr., quarter.

qt., quart(s).

R., Railway; Regina (Queen); Rex (King); River.

r., right.

R.A., Royal Academy.
R.A.F., Royal Air Force.
R.C., Red Cross, Roman Catholic.
R.D., refer (worthless cheque) to drawer.
Rd., road.
Re, rupee.
recd., received.
Regt., Regiment.
Rev., Reverend.
R.I.P., May he (she, they) be at rest.
R.N., Royal Navy.
R.P.M., revolutions per minute; resale price maintenance.
Rs., rupees.
R.S.V.P., Please reply.
Rt. Hon., Right Honourable.
Rt. Rev., Right Reverend.
Ry., Railway.

S., Saint; South. **S.E.,** south-east.
S.W., south-west.
s., second; shilling; singular; son.
S.A., Salvation Army; South Africa.
Sat., Saturday.
sch., school.
Sec., Secretary.
sec., second.
sect., section.
Sen., Senr., senior.
Sept., September.
Sergt., Sgt., Sergeant.
sh., shilling(s).
S.J., Society of Jesus.
S.O.S., (see dictionary).
S.P.C.K., Society for Promoting Christian Knowledge.
sq., square.
Sr., senior.
S.S., screw steamer; (also **s.s.**) steamship.
St., Saint; Strait; Street.
st., stone (14 lb.).
stg., sterling.
Sun., Sunday.
Supt., superintendent.

t., ton(s).
T.B., tuberculosis.
Thurs., Thursday.
T.O., turn over.
Treas., Treasurer.

T.T., total abstainer.
Tues., Tuesday.
TV, television.

U.A.R., United Arab Republic.
U.K., United Kingdom (England, Wales, Scotland, N. Ireland).
ult., of last month.
U.N., The United Nations.
U.N.E.S.C.O., United Nations Educational Scientific and Cultural Organization.
U.N.O., United Nations Organization.
Univ., University.
U.S., U.S.A., United States (of America).
U.S.S.R., Union of Soviet Socialist Republics.

v., see; verse; versus; volt(s).
V.A.T., value added tax.
V.C., Vice-Chancellor; Victoria Cross.
Ven., Venerable.
v.f., very fair.
v.g., very good.
V.I.P., very important person.
viz., namely.
vol., volume.
v.p.p., value payable (on delivery, by) post.
vv., verses.

W., West.
w., watt; wife; with.
W.C., West Central (London postal district).
w.c., water-closet.
W.D., War Department.
Wed., Wednesday.
W.H.O., World Health Organization.
Wm., William.
W.O., War Office; Warrant Officer.
w.p., weather permitting.
wt., weight.

Xmas, Christmas.

yd(s)., yard(s).
yr(s)., year(s); your(s).

IRREGULAR VERBS

Note : Words in italic type are old forms.

Infinitive	Past Tense	Past Participle
abide	abode	abode
arise	arose	arisen
awake	awoke	awaked, awoke
backslide	backslid	backslid
be (am, *art*, is ; are)	was, *wast*, *wert* ; were	been
bear	bore	borne, born
beat	beat	beaten
become	became	become
befall	befell	befallen
beget	begot, *begat*	begotten
begin	began	begun
behold	beheld	beheld
bend	bent	bent
beseech	besought	besought
beset	beset	beset
bet	bet, betted	bet, betted
betake	betook	betaken
bid	bid, *bade*	bid, *bidden*
bind	bound	bound
bite	bit	bitten
bleed	bled	bled
bless	blessed, blest	blessed, blest
blow	blew	blown
break	broke	broken
breed	bred	bred
bring	brought	brought
broadcast	broadcast	broadcast
browbeat	browbeat	browbeaten
build	built	built
burn	burnt, burned	burnt, burned
burst	burst	burst
buy	bought	bought
cast	cast	cast
catch	caught	caught
chide	chid	chided
choose	chose	chosen
cleave	clove, cleft	cloven, cleft
cling	clung	clung
clothe	clothed, *clad*	clothed, *clad*
come	came	come
cost	cost	cost
creep	crept	crept
crow	crowed, *crew*	crowed
cut	cut	cut
dare	dared, *durst*	dared
deal	dealt	dealt
dig	dug	dug
do	did	done
draw	drew	drawn

Infinitive	Past Tense	Past Participle
dream	dreamed, dreamt	dreamed, dreamt
drink	drank	drunk
drive	drove	driven
dwell	dwelt	dwelt
eat	ate	eaten
fall	fell	fallen
feed	fed	fed
feel	felt	felt
fight	fought	fought
find	found	found
flee	fled	fled
fling	flung	flung
fly	flew	flown
forbear	forbore	forborne
forbid	forbade	forbidden
forecast	forecast, forecasted	forecast, forecasted
forego	forewent	foregone
foresee	foresaw	foreseen
foretell	foretold	foretold
forget	forgot	forgotten
forgive	forgave	forgiven
forsake	forsook	forsaken
forswear	forswore	forsworn
freeze	froze	frozen
gainsay	gainsaid	gainsaid
get	got	got
gird	girded, girt	girded, girt
give	gave	given
go	went	gone
grind	ground	ground
grow	grew	grown
hang	hung, hanged	hung, hanged
have (hast, has)	had, hadst	had
hear	heard	heard
heave	heaved, hove	heaved, hove
hew	hewed	hewn
hide	hid	hidden
hit	hit	hit
hold	held	held
hurt	hurt	hurt
inlay	inlaid	inlaid
keep	kept	kept
kneel	knelt	knelt
knit	knitted	knitted
know	knew	known
lay	laid	laid
lead	led	led
lean	leant, leaned	leant, leaned
leap	leapt [lept], leaped	leapt [lept], leaped
learn	learnt, learned	learnt, learned
leave	left	left
lend	lent	lent
let	let	let
lie	lay	lain
light	lit	lit
lose	lost	lost
make	made	made

Infinitive	Past Tense	Past Participle
mean	meant	meant
meet	met	met
melt	melted	melted, molten
misdeal	misdealt	misdealt
mislay	mislaid	mislaid
mislead	misled	misled
mistake	mistook	mistaken
misunderstand	misunderstood	misunderstood
mow	mowed	mown
outbid	outbid	outbid
outdo	outdid	outdone
outgrow	outgrew	outgrown
outrun	outran	outrun
outshine	outshone	outshone
outspread	outspread	outspread
outwear	outwore	outworn
overbear	overbore	overborne
overcast	overcast	overcast
overcome	overcame	overcome
overdo	overdid	overdone
overdraw	overdrew	overdrawn
overeat	overate	overeaten
overfeed	overfed	overfed
overhang	overhung	overhung
overhear	overheard	overheard
overlay	overlaid	overlaid
override	overrode	overridden
overrun	overran	overrun
oversee	oversaw	overseen
oversleep	overslept	overslept
overtake	overtook	overtaken
overthrow	overthrew	overthrown
partake	partook	partaken
pay	paid	paid
put	put	put
read	read [red]	read [red]
rebuild	rebuilt	rebuilt
recast	recast	recast
relay	relaid	relaid
rend	rent	rent
repay	repaid	repaid
reset	reset	reset
retell	retold	retold
rid	ridded, rid	rid
ride	rode	ridden
ring	rang, rung	rung
rise	rose	risen
run	ran	run
saw	sawed	sawn
say	said	said
see	saw	seen
seek	sought	sought
sell	sold	sold
send	sent	sent
set	set	set
sew	sewed	sewn, sewed
shake	shook	shaken

Infinitive	Past Tense	Past Participle
shear	sheared	shorn
shed	shed	shed
shine	shone	shone
shoe	shod	shod
shoot	shot	shot
show	showed	shown
shrink	shrank	shrunk
shrive	shrove, shrived	shriven
shut	shut	shut
sing	sang	sung
sink	sank	sunk, sunken
sit	sat	sat
slay	slew	slain
sleep	slept	slept
slide	slid	slid
sling	slung	slung
slink	slunk	slunk
slit	slit	slit
smell	smelt	smelt
smite	smote	smitten
sow	sowed	sown, sowed
speak	spoke, spake	spoken
speed	sped	sped
spell	spelt, spelled	spelt, spelled
spend	spent	spent
spill	spilt, spilled	spilt, spilled
spin	spun, span	spun
spit	spat	spat
split	split	split
spoil	spoilt, spoiled	spoilt, spoiled
spread	spread	spread
spring	sprang	sprung
stand	stood	stood
stave	staved, stove	staved, stove
steal	stole	stolen
stick	stuck	stuck
sting	stung	stung
stink	stank, stunk	stunk
strew	strewed	strewn, strewed
stride	strode	
strike	struck	struck, stricken
string	strung	strung
strive	strove	striven
swear	swore	sworn
sweep	swept	swept
swell	swelled	swollen, swelled
swim	swam	swum
swing	swung	swung
take	took	taken
teach	taught	taught
tear	tore	torn
tell	told	told
think	thought	thought
thrive	throve	thriven
throw	threw	thrown
thrust	thrust	thrust
tread	trod	trodden, trod

Infinitive	Past Tense	Past Participle
unbend	unbent	unbent
undergo	underwent	undergone
undersell	undersold	undersold
understand	understood	understood
undertake	undertook	undertaken
underwrite	underwrote	underwritten
undo	undid	undone
upset	upset	upset
wake *acordar*	woke, waked	waked, woken, woke
waylay	waylaid	waylaid
wear *usa, vestir.*	wore	worn
weave	wove	woven
wed	wedded	wedded
weep *llorar*	wept	wept
win *ganar, vencer.*	won	won
wind [waind]	wound	wound
withdraw *retirar*	withdrew	withdrawn
withhold *negar*	withheld	withheld
withstand *resistir*	withstood	withstood
work *trabajar.*	worked, *wrought*	worked, *wrought*
wring *torcer.*	wrung	wrung
write *escribir.*	wrote	written

BRITISH (DECIMAL) COINAGE (£p)

(since 14 February 1971)

£1 = 100 pence.

Coins ½ penny (= 1·2d.) 5 pence (= 1s.)
1 penny (= 2·4d.) 10 pence (= 2s.)
2 pence (= 4·8d.) 50 pence (= 10s.)

Notes £1., £5., £10., £20.

£29·00   twenty-nine pounds
£29·26   twenty-nine pounds 26 (= twenty-six pence)
£0·08½ (or 8½p) eight and a half pence.

FORMER BRITISH COINAGE (£.s.d.)

(until 14 February 1971)

£1. = 20 shillings = 240 pence.

Coins	halfpenny	½d.	shilling	1/-, 1s.
	penny	1d.	two shillings (florin)	2/-, 2s.
	threepence	3d.	half-crown, half a crown	2/6, 2s. 6d.
	sixpence	6d.		
Notes	ten shillings	10/-, 10s.	five pounds	£5.
	one pound	£1.	ten pounds	£10.

MEASURES, WEIGHTS, ETC.

Long Measure

12 inches	= 1 foot	
3 feet	= 1 yard	
5½ yards	= 1 rod, pole, or perch	
22 yards	= 1 chain	
220 yards	= 1 furlong	
8 furlongs	= 1 mile	
1,760 yards	= 1 mile	
3 miles	= 1 league	

Surveyors' Measure

7·92 inches	= 1 link
100 inches	= 1 chain
10 chains	= 1 furlong
80 chains	= 1 mile

Nautical Measure

6 feet	= 1 fathom
608 feet	= 1 cable
6,080 feet	= 1 sea mile

Square Measure

144 sq. inches	= 1 sq. foot
9 sq. feet	= 1 sq. yard
484 sq. yards	= 1 sq. chain
4,840 sq. yards	= 1 sq. rod or pole
40 sq. rods	= 1 rood
4 roods	= 1 acre

Cubic Measure

1,728 cub. inches	= 1 cub. foot
27 cub. feet	= 1 cub. yard

Liquid Measure

4 gills	= 1 pint
2 pints	= 1 quart
4 quarts	= 1 gallon

Apothecaries' Fluid Measure

8 fluid drachms	= 1 fluid ounce (or drams)
20 fluid ounces	= 1 pint

Dry Measure

2 gallons	= 1 peck
4 pecks	= 1 bushel
8 bushels	= 1 quarter

Weight (Avoirdupois)

16 drams	= 1 ounce (437½ grains)
16 ounces	= 1 pound (7,000 grains)
14 pounds	= 1 stone
2 stones	= 1 quarter
4 quarters (or 112 pounds)	= 1 cwt. (hundredweight)
100 pounds	= 1 short cwt.
20 cwt.	= 1 ton
2,000 pounds	= 1 short ton
2,240 pounds	= 1 long ton

Troy Weight

24 grains	= 1 pennyweight (dwt.)
20 pennyweights	= 1 ounce
12 ounces	= 1 pound (5,760 grains)

THE METRIC SYSTEM

10 millimetres	= 1 centimetre (0·3937 inches)
100 centimetres	= 1 metre (39·37 inches)
1,000 metres	= 1 kilometre (0·62137 mile or about ⅝ mile)
10,000 sq. metres	= 1 hectare (2·471 acres)
1 acre	= 0·405 hectare
1 litre	= 1¾ pints (liquid measure)
10 milligrams	= 1 centigram
1,000 grams	= 1 kilo(gram)
1,000 kilograms	= 1 tonne
1 pound (avoirdupois)	= 0·454 kilogram
1 cwt.	= 50·8 kilos

GEOGRAPHICAL NAMES: CONTINENTS, COUNTRIES, OCEANS, ETC.

Afghanistan [æf'gænistæn]
Africa ['æfrikə]
Albania [æl'beinjə, -niə]
Algeria [æl'dʒiəriə]
America [ə'merikə]
Angola [æŋ'goulə]
Antarctic [ænt'ɑ:ktik]
Arabia [ə'reibjə, -biə]
Arctic ['ɑ:ktik]
Argentina [ˌɑ:dʒən'ti:nə]
Argentine (the) ['ɑ:dʒəntain]
Asia ['eiʃə]
Atlantic (the) [ət'læntik]
Australia [ɔ(:)s'treiljə]
Austria ['ɔstriə]
Bahamas (the) [bə'hɑ:məz]
Balkans (the) ['bɔ:lkənz]
Baltic (the) ['bɔ:ltik]
Bangladesh [ˌbæŋglə'deʃ]
Barbados [bɑ:'beidɔz]
Belgium ['beldʒəm]
Bermuda [bə'mju:də]
Bhutan [bu'tɑ:n]
Bolivia [bə'liviə]
Bosnia ['bɔzniə]
Botswana [bɔ'tswɑ:nə]
Brazil [brə'zil]
Britain ['britn]
Bulgaria [bʌl'gɛəriə]
Burma ['bə:mə]
Burundi [bu'rundi]
Cambodia [kæm'boudjə]
Cameroun [ˌkæmə'ru:n]
Canada ['kænədə]
Caribbean (the) [ˌkæri'bi(:)ən]
Caspian (the) ['kæspiən]
Celebes [se'li:biz, si-]
Ceylon [si'lɔn]
Chad [tʃæd]
Chile ['tʃili]
China ['tʃainə]
Colombia [kə'lɔmbiə]
Congo (the) ['kɔŋgou]
Corsica ['kɔ:sikə]
Costa Rica ['kɔstə 'ri:kə]
Crete [kri:t]
Crimea [krai'miə]
Cuba ['kju:bə]

Cyprus ['saiprəs]
Czechoslovakia ['tʃekouslou'vækiə]
Dahomey [dɑ:'houmi]
Denmark ['denmɑ:k]
Dominican Republic (Santo
    Domingo) [də'minikən ri'pʌblik]
Ecuador [ˌekwə'dɔ:*]
Egypt ['i:dʒipt]
Eire (= Republic of Ireland) ['ɛərə]
England ['iŋglənd]
Estonia [es'tounjə]
Ethiopia [ˌi:θi'oupjə]
Europe ['juərəp]
Finland ['finlənd]
Formosa [fɔ:'mousə]
France [frɑ:ns]
Gabon ['gæbən]
Galilee ['gælili:]
Gambia ['gæmbiə]
Germany ['dʒə:məni]
Ghana ['gɑ:nə]
Gibraltar [dʒi'brɔ:ltə*]
Greece [gri:s]
Greenland ['gri:nlənd]
Guadeloupe [ˌgwɑ:də'lu:p]
Guatemala [ˌgwæti'mɑ:lə]
Guinea ['gini]
Guyana [gi'ɑ:nə, gai'ænə]
Haiti ['heiti]
Hawaii [hɑ:'waii:]
Holland ['hɔlənd]
Honduras [hɔn'djuərəs]
Hong Kong [hɔn'kɔŋ]
Hungary ['hʌŋgəri]
Iceland ['aislənd]
India ['indjə]
Indonesia [ˌindou'ni:zjə]
Iran (Persia) [i'rɑ:n]
Iraq [i'rɑ:k]
Ireland ['aiələnd]
Israel ['izreiəl, -riəl]
Italy ['itəli]
Jamaica [dʒə'meikə]
Japan [dʒə'pæn]
Java ['dʒɑ:və]
Jordan ['dʒɔ:dn]
Kashmir [kæʃ'miə*]
Kenya ['kenjə]

Khmer Republic ['khmɛə* ri'pʌblik]
Korea [kə'riə]
Kuwait [ku'weit]
Laos [lauz, laus]
Latvia ['lætviə]
Lebanon ['lebənən]
Lesotho [lə'soutou]
Levant (the) [li'vænt, lə-]
Liberia [lai'biəriə]
Libya ['libiə, -jə]
Luxemb(o)urg ['lʌksəmbə:g]
Majorca [mə'dʒɔ:kə]
Malawi [mə'lɑ:wi]
Malaya [mə'leiə]
Malagasy [ˌmælə'gæsi]
Malaysia [mə'leiziə]
Mali ['mɑ:li]
Mallorca [mə'jɔ:kə]
Malta ['mɔ:ltə]
Manchuria [mæn'tʃuəriə]
Martinique [ˌmɑ:ti'ni:k]
Mauritania [ˌmɔri'teinjə]
Mediterranean [ˌmeditə'reinjən]
Mexico ['meksikou]
Minorca [mi'nɔ:kə]
Mongolia [mɔŋ'gouljə. -liə]
Montenegro [ˌmɔnti'ni:grou]
Morocco [mə'rɔkou]
Mozambique [ˌmouzəm'bi:k]
Nepal [ni'pɔ:l]
Netherlands (Holland) ['neðələndz]
New Zealand [nju: 'zi:lənd]
Nicaragua [ˌnikə'rægjuə]
Niger ['naidʒə*]
Nigeria [nai'dʒiəriə]
Normandy ['nɔ:məndi]
Norway ['nɔ:wei]
Oman [ou'mæn, -'mɑ:n]
Pacific (the) [pə'sifik]
Pakistan [ˌpɑ:kis'tɑ:n, -'tæn]
Palestine ['pælistain]
Panama [ˌpænə'mɑ:]
Papua ['pæpjuə]
Paraguay ['pærəgwai]
Patagonia [ˌpætə'gounjə]
Persia (Iran) ['pə:ʃə]
Philippines (the) ['filipi:nz]
Poland ['poulənd]
Polynesia [ˌpɔli'ni:zjə]
Portugal ['pɔ:tʃugəl]
Prussia ['prʌʃə]
Puerto Rico ['pwɛətou 'ri:kou]

Rhodesia [rou'di:zjə, -sje, -ʃiə]
R(o)umania [ru(:)'meinjə]
Russia ['rʌʃə]
Rwanda [ru'ændə]
Sabah ['sæbə]
Sahara (the) [sə'hɑ:rə]
Santo Domingo (Dominican Republic) ['sæntou də'miŋgou]
Sarawak [sə'rɑ:wək, sə'rɑ:wə]
Sardinia [sɑ:'dinjə]
Saudi Arabia ['saudi ə'reibjə]
Scandinavia [ˌskændi'neivjə]
Scotland ['skɔtlənd]
Senegal [ˌseni'gɔ:l]
Serbia ['sə:bjə]
Siberia [sai'biəriə]
Sicily ['sisili]
Sierra Leone ['siərə li'oun]
Silesia [sai'li:zjə]
Singapore [ˌsiŋgə'pɔ:*]
Somalia [sou'mɑ:liə]
Somaliland [sou'mɑ:lilænd]
Spain [spein]
Sri Lanka [ˌsri 'læŋkə]
Sudan [su(:)'dɑ:n, -'dæn]
Suez ['su(:)iz, 'sju(:)iz]
Sumatra [su(:)'mɑ:trə, sju(:)-]
Swaziland ['swɑ:zilænd]
Sweden ['swi:dn]
Switzerland ['switsələnd]
Syria ['siriə]
Tahiti [tɑ:'hi:ti]
Tanzania [ˌtænzə'niə]
Tasmania [tæz'meinjə]
Thailand (Siam) ['tailænd]
Tibet [ti'bet]
Togo ['tougou]
Trinidad ['trinidæd]
Tripoli ['tripəli]
Tunisia [tju(:)'niziə]
Turkey ['tə:ki]
Uganda [ju(:)'gændə]
Ulster ['ʌlstə*]
Uruguay ['urugwai]
Venezuela [ˌvene'zweilə]
Vietnam ['vjet'næm]
Wales [weilz]
Yemen ['jeimən]
Yugoslavia ['ju:gou'slɑ:vjə]
Zaire [zɑ'i:ə*]
Zambia ['zæmbiə]
Zanzibar [ˌzænzi'bɑ:*]

new = novo ≠ old = velho
next - próximo ≠ last - último

THE PROGRESSIVE ENGLISH DICTIONARY

By A. S. Hornby and E. C. Parnwell

A first dictionary in English for learners of
the language who have taken an elementary
course.

320 pages

AN ENGLISH-READER'S DICTIONARY

Second Edition

By A. S. Hornby and E. C. Parnwell

An intermediate dictionary for students of the
English language up to School Certificate
standard.

640 pages

THE ADVANCED LEARNER'S DICTIONARY OF CURRENT ENGLISH

Second Edition

By A. S. Hornby, E. V. Gatenby, and H. Wakefield

Designed to meet all general requirements at
an advanced stage.

1232 pages

OXFORD UNIVERSITY PRESS

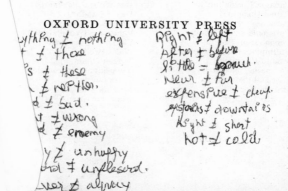

anything ≠ nothing   Right ≠ left
t ≠ those   after ≠ before
's ≠ these   little = branch.
≠ reption.   Near ≠ far
d ≠ bad.   expensive ≠ cheap.
t ≠ wrong   upstairs ≠ downstairs
d ≠ enemy   Right ≠ short
y ≠ unhappy   hot ≠ cold
d ≠ unpleased.
ver ≠ always